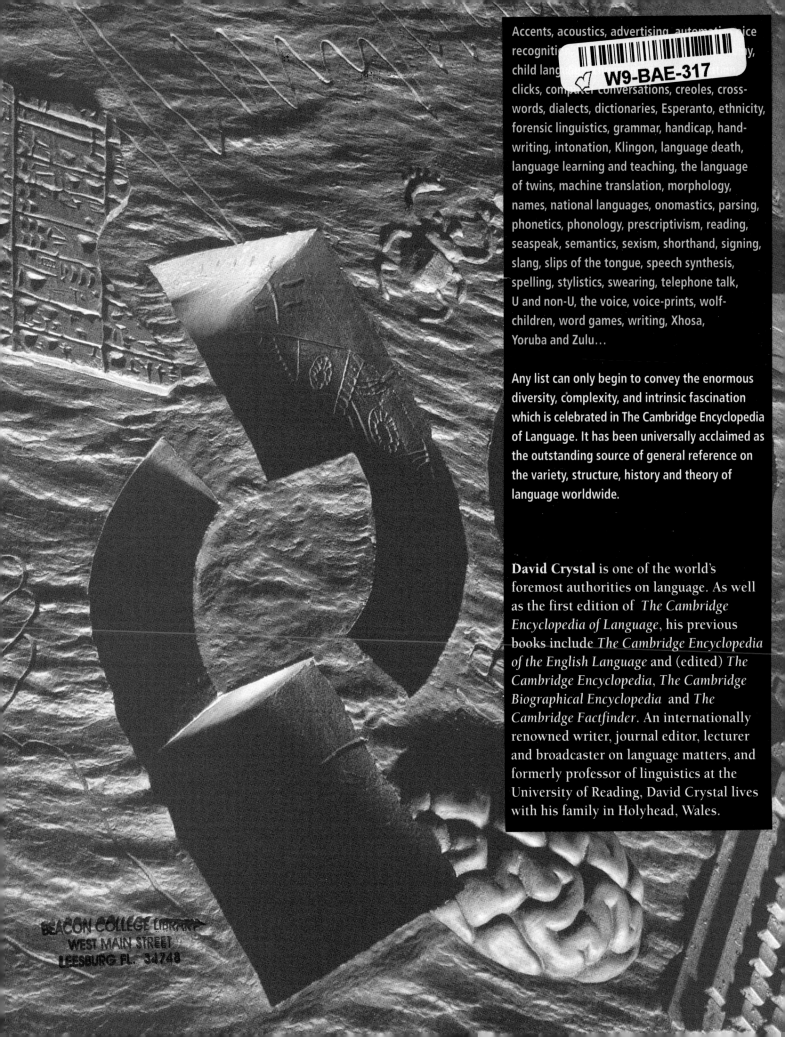

Accents, acoustics, advertising, automatic voice recognition, ..., child language, ..., clicks, computer conversations, creoles, crosswords, dialects, dictionaries, Esperanto, ethnicity, forensic linguistics, grammar, handicap, handwriting, intonation, Klingon, language death, language learning and teaching, the language of twins, machine translation, morphology, names, national languages, onomastics, parsing, phonetics, phonology, prescriptivism, reading, seaspeak, semantics, sexism, shorthand, signing, slang, slips of the tongue, speech synthesis, spelling, stylistics, swearing, telephone talk, U and non-U, the voice, voice-prints, wolf-children, word games, writing, Xhosa, Yoruba and Zulu…

Any list can only begin to convey the enormous diversity, complexity, and intrinsic fascination which is celebrated in The Cambridge Encyclopedia of Language. It has been universally acclaimed as the outstanding source of general reference on the variety, structure, history and theory of language worldwide.

David Crystal is one of the world's foremost authorities on language. As well as the first edition of *The Cambridge Encyclopedia of Language*, his previous books include *The Cambridge Encyclopedia of the English Language* and (edited) *The Cambridge Encyclopedia*, *The Cambridge Biographical Encyclopedia* and *The Cambridge Factfinder*. An internationally renowned writer, journal editor, lecturer and broadcaster on language matters, and formerly professor of linguistics at the University of Reading, David Crystal lives with his family in Holyhead, Wales.

THE CAMBRIDGE
ENCYCLOPEDIA OF
LANGUAGE

Published by the Press Syndicate of the University of Cambridge
The Pitt Building, Trumpington Street, Cambridge CB2 1RP
40 West 20th Street, New York, NY 10011-4211, USA
10 Stamford Road, Oakleigh, Melbourne 3166, Australia

© Cambridge University Press 1997

First published in 1997

First edition published in 1987

Printed in Great Britain at the University Press, Cambridge
Origination by Adroit

A catalogue record for this book is available from
the British Library

Library of Congress Cataloguing in Publication data
The Cambridge encyclopedia of language/David Crystal–2nd ed.
p.   cm.
Includes bibliographical references and index
ISBN 0 521 550505 HARDBACK
ISBN 0 521 559677 PAPERBACK
1. Language and languages–Dictionaries.
2. Linguistics–Dictionaries   I. Title
P29.C64   1997
403–dc20

Maps and diagrams: European Map Graphics Limited
and David Gregson
Picture Research: Paula Granados
Jacket: Unit 18 photography and Rob Lee
Typeset in Adobe Garamond and Frutiger

Note: It is inevitable that some of the maps in this book will
indicate international and other boundaries which may be the
subject of present or future dispute, and the publisher wishes to
make it clear that the form in which such boundaries happen to
appear here should not be taken as either an attempt to influence
any such dispute or as an expression of the publisher's preference.

THE CAMBRIDGE

ENCYCLOPEDIA OF

LANGUAGE

SECOND EDITION

DAVID CRYSTAL

CAMBRIDGE
UNIVERSITY PRESS

Contents

The *Cambridge Encyclopedia of Language* is organized in 11 parts, comprising 65 thematic sections. Each section is a self-contained presentation of a major theme in language study, with cross-references included to related sections and topics.

Preface to the first edition   VI

Preface to the second edition   VII

I   Popular ideas about language   1

Widely held linguistic beliefs and attitudes, and the basic functions of language.

1   **The prescriptive tradition**   2
Popular notions of linguistic authority and correctness; purism and language change; the role of linguistic description.

2   **The equality of languages**   6
Myths about primitive languages and language superiority.

3   **The magic of language**   8
Linguistic superstitions and verbal taboos; the mystical power of proper names.

4   **The functions of language**   10
The many cultural, social, and personal roles which language performs.

5   **Language and thought**   14
The complex relationship between language and thinking; the notion of language relativity.

II   Language and identity   17

The many ways in which language expresses a person's individuality or social identity.

6   **Physical identity**   18
The relationship between language and age, sex, physical type, and physical condition; voiceprints; male vs female speech.

7   **Psychological identity**   22
The relationship between language and personality, intelligence, and other psychological factors.

8   **Geographical identity**   24
The regional background of a speaker; accents, dialects, linguistic areas, and the study of dialectology.

9   **Ethnic and national identity**   34
Language, ethnicity, and nationalism; the problem of minority languages and dialects.

10   **Social identity**   38
Language and social stratification, class, status, role, solidarity, and distance; the problem of sexism.

11   **Contextual identity**   48
Situationally determined varieties of speech and writing; restricted and secret language; verbal play and art; word games.

12   **Stylistic identity and literature**   66
The concept of style; authorship identity and forensic linguistics; literary language in poetry, drama, and prose.

III   The structure of language   81

The dimensions of language analysis that underlie all forms of language, whether spoken, written, or signed.

13   **Linguistic levels**   82
The relationship between the main components of language analysis; models of linguistic structure.

14   **Typology and universals**   84
Analysing the structural similarities and differences among the languages of the world.

15   **The statistical structure of language**   86
The study of the statistical regularities found in language; the frequency of sounds, letters, and words.

16   **Grammar**   88
Syntax and morphology; the structure of words, phrases, clauses, and sentences.

17   **Semantics**   100
The study of meaning in language; the semantic analysis of words and sentences.

18   **Dictionaries**   108
The use and evaluation of dictionaries; the past, present, and future of lexicography.

19   **Names**   112
Patterns and trends in the use of personal names; place names and their history.

20   **Discourse and text**   116
The study of stretches of spoken and written language above the sentence; the nature of conversation; analysing textual structure.

21   **Pragmatics**   120
The factors that govern our choice of language in social interaction; speech acts and their analysis.

IV   The medium of language: speaking and listening   123

The study of the auditory-vocal channel of communication; the production, transmission, and reception of speech.

22   **The anatomy and physiology of speech**   124
The vocal tract and vocal organs; the nature of articulation.

23   **The acoustics of speech**   132
The nature of sound waves and the way they transmit speech; the sound spectrograph and its use in speech sound analysis.

24   **The instrumental analysis of speech**   138
Some of the techniques used in the analysis of speech acoustics and physiology.

25   **Speech reception**   142
The ear, and the process of hearing; speech perception and its investigation.

26   **Speech interaction with machines**   149
The principles and practice of automatic speech recognition and speech synthesis.

27   **The sounds of speech**   154
Phonetics; the description of vowels and consonants; kinds of phonetic transcription.

28   **The linguistic use of sound**   162
Phonology; phonemes, distinctive features, and other models; comparing the sound systems of languages.

29   **Suprasegmentals**   171
The prosody of speech; the structure of intonation; tone languages; the relationship between speech and music.

30   **Sound symbolism**   176
The relationship between sounds and meaning; the role of onomatopoeia.

V   The medium of language: writing and reading   179

The study of the development and functions of written language, in all its forms.

31   **Written and spoken language**   180
The relationship between speech and writing; how sound is portrayed in written language.

32   **Graphic expression**   184
The physical substance of written language; types of graphic expression; handwriting, print, typing, and electronic forms.

33   **Graphology**   196
The writing system of a language; the history of writing; the alphabet; spelling, punctuation, and other contrasts; systems of shorthand.

34   **The process of reading and writing**   210
Psychological accounts of the process of reading, writing, and spelling; spelling regularity and spelling reform.

VI   The medium of language: signing and seeing   221

The development and use of deaf sign languages.

35 Sign language 222
Popular fallacies about sign language; the development and use of signs by the deaf.

36 Sign language structure 224
The way signs are used to convey grammatical contrasts; American Sign Language.

37 Types of sign language 226
The range of contrived sign languages; finger spelling, cued speech, and other systems.

VII Child language acquisition 229
The study of the way children learn to understand and speak their mother tongue – methods, theories, and findings; later language learning in school.

38 Investigating children's language 230
Techniques for finding out about child language; speech production and comprehension; theories of language acquisition.

39 The first year 238
The development of infant vocalization; early speech perception and interaction.

40 Phonological development 242
The acquisition of the sound system; the learning of vowels, consonants, and intonation.

41 Grammatical development 244
The acquisition of grammar; growth in sentence length and complexity.

42 Semantic development 246
The acquisition of vocabulary; first words and their content; distinguishing the meanings of words.

43 Pragmatic development 248
The acquisition of conversational skills; the language of twins.

44 Language development in school 250
The study of language in school; later oral development; learning to read and write.

VIII Language, brain, and handicap 259
The neurological basis of language, and the range of physical or psychological problems that can give rise to disabilities in spoken, written, or signed language.

45 Language and the brain 260
Brain structure and function; hemispheric dominance and localization; slips of the tongue and critical periods.

46 Language handicap 266
Incidence, causation, and classification; deafness, aphasia, dyslexia, dysgraphia; disorders of voice, articulation, and fluency; language delay; alternative communication systems and aids.

IX The languages of the world 285
The range of languages in past or present use – numbers, speakers, sources; identifying and explaining linguistic change.

47 How many languages? 286
Identifying, counting, and classifying the languages of the world

48 How many speakers? 288
Determining how many people speak a language; the world's most widely used languages and families.

49 The origins of language 290
Myths and experiments about the origins of language; wolf children; humans and primates; the evidence of palaeontology.

50 Families of languages 294
Discovering the history of languages; comparative philology; the language families of the world.

51 The Indo-European family 298
The history of Indo-European languages, where they are spoken, and how they are classified.

52 Other families 306
The distribution, family grouping, and use of the world's languages (other than Indo-European).

53 Language isolates 328
Languages which cannot be related to any of the major families.

54 Language change 330
The identification of change in sounds, grammar, and vocabulary; glottochronology; explanations for language change.

55 Pidgins and creoles 336
The origins, distribution, and present-day use of the world's pidgins and creoles.

X Language in the world 343
The problems of communication posed by the diversity of the world's languages and varieties, and the search for solutions.

56 The language barrier 344
The problems caused by foreign languages in the field of international communication; language and the business world.

57 Translating and interpreting 346
The principles and practice of translating and interpreting; the role of machine translation.

58 Artificial languages 354
The history of artificial languages, and the present-day position; Esperanto, Basic English, and other systems.

59 World languages 359
The international use of languages; official languages; World English and its varieties.

60 Multilingualism 362
Causes and extent of bilingual attitudes and practice; language maintenance and shift; language switching.

61 Language planning 366
Government policies about language selection and use; endangered languages; bilingual educational programmes.

62 Foreign language learning and teaching 372
The role and status of foreign languages in school and society; theories of language learning, and methods of language teaching; language materials and laboratories.

63 Language for special purposes 382
The development of special varieties of language in science, medicine, religion, the law, the press, advertising, and broadcasting; the related problems of intelligibility and change.

XI Language and communication 399
The relationship between language and other systems of human and non-human communication, and the scientific study of language.

64 Language and other communication systems 400
Language defined; chimpanzee communication; semiotics; communication by non-linguistic sound, face, gesture, and touch.

65 Linguistics 408
The history of ideas in language study; domains and personalities in 20th-century linguistics; linguistic methods; natural language processing.

Appendices

I Glossary. 420

II Special symbols and abbreviations used in the encyclopedia. 438

III Table of the world's languages. 440

IV Further reading. 448

V References. 452

VI Index of languages, families, dialects, and scripts. 456

VII Index of authors and personalities. 460

VIII Index of topics. 462

Preface to the First Edition

My purpose in writing this book is to celebrate the existence of human language, and to provide a tribute to those who engage in its study. Its aim is to illustrate the enormous diversity of the world's languages, and the great range, complexity, and beauty of expression that can be encountered in any of them, whether spoken by millions or by hundreds - from the most polished formulations of respected literature to the most routine utterances of everyday conversation. At the same time, I want to convey something of the fascination and value of linguistic research, which has led to innumerable general findings about language structure, development, and use, and which has prompted so many important applications in relation to the problems of the individual and society.

The book therefore operates on two levels. It reflects the kind of interest in language history and behaviour that we encounter daily as we argue over the history of a word's meaning or listen in fascination to a young child's early attempts to talk. At the same time, it reflects a deeper level of interest, arising out of our attempt to make sense of what we observe, and to find patterns and principles in it – an interest that can lead to a professional career in linguistic research or in one of the language-related professions, such as language teaching or therapy.

I have certain practical aims also. I hope the book will help promote an informed awareness of the complexity of human language, draw attention to the range of human problems that have a linguistic cause or solution, and emphasize the fact that people have language rights which should not be neglected. In early 1987, in fact [as the first edition of this book was going to press], I received a copy of a plea for a 'Declaration of Individual Linguistic Rights', sponsored by Francisco Gomes de Matos of the Federal University of Pernambuco, Recife, Brazil. The plea points to the widespread occurrence of linguistic prejudice and discrimination around the world, and to the problems people face when they wish to receive special help in language learning and use. All people have the right to use their mother tongue, to learn a second language, to receive special treatment when suffering from a language handicap ... but in many parts of the world, these rights are absent or inadequately provisioned. Only concentrated public attention on the issues will promote the recognition of such rights, and it is my hope that this encyclopedia will play its part in helping to develop a climate where people will sense the importance of language in the individual and in society, and act accordingly.

I have used the term 'encyclopedia', but not without misgivings: if there were a term for 'embryo encyclopedia', it would be better. The subject of language is truly vast, and it is possible only to make a start in under 500 pages. In particular, because my background is in linguistics, I am conscious of paying insufficient attention to other traditions of thinking and research, such as in philosophy, psychology, and artificial intelligence. Also, although I write from a linguistic point of view, this book is not an introduction to linguistics: I have stopped short of a discussion of the many approaches to the analysis of language that linguistics provides, and I give few technical details about theoretical differences, hoping that my references will provide sources for those who wish to enquire into these matters further.

This is just one of many apologies scattered throughout the book. Facts about the use of language are extremely difficult to come by, and, when obtained, fall quickly out of date. Language changes rapidly, as do the techniques and theories that scholars devise to study it. On the other hand, few books can have been written with such an optimistic outlook - thanks largely to the backing and enthusiasm of the team of editorial advisors appointed by Cambridge University Press: Charles Ferguson (Stanford University), Victoria A. Fromkin (University of California), Shirley Brice Heath (Stanford University), Dell Hymes (University of Virginia), Stephen Levinson (University of Cambridge), John Marshall (The Radcliffe Infirmary, Oxford), Wilga Rivers (Harvard University), Sheldon Rosenberg (University of Illinois), Klaus Scherer (University of Geneva), Roland Sussex (University of Melbourne), Jan Svartvik (Lund University), Michael Twyman (University of Reading), and C. F. and F. M. Voegelin (Indiana University). To know that one's plans and material will be scrutinized by scholars of such eminence is immensely reassuring, and I have benefitted immeasurably from their advice while the book was being written. I am therefore delighted to acknowledge my debt of gratitude to these advisors: it has been a privilege to have their support, and I hope the result does them no disservice. Needless to say, the responsibility for what remains is mine alone.

Finally, it is my pleasant duty to thank members of the Department of Linguistic Science, University of Reading, and of the Centre for Information on Language Teaching, London, for help in researching aspects of the work; the editorial and design staff of the Press, for their invaluable advice during the period of this book's preparation; and, above all, the support and assistance of my wife, Hilary, in helping this project come to fruition.

DAVID CRYSTAL
Holyhead, March 1987

Preface to the Second Edition

The late 1980s was no time to be writing encyclopedias. I recall, at the end of the revolutionary year of 1989, reflecting on the remarkable political changes which had taken place, and gloomily wondering how to cope with the hundreds of places in this book where alterations would need to be made. In particular, social developments of such magnitude wreak havoc with language statistics: the figures for old countries are immediately out-of-date, and new countries usually have more on their mind than the task of publishing linguistic data. However, help proved to be not far away, in the form of the many encyclopedia projects in linguistics which came to fruition in the early or mid 1990s, and which contained the latest data on the languages of the world. Their findings, along with 1990s census data, where available, have helped inform the relevant sections of this new edition, especially in Part II, Part IX, and Appendix III.

In addition to a thorough socio-political revision of the text, I have felt it necessary to add extra sections in relation to three topics where progress in the last decade has been substantial. I have added an extra spread on speech synthesis and recognition to Chapter 26; a spread on the world's endangered languages to Chapter 61; and a spread on natural language processing to Chapter 65. The typography section has also been thoroughly revised. New proposals on the classification of some language families have been incorporated, largely following the frame of reference presented in the International Encyclopedia of Linguistics (ed. William Bright, 1992). The re-setting of the whole book in a new typeface has permitted the redesign of several pages, and allowed text to be added on a number of fresh topics, such as conversational misunderstandings, principles and parameters, and Klingon.

The availability of full colour has given me access to a much wider range of pictorial material than in the first edition: all the pictures in the book have been freshly researched, and most are new. This has meant, for example, that I could use illustrations in which colour is functionally integral, such as in images of cortical language processing, television sub-titles, and typographic design; and in general, the greater realism and depth of detail which a colour print can provide is a significant improvement, especially in the sections on phonetics and linguistic geography. All maps have been redrawn, and – with the benefit of four-colour printing – language information is now presented far more clearly than was possible using the two-colour shading of the first edition.

I have several people to thank for their help in updating parts of this new edition, especially Doug Arnold, Andrew Boag, Mark Gresham, Bill Hardcastle, and Keith Johnson. The in-house editorial team at Cambridge University Press have, as ever, been wonderfully supportive – Adrian du Plessis, Clare Orchard, and Geoff Staff – along with picture researcher Paula Granados. Many users of the first edition, too numerous to name individually, have taken the trouble to send in suggestions for improvement, and I have also benefitted greatly from the reviews the book received when it first appeared. To everyone I am most grateful.

DAVID CRYSTAL
Holyhead, February 1996

The cultural diversity of language, as reflected in exchanges between medieval merchants, a customary debate among three men of Irian Jaya, and the imposing dome of the French Academy building in Paris.

Popular ideas about language

PART I

Why does language provide such a fascinating object of study? Perhaps because of its unique role in capturing the breadth of human thought and endeavour. We look around us, and are awed by the variety of several thousand languages and dialects, expressing a multiplicity of world views, literatures, and ways of life. We look back at the thoughts of our predecessors, and find we can see only as far as language lets us see. We look forward in time, and find we can plan only through language. We look outward in space, and send symbols of communication along with our spacecraft, to explain who we are, in case there is anyone there who wants to know.

Alongside this, there is the importance we attach to language, as a means of understanding ourselves and our society, and of resolving some of the problems and tensions that arise from human interaction. No sector of society is unaffected, and all can benefit from the study of the linguistic factors that constitute a barrier, as well as a means of communication. But linguistic problems rarely admit simple solutions, and it is this elementary observation that has led to the present work.

The main aim of this encyclopedia is to provide information about all aspects of language structure and use, so that the complex forces which act upon language, and upon the people who use it, will be more readily understood. The work is founded on the belief that the systematic analysis and discussion of language in an objective way is an essential step forward towards any world in which mutual respect and tolerance is a reality. 'They don't speak like us; therefore they aren't like

us; therefore they don't like us.' This is the kind of logic that the information in this book seeks to deny.

But such a world is a long way off. The world we currently see displays many signs of linguistic intolerance and tension. They appear most noticeably in the language riots of India or Belgium, and in the disfigured road signs of Wales or northern Spain; but they are present in more subtle ways, in the unmotivated preservation of traditional purist linguistic practices in many schools, and in the regular flow of complaints on the world's radio channels and in the press about *other* people's usage.

In the opening part of this book, therefore, we look at the most important ideas that have influenced the nature of popular opinion about language, in both 'civilized' and 'uncivilized' societies. We begin with the idea of correctness, and the historical development of prescriptive attitudes to language. We look at the desire to keep language 'pure', as encountered in the movements in support of language academies, and the general concern over linguistic change. We address the proposition that all languages are equal, in the face of the widespread view that some are more equal than others. This is followed by a discussion of popular beliefs about the magical and mystical power of language, and a general investigation of the wide range of functions that language performs in everyday life. Part I then concludes by considering the intriguing but intricate question of the relationship between language and thought.

1 · THE PRESCRIPTIVE TRADITION

At the beginning of any book on language, readers have a distinct advantage over the author. More than in most areas of enquiry, they already 'know' the subject, in the sense that they already speak and read a language. Moreover, because in modern societies linguistic skills are highly valued, many readers will have definite views about the nature of language and how it should function. This is not the usual state of mind of someone who opens an encyclopedia on, say, astronomy, Roman mythology, or physics.

We must therefore begin our investigation by looking at the main opinions and beliefs people already hold about language as a result of the normal processes of education and social development. These views will provide a frame of reference familiar to many readers, and they will also act as a point of departure for the detailed, systematic, and objective study of the subject in the following pages.

AN EMOTIONAL SUBJECT

It is not easy to be systematic and objective about language study. Popular linguistic debate regularly deteriorates into invective and polemic. Language belongs to everyone; so most people feel they have a right to hold an opinion about it. And when opinions differ, emotions can run high. Arguments can flare as easily over minor points of usage as over major policies of linguistic planning and education (§61).

Language, moreover, is a very public behaviour, so that it is easy for different usages to be noted and criticized. No part of society or social behaviour is exempt: linguistic factors influence our judgments of personality, intelligence, social status, educational standards, job aptitude, and many other areas of identity and social survival. As a result, it is easy to hurt, and to be hurt, when language use is unfeelingly attacked.

The American linguist Leonard Bloomfield (1887–1949) discussed this situation in terms of three levels of response people give to language. The 'primary response' is actual usage. 'Secondary responses' are the views we have about language, often expressed in some kind of terminology. 'Tertiary responses' are the feelings which flare up when anyone dares to question these views. Bloomfield tells the story of visiting a doctor who was quite firm in his view that the Amerindian language Chippewa had only a few hundred words (p. 6). When Bloomfield attempted to dispute the point, the doctor turned away and refused to listen. Irrational responses of this kind are unfortunately all too common; but everyone is prone to them – linguist and non-linguist alike.

PRESCRIPTIVISM

In its most general sense, prescriptivism is the view that one variety of language has an inherently higher value than others, and that this ought to be imposed on the whole of the speech community. The view is propounded especially in relation to grammar and vocabulary, and frequently with reference to pronunciation. The variety which is favoured, in this account, is usually a version of the 'standard' written language, especially as encountered in literature, or in the formal spoken language which most closely reflects this style. Adherents to this variety are said to speak or write 'correctly'; deviations from it are said to be 'incorrect'.

All the main European languages have been studied prescriptively, especially in the 18th century approach to the writing of grammars and dictionaries. The aims of these early grammarians were threefold: (a) they wanted to codify the principles of their languages, to show that there was a system beneath the apparent chaos of usage, (b) they wanted a means of settling disputes over usage, (c) they wanted to point out what they felt to be common errors, in order to 'improve' the language. The authoritarian nature of the approach is best characterized by its reliance on 'rules' of grammar. Some usages are 'prescribed', to be learnt and followed accurately; others are 'proscribed', to be avoided. In this early period, there were no half-measures: usage was either right or wrong, and it was the task of the grammarian not simply to record alternatives, but to pronounce judgment upon them.

These attitudes are still with us, and they motivate widespread concern that linguistic standards should be maintained. Nevertheless, there is an alternative point of view that is concerned less with 'standards' than with the *facts* of linguistic usage. This approach is summarized in the statement that it is the task of the grammarian to *describe,* not *prescribe* – to record the facts of linguistic diversity, and not to attempt the impossible tasks of evaluating language variation or halting language change. In the second half of the 18th century, we already find advocates of this view, such as Joseph Priestley, whose *Rudiments of English Grammar* (1761) insists that 'the custom of speaking is the original and only just standard of any language'. Linguistic issues, it is argued, cannot be solved by logic and legislation. And this view has become the tenet of the modern linguistic approach to grammatical analysis.

In our own time, the opposition between 'descriptivists' and 'prescriptivists' has often become extreme,

George Orwell (1903–50)

In *Politics and the English Language* (1947), Orwell lists six rules 'that one can rely on when instinct fails'. These rules were not written with literary or scientific language in mind, but with the everyday need to foster language 'as an instrument for expressing and not for concealing or preventing thought'. In this way, Orwell hoped, it would be possible to halt the decline in the language, which he saw as intimately connected with the 'political chaos' of the time.

1 Never use a metaphor, simile or other figure of speech which you are used to seeing in print.
2 Never use a long word when a short one will do.
3 If it is possible to cut a word out, always cut it out.
4 Never use the passive where you can use the active.
5 Never use a foreign phrase, a scientific word or a jargon word if you can think of an everyday English equivalent.
6 Break any of these rules sooner than say anything outright barbarous.
(See further, p. 382.)

with both sides painting unreal pictures of the other. Descriptive grammarians have been presented as people who do not care about standards, because of the way they see all forms of usage as equally valid. Prescriptive grammarians have been presented as blind adherents to a historical tradition. The opposition has even been presented in quasi-political terms – of radical liberalism vs elitist conservatism.

If these stereotypes are abandoned, we can see that both approaches are important, and have more in common than is often realized – involving a mutual interest in such matters as acceptability, ambiguity, and intelligibility. The descriptive approach is essential because it is the only way in which the competing claims of different standards can be reconciled: when we know the facts of language use, we are in a better position to avoid the idiosyncrasies of private opinions, and to make realistic recommendations about teaching or style. The prescriptive approach provides a focus for the sense of linguistic values which everyone possesses, and which ultimately forms part of our view of social structure, and of our own place within it. After 200 years of dispute, it is perhaps sanguine to expect any immediate rapport to be achieved, but there are some grounds for optimism, now that sociolinguists (p. 414) are beginning to look more seriously at prescriptivism in the context of explaining linguistic attitudes, uses, and beliefs.

Where traditional grammatical rules come from

	Example of a prescriptive rule	Descriptive comment
Latin and Greek The unchanging form of these languages, the high prestige they held in European education, and the undisputed brilliance of classical literature led to their adoption as models of linguistic excellence by grammarians of other languages.	You should say or write *It is I* and not *It is me*, because the verb *be* is followed by the nominative case in Latin, not the accusative.	The Latin rule is not universal. In Arabic, for example, *be* is followed by the accusative. In English, *me* is the educated informal norm; *I* is felt to be very formal. In French, only *moi* is possible (*c'est moi,* etc.)
The written language Writing is more careful, prestigious and permanent than speech, especially in the context of literature. People are therefore often told to speak as they would write.	You should say and write *whom* and not *who,* in such sentences as – *did you speak to?*	*Whom* is common in writing, and in formal styles of speech; but *who* is more acceptable in informal speech. The rules which govern acceptable speech and writing are often very different.
Logic Many people feel that grammar should be judged insofar as it follows the principles of logic. Mathematics, from this viewpoint, is the ideal use of language.	You shouldn't say *I haven't done nothing* because two negatives make a positive.	Here, two negatives do not make a positive, but a more emphatic negative – a construction which is found in many languages (e.g. French, Russian). The example is not acceptable in standard English, but this is the result of social factors, not the dictates of logic.

MURRAY'S *GRAMMAR*

One of the most influential grammars of the 18th century was Robert Lowth's *Short Introduction to English Grammar* (1762). This was the inspiration for Lindley Murray's widely used *English Grammar* (1794). Both grammars went through over 20 editions in the decades following publication.

Murray's book had an enormous influence on school practice and popular attitudes, especially in the USA. His alliterative axiom contains several watchwords of prescriptivism: 'Perspicuity requires the qualities of purity, propriety and precision'.

Some of Murray's general linguistic principles were unexceptionable, such as 'Keep clear of double meaning or ambiguity' and 'Avoid unintelligible words or phrases.' But most of his analyses, and the detailed principles of his Appendix, 'Rules and observations for promoting perspicuity in speaking and writing', contain the kind of arbitrary rule and artificial, Latinate analysis which was to fuel two centuries of argument. In Rule 16, for example, we find the negation

principle illustrated: 'Two negatives, in English, destroy one another, or are equivalent to an affirmative.'

Murray's rules were widely taught, and formed the basis for much of the linguistic purism still encountered today. However, they were also fiercely attacked. One writer in the *American Journal of Education* (in 1826) compares the grammar to a

'foreign rack on which our simple language has been stretched'. Another (in 1833) insists that grammarians should 'discover' and not 'invent' rules. Long before the advent of modern linguistics, the battle lines of both descriptivism and prescriptivism had been clearly established.

Right: **Lindley Murray (1745–1826)**

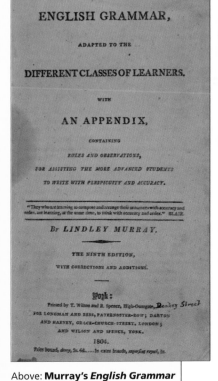

Above: **Murray's *English Grammar***

THE ACADEMIES

Some countries have felt that the best way to look after a language is to place it in the care of an academy. In Italy, the *Accademia della Crusca* was founded as early as 1582, with the object of purifying the Italian language. In France, in 1635, Cardinal Richelieu established the *Académie française,* which set the pattern for many subsequent bodies. The statutes of the *Académie* define as its principal function:

to labour with all possible care and diligence to give definite rules to our language, and to render it pure, eloquent, and capable of treating the arts and sciences.

The 40 academicians were drawn from the ranks of the church, nobility, and military – a bias which continues to the present day. The *Académie's* first dictionary appeared in 1694.

Several other academies were founded in the 18th and 19th centuries. The Spanish Academy was founded in 1713 by Philip V, and within 200 years corresponding bodies had been set up in most South American Spanish countries. The Swedish Academy was founded in 1786; the Hungarian in 1830. There are three Arabic academies, in Syria, Iraq, and Egypt. The Hebrew Language Academy was set up more recently, in 1953.

Kippers *sur* toast? Menus like this could be found, with the appropriate language change, in almost any European city. They illustrate the way English has permeated public life, despite the efforts of many countries to stop it. The German post office, for example, insisted for many years that *Fernsprecher* should be used on phone booths, though *Telefon* was far more common in speech; but in 1981 they made the change. In 1975, the French went so far as to pass a law banning the use of English loan words in official contexts, if an equivalent word exists in French (the *loi Bas-Lauriol*): a *corner* (in football) was to be replaced by *jet de coin,* or *collapser* by *s'évanouir*. However, it was a law honoured more in the breach than in the observance; and when a further attempt to impose French in a range of public contexts was made in 1994 (the *loi Toubon*), parts of the proposal were rejected on the grounds that they were contrary to the principle of freedom of speech, and thus against the constitution . Whether one approves or not, the academies seem to be no match for Franglais, Angleutsch, Swedlish, Spanglish, and all the other hybrids which have become so noticeable in recent years (§§55, 61).

In England, a proposal for an academy was made in the 17th century, with the support of such men as John Dryden and Daniel Defoe. In Defoe's view, the reputation of the members of this academy

would be enough to make them the allowed judges of style and language; and no author would have the impudence to coin without their authority ...There should be no more occasion to search for derivations and constructions, and it would be as criminal then to coin words as money.

In 1712, Jonathan Swift presented his *Proposal for Correcting, Improving and Ascertaining the English Tongue,* in which he complains to the Lord Treasurer of England, the Earl of Oxford, that

our language is extremely imperfect; that its daily improvements are by no means in proportion to its daily corruptions; that the pretenders to polish and refine it have chiefly multiplied abuses and absurdities; and that in many instances it offends against every part of grammar.

His academy would 'fix our language for ever', for,

I am of the opinion, it is better a language should not be wholly perfect, than it should be perpetually changing.

The idea received a great deal of support at the time, but nothing was done. And in due course, opposition to the notion grew. It became evident that the French and Italian academies had been unsuccessful in stopping the course of language change. Dr Johnson, in the Preface to his Dictionary, is under no illusion about the futility of an academy, especially in England, where he finds 'the spirit of English liberty' contrary to the whole idea:

When we see men grow old and die at a certain time one after another, century after century, we laugh at the elixir that promises to prolong life to a thousand years; and with equal justice may the lexicographer be derided, who being able to produce no example of a nation that has preserved their words and phrases from mutability, shall imagine that his dictionary can embalm his language, and secure it from corruption, and decay, that it is in his power to change sublunary nature, or clear the world at once from folly, vanity, and affectation.

From time to time, the idea of an English Academy continues to be voiced, but the response has never been enthusiastic. A similar proposal in the USA was also rejected. By contrast, since the 18th century, there has been an increasing flow of individual grammars, dictionaries, and manuals of style in all parts of the English-speaking world.

Daniel Defoe (1660?–1731)

Jonathan Swift (1667–1745)

LANGUAGE CHANGE

The phenomenon of language change probably attracts more public notice and criticism than any other linguistic issue. There is a widely held belief that change must mean deterioration and decay. Older people observe the casual speech of the young, and conclude that standards have fallen markedly. They place the blame in various quarters – most often in the schools, where patterns of language education have changed a great deal in recent years (§44), but also in state public broadcasting institutions, where any deviations from traditional norms provide an immediate focus of attack by conservative, linguistically sensitive listeners. The concern can even reach national proportions, as in the widespread reaction in Europe against what is thought of as the 'American' English invasion.

UNFOUNDED PESSIMISM

It is understandable that many people dislike change, but most of the criticism of linguistic change is misconceived. It is widely felt that the contemporary language illustrates the problem at its worst, but this belief is shared by every generation. Moreover, many of the usage issues recur across generations: several of the English controversies which are the focus of current attention can be found in the books and magazines of the 18th and 19th centuries – the debate over *it's me* and *very unique,* for example. In *The Queen's English* (1863), Henry Alford, the Dean of Canterbury, lists a large number of usage issues which worried his contemporaries, and gave them cause to think that the language was rapidly decaying. Most are still with us, with the language not obviously affected. In the mid-19th century, it was predicted that British and American English would be mutually unintelligible within 100 years!

There are indeed cases where linguistic change can lead to problems of unintelligibility, ambiguity, and social division. If change is too rapid, there can be major communication problems, as in contemporary Papua New Guinea – a point which needs to be considered in connection with the field of language planning (§§55, 61). But as a rule, the parts of language which are changing at any given time are tiny, in comparison to the vast, unchanging areas of language. Indeed, it is because change is so infrequent that it is so distinctive and noticeable. Some degree of caution and concern is therefore always desirable, in the interests of maintaining precise and efficient communication; but there are no grounds for the extreme pessimism and conservatism which is so often encountered – and which in English is often summed up in such slogans as 'Let us preserve the tongue that Shakespeare spoke'.

THE INEVITABILITY OF CHANGE

For the most part, language changes because society changes (§10). To stop or control the one requires that we stop or control the other – a task which can succeed to only a very limited extent. Language change is inevitable and rarely predictable, and those who try to plan a language's future waste their time if they think otherwise – time which would be better spent in devising fresh ways of enabling society to cope with the new linguistic forms that accompany each generation. These days, there is in fact a growing recognition of the need to develop a greater linguistic awareness and tolerance of change, especially in a multi-ethnic society. This requires, among other things, that schools have the knowledge and resources to teach a common standard, while recognizing the existence and value of linguistic diversity. Such policies provide a constructive alternative to the emotional attacks which are so commonly made against the development of new words, meanings, pronunciations, and grammatical constructions. But before these policies can be implemented, it is necessary to develop a proper understanding of the inevitability and consequences of linguistic change (§54).

Some people go a stage further, and see change in language as a progression from a simple to a complex state – a view which was common as a consequence of 19th-century evolutionary thinking. But there is no evidence for this view. Languages do not develop, progress, decay, evolve, or act according to any of the metaphors which imply a specific endpoint and level of excellence. They simply change, as society changes. If a language dies out, it does so because its status alters in society, as other cultures and languages take over its role: it does not die because it has 'got too old', or 'become too complicated', as is sometimes maintained. Nor, when languages change, do they move in a predetermined direction. Some are losing inflections; some are gaining them. Some are moving to an order where the verb precedes the object; others to an order where the object precedes the verb. Some languages are losing vowels and gaining consonants; others are doing the opposite. If metaphors must be used to talk about language change, one of the best is that of a system holding itself in a state of equilibrium, while changes take place within it; another is that of the tide, which always and inevitably changes, but never progresses, while it ebbs and flows.

WILLIAM CAXTON

One of the earliest English voices to complain about the problems of linguistic change was William Caxton (1422?–91). He was writing at a time when English had undergone its greatest period of change, which had resulted in a major shift in pronunciation, the almost total loss of Anglo-Saxon inflections, and an enormous influx of new vocabulary, mainly from French:

And certaynly our language now used varyeth ferre from that whiche was used and spoken whan I was borne... And that comyn Englysshe that is spoken in one shyre varyeth from a nother. In so moche that in my dayes happened that certayne marchauntes were in a shippe in Tamyse [Thames] for to have sayled over the see into Zelande, and for lacke of wynde thei taryed atte forlond, and wente to lande for to refreshe them. And one of theym named Sheffelde, a mercer, cam in to an hows and axed for mete, and specyally he axyd after 'eggys'. And the good wyf answerde that she coude speke no Frenshe. And the marchaunt was angry, for he also coude speke no Frenshe, but wold have hadde egges, and she understode hym not. And thenne at last a nother sayd that he wolde have 'eyren'. Then the good wyf sayd that she understod hym wel. Loo! What sholde a man in thyse dayes now wryte, 'egges' or 'eyren'? Certaynly, it is harde to playse every man by cause of dyversite & chaunge of langage.

(Preface to *Eneydos,* 1490; modernized punctuation)

Caxton's plaint echoes through the ages, though problems of linguistic change have never been so serious since, with the subsequent standardization of English, and the spread of the written language.

It comes near to stating the obvious that all languages have developed to express the needs of their users, and that in a sense all languages are equal. But this tenet of modern linguistics has often been denied, and still needs to be defended. Part of the problem is that the word 'equal' needs to be used very carefully. We do not know how to quantify language, so as to be able to say whether all languages have the same 'amounts' of grammar, phonology, or semantic structure (§§16, 17, 28). There may indeed be important differences in the structural complexity of language, and this possibility needs to be investigated. But all languages are arguably equal in the sense that there is nothing intrinsically limiting, demeaning, or handicapping about any of them. All languages meet the social and psychological needs of their speakers, are equally deserving of scientific study, and can provide us with valuable information about human nature and society. This view is the foundation on which the whole of the present book is based.

'PRIMITIVE' LANGUAGES

There are, however, several widely held misconceptions about languages which stem from a failure to recognize this view. The most important of these is the idea that there are such things as 'primitive' languages – languages with a simple grammar, a few sounds, and a vocabulary of only a few hundred words, whose speakers have to compensate for their language's deficiencies through gestures. Speakers of 'primitive' languages have often been thought to exist, and there has been a great deal of speculation about where they might live, and what their problems might be. If they relied on gestures, how would they be able to communicate at night? Without abstract terms, how could they possibly develop moral or religious beliefs? In the 19th century, such questions were common, and it was widely thought that it was only a matter of time before explorers would discover a genuinely primitive language.

The fact of the matter is that every culture which has been investigated, no matter how 'primitive' it may be in cultural terms, turns out to have a fully developed language, with a complexity comparable to those of the so-called 'civilized' nations. Anthropologically speaking, the human race can be said to have evolved from primitive to civilized states, but there is no sign of language having gone through the same kind of evolution (§48). There are no 'bronze age' or 'stone age' languages, nor have any language types been discovered

which correlate with recognized anthropological groups (pastoral, nomadic, etc.). All languages have a complex grammar: there may be relative simplicity in one respect (e.g. no word-endings), but there seems always to be relative complexity in another (e.g. word-position). People sometimes think of languages such as English as 'having little grammar', because there are few word-endings. But this is once again (§1) the unfortunate influence of Latin, which makes us think of complexity in terms of the inflectional system of that language.

Simplicity and regularity are usually thought to be desirable features of language; but no natural language is simple or wholly regular. All languages have intricate grammatical rules, and all have exceptions to those rules. The nearest we come to real simplicity with

The Roman goddess Fortuna, holding a cornucopia and a rudder – an appropriate deity to associate with the uncertain destinies of languages.

Juanita, a Navaho woman in the 1870s.

SIMPLE SAVAGES?

Edward Sapir was one of the first linguists to attack the myth that primitive people spoke primitive languages. In one study, he compared the grammatical equivalents of the sentence *he will give it* (a stone) *to you* in six Amerindian languages. (Hyphens separate the parts of the Indian sentences, and in the literal translations that follow they join words that are equivalent to a single Indian form. For phonetic symbols, see p. 442.)

Wishram
a-ċ-i-m-l-ud-a
will he him thee to give will

Takelma
ʔòk-t-xpi-nk

will-give to thee he-or-they-in-future

Southern Paiute
maˑya-vaania-aka-aŋa-'mi
give will visible-thing visible-creature thee

Yana
baˑ-ˑa-ma-si-wa-ʔnuma
round-thing away to does-or-will done-unto thou-in-future

Nootka
oʔ-yi-ʔaˑqƛ-ʔat-eʔic
that give will done-unto thou-art

Navaho
n-aˑ-yi-diho-ʔáˑl
thee to transitive-marker will round-thing-in-future

Among many fascinating features of these complex

grammatical forms, note the level of abstraction introduced by some languages (expressed by *round thing* and *visible*) – quite contrary to the claim that primitive peoples could only talk about concrete objects.

Sapir also gave part of the full Takelma verb paradigm:

ʔokúspi gives / gave it to you
ʔòspink will give to you
ʔòspi can give to you
ʔòspik evidently gave to you

He points out the similarity to the way the verb varies in Latin – a comparison which many traditional scholars would have considered to verge on blasphemy!

natural languages is in the case of pidgin languages (§55); and the desire for regularity is a major motivation for the development of auxiliary languages (§58). But these are the only exceptions. Similarly, there is no evidence to suggest that some languages are in the long term 'easier for children to learn' than others – though in the short term some linguistic features may be learned at different rates by the children of speakers of different languages (Part VIII).

None of this is to deny the possibility of linguistic differences which correlate with cultural or social features (such as the extent of technological development), but these have not been found; and there is no evidence to suggest that primitive peoples are in any sense 'handicapped' by their language when they are using it within their own community.

LANGUAGES OF EXCELLENCE

At the other end of the scale from so-called 'primitive' languages are opinions about the 'natural superiority' of certain languages. Latin and Greek were for centuries viewed as models of excellence in western Europe because of the literature and thought which these languages expressed; and the study of modern languages is still influenced by the practices of generations of classical linguistic scholars (p. 378).

The idea that one's own language is superior to others is widespread, but the reasons given for the superiority vary greatly. A language might be viewed as the oldest, or the most logical, or the language of gods, or simply the easiest to pronounce or the best for singing. Arabic speakers, for example, feel that their classical language is the most beautiful and logical, with an incomparable grammatical symmetry and lexical richness. Classical Arabic is strongly identified with religion (p. 388), as the language of the Qur'an is held to provide miraculous evidence of the truth of Islam. From this viewpoint, it would be self-evident that, as God chose Arabic as the vehicle of his revelation to his Prophet, this must be the language used in heaven, and thus must be superior to all others.

However, a similar argument has been applied to several other languages, such as Sanskrit and Classical Hebrew, especially in relation to claims about which language is the oldest (§49). For example, J. G. Becanus (1518–72) argued that German was superior to all other languages. It was the language Adam spoke in Eden, but it was not affected in the Babel event, because the early Germans (the Cimbrians) did not assist in the construction of the tower. God later caused the Old Testament to be translated from the original German (no longer extant) into Hebrew.

There have been many other spurious linguistic evaluations, reflecting the sociopolitical situation of the time. Charles V of Germany (who ruled from 1519 to 1558) is said to have spoken French to men, Italian to women, Spanish to God, and German to horses! The

Johann Herder (1744–1803)

Swedish writer, Andreas Kempe (1622–89), satirized contemporary clerical attitudes in presenting the view that in Paradise Adam spoke Danish, God spoke Swedish, and the serpent spoke French.

A LINGUISTIC MYTH

A belief that some languages are intrinsically superior to others is widespread, but it has no basis in linguistic fact. Some languages are of course more useful or prestigious than others, at a given period of history, but this is due to the preeminence of the speakers at that time, and not to any inherent linguistic characteristics. The view of modern linguistics is that a language should not be valued on the basis of the political or economic influence of its speakers. If it were otherwise, we would have to rate the Spanish and Portuguese spoken in the 16th century as somehow 'better' than they are today, and modern American English would be 'better' than British English. Yet when we make such comparisons, we find only a small range of linguistic differences, and nothing to warrant such sweeping conclusions.

At present, it is not possible to rate the excellence of languages in linguistic terms. And it is no less difficult to arrive at an evaluation in aesthetic, philosophical, literary, religious, or cultural terms. How, ultimately, could we compare the merits of Latin and Greek with the proverbial wisdom of Chinese, the extensive oral literature of the Polynesian islands, or the depth of scientific knowledge which has been expressed in English? Perhaps one day some kind of objective linguistic evaluation measure will be devised; but until then, the thesis that some languages are intrinsically better than others has to be denied.

Nationalism In the 18th and 19th centuries, language evaluations were often tied to questions of national identity (§9), especially in Germany, in a school of thought which can be traced back to the view of Johann Herder: 'Has a nation anything more precious than the language of its fathers?' Johann Gottlieb Fichte (1762–1814) praised the German language, and dismissed others, in his *Addresses to the German Nation* (1807), even to the extent of claiming that the native German speaker 'can always be superior to the foreigner and understand him fully, even better than the foreigner understands himself'. But comparable claims were made for French and Spanish; and English was similarly lauded by Thomas Macaulay (1800–59): in his *Minute on Education* (1835), referring to the languages of India, he wrote that English 'stands preeminent even among the languages of the West… It may safely be said that the literature now extant in that language is of greater value than all the literature which three hundred years ago was extant in all the languages of the world together.'

3 · THE MAGIC OF LANGUAGE

The magical influence of language is a theme which reverberates throughout the literatures and legends of the world. Language, especially in its written form, is thought to contain special powers, which only the initiated are allowed to understand or control. The beliefs are often linked to a myth about the divine origins of language (§49), but they extend beyond this, to influence religious activities of all kinds, and to reflect a widespread primitive superstition about objects and events which have a symbolic meaning and use.

The belief that words control objects, people, and spirits can be seen in the use of magical formulae, incantations, litanies of names, and many other rites in black and white magic and in organized religion. The language is thought to be able to cure sickness, keep evil away, bring good to oneself and harm to an enemy. Such language usually has to be used with great exactitude, if an effect is to be obtained: meticulous attention is paid to pronunciation, phraseology, and verbal tradition (a factor which appears, most notably, in the history of Sanskrit and Massoretic Hebrew). There often has to be a great deal of repetition, in order to intensify the power of the words. The language, however, does not have to be intelligible to have its effect: many magical formulae are meaningless to those who use them, but there is still great belief in their efficacy (p. 11).

Cases of linguistic superstition abound. To primitive peoples, the written language must appear to be omniscient, when encountered for the first time. Several stories tell of illiterate people stealing an object from a parcel, and being found out when they delivered the message which accompanied it. The writing, it would seem, had a voice of its own—or perhaps a god lived in the letters. Such ideas are found throughout history. The search for mystical meaning in alphabetic script can be seen in the use of runic charms, or in the systems, still in use, which relate letters to numbers, such as gematria (p. 61)

At another level, the mystique of language is something which we encounter throughout modern society, especially in the field of advertising (pp. 390–3). Conquerors, too, well know the power that exists in words. Napoleon, it is said, preferred newspapers to battalions. And what better way is there to remove a nation's influence than to burn its writings? Cortéz did this to the Aztecs in 1520; and the Nazis and Allies did it to each other in World War II.

VERBAL TABOOS

The word *taboo* has been borrowed from Tongan, where it means 'holy' or 'untouchable'. Taboos exist in all known cultures, referring to certain acts, objects, or relationships which society wishes to avoid – and thus to the language used to talk about them. Verbal taboos are generally related to sex, the supernatural, excretion, and death, but quite often they extend to other aspects of domestic and social life. For example, certain animals may be considered taboo: the Zuñi of New Mexico prohibit the use of the word *takka* ('frogs') during ceremonies; until recently, many southern Americans avoided the word *bull* in polite speech, replacing it by a euphemism, such as *he-cow* or *male beast*; in Lappish and Yakuts, the original name for *bear* is replaced by such phrases as *our lord* or *good father*; and wolves, weasels, rats, lice, snakes, and many other animals have been given name-taboos by various cultures. Even people can be affected: certain members of the family are considered taboo among Australian aborigines; either a special language has to be used to them, or they are not directly addressed at all (§10).

The use of a taboo word can lead to a variety of sayings, practices, and responses. The mention of a devil or unclean spirit can evoke a verbal or physical reaction, such as a divine invocation, or the sign of the cross. An obscenity can be the cause of shocked recrimination ('go and wash your mouth out'), physical violence (especially if 'ladies' are present), or legal action (as in the trial over the publication of the unexpurgated D. H. Lawrence novel, *Lady Chatterley's Lover* (p. 61)). The influence of taboo words can even extend across language boundaries. It has been noted that Creek Indians avoid their native words for 'earth' and 'meat' (*fákki* and *apíswa* respectively) because of their phonetic resemblance to English taboo words, which is the dominant language around them. A similar phenomenon has been recorded with Thai learners of English, where English *yet* closely resembles Thai *jēd* (an impolite word for 'to have intercourse'). And Chinese people called *Li* (a common family name) can find their name a source of embarrassment in Rangoon, in view of the Burmese word *li* ('phallus').

The usual way of coping with taboo words and notions is to develop euphemisms and circumlocutions. Hundreds of words and phrases have emerged to express basic biological functions, and talk about death has its own linguistic world, with its morticians, caskets, and innumerable ways of dying. English examples include *to pass on, pass over, make one's bow, kick the bucket, snuff the candle, go aloft,* and *cut the painter.* French has *fermer son parapluie* ('to close one's umbrella'), the indescribably final *n'avoir plus mal aux dents* ('to have no more toothache'), and many more.

A Jewish man wearing phylacteries (Hebrew *tefillin*) These are a pair of small leather boxes containing scriptural passages, traditionally worn by male Jews over 13 years of age, as a reminder of God's Law. They are worn on the left arm facing the heart, and on the forehead during morning weekday prayers. The bands of the phylacteries are knotted so as to form the Hebrew letters *daleth, yod* and *shin,* which form the divine name *Shaddai.*

Proper names

The use of words as personal labels is a matter of particular significance – a fact which is early learned by children, who are often anxious to conceal their own names, and who so easily hurt, and are hurt, by name-calling. Many primitive people do not like to hear their name used, especially in unfavourable circumstances, for they believe that the whole of their being resides in it, and they may thereby fall under the influence of others. The danger is even greater in tribes (in Australia and New Zealand, for example), where people are given two names – a 'public' name, for general use, and a 'secret' name, which is known only to God, or to the closest members of their group. To get to know a secret name is to have total power over its owner.

The Todas of southern India dislike uttering their own names, to the extent that, if they are asked for their name, they will ask someone else to give it. The Sakalavas of Madagascar do not communicate their own name, or the name of their village, to strangers, in case mischievous use should be made of it. In folklore, there are many examples of forbidden names which, when discovered, break the evil power of their owners – Tom-tit-tot, Vargaluska, Rumpelstiltskin.

The process of personal naming can even affect the whole of a language. Stories are common of tribal chiefs who change their name when they take office, as a result of which any everyday words which resemble that name have to be replaced, so that the name will not be used in inauspicious circumstances. It is reported, for example, that when Queen Rasoherina of the Anemerina tribe in Madagascar came to the throne, the word *sopherina* ('silk worm') was forbidden, and replaced by *zana dandy* ('silk's child').

Death can lead to major taboo effects on the use of names. Often, the names of the dead are not to be uttered – though this may well be out of fear rather than respect: while a name endures, it is believed, the dead person does also, and those who utter the name bring the evil of death upon themselves. In some cultures (such as the Polynesian), therefore, when a person dies, other people of the same name have to be renamed, or, if the name happens to correspond to a word in the language, that word would have to be changed. By contrast, some cultures (such as the Greenlandic) place great store by the names of dead people, who are thought to be unable to rest in peace, unless a child has been named after them. In yet others, if a child dies, the next by the same mother will be called by some evil name, to show the death spirit that the child is not worth bothering about.

Sophisticated societies have had their superstitions too. In the Roman levies, the authorities took good care to enrol first those men who had auspicious names, such as Victor and Felix. The names of Greek gods were carved on stone and sunk in the sea, to guard against profanation. In Plato's *Cratylus*, debaters worry about using the names of gods as etymological examples (p. 408), and in the Christian era there are long-standing prohibitions over taking the name of the Lord 'in vain' (p. 61). Older Hebrew names usually had meanings, such as Nathaniah ('Yahweh has given') or Azzan ('Strong'). When Adrian VI became pope, he was advised not to retain his own name on the grounds that all popes who had done so had died in the first year of their reign. People in the 20th century may find it easy to dismiss such attitudes, but things have not greatly changed. It is unlikely that popular opinion would ever allow a new ship to be named *Titanic*.

OUT WITH THE OLD, IN WITH THE NEW

The mystique of words can affect place names too, as a country searches to replace forms which have unhappy associations. In 1868, *Edo* was renamed *Tokyo* ('eastern residence'), symbolizing a new period in Japanese history. *St Petersburg* became *Petrograd*, then *Leningrad*, then reverted to *St Petersburg*; *Christiania* became *Oslo*. It is common practice for new nations to change their names, or the names of their major cities, to symbolize their independence and freedom from imperialist influence. Thus in recent times in Africa, for example, we have seen Upper Volta change its name to Burkina Faso (1985); Rhodesia was renamed as Zimbabwe (1980), with its capital city Salisbury renamed Harare (1982); Dahomey has become Benin (1975), French Sudan has become Mali (1960), and Gold Coast has become Ghana (1957).

The old and new Japan: the Imperial Palace in Tokyo, with the high-rise towers of Shinjuku behind.

THE NAME OF GOD

The true name of God, or of individual gods, is a closely guarded secret in many cultures, if indeed it is known at all. The real names of many Egyptian deities were never divulged.

Observant Jews do not pronounce the divine name as it occurred in the Hebrew of the Old Testament. It was written with four consonants, YHWH (the tetragrammaton), vowel points not being written in pre-Massoretic Hebrew (p. 204). In reading aloud, the forms '*Adonai* or '*Elohim* are substituted. The form *Yahweh* is a scholarly attempt at reconstruction, interpreting its meaning as part of the verb 'to be', to give the title 'the One who Is'. The name *Jehovah* has been traced back only to the 14th century; it is reached by inserting the vowels of '*Adonai* under the tetragrammaton, and arose from a misreading by Christian scholars of the two sources as one word. It is thus not of Scriptural origin, and the true pronunciation of YHWH is now quite lost.

The question 'Why do we use language?' seems hardly to require an answer. But, as is often the way with linguistic questions, our everyday familiarity with speech and writing can make it difficult to appreciate the complexity of the skills we have learned. This is particularly so when we try to define the range of functions to which language can be put.

'To communicate our ideas' is the usual answer to the question – and, indeed, this must surely be the most widely recognized function of language. Whenever we tell people about ourselves or our circumstances, or ask for information about other selves and circumstances, we are using language in order to exchange facts and opinions. The use of language is often called 'referential', 'propositional', or 'ideational'. It is the kind of language which will be found throughout this encyclopedia – and in any spoken or written interaction where people wish to learn from each other. But it would be wrong to think of it as the *only* way in which we use language. Language scholars have identified several other functions where the communication of ideas is a marginal or irrelevant consideration.

EMOTIONAL EXPRESSION

Mr X carefully leans his walking stick against a wall, but it falls over. He tries again, and it falls a second time. Mr X roundly curses the walking stick. How should we classify this function of language? It cannot be 'communication of ideas', for there is no-one else in the room.

Here we have one of the commonest uses of language – a means of getting rid of our nervous energy when we are under stress. It is the clearest case of what is often called an 'emotive' or 'expressive' function of language. Emotive language can be used whether or not we are alone. Swear words and obscenities are probably the commonest signals to be used in this way, especially when we are in an angry or frustrated state (p. 61). But there are also many emotive utterances of a positive kind, such as our involuntary verbal reactions to beautiful art or scenery, our expression of fear and affection, and the emotional outpourings of certain kinds of poetry.

The most common linguistic expressions of emotion consist of conventional words or phrases (such as *Gosh, My, Darn it,* and *What a sight*) and the semi-linguistic noises often called *interjections* (such as *Tut-tut, Ugh, Wow, Ow,* and *Ouch*). Also, an important function of the prosody of language (§29) is to provide an outlet for our attitudes while we speak. At a more sophisticated level, there are many literary devices of grammar and vocabulary which convey the writer's feelings (§12). However, in these more complex cases it becomes difficult to distinguish the emotional function of language from the 'ideational' function described above.

SOCIAL INTERACTION

Mrs P sneezes violently. Mrs Q says 'Bless you!' Mrs P says 'Thank you.' Again, this hardly seems to be a case of language being used to communicate ideas, but rather to maintain a comfortable relationship between people. Its sole function is to provide a means of avoiding a situation which both parties might otherwise find embarrassing. No factual content is involved. Similarly, the use of such phrases as *Good morning* or *Pleased to meet you*, and ritual exchanges about health or the weather, do not 'communicate ideas' in the usual sense.

Sentences of this kind are usually automatically produced, and stereotyped in structure. They often state the obvious (e.g. *Lovely day*) or have no content at all (e.g. *Hello*). They certainly require a special kind of explanation, and this is found in the idea that language is here being used for the purpose of maintaining rapport between people. The anthropologist Bronisław Malinowski (1884–1942) coined the phrase 'phatic communion' to refer to this social function of language, which arises out of the basic human need to signal friendship – or, at least, lack of enmity. For someone to withhold these sentences when they are expected, by staying silent, is a sure sign of distance, alienation, even danger.

These illustrations apply to English and to many European languages. But cultures vary greatly in the topics which they permit as phatic communion. The weather is not as universal a conversation-filler as the English might like to think! For example, Rundi

---

SNEEZING IN TONGA

When someone sneezes, the English stock response is *Bless you*. But there is no equivalent to such forms in many languages, and any remarks which might be made can have a totally different meaning and function. In German, one says *Gesundheit* ('health'); in Mende (Sierra Leone), the word to use is *biseh* ('thank you'); in Bembe (Congo), it is *kuma* ('be well'); and in Malagasy, it is *velona* ('alive'). In Tonga, a sneeze is often taken to be a sign that your loved one is missing you. It is quite common for someone to say jokingly, after a sneeze, *Ikai ke nofo noa mua!* – literally, 'Not to be nothing, alas.' The sense intended is that the loved one who has 'caused' the sneeze should be thinking about nothing, instead of about the one who has sneezed. A major difference with English is that the person who has sneezed may utter the phrase – a kind of *Bless me!*

women (in Burundi, Central Africa), upon taking leave, are quite often heard to say, routinely and politely, 'I must go home now, or my husband will beat me.' Moreover, phatic communion itself is far from universal: some cultures say little, and prefer silence, as in the case of the Paliyans of southern India, or the Aritama of Columbia.

THE POWER OF SOUND

In 1952, children skipping in a school playground were heard to chant: 'Shirley Oneple, Shirley Twople, Shirley Threeple ...' and so on up to 'Shirley Tenple' (i.e. Temple). The instance was recorded by Iona and Peter Opie in *The Lore and Language of Schoolchildren* (1959), and it clearly illustrates the 'phonetic' character of children's rhymes and games. It is largely nonsense, and yet it performs an important function: the repetitive rhythms help to control the game, and the children plainly take great delight in it.

There are many situations where the only apparent reason for a use of language is the effect the sounds have on the users or listeners. We can group together here such different cases as the rhythmical litanies of religious groups, the persuasive cadences of political speechmaking, the dialogue chants used by prisoners or slaves as they work, the various kinds of language games played by children and adults (p. 59), and the

voices of individuals singing in the kitchen or the bath. Perhaps the clearest cases are the lyrics of popular songs and the range of phonetic effects which can be encountered in poetry. Unintelligible words and phrases are commonplace in the oral poetry of many languages, and can be explained only by a universal desire to exploit the sonic potential of language.

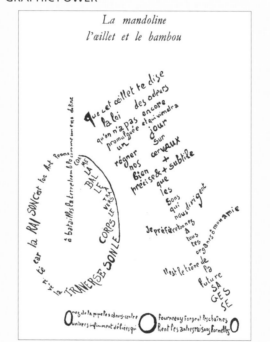

'I like coffee, I like tea, I like radio, and TV...' – a typical ball-bouncing monologue

---

SPEAKING IN TONGUES

paka bante rine sokuntare mare paka tore moti shalara tamere pakashara merime...

This is part of an utterance which occurred spontaneously at a religious service. It displays the repetitive, reduced range of syllabic and rhythmic patterns typical of tongue-speaking, or *glossolalia* – a widespread phenomenon within the Pentecostal tradition of Protestantism and charismatic Roman Catholicism.

Though many glossolalists believe they are speaking a real but unknown language, the utterance patterns are quite unlike ordinary language: the

sounds are simpler and more repetitive; there are few predictable structural units; and there is no systematic word- or sentence-meaning. When asked, glossolalists are usually unable to repeat utterances exactly, or give a detailed account of their meaning.

Glossolalic speech is interpreted in a general way. To speak in tongues is taken as a sign of the sincerity of a person's belief, or as evidence of conversion. The speakers treat it as a highly significant, emotional event, which reflects their new-found sense of the presence of God. In this respect, the phenomenon (or its written equivalent,

glossographia) must be classed along with other cases of functional pseudo-linguistic behaviour, such as jazz 'scat' singing.

Glossolalia needs to be distinguished from cases of *xenoglossia*, where people miraculously speak a language they have not previously learned or heard. Claims for such cases are rare, difficult to prove (e.g. to rule out the possibility that the speaker heard the language as a child), and usually turn out to involve chance effects – as when a few syllables happen to resemble a sequence in some language.

GRAPHIC POWER

La mandoline
l'œillet et le bambou

[handwritten calligramme text, arranged in the shape of a mandolin, bamboo stick, and flower]

Writing and print can exercise a purely visual effect upon the reader, over and above the linguistic content of the words (§32). This is best illustrated in poetry where the shape of the poem reflects its subject matter – as in this poem from Guillaume Apollinaire's *Calligrammes* (1918), showing a mandolin, a bamboo stick, and a flower.

ICELANDIC NAMES

The names of dwarfs in the 13th-century Icelandic Edda are like a painting in sound. A few of the names resemble words in the language, but most have no meaning. (ð and þ are the *th* sound in *this* and *thin* respectively.)

Nyi ok Niði,
Norðri, Suðri,
Austri, Vestri,
Al þjófr, Dvalinn,
Nár ok Náinn,
Nípingr, Dáinn,
Bifurr, Bofurr,
Bomburr, Nóri,
Óri, Ónarr,
Óinn, Mjoðvitnir,
Viggr ok Gandálfr,
Vindálfr, Þorinn,
Fíli, Kíli,
Fundinn, Váli,
Þrór, Þróinn,
Þekkr, Litr ok Vitr,
Nyr, Nyráðr,
Rekkr, Rádsviðr.

THE CONTROL OF REALITY

In the northern borderland of Nigeria, an Igbo man invokes the spirit powers in his ancestral prayers, using a formulaic curse: *Kwo, unu, kwosi okiro!* ('Wash, all of you, wash down upon all of our enemies!'). In an English church, a priest holds a baby over a font, and pours water on its head, saying *I baptize you....*

'Devil dancer' performing a healing ritual in Matara, Sri Lanka

All forms of supernatural belief involve the use of language as a means of controlling the forces which the believers feel affect their lives. The various prayers and formulae which are directed at God, gods, devils, spirits, objects, and other physical forces are always highly distinctive forms of language (p. 388). In some cases, the language might be regarded as a form of ideational communication, with a supernatural being as the recipient – but if so, it is a somewhat abnormal type of communication, for the response is usually appreciated only in the mind or behaviour of the speaker, and there may be no evident response at all.

In other cases, the function of the language is to control matter, or the reality which the matter is supposed to represent. For example, the gardening ritual of the Trobriand Islanders involves a series of formulae which 'charm' the axes, making them effective tools. At a Roman Catholic Mass, the speaking of the words *This is my body* is believed to identify the moment when the communion bread is changed into the body of Christ. Several other situations, apart from the magical and the religious, illustrate this 'performative' function of language – such as the words which name a ship at a launching ceremony.

RECORDING THE FACTS

A solicitor, preparing a case for a client, pulls down an old book of judgments from the shelf, and reads a report of a case which took place 25 years ago. What use of language is this? At first sight, it would appear to be 'ideational'; but the situation in which the communication takes place is quite different in several respects.

When information is stored for future use, it is impossible to predict who is likely to use it – indeed, much of the material may never be referred to again. There is therefore no 'dialogue' element in the communication. The information has to be as self-contained as possible, for it is impossible to predict the demands which may one day be made upon it, and in most cases there is no way in which the user can respond so as to influence the writer. Accordingly, when language is used for the purposes of recording facts, it is very different from that used in everyday conversation – in particular, it displays a much greater degree of organization, impersonality, and explicitness.

This function of language is represented by all kinds of record-keeping, such as historical records, geographical surveys, business accounts, scientific reports, parliamentary acts, and public databanks. It is an essential domain of language use, for the availability of this material guarantees the knowledge-base of subsequent generations, which is a prerequisite of social development.

THE DOMESDAY BOOK

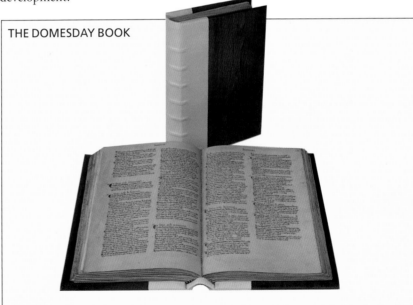

The two volumes which comprise Domesday Book This was the summarizing record of William I's survey of England, which was carried out in 1086. The smaller volume contains all the information returned about Essex, Norfolk, and Suffolk; the larger volume contains the abbreviated account of all other counties surveyed (the whole of England except some of the most northerly areas). The 'once-and-for-all' function of this kind of language is well symbolized by the popular label for the books, 'Domesday', which came to be widely used by the 12th century. From this record there would be no appeal!

THE INSTRUMENT OF THOUGHT

A woman sits alone at a workbench, staring at a piece of equipment with a puzzled frown. She says: 'So if I put red four there, and link it to blue three, that'll leave blue six free. Then I can use that for green four. Right.' She sets to work.

People often feel the need to speak their thoughts aloud. If asked why they do it, they reply that it helps their concentration. Authors often make similar remarks about the need to get a first draft down on paper, in order to see whether what they have written corresponds to what they had in mind. The French thinker, Joseph Joubert (1754–1824), once said: 'We only know just what we meant to say after we have said it.'

Perhaps the most common use of language as an instrument of thought is found when people perform mathematical calculations 'in their head'. Very often, this supposedly 'mental' act is accompanied by a verbal commentary. However, it is not essential that language used in this way should always be spoken aloud or written down. Often, people can be seen to move their lips while they are thinking, but no actual sound emerges. Language is evidently present, but in a 'sub-vocal' form.

Several theories have been proposed concerning the role of language as the instrument of thought – notably that of the Russian psychologist, Lev Semenovich Vygotsky (1896–1934), who argued for a concept of 'inner speech', a mental use of words to evoke a sequence of thoughts. Does all thought, then, require language? This complex question will be reviewed in §5.

THE EXPRESSION OF IDENTITY

The crowds attending President Reagan's pre-election meetings in 1984 repeatedly shouted in unison 'Four more years!' What kind of language is this?

Such language is hardly informative to those who use it, but it plainly has an important role in fostering a sense of identity – in this case, among those who share the same political views. Many social situations display language which unites rather than informs – the chanting of a crowd at a football match, the shouting of names or slogans at public meetings, the stage-managed audience reactions to television game shows, or the shouts of affirmation at some religious meetings.

Our use of language can tell our listener or reader a great deal about ourselves – in particular, about our regional origins, social background, level of education, occupation, age, sex, and personality. The way language is used to express these variables is so complex that it requires separate discussion (§§6–12), but the general point can be made here, that a major function of language is the expression of personal identity – the signalling of who we are and where we 'belong'.

These signals enter into the whole of our linguistic behaviour, so much so that it is often a problem distinguishing the identifying function of language from that used for the communication of ideas. In a public meeting, for instance, Mr A may make a speech in support of Mr B, and it may be difficult to decide whether the reason for his speech is to make a fresh point, or simply to demonstrate to all concerned that A is on B's side. The arena of political debate is full of such manoeuvrings, as individuals strive to express their solidarity with (or distance from) each other.

Jacques Inaudi (1867–1950)

There are two kinds of mental calculating prodigies: those who 'hear' numbers and those who 'see' them. Both rely on some kind of 'inner' language, especially when faced with a complex problem. Inaudi was one of the great 'auditory' calculators. Though he did not learn to read or write until he was 20, by the age of 7 he was able to multiply two 5-digit numbers in his head.

When he was studied by the psychologist Alfred Binet in 1894, Inaudi's auditory techniques clearly emerged – in his own words, 'I hear numbers... resound in my ear, in the way I pronounce them, with the sound of my own voice, and this interior audition stays with me a good part of the day.' In observing him perform on stage, he was usually seen to move his lips or mutter, and he often accompanied this by exaggerated gestures and pacing.

An interesting parallel is sometimes drawn between prodigious calculating abilities and language. Are these mental feats very far removed from our impressive everyday generative ability (§16) to manipulate the complex structure of a vast range of novel sentences?

GRAPHIC IDENTITY

The characteristic typefaces of several British newspapers provide an illustration of identity using the graphic medium (p. 187). These examples are all taken from the *Guardian's* spoof edition of 1 April 1978, in which news from the fictitious island of San Serriffe was presented in a series of typical formats and language styles lampooning actual British newspapers of the time. The joke relies totally on the reader being able to identify these formats immediately, using a mixture of typographic and linguistic cues.

5 · LANGUAGE AND THOUGHT

It seems evident that there is the closest of relationships between language and thought: everyday experience suggests that much of our thinking is facilitated by language (p. 13). But is there identity between the two? Is it possible to think without language? Or does our language dictate the ways in which we are able to think? Such matters have exercised generations of philosophers, psychologists, and linguists, who have uncovered layers of complexity in these apparently straightforward questions. A simple answer is certainly not possible; but at least we can be clear about the main factors which give rise to the complications.

KINDS OF THINKING

Many kinds of behaviour have been referred to as 'thinking', but not all of them require us to posit a relationship with language. Most obviously, there is no suggestion that language is involved in our emotional response to some object or event, such as when we react to a beautiful painting or an unpleasant incident: we may use language to explain our reaction to others, but the emotion itself is 'beyond words'. Nor do people engaged in the creative arts find it essential to think using language: composers, for example, often report that they 'hear' the music they wish to write. Also, our everyday fantasies, day-dreams, and other free associations can all proceed without language.

The thinking which seems to involve language is of a different kind: this is the reasoned thinking which takes place as we work out problems, tell stories, plan strategies, and so on. It has been called 'rational', 'directed', 'logical', or 'propositional' thinking. It involves elements that are both deductive (when we solve problems by using a given set of rules, as in an arithmetic task) and inductive (when we solve problems on the basis of data placed before us, as in working out a travel route). Language seems to be very important for this kind of thinking. The formal properties of language, such as word order and sentence sequencing, constitute the medium in which our connected thoughts can be presented and organized.

INDEPENDENCE OR IDENTITY?

But how close is this relationship between language and thought? It is usual to see this question in terms of two extremes. First, there is the hypothesis that language and thought are totally separate entities, with one being dependent on the other. At the opposite extreme, there is the hypothesis that language and thought are identical – that it is not possible to engage in any rational thinking without using language. The truth seems to lie somewhere between these two positions.

Within the first position, there are plainly two possibilities: language might be dependent upon thought, or thought might be dependent upon language. The traditional view, which is widely held at a popular level, adopts the first of these: people have thoughts, and then they put these thoughts into words. It is summarized in such metaphorical views of language as the 'dress' or 'tool' of thought. The view is well represented in the field of child language acquisition (§38), where children are seen to develop a range of cognitive abilities which precede the learning of language.

The second possibility has also been widely held: the way people use language dictates the lines along which they can think. An expressive summary of this is Shelley's 'He gave men speech, and speech created thought, /Which is the measure of the universe' (*Prometheus Unbound*). This view is also represented in the language acquisition field, in the argument that the child's earliest encounters with language are the main influence on the way concepts are learned. The most influential expression of this position, however, is found in the Sapir–Whorf hypothesis (see facing page).

A third possibility, which is also widely held these days, is that language and thought are interdependent – but this is not to say that they are identical. The identity view (for example, that thought is no more than an internalized vocalization) is no longer common. There are too many exceptions for such a strong position to be maintained: we need think only of the various kinds of mental operations which we can perform without language, such as recalling a sequence of movements in a game or sport, or visualizing the route from home to work. It is also widely recognized that pictorial images and physical models are helpful in problem-solving, and may at times be more efficient than purely verbal representations of a problem.

On the other hand, these cases are far outnumbered by those where language does seem to be the main means whereby successful thinking can proceed. To see language and thought as interdependent, then, is to recognize that language is a regular part of the process of thinking, at the same time recognizing that we have to think in order to understand language. It is not a question of one notion taking precedence over the other, but of both notions being essential, if we are to explain behaviour. Once again, people have searched for metaphors to express their views. Language has been likened to the arch of a tunnel; thought, to the tunnel itself. But the complex structure and function of language defies such simple analogies.

NON-VERBAL AND VERBAL THOUGHT

The two dimensions to rational thinking – linguistic and non-linguistic – can be discovered in a simple experiment, which anyone can perform.

1. Think of where you work. Now visualize the route you follow, as if you were driving along in a car, as you proceed from work to your home. The sequence of visual images which you bring to mind will be largely independent of language.

2. Now imagine you have to explain to a visitor how to reach your house from work. Think out the steps of your explanation, as you would present them, without saying anything aloud. The sequence of ideas will be expressed internally using language.

THE SAPIR–WHORF HYPOTHESIS

The romantic idealism of the late 18th century, as encountered in the views of Johann Herder (1744–1803) and Wilhelm von Humboldt (1762–1835), placed great value on the diversity of the world's languages and cultures. The tradition was taken up by the American linguist and anthropologist Edward Sapir (1884–1939) and his pupil Benjamin Lee Whorf (1897–1941), and resulted in a view about the relation between language and thought which was widely influential in the middle decades of this century.

The 'Sapir–Whorf hypothesis', as it came to be called, combines two principles. The first is known as *linguistic determinism*: it states that language determines the way we think. The second follows from this, and is known as *linguistic relativity*: it states that the distinctions encoded in one language are not found in any other language. In a much-quoted paragraph, Whorf propounds the view as follows:

We dissect nature along lines laid down by our native languages. The categories and types that we isolate from the world of phenomena we do not find there because they stare every observer in the face; on the contrary, the world is presented in a kaleidoscopic flux of impressions which has to be organized by our minds – and this means largely by the linguistic systems in our minds. We cut nature up, organize it into concepts, and ascribe significances as we do, largely because we are parties to an agreement to organize it in this way – an agreement that holds throughout our speech community and is codified in the patterns of our language. The agreement is, of course, an implicit and unstated one, *but its terms are absolutely obligatory*; we cannot talk at all except by subscribing to the organization and classification of data which the agreement decrees.

Whorf illustrated his view by taking examples from several languages, and in particular from Hopi, an Amerindian language. In Hopi, there is one word (*masa'ytaka*) for everything that flies except birds – which would include insects, aeroplanes and pilots. This seems alien to someone used to thinking in English, but, Whorf argues, it is no stranger than English-speakers having one word for many kinds of snow, in contrast to Eskimo, where there are different words for falling snow, snow on the ground, snow packed hard like ice, slushy snow (cf. English *slush*), and so on. In Aztec, a single word (with different endings) covers an even greater range of English notions – snow, cold, and ice. When more abstract notions are considered (such as time, duration, velocity), the differences become yet more complex: Hopi, for instance, lacks a concept of time seen as a dimension; there are no forms corresponding to English tenses, but there are a series of forms which make it possible to talk about various durations, from the speaker's point of view. It

would be very difficult, Whorf argues, for a Hopi and an English physicist to understand each other's thinking, given the major differences between the languages.

Examples such as these made the Sapir–Whorf hypothesis very plausible; but in its strongest form it is unlikely to have any adherents now. The fact that successful translations between languages can be made is a major argument against it, as is the fact that the conceptual uniqueness of a language such as Hopi can nonetheless be explained using English. That there are some conceptual differences between cultures due to language is undeniable, but this is not to say that the differences are so great that mutual comprehension is impossible. One language may take many words to say what another language says in a single word, but in the end the circumlocution can make the point.

Similarly, it does not follow that, because a language lacks a word, its speakers therefore cannot grasp the concept. Several languages have few words for numerals: Australian aboriginal languages, for example, are often restricted to a few general words (such as 'all', 'many', 'few'), 'one' and 'two'. In such cases, it is sometimes said that the people lack the concept of number – that Aborigines 'haven't the intelligence to count', as it was once put. But this is not so, as is shown when these speakers learn English as a second language: their ability to count and calculate is quite comparable to that of English native speakers.

However, a weaker version of the Sapir–Whorf hypothesis is generally accepted. Language may not determine the way we think, but it does influence the way we perceive and remember, and it affects the ease with which we perform mental tasks. Several experiments have shown that people recall things more easily if the things correspond to readily available words or phrases. And people certainly find it easier to make a conceptual distinction if it neatly corresponds to words available in their language. A limited salvation for the Sapir–Whorf hypothesis can therefore be found in these studies, which are carried out within the developing field of psycholinguistics (p. 418).

HAVING A WORD FOR IT

There is nothing in everyday English to correspond to the many Arabic words for *horse* or *camel*, the Eskimo words for *snow,* or the Australian languages' words for *hole* or *sand.* Speakers of English have to resort to circumlocutions if they want to draw the distinctions which these languages convey by separate words – such as the size, breed, function, and condition of a camel. On the other hand, several languages cannot match the many words English has available to identify different sizes, types, and uses of vehicles – *car, lorry, bus, tractor, taxi, moped, truck,* and so on – and might have just one word for all of these.

There is in fact no single word in English for the driver of all kinds of motor vehicles – *motorist* being restricted to private cars, and *driver* being unacceptable for motorcycles – a lexical gap which greatly worried the British Automobile Association in 1961. It was felt that such a word would be useful, and they therefore asked for suggestions. Among the 500 they received were:

autoist	autonaut
roadist	vehiclist
chassimover	murderist
mobilist	roadent
wheelist	vehicuwary

doice (Driver Of Internal Combustion Engine)
pupamotor (Person Using Power-Assisted Means of Travel on Roads)
licentiat (Licensed Internal Combustion Engine Navigator Trained in Automobile Tactics)

However, none of these ingenious ideas has survived.

WORDS FOR *HOLE* IN PINTUPI

It takes between three and 14 English words to distinguish the various senses of *hole* in this Australian aboriginal language, but the distinctions can nonetheless be conveyed.

yarla a hole in an object

pirti a hole in the ground

pirnki a hole formed by a rock shelf

kartalpa a small hole in the ground

yulpilpa a shallow hole in which ants live

mutara a special hole in a spear

nyarrkalpa a burrow for small animals

pulpa a rabbit burrow

makarnpa a goanna burrow

katarta the hole left by a goanna when it has broken the surface after hibernation

The linguistic reflection of cultural identity, here seen in the thousands of Quebecers taking to the streets in support of Québec sovereignty (and thus, of French), during the Fête Nationale day parade in Montreal, 1995.

PART II

Language and identity

'Who are you? How old are you? Where are you from? What do you do? What are you doing now?…' We would only have to speak, to provide our interrogator with innumerable clues about our personal history and social identity. The linguistic signals we unwittingly transmit about ourselves every moment of our waking day are highly distinctive and discriminating. More than anything else, language shows we 'belong', providing the most natural badge, or symbol, of public and private identity. The reports and discussion in this part of the encyclopedia plainly demonstrate this fact and illustrate how our perception of our own and others' language can become, in varying degrees, a source of pleasure, pride, anxiety, offence, anger, and even violence.

The various sections of Part II explore this relationship between language and the many 'faces' of our identity as we interact with others. We begin with the relatively permanent features of language that express aspects of a person's physical or psychological identity – factors such as age, sex, body type, personality, and intelligence. Next, we look at the linguistic facts and issues surrounding the notion of geographical background, and the way this is manifested in regional accent and dialect. This leads, in particular, to a consideration of the world of dialectology, with its atlases and questionnaires, which has attracted widespread interest.

The following sections review the complex set of factors that enter into the definition of ethnic and social identity: racism and nationalism, stratification into classes and castes, status and role, solidarity and distance, social stereotypes – it emerges that all have an influence on the way in which language is used, and that language, in turn, exercises a dominant influence on our perception of social structure, whatever our mother tongue.

An even wider range of linguistic variation is subsumed under the heading of contextual identity. Here we examine how the immediate situation in which people communicate can influence the kind of language they use. Three main features of context are distinguished – the setting, the participants, and the type of activity in which they engage. This leads us to consider such divergent topics as greetings, news-readings, speech making, everyday conversation, proverbial expressions, and slang. In addition, there are separate sections devoted to visual varieties, restricted languages, hidden and secret languages, word games, humour, and the many forms of verbal art.

These last topics lead naturally to the final subject of Part II: personal linguistic identity, with its reliance on the concept of 'style'. We begin by identifying different kinds of approach to stylistic study, and look in detail at one of them, stylo-statistics, where we encounter linguistic detective work in areas as far apart as literary authorship and the investigation of murder. The concept of stylistic distinctiveness then leads us to examine the relationship between literary and non-literary uses of language, with particular reference to the traditional study of rhetoric and to each of the major literary genres – poetry, drama, and the novel. Part II then concludes with a summary of recent trends in literary theory that have focused on the role of language in the interpretation of texts: the antecedents and consequences of structuralism.

6 · PHYSICAL IDENTITY

Several factors define a person's physical identity, the most obvious being age, sex, physical type (height, build, facial features, type of hair, and so on), and physical condition. These factors, supplemented by the criteria made available through modern genetic techniques, are also taken into account when identifying the broad, biologically defined groups of human beings known as 'races'. Such considerations naturally lead to several questions. Are there any correlations between language and the physical characteristics of an individual or race? Can any of the differences between languages, or the variations within a language, be explained by referring directly to the physical constitution of the users?

PHYSICAL TYPE

There seems to be little clear relationship between speech and such physical characteristics as height, weight, head size, and shape. That there is some correlation is evident from our surprise when we hear a large, fat person come out with a thin, high-pitched voice. There is a general expectation that size relates to loudness and pitch depth. However, there is no conclusive way of predicting from physical appearance alone whether a person's vocal range is going to be soprano, contralto, tenor, or bass.

There is little in the anatomy of the human vocal tract to account for the linguistic differences between people and groups. The proportions of the various vocal organs (§22) seem to be very similar in all human beings. Individual variations do exist in size and shape: for example, the height of the palate varies a great deal, as does the length and flexibility of the tongue. Some people can make the tip of their tongue touch their uvula; others can hardly make their tongue touch their hard palate. More men than women can make the edges of their tongue curl upwards. But, pathological cases aside (§46), these differences do not seem to add up to much, as far as spoken language is concerned. There is no evidence to suggest that anatomical variations have any effect on the ability of a person to learn or use speech.

We have to reach a similar conclusion when we consider the kinds of anatomical variation that distinguish the world's racial groups. Certainly several differences could be relevant for speech – for example, the considerable variation in the length of the tongue. In one study (F. Brosnahan, 1961), the tongues of Japanese, Melanesians, and blacks were measured: blacks had the longest tongues on average (a mean of 97 mm, with

individual variation from 72–123 mm); Melanesians had a mean of 84 mm (variation from 70–110 mm); and the Japanese had a mean of 73 mm (variation from 55–90 mm). People have speculated whether this factor would make it more difficult for someone to speak a language of a racially different group; it is highly unlikely (one would expect there to be a constant relationship between the size of the articulating organs and the overall size of the head and neck), but it is not possible to reach a firm conclusion – especially as only very small samples of speakers have so far been used.

It is difficult to be sure what effect this kind of genetically determined difference could have on a language. It might have no effect at all. People might compensate for the 'lack' of one anatomical feature by making greater use of some other feature. Here too, the information is not available, as detailed comparative studies of racial vocal anatomy are lacking. Certainly, everyday experience suggests that the effects are minimal. One indication of this is the language-learning ability of second-generation immigrants, whose accents may be indistinguishable on tape from those of the indigenous population. A widely recognized experience is for London bus passengers to hear behind them a perfectly articulated Cockney *Any more fares please?*, only to find a conductor who is plainly West Indian or African in racial origin.

Despite the superficial differences, it has generally been concluded that vocal tracts the world over are sufficiently similar that we can regard them as variants of a single, universal type. Work in phonetics (§27) proceeds

BODIES, MINDS, AND VOICES

The German psychiatrist, Ernst Kretschmer (1888–1964) proposed a threefold classification of body types, claiming that these correlated with certain mental conditions. The *pyknic* type (thick trunk, short limbs) were thought to be more prone to manic-depressive psychosis; the *leptosomic* type (thin trunk, long legs) more prone to schizophrenia; and the *athletic* type (broad shoulders, thin hips) prone to neither.

While these distinctions proved in due course to be too simplified for practical application, certain general correlations between body type and voice have been observed. In one study, which matched voices with photographs of these types, the pyknic type were matched most accurately, followed by the leptosomic, with the athletic type least well predicted. Other studies have also shown significant correlations between voices and photographs of the speakers, doubtless because of the general physical relationship between a person's size and physique, and the dimensions of the larynx and vocal tract. There are, however, wide margins of error in these studies.

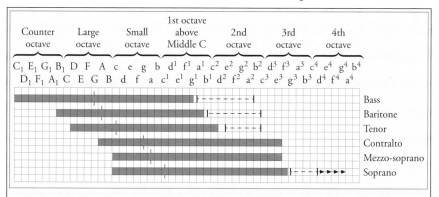

Voice types Probably the most common way of talking about human voices is the classification into six basic types: soprano, mezzo-soprano, contralto, tenor, baritone, and bass. Generally, the individual range of each type is around two octaves, with good singers achieving three octaves or more. Exceptional cases have been recorded, with coloratura sopranos reaching as high as e^4 (2637 Hz), and basses as low as 'contra' F^1 (44 Hz). The diagram shows the average ranges for each type of voice (after M. Nadoleczny, 1923). Speaking level tends to be towards the bottom of the singing range, as shown by cross bars.

on this assumption. But we still know very little about the general potential for sound production in human beings – a subject that the Polish linguist Jan Baudouin de Courtenay (1845–1929) christened *anthropophonics*.

PHYSICAL CONDITION

That there must be some kind of relationship between physical condition and language is plain from the way language can be affected in cases of physical handicap. Several disorders of constitutional origin have a direct effect on a person's ability to use language, variously affecting the ability to comprehend and produce speech, read, and write. Temporary handicaps may have minor but quite noticeable effects – such as the change in voice quality that accompanies a cold or a sore throat, or the alterations in pronunciation that may follow a visit to the dentist. At a much more serious level, there are such cases as the child with cleft palate, or the adult with *myaesthenia gravis*, where speech can be fundamentally and dramatically affected. Here, it is often possible to make deductions about the nature of the person's handicap solely from a tape recording. Voice quality, individual sounds, grammar, vocabulary, and other features of language can all be affected. It is thus a complex field of study, which needs a separate review to do it justice (Part VIII).

AGE

What can be said of the normal process of aging, from a linguistic point of view? In general terms, there is a clear and unmistakeable relationship: no-one would have much difficulty identifying a baby, a young child, a teenager, a middle-aged person, or a very old person from a tape recording. With children, it is possible for specialists in language development, and people experienced in child care, to make very detailed predictions about how language correlates with age in the early years – a research field treated separately in Part VII.

Little is known about the patterns of linguistic change that affect older people. It is plain that our voice quality, vocabulary, and style alter as we grow older, but research into the nature of these changes is in its earliest stages. However, a certain amount of information is available about the production and comprehension of spoken language by very old people, especially regarding the phonetic changes that take place.

Speech is likely to be affected by reductions in the efficiency of the vocal organs (§22). The muscles of the chest weaken, the lungs become less elastic, the ribs less mobile: as a result, respiratory efficiency at age 75 is only about half that at age 30, and this has consequences for the ability to speak loudly, rhythmically, and with good tone. The cartilages, joints, muscles, and tissues of the larynx also deteriorate, especially in men; and this affects the range and quality of voice pro-

THE VOICE 'BREAKS'

Cutting across the distinctions between age, sex, and physical type is the phenomenon of *voice mutation*, which accompanies the development of secondary sex characteristics during puberty. At this time, the child voice differentiates into male and female types, due mainly to the rapid growth of the larynx.

The development is far more noticeable in boys: male vocal folds become about 1cm longer, whereas with girls the increase is only around 3–4 mm. As a consequence, in boys, the entire vocal range is both broadened and lowered by about one octave. In girls, there is no such 'octave shift', and the increase in voice range is much less marked: the lower limit of their range extends by only one-third of an octave, and the upper limit by only a few tones.

As well as the pitch change, certain other vocal features usually mark the onset of puberty. The voice is often husky and weak, with poorly controlled vocal fold vibration (§22). Subsequently, in males, the voice depth is the most noticeable feature; in females, the voice becomes louder, and it changes in timbre – the thin childlike voice becomes fuller and more vibrant.

The term 'break' is not always an accurate way of describing the changes that take place. The change from infantile to adult voice is often a gradual transition, rather than a sudden shift, especially in females. Moreover, the speaking voice and the singing voice may be differently affected. The muta-tional change of the former usually takes between 3 and 6 months, whereas the latter may take much longer. For this reason, it is generally felt to be wise to delay adult singing instruction until well after the change in speaking voice has taken place, to avoid the risk of vocal strain (p. 278).

There is no predictable rule relating adult singing registers to child voices. Whether a boy is soprano or alto, he will develop a bass or baritone singing voice in about two-thirds of cases – a phenomenon that accounts for the common complaint among conductors about the shortage of tenors, and the fact that operatic tenors receive the higher salaries! Similarly, sopranos are far more common than other female voices.

duced by the vocal folds, which is often rougher, breathier and characterized by tremor. In addition, speech is affected by poorer movement of the soft palate and changes in the facial skeleton, especially around the mouth and jaw.

There are other, more general signs of age. Speech rate slows, and fluency may be more erratic. Hearing deteriorates, especially after the early fifties. Weakening faculties of memory and attention may affect the ability to comprehend complex speech patterns. But it is not all bad news: vocabulary awareness may continue to grow, as may stylistic ability – skills in narration, for example. And grammatical ability seems to be little affected.

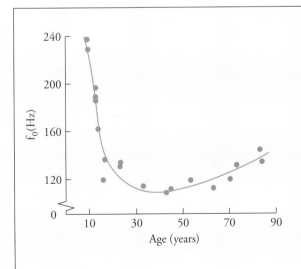

The aging voice The fundamental frequency of the voice (§23) changes quite markedly with age. The graph shows the change that takes place in males: the level drops sharply at adolescence, continues to decrease until middle age, and then increases into senescence. The data points are a composite of averages taken from various published studies. For females, the level is stable during middle age, decreasing later. (After R. D. Kent & R. Burkard, 1981.)

VOICEPRINTS

The traditional method of identifying a person is through fingerprint patterns, which seem to be unique to each person. In recent years, several attempts have been made to provide an analogous technique using the voice. One approach, which received widespread publicity in the 1960s, was developed by an American acoustic scientist, Lawrence Kersta (1907–).

'Voiceprints' are made from an acoustic analysis of speech by a sound spectrograph (p. 136). It is assumed that no two people will have identical vocal tracts, and therefore the patterns of sound vibration they produce when they speak will be different. Kersta claimed it was possible to tell people apart by analysing the visual patterns shown on the spectrograms of ten common words (cf. the ten fingerprints). The patterns were displayed both as bar voiceprints and as contours.

The approach attracted considerable interest among law enforcement agencies, who saw its potential value in crime detection, and voiceprints were soon used as evidence in US courts. In 1965, for example, a youth boasted on a television programme of having set fire to several shops in Los Angeles. His face was concealed, and the television company exercised its legal right not to say who he was. Using other clues in the broadcast, detectives were able to trace a youth, who was brought to trial. Voiceprint evidence established that the voice of the youth in court and that of the youth in the programme were the same. Despite an attack by defence lawyers on the voiceprint evidence, the youth was found guilty.

Critical reactions

After several cases, criticism of the technique began to grow. In 1976, a special committee of the Acoustical Society of America expressed its concern that voiceprints were being admitted as legal evidence when there had been insufficient scientific evaluation of the technique.

The main thrust of the criticism was directed at the fingerprint analogy. Fingerprint patterns are established in the fetus; they change in size, as people grow, but not in form. Voices, however, are partly the result of learning, and they vary: speakers can utter sounds in different ways on different occasions. Also, speakers might produce voiceprints that would not be distinguishable (at the level of detail shown on a spectrogram).

Professional impersonators were invoked. In Britain, a television programme showed a spectrogram of John Bird impersonating the then Prime Minister, Harold Wilson, and compared it with one of Wilson's own voice. The similarities were thought to be much greater than those seen on spectrograms both of Bird's impersonation compared with his normal voice, and of Wilson's voice on that occasion compared with other occasions. On the other hand, in the US, people who could not hear the difference between President Kennedy and Elliot Reid's impersonation were able to see from the voiceprints that the two voices were not the same.

The technique remains controversial. On the positive side, it is accepted that some features of the voice are indicative of speakers rather than of languages (e.g. the higher formants, §23). Also, more refined techniques in spectrography and more sophisticated methods of pattern recognition using computers are now circumventing some of the first criticisms. Interest in the possibilities remains high, because the potential value of the approach is very great – not only in forensic science, but in such fields as commerce (identifying people over the phone), medicine (distinguishing abnormal body noises), and engineering (identifying abnormal moving parts in machinery). On the negative side, the error rate among analysts is still high, and many people doubt whether the properties of the vocal tract are in principle capable of making the discriminations required by the theory. As a result, speech scientists have been extremely cautious about making claims for voiceprinting procedures.

A contour representation of bar voiceprint (a) (below)

Voiceprints. The bar voiceprints of four male speakers uttering *you*, taken from Kersta's paper in *Nature*, 1962. One speaker has uttered the word a second time. Can you tell which two voiceprints are from the same person? (*See foot of facing page for answer.)

(a) 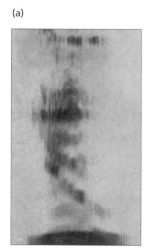 (b) 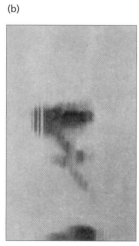 (c)  (d)  (e)

SEX

Phonetic differences (p. 19) are the most obvious measures of sexual identity; but languages provide many instances of males and females *learning* different styles of speech – as in Japanese, Thai, Carib, Chukchi, and Yana. Pronunciation, grammar, vocabulary, and context of use can all be affected. In Koasati, certain verb forms differ according to the sex of the speaker. If the form ends in a vowel, or /tʃ/, there is no difference; but in cases where the woman's form ends in a nasalized vowel, or in certain consonants, the man's form substitutes /s/. This can be seen in the following examples (after M. R. Haas, 1944):

Female	Male	
iskó	*iskó*	he drank
lakáwč	*lakáwč*	you are lifting it
kạ̀	*ká·s*	he is saying
molhîl	*molhís*	we are peeling it
tačwân	*tačilwâ·s*	don't sing!

When Haas carried out her study, only middle-aged and elderly women used the female forms; younger women were beginning to use the forms typical of male speech. But members of each sex were quite familiar with both speech styles, and could use either upon occasion. If a man were telling a story involving a female character, he would use women's forms when quoting her speech.

JAPANESE MALE AND FEMALE SPEECH

A clear case of linguistic sex-differentiation is Japanese, where well-defined styles of speech have been known since the early 11th century. Females have used a style known as *joseigo* or *onnakotoba*, which evolved among upper-class women as a sign of their special position in society. Books on feminine etiquette fostered the use of special vocabulary and grammar, alongside norms of gentle and submissive behaviour. This traditional view is undergoing considerable change today; but clearly defined sexual roles still predominate, and distinct linguistic forms are widely encountered.

Japanese female speech is a style over which women have conscious control. It is used when women wish to emphasize their femininity; on other occasions, they adopt a sexually neutral style. Thus a women may use feminine style in talking to her friends about her children but use neutral style when talking to business colleagues. It is also possible for women to use the masculine speech style if they wish to express themselves in an assertive way – and this is often done these days by many who are concerned to promote notions of sexual equality. A particular example is the increasing use of *boku* ('I') among schoolgirls – traditionally used only by males.

There are also frequency differences in the use of forms. Both males and females use the formal and the honorific (p. 99) varieties of speech, but females use them much more commonly and in a wider range of situations. For example, a man might use a certain honorific form only in talking to a superior, whereas a woman might use it for a social equal as well. The polite forms of nouns, verbs, and adjectives are also used more frequently by women.

There have been fewer studies of male speech style, reflecting a tradition that sees female speech as the 'special' variety; and a separate label for the male style is not often used. But the style can be clearly defined, and is heard in contexts where traditional notions of masculinity are to be found (assertiveness, toughness, etc.). By no means all male language is distinctive, however: as in the case of women, sex-neutral speech will often be used, and on occasion there may be the use of feminine features, as signals of gentleness or consideration.

ENGLISH MALE AND FEMALE SPEECH

In English, the situation is less clear. There are no grammatical forms, lexical items, or patterns of pronunciation that are used exclusively by one sex, but there are several differences in frequency. For example, among the words and phrases that women are supposed to use more often are such emotive adjectives as *super* and *lovely*, exclamations such as *Goodness me* and *Oh dear*, and intensifiers such as *so* or *such* (e.g. *It was so busy*). This use of intensifiers has been noted in several languages, including German, French, and Russian.

More important are the strategies adopted by the two sexes in cross-sex conversation. Women have been found to ask more questions, make more use of positive and encouraging 'noises' (such as *mhm*), use a wider intonational range and a more marked rhythmical stress, and make greater use of the pronouns *you* and *we*. By contrast, men are much more likely to interrupt (more than three times as much, in some studies), to dispute what has been said, to ignore or respond poorly to what has been said, to introduce more new topics into the conversation, and to make more declarations of fact or opinion.

Most interpretations of these differences refer to the contrasting social roles of the sexes in modern society. Men are seen to reflect in their conversational dominance the power they have traditionally received from society; women, likewise, exercise the supporting role that they have been taught to adopt – in this case, helping the conversation along and providing men with opportunities to express this dominance. The situation is undoubtedly more complex than this, as neither sex is linguistically homogeneous, and considerable variation exists when real contexts of use are studied. The risk, as some commentators have pointed out, is that in the process of criticizing old sexual stereotypes, researchers are in danger of creating new ones (p. 46).

(p. 46)

SOME MARKERS OF JAPANESE FEMALE STYLE

- Use of *atashi* ('I'), instead of *watakushi*.
- Sentence particle *wa* used at the end of sentences with rising intonation, instead of with falling intonation.
- Interjections of surprise, such as *ara, mā, uwā*.
- Less frequent use of such interjections as *ā* or *ē*.
- Use of sentence particle *yo* following a noun, instead of *da* (male) or *desu yo* (sex-neutral).
- Use of *no* ('matter') at the end of statements, instead of *n da* (male) or *n desu* (sex-neutral), e.g. *Dekinai no* ('It's [a matter of being] impossible') vs *Dekinai n da*.
- Use of polite forms of nouns, such as *osakana* ('fish') for *sakana* (sex-neutral).
- More frequent use of particle *ne* ('right?', 'Okay') at the end of sentences.
- Less frequent use of the assertive particles *ze* and *zo* at the end of statements.
- Use of *jodai* (female) and *kudusai* (male) for 'please'.

* (a) and (e)

It is common practice to identify individuals, or groups of people, in terms of their psychological attributes – whether they have high intelligence, good concentration, an aggressive personality, a poor memory, and so on. We generally make these judgments on the basis of the non-linguistic way in which people behave when they carry out tasks and interact in specific situations. For example, we do not need to refer to language in order to see whether someone can pay attention, remember which route to take, fix a piece of equipment, or behave in a friendly manner. But very often we do rely on language in order to evaluate such matters, and this forms an important part of the study of identity.

Any of the fields of academic psychology can prompt a linguistic enquiry of this kind. We might investigate whether there is a relationship between language structures or skills and such notions as memory, attention, perception, personality, intelligence, learning, or any other recognized psychological domain. These studies have both theoretical and practical implications. They suggest ways of constructing models of our mental processes – a major preoccupation of the field of psycholinguistics (p. 418). And they relate to several issues of language learning – both normal (in such contexts as mother-tongue education and foreign language learning) and pathological (in such contexts as speech and hearing disorders). The main findings are thus more appropriately reviewed in other sections (§§25, 34, 38, 45). Furthermore, any linguistic medium (speech, writing, signing) can be the focus of enquiry, though only spoken language characteristics are considered here (for handwriting and signing, see §§32, 35).

This cluster of cross-references shows how the topic of psycholinguistic identity extends well beyond the subject matter of the present section. It is also somewhat arbitrary dealing with it next to the section on physical identity instead of later, as part of the section that deals with the distinctive features of 'style' (§12). However, this decision should not be construed as taking sides in the controversies that have raged over the role of 'nature' and 'nurture' in the formation of such attributes as personality and intelligence. From a linguistic point of view, it is simply to recognize the fact that, once adulthood is achieved, any features of language that can be related to psychological attributes seem to be relatively permanent, and thus have more in common with the long-term characteristics of physical constitution, than with the temporary and consciously controllable features that form the basis of stylistic study.

LANGUAGE AND INTELLIGENCE

Decades of controversy over the nature and assessment of intelligence preclude any straightforward statement about its relationship to language. It is evident that people are judged as more or less intelligent, based on how they behave in certain situations, and in response to certain tasks. There is a long tradition of intelligence testing, in which sets of tasks are presented in order to ascertain levels of achievement, and to demonstrate individual differences; the scores that result are widely used in educational, clinical, and other contexts.

Most research has been carried out in relation to the development of children's intellectual processes, as they learn about the world, react to situations, solve problems, and carry out all kinds of tasks. Several theoretical positions exist, which are reviewed in Part VII. Studies with mentally handicapped children have shown that a certain minimum level of intelligence, as measured on conventional tests, is a prerequisite for language development. However, this need not be very high, and there is no clear relationship between intelligence and the ability to use particular language structures. Attempts have been made to relate intelligence to quantity of infant babbling, amount of vocabulary, grammatical complexity, the prosodic features of speech, the use of figurative expressions, and other variables. In no case is there a neat correlation, though stereotypes of performance undoubtedly exist, and here the psycholinguistic study of intelligence overlaps with that of personality.

VERBAL VS NON-VERBAL IQ

Some intelligence tests do not contain any tasks that require a knowledge of language in order to solve them. A person is asked to carry out such activities as building an object, matching shapes, finding a way through a maze, detecting picture similarities and differences, or deciding which entities 'go together'. These 'non-verbal' tests contrast with 'verbal' tests, which rely on a prior awareness of language comprehension or production – for example, tests of general knowledge, memory for digits, arithmetic, vocabulary comprehension, and similarities between words. Several kinds of material have been devised to help promote non-verbal skills. The picture below shows a child playing with Fluorescent Octons, developed by Galt as a medium through which children can develop their skills in coordination as well as their understanding of 3-dimensional shapes.

PERSONALITY

This complex field deals with the characteristics that enable us to distinguish between people, and to make predictions about their behaviour – characteristics generally classified as personality *traits* and *types*. Traits are styles of behaviour that an individual displays, whatever the stimulus, in many different circumstances. Types involve the identification of a salient feature that is then used as a label for the whole personality. In one study (G. W. Allport & H. S. Odbert, 1936), nearly 18,000 trait labels were found to be available in English to distinguish one person's behaviour from another (honest, tidy, shy, thoughtful, stupid…), but of course many of these overlap in meaning, and most studies classify traits into much smaller sets of basic dimensions, such as dominance, extraversion, or likeability.

Several interesting inferences have been drawn about the relationship between personality traits or types and aspects of speech, especially in 'matched-guise' experiments. The first of these studies (W. E. Lambert *et al.*, 1960) aimed to show how English- and French-speaking Canadians viewed each other. English-speaking college students in Montreal were asked to listen to recordings of a passage being read aloud in English and in French, and to mark on a checklist what the personality traits of the speakers were. They were told to disregard language, and to concentrate solely on voice and personality. However, the students were *not* told that the voices were in fact those of perfectly bilingual speakers, each of whom read the passage both in an English and a French 'guise'.

The results were illuminating. The English guises of the speakers were evaluated much more favourably that were the French guises: for example, they were thought to be better looking, more intelligent, kinder, and more ambitious. But in a second part to the study, there was an even more interesting finding. When French-speaking Canadians were given the same test, they too rated the English guises as higher, in almost all respects, indicating the low esteem in which the French language was held at that time.

There is of course no correlation between such attributes as intelligence or attractiveness and the speaking of English or French. But it is a fact that people do form such stereotyped impressions on the basis of linguistic features (especially prosody, §29). Moreover, *all* accents, dialects, and languages are affected by evaluations of this kind. If speakers use a standard accent, speak quickly and fluently, and use few hesitations, they are likely to be rated as more competent, dominant, and dynamic. The use of regional, ethnic, or lower-class varieties, on the other hand, is associated with greater speaker integrity and attractiveness. Even national personalities can be perceived: British speakers rate French as a more romantic language, it seems, and German as a more businesslike one.

Vocal stereotypes

Listeners are very ready to make stereotyped judgments about personality: comments such as *You can tell he's anxious from his voice* or *She sounds very strong minded* are often to be heard. Systematic information has been obtained in social psychology experiments since the 1930s, when researchers began to use the new broadcasting medium to get large-scale listener judgments of different voices. In one study (T. H. Pear, 1931), 4,000 listener judgments were obtained about nine speakers played over the air. Age and sex proved easiest to identify, and among the vocations represented, actors and clergy were most frequently recognized. But even when the listeners made the wrong decisions about vocation, they were extremely consistent in their errors. People who sound like priests, it appears, will be rated as if they are priests, whether they are or not.

Stereotypes of this kind markedly colour interpersonal and intergroup relationships. They are widespread, with similar results being found in several other areas where accent, dialect, or language conflicts exist, such as between speakers of white and black American English, Canadian and European French, Hebrew and Arabic in Israel, and urban and rural accents of British English. They are also seen in social and occupational contexts (e.g. affecting the way in which a jury judges the credibility of witnesses in court, p. 391), and in education (where teachers' evaluations of a pupil's capabilities can be more influenced by speech style than by written composition, artistic work, or personal appearance). Our impressions of a person's guilt, innocence, intelligence, or stupidity are, it seems, much affected by phonetic and linguistic factors. A more informed popular awareness of the dangers of vocal stereotyping is thus an important aim of this branch of sociopsychological research.

PSYCHOPATHOLOGY

Voice characteristics are also an important diagnostic feature of abnormal personalities. Patients suffering from schizophrenia, depression, and other such conditions often speak with voices that are monotonous, weak, hesitant, slow, and deviant in timbre. Abnormal intonation, loudness, rhythm, and timbre can also be heard in the voices of many autistic children. Some clinicians have maintained that psychopathological syndromes can be detected on the basis of the voice alone; but this seems exaggerated. Even experienced clinicians find it difficult to make predictions about some types of mental state solely from audio recordings.

PERSONALITY TRAITS AND VOICE STEREOTYPES

This graphic presentation of personality traits was devised by the British psychologist Hans Eysenck (1916–). The inner ring shows the four ancient Greek temperaments, based on the predominance of one of the four 'body fluids'. The outer ring represents the location of different traits, grouped on a statistical basis, and related to two principal dimensions: instability/stability and extraversion/introversion. But would it always follow that if someone *sounds* reliable (sober, etc.) then he/she *is* reliable (sober, etc.)?

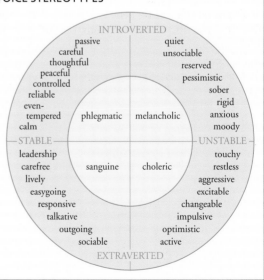

The most widely recognized features of linguistic identity are those that point to the geographical origins of the speakers – features of *regional dialect*, which prompt us to ask the question 'Where are they from?' But there are several levels of response to this question. We might have a single person in mind, yet all of the following answers would be correct 'America', 'The United States', 'East Coast', 'New York', 'Brooklyn'. People belong to regional communities of varying extent, and the dialect they speak changes its name as we 'place' them in relation to these communities.

Languages, as well as dialects, can convey geographical information about their speakers, but this information varies greatly, depending on the language of which we are thinking. The variation can be seen if we complete a test sentence using different language names: 'If they speak —, they must be from —.' If the first blank is filled by 'Swedish', the second blank will almost certainly be filled by 'Sweden'. But 'Portuguese' would not inevitably lead to 'Portugal': the second blank could be filled by 'Brazil', 'Angola', 'Mozambique', and several other countries. 'French' would give us the choice of about 40 countries, and 'English' well over 50. 'Dialect', by contrast with 'language', is a much more specific geographical term.

POPULAR NOTIONS OF DIALECT

It is sometimes thought that only a few people speak regional dialects. Many restrict the term to rural forms of speech – as when they say that 'dialects are dying out these days'. They have noticed that country dialects are not as widespread as they once were, but they have failed to notice that urban dialects are now on the increase (p. 32). Another view is to see dialects as substandard varieties of a language, spoken only by low-status groups – implicit in such comments as 'He speaks correct English, without a trace of dialect'. Comments of this kind fail to recognize that standard English is as much a dialect as any other variety – though a dialect of a rather special kind (p. 39). Or again, languages in isolated parts of the world, which may not have been written down, are sometimes referred to pejoratively as dialects, as when someone talks of a tribe speaking 'a primitive kind of dialect'. But this fails to recognize the true complexity and range of all the world's languages (§47).

In this encyclopedia, as is standard practice in linguistics, dialects are seen as applicable to all languages and all speakers. In this view, all languages are analysed into a range of dialects, which reflect the regional and social background of their speakers. The view maintains that everyone speaks a dialect – whether urban or rural, standard or non-standard, upper class or lower class. And no dialect is thought of as 'superior' to any other, in terms of linguistic structure – though several are considered prestigious from a social point of view.

WHERE ARE YOU FROM?

How easy is it to tell where someone is from? A few years ago, it would have been relatively straightforward for a specialist to work out from a sample of speech the features that identified someone's regional background. Some dialect experts have been known to run radio shows in which they were able to identify the general regional background of members of their audience with considerable success. But it is doubtful whether anyone has ever developed the abilities of Shaw's Henry Higgins: '*I* can place any man within six miles. I can place him within two miles in London. Sometimes within two streets' (*Pygmalion*, Act 1).

These days, dialect identification has become much more difficult, mainly because of increased social mobility. In many countries, it is becoming less common for people to live their whole lives in one place, and 'mixed' dialects are more the norm. Also, as towns and cities grow, once-distinct communities merge, with a consequent blurring of speech patterns. And nowadays, through radio and television, there is much more exposure to a wide range of dialects, which can influence the speech of listeners or viewers even within their own homes. A radio dialect show would be much less impressive today. On the other hand, meticulous analysis can bring results, and there have been several notable successes in the field of forensic linguistics (p. 69).

DIALECT OR ACCENT?

It is important to keep these terms apart, when discussing someone's linguistic origins. *Accent* refers only to distinctive pronunciation, whereas *dialect* refers to grammar and vocabulary as well. If we heard one person say *He done it* and another say *He did it*, we would refer to them as using different dialects, because a grammatical difference is involved. Similarly, the choice between *wee bairn* and *small child* is dialectal, because this is a contrast in vocabulary. But the difference between *bath* with a 'short a' [a] and *bath* with a 'long a' [ɑː] is to do with accent, as this is solely a matter of pronunciation (or phonology, §28).

Usually, speakers of different dialects have different accents; but speakers of the same dialect may have different accents too. The dialect known as 'standard English' is used throughout the world, but it is spoken in a vast range of regional accents.

DIALECT, IDIOLECT, AND LECT

Probably no two people are identical in the way they use language or react to the usage of others. Minor differences in phonology, grammar, and vocabulary are normal, so that everyone has, to a limited extent, a 'personal dialect'. It is often useful to talk about the linguistic system as found in a single speaker, and this is known as an *idiolect*. In fact, when we investigate a language, we have no alternative but to begin with the speech habits of individual speakers: idiolects are the first objects of study. Dialects can thus be seen as an abstraction, deriving from an analysis of a number of idiolects; and languages, in turn, are an abstraction deriving from a number of dialects.

It is also useful to have a term for *any* variety of a language which can be identified in a speech community – whether this be on personal, regional, social, occupational, or other grounds. The term *variety* is itself often used for this purpose; but in recent years, many sociolinguists (p. 418) have begun to use *lect* as a general term in this way.

LANGUAGE VS DIALECT

One of the most difficult theoretical issues in linguistics is how to draw a satisfactory distinction between language and dialect. The importance of this matter will be repeatedly referred to in Part IX, where we have to make judgments about the number of languages in the world and how they are best classified.

At first sight, there may appear to be no problem. If two people speak differently, then, it might be thought, there are really only two possibilities. Either they are not able to understand each other, in which case they can be said to speak different languages; or they do understand each other, in which case they must be speaking different dialects of the same language. This criterion of *mutual intelligibility* works much of the time; but, unfortunately, matters are not always so simple.

MUTUAL INTELLIGIBILITY

One common problem with this criterion is that dialects belonging to the same language are not always mutually intelligible in their spoken form. It can be very difficult for someone speaking a regional dialect in one part of Britain to understand some of the regional dialects of other areas; and the degree of intelligibility can be even worse when people attempt to communicate with English speakers from other countries. However, at least all of these speakers have one thing in common: they share a common written language. On this count, the varieties they speak could justly be called dialects of the same language.

A rather more serious problem arises in cases where there is a geographical *dialect continuum*. There is often a 'chain' of dialects spoken throughout an area. At any point in the chain, speakers of a dialect can understand the speakers of other dialects who live in adjacent areas to them; but they find it difficult to understand people who live further along the chain; and they may find the people who live furthest away completely unintelligible. The speakers of the dialects at the two ends of the chain will not understand each other; but they are nonetheless linked by a chain of mutual intelligibility.

This kind of situation is very common. An extensive continuum links all the dialects of the languages known as German, Dutch, and Flemish. Speakers in eastern Switzerland cannot understand speakers in eastern Belgium; but they are linked by a chain of mutually intelligible dialects throughout the Netherlands, Germany, and Austria. Other chains in Europe include the Scandinavian continuum, which links dialects of Norwegian, Swedish, and Danish; the West Romance continuum, which links rural dialects of Portuguese, Spanish, Catalan, French, and Italian; and the North Slavic continuum, which links Slovak, Czech, Ukrainian, Polish, and Russian.

The theoretical problem should be clear. At what point in the chain can we say that one language ends and the next begins? On what basis can we draw boundary lines between Portuguese, Spanish, French, and so on? We are used to thinking of these languages as quite different from each other, but this is only because we are usually exposed to their standard varieties, which are not mutually intelligible. At the local level, it is not possible to make a clear decision on linguistic grounds.

But decisions are of course made on other grounds. As one crosses a well-established national boundary, the variety of speech will change its name: 'Dutch' will become 'German', 'Spanish' will become 'Portuguese', 'Swedish' will become 'Norwegian'. It is important to appreciate that the reasons are political and historical, not linguistic (§47). Arguments over language names often reduce to arguments of a political nature, especially when there is a dispute over national boundaries. For example, in the South Slavic continuum, varieties spoken on the western side of the border between the Former Yugoslav Republic of Macedonia and Bulgaria are called dialects of Macedonian by the former country, but dialects of Bulgarian by the latter – reflecting a claim to the territory. However, because there is a dialect chain in the area, linguistic criteria will never be able to solve conflicts of this kind.

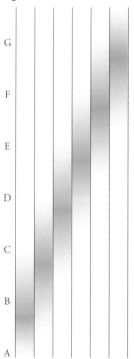

A schematic dialect continuum between dialects A and G. The possible degrees of mutual intelligibility are represented by different shading, from maximum (dark) to zero (light).

DIALECT CONTINUA IN EUROPE

DIALECTOLOGY

The systematic study of regional dialects is known variously as *dialectology*, *dialect geography*, or *linguistic geography*; but these terms are not exact equivalents. In particular, the latter terms suggest a much wider regional scope for the subject. Dialect specialists who spend their lives researching the local usage of a single Yorkshire village can hardly be called 'linguistic geographers', though they are certainly 'dialectologists'. By contrast, the 'geographer' designation would be quite appropriate for anyone involved in plotting the distribution of forms over a large area, such as Scotland, or the eastern United States.

There is another difference between these terms. Traditionally, dialectology has been the study of regional dialects, and for many people that is still its main focus. But in recent years, dialectologists have been paying more attention to social as well as geographical space, in order to explain the extent of language variation (§§9–10). Factors such as age, sex, social class, and ethnic group are now seen as critical, alongside factors of a purely regional kind.

But whatever the approach, the contemporary fascination with dialects seems no less than that shown by previous generations. Radio programmes on dialect variations are popular in several countries, and compilations of dialect data continue to be produced in the form of grammars, dictionaries, folk-lore collections, and guides to usage. Local dialect societies thrive in many parts of the world. Dialects continue to be seen as a major source of information about contemporary popular culture and its historical background; and dialect variation forms part of the study of change (§54).

Probably the most important application of dialectology these days is in education, where the development of dialect 'awareness' in children is widely recognized as a way of getting them to see the heterogeneity of contemporary society, and their place within it (§§44, 61). Teachers are often faced with a conflict between the child's spontaneous use of dialect forms and the need to instil a command of the standard language, especially in writing. The conflict can be resolved only by developing in children a sense of the relationships between the two kinds of language, so that the value of both can be better appreciated. There needs to be an awareness of the history, structure, and function of present-day dialects – and this is what dialectology can provide.

THE HISTORY OF REGIONAL DIALECTOLOGY

While there has been sporadic interest in regional dialects for centuries, the first large-scale systematic studies, in Germany and France, did not take place until the end of the 19th century. In 1876, Georg Wenker (1852–1911) began sending out questionnaires to all the school districts in the German Empire. It took him ten years to contact nearly 50,000 local teachers, who were asked to provide equivalents for 40 sentences in the local dialect. An enormous amount of data was received, and this led to the publication in 1881 of the first linguistic atlas, *Sprachatlas des Deutschen Reichs*. A larger series of works, based on Wenker's files, appeared between 1926 and 1956; but even today, much of the original material has not been published.

The postal questionnaire method enables a large amount of data to be accumulated in a relatively short time, but it has several limitations – chiefly that dialect pronunciations cannot be accurately recorded. The alternative, to send out trained field workers to observe and record the dialect forms, was first used in the linguistic survey of France, which began in 1896. The director, Jules Gilliéron (1854–1926), appointed Edmond Edmont (1849–1926) – a grocer with a very sharp ear for phonetic differences – to do the field work. For four years, Edmont went around France on a bicycle, conducting interviews with 700 informants using a specially devised questionnaire of nearly 2,000 items. The *Atlas linguistique de la France* was subsequently published in 13 volumes between 1902 and 1910. It stands as the most influential work in the history of dialectology.

In the first half of this century, major projects were initiated in many parts of Europe, such as Romania, Italy, Holland, Spain, and Denmark, and there have been several impressive publications. In due course the large-scale dialect surveys of the United States and England began (p. 30). A great deal of dialect work has also been undertaken in Japan and China, as well as in parts of Africa, Australia, Canada, and South America. In some countries, even, surveys leading to a 'second generation' of linguistic atlases have begun. Direct interviewing and postal questionnaires continue to be used today, as does the tradition of presenting the linguistic material in the form of maps; and in recent years, dialectology has benefited enormously from the development of techniques using tape recorders. The field is also now being influenced by the electronic revolution, with computers helping to 'crunch' the data provided by questionnaires, and making large databases of regional variants more available, accessible, and analysable – and even more visible, using computer graphic techniques.

However, nowadays there are fewer big regional dialect projects, and some of those that have begun may never be completed. This is mainly because of the large costs involved in collecting, analysing, and publishing dialect data; but it is also partly because of the new direction dialect studies have taken. Younger scholars are these days more likely to be attracted by the sociolinguistically inspired approaches that developed in the 1970s. with their focus on social factors, and on urban rather than on rural dialects (p. 32).

THE EARLIEST USE OF DIALECTOLOGY?

Then Gilead cut Ephraim off from the fords of the Jordan, and whenever an Ephraimite fugitive said 'Let me cross', the men of Gilead asked him, 'Are you an Ephraimite?'. If he answered 'No', they said, 'Then say "Shibboleth".' He would say 'Sibboleth', since he could not pronounce the word correctly. Thereupon they seized and slaughtered him by the fords of the Jordan.
(Judges XII, 4–6)

The Ephraimites were betrayed by their regional pronunciation. As a result of this story, *shibboleth*, which then meant 'ear of corn' or 'flowing stream', has in modern use come to mean 'distinguishing mark' or 'criterion'.

Jules Gillieron (1854–1926)

THE FARM

THE FARMSTEAD

Show an aerial photograph of a farmstead and surrounding fields @.

1   ... these? **Fields**
2   ... this? **Farmstead.**
3   ... this? **Farmyard.**
4   ... this? **Stackyard.**
     ... the various buildings?

     If necessary, ask the relevant question below.

5   ... the place where you keep pigs? **Pigsty.**–
     April 1953, *the animals that go* (*i. grunting*)
     replaced *pigs*.
6   ... the place where you keep hens? **Hen-
     house.**–April 1953, *the birds that lay eggs
     for you* replaced *hens*.
7   ... *the place where you keep pigeons?* **Dove-
     cote.**–April 1953, *the birds that go (i.
     cooing)* replaced *pigeons*.
8   ... the place where you keep cows? **Cow-
     house.**–April 1953, *the animals that
     give you milk* replaced *your cows*.
9   ... the yard in which cattle are kept,
     especially during the winter, for fattening,
     and for producing dung? **Straw-yard.**
     (Verify the kind of cattle and the purpose).
10   ... the small enclosed piece of pasture near
     the farmhouse, the place where you might
     put a cow or a pony that's none too well?
     Paddock.
11   What's the **barn** for and where is it?

COW-HOUSE

Q.   *What do you call the place where you keep
      your cows? – April 1953, the animals that
      give you milk* replaced *your cows.*

Rr.   BEEF-HOUSE (COW-)BYRE, COW-
      HOLE/HOUSE/HULL/SHADE/SHED,
      LATHE, MISTALL, SHIPPON

1 Nb 1 baɪɔʳ   2 baɪɔʳ [baɪɔʳmən¹ *byre-man*
      (= *cowman*) I.2.3]   3 ku:baɪɔʳ
      4–5 baɪɔʳ   6 baɪɔʳ   7 baɪɔʳ,
      °▫baɪɔʳz¹   8 baɪɔʳ   9 baɪə

2 Cu 1 baɪər   2 baɪər   3 baɪə, ku:əs
      4 baɪə,°▫baɪəz¹   5 ku:baɪɹ   6 baɪə,
      kᵊu:əs ["old name"]

3 Du 1 ku:baɪɔʳ, °ku:ʃɪəd³   2 bɛ̌ɪəʳ   3
      baɪər   4–5 baɪə   6 baɪə °▫baɪəz¹

4 We 1 baɪɹ, °baɪə¹   2–3 baɪə   4 ʃɷpm

5 La 1–3 ʃɷpm   4 ʃɪpn, °ʃɷpn¹
      5 ʃɪpn   6 ʃɪpm, ʃɷpm ["older"], °ʃɪpən¹
      III.11.3,°▫ʃɪpmz¹   7 ʃɪpn,
      °▫ʃɪpənz¹   8–9 ʃɪpn   10 ʃɪpən
      11 ʃɪppɷn   12 ʃɪpɷn, °ʃɷpɷn¹
      13 ʃɪpən, °ʃɪpɪn²   14 ʃɪpɷn

QUESTIONNAIRES

In a large dialect survey, there will be many infor-mants and several investiga-tors. One way of ensuring that the results of all the interviews will be compara-ble, while also saving a great deal of time, is through the use of questionnaires. On the other hand, unless the questions are particularly ingenious, the responses will lack the spontaneity of informal speech. Results thus have to be interpreted with caution.

Opposite is an extract from the questionnaire used in the English Dialect Survey (p. 30). The dots at the beginning of each line stand for 'What do you call ...', *i* = imitate. The second extract illustrates the depth of phonetic detail recorded by the field work-ers. Abbreviations after each number stand for the different northern counties of England.

PAUSY, *adj.* n.Lin.¹ [pō·zi.] Slightly intoxicated.
Slightly the worse for drink; said of persons who combine an amiable desire to impart information with an incapacity to call to mind all the necessary words. 'Drunk ! naw he was n't what you'd call drunk, nobbud he was pausy like.'
PAUT, *v.* and *sb.* Sc. Nhb. Dur. Lakel. Yks. Lan. Chs. Der. Not. Lin. Wor. Suf. Also written **pawt** Sc. Lakel.² Cum.¹⁴ n.Yks.² e.Yks.¹ m.Yks.¹ w.Yks. ne.Lan.¹ Der.¹ Not.¹³ n.Lin.¹ sw.Lin.¹; **pawte** w.Yks.; port w.Yks. Not.³; and in forms **paat** Cai.¹ Nhb.¹ Cum.¹⁴; **paout** se.Wor.¹; **pout** Sc. (JAM.) N.Cy.¹ s.Wor.¹; **powt** Sc. (JAM.) Bnff.¹ n.Cy Suf.¹ [pōt, pǫ·t, pāt.] 1. *v.* To poke or push with the hand or a stick; to stir up; to paw, handle, or finger things. Cf. **pote**.
Sc. To search with a rod or stick in water, or in a dark or confined place. To make a noise when searching or poking in water (JAM.). **n.Cy.** GROSE (1790). **Nhb.**¹ Divent paat on wi'd, or ye'll spoil'd. **Cum.** Children pawt when they make repeated attempts to get things with their hands (E.W.P.) **Cum.**⁴ A dog pawts at the door when it wants to get in, and children pawt when they make repeated attempts to get hold of things with their hands. **n.Yks.**¹; **n.Yks.**² Kneading with the fingers into a soft mass. **n.Lin.** SUTTON *Wds.* (1881); **n.Lin.**¹ I wish we hed n't noä cats, really, thaay're alus pawtin' at one, when one's gettin' one's meät. **sw.Lin.**¹ Some lasses are always pawting things about they've no business with. **s.Wor.** To beat down apples, PORSON *Quaint Wds.* (1875) 15.
Hence (1) **Pouting**, *vbl. sb.* the practice of spearing salmon ; also used *attrib.* ; (2) **Pout-net**, *sb.* a net fastened

An extract from the *English Dialect Dictionary*
Joseph Wright (1855–1930), published this dictionary in six volumes between 1898 and 1905; it contained 100,000 entries. Wright was largely self-taught, and did not learn to read until he was a teenager – a fact that may have been an advantage to him in his later studies, as his early awareness of dialect differences would not have been influenced by the forms of the standard written language.

FROM STRINE TO SCOUSE

The contrast between regional dialect and stan-dard English usage has been a source of humour the world over. In *Let Stalk Strine* (1965), Afferbeck Lauder (said to be Professor of Strine Studies at the University of Sinny) uses standard spellings to represent the popular impression of an Australian accent, with bizarre results:

Egg Nishner: A mechanical device for cooling and puri-fying the air of a room.
Jezz: Articles of furniture. As in: 'Set the tible, love, and get a coupler jezz'.
Money: The day following Sunny. (Sunny, Money, Chewsdy, Wensdy, Thursdy, Fridy, Sairdy.)
Scone: A meteorological term. As in: 'Scona rine'.

Sly Drool: An instrument used by engineers for dis-covering Kew brutes and for making other calculations.
Tiger: Imperative mood of the verb to take. As in: 'Tiger look at this, Reg...'
X. The twenty-fourth letter of the Strine alphabet; also plural of egg; also a tool for chopping wood.

Some of the colloquial pronunciations here are found in many dialects. For example, *Gissa* ('Please give me ...') is a feature of Strine, but it is also well known in Liverpool, as can be seen from the section on 'Forms of Address' in *Lern Yerself Scouse* (1966), by Frank Shaw, Fritz Spiegl, and Stan Kelly (whose standard English translations are given in parentheses):

Ullo dur! ('Greetings; I am pleased to make your acquaintance.')
Gisalite ('Could you oblige me with a match, please?')
Ay-ay ('I say!')
La ('I say, young man.')
Ere, tatty-head! ('I say, young woman!')

In the Appendix to this work, selected verses from *The Rubáiyat of Omár Khayyám* are translated into Scouse by Stan Kelly:

Gerrup dere La! De
  knocker-up sleeps light;
Dawn taps yer winder,
  ends anudder night;
And Lo! de dog-eared mog-
  gies from next-door
Tear up de jigger fer an
  early fight.

LINES ON MAPS

Once the speech of dialect informants has been collected, it is analysed, and the important features are marked on a map of the area in which the informants live. When several points on the map have been located, it is then possible to see whether there is a pattern in the way these features are used. The usual way of identifying dialect patterns is to draw lines around the places where the people use a linguistic feature in the same way. These boundary lines are known as *isoglosses*. For example, one famous isogloss runs across England, from the Severn to the Wash: it distinguishes northern speakers who pronounce a rounded *u* /ʊ/ in words like *cup* from southern speakers who keep the vowel open and unrounded, /ʌ/. A series of lexical isoglosses, identifying various words for *snack*, is illustrated on p. 30.

When isoglosses were first introduced (in 1892), it was expected that they would provide a clear method for identifying dialect areas. Because people from a particular part of a country 'speak in the same way', it was assumed that the isoglosses for many linguistic features would coincide, and form a neat 'bundle', demarcating one dialect from another. However, early dialectology studies soon discovered that the reality was very different. Isoglosses crisscrossed maps in all directions, and very few actually coincided. There seemed to be no clear dialect boundaries at all – a finding which made some scholars go so far as to argue that the whole idea of a dialect was meaningless.

In due course, however, supplementary notions were developed to make sense of the data. It was noted that, while isoglosses rarely coincided, they did often run in the same general direction. Some areas, called *focal areas*, were seen to be relatively homogeneous, containing few isoglosses. Where focal areas merged, there was a great deal of linguistic variation, with many isoglosses present: these became known as *transition areas*. Often, a feature might be left isolated, as a result of linguistic change affecting the areas around it: these 'islands' of more conservative usage were called *relic areas*.

Dialectologists have mixed feelings about isoglosses. There is often too much variability in the way a linguistic feature is used for the data to be easily summarized in a single isogloss. Also, the relative significance of different isoglosses remains to be interpreted. Some isoglosses mark distinctions that are considered to be more important than others (such as the contrast between short and long *a* in words like *bath* in British English, which has long been the focus of special comment). Isoglosses are an important visual guide, but they need to be supplemented by other criteria if they are to display, and not to obscure, the true complexity of regional variation.

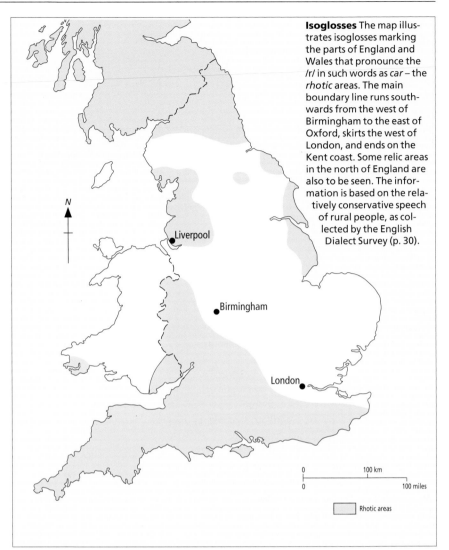

Isoglosses The map illustrates isoglosses marking the parts of England and Wales that pronounce the /r/ in such words as *car* – the *rhotic* areas. The main boundary line runs southwards from the west of Birmingham to the east of Oxford, skirts the west of London, and ends on the Kent coast. Some relic areas in the north of England are also to be seen. The information is based on the relatively conservative speech of rural people, as collected by the English Dialect Survey (p. 30).

0   100 km
0   100 miles

Rhotic areas

The main kinds of isogloss

Term	Separates	Examples
isolex	lexical items	*nunch* vs *nuncheon* (p. 30)
isomorph	morphological features	*dived* vs *dove*
isophone	phonological features	*put*/pʊt/ vs /pʌt/
isoseme	semantic features	*dinner* (mid-day meal) vs (evening meal)

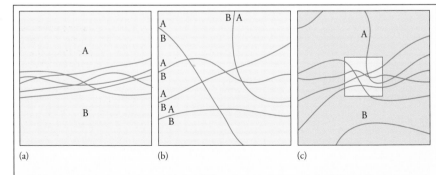

(a)

(b)

(c)

The expectation Isoglosses will form neat bundles, demarcating dialect A from dialect B.

The reality Isoglosses crisscross an area, with no clear boundary between A and B.

Focal and transitional On a larger scale, the isoglosses are seen to constitute a transitional area between the focal areas A and B.

THE RHENISH FAN

One of the best examples of the way isoglosses fail to group themselves into bundles is in northern Europe. A set of isoglosses runs east–west across Germany and Holland, separating Low German, in the north, from High German, in the south. They reflect the different ways in which these dialects have developed the voiceless plosive consonants of Indo-European (p. 330). In Low German, the sounds have remained plosives (/p, t, k/); but in High German, these have generally become fricatives. For example, 'village' is [dorp] in the north, [dorf] in the south; 'that' is [dat], as opposed to [das]; 'make' and 'I' are [makən] and [ik] respectively, rather than [maxən] and [iç].

The map shows the location of the isoglosses that distinguish these words. Through most of Germany, they are close together, displaying only minor variations; but where they meet the River Rhine, the isoglosses move in quite different directions, in a pattern that resembles the folds in a fan. It thus becomes impossible to make simple generalizations about dialect differences in this area. A speaker in a village near Cologne, for example, would say [iç] and [maxən], as in High German, but say [dorp] and [dat], as in Low German.

What accounts for the Rhenish fan? It has been suggested that several of the linguistic features could be explained with reference to certain facts of social history. For example, the area between the [dorp/dorf] and [dat/das] isoglosses was coextensive with the old diocese of Trier; the area immediately north was coextensive with the old diocese of Cologne. The linguistic innovations seem to have spread along the Rhine from southern Germany to the cities, and then 'fanned out' throughout the administrative areas these cities controlled. Rural speakers were naturally influenced most by the speech of their own capital cities, and political and linguistic boundaries gradually came to coincide. (After L. Bloomfield, 1933.)

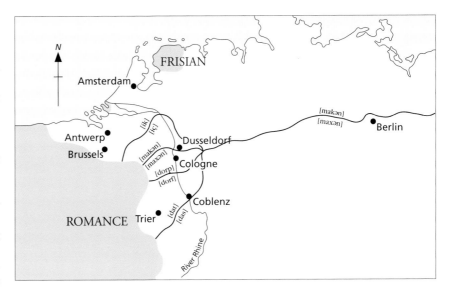

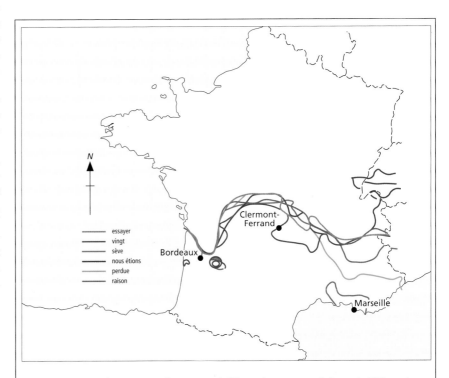

The two halves of France
One of the main findings of the *Atlas linguistique de la France* (p. 26) was the bundle of isoglosses that runs across France from east to west, dividing the country into two major dialect areas. The areas are traditionally known as *langue d'oïl* (in the north) and *langue d'oc* (in the south) – names based in the words for 'yes' current in these areas during the 13th century, when the division was first recognized. The map shows six items that are used differently on either side of an isogloss (J. K. Chambers & P. Trudgill, 1980, p. 111).

The distinction corresponds to several important social and cultural differences, some of which can still be observed today. For example, to the south of the isogloss bundle (roughly where the Provençal region begins), a biennial (as opposed to a triennial) method of crop rotation is traditionally used. A different legal system existed until the early 19th century, using a written code inspired by Roman traditions. And there is a major difference in architectural style, the roofs being generally flat, and not steeply pitched (as they are to the north of the bundle). Such clear correlations between language and cultural identity illustrate the way in which dialect studies form an important part of the study of social history.

THE LINGUISTIC ATLAS OF ENGLAND

Three of the maps from the English Dialect Survey, carried out by Harold Orton (1898–1975) and Eugene Dieth (1893–1956), are illustrated here. The field survey was undertaken between 1950 and 1961 in 313 localities throughout England. The localities were usually not more than 15 miles apart, and generally consisted of villages with a fairly stable population. The informants were natives of the locality, mainly male agricultural workers, with good mouths, teeth, and hearing, and over 60 years of age.

The principal method was a questionnaire that elicited information about phonological, lexical, morphological, and syntactic features. Tape recordings of informal conversation were also made. Questionnaire responses were transcribed using the International Phonetic Alphabet (p. 158). Over 1,300 questions were used, on such themes as farming, animals, housekeeping, weather, and social activities; and over 404,000 items of information were recorded.

Between 1962 and 1971 the basic material of the survey was published in an introduction and four separate volumes; in 1977 the *Linguistic Atlas of England* was published, containing an interpretation of a selection of the data. The maps below provide an example of the Survey's basic material for the item *snack* and two interpretive maps, based on this material. The first map is a display of all the responses obtained, which are listed in the top right-hand corner. The other maps pick out various trends in usage, and are a considerable simplification. (After H. Orton, S. Sanderson & J. Widdowson, 1978.)

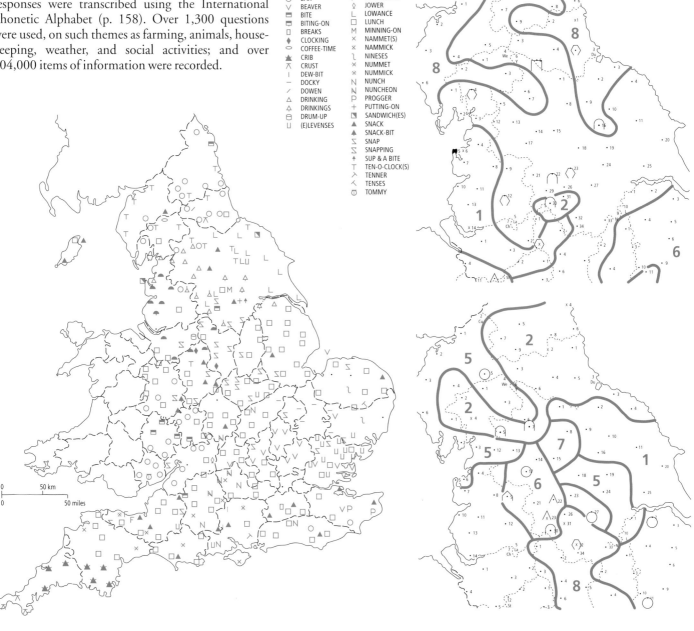

THE LINGUISTIC GEOGRAPHY OF WALES

One of the most recent dialect surveys was carried out in Wales in the 1960s under the direction of Alan R. Thomas (1935–) and published in 1973. It was based on 180 points of enquiry in the Welsh-speaking areas, the localities being selected on the basis of their position relative to the physical geography of the country and to the main communication routes.

The survey was based on a postal questionnaire, with questions using both Welsh and English. There were over 500 questions, which dealt largely with domestic, rural, and farming vocabulary; about 130,000 responses were received. The questionnaire was sent to a person of educated background, who supervised its completion by local informants, using spelling that reflected regional pronunciation. Informants were of the older generation, with little formal education, and had spent no prolonged periods away from their native area.

The main part of the atlas discusses the distribution of regional words for around 400 items, on the basis of which the main Welsh speech areas are drawn up. The illustration (right) shows the distribution of Welsh words for *pane of glass*, an item in which two distinct patterns of use can be clearly seen: *paen* and its variants in the north-east and the midlands, *cwalar* and its variants in most other places. (After A. R. Thomas, 1973.)

THE LINGUISTIC ATLAS OF THE UNITED STATES

This survey began in 1931, under the direction of Hans Kurath (1891–1992), as part of an ambitious programme to establish a linguistic atlas of the United States and Canada. The region was divided into survey areas, and the first atlas to appear, dealing with New England, was published in 1939–43. The project is ongoing, with informant interviews complete in many areas, but the amount of work involved means that publication is a slow and irregular process.

The illustration (right) is taken from Kurath's *Word Geography of the Eastern United States* (1949) – a survey area that included the coastal Atlantic states from Maine to Georgia, Pennsylvania, West Virginia, and eastern Ohio. Dialectologists went to nearly every county in these states and interviewed two people in each – one older-generation and unschooled, the other a member of the middle class with some degree of education. In the larger cities, people with a more cultured background were also interviewed. All were natives of their area, and had not moved much outside it. Interviewers spent from 10 to 15 hours with each informant, dealing with over 1,000 points of usage. More than 1,200 people were interviewed, and information was obtained about the diffusion of around 400 regional expressions for domestic and agricultural items.

The map records the distribution of words for *dragonfly*.

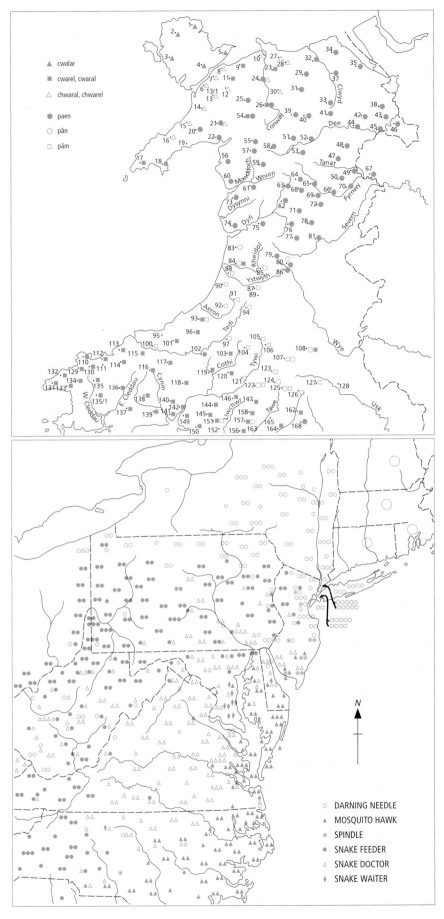

MODERN DIALECT STUDIES

Traditional dialectology studied geographical variation, generally using elderly, untravelled, and uneducated speakers from rural areas. Modern dialectology has moved in other directions.

Social factors now provide the focus of investigation. Speech variation can be partly understood with reference to regional location and movement, but social background is felt to be an equally if not more important factor in explaining linguistic diversity and change. Modern dialectologists therefore take account of socio-economic status, using such indicators as occupation, income, or education, alongside age and sex. Ideally informants are found in all social groups, and the traditional focus on the language of older people of working-class backgrounds has been replaced by the study of speakers of all ages and from all walks of life (§10).

Dialect studies have moved from the country to the city. The description of rural dialects led to fascinating results, but only a small proportion of a country's population was represented in such studies. In many countries, over 80% of the population live in towns and cities, and their speech patterns need to be described too – especially as linguistic change so often begins when people from the country imitate those from urban areas. This approach, accordingly, is known as *urban dialectology.*

Informants are now randomly selected. In the older studies, small numbers of speakers were carefully chosen to represent what were thought of as 'pure' forms of dialect. Today, larger numbers of people are chosen from the whole population of a city – perhaps using the electoral register or a telephone directory. Also, the earlier approach generally asked for one-word responses to a range of carefully chosen questions. This produced useful data, but these speech patterns were unlikely to have been typical. When people have their attention drawn to the way they speak, they usually adopt a more careful and unnatural style. Attempts are therefore now made to elicit speech that is more spontaneous in character by engaging informants in topics of conversation that they find interesting or emotionally involving (p. 334). The questionnaire has been largely replaced by the tape recorder.

LINGUISTIC VARIABLES

Traditional dialectology studied the fact that different people do not speak in the same way. Contemporary dialectology adds to this study the fact that the same person does not speak in the same way all the time. Individuals vary in their pronunciation, grammar, and vocabulary. Is there a reason for this variation, or is it random – 'free' variation, as it is often called? The current belief is that most of the variation is systematic, the result of the interplay between linguistic and social factors.

In the 1970s, the notion of the *linguistic variable* was developed, as a means of describing this variation. A linguistic variable is a unit with at least two variant forms, the choice of which depends on other factors, such as sex, age, social status, and situation. For example, in New York City, speakers sometimes pronounce /r/ in words like *car* and sometimes they do not. This unit can thus be seen as a variable, (r), with two variant forms, /r/ and zero. (It is usual to transcribe linguistic variables in parentheses.) It is then possible to calculate the extent to which individual speakers, or groups of speakers, use /r/, and to determine whether there is a correlation between their preferences and their backgrounds. Several interesting correlations have in fact been found (see also p. 334).

DROPPING THE /h/

In British English, the accent which carries most prestige (p. 39) pronounces /h/ at the beginnings of words such as *head*. But in most other accents of England and Wales, it is common to omit /h/ in this position. Regions do not pronounce or omit /h/ with total consistency, however, as can be seen from the results of two studies of this variable carried out in Norwich and Bradford.

The speakers were grouped into five social classes, based on such factors as their occupation, income, and education. The proportion of /h/-dropping was calculated, with the following results:

Class	Bradford	Norwich
Middle middle (MMC)	12%	6%
Lower middle (LMC)	28%	14%
Upper working (UWC)	67%	40%
Middle working (MWC)	89%	60%
Lower working (LWC)	93%	60%

The correlation is clear. In both areas, there is more /h/-dropping as one moves down the social scale. Moreover, the proportion is always greater in Bradford, suggesting that the phenomenon has been longer established in that area. (After J. K. Chambers & P. Trudgill, 1980.)

READING ALOUD IN NORWICH

People of different social levels were asked to read aloud a list of isolated words (A) and a piece of continuous text (B), and their pronunciations when reading were compared with their formal (C) and casual (D) speech.

The table shows whether the variable (ng) in such words as *walking* was pronounced /ŋ/ or /n/. (0 = no use of /n/; 100 = 100% use of /n/.)

Class	A	B	C	D
MMC	0	0	3	28
LMC	0	10	15	42
UWC	5	15	74	87
MWC	23	44	88	95
LWC	29	66	98	100

The consistency with which speakers increase their use of /n/ as their language becomes more spontaneous and casual is reflected at every social level. (After P. Trudgill, 1974.)

/l/ -DROPPING IN MONTREAL

The consonant /l/ is often dropped in the pronunciation of *il* ('he, it'), *elle* ('she, it'), *ils* ('they'), *la* ('her, it, the'), and *les* ('the, them'). The prestige forms retain the /l/. When usage is analysed by sex of speaker, a clear pattern emerges. (The numbers represent the percentage of /l/-dropping.)

	Male	Female
il (impersonal)	99	97
ils	94	90
il (personal)	94	84
elle	67	59
les (pronoun)	53	41
la (article)	34	25
la (pronoun)	31	23
les (article)	25	15

Women are much more likely to use the higher-prestige variant than men – a pattern of differentiation that has often been found in studies of urban dialectology. (After G. Sankoff & H. Cedergren, 1971.)

LINGUISTIC AREAS

Geographical identity can sometimes be established within a broader context than that provided by rural or urban dialectology. Certain features of speech can identify someone as coming from a particular part of the world, but the area involved may extend over several countries, languages, or even language families (§50). The study of 'areal features' of this kind is sometimes referred to as *areal linguistics*.

Features of pronunciation are often shared by adjacent, but historically-unrelated languages. In the indigenous languages of southern Africa (p. 317), the use of click sounds in speech identifies speakers of the Khoisan languages as well as of local Bantu languages, such as Zulu and Xhosa. In the Indian sub-continent (p. 310), languages that belong to different families (such as Indo-European and Dravidian) have several important phonological features in common – the use of retroflex consonants (p. 157) is particularly widespread, for example. In Europe the distribution of the affricate [tʃ] is interesting: it is found in many of the languages on the periphery of the area, such as Lapp, Romanian, Hungarian, Spanish, Galician, Basque, Italian, Gaelic, English, and the Slavic languages. The languages within this periphery, such as Danish, German, and French, do not use it.

Grammatical features can also cross linguistic and national boundaries. The use of particles to mark different semantic classes of nouns (§16) can be found throughout South-east Asia. In Europe, the Balkans constitutes a particularly well-defined linguistic area. For example, Albanian, Romanian, Bulgarian, and Macedonian all place the definite article *after* the noun, as in Romanian *lup* ('wolf') and *lupul* ('the wolf'), whereas historically-related languages outside of the Balkans area (such as Italian) do not.

How do areal features develop? In some areas, dialect chains (p. 25) have probably helped to diffuse a linguistic feature throughout an area. Concentrations of bilingual speakers along lines of communication would also play a part, and political factors will have exercised their influence. Sometimes, the progress of an areal feature can be traced – an example being the uvular pronunciation of /r/. Originally, speakers of European languages pronounced /r/ with the front of their tongue; but, in the 17th century, Parisians began to use a uvular variant. The variant caught on, spreading first throughout most of France, then to parts of Italy, Switzerland, Luxembourg, Belgium, Holland, Germany, Denmark, and (by the end of the 19th century) to southern Norway and Sweden. Spain, Austria, England, and other countries were not affected. The historical reasons for this complex state of affairs are little understood, and require investigation on several fronts. In such cases, the facts of dialectology, social history, and political history merge.

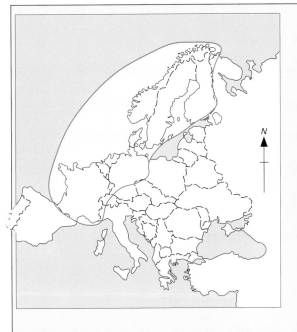

Front-rounded vowels
These vowels, such as in German *müde* ('tired') or French *soeur* ('sister'), are found along an axis which runs diagonally across northern Europe. They are heard in French, Dutch, German, Danish, Norwegian, Swedish, and Finnish. The feature cannot be explained on historical grounds: German and English are closely related, but the latter does not have front-rounded vowels; nor does Spanish, which is closely related to French. The main factor seems to be geographical proximity – as further illustrated by the way in which many south German dialects lack these vowels, whereas they are found in north-west Italy.
(J. K. Chambers & P. Trudgill, 1980, p. 185.)

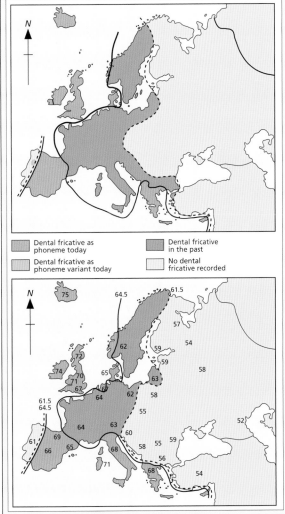

Dental fricative as phoneme today

Dental fricative as phoneme variant today

Dental fricative in the past

No dental fricative recorded

A genetic explanation?
The distinctive European distribution of such sounds as front-rounded vowels, affricates, and dental fricatives has been studied from a genetic point of view. The geneticist C. D. Darlington (1903–) proposed in the 1940s that the genetic composition of a community would partly determine its preferences for types of sound. The maps show the distribution of dental fricatives in western Europe (above, left), and the frequency with which the O blood-group gene is distributed in the population (below, left). There seems to be an intriguing correlation: in populations where fewer than 60% have the gene, there is no history of these sounds; and in those where more than 65% have the gene, the sounds are well represented. Unfortunately, proposals of this kind have not been followed up, and remain only suggestive. There are also exceptions (e.g. /θ/ is used in Galician, in NW Spain). Social explanations of such distributions are currently felt to be far more likely. (After L. F. Brosnahan, 1961.)

9 · ETHNIC AND NATIONAL IDENTITY

Nowhere does the issue of personal linguistic identity emerge more strongly than in relation to questions of ethnicity and nationhood. Ethnic identity is allegiance to a group with which one has ancestral links. It is a general notion, which applies to everyone, and not just to those who practise a traditional rural culture (a current usage of the term 'ethnic'). However, questions of ethnolinguistic identity in fact arise most often in relation to the demands and needs of those who are in an ethnic minority within a community, such as the many groups of immigrants, exiles, and foreign workers in Europe and the USA, or the tribal divisions that characterize several African countries.

Questions of ethnicity are closely related to those of national identity. Once a group becomes aware of its ethnic identity, it will wish to preserve and strengthen its status, and this often takes the form of a desire for political recognition, usually self-government. Political commentators have stressed the subjective element in the idea of a 'nation' – the difficulty of defining the psychological bond that motivates a nationalistic movement, or predicting which elements will contribute most to a group's sense of identity. Religious practices, long standing institutions, and traditional customs are all important in this respect; but perhaps the most widely encountered symbol of emerging nationhood is language. In the 18th and 19th centuries, in particular, linguistic nationalism was a dominant European movement, with language seen as the primary outward sign of a group's identity (§§10, 61). Today, a comparable concern can be observed in many areas of the world, as part of separatist political demands.

It is important to recognize the extent to which national diversity can give rise to linguistic issues. Political entities that comprise a homogeneous national group are quite rare. A study of the 132 states existing in 1971 found that only 12 were true nation-states; 50 contained a major ethnic group comprising more than three-quarters of the population; and in 39 states, the largest ethnic group comprised less than half the population (W. Connor, 1978). National and state loyalties thus rarely coincide, and when different languages are formally associated with these concepts, the probability of conflict is real.

Linguistic conflicts due to divided ethnic and national loyalties are often bitter and violent. In recent years, there have been major incidents in several countries, such as India (p. 310), Spain, Canada (p. 369), Belgium, Corsica, the USA, South Africa, and the Celtic-speaking areas (p. 305). The reasons for conflict vary greatly: in some cases, the use of a language is declining, and the reaction is a desperate attempt to keep it, and the community it represents, alive; in others, a minority group may be rapidly growing in numbers, so that its language begins to compete with the established languages of the country for educational, media, and other resources; in still others, the number of speakers may be stable, but there has been an awakening (or reawakening) of cultural identity, with a subsequent demand for recognition and (usually) territorial independence. These situations are discussed further in §61.

Why should language be such a significant index of ethnic or nationalistic movements? One reason is undoubtedly that it is such a widespread and evident feature of community life. To choose one language over another provides an immediate and universally recognized badge of identity. Another reason is that language provides a particularly clear link with the past – often the only detailed link, in the form of literature. This link exists even after ability in the language has been lost; for example, many present-day Italian-Americans and -Australians know very little Italian, but they still see Italian as a symbol of their ethnic identity. There is also a tendency for language to act as a natural barrier between cultural groups, promoting conflict rather than cooperation – as has often been seen in political meetings between opposed groups, when the question of which language to use in the discussion has become a major procedural decision. In bilingual communities, or areas where there is a recognized lingua franca, this factor is less important; but even here, language can focus the sense of political grievance in a clearer way than any other factor. There is no more awesome testimonial to the power of language than the fact that there have been so many people ready to die, if their demands for linguistic recognition were not met (p. 310).

Religious identity Perhaps the clearest case of a language fulfilling the need to define a national identity in modern times is Hebrew. When the state of Israel was established in 1948, there was an urgent need to unify its linguistically heterogeneous population. Classical Hebrew was the obvious candidate, in view of its ancient history and continued use as the religious language of Judaism (and even as a secular language for some purposes among eastern European Jews). The complex stages that led to the successful revival of Hebrew provide a particularly clear example of the nature and procedures of language planning (§61).

The picture shows a fragment of one of the Dead Sea Scrolls.

BASQUE

The way language can become a symbol of national identity is very clearly seen in the history of Basque (*Euskera*), and the attitude towards it of the Spanish government under Franco, from 1937 until the mid-1950s. The teaching of the language in schools was forbidden, as was its use in the media, church ceremonies, and all public places. Books in the language were publicly burnt. Basque names were no longer allowed in baptism, and all names in the language on official documents were translated into Spanish. Inscriptions on public buildings and tombstones were removed.

By the early 1960s, official policy had changed. Basque came to be permitted in church services, and then in church schools and broadcasts. In 1968, a government decree authorized the teaching of regional languages in Spain. By 1979, the Ministry of Education had accepted responsibility for Basque teaching programmes at all levels of education. In March 1980, the first Basque Parliament was elected, with Euskera recognized as an official language along with Spanish in the Basque provinces. Current discontent, as a consequence, is focused more on the region's future socioeconomic development, associated with persistent demands for political autonomy.

ETHNIC VARIETIES

Varieties of language can also signal ethnic identity. In fact, probably the most distinctive feature of ethnicity in immigrant groups is not their mother tongue (which may rarely be heard outside the home), but the foreign accent and dialect that characterizes their use of the majority language. In the course of time, many of these features have become established, resulting in new varieties of the majority language. Well-known cases include the range of English accents and dialects associated with speakers from the Indian sub-continent, from the West Indies, or from Puerto Rico. A non-regional example would be people with a Jewish background, whose speech has had a distinctive influence on many European languages.

BLACK ENGLISH VERNACULAR

One of the clearest examples of ethnic linguistic variety is provided by the contrast between the speech of black and white Americans. There is no simple correlation between colour and language, because there is considerable linguistic variation within both racial groups, and it is perfectly possible for black speakers to 'sound' white, and vice versa, depending on educational, social, and regional factors (p. 18). The term 'Black English' has been criticized, therefore, because of its suggestion that all blacks use the same variety, and has been replaced in academic study by 'Black English Vernacular' (BEV), or 'African-American English Vernacular', referring to the speech of the group most often studied in this context – the non-standard English spoken by lower-class African-Americans in urban communities.

Some features of BEV are given below. It is not clear just how widespread these features are amongst the black community; nor is it obvious where they come from. In one view, all BEV features can be found in white English dialects (especially those of the southern USA), suggesting that black English historically derived from white. The association with blacks is then explained as a result of their emigration to the northern cities, where these features were perceived as a distinctive marker of ethnic, as opposed to regional, identity. With the development of urban ghettos, the contrast became more marked over time. The alternative view argues that the origins of BEV lie in the use of a creole English (p. 338) by the first blacks in America. This language, originally very different from English as a result of its African linguistic background, has been progressively influenced by white English so that it now retains only a few creole features.

It is often difficult to obtain an objective discussion and evaluation of the linguistic evidence because of the existence of strong emotions around the subject, and the colour prejudice which has promoted the view that black English is necessarily inferior to white – a view that has no linguistic validity (§2). During the early 1970s, there were fierce arguments surrounding two viewpoints. Some argued that BEV was nothing more than a restricted code (p. 40), the result of verbal deprivation. Others, that the whole thing was a myth devised by white liberals, or an attempt to further discredit blacks. But in the late 1970s, these arguments were largely resolved – at an academic level, at least. Most contemporary linguists who have studied this topic accept a version of the creole hypothesis, because of the striking phonological and grammatical similarities between BEV and other creoles, such as those of the West Indies; but they allow for the probability that some features of BEV may have arisen partly or wholly as the result of white dialects.

There is a continuing need to disseminate the facts about the relationship between standard English and non-standard varieties, such as BEV, because the principle of mutual recognition and respect is constantly being challenged. In particular one has to anticipate the severe linguistic disadvantage that affects children from these dialect backgrounds when they go to school, where the medium of instruction and criterion of successful performance is standard English. These days there is an increasing understanding of the educational issues (§44); but an enlightened approach to the problem is by no means universal.

Some grammatical features of BEV

- No final *s* in the third-person singular present tense, e.g. *he walk, she go.*
- No use of forms of the verb *be* in the present tense, when it is used as a *copula*, or 'linking' verb, within a sentence, e.g. *They real fine, If you interested.*
- The use of the verb *be* to mark habitual meaning, but without changing its grammatical form ('invariant *be*'), e.g. *Sometimes they be walking round here.*
- Use of *been* to express a meaning of past activity with current relevance, e.g. *I been known your name.*
- Use of *be done* in the sense of 'will have', e.g. *We be done washed all those cars soon.*
- Use of *it* to express 'existential' meaning (cf. standard English *there*), e.g. *It's a boy in my class name Mike.*
- Use of double negatives involving the auxiliary verb at the beginning of a sentence, e.g. *Won't nobody do nothing about that.*

THE ANN ARBOR TRIAL

In 1977, an important case was brought by the children of the Martin Luther King Elementary School in Ann Arbor, Michigan, against the Ann Arbor School District Board. The racial balance of children attending the school at the time was 80% white, 13% black, and 7% Asian and Latino. Some of the black children, who came from a local low-income housing area, were found to be doing extremely badly in the school.

The mothers of these children believed that this situation was due to the school's failure to take into account the children's racial and sociocultural background. It was argued that there was a 'linguistic barrier', in the form of BEV, which impeded their academic performance, and that this barrier prevented the children having the equal educational opportunity that was their right under Title 20 of the US Code. Alternative educational programmes should have been provided to cater for their unique linguistic needs.

The case thus depended on whether BEV was so different from standard English as to constitute a barrier. Other considerations, of a cultural and economic kind, were judged irrelevant. Recordings were played in court of the children's spontaneous speech, which was shown to be similar to the BEV used by black children elsewhere; and a team of linguistics experts testified to the extent of the language differences, and to the creole history of BEV, which indicated that these differences were the result of racial segregation.

The plaintiffs won their case, and the School Board was directed to take steps to help the teachers identify children speaking BEV, and to use that knowledge in teaching the children to read Standard English. Since then, several other school districts have developed programmes, influenced by this decision. The Ann Arbor judgment can therefore be seen as a landmark in the slow process towards the public recognition of ethnic linguistic identity. (After W. Labov, 1982.)

GASTARBEITER

There are now over 24 million migrant workers (often called *Gastarbeiter*, 'guest workers') and their dependants in north-west Europe. They come from several countries, such as Turkey, Greece, Italy, Japan, the new Balkan states, and the Arabic-speaking countries. The demands of their new life require a level of adaptation that transcends language frontiers, and these workers often do not make an issue of their linguistic identity. On the other hand, their communication skills are usually limited, and the social and educational problems of the receiving country are considerable.

In the early 1990s, for example there were over 750,000 foreign pupils in German schools, and about 1 million in French schools. In 1995, minority languages being taught in French schools included German, English, Spanish, Italian, Portuguese, Arabic, Hebrew, Russian, Japanese, Dutch, Chinese, and Turkish. Even in a small country, significant minority language problems exist: in Denmark, for example, migrants from the Balkan States, Turkey, and the Nordic countries have to be catered for; in Luxemburg, there are many Italians and Portuguese. In Britain, there are around 100 minority languages, about a quarter of which are taught in schools to over half a million pupils.

The situation is likely to become yet more complex in Europe with increasing international mobility within the European Union, where member-states are still investigating solutions to the problem of language teaching and learning (§62). But at least the problem is now formally recognized. In 1977, the Council of the European Economic Community issued a directive on the education of children of migrant workers in Europe. The directive applied only to member-states, but the Council resolved to extend the measures to include all immigrant children within the Community (over 1.5 million). The aim of the exercise was to adapt school structures and curricula to the specific educational needs of these children without losing sight of their cultural and linguistic identity (see further, p. 371).

THE ETHNICITY BOOM

Between the mid-1960s and the mid-1970s, western Europe and North America experienced an 'ethnicity boom'. Considerable progress was made in integrating minority indigenous or immigrant groups within their host communities, and there was a widespread raising of consciousness about ethnicity issues. This was especially noticeable in the USA, where 1970 census data showed that 17% of the American population (over 33 million) claimed a mother tongue other than English – the largest claims relating to Spanish, German, Italian, French, Polish, and Yiddish. This was a dramatic increase of 71% compared with 1960 (though the total population increased by only 13% during that decade) and a marked reversal of the decline seen in the period 1940–60.

However, during the 1970s a further change took place. There was still an overall increase in the number of people claiming a mother tongue other than English, but this increase was largely due to Spanish. For many other languages, especially German, Yiddish, and the Scandinavian languages, there was a notable decline. Evidently, large numbers of the younger generation, from mainly North European backgrounds, were ceasing to claim these languages as their mother tongue. On the other hand, the claims increased for some South European languages (e.g. Greek and Portuguese, as well as Spanish) and for most Asian languages. (After J. A. Fishman, 1984.) In the 1990 census, the proportion of the US population claiming to speak a language other than English at home has declined somewhat (14%, or 31,845,000). However, the trends for particular languages are the same, with Spanish accounting for over half this total (over 17 millions), and only French, German, Italian, and Chinese achieving more than 1 million each).

WHY THE CHANGE?

It is perhaps too early for these changes to be given a social interpretation. One analysis has drawn attention to the contrast between the (decreasing) languages of white North and Central European Christendom, which were among the earliest settlers, and the (increasing) non-European languages associated with largely eastern religious groups, whose arrival in the USA is more recent. The former have now become a part of the American mainstream, it is argued, whereas the latter have still to find their identity within that culture. Because they are less accepted, they are more aware of the importance of maintaining traditional linguistic ties.

These trends can be further seen in the 1990 census results, where all the Scandinavian and S Slavic languages have fallen to below 100,000; French, German, Italian, Polish, Yiddish, Hungarian, and Dutch are down by at least a third; Arabic, Armenian, and Hebrew are up by a corresponding proportion; and the SE Asian languages are making their presence increasingly felt: Korean, Vietnamese, Hindi, Thai, Persian, Mon-Khmer, and Gujarati are now over 100,000 speakers, and there have been particularly marked increases in the numbers using Chinese and Tagalog.

MOTHER-TONGUE CLAIMING

The first line, after each language, shows the number of people who claimed this language as a mother tongue in the USA in 1970, with an estimate of the percentage increase (+) or decrease (–) in 1979 in parentheses (after J. A. Fishman, 1984). The second line shows the 1990 census total for foreign languages used at home; the increase or decrease since 1970 is also given in parentheses. Only languages which have or had over 100,000 speakers are listed, and all totals have been rounded to the nearest thousand.

Language	1970 / 1990		Language	1970 / 1990		Language	1970 / 1990	
English	160,717,000	(+6%)	Italian	4,144,000	(+5%)	Japanese	409,000	(+30%)
	198,601,000	(+24%)		1,309,000	(–68%)		428,000	(+5%)
Spanish	7,824,000	(+46%)	French	2,598,000	(+7%)	Portuguese	365,000	(+30%)
	17,339,000	(+122%)		1,702,000	(–35%)		430,000	(+18%)
German	6,093,000	(–10%)	Polish	2,438,000	(+5%)	Chinese	345,000	(+87%)
	1,547,000	(–75%)		723,000	(–70%)		1,249,000	(+262%)
			Yiddish	1,594,000	(–24%)	Russian	335,000	(+17%)
				213,000	(–86%)		242,000	(–28%)
			Swedish	626.000	(–11%)	Lithuanian	293,000	(+6%)
				1990: below 100,000			*1990: below 100,000*	
			Norwegian	613,000	(–2%)	Ukrainian	249,000	(+6%)
				1990: below 100,000			*1990: below 100,000*	
			Slovak	510,000	(+17%)	Serbo-Croatian	239,000	(+17%)
				1990: below 100,000			*1990: below 100,000*	
			Greek	459,000	(+25%)	Tagalog	218,000	(+75%)
				388,000	(–15%)		843,000	(+287%)
			Czech	453,000	(+15%)	Finnish	214,000	(–10%)
				1990: below 100,000			*1990: below 100,000*	
			Hungarian	447,000	(+17%)	Danish	194,000	(–10%)
				148,000	(–67%)		*1990: below 100,000*	
			Dutch	413,000	(–6%)	Arabic	194,000	(+17%)
				143,000	(–65%)		355,000	(+83%)

Language	1970 / 1990	
Hebrew	102,000	(+500%)
	144,000	(+41%)
Armenian	100,000	(+17%)
	150,000	(+50%)
Korean	*1970: below 100,000*	
	626,000	
Vietnamese	*1970: below 100,000*	
	507,000	
Hindi	*1970: below 100,000*	
	331,000	
Thai	*1970: below 100,000*	
	206,000	
Persian	*1970: below 100,000*	
	202,000	
French Creole	*1970: below 100,000*	
	188,000	
Navaho	*1970: below 100,000*	
	149,000	
Mon-Khmer	*1970: below 100,000*	
	127,000	
Gujarati	*1970: below 100,000*	
	102,000	

MINORITY LANGUAGES IN EUROPE

1. Britain The dramatic increase in immigrant numbers in the 1960s has resulted in over 100 languages being used in Britain by ethnic minority communities. The most widely spoken immigrant languages appear to be Panjabi, Bengali, Urdu, Gujarati, German, Polish, Italian, Greek, Spanish, and Cantonese. For the situation of the Celtic languages, see p. 305.

2. France There are several minority languages indigenous to France – Basque, Breton, (p. 304), Catalan, Corsican, Alsatian, Flemish, and Occitan. In a 1978 survey, three-quarters of the population wished to retain this diversity, but only 35% actually understood or spoke one of these languages. There are also many immigrant languages.

3. Luxembourg Letzebuergesch, related to German, is spoken as a mother tongue, and it is taught in schools, along with French and Standard German. It retains a strong popular appeal as a symbol of national identity.

4. Spain The history of Catalan, centred on the Barcelona area, is similar to Basque (p. 34), with an early history of repression, and the recent acquisition of a degree of autonomy. In the north-west corner of the country, Galician, closely related to Portuguese, provides a link with the old Kingdom of Galicia.

5. Switzerland German is spoken by nearly 70% of the Swiss population, French by around 19%, and Italian by 10% (most of the latter living in the canton of Ticino). This leaves Romansch, spoken by fewer than 50,000 in the canton of the Grisons (Graubünden). The language is rapidly declining, under the influence of German, though it continues to be the early medium of education in the region, and there has been a recent attempt at cultural revival. The Romansch League looks after all conservation measures relating to the language.

6. Malta Maltese is the national language of Malta, but English also has official status, and Arabic and Italian are widely known. Since receiving official status (1934), its role in written contexts has increased, and the island's television channel broadcasts in Maltese. Its status as a symbol of Maltese identity is widespread. (See further, p.318.)

7. Belgium A linguistic and cultural boundary runs across Belgium. In the north and west are the Flemings, descendants of the Franks, who speak dialects of Dutch (known as Flemish, or Vlaams). In the south and east are the Walloons, descendants of the Romano-Celts, who speak dialects of French. There is also a small German-speaking area in the east. The capital, Brussels, is officially bilingual, though predominantly French.

Early Belgian history saw French as the dominant language, and this situation continued until the 1930s, when official status was given to Flemish. Since then, linguistic issues have come to dominate Belgian politics, as efforts were made to establish language frontiers, and to provide satisfactory political representation and educational resources. In 1968 serious rioting over plans to expand the French-speaking section of the University of Louvain (Leuven) brought down the government. The four linguistic areas have now been officially recognized, with each responsible for its own affairs; but the complex social situation is by no means resolved, and several further governments have fallen as a result of linguistic policies.

8. Netherlands Frisian is accepted as an official language in the Netherlands, and it has its own academy. It is used in schools and courts, especially in the Friesland area; but generally its use is diminishing, under the influence of Dutch. The minority population consists mainly of over a million Surinamese, Indonesians, Moluccans, and Frisians – with a sizeable *Gastarbeiter* group.

9. Germany In North Frisia, Low and High German are used, alongside Danish, Jutish, and Frisian – the latter in several divergent dialects (p. 367). There are both German and Danish Frisians, but the most active group is oriented towards Denmark, with the result that there is local German concern about future separatist developments. Sorbian, a Slavic language, is

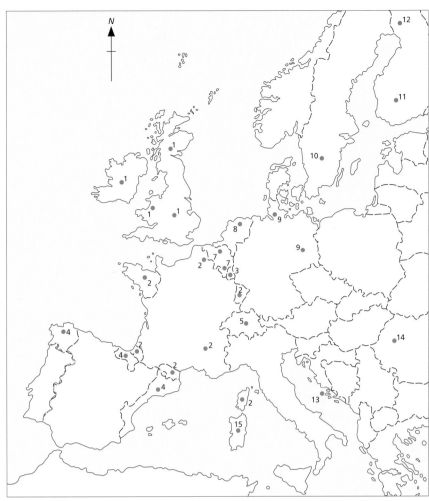

spoken SE of Berlin. There is also a large *Gastarbeiter* population.

10. Sweden Until the 1930s, Sweden was ethnically homogeneous; but following the Second World War, there was a large influx of refugees, mainly from Finland, but also from Italy, Hungary, Austria, West Germany, Greece, and Yugoslavia. Immigration has been controlled since 1967, but there are still around a million people from non-Swedish backgrounds – about 10% of the population. In 1975, Parliament recognized that these groups should have freedom of choice to retain their identity. There is an active bilingualism policy. Foreign children may have some educational instruction in their mother tongue, if their parents request it; and these classes are growing. By 1980, in comprehensive schools, about 50,000 students were being taught in 60 different languages.

11. Finland There were around 300,000 Swedish speakers in Finland in the early 1990s– about 6% of the population. Swedish is an official language, alongside Finnish, and education is available in Swedish at all levels; but most Swedish speakers are bilingual, and the language generally seems to be in decline.

12. Lapland Around 50,000 Same (Lapps) live in Norway, Sweden, Finland, and the USSR. The Lappish language has no official status in any of these countries, and educational practice is primarily concerned with the majority languages. However, a Language Board was set up in 1971.

13. Balkan states Current information about the minority languages in the states formerly comprising Yugoslavia is unavailable, due to the changing political situation since 1991. Varieties of the former union language, Serbo-Croatian, are still usable as a lingua franca, but the differences between Serbian and Croatian are now strongly emphasized. Slovene is used by c.8% in Slovenia, and Macedonian by c.6% in the Former Yugoslav Republic of Macedonia. Albanian (c.5%) has official status in the autonomous province of Kosovo, and Hungarian (c.2%) in Voivodina. Several other languages are in use in the region, such as Romani, Ukrainian, and Slovak.

14. Romania The many minority languages of this country include Hungarian (c.2 million), German, Ukrainian, Romani, Russian, Serbo-Croatian, Yiddish, Tatar, Slovak, Turkish, Bulgarian, and Czech. The larger languages have media coverage; but all have some official status.

15. Sardinia Sardinian is a variety of Romance, closely related to Italian, spoken by an uncertain number (perhaps over 1 million) on the island of Sardinia. Although written materials date from the 11th century, none of the dialects has emerged as a standard, and Italian is the official language.

In addition to the questions 'Who are you?' and 'Where are you from?', which have been addressed from a linguistic viewpoint in §§6–9, there is also '*What* are you, in the eyes of the society to which you belong?' It is a complex and multi-faceted question, to which there is no easy answer. People acquire varying status as they participate in social structure; they belong to many social groups; and they perform a large variety of social roles. As a consequence, no single system of classification is likely to do justice to the task of defining a person's social identity in linguistic terms, especially when the vast range of the world's cultural patterns is taken into account. This section, therefore, has to be extremely selective, in order to represent the range of sociolinguistic and ethnolinguistic variables involved.

SOCIAL STRATIFICATION

One of the chief forms of sociolinguistic identity derives from the way in which people are organized into hierarchically ordered social groups, or *classes*. Classes are aggregates of people with similar social or economic characteristics. Within sociology, the theoretical basis of social class has been a controversial subject, and it has not always proved easy to work consistently with the notion, especially when cross-cultural comparisons are involved. Factors such as family lineage, rank, occupation, and material possessions often conflict or are defined with reference to different criteria. But for most sociolinguistic purposes to date, it has been possible to make progress by recognizing only the broadest distinctions (such as high vs low, or upper vs middle vs lower) in order to determine the significant correlations between social class background and language. Examples of some of these correlations are given below and also on p. 32.

One does not need to be a sociolinguist to sense that the way people talk has something to do with their social position or level of education. Everyone has developed a sense of values that make some accents seem 'posh' and others 'low', some features of vocabulary and grammar 'refined' and others 'uneducated'. We have a large critical vocabulary for judging other people's language in this way. But one does need to be a sociolinguist to define precisely the nature of the linguistic features that are the basis of these judgments of social identity. And it is only as a result of sociolinguistic research that the pervasive and intricate nature of these correlations has begun to be appreciated.

CASTES

Probably the clearest examples of social dialects are those associated with a caste system. Castes are social divisions based solely on birth, which totally restrict a person's way of life – for example, allowing only certain kinds of job, or certain marriage partners (p. 405). The best-known system is that of Hindu society in India, which has four main divisions, and many sub-divisions – though in recent years, the caste barriers have been less rigidly enforced. The Brahmins (priests) constitute the highest class; below them, in descending order, are the Kshatriyas (warriors), Vaisyas (farmers and merchants), and Sudras (servants). The so-called 'untouchables', whose contact with the other castes is highly restricted, are the lowest level of the Sudra caste.

Linguistic correlates of caste can be found at all levels of structure. For example, in Tamil, there are several clear-cut distinctions between the phonology, vocabulary, and grammar of Brahmin and non-Brahmin speech. The former also tends to use more loan words, and to preserve non-native patterns of pronunciation.

Brahmin		**Non-Brahmin**
	Vocabulary	
tūngu	'sheep'	orangu
alambu	'wash'	kaluyu
jalō	'water'	taṇṇi
	Phonology	
krāfu	'haircut'	krāppu
jīni	'sugar'	cīni
vārepparo	'banana'	vāreppolo
		vāleppolo
	Grammar	
–du	'it'	–ccu
vandudu	'it came'	vanduccu
paṇra	'he does'	pannuhā

(After W. Bright & A. K. Ramanujan, 1964.)

SPEECH AND SILENCE IN KIRUNDI

In the Central African kingdom of Burundi, age and sex combine with caste to constrain the nature of linguistic interaction in several ways. Seniority (*ubukuru*) governs all behaviour. There are clear caste divisions; older people precede younger; and men precede women. The order in which people speak in a group is strictly governed by the seniority principle. Males of highest rank must speak first, regardless of age. Females do not speak at all, in the presence of outsiders, unless spoken to.

Upper-caste speakers seem never to raise their voices, or allow emotion to show. In group discussion, for the senior person to be silent implies disapproval. As others must then also stay silent, any further proceedings are effectively negated.

To speak well is considered a mark of good breeding in men. From their tenth year, boys in the upper castes are given formal speech training – how to use social formulae, talk to superiors and inferiors, and make speeches for special occasions. Upper-caste girls do not take part in public speaking, but they do develop effective bargaining skills, for use behind the scenes. They are also trained to listen with great care, so that they can accurately recount to the men of the family what has been said by visitors. (After E. M. Albert, 1964.)

The John Betjeman poem, 'How to get on in society', originally set as a competition in *Time and Tide,* was included in the book *Noblesse Oblige* as part of the U/non-U debate (see facing page).

HOW TO GET ON IN SOCIETY

Phone for the fish-knives, Norman,
As Cook is a little unnerved;
You kiddies have crumpled the serviettes
And I must have things daintily served.

Are the requisites all in the toilet?
The frills round the cutlets can wait
Till the girl has replenished the cruets
And switched on the logs in the grate.

It's ever so close in the lounge, dear,
But the vestibule's comfy for tea,

And Howard is out riding on horseback
So do come and take some with me.

Now here is a fork for your pastries
And do use the couch for your feet;
I know what I wanted to ask you –
Is trifle sufficient for sweet?

Milk and then just as it comes, dear?
I'm afraid the preserve's full of stones;
Beg pardon, I'm soiling the doilies
With afternoon tea-cakes and scones.

SOME ENGLISH MARKERS OF SOCIAL CLASS

Long before the days of 20th-century linguistics and phonetics, English novelists and dramatists, especially in the 18th and 19th centuries, were observing the relationship between language and social class in Britain and using it as a basis for characterization and social comment.

• George Gissing, about Mrs Yule, in his *New Grub Street* (1891, Chapter 7).

Mrs Yule's speech was seldom ungrammatical, and her intonation was not flagrantly vulgar, but the accent of the London poor, which brands as with hereditary baseness, still clung to her words, rendering futile such propriety of phrase as she owed to years of association with educated people.

• Mrs Waddy, about Harry Richmond's father, in George Meredith's *The Adventures of Harry Richmond* (1871, Chapter 3).

'More than his eating and his drinking, that child's father worrits about his learning to speak the language of a British gentleman ... Before that child your "h's" must be like the panting of an engine – to please his father ... and I'm to repeat what I said, to make sure the child haven't heard anything ungrammatical ...'

• Pip to Biddy, in Charles Dickens' *Great Expectations* (1861, Chapter 35).

'Biddy', said I, in a virtuously self-asserting manner, 'I must request to know what you mean by this?'
'By this?' said Biddy.
'No, don't echo,' I retorted. 'You *used not* to echo, Biddy.'
'*Used not!*' said Biddy. 'O Mr Pip! *Used!*'

• Elfride Swancourt to Mrs Swancourt, in Thomas Hardy's *A Pair of Blue Eyes* (1873, Chapter 14).

'I have noticed several ladies and gentlemen looking at me.'
'My dear, you mustn't say "gentlemen" nowadays ...
We have handed "gentlemen" to the lower classes, where the word is still to be heard at tradesmen's balls and provincial tea-parties, I believe. It is done with here.'
'What must I say then?'
'"Ladies and men" always.'

Dropping the *g*

'Where on earth did Aunt Em learn to drop her g's?'
'Father told me once that she was at a school where an undropped "g" was worse that a dropped "h". They were bringin' in a country fashion then, huntin' people, you know.'

This conversation between Clare and Dinny Cherrel, in John Galsworthy's *Maid in Waiting* (1931, Chapter 31), illustrates a famous linguistic signal of social class in Britain – the two pronunciations of final *ng* in such words as running, [n] and [ŋ]. But it also brings home very well the arbitrary way in which linguistic class markers work. The [n] variant is typical of much work-ing-class speech today (p. 32), but a century ago this pronunciation was a *desirable* feature of speech in the upper middle class and above – and may still occasionally be heard. The change to [ŋ] came about under the influence of the written form: there was a *g* in the spelling, and it was felt (in the late 19th century) that it was more 'correct' to pronounce it. As a result, 'dropping the *g*' in due course became stigmatized.

U AND NON-U

In 1954, the British linguist A. S. C. Ross published an article entitled 'Linguistic class-indicators in present-day English' in a Finnish philological journal. It was read by Nancy Mitford , who wrote an *Encounter* article based upon it. The result was an enormous public reaction, with immediate recognition for the terms *U* and *non-U*. Two years later, Ross's essay was reprinted, with some modifications and a new title ('U and Non-U: an essay in sociological linguistics'), in *Noblesse Oblige,* which included contributions on the same subject by Nancy Mitford, Evelyn Waugh, and John Betjeman.

The essay's aim was to investigate the linguistic demarcation of the British upper class. *U* stood for 'upper class' usage; *non-U* stood for other kinds of usage. It looked at distinctive pronunciation and vocabulary, as well as written language conventions, such as how to open and close letters. It was a personal account containing many subjective judgments and disregarding the subtle gradations in usage intermediate between the two extremes; but it was also highly perceptive, drawing attention to a large number of distinguishing features. The nature of upper-class language has changed over 30 years later, but the terms *U* and *non-U* are still well known.

Some of the lexical oppositions proposed by Ross:

U	non-U
have a bath	take a bath
bike, bicycle	cycle
luncheon	dinner
riding	horse riding
sick	ill
knave	jack
mad	mental
looking-glass	mirror
writing-paper	note-paper
jam	preserve
wireless	radio
table-napkin	serviette
lavatory-paper	toilet-paper
rich	wealthy
vegetables	greens
pudding	sweet
telegram	wire
England	Britain
Scotch	Scottish

SOCIAL IDENTITY AND OTHER FACTORS

It is never possible to make a simple statement about language variation and social class because other influential factors are involved, such as the sex of the speaker, and the formality of the situation (p. 42). There is also an important interaction between social and regional factors (§8), as illustrated below for British English.

The two pyramids deal with differences of accent and dialect, and represent the relationship between 'where' a speaker is, both socially (the vertical dimension) and geographically (the horizontal dimension). At the top are the speakers of the highest social class: they speak the standard dialect with very little regional variation. Also at the top are those who speak Received Pronunciation (RP), the educated accent which signals no regional information at all (within Britain). The further we move down the class scale, the more we encounter regional accent and dialect variation. And when we reach the lowest social class, we encounter the widest range of local accents and dialects.

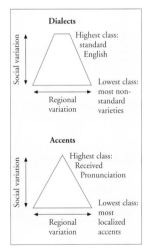

Thus, for example, speakers from the top social class will all use the same word *headache*, and give it the same (RP) pronunciation, but speakers from the lowest class will use *skullache, headwarch, sore head,* and other forms, in a variety of pronunciations, depending on where they are from. (After P. Trudgill, 1983.)

RESTRICTED AND ELABORATED CODES

Do people from different social classes display different abilities in their use of language? This was one of the questions widely discussed in the 1970s, as a result of a distinction proposed by the sociologist Basil Bernstein (1924–). The concepts of 'elaborated code' and 'restricted code' attempt to explain how a society's distribution of power and its principles of control shape and enter different modes of communication which carry the cultures of different social classes and that of the school, and so reproduce unequal educational advantages. The theory proposes that the sets of social relationships in which people are embedded act selectively on the production of meanings, and so upon choices within common linguistic resources.

Codes are said to have their origins in different family structures, associated (but not inevitably) with social classes, and are relayed through crucial socializing contexts, instructional and regulative, which differently orient children to the roles, meanings, and values of the school. Restricted codes arise where meanings are particular to and embedded in a local context, and the need to make meanings specific and explicit is reduced by the foregrounding of shared understandings, values, and identifications. By contrast, the forms of elaborated codes arise out of social relations where less is taken for granted, where shared understandings, values, and identifications are less foregrounded, and so where explicitness and specificity are more likely to be demanded. Middle-class children are said to have access to both codes, whereas lower-working-class children are more likely to be initially limited to a restricted code, and to experience difficulty in acquiring the form of the elaborated code required by the school, and thus the meanings and pedagogical practices regulated by that code.

The complexities of this theory were sometimes reduced to the proposition that middle-class children are able to abstract, but working-class children are not; this difference was then attributed to differences in the children's linguistic resources. Bernstein argues strongly that there is no basis for either of these propositions in his theory. Misreadings of the theory can also occur through a too-ready association of codes with language varieties or registers. Certainly, it is possible to show that a lower-class speaker can handle abstract concepts in restricted code. For example, in one of the recordings made by William Labov (1927–), a black 15-year-old was asked why he thought a God would be white. He replied: 'Why? I'll tell you why! Cause the average whitey out here got everything, you dig? And the nigger ain't got shit, y'know? Y'understan'? So – um – for in order for *that* to happen, you know it ain't no black God that's doin' that bullshit.' There is plainly abstract reasoning here, despite the non-standard language, and the restricted code.

Studies of this kind show that the correlation between the use of language and social class is evidently not simple: other factors intervene, such as the context in which learning takes place, and the way family life is structured. These factors always need to be borne in mind when debating levels of linguistic 'deficiency' or 'difference' between people of different social classes.

THE LANGUAGE OF RESPECT

Many communities make use of a complex system of linguistic levels in order to show respect to each other. The levels will partly reflect a system of social classes or castes, but the choice of forms may be influenced by several other factors, such as age, sex, kinship relationships, occupation, religious affiliation, or number of possessions. In Javanese, for example, choice of level can in addition be affected by the social setting of a conversation, its subject matter, or the history of contact between the participants. Other things being equal, people would use a higher level at a council meeting than in the street; in talking about religious matters than about buying and selling; and when addressing someone with whom they had recently quarrelled. Similar constraints have been noted for several languages, such as Japanese (p. 99), Korean, Tibetan, Samoan, and Sundanese.

Devices for conveying relative respect and social distance can be found in all languages. What is distinctive about 'respect' languages is the way differences of social level have been so extensively coded in the grammar and vocabulary. In Javanese, the differences between levels are so great that equivalent sentences may seem to have very little in common.

WOLOF GREETINGS

Greeting behaviour has a special place among the Wolof of Senegal, and well illustrates the link between language and social identity. Every interaction *must* begin with a greeting.

In the country, a greeting occurs between any two persons who are visible to each other – even if one person has to make a detour to accomplish it. In crowded areas, everyone close to the speaker must be greeted. In a conversational gathering, everyone must be greeted at the outset; and if, in the course of the conversation, someone leaves and then returns, it is often necessary to pause while all are greeted individually again.

Wolof society is divided into several castes, and a person's social identity is involved in every greeting. The most senior people present are greeted before those of lower rank; and in any meeting, those of lower rank must speak first. When two people meet, they must reach a tacit agreement about their relative status: the one who talks first accepts the lower role. Variations in status also occur. For example, an upper-caste person may not wish to adopt the higher-ranking position, because that would oblige him to support the lower-ranking person with a gift at some future point. He would therefore attempt to lower himself by speaking first in a conversation.

A Wolof proverb sums up this principle of social inequality: *sawaa dyi, sawaa dyi, gatyangga tya, ndamangga ca*, 'When two persons greet each other, one has shame, the other has glory'. (After J. T. Irvine, 1974.)

Five status levels, in one Javanese dialect (after C. Geertz, 1968), using the sentence *Are you going to eat rice and cassava now?* The names *krama*, *madya*, and *ngoko* refer to 'high', 'middle', and 'low' respectively. In addition, the high and low levels each have two divisions, depending on whether honorific words are used, to produce *krama inggil* vs *krama biasa*, and *ngoko madya* vs *ngoko biasa*.

Level	are	you	going	to eat	rice	and	cassava	now	Complete
krama inggil	menapa	pandjenengan	badé	ḍahar	sekul	kalijan	kaspé	samenika	*Menapa pandjenengan badé ḍahar sekul kalijan kaspé samenika?*
krama biasa		sampéjan		neda					*Menapa sampéjan badé neda sekul kalijan kaspé samenika?*
madya	napa		adjeng			lan		saniki	*Napa sampéjan adjeng neda sekul lan kaspé saniki?*
ngoko madya	apa		arep		sega			saiki	*Apa sampéjan arep neda sega lan kaspé saiki?*
ngoko biasa		kowé		mangan					*Apa kowé arep mangan sega lan kaspé saiki?*

SOCIAL STATUS AND ROLE

'Status' is the position a person holds in the social structure of a community – such as a priest, an official, a wife, or a husband. 'Roles' are the conventional modes of behaviour that society expects a person to adopt when holding a particular status. Public roles often have formal markers associated with them, such as uniforms; but among the chief markers of social position is undoubtedly language. People exercise several roles: they have a particular status in their family (head of family, first-born, etc.), and another in their place of work (supervisor, apprentice, etc.); they may have a third in their church, a fourth in a local sports centre, and so on. Each position will carry with it certain linguistic conventions, such as a distinctive mode of address, an 'official' manner of speech, or a specialized vocabulary. During the average lifetime, people learn many such linguistic behaviours.

It is only occasionally that the adoption of a social role requires the learning of a completely different language. For instance, a knowledge of Latin is required in traditional Roman Catholic practice; a restricted Latin vocabulary was once prerequisite for doctors in the writing out of prescriptions; students in some schools and colleges still have to speak a Latin grace at meal-times; and Latin may still be heard in some degree ceremonies. More usually, a person learns a new *variety* of language when taking up a social role – for example, performing an activity of special significance in a culture (such as at a marriage ceremony or council meeting), or presenting a professional image (as in the case of barristers, the police, and drill sergeants). The use of new kinds of suprasegmental feature (§29) is particularly important in this respect. One of the most distinctive indications of professional role is the intonation, loudness, tempo, rhythm, and tone of voice in which things are said.

In many cases, the linguistic characteristics of social roles are fairly easy to identify; but often they are not, especially when the roles themselves are not clearly identifiable in social terms. With unfamiliar cultures and languages, too, there is a problem in recognizing what is really taking place in social interaction or realizing how one should behave when participating in an event. How to behave linguistically as a guest varies greatly from culture to culture. In some countries, it is polite to comment on the excellence of a meal, as one eats it; in others, it is impolite to do so. In some countries, a guest is expected to make an impromptu speech of thanks after a formal meal; in others there is no such expectation. Silence, at times, may be as significant as speech (p. 38).

CEREMONIAL LANGUAGE

Probably all communities have developed special uses of language for ritual purposes. Distinctive forms are employed by those who have official status in the ceremony, as well as by those who participate. This may extend to the use of totally different languages (without regard for listener intelligibility), or be no more than selective modifications of everyday speech – such as prayers and speeches that are distinguished only by a more careful articulation, abnormal prosody, and the occasional use of exceptional vocabulary and grammatical forms.

Among the Zuñi, for example, 'sacred words' (*téwusu péna· we*), usually prayers, are pronounced in rhythmical units, resembling the lines of written poetry, with a reversal of the expected patterns of stress and intonation: strongly stressed syllables become weak, and the weakest syllable in the unit is pronounced most strongly. Ceremonial speech among the Kamsá Indians of Colombia also involves distinctive intonation and timing, reminiscent of chant, but in addition there are grammatical and lexical changes. They use many more Spanish loan words than in everyday speech (60%, compared with 20%), and there is a marked increase in the number of affixes in a word (as many as 11 attached to a root, compared to the six or fewer heard in ordinary use).

Often, ceremonial genres are marked by considerable verbal ingenuity. For example, among the Ilongot of the northern Philippines there is a speech style known as 'crooked language'(*qambaqan*), used in oratory, play, song, riddles, and public situations, such as debates. It is a style rich in witty repartee, puns, metaphor, elaborate rhythms, and changes in words. In Malagasy, there is a contrast between every-day talk (*resaka*) and orato-rial performance (*kabary*), which is used in ceremonial situations such as marriages, deaths, and bone-turnings, and also in formal settings, such as visits. An obligatory feature of *kabary* is 'wind-ing' speech, in which male speakers perform a dialogue in a roundabout, allusive manner, using many stylistic devices, such as metaphors, proverbs, and comparisons. The genre uses traditional ways of speech, handed down from ancestors. To speak Malagasy well means to be in command of this style; and it is common to hear speakers' abilities discussed and evaluated.

In a marriage request ceremony, for example, the girl's family gather in her village, and await the arrival of the boy's family. Each is represented by a speech-maker. As the boy's family approaches, no official notice is taken of them until their speech-maker makes a series of requests to enter the village. Unless the girl's speech-maker judges that these speeches are per-formed adequately, accord-ing to the traditional standards of the *kabary*, they will not be allowed to proceed to the formal mar-riage request, and the speech-maker must redou-ble his efforts. Subsequent steps in the ceremony are evaluated in the same way. (After E. Keenan, 1974.)

Kabary in progress An orator at a Malagasy marriage ceremony.

SOCIAL SOLIDARITY AND DISTANCE

One of the most important functions of language variation is to enable individuals to identify with a social group or to separate themselves from it. The markers of solidarity and distance may relate to family, sex (p. 46), ethnicity, social class (p. 38), or to any of the groups and institutions that define the structure of society. They may involve tiny sections of the population, such as scout groups and street gangs, or complete cross-sections, such as religious bodies and political parties. The signals can be as small as a single word, phrase, or pronunciation, or as large as a whole language.

DIFFERENT LANGUAGES

Probably the clearest way people have of signalling their desire to be close to or different from those around them is through their choice of languages. Few societies are wholly monolingual, and it is thus possible for different languages to act as symbols of the social structure to which their speakers belong. The test sentence 'If they speak LANGUAGE NAME, they must be — ' can be completed using geographical terms (p. 24), but social answers are available as well: the blank can be filled by such phrases as 'my tribe', 'my religion', 'immigrants', 'well educated', 'rich', 'servants', and 'the enemy'.

The use of a different language is often a sign of a distinct religious or political group – as in the cases of Basque, Latin, Welsh, the many official languages of the Indian sub-continent, and the pseudolinguistic speech known as glossolalia (p. 11). Switching from one language to another may also be a signal of distance or solidarity in everyday circumstances, as can be seen in strongly bilingual areas, such as Paraguay. Here, the choice of Spanish or Guaraní is governed by a range of geographical and social factors, among which intimacy and formality are particularly important. In one study (J. Rubin, 1968), bilingual people from Itapuami and Luque were asked which language they would use in a variety of circumstances (e.g. with their spouse, sweetheart, children, boss, doctor, priest, etc.). For most, Guaraní was the language of intimacy, indicating solidarity with the addressee. The use of Spanish would indicate that the speaker was addressing a mere acquaintance or a stranger. Spanish was also the language to use in more formal situations, such as patient–doctor, or student–teacher. Jokes would tend to be in Guaraní. Courtship often began in Spanish, and ended in Guaraní.

The adoption of a local language as an emblem of group identity is well illustrated by the Vaupés Indians of Colombia, who live in more than 20 tribal units, each of which is identified by a separate language. Despite the existence of a lingua franca (Tukano), a homogeneous culture throughout the region, and the small numbers of speakers (around 5,000 in total, in the early 1960s), the Indians all learn at least three languages – some, as many as ten. The identity of the different languages is sharply maintained – for instance, several places have separate names in all the languages, and the Indians themselves emphasize their mutual unintelligibility. In such circumstances, the languages act as badges of membership of the tribal units. An Indian will often speak initially in his own father language to acknowledge publicly his tribal affiliation. And language acts as a criterion for all kinds of social behaviour. For example, when the investigator asked a Bará Indian about marriage sanctions, she was told: 'My brothers are those who share a language with me. Those who speak other languages are not my brothers, and I can marry their sisters.' On another occasion, when she asked an Indian why they spoke so many languages instead of using the lingua franca, she received the reply: 'If we were all Tukano speakers, where would we get our women?' (After J. Jackson, 1974.)

DIFFERENT VARIETIES

In monolingual communities, a major way of marking factors such as solidarity, distance, intimacy, and formality is to switch from one language variety to another. A Berlin business manager may use standard German at the office and lapse into local dialect on returning home. A conference lecturer in Paris may give a talk in formal French, and then discuss the same points with colleagues in an informal variety. A London priest may give a sermon in an archaic, poetic style, and talk colloquially to the parishioners as they leave. During the service, the priest might have used a modern English translation of the Bible, or one which derives from the English of the 16th century.

Languages have developed a wide range of varieties for handling the different kinds and levels of relationship which identify the social structure of a community. These varieties are discussed in other sections (§§11, 63), because they partly reflect such factors as occupation, subject matter, social status, and setting; but it is important to note that they may also be used as symbols of social identity. In English, for example, forms such as *liveth and reigneth, givest, vouchsafe,* and *thine* have long been distinctive in one variety of religious language; but in the 1960s, as proposals for the modernization of Christian liturgical language were debated, this variety came to be seen as a symbol of traditional practice with which people chose to identify or from which they dissociated themselves. The case is worth citing because the world-wide status of Christianity meant that many speech communities were involved, and over a quarter of the world's population was affected. No other linguistic change can ever have raised such personal questions of linguistic identity on such a global scale.

AVOIDANCE LANGUAGES

Among Australian aborigines, it is common for a man to 'avoid' certain relatives – often his wife's mother and maternal uncles, sometimes her father and sisters as well. Brothers and sisters, too, may not be allowed to converse freely, once they grow up. In some tribes, avoidance of taboo relatives means total lack of contact; in others, a degree of normal speech is tolerated; but the most interesting cases are those where special languages have developed to enable communication to take place. These are usually referred to as 'mother-in-law' languages, but all taboo relatives are included under this heading.

In Dyirbal (now almost extinct), the everyday language is known as Guwal, and the mother-in-law language is called Dyalnguy. The latter would be used whenever a taboo relative was within earshot. The two languages have virtually the same grammar, but no vocabulary in common. Dyalnguy also has a much smaller vocabulary than Guwal.

In Guugu-Yimidhirr, there is no contact at all with the mother-in-law, and a strong taboo also affects speech to brothers- and fathers-in-law. There are important differences in vocabulary, style, and prosody. Sexual topics are proscribed. One must speak to these relatives slowly, in a subdued tone, without approaching closely or facing them. The style is sometimes described as *dani-man-aarnaya*, 'being soft/slow', or *diili yirrgaalga*, speaking 'sideways'. (After J. B. Haviland, 1979.)

The avoidance languages of Australia illustrate yet another means of marking social distance. The people turn away, linguistically and physically, from their taboo relatives. Similar taboos have also been observed in many other parts of the world, such as among the Plains Indians of North America. These languages can therefore be contrasted with those (in South-east Asia, for example) where social relations are expressed by adding complexity to ordinary speech (p. 40).

Diglossia

Perhaps the clearest use of varieties as markers of social structure is in the case of *diglossia* – a language situation in which two markedly divergent varieties, each with its own set of social functions, coexist as standards throughout a community. One of these varieties is used (in many localized variant forms) in ordinary conversations; the other variety is used for special purposes, primarily in formal speech and writing. It has become conventional in linguistics to refer to the former variety as 'low' (L), and the latter as 'high' (H).

Diglossic situations are widespread, some of the better-known ones including Arabic, Modern Greek, and Swiss German. These speech communities recognize the H/L distinction and have separate names for the two varieties:

	High	**Low**
Greek	Katharévousa	Dhimotiki (Demotic)
Arabic	ʾal-fuṣḥā (Classical)	ʾal-ʿāmmiyyah (Colloquial)
Swiss German	Hochdeutsch (High German)	Schweitzerdeutsch (Swiss German)

The functional distinction between H and L is generally clear-cut. H is used in such contexts as sermons, lectures, speeches, news broadcasts, proverbs, newspaper editorials, and traditional poetry. It is a language that has to be learned in school. L is used in everyday conversation and discussion, radio 'soap operas', cartoon captions, folk literature, and other informal contexts.

H and L varieties can display differences in phonology, grammar, and vocabulary. For example, the sound systems of the two Swiss German varieties are strikingly different. Classical Arabic has three noun cases, whereas Colloquial Arabic has none. And in Greek there are many word pairs, such as *ínos* (H) and *krasí* (L) ('wine'): the H word would be written on Greek menus, but diners would ask for their wine using the L word. All three kinds of distinctiveness are illustrated in the following sentence given first in Hochdeutsch (H) and then in Schweitzerdeutsch (L): *Nicht nur die Sprache hat den Ausländer verraten, sondern auch seine Gewohnheiten;* and *Nüd nu s Muul häd de Ussländer verraate, au syni Möödeli.* 'It was not only his language that showed he was a foreigner, his way of life showed it too.' (After P. Trudgill, 1983.)

In diglossic situations, the choice of H vs L can easily become an index of social solidarity. A Swiss German speaker who used Hochdeutsch in everyday conversation would be considered snobbish or artificial – and if the context were a political discussion, it could even raise questions of national loyalty, as Hochdeutsch is used as the everyday language by people outside the country. Religious as well as political attitudes may be involved. The H form is often believed to be the more beautiful and logical, and thus the more appropriate for religious expression – even if it is less intelligible. In Greece, there were serious riots in 1903, when the New Testament was translated into Dhimotiki. And strong views are always expressed by Arabic speakers about Classical Arabic, which, as the language of the Qur'an, belongs to God and heaven (p. 388).

Diglosssic situations become unstable in the face of large-scale movements for a single standard – such as might be found in programmes of political unification, national identity, or literary reform. In such circumstances, there are arguments in favour of either H or L varieties becoming the standard. Supporters of H stress its link with the past, and its claimed excellence, and they contrast its unifying function with the diversity of local dialects. Supporters of L stress the need to have a standard which is close to the everyday thoughts and feelings of the people, and which is a more effective tool of communication at all levels. 'Mixed' positions, setting up a modified H or L, are also supported; and the steady emergence of L-based standards has been noted in Greece, China, Haiti, and several other areas.

A personal column from the Basel daily newspaper *Basler Zeitung* This item shows an interesting contrast between High German and Swiss German. The rest of the newspaper is written in High German, but in the *Perseenlig* column (High German *persönlich*), the last two items are entirely in Swiss German (apart from the words in English). One is a humorous announcement of the opening of a medical practice; the other is a birthday greeting.

Why are the remaining ads not in Swiss German? This is probably because of their content and level: the first item expresses the thanks of an old married couple to their neighbours for all they did at their golden wedding celebration; the second announces the assembly point and time for a meeting of the fire service association. Even so, the second item has one distinctive feature: *Besammlung* ('meeting') is an example of 'Swiss High German', midway between High German (*Versammlung*) and Swiss German (*Besammlig*).

DIFFERENT WORDS AND PHRASES

We recognize varieties of language as a result of perceiving several distinctive linguistic features being used together in a social situation. But often a single linguistic feature is enough to indicate social distance – such as the particular words or phrases used when people meet, address each other by name, or select pronouns for talking to or about each other.

Modes of address

One of the most significant ways of signalling social intimacy and distance is through the use of a person's name in direct address. In English, the basic choice is between first name (FN) or title with last name (TLN), but several other conventions are possible in certain contexts, such as the use of LN in business or military settings (*Come in, Smith...*), or the use of abbreviations (*Is JM in?*). The range of possible forms is easy to state; but the factors that govern the choice of forms are often complex and difficult to summarize. When would two people use FNs or TLNs reciprocally to each other? When would one speaker use FN and the other TLN?

Charting address relationships   Several studies have attempted to explicate these factors. The flowchart (right) was devised by Susan Ervin-Tripp (1927–) as a means of specifying the factors that condition a speaker's choice of address in American English. The chart is simply a logical statement of the various possibilities, given a context such as 'Look, — , it's time to leave'; it is not an account of what goes on in the speaker's mind. The knowledge structure represented is that of an American academic; but dialect differences, idiosyncratic preferences, and other variants are not taken into account.

The entrance point to the diagram is at the bottom left. Each path through the diagram leads to one of the possible modes of address, listed vertically at the right. Alternative realizations of these address modes are not given (e.g. a first name may alternate with a nickname). For example, as one enters the diagram, the first choice which has to be made is whether the addressee is a child (– Adult) or an adult (+ Adult). If the former, one follows the line downwards, where the only distinction drawn is that between name known (+) or not (–). If the child's name is known, one uses the first name; if not, one does not use a name at all (Ø). The diagram does not give criteria for deciding when a child becomes an adult.

Along the adult path, several decisions have to be made. 'Status-marked setting' refers to special occasions (such as a courtroom) where forms of address are rigidly prescribed (e.g. *your honour, Mr Chairman*). The 'identity set' refers to the list of occupational or courtesy titles that may be used alone to mark social identity (e.g. *Father, Doctor, Mr, Miss*).

In addressing people whose names are known, kinship is a major criterion. If the speaker is related to the addressee ('alter'), two factors are relevant: 'ascending generation' (e.g. aunt as opposed to cousin) and age. If the speaker is not related to alter, the factor of familiarity is relevant: whether or not alter is a friend or colleague. If familiarity applies, the next factor is social rank, here defined with reference to a professional hierarchy. A senior alter has the option of offering or accepting FN, instead of TLN ('dispensation' – *Call me Mike*), though this situation is often ambiguous. Age difference is not significant until there is a gap of nearly a generation.

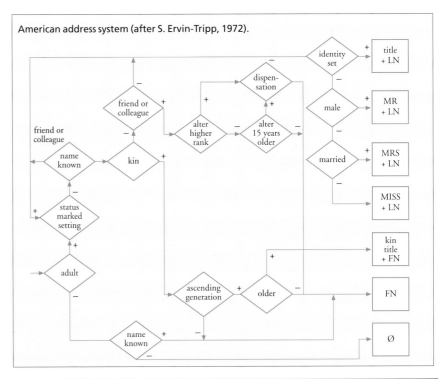

American address system (after S. Ervin-Tripp, 1972).

NUER MODES OF ADDRESS

Address systems vary greatly from culture to culture. Among the Nuer (Sudan), a system of multiple names and titles marks a person's place in social structure. Every Nuer is given a personal name, shortly after birth, which he retains through life; but as an adult, it is used only by close relatives and friends. These names usually refer to the place of birth, or to events that took place at the time, such as *Nhial* 'rain', *Duob* 'path'. Maternal grandparents often give the child a second personal name, which is used by kinsfolk on the maternal side. Twins are given special personal names, which immediately identify their status, such as

Both 'the one who goes ahead' and *Duoth* 'the one who follows'.

The social setting is an important factor in the selection of a mode of address. Every child inherits an honorific, or clan name, which tends to be used only in ceremonies or on special occasions (such as a return after a long absence). When a boy is initiated to manhood, he is given an ox, and from the distinctive features of this animal he takes his 'ox-name', which is used only by people of the same or similar ages. There are also 'dance-names' – more elaborate versions of oxnames that are used only at dances.

Kinship roles also play

their part. A man would normally be addressed using the name of his father (his patronymic). But a man visiting maternal relatives will be greeted primarily by his mother's name (his matronymic). The naming of people after their eldest child (teknonymy) is also heard, especially when talking to in-laws. For example, a woman's status in her husband's home is based on her having borne him a child, and this is the link that binds her to her husband's social group. It is therefore natural for that group to address her using the child's name. (After E. E. Evans-Pritchard, 1948.)

T or V?

A well-studied example of address is the use of the familiar and polite pronouns found in many languages, as in French *tu/vous*, German *du/Sie*, Welsh *ti/chwi*, and so on. These forms (generally referred to as *T* forms and *V* forms, respectively, from Latin *tu* and *vos*) follow a complex set of rules that foreigners never find easy to master. Terms such as 'familiar' and 'polite' capture aspects of their use, but are inadequate summaries of all their social functions, and ignore important differences between languages.

In Latin, the T forms were used for addressing one person, and the V forms for more than one; but from around the 4th century AD, the convention developed of referring to the Roman Emperor using the plural form *vos*. Gradually, this 'royal *you*' extended to others who exercised power, so that by medieval times, the upper classes were showing mutual respect through the use of V forms only. The historical picture is complicated and not entirely understood, but medieval nobles would generally address each other as V, whether talking to one person or more than one, and would address the lower classes as T. By contrast, the lower classes would use T to each other, and V to their superiors.

Later the V forms began to be used in other circumstances, not simply as a mark of respect due to those with power but as a sign of any kind of social distance. T forms, correspondingly, began to be used as markers of social closeness and intimacy. Thus, between equals, it became possible to use either T or V, depending on the degree of solidarity one wished to convey. Lower-class friends would address each other as T, and use V to strangers or acquaintances. Upper-class people would do likewise.

In these circumstances, where there is a power relationship motivating one usage (T = lack of respect), and a solidarity relationship motivating another (T = social closeness), situations of uncertainty would often arise. For example, during a meal, should diners address servants as T or V? The diners are more 'powerful' (and so should use T), but they are also socially distant from the servants (and so should use V). Similarly, should children address their parents as T (because they are intimates) or V (because there is a power difference)? By the 20th century, such conflicts had in most cases been resolved by following the dictates of the solidarity dimension: these days, diners address waiters as V, and children address parents as T.

But some fascinating differences remain. In the first systematic T/V study, male students from different linguistic backgrounds were asked about their pronoun preferences. The sample was relatively small, but it clearly emerged that Italians used T more than the French, and the French more than the Germans. There were several interesting points of detail: for example, Germans used T more to distant relations than did the French; Italians were more likely to use T to fellow female students than either French or Germans. There were psychological as well as geographical differences. Radical students used more T forms than did conservatives. One of the conclusions of the study was that 'a Frenchman could, with some confidence, infer that a male university student who regularly said T to female fellow students would favour the nationalization of industry, free love, trial marriage, the abolition of capital punishment, and the weakening of nationalistic and religious loyalties'. Inferences like these are difficult to confirm on a larger scale, partly because of the speed of linguistic change (since the early 1960s, when this study was done, student use of T has become much more widespread). But hypotheses of this kind are well worth following up, as they bear directly on the task of establishing the basis of sociolinguistic identity. (After R. Brown & A. Gilman, 1968.)

Flow-charts These charts provide an opportunity to make hypotheses about naming practice precise, and help to clarify interlanguage differences. For example, this kind of diagram has been used to identify the factors governing the use of T or V forms in Yiddish (S. Ervin-Tripp, 1972).

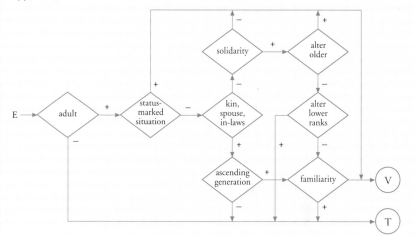

Farr's Law of Mean Familiarity
… as discovered by Lumer Farr, one of the senior life-men in Stephen Potter's *One-upmanship* (1952), identifies a well-known inverse naming relationship in the following way:

The Guv'nor addresses:

Co-director Michael Yates as	Mike
Assistant director Michael Yates as	Michael
Sectional manager Michael Yates as	Mr Yates
Sectional assistant Michael Yates as	Yates
Indispensable secretary Michael Yates as	Mr Yates
Apprentice Michael Yates as	Michael
Night-watchman Michael Yates as	Mike

SEXISM

The relationship between language and sex has attracted considerable attention in recent years, largely as a consequence of public concern over male and female equality. In many countries, there is now an awareness, which was lacking a generation ago, of the way in which language can reflect and help to maintain social attitudes towards men and women. The criticisms have been directed almost exclusively at the linguistic biases that constitute a male-orientated view of the world, fostering unfair sexual discrimination, and, it is argued, leading to a denigration of the role of women in society. English has received more discussion than any other language, largely because of the impact of early American feminism.

Several areas of grammar and vocabulary have been cited. In grammar, the issue that has attracted most attention is the lack of a sex-neutral, third-person singular pronoun in English, especially in its use after indefinite pronouns, e.g. *If anyone wants a copy, he can have one.* (In the plural, there is no problem, for *they* is available.) No natural-sounding option exists: *one* is considered very formal, and forms such as *he or she* are stylistically awkward. As a result, there have been many proposals for the introduction of a new English sex-neutral pronoun – including *tey, co, E, ne, thon, mon, heesh, ho, hesh, et, hir, jhe, na, per, xe, po,* and *person.* None of these proposals has attracted widespread support, but *co,* for example, has been used in some American communes, and *na* and *per* have been used by some novelists. Less radical alternatives include advice to restructure sentences to avoid the use of *he*-forms.

Many other examples of linguistic bias have been given. In the lexicon, particular attention has been paid to the use of 'male' items in sex-neutral contexts, such as *man* in generic phrases (*the man in the street, stone-age man,* etc.), and the potential for replacing it by genuinely neutral terms (*chairman → chairperson, salesman → sales assistant,* etc.). Another lexical field that is considered problematic is marital status, where bias is seen in such phrases as X's *widow* (but not usually Y's *widower),* the practice of changing the woman's surname at marriage, and the use of *Mrs* and *Miss* (hence the introduction of *Ms* as a neutral alternative). The extent of the bias is often remarked upon. In one computer analysis of child school books, male pronouns were four times as common as female pronouns. In another study, 220 terms were found in English for sexually promiscuous women, and only 22 for sexually promiscuous men. It is easy to see how sexual stereotypes would be reinforced by differences of this kind.

THE PROPER STUDY OF MANKIND IS MAN?

What has happened to sexist language, as a result of feminist criticism? So far, the effect has been far more

---

MAINTAINING SEXUAL STEREOTYPE LANGUAGE

This was the list of lecturers from the University of Reading's Department of Linguistic Science in 1983, as printed in the University calendar. Although gender is irrelevant to the job, the women in the Department were clearly identified by the use of a full first name, and/or by the use of *Mrs*. It is not possible to tell if the male members of staff are married.

Lecturers:

C. Biggs, *MA, Oxford; PhD Cambridge; Diploma in Linguistics, Cambridge*

R. W. P. Brasington, *MA, Oxford*

A. R. Butcher, *MA, Edinburgh; MPhil, London; Dr phil, Kiel*

F. Margaret Davison, *BA, Sussex; MA, Reading; Cert T Deaf, Manchester*

P. J. Fletcher, *BA, Oxford; MPhil, Reading; PhD, Alberta*

M. A. G. Garman, *BA, Oxford; PhD Edinburgh; Diploma in General Linguistics, Edinburgh*

G. A. Hughes, *BA, Montreal; Diploma in English as Second Language, Wales*

K. Johnson, *BA, Oxford; MA, Essex*

Carolyn A. Letts (Mrs Letts), *BA, Wales; MCST*

K. M. Petyt, *MA, Cambridge; MA, PhD, Reading; Diploma in Public and Social Administration, Oxford (Director of Extramural and Continuing Education)*

Marion E. Trim (Mrs Trim), *MSc, London; LCST*

Irene P. Warburton (Mrs Warburton), *BA, Athens; PhD, Indiana*

SEXIST LANGUAGE

People would bring their wives, mothers, and children.
Rise Up, O Men of God ...
Man, being a mammal, breastfeeds his young.
Mind that child – he may be deaf!
Man overboard!

These randomly selected cases of sexist language may provoke ridicule, anger, or indifference, but they would be unlikely to warrant a legal action to determine their meaning. However, there are other examples where a legal decision could hang on the sex-specific vs sex-neutral senses of *man*. In the USA, for example, there has been legal controversy over the application of the generic male pronoun in cases where it was disputed whether such phrases as 'a reasonable man' could legitimately be applied to women. And in a case heard in 1977, an appeal was made against a woman's murder conviction on the grounds that instructions to the jury were phrased using the generic male form; this, it was argued, could have biased the jury's response, giving them the impression that the objective standard to be applied was that applicable to an altercation between two men. Traditional safeguard phrases such as 'the masculine pronoun shall import the feminine' have turned out to be less than satisfactory in resolving such issues.

SEX-ROLE STEREOTYPING IN SCHOOLBOOKS

Sexual stereotyping has been especially noted in traditional children's reading books and textbooks. There were always more male characters than female, and they took part in a greater variety of roles and activities. In early reading books, it was always the boys who were daring, the girls who were caring. Pictures in science books would show experiments being conducted by boys, while girls looked on. There is now a widespread trend to avoid sex-role stereotypes in children's books, and to prepare children for a more egalitarian society.

noticeable in writing than in speech. Several publishing companies have issued guidelines about ways of avoiding its use, and several writers and editors, in many important areas, now make a conscious effort to avoid unintentional biases – including such well-known bodies as the American Library Association, and writers such as Dr Benjamin Spock and the present author. Legal changes, such as the Sex Discrimination Act in Britain (1975), have caused job titles and much of the associated language to be altered. But is there any evidence of a significant change in practice throughout the language as a whole.

In 1984, an American study investigated the use of *man* and its compounds to refer to all humans, and the use of *he* and its inflected forms to refer to females as well as males, in a selection of publications taken at intervals between 1971 and 1979. The texts were samples of 75,000 running words from American women's magazines, science magazines, several newspapers, and both prepared and spontaneous remarks from the *Congressional Record;* a sample from *The Times Literary Supplement* was used, as a British comparison. The total sample was over half a million words.

The results were dramatic. In the American corpus, the use of these forms fell from 12.3 per 5,000 words in 1971 to 4.3 per 5,000 in 1979. Women's magazines showed the steepest decline, followed by science magazines. By contrast, results for congressmen showed no decline at all, and results for congresswomen were mixed. There was no clear decline in the British publication, but rates were very low, and little can be deduced from such a small sample. (After R. L. Cooper, 1984.)

What took the place of these forms? There was no evidence that a straightforward replacement by such forms as *he or she* was taking place. Rather, it seems likely that people were using alternative linguistic devices to get round the problem, such as *they* along with a plural noun. (This is the solution I have found most congenial in the present work, in fact.)

There is thus clear evidence that the feminist movement had an observable impact in the 1970s on several important genres of written language – publications aimed at general audiences, not solely at women. Plainly, there has been a general raising of consciousness about the issue of linguistic sexism, at least as regards the written language. Whether this same consciousness would be found in everyday speech is unclear, as is the question of how long-term these linguistic effects will be. A great deal of social change has taken place in two decades, and this could be enough to make the associated linguistic changes permanent; but a decade or two is as nothing within the large time-scale of language change, and it remains to be seen whether the new trends in usage will continue, or whether there will be a reversal, with public opinion reacting against the extreme positions taken by some militant feminists.

Dear God,
Are boys better than girls. I know you are one but try to be fair.
Sylvia.

Child's letter from *Children's Letters to God.*

The question 'Where are you from?', which signals geographical identity (§8), can be balanced by another locational question, 'Where are you now?'. Many features of language correlate directly with the characteristics of the context, or situation, in which a communicative event takes place. Classifications vary, but most approaches recognize the central role played by the following factors:

- *Setting.* The time and place in which a communicative act occurs, e.g. in church, during a meeting, at a distance, and upon leave-taking.
- *Participants.* The number of people who take part in an interaction, and the relationships between them, e.g. addressee(s), bystander(s).
- *Activity.* The type of activity in which a participant is engaged, e.g. cross-examining, debating, having a conversation.

The interaction between these factors produces a set of constraints on several features of language (discussed in Parts III–VI, and X), notably:

- *Channel.* The medium chosen for the communication (e.g. speaking, writing, drumming) and the way it is used.
- *Code.* The formal systems of communication shared by the participants (e.g. spoken English, Russian, etc., deaf sign languages).
- *Message form.* The structural patterns that identify the communication, both small scale (the choice of specific sounds, words, or grammatical constructions) and large scale (the choice of specific genres).
- *Subject matter.* The content of the communication, both explicit and implicit.

Each of these plays a crucial part in the identification of a communicative event. For example, a sermon (activity) is normally given in a church (setting), by a preacher addressing a congregation (participants), primarily using speech (medium), in a monologue in a single language (code), involving religious forms and genres (message form), and about a spiritual topic (subject matter). This kind of characterization needs immediate refinement, of course. Some sermons permit dialogue as well as monologue; some use chant and song alongside speech; some introduce different languages. But an initial simplified analysis is useful, because it enables a comparison to be made between different kinds of communicative event, which points the way towards a typology of communication. Several contextually distinctive uses of language are illustrated in §63.

SETTING

The particular time and place in which people interact will exercise its influence on the kind of communication that may occur – or whether communication is permitted at all. In institutionalized settings, such as a church or a court of law, the effect on language use is clear enough. But in many everyday situations, and especially in cultures we find alien, the relationship between setting and language can be very difficult to discover. At dinner parties, funerals, interviews, council meetings, weddings, and on other occasions, linguistic norms of behaviour need to be intuitively recognized if people are to act appropriately, but they are not always easy to define. For example, how would one begin to define the optimum length of an after-dinner speech, or the proportion of humour its subject matter should contain? In different times and places we may be obliged, permitted, encouraged, or even forbidden to communicate; and the quality or quantity of the language we use will be subject to social evaluation and sanction. The extent to which people recognize, submit to, or defy these sanctions is an important factor in any study of contextual identity.

HOW TO ANSWER THE TELEPHONE

Telephone conversations provide one of the clearest examples of the influence of setting upon language, because of the lack of visual feedback, and the constraints of time and money. The opening and closing phases of such conversations are particularly distinctive, with rules governing sequences of acceptable and unacceptable utterances. Certain features of the language are universal, but there are also interesting cultural differences, which often make themselves felt whenever one attempts to telephone someone abroad.

In British English, for example, the normal sequence for a call to a private residence is as follows:
1. Telephone rings.
2. Answerer gives number.
3. Caller asks for intended addressee.
By contrast, in French, the

following practice seems to be more usual (after D. Godard, 1977):
1. Telephone rings.
2. Answerer: 'Allo.'
3. Caller verifies number.
4. Answerer: 'Oui.'
5. Caller identifies self, apologizes, and asks for intended addressee.

The different conventions can have several consequences – not least, the possibility (which has been seriously mooted) that French people have greater difficulty remembering their own telephone number, because they do not have to verify it themselves when they pick up their phone! An English caller in France could unintentionally offend, by using the British pattern, which lacks the caller's self-identification and apology for troubling the answerer. And, conversely, English answerers can be irritated

when a French caller checks their number, when they themselves have just said it. Or again, in trying to reach a third party, a French caller would expect French answerers to reciprocate with a self-identification or some degree of small talk, before going to get the third party, whereas an English answerer would have no such expectation. The sequence:
1. Telephone rings.
2. Answerer gives number.
3. Caller asks for third party.
4. Answerer: 'I'll get her.' (Leaves phone.)
is normal in England, but abnormal in France, where there would be a further interaction before the answerer left the phone. Several such differences exist, which, if not correctly understood, can easily lead to unfortunate stereotypes about foreign attitudes.

MAORI GREETINGS

In some cultures, rituals of greeting or leave-taking are marked by elaborate and highly conventionalized forms of expression, often reflecting the social standing of the speakers (§10). Among the Maori, for example, distinctive behaviour and language identify the ritual encounter at the beginning of the ceremonial gathering (or *hui*) which takes place on such occasions as weddings, funerals, and visitations by dignitaries.

There may be as many as seven stages in the encounter ritual, all but two involving language. In each case, accuracy of expression is essential, otherwise evil will result. (After A. Salmond, 1974):

• The *waerea* is a protective incantation chanted upon entry to a gathering. Its words are archaic, and are often not understood.

• The *wero* is a ritual challenge, involving noise and actions, but no language.

• The *karanga* is an exchange of high, chanted calls of greeting, and invocations to the dead, between the old women of the local and visiting parties.

• The *poowhiri* is an action chant of welcome, using rhythmical actions and loud shouts.

• The *tangi* is a high wailing and sobbing, on a single vowel, uttered for the dead.

• The *whaikoorero* is the oratory that is the main part of the ritual. The locals and each group of visitors have a 'team' of orators. Speeches alternate, each speech beginning with a warning shout, and being followed by an archaic chant, greetings for the dead and living, perhaps a topic for discussion, and concluding with a traditional song by the group as a whole.

• The *hongi*, or pressing of noses, concludes the ritual.

When high-ranking foreigners make an official visit to New Zealand, they are usually greeted by the elaborate leaping and grimacing of a Maori ceremonial challenge (*wero*). Such ritual displays of strength were always customary on the first encounter with strangers – though early settlers often took them for displays of real belligerence, with deadly results!

Maori ceremony, Waitangi Day 1984, New Zealand.

A Maori *karanga* exchange
LOCAL: *Haere mai ra e te mana ariki e, mauria mai o taatou tini aituaa!*
Welcome, prestige of chiefs, bring our many dead!
Haere mai, haere mai!
Welcome, welcome!
VISITOR: *Karanga ra te tupuna whare ki te kaahui pani!*
Call, ancestral house, to those who mourn!
Ki ngaa iwi e, karanga ra!
Call to the tribes!
LOCAL: *Nau mai ngaa karanga maha o te motu!*
Draw near from all corners of the island!
Mauria mai ngaa mate kua ngaro ki te poo!
Bring the dead who have gone into the night!
VISITOR: *Hoki wairua mai raa e koro e!*
Return in spirit, old man!
Ki te karanga ki te poowhiri i taa koutou kaahui pani!
To the call and welcome of those who mourn you!
Hoki wairua mai e Paa e!
Return in spirit, father!

A Maori greeting (hongi), Rotorua, New Zealand

SPEECH-MAKING IN SAMOAN

A study of formal speech-making in the village of Falefa, in Western Samoa, provides a good illustration of the effect of setting on language. The village council (*fono*) consists of around 100 adults (*matai*), who are chiefs and orators, all with special titles. Meetings of the *fono* are called to discuss crises in village life; but before the main issue is discussed, orators make one or more formal speeches (*lāuga*). The *lāuga* seems to function as an affirmation of the need for a stable society, at a time when conflict and dissent are present. It contains seven distinct parts (though these may be reduced in number, and their performance varies from one type of social event to another).

• *Kava*: an acknowledgement of the person who has called out the titles of those who were served kava roots in the opening ceremony.

• *Thanksgiving to God*: for allowing the people to gather in this way.

• *Mornings*: a metaphor for important events, which symbolizes the performing of good deeds, and focuses attention on the present meeting.

• *Dignity of the sacred names*: an acknowledgement of the dignity of the *matai* and their titles.

• *Formal greeting*: praise and greeting for all the *matai* titles.

• *Agenda of the fono*: the official reason for the meeting, stated in very general terms.

• *Clearing of the sky*: the speaker wishes a good and long life to all present, using this metaphor, which represents a life with no problems.

As an example of the speech style, part of the *Mornings* section of one *lāuga* is given below (from A. Duranti, 1983):

…O ikū i kaeao…	Moving on to the mornings…
la 'o kaeao masagi lava	well (they) are very well-known mornings
o le aukuguʻu	of our country
kaeao (o) le Loku	the morning of the Church
ma kaeao- le Kusi Paʻia	and the morning (of) the Bible
la…o kaeao lava…	Yes…real mornings…
Ua kuagaʻi ia kaeao	Those mornings have gone
ma kaeao- foʻi sa faʻ asilisiliga	and the mornings that have been indicated
i o(u)kou figagalo	by the wish of you (chiefs)
ma o kakou faʻamoemoe…	and the hope of us (orators)…
la ʻae o le kaeao sili a legei	well this is the most important morning
ua kākou aulia maguia	when we meet in good spirit
legei kaeao fou	(on) this new morning
ma legei asa fou…	and this new day…
faʻakauguʻuiga ai	to accomplish
le- le kōfā ma le faʻ aukaga.	the decision of the chiefs and of the orators.

PARTICIPANTS

The simple opposition of message 'sender' and message 'receiver' needs considerable refinement if we are to classify communicative events satisfactorily. Normally a single person acts as sender, or addressor; but we have to allow for unison speech, as in the case of liturgical responses in church or other rituals, group teaching (where the whole class may respond together), popular acclamations (such as during a political address, or in a sports arena), and speeches by the players in a theatrical presentation. The linguistic characteristics of such speech (especially the prosody (§29)) will obviously be very different from those found when a person speaks alone.

Similarly, a single person is the usual receiver, or addressee, of a message; but here too we must allow for variations. We may address someone directly, or through an intermediary, such as a secretary, interpreter, or spokesperson. A third party may overhear what we are saying, or see what we have written, and we may consider this desirable or undesirable. And speech addressed to a group of people is common enough in everyday conversation, as well as in more formal contexts, such as sermons, toasts, and lectures, and the whole range of circumstances that define the world of spoken and written mass communication (§63).

All of these contexts can influence the language used by the speaker. For example, to know that one is being overheard by one's superior can lead to marked alterations in speech, even to the extent of adopting a completely different stylistic level (as has been observed in Persian). One may need to defer to the broader audience by altering pronoun forms and using various politeness strategies, as well as by modifying non-linguistic behaviour (such as body movements and eye contact). In some circumstances, the knowledge that one is being (or even, is likely to be) overheard may lead to nonfluency or a breakdown in communication, as in patient–doctor conversation, or the well-known effects that take place when people are asked to speak into a microphone.

In multilingual environments, there will usually be language switching (p. 365) when a conversation is joined by a third party who is not at ease in the language being used. However, language switching may not take place if the participants wish to exclude the third party – a common reaction to tourists visiting rural communities abroad. Nevertheless, circumstances vary greatly, and reactions are difficult to predict. One empirical study encountered a group of bilinguals at an inn in Austria who switched from Hungarian to German when asked to do so by people at a nearby table; but the study of a similar situation in Scotland found that a request to switch from Gaelic to English was refused.

CUNA CURING RITUAL

Some cultures introduce unusual participants into the speech event, especially where special powers need to be invoked. For example, in Cuna (Panama), language combines with medicine to help cure disease. There are many speech forms (*ikar*) that are thought to effect cures. These vary according to the nature of the ailment, but all have the same basic structure.

The sick person lies on a hammock, under which is a box of wooden dolls; it is the dolls which are thought to carry out the curing, and someone who knows the appropriate *ikar* is used to instruct them. The sick are not themselves active participants in the event: they may be asleep, or unaware of what is taking place around them, or even absent. Nor would they (or other onlookers) usually understand the special language of the *ikar*. In several ways, this ritual is similar to the western religious tradition of praying over or for the sick.

Other objects of medicinal value, such as tree bark or plants – or even western medicines – can be addressed in this way, as can be seen in the following extract (from J. Sherzer, 1974), in which the *ikar* calls on certain trees to use their strength to help someone suffering from severe headaches. The italicized words are used only in this particular type of *ikar*, whose fixed pattern must be accurately repeated in order to be effective. As curing *ikar* generally last for about 1½ hours, those who speak them need to have great powers of memory.

*kurkin ipe*kantiye olopillise *pupawala*kan akkuek^wiciye,
*kurkin ipe*kantiye olopillise pe maliwaskakan upoek^wiciye,
*kurkin ipe*kantinaye olopillise pe maliwaskakana pioklekek^wiciye,
*kurkin ipe*kantinaye olopillipiye apikaek^wiciye...
'trees, your roots reach the level of gold,
trees, your small roots are placed into the level of gold,
trees, your small roots are nailed into the level of gold,
trees, within the very level of gold you are resisting...'

READING THE NEWS

The effects of a mass audience on speaker style can be illustrated from studies of variation in the speech of radio newscasters. In New Zealand, for example, the same group of newscasters read the news on a number of different radio stations that share the same suite of studios. In one study, individual newscasters were monitored when they read the news on a higher-status station (YA) and on a lower-status station (ZB). In every case their pronunciation changed in the same direction. For example, /t/ between vowels (as in *butter*) was produced with voicing far more on ZB than on YA, as shown in the diagram (after A. Bell, 1984):

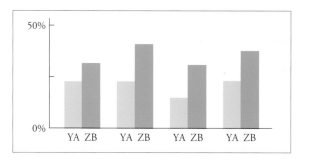

Because the voiced variant is normal in New Zealand, the announcers' use of the alternative must be demonstrating the external influence of a model of acceptable public speech (in this case, Received Pronunciation) – an instance of positive accommodation to an audience (p. 51).

NEW LANGUAGE FOR OLD

Varieties of language can alter completely if there is a change in one's view of audience needs. In recent years, for example, there has been a radical shift in the way theologians have begun to talk about God, in the light of their perception that people have become dissatisfied with traditional images and are searching for new ones. Such images covered a wide area of language, including terms that were highly abstract and mystical (*supreme being, infinite one, the unknowable, essence*), metaphorical and personal (*father, lord, judge, saviour*), psychological and ethical (*forgiveness, love, compassion*).

The dissatisfaction is well illustrated by the success of Bishop John Robinson's *Honest to God* (1963), which sold over a million copies. This book questioned the tradition of talking about God in crude spatial metaphors, as if he were 'up there', or 'out there'. It argued that, to modern audiences, such language was outmoded and acted as a barrier to understanding, whereas images such as 'ground of our being' could more easily be related to current ways of thinking. Several experiments in religious communication followed, in the spirit of this approach, and a new academic discipline has even been proposed to study this area – *theography*, a term coined on analogy with 'geography', which aims to 'draw the map' of language that people use to talk about God.

LINGUISTIC ACCOMMODATION

When two people with different social backgrounds meet, there is a tendency for their speech to alter, so that they become more alike – a process known as *accommodation,* or *convergence*. Modifications have been observed in several areas of language, including grammar, vocabulary, pronunciation, speech rate, use of pause, and utterance length. Everyday examples are the slower and simpler speech used in talking to foreigners or young children; the way technical information is presented in a less complex manner to those who lack the appropriate background; the rapid development of catch phrases within a social group; and the way many people cannot stop themselves unconsciously picking up the accent of the person they are talking to. The process has even been observed with babies 'talking' to adults: at 12 months, they were babbling at a lower pitch in the presence of their fathers, and at a higher pitch with their mothers.

These shifts take place in order to reduce the differences between participants, thus facilitating interaction, and obtaining the listener's social approval (p. 23). It should be noted that linguistic accommodation also has its risks, such as the loss of personal (and sometimes group) identity, or the perceived loss of integrity, such that the listener may react against the speaker's new style. Much depends on how speakers view themselves and the group to which they belong (the 'in group') in comparison with the group to which the listener belongs (the 'out group'). But on the whole, the benefits of convergence seem to outweigh these risks, with several social psychological studies showing that people react more favourably to those who move linguistically closer to them.

Divergence

Speech divergence also takes place when people wish to emphasize their personal, social, religious, or other identity. There may be quite elementary reasons for the divergence, such as a dislike of the listener's appearance or behaviour; or there may be more deep-rooted reasons, such as the deliberate use of a minority language or ethnically distinctive accent or dialect (§9). Threatening contexts readily result in divergence, as has been demonstrated experimentally. In one study, a group of people in Wales were learning Welsh in a language laboratory. During one of the sessions, they were asked to answer some questions about language learning. The questions were presented to them in their individual booths by an English speaker with an RP accent (p. 39), who at one point arrogantly challenged their reasons for learning what he called 'a dying language with a dismal future'. The accents used in their replies were then compared with those used in responding to a previous question that was emotionally neutral. The test sentence replies showed immediate divergence (as well as an aggressive tone of voice): speakers used a broader Welsh accent, and some introduced Welsh words into their speech. In a similar study, in Belgium (p. 37), the divergence took the form of a complete language shift. Here, the aggressive question was spoken by an unsympathetic Walloon (French) speaker to Flemish learners of English. Although replies to other questions were in English, half the learners switched into Flemish in their replies to the question which threatened their ethnic identity.

GOD IS FOR REAL, MAN

This is the title of a book by Carl Burke, an American prison chaplain, who hoped to make the biblical message meaningful to people from New York's toughest areas, by 'translating' passages into their everyday style of speech. The first three commandments read:
1. *You shall have no other gods before me...* Means God's the leader – nobody, but nobody, man, gets in the way. This is the top. He is Mr. Big, real big.
2. *You shall not make for yourself a graven image...* This means no making things that look like God in the craftshop at the settlement house. No worshipping things like rabbits' foots and lucky dice and, damn it, dolls.
3. *You shall not take the name of the Lord your God in vain...* It means knock off the swearing or you better watch out.

ACTIVITY

The kind of activity in which we engage will directly influence the way we communicate. At one level, our activities reflect the social status we have and the roles we perform (§10). But status and role are very general notions, within which it is possible to recognize a much more specific notion of 'activity type'. For example, priests have a well-defined status and role within a community; but while exercising their role as priests, they engage in a wide range of activities, such as leading a service, giving a sermon, exorcizing spirits, hearing confession, baptizing, and visiting the sick. Many other occupations involve a similar variety; and in all cases there are linguistic consequences of the shift from one activity to another. Linguistically-distinct activities are often referred to as *genres* or *registers,* though these terms are sometimes used to refer to all the contextually influenced varieties presented in this section.

Activity influence is not restricted to occupational environments. We also engage in many kinds of activity in everyday speech and writing, such as gossiping, discussing, quarrelling, petitioning, visiting, telephoning, and writing out lists. Here too there are linguistic norms and conventions, although they are usually more flexible, and the genres are not always as easy to define as those associated with more formal activities.

SPOKEN VARIETIES

Conversation

Everyday conversation is so habitual that it is easy to forget its status as a genre, with its own norms and conventions, often very different from those used in written language (§31).

- The language is often inexplicit, because the participants can rely on context to clarify their meaning e.g. A: *That's a nice one.* B: *It sure is.*
- There is no careful thematic planning governing the way a conversation proceeds; there are often changes of subject matter, and alterations in level (even, in multicultural contexts, switching between dialects or languages, p. 365).
- A degree of non-fluency is normal, while participants spontaneously construct their sentences; one expects to hear false starts, hesitation noises (*er, um*), pauses, repetitions, and other 'errors' of performance.
- Speech is usually quite rapid, with many of the sounds of careful pronunciation being omitted or altered in the interests of preserving naturalness and fluency; a wide range of prosodic effects (§29) is heard, signalling the diverse emotions which are encountered in conversations.
- The clear-cut sentence patterns known from the

written language are often missing; in their place are more loosely-connected constructions, frequently requiring the application of different grammatical rules from those found in good writing or recommended by traditional grammars (§1).
- The vocabulary of everyday speech tends to be informal and domestic, limited and inexplicit, as speakers cope with difficulties of memory, attention, and perception. In extreme (though not uncommon) cases, empty nonsense words may be used, e.g. *thingummajig, whatchamacallit, doo-da.*
- There is a great deal of usage variation on the part of individual speakers, often involving the unconscious use of non-standard or deviant forms.

Certain other features of this activity are included in §31. The subject of 'conversation analysis', which deals with the rules governing turn-taking between speakers, is introduced in §20.

Courtesy expressions

Ritual expressions of politeness are a common feature of social interaction in all forms of spoken and written dialogue, but especially in conversation. They are of considerable importance in accounting for the way people judge each other, and in explaining the success or failure of an interaction. The omission of a politeness formula, when one is expected, or the failure to acknowledge one appropriately, can lead to a tense atmosphere, or even social sanctions – as children who fail to say *please* sometimes find to their cost. In some languages, complex formulaic politeness sequences reflect levels of social structure and long-standing social traditions, as in the case of Wolof or Maori greetings (pp. 40, 49). English has only a small number of expressions, by comparison.

Languages display many differences in politeness expression. For example, phrases such as *good morning* and *good evening* are by no means universal: salutations related to time of day are normal in many languages, but not, say, in Bengali or Wolof; and the distinctions found in English are lacking in French (which uses one expression, *bonjour*, more widely). Foreigners do not always find it easy to work out the pragmatic rules that govern the use of these expressions, for arbitrary conventions are often involved. For example, the 'morning' in *good morning* does not coincide with the chronological period from midnight to noon: in normal use, it does not extend from midnight, but only from waking up; and it may extend beyond midday, until the midday meal. Outside of this period, its use is ironic, as when it is said late at night to someone who was expected earlier, or said mid-afternoon to someone who has overslept. Moreover, it may be used only once to a person during the day (unlike *Hello*), and an echo of the greeting is expected (unlike *Thank you*). But *good morning* is simple compared with *good evening*, where use is affected by variations in social background, habits of work, and the onset of darkness.

SOME ENGLISH POLITENESS FORMULAE

Greetings   Good morning, Hello, Hi
Farewells   Good night, Bye, See you, Cheers
Introductions   How do you do?, How's things?, Hi
Thanks   Thank you, Ta, Thanks a lot
Toasts   Good health, Cheers, Here's to...
Seasonal greetings   Merry Christmas, Happy Birthday
Apologies   Sorry, I beg your pardon, My mistake
Responses to apologies That's OK, Don't mention it, Never mind
Congratulations   Well done, Right on, Congratulations
Public noises   Encore, Hear hear, Goal
Body noises   Excuse me, Bless you, Pardon me

AN ARABIC FAREWELL

The normal exchange of farewells in Syrian Arabic is a three-part sequence. If A is said first, the addressee must reply with B, and the first speaker may then use C; but if B is said first, C is obligatory.

A. *(b)xātrak* 'by your leave'
B. *maⁿssalame* 'with peace'
C. *ⁿallaysallmak* 'God keep you'

This language also illustrates the principle of replying to greetings by 'adding' to the original, as in

A. *marħaba* 'hello'
B. *marħabtēn* 'two hellos' or *mīt marħaba* '100 hellos'.

The Qur'an in fact says at one point (Surah IV, verse 86): 'If someone greets you, either return the greeting or greet him better, for God takes everything into account.' (After C. A. Ferguson, 1976.)

PROVERBIAL EXPRESSIONS

In every culture there are nuggets of popular wisdom, expressed in the form of succinct sayings. These are usually referred to as *proverbs*, though several other terms are also used (e.g. *adage, maxim, precept*). Proverbs are not commonly encountered in everyday speech in English, but in many cultures (e.g. in most parts of Africa) they are an important and frequent element in ordinary conversation.

Several extensive collections of proverbs have been made, which provide evidence for considerable similarities across cultures – similarities that are largely due to the universality of human experience (though there are often signs of linguistic borrowing). For example, many languages have parallels for such proverbs as the Somali *Kaadsade ma kufo* 'He who takes his time does not fall.' Structurally, also, proverbs display interlanguage similarities with their reliance on vivid images, domestic allusions, and word play. One of the most interesting features is the way many can be divided into two parts that balance each other, often displaying parallel syntax and rhythm, and links of rhyme and alliteration.

- *English:* Least said, soonest mended.
- *Maori: Ka whakaiti koe i te manuhiri, ka whakaiti koe i a koe.* 'In demeaning the visitor, you lower yourself.'
- *Latin: Praemonitus, praemunitus.* 'Forewarned is forearmed.'
- *Somali: Beeni marka hore waa malab, marka dambe na waa malmal.* 'Lies are honey at first, later they are myrrh.'
- *Chinese: ái wū jí wū.* 'If you love a house, you love its crows.' (cf. 'Love me, love my dog.')
- *Samoan: E mafuli le ului, ae tupu le suli.* 'The parent tree has fallen over, but one of its saplings is growing.'
- *Welsh: Cenedl heb iaith, cenedl heb galon.* 'A nation without a language is a nation without a heart.'

THE CHIEF USE OF SLANG ...

Is to show that you're one of the gang! In fact, slang has so many uses that it is difficult to choose one as central. Eric Partridge (1894–1979) was able to distinguish as many as 15 different reasons for the use of slang:

for the fun of it
as an exercise in wit or ingenuity
to be different
to be picturesque
to be arresting
to escape from cliches
to enrich the language
to add concreteness to speech
to reduce seriousness
to be colloquial
for ease of social interaction
to induce intimacy
to show that one belongs
to exclude others
to be secret

But one theme recurs among all these reasons: the use of slang as a means of marking social or linguistic identity. In Partridge's book *Slang: Today and Yesterday* (1933), the group-identifying function in fact provides the basis for most of the detailed illustrations, which come from a wide range of geographical areas and occupational activities. Slang is, by definition, a colloquial departure from standard usage; it is often imaginative, vivid, and ingenious in its construction – so much so that it has been called the 'plain man's poetry'. It thus especially attracts those who, for reasons of personality or social identity, wish to be linguistically different – to be 'one of the gang', whether the 'gang' in question be soldiers, nurses, actors, footballers, prisoners, warders, linguists, gays, or pop singers (see also pp. 56, 59).

SLANG SAMPLES

Cockney rhyming slang
Cain and Abel table
Cows and kisses the missus
Gawd forbids kids
Hampstead Heath teeth
lean and lurch church

U.S. hospital slang
crispy critter severe burn patient
pre-stiff close to death
prune old, dehydrated patient
Zorro belly someone with surgical scars on abdomen
(From D. P. Gordon, 1983.)

British prison slang
filth detectives
LTI long-term inmate
nick prison
screw prison warder
snout tobacco

But remember...
The slang of one generation can be the standard English of the next:
bus from *omnibus*
zoo from *zoological garden*
piano from *pianoforte*

FROM SPEECH TO POETRY

In several speech situations, contextual factors combine with the skill of the speaker to produce genres that display many of the characteristics of poetry. The main comparison is with the techniques used in the oral formulaic poetry of early European culture (in the Homeric epics, in particular), and still found earlier this century in the singing of oral epics by the Serbo-Croatian *guslars*. The rhythm and intonation changes from that of normal speech, so that prosodic 'lines' can be heard. The speech contains many memorized formulae, which can be embellished or modified as occasion arises.

Sermons
An example of this intermediate stage between speech and oral poetry is in the spontaneous sermons of black preachers in the southern United States. The text below has been transcribed in lines (from B. A. Rosenberg, 1970), identified by the preacher's own rhythms and the oral response of the congregation (*Amen, Hallelujah,* etc.). The heavy use of formulae is clear.

Keep your hand in God's hand,
And your eyes on the star-posts in glory.
Lord said he would fight your battles,
If you'd only be still.
You may not be a florist.
Am I right about it?
But you must tell them, that He's the Rose of Sharon.
I know that's right.
You may not be a geologist.
But you must tell them, that He's the Rock of Ages.
I know that's right.
You may not be a physician.
But you must tell them, that He's the Great Physician.
Am I right about it?
You may not be a baker.
But you must tell them, that He's the Bread of Life.
Am I right about it?...

Auctioneer speech
Auctioneers all over the world impress lay audiences with their fluent verbal skills; but much of their performance is based on the use of linguistic formulae, uttered in a distinctive prosodic form. Repeated phrases and an absence of pauses contribute to an impression of rapid speech – though in fact their speed (as measured in syllables per second) only occasionally exceeds that found in a normal conversation on a familiar topic. The special prosody has been studied, for example, in the monologues of New Zealand livestock auctioneers. During the opening phrase of the auction, the stock is described using a loud, high-pitched drone. When the bids begin, many of the speaker's rhythm units start with a stylized shout. The last bid generally has its own tune – a prosodic warning that the auction is about to end. Then the gavel falls, and the auctioneer's speech returns to a normal mode. Extracts from one auction illustrate its formulaic character (from K. Kuiper & D. Haggo, 1984):

What do you think Sir?
Sell 'em Sir?
Are they on the market, Sir?...
I'll sell 'em.
Right, I'll sell 'em.
Right, I'll sell.
We'll sell 'em.
Right, we'll sell 'em.
I'm gonna sell 'em...
I got twenty dollar twenty bid twenty bid twenty got twenty bid forty twenty dollar forty twenty forty I'm bid...

VISUAL VARIETIES

Ethnographers of communication have largely focused on the study of *speech* events in a wide range of cultural contexts, because of a previous lack of research in these domains. But it must not be forgotten that the various activities of the *written* language also display the influence of context – often in a highly distinctive manner, because of the visual contrasts available in the written medium, especially in print (§31). With thousands of stylistically distinct varieties available in a literate culture, there is space here to select only a tiny fraction, in order to illustrate the range of variability and some of the linguistic features involved. Further illustration of contextually influenced visual language activities will be found in §63, in relation to advertising, law, science, the press, and other specialized fields, and in §32, in relation to the field of typography.

Information materials

This is an enormous field, including works of reference (dictionaries, catalogues, almanacs, government leaflets, etc.), instructional material (phrase books, recipe books, do-it-yourself manuals, etc.), newspapers, documents, reports, teletext, and all kinds of academic publication. Some of these materials are so wide ranging and diverse that it is impossible to make simple generalizations about their linguistic distinctiveness. Newspapers, for example, constitute a clearly identifiable linguistic variety but one that is made up of a large number of 'sub-varieties' such as news reports, letters, editorials, and crosswords (p. 392). But at the opposite extreme, there are many informational linguistic activities that are limited in scope and fairly homogeneous in content and structure – some so severely constrained that they fall within the category of 'restricted language' (p. 56) – as with cooking recipes, phrase books, and commercial advertising.

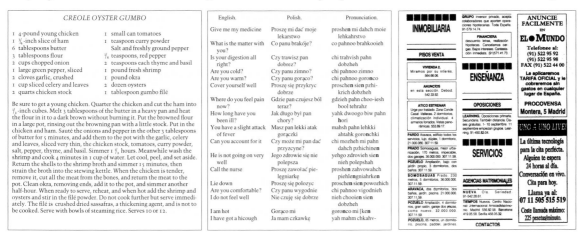

Ceremonial materials

Some of the most ornate forms of visual language will be found in materials intended for use on religious and ceremonial occasions, such as in books of religious significance, memorial plaques, certificates (examination, birth, marriage, etc.), and inscriptions. Formal and often archaic language is usual, reflecting the special significance society attributes to these activities. A birth certificate, a tombstone inscription, and part of a religious service leaflet illustrate this.

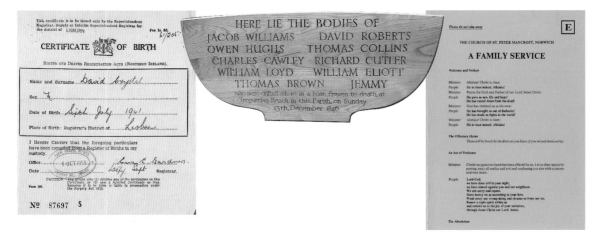

Dialogue materials

There are many linguistic activities where the identity of the visual variety is partly dependent on the active participation of the user. Either space is left for the users to fill in, or opportunity is given for them to reply in their own terms. Included in the first category are questionnaires, official forms, diaries, and various kinds of stationery; in the second are postcards, circulars, letters, and graffiti.

In the illustration (right), typographical design, technical vocabulary, and reduced syntax provide an unmistakeable linguistic identity for a German income-tax form, which is little different from its counterparts in other languages, and which would doubtless provide its taxpayers with a commensurate degree of difficulty. In recent years, government departments in several countries have tried to make such forms easier to use, with some success (§63). It is possible to make progress in clarifying layout and question structure, but there is a limit to the degree of simplification one can introduce when dealing with such a complex area of human activity.

Identifying materials

Probably the most widely encountered variety of visual language is that used for identifying persons, places, and objects. This includes street names, public signs, name tags, compliment slips, publication titles, identity cards, product labels, house numbers, registration plates, letter headings, tickets, shop facias, and much more. Typographical clarity and distinctiveness are the main characteristics, along with considerable grammatical abbreviation and the use of specialized vocabulary. There are marked linguistic similarities between languages. Internationally used symbols, such as numerals and trade marks, are routinely involved. A bilingual (Welsh/English) membership card, road signs, and car registration plates illustrate several of these features.

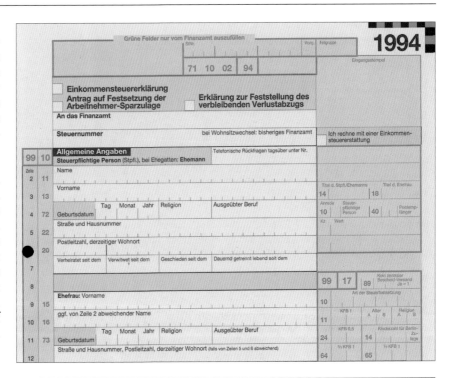

SOME LINGUISTICALLY DISTINCTIVE GRAFFITI

Scots rule, och aye!
French diplomats rule, au quai.
Oedipus was a nervous rex.
Mort au Shah – et aux souris (Paris).
Town criers rule, okez, okez, okez.
Ave Maria – I don't mind if I do.
Synonyms govern, all right.
Roget's Thesaurus dominates, regulates, rules,
OK, all right, agreed.

"I suppose it makes a change to see all that foreign graffiti."

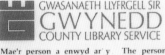

RESTRICTED LANGUAGES

The British linguist J. R. Firth (1890–1960) introduced the phrase 'restricted language' to refer to a severely reduced linguistic system used for a special activity. The language is so tightly constrained by its context that only a small degree of linguistic variation is permitted. These 'languages' are both spoken and written, and can be found in everyday as well as specialized contexts. They usually consist of routinely used formulaic constructions, with a conventionalized prosody or typographical layout, and a limited vocabulary.

BROADCASTING SCORES

The reporting of sports scores and stages of play is always a highly stereotyped activity. For example, in American baseball, there is the 'count' routine, which specifies first the number of balls (0–4) and then the number of strikes (0–3) of a player at bat, as in the following sequence:
One and one.
Count of one and one to M.
One and oh.
Two and oh.
Oh and one.
It's one and one.
Nothing and one count...
This can be compared with the equivalent reporting in Japanese sportscasts, where the English vocabulary continues to be used, although in Japanese pronunciation (e.g. *three* is *surii, strike* is *sutoraiku*). The conventions are different (the order is strikes before balls, and there are no plural endings or connecting words), but the stereotyped nature of the language is maintained:
Two strike two ball.
No strike two ball.
Two strike nothing.
Two nothing.
Two two.
(After C. A. Ferguson, 1983.)
   In reporting final scores, the convention in America, Japan, and many other countries is to read the higher score first; whereas in such countries as Britain and Germany, the home team is read first, with intonation being the signal of which team has won. Another common convention is for the two team names to be read together, followed by the two scores.

HERALDRY

The description of the symbols used on shields, flags, seals, and other objects involves an archaic grammar and vocabulary, much influenced by French, to produce phrases such as 'three bars gemel sable surmounted of a lion rampant gules, armed and langued azure'. Heraldic glossaries often contain around 800 terms, but only a few of these are in frequent use.

The distinctive terminology can be illustrated from some of the main features of a shield. The ground of the shield can be a colour, metal, or fur, involving contrasts such as *argent* (silver), *or* (gold), *gules* (red), *azure* (blue), *sable* (black), *vert* (green), *purpure* (purple), and *vair* (squirrel). The device on a shield is known as a *charge*, traditionally an animal or geometric shape,

but these days an increasing set of modern objects is used, as new coats of arms come to be devised. The main shield positions have their own terms (such as *chief* = top third; *dexter* = right side, as seen by the bearer; *pale* = vertical centre), and some of the patterns are shown below.

INDEXING

Alphabetical organization is a crucial feature of indexing style, but there are two competing principles in regular use – letter-by-letter and word-by-word. The difference can be seen by comparing two small sections of an index:

dialect 16, 42, 70–90
   accent vs 3
dialectic 40
dialect mixture 80–1
dialectology 36
dialect standards 65, 84–5
   research into 77

dialect 16, 42, 70–90
   accent vs 3
dialect mixture 81
dialect standards 65, 84–5
   research into 77
dialectic 40
dialectology 36

These samples show some of the idiosyncratic features of grammar that characterize this style, especially the inverted and telegraphic syntax.

TRUCKER TALK

The jargon of American truck drivers using citizen band (CB) radio has been widely publicized since the medium became available in 1958. The language contains a large number of stereotyped phrases for communicating routine messages, using a special numerical code (the CB-10 system). More complex messages use everyday English, peppered with CB slang, which makes it attractive to initiates and largely unintelligible to outsiders. In this special lexicon are such items as: *affirmative* (yes), *bears* (police), *anklebiters* (children), *doughnuts* (tyres), *eyeballs* (headlights), *five finger discount* (stolen goods), *grandma lane* (slow lane), *handle* (CBer nickname), *mobile mattress* (caravan), *motion lotion* (fuel), *rubber duck* (the first vehicle in a convoy), *smokey* (policeman), and *super cola* (beer). Some of the main CB-10 codes are given below.

10–1	Poor reception
10–2	Good reception
10–3	End transmission
10–4	Message understood
10–5	Relay message
10–6	Stand by
10–7	Leaving air
10–8	In service
10–9	Repeat
10–10	Monitoring without transmitting
10–20	My position is
10–100	Stop at lavatory
10–200	Police needed

LANGUAGE BOUNDARIES

Two knitting pattern extracts, one English, one Swedish, illustrate the way in which the features of restricted language cut across linguistic boundaries.

1st row–(K.1, P.1) twice, *K.1, w.f., K.3, w.f., sl.1, K.1, p.s.s.o., K.1, K.2 tog., w.f., K.3, w.f., (K.1, P.1) 4 times, rep. from * to last st., K.1.
2nd row–K.1, P.1, *(K.1, P.1) 3 times, P.16, rep. from * to last 3 sts., K.1, P.1, K.1.
3rd row–(K.1, P.1) twice, *K.1, w.f., sl.1, K.1, p.s.s.o., K.1, K.2 tog., w.f., sl.1, K.2 tog., p.s.s.o., w.f., sl.1, K.1, p.s.s.o., K.1, K.2 tog., w.f., (K.1, P.1) 4 times, rep. from * to last st., K.1.

Lägg upp 90 (98) 106 m på st 3½. Byt till st 2 och sticka 8 cm resår 2 am, 2 rm. Första v är avigsida. Byt till st 3½, sticka rätst (= alla v stickas räta) och öka jämnt över första v till 99 (107) 115 m. När arb mäter 46 (47) 48 cm avmaskas den mittersta m för v-ringn och var sida stickas för sig. Minska 1 m för v-ringn = på höger sida stickas 2 rm tills. och på vänster sida stickas 2 rm tills. bakifrån. Denna hoptagn görs vartannat v 21 ggr = 28 (32) 36 m kvar för axel.

SEASPEAK

There have been major changes in modern sea transport in recent years. Larger and faster ships pose greater navigational hazards. Shipping routes alter and present fresh problems of traffic flow. VHF radio permits direct communication between ship, shore, and aircraft, and satellite systems extend a ship's communicative range indefinitely. In such circumstances, mariners need to make their speech as clear and unambiguous as possible. Bridge officers, however, come from a variety of language backgrounds.

Although English is already recognized as the international language of the sea, it is essential that the language should follow clear rules, so as to reduce the possibilities of ambiguity and confusion in the sending and receiving of messages. In 1980, a project was set up to produce Essential English for International Maritime Use (referred to as Seaspeak) in Britain. The recommendations relate mainly to communication by VHF radio, and include procedures for initiating, maintaining, and terminating conversations, as well as a recommended grammar, vocabulary, and structure for messages on a wide range of maritime subjects. The language thus has considerable expressive power, though it is far more restricted than everyday language.

Call-signs

When sending call-signs in Seaspeak, as in air-traffic control, police communication, and other radio contexts, the NATO phonetic alphabet is used to spell a word or speak out individual letters. Each letter has its own name and pronunciation (italics mark the stress), which is given as follows in the Seaspeak manual.

A	Alpha	*AL*-FAH	N	November	NO-*VEM*-BER
B	Bravo	*BRAH*-VOH	O	Oscar	*OSS*-CAH
C	Charlie	*CHAR*-LEE	P	Papa	PAH-*PAH*
D	Delta	*DELL*-TAH	Q	Quebec	KEY-*BECK*
E	Echo	*ECK*-OH	R	Romeo	*ROW*-ME-OH
F	Foxtrot	*FOKS*-TROT	S	Sierra	SEE-*AIR*-RAH
G	Golf	*GOLF*	T	Tango	*TANG*-GO
H	Hotel	HOH-*TELL*	U	Uniform	*YOU*-NEE-FORM
I	India	*IN*-DEE-AH	V	Victor	*VIK*-TAH
J	Juliet	*JEW*-LEE-*ETT*	W	Whiskey	*WISS*-KEY
K	Kilo	*KEY*-LOH	X	Xray	*ECKS*-RAY
L	Lima	*LEE*-MAH	Y	Yankee	*YANG*-KEY
M	Mike	*MIKE*	Z	Zulu	*ZOO*-LOO

Similarly, some numbers change their pronunciation, so that they will be more clearly received. Large numbers have their own grammar.

0	zero	*ZERO*	8	eight	*AIT*
1	one	*WUN*	9	nine	*NINER*
2	two	*TOO*	15	one-five	WUN-FIFE
3	three	*TREE*	215	two-one-five	TOO-WUN-FIFE
4	four	*FOWER*	1,000	thousand	*TOUSAND*
5	five	*FIFE*	24,000	two-four-	
6	six	*SIX*		thousand	TOO-FOWER-
7	seven	*SEVEN*			TOUSAND

A conversation in Seaspeak

Western Sky (WS) is approaching Singapore (SPO).

WS: Singapore Port Operations. *This is* Western Sky. Information: My ETA* position: East Johore pilot station is time: one-three-four-five UTC. † *Over.*

SPO: Western Sky. *This is* Singapore Port Operations. *Mistake.* Time is: one-four-three-zero UTC now. *Stay on. Over.*

WS: Singapore Port Operations. *This is* Western Sky. *Correction.* My ETA is one-five-four-five UTC. *Over.*

SPO: Western Sky. *This is* Singapore Port Operations. Information-received: Your ETA position: East Johore pilot station is time: one-five-four-five UTC. Instruction: anchor in the General Purpose Anchorage, reason: your berth is occupied. *Over.*

WS: Singapore Port Operations. *This is* Western Sky. Instruction-received: anchor in the General Purpose Anchorage. *Nothing more. Over.*

SPO: Western Sky. *This is* Singapore Port Operations. *Out.*

* ETA = estimated time of arrival

† UTC = coordinated universal time

SOME RULES OF SEASPEAK

• A set of standard phrases is recommended, to avoid the many alternative ways there are in everyday language of expressing the same meaning. For example, *Say again* means 'What did you say?', 'I can't hear you', 'Would you repeat that?' These phrases are italicized in the transcribed conversation above.

• There are fixed syntactic and lexical routines for giving information. For example, bearings and courses using the 360-degree figure notation must give three-figure values: *009 degrees*, not *9 degrees*, etc. Dates are signalled using prefixes, e.g. 'day one-three, month zero-five, year one-nine-nine-five'. Days of the week are never used. When giving reasons, sentence construction is simplified. Everyday English has such connectives as *since, because, so that, in order to,* and *as,* but in Seaspeak, only *reason* is used, e.g. 'I intend to enter stern first, reason: my port thruster is damaged'.

• It is widely known that *Mayday* is the marker word for Distress; but there are also marker words for Urgency (*pan-pan*) and Safety (*Securité*, say-cure-e-tay), the latter being used when sending a message containing an important navigational or meteorological warning. Initial distress messages are repeated three times, and take priority over all other communications.

• Special markers indicate message type. The opening word is spoken aloud, e.g. *Question, Instruction, Advice, Warning, Intention,* and each has its own reply marker, e.g. *Answer, Instruction-received, Advice-requested.* Each form has its own rules. For example, only certain question-forms are allowed: rising intonations and tag questions (e.g. *isn't it?*) are not permitted. Use is also made of turn-taking devices, to check or correct messages, mark speaker-change, and so on, e.g. *Understood, Mistake, Over, Out.*

In addition to the equipment required for routine radio communications, several special-function aerials can be seen on *HMS Edinburgh*, a type 42 destroyer, including links with the marine communications satellite, Marisat.

HIDDEN AND SECRET LANGUAGE

Why should people deliberately use language that is unintelligible to all but a few initiates? There are three general reasons: to mark a person's membership of a group, to provide a pastime, and to ensure secrecy when performing a particular activity. When viewed as linguistic games, they are often seen as a creative form of play (e.g. by the Cuna of Panama), or even as a means of improving competence in speaking and language learning (as in Thai). Genres of secret language can thus be found in many cultures and in a wide range of human contexts, especially those where there is a concern to avoid detection (as in criminal argot, or cant), or to keep something hidden from lay people (as in magical formulae). Apart from the cases presented below, therefore, reference should also be made to several other instances of hidden language described in this book: glossolalia (p. 11), in-law taboos (p. 42), trucker talk (p. 56), whistle speech (p. 404), and various forms of slang (p. 53).

CRIMINAL CODES

There have been few studies of the secret languages used by underworld groups – for obvious reasons: it is not difficult to imagine the problems faced by academic researchers who have entered dens, parlours, and red-light areas, armed only with a tape recorder and an innocent smile! And even if they can extricate themselves safely, the risk continues. One scholar, who studied an underworld language in a city in India, was severely beaten at a later date for publishing something its speakers did not like.

In a study of the Vanarasi *Pandas* (those who look after Hindu pilgrims to the city), it was found that they use an argot alongside Sanskrit and Hindi during transactions with the pilgrims. A great deal of code-switching (p. 365) takes place, as can be seen in this sequence where a *Panda* talks to both an associate and a pilgrim about to bathe:

To associate (in argot): Martī jabrī hō. Khalag thilāv. ('The client is rich. Make him sit separate.')
To client (in Hindi): Hān, hāth joriye. ('Yes, fold your hands.')
(Sanskrit verses are then said, while the client takes his bath.)

The argot words are sometimes of unknown origin (e.g. *ragul* 'thief', *khotar* 'policeman'), but often they are distortions of everyday words (e.g. *mandir* 'temple' → *jhandir*, *ghar* 'house' → *ragha)* or common words that have been given a special meaning (e.g. *bājā* 'musical instrument' is used for 'gun').

Secret names for numbers are especially common because of their role in financial transactions. Within a radius of one kilometre around the Vishwanath temple in Vanarasi, one investigator found several distinct sets of secret number-names, used by such people as diamond dealers (A), silk merchants (B), fruit and vegetable merchants (C), and *Pandas* (D). Numbers 1–5 are given here, with Hindi numbers for comparison (after R. R. Mehrotra, 1977):

No	A	B	C	D	Hindi
1	airan pā	sāng	nimā	sāng	ek
2	thāl pā	swān	jōr	javar	do
3	bābar pā	ikwāi	rag	singhārā	tin
4	āirvan	fok	fok	fok	cār
5	sūt pā	bud	bud	pānro	pānc

The most noticeable kinds of criminal argot, or 'speech disguise' as it is sometimes called, are those where utterances are totally or partially unintelligible to the outsider because of the distinctive sounds, grammar, or vocabulary. But a great deal of argot occurs that appears to be in ordinary language, though in fact the utterances have a special meaning. An example of the latter was recorded in another study in India when the sentence *Jāo katori manj lo* 'Go, clean the bowl' was used by a murderer to an associate in front of his victim. The intended sense was: 'Prepare a grave'!

A ciphering machine The famous *Enigma*, which played a major role in World War 2 cryptology. The lid of the machine is raised, showing the rotors that control the letter permutations.

CRYPTOLOGY

It is a short step from the secret languages of children and the underworld to the world of secret intelligence, with its dual concern to preserve the military, commercial, and scientific security of one side, and to penetrate the corresponding security systems of the other. Cryptology is essentially a two-part science. One branch of the subject, *cryptography*, deals with the task of making messages secure, so that they cannot be understood by an enemy. The other branch, *cryptanalysis*, is concerned with extracting the meaning from enemy messages that have been intercepted.

The two branches are often referred to as 'code-making' and 'code-breaking'; but these popular names are inadequate, because they fail to distinguish the special sense of 'code' in this field. In cryptology, *code* has to be distinguished from *cipher*. A code is a system of phrases, words, syllables, or letters, each of which has an associated 'code word' or 'code number'; it may be 'decoded' using a 'code book'. A cipher, by contrast, is a system in which a message is 'enciphered' by transforming its letters is various ways, by substitution or transposition; it may be 'deciphered' using a 'key'. For example, the message *Crystal escape planned Friday* could be encoded as follows:
182   636   24   812
where each code number would correspond to the words as listed in a code book. It could also be enciphered as follows:
NLGHCZM   YHNZPY
PMZEEYV   SLAVZG
using a simple 'cipher alphabet' in which each letter has been substituted (a = z, b = d, etc.).

The history of cryptology illustrates the many ingenious methods that have been devised to maintain secrecy. Cipher alphabets, for example can be made more complex by using several equivalents for a letter ('homophones'), as when c is replaced by *dx*, *re*, or *pj*. Several such alphabets can be used at once: a message can be enciphered using alphabet A, and the result further changed using alphabet B, and so on; or certain letters of the message can be enciphered using A, others using B. Modern cipher machines can produce these 'polyalphabetic' ciphers using millions of such transformations. It is also possible to use codes and ciphers simultaneously. The result of all this ingenuity is the secret message, or *cryptogram*.

These days, there are several other aspects to signal security and intelligence, such as altering radio and radar frequencies, radio silence, and *steganography* – the use of techniques that conceal the existence of a message, such as invisible inks, microdots, or the use of electronic devices which hide a message in a signal. But these are of more interest to spies than linguists!

PLAYING WITH SOUNDS AND LETTERS

There are several 'languages' in which words are systematically altered, through the addition, subtraction, substitution, or transposition of sounds. Some are purely phonetic changes; others require a knowledge of spelling and alphabet order. Even in the more complex cases, practitioners can teach themselves to talk at great speed.

Records of some of the languages go back over 100 years in many parts of Europe. They have mainly been found among children, but there are also reports of their use among adults, especially in contexts where secrecy is required (e.g. in front of customers or small children).

• In *back slang,* words are spelled backwards, and then the new arrangement of letters is given a plausible pronunciation. It has been observed in the UK among soldiers, barrow-boys, shopkeepers, thieves, and public school pupils. First World War examples include *kew* 'week', *neetrith* 'thirteen', *tekram* 'market', and *tenip* 'pint'. In French, *parler a l'envers* ('speaking backwards') is found in several variants, e.g. *copains* 'friends' → *painsco, mari* 'husband' → *rima, l'envers* 'backwards' → *verlen.* The same game also appears in Javanese, e.g. *Bocah iku dolanan asu* 'The boy is playing with a dog' → *hacob uki nanalod usa.* In Thai, there are several variants involving consonants, vowels, and even tones, e.g. *kràb bâan* 'return home' → *kâan bàb, yàak kin khâw* 'I'd like to eat' → *yâw kin khàak.*

• In what is sometimes called *centre slang,* the central vowel of a word, along with its following consonant, is placed at the beginning, and a nonsense syllable added, e.g. *eekcher* 'cheek', *hoolerfer* 'fool', *ightri* 'right'.

• In *eggy-peggy* or *aygo-paygo* speech, an extra syllable is added, e.g. *Pugut thagat begook dowgun.* Similar are cases when an extra vowel or consonant is inserted between each syllable: using *f,* for example, *Where are you going* becomes *Wheref aref youf gofing.* In Cuna (Panama), there is a form in which *pp* or *r* is inserted, along with the vowel of the preceding syllable, e.g. *ua* 'fish' → *uppuappa, tanikki* 'he's coming' → *taranirikkiri.* In another Cuna game, *ci* is prefixed to every syllable, e.g. *maceret* 'man' → *cimaciceciret.* In Javanese, games using an inserted *f* for *p* plus vowel repetition have been recorded, e.g. *Aku arep tuku klambi* 'I want to buy a dress' → *afakufu afarefep tufukufu klafambifi* (after J. Sherzer, 1974).

• In *Pig Latin,* the first consonants are put at the end of the word, and *ay* or *e* added, e.g. *Utpay atthay ookbay ownday* 'Put that book down'. In a variant of this, last consonants are put at the beginning of the word, with extra sounds to aid the pronunciation, e.g. *Tepu tatha keboo nadaw.* A similar phenomenon has been studied in Cuna, where it is known as *arepecunmakke* (from Spanish *al revés* 'backwards' and Cuna *sunmakke* 'to speak'). Here, the first syllable is placed at the end, e.g. *takke* 'to come' → *ketak, ipya* 'eye' → *yaip.*

• In another form, there is a switch of initial and final consonants, and of initial consonants and consonant clusters of successive syllables, e.g. in a French version, *parler* 'speak' → *larper, boire* 'drink' → *roib.* Not all classes of words are affected, however, e.g. *Je bouffe pas* 'I'm not eating' → *Je foub pas.* A similar game has been found in Javanese, e.g. *rupiah* 'rupees' → *puriah, nduwe* 'have' → *wunde.*

• Some secret languages involve sound substitutions that resemble written language codes. One Javanese game is based on the order of the 20 consonant letters of the alphabet. The first ten letters (*h, d, p, m, n, t, ḍ, g, c, s*) are matched against the second ten (*j, b, r, w, y, ṭ, k, l, ñ, ŋ*), in reverse order; and the members of each pair are made to substitute for each other (*h* for *ŋ* and vice versa, *d* for *ñ* and vice versa, and so on), Thus the sentence (*h*)*aku gawe layaŋ* 'I'm writing a letter' emerges as *ŋamu rade patan*. It is reported that some speakers develop great skill in producing such forms at speed.

• 'T-ing in i' (talking in initials) has been reported, in which certain words are replaced by their first letters. A case from a school in Texas showed examples such as *Some p l-ed the m* 'Some people liked the movie', *She's a v p g* 'She's a very pretty girl'. Parents also sometimes use this form of abbreviation in front of their young children, along with the other spelling conventions, such as *It's time for b, e, d.*

MYSTICAL LETTERS

In the Middle Ages, there arose a Jewish (later a Christian) system of mystical practices based on an esoteric interpretation of Old Testament texts, known as the *Kabbala* (from Hebrew *qabbalah* 'something received'). It was thought that language in general, and biblical language in particular, contained coded secrets about God and the world, based on the way the letters of the text were arranged, and the numerical values which could be assigned to them. Some books, such as the 13th-century *Sefer ha-zo-har* (Book of Splendour), viewed by many as a sacred book, went into the Torah texts in minute detail, in a search for mystical values. Every word, letter, vowel point, and accent mark was evaluated, to determine its hidden meaning. The method lost its religious popularity by the 18th century.

One exegetical technique, which can be traced back to the early Christian era, was known as *gematria.* Here,

numbers were substituted for letters, and values compared in order to provide fresh insights into the meaning of texts. In the most commonly used system, the first ten letters of the Hebrew alphabet are numbered from 1 to 10; the next eight are given the values 20, 30, etc.; and the last four letters have the values 100, 200, 300, and 400. In English, the 26 letters are valued 1 to 26, in order. On this basis, all kinds of curious and (some still believe) significant correlations can be obtained.

Linguists take note: *tongue* and *lexicon* = 82. *sibilant* and *hissing* are adjacent numbers. *etymology, Indo-European* and *West Germanic* all = 137.

Those interested in deeper matters will note that: *man* and *Eden* = 28. *Bible* and *Holy Writ* are separated by 100. *Mount Sinai* and *the laws of God* = 135. *Jesus, Messiah, son, God, cross* and *gospel* all = 74.

Gematria is also occasionally practised outside of the religious context. For example, in deciding whether one should carry out a certain activity at a certain time, believers may look to see whether the numerical value of their name and that of the day or date correspond in any way.

MYSTICAL SUMS

Part of the arithmetic used by those who argue for the validity of gematria.

Bad
+ Language
Profane

Arm
+ Bend
Elbow

Not
+ Same
Different

Good
+ Deeds
Scout

Hide
+ Listen
Eavesdrop

All
+ Vote
Democracy

King
+ Chair
Throne

Keep
+ Off
Grass

VERBAL ART

Oe No Dain Biin	The goat of Oe No from Dai	1
Na biï ma-pau henuk	The goat has a yellow-necklaced beard	2
Ma Kedi Poi Selan manun	And the cock of Kedi Poi from Sela	1
Na manun ma-kao lilok.	The cock has gold-stranded tailfeathers	2
De ke heni pau biin	Cut away the goat's beard	3
Te hu ela lesu biin	Leaving but the goat's throat	4
De se lesun na pau seluk	That throat will beard again	5
Fo na pau henu seluk;	And the beard will be a yellow necklace again;	6
Ma feä heni koa manun	And pluck out the cock's tailfeathers	3
Te sadi ela nggoti manun	Leaving only the cock's rear	4
Fo nggotin na koa seluk	That rear will feather again	5
Fo na koa lilo seluk.	And the tailfeathers will be gold strands again.	6
Fo bei teman leo makahulun	Still perfect as before	7
Ma tetu leo sososan.	And ordered as at first.	7

SPEAKING IN PAIRS

The use of parallelism to mark certain kinds of speech activity is widely known. Semantic couplets are found extensively in the Indian languages of Middle America, such as Nahuatl and Yucatec, as part of formal speech genres. In Rotinese (eastern Indonesia), for example, parallel speech (or *bini*) is used as a form of ritual language, in which past events are recounted following a fixed ancestral pattern. *Bini* involves speaking in pairs of formulaic phrases, which may be in sequence or separated by several other 'lines'. The genre includes proverbs, songs, and chants and is used in relation to many formal activities, such as greetings, farewells, petitions, courtship, funerals, negotiations, and ceremonies of all kinds. *Bini* varies in length from two to several hundred 'lines'. The example right is of a 'succession' *bini*, in which imagery of renewal is used to express the continuation of lineage. The numbers refer to the lines that are in parallel. (After J. J. Fox, 1974.)

VERBAL DUELLING

Informal linguistic contests, in which people attack each other through their forceful or ingenious use of language, can be found in all parts of the world, and in all kinds of social settings. In everyday conversation there are numerous occasions where people have to fight to speak first, avoid interruption, and have the last word. The subject matter ranges from subtle forms of intellectual sarcasm and humour to the crudest possible attacks on a person's courage, sexual prowess, or relatives. At one level, attacks may be subtle and indirect, involving allusion and figurative speech; at another, there may be explicit taunts, boasts, name calling, and jokes at the other's expense.

Often these duels take the form of set sequences of challenges and replies according to certain rules. They involve a great deal of skill, as participants have to master special techniques of sentence construction, remember a large number of fixed phrases, and be able to modify them in ingenious ways as they come under verbal attack. These duels have been studied in places as far afield as Africa, the Near East, Greenland, and the Americas. They seem to function as a means of discovering the rules governing the social structure of the peer group. One can discover and test the dominance of others, without recourse to fighting and bloodshed.

Politeness duels and boasting contests have been recorded in early Chinese and Germanic languages. Among the Eskimo there are song duels, in which all forms of insults are exchanged. The West Indian calypso was originally a type of verbal insult directed at political figures. Among African-American youths in ghetto areas, various kinds of exchange are known as 'sounding', 'signifying', 'woofing', or 'playing the dozens' – a sequence of ritual insults (or 'raps') followed by replies ('caps'). Among Turkish boys, from around ages 8 to 14, the exchanges are phonologically linked: the retort must rhyme with the insult, and each new insult must be linked in some way with a previous part of the sequence. The exchanges are all to do with virility and homosexuality. They are delivered with great fluency and speed, and may continue for some time. A fragment from one exchange illustrates the rhyming pattern:

A: *Üstüne binek* Let me ride you
B: *Halebe gidek* Let's go to Aleppo
A: *Halep yikildi* Aleppo was flattened
B: *İçine tikildi* It was crammed inside (you)

In such sequences, A can win only if B fails to reply with an appropriate retort. If B succeeds, A must continue with more taunts. The more rhymes B has memorized, the more he is safe from sudden verbal attacks. He loses the contest if he answers without rhyme, or fails to answer at all. (See further, riddles, p. 63.)

FLYTING

Among the Germanic peoples, ritual cursing and boasting, known as *flyting*, often took place between poets or chiefs. One of the earliest exchanges of this kind is recorded between the English and Viking leaders in the Anglo-Saxon poem *The Battle of Maldon* (AD 991). The form is also found in Gaelic tradition, being best developed among the Scottish poets (*makaris*) of the 15th and 16th centuries. Their ferocious exchanges of extravagant invective are well illustrated in *The Flyting of Dunbar and Kennedie* by William Dunbar (1460–1521?). The exact meaning of some of the words is uncertain, but there is no doubting their malicious intent!

Mauch muttoun, byt buttoun, peilit gluttoun, air to Hilhous:

Rank beggar, ostir, dregar, foule fleggar in the flet;

Chittirlilling, ruch lilling, lik schilling in the milhous;

Baird rehator, theif of natur, fals tratour, feyindis gett...

(ll. 145–8)

A verbal confrontation.

CURSING AND SWEARING

A remarkable variety of linguistic forms can be considered as cursing and swearing. At one extreme there are the complex and sophisticated expressions that may be found in religious, legal, and other formal contexts. At the other, there are the many daily examples of taboo speech, usually profanities or obscenities, that express such emotions as hatred, antagonism, frustration, and surprise. The most common utterances consist of single words or short phrases (though lengthy sequences may occur in 'accomplished' swearers), conveying different levels of intensity and attracting different degrees of social sanction. English examples range from 'mild' expletives, such as *heck* and *dash*, to the two maximally taboo words, *fuck* and *cunt*.

The functions of swearing are complex. Most obviously, it is an outlet for frustration or pent-up emotion and a means of releasing nervous energy after a sudden shock (§4). It has also been credited with various social functions as a marker of group identity and solidarity (§10), and as a way of expressing aggression without resort to violence. In these social contexts swearing can become a dominant linguistic trait, with sentences often containing many taboo words.

Sex, excretion, and the supernatural are the main sources of swear-words. One important class of items deals with words to do with body parts and functions that society considers taboo, such as *merde, balls,* and

Roman lead tablet of 2nd to 4th century BC Cursing tablets were commonplace among the ancient Greeks and Romans. A curse would be inscribed on a tablet, which would then be buried or thrown into deep water. The lengthy inscription on one such tablet begins (after W. Sherwood Fox, 1919):

Good and beautiful Proserpina (or Salvia, shouldst thou prefer), mayest thou wrest away the health, body, complexion, strength and faculties of Plotius and consign him to thy husband, Pluto. Grant that by his own devices he may not escape this penalty. Mayest thou consign him to the quartan, tertian and daily fevers to war and wrestle with him until they snatch away his soul ... I give thee his ears, nose, nostrils, tongue, lips, and teeth, so he may not speak his pain; his neck, shoulders, arms, and fingers, so that he may not aid himself ...

and the curse continues through the whole anatomy of poor Plotius, in a most comprehensive way.

A similar curse was levelled against a Parisian woman, and published in a Nancy newspaper, as recently as 1910!

***Punch* cartoon of 2 April 1913** Old Lady: I shouldn't cry if I were you, little man.
Little Boy: Must do sumping; I bean't old enough to swear.

other 'four-letter' words. The other class deals with the names of gods, devils, sacred places, the future life, and anyone or anything that holds a sacred place in the belief systems of the community: *God, Dear Lord, By the beard of the prophet, By the holy sacrament, Heavens, Hell* ... Sometimes expressions from other belief systems are used (e.g. *by Jove*). In the course of time, euphemistic forms of words can obscure their original meaning (*hell → heck, bloody → blooming*, and such ingenious distortions as *Geraniums* and *Gee Whiskers* from *Jesus*). In fact, it can be argued that the real meaning of the expressions used in swearing is rarely a factor governing their use (thus allowing a contrast to be drawn with blasphemy, where the speaker has a definite intention to vilify religious matters).

It is never possible to predict the range of experience a culture will use to curse or swear by. It may be the name of a dead relative, a ruler or famous person, symbols of power, natural forces (*Donnerwetter*), a part of the body (*Stap me vitals*), an animal (*Rats*), or even a plant. One of the most famous oaths of ancient Ionia was *ma tin krambin* 'By the cabbage!' – an expression that seems to have originated in the special status of this vegetable as an antidote to hangovers! Socrates swore *ni ton kuna* 'By the dog'; and Pythagoras is said to have sworn *ma tin tetrakton* 'By the number four'. Even nonsense words can be invoked: Roberts Southey (1744–1843) swore by the great decasyllabon *Aballiboozobanganovribo*. Some languages, such as Arabic and Turkish, are famous for the range and imagination of their swearing expressions ('You father of 60 dogs', 'You ride a female camel', etc.). By contrast, several peoples, such as the Amerindians, Polynesians, and Japanese, swear very little, or not at all.

FOUR LETTERS AND THE LAW

In 1936, Eric Partridge (1894–1979) included *fuck* in his *Dictionary of Slang and Unconventional English.* Despite his use of an asterisk for the vowel, the result was a storm of complaints to schools, libraries, and the police. Even today, the book is not always available on the open shelves of public libraries.

An even greater furore took place in 1959, when Grove Press of New York published the unexpurgated edition of D. H. Lawrence's *Lady Chatterley's Lover,* which contained several instances of the word. The edition was banned on grounds of obscenity, and court cases followed, first in the U.S., then in Britain. The trial of the British publishers, Penguin Books, at the Old Bailey, took place in October 1960, and a verdict of not guilty was returned. As a result, the word quickly appeared in the daily press, and it has since become widespread in literary work. In the context of public speech, however, a strong prohibition remains.

Despite the development of liberal attitudes, there is still a strong antagonism to the use of four-letter words in public speech; and they are still not always to be found in dictionaries. There was nothing between *fuchsite* and *fucoid* in *Webster's Third New International Dictionary* (1961), for example; but the gap was filled in the 1983 addendum.

RABELAISIAN CURSES

Gargantua and *Pantagruel* (both 1532), by François Rabelais (c. 1495–1553), contain swearing performances that have never been surpassed. In the 1694 English translation by Peter Motteux (1660–1718), Book IV begins:

Ods-bodikins. What a devil. Codzooks. By the mass. With a pox to them. I vow and swear by the handle of my paper lantern. Adzookers. Zwoons. A pox on it. A murrain seize thee for a blockheaded booby ... By the worthy vow of Charroux. By St Winifred's pocket. By St Anthony's hog. By St Ferreol of Abbeville. By St Patrick's slipper. By our Lady of Riviere ...

LANGUAGE AND HUMOUR

The story is told of a man who was carrying out research into the language of jokes in the Reading Room of the British Library but who had to be expelled for laughing too loud. The story is improbable. Nothing is more likely to kill a good joke than a linguistic analysis. The examples in this section, therefore, are not offered by way of entertainment but solely to illustrate some of the conventions that make the expression of humour one of the most distinctive of all linguistic contexts.

The choice of funny or silly words, grammatical patterns, pronunciations, and tones of voice is a normal part of informal conversation. In one study of an evening's conversation, the participants 'tampered with' several linguistic features, for humorous effect: one person talked of climbing 'an Ande'; another coined a false gender, saying 'a customs officer-ess'; and a third speaker, talking about football, adopted a mock-American accent, commenting 'We wuz robbed.' In a recent conversation between several teenage boys, this kind of word- and pronunciation-play proved to be a dominant motif, acting more as a marker of solidarity than of humour – for the linguistic changes *per se* provoked little laughter.

JOKES

Modifications of these kinds happen so often that we hardly notice them; but they use the same principle, of deviating from language norms, as is found in more structured forms of humour, such as jokes and riddles, where the 'punch-line' frequently relies on breaking the linguistic expectations of the listener. This can be observed even in jokes that are (fortunately) quite short, especially those with highly stereotyped openings:

What do you get if you cross...
    an elephant with a mouse?
    Large holes in the skirting board.

Where is Felixstowe?
    On the end of Felix' foot.

It is important that jokes have some degree of initial stereotyping, in everyday contexts, for otherwise it would not be clear what the speaker's intentions were. Common markers in English are such phrases as 'Did you hear the one about ...' and 'There was this man ...' Often, a sub-genre of joke is established through the use of a specific opening, such as 'There was an Englishman, an Irishman, and a Scotsman ...', or 'Waiter, there's a fly in my soup.' Children's jokes in particular rely on a small number of set openings, or fixed internal structures, which permit a large number of follow-up sequences – witness the traditional success of such patterns as 'What's the difference between a NOUN and a NOUN?', 'What did the NOUN say to the NOUN?', 'Why did the NOUN VERB?', and, above all, the

'Knock knock' jokes with their fixed sentence sequence and final-line word play:

A: Knock, knock!
B: Who's there?
A: NAME. (*Fred*)
B: NAME who? (*Fred who?*)
A: NAME + EXTENSION. (*Fred* (= *afraid*) *I can't tell you!*)

A classification of the types of linguistic deviation and incongruity would be hard to achieve, for probably all aspects of language structure have been used as the basis of an effect at one time or other. Further examples would include effects based on word-structure and word-class ('Can the match box? No, but the tin can.'), idiomatic shifts ('A: Who's that at the door? B: The invisible man. A: Tell him I can't see him.'), incongruous themes (such as the 'elephant' jokes, which must now number thousands), as well as the many puns and riddles, which are discussed on the facing page. For the *cognoscenti*, there are even jokes that cross the boundary between languages, such as 'Pas de deux. Father of twins', and 'Coq au vin. Chicken on lorry.' A good joke classification would also have to deal with the contexts in which jokes are used (or not used), the attitudes and expectations of the people who use them, and the conventions that listeners have to follow while a joke is being told – such as not interrupting, not anticipating the punch-line, and (if the joke is truly 'awful') making a disparaging remark when it is all over.

Comic alphabets

There are hundreds of poems and puns based on reciting the letters of the alphabet. Widely known in the 19th century, they seem to have originated as an adult reflex of the rhyming alphabets that came to be used in schools ('A for an Apple, an Archer, and Arrow; B for a Bull, a Bear, and a Barrow', etc.) One of the alphabets reproduced in Eric Partridge's *Comic alphabets* (1961) runs as follows (with explanatory glosses added here):

A for 'orses. ('hay')	Q for the bus.
B for mutton. ('beef')	R for mo'. ('half ['arf] a
C for yourself. ('see')	mo[ment]')
D for dumb. ('deaf or')	S for you. ('as for')
E for brick. ('heave a brick')	T for two. ('tea')
F for vescence. ('effervescence')	U for me. ('you')
G for police. ('chief of')	V for la compagnie. ('Viva')
H for beauty. ('age before')	W for a quid. ('double you' in betting)
I for Novello. ('Ivor')	X for breakfast. ('eggs')
J for oranges. ('Jaffa')	Y for mistress. ('wife or')
K for teria. ('cafeteria')	Z for the doctor. ('send for
L for leather. ('hell')	...': the speaker has a
M for sis. ('emphasis')	cold: the joke works
N for mation. ('information')	only for British
O for the rainbow. ('over')	English, where *z* is
P for soup. ('pea')	pronounced /zed/)

UNIVERSAL JOKES?

Many cultural differences exist in joke telling and subject matter. It is a fairly common experience not to see why a foreign language joke is funny. On the other hand, certain themes are found in many languages. An example is the way certain social or regional groups are stereotyped as stupid, so that merely by saying 'There was this man from X', the listener knows that a foolish action is to follow. 'Irish jokes' illustrate the tradition in England, but the Irish should not take this personally, for they too have Irish jokes. In Dublin, such jokes are often made about people from Cork; and in Cork, the jokes are often made about people from Galway. (I have no data on who Galway people joke about!)

Similarly, in Tonga, such jokes are made about people from Ena, an island off the coast of Tongatapu. In Jordan, there are jokes about people from the village of Al-Sareeh. Several Central African tribes refer to pygmy groups in this way. What is interesting is the way in which the same joke turns up in very different cultures. For example, there's the one about the Sareehi boy who chased a bus all the way home, then boasted to his mother that he had saved 20 pence. But his mother called him foolish, saying that if he had followed a taxi, he would have saved over a pound! Of course, the joke was originally told in Arabic, and the monetary units were in local currency, but the same joke is familiar in English, and is heard, with minor variants, in several other languages.

RIDDLES

Riddling is a kind of intellectual linguistic game or contest, which in some ways is similar to verbal duelling (p. 60). It is found in many cultures, in all continents, and throughout history, but it is not universal (observers have reported no riddles in Manus, Miao, and Pukapuka, for example). A satisfactory definition encompassing the whole of the genre is difficult to achieve because riddles come in several linguistic forms and are used for a variety of purposes. It is also not easy to draw a clear distinction between riddles and other kinds of linguistic game, such as puns, and 'catch' questions. But essentially, riddles are traditional utterances intended to mystify or mislead: objects, animals, people, and events are deliberately described in such a way that their description suggests something quite different. The task of the listener is to resolve the ambiguity and arrive at an appropriate interpretation.

In Europe, riddles usually take the form of short questions, generally with humorous intent. In English, the genre is found largely in children's games and conversation, from around 7 to 10 years of age, and there are few things that make more demands on parental patience than learning to cope with the persistent riddle. In Africa, by contrast, riddles are widely used by adults: they are often cryptic statements, of a poetic or philosophical character, which do not contain any question element. In the ancient world, riddles had a serious purpose, being used by kings, judges, oracles, and others to test a person's wisdom or worthiness.

Riddles vary greatly in grammatical and phonological form. They may be single phrases, or have several short lines. They may be introduced by special formulae, such as *What is it?*, *A noun*, *A four-letter word*. They may display rhymes, parallel rhythms, and other special effects, often (as during the Renaissance) involving intricate and sophisticated forms of expression. This three-line Persian riddle from Teheran has an equivalent number of syllables in each 'line' (after C. T. Scott, 1965):

/ dóta bæradǽrænd / hǽrče bedævǽnd / behǽm némiræ sǽnd / 'They are two brothers. However much they run, they do not reach each other.'
/ čærxáye dočǽrxél 'Wheels of a bicycle.'

Examples such as this also illustrate the way in which riddles can cut across linguistic boundaries, for the same subject matter will be found in the riddle collections of many languages.

IN THE BEGINNING WAS THE PUN

This heading is a quotation from *Murphy* (Samuel Beckett) and represents one view about the importance of puns; John Dryden's comment, that they are 'the lowest and most grovelling kind of wit' represents the other. There is truth in both. Puns have always been known, and some have achieved great fame – notably the *Peter/rock* play on words in the New Testament

(clearer in French, where *pierre* is used for both), or the puns used by the oracle at Delphi (such as the ambiguous reply to the general who wished to know whether he should go on a journey: *Domine, stes* vs *Domi ne stes* 'Master, stay' vs 'At home do not stay'). Shakespeare was one of the greatest users of puns. In France, one of the most famous punsters was the Marquis de Bièvre, in whose never-acted play *Vercingétorix* (1770) there is an italicized pun in every line.

Puns are a feature of many linguistic contexts, such as black comedy, sick humour, T-shirts, lapel badges, car stickers, trade names, book titles, and graffiti (p. 55). The world of advertising (p. 394) makes great use of the economical impact and freshness of a pun (e.g. the slogan for a new kind of adhesive, 'Our word is your bond'). But the best and worst of them are found in everyday conversation. Puns that have been justly lauded include the response of the disappointed recipient of a gift of poor quality flowers ('With fronds like these, who needs anemones?'), the comment made by the circus manager to the human cannonball who wanted to leave ('Where will I find another man of your calibre?'), and the comment about the Spanish girls in a certain town, that they are 'senoreaters'.

Puns have been called verbal practical jokes, and are either loved or hated according to temperament. Their popularity varies greatly between languages and cultures, though the reasons for this are unclear; it has been said, for example, that they are far more popular in Britain than in the USA, and in France than in Germany. But punning is not without its dangers. The Gnat, in Lewis Carroll's *The Hunting of the Snark*, dies of a pun. And punsters should beware the phenomenon of compulsive punning, first recorded by a German surgeon in 1939, and now known as 'Förster's syndrome'.

THE OLDEST ENGLISH RIDDLES

In the oldest collection of Anglo-Saxon poetry, the Exeter Book, there are 95 riddles, which probably date from the 8th century. The riddles are generally in the first person, as illustrated by the opening lines of the 'book' riddle (translation R. K. Gordon):

A foe deprived me of life, took away my bodily strength; afterwards wet me, dipped me in water, took me out again, set me in the sun where I quickly lost the hairs I had. Afterwards the hard edge of the knife cut me ...

The riddle ends:

Ask what is my name, useful to men; my name is famous, of service to men, sacred in myself.

A page from the Exeter Book

WORD GAMES

Playing with words is a universal human activity, but it is particularly noticeable in the way literate societies have devised word games, based largely on the written language. People delight in pulling words apart and reconstituting them in a novel guise, arranging them into clever patterns, finding hidden meanings inside them, and trying to use them according to specially invented rules. Word puzzles and competitions are to be found in newspapers, at parties, in schools, on radio and television, and in all kinds of individual contexts – as when an adult completes a crossword, or a child plays a game of Hangman. Something of the enormous diversity of the 'ludic' function of language is illustrated in this section (see also pp. 59, 62–3).

ACROSTICS

These are compositions, usually in verse, in which certain letters within the text form a word, phrase, or special pattern. Some are written as puzzles; in others, there is no attempt to conceal the 'answer'. Generally the initial letter of each line provides the clue, but sometimes it is based on the last letter of the line (a 'telestich'), combinations of first and last letters (a 'double acrostic'), or more complex sequences.

A 'triple acrostic' The solution is based on initial, medial, and final letters in each clue word.
 Left, middle, and right
Give us a choice of a light.

1. The kind of glance which he who's lost his heart
   Bestows on her who wears the latter part.
2. Here is one
   With a gun.
3. This is bound
   To go round.
4. Simplify taste
   And eliminate waste.
5. My meaning is made plain
   By my saying it again.

Ado	Rin	G
Musk	Etee	R
Ban	Dag	E
Econ	Omiz	E
Reite	Ratio	N

CHRONOGRAMS

A date is hidden in a series of words, by using the letters for Roman numerals, C, D, I, L, M, V (used for U), and X. The significant letters are usually written in capitals, producing an odd graphic appearance to the line. Chronograms were often used on medals, tombstones, foundation stones, bells, and title pages of books, to mark the date of an event.

In the chronogram used in the tower vaulting of Winchester Cathedral, the verse of scripture reads: 'sInt DoMVs hVIVs pII reges nVtrItII, regInae nVtrICes plae' (Isaiah 49:23, 'Kings shall be the nursing fathers and queens the nursing mothers of thy house'). MDCVVVVVIIIIIIIIII = 1635, the date of completion of the roof.

GRID GAMES

There are now innumerable games that all operate on the principle of building up words on a predetermined grid. Some are intended for individual use, such as Word Search (a large letter grid in which words have to be found by moving from one square to the next, in any direction). Others are for several players, such as Lexicon, Kan-U-Go, and Boggle. In Scrabble – the most famous game of this type – points are assigned based upon how many letters are used, with higher points for the rarer letters, and with certain squares in the grid more valuable than others. This game now has its own national championships, in which expert players display rare feats of lexical awareness to achieve high scores. Clement Wood's *Death of a Scrabble Master* cleverly portrays some of the special knowledge required to keep on winning:

This was the greatest of the game's great players:
If you played BRAS, he'd make it HUDIBRASTIC.
He ruled a world 15 by 15 squares,
Peopled by 100 letters, wood or plastic.

He unearthed XEBEC, HAJI, useful QAID,
Found QUOS (see pl. of QUID PRO QUO) and QUOTHA,
Discovered AU, DE, DA all unitalicized
(AU JUS, DA CAPO, ALMANACH DE GOTHA).

Two-letter words went marching through his brain,
Spondaic-footed, singing their slow litany:
AL (Indian Mulberry), AI (a sloth), EM, EN,
BY, MY, AX, EX, OX, LO, IT, AN, HE...

The day his adversary put down GNASHED,
He laid – a virtuoso feat – beneath it GOUTIER,
So placed, that six more tiny words were hatched:
GO, NU, AT, SI, then (as you've seen, no doubt) HE, ER.

DECODING CROSSWORD CLUES

The crossword is undoubtedly the most popular of all word games. Its origins are unclear, but it became widely known in 1913, when a U.S. journalist, Arthur Wynne, devised a newspaper puzzle, called a 'word cross', which quickly became a craze. But for anyone who has tried it, writing a good puzzle turns out to be far more difficult than solving it. The construction of the interlocking words within the puzzle is not the issue: the main problem is devising clues which are ingeniously ambiguous, but do not unintentionally mislead.

The more difficult puzzles make use of cryptic clues, which require the solver to understand several special conventions. An anagram might be signalled by a figure of speech expressing disorder, such as 'A youth is all mixed up...' 'Used in' may mean that the required word is hidden within a phrase forming part of the clue. If the clue contains a parenthetic phrase such as 'we hear', two similar-sounding words are involved. Punning clues often end with an exclamation or question mark. And a large number of conventional expressions are used to symbolize certain letters, such as 'left' (= *l*), 'north' (=*n*), 'a sailor' (=*ab*), or 'a thousand' (=*m*).

In the specialized world of the 'serious' crossword compilers, the rules governing the construction of clues are strictly adhered to, and much pleasure is obtained by making them really difficult and ingenious. In Britain, the symbol of this state of mind has been the choice of pseudonyms of some of the great compilers: Torquemada, Ximenes, and Azed (Deza in reverse) – all names of leaders of the Spanish Inquisition!

WORD-SQUARES

A square of letters is constructed, using words of equal length, which read in horizontal, vertical, and occasionally diagonal directions. Usually the words are the same in each direction, but in 'double word-squares', they read differently, as in:

```
O R A L
M A R E
E V E N
N E A T
```

A famous Roman word-square was part acrostic, part palindrome. It may be read in four directions.

```
S A T O R
A R E P O
T E N E T
O P E R A
R O T A S
```

Its literal translation is 'The sower, Arepo, guides wheels with care', but it may well have had special significance to Christians of the time: the middle lines form a cross, and the letters can be rearranged to form several significant messages, like

```
            A
            P
            A
            T
            E
            R
A  P A T E R N O S T E R  O
            O
            S
            T
            E
            R
            O
```

(where A and O stand for ALPHA and OMEGA).

Other intriguing word-shapes have been invented, such as diamonds, pyramids, and half-squares. Also of interest is the maximum size of such shapes. In English, nine-word squares have been completed, containing several rare words and places, but so far no ten-word squares using ten different words have been completed – even with the help of a computer. A nine-word square:

```
Q U A R E L E S T
U P P E R E S T E
A P P O I N T E R
R E O M E T E R S
E R I E V I L L E
L E N T I L L I N
E S T E L L I N E
S T E R L I N G S
T E R S E N E S S
```

ANAGRAMS

The letters of words and phrases are rearranged to make new words – a procedure which at one time was thought to disclose significant information about a person's character or future, and even to carry mystical meaning or magical power (p. 59). People would sometimes live according to the 'real' meaning of their names, and in post-Renaissance Europe, it was commonplace to work out laudatory anagrams from the names of the famous. Louis XIII of France even had an official anagrammatist within his court. Jonathan Swift, on the other hand, was one of many who ridiculed the pomposity and superstition of those who dealt in anagrams. In *Gulliver's Travels,* natives of Tribnia (= Britain) discover plots using the 'anagrammatic method':

By transposing the letters of the alphabet in any suspected paper, they can lay open the deepest designs of a discontented party. So, for example, if I should say, in a letter to a friend, 'Our brother Tom has just got the piles', a skilful decipherer would discover that the same letters that compose that sentence, may be analysed into the following words, 'Resist – a plot is brought home – the tour'.

As a game, however, anagrams can provide a great deal of fun, especially when an anagram relates to the meaning of the original in some way:

astronomers → moon-starers
conversation → voices rant on
Margaret Thatcher →
  Meg, the arch-tartar
  that great charmer
parishioners → I hire parsons
revolution → to love ruin
sweetheart → there we sat
total abstainers → sit not at
  ale bars

LIPOGRAMS

These are compositions which contain no instances of a particular letter of the alphabet. An early master of the genre was the 5th-century BC Greek poet Tryphiodorus, who wrote an epic of 24 books, each omitting a different letter of the Greek alphabet. One of the most famous lipograms of recent times is *Gadsby* (1939), a 50,000-word novel by Ernest Wright, which makes no use of the most frequent letter of the English alphabet, e. A tiny extract from this remarkable work illustrates how it can be done:

Upon this basis I am going to show you how a bunch of bright young folks did find a champion; a man with boys and girls of his own; a man of so dominating and happy individuality that Youth is drawn to him as is a fly to a sugar bowl. It is a story about a small town...

PALINDROMES

There are words or phrases – and sometimes much larger units of language – that read the same in both directions. Simple examples are found in such everyday words as *madam* and *Eve;* but the real challenge is to construct long sequences that make sense, such as:

Draw, o coward!
Sex at noon taxes.
Eh, ça va, la vache?

or the palindromes attributed to Napoleon:

Able was I ere I saw Elba.

Longer sequences tend to deteriorate into nonsense, though there are exceptions:

Doc, note, I dissent. A fast never prevents a fatness. I diet on cod.

The longest palindrome is reputedly over 65,000 words.

TONGUE TWISTERS

One of the few word games that relate purely to the spoken medium. Words that contain the same or similar sounds are juxtaposed, and the exercise is to say them as rapidly as possible, as in:

The Leith police dismisseth us.
The sixth sheikh's sixth sheep's sick.
She sells sea-shells on the sea-shore.

This fine Italian specimen is worth recording.

Se l'Arcivescovo di Constanti-nopoli si volesse disarcivesco-viscostantino politannizzare, vi disarcivescoviscostantino politannizzereste voi per non fare disarcivescoviscostantino politannizzare lui?

(If the Archbishop of Constantinople wished to give up his archbishopric, would you do the same in order that he may not give up his archbishopric?)

Sign outside The Plough at East Hendred, Oxfordshire. Hiding words within other words, or spreading them across the words in a sentence (e.g. *maniac* within *the man I accuse*) is a well-known feature of crossword puzzle clues, and it can become a game in its own right. Altering word boundaries can also lead to initially confusing results, as is shown by this sign.

REBUSES

A rebus mixes letters, pictures and logograms (p. 202) to make words and sentences. Often, the sentences make sense only when read aloud in a certain way, as in this famous rebus:

YY U R	*Too wise you are.*
YY U B	*Too wise you be.*
I C U R	*I see you are.*
YY 4 ME	*Too wise for me.*

Other conventions are shown in H& (= hand), XQQ (= excuse), and in such ingenious forms as *timing tim ing* (= split-second timing) and FECpoxTION (= smallpox infection).

A typical rebus game from a children's annual

UNIVOCALICS

By contrast with lipograms, univocalics are compositions that use only one vowel. The possibilities for expression are much more limited, but several clever poems have been constructed in this way, as is illustrated by this couplet from a 16-line work by C. C. Bombaugh (1890):
No cool monsoons blow soft on Oxford dons, Orthodox, jog-trot, book-worm Solomons!

DOUBLETS

One word is changed into another in a series of steps, each intervening word differing from its neighbours in only one letter. The challenge is both to form the chain of linked words, and to do so in as few steps as possible. The game was invented by Lewis Carroll, who gave as one of his first examples, 'Drive *pig* into *sty.*' His answer involved five steps: *pig–wig–wag–way–say–sty.*

PANGRAMS

These are sentences that contain every letter of the alphabet – ideally, a single instance of each. *The quick brown fox jumps over the lazy dog* satisfies the first criterion, but has several duplications. A 26-letter pangram devised in 1984 is *Veldt jynx grimps Waqf zho buck* (all words to be found in a large dictionary). In French, the shortest pangram is listed as *Whisky vert: jugez cinq fox d'aplomb,* but there are three duplications.

The way people use language gives us information about their physical type, their geographical, ethnic, and social background, and the type of context in which they are communicating (§§6–11). In each case, the distinctive features mark someone as belonging to a group, or performing a particular type of activity along with others – 'female', 'upper class', 'from Glasgow', 'black', 'praying', and so on. But in addition, a person's language use conveys information of a purely idiosyncratic kind. We observe the language and conclude that it is 'William Brown' communicating – or, of course, William Wordsworth, or William Shakespeare.

In everyday life, unless cognitive faculties are impaired, people have an ability to recognize individual voices and handwriting style, and this facility has prompted a great deal of research into voiceprints (p. 20) and graphology (§33). But adult voice quality and handwriting are relatively permanent, background features of communication – general physiological and psychological reflexes over which there is little conscious control. They therefore contrast with those personal linguistic characteristics that are relatively temporary, in the foreground, changing and changeable as people make conscious choices about what they want to express and the way they want to express it. It is these characteristics that provide the subject matter of this section, often referred to cumulatively under the heading of *style*.

STYLE

Style is one of the thorniest concepts to be dealt with in this encyclopedia. To Samuel Wesley, it was 'the dress of thought'; to Jonathan Swift, it was 'proper words in proper places'; to W. B. Yeats, it was 'high breeding in words and in argument'. And so we could continue, through several hundred definitions and characterizations. It is a remarkable career for a word that originally meant no more than a 'writing-implement' – a pointed object, or *stilus*, for inscribing wax.

The many senses of style can be classified into two broad types: the *evaluative* and the *descriptive*. Under the first heading, style is thought of in a critical way: the features that make someone or something stand out from an 'undistinguished' background. In this sense, it implies a degree of excellence in performance or a desired standard of production, as when someone is complimented for 'having style', or condemned for writing 'without style'. The second

sense lacks these value judgments and simply describes the set of distinctive characteristics that identify objects, persons, periods, or places. In this sense, we talk of 'Shakespearean style', the 'house style' of an institution, and all the variations in expression that relate to psychological or social states ('informal style', 'legal style', etc.).

Both these general senses are widely used in language study. Evaluative notions are an essential part of aesthetic approaches to language, and are implicit in such areas as elocution, oratory, and literary criticism. Descriptive approaches are found more in scientific studies, such as the various branches of linguistics, where there is a concern for objective identification without evaluation. But there is a common strand running through these various traditions: style always involves an appreciation of *contrast* between alternative locations, periods, appearances, or behaviour. As language observers, we distinguish 'Shakespearean' from 'not Shakespearean', 'formal' from 'informal', 'scientific' from 'religious', and so on. And as producers of language ourselves, we can to a large extent *choose* the linguistic 'guise' in which we wish to appear.

This concept of choice is central to stylistic study, whatever our approach. Style is seen as the (conscious or unconscious) selection of a set of linguistic features from all the possibilities in a language. The effects these features convey can be understood only by intuitively sensing the choices that have been made (as when we react to the linguistic impact of a religious archaism, a poetic rhyme scheme, or a joke), and it is usually enough simply to respond to the effect in this way. But there are often occasions when we have to develop a more analytical approach, as when we are asked our opinion about a particular use of language. Here, when we need to explain our responses to others, or even advise others how to respond (as in the teaching of literature), our intuition needs to be supplemented by a more objective account of style. It is this approach which is known as *stylistics*.

The notion of stylistic choice could be used to explain many of the effects used in the expression of social and contextual identity (§§10, 11); and indeed, several stylisticians do adopt this wider approach. For them, 'style' is *any* situationally distinctive use of language – a characteristic of groups as well as individuals. In the present volume, however, a narrower definition is used: 'style' is viewed as the set of language features that make people distinctive – the basis of their personal linguistic identity.

WHO'S WHO?

The importance of personal linguistic identity is often recognized in the study of literature, where an author's expression may be analysed in detail by literary critics to determine its specific effect, meaning, and significance. But critics are not the only professionals involved in the study of language individuality.

• Lawyers have a particular interest in the language of their clients, especially when questions of libel, slander, perjury, and mistaken identity are raised. In recent years there have been several stylistic analyses of speech samples, where the aim has been to establish the similarities between an accused person's language and that heard in a tape recording (p. 69). However, such 'forensic linguistic' enquiries are persuasive only when the stylistic features are particularly clear-cut.

• Psychiatrists, especially those practising psychotherapy, spend a great deal of their professional lives attempting to understand the idiosyncratic linguistic behaviour of their patients – an approach that stems from the detailed analyses of Sigmund Freud (1856–1939). By studying patients' favourite words and sense associations, their errors, and the words they avoid, analysts may draw up a linguistic picture of the disorder and use it as a basis for treatment. Psychotherapy, indeed, has been called the 'talking cure'.

STATISTICS AND STYLE

The recognition and analysis of all forms of linguistic variation depends on the making of comparisons. We intuitively sense that individuals and groups differ and develop, and we seek to explain our intuition by systematically comparing the way in which they make use of specific linguistic features. If we wish to make our account objective, sooner or later we need to count the frequency of these features, plot their distribution in controlled samples, and quantify the extent of the difference – at which point, we would be engaging in *stylostatistics*, or *stylometrics*. Such studies comprise a major part of the field of *statistical linguistics* (§15) – a field which investigates not only the differences between samples or texts, but also the properties that samples (and, ultimately, whole languages, and all languages) have in common, as part of the search for linguistic universals (§14).

Nobody can count everything; and even if modern computers printed out comprehensive accounts of the linguistic structure of texts, there would not be enough time available to analyse them. On the other hand, the larger the sample of data analysed, the more confident our conclusions will be. Stylostatistical studies thus tend to use a small number of carefully chosen textual features and to search for these in as large a body of text as is practicable. Where possible, comparisons are made with statistical data available for the whole language (such as large-scale counts of word frequency). In this way the language acts as a 'norm' against which the idiosyncratic features are made to stand out.

Typically, stylostatistics investigates matters of frequency and distribution in three main areas:

- formal characteristics that do not relate directly to the meaning of a text, such as parts of speech, source of vocabulary (e.g. Romance vs Germanic), and the length of words, sentences, or lines;
- characteristics that relate directly to meaning, such as the size and diversity of an author's vocabulary; and
- the detailed study of single words, or small sets of words, such as *and,* or the use of *on* vs *upon*; particular attention is paid to words that occur only once in a text, in the works of an individual author, or in the language as a whole (*hapax legomena*).

Quantitative studies using these variables date from the 19th century. Much effort was devoted to devising measures that were statistically satisfactory as well as stylistically interesting.

Stylostatistics would not normally analyse those features over which individuals have little or no control because they are part of the obligatory structure of a language – such as the letter sequence $q + u$ in English, or the use of the article before the noun. Where there is no choice, there is no basis for making a stylistic contrast. Style is thus seen as an author's regular selections from the *optional* features of language structure.

Institutions, as well as people, need to be considered in relation to the definition of style as 'individual identity'. There are certain distinctive linguistic characteristics of newspaper language, for example, which will be found in all instances of the genre (p. 392); but each paper has its own linguistic identity too, which make it different from the others. The same principle applies to the study of banks, commercial products, broadcasting channels, and any organization which requires an identity and public image. House styles, letter-heads, newspaper titles, advertising slogans, and many kinds of trade mark illustrate some of the ways in which institutions rely on stylistic features as a means of promoting corporate identity (p. 13).

Groucho Marx The success of a public entertainer may depend on linguistic idiosyncrasy. Public recognition can come from the clever use of a single catch phrase. In many cases, the image involves an entire way of speaking, a well-known example being the professional tone of voice of Groucho Marx.

YULE'S CHARACTERISTIC

George Udny Yule (1871–1951) was a Cambridge statistician who pioneered several important stylostatistical measures. His main concern was to devise a criterion which would apply largely independently of sample size. 'Yule's Characteristic' (K) is a measure of the chance that any two nouns selected at random from a text will be identical. It is thus a means of measuring the repetitiveness of a work's vocabulary, expressed as a single value.

George Udny Yule

AUTHORSHIP IDENTIFICATION

One of the most important applications of stylostatistical studies has been in relation to cases of disputed or unknown authorship. The frequency and distribution of a small number of linguistic features in a problem text is compared with the corresponding features in texts where the authorship is known. Given a judicious selection of features for comparison, it is often possible to make an identification, though with varying levels of confidence. In this way, several important authorship questions have been illuminated or solved.

Sometimes a conclusion can be reached using a very small number of variables. For example, in one study (E. L. Moerk, 1970), as few as 20 grammatical features proved enough to distinguish between 1,000-word samples of six Greek and Roman writers (Herodotus, Thucydides, Xenophon, Tacitus, Caesar, Livy). The measures included counts of main and subordinate clauses, certain types of connecting word, nouns in various cases, and several other word classes. However, it is often necessary to use much larger textual samples (samples of over 10,000 words are common), where special attention has to be paid to their homogeneity; sophisticated statistical measures may have to be used; and a wider range of linguistic criteria may need to be involved, and given a precise definition.

There are several technical problems. If we are counting word classes, then it is important to use clear criteria of identification (are *London, boy,* and *the rich* all called nouns? (p. 91)). If a word count is being made, a precise definition of 'word' is of paramount importance (how are hyphenated forms to be handled? are *bear* 'carry' and *bear* 'animal' counted as one word or two? is *The Hague* one word or two?) (p. 104). Certain kinds of data may need to be excluded from the sample (e.g. quotations, translated forms, proper names). And a decision must be made about the range of stylistic variation to be permitted within the supposedly 'homogeneous' sample (e.g. how to take account of different levels of intimacy and formality, or dialect mixing?). Above all, the basic question must be addressed: is the text too small to warrant any kind of stylostatistical study – as is often the case with poems, letters, or police statements?

It is difficult to take account of all these technical factors, and even more difficult to anticipate the range of external factors that interfere with linguistic judgments. A text might have been written by more than one person. It might be a deliberate imitation or forgery. And there may be a large number of potential candidates for authorship, all of whom need to be systematically compared. But with meticulous care and a great deal of motivation, it is possible to reach reliable conclusions, and several fascinating and successful studies have been carried out. Moreover, there is well-founded optimism for the future, now that specially designed computer programs are becoming available for the study of stylistic differentiation.

WHO WAS JUNIUS?

If we see them [the people] obedient to the laws, prosperous in their industry, united at home, and respected abroad, we may reasonably presume that their affairs are conducted by men of experience, abilities and virtue. If, on the contrary, we see an universal spirit of distrust and dissatisfaction, a rapid decay of trade, dissensions in all parts of the empire, and a total loss of respect in the eyes of foreign powers, we may pronounce, without hesitation, that the government of that country is weak, distracted and corrupt.

This is an extract from a series of political letters written under the pseudonym Junius, which appeared in the London daily newspaper, *The Public Advertiser,* between 1769 and 1772. The letters were much appreciated and were reprinted in pamphlet form several times. During the years that followed, and throughout the 19th century, hunting for the identity of Junius became a popular sport, with several well-known names being proposed.

An investigation in 1962 by the Swedish linguist, Alvar Ellegård (1919–) counted the words in the letters (over 80,000) and compared them with a million-word norm of political literature from the same period. Some words were found to be more common in the letters than in the norms, and some were found to be less common. Altogether, 458 lexical features were used, along with 51 synonym choices (such as whether Junius used *on* or *upon, commonly* or *usually, till* or *until, know not how* or *do not know how*). For example, Junius preferred *until* to *till* in 78% of possible instances – a feature shared by only one in seven contemporary writers in Ellegård's sample. These features were then compared with a sample of over 230,000 words taken from the known works of the most likely contender for authorship, Sir Philip Francis. The similarities were so significant that Ellegård was able to conclude with confidence (p. 15), 'We have identified Junius with Francis.'

Junius: Sir Philip Francis by James Lonsdale, 1810

Augustus de Morgan

MIND, I TOLD YOU SO!

Augustus de Morgan (1806–71), British mathematician and logician, who first saw the possibility of stylostatistic authorship identification, wrote in a letter in 1851: 'I should expect to find that one man writing on two different subjects agrees more nearly than two different men writing on the same subject. Some of these days spurious writings will be detected by this test. Mind, I told you so.'

The letter was not published until 1882, when it was read by the American geophysicist, T. C. Mendenhall (1841–1924). He likened the frequency distribution of words of different lengths to the spectrum of light, and began to search for word-length profiles in several English authors – 'word spectra', which he thought could be as specific as metallurgical spectrograms. He made several pioneering contributions to authorship studies, including the Bacon/Shakespeare controversy.

FORENSIC LINGUISTICS

Most stylostatistical studies are of literary works; but the same techniques can be applied to any spoken or written sample, regardless of the 'standing' of the user. In everyday life, of course, there is usually no reason to carry out a stylistic analysis of someone's usage. But when someone is alleged to have broken the law, stylisticians might well be involved, in an application of their subject sometimes referred to as 'forensic' linguistics.

Typical situations involve the prosecution arguing that incriminating utterances heard on a tape recording have the same stylistic features as those used by the defendant – or, conversely, the defence arguing that the differences are too great to support this contention. A common defence strategy is to maintain that the official statement to the police, 'written down and used in evidence', is a misrepresentation, containing language that would not be part of the defendant's normal usage.

Arguments based on stylistic evidence are usually very weak, because the sample size is small, and the linguistic features examined are often not very discriminating. But in several cases they have certainly influenced the verdict; and in one well known case subsequent analysis definitely supported the contention that there had been a miscarriage of justice.

10 Rillington Place

In 1950, Timothy Evans was hanged for the murder of his wife and child at this address in London. Three years later, following the discovery of several bodies at the house, John Christie was also hanged. After considerable discussion of the case, a public enquiry was held, which led to Evans being granted a posthumous pardon in 1966.

A central piece of evidence against Evans was the statement he made to the police in London on 2 December 1949, in which he confessed to the murders. Evans was largely illiterate, so the statement was made orally, and written down by the police. At the trial, he denied having anything to do with the murders, claiming that he was so upset that he did not know what he was saying, and that he feared the police would beat him up if he did not confess.

In an analysis of the Evans statements, amounting to nearly 5,000 words, it proved possible to show that the language contained many conflicting stylistic features, such as those italicized below:

Type 1: I *done* my day's work and then had an argument with the *Guvnor* then I left the job. He *give* me my wages before I went home.

Type 2: She was *incurring* one debt after another and I could not stand it any longer so I strangled her with a piece of rope and took her down to the flat below the same night *whilst* the old man was in hospital.

The incriminating statement was analysed in five sections, three of which contained background informa-tion (Type 1), two of which contained the details of the murders (Type 2). Six grammatical features were examined, all to do with the way Evans connected his clauses: (*a*) clauses lacking any formal linkage; and clauses linked by (*b*) words like *and*, (*c*) words like *then*, (*d*) ellipsis, (*e*) words like *if*, and (*f*) words like *which*. The results were as follows (after J. Svartvik, 1968):

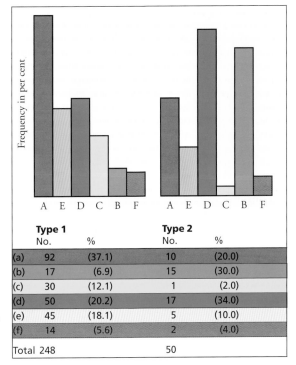

	Type 1		Type 2	
	No.	%	No.	%
(a)	92	(37.1)	10	(20.0)
(b)	17	(6.9)	15	(30.0)
(c)	30	(12.1)	1	(2.0)
(d)	50	(20.2)	17	(34.0)
(e)	45	(18.1)	5	(10.0)
(f)	14	(5.6)	2	(4.0)
Total	248		50	

The differences turn out to be highly significant.

With so few criteria, and a small sample, conclusions must be tentative; but the analysis undoubtedly corroborates Evans's denial: from a linguistic point of view, the paragraphs that he later claimed were untrue are very different indeed from the rest of his statement, which to the end he continued to assert was the truth.

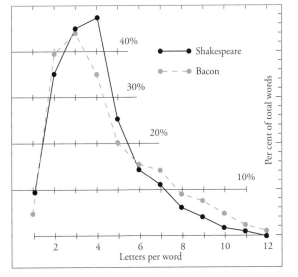

Histographic presentation of Type 1 and Type 2 sentences in the Evans statements.

SHAKESPEARE – OR BACON?

The question of whether the works of Shakespeare could be attributed to Bacon attracted particular interest towards the end of the 19th century. T. C. Mendenhall (p. 68) counted the lengths of about 400,000 words from Shakespeare's plays, and an unspecified but large sample from the writings of Bacon. These large totals were made up of a number of separate counts, based on single works. He found that in each single count from Shakespeare there were more four-letter than three-letter words, whereas the reverse was the case with Bacon. Bacon also has a much higher proportion of longer words than Shakespeare. The graph (left) shows the frequency distributions, using data derived from Mendenhall's original graphs (after C. B. Williams, 1970).

However, statistical evidence convinces only those who wish to be convinced. As one sceptic remarked, in 1901, following the publication of Mendenhall's findings: if Bacon could not have written the plays, 'the question still remains, who did?'!

STYLISTIC DISTINCTIVENESS

How do we set about the task of isolating and identifying the linguistic features that constitute a person's style? Traditionally, this activity was carried out as part of the field of *rhetoric*, the study of persuasive speech or writing (especially as practised in public oratory). Several hundred 'rhetorical figures' were introduced by classical rhetoricians, classifying the way words could be arranged in order to achieve special stylistic effects. Many were restricted to the patterns found in Latin or Greek, but some achieved a broader currency, especially after the Renaissance, in studies of poetry.

The traditional classification of rhetorical figures distinguished between *schemes* and *tropes*. Schemes (such as alliteration) were considered to alter the formal structure of language to create stylistic effects, without altering the meaning. Tropes (such as metaphor) were thought to alter the meaning of the language in some way. However, the theoretical principle on which this distinction relies (the relationship between form and meaning, §13) is not straightforward, and its application to the vast range of literary effects led to controversy, especially over the extent to which changes of form inevitably result in changes of meaning.

In present-day stylistic analysis (e.g. in schools), the distinction is usually not made; inventories or simple classifications of 'figures of speech' are used instead. Also, only a tiny number of the traditional labels (alliteration, simile, hendiadys, homoioteleuton, epanalepsis, etc.) continue to be taught. It is recognized that the task of mastering long lists of labels can alienate readers and encourage them to go in for mechanical 'figure spotting' ('Ah, I can see three similes in that poem'), without pausing to reflect on the role the figures play in the meaning of a text. But a selective and sensitive introduction to figures of speech retains its value, in helping students of style to see the many ways in which a text is linguistically distinctive.

FIGURES OF SPEECH

Metaphor and simile are the most widely recognized figures of speech, being commonly used in many everyday varieties of language as well as in rhetorical and literary contexts. Some analysts consider metaphor, in particular, to be the core of linguistic (and especially poetic) creativity. Both categories are illustrated here, along with a selection of other kinds of figurative expression.

- *metaphor* Two unlike notions are implicitly related, to suggest an identity between them:

When I have seen the hungry ocean gain
Advantage on the kingdom of the shore
(William Shakespeare, *Sonnet 64*)

- *simile* Two unlike things are explicitly compared, to point a similarity, using a marker such as *like* or *as*:

I wandered lonely as a cloud
That floats on high o'er vales and hills
(William Wordsworth, *Daffodils*)

- *personification* A type of metaphor in which an object or idea is represented in human terms:

And all the little roofs of the village bow low, pitiful, beseeching, resigned...
(D. H. Lawrence, *End of Another Home Holiday*)

- *paradox* A statement that is contradictory or absurd on the surface, which forces the search for a deeper level of meaning:

War is peace. Freedom is slavery. Ignorance is strength.
(George Orwell, *1984*)

- *metonymy* The use of an attribute in place of the whole, e.g. *the stage* (the theatrical profession), *the bench* (the judiciary).

- *oxymoron* Two semantically incompatible expressions are brought together, thus forcing a non-literal interpretation, e.g. Emerson's *delicious torment*, Milton's *living death*.

- *apostrophe* Objects, ideas, places, dead or absent people are directly addressed:

Milton! Thou should'st be living at this hour
(William Wordsworth, *London, 1802*)

- *chiasmus* A balanced structure, in which the main elements are reversed:

Love's fire heats water, water cools not love
(William Shakespeare, *Sonnet 154*)

- Combinations of figurative effects are also common, especially in literary writing.

The silted flow
Of years on years
Is marked by dawns
As faint as cracks on mud-flats of despair
(Stephen Spender, *The Prisoners*)

CLASSICAL RHETORIC

Rhetorical ability was prized in classical times, when several major works were written on the art of public speaking, including Aristotle's *Rhetorica*, Quintilian's *Institutio oratoria*, and Cicero's *De oratore*. Five steps were thought to be involved in successful rhetorical composition, identified here with their Latin and (in parenthesis) Greek labels.

- *inventio* (*heuresis*) Relevant subject matter is brought together (a process of 'invention').
- *dispositio* (*taxis*) The material is organized into a structural form appropriate for oratory ('disposition').
- *elocutio* (*lexis*) Language is chosen to suit the subject matter, speaker, and occasion ('style' or 'elocution').
- *memoria* (*mneme*) The various elements of the discourse have to be retained in memory.
- *actio* (*hypocrisis*) The speech is delivered using the most effective techniques ('delivery' or 'pronunciation').

In the middle ages, the study of rhetoric became part of the scholastic *trivium*, along with grammar and logic (§65). Post-Renaissance theorists reduced the five parts to two, 'style' and 'delivery', and the subject, as a result, became particularly associated with techniques of verbal expression, especially in relation to reading aloud (the concern of 'elocution'). Because of this influential tradition, many people think of rhetoric as essentially a matter of 'verbal ornament'.

The modern academic view of the subject, however, involves far more than the special effects of language production. It deals with the whole study of creative discourse, in both speech and writing, including the use of language in the mass media, and the way in which audiences react to and interpret communications directed at them (p. 397). In effect, it is the analysis of the theory and practice of techniques of argumentation, involving listeners as well as speakers, readers as well as writers. In its broadest sense, therefore, modern rhetoric studies the basis of all forms of effective communication.

EMOTIONAL APPEALS

The complex universe of traditional rhetoric is clearly illustrated from this small selection of classical terms which described the types of emotional appeal.
- *amphidiorthosis* modifying a charge made in anger;
- *anacoenosis* asking the opinion of listener or reader;
- *asphalia* offering oneself as surety for a bond;
- *bdelygma* expressing abhorrence;
- *cataplexis* threatening punishment or disaster;
- *comprobatio* complimenting one's listeners or judges;
- *diabole* predicting or denouncing future events;
- *diasyrmus* disparaging the arguments of one's opponent;
- *ecphonesis* using an emotional exclamation;
- *eucharistia* giving thanks;
- *eulogia* commending or blessing a person or thing;
- *hypocrisis* mocking an opponent by exaggerating speech or gestures;
- *mempsis* complaining against one's injuries;
- *ominatio* prophesying evil;
- *paramythia* consoling those who grieve;
- *peroration* summarizing in an impassioned manner;
- *thaumasmus* exclaiming in wonder.

LITERARY VS NON-LITERARY LANGUAGE

In principle, a detailed stylistic study could be made of a press report, a television commercial, or any other 'everyday' use of language, and examples of this 'general' approach to stylistics can be found in §§11 and 63. In practice, most stylistic analyses have attempted to deal with the more complex and 'valued' forms of language found in works of literature ('literary stylistics'). Moreover, it is possible to see in several of these studies a further narrowing of scope, with analysts concentrating on the more striking areas of literary language. Poetic language has attracted most attention, and within this there has been a marked predilection to investigate authors who make use of highly abnormal or 'deviant' features of language (such as Dylan Thomas or E. E. Cummings). The bias is less obvious in contemporary stylistic work, but it is still present.

This concentration on the more distinctive forms of literary expression is not difficult to explain. It reflects the fact that linguistic analytic techniques, as developed during this century, are more geared to the analysis of the detailed features of sentence structure than of the broader structures found in whole texts or discourses (Part III). The more compact and constrained language of poetry is far more likely to disclose the secrets of its construction to the stylistician than is the language of plays and novels, where the structuring process is less evident, and where dialogue and narrative is often indistinguishable from the norms of everyday speech. Most work, accordingly, has been in the area of poetic language.

Bottom up vs top down

A more balanced account of the language of literature is gradually emerging in contemporary stylistics, with two main approaches to the subject plainly in evidence. The first approach begins by identifying the smallest features felt to be distinctively used in a work – minimal contrasts of sound, grammar, or vocabulary – and proceeds to build up more complex patterns of use. The second moves in the opposite direction, beginning with the broadest possible statements about an author's style, then studying particular aspects of the language in detail.

In the first approach, we might start by considering the distinctive way in which a novelist, for example, favours certain adjectives, varies tenses, or coins idiosyncratic words. We might count the frequency with which these features are used in a particular novel, and contrast them with the frequencies found in other works, by the same or different authors. In the second approach, we might start by discussing the structure of the novel as a whole, with reference to plots and sub-plots, favourite themes, and the way characters interrelate. In due course, we might proceed to look more closely at how particular linguistic features signal the author's intentions, and again make comparisons with other works.

The two approaches – sometimes referred to as the 'bottom up' and 'top down' (or 'micro' and 'macro') approaches – can both be illuminating, and neither excludes the other. Quite often, micro- and macro-stylistic procedures are simultaneously used in investigating the same work. To some extent, the approaches are complementary, and it might be thought that they would meet 'in the middle'. In practice, because of the multifaceted nature of stylistic analyses, and the different theories used by stylisticians, this hardly ever happens.

A linguistic perspective

Linguistic approaches to the study of literary style stress the importance of seeing an individual author's use of language in the context of the language as a whole. It is pointed out that this language cannot be studied in isolation from other varieties. Literature reflects the whole of human experience, and authors thus find themselves drawing on all varieties of language (or even on different languages) as part of their expression. In a single work, they might make considerable use of a non-literary variety, or allude to several such varieties. This happens most markedly in drama and the novel, as can be readily observed from the vast linguistic range of Shakespeare or Molière, or the regional and class varieties found throughout the writing of Dickens or Hardy. But the tapping of language varieties can be found in poetry too, as in *The Waste Land*, where T. S. Eliot draws on linguistic features belonging to conversational, religious, medieval, and musical varieties, as well as a wide range of literary forms. Indeed, this work clearly illustrates the way literature knows no linguistic bounds, for it also includes lines in French, German, Italian, and Sanskrit (p. 73).

Nor can literary language be isolated from the least situationally specific language variety of all – conversation (p. 52). When an author uses language ingeniously, we instinctively relate the special features to our own spoken norms, and any explanation of the effect ultimately depends on our awareness of these norms, and of how the features relate to them. To use modern stylistic terms, we see how the features have been 'foregrounded' – made to stand out from the background of normal, unremarkable usage. Robert Graves recognized the importance of this principle when he said that a poet should 'master the rules of grammar before he attempts to bend or break them'. So too critics – and indeed all who enjoy literature – need to be aware of the normal constraints on language use before they can explain the effects authors achieve when rules are bent or broken.

T. S. Eliot (1888–1965)

BRIDGING THE GAP

That there is a continuum between literary and non-literary discourse is clear when we consider the widespread use of such notions as metaphor, personification, and alliteration in advertising, journalism, commentary, ordinary conversation, and other varieties. Metaphor, in particular, permeates everyday speech. Our arguments are couched in terms of battle: they are 'won', 'attacked', 'defended', 'destroyed'; our economies are described as if they were bodies ('healthy', 'ailing', 'restoring') or buildings ('shore up', 'support', 'weak', 'collapse'). This short selection illustrates the way our daily idiomatic expression is rooted in metaphor:

> can't believe my ears
> a piece of cake
> at the back of my mind
> dressed to kill
> drive a hard bargain
> make him eat his words
> fit as a fiddle
> got the sack
> hold your horses
> got cold feet
> you're pulling my leg
> scream blue murder
> under my thumb
> got the picture?

Robert Graves (1895–1985)
by John Aldridge, 1968.

THE EDGES OF LANGUAGE

Authors take risks when they push language to its limits. If they break too many rules, they can fall over the edge of language into unintelligibility. Even well-known authors, such as James Joyce and Dylan Thomas, have been criticized for verbal excesses – for sacrificing meaning to the seductive patterns of sound or graphic form. It is possible to arrive at a satisfactory explanation of all the distinctive graphic features in E. E. Cummings's *Four III*, for instance?

The move from centre to edge of language is a gradual one. We can take an everyday construction, and manipulate its use to show increasing levels of inventiveness – and thus increasing difficulties of interpretation. One construction that has been well studied from this point of view is the use of *ago* with a noun phrase to express various temporal meanings. It is possible to construct a continuum that has mundane uses at one end and bizarre uses at the other, as in this example (from G. N. Leech, 1969):

several hours ago	MUNDANE
many moons ago	
ten games ago	
several performances ago	
a few cigarettes ago	
three overcoats ago	
two wives ago	
a grief ago (Dylan Thomas)	
a humanity ago	ABNORMAL

We might dispute the particular ordering of items on this scale, but the general move away from literal meaning is clear enough, as is the growing difficulty we encounter as we attempt to provide a plausible context for each use. It would also be possible to construct even more bizarre examples (*an incompleteness ago*), and thus to suggest how, with the more deviant kinds of poetic language, a reader might simply give up the struggle to decode its meaning. There is nothing more likely to crush the desire to read poetry than having to resort to cryptanalysis.

Poets are not the only ones who push language beyond its normal limits. All who engage in literary or quasi-literary activity, from novelists and dramatists to journalists and commentators, face similar problems. Nor is the wrestle with words restricted to literature. Humorists, both amateur and professional, are another group who constantly tease new effects out of old words, in their search for good punch-lines. And a further example is provided by the heading of the present section, which is the title of a book by the German theologian, Paul van Buren, about how people use the word 'God' as part of religious discourse (p. 388). In his view, theistic language is 'a case of walking language's borders' – an attempt to express insight at the very edge of the 'platform of language', where, if we try to go further, 'we fall off into a misuse of words, into nonsensical jabbering, into the void where the rules give out'. Theologians, like poets, it seems, are continually striving to say what cannot be said.

FOUR III

here's a little mouse) and
what does he think about, i
wonder as over this
floor (quietly with

bright eyes) drifts (nobody
can tell because
Nobody knows, or why
jerks Here &, here,
gr(oo)ving the room's Silence) this like
a littlest
poem a
(with wee ears and see?

tail frisks)
            (gonE)
'mouse',
            We are not the same you and

i, since here's a little he
or is
it It
? (or was something we saw in the mirror)?

therefore we'll kiss; for maybe
what was Disappeared
into ourselves
who (look). ,startled.

E. E. Cummings (1894–1962), whose ingenious typographic configurations frequently reflect the distinctive rhythms and tones of voice that can be heard in speech (p. 182).

BENDING THE RULES

Dylan Thomas's poetry repeatedly illustrates the way in which some poets bend grammatical rules as they strive to express their insights. A feature of his stylistic technique is the use of unexpected associations between words (p. 105) – as well as *a grief ago*, examples (from *Fern Hill*) include *happy as the heart was long, all the sun long,* and *once below a time*. Such effects can be formally identified only by drawing attention to the everyday meaning of the underlying phrase. In such cases, usage norms provide a relevant perspective for the discussion of stylistic effects, and often act as a stimulus to critical thinking.

Dylan Thomas (1914–53) by Augustus John.

LITERARY GENRES

Genres of literature are established categories of composition, characterized by distinctive language or subject matter. The most widely recognized are poetry, drama, and the novel, but several other categories exist, such as the short story, autobiography, and essays. Each major category can be further classified – for example, epic, lyrical, and narrative genres within poetry; comedy, tragedy, and farce within drama; and romance, crime, and science fiction within the novel.

POETRY

There has always been controversy over the nature of poetic language. To some, poetic language should be special, removed from the language of everyday (thus, Thomas Gray's dictum, 'The language of the age is never the language of poetry'). To others, it should be closely in touch with everyday, or, perhaps, be 'current language heightened' (Gerard Manley Hopkins). To Ralph Waldo Emerson, the whole of language is in any case 'fossil poetry'.

Statements of this kind to some extent miss the point, which is to stress the enormous range of linguistic expression that is found under the heading of poetry. At one extreme, there are poems that are as far removed from everyday speech as it is possible to imagine; at the other, there are poems that, if it were not for the division into lines, would closely resemble prose. Poetic movements often swing between these poles, as people respond to the competing linguistic influences of old traditions and contemporary realities. It is not possible to make simple general statements about the form of poetic language, therefore; all one can do is identify a number of recurrent notions that are part of the traditional image of poetic language, and that enter into what is often called 'poetic licence'.

The creativity poets seek takes many forms. It may involve the invention of totally new linguistic features, as in the neologistic vocabulary of James Joyce, or the typographical design of a poem by E. E. Cummings. But it more often takes the form of a fresh use of familiar language, as when John Donne compares himself and his mistress to the legs on a pair of compasses, or T. S. Eliot's Prufrock compares the evening laid out against the sky to a 'patient etherised upon a table'. Above all else, poets fear banality. Whatever the literary era or tradition in which they find themselves, they are concerned to avoid what is linguistically boring or predictable, and to discover ways in which words can come alive, to convey fresh worlds of meaning. T. S. Eliot's phrase vividly captures the essence of their predicament: 'the intolerable wrestle with words and meanings'.

GRAMMAR AND VOCABULARY

• *archaisms* The use of grammar and vocabulary no longer current is a well-established feature of poetry (though not so common today). Examples include the use of grammatical forms such as *'twas* and *quoth,* words such as *e'en, fain,* and *wight,* and spellings such as *daunsynge* and *olde.*

• *neologisms* The invention of new words is perhaps the most obvious way to go beyond the normal resources of a language: completely fresh creations, such as Shakespeare's *incarnadine*: new constructions, such as Hopkins's 'widow-making unchilding unfathering deeps' (*The Wreck of the Deutschland*); and new parts of speech, as in Othello's verb *lip* (= kiss), 'To lip a wanton in a secure couch.'

• *poetic diction* In a narrow sense, this term refers to vocabulary that is typically poetic, and that would rarely be used in other contexts; more broadly, it can mean any use of words thought to be effective by the poet, whether or not it occurs elsewhere. The traditional sense can be illustrated by *nymph, slumber, woe,* and *billows,* or many lines from 18th-century poetry, such as the opening of Thomas Gray's *Elegy in a Country Churchyard:*

The curfew tolls the knell of parting day,
The lowing herd winds slowly o'er the lea

For the broader sense, there is the beginning of Stephen Spender's *The Exiles:*

History has tongues
Has angels has guns – has saved has praised –
Today proclaims
Achievements of her exiles long returned.

• *word order* Abnormal word order is common, as when adjectives are placed after nouns (e.g. Milton's 'Anon out of the earth a fabric huge / Rose like an exhalation' (*Paradise Lost*), or the normal order of elements in a clause is reversed (e.g. Hamlet's 'I might not this believe ...').

MULTILINGUAL POETRY

Lexical effects may even cross language boundaries. In Verlaine's *Sonnet boiteux,* English words heard in a London fog are interspersed within the French text:

Tout l'affreux passé saute,
    piaule, miaule et glapit
Dans le brouillard rose et
    jaune et sale des sohos
Avec des indeed *et des* all
    rights et des haôs.
(The whole hideous past jumps, whines, mews and yelps in the pink and yellow and dirty fog of the *sohos,* with *indeeds* and *all rights* and *hey-o's.*)

But one of the best-known examples is the cluster of foreign language elements in the closing lines of T. S. Eliot's *The Waste Land:*

I sat upon the shore
Fishing, with the arid plain
    behind me
Shall I at least set my lands in
    order?
London Bridge is falling
    down falling down falling
    down
Poi s'ascose nel foco che gli
    affina
Quando fiam uti chelidon –
    O swallow swallow
Le Prince d'Aquitaine à la
    tour abolie
These fragments I have
    shored against my ruins
Why then Ile fit you.
    Hieronymo's mad againe.
Datta. Dayadhvam. Damyata.
    Shantih shantih shantih

William Wordsworth in 1842, after B. R. Haydon.

THE VERY LANGUAGE OF MEN

William Wordsworth made a strong statement about the relationship of poetry to prose. In the Preface to the *Lyrical Ballads* (1800), he wrote:

My purpose was to imitate, and, as far as is possible, to adopt the very language of men ... There will be found in these volumes little of what is usually called poetic diction; as much pains has been taken to avoid it as is ordinarily taken to produce it ... It may be safely affirmed that there neither is, nor can be, any *essential* difference between the language of prose and metrical composition.

SOUNDS AND RHYTHMS

For many people, it is the sound or 'music' of poetry that chiefly identifies the genre – the distinctive use of vowels, consonants, cadences, and rhythms. Several different phonetic and phonological stylistic features contribute to the total effect, which is often studied under the separate heading of *phonostylistics*.

• Individual sounds can be used in an onomatopoeic or symbolic way (§30) for expressive purposes. Poetry sometimes uses vowels and consonants to reflect the noises of real life, or to symbolize other sensory or abstract notions, such as colour, texture, character, or mood (e.g. Milton's 'The serpent subtlest beast of all the field'). Poetic rhythms, too, can directly evoke real world sounds and events, as in

I sprang to the stirrup, and Joris, and he;
I galloped, Dirck galloped, we galloped all three.
(Robert Browning, *How They Brought the Good News from Ghent to Aix*)

• A network of associations can be built up between sounds. By repeating vowels or consonants at different points, words and phrases can be formally linked, sometimes to achieve a purely aesthetic effect, sometimes to force the listener to consider their possible relationships of meaning. Three cases are usually recognized, involving the repetition of initial consonants (*alliteration*, as in *fine friend*), vowels (*assonance*, as in *roll/moan*), and final syllables (*rhyme*, e.g. *gladness/madness*). But other effects are possible, such as the repetition of initial syllables, as in *state/stayed* (*reverse rhyme*), or the simultaneous repetition of initial and final consonants, as in *bend/bound* (*pararhyme*). The opening lines of Coleridge's *Kubla Khan* illustrate the overlapping use of several of these effects.

• The language is organized into rhythmical units, which appear in print as lines. In European poetry, the traditional study of versification, or *prosody*, was based on the rules of Latin scansion, and many generations of schoolchildren have had to learn to scan verse on the assumption that poetry in their language used similar rhythms to those of Latin. But the quantitative metrical system of Latin, based on a classification of syllables into long and short durations, is by no means universal. English and German use an accentual system, in which heavy and light syllables alternate. Classical Chinese used a tonal system, which alternated classes of even and changing tones. Sometimes only the number of syllables in a unit is critical, regardless of their pitch, loudness, or duration, as in Mordvinian. And several 'mixed' metrical systems have been found, such as French, where syllable number and accentuation combine.

Traditional analyses of English metre divide poetic lines into combinations of stressed (´) and unstressed (˘) syllables known as 'feet'. Four types are prominent in English verse: the *iamb* (˘´), *trochee* (´˘), *anapaest* (˘˘´), and *dactyl* (´˘˘). A line is classified on the basis of the number of stressed syllables it contains, such as the monometer (1), dimeter (2), trimeter (3), tetrameter (4), pentameter (5), and hexameter (6). Combination of foot-type and line-length produce such designations as 'iambic pentameter' – the so-called 'backbone' of English metre.

I come not, friends, to steal away your hearts
(William Shakespeare, *Julius Caesar*)
The rising world of waters dark and deep
(Milton, *Paradise Lost*)

Many famous studies (such as G. Saintsbury's three-volume *A History of English Prosody*, 1906–10) have been devoted to plotting the metrical norms in a language's poetry, and evaluating the kinds of deviations from these norms that poets use. As systems of description, they work quite well in analysing the regular lines of traditional poetry. But they have been criticized on several points. They tend to be applied in too mechanical a way; it is often difficult to decide which analysis to assign to a line containing an abnormal rhythm; and they break down completely when they encounter the markedly irregular lines of modern 'free verse':

What is the use of talking, and there is no end of talking,
There is no end of things in the heart.
I call in the boy,
Have him sit on his knees here
          To seal this,
And send it a thousand miles, thinking
(Ezra Pound, *Exile's Letter*)

In such cases, it is necessary to devise alternative metrical models, using different analyses of stress, and introducing other prosodic notions, such as tempo, pause, and intonation (§29), to identify the patterns that emerge when readers utter the lines.

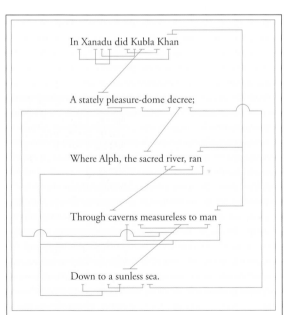

Sound-patterns in the opening lines of Coleridge's *Kubla Khan*

In Xanadu did Kubla Khan

A stately pleasure-dome decree;

Where Alph, the sacred river, ran

Through caverns measureless to man

Down to a sunless sea.

THE SOUND OF SILENCE

Lateral consonants (p. 159) are used by poets in several languages to suggest softness and silence:

Wi*l*d thyme and va*ll*ey- *l*i*l*ies whiter sti*ll*
Than *L*eda's *l*ove, and cresses from the ri*ll*
(Keats, *Endymion*)

Les souff*l*es de *l*a nuit f*l*ottaient sur Ga*l*ga*l*a.
(Victor Hugo, *Booz Endormi*)
'The breezes of the night floated over Galgala.'

Dir in *L*iedern, *l*eichten, schne*ll*en,
Wa*ll*et küh*l*e F*l*uth.
(Goethe,*West-östlicher Divan*)
'For you the cool waves lap in songs light and nimble.'

Ah! *L*ágyan ké*l* az éji szé*l* Mi*l*ford öbö*l*fe*l*é.
(János Arany, *A Walesi bardok*)
'Oh! The night breeze rises softly towards Milford Haven.'
(After S. Ullmann, 1964.)

THE POET'S STRUGGLE

T. S. Eliot's lines, in *East Coker*, sum up what for many is the essence of the linguistic task facing the poet.

So here I am, in the middle way, having had twenty years...
Trying to learn to use words, and every attempt
Is a wholly new start, and a different kind of failure
Because one has only learnt to get the better of words
For the thing one no longer has to say, or the way in which
One is no longer disposed to say it. And so each venture
Is a new beginning, a raid on the inarticulate
With shabby equipment always deteriorating
In the general mess of imprecision of feeling
Undisciplined squads of emotion.

CONCRETE POETRY

This 1950s movement produced a form of poetry variously known as 'shaped', 'pattern', 'concrete', or 'Cubist' poetry, which blurred the boundary between literature and the visual arts. In concrete poems, the primary consideration is the way in which letters and words are arranged on the page, so that they visually reinforce, or act as a counterpoint to, the verbal meaning.

Shaped poems can in fact be traced to classical Greek times, and they emerge over the centuries in the work of several Western writers, such as Apollinaire (p. 11), Mallarmé, Mayakovsky, Dylan Thomas, and Cummings (p. 72), as well as being very popular in Eastern literature, where they may have originated. One of the best-known examples is *The Altar*, by the 17th-century poet George Herbert. Representative of the more recent movement is *Au Pair Girl* by Ian Hamilton Finlay.

Ian Hamilton Finlay's
Au Pair Girl

```
        pair g
     rl au pair
    )air girl au
    au pair girl
   au pair girl a
  rl au pair girl a
 )air girl au pair gir
jirl au pair girl au pair
)air girl au pair girl au pa
air girl au pair girl au pair
pair girl au pair girl au pa
1u pair girl au pair girl a
 irl au pair girl au pair
  1irl au pair girl
```

George Herbert's *The Altar*

A broken ALTAR, Lord, thy servant rears,
Made of a heart, and cemented with tears;
　Whose parts are as thy hand did frame;
　No workman's tool hath touch'd the same.
　　　　A　HEART　alone
　　　　Is　such　a　stone,
　　　　As　nothing　but
　　　　Thy　pow'r　doth　cut.
　　　Wherefore each part
　　　Of　my　hard　heart
　　　Meets　in　this　frame,
　　　To　praise　thy　name.
That if I chance to hold my peace,
These stones to praise thee may not cease.
O　let　thy　blessed　SACRIFICE　be　mine,
And　sanctifie　this　ALTAR　to　be　thine.

DRAMA

There has been remarkably little study of the genre of drama from a linguistic point of view. This is partly because so much of the language it contains is traditionally analysed under other headings – reference is often made to the 'poetry' of Shakespeare's plays, for instance, which is then investigated using metrical and rhetorical techniques. And if the language of drama is not poetry (it might be argued), then it is prose, and thus analysable using the techniques of other prose genres, such as the novel or short story.

But drama is neither poetry nor novel. It is first and foremost dialogue in action. With few exceptions, there is no narrative framework other than that provided by the language of the characters and by the visual setting in which they act. The author cannot step back and provide an opinion or manipulate our point of view, as happens routinely in novels. The dialogue must do everything.

Dramatic dialogue also has to be convincing, as a representation of conversation. But to be convincing is not to be real. No dramatist presents us with the equivalent of a tape recording of everyday speech, with all its hesitations, broken syntax, and inexplicit vocabulary (p. 52). Even the most colloquial of dramatic conversations, whether it is written by Harold Pinter, Arthur Miller, or Shakespeare, presents us with an exercise in linguistic artifice, the extent of which is only beginning to be appreciated, as techniques become available that allow us to make comparisons with real conversation.

SIGNIFICANT SILENCE

Even pauses can be manipulated for special dramatic effect, as is well illustrated by this extract from Harold Pinter's *The Caretaker* (1959), where three degrees of pause are written into the dialogue. Apart from controlling the pace of the drama, the pauses also underline the uncertain relationship between the characters, keep the atmosphere tense, and help to promote our sense of apprehension.

DAVIES: You sleep here, do you?
ASTON: Yes.
DAVIES: What, in that?
ASTON: Yes.
DAVIES: Yes, well, you'd be well out of the draught there.
ASTON: You don't get much wind.
DAVIES: You'd be well out

of it. It's different when you're kipping out.
ASTON: Would be.
DAVIES: Nothing but wind then.
(*Pause.*)
ASTON: Yes, when the wind gets up it ...
(*Pause.*)
DAVIES: Yes ...
ASTON: Mmnn ...
(*Pause.*)
DAVIES: Gets very draughty.
ASTON: Ah.
DAVIES: I'm very sensitive to it.
ASTON: Are you?
DAVIES: Always have been.
(*Pause.*)
You got more rooms then, have you?
ASTON: Where?
DAVIES: I mean, along the landing here ... up the landing there.
ASTON: They're out of commission.

Peter Howitt (left) and Donald Pleasence (right) in *The Caretaker*, 1991.

DAVIES: Get away.
ASTON: They need a lot of doing to.
(*Slight pause.*)
DAVIES: What about downstairs?
ASTON: That's closed up. Needs seeing to ... The floors ...
(*Pause.*)

CONTROLLING THE DIALOGUE

The stylistic distinctiveness of a dramatic text lies primarily in the conventions of layout, abbreviation, and direction that the dramatist employs to indicate the nature of the action, and the movement and interpretation of the dialogue. But there are great variations in approach. Some authors restrict themselves to the essential directions about the actions of the characters, leaving it to the actors and producer to infer interpretations about character or tone of voice from the text. In Shakespeare, for example, we find the bare minimum of comment, as in this scene from *Hamlet*:

SCENE 1. *Elsinore. The guard-platform of the Castle.*

[FRANCISCO *at his post. Enter to him* BERNARDO.]

BER: Who's there?
FRAN: Nay, answer me. Stand and unfold yourself.
BER: Long live the King!
FRAN: Bernardo?
BER: He.
FRAN: You come most carefully upon your hour.
BER: 'Tis now struck twelve; get thee to bed, Francisco.

By contrast, some authors make great use of stage directions – in effect, giving the reader a partial interpretation of events. Along with the formal indications of dialogue, they provide the chief marker of linguistic identity of the genre in its written form. Extracts from Act I of Tom Stoppard's *Rosencrantz and Guildenstern Are Dead* (1967) illustrate (to the point of parody) the way stage directions can give information about character, setting, and plot.

ACT I

Two ELIZABETHANS *passing the time in a place without any visible character.*
They are well dressed – hats, cloaks, sticks and all.
Each of them has a large leather money bag.
GUILDENSTERN'*s bag is nearly empty.*
ROSENCRANTZ'*s bag is nearly full..*
The reason being: they are betting on the toss of a coin, in the following manner: GUILDENSTERN *(hereafter* 'GUIL') *takes a coin out of his bag, spins it, letting it fall.* ROSENCRANTZ *(hereafter* 'ROS') *studies it, announces it as 'heads' (as it happens) and puts it in his own bag. Then they repeat the process. They have apparently been doing this for some time.*
The run of 'heads' is impossible, yet ROS *betrays no surprise at all – he feels none. However, he is nice enough to feel a little embarrassed at taking so much money off his friend. Let that be his character note.*

...   .

ROS: Now why exactly are you behaving in this extraordinary manner?
GUIL: I can't imagine! (*Pause.*) But all that is well known, common property. Yet he sent for us. And we did come.
ROS: (*alert, ear cocked*): I say! I heard music –
GUIL: We're here.
ROS: – Like a band – I thought I heard a band.
GUIL: Rosencrantz ...

ROS: (*absently, still listening*): What?
  (*Pause, short.*)
GUIL: (*gently wry*): Guildenstern ...
ROS: (*irritated by the repetition*): What?
GUIL: Don't you discriminate at all?
ROS: (*turning dumbly*): Wha'?
  (*Pause.*)

FROM DRAMA TO NOVEL

A play for voices

In Dylan Thomas's *Under Milk Wood* (1954), the narrator's voice interweaves with the voices of the characters to produce a work that, though cast in dramatic form, permits several of the effects of the novel.

ACT I

FIRST VOICE: In the blind-drawn dark dining-room of School House, dusty and echoing as a dining-room in a vault, Mr and Mrs Pugh are silent over cold grey cottage pie. Mr Pugh reads, as he forks the shroud meat in, from *Lives of the Great Poisoners*. He has bound a plain brown-paper cover round the book. Slyly, between slow mouthfuls, he sidespies up at Mrs Pugh, poisons her with his eye, then goes on reading. He underlines certain passages and smiles in secret.
MRS PUGH: Persons with manners do not read at table,
FIRST VOICE: says Mrs Pugh. She swallows a digestive tablet as big as a horse-pill, washing it down with clouded peasoup water.
  [*Pause*]
MRS PUGH: Some persons were brought up in pigsties.
MR PUGH: Pigs don't read at table, dear.
FIRST VOICE: Bitterly she flicks dust from the broken cruet. It settles on the pie in a thin gnat-rain.
MR PUGH: Pigs can't read, my dear.
MRS PUGH: I know one who can.

CHARLES DICKENS

In a speech made in 1858 (*For the Royal Theatrical Fund*), Dickens made a remark which underscores the problem facing anyone who wishes to argue for a definite boundary between plays and novels: 'Every writer of fiction, though he may not adopt the dramatic form, writes in effect for the stage.'

Charles Dickens (1812–70)

A NOVEL FOR VOICES

It would take only the addition of character names and a change to present tense in the last line to turn the following extract into a play. It is the whole of a chapter from Hank Stine's *The Prisoner* (1970, p. 63), a novel based on the cult television series starring Patrick McGoohan. The Prisoner is under arrest.

  'On what charge?'
  'A complaint has been brought against you.'
  'By whom?'
  'By a party who considers himself aggrieved.'
  'In what way?'
  'It is not my place to know.'
  'Whose place is it?'
  'Those whose place it is to know such things.'
  'And when will I be advised of the nature of the charge?'
  'At the proper time.'
  'And when will that be?'
  'When it is deemed necessary.'
  'And who will decide it is necessary?'
  'The proper authorities.'
  'Just who are these "proper authorities"?'
  'Those who have been duly constituted.'
  'And who constituted them?'
  'The people.'
  'Which people?'
  'The people of this village. Now, you will come with me. There will be no further arguments.'
  They went out into the rain.

THE NOVEL

Since the 18th century, the novel has become the major genre of literature in most literate societies. It has attracted a vast range of literary criticism, but few large-scale linguistic investigations. Enormous variations in the size and scope of different novels make it difficult to arrive at satisfactory generalizations about linguistic form and content, other than to identify its essentially *narrative* purpose. The problem has long been recognized: indeed, it was present from the earliest years of the genre, when authors searched for a label to identify their new product. Henry Fielding, for example, called his *Joseph Andrews* (1742) 'a comic Epic-Poem in Prose'.

Part of the analytical problem lies in the way novels contain so much variety mixing. They tap the resources of a language's stylistic range more than does any other genre. In principle, no character, situation, theme, plot, or point of view is excluded. All language varieties might expect to be represented in a novel sooner or later, from the most colloquial to the most formal, from the most mundane to the most arcane. Even other major genres come to be swallowed up by the novel, as may be seen in an early work, Samuel Richardson's *Clarissa* (1747–8), where one of the letters from Lovelace to Belford opens with the heading 'Act II, Scene: Hampstead Heath, continued. Enter my Rascal', and continues in dialogue form with stage directions interspersed. James Joyce's *Ulysses* has over 100 pages in dramatic form, representing the fantasy world of one of the characters. And D. M. Thomas's *The White Hotel* (1981) contains long extracts of poetry, alongside documentary prose, imaginative prose, postcards, letter-writing, scholarly writing, and even footnotes!

In recent years, linguistic (or textual) analysis has examined several aspects of the way language is used to identify the various themes, characters, settings, plots, and viewpoints which are introduced into the narrative. There have been several studies of the experiments in linguistic technique that have been a major feature of novel-writing during the past century, especially in relation to the ways in which a character's consciousness might be portrayed (p. 78). Authors such as Henry James, Virginia Woolf, and James Joyce have attracted particular attention from this point of view. Another well-investigated area is the author's use of linguistic devices to maintain realistic dialogue and to identify character. And a third area is the study of the movement and direction of plot, which can be illuminated by the detailed study of patterns of sentence and paragraph connectivity – a major feature of the emerging field of textlinguistics (§20), and a preoccupation of structuralist approaches to literature (p. 79).

WHO SPOKE?

The characters in a novel can be presented in several ways: the author can describe them directly, other characters can talk about them – and they can talk for themselves. One of the most important linguistic techniques of characterization is through the use of a distinctive style of speech, which emphasizes features of regional or class background, or personal idiosyncrasies. The effect may be conveyed by the habitual use of a single word (as in the first extract below), by more fundamental changes in grammatical construction (as in the second and third extracts), or by a completely different orthographic system, specially devised to capture features of pronunciation (as in the fourth extract).

'I think you are wrong. Uriah,' I said, 'I dare say there are several things I could teach you, if you would like to learn them.'

'Oh I don't doubt that, Master Copperfield,' he answered; 'not in the least. But not being umble yourself, you don't judge well, perhaps, for them that are. I won't provoke my betters with knowledge, thank you. I'm much too umble. Here is my umble dwelling, Master Copperfield.' (Charles Dickens, *David Copperfield*, 1849–50, Ch. 17)

'No,' El Sordo said and patted his shoulder. 'Joke. Comes from La Granja. Heard last night comes English dynamiter. Good. Very happy. Get whisky. For you. You like?' (Ernest Hemingway, *For Whom the Bell Tolls*, 1940, Ch. 11)

While narrating these things, every time Queequeg received the tomahawk from me, he flourished the hatchet-side of it over the sleeper's head. 'What's that for, Queequeg?' 'Perry easy, kill-e; oh! perry easy!' (Herman Melville, *Moby Dick*, 1851, Ch. 21)

'Noa!' said Joseph … 'Noa! that manes nowt – Hathecliff makes noa 'cahnt uh t'mother, nur yah norther – bud he'll hev his lad; und Aw mun tak him – soa now ye knaw!' (Emily Brontë, *Wuthering Heights*, 1847, Ch. 19)

SPEECH PRESENTATION

In traditional grammars, a basic distinction is drawn between 'direct' and 'indirect' (or 'reported') speech. In direct speech, someone's words are quoted exactly as they were said (e.g. *'Did the man see you yesterday?' Mary asked John.*); in indirect speech, we express what was said in our own words (e.g. *Mary asked John if the man had seen him the day before.*). Several important linguistic changes take place in moving from direct to indirect speech, such as the removal of inverted commas, the change of pronouns, and the 'back-shift' in tense forms and associated adverbs. Both styles of speech presentation are widely used in the novel.

But there are several other, more subtle modes of presenting speech, where the distinction between direct and indirect does not easily apply. 'Free indirect speech' (*le style indirect libre*, or *erlebte Rede*) is one such mode, in which, typically, the reporting clause of indirect speech is dropped, but the other conventions are retained (e.g. *Had the man seen John the day before?*). But there may be further variants, in which only some forms are altered (e.g. *Had the man seen John yesterday?*). And there is also a category of 'free direct speech', in which the writer moves from narrative to direct speech without the use of the usual markers (e.g. *Mary approached John. Did the man see you yesterday? John looked away.*).

Charles Dickens was one who experimented successfully with modes of speech presentation – especially the use of free indirect speech. The Coroner's interrogation of the crossing sweeper, Jo, in *Bleak House* (Ch. 11) is a good illustration of the way this style can add speed and economy to a narrative, as characters interact without the cumbersome use of such conventions as 'said X … said Y'. It also conveys something of the character's typical speech style, and his unspoken process of reflection:

Name, Jo. Nothing else that he knows on. Don't know that everybody has two names. Never heard of sich a think.

Don't know that Jo is short for a longer name. Thinks it long enough for *him. He* don't find no fault with it. Spell it? He can't spell it. No father, no mother, no friends. Never been to school …

SOME WAYS OF TELLING A STORY

• The author, in the first person, takes on the *persona* of someone in the story. This convention allows a great sense of involvement and immediacy, and a personal relationship to develop with the reader; but inevitably there is a limited perspective:

1801. – I have just returned from a visit to my landlord – the solitary neighbour that I shall be troubled with. This is certainly a beautiful country! In all England, I do not believe that I could have fixed on a situation so completely removed from the stir of society. A perfect misanthropist's Heaven – and Mr Heathcliff and I are such a suitable pair to divide the desolation between us. A capital fellow!
(Emily Brontë, *Wuthering Heights*, 1847, Ch. 1)

• A third-person narrative, with an omniscient narrator, can provide a comprehensive account of all aspects of the story, including the characters' motivations, without personal involvement:

Emma Woodhouse, handsome, clever, and rich, with a comfortable home and happy disposition, seemed to unite some of the best blessings of existence; and had lived nearly twenty-one years in the world with very little to distress or vex her.
(Jane Austen, *Emma*, 1816, Ch. 1)

• The author may cease to be omniscient, adopting the point of view of the reader, or of another character in the novel. In this extract, the author breaks the usual third-person convention, adopting the viewpoint of the people in the vicinity, first through the use of question-forms, then through speculative commentary:

A fine night, and a bright large moon, and multitudes of stars. Mr Tulkinghorn, in repairing to his cellar, and in opening and shutting those resounding doors, has to cross a little prison-like yard, He looks up casually, thinking what a fine night, what a bright large moon, what multitudes of stars! A quiet night, too.

... ...

What's that? Who fired a gun or pistol? Where was it?
The few foot-passengers start, stop, and stare about them. Some windows and doors are opened, and people come out to look. It was a loud report, and echoed and rattled heavily. It shook one house, or so a man says who was passing ... Has Mr Tulkinghorn been disturbed? His windows are dark and quiet, and his door is shut. It must be something unusual indeed, to bring him out of his shell ...
(Charles Dickens, *Bleak House*, 1853, Ch. 48)

• The author may switch from third-person to first-person and back again, often in a highly indirect and subtle manner. In this extract, the two viewpoints continue almost simultaneously, as first-person words like *yesterday* and the reflective *yes* combine with third-person words such as *he*, and words that could represent either viewpoint, such as *might* and *could*:

It cheered Pavel Nikolayevich to think that his wife was coming to see him. There was nothing concrete she could do to help him, of course, but it would mean a lot to be able to unburden himself, to tell her how awful he felt, how the injection hadn't done him any good, and how horrible the people in the ward were. She would sympathise with him, and he would feel better. He might ask her to bring him a book, some cheerful modern book, and his fountain pen, so there'd be no recurrence of that ridiculous situation yesterday when he'd had to borrow the young boy's pencil to write down the prescription. Yes, and most important of all, he could get her to find out about that fungus for him, the birch fungus.
(Alexander Solzhenitsyn, *Cancer Ward*, 1968, Ch. 13)

• The story may be told by the characters themselves, in the form of a representation of their stream of consciousness. In its most extreme form, there are no quotation marks or reporting verbs; sentences are short and elliptical; topics change suddenly:

O, look we are so! Chamber music. Could make a kind of pun on that. It is a kind of music I often thought when she. Acoustics that is. Tinkling. Empty vessels make most noise. Because the acoustics, the resonance changes according as the weight of the water is equal to the law of falling water. Like those rhapsodies of Liszt's, Hungarian, gipsyeyed. Pearls. Drops. Rain. Diddle iddle, addle addle, oodle oodle. Hissss. Now. Maybe now. Before.
(James Joyce, *Ulysses*, 1922, p. 281 (Penguin edn.))

Leo Spitzer (1887–1960)

This Austrian-born literary theorist provided an early account of the link between stylistic features and aesthetic response. His approach to stylistic study involved the use of what he called a 'philological circle' (right) of reasoning. The first step is to use our intuition to identify stylistic features. The second step is to analyse these features and find a pattern. As a result, we confirm the validity of our original intuition.

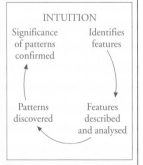

INTUITION

Significance of patterns confirmed → Identifies features

Patterns discovered ← Features described and analysed

TAKING TEXTS TO PIECES

The present century has witnessed a series of academic approaches to the study of style, deriving partly from linguistics and partly from literary theory. It is a complex period, raising questions about literary interpretation and evaluation that go well beyond the scope of this encyclopedia. In this section, therefore, it is possible only to hint at the overlap that exists between the study of language and this broader domain.

The end of the 19th century saw a reaction against the traditional view of a literary work as the product of an author's way of thinking about the world, in which the writer's personal history and culture milieu were crucial factors in arriving at an interpretation. To some critics, this view of literature was too subjective and 'mystical', and drew attention away from what they saw to be the one definite fact about a work: the language in which it was written. Only a close analysis of textual language, it was felt, would place the study of literary texts on a firm, objective footing.

The first method to attempt this task developed in France, and came to be known as *explication de texte.* This used analytical techniques deriving from the study of classical languages. Tests were seen as unique, autonomous units of meaning, with a complex internal structure that could be discovered only through a meticulous language analysis. The linguistic features identified (such as figurative language or metrical structure) were then related to the text's historical background and to the reader's aesthetic response.

The 'formalist' school of Russian (later Czech) critics in the early 20th century focused on the analysis of the literary text as an end in itself, without reference to social history, the writer's intention, or the reader's reaction. In this approach, literary language was seen as a special variety, whose aesthetic effects could be explained by a systematic technical analysis.

These principles were introduced into modern English criticism in the 1920s, through the work of I. A. Richards (1893–1979), William Empson (1906–84), and Cleanth Brooks (1906–), and in due course became associated with the American school of critical theory known as 'New Criticism'. In linguistics, the ideas of the Russian emigré linguist Roman Jakobson (1896–1983) were influential in the development of a specifically linguistic approach to the study of style, which later came to be called *linguistic stylistics* (sometimes *stylolinguistics*). In its early period, this was much taken up with microanalytical studies of word use, metrics, and sentence structure. In recent years, efforts have been made to broaden the scope of the subject, through the study of patterns above the sentence (§20).

STRUCTURALISM AND AFTER

Formalist approaches displayed several limitations. They were unable to handle types of literature that did not use specifically 'literary' language (p. 71), and their microanalytic techniques were not suitable for larger texts, such as the novel. As a result, an alternative approach developed during the 1950s based on the principles of structural linguistics (§§16, 65). This provided a fresh focus for textual analysis, concentrating on the *function* of the various elements in a text. The insights of the founder of modern linguistics, Ferdinand de Saussure (p. 411), were used to hypothesize rules governing the underlying system of meaning that a literary text expressed. The aim was not to interpret texts, in the traditional way, but to define universal principles of literary structure using linguistic techniques. As one critic put it, the aim was to 'transform literary studies into a scientific discipline' (T. Todorov).

The approach used by the French anthropologist Claude Lévi-Strauss (1908–) and others was to take the basic notion of a contrastive unit (or '-eme', as in 'phoneme', p. 162), and apply it to the analysis of behaviour (kinship, eating, etc.). In literary studies, research focused on finding a common structure underlying the many kinds of narrative text (e.g. folk tales, myths, detective stories). For example, significant basic units of myth ('mythemes') were recognized, and organized as a set of binary oppositions, in the same way as phonemes. In one study (A. J. Greimas, 1966), it was suggested that three basic thematic contrasts occur in all narrative:

- 'Subject' vs 'Object', which relate to the desire or search that motivates a character at the beginning of the story (e.g. a detective searching for a murderer).
- 'Sender' vs 'Receiver', as people communicate with each other about relevant events (e.g. establishing various facts about the murder).

- 'Helper' vs 'Opponent', as characters assist or hinder the course of events.

These notions, it was argued, identified a common structure of themes, actions, and character types underlying all kinds of narrative.

Structuralism paid little attention in its analyses to the role of the human mind or social reality. A poem, for example, was to be understood not by studying the experience of the poet, the reader, or the world, but by studying the text. The author was no longer the authority for interpretation; the meaning of a text was to be found in its individual use of language. This meaning was accessible to the critic because author and critic both belonged to the same community language system (or *langue*, p. 411). Language had been handed down to an author, who used it to construct a text. In this view, language did not reflect reality, but created it.

Structuralism brought a valuable objectivity into literary analysis, but at the expense of the total neglect of an author's individuality, the social context, and the varying historical situation. In the late 1960s, accordingly, there developed a reaction to this 'logocentric' view, which came to be known as 'post-structuralism' – a set of ideas whose implications have still to be fully explored. Here, language is seen not as a static structure, existing regardless of social, historical, or personal considerations, but as a system whose values shift in response to these factors, and whose meaning is too complex to be demonstrable by structuralist techniques. A range of post-structuralist viewpoints has developed which emphasize the limitations of binary analyses, draw attention to the multiple and overlapping meanings of words, and stress the role of mental processes in interpreting linguistic relationships. The approach is highly critical of the scientific aims of structuralism, denying the possibility of objectivity in textual interpretation.

Roland Barthes French theorist Barthes (1915–80) was a major influence on early structuralist thought, and he continued to play an important role in the post-structuralist period. In his later thinking, the focus on a text's formal structure is replaced by an emphasis on the active, creative processing carried out by the reader (cf. Chomsky's emphasis, in the same decade, on the creative abilities of the speaker (p. 413)).

Several reader-oriented approaches to literature have now been proposed, and a number of controversial issues have emerged or re-emerged as to whether readers can be credited with a 'literary competence' capable of handling the special properties of literary language. But there is a common emphasis on the opinion that meaning is not to be found in the language of the text. Rather, it is the reader who constructs the text's meaning, always *reading in* meanings which cannot be found within the text itself. Texts, in this view, have no separate identity: they exist only when they are read.

DECONSTRUCTION

The methods and principles of structuralism come under most severe attack in the approach known as 'deconstruction', associated primarily with the writing of Jacques Derrida (1930–). This approach aims to show inherent contradictions and paradoxes in the way that structuralism demonstrates the rules governing the structure of texts, especially its reliance on binary oppositions.

The task of deconstruction begins by isolating a specific structural relationship (e.g. 'speech' vs 'writing'), and identifying the priorities that give the structure its centre (in structuralist think- ing, speech is held to be more fundamental, closer to thought, expressing the 'presence' of the author more directly; writing is a derived medium, with an independent existence on paper that makes it less able to maintain the author's presence). In order to deconstruct the opposition, the critic reverses the expected priorities (showing that, in certain respects, writing might be closer to self-consciousness than speech, and speech less so). The result, however, is not to see the alternative term as in some way superior (to see writing as fundamental, and speech as derived). Rather, the whole basis of the opposition is called into question (*both* speech and writing can be shown to lack presence, *both* can be seen as derived). In this way, readers are forced to rethink the validity of the sets of oppositions they use to think about the world.

The approach has attracted a great deal of interest among literary theorists in recent years. Whether a coherent critical position can ultimately emerge from such radical questioning is a major theme of contemporary critical debate. The issues, of course, extend well beyond literature. Many philosophers have grappled with the paradox that, in order to discuss language, we have to use language, and argued that any claim to 'understanding' rests on a foundation which is uncertain and shifting. The more cross-linguistic our perspective (as in comparative literature or international law), the more the problem grows. The limitations on the average person's ability to learn, with real depth, more than a tiny number of foreign languages raises serious questions about our ability to form linguistically sophisticated global judgments.

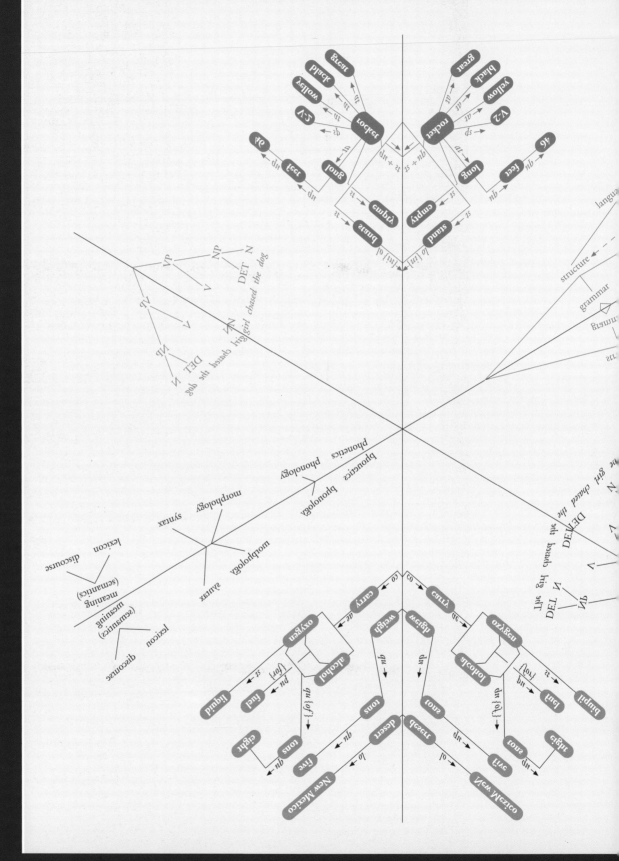

Fragments of the
grammatical and semantic
structure of language.

PART III

The structure of language

The structure of language is something most of us take completely for granted. We are so used to speaking and understanding our mother tongue with unselfconscious ease that we do not notice the complex linguistic architecture that underlies almost every sentence. We forget the years we expended in mastering this skill, so that when we encounter the structural complexity of a foreign language as an adult, we are often amazed at the level of difficulty involved. Similarly, when we hear of people whose ability to control the structures of their language has broken down, as in the case of aphasia (p. 272), we can be surprised at the amount of structural planning involved in the linguistic analysis and treatment of their handicap. Such instances suggest the central importance of the field of linguistic structure, not only to such specialists as teachers or therapists, but to all who wish to further their understanding of the phenomenon of language.

A simple but effective way of sensing the variety and complexity of language structure is to turn a radio dial slowly from one end of a waveband to the other. The first reaction to the auditory tangle of sounds and words must be one of confusion; but if we stop and listen for a while to one of the foreign-language stations, a pattern will gradually emerge. Some words will stand out, and some (such as international products or political names) may be recognizable. The pronunciation will become less alien, as we detect the melodies and rhythmical patterns that convey such information as 'stating' and 'questioning'. We may even find ourselves distinguishing familiar from unfamiliar sounds.

The same kind of reaction takes place when we scan an array of foreign-language publications. Instead of sounds and rhythms, we are now dealing with shapes and spaces; but the principle is the same. The multifarious variety of visual forms, many of which are expressing similar meanings, is a striking manifestation of the diversity and depth of language structure.

In this part of the encyclopedia, we therefore examine the factors involved in carrying out a structural analysis of language, whether spoken, written, or signed, and illustrate the main components, or levels, that linguists have proposed in order to elucidate the way languages operate. The largest section will be devoted to the field of grammar, which is at the centre of most linguistic investigation, but several pages will also be given to semantics, the study of meaning in language, and to the associated themes of dictionaries, place names, and personal names. We begin with a review of some general issues that form part of any structural study of language, and address the question of whether all languages have properties in common. Part III concludes with a discussion of some of the more recent movements in linguistic study which analyse conversations, narratives, and other kinds of spoken or written discourse.

13 · LINGUISTIC LEVELS

There is too much going on in a piece of speech, writing, or signing to permit us to describe its characteristics in a single, simple statement. Even in a short spoken sentence such as *Hello there!*, several things are taking place at once. Each word conveys a particular meaning. There is a likely order in which the words may appear – we would not say *There hello!* Each word is composed of a specific sequence of sounds. The sentence as a whole is uttered in a particular tone of voice (poorly signalled in writing through the exclamation mark (§29)). And the choice of this sentence immediately constrains the occasions when it might be used – on a first meeting (and not, for example, upon leave-taking). While we say or hear the sentence, we are not consciously aware of all these facets of its structure, but once our attention is drawn to them, we easily recognize their existence. We could even concentrate on the study of one of these facets largely to the exclusion of the others – something that takes place routinely in language teaching, for instance, where someone may learn about aspects of 'pronunciation' one day, and of 'vocabulary' or 'grammar' the next.

Selective focusing of this kind in fact takes place in all linguistic studies, as part of the business of discovering how language works, and of simplifying the task of description. The different facets are usually referred to as *levels* of linguistic organization. Each level is studied using its own terms and techniques, enabling us to obtain information about one aspect of language structure, while temporarily disregarding the involvement of others. The field of pronunciation, for example, is basically analysed at the level of *phonetics*, using procedures that are quite distinct from anything encountered at other linguistic levels. When we do phonetic research, we try to disassociate ourselves from the problems and practices we would encounter if we were carrying out a study at the level of, say, *grammar*. Similarly, grammatical study takes place using approaches that are in principle independent of what goes on in phonetics. And other levels, likewise, provide us with their own independent 'slant' on the workings of language structure.

The notion of levels is widely applicable, especially when we engage in the analysis of a range of languages, as it enables us to see and state patterns of organization more clearly and succinctly than any other way that has so far been devised. Levels appear to have a certain empirical validity in psychological and neurological contexts also (§45). At the same time, we must never forget that, when we isolate a level for independent study, we are introducing an artificial element into our enquiry, whose consequences must be anticipated. The sounds of speech that we study via phonetics are, after all, the substance through which the patterns of grammar are conveyed. There will therefore be interrelationships between levels that need to be taken into account if we wish to understand the way language as a whole is organized. As with any structure, the whole cannot be broken down into its constituent parts without loss; and we must therefore always recollect the need to place our work on individual levels within a more general structural perspective.

HOW MANY LEVELS?

It is not difficult to sense the complexity of language structure, but it is not so easy to say how many levels should be set up in order to explain the way this structure is organized. Some simple models of language recognize only two basic levels: the set of physical *forms* (sounds, letters, signs, words) contained in a language, and the range of abstract *meanings* conveyed by these forms. More commonly, the notion of *forms* is subdivided, to distinguish different kinds of abstractness. In speech, for example, the physical facts of pronunciation, as defined by the processes of articulation, acoustic transmission and audition, are considered to be the subject matter of *phonetics* (§27). The way different languages organize sounds to convey differences of meaning is the province of *phonology* (§28). And the study of the way meaningful units are brought into sequence to convey wider and more varied patterns of meaning is the province of *grammar*. The term *semantics* is then used for the study of the patterns of meaning themselves.

Four-level models of language (phonetics / phonology / grammar / semantics) are among the most widely used, but further divisions within and between these levels are often made. For example, within the level of grammar, it is common to recognize a distinction between the study of word structure (*morphology*) and the study of word sequence within sentences (*syntax*) (§16). Within phonology, the study of vowels, consonants, and syllables (*segmental* phonology) is usually distinguished from the study of prosody and other tones of voice (*suprasegmental* phonology) (§29). Within semantics, the study of vocabulary (or *lexicon*) is sometimes taken separately from the study of larger patterns of meaning (under such headings as *text* or *discourse*) (§20). All of these are regularly referred to as 'levels' of structure.

We could continue, making divisions within divisions, and recognizing more subtle kinds of structural

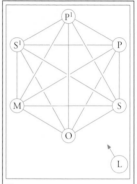

organization within language. We could extend the notion to include other aspects of language functioning apart from structure (as when some scholars talk of a *pragmatic* 'level' (§21)). But there comes a point when the notion ceases to be helpful. When a theory sets up a large number of levels, it becomes difficult to plot the relationships between them, and to retain a sense of how they integrate into a single system. At that point, alternative models need to be devised.

WHICH LEVEL FIRST?

Is there a 'best' direction for the study of a language, using the framework of levels? The American linguist Leonard Bloomfield (1887–1949) recommended an approach in which one worked through the various levels in a particular order, beginning with a phonetic description, proceeding through phonology, morphology, and syntax, and concluding with semantics. In this view, the analysis at each level apart from the first is dependent on what has gone before. Workers in the Bloomfieldian tradition would talk about starting at the 'bottom', with the phonetics, and working 'up' to the semantics – though in view of the complexity of the task facing phoneticians, phonologists, and grammarians, it is a moot point whether anyone who strictly followed this approach would ever arrive there. Apocryphal stories abound of informants in field studies who have died before the investigating linguist got around to studying the meaning of the speech patterns that had been so painstakingly transcribed!

In any case, it is now recognized that it is possible to carry out an analysis at one level only if we make certain assumptions about other levels. Our choice of sounds to describe phonetically depends to some extent on our awareness of which sounds play an important role in a language (phonology), which in turn depends on our awareness of the way sounds distinguish words (grammar) enabling them to convey differences in meaning (semantics). Similarly, when we study grammatical patterns, such as sentence structure, we need to be aware of both semantic factors (such as the relationships of meaning that bring the patterns together) and phonological factors (such as the features of intonation that help to identify sentence units in speech). In a sense, when we work with levels, we need to be able to move in all directions at once. The British linguist J. R. Firth (1890–1960) once likened the business to a lift that moves freely from one level to another, in either direction, without giving priority to any one level. The simile makes its point, but the two-dimensional analogy is still misleading. To capture the notion of levels, multidimensional geometries are required.

MODELS OF SPOKEN LANGUAGE STRUCTURE

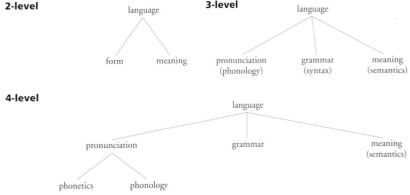

5-level This model (after M. A. K. Halliday, 1961) recognizes three primary levels (substance, form, context); substance and form are related by the 'interlevel' of phonology; form is divided into grammar and lexis.

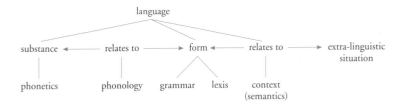

6-level In this approach (after S. M. Lamb, 1966), the various levels are referred to as *strata*, and the model as a whole is known as *stratificational grammar*.

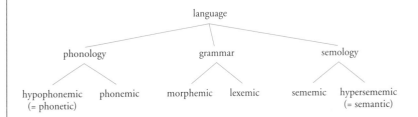

The present work In this encyclopedia, we shall be making most use of a 6-level model of structure which uses three basic notions (*transmitting medium, grammar, semantics*), each containing a twofold division. The model also incorporates the dimension of language *in use*, which is related to the concerns of language structure through the notion of *pragmatics*. The diagram gives only the distinctions required for the spoken medium of transmission: these are reviewed in detail in Part IV. The properties of the written medium are reviewed in Part V, and of the signing medium in Part VI. The various facets of language in use are discussed in Part II and §63. The remaining levels, including pragmatics, are dealt with in later sections of Part III.

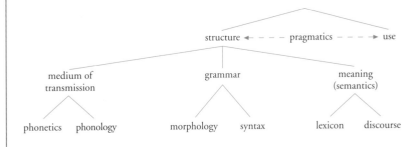

The languages of the world present us with a vast array of structural similarities and differences. Why should this be so? One way of answering this question is to adopt a historical perspective, investigating the origins of language, and pointing to the importance of linguistic change – a perspective that is discussed in Part IX. An alternative approach is to make a detailed description of the similarities or differences, regardless of their historical antecedents, and proceed from there to generalize about the structure and function of human language.

There are two main ways of approaching this latter task. We might look for the structural features that all or most languages have in common; or we might focus our attention on the features that differentiate them. In the former case, we are searching for language *universals*; in the latter case, we are involving ourselves in language *typology*. In principle, the two approaches are complementary, but sometimes they are associated with different theoretical conceptions of the nature of linguistic enquiry.

SIMILARITY OR DIFFERENCE?

Since the end of the 18th century, the chief concern has been to explain the nature of linguistic diversity. This was the focus of comparative philology and dialectology, and it led to early attempts to set up genetic and structural typologies of languages (§50). The emphasis carried through into the 20th century when the new science of linguistics continually stressed the variety of languages in the world, partly in reaction against the traditions of 19th-century prescriptivism, where one language, Latin, had been commonly regarded as a standard of excellence (§1).

Since the 1950s, the focus on diversity has been replaced by a research paradigm, stemming from the work of the American linguist Noam Chomsky (1928–), in which the nature of linguistic universals holds a central place. Chomsky's generative theory of language proposes a single set of rules from which all the grammatical sentences in a language can be derived (p. 97). In order to define these rules in an accurate and economical way, a grammar has to rely on certain general principles – abstract constraints that govern the form it takes and the nature of the categories with which it operates. In this approach, these principles are conceived as universal properties of language – properties that are biologically necessary and thus innate (p. 236). The notion of universals is important, it is argued, not only because it deepens our understanding of language in its own right, but because it provides an essential first step in the task of understanding human intellectual capacity.

In Chomsky's view, therefore, the aim of linguistics is to go beyond the study of individual languages, to determine what the universal properties of language are, and to establish a 'universal grammar' that would account for the range of linguistic variation that is humanly possible. The question is simply: What are the limits on human language variability? Languages do not make use of all possible sounds, sound sequences, or word orders. Can we work out the reasons? It might be possible to draw a line between the patterns that are essential features of language, and those that no language ever makes use of (p. 97). Or perhaps there is a continuum between these extremes, with some features being found in most (but not all) languages, and some being found in very few. Questions of this kind constitute the current focus of many linguists' attention.

EXPRESSING
COMPARISON

The English comparative construction, 'X is *bigger than* Y' involves three parts: the adjective (*big*), the markers of comparison (*-er* and *than*), and the standard of comparison (*Y*). This way of putting it is shared by many languages, including Berber, Greek, Hebrew, Malay, Maori, Songhai, Swahili, Thai, Welsh, and Zapotec.

However, the opposite order, in which the standard of comparison is expressed first, is also common. In Japanese, for example, it is 'Y *yori okii*' (literally 'Y than big'), and this way of putting it is shared by Basque, Burmese, Chibcha, Guaraní, Hindi, Kannada, and Turkish, among others. Finnish is a language which uses both constructions.

THE PORT-ROYAL GRAMMAR

Contemporary ideas about the nature of linguistic universals have several antecedents in the work of 17th-century thinkers. The *Grammaire générale et raisonnée* (1660) is widely recognized as the most influential treatise of this period. It is often referred to as the 'Port-Royal grammar', because it was written by scholars who belonged to the community of intellectuals and religious established between 1637 and 1660 in Port-Royal, Versailles.

Although published anonymously, the authorship of the grammar has been ascribed to Claude Lancelot (1615–95) and Antoine Arnauld (1612–94). Its subtitle, referring to 'that which is common to all languages, and their principal differences ...' provides a neat summary of the current preoccupation with universals and typology. However, the approach of modern linguistics is less concerned with how language relates to logic and reality, and more with its arbitrary properties.

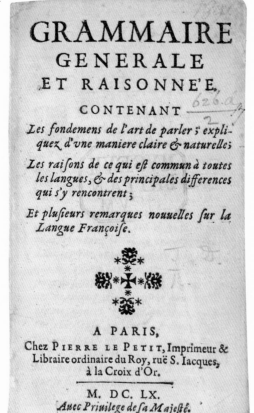

BREADTH OR DEPTH?

The distinction between typological and universalist approaches to language study is doubtless ultimately an arbitrary one; and both have considerable insights to offer. But the two approaches, as currently practised, differ greatly in their procedures. Typologists typically study a wide range of languages as part of their enquiry, and tend to make generalizations that deal with the more observable aspects of structure, such as word order, word classes, and types of sound. In contrast with the empirical breadth of such studies, universalists rely on in-depth studies of single languages, especially in the field of grammar – English, in particular, is a common language of exemplification – and tend to make generalizations about the more abstract, underlying properties of language.

This focus on single languages might at first seem strange. If we are searching for universals, then surely we need to study many languages? Chomsky argues, however, that there is no paradox. Because English is a human language, it must therefore incorporate all universal properties of language, as well as those individual features that make it specifically 'English'. One way of finding out about these properties, therefore, is the detailed study of single languages. The more languages we introduce into our enquiry, the more difficult it can become to see the central features behind the welter of individual differences.

On the other hand, it can be argued that the detailed study of single languages is inevitably going to produce a distorted picture. There are features of English, for example, that are *not* commonly met with in other languages, such as the use of only one inflectional ending in the present tense (third-person, as in *she runs*), or the absence of a second-person singular / plural distinction (cf. French *tu / vous*). Without a typological perspective, some say, it is not possible to anticipate the extent to which our sense of priorities will be upset. If languages were relatively homogeneous entities, like samples of iron ore, this would not be a problem. But, typologists argue, languages are unpredictably irregular and idiosyncratic. Under these circumstances, a focus on breadth, rather than depth, is desirable.

RELATIVE OR ABSOLUTE?

The universalist ideal is to be able to make succinct and interesting statements that hold, without exception, for all languages. In practice, very few such statements can be made: the succinct ones often seem to state the obvious (e.g. all languages have vowels); and the interesting ones often seem to require considerable technical qualification. Most of the time, in fact, it is clear that 'absolute' (or exceptionless) universals do not exist. As a result, many linguists look instead for trends or tendencies across languages – 'relative' universals – which can be given statistical expression. For example, in over 99% of languages whose word order has been

studied, grammatical subjects precede objects. And in a phonological study of over 300 languages (p. 167), less than 3% have no nasal consonant. Linguistic features that are statistically dominant in this way are often referred to as 'unmarked'; and a grammar that incorporates norms of this kind is known as a 'core grammar' (p. 97).

THREE TYPES OF UNIVERSALS

Substantive
Substantive universals comprise the set of categories that is needed in order to analyse a language, such as 'noun', 'question', 'first-person', 'antonym', and 'vowel'. Do all languages have nouns and vowels? The answer seems to be yes. But certain categories often thought of as universal turn out not to be so: not all languages have case endings, prepositions, or future tenses, for example, and there are several surprising limitations on the range of vowels and consonants that typically occur (§28). Analytical considerations must also be borne in mind. Do all languages have words? The answer depends on how the concept of 'word' is defined (p. 91).

Formal
Formal universals are a set of abstract conditions that govern the way in which a language analysis can be made – the factors that have to be written into a grammar, if it is to account successfully for the way sentences work in a language. For example, because all languages make statements and ask related questions (such as *The car is ready* vs *Is the car ready?*), some means has to be found to show the relationship between such pairs. Most grammars derive question structures from statement structures by some kind of transformation (in the above example, 'Move the verb to the beginning of the sentence'). If it is claimed that such transformations are necessary in order to carry out the analysis of these (and other kinds of) structures, as one version of Chomskyan theory does, then they would be proposed as formal universals. Other cases include the kinds of rules used in a grammar, or the different levels recognized by a theory (§13).

Implicational
Implicational universals always take the form 'If X, then Y', their intention being to find constant relationships between two or more properties of language. For example, three of the universals proposed in a list of 45 by the American linguist Joseph Greenberg (1915–) are as follows:

Universal 17. With overwhelmingly more-than-chance frequency, languages with dominant order VSO [=Verb–Subject–Object] have the adjective after the noun.

Universal 31. If either the subject or object noun agrees with the verb in gender, then the adjective always agrees with the noun in gender.

Universal 43. If a language has gender categories in the noun, it has gender categories in the pronoun.

As is suggested by the phrasing, implicational statements have a statistical basis, and for this reason are sometimes referred to as 'statistical' universals (though this is a somewhat different sense from that used in §15).

HOW MANY LANGUAGES?

It is impossible in principle to study all human languages, in order to find out about universals, for the simple reason that many languages are extinct, and there is no way of predicting what languages will emerge in the future. To be practical, typological or universal studies therefore need to be based on a sample of the 6,000 or so current languages of the world (§47). But how should a representative sample be achieved?

Several projects on language universals have had to address this basic question. The aim is to include as many different kinds of language as possible. Languages are selected from the main branches of every language family, insofar as these are known. They are not selected from the same local geographical area, in case they display a high degree of mutual influence. And the number of languages within each family has to be carefully considered. It would not be right to select an arbitrary five languages from each family – bearing in mind that Indo-Pacific, for example, has over 700 languages, whereas Dravidian has only about 25 (§52). The languages of New Guinea ought, statistically speaking, to constitute about 20% of any sample.

In practice, surveys have to be satisfied with what they can get. As few of the New Guinea languages have been studied in depth, for instance, it is currently impracticable to achieve the target of 20%. For such reasons, even the largest surveys work under considerable limitations. For example, in an American study of phonological universals (§28), the database was provided by a total of only 317 languages – about 5% of the whole. But the study nonetheless provided an enormous amount of valuable information (I. Maddieson, 1984).

Within any level of linguistic structure (§13), it is possible to count the different units that occur, and interrelate the frequencies we obtain, to see if there are statistical regularities governing their use. Many aspects of grammar, vocabulary, sound system, and writing system have been studied in this way, and several interesting patterns have emerged. It has even been possible to propose statistical properties that are in common to all languages; these are sometimes referred to as statistical *laws* or 'universals'.

Statistical regularities are independent of speaker or writer, or subject matter. While in a sense we are free to say whatever we want, in practice our linguistic behaviour conforms closely to statistical expectations. We can say with confidence that if we write a *q* in English, it is almost always going to be followed by *u* (though not always, because of *Iraq*, and other exceptions). Less obviously, but equally confidently, it emerges that just over 60% of everything we say will be made up of consonants, and just under 40% of vowels. About a third of all the syllables we use in everyday speech will have the structure of consonant + vowel + consonant, as in *cat*. The 50 most commonly used words in the language will make up about 45% of everything we write.

The remarkable thing about such facts is that, while we are engaged in communication, we do not consciously monitor our language to ensure that these statistical properties obtain. It would be impossible to do so. Yet, without any deliberate effort on our part, we will find the same underlying regularities in any large sample of our speech or writing. The study of these regularities, and of the factors that constrain them, is the province of *statistical linguistics*.

LETTER FREQUENCY

One of the simplest demonstrations of statistical regularity within a language is the frequency of occurrence of the letters of the alphabet. Here is a selection of frequency orders found in one comparative study of different styles of American English (after A. Zettersten, 1969, p. 21): (a) press reporting, (b) religious writing, (c) scientific writing, (d) general fiction. The average rank order, based on a description of 15 categories of text totalling over a million words, is given as (e). Column (f) gives the order used by Samuel Morse (1791–1872) in compiling the Morse Code. His frequency ordering was based on the quantities of type found in a printer's office (see column (g)).

(a)	(b)	(c)	(d)	(e)	(f)	(g)
e	e	e	e	e	e	12,000
t	t	t	t	t	t	9,000
a	i	a	a	a	a	8,000
o	a	i	o	o	i	8,000
n	o	o	h	i	n	8,000
i	n	n	n	n	o	8,000
s	s	s	i	s	s	8,000
r	r	r	s	r	h	6,400
h	h	h	r	h	r	6,200
l	l	l	d	l	d	4,400
d	d	c	l	d	l	4,000
c	c	d	u	c	u	3,400
m	u	u	w	u	c	3,000
u	m	m	m	m	m	3,000
f	f	f	c	f	f	2,500
p	p	p	g	p	w	2,000
g	y	g	f	g	y	2,000
w	w	y	y	w	g	1,700
y	g	b	p	y	p	1,700
b	b	w	b	b	b	1,600
v	v	v	k	v	v	1,200
k	k	k	v	k	k	800
j	x	x	j	x	q	500
x	j	q	x	j	j	400
q	q	j	z	q	x	400
z	z	z	q	z	z	200

Rank	French	German	Written English	Spoken English
1	de	der	the	the
2	le (a.)	die	of	and
3	la (a.)	und	to	I
4	et	in	in	to
5	les	des	and	of
6	des	den	a	a
7	est	zu	for	you
8	un (a.)	das	was	that
9	une (a.)	von	is	in
10	du	für	that	it
11	que (p.)	auf	on	is

a. article p. pronoun

Rank	French	German	Written English	Spoken English
12	dans	mit	at	yes
13	il	sich	he	was
14	à	daß	with	this
15	en	dem	by	but
16	ne	sie	be	on
17	on	ist	it	well
18	qui	im	an	he
19	au	eine	as	have
20	se	DDR	his	for

MONOSYLLABIC OR POLYSYLLABIC?

The most frequent words are monosyllabic. This effect is clearly seen in a study of telephone conversation. There were few words of 3 or more syllables in the 800 most frequently occurring words. (After N. R. French, et al., 1930.)

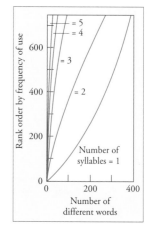

LEXICAL TOP TWENTIES

The 20 most-frequently occurring words in studies of newspaper writing in English, French, and German are shown (after P. M. Alexejew et al., 1968). For comparison, the last column lists the most-frequent words in the London–Lund corpus of spoken conversation (p. 417). The importance of the speech / writing distinction is evident: note the frequency of *I*, *yes*, and *well* in spoken English, and the occurrence of *DDR* ('German Democratic Republic') in the German list.

ZIPF'S LAWS

One of the first demonstrations of the existence of major statistical regularities in language was carried out by the American philologist George Kingsley Zipf (1902–50). His best known 'law' proposes a constant relationship between the rank of a word in a frequency list, and the frequency with which it is used in a text. If you want to test the validity of the law, you have to carry out the following operations:

1. Count all the instances (tokens) of different words (types) in a text – *the* 364, *is* 251, *table* 4, etc.
2. Put them in descending rank order of frequency, and give each rank a number – (1) *the* 364, (2) *is* 251, (3) *of* 166, etc.
3. Multiply the rank number (r) by the frequency (f), and the result is approximately constant (C).

For example, the list below gives the 35th, 45th, 55th, 65th, and 75th most-frequently occurring words in one category of the London–Lund corpus of spoken conversation. The values come out at around 30,000 each time.

r	×	f	=	C
35	*very*	836	=	29,260
45	*see*	674	=	30,330
55	*which*	563	=	30,965
65	*get*	469	=	30,485
75	*out*	422	=	31,650

In other words, the relationship is inversely proportional, and it was thought to obtain regardless of subject matter, author, or any other linguistic variable. However, it was subsequently shown that the relationship does not obtain for words of highest and lowest frequencies. In the same corpus, for example, the most frequent word, *I*, occurs 5,920 times (r.f = 5,920), and the 100th word, *he's*, occurs 363 times (r.f = 36,300). The size of the sample is also a critical factor.

Nonetheless, the 'standard curve' of word frequency, summarized as *f.r = C* is an interesting observation about language patterns. Moreover, the same kind of curve has been found in many languages. For example, in a French word-frequency book, the 100th word was used 314 times (= 31,400), the 200th, 158 times (31,600), and the 1,000th, 31 times (31,000).

OTHER RELATIONSHIPS

Zipf also showed that there is an inverse relationship between the length of a word and its frequency. In English, for example, the majority of the commonly used words are monosyllables. The same relationship obtains even in a language like German, which has a marked 'polysyllabic' vocabulary. This effect seems to account for our tendency to abbreviate words when their frequency of use rises, e.g. the routine reduction of *microphone* to *mike* by radio broadcasters. It would also seem to be an efficient communicative principle to have the popular words short and the rare words long.

Factors such as efficiency and ease of communication appealed strongly to Zipf, who argued for a principle of 'least effort' to explain the apparent equilibrium between diversity and uniformity in our use of sounds and words. The simpler the sound and the shorter the word, the more often will human beings want to use it. There are, however, several difficulties facing this explanation (e.g. how to quantify the 'effort' involved in articulating sounds, and the exceptions to the law referred to above), and today a more conventional explanation in terms of probability theory is accepted.

G. K. Zipf (1902–50)

SYLLABLES

Take a tape recording of some spoken English, and transcribe it. Mark the boundaries between the syllables. You should find that 12 syllables make up 25% of the speech: /ðə/, /əv/, /ɪn/, /ænd/, /ɪ/, /ə/, /tʊ/, /ɪŋ/, /ə/, /rɪ/, /ɪt/, /ðæt/ (see Appendix II for transcription). Half the speech will use only 70 different syllables. But to account for 90% of the speech, you will need to recognize over 1,300 syllable types. /ðə/ alone makes up 7% of all spoken syllables; it turns up on average every 14 syllables. (After G. Dewey, 1923.)

LENGTH / FREQUENCY RELATIONSHIP

The relationship of syllable length and frequency of occurrence was chartered in a study of nearly 11 million German words (after F. W. Kaeding, 1898).

Number of syllables in word	Number of word occurrences	Percentage of whole
1	5,426,326	49.76
2	3,156,448	28.94
3	1,410,494	12.93
4	646,971	5.93
5	187,738	1.72
6	54,436	0.50
7	16,993	
8	5,038	
9	1,225	
10	461	
11	59	0.22
12	35	
13	8	
14	2	
15	1	

TAKE A TEXT, ANY TEXT...

Take a text, in any language, and count the words. Order the words in terms of decreasing frequency. According to one statistical prediction, the first 15 words will account for 25% of the text. The first 100 words will account for 60%; and the first 1,000 for 85%. The first 4,000 will account for 97.5%. In short samples, however, considerable variation from these proportions will be found. Also, the type of text in a corpus will affect the results: in the Lancaster Oslo / Bergen corpus, for example, the 25% figure is reached after only 12 words. (After S. Johansson & K. Hofland, 1989, p. 415).

DICTIONARIES

Take a dictionary and count the meanings of each word, as indicated by the sub-entries. The number of words (n) that have a particular number of meanings (m) is inversely proportional to the square of the number of meanings ($n.m^2 = C$).

16 · GRAMMAR

It is difficult to capture the central role played by grammar in the structure of language, other than by using a metaphor such as 'framework' or 'skeleton'. But no physical metaphor can express satisfactorily the multifarious kinds of formal patterning and abstract relationship that are brought to light in a grammatical analysis.

Two steps can usually be distinguished in the study of grammar. The first step is to identify units in the stream of speech (or writing, or signing) – units such as 'word' and 'sentence'. The second step is to analyse the patterns into which these units fall, and the relationships of meaning that these patterns convey. Depending upon which units we recognize at the beginning of the study so the definition of grammar alters. Most approaches begin by recognizing the 'sentence', and grammar is thus most widely defined as 'the study of sentence structure'. A grammar of a language, from this point of view, is an account of the language's possible sentence structures, organized according to certain general principles. For example, in the opening pages of the most influential grammatical treatise of recent times, the American linguist Noam Chomsky (1928–), writes that a grammar is a 'device of some sort for producing the sentences of the language under analysis' (1957, p. 11), to which is added the rider that the sentences produced must be grammatical ones, acceptable to the native speaker.

Within this general perspective there is room for many different positions. In particular, there are two quite distinct applications of the term 'grammar', yielding a specific sense and a general one. The specific sense is the more traditional: here, grammar is presented as just one branch of language structure, distinct from phonology and semantics. This is the approach used in this encyclopedia (§13):

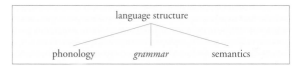

The general sense of the term, popularized by Chomsky, subsumes *all* aspects of sentence patterning, *including* phonology and semantics, and introduces the term 'syntax' as the more specific notion:

SIX TYPES OF GRAMMAR

Descriptive grammar   An approach that describes the grammatical constructions that are used in a language, without making any evaluative judgments about their standing in society. These grammars are commonplace in linguistics, where it is standard practice to investigate a 'corpus' of spoken or written material, and to describe in detail the patterns it contains (p. 414).

Pedagogical grammar   A book specifically designed for teaching a foreign language, or for developing an awareness of the mother tongue. Such 'teaching grammars' are widely used in schools, so much so that many people have only one meaning for the term 'grammar': a grammar book.

Prescriptive grammar   A manual that focuses on constructions where usage is divided, and lays down rules governing the socially correct use of language (§1). These grammars were a formative influence on language attitudes in Europe and America during the 18th and 19th centuries. Their influence lives on in the handbooks of usage widely found today, such as *A Dictionary of Modern English Usage* (1926) by Henry Watson Fowler (1858–1933).

Reference grammar   A grammatical description that tries to be as comprehensive as possible, so that it can act as a reference book for those interested in establishing grammatical facts (in much the same way as a dictionary is used as a 'reference lexicon' (§18)). Several north European grammarians compiled handbooks of this type in the early 20th century, the best known being the seven-volume *Modern English Grammar* (1909–49) by the Danish grammarian Otto Jespersen (1860–1943), and *A Comprehensive Grammar of the English Language* (1985) by Randolph Quirk (1920–) *et al.*

Theoretical grammar   An approach that goes beyond the study of individual languages, to determine what constructs are needed in order to do any kind of grammatical analysis, and how these can be applied consistently in the investigation of a human language. It is thus a central notion in any investigation of linguistic universals (§14).

Traditional grammar   A term often used to summarize the range of attitudes and methods found in the period of grammatical study before the advent of linguistic science (§65). The 'tradition' in question is over 2,000 years old, and includes the work of classical Greek and Roman grammarians, Renaissance writers, and 18th-century prescriptive grammarians. It is difficult to generalize about such a wide variety of approaches, but linguists generally use the term pejoratively, identifying an unscientific approach to grammatical study, in which languages were analysed in terms of Latin, with scant regard for empirical facts. However, many basic notions used by modern approaches can be found in these earlier writings, and there is now fresh interest in the study of traditional grammar, as part of the history of linguistic ideas.

* ?

Two of the most important symbols in modern grammatical analysis. An asterisk is placed before a construction to show that it is ungrammatical. A question-mark placed before a construction shows that it is of doubtful grammaticality. For example, there is no doubt about the ungrammaticality of

*Who and why came in?

*That book looks alike.

But the status of the following sentence is less certain. Both are in use, yet there is something odd about them.

?Don't forget yours and my books.

?This is the car of the family.

One of the main aims of linguistic analysis is to discover the principles enabling us to decide the grammaticality of a sentence.

SO MUCH GRAMMAR IN A LANGUAGE

Probably the largest grammar produced for any language: *A Comprehensive Grammar of the English Language* (1985), by Randolph Quirk, Sidney Greenbaum, Geoffrey Leech, and Jan Svartvik. The amount of detail in its 1,779 pages comes as a surprise to many people who, because of the traditional focus on grammar as a matter of word-endings, have been brought up to think of English as a language lacking in grammar. But this book stands on the shoulders of even more detailed treatments of areas of the language; for example, *a* and *the* alone have warranted a 200-page study (P. Christopherson, 1939).

PARSING vs CREATING

Traditional grammars taught people to 'parse', or analyse, a sentence, by making a series of divisions within it. *The man saw the cow,* for example, would be divided into a 'subject' (*the man*), and a 'predicate' (*saw the cow*). The predicate would then be divided into its verb (*saw*) and the 'object' (*the cow*). Other divisions would not be made until all the features of the sentence had been identified. It is an approach to language that many people recall with distaste. Grammar, for them, was a dry, boring, and frustrating subject. Why should this have been so?

There were several reasons. All too often, in the traditional grammars, insufficient reasons were given for making a particular sentence analysis. As a consequence, it was common to find children learning analyses and definitions off by heart, without any real understanding of what was going on. In particular, they had to master the cumbersome, Latin-based grammatical terminology as an end in itself (terms such as 'accusative', 'complement', 'apposition'), and apply it to examples of language that were either artificially constructed, or taken from abstruse literature. It was all at a considerable remove from the child's real language world, as found in conversation or the media. Little attempt was made to demonstrate the practical usefulness of grammatical analysis in the child's daily life, whether in school or outside. And there was no interest shown in relating this analysis to the broader principles of grammatical patterning in the language as a whole. It is not surprising, then, that most people who were taught parsing in school ended up unable to see the point of the exercise, and left remembering grammar only as a dead, irrelevant subject.

The reality is quite the opposite. The techniques of grammatical analysis can be used to demonstrate the enormous creative power of language – how, from a finite set of grammatical patterns, even a young child can express an infinite set of sentences. They can help us all to identify the fascinating 'edges' of language, where grammaticality shades into ungrammaticality, and where we find the many kinds of humorous and dramatic effects, both in literature and in everyday language (p. 72). As we discover more about the way we each use grammar as part of our daily linguistic survival, we inevitably sharpen our individual sense of style, and thus promote our abilities to handle more complex constructions, both in speaking/listening and in reading/writing. We become more likely to spot ambiguities and loose constructions, and to do something about it. Moreover, the principles of grammatical analysis are general ones, applicable to the study of any language, so that we find ourselves developing a keener sense of the similarities and differences between languages. And many kinds of specialized problems can be illuminated through the study of grammar – such as the difficulties facing the language-handicapped, the foreign-language learner, or the translator.

Grammar need not be dry, unreal, arcane; it can be alive, relevant, entertaining. As with so many subjects, it depends only on how it is put across.

GRAMMATICAL NATURE RAMBLES?

Imagine teaching a child about the structure of a flower in the following way. A hypothetical plant is drawn on the board, and its parts labelled: stamen, pistil, stalk, etc. Each term is defined, and the children write them in their books. They have to learn them off by heart, and until they do they will *not* be allowed to see or work with any real plant!

It is unlikely that anyone in a modern biology class would be taught this topic through such an approach. The teacher would arrive armed with real plants, and give them out; then the children would search for the parts, all the while meeting problems, and asking for help with the labels as they went along. Later, the teacher would get them to write up their project in a book, and then might ask for some terms to be learned.

That is the modern way: discovery first, definitions of terms last. But grammar has continued to suffer, in many schools, by being taught the other way round (when it was taught at all!). A hypothetical sentence would be put on the board, and the required grammatical terminology had to be learned, before any attempt would be made to grapple with real sentences in a real world. Often, even, no attempt at all would be made to go searching for interesting, real sentence specimens. It is as if the children's knowledge of plants were to remain forever solely on the blackboard. No one would tolerate such a silly pedagogical approach for biology. But for many decades, just such an approach was actively practised for grammar – and it is by no means extinct.

A page from Maureen Vidler's *Find a Story* (1974) The page is cut horizontally, so that as each strip is turned over, a new sentence and picture results. On the next page, for instance, the top strip reads 'Meg has a gay bonnet', and the bottom one 'and long, sharp teeth'. There are only 12 pages in the book, but there are over 20,000 possible grammatical combinations. In a similar approach ('Roll a Story'), the child makes a sentence by rolling a series of blocks on which words have been printed. Such approaches are an entertaining means of drawing young children's attention to sentence structure. Grammar can, at times, be fun.

Jake has a black hat,

one good eye

and too much lipstick.

POODLES WEARING JEANS?

It is not difficult to think up dramatic or entertaining sentences that would motivate a child to carry out a grammatical analysis, because of their ambiguity or stylistic effect. Here are some nice cases of ambiguity, taken from W. H. Mittins, *A Grammar of Modern English* (1962), all of which can be explained through a single principle:

The girl was followed by a small poodle wearing jeans.

Next came a mother with a very small baby who was pushing a pram.

I always buy my newspapers at the shop next to the police station in which cards, magazines, and fancy goods are displayed.

A sailor was dancing with a wooden leg.

In each case, the construction at the end of the sentence has been separated from the noun to which it belongs. If one wished to avoid the unintentionally humorous effects, the sentences would need to be reformulated with this construction immediately following, or 'postmodifying', the noun ('The girl wearing jeans ...').

BASIC GRAMMATICAL NOTIONS

The range of constructions that is studied by grammar is very large, and grammarians have often divided it into sub-fields. The oldest and most widely-used division is that between morphology and syntax.

MORPHOLOGY

This branch of grammar studies the structure of words. In the following list, all the words except the last can be divided into parts, each of which has some kind of independent meaning.

unhappiness	*un- -happi- -ness*
horses	*horse- -s*
talking	*talk- -ing*
yes	*yes*

Yes has no internal grammatical structure. We could analyse its constituent sounds, /j/, /e/, /s/, but none of these has a meaning in isolation. By contrast, *horse*, *talk*, and *happy* plainly have a meaning, as do the elements attached to them (the 'affixes'): *un-* carries a negative meaning; *-ness* expresses a state or quality; *-s* expresses plural; and *-ing* helps to convey a sense of duration. The smallest meaningful elements into which words can be analysed are known as *morphemes*; and the way morphemes operate in language provides the subject matter of *morphology*.

It is an easy matter to analyse the above words into morphemes, because a clear sequence of elements is involved. Even an unlikely word such as *antidisestablishmentarianism* would also be easy to analyse, for the same reason. In many languages (the so-called 'agglutinating' languages (p. 295)), it is quite normal to have long sequences of morphemes occur within a word, and these would be analysed in the same way. For example, in Eskimo the word *angyaghllangyugtuq* has the meaning 'he wants to acquire a big boat'. Speakers of English find such words very complex at first sight; but things become much clearer when we analyse them into their constituent morphemes:

angya-	'boat'
-ghlla-	an affix expressing augmentative meaning
-ng-	'acquire'
-yug-	an affix expressing desire
-tuq-	an affix expressing third person singular.

English has relatively few word structures of this type, but agglutinating and inflecting languages, such as Turkish and Latin, make widespread use of morphological variation. Many African languages, such as Swahili or Bilin, have verbs which can appear in well over 10,000 variant forms.

MORPHEME PROBLEMS

Not all words can be analysed into morphemes so easily. In English, for example, it is difficult to know how to analyse irregular nouns and verbs: *feet* is the plural of *foot*, but it is not obvious how to identify a plural morpheme in the word, analogous to the *-s* ending of *horses*. In the Turkish word *evinden* 'from his/her house', there is the opposite problem, as can be seen from the related forms:

ev	house
evi	his / her / its house
evden	from the house

It seems that the *-i* ending marks 'his / her / its', and the *-den* ending marks 'from' – in which case the combination of the two ought to produce *eviden*. But the form found in Turkish has an extra *n*, which does not seem to belong anywhere. Its use is automatic in this word (in much the same way as an extra *r* turns up in the plural of *child* in English – *child-r-en*). Effects of this kind complicate morphological analysis – and add to its fascination. Explanations can sometimes be found in other domains: it might be possible to explain the *n* in *evinden* on phonetic grounds (perhaps anticipating the following nasal sound), and the *r* in children is certainly a fossil of an older period of usage (Old English *childru*). To those with a linguistic bent, there is nothing more intriguing than the search for regularities in a mass of apparently irregular morphological data.

Another complication is that morphemes sometimes have several phonetic forms, depending on the context in which they occur. In English, for example, the past-tense morpheme (written as *-ed*), is pronounced in three different ways, depending on the nature of the sounds that precede it. If the preceding sound is /t/ or /d/, the ending is pronounced /id/, as in *spotted*; if the preceding sound is a voiceless consonant (p. 128), the ending is pronounced /t/, as in *walked*; and if the preceding sound is a voiced consonant or a vowel, the ending is pronounced /d/, as in *rolled*. Variant forms of a morpheme are known as *allomorphs*.

INFLECTIONAL AND DERIVATIONAL

Two main fields are traditionally recognized within morphology. *Inflectional morphology* studies the way in which words vary (or 'inflect') in order to express grammatical contrasts in sentences, such as singular/plural or past/present tense. In older grammar books, this branch of the subject was referred to as 'accidence'. *Boy* and *boys*, for example, are two forms of the 'same' word; the choice between them, singular vs plural, is a matter of grammar, and thus the business of inflectional morphology. *Derivational morphology*, however, studies the principles governing the construction of new words, without reference to the specific grammatical role a word might play in a sentence. In the formation of *drinkable* from *drink*, or *disinfect* from *infect*, for example, we see the formation of different words, with their own grammatical properties.

NEW WORDS OUT OF OLD

There are four normal processes of word formation in English:

• *prefixation* an affix is placed before the base of the word, e.g. *disobey*;
• *suffixation* an affix is placed after the base of the word, e.g. *kindness*;
• *conversion* a word changes its class without any change of form, e.g. *(the) carpet* (noun) becomes *(to) carpet* (verb);
• *compounding* two base forms are added together, e.g. *blackbird*.

There are also some less usual ways of making new words.

• *reduplication* a type of compound in which both elements are the same, or only slightly different, e.g. *goody-goody, wishy-washy, teeny-weeny*;
• *clippings* an informal shortening of a word, often to a single syllable, e.g. *ad, gents, flu, telly*;
• *acronyms* words formed from the initial letters of the words that make up a name, e.g. NATO, UNESCO, *radar* (= radio detection and ranging); a sub-type is an *alphabetism*, in which the different letters are pronounced, e.g. *VIP, DJ*;
• *blends* two words merge into each other, e.g. *brunch* (from 'breakfast' + 'lunch'), *telex* ('teleprinter' + 'exchange'.)

ABSO-BLOOMING-LUTELY

Morphemes can be classified into 'free' and 'bound' forms. Free morphemes can occur as separate words, e.g. *car, yes*. Bound morphemes cannot occur on their own, e.g. *anti-, -tion*. The main classes of bound morphemes are the prefixes and suffixes; but *infixes* are also possible – an affix which is inserted *within* a stem. The nearest we get to this in English is emphatic forms such as *abso-blooming-lutely awful*; but in many languages, infixation is a normal morphological process. In Tagalog, for example, the form /um/ 'one who does' is infixed within the form /piːlit/ 'effort' to produce /pumiːlit/, which means 'one who compelled'.

WORDS

Words sit uneasily at the boundary between morphology and syntax. In some languages – 'isolating' languages, such as Vietnamese (p. 295) – they are plainly low-level units, with little or no internal structure. In others – 'polysynthetic' languages, such as Eskimo – word-like units are highly complex forms, equivalent to whole sentences. The concept of 'word' thus ranges from such single sounds as English *a* to *palyamunurringkutjamunurtu* ('he/she definitely did not become bad') in the Western Desert language of Australia.

Words are usually the easiest units to identify, in the written language. In most writing systems, they are the entities that have spaces on either side. (A few systems use word dividers (e.g. Amharic), and some do not separate words at all (e.g. Sanskrit).) Because a literate society exposes its members to these units from early childhood, we all know where to put the spaces – apart from a small number of problems, mainly to do with hyphenation. Should we write *washing machine* or should it be *washing-machine? Well informed* or *well-informed? No one* or *no-one?*

It is more difficult to decide what words are in the stream of speech, especially in a language that has never been written down. But there are problems, even in languages like English or French. Certainly, it is possible to read a sentence aloud slowly, so that we can 'hear' the spaces between the words; but this is an artificial exercise. In natural speech, pauses do not occur between each word, as can be seen from any acoustic record of the way people talk. Even in very hesitant speech, pauses come at intervals – usually between major grammatical units, such as phrases or clauses (p. 95). So if there are no audible 'spaces', how do we know what the words are? Linguists have spent a great deal of time trying to devise satisfactory criteria – none of which is entirely successful.

There are no word spaces in the 4th century AD Greek *Codex Sinaiticus.* Word spaces were a creation of the Romans, and became widespread only in the Middle Ages.

KͤΤΙϹΕϹΤΙΝΟΠΛ
ΡΛΛΙΛΟΥϹϹΕΤΟΥϮ
ΟΥΝΙΛΩΝΟΠΙΕϮ
ΕΙΤΙΕΝΤΩΙϮΟΥϮ

FIVE TESTS OF WORD IDENTIFICATION

Potential pause
Say a sentence out loud, and ask someone to 'repeat it very slowly, with pauses'. The pause will tend to fall between words, and not within words. For example, *the / three / little / pigs / went / to / market.* But the criterion is not foolproof, for some people will break up words containing more than one syllable, e.g. *mar / ket.*

Indivisibility
Say a sentence out loud, and ask someone to 'add extra words' to it. The extra items will be added between the words and not within them. For example, *the pig went to market* might become *the big pig once went straight to the market,* but we would not have such forms as *pi-big-g* or *mar-the-ket.* However this criterion is not perfect either, in the light of such forms as *absobloominglutely.*

Minimal free forms
The American linguist Leonard Bloomfield (1887–1949) thought of words as 'minimal free forms' – that is, the smallest units of speech that can *meaningfully* stand on their own. This definition does handle the majority of words, but it cannot cope with several items which are treated as words in writing, but which never stand on their own in natural speech, such as English *the* and *of,* or French *je* ('I') and *de* ('of').

Phonetic boundaries
It is sometimes possible to tell from the sound of a word where it begins or ends. In Welsh, for example, long words generally have their stress on the penultimate syllable, e.g. (*cartref* 'home', *car'trefi* 'homes'. In Turkish, the vowels within a word harmonize in quality (p. 163), so that if there is a marked change in vowel quality in the stream of speech, a new word must have begun. But there are many exceptions to such rules.

Semantic units
In the sentence *Dog bites vicar,* there is plainly three units of meaning, and each unit corresponds to a word. But language is often not as neat as this. In *I switched on the light, the* has little clear 'meaning', and the single action of 'switching on' involves two words.

WORD CLASSES

Since the early days of grammatical study, words have been grouped into *word classes*, traditionally labelled the 'parts of speech'. In most grammars, eight such classes were recognized, illustrated here from English:

nouns	*boy, machine, beauty*
pronouns	*she, it, who*
adjectives	*happy, three, both*
verbs	*go, frighten, be*
prepositions	*in, under, with*
conjunctions	*and, because, if*
adverbs	*happily, soon, often*
interjections	*gosh, alas, coo*

In some classifications, participles (*looking, taken*) and articles (*a, the*) were separately listed.

Modern approaches classify words too, but the use of the label 'word class' rather than 'part of speech' represents a change in emphasis. Modern linguists are reluctant to use the notional definitions found in traditional grammar – such as a noun being the 'name of something'. The vagueness of these definitions has often been criticized: is *beauty* a 'thing'? is not the adjective *red* also a 'name' of a colour? In place of definitions based on meaning, there is now a focus on the structural features that signal the way in which groups of words behave in a language. In English, for example, the definite or indefinite article is one criterion that can be used to signal the presence of a following noun (*the car*); similarly, in Romanian, the article (*ul*) signals the presence of a preceding noun (*avionul* 'the plane').

Above all, the modern aim is to establish word classes that are coherent: all the words within a class should behave in the same way. For instance, *jump, walk,* and *cook* form a coherent class, because all the grammatical operations that apply to one of these words apply to the others also: they all take a third person singular form in the present tense (*he jumps/walks/cooks),* they all have a past tense ending in *-ed* (*jumped/walked/cooked*), and so on. Many other words display the same (or closely similar) behaviour, and this would lead us to establish the important class of 'verbs' in English. Similar reasoning would lead to an analogous class being set up in other languages, and ultimately to the hypothesis that this class is required for the analysis of all languages (as a 'substantive universal', §14).

CLASSIFYING NOUNS

Distinctions such as masculine / feminine and human / non-human are well known in setting up sub-classes of nouns, because of their widespread use in European languages. But many Indo-Pacific and African languages far exceed these in the number of noun classes they recognize. In Bantu languages, for example, we find such noun classes as human beings, growing things, body parts, liquids, inanimate objects, animals, abstract ideas, artefacts, and narrow objects.

However, these labels should be viewed with caution, as they are no more exact semantically than are the gender classes of European languages. In Swahili, for example, there are sub-classes for human beings and insect / animal names, but the generic words 'insect' and 'animal' in fact formally belong to the 'human' class!

Gradience

Word classes should be coherent. But if we do not want to set up hundreds of classes, we have to let some irregular forms into each one. For example, for many speakers *house* is the only English noun ending in /s/, where the /s/ becomes /z/ when the plural ending is added (*houses*). Although in theory it is 'in a class of its own', in practice it is grouped with other nouns, with which it has a great deal in common.

Because of the irregularities in a language, word classes are thus not as neatly homogeneous as the theory implies. Each class has a core of words that behave identically, from a grammatical point of view. But at the 'edges' of a class are the more irregular words, some of which may behave like words from other classes. Some adjectives have a function similar to nouns (e.g. *the rich*); some nouns behave similarly to adjectives (e.g. *railway* is used adjectivally before *station*).

The movement from a central core of stable grammatical behaviour to a more irregular periphery has been called *gradience*. Adjectives display this phenomenon very clearly. Five main criteria are usually used to identify the central class of English adjectives:

(A) they occur after forms of *to be*, e.g. *he's sad*;
(B) they occur after articles and before nouns, e.g. *the big car*;
(C) they occur after *very*, e.g. *very nice*;
(D) they occur in the comparative or superlative form e.g. *sadder / saddest, more / most impressive*; and
(E) they occur before *-ly* to form adverbs, e.g. *quickly*.

We can now use these criteria to test how much like an adjective a word is. In the matrix below, candidate words are listed on the left, and the five criteria are along the top. If a word meets a criterion, it is given a +; *sad*, for example, is clearly an adjective (*he's sad, the sad girl, very sad, sadder / saddest, sadly*). If a word fails the criterion, it is given a – (as in the case of *want*, which is nothing like an adjective: **he's want, *the want girl, *very want, *wanter / wantest, *wantly*).

	A	B	C	D	E
happy	+	+	+	+	+
old	+	+	+	+	–
top	+	+	+	–	–
two	+	+	–	–	–
asleep	+	–	–	–	–
want	–	–	–	–	–

The pattern in the diagram is of course wholly artificial because it depends on the way in which the criteria are placed in sequence; but it does help to show the gradual nature of the changes as one moves away from the central class, represented by *happy*. Some adjectives, it seems, are more adjective-like than others.

WHAT PART OF SPEECH IS *ROUND*?

You cannot tell what class a word belongs to simply by looking at it. Everything depends on how the word 'behaves' in a sentence. *Round* is a good illustration of this principle in action, for it can belong to any of five word classes, depending on the grammatical context.

Adjective
Mary bought a round table.

Preposition
The car went round the corner.

Verb
The yacht will round the buoy soon.

Adverb
We walked round to the shop

Noun
It's your round. I'll have a whiskey.

A DUSTBIN CLASS?

Several of the traditional parts of speech lacked the coherence required of a well-defined word class – notably, the adverb. Some have likened this class to a dustbin, into which grammarians would place any word whose grammatical status was unclear. Certainly, the following words have very little structurally in common, yet all have been labelled 'adverb' in traditional grammars:

tomorrow	very	no
however	quickly	when
not	just	the

The, an adverb? In such contexts as *The more the merrier.*

NOUN TENSES?

Some languages formally mark the expression of time relations on word classes other than the verb. In Japanese, adjectives can be marked in this way, e.g. *shiroi* 'white', *shirokatta* 'was white', *shirokute* 'being white', etc. In Potowatomi, the same ending that expresses past time on verbs can be used on nouns

/nkašatəs/	I am happy
/nkəšatsəpən/	I was once happy
/nos·/	my father
/nospˑən/	my dead father
/nčiman/	my canoe
/nčimanpən/	my former canoe (lost, stolen)

(After C. F. Hockett, 1958, p. 238.)

FIVE MOODS

A range of attitudes can be expressed by the mood system of the verb. In Fox, one mood expresses the meaning 'God forbid that this should happen!'; another, 'What if it did happen! What do I care!' In Menomini, there is a five-term mood system:

/piˑw/	he comes / is coming / came
/piˑwen/	he is said to be coming / it is said that he came
/piˑʔ/	is he coming / did he come?
/piasah/	so he *is* coming after all!
/piapah/	but he was going to come! (and now it turns out he is not)

(After C. F. Hockett, 1958, p. 237.)

DUAL AND TRIAL NUMBER

Four numbers are found in the language spoken on Aneityum Island (Melanesia): singular, dual, trial, plural. The forms are shown for 1st and 2nd person: /ñ/ is a palatal nasal; /j/ is a palatal affricate or stop; excl./incl. = exclusive/inclusive of speaker:

/añak/	I
/akaja/	we (incl.)
/ajama/	we (excl.)
/akajau/	we two (incl.)
/ajamrau/	we two (excl.)
/akataj/	we three (incl)
/ajamtaj/	we three (excl.)
/aek,aak/	you
/ajourau/	you two
/ajoutaj/	you three
/ajowa/	you (pl.)

A FOURTH PERSON

A fourth-person contrast is made in the Algonquian languages, referring to non-identical animate third persons in a particular context. In Cree, if we speak of a man, and then (secondarily) of another man, the forms are different: /ˈnaːpeˑw/ vs /ˈnaːpewa/. This fourth person form is usually referred to as the 'obviative'.
(After L. Bloomfield, 1933, p. 257.)

FIFTEEN CASES

Nominative (subject), *genitive* (of), *accusative* (object), *inessive* (in), *elative* (out of), *illative* (into), *adessive* (on), *ablative* (from), *allative* (to), *essive* (as), *partitive* (part of), *translative* (change to), *abessive* (without), *instructive* (by), and *comitative* (with).

The Finnish case system seems fearsome to those brought up on the six-term system of Latin. But the less familiar cases are really quite like prepositions – except that the forms are attached to the end of the noun as suffixes, instead of being separate words placed before, as in English.

GRAMMATICAL CATEGORIES

In many languages, the forms of a word vary, in order to express such contrasts as number, gender, and tense. These categories are among the most familiar of all grammatical concepts, but their analysis can lead to surprises. In particular, it emerges that there is no neat one-to-one correspondence between the grammatical alterations in a word's form and the meanings thereby conveyed. Plural nouns do not always refer to 'more than one'; a first-person pronoun does not always refer to the person who is talking; and masculine nouns are not always male.

Category	Typical formal contrasts	Typical meanings conveyed	Examples	But note...
aspect (verbs)	perfect(ive), imperfect(ive)	completeness, habituality, continuousness, duration, progressiveness	Russian *ya pročital* (pf.) vs *ya čital* (impf.), roughly 'I read' vs 'I used to read / was reading'; English *she sings* (as a job) vs *she's singing* (now).	Adverbs can change the meaning, as when *always* changes the 'in progress' meaning of *John is driving from London* to a habitual (and often irritated) meaning: *John's always driving from London.*
case (nouns, pronouns, adjectives)	nominative, vocative, accusative, genitive, partitive	actor, possession, naming, location, motion towards	English gen. *boy's, girls'*; Latin nom. *puella* 'girl', gen. *puellae* 'of the girl'; Serbo-Croat *grad* 'town', loc. *gradu* 'at a town'.	Cases may have several functions. The English genitive is sometimes called the 'possessive', but it can express other meanings than possession, e.g. *the man's release, a week's leave, a summer's day.*
gender (nouns, verbs, adjectives)	masculine, feminine, neuter, animate, inanimate	male, female, sexless, living	Spanish masc. *el muchacho* 'boy', fem. *la muchacha* 'girl'; German masc. *der Mann* 'the man', fem. *die Dame* 'the lady', neut. *das Ende* 'the end'; Russian past tense singular masc. *čital*, fem. *čitala*, neut. *čitalo* 'read'.	There is no necessary correlation between grammatical gender and sex. In German, 'spoon' is masculine (*der Löffel*); 'fork' is feminine (*die Gabel*); 'knife' is neuter (*das Messer*). French 'love' *amour* is masculine in the singular, but often feminine in the plural.
mood (verbs)	indicative, subjunctive, optative	factuality, possibility, uncertainty, likelihood	Latin *requiescit* 'he / she / it rests' vs *requiescat* 'may he / she rest'; English *God save the Queen, if I were you.*	Although a major section in traditional grammars, many European languages no longer make much use of the subjunctive. It is often restricted to formulaic phrases or very formal situations.
number (nouns, verbs, pronouns)	singular, dual, trial, plural	one, two, more than one, more than two, more than three	Swedish *bil* 'car', *bilar* 'cars'; Dutch *ik roep* 'I call', *wij roepen* 'we call'; Samoan *ʔoe* 'you' (sing.), *ʔoulua* 'you two', *ʔoutou* 'you' (pl.).	Nouns plural in form may refer to singular entities (e.g. *binoculars, pants*), and some nouns functioning as singulars refer to several events (e.g. *athletics, news*). The two crops known as *wheat* and *oats* look very similar; but in English one is singular and the other is plural.
person (pronouns, verbs)	first person, second person, third person, fourth person	speaker, addressee, third party, fourth party	Welsh *mi* 'I', *ni* 'we'; Menomini /nenah/ 'I' /kenah/ 'thou', /wenah/ 'he'; Latin *amo* 'I love', *amas* 'you love' (sing.), *amat* 'he / she / it loves'.	First person can refer to addressee (Doctor (to patient): *How are we today?*) or to a third party (Secretary – to friend, about the boss: *We're not in a good mood today*). Third person can refer to self (Wife: *How's my husband?* Husband: *He's hungry*).
tense (verbs)	present, past, future	present time, past time, future time	Italian *io parlo* 'I speak', *io ho parlato* 'I have spoken', *io parlavo* 'I was speaking'; Gaelic *chuala mi* 'I heard', *cluinneadh mi* 'I'll hear'.	Tense and time do not always correspond. Present tense–past time: *Minister dies* (headline). Present tense–future time: *I'm leaving tomorrow.*
voice (verbs)	active, passive middle, causative	who did action what was acted upon, what caused action	Classical Greek active *didàsko* 'I teach', middle *didàskomai* 'I get myself taught'; Portuguese active *cortou* 'cut', passive *foi cortada* 'was cut'; Tigrinya active *qätäle* 'he killed', causative *ʔaqtäle* 'he caused to kill'.	There are several active verbs in English which have no passive (e.g. *She has a car* will not transform into **A car is had by her*), and several passives which have no active (e.g. *He was said to be angry* will not transform into **Someone said him to be angry*).

SYNTAX

Syntax is the way in which words are arranged to show relationships of meaning within (and sometimes between) sentences. The term comes from *syntaxis,* the Greek word for 'arrangement'. Most syntactic studies have focused on sentence structure, for this is where the most important grammatical relationships are expressed.

THE SENTENCE

Traditionally, grammars define a sentence in such terms as 'the complete expression of a single thought'. Modern studies avoid this emphasis, because of the difficulties involved in saying what 'thoughts' are. *An egg* can express a thought, but it would not be considered a complete sentence. *I shut the door, as it was cold* is one sentence, but it could easily be analysed as two thoughts.

Some traditional grammars give a logical definition to the sentence. The most common approach proposes that a sentence has a 'subject' (= the topic) and a 'predicate' (= what is being said about the topic). This approach works quite well for some sentences, such as *The book is on the table,* where we can argue that *the book* is what the sentence is 'about'. But in many sentences it is not so easy to make this distinction. *It's raining* is a sentence, but what is the topic? And in *Michael asked Mary for a pen,* it is difficult to decide which of Michael, Mary, or the pen is the topic – or whether we have *three* topics! Also, some modern grammars treat subjects and topics in completely different ways.

In some written languages, it is possible to arrive at a working definition of 'sentence' by referring to the punctuation one is taught to use in school. Thus, an English sentence for many people 'begins with a capital letter and ends with a full stop' (or some other mark of 'final' punctuation). The problem is that many languages (e.g. in Asia) do not make use of such features; and even in those that do, punctuation is not always a clear guide. It may be omitted (in notices and legal documents, for example); and it proves difficult to prescribe rules governing its use other than 'good practice'. People therefore often disagree about the best way to punctuate a text. In some manuals of style, it is recommended that one should not end a sentence before a coordinating conjunction (*and, or, but*). But there are often cases where an author might feel it necessary – for reasons of emphasis, perhaps – to do the opposite.

It is even more difficult to identify sentences in speech, where the units of rhythm and intonation often do not coincide with the places where full stops would occur in writing. In informal speech, in particular, constructions can lack the careful organization we associate with the written language (p. 52). It is not that conversation lacks grammar: it is simply that the grammar is of a rather different kind, with sentences being particularly difficult to demarcate. In the following extract, it is not easy to decide whether a sentence ends at the points marked by pauses (–), or whether this is all one, loosely constructed sentence:

when they fed the pigs/ they all had to stand well back/ – and they were allowed to take the buckets/ – but they weren't allowed to get near the pigs/ you see/ – so they weren't happy ...

Linguistic approaches

Despite all the difficulties, we continue to employ the notion of 'sentence', and modern syntacticians try to make sense of it. But they do not search for a satisfactory definition of 'sentence' at the outset – an enterprise that is unlikely to succeed, with over 200 such definitions on record to date. Rather, they aim to analyse the linguistic constructions that occur, recognizing the most independent of them as sentences. Thus, because the following constructions can stand on their own as utterances, and be assigned a syntactic structure, they would be recognized as sentences:

she asked for a book/
come in/
the horse ran away because the train was noisy/

The following combination of units, however, could not be called a sentence:

will the car be here at 3 o'clock/ it's raining/.

The syntax of the first unit and that of the second do not combine to produce a regular pattern. It would be just as possible to have:

it's raining / will the car be here at 3 o'clock /

or either unit without the other. Within each unit, however, several kinds of rules of syntactic order and selection are apparent. We may not say:

*will be here at 3 o'clock the car/
*will be here the car/
*car at 3 o'clock/.

Each unit in the sequence, then, is a sentence; but the combination does not produce a 'larger' syntactic unit.

A sentence is thus the largest unit to which syntactic rules apply – 'an independent linguistic form, not included by virtue of any grammatical construction in any larger linguistic form' (L. Bloomfield, 1933, p. 170). But this approach has its exceptions, too. In particular, we have to allow for cases where sentences are permitted to omit part of their structure and thus be dependent on a previous sentence (*elliptical* sentences), as in:

A: Where are you going?
B: To town.

Several other types of exception would be recognized in a complete grammatical description.

MINOR SENTENCE TYPES

A language contains many sentence-like units which do not conform to the regular patters of formation. Here is a selection from English:

Yes
Gosh!
Least said, soonest mended.
How come you're early?
Oh to be free!
All aboard!
Down with racism!
No entry.
Taxi!
Good evening.
Happy birthday!
Checkmate.

A sign like this has a regular syntactic structure, but it does not use normal sentence punctuation.

ASPECTS OF SENTENCE SYNTAX

Hierarchy

Hilary couldn't open the windows.

One of the first things to do in analysing a sentence is to look for groupings within it – sets of words (or morphemes, p. 90) that hang together. In this example, we might make an initial division as follows:

Hilary / couldn't open / the windows.

Units such as *couldn't open* and *the windows* are called *phrases*. The first of these would be called a *verb phrase*, because its central word (or 'head') is a verb, *open*; the second would be called a *noun phrase*, because its head is a noun, *windows*. Other types of phrase also exist – adjective phrases, for example, such as *very nice*.

Phrases may in turn be divided into their constituent *words* (p. 91):

couldn't + open   the + windows

And words may be divided into their constituent *morphemes*, if there are any:

could + n't   window + s

This conception of sentence structure as a hierarchy of levels, or ranks, may be extended 'upwards'. The sentence can be made larger by linking several units of the same type:

Hilary opened the windows, but David couldn't open the doors.

Here, too, we have a sentence, but now we have to recognize two major units within it – each of which has a structure closely resembling that of an independent sentence. These units are traditionally referred to as *clauses*. In the above example, the clauses have been 'coordinated' through the use of the conjunction *but*. An indefinite number of clauses can be linked within the same sentence.

A five-rank hierarchy is a widely used model of syntactic investigation:

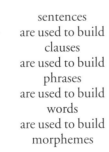

sentences	sentences
are analysed into	are used to build
clauses	clauses
are analysed into	are used to build
phrases	phrases
are analysed into	are used to build
words	words
are analysed into	are used to build
morphemes	morphemes

Morphemes are the 'lower' limit of grammatical enquiry, for they have no grammatical structure. Similarly, sentences form the 'upper' limit of grammatical study, because they do not usually form a part of any larger grammatical unit.

CLAUSES

The various units that make up the structure of a clause are usually given functional labels, such as *Subject* (S), *Verb* (V), *Complement* (C), *Object* (O), and *Adverbial* (A). A number of clause types can be identified in this way, such as:

S + V	The dog + is running.
S + V + O	The man + saw + a cow.
S + V + C	The car + is + ready.
S + V + A	A picture + lay + on the ground.
S + V + O + O	I + gave + John + a book.
S + V + O + C	He + called + John + a fool.
S + V + O + A	Mary + saw + John + yesterday.

Several approaches to grammatical analysis make use of elements of this kind, though there is considerable variation in definition and terminology. Languages also vary greatly in the way in which these elements are identified. In English, for example, word order is the main factor, with only occasional use being made of morphology (e.g. *he* (subject) *saw* (verb) *him* (object)). In Latin, word-endings provide the main clues to element function, word order being irrelevant (e.g. *puer puellam vidit* 'the boy saw the girl'). In Japanese, basic grammatical relations are marked by special particles: *ga* (subject), *o* (direct object), *ni* (indirect object), and *no* (genitive). For example,

kodomo ga	*tomodachi no*	*inu ni*	*mizu o*	*yaru*
the child	friend's	to dog	water	gives

'The child gives water to his / her friend's dog.'

PHRASES

Most phrases can be seen as expansions of a central element (the *head*), and these are often referred to as 'endocentric' phrases:

```
            cars
        the cars
      the big cars
   all the big cars
all the big cars in the garage
```

Phrases which cannot be analysed in this way are then called 'exocentric': *inside / the cars*.

The internal structure of an endocentric phrase is commonly described in a three-part manner:

all the big	*cars*	*in the garage*
PREMODIFICATION	HEAD	POSTMODIFICATION

COORDINATION VS SUBORDINATION

Coordination is one of two main ways of making sentences more complex; the other is known as *subordination,* or 'embedding'. The essential difference is that in the former the clauses that are linked are of equal grammatical status, whereas in the latter, one clause functions as part of another (the 'main' clause). Compare:

Coordinate clause:
The boy left on Monday   and the girl left on Tuesday.

Subordinate clause:
The boy left on Monday   when John rang.

The phrase *on Monday* is part of the clause, giving the time when the action took place. Similarly, the unit *when John rang* is also part of the clause, for the same reason. But *when John rang* is additionally a clause in its own right.

CONCORD

Grammatical links between words are often signalled by concord or 'agreement'. A form of one word requires a corresponding form of another, as when in English a singular noun 'agrees with' a singular verb in the present tense: *the man walks* vs *the men walk*.

The purpose of concord varies greatly between languages. In Latin, it is an essential means of signalling which words go together. In the absence of fixed word-order patterns, sentences would otherwise be uninterpretable. For example, in *parvum puerum magna puella vidit* 'the tall girl saw the small boy', we know that the boy is small and the girl is tall only through the agreement of the endings, *-um* vs *-a.*

On the other hand, concord plays much less of a role in modern French, in cases such as *le petit garçon et la grande fille* 'the little boy and the big girl'. Because the position of adjectives is fixed (before the noun, in these cases), it would not pose any problems of intelligibility if there were no difference between the masculine and feminine forms:

le petit garçon
*la petit fille
*le petite garçon
la petite fille

If French allowed free word order, as in Latin, so that one could say **le garçon et la fille petit grande,* then concord would be needed to show which adjective should go with which noun – but this does not happen. The gender system is thus of limited usefulness, though it still has a role to play in certain syntactic contexts, such as cross-reference (*J'ai vu **un** livre et une plume. **Il** était **nouveau**.* 'I saw a book and a pen. It [i.e. the book] was new.').

IMMEDIATE CONSTITUENT DIAGRAMS

One of the most widely used techniques for displaying sentence structure is the use of *immediate constituent* (IC) analysis. This approach works through the different levels of structure within a sentence in a series of steps. At each level, a construction is divided into its major constituents, and the process continues until no further divisions can be made. For example, to make an IC analysis of the sentence *The girl chased the dog,* we carry out the following steps:

1. Identify the two major constituents, *the girl* and *chased the dog.*
2. Divide the next-biggest constituent into two, *viz. chased the dog* into *chased* and *the dog.*
3. Continue dividing constituents into two until we can go no further, *viz. the girl* and *the dog* into *the + girl, the + dog,* and *chased* into *chase + the -ed* ending.

The order of segmentation can be summarized using lines or brackets. If the first cut is symbolized by a single vertical line, the second cut by two lines, and so on, the sentence would look like this:

the /// girl / chase /// -ed // the /// dog

However, a much clearer way of representing constituent structure is through the use of 'tree diagrams':

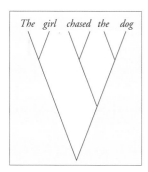 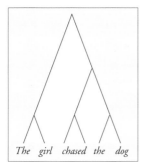

The second kind of tree diagram is in fact the normal convention in modern linguistics.

Such representations of structure are very helpful, as far as they go. But not all sentences are as easy to analyse in IC terms as this one. It is sometimes not clear where the cuts should be made (e.g. whether to divide *the three old men* into *the + three old men* or *the three old + men,* or *the three + old men*). More important, the process of segmenting individual sentences does not take us very far in understanding the grammar of a language. IC analyses do not inform us about the identity of the sentence elements they disclose, nor do they provide a means of showing how sentences relate to each other grammatically (as with statements and questions, actives and passives). To develop a deeper understanding of grammatical structure, alternative approaches must be used.

PHRASE STRUCTURE

A good way of putting more information into an analysis would be to name, or *label,* the elements that emerge each time a sentence is segmented. It would be possible to use functional labels such as 'subject' and 'predicate', but the approach that is most widely practised has developed its own terminology and abbreviations, so these will be used here. Taking the above sentence (S), the first division produces a 'noun phrase' (NP) *the girl* and a 'verb phrase' (VP) *chased the dog.* (This is a broader sense of 'verb phrase' than that used on p. 95, as it includes both the verb and the noun phrase that follows.) The second division recognizes a 'verb' (V) *chased* and another noun phrase *the dog.* The next divisions would produce combinations of 'determiner' (DET) and 'noun' (N) *the + girl, the + dog.* This is the 'phrase structure' of the sentence, and it can be displayed as a tree diagram:

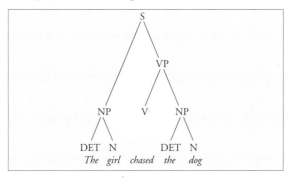

This kind of representation of the phrase structure of a sentence is known as a 'phrase marker' (or 'P-marker'). Phrase structures are also sometimes represented as labelled sets of brackets, but these are more difficult to read:

$[_S[_{NP}[_{DET}the][_Ngirl]][_{VP}[_Vchased][_{NP}[_{DET}the][_Ndog]]]]$

DIAGRAMMING

A frequent practice in American schools is the use of a system of vertical and slanting lines to represent the various relationships in a sentence. The representations are often called 'Reed & Kellogg' diagrams, after the authors of a 19th-century English textbook. A long vertical line marks the boundary between subject and predicate; a short vertical line divides verb and direct object; and a short slanting line marks off a complement. Other items are drawn in beneath the main parts of the sentence.

The old man called me a crazy inventor.

The approach shows the relationships between words clearly, but it cannot handle variations in word order: both *I turned off the light* and *I turned the light off* would be diagrammed in the same way.

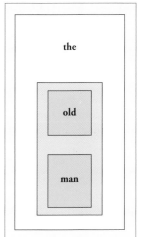

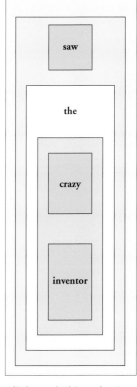

A little-used 'Chinese box' representation of sentence structure

RULES

Analyses of single sentences are illuminating, as far as they go, but grammarians are concerned to move beyond this point, to see whether their analyses work for other sentences in the language. To what other sentences might the above sequence of steps, and the resulting P-marker, also apply? In Noam Chomsky's approach, first outlined in *Syntactic Structures* (1957), the jump from single-sentence analysis is made by devising a set of rules that would 'generate' tree structures such as the above. The procedure can be illustrated using the following rules (but several details from the original approach are omitted for clarity):

$$S \rightarrow NP + VP$$
$$VP \rightarrow V + NP$$
$$NP \rightarrow DET + N$$
$$V \rightarrow chased$$
$$DET \rightarrow the$$
$$N \rightarrow girl, dog$$

The first rule states that a sentence can consist of a noun phrase and a following verb phrase; the second, that a verb phrase can consist of a verb plus a following noun phrase; the third, that a noun phrase can consist of a determiner plus a noun. Each abstract category is then related to the appropriate words, thus enabling the sentence to be generated. Grammars that generate phrase structures in this way have come to be called 'phrase structure grammars' (PSGs).

If we follow these rules through, it can be seen that there is already a significant increase in the 'power' of this grammar over the single-sentence analysis used previously. If we choose *the girl* for the first NP, and *the dog* for the second, we generate *the girl chased the dog*; but if the choices are made the other way round, we generate the sentence *the dog chased the girl*. By the simple device of adding a few more words to the rules, suddenly a vast number of sentences can be generated:

$$V \rightarrow chased, saw, liked \dots$$
$$DET \rightarrow the, a$$
$$N \rightarrow girl, man, horse \dots$$

the girl chased the horse
the man saw the girl
the horse saw the man etc.

However, if *went* were introduced into the rules, as a possible V, ungrammatical sentences would come to be generated, such as **the girl went the man*. In working out a generative grammar, therefore, a means has to be found to block the generation of this type of sentence, at the same time permitting such sentences as *the man went* to be generated. The history of generative syntax since 1957 is the study of the most efficient ways of writing rules, so as to ensure that a grammar will generate all the grammatical sentences of a language and none of the ungrammatical ones.

Transformations

This tiny fragment of a generative grammar from the 1950s suffices only to illustrate the general conception underlying the approach. 'Real' grammars of this kind contain many rules of considerable complexity and of different types. One special type of rule that was proposed in the first formulations became known as a *transformational* rule. These rules enabled the grammar to show the relationship between sentences that had the same meaning but were of different grammatical form. The link between active and passive sentences, for example, could be shown – such as *the horse chased the man* (active) and *the man was chased by the horse* (passive). The kind of formulation needed to show this is:

$$NP_1 + V + NP_2 \rightarrow NP_2 + Aux + Ven + by + NP_1$$

which is an economical way of summarizing all the changes you would have to introduce, in order to turn the first sentence into the second. If this formula were to be translated into English, four separate operations would be recognized:

(i) The first noun phrase in the active sentence (NP_1) is placed at the end of the passive sentence.
(ii) The second noun phrase in the active sentence (NP_2) is placed at the beginning of the passive sentence.
(iii) The verb (V) is changed from past tense to past participle (V*en*), and an auxiliary verb (Aux) is inserted before it.
(iv) A particle *by* is inserted between the verb and the final noun phrase.

This rule will generate all regular active-passive sentences.

In subsequent development of generative grammar, many kinds of transformational rules came to be used, and the status of such rules in a grammar has proved to be controversial (§65). Recent generative grammars look very different from the model proposed in *Syntactic Structures*. But the fundamental conception of sentence organization as a single process of syntactic derivation remains influential, and it distinguishes this approach from those accounts of syntax that represent grammatical relations using a hierarchy of separate ranks (p. 95).

RULES AND 'RULES'

The 'rules' of a generative grammar are not to be identified with the prescriptive 'rules' that formed part of traditional grammar (p. 3). A prescriptive grammatical rule is a statement – such as 'You should never end a sentence with a preposition' – that tells us whether we are right or wrong to use a particular construction. Generative rules have no such implication of social correctness. They are objective descriptions of the grammatical patterns that occur.

GENERATIVE NOTATION

A major feature of generative grammar is the way special notations have been devised to enable rules to be expressed in an economical way. In particular, different types of brackets, such as ( ), [ ], and { } are given different meanings. Round brackets, for example, enclose a grammatical element that is *optional* in a sentence; that is, the sentence would be grammatical even if the element were left out. The rule

$$NP \rightarrow DET (ADJ) N$$

means that a noun phrase can consist of *either* a determiner, adjective, and noun *or* simply a determiner and noun (*the old man* or *the man*). A grammar could, of course, list the two possibilities separately, as

$$NP \rightarrow DET + N$$

$$NP \rightarrow DET + ADJ + N$$

but collapsing them into a single rule, through the use of the ( ) convention, saves a great deal of space, and represents something we all 'know' about the structure of the noun phrase.

PRINCIPLES AND PARAMETERS

Government and binding theory is an approach to generative grammar which developed in the 1980s. It takes its name from the way it focuses on the conditions which formally relate (or 'bind') certain elements of a sentence, and on the structural contexts within which these binding relationships apply ('govern').

The approach holds that the same *principles* of syntax operate in all languages, though they can differ slightly (along certain *parameters*) between languages (§14). For example it is a syntactic principle that in a noun phrase there is a chief element (the *head*), which will be the noun (*the new President*), and that other nouns may accompany it (*the President of America*). But whether the accompanying nouns occur before or after the head varies between languages: they occur after it in English, but before it in Japanese (*Amerika no Daitoryo*).

WORD ORDER

The term 'word order' is somewhat ambiguous, for it can refer both to the order of words in a phrase, and to the order of multi-word units within a sentence. Given the sentence

The cat sat on the mat

both the following involve word-order problems – but they are of very different kinds:

*cat the	sat	mat the on
*sat	the cat	on the mat

In linguistic description, word-order studies usually refer to the second type of problem – that is, the sequence in which grammatical elements such as Subject, Verb, and Object occur in sentences. A great deal of attention has been paid to the way in which languages vary the order of these elements, as part of typological studies (§14). Word order, it is hoped, will be a more satisfactory way of classifying languages than the older morphological method (which recognized such types as isolating and inflecting, p. 295), into which many languages do not fit neatly.

In comparing word orders across languages, it is important to appreciate that what is being compared is the 'basic' or 'favourite' pattern found in each language. For example, in English, we will encounter such sequences as:

SVO   *the boy saw the man*
OVS   *Jones I invited – not Smith*
VSO   *govern thou my song* (Milton)
OSV   *strange fits of passion have I known*
          (Wordsworth)
SOV   *pensive poets painful vigils keep* (Pope)

However, only the first of these is the natural, usual, 'unmarked' order in English; the others all convey special effects of an emphatic or poetic kind. The same principle must apply in studying word order in all languages, but it is often not so easy to establish which is the normal word-order pattern and which is the pattern that conveys the special effect. The mere fact of talking to a foreigner, for instance, might motivate a native speaker to change from one order to another, and it often requires great ingenuity on the part of the linguist to determine whether such stylistic changes are taking place.

Typology

Apart from cases of free word order (e.g. Latin, Quechua, Navajo, Fore), there are six logical possibilities: SVO, SOV, VSO, VOS, OSV, OVS. Of these, over 75% of the world's languages use SVO (as in English, French, Hausa, Vietnamese) or SOV (as in Japanese, Amharic, Tibetan, Korean). A further 10–15% use VSO (e.g. Welsh, Tongan, Squamish). Examples of VOS are Malagasy, Tzotzil, and Houailou.

Until recently, Object-initial languages were conspicuous by their absence, and it was thought that perhaps these did not exist. But a group of OVS languages have now been found, all in the Amazon basin, mainly belonging to the Carib family, e.g. Hixkaryana, Apalai, Bacairi, Makusi. A few other languages (e.g. Jamamadi, Apurina) seem to be OSV. But there is some variability in the data that have been collected so far, with both OVS and OSV being used by some languages.

Word-order generalizations often need careful qualification. Latin, for example, is said to have a free word order, but in fact SOV is a very common pattern in that language. Modern Hebrew is SVO, but Classical Hebrew seemed to favour VSO. German prefers SVO in main clauses, but SOV in subordinate clauses. In Tagalog, the V usually comes first, but there is great variation in what follows, with both OS and SO being widely used. In Japanese, SOV is favoured, but OSV is also very common.

LISU

This Lolo-Burmese language seems to have free word order, yet it has no morphological cases to mark Subject and Object. A sentence Noun–Verb–Noun might therefore mean either 'N1 did V to N2' or 'N2 did V to N1'. In theory, such a language ought to be unintelligible! But in fact the speakers survive, by relying on context, the use of alternative grammatical constructions, and a modicum of common sense.

OSV IN SPACE

Sick have I become.
Strong am I with the Force.
Your father he is.
When nine hundred years
   old you reach, look as
   good you will not.

The rarity of OSV constructions and languages perhaps explains the impact of this strange speech style, used by the Jedi Master, Yoda, in the film *The Empire Strikes Back* (1983).

DEEP AND SURFACE STRUCTURE

In the standard approach to generative grammar, sentences are analysed in terms of two levels of organization, known as *deep structure* and *surface structure*. At the 'deep' (or 'underlying') level, a sentence structure is represented in an abstract way, displaying all the factors that govern how it should be interpreted. At the 'surface' level, there is a more concrete representation, giving the string of morphemes that closely corresponds to what we would hear if the sentence were spoken.

This distinction was used to explain sentence ambiguities, by arguing that in such cases a single surface structure correlates with more than one deep structure. An early Chomskyan example was *Flying planes can be dangerous*, which can be related to two underlying sentences: *Planes which fly can be dangerous* and *To fly planes can be dangerous*.

The distinction was also used to relate sentences that have different surface forms but the same underlying structure, as in the case of active and passive sentences. *Cats chase mice* and *Mice are chased by cats* were said to have different surface structures, but the same deep structure.

The interpretation and status of the two notions has altered greatly in generative theory over the years (§65), but the basic insight is one that has achieved widespread recognition in linguistics.

Honorific grammar

Several languages make use of a special set of grammatical contrasts, in which different levels of politeness or respect are expressed, according to the mutual status of the participants (§10). An 'honorific' system, as it is often called, is well developed in several oriental languages, such as Korean, Javanese, Tibetan, and Japanese; and although its use is changing, especially among younger generations of speakers, it still plays an important role in the marking of social relationships.

Japanese honorific expression shares with many other languages certain characteristics of formal speech. Local dialect forms are avoided; loan words are often used (Chinese loans, in the case of Japanese); sentences are longer and involve more circumlocution and negative expression (cf. English 'I wonder whether you mightn't …'). What differentiates Japanese from European languages is the way in which pronouns, verbs, adjectives, and many types of grammatical construction change their form depending on their honorific status. A large number of special forms are permitted, which are classified into 'respect words' (*sonkeigo*), 'condescending words' (*kenzjo-go*), and 'polite words' (*teinei-go*).

Honorific markers in the morphological system include: (a) a specific honorific prefix, *o-* or *go-*; (b) the complete replacement of a word, e.g. *iu* 'say' becomes *ossharu*; and (c) a complex system of titular forms (where English would say 'Mr, Mrs, Miss'), all suffixes attached to the name:

-sama	very polite
-san	neutral
-chan	diminutive
-kun	for men only
sensei	traditionally used to a person who was 'born earlier', but now used to someone whose capabilities are respected, especially a teacher or politician

A wide range of pronoun forms is used. Among the first-person forms, we find:

watakushi	very formal male; less formal female
watashi	formal male; neutral female
atakushi	rare male; snobbish female
atashi	chiefly female, colloquial
washi	dialectal, chiefly male, older generation
boku	exclusively male, proscribed in talking to superiors (but cf. p. 21)
ore	colloquial male

Among the second-person forms, we find:

anata	standard, polite, not used to superiors
anta	informal
sochira	polite, very formal
kimi	chiefly men to men of equal or lower status
omae	informal, colloquial, somewhat pejorative
kisama and *temē*	derogatory, very impolite

(After S. I. Harada, 1976.)

"I miss the good old days when all we had to worry about was nouns and verbs."

Semantics is the study of meaning in language. The term did not come to be widely used until the 20th century, but the subject it represents is very old, reaching back to the writings of Plato and Aristotle, and attracting the special interest of philosophers, logicians, and (these days) linguists (§65). The linguistic approach aims to study the properties of meaning in a systematic and objective way, with reference to as wide a range of utterances and languages as possible. It is thus broader than the approach taken by many logicians and philosophers, who have tended to concentrate on a restricted range of sentences (typically, statements, or 'propositions') within a single language. But logical analysis nonetheless exercises a major influence on contemporary linguistic semantics (p. 107).

Any scientific approach to semantics has to be clearly distinguished from a pejorative sense of the term that has developed in popular use, when people talk about the way language can be manipulated in order to mislead the public. A newspaper headline might read 'Unemployment reduced to semantics' – referring to a new way of counting the unemployed which makes it appear that there are fewer of them. Or someone might say in an argument, 'That's just semantics', implying that the point is purely a verbal quibble, bearing no relationship to anything in the real world. This kind of nuance is absent when we talk about semantics from the objective viewpoint of linguistic research.

THE MEANINGS OF MEANING

In an important early book on the subject, C. K. Ogden & I. A. Richards's *The Meaning of Meaning* (1923), 16 different meanings of the words 'mean / meaning' were distinguished. Here are some of them:

John means to write. 'intends'
A green light means go. 'indicates'
Health means everything. 'has importance'
His look was full of meaning. 'special import'
What is the meaning of life? 'point, purpose'
What does 'capitalist' mean to you? 'convey'
What does 'cornea' mean? 'refer to in the world'

It is the last kind of use that comes closest to the focus of linguistic semantics; but even this is a special kind of enquiry. The question asks for a definition, which is a somewhat unusual form of reply, found more in dictionaries than in everyday speech, that involves the 'translation' of the difficult word into 'easier' words. The study of the properties of definitions is an important part of semantics, but it is only a part. Of greater importance is the study of the way in which words and sentences convey meaning in everyday situations of speech and writing.

THREE CONCEPTIONS OF MEANING

Words → things

A popular view is that words 'name' or 'refer to' things – a view that can be found in the pages of Plato's *Cratylus*. Proper names like *London, Bill Brown,* and *Daddy* illustrate this conception, as do several other words and phrases – the labels attached to objects for sale in a shop, or those found on a paint colour chart. But there are large numbers of words where it is not possible to

SEMANTICS AND ALICE

One of the favourite quotations of semanticists is from Lewis Carroll's *Through the Looking Glass* (1872, Chapter 6), in which Humpty Dumpty turns our conventional understanding of meaning on its head, and thus makes us see more clearly what it has to be about. If everyone were to use words in an idiosyncratic way, as Humpty suggests, the result would be communication anarchy. Only in certain fields – such as literature (§12) – do we tolerate personal deviations from the semantic norms of the language.

'There's glory for you!'
'I don't know what you mean by "glory,"' Alice said.

Humpty Dumpty smiled contemptuously. 'Of course you don't – till I tell you. I meant "there's a nice knock-down argument for you!"'

'But "glory" doesn't mean "a nice knock-down argument,"' Alice objected.

'When *I* use a word,' Humpty Dumpty said, in rather a scornful tone, 'it means just what I choose it to mean – neither more nor less.'

'The question is,' said Alice, 'whether you *can* make a word mean so many different things.'

'The question is,' said Humpty Dumpty, 'which is to be master – that's all.'

Alice was too much puzzled to say anything: so after a minute Humpty Dumpty began again. 'They've a temper, some of them – particularly verbs, they're the proudest – adjectives you can do anything with, but not verbs – however, *I* can manage the whole lot of them! Impenetrability! That's what *I* say!'

'Would you tell me, please,' said Alice, 'what that means?'

'Now you talk like a reasonable child,' said Humpty Dumpty, looking very much pleased. 'I meant by "impenetrability" that we've had enough of that subject, and it would be just as well if you'd mention what you mean to do next, as I suppose you don't mean to stop here all the rest of your life.'

'That's a great deal to make one word mean,' Alice said in a thoughtful tone.

'When I make a word do a lot of work like that,' said Humpty Dumpty, 'I always pay it extra.'

'Oh!' said Alice. She was too much puzzled to make any other remark.

'Ah, you should see 'em come round me of a Saturday night,' Humpty Dumpty went on, wagging his head gravely from side to side, 'for to get their wages, you know.'

see what 'thing' the word refers to: verbs such as *ask* or *find*; adjectives such as *difficult* or *popular*; nouns such as *consistency* or *tradition*. In fact, the majority of words seem unable to be related to things, in any clear way.

Words → concepts → things

This view denies a direct link between words and things, arguing that the relationship can be made only through the use of our minds. For every word, there is an associated concept. One of the best-known formulations of this position is the 'semiotic triangle' of Ogden and Richards (1923, p. 99):

The main criticism of this approach is the insuperable difficulty of identifying 'concepts'. The 'concept' underlying a word such as *tradition* is no easier to define than the 'thing' referred to by *tradition*. Some words do have meanings that are relatively easy to conceptualize, but we certainly do not have neat visual images corresponding to every word we say. Nor is there any guarantee that a concept which might come to mind when I use the word *table* is going to be the same as the one you, the reader, might bring to mind.

Stimuli → words → responses

Leonard Bloomfield (1887–1949) expounded a behaviourist view of meaning in his book *Language* (1933): meaning is something that can be deduced solely from a study of the situation in which speech is used – the stimulus (S) that led someone to speak (r), and the response (R) that resulted from this speech (s). He draws this as follows:

In Bloomfield's example, Jill is hungry, sees an apple (S), and asks Jack to get it for her (r); this linguistic stimulus (s) leads to Jack getting the apple (R). Bloomfield argues that you can tell what the meaning of r ... s must be just be observing the events that accompanied it. However, in very many situations it is difficult to demonstrate what the relevant features of the stimulus / response are – a real problem when events are not clearly visible in physical terms (as in the expression of feelings). And it proves even more difficult to handle cases where people do not act in the 'predicted' way (if Jack did not fetch the apple, perhaps because of a quarrel with Jill at Monte Carlo two years before).

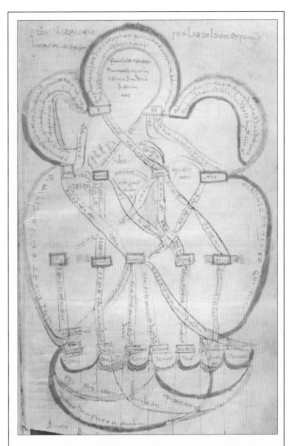

A design by Isidore of Seville (c. AD 555–636) The design attempts to show a link between a word's shape and its meaning. Isidore believed that the basic meaning of a word could be found if it could be traced back to its primitive shape. The discussion is found in the ninth book of his *Originum sive etymologiarum libri XX*, which is largely about questions of semantic history and the origins of language.

NATURAL OR CONVENTIONAL?

The Greek philosophers were the first to debate the nature of meaning, from which two main views emerged. The *naturalist* view, deriving largely from Plato (427–347 BC), maintained that there was an intrinsic connection between sound and sense. The *conventionalist* view, largely Aristotelian, held that this connection was purely arbitrary (§65).

In their extreme forms, both views are untenable. If the naturalist view were valid, we would be able to tell the meaning of words just by hearing them. Only onomatopoeic words (§30), such as *bow wow* and *splash*, come close to this,

and even they change greatly from language to language. But naturalistic thinking is still widely encountered, especially in the concern many people have over the use of certain words (to do with death or sex, for example, p. 61), or in the readiness with which they make judgments about the appropriateness of words. 'Look at them, sir,' says Aldous Huxley's character Old Rowley, pointing to swine wallowing in the mud, 'Rightly is they called "pigs".' (*Crome Yellow*, 1921).

The conventionalist position is nearer the truth, as it emphasizes the arbitrary relationship between words

and things – a principle accepted by modern semanticists. There is nothing in the form of the word *pig* that bears any direct relationship to the 'thing'. But it is equally untenable to think of language, as the conventionalists did, solely as the result of an *agreement* between people to use a word in a certain way. Such a procedure would presuppose the prior existence of language, to formulate the agreement in the first place. Diodorus of Megara (4th century BC) nonetheless supported the conventionalist position to the extent of calling his slaves by the names of Greek particles!

MODERN SEMANTICS

In the past, semantic debate has been largely concerned with discovering what 'meaning' is, as a concept in its own right. The enquiries have undoubtedly increased our understanding of the nature of the problem, but an accepted definition of 'meaning' is as far away today as it was in Plato's time. Why should this be so?

It is now widely held that 'meaning' is not some kind of 'entity' separate from language – any more than measures such as 'height' or 'length' have some kind of independent existence. To say that objects 'have height' means only that they are so many units high; it does not mean that there is an abstract property of 'height' that exists independently of objects. In the same way, it is argued, to say that words 'have meaning' means only that they are used in a certain way in a sentence. We can examine the meaning of individual words and sentences – but there is no 'meaning' beyond that.

In modern linguistics, then, meaning is studied by making detailed analyses of the way words and sentences are used in specific contexts. It is an approach shared by several philosophers and psychologists (p. 418). Ludwig Wittgenstein (1889–1951), in particular, stressed its importance in his dictum: 'the meaning of a word is its use in the language'.

SENSE vs REFERENCE

Semantics is not directly concerned with the study of the external world, or its conceptualization. The world of non-linguistic experience is the province of physicists, geographers, psychologists, and others. Nor, as we have seen (p. 101), is semantics easily able to cope with the study of how language *refers* to this external world – the notion of 'reference'. Rather, the primary focus of the modern subject is on the way people relate words to each other within the framework of their language – on their 'sense', rather than their reference.

The distinction between sense and reference is a critical one, because it allows us to study the many cases where we happily use words, even though they do not naturally correspond to the way things are in the world. This may be difficult to see if we restrict our study to a single language, but when we look at how different languages 'parcel out' the world, the distinction is forced upon us. For example, in the 'real' world, mothers and fathers have brothers and sisters. In English, there are no single words expressing the notions 'mother's brother', 'father's brother', 'mother's sister', or 'father's sister', and we have to use a circumlocution to make the distinction. In the Australian language Pitjanjatjara, however, we have a different situation: *ngunytju* = 'mother's sister', *kamuru* = 'mother's brother', *kurntili* = 'father's sister', and *mama* = 'father's brother'. There is also a complication (to English ways of thinking): *mama* also means 'father', and *ngunytju*

also means 'mother'. What is plain, though, is that the same biological relationships are given quite different linguistic treatment between the two languages. Family photographs would look the same, but the words would have different senses (see below).

But even within a single language, we need to distinguish sense from reference, to explain the way language makes divisions where there are none in reality. The neat scientific classifications of fauna and flora, where each name has its place in a system of terms, are not typical of language. In everyday life, we use such words as *hill* and *mountain, cup* and *glass,* or *stream* and *river,* where the real-world notions are quite indeterminate. When does a stream become a river, or a hill a mountain? And would all agree about which of the pictures (right) count as a *chair*?

There is also the problem of how we explain what a word's meaning is. Let us imagine someone who had encountered the word *chair* and did not know what it meant. One procedure would be to explain its reference: we could take the person to a chair and point to it. But this would be of limited help, for how would the person know from that experience which *other* objects in the world should also be called chairs? The wrong deduction might also be made, that what we were pointing at was the quality 'wooden', or the concept of 'furniture' – the kind of error children make when they learn vocabulary (§42). A better procedure would be to explain the sense of the word, using a rough definition such as a 'seat with four legs and a back'. Such a definition would enable the person to look out for other objects with similar properties, and thus use the word appropriately. The definition could then be sharpened, as related words were met (e.g. *armchair, stool*). But this whole process of vocabulary learning continues without any direct reference to the objects in the real world: there is total reliance on the use of words to explain the sense of other words – a process that reaches its logical conclusion in a dictionary (§18).

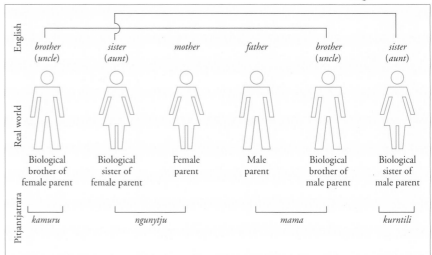

SEMANTIC SPACE

Psychologists also share the concern to establish the semantic properties of individual words, and several approaches have been proposed to plot differences and quantify the psychological 'distance' between words.

A pioneering work in this field was C. E. Osgood, G. Suci, & P. Tannenbaum, *The Measurement of Meaning* (1957), which was a study of 'affective' meaning – the emotional reactions attached to a word. Each word was subjected to a test that they called a 'semantic differential' – the name reflecting the view that it was possible to analyse meaning into a range of different dimensions. Osgood likened his procedure to a game of Twenty Questions, in which each question (e.g. 'Is it good or bad? fast or slow? small or large?') would aim to locate a concept in semantic space. The questions were presented as seven-point scales, with the opposed adjectives at each end, such as

good — — — — — — bad

and subjects were asked to rate words in terms of where they would fall on these scales. If they felt that *car* was 'good', for example, they would place a mark towards the 'good' end of the first scale; if 'bad', towards the other end. The seven positions allowed for variations in degree of feeling. Ten of the scales are illustrated below, giving the average responses from the two groups of 20 subjects to the word *polite* (after C. E. Osgood, 1952):

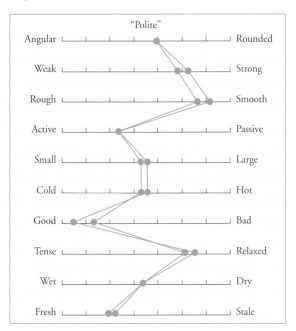

The method was also used to make comparisons between cultural groups. For example, *noise* is a highly affective concept for the Japanese, who tended to react to it using the extremes of the polar scales; it is not so for Americans or Kannada-speaking Indians. The word *male* varies in its connotations between Hopi (H), Zuñi (Z), and Navaho (N) Indians, the first two groups being fairly close together (after H. Maclay & E. E. Ware, 1961).

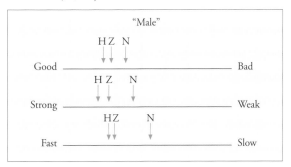

Charles E. Osgood (1916–)

The semantic differential procedure is a limited one. It does not provide information about the basic meaning of a word but only about the emotions the word generates. It tells us, for example, that *mother* might be 'very good', 'slightly strong', etc., but it does not tell us that the word means 'adult female parent'. To display this kind of information, other ways of working with semantic space are required. We can illustrate this using the results of a technique in which people judge the similarities between words. In the diagram, mammal names are located in a space where the horizontal dimension represents size and the vertical dimension represents ferocity (after L. J. Rips *et al.*, 1973). Larger animals are on the left; more ferocious animals are towards the bottom. The more similar any two animals are thought to be, the closer they are placed in the space. (There is no necessary correspondence with zoological reality, as can be seen from the closeness between cats and mice.)

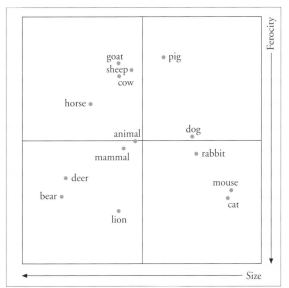

This is a very simple analysis, which it would be more difficult to make for words where the relevant dimensions of meaning are less clear-cut (items of furniture, for example). But the general approach is illuminating, with considerable research potential.

SEMANTIC STRUCTURE

One of the most productive approaches to the semantic analysis of vocabulary has come from the application of structuralist ideas (§65). From this viewpoint, language is a network of systematic relationships between units. In phonology, for example, the relationships exist between sounds – or phonemes (§28). What are the equivalent semantic units, and how are they related?

Lexemes

So far in this section, we have used the term 'word' to discuss semantic units, and this is the traditional use. People readily talk about the 'meaning of words'. However, if we wish to enquire precisely into semantic matters, this term will not do, and an alternative must be found. There are three main reasons.

1. The term *word* is used in ways that obscure the study of meaning. The forms *walk, walks, walking,* and *walked* could all be called 'different words'; yet from a semantic point of view, they are all variants of the same underlying unit, 'walk'. If the variants are referred to as 'words', though, what should the underlying unit be called? It would not be particularly clear to say that 'these four words are different forms of the same word'.

2. The term *word* is useless for the study of idioms, which are also units of meaning. A much-used example is *kick the bucket* (= 'die'). Here we have a single unit of meaning, which happens to consist of three words. Again, it would hardly be clear to talk of this unit as a 'word', if we then go on to say that this word consists of three words.

3. The term *word* has in any case been appropriated for use elsewhere in linguistic study – in the field of grammar, where it does sterling service at the junction between syntax and morphology (p. 90).

For such reasons, most linguists prefer to talk about the basic units of semantic analysis with fresh terminology, and both *lexeme* and *lexical item* are in common use. We may now avoid the lack of clarity referred to above, and say that the 'lexeme' WALK occurs in several variant forms – the 'words' *walk, walks,* etc. Similarly, we can say that the 'lexeme' KICK THE BUCKET contains three 'words'; and so on. It is lexemes that are usually listed as headwords in a dictionary. Accordingly, we shall put this term to use in the remaining parts of this section.

SEMANTIC FIELDS

One way of imposing some order on vocabulary is to organize it into 'fields' of meaning. Within each field, the lexemes interrelate, and define each other in specific ways. For example, the various lexemes for 'parts of the body' (*head, neck, shoulders,* etc.) form a semantic field, as do the different lexemes for 'vehicles', 'fruit', 'tools', or 'colour'. It has been argued that the whole of

a language's vocabulary is structured into fields; but there is in fact a great deal of variation as we move from one part of the language to another. There would be little difficulty gathering together all the English lexemes for 'body parts', for example; but it would be very difficult to do the same job for 'noise' or 'ornaments'.

There have been many philosophical and linguistic attempts to classify the concepts or words in a language – notably, those associated with the 17th-century quest for a universal language (§58). In recent times, the most influential and popular work has been the *Thesaurus* of Peter Mark Roget (1779–1869), first published in 1852. Roget divided the vocabulary into six main areas: *abstract relations, space, matter, intellect, volition,* and *affections.* Each area was given a detailed and exhaustive sub-classification, producing 1,000 semantic categories in all. One path through the thesaurus is illustrated below:

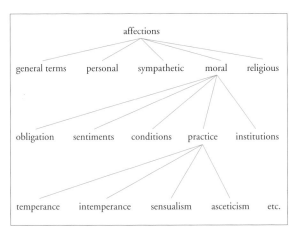

Groups of words are then listed under each of these headings and classified into the main parts of speech. For example, in the 1962 edition of the work (p. 625), we find the following items listed as a section within *temperance* (numbers refer to other thesaurus sections; keywords are in italics):

abstainer, total a., teetotaller 948n. *sober person;* prohibitionist, pussyfoot; vegetarian, fruitarian, Pythagorean; Encratite; dieter, banter, faster; enemy of excess, Spartan 945n. *ascetic.*

Thesauri of this kind have now been produced for several languages, and prove to be a useful adjunct to many practical linguistic activities, such as professional writing, translating, and setting or solving crosswords. For the semanticist, however, their value is limited, as they contain no information about the sense relationships between individual lexemes, and items that come from different regional, social, or professional varieties (§§8–11) are juxtaposed without comment. To study the structure of a semantic field, more precise means of plotting the sense relations between lexemes need to be used.

Roget (1779–1869) by William Brockedon, 1835

SEMANTIC CHANGE

The linguistic approach to semantic fields was first propounded by German scholars in the 1930s. In one of the earliest studies (J. Trier, 1934), the approach showed how the structure of a semantic field can change over time. Middle High German terms for 'knowledge' changed greatly between 1200 and 1300. In 1200, a German had no separate lexeme for the quality of cleverness. The language contained *kunst* ('courtly skills') and *list* ('noncourtly skills'), and there was also *wîsheit* for any form of knowledge, whether courtly or not, mundane or divine.

A hundred years later, everything was different. *Wîsheit* had developed the restricted meaning of 'religious experience'; *kunst* was beginning to take on the meaning of 'art / skill', and *wizzen* (modern *Wissen*) had more the meaning of 'knowledge'. *List* had left the field entirely, as it had begun to develop pejorative connotations (cf. its sense of 'cunning' or 'trick' in Modern German). The whole of this change can be summarized in the form of two diagrams:

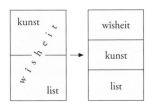

For a similar use of diagrams in the comparison of modern languages, see p. 106.

SENSE RELATIONSHIPS

How are the lexemes of a language organized? To think of them as a list, such as we might find in a dictionary, is highly misleading. There is no semantic reality in alphabetical order; on the contrary, alphabetical order destroys semantic structure, keeping apart lexemes that should belong together (such as *aunt* and *uncle*, or *big* and *little*). Rather, we need to develop an alternative conception, based on our intuitions that groups of lexemes are related in sense.

Accounts of semantic structure recognize several kinds of sense relations between lexemes. Some result from the way lexemes occur in sequences (*syntagmatic* relations); others from the way in which lexemes can substitute for each other (*paradigmatic* relations) (§65). For example, in the sentence *It was a very auspicious —*, English speakers 'know' that the omitted word will be one of a very small set (e.g. *occasion, event*) – unless, of course, a literary or humorous point is being made (*It was a very auspicious kilt*). This would be a syntagmatic semantic relationship. By contrast, the relationship between the following two sentences is a paradigmatic one: *Is that a new radio? No, it's an old radio*. The substitution of *old* for *new* results in a change of meaning that we recognize as an 'opposite'.

Several types of paradigmatic relationship have been recognized, some of which form a familiar part of language syllabuses in school. These include:

• *Synonymy* This is the relationship of 'sameness' of meaning, e.g. *kingly / royal / regal, pavement / sidewalk, youth / youngster*. The search for synonyms is a long-standing pedagogical exercise, but it is as well to remember that lexemes rarely (if ever) have *exactly* the same meaning. There are usually stylistic, regional, emotional, or other differences to consider. And context must be taken into account. Two lexemes might be synonymous in one sentence but different in another: *range* and *selection* are synonyms in *What a nice — of furnishings*, but not in *There's the mountain —*.

• *Hyponymy* This less familiar relationship refers to the notion of 'inclusion', whereby we can say that 'an X is a kind of Y'. For example, *rose* is a hyponym of *flower*, *car* of *vehicle*. Several lexemes will be 'co-hyponyms' of the same superordinate term: *rose, pansy, tulip ...* Once again, it must be stressed that this is a linguistic, and not a real-world classification. Languages differ in their superordinate terms, and in the hyponyms they accept under one such term. For instance in classical Greek the lexemes for 'carpenter', 'doctor', 'flautist', and other occupations are all hyponyms of *demiourgos*; but there is no equivalent superordinate term in English. We simply do not have a single 'occupational' term that would allow us to say 'A carpenter / doctor / flautist, etc is a kind of —'. Likewise, *potato* is a hyponym of *vegetable* in English, but *Kartoffel* is not included among *Gemüse* in German (after J. Lyons, 1963).

THE 'ANIMAL' KINGDOM

Animal is a strange lexeme in English, because it can be used at three levels in a hierarchy of inclusion:

1. in a classification of living things, it contrasts with *vegetable*, to include birds, fishes, and insects;
2. it contrasts with *bird, fish*, and *insect* to include humans and beasts;
3. it contrasts with *human*.

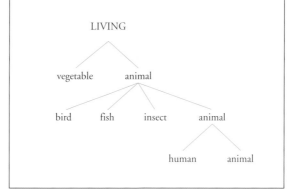

• *Antonymy* This is the relationship of 'oppositeness' of meaning'. Antonyms are often thought of in the same breath as synonyms, but they are in fact very different. There may be no true synonyms, but there are several kinds of antonyms. Some of the most important types are:

– *gradable* antonyms, such as *big / small, good / bad*, which permit the expression of degrees (*very big, quite small*, etc.);
– *nongradable* antonyms (also called *complementary* terms), which do not permit degrees of contrast, such as *single / married, male / female*; it is not possible to talk of *very male, quite married*, etc., except in jest; and
– *converse* terms: two-way contrasts that are interdependent, such as *buy / sell* or *parent / child*; one member presupposes the other.

• *Incompatibility* Under this heading are grouped sets of lexemes that are mutually exclusive members of the same superordinate category. For example, *red, green*, etc. are incompatible lexemes within the category *colour*: it would not be possible to say 'I am thinking of a single colour, and it is green and red.' On the other hand, *red* is not incompatible with such lexemes as *round* or *dirty* (something can be at once 'red and round'). Terms for fruit, flowers, weekdays, and musical instruments illustrate other incompatible sets. Once again, we must be prepared for some unexpected usages – as in English, where *black, white*, and *grey* are not always included within the category of colour (as with *black-and-white* films and TV sets), and where *red* can be excluded from this category (as with snooker, where one may proceed to play the 'coloured' balls only after all the red balls have been potted).

THE COMPANY LEXEMES KEEP

'You shall know a word by the company it keeps', said the British linguist J. R. Firth (1890–1960) in 1957, referring to the syntagmatic tendency of lexemes to work together ('collocate') in predictable ways. *Blond* collocates with *hair*, *flock* with *sheep*, *neigh* with *horse*. Some collocations are totally predictable, such as *spick* with *span*, or *addled* with *brains* or *eggs*. Others are much less so: *letter* collocates with a wide range of lexemes, such as *alphabet* and *spelling*, and (in another sense) *box, post* and *write*. Yet other lexemes are so widely used that they have no predictable collocates at all, such as *have* and *get*.

Collocation should not be confused with 'association of ideas'. The way lexemes work together may have nothing to do with 'ideas'. We say in English *green with jealousy* (not *blue, red*, etc.), though there is nothing literally 'green' about 'jealousy'. *Coffee* can be *white*, though the colour is brown. Both lads and lasses may be well rounded enough to be called *buxom*, but this lexeme is used only with the latter.

Collocations differ greatly between languages, and provide a major difficulty in mastering foreign languages. In English, we 'face' problems and 'interpret' dreams; but in modern Hebrew, we have to 'stand in front of' problems and 'solve' dreams. In Japanese the verb for 'drink' collocates with water and soup, but also with tablets and smoking.

The more fixed a collocation is, the more we think of it as an 'idiom' – a pattern to be learned as a whole, and not as the 'sum of its parts'. Thus we find French *broyer du noir* (lit. 'grind' + 'black'), meaning to 'have the blues' or 'be browned off' – a nice instance of the arbitrary use of colour terms.

Collocations are quite different from the idiosyncratic links between ideas that can be verbally expressed. On a psychiatrist's couch, we may 'free associate', responding to *farm* with *Easter*, or *jam* with *mother*. This is not collocation, which is a link between lexemes made by *all* who speak a language.

COLOUR LEXEMES

The range of colours is a continuous band, lacking any clear physical boundaries. The semantic field of colour has therefore attracted particular attention because it demonstrates very clearly the different patterns of lexical use in a language. English has 11 basic colour lexemes: *white, black, red, green, yellow, blue, brown, purple, pink, orange,* and *grey.* In contrast:

- There were no generic lexemes for 'brown' or 'grey' in Latin; modern Romance forms (such as French *brun, gris*) have been borrowed from Germanic. Navaho has a single lexeme for both.
- Navaho also makes no lexical distinction between 'blue' and 'green'. On the other hand, it has two terms for 'black', distinguishing the black of darkness from the black of such objects as coal.
- Russian makes a distinction between two kinds of 'blue', *sinij* vs *goluboj,* where English has to use circumlocutions: 'dark blue' vs 'sky blue'. Hungarian has two terms for 'red'.
- Japanese *ao* can mean 'green', 'blue', or 'pale', depending on context (e.g. vegetables, sea, clouds).
- In Hanunóo, there are just four basic colour terms, 'black', 'white', 'red', and 'green'.
- Some New Guinea Highland languages have terms only for 'black' and 'white' – perhaps better translated as 'dark' vs 'light'.
- In some languages the situation is more difficult to express in words, and a field diagram is clearer. Literary Welsh, for example, divides the green–brown part of the spectrum quite differently from English:

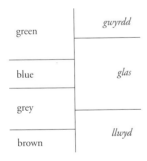

Modern Welsh is similar to English, but even so, *glas* is used for the colour of growing things (though it otherwise is equivalent to *blue*).

Colour universals?

The differences between the colour terms of various languages are striking, and might lead us to conclude that each language has worked out a unique system in a totally arbitrary way. A 1969 study by B. Berlin & P. Kay, however, argued the opposite. After studying the colour systems of 98 languages, they concluded that there is a universal inventory of only 11 basic colour categories, and all languages use either these 11 or fewer. 'Basic' was interpreted to mean that the terms

used only a single morpheme (excluding *light brown,* etc.), were in common use (excluding *indigo*), applied to many objects (excluding *blond*), and were not contained within another colour (excluding *scarlet*). They also claimed (p. 25) that these basic terms were ordered, as follows:

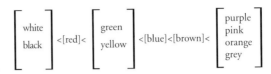

If a language has a term to the right of the sign <, it will also have all the terms to the left.

These claims are not without controversy. Obtaining reliable data from native speakers about such matters is a problem, especially as their judgments might have been coloured by their exposure to other languages. Some languages, also, seem to have 12 basic terms (e.g. Russian). But the research has demonstrated some impressive similarities across a wide range of languages.

POLYSEMY OR HOMONYMY?

- *Polysemy* refers to cases where a lexeme has more than one meaning: for example, *chip* can mean a piece of wood, food, or electronic circuit. People see no problem in saying that 'the word *chip* has several different meanings in English'.
- *Homonymy* refers to cases where two (or more) different lexemes have the same shape: for example, *bank* is both a building and an area of ground. Again, people see no problem in saying that 'these are two different words in English'.

This second reaction would also be given to those cases where lexemes were only 'half' identical in shape:

– *homophones,* which have the same pronunciation, but different spelling (e.g. *threw* vs *through*);
– *homographs,* which have the same spelling, but different pronunciation (e.g. *wind* – air movement vs bend).

The distinction seems clear enough, and dictionaries treat cases of multiple meaning either as polysemy or as homonymy. But in fact it is not always easy to decide which we are dealing with, and dictionaries sometimes differ in their decisions. Are *table* (furniture) and *table* (arrangement of data) two different words, or the same word with two meanings? Dictionaries usually go for the latter solution, on grounds of a shared etymology. On the other hand, *pupil* (in school) and *pupil* (of the eye) are usually listed as different words – though in fact they have the same historical origin. French *voler* 'fly' and *voler* 'steal' are similar: they are now thought of as different words, but both derive from Latin *volare.* There is often a conflict between historical criteria and present-day intuition, in sorting out cases of polysemy and homonymy.

KINSHIP CONTRASTS

Another semantic field which has been much studied is that of kinship. Here too there are interesting differences between languages:

- Hungarian had no terms for 'brother' or 'sister' until the 19th century, though it did have separate terms for 'elder' and 'younger' brothers and sisters.
- Malay has a generic term for both 'sibling' and 'cousin'.
- There is no single term for 'grandfather' or 'grandmother' in Swedish: *farfar* = 'father's father', *morfar* = 'mother's father', *farmor* = 'father's mother', *mormor* = 'mother's mother'.
- In Njamal (Australia), some terms express generation distance, e.g. a man can use *maili* both for 'father's father' and 'daughter's son's wife's sister' – both are two generations away.
- Latin distinguished 'father's brother' (*patruus*), 'father's sister' (*matertera*), 'mother's brother' (*avunculus*), and 'mother's sister' (*amita*), but modern Romance languages have reduced these to two (e.g. French *oncle* and *tante*, derived from the maternal terms).

DEIXIS

Every language has a set of lexemes which can be interpreted only with reference to the speaker's position in space or time. These are known as *deictic* forms (from the Greek word for 'pointing'), and the conditions governing their use have attracted especial attention in recent semantics. They fall into three main types.

- *Personal deixis* The use of pronouns, such as *I* and *you,* which identify who is taking part in the discourse.
- *Spatial deixis* Forms that distinguish the position of the speaker in relation to other people or objects, such as *this / that, here / there* (p. 99), *bring / take, come / go. Come,* for example, implies direction towards the speaker – *Come here!* (but not **Go here!*).
- *Temporal deixis* Forms that distinguish time with reference to the speaker, such as *now, yesterday, then,* and the various kinds of tense marker.

SEMANTIC COMPONENTS

A further way to study lexical meaning is by analysing lexemes into a series of semantic features, or components. *Man,* for example, could be analysed as ADULT, HUMAN, and MALE. The approach was originally devised by anthropologists as a means of comparing vocabulary from different cultures, and it has been developed by semanticists as a general framework for the analysis of meaning.

Whole systems of relationships can be established, using a small set of components. For example, the components ADULT/NON-ADULT and MALE/FEMALE can be used for the following:

man (ADULT, MALE), woman (ADULT, FEMALE)
boy (NON-ADULT, MALE), girl (NON-ADULT, FEMALE).

Many animals display a similar pattern (though lacking a male / female non-adult distinction):

MALE	FEMALE	NON-ADULT
bull	cow	calf
ram	ewe	lamb
boar	sow	piglet

In componential analysis, contrasts are usually presented in terms of + or −, and often drawn in a matrix. Thus, we could use +MALE and −MALE (or, of course +FEMALE and −FEMALE) to summarize the above possibilities:

	bull	ram	boar	cow	ewe	sow	calf	lamb	piglet
MALE	+	+	+	−	−	−	+-	+-	+-
FEMALE	−	−	−	+	+	+	+-	+-	+-

The analyses become more interesting, as the lexemes become more complex. Here, for instance, is a possible matrix for some human motion verbs.

	NATURAL	HURRIED	FORWARD	ONE FOOT ALWAYS ON GROUND
walk	+	−	+	+
march	−	+	+	+
run	−	+	+	−
limp	−	−	+	+

It is easy, using a system of this kind, to see what lexical gaps there are in a language. For example, this matrix suggests there is no single English lexeme expressing the notion of 'human using legs to move backwards'. On the other hand, it is not always so easy to decide which are the relevant components of a lexeme and whether they can be applied in a binary (+/−) way. Would *swim* be +HURRIED or −HURRIED in this matrix? Or, in other fields, would *soup* be +EAT or −EAT, and *porridge* +LIQUID or −LIQUID?

SENTENCE MEANING

The study of meaning takes us by degrees through the whole of a language, and it proves difficult to draw a neat line around the semantic component of any linguistic framework (§13). Much of the focus of traditional semantics has been on vocabulary, but contemporary semantics is increasingly concerned with the analysis of sentence meaning – or, at least, of those aspects of sentence meaning that cannot be predicted from the 'sum' of the individual lexemes.

- *Prosodic meaning* The way a sentence is said, using the prosody of the language (§29), can radically alter the meaning. Any marked change in emphasis, for example, can lead to a sentence being interpreted in a fresh light. Each of these sentences carries a different implication, as the stress (indicated by capitals) moves:

John's bought a red CAR (not a red bicycle).
John's bought a RED car (not a green one).
JOHN's bought a red car (not Michael).

The prosody informs us of what information in the sentence can be taken for granted (is 'given') and what is of special significance (is 'new').

- *Grammatical meaning* The categories that are established by grammatical analysis can also be analysed from a semantic point of view. A sentence such as *John read a book yesterday* consists of Subject + Verb + Object + Adverbial (p. 95); but it can also be analysed as an 'actor' performing an 'action' on a 'goal' at a certain 'time'. There is a great deal to be said about the 'semantic roles' played by syntactic elements – an area of study that falls uneasily between semantics and grammar.

- *Pragmatic meaning* The function performed by the sentence in a discourse needs to be considered. The meaning of the sentence *There's some chalk on the floor* seems plain enough; but in some situations it would be interpreted as a statement of fact ('Have you seen any chalk?') and in others as a veiled command (as when a teacher might point out the chalk to a child in class). The pragmatic study of sentence function is reviewed in §21, but it overlaps greatly with the field of semantics—especially the 'semantics of misunderstanding'.

- *Social meaning* The choice of a sentence may directly affect the social relationships between the participants. We may convey such impressions as politeness, rudeness, competence, or distance, and this will affect our status and role within a community. 'What do you mean by talking to me like that?' is a question that raises larger issues than the meaning of the individual lexemes and sentences that have been used.

- *Propositional meaning* Perhaps the most important trend in modern semantics is the investigation of sentence meaning using ideas derived from philosophy and logic. In this kind of approach, a careful distinction is drawn between sentences (grammatical units, p. 94) and propositions. A proposition is the unit of meaning that identifies the subject matter of a statement; it describes some state of affairs, and takes the form of a declarative sentence, e.g. *Mary loves Michael.* In such theories as 'truth-conditional semantics', sentences are analysed in terms of the underlying propositions they express, and these propositions are then tested to see whether they would be true or false, in relation to the real world. The theories are controversial, and require not a little expertise in formal logic to be understood. But they may in due course provide a level of general explanation for semantic observations that the subject has hitherto lacked.

GRAMMAR OR SEMANTICS

The uncertain boundary between semantics and grammar is a classic problem in linguistic theory. It can be illustrated by the many sentences that are used in a habitual manner, and are thus semi-idiomatic in type, falling midway between the 'straightforward' idioms such as *raining cats and dogs* and clear cases of sentences which follow the normal rules of grammar, such as *The man kicked the ball.*

In one study, a large number of habitually used expressions were collected, based on the lexeme *think.* They included:

Come to think of it ...
What do you think?
I thought better of it.
Think nothing of it.
Think it over.
It doesn't bear thinking about.
I thought you knew.
I think so.
What I think is ...
I was just thinking aloud.
Who'd have thought it?
Who do you think you are?
(After A. Pawley & F. H. Syder, 1983, pp. 213–14.)

It is argued that people have memorized expressions of this kind, as part of the process of building up fluent connected speech (the phenomenon is less obvious in the written language). On the other hand, these 'lexicalized sentence stems', as they were called, are plainly not as 'fixed' in their structure as conventional idioms, and their meaning can be predicted quite accurately from their constituent lexemes (unlike, say *raining cats and dogs*). The result is an area of usage that lies midway between the domain of grammar, which focuses on productive sentence types, and that of the lexicon, which focuses on the properties of particular lexical items.

A dictionary is a reference book that lists the words of one or more languages, usually in alphabetical order, along with information about their spelling, pronunciation, grammatical status, meaning, history, and use. The process of compiling dictionaries is known as *lexicography*, and the people who carry out this task are *lexicographers* – 'harmless drudges', as Dr Johnson defined them.

In literate societies, most homes have a dictionary, but there is enormous variation in the way this is used. Some people constantly use them as a serious educational tool, aiming to improve their own or their children's 'word power'. Others use them only for fun – as the arbiter in a game of Scrabble, for instance (p. 64). Others do not use them at all and do not replace them when they fall badly out of date. The continued use of 10- or 20-year-old dictionaries is by no means uncommon.

For a book that is viewed with a level of respect normally accorded only to the Bible, it is remarkable how casually dictionary-users treat their dictionaries. When people are asked what factors govern their choice of dictionary, most cite linguistically irrelevant matters, such as price, pictorial content, and size – not in terms of number of entries, but whether it would fit on a shelf, or in a pocket. Many people expect a dictionary to contain encyclopedic information about historical events, people, and places. Most admit they have never bothered to read the Preface to their dictionary – the place where the layout and conventions of the book are systematically explained. As a consequence they are unable to say what the various abbreviations and symbols mean, or why they are there. The general conclusion is inescapable: most people who would check out every tiny feature of their new car before buying it are unaware of the power that lies under the bonnet of their dictionary.

THE RANGE OF DICTIONARIES

Dictionaries come in all shapes and sizes, from the massive unabridged works, such as the 2,662-page Merriam-Webster *Third New International Dictionary of the English Language* (1961), to the tiniest of pocket-size works, such as the 386-page Nimmo's *Thumb English Dictionary*, each page of which is less than 9 cm high. Coverage (the number of headwords the work contains) and treatment (the kind of information provided under each headword) thus vary enormously. The simplest way of showing this is to compare the amount of detail given for the same word in dictionaries of different sizes. Here are the entries for *insular* in a large, medium-sized, and small dictionary:

A page from the
'thumb' dictionary (75% of real size)

The Random House Dictionary of the English Language (c. 260,000 headwords, 1987)

(inʹsə lər, insʹyə-), *adj.* **1.** of or pertaining to an island or islands: *insular possessions.* **2.** dwelling or situated on an island. **3.** forming an island: *insular rocks.* **4.** detached; standing alone; isolated. **5.** of, pertaining to, or characteristic of islanders. **6.** narrow-minded or illiberal; provincial: *insular attitudes towards foreigners.* **7.** *Pathol.* occurring in or characterized by one or more isolated spots, patches, or the like. **8.** *Anat.* pertaining to an island of cells or tissue, as the islets of Langerhans. –*n.* **9.** an inhabitant of an island; islander. [1605–15; <LL *insulār* (*is*). See INSULA, -AR¹] –inʹsu . lar . ism, *n.* –inʹsu . larʹi . ty, *n.* –inʹsu . lar . ly, *adv.*

Longman Dictionary of the English Language (c. 90,000 headwords, 1984)

/ ˈinsyoolə/ *adj* **1a** of or being an island **b** living or situated on an island <~*residents*> **2** *of a plant or animal* having a restricted or isolated natural range or habitat **3a** of island people <*surviving customs*> **b** that results (as if) from lack of contact with other peoples or cultures; narrow-minded, illiberal **4** *anatomy* of an island of cells or tissue [LL *insularis*, fr L *insula* island] – **insularism** *n*, **insularly** *adv*, **insularity** *n*

Penguin English Dictionary (c. 40,000 headwords, 2nd edn, 1969)

[*insewler*] *adj* of or like an island; of or like inhabitants of an island; cut off from general currents of thought; narrow-minded, smugly intolerant.

For further comparison, Nimmo's tiny book says simply: '*a.* surrounded by water'.

Apart from variations of format – the use of bold face, numbered senses, etc. – there are major differences in the range and depth of information provided. It is worth spending five minutes making a point-by-point comparison, to see exactly how much information is lost as the dictionaries become smaller. And the moral is plain: for serious study of a language's word-hoard, only the largest dictionaries will suffice.

HOW BIG IS A DICTIONARY?

Dictionaries usually claim to contain 'X,000' words. But this grand total can mean several different things. It might refer just to the number of *headwords* in the dictionary – that is, the bold-face items that occur at the beginning of each entry. Or it might include in addition all the subsidiary bold-face items that occur within an entry: under *quick*, for example, there will be ~*ly* and ~*ness*. Different word classes might be counted separately (e.g. *play* noun vs *play* verb), as might idioms, and irregular grammatical forms (e.g. *go, went*). Depending on what you decide to count, you can end up with two very different totals for the same dictionary. Claims about size should therefore be viewed with caution.

The best way to evaluate the coverage of a dictionary is to compare the words and senses it includes with another dictionary of about the same size. It is notable how even the largest dictionaries present great differences in their coverage – the variation being particularly noticeable in the way they treat world regional vocabulary (how many Australian, South African, or West Indian forms does an English dictionary include, for example?), local dialect words, abbreviations, slang and sub-standard forms, new coinages and borrowings. The use of illustrations and the inclusion of encyclopedic information (names of people, places, historical events, etc.) is also a major source of difference, especially between British and American dictionaries. It has been estimated that the lack of correspondence in large English dictionaries can be as great as 50% – indicating that a truly comprehensive dictionary of the language has yet to be compiled.

Dr Samuel Johnson (1709–84) by Joshua Reynolds, 1775.

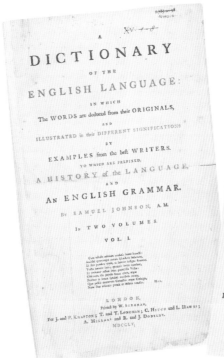

The title page, together with an extract from Dr Samuel John-son's *Dictionary of the English Language*

JOHNSON'S DICTIONARY

This great dictionary was published in two volumes in 1755, and its influence on subsequent lexicography was unequalled. Noah Webster went so far as to compare Johnson's contribution to Newton's in mathematics. The dictionary had four main features that set it off from previous English works:

• It aimed to be a scholarly record of the whole of a language – a marked contrast with the haphazard dictionaries of 'hard words' previously compiled.

• It was based on a corpus of examples of usage, largely from the period 1560 to 1660; certain types of words were excluded (e.g. proper names – a decision which resulted in a major difference between British and American dictionaries, for while the former followed Johnson, the latter did not).

• It introduced a literary dimension, departing from the previous concentration on technical language. Half of all Johnson's quotations come from Shakespeare, Dryden, Milton, Addison, Bacon, Pope, and the Bible.

The dictionary is very much the language of the 'best' authors.

• Dictionaries become more authoritative – and authoritarian – as a consequence. They became increasingly used in a normative way, as guides to *good* usage – a bias which 20th-century dictionaries are only just beginning to correct.

However, Johnson's was not the first monolingual English dictionary. The credit for this must go to Robert Cawdrey's *A Table Alphabeticall ...*, a 2,500-entry work printed in 1604.

From Johnson's Preface

My purpose was to admit no testimony of living authors, that I might not be misled by partiality, and that none of my contemporaries might have reason to complain ... I have studiously endeavoured to collect examples and authorities from the writers before the restoration, whose words I regard as *the wells of English unde-filed,* as the pure sources of genuine diction.

James Murray (1837–1915) The first editor of the *Oxford English Dictionary* is seen at work in his Scriptorium. Murray, the son of a village tailor from Hawick, Scotland, was largely self-educated. He left school at 14, and was a teacher and bank clerk before becoming a lexicographer. His Scriptorium, where most of the editing took place, was built in the back garden of his house in Oxford. Murray planned the whole of the New English Dictionary, and he edited more than half of its first edition himself. The first instalment was published in 1884: A–ANT, 352 pages, price 12s. 6d. (or 62½p today. It took 44 years to complete the dictionary, in 125 instalments – four times longer than had been expected. The complete work, totalling 424,825 entries, was then published as the *Oxford English Dictionary (OED)* from 1933 onwards, with four supplements issued from 1972. An integrated edition appeared in 1989, and was also released on compact disk; a third edition is planned for 2005.

Noah Webster (1758–1843)

Webster's works on spelling, grammar, and lexicon constituted the first major account of American English, and gave the variety a clear identity and status. His *An American Dictionary of the English Language*, published in two volumes in 1828, consisted of around 70,000 entries. Particular attention was paid to the inclusion of scientific terms, and to etymological background. The latest revision is the *Third New International Dictionary* (Merriam, 1961), containing over 450,000 entries, which took 757 editor-years to complete. Supplements appeared in 1976, 1983, and 1986.

THE HISTORY OF LEXICOGRAPHY

The earliest dictionaries had a practical aim. They were often bilingual or polyglot word-lists aimed at the traveller and the missionary, or glossaries written to help people understand words which were dialectal, technical, or rare. From as early as the 5th century BC, the Greeks were compiling *glossai*, explaining difficult words in such authors as Homer. The first vocabulary lists in English were similar: these were 8th-century Anglo-Saxon glosses, in which English words were written between the Latin lines. Later, these glosses were collected together as lists. But random collections of words or glosses are not dictionaries: to count as a dictionary, the words need to be organized in a systematic way – such as through the use of the alphabetical principle.

The history of lexicography goes back over 2,000 years, to ancient China, Greece, and Rome. But there has never been a time when some kind of lexicographical work was not in progress. Some periods were particularly fruitful.

- Arabic dictionaries flourished from around the 8th century onwards.

Left: a page from the *Grand Larousse Universel* (1982) It shows the mixture of lexical, literary, and encyclopedic information which is the hallmark of this tradition.

Below: a page from a German–Latin school book, *Teutsch lateinisches Wörter-Büchlein* Printed around 1722, it contains about 6,000 words, each of which is illustrated.

16 der Wasserkessel (Flötenkessel)
– kettle (whistling kettle)
17 der Wrasenabzug (Dunstabzug)
– cooker hood
18 der Topflappen
– pot holder
19 der Topflappenhalter
– pot holder rack

16 der Wasserkessel (Flötenkessel)
– el hervidor (el hervidor de silbato m; Amér.: la pava)
17 der Wrasenabzug (Dunstabzug)
– la campana
18 der Topflappen
– la manopla (el agarrador)
19 der Topflappenhalter
– el cuelgamanoplas

16 der Wasserkessel (Flötenkessel)
– la bouilloire, la bouilloire à sifflet m
17 der Wrasenabzug (Dunstabzug)
– la hotte
18 der Topflappen
– la manique, le protège-main
19 der Topflappenhalter
– l'accroche-manique m, le crochet à protège-main

16 der Wasserkessel (Flötenkessel)
– il bollitore dell'acqua
17 der Wrasenabzug (Dunstabzug)
– la cappa aspirante
18 der Topflappen
– la presina da cucina
19 der Topflappenhalter
– il portapresine (l'appendipresine m)

Above: a page from the *Duden pictorial Encyclopedia in Five Languages* (1958 edition)

- There was a flurry of activity in several languages following the invention of printing.
- The Accademia della Crusca produced its dictionary in 1612 (the first to be compiled by a team of people), and prompted several other national dictionary projects.
- Polyglot dictionaries were particularly numerous in the 17th century, with the development of trade and missionary activities around the world.
- The 18th century saw a fresh direction in lexicography, following the discoveries of the comparative philologists (§50), and the first major historical dictionaries began to be compiled.
- The 19th century saw many large-scale dictionary projects, produced by teams of compilers, and several specialized dictionaries (such as of dialect or technical words). Different kinds of dictionaries began to be produced, notably the Larousse series (from 1856), with its distinctive pictorial and encyclopedic character.
- The 20th century has seen the development of lexicography as a scholarly subject, largely under the influence of linguistics, and promoted especially by the growth of academic societies, such as the Dictionary Society of North America (1975), and the European Association for Lexicography (EURALEX, 1983)

THE PRESENT ... THE FUTURE ...

Since the 1970s, the flow of dictionaries has been unabated, as publishers try to meet the needs of an increasingly language-conscious age. In English, for example, new editions and supplements to the well-known dictionaries have appeared, and several publishers have launched new general series. Reader's Digest produced its *Great Illustrated Dictionary* in 1984, the first full-colour English dictionary, in the encyclopedic tradition of Larousse. Prominent also have been the dictionaries for special purposes (foreign language teaching, linguistics, medicine, chemistry, etc.). For the first time, spoken vocabulary has begun to find its way into dictionaries (though by no means all are yet willing to include the more colloquial words and uses).

But this outpouring is as nothing compared with the flood yet to come. The 1980s will one day be seen as a watershed in lexicography – the decade in which computer applications began to alter radically the methods and the potential of lexicography. Gone are the days of painstaking manual transcription and sorting on paper slips: the future is on disk, in the form of vast lexical databases, continuously updated, that can generate a dictionary of a given size and scope in a fraction of the time it used to take. Special programs are already available enabling people to ask the dictionary special questions (such as: 'find all words that entered the language in 1964' or 'find all words ending in -esse'). Access to large machine-dictionaries will become routine in offices and homes. One day, we shall not look up a word in a dictionary on a shelf but ask our home computer for the information we need. That day is not far off.

TWENTY QUESTIONS TO ASK WHEN YOU BUY A DICTIONARY

1 Is the paper of good, hard-wearing quality?
2 Will the binding allow it to be opened flat?
3 Are (especially long) entries clearly laid out?
4 Does it have the words you most want to look up? (Keep a note of some words which have caused you problems, and use them as a quick check.)
5 Does it have good international coverage?
6 Does it contain encyclopedic information?
7 Does it have illustrations of difficult concepts?
8 Are the definitions clearly distinguished, and organized on a sensible principle?
9 Are the definitions easy to understand, and helpful (e.g. avoiding vicious circularity, as when X is defined as Y, and Y is then defined as X)?
10 Does it give citations (examples of usage), and are they real or artificial?
11 Does it give guidance about usage?
12 Does it use a good set of stylistic labels (e.g. formal, slang, medical, archaic)?
13 Does it give etymological information?
14 Does it give guidance about capitalization, spelling variation, and where syllable boundaries go (i.e. where to hyphenate)?
15 Does it give pronunciation variants, and is the phonetic transcription easy to follow?
16 Does it contain idioms, phrases, proverbs, etc.?
17 Does it contain lists of synonyms and antonyms?
18 Does it give useful cross-references to other words of related meaning?
19 Does it give information about word class, inflectional endings, and other relevant features of grammar?
20 Are there useful appendices (e.g. abbreviations, measures)?

SOME IMPORTANT EVENTS BJ (BEFORE JOHNSON)

5th c. BC Protagoras of Abdera compiled a glossary of unfamiliar words in Homer.
3rd c. BC The poet Philetas of Cos compiled a glossary of unusual poetic, technical, and dialect words.
2nd c. BC Aristophanes of Byzantium compiled a dictionary of current and obsolete words.
1st c. BC Marcus Verrius Flaccus compiled the first Latin lexicon, *Libri de significatu verborum*.
1st c. Valerius Harpocration compiled a lexicon of the Attic orators.
2nd c. First systematic Chinese dictionary, *Hsuo Wên*, compiled by Hsü Shên.
5th c. Hesychius of Alexandria compiled a large lexicon of Classical Greek.
6th c. Compilation of a Sanskrit dictionary by the Hindu grammarian, Amarasimha.
8th c. The first general Arabic dictionary, *Kitāb al-'ayn*, compiled by Al-Khalīl Ibn Ahmad.
10th–11th c. Compilation of a Byzantine encyclopedic dictionary, the *Suda*.
11th c. First Chinese–Japanese encyclopedic dictionary, by Minamoto no Shitagô.
12th c. Compilation of the Greek *Etymologicon magnum*, author unknown.
13th c. Johannes Balbus Januensis compiled the encyclopedic dictionary, the *Catholicon*, one of the most influential dictionaries of the middle ages, and the first to be printed (in 1460).
1477 The earliest printed bilingual dictionary: the *Vocabolista italiano-tedesco* (Venice).
1499 Probably the first dictionary to be printed in England: the Latin–English *Promptuorium parvulorum* (London, Richard Pynson).
1511 The first printed Dutch dictionary: Noël de Berlaimont's *Vocabulaire*.
1539 Compilation of Robert Estienne's *Dictionnaire françois-latin*.
1596 The first published Russian dictionary: Laurentii Zizanii's *Leksys ... synonima sloveno-rosskaia*.
1606 Publication of Jean Nicot's *Thresor de la langue francoyse*, the first systematic French dictionary.
1611 Publication of the first major Spanish dictionary, *Tesoro de la lengua castellana o española* of Covarrubias y Horozco.
(After R. L. Collison, 1982.)

A name is a word or phrase that identifies a specific person, place, or thing. We see the entity as an individual, and not as a member of a class: *Everest,* for example, is a unique name (a 'proper noun'), whereas *mountain* applies to a whole class of objects (a 'common noun'). In the written language, European languages generally recognize the distinction by writing names with an initial capital letter. But most other writing systems do not distinguish upper- and lower-case letters (§33), and even in Europe there are several arbitrary conventions and points of uncertainty. English, for example, is idiosyncratic in its use of capitals for days of the week and proper adjectives (as in *the Chinese language*) (p. 196). And decisions have to be made over whether one writes *catholic* or *Catholic, the church* or *the Church, bible* or *Bible.*

The science that studies names is known as *onomastics,* usually divided into the study of personal names *(anthroponomastics)* and place names *(toponomastics).* In more popular usage, however, the term *onomastics* is used for the former, and *toponymy* for the latter. The division is ultimately an arbitrary one, as places are often named after people (e.g. *Washington*) and vice versa (e.g. *Israel* is sometimes used as a first name). Other categories of name (e.g. ships, trains, yachts, domestic pets, race horses, commercial products) also need to be taken into account. But most name studies fall under one of the two major headings.

PERSONAL NAMES

Most people are familiar with only one personal naming system, and are surprised to learn that practices differ greatly from language to language. Even such a basic distinction as 'given name' (or 'Christian name') and 'family name' (or 'surname') is not universal (in Europe, it began to be used in the late middle ages, reaching some areas only as recently as the 19th century). These names are also often referred to as 'first' and 'last' names; but this nomenclature is ambiguous when comparing languages, as there is considerable variation in the order in which such names occur. In most European languages, the family name follows the given name; but the reverse is the case in, say, Hungarian and Chinese (e.g. *Mao Zedong).*

In some societies, a middle name is also regularly used. This is the case in America, for instance, where an initial is especially favoured (e.g. *John H. Smith).* In Europe, middle names are less common, unless acquired at a special occasion (such as the Catholic ceremony of Confirmation). Where there is a sequence of names, there may also be variation in levels of importance. In Britain, for example, the first name is the important one – David Michael Smith would usually be referred to as 'David'; in Germany, the name nearest to the surname is more important – Johann Wolfgang Schmidt would usually be referred to as Wolfgang.

Some languages make use of *patronymics* – a name derived from the father's given name: in Russian, *Ivan's* son would be known as *Ivanovich,* and his daughter as *Ivanovna.* The opposite practice, of naming a parent after a child *(teknonymy),* is less common, but is widespread in the Arab world, for example, where a parent is often called 'father of' or 'mother of' the eldest son. In Russian, the patronymic is placed between the child's given and family names. In Icelandic, the patronymic serves as the surname, which then changes with each generation. Amharic names consist simply of the child's given name plus the father's given name. In English, patronymic prefixes and suffixes are used only in family names (e.g. *Robertson),* and this is common throughout Europe (e.g. 'son of' appears in Scots *Mac / Mc-,* Irish *O',* Welsh *Ap,* Polish *-ski,* Russian *-ovich).*

SIMILARITIES AND DIFFERENCES

There are some impressive similarities in naming practice across different languages, such as the use of names based on professions. *Smith,* and its foreign-language equivalents, is the best-known case, being the most common surname in many parts of Europe: Arabic *Haddad,* Hungarian *Kovács,* Russian *Kuznetsov,* Portuguese *Ferreiro,* German *Schmidt,* Spanish *Hernández / Fernández,* French *Le Fèvre / La Forge,* and so on. But the differences in naming practices are far more striking.

The possibilities of variation seem endless. We find the tripartite personal names of the Romans (e.g. *Gaius Julius Caesar),* the compound names of early Germans and Celts (e.g. *Orgetorix* 'king of killers'), and the use of 'by-names' to distinguish people who have the same name (e.g. Welsh *Dai Jones-the-milk* vs *Dai Jones-the-post).* In Europe, there is a great diversity of given and family names; by contrast, in several oriental societies the possibilities are highly restricted – for example, just three family names, Kim, Pak, and Yi, are used by most of the people of Korea.

We find children named after saints, events, places, omens, personal traits – even animals (as with North American Indians, e.g. *Little Bear).* In some societies, divine names can be used ('theophoric' names, such as Greek *Herodotus* 'given by Hera' or Arabic *Abd Allāh*

I NAME THIS SHOP ...

Shops and streets, as well as babies and ships, can receive their names in a formal ceremony. Before the event, the proposed name may be widely known, but there is no official reality until the proper words are said on the proper occasion. Naming ceremonies are one type of *performative* speech act (p. 121): the very act of saying the words sanctions the linguistic status of the named object, in the eyes of society.

'slave of Allah'). At the opposite extreme, children might be named after unpleasant notions to make them undesirable to evil spirits ('apotropaic' names, such as 'cripple' or 'ugly', p. 9). Where personal names are concerned, there seems to be no limit to parental idiosyncrasy and invention, two fine examples being the Puritan given name *Kill Sin,* and the Russian concoction *Mels* – an acronym for 'Marx-Engels-Lenin-Stalin'.

FIRST NAMES

In 1623, the historian and antiquary William Camden (1551–1623) published an appendix to his guide book to Britain, in which he included a long list of the most popular given names and surnames of his time. Since then, there have been several academic studies of given names in a wide range of European languages, and many popular accounts, aimed especially at providing information for parents who do not know what to call their baby.

The studies are both etymological and statistical. The former have universal appeal. People are fascinated by the history of names – in particular, where their own name comes from and how its usage has changed over the centuries. For example, *Hilary* is from Latin *hilarius,* meaning 'cheerful'. It has been used by three male saints (including one Pope), and it has continued as a male name in Europe. However, in Britain, it fell out of use in the 17th century, and when it revived in the 1890s, it was usually as a female name. Its peak British usage was during the 1950s and 1960s.

Interesting though the origin of a name may be, it exercises very little influence on most parental choice and is of little value in the study of naming trends. Far more important is the recent history of the name in a society – whether it has been used by the parents or near relatives, or by famous individuals such as film stars, pop stars, or members of a royal family. Nations have different traditions in this respect. Britain and America permit all possible names, whereas in France and Germany there are approved lists of names that must be used if a child is to be legally recognized. The influence of a religious tradition (as in the Catholic use of saints' names) is often apparent. Statistical studies of name use are thus of particular significance.

Information about name use over the years comes from a variety of sources such as parish records, national censuses, newspaper birth announcements, and special surveys by name scholars and enthusiasts. There has, for example, been a survey of every first name used by the Smiths in England and Wales since 1837. In the case of English, it is also important to consider all parts of the English-speaking world to discover whether there have been directions of influence.

General findings about first names are tentative but intriguing. Names are much influenced by fashion, and very few names retain great popularity from one generation to the next. There is much greater variation in girls' names: in the lists (right), hardly any girls' names carry over from one generation to the next, whereas several boys' names do. The white / non-white difference in the USA is noticeable for girls, also. And in English, it seems that traditionally-male names are likely to be used for girls at any time, whereas female names are rarely used for boys (after L. Dunkling, 1995).

TOP TEN FIRST NAMES

BOYS (*England and Wales*)		BOYS (*USA*)		GIRLS (*England and Wales*)		GIRLS (*USA*)	
1925	1950	1925	1950	1925	1950	1925	1950
1 John	David	1 Robert	Robert	1 Joan	Susan	1 Mary	Linda
2 William	John	2 John	Michael	2 Mary	Linda	2 Barbara	Mary
3 George	Peter	3 William	James	3 Joyce	Christine	3 Dorothy	Patricia
4 James	Michael	4 James	John	4 Margaret	Margaret	4 Betty	Susan
5 Ronald	Alan	5 Charles	David	5 Dorothy	Carol	5 Ruth	Deborah
6 Robert	Robert	6 Richard	William	6 Doris	Jennifer	6 Margaret	Kathleen
7 Kenneth	Stephen	7 George	Thomas	7 Kathleen	Janet	7 Helen	Barbara
8 Frederick	Paul	8 Donald	Richard	8 Irene	Patricia	8 Elizabeth	Nancy
9 Thomas	Brian	9 Joseph	Gary	9 Betty	Barbara	9 Jean	Sharon
10 Albert	Graham	10 Edward	Charles	10 Eileen	Ann	10 Ann(e)	Karen
1965	1975	1970	1993 (*white*)	1965	1975	1970	1993 (*white*)
1 Paul	Stephen	1 Michael	Michael	1 Trac(e)y	Claire	1 Michelle	Ashley
2 David	Mark	2 Robert	Joshua	2 Deborah	Sarah	2 Jennifer	Jessica
3 Andrew	Paul	3 David	Matthew	3 Julie	Nicola	3 Kimberly	Sarah
4 Stephen	Andrew	4 James	Jacob	4 Karen	Emma	4 Lisa	Brittany
5 Mark	David	5 John	Zachary	5 Susan	Joanne	5 Tracy	Kaitlyn
6 Michael	Richard	6 Jeffrey	Christopher	6 Alison	Helen	6 Kelly	Taylor
7 Ian	Matthew	7 Steven	Tyler	7 Jacqueline	Rachel	7 Nicole	Emily
8 Gary	Daniel	8 Christopher	Brandon	8 Helen	Lisa	8 Angela	Megan
9 Robert	Christopher	9 Brian	Andrew	9 Amanda	Rebecca	9 Pamela	Samantha
10 Richard	Darren	10 Mark	Nicholas	10 Sharon	Karen	10 Christine	Katherine
1993		1993 (*non-white*)		1993		1993 (*non-white*)	
1 Daniel		1 Christopher		1 Rebecca		1 Jasmine	
2 Thomas		2 Michael		2 Amy		2 Brianna	
3 Matthew		3 Brandon		3 Sophie		3 Brittany	
4 Joshua		4 Joshua		4 Charlotte		4 Ashley	
5 Adam		5 James		5 Laura		5 Alexis	
6 Luke		6 Anthony		6 Lauren		6 Jessica	
7 Michael		7 Devonte		7 Jessica		7 Chelsea	
8 Christopher		8 Jonathan		8 Hannah		8 Courtney	
9 Ryan		9 William		9 Jade		9 Kayla	
10 Jack		10 Justin		10 Emma		10 Sierra	

PLACE NAMES

The names people give to their surroundings provide a unique source of information about a society's history, beliefs, and values. There are so many aspects of a country's development that achieve linguistic recognition in its place names. The various steps in the exploration of America, for example, can be seen reflected in the 'layers' of Spanish, French, Dutch, Indian, and English names introduced by different groups of explorers; and Celtic, Roman, Anglo-Saxon, Scandinavian, and Norman names provide a similar insight into British history. Often, a place name is the only record of a historical event or of a person's existence. The name of Rēada, 'the red', lives on in the town of Reading, in Berkshire ('the people of Rēada'); but of his life and deeds, nothing else is known.

The study of place names includes the 'small' places and institutions (such as names of streets, houses, inns, and fields) as well as the main geographical features of the world (such as seas, rivers, mountains, cities, and towns); but most academic study has been in relation to the latter. Place names are sometimes fanciful and idiosyncratic (e.g. USA *Rabbit Hash*, Britain *Thertheoxlaydede* 'there the ox lay dead', or jocular house names such as *Webiltit* and *Noname*), but the vast majority can be explained with reference to a small set of creative processes. With geographical names, some of the most widespread types of derivation include the following:

- natural features, such as hills, rivers, and coastlines, e.g. *Dover* (water), *Staines* (stones), *Honolulu* (safe harbour), *Rotorua* (two lakes), *Kalgoorlie* (a native shrub), *Twin Forks, South Bend*;
- special sites, such as camps and forts, e.g. *Doncaster* (camp on the Don), *Barrow* (burial mound);
- religious significance, such as gods, saints, and churches, e.g. *Providence, Godshill, Axminster, St Neots, Sacramento, Santa Cruz, Thorsley* (from Thor);
- royalty, e.g. *Queensland, Victoria Falls, Carolina, Kingston, Louisiana, Maryland, Fredericksburg*;
- explorers, e.g. *America, Cookstown, Columbus, Flinders*;
- famous local people, such as presidents, politicians, tribesmen, e.g. *Delaware, Baltimore, Washington,*

Everest, Reading, London (town of Londinos – 'the bold one');
- memorable incidents or famous events, such as a battle, e.g. *Waterloo, Crimea, Blenheim, Cape Catastrophe, Anxious Bay, Manhattan* ('the place of great drunkenness'); and
- other place names, such as a famous city, or a town from an immigrant's home-land, e.g. USA *Paris, Memphis, Troy, Hertford, London*.

Many other factors have been recognized. There are the appealing names introduced by explorers as they encountered good and bad fortune on their travels (e.g. *Cape Tribulation* and *Weary Bay* in Australia). Animal names are sometimes used (e.g. *Beaver City, Buffalo*). And there are many names of a purely descriptive type, such as *North Sea, South Island*, and – perhaps the most common place name of all – the 'new town' (*Newtown, Neuville, Naples, Villanueva, Novgorod, Neustadt*, and – less obviously, because of its Phoenician origin – *Carthage*). By contrast, there seem to be few names derived from famous writers and artists: there is a distinct paucity of towns called Shakespeare, Voltaire, or Tolstoy.

Place names have an intrinsic fascination, and many specialized studies have been undertaken. But it must not be forgotten that many thousands of names have an unclear or unknown etymology, and it is this which provides a continuing motivation for place-name study, such as is carried on by the English Place-Name Society, the American Name Society, and similar bodies. These studies also relate to matters of practical import. To facilitate international communication by post, telex, and telephone, the various problems posed by linguistic place-name variation need to be anticipated. Place names can vary greatly between languages (e.g. *Munich* vs *München*) and be unrecognizable in different scripts. Names can change along with governments (p. 9). New systems of naming may need to be introduced for special purposes, such as the means of designating stellar objects (e.g. *NGC 4565, M101*). There is thus a pressing need for international cooperation in the coining and use of place names – a need that can only become more urgent as the exploration of space proceeds.

THE OLD AND THE NEW

The two faces of the moon present a marked contrast in place names. The near side reflects 2,000 years of study, with most of the prominent features being of Latin or Greek origin. The far side reflects the results of 20th-century space exploration. Though some traditional labels are used (such as *Mare* 'sea'), the majority of new names are those of Soviet and American astronauts, astronomers, and scientists.

1 Mare Tranquillitatis
2 Montes Apennini
3 Clavius
4 Lacus Somniorum
5 Cleomedes
6 Archimedes

Near side

Far side

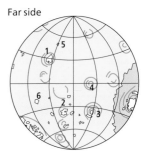

1 Mare Moscoviense
2 Gagarin
3 Apollo
4 Korolev
5 Campbell
6 Tsiolkovskiy

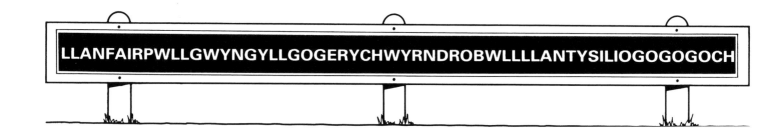

SOME COMMON PLACE-NAME ELEMENTS IN ENGLISH

Source	Language	Meaning	Common modern forms
āc	Anglo-Saxon	oak	Ac-, Aik-, Oak-, Oke-, -ock
baile	Gaelic	farm, village	Bally-, Balla-, Bal-
bearu	Anglo-Saxon	grove, wood	Barrow-, -bere, -beare, -ber
beorg	Anglo-Saxon	hill, burial-mound	Bar-, Berg-, -borough, -burgh
brycg	Anglo-Saxon	bridge	Brig-, -bridge, -brig
burh	Anglo-Saxon	fortified place	Bur-, -borough, -burgh, -bury
burna	Anglo-Saxon	stream, spring	Bourne-, Burn-, -burn, -borne
by	Old Norse	farm, village	-by
caer	Welsh	fortified place	Car-
ceaster	Latin castra	Roman town, fort	Chester-, -caster, -c(h)ester
cot	Anglo-Saxon	shelter, cottage	Coat-, Cote, -cot, -cote
cwm	Welsh	deep valley	Coombe-, Combe-, Comp-, -combe
daire	Gaelic	oak wood	Derry-, -derry, -dare
dair	Old Norse	dale, valley	Dal-, -dale
denn	Anglo-Saxon	swine pasture	-dean, -den
dūn	Anglo-Saxon	hill, down	Dun-, Down-; -down, -don, -ton
ēa	Anglo-Saxon	water, river	Ea-, -ey, Ya-, -eau
ēg	Anglo-Saxon	island	Ea-, Ey-, -ey, -y
ey	Old Norse	island	-ey, -ay
gleann	Gaelic	narrow valley	Glen-
graf	Anglo-Saxon	grove	Graf, -grave, -greave, -grove
hām	Anglo-Saxon	homestead, village	Ham-, -ham
hyrst	Anglo-Saxon	wooded hill	Hurst-, -hurst, -hirst
-ing	Anglo-Saxon	people / descendant of	-ing
lēah	Anglo-Saxon	glade, clearing	Leigh, Lee, -leigh, -ley, -le
loch	Gaelic	lake, inlet	Loch-, -loch
mere	Anglo-Saxon	lake, pool	Mer-, Mar-, -mer, -mere, -more
nes	Old Norse	cape, headland	-ness, Nas-, Nes-
pwll	Welsh	pool, anchorage	Pol-, -pool
rhos	Welsh	moorland	Ros-, Ross, -rose
stān	Anglo-Saxon	stone	Stan-, Ston-, -stone, -ston
stede	Anglo-Saxon	place, site	-sted, -stead
stoc	Anglo-Saxon	meeting place	Stoke-, Stock-, -stock, -stoke
stōw	Anglo-Saxon	meeting place	Stow(e)-, -stow(e)
strǣt	Latin strata	Roman road	Strat-, Stret-, Streat-, -street
tūn	Anglo-Saxon	enclosure, village	-ton, -town, Ton-
þorp	Old Norse	farm, village	Thorp(e), -thorpe, -throp, -trop
þveit	Old Norse	glade, clearing	Thwaite, -thwaite
wic	Anglo-Saxon	dwelling, farm	Wick-, Wig-, -wick, -wich

INTERNATIONAL BRAND NAMES

International companies are finding it increasingly important to develop brand names that can be used in a wide range of countries. To have a product with a single, universally recognized name can lead to major savings in design, production, and promotion costs – especially now that satellite television has made world advertising a reality in such contexts as major sporting events. Also, from a legal point of view, an international trade mark has a clearer status than a national one, in cases of dispute.

It is said that more time is spent deciding the name of a new product than on any other aspect of its development. The problem is not easily solved. In the European Union alone, there are over 5 million registered trade marks, and inventing a new name that does not conflict with existing practice is a highly complex and time-consuming process. Several hundred names may need to be proposed, each of which has to be checked from a linguistic, marketing, and legal viewpoint. In such fields as cars, perfumes, and soft drinks, thousands of possible names may need to be investigated to find one that is internationally acceptable and registrable.

An indication of the scope of the problem can be seen from the experience of Dunlop, who spent over two years researching a name for a new tyre, to no avail. They then launched an international competition amongst their employees, receiving over 10,000 entries. Around 30 names were selected from the enormous number submitted – but not one was found to be legally available in more than a small number of countries. After further work, a viable name was found (the tyre was called Denovo); but often companies are not so successful, ending up with a name that is unusable for legal or linguistic reasons. A word that is pronounceable in one language may be quite impossible to say in another; and there is always the danger of unfortunate connotations creeping in, because of the name overlapping with words of an irrelevant or taboo meaning.

COUNTRY ETYMOLOGIES

Argentina (Spanish) 'the silver republic'
Canaries (Latin) 'dogs' (*not* canaries)
Chile (Araucanian) 'end of the land'
Cyprus (Greek) 'copper'
Ethiopia (Greek) 'burnt face'
Jamaica (Carib) 'well watered'
Japan (Chinese) 'sun-root' (the sun rose over Japan)
Mexico (Aztec) 'war god, Mextli'
Pakistan (an acronym) P(unjab) + A(fghan tribes) + K(ashmir) + S(ind) + (Baluchis)tan

THE LONGEST PLACE NAME

A long place name would appear to be an unnecessary complication, and it is usually shortened to a more speakable and writable size. In this way, 'El Pueblo de Nuestra Señora la Reina de los Ángeles de Porciúncula' has been reduced to the more manageable 'Los Angeles'.

However, an exceptionally long place name proves to be a tourist attraction, and in 1984 a new candidate for longest place name emerged. A station on the Fairbourne narrow track railway in North Wales was deliberately renamed, so as to be longer than the previous British record-holder. The new name has 66 letters, thus beating the Anglesey village whose unofficial name of 58 letters had also been artificially constructed (in the 19th century). But the unofficial name of a 300 m hill in Southern Hawke's Bay, New Zealand, has 85 letters.

Gorsafawddacha'idraigodanheddogleddolônpenrhynareurdraethceredigion
'The Mawddach station and its dragon teeth at the Northern Penrhyn Road on the golden beach of Cardigan Bay'

Llanfairpwllgwyngyllgogerychwyrndrobwllllantysiliogogogoch
'St Mary's Church in a hollow by the white hazel, close to the rapid whirlpool, by the red cave of St Tysilio'

Taumatawhakatangihangakoauauotamatea(turipukakapikimaungahoronuku)pokaiwhenuakitanatahu
'The place where Tamatea, the man with the big knee who slid, climbed and swallowed mountains, known as Land-eater, played on his flute to his loved one'

20 · DISCOURSE AND TEXT

The traditional concern of linguistic analysis has been the construction of sentences (§16); but in recent years there has been an increasing interest in analysing the way sentences work in sequence to produce coherent stretches of language.

Two main approaches have developed. *Discourse analysis* focuses on the structure of naturally occurring spoken language, as found in such 'discourses' as conversations, interviews, commentaries, and speeches. *Text analysis* focuses on the structure of written language, as found in such 'texts' as essays, notices, road signs, and chapters. But this distinction is not clear-cut, and there have been many other uses of these labels. In particular, both 'discourse' and 'text' can be used in a much broader sense to include *all* language units with a definable communicative function, whether spoken or written. Some scholars talk about 'spoken and written discourse'; others about 'spoken and written text'. In Europe, the term *text linguistics* is often used for the study of the linguistic principles governing the structure of all forms of text.

The search for larger linguistic units and structures has been pursued by scholars from many disciplines. Linguists investigate the features of language that bind sentences when they are used in sequence. Ethnographers and sociologists study the structure of social interaction, especially as manifested in the way people enter into dialogue. Anthropologists analyse the structure of myths and folk-tales. Psychologists carry out experiments on the mental processes underlying comprehension. And further contributions have come from those concerned with artificial intelligence, rhetoric, philosophy, and style (§12).

These approaches have a common concern: they stress the need to see language as a dynamic, social, interactive phenomenon – whether between speaker and listener, or writer and reader. It is argued that meaning is conveyed not by single sentences but by more complex exchanges, in which the participants' beliefs and expectations, the knowledge they share about each other and about the world, and the situation in which they interact, play a crucial part.

CONVERSATION

Of the many types of communicative act, most study has been devoted to conversation, seen as the most fundamental and pervasive means of conducting human affairs (p. 52). These very characteristics, however, complicate any investigation. Because people interact linguistically in such a wide range of social situations, on such a variety of topics, and with such an unpredictable set of participants, it has proved very difficult to determine the extent to which conversational behaviour is systematic, and to generalize about it.

There is now no doubt that such a system exists. Conversation turns out, upon analysis, to be a highly structured activity, in which people tacitly operate with a set of basic conventions. A comparison has even been drawn with games such as chess: conversations, it seems, can be thought of as having an opening, a middle, and an end game. The participants make their moves and often seem to follow certain rules as the dialogue proceeds. But the analogy ends there. A successful conversation is not a game: it is no more than a mutually satisfying linguistic exchange. Few rules are ever stated explicitly (some exceptions are 'Don't interrupt!', and 'Look at me when I talk to you'). Furthermore, apart from in certain types of argument and debate, there are no winners.

Conversational success

For a conversation to be successful, in most social contexts, the participants need to feel they are contributing something to it and are getting something out of it. For this to happen, certain conditions must apply. Everyone must have an opportunity to speak: no one should be monopolizing or constantly interrupting. The participants need to make their roles clear, especially if there are several possibilities (e.g. 'Speaking as a mother / linguist / Catholic ...'). They need to have a sense of when to speak or stay silent; when to proffer information or hold it back; when to stay aloof or become involved. They need to develop a mutual tolerance, to allow for speaker unclarity and listener inattention: perfect expression and comprehension are rare, and the success of a dialogue largely depends on people recognizing their communicative weaknesses, through the use of rephrasing (e.g. 'Let me put that another way') and clarification (e.g. 'Are you with me?').

There is a great deal of ritual in conversation, especially at the beginning and end, and when topics change. For example, people cannot simply leave a conversation at any random point, unless they wish to be considered socially inept or ill-mannered. They have to choose their point of departure (such as the moment when a topic changes) or construct a special reason for leaving. Routines for concluding a conversation are particularly complex, and cooperation is crucial if it is not to end abruptly, or in an embarrassed silence. The parties may prepare for their departure a

CONVERSATION ANALYSIS

In recent years, the phrase 'conversation analysis' has come to be used as the name of a particular method of studying conversational structure, based on the techniques of the American sociological movement of the 1970s known as *ethnomethodology*.

The emphasis in previous sociological research had been deductive and quantitative, focusing on general questions of social structure. The new name was chosen to reflect a fresh direction of study, which would focus on the techniques (or 'methods') used by people themselves (oddly referred to as 'ethnic'), when they are actually engaged in social – and thus linguistic — interaction. The central concern was to determine how individuals experience, make sense of, and report their interactions.

In conversation analysis, the data thus consist of tape recordings of natural conversation, and their associated transcriptions. These are then systematically analysed to determine what properties govern the way in which a conversation proceeds. The approach emphasizes the need for empirical, inductive work, and in this it is sometimes contrasted with 'discourse analysis', which has often been more concerned with formal methods of analysis (such as the nature of the rules governing the structure of texts).

long way in advance, such as by looking at their watches or giving a verbal early warning. A widespread convention is for visitors to say they must leave some time before they actually intend to depart, and for the hosts to ignore the remark. The second mention then permits both parties to act.

The topic of the conversation is also an important variable. In general it should be one with which everyone feels at ease: 'safe' topics between strangers in English situations usually include the weather, pets, children, and the local context (e.g. while waiting in a room or queue); 'unsafe' topics include religious and political beliefs and problems of health. There are some arbitrary divisions: asking what someone does for a living is generally safe: asking how much they earn is not. Cultural variations can cause problems: commenting about the cost of the furniture or the taste of a meal may be acceptable in one society but not in another.

It is difficult to generalize about what is normal, polite, or antisocial in conversational practice, as there is so much cultural variation. Silence, for example, varies in status. It is an embarrassment in English conversations, unless there are special reasons (such as in moments of grief). However, in some cultures (e.g. Lapps, Danes, the Western Apache) it is quite normal for participants to become silent. Often, who speaks, and how much is spoken, depends on the social status of the participants – for example, those of lower rank may be expected to stay silent if their seniors wish to speak (p. 38). Even the basic convention of 'one person speaks at a time' may be broken. In Antigua, for example, the phenomenon of several people speaking at once during a whole conversation is a perfectly normal occurrence.

CONVERSATIONAL MAXIMS

The success of a conversation depends not only on what speakers say but on their whole approach to the interaction. People adopt a 'cooperative principle' when they communicate: they try to get along with each other by following certain conversational 'maxims' that underlie the efficient use of language. Four basic maxims have been proposed (after H. P. Grice, 1975):

- The *maxim of quality* states that speakers' contributions to a conversation ought to be true. They should not say what they believe to be false, nor should they say anything for which they lack adequate evidence.
- The *maxim of quantity* states that the contribution should be as informative as is required for the purposes of the conversation. One should say neither too little nor too much.
- The *maxim of relevance* states that contributions should clearly relate to the purpose of the exchange.
- The *maxim of manner* states that the contribution should be perspicuous – in particular, that it should be orderly and brief, avoiding obscurity and ambiguity.

Other maxims have also been proposed, such as 'Be polite', 'Behave consistently'. The principle of relevance has recently attracted most attention, as it has been proposed as a fundamental explanatory principle for a theory of human communication (D. Sperber & D. Wilson, 1986).

Listeners will normally assume that speakers are following these criteria. Speakers may of course break (or 'flout') these maxims – for example, they may lie, be sarcastic, try to be different, or clever – but conversation proceeds on the assumption that they are not doing so. Listeners may then draw inferences from what speakers *have* said (the literal meaning of the utterance) concerning what they have *not* said (the implications, or 'implicatures' of the utterance). For example,

A: I need a drink.   B: Try The Bell.

If B is adhering to the cooperative principle, several implicatures arise out of this dialogue: for example, The Bell must be a place that sells drinks; it must be open (as far as B knows); it must be nearby. If B is not being cooperative (e.g. if he knows that The Bell is closed, or is the name of a greengrocer's), he is flouting the maxims of quality and relevance.

Deliberate flouting of this kind is uncommon, of course, and only occurs in such special cases as sarcasm, joking, or deliberate unpleasantness. More likely is the inadvertent flouting of conversational maxims – as would happen if B genuinely did not know that The Bell was closed, and accidentally sent A on a wild goose chase. In everyday conversation, misunderstandings often take place as speakers make assumptions about what their listeners know, or need to know, that turn out to be wrong. At such points, the conversation can break down and may need to be 'repaired', with the participants questioning, clarifying, and cross-checking. The repairs are quickly made in the following extract, through the use of such pointers as 'I told you' and 'sorry'.

A: Got the time?   B: No, I told you, I lost my watch.   A: Oh, sorry, I forgot.

But it is quite common for participants not to realize that there has been a breakdown, and to continue conversing at cross purposes.

Bob Newhart
Newhart's comedy routines often rely on the audience's awareness of discourse conventions. His 'driving instructor' sketch, for example, gives us only half of the conversation, from the instructor's viewpoint, leaving the responses of the learner driver to our imagination. Joyce Grenfell's 'teaching young children' sketches were based on the same principle.

GEORGE – DON'T DO THAT

This extract from one of Joyce Grenfell's nursery school monologues shows how the reader can survive using just one side of a dialogue. The task is made easier here by the fact that it is a standard teaching technique to reinforce what a young child has just said by repeating or expanding it (as do parents: see p. 233).

Now then, let's all put on our Thinking Caps, shall we, and think what flowers we are going to choose to be.
Lavinia? – What flower are you?
A bluebell. Good.
Peggy?
A red rose. That's nice.
Neville?
A *wild* rose. Well done, Neville!

Sidney? – Sidney, pay attention, dear, and don't pummel Rosemary – what flower are you going to choose to be?
A *horse* isn't a flower, Sidney.
(From J. Grenfell, 1977, p. 30.)

Joyce Grenfell (1910–79)

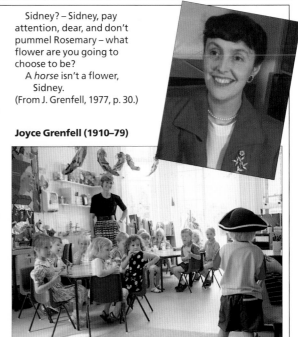

CONVERSATIONAL TURNS

Probably the most widely recognized conversational convention is that people take turns to speak. But how do people know when it is their turn? Some rules must be present, otherwise conversations would be continually breaking down into a disorganized jumble of interruptions and simultaneous talk. In many formal situations, such as committee meetings and debates, there are often explicit markers showing that a speaker is about to yield the floor, and indicating who should speak next ('I think Mr Smith will know the answer to that question'). This can happen in informal situations too ('What do you think, Mary?'), but there the turn-taking cues are usually more subtle.

People do not simply stop talking when they are ready to yield the floor. They usually signal some way in advance that they are about to conclude. The clues may be semantic ('So anyway, ...', 'Last but not least ...'); but more commonly the speech itself can be modified to show that a turn is about to end – typically, by lowering its pitch, loudness, or speed. Body movements and patterns of eye contact are especially important. While speaking, we look at and away from our listener in about equal proportions; but as we approach the end of a turn, we look at the listener more steadily. Similarly, when talking to a group of people, we often look more steadily at a particular person, to indicate that in our view this should be the next speaker.

Listeners are not passive in all of this. Here too there are several ways of signalling that someone wants to talk next. Most obviously, the first person in a group actually to start speaking, after the completion of a turn, will usually be allowed to hold the floor. More subtly, we can signal that we want to speak next by an observable increase in body tension – by leaning forward, or producing an audible intake of breath. Less subtly, we can simply interrupt – a strategy which may be tolerated, if the purpose is to clarify what the speaker is saying, but which more usually leads to social sanctions.

EXCHANGES

Because conversational discourse varies so much in length and complexity, analysis generally begins by breaking an interaction down into the smallest possible units, then examining the way these units are used in sequences. The units have been called 'exchanges' or 'interchanges', and in their minimal form consist simply of an initiating utterance (I) followed by a response utterance (R), as in:

I: What's the time?
R: Two o'clock.

Two-part exchanges (sometimes called 'adjacency pairs') are commonplace, being used in such contexts as questioning / answering, informing / acknowledging, and complaining / excusing. Three-part exchanges are also important, where the response is followed by an element of feedback (F). Such reactions are especially found in teaching situations:

TEACHER: Where were the arrows kept? (I)
PUPIL: In a special kind of box. (R)
TEACHER: Yes, that's right, in a box. (F)

What is of particular interest is to work out the constraints that apply to sequences of this kind. The teacher–feedback sequence would be inappropriate in many everyday situations:

A: Did you have a good journey?
B: Apart from a jam at Northampton.
A: *Yes, that's right, a jam at Northampton.

Unacceptable sequences are easy to invent:

A: Where do you keep the jam?
B: *It's raining again.

On the other hand, with ingenuity it is often possible to imagine situations where such a sequence could occur (e.g. if B were staring out of the window at the time). And discourse analysts are always on the lookout for unexpected, but perfectly acceptable, sequences in context, such as:

A: Goodbye.
B: Hello.

(used, for example, as A is leaving an office, passing B on the way in). Many jokes, too, break discourse rules as the source of their effect:

A: Yes, I can.
B: Can you see into the future?

MISUNDERSTANDINGS

An important aim of discourse analysis is to find out why conversations are not always successful. Misunderstanding and mutual recrimination is unfortunately fairly common. Participants often operate with different rules and expectations about the way in which the conversation should proceed – something that is particularly evident when people of different cultural backgrounds interact. But even within a culture, different 'rules of interpretation' may exist.

It has been suggested, for example, that there are different rules governing the way in which men and women participate in a conversation (pp. 21, 120). A common source of misunderstanding is the way both parties use head nods and *mhm* noises while the other is speaking – something that women do much more frequently than men. Some analysts have suggested that the two sexes mean different things by this behaviour. When a woman does it, she is simply indicating that she is listening, and encouraging the speaker to continue, but the male interprets it to mean that she is agreeing with everything he is saying. By contrast, when a man does it, he is signalling that he does not necessarily agree, whereas the woman interprets it to mean that he is not always listening. Such interpretations are plausible, it is argued, because they explain two of the most widely reported reactions from participants in cross-sex conversations – the male reaction of 'It's impossible to say what a woman really thinks', and the female reaction of 'You never listen to a word I say.' (After D. N. Maltz & R. A. Borker, 1982.)

CONVERSATION MANOEUVRES

Conversational turn-taking is often marked by clear signals of direction

Openings
Guess what ...
Sorry to trouble you ...
Lovely day!
Got a match?

Can I help you?
Good morning.
Excuse me ...
Did you hear the one about ...
Can you spare a minute?
Halt! Who goes there?
But not: *How much do you earn?

Ongoing checks
By the speaker:
Do you see?

Can you guess what he said?
Are you with me?
Do I make myself clear?
Don't you think?
Let me put it another way ...
Don't get me wrong ...
What I'm trying to say is ...
By the listener:
You mean ...
Have I got you right?
Mhm.
I don't get you.

Let's get that straight ...

Changing topic
Introducing a new topic:
That reminds me ...
Incidentally ...
That's a good question.
By the way ...
Speaking of John ...
Where was I?
Concluding a topic:
So it goes.

That's life.
Makes you think, doesn't it.
Let's wait and see.

Ending
Sorry, but I have to go now.
Nice talking to you.
Well, must get back to work.
Gosh, is that the time?
I mustn't keep you.
Gotta run. (*especially US*)

TEXTUAL STRUCTURE

To call a sequence of sentences a 'text' is to imply that the sentences display some kind of mutual dependence; they are not occurring at random. Sometimes the internal structure of a text is immediately apparent, as in the headings of a restaurant menu; sometimes it has to be carefully demonstrated, as in the network of relationships that enter into a literary work. In all cases, the task of textual analysis is to identify the linguistic features that cause the sentence sequence to 'cohere' – something that happens whenever the interpretation of one feature is dependent upon another elsewhere in the sequence. The ties that bind a text together are often referred to under the heading of *cohesion* (after M. A. K. Halliday & R. Hasan, 1976). Several types of cohesive factor have been recognized:

• *Conjunctive relations* What is about to be said is explicitly related to what has been said before, through such notions as contrast, result, and time:

I left early. *However,* Jean stayed till the end.

Lastly, there's the question of cost.

• *Coreference* Features that cannot be semantically interpreted without referring to some other feature in the text. Two types of relationship are recognized: *anaphoric* relations look backwards for their interpretation, and *cataphoric* relations look forwards:

Several people approached. They seemed angry.

Listen to this: *John's getting married.*

• *Substitution* One feature replaces a previous expression:

I've got a pencil. Do you have *one*?

Will we get there on time? I think *so*.

• *Ellipsis* A piece of structure is omitted, and can be recovered only from the preceding discourse:

Where *did you see the car*? ∧ In the street.

• *Repeated forms* An expression is repeated in whole or in part:

Canon Brown arrived. Canon Brown was cross.

• *Lexical relationships* One lexical item enters into a structural relationship with another (p. 105):

The *flowers* were lovely. She liked the *tulips* best.

• *Comparison* A compared expression is presupposed in the previous discourse:

That house was *bad*. This one's far *worse*.

Cohesive links go a long way towards explaining how the sentences of a text hang together, but they do not tell the whole story. It is possible to invent a sentence sequence that is highly cohesive but nonetheless incoherent (after N. E. Enkvist, 1978, p. 110):

> A week has seven *days*. Every *day* I feed my *cat*. *Cats* have four legs. *The cat* is on the *mat. Mat* has three letters.

A text plainly has to be *coherent* as well as cohesive, in that the concepts and relationships expressed should be relevant to each other, thus enabling us to make plausible inferences about the underlying meaning.

TWO WAYS OF DEMONSTRATING COHESION

Paragraphs are often highly cohesive entities. The cohesive ties can stand out very clearly if the sentences are shuffled into a random order. It may even be possible to reconstitute the original sequence solely by considering the nature of these ties, as in the following case:
1. However, nobody had seen one for months.
2. He thought he saw a shape in the bushes.
3. Mary had told him about the foxes.
4. John looked out of the window.
5. Could it be a fox?
(The original sequence was 4,2,5,3,1.)

We can use graphological devices to indicate the patterns of cohesion within a text. Here is the closing paragraph of James Joyce's short story 'A Painful Case'. The sequence of pronouns, the anaphoric definite articles, and the repeated phrases are the main cohesive features between the clauses and sentences. Several of course refer back to previous parts of the story, thus making this paragraph, out of context, impossible to understand.

He turned back the way he had come, the **rhythm** of the engine pounding in his ears. He began to doubt the reality of what memory told him. He halted under a tree and allowed **the rhythm** to die away. He could not feel her near him in the DARKNESS nor her *voice* touch his ear. He waited for some minutes *listening*. He could *hear* **NOTHING**: the NIGHT was **perfectly silent**. He *listened* again: **perfectly silent**. He felt that he was **ALONE**.

MACROSTRUCTURES

Not all textual analysis starts with small units and works from the 'bottom up' (p. 71); some approaches aim to make very general statements about the macrostructure of a text. In psycholinguistics, for example, attempts have been made to analyse narratives into schematic outlines that represent the elements in a story that readers remember. These schemata have been called 'story-grammars' (though this is an unusually broad sense of the term 'grammar', cf §16).

In one such approach (after P. W. Thorndyke, 1977), simple narratives are analysed into four components: *setting, theme, plot,* and *resolution.* The setting has three components: the *characters*, a *location*, and a *time*. The theme consists of an *event* and a *goal*. The plot consists of various *episodes*, each with its own *goal* and *outcome*. Using distinctions of this kind, simple stories are analysed into these components, to see whether the same kinds of structure can be found in each (p. 79). Certain similarities do quickly emerge; but when complex narratives are studied, it proves difficult to devise more detailed categories that are capable of generalization, and analysis becomes increasingly arbitrary.

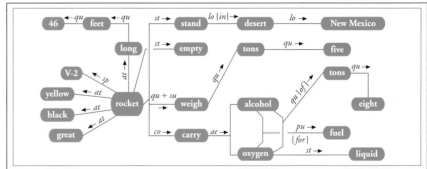

Conceptual structure One way of representing the conceptual structure of a text (after R. de Beaugrande & W. Dressler, 1981, p. 100). This 'transition network' summarizes the following paragraph:

A great black and yellow V-2 rocket 46 feet long stood in a New Mexico desert. Empty, it weighed five tons. For fuel it carried eight tons of alcohol and liquid oxygen.

The abbreviations identify the types of semantic links which relate the concepts (following the direction of the arrows):

ae	affected entity
at	attribute of
co	containment of
lo	location of
pu	purpose of
qu	quantity of
sp	specification of
st	state of
su	substance of

Pragmatics studies the factors that govern our choice of language in social interaction and the effects of our choice on others. In theory, we can say anything we like. In practice, we follow a large number of social rules (most of them unconsciously) that constrain the way we speak. There is no law that says we must not tell jokes during a funeral, but it is generally 'not done'. Less obviously, there are norms of formality and politeness that we have intuitively assimilated, and that we follow when talking to people who are older, of the opposite sex, and so on. Writing and signing behaviour are constrained in similar ways.

Pragmatic factors always influence our selection of sounds, grammatical constructions, and vocabulary from the resources of the language. Some of the constraints are taught to us at a very early age – in British English, for example, the importance of saying *please* and *thank you*, or (in some families) of not referring to an adult female in her presence as *she* (p. 248). In many languages, pragmatic distinctions of formality, politeness, and intimacy are spread throughout the grammatical, lexical, and phonological systems, ultimately reflecting matters of social class, status, and role (§10, p. 99). A well-studied example is the pronoun system, which frequently presents distinctions that convey pragmatic force – such as the choice between *tu* and *vous* in French.

Languages differ greatly in these respects. Politeness expressions, for instance, may vary in frequency and meaning. Many European languages do not use their word for *please* as frequently as English does; and the function and force of *thank you* may also alter (e.g. following the question 'Would you like some more cake?', English *thank you* means 'yes', whereas French *merci* would mean 'no'). Conventions of greeting, leave-taking, and dining also differ greatly from language to language. In some countries it is polite to remark to a host that we are enjoying the food; in others it is polite to stay silent. On one occasion, at a dinner in an Arabic community, the present author made the mistake of remarking on the excellence of the food before him. The host immediately apologized, and arranged for what was there to be replaced!

Pragmatic errors break no rules of phonology, syntax, or semantics. The elements of *How's tricks, your majesty?* will all be found in English language textbooks and dictionaries, but for most of us the sequence is not permissible from a pragmatic viewpoint. Pragmatics has therefore to be seen as separate from the 'levels' of language represented in linguistic models of analysis (§13). It is not a 'part' of language structure, but its

domain is so closely bound up with structural matters that it cannot be ignored in this section of the encyclopedia.

THE IDENTITY OF PRAGMATICS

Pragmatics is not at present a coherent field of study. A large number of factors govern our choice of language in social interaction, and it is not yet clear what they all are, how they are best interrelated, and how best to distinguish them from other recognized areas of linguistic enquiry. There are several main areas of overlap.

Semantics (§17) Pragmatics and semantics both take into account such notions as the intentions of the speaker, the effects of an utterance on listeners, the implications that follow from expressing something in a certain way, and the knowledge, beliefs, and presuppositions about the world upon which speakers and listeners rely when they interact.

Stylistics (§12) *and sociolinguistics* (§§10, 63) These fields overlap with pragmatics in their study of the social relationships which exist between participants, and of the way extralinguistic setting, activity, and subject-matter can constrain the choice of linguistic features and varieties.

Psycholinguistics (§§7, 38) Pragmatics and psycholinguistics both investigate the psychological states and abilities of the participants that will have a major effect upon their performance – such factors as attention, memory, and personality.

Discourse analysis (§20) Both discourse analysis and pragmatics are centrally concerned with the analysis of conversation, and share several of the philosophical and linguistic notions that have been developed to handle this topic (such as the way information is distributed within a sentence, deictic forms (p. 106), or the notion of conversational 'maxims' (p. 117)).

As a result of these overlapping areas of interest, several conflicting definitions of the scope of pragmatics have arisen. One approach focuses on the factors formally encoded in the structure of a language (honorific forms, *tu / vous* choice, and so on). Another relates it to a particular view of semantics: here, pragmatics is seen as the study of all aspects of meaning other than those involved in the analysis of sentences in terms of truth conditions (p. 107). Other approaches adopt a much broader perspective. The broadest sees pragmatics as the study of the principles and practice underlying *all* interactive linguistic performance – this including all aspects of language usage, understanding, and appro-

UNDERSTANDING MISUNDERSTANDING

The 1990s has seen the growth of a domain which can perhaps best be labelled 'applied pragmatics' – the use of a pragmatic perspective to analyse situations in which a conversation has not been successful, and to suggest solutions (p. 118). The general interest of this approach has been well illustrated by the success of Deborah Tannen's *That's Not What I Meant!* (1986) and *You Just Don't Understand* (1990), which focus on the different strategies and expectations people use when they try to talk to each other. There are a surprising number of everyday notions which can be illuminated by this kind of analysis, such as 'nagging', 'accusing', and 'being at cross-purposes'.

Here is one of Tannen's anecdotes and part of her associated commentary:
Loraine frequently compliments Sidney and thanks him for doing things such as cleaning up the kitchen and doing the laundry. Instead of appreciating the praise, Sidney resents it. 'It makes me feel like you're demanding that I do it all the time', he explains. ...

'In all these examples, men complained that their independence and freedom were being encroached on. Their early warning system is geared to detect signs that they are being told what to do ... Such comments surprise and puzzle women, whose early warning systems are geared to detect a different menace. ... If a man struggles to be strong, a woman struggles to keep the community strong.'

Applied pragmatics is not limited to family arguments. The same issues arise in the attempt to achieve successful communication in any setting at any level. A course in problems of business communication, advertising itself with the slogan 'Are you getting through to your customer?' is, in effect, an exercise in applied pragmatics.

priateness. Textbooks on pragmatics to date, accordingly, present a diversity of subject matter, and a range of partially conflicting orientations and methodologies, which proponents of the subject have yet to resolve. However, if we take diversity of opinion to be a sign of healthy growth in a subject, it must be said that few other areas of language study have such a promising future.

SPEECH ACTS

The British philosopher J. L. Austin (1911–60) was the first to draw attention to the many functions performed by utterances as part of interpersonal communication. In particular, he pointed out that many utterances do not communicate information, but are equivalent to actions. When someone says 'I apologize ...', 'I promise ...', 'I will' (at a wedding), or 'I name this ship ...', the utterance immediately conveys a new psychological or social reality. An apology takes place when someone apologizes, and not before. A ship is named only when the act of naming is complete. In such cases, to say is to perform. Austin thus called these utterances *performatives*, seeing them as very different from statements that convey information (*constatives*). In particular, performatives are not true or false. If A says 'I name this ship ...', B cannot then say 'That's not true'!

In speech act analysis, we study the effect of utterances on the behaviour of speaker and hearer, using a threefold distinction. First, we recognize the bare fact that a communicative act takes place: the *locutionary* act. Secondly, we look at the act that is performed as a result of the speaker making an utterance – the cases where 'saying = doing', such as betting, promising, welcoming, and warning: these, known as *illocutionary* acts, are the core of any theory of speech acts. Thirdly, we look at the particular effect the speaker's utterance has on the listener, who may feel amused, persuaded, warned, etc., as a consequence: the bringing about of such effects is known as a *perlocutionary* act. It is important to appreciate that the illocutionary force of an utterance and its perlocutionary effect may not coincide. If I warn you against a particular course of action, you may or may not heed my warning.

There are thousands of possible illocutionary acts, and several attempts have been made to classify them into a small number of types. Such classifications are difficult, because verb meanings are often not easy to distinguish, and speakers' intentions are not always clear. One influential approach sets up five basic types (after J. R. Searle, 1976):

- *Representatives* The speaker is committed, in varying degrees, to the truth of a proposition, e.g. *affirm, believe, conclude, deny, report.*
- *Directives* The speaker tries to get the hearer to do something, e.g. *ask, challenge, command, insist, request.*

- *Commissives* The speaker is committed, in varying degrees, to a certain course of action, e.g. *guarantee, pledge, promise, swear, vow.*
- *Expressives* The speaker expresses an attitude about a state of affairs, e.g. *apologize, deplore, congratulate, thank, welcome.*
- *Declarations* The speaker alters the external status or condition of an object or situation solely by making the utterance, e.g. *I resign, I baptize, You're fired, War is hereby declared.*

FELICITY CONDITIONS

Speech acts are successful only if they satisfy several criteria, known as 'felicity conditions'. For example, the 'preparatory' conditions have to be right: the person performing the speech act has to have the authority to do so. This is hardly an issue with such verbs as *apologize, promise,* or *thank,* but it is important constraint on the use of such verbs as *fine, baptize, arrest,* and *declare war,* where only certain people are qualified to use these utterances. Then, the speech act has to be executed in the correct manner: in certain cases there is a procedure to be followed exactly and completely (e.g. *baptizing*); in others, certain expectations have to be met (e.g. one can only *welcome* with a pleasant demeanour). And, as a third example, 'sincerity' conditions have to be present: the speech act must be performed in a sincere manner. Verbs such as *apologize, guarantee,* and *vow* are effective only if speakers mean what they say; *believe* and *affirm* are valid only if the speakers are not lying.

Ordinary people automatically accept these conditions when they communicate, and they depart from them only for very special reasons. For example, the request *Will you shut the door?* is appropriate only if (a) the door is open, (b) the speaker has a reason for asking, and (c) the hearer is in a position to perform the action. If any of these conditions does not obtain, then a special interpretation of the speech act has to apply. It may be intended as a joke, or as a piece of sarcasm. Alternatively, of course, there may be doubt about the speaker's visual acuity, or even sanity!

INDIRECT SPEECH ACTS

Some speech acts directly address a listener, but the majority of acts in everyday conversation are indirect. For example, there are a very large number of ways of asking someone to perform an action. The most direct way is to use the imperative construction (*Shut the door*), but it is easy to sense that this would be inappropriate in many everyday situations – too abrupt or rude, perhaps. Alternatives stress such factors as the hearer's ability or desire to perform the action, or the speaker's reasons for having the action done. These include the following:
  I'd be grateful if you'd shut the door.
  Could you shut the door?
  Would you mind shutting the door?
  It'd help to have the door shut.
  It's getting cold in here.
  Shall we keep out the draught?
  Now, Jane, what have you forgotten to do?
  Brrr!
Any of these could, in the right situation, function as a request for action, despite the fact that none has the clear form of an imperative. But of course, it is always open to the hearer to misunderstand an indirect request – either accidentally or deliberately.
Teacher: Johnny, there's some chalk on the floor.
Johnny: Yes, there is, sir.
Teacher: Well, pick it up, then!

Each part of this notice conveys the directive illocutionary force intended by the writer. The perlocutionary effect, however, is not as anticipated!

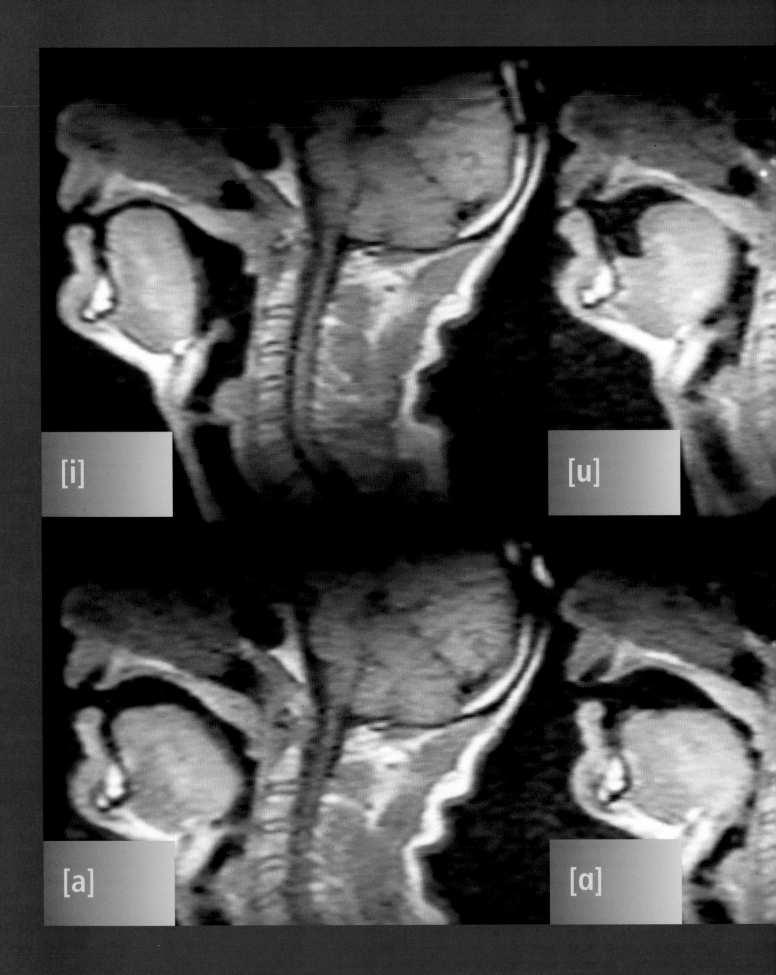

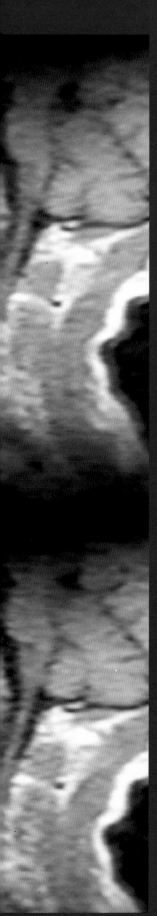

The medium of language: speaking and listening

PART IV

The core of language study is the analysis of meaning and its grammatical expression – matters that are treated under the heading of 'The Structure of Language' in Part III. These properties of language underlie all forms of linguistic communication, and must be recognized whether we choose to communicate through the medium of speech, writing, signing, or any other. At the same time, each medium has its own distinctive properties that require independent study. These are the subject matter of Parts IV–VI.

We begin with the study of sound, which is the most universal and natural medium for the transmission and reception of language. Writing holds a less central place, in the history of both the individual and the human species. No community has ever been found to lack spoken language, but only a minority of languages have ever been written down. Likewise, the vast majority of human beings learn to speak (for those who do not, see Part VIII); but it is only in recent years that some of these people have learned to write.

Part IV provides an account of the chief factors involved in the production, transmission, and reception of speech. It begins with a description of the aspects of human anatomy and physiology involved in speech production – the vocal organs

(§22). This is followed by an account of the acoustic properties of speech – the nature of the sound waves that are set in motion as a result of vocal organ activity (§23). Some of the main instruments used in the study of speech physiology and acoustics are reviewed in §24. The process of speech reception is then introduced (§25), with reference to both the mechanism of hearing and the little-understood task of speech perception. And all three stages – production, transmission, and reception – are brought together, in order to attack the problem of how to promote speech interaction with machines (§26).

Phonetics, the science of speech sounds, provides the framework for §27, which reviews the whole range of sounds that the vocal tract can produce, and presents the symbols used in making a phonetic transcription. This leads naturally to a discussion of the kinds of sound most commonly used in the world's languages, and of the way sounds interrelate as part of a language system (§28). The main notions in the subject of phonology, which studies the properties of sound systems, are introduced during this section. Part IV then concludes with an account of such effects as intonation, rhythm, and tones of voice – the 'suprasegmental' aspects of spoken language (§29) – and a discussion of sound symbolism (§30).

An MRI (magnetic resonance image) of a speaker pronouncing [i], [u], [a], and [ɑ] vowels.

THE VOCAL ORGANS

The vocal organs are those parts of the body that are involved in the production of speech. The name 'vocal organs' is not entirely appropriate, as their main function is in fulfilling the basic biological needs of breathing and eating. But there seems to have been considerable evolutionary development in their form, which enables them to function efficiently for the act of speech (§49).

Perhaps the most striking feature of any diagram of the vocal organs is the amount of the body involved in speech. It is not simply the mouth and throat; we have to show the involvement of the *lungs*, the *trachea* (or windpipe) and the *nose*. Inside the mouth, we have to distinguish the *tongue*, and the various parts of the *palate*. Inside the throat, we need to distinguish the upper part, or *pharynx*, from the lower part, or *larynx*, which contains the *vocal folds* – commonly called the vocal 'cords'. The pharynx, mouth, and nose form a system of hollow areas, or *cavities*, known as the *vocal tract* (though this term sometimes includes larynx and lungs as well). When we move the organs in the vocal tract, we alter its shape, and it is this which enables the many different sounds of spoken language to be produced.

THE LUNGS

Before any sound can be produced at all, there has to be a source of energy (p. 132). In speech, the energy takes the form of a stream of air, which has in normal circumstances been set in motion by the lungs.

The lungs are found in a cavity in the chest (or *thorax*) known as the *thoracic cavity*. This cavity is bounded at the back by the spinal column, at the front by the ribs and breastbone (or *sternum*), and at the bottom by the dome-shaped muscle known as the *diaphragm*, which separates the lungs from the lower cavities of the abdomen. The structure surrounding the thoracic cavity is referred to as the thoracic *cage*. The act of respiration takes place through the action of the thoracic cage, which enables the lungs to act as a kind of bellows, allowing air to flow inwards and outwards.

In order to speak, we must first inhale. Signals from the nerve centre in the brain stem (where respiration is controlled) cause the muscles of the thoracic cage to contract: in particular, the muscles between the ribs (the *intercostal* muscles) cause the ribs to move upwards and outwards, and the diaphragm to move

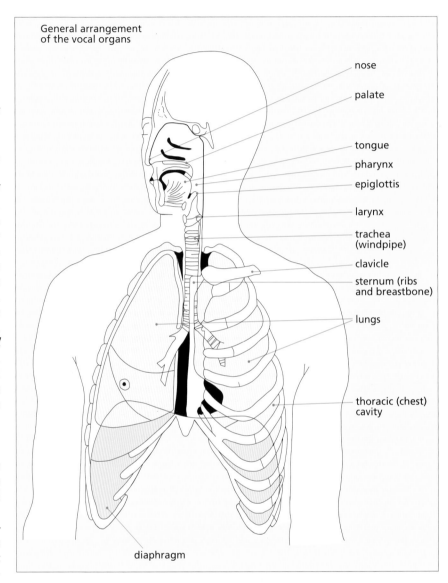

General arrangement
of the vocal organs

nose

palate

tongue

pharynx

epiglottis

larynx

trachea
(windpipe)

clavicle

sternum (ribs
and breastbone)

lungs

thoracic (chest)
cavity

diaphragm

downwards. The result is to expand the chest, and thus the lungs, temporarily causing the air pressure in the lungs to be reduced. Air immediately flows into the lungs, in order to equalize the pressure with that of the atmosphere outside the body.

We then exhale. We contract the chest, and thus the lungs, by lowering the ribs and raising the diaphragm, forcing the air out. But we never exhale all the air. Only about a quarter of the air in the lungs is used while we are engaged in normal conversation – though the amount increases to some extent if our speech becomes loud or effortful, as in shouting, acting, public speaking, or producing a 'stage whisper'.

USING THE LUNGS FOR SPEECH

Lung air is often referred to as *pulmonic* air. When pulmonic air flows outwards, it is said to be *egressive*. The vast majority of speech sounds are made using pulmonic egressive air.

It is also possible – though not usual – to speak while the air stream is flowing inwards to the lungs (pulmonic *ingressive* air). We occasionally hear this air stream used in a language when someone is trying to talk while laughing or crying, or when out of breath. Words such as *yes* and *no* are sometimes said with an ingressive air stream, when we use a 'routine' tone of voice to acknowledge what someone is saying. An alternate use of egressive and ingressive air streams is sometimes heard when people are counting rapidly, 'under their breath'. But ingressive speech is of poor quality, muffled, and croaky, and many people find it unpleasant to listen to. It is never put to routine use in everyday speech.

Spirometer (Right) The spirometer measures the volume of air produced by the lungs.

Pneumotachograph (Below) Inside the face mask of this instrument there are separate meters for monitoring the volume of air flow from the mouth and the nose.

The respiratory cycle

The sequence of events involved when we breathe in (*inspiration*) and out (*expiration*) is known as the *respiratory cycle*. Normally, the two halves of this cycle are nearly equal in duration; but when we speak, the pattern changes to one of very rapid inhalation and very slow exhalation. The rate at which we breathe also changes. When we are silent and at rest, our average rate is 12 breaths a minute, so the time we take to inhale and exhale is about $2\frac{1}{2}$ seconds each. During speech, we cut down the time for inhaling to as little as a quarter of a second, and we regularly extend the time for exhaling to 5 or 10 seconds – even 20 seconds is possible, depending on the speaker's voice control, emotional state, and other such factors. This altered pattern of breathing enables our exhalations to 'carry' much larger amounts of speech than would otherwise be the case. In everyday conversation, it is quite normal to produce from 250 to 300 syllables in a minute.

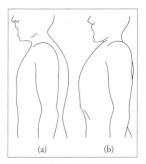

RIGHT AND WRONG WAYS TO BREATHE

Techniques of breath control form an essential part of any training programme to improve the use of the voice – as in singing, drama, or speech therapy (§46). The most efficient breathing requires a rapid inspiration and a measured expiration that exactly meets the needs of the voice. The careful control of rib and diaphragm movement is the main feature of the *intercostal diaphragmatic* method of breathing, which specialists consider to be the most efficient for most purposes. It contrasts with several less efficient methods, such as the tense, nervous form of breathing in the upper part of the chest, known as *clavicular* breathing. If it is habitually used during speech, the excessive muscular tension required to maintain this breathing pattern can strain the vocal folds, causing hoarseness and other abnormal voice qualities. The diagrams above show correct (a) and incorrect (b) body positions for singing.

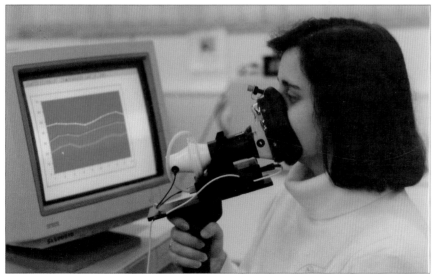

An 18th-century plethysmograph Plethysmography is a technique for determining the size of a part of the body, and it can be used to investigate the lung volume. This plethysmograph was simply a barrel with an airtight collar at the neck. The act of breathing alters the subject's body volume, which in turn alters the amount of air in the barrel. A small pipe at the top of the barrel permits the passage of air. Monitoring the changes in airflow through the pipe thus provides a measure of the changes in lung volume. A development of the same technique is still used today.

SPEAKING WITHOUT THE LUNGS

The vowels and consonants of English, as of most languages, are all made using pulmonic egressive air. But there are several other types of speech sound which do not use an air-stream from the lungs, and these are encountered in many languages of the world.

CLICKS

One of the most distinctive types of non-pulmonic sound is the click. Click sounds are sharp, suction noises, made by the tongue or lips. For example, the noise we write as *tut tut* (or *tsk tsk*) is a pair of click sounds, made by the tongue against the top teeth. While making a click sound, it is possible to breathe in and out, quite independently, showing that the lungs are not involved in their production.

In European languages, isolated click sounds are often heard as meaningful noises, but they are not part of their system of vowels and consonants (§28). The *tut tut* click, for example, expresses disapproval in English, but the sound is not used as part of a word, in the way that /t/ and /p/ are. However, in many other languages, clicks are used as consonants. Most well known are some of the languages of southern Africa, often referred to as 'click languages'. !Xū is one such language, with as many as 48 clicks (p. 170). The Khoisan languages, which include the languages of the Khoikhoin (Hottentot) and San (Bushmen) tribes, have the most complex click systems, using many different places of articulation in the mouth, and involving the simultaneous use of other sounds made in the throat or nose.

GLOTTALIC SOUNDS

The space behind the Adam's apple, between the vocal folds, is known as the *glottis*. We can use the glottis to start an air-stream moving, and several languages make use of sounds based on this principle, referred to as the *glottalic* air-stream mechanism. When the glottis makes the air move inwards, the sounds are called *implosives*. An implosive consonant is a glottalic ingressive sound. When the air is made to move outwards, the sounds are called *ejectives*. An ejective consonant is a glottalic egressive sound.

Implosive consonants occur in many languages, but are particularly common in American Indian and African languages (such as Shona and Ijo). Ejective consonants are widely used in the languages of the Caucasian family, and also in many American Indian and African languages (such as Hausa and Amharic). They may even be heard in certain accents and styles of English. Speakers from the north of England quite often use them at the ends of words, in place of the usual pulmonically produced [p], [t], or [k]. And regardless of the accent we use, if we speak in a tense, clipped manner, these sounds will often be 'spat' out at the end of a word.

Miriam Makeba Her recordings of 'click songs' were popular in the 1960s. A native speaker of Xhosa, she used words containing click consonants in her songs, achieving notable effects by articulating them with great resonance.

HOW CLICK SOUNDS ARE MADE

A click sound is produced solely in the mouth. The air flow is controlled by movements which take place against the back part of the roof of the mouth, known as the *velum* (p. 130). Because of this, click sounds are described as using a *velaric* air-stream mechanism.

Tut-tut is an example of a double *dental* click (phonetic symbol [ǀ]), because the teeth have been involved in its production. A single dental click is widely used as a noise expressing negation throughout the Near East. *Lateral* clicks (phonetic symbol [ǁ]) are made with the sides of the tongue, and are heard in the noises of encouragement to horses or other animals (including the human). A click made against the alveolar ridge is symbolized by [!]. A click sound made at the lips would be known as a *bilabial* click – made with the lips puckered, it is often used as a 'kiss at a distance'. There are six clicks recognized on the IPA chart (p. 161).

1. The back of the tongue is raised so that it presses against the velum. At the same time, a closure is made at the front of the mouth, using the tongue or lips. This forms a cavity in the mouth, cut off from the air outside.

2. The body of the tongue is moved slightly downwards and backwards, so as to form a partial vacuum inside the cavity.

3. When the tongue is suddenly lowered, or the lips opened, air rushes in from outside, to produce the sound we hear as a click.

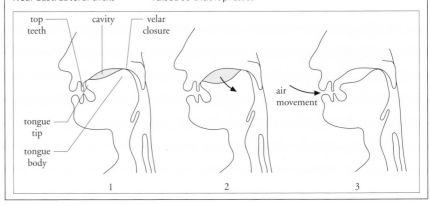

HOW EJECTIVE SOUNDS ARE MADE

The essential feature of an ejective sound is that the glottis is tightly closed, so that no air can get to or from the lungs. We are, in effect, 'holding our breath' for a brief moment.

1. At the same time as the glottis closes, we make ready to articulate a consonant sound – for [p'] we close the lips, for [t'] or [k'] we raise the tongue. A body of air is thus trapped in the cavity between the glottis

and the closure higher up the vocal tract.

2. We contract some of the muscles of the larynx, so as to make the glottis move in an upwards direction – a movement which compresses the air in the cavity.

3. The increased pressure is suddenly released by removing the closure in the mouth – opening the lips, or lowering the tongue – and the sound 'pops' out.

4. The glottis opens, and lung air rushes up the vocal tract, to act as a source of power for the next speech sound.

The whole process, from initial glottal closure to final glottal release takes on average only a twentieth of a second, though there is a great deal of timing variation among languages. There are six ejectives recognized on the IPA chart (p. 161).

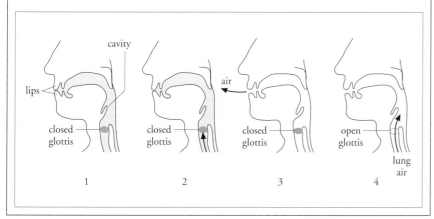

HOW IMPLOSIVE SOUNDS ARE MADE

Implosive sounds use a process that is to a large extent the reverse of that used for ejectives.

1. We make a closure in the vocal tract – for [ɓ] at the lips, for [ɗ] or [ɠ] with the tongue. Note the special phonetic symbols, to distinguish these sounds from pulmonic [b], [d], and [g].
2. The muscles of the larynx

are used to partially close the glottis, and move it in a downwards direction, so that air pressure in the cavity above the glottis is somewhat reduced. The glottis is not closed completely (unlike ejective sounds), so that a certain amount of lung air is still able to move between the vocal folds, causing them to vibrate.
3. When we open the lips, or lower the tongue, we

release the vocal tract closure, and outside air is sucked into the mouth. This mixes with the lung air in the glottis, to produce a sound which has a muffled, hollow resonance. There are ten implosives recognized on the IPA chart (p. 161).

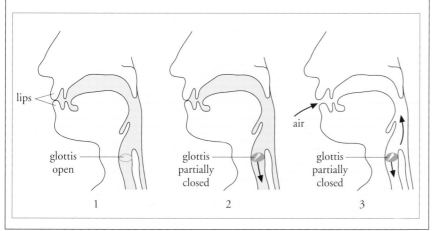

OTHER TYPES OF SOUND

The vocal tract can produce many other kinds of sound, but they do not seem to be used with any regularity in spoken language. Scraping the teeth together, flapping the tongue against the floor of the mouth, or making a sucking noise with the tongue against the inside of the cheek – sounds like these are perceived as idiosyncrasies of the speaker. The listener does not usually interpret them as attempts at communication.

On the other hand, other air-stream mechanisms are occasionally used when people communicate. A velaric egressive sound (the same mechanism as for a click, but with the sound sent outwards rather than sucked inwards), made with the lips, is fairly common in French, where, along with a distinctive hand gesture and shrug of the shoulders, it means roughly 'I couldn't care less' or 'It's not my fault.' The similar sound, but with the tongue protruding slightly, is a signal of contempt in many languages – what in Britain is called a 'raspberry'.

Abnormal air-stream mechanisms are also used in special circumstances. It is possible to compress air within the cheek-space and use it to carry speech – so-called *buccal* voice, most well-known through the voice of Walt Disney's Donald Duck. It is also possible to make sounds using air rising from the stomach or oesophagus (the pipe leading from the pharynx to the stomach), as in a belch. *Oesophageal* voice is used in a sophisticated way by many people whose diseased larynx has been surgically removed (p. 278).

It is usual for a language to use only one or two air-stream mechanisms for the production of vowels and consonants. All languages make use of pulmonic egressive air. Glottalic egressive air (for ejectives) is also widely used (though not in European languages). Glottalic ingressive air (for implosives) is much rarer; and velaric air (for clicks) is used only in a small number of African languages. It is uncommon to find a language using more than one or two of these mechanisms regularly. A few languages use three. Damin, a ritual language of a north Australian aboriginal tribe, the Lardil, is unique in that it is reported to use no fewer than five air-stream mechanisms. Pulmonic egressive, glottalic egressive, and velaric ingressive sounds are used, but this language also has a pulmonic *ingressive* [l] sound, and a velaric *egressive* [p] sound. No other languages have been discovered with consonants involving these latter types of sound, which has led some scholars to speculate that perhaps the sound system of this language was specially invented to perform some ritual function.

THE LARYNX

Before we can speak, lung air has to be converted into audible vibrations, using the various organs within the vocal tract. The most important source of vibration for the production of speech sounds is in the lower region of the tract, at the larynx.

The larynx is located in the upper part of the trachea. It is a tube consisting of cartilages with connecting ligaments and membranes, within which are housed the two bands of muscular tissue known as the vocal folds. The location of the larynx can be easily felt because its front part, the *thyroid* (or 'shield-like') cartilage, forms a prominent angle in the neck, known as the 'Adam's apple' (it stands out more sharply in men). Two other cartilages work along with the thyroid to define the area of the larynx – the *cricoid* (or 'ring-like') cartilage, and the two *arytenoid* (or 'ladle-shaped') cartilages. The movements of all three help to control the way the vocal folds vibrate. Their anatomical arrangement is shown (right).

The opening between the vocal folds, known as the *glottis*, is quite a small area. In men, the inner edge of the folds is usually between 17 and 24 mm; in women it is even smaller, from about 13 to 17 mm. The folds at the glottis are often referred to as the 'true' vocal folds because slightly above them in the larynx is a second constriction, called the 'false' vocal folds, or 'ventricular' folds. It is uncommon to hear these used in speech sound production, though they are often involved in certain types of voice quality (a notable example being the 'gravelly' voice of the jazz musician, Louis Armstrong), and the effect of 'two-toned' voice is heard in certain types of voice disorder (p. 278).

The vocal folds

The vocal folds are remarkably versatile. Their tension, elasticity, height, width, length, and thickness can all be varied, owing to the complex interaction of the many sets of muscles controlling laryngeal movement. These movements take place very rapidly during speech, and account for several kinds of auditory effect.

Voicing   The most important effect is the production of audible vibration – a buzzing sound, known as *voice* or *phonation*. All vowels, and most of the consonants (e.g. [m], [b], [z]) make use of this effect. It is in fact possible to feel the vibration – for example, by placing the forefinger and thumb on either side of the Adam's apple, and comparing the effect of saying [zzz] and [sss] loudly. Alternatively, the resounding effect of vocal fold vibration can be sensed by making these sounds while closing one's ears with the fingers.

Each pulse of vibration represents a single opening and closing movement of the vocal folds. In adult male voices, this action is repeated on average about 120 times (or 'cycles') a second – corresponding to a note on the piano about an octave below middle C. In women, the average is just less than an octave higher, about 220 cycles a second. The higher the pitch of the voice, the more vibrations there will be (p. 133). A new-born baby's cry averages 400 vibrations a second.

Pitch   We are able to alter the frequency of vocal fold vibration at will, within certain limits, to produce variations in pitch and loudness. The linguistic use of these features (in connection with 'intonation', 'stress', and the 'tones' of tone languages) are described separately in §29.

Glottal stop   The vocal folds may also be held tightly closed (when holding one's breath, for example). When they are opened, the released lung air causes the production of a glottal stop [ʔ], heard most clearly in the sharp onset to a cough, but also commonly used as a sound unit in many languages and dialects (§27). In British English, for example, the glottal stop is most commonly heard in those dialects that have been influenced by London speech (in such words as *bottle*, where it replaces the sound [t]).

Glottal friction   If the vocal cords are kept wide apart, air expelled with energy will produce audible glottal friction – an effect that is often used as an [h] sound in languages.

Voice qualities   Other vocal fold movements can be initiated to produce such sound effects as *whisper*, *breathy* voice (heard in the so-called 'bedroom' voice of many female film stars and singers), and *creaky* voice (heard, for example, in the menacing low tones of the horror-film actor, Vincent Price), where the vibrations are extremely slow (about 30 times a second). These and other similar effects involve complex patterns of vibration, and their physiological mechanism is not entirely understood.

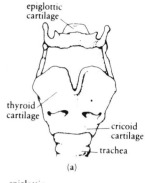

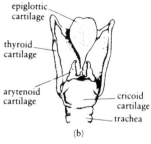

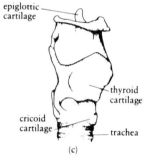

The structure of the larynx
(a) front view
(b) back view
(c) side view

AN EVOLUTIONARY PERSPECTIVE

From a biological point of view, the larynx acts as a valve, controlling the flow of air to and from the lungs, and preventing food, foreign bodies, or other substances from entering the lungs. Also, by closing the vocal folds, it is possible to build up pressure within the lungs, such as would be required for all forms of muscular effort (e.g. lifting, defecation, coughing).

In the course of evolution, the larynx has come to be adapted to provide the main source of sound for speech. However, its position in front of the lower pharynx (which leads to the stomach) presents a complication, because food and liquids must therefore pass the entrance to the trachea on their way to the stomach. (This complication does not exist in other animals, where the larynx is positioned higher up (§49).) To solve the problem, a leaf-shaped cartilage known as the *epiglottis* is pulled across the entrance to the larynx as part of the mechanism of swallowing, thus preventing these substances going in the wrong direction.

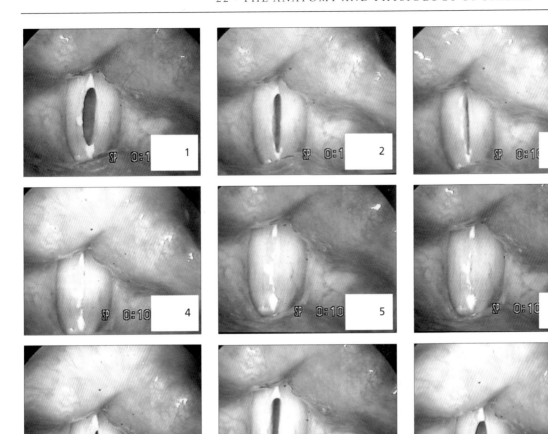

The movement of the vocal folds, filmed by a high-speed camera (10,000 frames per second) as the vocal folds are in the process of closing (above) then opening (below). The posterior part of the folds is towards the bottom of each frame.

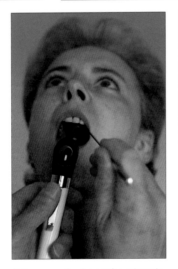

A laryngeal mirror The mirror is carefully inserted through the mouth until it is above the larynx. The angle of the mirror then permits a clear view. The investigator needs to hold down the tongue, and must be careful not to let the mirror touch the walls of the throat, which would produce a 'gagging' reflex in the subject.

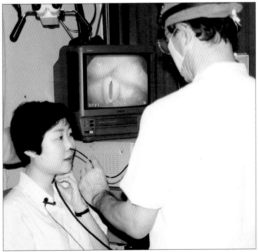

A fibre-optic laryngoscope The flexible tube is inserted up through the nose and nasal cavity until it hangs down behind the soft palate. Some of the glass filaments in the tube provide a strong light source; others bring an image back to the eye-piece (which can be linked to a camera, p. 141). The main advantage of this approach, compared with the laryngeal mirror, is that the subject is able to speak with the device in place.

HOW IS VOCAL FOLD VIBRATION PRODUCED?

It is possible to see vocal fold vibration using a laryngeal mirror or a fibre-optic laryngoscope. Rapid vibrations appear as a trembling movement, somewhat like that of a vibrating guitar string. To study the effects in detail, the vibrations need to be filmed, and observed in slow motion, and this is now routinely done in instrumental phonetics (§24).

Several theories of vocal cord vibration have been proposed. At first, it was thought that the vocal folds vibrated in the manner of a stringed instrument – the direct result of nerve impulses moving the muscles of the larynx (a theory that in more recent times has been called the 'neurochronaxiac' theory). The contemporary view, however, explains vocal fold activity in terms of the way the laryngeal muscles change the folds' tension and elasticity in response to the air stream from the lungs: the 'myoelastic aerodynamic' theory of phonation.

In this view, air pressure causes the vocal folds to open for each vibration; they then close, partly because the natural elasticity of the folds makes them 'bounce back', and partly because the folds are 'sucked' together, due to a sudden drop in air pressure in the glottis, as the air rushes through the narrowed larynx (the 'Bernoulli effect', named after the Swiss mathematician Daniel Bernoulli (1700–82)).

ARTICULATION

Once the air stream passes through the larynx, it enters the long tubular structure known as the vocal tract. Here it is affected by the action of several mobile vocal organs – in particular, by the tongue, soft palate, and lips – which work together to make a wide range of speech sounds. The production of different speech sounds through the use of these organs is known as *articulation*.

In addition, sounds produced within the larynx or vocal tract are influenced by the inherent properties of the cavities through which the air stream passes – the pharyngeal, oral, and (from time to time) nasal cavities. These cavities give sounds their resonance. Several kinds of resonance can be produced because the vocal tract is able to adopt many different shapes.

In describing articulation, it is usual to distinguish between those parts of the vocal tract that are immobile ('passive articulators') and those that can move under the control of the speaker ('active articulators'). Within the first category, we need to recognize:

- the upper teeth, especially the incisors, which are used to form a constriction for several sounds, such as the first sound of *thin* [θ];
- the ridge behind the upper teeth, known as the *alveolar ridge*, against which many speech sounds are made, such as [t], [s]; and
- the bony arch behind the alveolar ridge, known as the *hard palate*, which is used in the articulation of a few sounds, such as the first sound of *you* [j].

All other organs are mobile, to a greater or lesser extent.

Active articulators

Pharynx   This is a long muscular tube leading from the laryngeal cavity to the back part of the oral and nasal cavities. The areas adjacent to these cavities provide a means of dividing the pharynx into sections: the laryngopharynx, oropharynx, and nasopharynx. The pharynx can be narrowed or widened. Certain types of consonant can be produced by making a constriction here (p. 157), and movements of the larynx, soft palate, and tongue may also involve pharyngeal modifications that affect the quality of a sound. 'Pharyngealized' consonants and vowels can be heard in several languages (e.g. Arabic).

Soft palate, or **velum**   This is a broad band of muscular tissue in the rear upper region of the mouth, whose most noticeable feature is the uvula – an appendage that hangs down at the back of the mouth, easily visible with the aid of a mirror.

In normal breathing, the soft palate is lowered, to permit air to pass easily through the nose – though of course the mouth may be open as well. In speech, there are three main positions that affect the quality of sounds:

(i)   The soft palate may be raised against the nasopharyngeal wall to make a 'velopharyngeal closure', so that air escapes only through the mouth. This produces a range of *oral* sounds – such as all the vowels and most of the consonants of English.

(ii)   The soft palate may be lowered to allow air to escape through the mouth and nose. This is the position required to produce *nasalized vowels,* as in French (e.g. *bon* 'good'), Portuguese, and many other languages.

(iii)   The soft palate may be lowered, but the mouth remains closed. In this case, all the air is released through the nose, as in such *nasal consonants* as [m] and [n].

Lips   The *orbicularis oris* ('muscle that encircles the mouth') is the main muscle controlling lip movement, though several other facial muscles are also involved. The lips may be completely closed (as for [p] or [m]), or held apart in varying degrees to produce the different kinds of rounding or spreading used on vowels (e.g. [u] vs [i], p. 155) or the friction of certain kinds of consonant (as in the *b* of Spanish *saber* 'know'):

Jaw   The mandible bone permits a large degree of movement. It controls the size of the gap between the teeth, and strongly influences the position of the lips. Speakers sometimes adopt open or closed jaw positions – as when someone speaks 'through gritted teeth'.

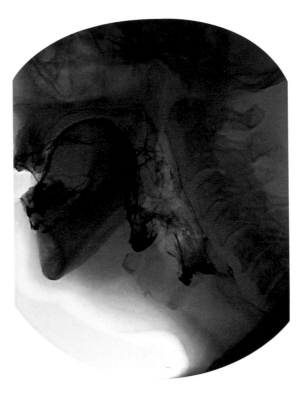

An X-ray radiograph giving a side view of the organs of speech during the articulation of an [i] vowel. The 'humped' outline of the tongue can be clearly seen. For a traditional anatomical diagram of this area, see p. 387.

The tongue

Of all the mobile organs, the tongue is the most versatile. It is capable of adopting more shapes and positions than any other vocal organ, and thus enters into the definition of a very large number of speech sounds: all vowels, and the majority of consonants. The tongue is a three-dimensional muscle, the whole of which can move in any of three main directions through the action of the various 'extrinsic' muscles: upwards / forwards (e.g. for [i]); upwards / backwards (e.g. for [u]); and downwards / backwards (e.g. for [a]). In addition, several 'intrinsic' muscles determine the shape of the tongue, in any position. For example, some muscles raise or lower the tongue tip, or move it to the left or the right. Others move the tongue sideways, or form a groove along the middle (as is needed for the articulation of [s]).

There are no obvious anatomical sections to the tongue, so to classify sounds, arbitrary divisions have to be made using the position of the tongue in relation to the upper part of the mouth. The main areas are best located when the tongue is at rest, with its tip behind the lower teeth.

- *front* the part opposite the hard palate
- *back* the part opposite the soft palate
- *centre* the part opposite where the hard and soft palate meet

(Front, back, and centre are often jointly called the *dorsum* of the tongue.)

- *blade* the tapering part opposite the teeth ridge
- *tip* or *apex* the front extremity
- *rims* the edges of the tongue

(Variations in tongue size are discussed in §6.)

The structures of the oral cavity

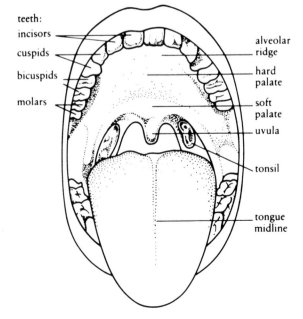

teeth:
incisors
cuspids
bicuspids
molars

alveolar ridge
hard palate
soft palate
uvula
tonsil
tongue midline

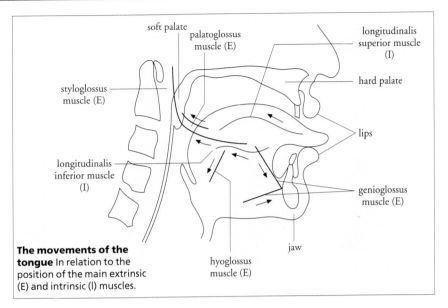

soft palate
palatoglossus muscle (E)
longitudinalis superior muscle (I)
hard palate
styloglossus muscle (E)
lips
longitudinalis inferior muscle (I)
genioglossus muscle (E)
hyoglossus muscle (E)
jaw

The movements of the tongue In relation to the position of the main extrinsic (E) and intrinsic (I) muscles.

THE NERVES THAT CONTROL THE VOCAL ORGANS

There are twelve pairs of *cranial* nerves, whose role is to link the brain with the head and neck. Some perform a 'motor' function, controlling the action of muscles; others perform a 'sensory' function, sending signals to the brain. (The main areas of the brain involved in the production and perception of speech are introduced in §45.) Seven of the cranial nerves are brought into service as part of the process of speech and hearing, and the relevant functions of these nerves are listed below. (It is usual to use roman numerals when listing cranial nerves.)

V The *trigeminal* nerve acts as a motor nerve to the muscles of the jaw and to one of the muscles controlling the soft palate. It also acts as a sensory nerve from the back two-thirds of the tongue.
VII The *facial* nerve is a motor nerve supplying the muscles of the lips.
VIII The *auditory* or *acoustic* nerve acts as a sensory nerve from the ear (p. 143).
IX The *glossopharyngeal* nerve acts both as a motor nerve to the pharynx, and as a sensory nerve from the back of the tongue.
X The *vagus* nerve is a motor nerve that supplies the muscles of the pharynx and larynx.
XI The *accessory* nerve acts as a motor nerve to the muscle that controls the raising of the soft palate.
XII The *hypoglossal* nerve is a motor that supplies the muscles of the tongue.

In addition, the relevance of several *spinal* nerves should be noted, some of which control the chest muscles involved in respiration (p. 124).

The main parts of the tongue

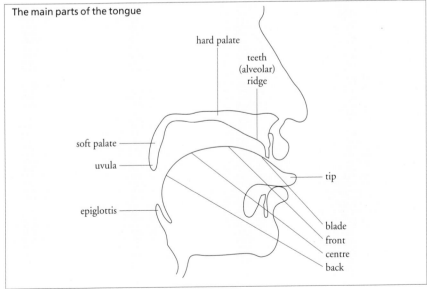

hard palate
teeth (alveolar) ridge
soft palate
uvula
tip
epiglottis
blade
front
centre
back

23 · THE ACOUSTICS OF SPEECH

Sound energy is a pressure wave consisting of vibrations of molecules in an elastic medium – such as a gas, a liquid, or certain types of solid. For the study of speech production, we usually deal with the propagation of sound through the air: air particles are disturbed through the movements and vibrations of the vocal organs, especially the vocal folds (§22). But when we study speech reception (§25), air is not the only medium involved. The process of hearing requires the sound vibrations in air to be transformed into mechanical vibrations (through the bony mechanism of the middle ear), hydraulic changes (through the liquid within the inner ear), and electrical nerve impulses (along the auditory nerve to the brain).

When an object vibrates, it causes to-and-fro movements in the air particles that surround it. These particles affect adjacent particles, and the process continues as a chain reaction for as long as the energy lasts. If there is a great deal of energy in the original vibration, the wave of sound that is produced may be transmitted a great distance, before it dies away. But the air particles themselves do not travel throughout this distance. The movement of each particle is purely local, each one affecting the next, in much the same way as a long series of closely positioned dominoes can be knocked over, once the first domino is moved. However, unlike dominoes, air particles move back towards their original position once they have transmitted their movement to their neighbours.

The movement of sound waves in air is sometimes explained by analogy with a stone dropped into a pool of water, causing ripples, or waves; but this ignores the essentially three-dimensional nature of the activity. The domino simile, likewise, gives only a limited impression of the movement involved. A better parallel would be with an expanding balloon, which grows in all directions at once. Sound waves, too, move simultaneously in all directions from their source.

WAVEFORMS

The way air particles move can be compared to a pendulum or a swing. At rest, a swing hangs down vertically. When it is put in motion, a backwards movement is followed by a forwards movement, on either side of the rest point, as long as there is energy available to keep the swing moving. This to-and fro movement is known as *oscillation*. Similarly, air particles oscillate around their rest point. As a particle moves forward, it compresses the adjacent particles and causes a tiny increase in the air pressure at that point. As it moves back, it decompresses these particles

and causes a decrease in pressure. The motion is wave-like, as can be seen if we follow the progress of a series of particles, once they have been set in motion by a source of vibration. In the following diagram, the movement of each particle is plotted at successive moments of time ($X+1$, $X+2$, etc.), imagining the source of vibration to be on the left.

Source of vibration	Air particles P1 P2 P3 P4 P5 P6 ...(etc.)	
Air particles (P) at rest	○ • ○ • ○ •	
I Vibration starts at time X	○• ○ • ○ •	I P1 hits P2.
II Time $X+1$	○ •○ • ○ •	II P2 hits P3; P1 returns towards its rest point.
III Time $X+2$	○ • ○• ○ •	III P3 hits P4; P2 returns towards its rest point; P1 has passed its rest point.
IV Time $X+3$	○ • ○ •○ •	IV P4 hits P5; P3 returns towards its rest point; P2 has passed its rest point; P1 returns towards its rest point.

If we draw a line between the position of each particle, the wave-like motion will be apparent, here presented vertically.

	Air particles P1 P2 P3 P4 P5 P6 ...(etc.)
At rest	
Time X	
Time $X+1$	
Time $X+2$	
Time $X+3$	
Time $X+4$	
Time $X+5$	
Time $X+6$	
Time $X+7$	
(etc.)	

A graph can be drawn of the pressure wave that is built up when particles move in this way, and this is known as a *waveform*. It is usual to draw waveforms as patterns from left to right, on either side of a horizontal line representing the passage of time. The simple movement of a single particle would look like this:

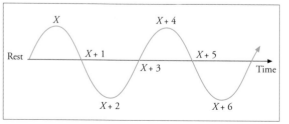

PURE TONES

The simplest waveforms, such as those illustrated on this page, are sinusoidal in shape, and known as *sine waves*. They consist of a single pulse of vibration that repeats itself at a constant rate and produces a *pure tone*.

Pure tones are rarely heard in everyday life. Most sounds are complex, consisting of several simultaneous patterns of vibration. To produce a pure tone, you need a special electronic machine, or a device such as a tuning fork.

When a tuning fork (below) is struck, it vibrates with a single tone. The prongs of the fork move to and fro at a fixed rate. When the fork is held to the ear, a pure tone can be heard.

FREQUENCY

A single to-and-fro movement of an air particle is called a *cycle*, and the number of cycles that occur in a second is known as the *frequency* of a sound. Frequency used to be measured in 'cycles per second' (cps), but this unit has been renamed *hertz* (after the German physicist, Heinrich Rudolf Hertz (1857–94), who first broadcast and received radio waves), and abbreviated as Hz. The basic frequency at which a sound vibrates is known as the *fundamental* frequency, generally abbreviated as F_0 and pronounced 'F nought'.

The range of frequencies that a young normal adult can hear is extremely wide – from about 20 to 20,000 Hz. It is not possible to hear vibrations lower ('infrasonic') or higher than this ('ultrasonic'). However, the frequencies at both ends of this range are of little significance for speech: the most important speech frequencies lie between 100 and 4,000 Hz. The fundamental frequency of the adult male voice, for example, is around 120 Hz; the female voice, around 220 Hz (p. 128).

The frequency of a pure tone correlates with the sensation of pitch – our sense that a sound is 'higher' or 'lower'. On the whole, the higher the frequency of a sound, the higher we perceive its pitch to be. But our perception of pitch is also affected by the duration and intensity of the sound stimulus. The notions of 'frequency' and 'pitch' are not identical: frequency is an objective, physical fact, whereas pitch is a subjective, psychological sensation (p. 144).

WAVELENGTH

The rate at which sound energy travels through air is known as its *velocity*, and this is a constant – usually (depending on temperature conditions) about 343 metres per second. All sounds are propagated at the same velocity. Low-energy sounds will fade sooner than high-energy sounds, but they do not travel any slower.

During the time it takes for there to be a single cycle of vibration, a sound wave travels a certain distance. This is known as the *wavelength* of the sound. Because of the constant rate of sound travel, it thus follows that the higher the frequency of a tone, the shorter its wavelength will be. A simple formula expresses this relationship: $\lambda = (C / F)$, where C is sound velocity, F is frequency, and λ is the wavelength. Thus, a tone of 500 Hz has a wavelength of (343 m / 500 m) = 69 cm; a tone of 1,000 Hz would be 34 cm.

The importance of wavelength can be seen in relation to the way we receive sound. When a sound wave approaches an object, if its wavelength is greater than the size of the object, it will tend to 'bend' around it; if the wavelength is smaller, it will tend to be reflected. Thus, for example, as sound waves approach the head, the lower frequencies, having a longer wavelength, will be more likely to be retained, whereas the higher frequencies will not – a factor that may be of considerable significance when considering how to assist people whose hearing is impaired (p. 268).

COMPLEX TONES

Most sources of sound produce complex sets of vibrations, and this is always the case with speech. Speech involves the use of complex waveforms because it results from the simultaneous use of many sources of vibration in the vocal tract (§22). When two or more pure tones of different frequencies combine, the result is a *complex tone*.

There are two kinds of complex tone. In one type, the waveform repeats itself: a *periodic* pattern of vibration. In the other, there is no such repetition: the vibrations are random, or *aperiodic*. Speech makes use of both kinds. The vowel sounds, for example, display a periodic pattern; sounds such as [s] are aperiodic.

Harmonics

The sound produced by an object vibrating in a periodic way involves more than the simple sine wave (p. 132). Other amounts of energy are also generated by the same vibration, all of which are correlated with the basic sine wave in a simple mathematical relationship: they are all multiples of the fundamental frequency. Thus an F_0 of 200 Hz will set up a 'sympathetic' set of frequencies at 400 Hz, 600 Hz, and so on. These multiples are known as *overtones*, or *harmonics*, and numbered in sequence. In physics (but not in music), F_0 counts as the first harmonic. So, in this example, 400 Hz would be the 'second harmonic', 600 Hz the 'third harmonic', and so on. This kind of framework is especially useful in analysing vowels, certain consonants, and intonation patterns (pp. 135–7).

Depending on the nature of the vibrating object (for example, the material it is made of, or its thickness), different sets of harmonics are established, and these are heard as differences in sound *quality*, or *timbre*. The difference we hear between two voices, or two musical instruments, when they produce a sound of the same pitch and loudness, is a contrast of timbre caused by the different harmonics.

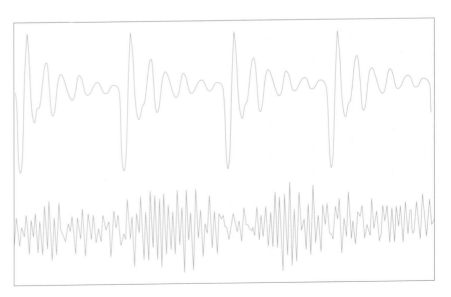

FAMILIAR FREQUENCIES

One way of relating the physical notion of frequency to our sense of pitch is to relate familiar musical notes to fundamental frequency. Middle C has a frequency of 264 Hz, and the notes above it in the diatonic scale of C have frequencies as follows:

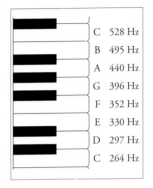

C	528 Hz
B	495 Hz
A	440 Hz
G	396 Hz
F	352 Hz
E	330 Hz
D	297 Hz
C	264 Hz

A is the note sounded by the oboe when an orchestra is tuning up. By comparison, the top note of a seven octave piano is 3,520 Hz, and the bottom note is 27.5 Hz.

VOCAL WAVEFORMS

A typical waveform of the vowel [a:] and of the consonant [s]. The time segments displayed are the same for each sound. The periodic pattern can clearly be seen in the case of the vowel sound, but no pattern is visible in the case of [s].

AMPLITUDE AND INTENSITY

The extent to which an air particle moves to and fro around its rest point is known as the *amplitude* of the vibration. The greater the amplitude, the greater the intensity of the sound, and along with other factors (such as frequency and duration) the greater our sensation of loudness. In the following diagram, we see three sine waves of equal frequency but of different amplitude. In each case, one complete vibration lasts 10 msec (the frequency is thus 100 per second, or 100 Hz). But (a) has twice the amplitude of (b), and (b) twice that of (c).

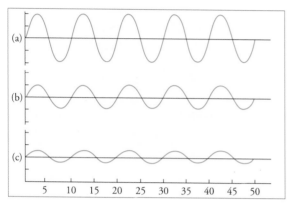

To measure the loudness of a sound, we need to take into account the contribution of both amplitude and frequency – factors that relate to the energy with which the sound is produced. The term *intensity* is used to refer to the overall power of a sound – a useful notion for the study of speech, where sound waves are complex, and the loudness of a sound does not relate clearly to any one of its acoustic components.

Decibels

To measure sound intensity, we need a basic, internationally accepted reference level for sound pressure in air. This reference sound pressure level (or SPL) identifies the threshold at which a sound can be heard (it is traditionally defined as 0.0002 dynes per square centimetre, *dyne* being the unit of measurement for force). Departures from this reference level are then measured in units known as *decibels* (dB) (named after Alexander Graham Bell (1847–1922), the American inventor of the telephone). Thus, to say that a sound is 90 dB means that it has an intensity which is 90 dB greater than the reference level.

THE SOUND AROUND US

The time it takes for sound waves to die away to an inaudible level is known as the 'reverberation time'. In a room, the walls and furnishings cause the energy to be absorbed. Fibrous materials, such as curtains and carpets, absorb sound well, whereas hard, dense surfaces cause sound to be reflected. Modern classrooms tend to use the latter material, thus producing high levels of noise ('ambient noise') that can often make it difficult for children to hear what is being said.

We are able to hear a vast range of sound intensities. A loud shout is a million times more powerful than a whisper. It has been estimated that the human ear is sensitive to about 10 million million (10^{13}) units of intensity. To enable analysts to cope with such large amounts, sound intensities are related to each other as ratios, using a logarithmic scale, and these are then related to our perception of loudness. An increase of 10 dB is roughly equivalent to a *doubling* of loudness. 30 dB is twice as loud as 20 dB, 40 dB is twice as loud as 30 dB, and so on. In this way, 10^{13} units can be 'reduced' to a scale of 130 decibels – a scale that more accurately reflects the way in which we sense differences of loudness between sounds.

It is possible to work out average intensity values for individual speech sounds. In the following table (after D. B. Fry, 1979, p. 127), the values for English sounds, expressed in decibels, have been related to the sound with the lowest intensity, [θ] (as in *thin*), which is given the value 0. Open vowels are the most intense sounds, followed by close vowels and continuants; the weak fricatives and plosives occur at the opposite end of the scale (§27; for transcription conventions, see Appendix 2). In a word like *thorn*, accordingly, the increase in intensity from the first sound to the second is nearly 30 dB.

ɔː	29	e	23	l	20	ʒ	13	ð	10
ɒ	28	iː	22	ʃ	19	z	12	b	8
ɑː	26	uː	22	ŋ	18	s	12	d	8
ʌ	26	ɪ	22	m	17	t	11	p	7
ɜː	25	w	21	tʃ	16	g	11	f	7
a	24	r	20	n	15	k	11	θ	0
ʊ	24	j	20	dʒ	13	v	10		

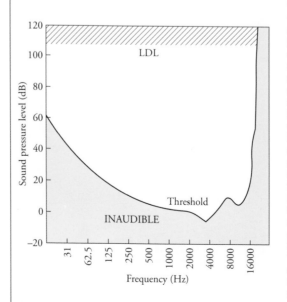

SPEECH AND EVERYDAY SOUNDS

The relative intensity of different kinds of speech can be seen by relating them to the average intensities of some everyday sounds (after D. B. Fry, 1979).

  0 threshold of audibility

 10 rustle of leaves

 20 ticking of watch (at ear); radio studio

 30 quiet garden; whispered conversation

 40 residential area, no traffic

 50 quiet office; typewriter

 60 conversation at 1 m; car at 10 m

 70 very busy city traffic at 30 m

 75 telephone bell at 3 m; shouting

 80 noisy tube train; loud radio music

 90 pneumatic drill at 1 m

100 car horn at 5 m; orchestra fortissimo

110 boilermakers' shop

120 pneumatic hammer, 1 m; amplified rock band

130 four-engined jet aircraft, 30 m

At around 120 dB, the sensation of hearing is replaced by that of pain.

The threshold of audibility for normal young adults has a characteristic 'U' shape, when it is presented in the form of a graph. The vertical scale represents increments in sound pressure level, measured in decibels. The horizontal scale represents increments in the frequency of a sound, measured in hertz. The diagram shows, for example, that the ear will pick up a sound of 250 Hz at around 15 dB, and will hear it throughout the whole decibel range, until the loudness discomfort level (LDL) is reached. The area of greatest sensitivity to sound is between 500 and 5000 Hz. The audiogram, used in the study of hearing impairment, is based on this kind of representation (p. 268).

SPECTRA

It is possible to make an acoustic analysis of a complex wave and present its various components in the form of a sound *spectrum*. A spectral analysis is a graph in which the horizontal axis represents frequency and the vertical axis represents amplitude. For example, the many acoustic components of the vowel [i:], representing the way the vocal tract resonates during its articulation, can be shown as a *spectrogram* in the following manner:

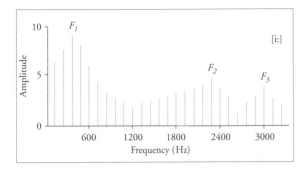

The vowel [a:] has a quite distinct spectral character, reflecting the very different configuration of the vocal tract.

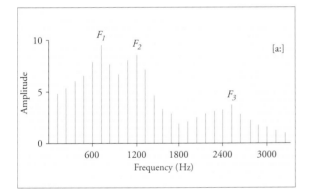

Note that, in these spectra, the amplitude of some frequencies is much greater than others. In fact, it is possible to see various 'peaks' of acoustic energy in each case, reflecting the main points of resonance in the vocal tract. These peaks are known as *formants*, and they are numbered from lowest to highest: the 'first formant' (F_1), the 'second formant' (F_2), and so on. In the spectrum of [i] above (which was spoken by a man at a fundamental frequency of 120 Hz), F_1 peaks at 360 Hz, F_2 at 2,280 Hz, and F_3 at 3,000 Hz.

Formant structure is a major feature of speech sounds. All vowels and some consonants have formants. It is the formant pattern (especially the disposition of the first two formants) that enables us to differentiate vowels, or to recognize repetitions of a vowel as being the 'same', even when produced by different speakers. And vowel formants can also help in identifying the character of adjacent consonant sounds.

RELATING ACOUSTICS TO ARTICULATION

By studying several speakers, it is possible to work out the mean frequencies of the first and second formants of the vowels in a language. This has been done for British English, with the following results (after J. C. Wells, 1962):

		F_1	F_2
i:	*heed*	300 Hz	2300 Hz
ɪ	*hid*	360 Hz	2100 Hz
e	*head*	570 Hz	1970 Hz
a	*had*	750 Hz	1750 Hz
ɑ:	*hard*	680 Hz	1100 Hz
ɒ	*hod*	600 Hz	900 Hz
ɔ:	*hoard*	450 Hz	740 Hz
ʊ	*hood*	380 Hz	950 Hz
u:	*who*	300 Hz	940 Hz
ə	*hub*	720 Hz	1240 Hz
ɜ:	*herb*	580 Hz	1380 Hz

We may now transfer such figures onto a graph in which the frequency of F_1 is displayed vertically and F_2 horizontally. The resulting pattern is remarkably similar to that displayed when vowels are described according to their place of articulation in the vocal tract (the vowel 'quadrilateral', p. 156). However, the match is not exact because the articulatory chart is based only on the point of greatest tongue constriction, whereas the acoustic chart derives from the resonances of the whole vocal tract.

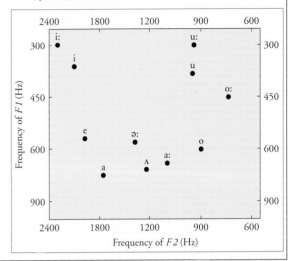

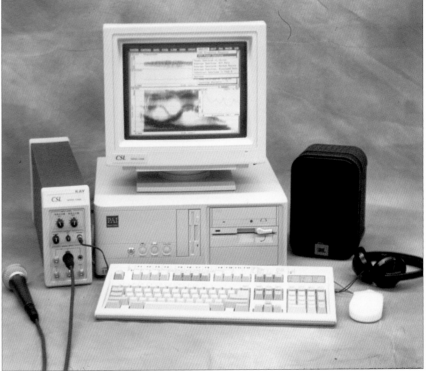

Speech analysis in the 1990s This Computerized Speech Lab, produced by the Kay Elemetrics Corporation, includes an extensive library of speech display and analysis features, including the ability to edit speech samples electronically, add phonetic transcription, represent speech data graphically and numerically, and provide simultaneous displays of acoustic and articulatory results. Optional programs are also available (e.g. real-time biofeedback programs) to facilitate use by speech professionals in teaching or therapy.

THE SOUND SPECTROGRAPH

During the 1940s, the *sound spectrograph* was designed to analyse and display speech spectra. This machine recorded speech, analysed the sound waves into their different frequencies using an array of electronic filters, measured the intensity of each frequency, and then presented the result as a visual display, using a stylus to make marks on a strip of specially coated paper placed round a drum. Today, the drum spectrograph is obsolete, having been replaced by digital electronic displays and laser printouts, but these retain the features of the earlier format. Spectrograms illustrating a variety of sounds are shown on this and the opposite page.

Three dimensions of sound are represented on a spectrogram.

1. Time is displayed horizontally: using the drum spectrograph it was possible to record 2.4 seconds of speech on the paper strip, which was then 'read' from left to right. Each horizontal half-inch of paper thus displayed a tenth of a second of speech. On a screen, it is possible to show a continuous spectral display in real time.
2. The vertical dimension displays information about frequency – from 0 Hz (the bottom line) to 8,000 Hz. The scale is linear: on the drum spectrograph, each vertical inch of paper represented 2,000 Hz.
3. The third dimension is intensity, represented in black-and-white displays by the degree of darkness of the marks. The more intense the signal, the blacker the mark. Frequencies of little or no intensity thus appear as areas of clear paper/screen.

The limitations of the drum spectrograph never allowed perfect accuracy of measurement from the paper strip, but the visual display gave an immediacy of recognition, to anyone trained in acoustic analysis, which made it a popular research tool. Contrasts between individual sounds could be clearly shown, as could the way sounds influence each other as they combine in connected speech. Nowadays, the early limitations have been largely overcome: modern digital spectrographs permit accurate and extensive acoustic analyses, using computational and statistical techniques, including the ability to store a number of spectrograms and to provide correlations with other kinds of display, thus enabling systematic and precise comparisons to be made.

TYPES OF SPECTROGRAM

It is possible to choose one of two settings when making a spectrogram. If the machine is set to 'narrow', it will analyse the range of speech frequencies into small bands (usually 45 Hz), and this will make individual harmonics show up very clearly. If the machine is set to 'wide', an analysis is made using much broader bands of frequency (usually 300 Hz), and this will make the formants stand out clearly. For most purposes, wide-band analysis is more useful in speech science.

Narrow-band and wide-band versions of the sentence 'This is a spectrogram' are shown below, with intensity represented by colour variation. Format activity (in blue) can be clearly seen.

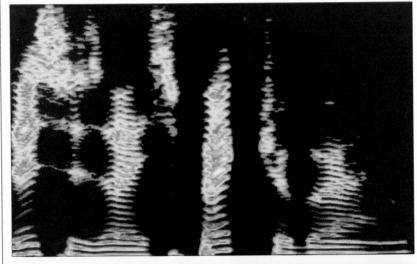

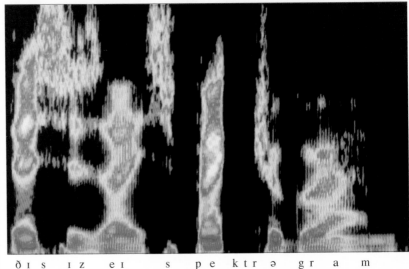

ð ɪ s   ɪ z   eɪ   s   pe   ktr ə   gr a m

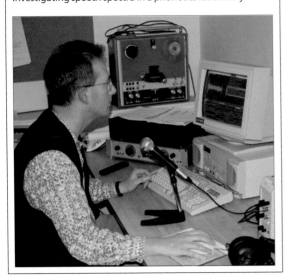

Investigating speech spectra in a phonetics laboratory

THE ACOUSTIC FEATURES OF VOWELS AND CONSONANTS

Vowels All vowel sounds in normal speech display two, and usually three, formants. These appear on a wide-band spectrogram as thick dark bars. They can be clearly seen in the spectrograms of the long vowels [iː], [ɑː], and [uː], said in isolation. The vertical striations represent vocal fold vibration.

Semi-vowels The sounds [j] and [w] (as in *you* and *we*) function as consonants in many languages, but they have the acoustic features of vowels – [i] and [u] respectively – and are thus often called 'semi-vowels' (p. 155). Their vowel-like character can be clearly seen on a spectrogram where they are articulated between [ɑ] vowels. In both cases, the formants are bent as the vowel changes its quality. For example, during [ɑjɑ], the first formant bends downwards, and the second formant bends upwards as the tongue moves from [ɑ] to [j]; they then bend back as the tongue resumes its original position. The bend also affects the third formant; but a fourth formant, higher up, is much less affected.

Plosive consonants A plosive consonant is typically identified by a short period of silence, while a closure is made in the mouth, followed by a short burst of noise, when the closure is released (p. 159). Both of these features can be clearly seen on a spectrogram, especially when these consonants are articulated between vowels. The silence is shown by the vertical strip of clear paper; and the release by a thin 'spike' of marks spread quite widely across the spectrum. The onset of the following vowel is shown by the appearance of the black formant bands.

The differences between voiceless [p, t, k] and voiced [b, d, g] plosives (p. 128) can be clearly seen.

• In the voiced sounds, the intensity of the noise burst is much less than in the voiceless sounds.

• The duration of the silence is shorter for voiced sounds.

• An important variable is the time between the release of the plosive and the onset of vocal cord vibration (which is represented by the formants). This is known as 'voice onset time', or VOT. There is a noticeable VOT gap in the case of each voiceless plosive (marked as *X* on the spectrograms); but the voiced plosives have little or no gap. In such cases, the voicing may actually begin *before* the noise burst.

The different places of articulation of plosive consonants can also be seen from spectrograms. The bilabial sounds [p, b] have a burst of noise at low frequencies; the alveolar sounds [t, d] have the burst at high frequencies; and the velar sounds [k, g] have the burst within the middle range. There is also a clear difference at the point of transition between consonant and vowel: a rapid articulatory movement is involved, and this is reflected in the sharp bend in the formants at the onset of the vowel – a bend that varies in direction between each pair of consonants.

Fricative consonants These consonants make use of random acoustic energy, or *noise*, which is represented on the spectrogram as a broad area of disturbance at certain frequencies. This is most clearly seen in the case of sibilant fricatives, such as [s] and [ʃ], which are high-energy sounds. The energy for [s] is largely above 4000 Hz; that for [ʃ] begins lower, at around 2500 Hz. The contrast is presented here between [ɑ] vowels.

CONNECTED SPEECH

The spectrograms to the right are of carefully articulated sound units, said in isolation. In connected speech, the sounds are produced more rapidly, they influence each other, and the boundaries between them become more difficult to distinguish. Spectrograms of connected speech (see facing page) emphasize the essential continuity of spoken language – the fact that articulation is a process of continuous change. It is a fact we should always bear in mind as we read the neat, separate symbols of a phonetic transcription.

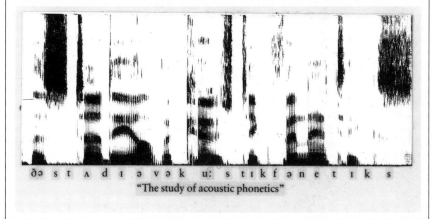

ð ə   s t ʌ d ɪ ə v ə k   uː s t ɪ k f ə n e t ɪ k s

"The study of acoustic phonetics"

The vowels

Semi-vowels

Plosive consonants

Fricative consonants

A vast array of instruments is today available for the study of speech production. A well-equipped phonetics laboratory includes equipment for recording speech, analysing the acoustic properties of the sound signal (§23), and investigating the physiology of the vocal organs (§22). Related techniques are available for the study of hearing and speech reception (§25). The field as a whole is known as *instrumental* (or *experimental*) *phonetics*.

RECORDING SPEECH

Any scientific investigation into the nature of speech requires the keeping of permanent records. The speech signal itself can be recorded on audiotape or digitally on a computer, and displayed in visual form on a paper chart, visual display unit, or computer printout. Similarly, photographic and other techniques are available for recording and displaying the speaker's physiological activity.

The careful choice of methods and instruments is of the highest priority in acoustic research. Unless special precautions are taken, recordings may not be sufficiently clear to enable accurate acoustic analysis to be carried out. If a recording contains a lot of background noise, or if the signal is weak or distorted, the speech sound waves will be obscure. Particular attention must therefore be paid to the limitations of the recording instrument (usually a tape recorder), the microphone, the playback system, and the location in which the recording is made.

For best results, recordings should be made in a special studio, which has been shielded from external sounds and which has sound-absorbent walls. If this is not available, recordings should be made in a quiet room containing sound-absorbent material (such as soft furnishings). In this way, it should be possible to minimize problems of echo and other interference.

DISPLAYING SPEECH SIGNALS

The most commonly used instrument for observing sound waves has long been the *oscilloscope*, which displays the frequency and amplitude of a waveform. Some scopes provide only a temporary image; others (storage oscilloscopes) are able to hold a waveform on the screen for more detailed study. In these cases, the images can be photographed directly, or some kind of chart recorder can be used to obtain a visual trace on paper. Most oscillographic displays are now incorporated within a computer system, given a digital analysis, and processed in a wide variety of ways.

Chart recorders reflected various technologies. All involved the use of a mechanically unrolling sheet of paper, on which a trace could be made with one or more ink jets or pens (depending on how many channels were being recorded simultaneously), or using a system based on heat recording, fibre-optics, or ultraviolet light. They are now largely superseded by techniques of electronic processing, in which information is rapidly displayed on screen in graphic or numerical form, stored on disk, and printed out as required.

The sound spectrograph, the most valuable of all instruments for the visual display of speech, is illustrated on p. 136.

Displaying the acoustics of speech Modern electronic and computational techniques have revolutionized speech analysis. This is one of the displays available using the Computerized Speech Lab (p. 135): up to four channels of signal acquisition can be shown simultaneously, each of which can be analyzed and displayed as time-synchronized data. Each channel can be AC or DC coupled, which is especially important when analyzing both acoustic and physiological signals.

Making a recording in an anechoic chamber (below). The ceiling, walls, and floor have been covered with a material designed to absorb sound and cut out reverberation.

PHYSIOLOGICAL INVESTIGATIONS

Speech physiology studies all aspects of the disposition and use of the vocal organs during the act of speaking. Precise information can be obtained about the functioning of the larynx, soft palate, tongue, and lips, and the role of other organs and cavities in the production of individual sounds and in connected speech. Particular attention is paid to patterns of air pressure, volume, and flow, and to the activity of the underlying muscles and nerves – including the way in which speech movements are controlled by the brain (§45). The work involves both the analysis of natural speech samples and the experimental investigation of sound production under carefully controlled conditions.

AIR FLOW

How is breathing modified in order to facilitate speech? What happens to the air stream as it passes through the vocal tract? The field of *aerometry* investigates these questions, and some of its most important instruments are illustrated on p. 125.

Several instruments provide air-flow data, such as the *electroaerometer* and the *pneumotachograph*. In pneumotachography, for example, a specially designed face-mask provides separate measures of air flow from the mouth and nose. For example, the following traces were obtained from a speaker uttering the word *smile*. Trace (a) shows the amount of nasal air flow, measured in litres per minute (1/m) – absent for [s], strong for [m], then gradually reducing during the rest of the word. Trace (b) shows the corresponding amount of oral air flow – strong at the beginning and end, but completely absent for [m], where the lips are closed. What is interesting, in this speaker, is the continued nasality throughout the vowel, which shows the influence of the preceding [m].

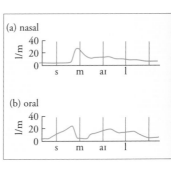

Muscle movement A hooked-wire electrode, as fine as a human hair, is used to monitor the activity of a laryngeal muscle. This is one of the techniques available for use in *electromyography* (EMG).

    Muscles produce tiny amounts of electrical activity when they contract. This can be monitored by placing an electrode on the skin, or (to produce a clearer and more specific signal) directly into a muscle. If the muscle is involved in the production of a speech sound, it sends signals to a monitoring device; the signals are amplified and then displayed on an oscilloscope or on paper.

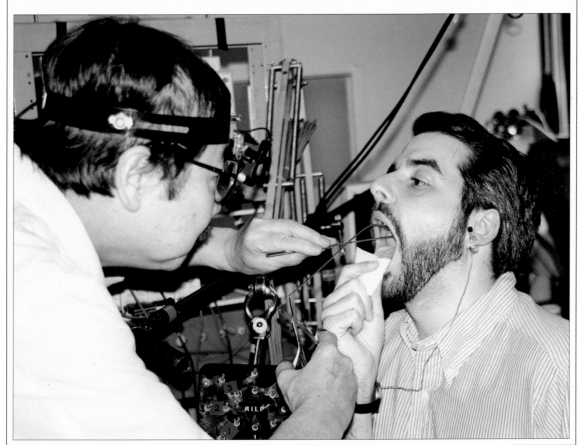

THE TONGUE AND PALATE

It is easy enough to see the tongue in a mirror, but it is one of the most difficult organs to monitor during speech. Many techniques have been tried, with varying levels of success: the first two below are of historical interest only.

Direct photography   This has been possible in a few cases where a subject has had an operation involving the partial removal of the cheek. The movements of the tongue can be clearly seen, but the data are of limited value, because a subject's speech is never normal in such circumstances.

Intraoral devices   A mechanical device can be placed inside the mouth to monitor aspects of tongue movement, such as a miniature camera, a pneumatic bulb, a wire electrode, or an instrument for recording pressure. The main problem with such procedures is that the presence of a sizeable foreign body inside the mouth is likely to interfere with normal articulation. Similar difficulties affect the use of plaster casts and plastographic techniques (a material, such as tinfoil, which deforms using tongue contact).

X-rays   Several X-ray studies have been made using static, cine, and video photography, and there are many specialized techniques. For example, in *cinefluorography*, X-ray images are photographed after being projected onto a fluorescent screen. However, the radiation hazard severely limits the amount of data that can be obtained, and it is not always easy to identify soft-tissue areas clearly, even when the surface of the tongue is outlined with a radio-opaque material. This difficulty can be overcome to some extent through the use of *tomographic* (or *laminagraphic*) techniques, which enable an X-ray to be taken of a predetermined layer of body structure. Recently, too, computer-controlled *X-ray microbeams* have been devised, which track the movements of the tongue through the use of small lead pellets fixed to its surface. This technique involves very low doses of radiation. An increasingly popular alternative is magnetic resonance imaging (for static positions of the vocal organs: see p. 123). But even the best pictures cannot provide a sense of the three dimensions involved in tongue movement (p. 131).

Electromagnetic midsagittal articulography   This is a transmitter system in which tiny receivers placed at various points (e.g. lips, teeth, parts of the tongue) send movement signals which are accurately plotted as articulatory trajectories, using a system of absolute coordinates. For example, the technique can be used to show that vertical tongue body movements during the articulation of a consonant are affected by such factors as voicing and the nature of adjacent vowels.

Palatography   This is the main technique for obtaining information about the exact location of tongue contact with the palate. In 'direct' palatography, the palate is painted with a special mixture; if the tongue makes contact with the palate during the articulation of a sound, some of the mixture will be wiped off, and the pattern can then be photographed. 'Indirect' palatography uses an artificial palate, which fits over the subject's palate, and is painted with material that adheres to the tongue after a contact is made. The palate can then be removed from the mouth for a detailed examination. A great deal of data about individual articulations can be obtained using these approaches, but the technique can provide no information about the movement of the articulators in connected speech.

Electropalatography   By contrast, this technique gives detailed information in real time about the location and sequence of tongue-palate contacts. An artificial palate is used, which incorporates an array of metal contacts. When the tongue touches a contact, a signal is sent to a recording device. Different patterns of contact can then be displayed on a screen or printed out on paper. Computer processing enables large quantities of data to be quickly analysed (see illustration [facing page]).

Ultrasonics   In recent years, researchers have begun to use ultrasound techniques, in which a beam of very high frequency sound waves is used to monitor the position and movement of internal structures. The safety of this approach makes it one of the most promising avenues for future speech research.

Positioning the sensor before monitoring an ultra-sonic echo of the vocal tract (p. 229).

THE LARYNX

The larynx can be observed through a laryngeal mirror or a fibre-optic laryngoscope (both illustrated on p. 129). High-speed films can then be made of the vocal fold vibrations and replayed at normal speed to give a slow-motion effect, or analysed frame by frame. A similar effect can be obtained by using a *stroboscope* to illuminate the folds: the frequency of its flashing light is adjusted until it is close to that of the fold vibrations, at which point the folds appear to vibrate slowly. A *glottograph* can also be used – a device that monitors the amount of light passing through the glottis, and thus indicates the extent of glottal opening during speech.

The main disadvantage of laryngoscopic techniques arises from their invasive character: they are introduced into the vocal tract and thus to a greater or lesser extent interfere with the comfort of the speaker and the naturalness of speech. A technique of larynx observation that avoids this problem is provided by *electrolaryngography*. Two small electrodes are applied to the skin of the neck on either side of the thyroid cartilage (p. 128). During speech, information about the way the vocal folds come together is displayed on a screen as a waveform (*Lx*). Here is the *Lx* waveform of an adult female speaker producing a steady [ɑ] vowel; the full speech waveform is also given for comparison.

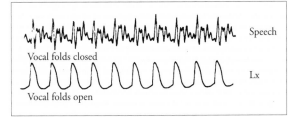

Speech

Vocal folds closed

Lx

Vocal folds open

When the electrolaryngograph is incorporated into a device known as a Voiscope®, it is possible to display fundamental frequency (*Fx*) on an oscilloscope screen in a manner that corresponds to our perception of pitch. High fundamentals appear towards the top of the screen; low ones towards the bottom. The *Fx* contour of an utterance is given below, showing two falling-rising pitch patterns on the first four words, and a falling pitch at the end. The breaks in the trace are due to the occurrence of the sounds [st] and [h], where there is no vocal fold vibration.

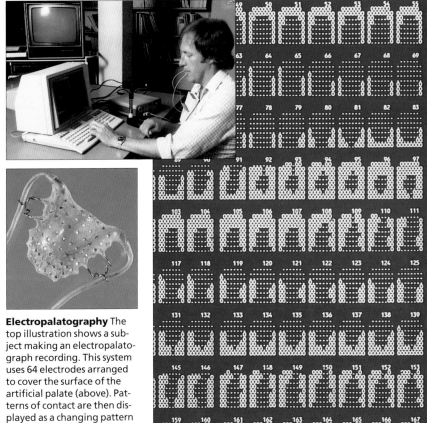

Electropalatography The top illustration shows a subject making an electropalatograph recording. This system uses 64 electrodes arranged to cover the surface of the artificial palate (above). Patterns of contact are then displayed as a changing pattern of lights on a display screen.

Alternatively, a computer printout can be made, in which tongue contacts are represented by zeros (see illustration above right). The velar area of the palate is at the top of each small diagram, and the alveolar area is at the bottom. The printout is read from left to right, with samples occurring at 10 msec intervals. The illustration shows the articulation of the word *tactics*. The sequence of tongue–palate contacts made during the word can be clearly seen. (After W. J. Hardcastle & R. A. Morgan, 1982, p. 51.)

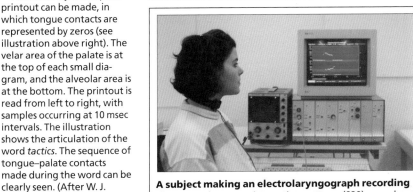

A subject making an electrolaryngograph recording The screen shows two intonation patterns (§29), one above the other, for the sentence 'It's easy, isn't it?' The contrast between rising and falling tones can be clearly seen. Below: Lying in front of the equipment are the guard-ring electrodes used, which are held in place by an elastic band.

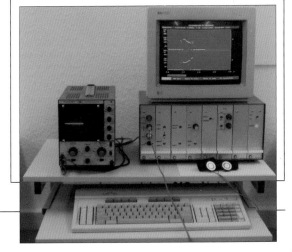

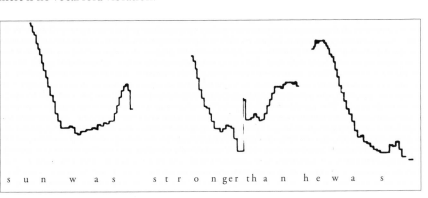

s u n w a s   s t r o n g e r t h a n   h e w a s   s

25 · SPEECH RECEPTION

THE EAR

The first step in the reception of speech takes place when sound waves arrive at the ear. From there, sound is transmitted along the auditory nerve to the brain (§45). The process is a complex one, involving several distinct stages which reflect the main anatomical division of the ear into *outer ear, middle ear,* and *inner ear.*

THE OUTER EAR

The outer ear consists of two parts. The visible part is known as the *auricle,* or *pinna* – a structure consisting of several rounded prominences formed mainly from cartilage. The pinna has a minor role to play in the reception of sound: it helps to focus sound waves into the ear, and assists our ability to detect the source of a sound. It also protects the entrance to the auditory canal, both from physical attacks and from excessive amounts of sound. By pressing the central part of the pinna with the finger, it is possible to cover the entrance to the canal, thus considerably reducing the amount of sound entering the ear.

From here, the *external auditory canal* leads to the eardrum. The canal is about 2.5 cm long and contains hairs and glands that secrete wax (*cerumen*), a substance that acts as a filter for dust, insects, and other tiny substances that might approach the eardrum. The

canal acts as a small amplifier for certain sound frequencies (between 3,000 and 4,000 Hz, p. 135), thus making weak sounds at these frequencies more perceptible. It also helps to protect the eardrum to some extent from changes in temperature and humidity as well as from physical damage (though no canal has yet proved capable of withstanding the ingenious attempts of young children to insert all kinds of implements inside their ears!).

THE MIDDLE EAR

The eardrum, or *tympanic membrane*, separates the outer ear from the middle ear. It is roughly circular in shape, lying at an angle of about 55° across the whole of the external auditory canal. It consists of a fibrous tissue with important elastic properties that enable it to vibrate when sound waves reach it. The shape and tension of the eardrum cause the vibrations to be focused at a prominence near its centre, from where they are transferred to the first of the bones of the middle ear, which is firmly attached to the membrane.

The chamber of the middle ear, known as the *tympanic cavity,* lies within the bones of the skull, about 15 mm high. It is filled with air, because there is a direct connection to the nose and throat via the Eustachian tube (named after the Italian anatomist, G. E. Eustachio (1520–74)). This tube is normally closed, but such activities as yawning or swallowing

DO WE NEED TWO EARS?

Two ears – *bilateral* hearing – are a great asset. They enable us to be more precise in our judgment of the position of a sound source – an important factor in listening to people in a group, or heeding the direction of a vocal warning. This happens because a sound source is usually nearer one ear than the other; as a result, the signals to each ear will be slightly out of phase, and one will be more intense. The brain resolves these differences and makes a judgment about localization. Sometimes there is ambiguity (when a sound is reflected by a nearby object, for example), in which case we have to 'search' for the sound source by moving the head.

The value of two ears is most evident in cases of hearing loss in one ear (*unilateral* loss, p. 268). The 'good' ear copes well with a single speaker in a quiet room; but in contexts where sound is coming in from several directions (such as in a meeting), the listener finds localizing the source of sound very difficult, and may look for the speaker in the wrong direction.

We should also note that the brain uses our two ears in different ways. One ear may have an advantage over the other for certain types of sound. This can be shown in tests of *dichotic* listening, where different signals are presented simultaneously to each ear, and listener responses show that one ear transmits a sound to the brain more readily than the other (p. 261).

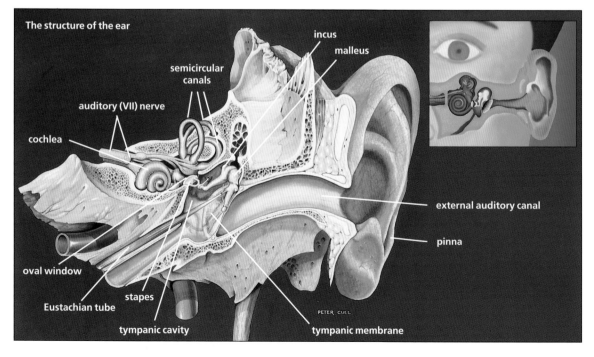

The structure of the ear

incus
malleus
semicircular canals
auditory (VII) nerve
cochlea
external auditory canal
pinna
oval window
stapes
Eustachian tube
tympanic cavity
PETER CULL
tympanic membrane

open it. In this way, the air pressure level on either side of the eardrum is maintained.

The primary function of the middle ear is to turn the sound vibrations at the eardrum into mechanical movement – which will in turn be transmitted to the fluid-filled inner ear. It does this using a system of three tiny bones, known as the auditory *ossicles*. These bones are the smallest in the body and are the only bones to be fully formed at birth. They are suspended from the walls of the tympanic cavity by ligaments, and are delicately hinged together so that vibrations can pass smoothly between them into the inner ear. The three bones have been named according to their shape: the *malleus* ('hammer'), which is attached to the eardrum, the *incus* ('anvil'), and the *stapes* ('stirrup'). The stapes fits into the *oval window* – an opening in the bony wall separating the middle ear from the inner ear.

This may seem an unnecessarily complicated system of getting vibrations from point A to point B, but it is known to have several advantages. In particular, the process acts as a kind of leverage system, enabling the vibrations to be greatly amplified (by a factor of over 30 dB) by the time they reach the inner ear. As the inner ear is filled with fluid, vibrations would very readily get lost without this amplification. Also, the bony network of the middle ear helps to protect the inner ear from sudden, very loud sounds. The muscles that control the movement of the eardrum and the stapes function in such a way that they lessen the chances of massive vibrations damaging the inner ear (the 'acoustic reflex'). However, the time it takes for these muscles to react is not so rapid that the inner ear can be protected from all such sounds; and cases of damage to the eardrum or inner ear do occur.

THE INNER EAR

This is a system of small interconnecting cavities and passageways within the skull. It contains the *semicircular canals*, which control our sense of balance, and the *cochlea*, a coiled cavity about 35 mm long, resembling a snail's shell. The main function of the cochlea is to turn the mechanical vibrations produced by the middle ear into electrical nerve impulses capable of being transmitted to the brain.

The cochlea is divided along most of its length into an upper chamber (the *scala vestibuli*) and a lower chamber (the *scala tympani*), separated by the *cochlear duct*. Both chambers are filled with a clear, viscous fluid known as *perilymph*. Vibrations enter this fluid via the oval window and the scala vestibuli, and are transmitted all the way around the cochlea. They pass from upper to lower chamber through an opening in the cochlear duct at its apex, and finish at a sealed opening in the wall of the middle ear, called the *round window*. This structure can be clearly seen in a diagram of an uncoiled cochlea (above right).

The cochlear duct is separated from the scala tympani by the *basilar membrane*, and is filled with fluid known as *endolymph*. This membrane is very thin at the base of the cochlea (about 0.04 mm) and gets thicker as it approaches the apex (about 0.5 mm). It is thus able to respond differentially to incoming vibratory pressures: high frequencies primarily affect the narrow end; certain low frequencies activate the entire membrane (p. 144).

Resting on this membrane is the highly sensitive organ of hearing, called the *organ of Corti* (discovered by the Italian anatomist, Alfonso Corti (1822–76)), which translates the mechanical movements of the membrane into nerve impulses. It contains a systematic arrangement of cells covered with very fine hairs, distributed in rows and layers along the membrane. These *hair cells* act as sensory receptors, picking up the pressure movements in the endolymph. Electrochemical changes take place, which activate the fibres of the auditory nerve (the VIII cranial nerve, p. 131). The signals are then sent the short distance along this nerve to the temporal lobe, via the brain-stem and mid-brain (p. 260).

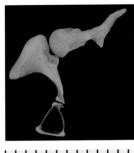

mm

A coloured X-ray of the three bones of the middle ear. At upper right is the *malleus* (hammer, 8mm long) Which strikes the *incus* (anvil, 9mm long) at centre; the *incus* is joined to the *stapes* (stirrup, 3mm long) at bottom.

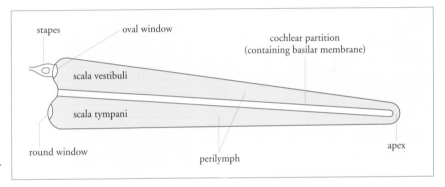

A schematic view of an uncoiled cochlea The movement of the stapes at the oval window is transmitted to the cochlear duct via the fluid (perilymph) in the two chambers.

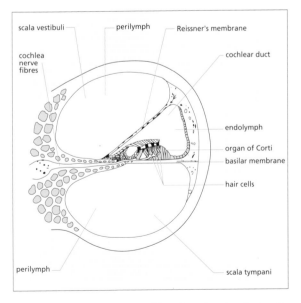

A cross-section through one cochlear duct, showing the location of the organ of Corti.

THEORIES OF HEARING

Pitch perception

How does the frequency information in a sound wave as it enters the cochlea (p. 143) come to be transformed into a pattern of nerve impulses that will enable the sound to be perceived? Several theories have been proposed since the matter was first systematically investigated in the mid-19th century.

Resonance or **place theory** This is the classical theory of pitch perception, deriving from the work of the German scientist, Hermann von Helmholtz (1821–94). In this approach, individual fibres in the cochlea were thought to resonate to a particular frequency. As the frequency changed, so the place of vibration along the basilar membrane would change. However, it has since been demonstrated that the basilar membrane vibrates, not at single points, but along most of its length.

Temporal or **frequency theory** In this view, first proposed by William Rutherford in 1886, the frequency of a wave was thought to be transmitted by the number of pulses per second in a nerve fibre. Every hair cell was thought to respond to every tone, the cochlea acting as a kind of telephone transmitter, directly passing on frequency information to the auditory nerve. This view had to be modified when it was discovered that no nerve fibre is capable of firing at more than 1,000 Hz, and that most firings take place at much lower rates. As humans can respond to speech frequencies ranging up to 20,000 Hz, a purely temporal theory is inadequate.

Volley theory This view, proposed by E. G. Wever in 1949, represents a compromise between place and temporal theories. It proposes that below 5,000 Hz temporal patterning is important, with pitch perception being dependent on the synchronized action of several nerve fibres, firing in volleys. Above 5,000 Hz, place analysis is well preserved.

Travelling wave theory This account was proposed by the Hungarian physiologist Georg von Békésy (1899–1972). By illuminating the vibrating basilar membrane with a stroboscope light, he was able to show that sound vibrations move through the cochlea in the form of a wave. The point on the basilar membrane at which the wave amplitude is greatest corresponds to the frequency of the signal.

After a century of debate and experimentation, it is still not possible to be sure about the relative roles of spatial and temporal factors in the hearing process. The acoustic and physiological aspects of the speech signal do not seem to interact in a simple or direct way; the patterns of fluid movement in the cochlea do not relate clearly to patterns of nerve impulses. More complex theories of pattern-recognition seem to be required,

involving both place and temporal elements, and perhaps involving central as well as peripheral neural processes. A great deal of research therefore continues to be devoted to this topic.

Loudness perception

It is unclear how the cochlea detects the loudness of a sound. One factor is the rate at which individual nerve fibres fire: the louder a sound stimulus, the faster the rate of firing. But this cannot be the whole explanation, as individual fibres seem able to cope with changes of only around 40 dB. Other mechanisms have to be involved. One proposal arises out of the finding that some of the hair cells are tuned to respond to certain frequencies. A very loud sound at a given frequency would quickly 'use up' the coding potential of that fibre; and other fibres might then be brought in as 'reinforcement', thereby transmitting a proportionately greater stimulus to the brain. The study of such matters provides another important focus of contemporary research into auditory perception.

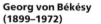

The basilar membrane A schematic diagram showing the points at which tones of different frequencies cause maximum amplitude of vibration (from O. Stuhlman, 1952).

Width at apex 0.50 mm
Average width 0.21 mm basal turn
0.34 mm middle turn
0.36 mm apical turn
Length 32 mm
Base 0.04 m

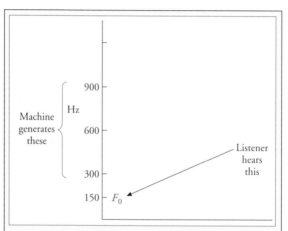

The case of the missing fundamental The place theory of pitch perception encounters a problem with the case of the missing fundamental. If a complex tone is generated, consisting (for example) of three pure tones at 300, 600, and 900 Hz, a listener will perceive the tone as having a pitch which corresponds to the fundamental frequency of these harmonics – 150 Hz – despite the fact that no energy has been generated at that frequency.

Hermann von Helmholtz (1821–94)

Georg von Békésy (1899–1972)

SPEECH PERCEPTION

Just as the vocal organs have evolved to facilitate the production of speech, so the auditory system seems 'tuned' to receive speech patterns. When we hear sounds, we hear them as either speech or non-speech; there seems to be no middle ground. No matter how hard we try, we cannot hear speech as a series of acoustic hisses and buzzes, but only as a sequence of speech sounds. This is the kind of observation that has motivated the field of *speech perception* – the study of the way speech sounds are analysed and identified by ears and brain.

Even after several years of research, the process of speech perception is little understood. Several questions illustrate the problems faced by researchers in this area.

• We hear a sequence of sounds, words, and other units in speech; but when we look for these units in the speech waveform, it is difficult to see them. The linguistic units are not neatly demarcated by pauses or other boundary markers: the speech signal varies continuously (p. 137). How, then, is the brain able to analyse this signal so that the language units can be identified?

• When several people are talking at once in a crowded room, we are able to 'tune in' to one speaker and to ignore the others. How does the brain select auditory information so impressively?

• When we hear different instances of a sound, we have no difficulty recognizing them as 'the same'; but when we examine the waveforms, we find that they are not physically identical. A [b] before an [i] vowel does not have exactly the same waveform as [b] before [a], or [b] at the end of a word. Moreover, the articulation of [b] by different people will result in different waveforms because their regional accents and individual voice qualities will not be the same (p. 20). It will vary, further, when people adopt different tones of voice (such as a whisper), or when it is said in a noisy situation. How does the brain recognize sounds when there is so much variation?

• Many pairs of words differ by only one sound – *cap* and *cab*, for instance; but when we examine the waveforms of such words, we find that the differences between them are often simultaneously located in several parts of the speech signal. The contrast between *cap* and *cab* is partly due to acoustic differences found at the ends of these words, but it is also due to differences between the vowels – the [a] of *cab* being much longer than that of *cap*. Yet in listening to speech we ignore the vowel difference and 'hear' only the consonant difference. How does the brain bring this information together?

• In normal speech, people produce sounds very quickly (12 or more segments per second), run sounds together, and leave sounds out. Nonetheless, the brain is able to process such rapid sequences, and cope with these modifications. For example, in the word *handbag*, the *nd* is pronounced as [m], because of the influence of the following [b] (p. 166); but the word is still interpreted as *hand* and not *ham*. How does the brain carry out such partial identifications?

Indirect procedures

A further difficulty is that the link between speech and listener perception cannot be studied in a direct manner. The movements within the ear and auditory nerve cannot easily be observed, nor can the associated activity taking place in the brain. Speech perception studies therefore have to rely on a range of indirect methods.

• The acoustic properties of the speech signal are analysed and related to the way in which people judge sounds to be the same or different.

• Experiments are devised in which sounds are obscured or distorted in various ways, to see how far identification continues to be possible.

• Speech sounds are created artificially using special instruments (p. 146), and systematically varied to see what effect this has on our perception – a procedure that also helps to determine whether our assumptions about speech analysis have been correct.

In all cases, problems of experimental design and data interpretation have caused progress to be painstakingly slow. Research into infant speech perception is especially difficult (p. 240). But a substantial core of theoretical and empirical research is now available.

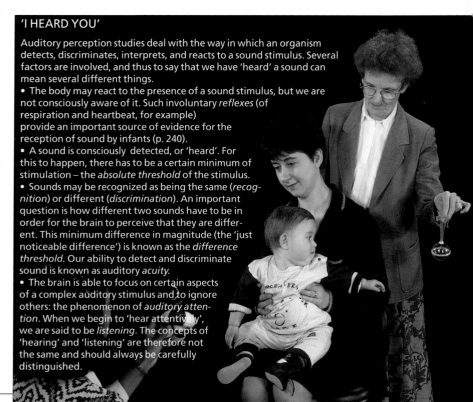

'I HEARD YOU'

Auditory perception studies deal with the way in which an organism detects, discriminates, interprets, and reacts to a sound stimulus. Several factors are involved, and thus to say that we have 'heard' a sound can mean several different things.

• The body may react to the presence of a sound stimulus, but we are not consciously aware of it. Such involuntary *reflexes* (of respiration and heartbeat, for example) provide an important source of evidence for the reception of sound by infants (p. 240).

• A sound is consciously detected, or 'heard'. For this to happen, there has to be a certain minimum of stimulation – the *absolute threshold* of the stimulus.

• Sounds may be recognized as being the same (*recognition*) or different (*discrimination*). An important question is how different two sounds have to be in order for the brain to perceive that they are different. This minimum difference in magnitude (the 'just noticeable difference') is known as the *difference threshold*. Our ability to detect and discriminate sound is known as auditory *acuity*.

• The brain is able to focus on certain aspects of a complex auditory stimulus and to ignore others: the phenomenon of *auditory attention*. When we begin to 'hear attentively', we are said to be *listening*. The concepts of 'hearing' and 'listening' are therefore not the same and should always be carefully distinguished.

ACOUSTIC CUES

One reason why we are able to recognize speech, despite all the acoustic variation in the signal, and even in very difficult listening conditions, is that the speech situation contains a great deal of *redundancy* – more information than is strictly necessary to decode the message. There is, firstly, our general ability to make predictions about the nature of speech, based on our previous linguistic experience – our knowledge of the speaker, subject matter, language, and so on. But in addition, the wide range of frequencies found in every speech signal presents us with far more information than we need in order to recognize what is being said. As a result, we are able to focus our auditory attention on just the relevant distinguishing features of the signal – features that have come to be known as *acoustic cues*.

What are these cues, and how can we prove their role in the perception of speech? It is not possible to obtain this information simply by carrying out an acoustic analysis of natural speech (as in §23): this would tell us what acoustic information is present but not which features of the signal are actually used by listeners in order to identify speech sounds. The best an acoustic description can do is give us a rough idea as to what a cue *might* be – for example, a formant (p. 135) at a certain frequency, or the duration of a burst of noise. But to learn about listeners' perception, we need a different approach.

The main technique has been to create artificial sounds using a *speech synthesizer* – an electronic device that generates sound waves with any required combination of frequency, intensity, and time (§§23, 26). In the classic experiments using this device, the synthesizer was fed simplified patterns of the kind produced by a sound spectrograph (p. 136). For example, it could be programmed to produce a sound with two formants at certain frequencies, and one could then see whether the sound that emerged was recognizable as a certain vowel. Or, a sequence of formants, formant transitions, and bursts of noise could be synthesized, to see if listeners would perceive a particular sequence of consonant and vowel.

Using this technique, in the 1960s researchers at Haskins Laboratories in the USA found it was possible to establish the crucial role of the first two formants for the recognition of vowels. Similarly, the technique confirmed the importance of voice onset time (p. 137) for discriminating voiceless and voiced consonants. And, in an important series of experiments, it was shown how the transitions of the second formant are especially important as a cue for place of articulation. The 14 patterns (above right) represented 300 msec syllables differing from each other only in their second formant transition. F_1 was held steady, and F_2 was made to vary, as shown. These sounds were then generated in a speech synthesizer and presented to listeners in random order. It was found that patterns 1 and 2 were heard as [b]; patterns 6 and 7 as [d]; and patterns 13 and 14 as [g] (after A. M. Liberman, et al., 1957).

Such findings have laid the foundation for speech perception studies; but a great deal still remains to be explained. For example, it is not obvious how listeners handle the difference between stressed and unstressed sounds, or other modifications that result from the speed of connected speech. Moreover, the acoustic values cited for the various sounds are averages, and do not take into account the many differences between speakers. Males, females, and children will produce the same vowel with very different formants, and it is not yet clear how listeners make allowances for these differences – for example, enabling them to judge that a male [a] and female [a] are somehow the 'same'. Presumably, they work out some way of relating vowel values to the dimensions of the speaker's vocal tract; but experiments have not yet been able to establish exactly what this might be.

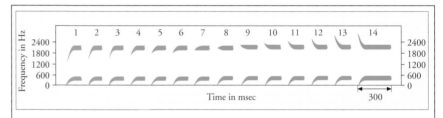

A series of control patterns for a speech synthesizer, in which F_2 transitions are systematically varied.

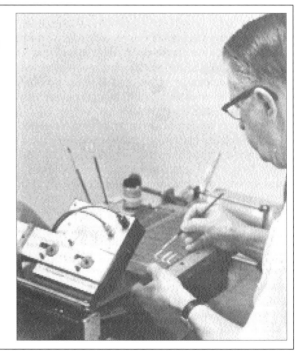

Early speech synthesis
A member of the Haskins Laboratories research team is shown using one of the early speech synthesizers, the Pattern Playback. A syllable was painted onto an acetate film loop. The pattern was then read photoelectrically, and converted into an acoustic signal.

CATEGORICAL PERCEPTION

When [pa] and [ba] are pronounced in isolation, the consonants clearly differ in voice onset time (VOT) – the time between the release of the lips and the onset of vocal cord vibration (p. 137). The average VOT value for [p] is +0.06 sec, and for [b] is 0.0. What would happen to a consonant that was syn-

syllables were synthesized with VOT values ranging from –0.15 sec to +0.15 sec in steps of 0.01 secs. They were played randomly to listeners, who had to say whether they were [pa] or [ba]. The graph below gives the results.

When VOT was less than +0.03, the syllable was usu-

narrow boundary region was there any confusion. What is significant is the very sharp nature of this boundary (a differential of only 0.05 sec). It seems that listeners hear two possible types of sound, regardless of VOT variation. There is very little room for uncertainty.

Several experiments on other sound contrasts have shown the generality of this finding, especially for consonants. It is even present in infants (p. 240). Listeners seem able to discriminate items on an acoustic continuum in a categorical manner. Sounds near a boundary area are interpreted as belonging to one or other of the categories, and are not felt to be uncertain cases. *Categorical perception* is plainly an important characteristic speech perceptual ability – and seems to be important for other aspects of sound discrimination too.

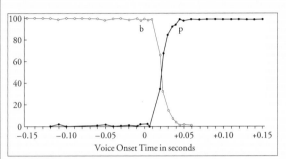

Voice Onset Time in seconds

thesized midway between these values? Would it be identified as [p] or as [b]?

In one study (L. Lisker & A. Abramson, 1970), artificial

ally identified as [ba]; when it was more than +0.03, it was heard as [pa]. For most of the study, listeners were in total agreement; only in a

SELECTIVE LISTENING

When listening to someone in a crowded room full of other conversations, we are able to attend to the speaker and ignore the others. However, if we hear our name spoken nearby, we readily tune in to that conversation, at the risk of ignoring the person we are supposed to be listening to. Such 'cocktail-party phenomena' illustrate the human ability to pay attention to some incoming sound stimuli and to ignore others – what is known as *selective listening*.

In early studies of selective listening, listeners were presented with two spoken messages at once. They were instructed to ignore one and to repeat the other while listening to it at the same time ('shadowing'). It turned out that people were able to do this very well. Moreover, afterwards they had hardly any memory for the ignored message – not even noticing when it was changed from a male to a female speaker, or from one language to another.

This kind of study can be used to help demonstrate the fundamental role that meaning plays in the process of speech perception. For example, if one message is semantically similar to the other, or consists of strings of clichés, listeners switch from one message to the other without realizing it; whereas if the two messages are semantically quite distinct, there is no interference.

This point also emerges from studies of people shadowing a single speech message. They can do this very quickly – sometimes being only a quarter of a second behind the speaker (no more than a syllable or two). If errors are then deliberately put into the speech stimulus (e.g. *tomorrance* for *tomorrow*, or *penknife* for *petrol*), they are often spontaneously corrected by the shadower. This too suggests that linguistic factors have an important part to play in the perception of continuous speech.

PERCEIVING CONTINUOUS SPEECH

A great deal of research has been carried out on the perception of isolated sounds, syllables, or words. In connected speech, however, very different processes seem to operate. We do not perceive whole sentences as a sequence of isolated sounds. Grammar and meaning (§§16–17) strongly influence our ability to identify linguistic units.

Several experiments have pointed to these differences. In one study, acoustically distorted words were presented to listeners in isolation and in context: the isolated words were identified far less accurately. In another study, single words were cut out of a tape recording of clear, intelligible, continuous speech: when these were played to listeners, there was great difficulty in making a correct identification. Normal speech proves to be so rapidly and informally articulated that in fact over half the words cannot be recognized in isolation – and yet listeners have little trouble following it, and can repeat whole sentences accurately.

Another feature of continuous speech perception is that people 'hear' sounds to be present, even if they are not. In one experiment, sentences were recorded with a sound electronically removed, and replaced with a cough or buzz. Most listeners, when asked if there were any sounds missing, said no; and even if told that a substitution had been made, most were unable to locate it. In another study, people were presented with one of

four sentences, in which a sound (marked =) had been replaced by a cough, and were asked to identify the word = *eel*.

It was found that the = eel was on the axle.
It was found that the = eel was on the shoe.
It was found that the = eel was on the orange.
It was found that the = eel was on the table.

People responded with *wheel*, *heel*, *peel*, and *meal* respectively, demonstrating the influence of grammatical and semantic context in perceptual decision-making (after R. M. Warren & R. P. Warren, 1970).

Results of this kind suggest that speech perception is a highly active process, with people making good the inadequacies of what they hear, arising out of external noise, omitted sounds, and so on. A further implication is that models of speech perception based on the study of isolated sounds and words will be of little value in explaining the processes that operate in relation to connected speech.

THEORIES OF SPEECH PERCEPTION

Theories of speech perception are usually classified into two general types, in which listeners adopt very different roles.

Listeners are active

In this view, listeners are thought to play an *active* role in speech perception, in the sense that when they hear a message, the sounds are decoded with reference to how they would be produced in speech. The listener's knowledge of articulation (§22) acts as a bridge between the acoustic signal and the identification of linguistic units.

One major view, proposed in the 1960s, is called the 'motor theory' of speech perception. This theory argues that people internally model the articulatory movements of a speaker. They identify sounds by sensing the articulatory gestures that must have produced them – as if they were 'saying' words to themselves to match the incoming speech.

Another approach is known as 'analysis by synthesis'. Here, listeners use a set of rules to analyse an incoming acoustic signal into an abstract set of features. The same rules are used to synthesize a matching version in production. The listener's perceptual system then compares the acoustic features of the incoming signal with the ones it has generated itself, and makes an identification.

Listeners are passive

In this view, listeners play a *passive* role. They hear a message, recognize the regular distinctive features of the waveform, and decode it. Listening is therefore essentially a sensory process, with the pattern of information in the acoustic stimulus directly triggering the neural response. No reference is made to a mediating process of speech production (except in difficult conditions, such as noisy speech situations).

Several mechanisms have been proposed. One approach proposes a system of 'template matching' – listeners match incoming auditory patterns to a set of abstract speech patterns (such as phonemes and syllables, §28) that have already been stored in the brain. Another postulates the use of 'feature detectors' – special neural receptors (analogous to those known to exist in visual processing) that are capable of responding to specific features of the sound stimulus, such as a particular formant, noise burst, or other universal feature.

Compromise

Both approaches have their strengths and weaknesses. Active approaches plausibly explain how listeners are able to adjust for such differences as speaker accent, voice quality, and speed of speech. And several kinds of experiment can be interpreted to support this view. In 'shadowing' studies for example, people are asked to repeat what someone says as quickly as possible, without waiting for the speaker to finish (p. 147). Listeners are evidently able to carry out this task at great speed, copying sounds even before they have heard all the acoustic cues. To do this, they must be making active use of their knowledge of linguistic structure.

However, there are arguments against a wholly active view of speech perception. There are many cases of people who cannot speak, for pathological reasons (§46), but who can understand well. And it is possible to understand the speech of stutterers, foreigners, young children, and others where it is not possible to make a simple articulatory match. The passive approach does not encounter the problems introduced by postulating an intermediate, articulatory step in speech perception. On the other hand, it has in turn been criticized for underestimating the variability of the link between acoustic signals and linguistic units (p. 145) and for presenting an account in which the processes of speech production and those of speech perception are seen as entirely separate. It therefore seems likely that some combination of active and passive theories will be required, in order to provide a satisfactory explanation of the process of speech perception.

A model of the hypothetical brain mechanisms used in speech perception and production (after G. Fant, 1967). This is a passive model, in which speech perception proceeds along the route ABCDE. In an active model, by contrast, the route would be ABCKFE.

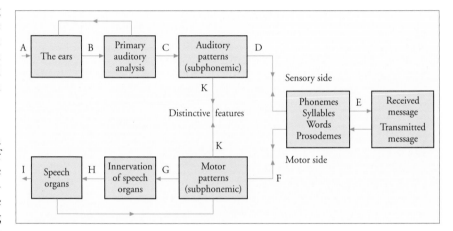

NATURAL VS. SYNTHETIC SPEECH

The 1990s has seen renewed interest in speech perception research as part of the growing programme of work on speech synthesis, especially in relation to automatic speech recognition (§26). The quality of synthetic speech has improved greatly in recent years, but the differences between synthetic and natural speech are still sufficiently large – particularly in relation to such characteristics as segment coarticulation and utterance prosody (pp. 158, 171) – that listeners usually find it easy to distinguish them. Natural speech, moreover, is highly redundant (p. 146), with more acoustic cues available for each segmental contrast than in synthetic speech, where the cues have been reduced to the bare minimum necessary to make a phonemic distinction. Do these differences affect the ability of listeners to perceive synthetic speech?

Certainly, if acoustic cues are missing or misleading, there are likely to be consequences. A problem of misperception in synthetic speech (e.g. because of a noisy environment) is less likely to be resolved if other acoustic cues are not there for the listener to fall back on. Repeating the utterance will not help, because no new information will be derived from hearing each repetition. It also appears to be much more difficult to identify phonemes (and thus words) in synthetic speech: people take longer, are less accurate, and find it more difficult to carry out other language tasks at the same time. Some studies have shown that listeners need to hear more of a synthesized word before they are able to identify it; and it proves to be more difficult recalling information when this is presented in synthetic speech.

The process of language comprehension, of course, involves factors (such as the use of context) which in some measure compensate for these problems, but these factors are not sufficient to eliminate all the difficulties. The current state of speech synthesis thus has several similarities with other kinds of speech where quality differs from normal, and where perceptual problems also arise, as in the case of foreign accents and speech handicaps (p. 279). (After S.A. Duffy & D.B. Pisoni, 1992.)

Is it possible to construct machines that will talk and understand speech? As early as the 18th century, attempts were being made to devise ways of mechanically reproducing the human voice. The Austrian inventor Wolfgang von Kempelen (1734–1804) built one such machine, consisting of a bellows to produce air flow, and other mechanisms to simulate parts of the vocal tract. Alexander Bell (1847–1922) also constructed a 'talking head', made out of various synthetic materials, that was able to produce a few distinct sounds.

Modern techniques have led to massive progress in this field. It is no longer necessary to build physical models of the vocal tract; sound waves can be generated electronically by synthesizing the different components of the sound wave. Early results sounded very much like machines; more recently, thanks to progress in computational technology, the quality of synthesized speech has greatly improved – so much so, that with some devices it is actually difficult to tell whether a machine or a human being is talking. In most cases, however, there are still problems of intelligibility and naturalness to be overcome, especially in producing speech with an acceptable intonation and rhythm (p. 148).

In general, automatic talkers are programmed with what to say. But current work in artificial intelligence has led to speech that has been synthesized on the basis of concepts derived from a machine's own internal knowledge structure (p. 416). This is a major area of contemporary research, which draws greatly on the fields of psychology, computer science, and linguistics. It is also hampered by the limitations of these fields – for example, the primitive accounts of human discourse structure available in linguistics (§20) make it difficult to devise satisfactory question-answering systems for use with machines. Spoken discourse is much harder to model than written discourse (p. 181) because of its use of prosody, hesitation, ellipsis, self-correction, and other dynamic features.

SPEECH RECOGNITION

The problem of automatic speech recognition is a complex one. It requires the automation of the processes of auditory perception and comprehension – neither of which is well understood in its own right (§25). Also, it has to cope with the large amount of variation in speech (such as regional accent and voice quality) and the noise found in everyday speech situations. However, there are now several devices that can recognize a small vocabulary of words spoken clearly and in isolation, or separated by pauses (as in a list of telephone numbers), in a quiet environment. The

machines are more likely to succeed if they have been given some information about the speaker's voice characteristics in advance (a 'template' of the speaker). It is also becoming increasingly possible to recognize chunks of continuous speech by single speakers, as long as the speech is not too rapid, and informal modifications are avoided. The amount of vocabulary that a system can cope with is gradually increasing, and large vocabulary recognition (LVR) systems are now being tested in continuous speech, in such domains as air travel and telephony. More advanced techniques of pattern matching are available as a result of research into artificial intelligence (p. 150), and projects are under way to use the new generation of computers to tackle these problems – but progress also depends on filling the gaps in our understanding of the acoustics of speech (§23), especially in relation to features of voice quality. Speaker-dependent approaches are still much more successful than speaker-independent ones.

Speech interaction with machines is unlikely to become routine (in homes and offices) until the 21st century, though some devices will be available sooner. For example, currently being developed is a 10,000-word, voice-activated typewriter, for which the manufacturers claim 97% accuracy in word recognition. The core vocabulary in this machine can be used by any speaker; but the machine has to be trained by individual speakers before they can get access to the whole vocabulary store. However, it remains to be seen whether such devices can cope with the biggest problem facing routine office use – the level of background noise.

A surviving fragment of Alexander Graham Bell's 'talking head', made around 1863, and discovered many years later in the attic of Bell's house in Washington DC.

RECOGNIZING SPEECH OR SPEAKERS?

Approaches to automatic speech recognition traditionally focus on the shared, linguistic elements in speech, and play down the non-linguistic – the features which comprise background voice quality or speaker individuality (§6). These are seen as obstacles in the way of efficient communication, and techniques of speaker normalization have been devised to eliminate such idiosyncrasy. But in a sociolinguistically real world, speaker identity and variety are important variables, and these days a great deal of attention is being paid to ways of incorporating these features into speech recognition and synthesis.

There are several domains where automatic speech recognition needs to take voice individuality into account. Speaker identification is one application, using such techniques as voiceprinting (p. 20) to determine whether the speech on a tape recording is the same as that of a suspect. Another is speaker verification, where the system uses the individuality present in voices to establish whether speakers are whom they claim to be.

Both applications present the analyst with major technical problems. A balance needs to be obtained between the need to accept a degree of normal variation (e.g. a temporary husky voice quality because the speaker has a sore throat) and the need to exclude others (a different person whose normal voice quality is husky). Another difficulty is in obtaining the minimum of data required to enable the system to establish an identity. For example, in the field of access control, such as a door entry system to a high security area, it is possible in principle to have someone provide as much speech as is needed to enable the recognizer to do its work; such flexibility is not present in the world of telephone banking, where people want to access their accounts quickly and with the minimum of fuss.

The problem of relevance

The essential problem facing speech recognition researchers is one of relevance: which features of the speech signal relate specifically to intelligibility (in the case of speech recognition), which to identity (in the case of speaker recognition), and which to neither (e.g. features of background noise)? Several acoustic parameters are involved, deriving from the characteristics of the vocal folds and vocal tract (§ 23). In relation to the vocal folds, particular attention needs to be paid to average fundamental frequency, frequency contour, frequency fluctuation, and glottal wave shape. Influential vocal tract features are the shape of the spectral envelope, the absolute values of the formant frequencies, formant bandwidth, formant trajectories, and the long-term average speech spectrum. A difficulty is that the significance of any one of these variables differs between speakers, and may also be affected by the speech situation and other factors. No single acoustic parameter is decisive in speech or voice recognition.

Most approaches, these days, are based on pattern recognition, in which subword units are modelled statistically. The most widely used is the Hidden Markov Model (HMM) method, named after Russian mathematician A. A. Markov (1856–1922), who helped develop the theory of stochastic processes. In a sequence of variable events (such as the sounds which comprise the pronunciation of a word), the probabilities at each step are seen as depending on the outcome of previous steps. HMM approaches specify the likelihood that a feature of the speech signal will occur at any given point. These models (there are several variants) are currently the most widely used in speech recognition: they do however require that a recognition system implements an efficient training procedure.

There are two critical issues. One is to solve the problem of the variability of speech. Individuals routinely vary the pronunciation of words when they speak, and this poses a major difficulty for any recognition system which contains a single transcription in its lexicon. The duration of syllables, in particular, varies enormously, depending on such factors as hesitancy and emphasis. The other critical issue is to improve the robustness of speech processing under adverse conditions (e.g. the noisy ambience of cars, cockpits, and military situations). Human perception and recognition of speech is highly robust and very flexible: humans can immediately adapt to a new sentence, even if it is spoken by a previously unknown speaker over a new instrument. Machines as yet cannot.

WHAT TIME IS IT?

Speech recognition technology is now sufficiently advanced that it is possible to introduce voice-activated services over a telephone network. In the early 1990s, one such service was being developed at a centre in Sydney, Australia: the World Time Information Service (WTIS). Callers use voice commands to access information about countries overseas (the time and day of the destination, the international direct-dial code, the country code, and the call charge rate). They dial a number, then name a country. If there is a good degree of recognition, the information contained in the database is transmitted, using digitized speech; if the recognition is poor, the system asks the caller to confirm the name of the country selected.

This kind of operation seems very simple, but the technical problems are considerable. We have only to reflect on the amount of variability in the speech signal with which any such system has to cope. In addition to the usual problems of variation in speaker accents and voice qualities, interference from the hardware needs to be taken into account. Telephone handsets vary greatly, as does the vocal behaviour of people when they use a handset (loudness and duration levels are especially prone to alteration). There are many unpredictable elements in background noise (passing cars and planes, ambulance sirens, office hubbub). Also, telephone networks have different characteristics, and quality can vary greatly between local and long-distance situations.

The WTIS database had a vocabulary of 55 words – 41 country names and their variations, along with five control words. The recognition system used a variant of the Hidden Markov Modelling approach. A test of this system on 50 male and 50 female speakers produced an average recognition rate of 96.8% for the first word chosen by the system – a figure which increased to 98.8% when a second word choice was allowed. Some names achieved 100% recognition first time. Many of the misrecognized words were due to a strong foreign accent, high background noise, or being spoken too softly or loudly. The most frequent errors related to the four items *Holland*, *Poland*, *Ireland*, and *Thailand*, which have a very similar phonological structure. When the researchers carried out some additional analysis (modify-

ing the system so that it recognized two subwords within each of these names), accuracy significantly improved, and produced an overall recognition rate of 97.3%.

Studies of this kind show the state of the art very clearly. A good speaker-independent result is obtained on a limited vocabulary set of isolated words, and a series of specific problems are identified which warrant further investigation using a more refined acoustic analysis. Extending the empirical range of such studies, in the light of increasingly sophisticated methodologies, is now the major goal of speech recognition research. (After J. Song & A. Samouelian, 1993.)

WORD ACCURACY TEST RESULTS

Word	Accuracy (%)	Word	Accuracy (%)	Word	Accuracy (%)
America	99.5	Indonesia	99.0	Sri Lanka	99.5
Australia	96.5	Ireland	84.0	States	94.0
Austria	99.0	Israel	99.0	Stop	98.5
Britain	96.5	Italy	94.5	Sweden	97.0
Canada	97.0	Japan	95.0	Switzerland	96.0
Cancel	99.0	Korea	99.0	Taiwan	96.5
Central	98.0	Lebanon	98.0	Thailand	86.0
Chile	97.0	Malaysia	98.0	Turkey	93.5
China	94.5	New Zealand	99.5	UK	95.6
Denmark	99.5	Netherlands	95.5	US	99.5
Eastern	98.0	No	92.4	USA	99.5
Fiji	99.5	Operator	100.0	United States	99.0
France	98.0	Papua New Guinea	99.5	United Kingdom	100.0
Germany	96.0	Philippines	96.5	Vietnam	97.5
Greece	97.5	Poland	83.4	Western	98.5
Hawaii	99.5	Russia	99.5	Yes	96.5
Holland	87.9	South Africa	100.0	Yugoslavia	100.0
Hong Kong	99.5	Singapore	100.0		
India	98.0	Spain	94.0	Average	96.8

SPEECH SYNTHESIS

Different techniques are available for providing a machine with a voice. The voices (human or synthesized) can be prerecorded, so that they can be produced at a predetermined point (when an engine requires servicing, for example), or when a button is pressed (as in many children's toys, such as 'Speak and Spell'). They are also widely used in aids for the handicapped, and in computer-assisted terminals. But the approach has several serious limitations. The linguistic needs have to be precisely anticipated, and changes are difficult to introduce. Also, accessing the data takes a lot of time, especially if a large vocabulary has been stored in the machine.

Modern speech synthesis systems work by using a model of the relevant properties of speech to generate artificial signals.

• Most approaches are *acoustic* or *terminal analogues*, representing the acoustic properties of the output of the vocal tract, which is viewed essentially as a combination of source (voice or noise) and filter (the frequency responses which relate to the sequence of articulatory movements). The channel vocoder was the earliest acoustic analogue system, to be followed by formant synthesis, using spectrographic input (p. 146) and more recently by linear prediction coefficient (LPC) synthesis, in which the aim is to predict the speech signal through a set of coefficients representing its spectral properties.

• *Articulatory analogues* are based on the physical geometry (the anatomy and physiology) of the vocal tract. They have considerable potential, but their development has been limited by the difficulty of obtaining reliable, non-invasive data about the properties of the vocal tract during the act of speech.

• A further alternative is to avoid the problems of acoustic and articulatory synthesis altogether, by devising a system which generates speech by stringing together ('concatenating') natural speech segments, later imposing prosodic features.

The above approaches work on the basis of an analysis of the parameters of natural speech, whether acoustic or articulatory. By contrast, it is possible to synthesize speech through the use of rules operating on an input consisting solely of written symbols, whether a phonetic transcription or everyday orthography (typewritten or printed). These 'text-to-speech' (or 'grapheme-to-phoneme') systems have special potential in areas which have to rely on orthographic input, such as in human–machine interfaces in information technology (in the absence of satisfactory speech recognition systems, p. 150) or in the development of reading machines for the blind.

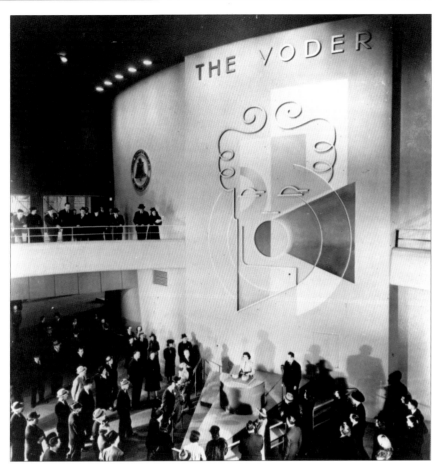

The Voder Speech Synthesizer being demonstrated at the 1939 World's Fair by Bell Telephones

VOICE CONVERSION

Voice conversion starts with the speech signal of one speaker and alters it to sound like another. It is a technique which is likely to be an important element in future text-to-speech systems, as it would reduce the time and expense involved in developing a new synthesized voice from scratch. Starting with a given voice, it would be possible to alter its properties so that it conveyed a different sex, age, or accent, depending on the needs of the users.

There are many areas of possible application. People could in principle choose a particular type of voice from a machine, in much the same way that they can now choose shades of paint by mixing constituent basic colours. Speech-handicapped people would be able to buy a machine with a 'standard' voice, and then modify this to suit their sex, age, and circumstances. Other areas of application include telephony, forensic science, security situations, and the selection and synchronization of voices on film soundtracks.

Speech morphing One day film directors will be able to shape and edit speech signals as easily as they can currently manipulate the morphology of shapes, using electronic technology. If a voice turns out not to be hoarse enough, or gravelly enough, the qualities could be added painlessly in post-production. The voices of Boris Karloff or Vincent Price could be heard alive again. The film personae of these actors might well approve of such beyond-the-grave developments, but whether modern undead actors will is quite another matter!

Boris Karloff (1887–1969) in *The Ghoul*, 1933

Text-to-speech systems

A text-to-speech system involves a complex sequence of steps, whose interaction is still not fully understood. Synthesis here refers to the whole process from input to output, and not just the final step of sound generation. Typically, the text needs to be processed in a preliminary way, to ensure that errors and irrelevant symbols are eliminated. The input words need to be analysed into their component parts (morphemes, p. 90), and any irregular items matched with those in the system's lexical store. Words whose sound–spelling correspondence is regular will be given a phonological shape generated by a system of letter-to-sound rules. Further rules will add information relating to word sequences, both segmental (e.g. assimilation, p. 166) and prosodic (e.g. rhythm and intonation), and a phonetic representation will be generated. These phonetic strings will then be given an acoustic synthesis, using one of the above methods (p. 151).

Speech synthesis continues to be an important goal of research in phonetics and technology. Apart from its potential applicability for machine interaction, it is needed by people (such as those with paralysis of the vocal organs, p. 282) who have to rely on a portable synthesizer to speak. In several automatic translation projects (p. 352), such as Japanese work on the translation of telephone messages, the goal is to ensure that the translated speech should be synthesized. Increasing the acceptability of such speech continues to be an important goal: the quality of synthesized output by well-known figures (such as the speech of UK professor Stephen Hawking) has achieved an unprecedented level of public recognition, and brought home to many the distance which has still to be travelled. The demands of these and other applications will motivate continued growth in the field, advances in speech technology will continue to broaden horizons, and progress is likely to be enhanced as the research directions in the fields of speech recognition and speech synthesis are brought closer together.

THREE WAYS IN

Three main methods of language analysis are commonly encountered in a 'synthesis by rule' system.

• The machine can translate whole words, by looking them up in a table in which each word has been given a synthesizer code. The words are then pronounced as wholes, in a kind of 'look and say' approach (§34). This is easily done when the vocabulary is small; but when many words are involved, the approach becomes cumbersome and restricting. Retrieving the words is very time-consuming, and the system cannot cope with new or unusual words (such as proper names).

• The machine analyses words into their constituent parts (morphemes, p. 90), and links these with appropriate speech sounds. It has been estimated that a dictionary of only 8,000 morphemes is sufficient to handle 95% of texts. However, a large computer system is needed in order to achieve real-time performance.

• The machine analyses words letter-by-letter, and matches the patterns with a stored list of sound correspondences, using a predetermined set of rules (about 400, in one approach). The usual method synthesizes speech on the basis of the acoustic features of sounds (§23), which are then combined into the vowel and consonant segments, words, and sentences, according to the language's phonological rules (§28). Some approaches use a database of already synthesized segments. This is a kind of 'phonic' decoding (§34) – essential if the system is to handle all the words in a language. But it is difficult to devise satisfactory rules to handle stress and intonation.

THE FEMALE VOICE

The vast majority of projects in speech synthesis have used male voices. The early synthesizers of the 1950s were very limited in the kind of speech they could cope with. The Haskins Laboratories Pattern Playback, for example, could only produce a fundamental frequency of 120 Hz. Moreover, very little information was available on the acoustics of female speech. Although several efforts were made to produce female-sounding speech, none of them was convincing. However, since the 1980s, the use of more sophisticated acoustic analyses and equipment has led to the synthesis of several utterances with an acceptable female quality.

Most versions have been based on conversion from a male voice, and not on the analysis of natural female speech. In an experiment by Denis Klatt (1987), this conversion was achieved chiefly by scaling up the fundamental frequency (by a factor of 1.7) and the formants (by 1.175), and by removing the fifth formant. However, the author concluded that the transformation was not entirely successful. Further progress has since been made, for example by a Swedish system known as GLOVE. This approach analyses a natural female utterance, then uses a text-to-speech system and a formant synthesizer to produce a female voice of acceptable quality. (After I. Karlsson, 1991.)

It evidently takes much more than an octave jump (p. 19) before the different sexual resonances of male and female speech can be achieved. It is important also to maintain a differential between the immature voice of the child and the voice of the mature female. Differences in voice quality (e.g. breathiness) are likely to be critical.

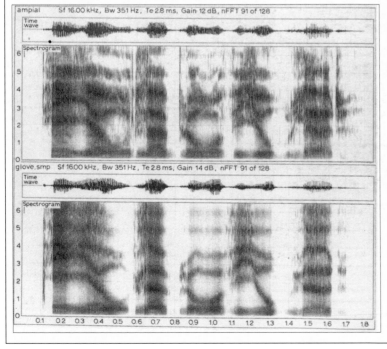

Time-wave and broad-band spectrograms of a Swedish sentence uttered by a female speaker (top) and produced by the GLOVE synthesizer (bottom). The differences are chiefly due to a limited copying of the voice source.

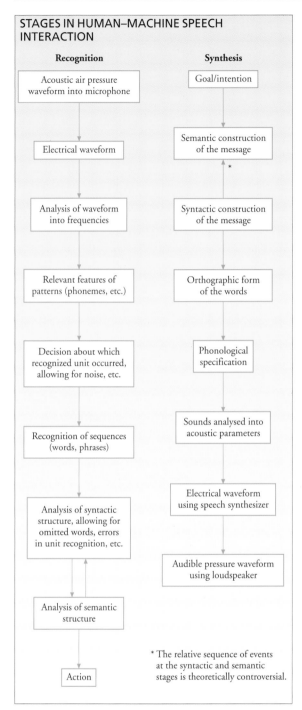

STAGES IN HUMAN–MACHINE SPEECH INTERACTION

Recognition

Acoustic air pressure waveform into microphone

↓

Electrical waveform

↓

Analysis of waveform into frequencies

↓

Relevant features of patterns (phonemes, etc.)

↓

Decision about which recognized unit occurred, allowing for noise, etc.

↓

Recognition of sequences (words, phrases)

↓

Analysis of syntactic structure, allowing for omitted words, errors in unit recognition, etc.

↓

Analysis of semantic structure

↓

Action

Synthesis

Goal/intention

↓

Semantic construction of the message

↓ *

Syntactic construction of the message

↓

Orthographic form of the words

↓

Phonological specification

↓

Sounds analysed into acoustic parameters

↓

Electrical waveform using speech synthesizer

↓

Audible pressure waveform using loudspeaker

* The relative sequence of events at the syntactic and semantic stages is theoretically controversial.

WHY BOTHER?

We are so used to hearing human voices emerging from robots and computers in science fiction films that the desirability of human–machine speech interaction is often taken for granted. However, this field of research has not been without its critics. The arguments have been based on several theoretical and commercial considerations.

- The research (into speech recognition, in particular) is unnecessary to social needs, and the money would be better spent elsewhere.

- Speech interaction may be more expensive in running costs than using written or coded text. It is unclear whether these costs are outweighed by the advantages.
- The commercial demand for quick results has led to some poor-quality research and development.
- The ability to produce hardware is now far ahead of the relevant theoretical research fields, especially in speech perception and acoustics.
- Speech input to machines will be unreliable for the foreseeable future because of interference from other speech in the environment.
- Routine speech input to machines leaves no permanent record, whereas written or coded input does.
- The concern to make machines sound human is unnecessary. Sometimes mechanical voices are more easily understood, especially in noisy work conditions. And 'friendly' voice systems may persuade non-expert users that the machines are capable of more than they really are.
- Many people do not like talking machines because this suggests they have intelligence (a currently controversial issue, in its own right).

In favour

At the same time, the field of human–machine speech interaction has had many defenders, whose arguments have been of the following kind.

- Speech interaction is the easiest and most natural approach, and is less prone to errors than typing.
- It permits other activities to proceed at the same time.
- It is more convenient in many respects. Interaction can take place even when the user is out of sight or reach of the machine. An interaction can be easily monitored by third parties and is compatible with other everyday methods of communication (e.g. by telephone).
- There are a large number of social and business applications that promote accuracy, efficiency, and cost-effectiveness.

The future

These arguments will doubtless continue, but they are somewhat academic. Machine speech, of varying quality, it rapidly becoming a routine part of everyday life, as the various technical problems are overcome. We can hear automatic talkers in elevators, announcing systems, assembly lines, calculators, children's toys, cars, speaking clocks, telephone answering services, and business offices (in providing stock quotation reports). The potential of human–machine speech interaction is also being actively researched in such areas as air-traffic control, airline connection information, shop checkout monitoring, medical screening, robotics, and communication aids for the handicapped. There are still many problems to be solved, but a world in which speech interaction with machines is routine may now be only a generation away.

The description and classification of speech sounds is the main aim of phonetic science, or *phonetics*. Sounds may be identified with reference to their production (or 'articulation') in the vocal tract, their acoustic transmission, or their auditory reception. The most widely used descriptions are articulatory, because the vocal tract provides a convenient and well-understood reference point (§22); but auditory judgments play an important part in the identification of some sounds (vowels, in particular). The more precise and comprehensive possibilities of acoustic description are outlined in §23.

An articulatory phonetic description generally makes reference to six main factors.

Air stream   The source and direction of air flow identifies the basic class of sound. The vast majority of speech sounds are produced using pulmonic egressive air (p. 125). Non-pulmonic sounds include the clicks, implosives, and ejectives described on pp. 126–7.

Vocal folds   The variable action of the vocal folds must be considered – in particular, the presence or absence of vibration (p. 128). *Voiced* sounds are produced when the vocal folds vibrate; *voiceless* sounds are produced when there is no vibration, the folds remaining open. Other vocal fold actions are sometimes referred to (e.g. the closed glottis used to produce the glottal stop).

Soft palate   The position of the soft palate (p. 130) must be noted. When it is lowered, air passes through the nose, and the sound is described as *nasal* or *nasalized*; when it is raised, air passes through the mouth, and the sound is *oral*.

Place of articulation   This parameter can be used to make several precise phonetic distinctions. It refers to the point in the vocal tract at which the main closure or narrowing is made, such as at the lips, teeth, or hard palate. Accompanying 'secondary' constrictions or movements may need to be taken into account as well.

Manner of articulation   This is also a major descriptive parameter, referring to the type of constriction or movement that occurs at any place of articulation, such as a marked degree of narrowing, a closure with sudden release, or a closure with slow release.

Lips   The position of the lips is an important feature of the description of certain sounds (especially vowels), such as whether they are rounded or spread, closed or open.

In very precise descriptions of speech sounds, other factors may also be noted, such as the relative position of the jaw or the overall shape of the tongue.

VOWELS AND CONSONANTS

These two labels are probably the most familiar of all the terms used in the description of speech, but they nonetheless need to be used with great care, to avoid mixing up two different kinds of definition.

In a *phonetic* definition, vowels are distinguished from consonants in terms of how they are articulated in the vocal tract, and the associated patterns of acoustic energy. In this approach, consonants are defined as sounds made by a closure in the vocal tract, or by a narrowing which is so marked that air cannot escape without producing audible friction. Vowels are sounds that have no such stricture: air escapes in a relatively unimpeded way through the mouth or nose. It is therefore relatively easy to 'feel' the articulation of consonants; whereas vowels, involving only slight movements of the tongue and lips, are difficult to locate in this way, and are easier to distinguish on auditory grounds.

In a linguistic – strictly, a *phonological* – definition (§28), vowels are distinguished from consonants in terms of how these units are used in the structure of spoken language. In this approach, consonants (C) are defined as the units that typically occur at the margins of syllables (p. 166); vowels (V) are the units that typically occur at the centre of syllables. For example, in the syllables *pet* /pet/, *cat* /kat/, and *bus* /bʌs/, the syllable structure in each case consists of a central unit and two marginal units, to produce the pattern CVC.

In the case of most sounds, the phonetic and the phonological approaches coincide. For example [p], [f], and [m] are 'consonants' from both points of view. Phonetically, they involve closure or audible friction. Phonologically, they function at syllable margins, e.g. *map* /map/, *puff* /pʌf/; there are no such syllables as */mpf/ or */mfp/. Similarly, [a], [i], and [o] are 'vowels' from both points of view: phonetically, they are produced without audible friction; and phonologically, they occur at the centres of syllables, in such words as *cap* /kap/, *hit* /hɪt/, and *hot* /hɒt/.

The problem cases
In such cases as English [l], [ɹ], [w], and [j], the two sets of criteria conflict. From a phonological point of view, these units typically occur at the margins of syllables, as in *let* /let/, *rat* /rat/, *wet* /wet/, and *you* /juː/ and they must therefore be considered as consonants. But

Kenneth L Pike

from a phonetic point of view, they are articulated without audible friction, and acoustically they display a similar energy pattern to that displayed by [a], [i], etc. (p. 137). They must therefore be considered as vowels.

There are only two ways out of this problem. One is to say that these four units are neither consonants nor vowels but midway between these categories. The terms *semi-consonant* or *semi-vowel* have often been introduced for this purpose, and this is the usual solution. The other, more radical solution is to introduce two completely different sets of labels for talking about these units. The American phonetician Kenneth Pike (1912–) suggested the terms *vocoid* and *contoid* for the phonetic distinction, reserving *vowel* and *consonant* for the phonological one. Thus, all vowels are vocoids; but consonants may be either contoids ([p], [f], [h], etc.) or vocoids ([l], [ɹ], [w], [j]). (The further possibility of a contoid acting as a vowel is of marginal linguistic significance, e.g. the [s] of *psst*.)

It is certainly helpful to have two sets of terms to make it clear whether we are talking about sound units from a phonetic or a phonological point of view. However, as only a small number of units raise the problem in a severe form, the distinction has not been universally adopted. Moreover, it needs further interpretation in the light of the way a language's phonological system is organized (§28).

VOWELS

Vowels are normally described with reference to four criteria:

- The part of the tongue that is raised – front, centre, or back (p. 131).
- The extent to which the tongue rises in the direction of the palate. Normally, three or four degrees are recognized: *high, mid* (often divided into *mid-high* and *mid-low*), and *low*. Alternatively, tongue height can be described as *close, mid-close, mid-open* and *open*.
- The position of the soft palate – raised for oral vowels, and lowered for vowels which have been nasalized.
- The kind of opening made at the lips – various degrees of lip rounding or spreading.

It is difficult to be precise about the exact articulatory positions of the tongue and palate because very slight movements are involved, which give us very little internal sensation. Absolute values are not possible (such as saying that the tongue has moved *n* millimetres in a certain direction), because the mouth dimensions are not the same between speakers. Vowel judgments therefore tend to be made on the basis of auditory criteria, in association with a limited amount of visual and tactile information.

WAYS OF TRANSCRIBING ENGLISH VOWELS

Several phonetic transcriptions for English vowels have been devised. The changes in symbol reflect different interpretations by the authors of the relationships between the sounds. For example, Daniel Jones (p. 156) represents the difference between *seat* and *sit* as essentially a contrast of vowel length, using the symbols [ɪ] and [i] respectively; whereas A.C. Gimson (1917–85) represents it as a contrast of both length and quality, using a different symbol as well as a length mark, [i:] and [ɪ] respectively. It is important to realize that all the authors are transcribing the *same* set of contrasts (apart from the case of the back open vowels, where American and British English accents differ). Their symbols simply draw our attention to different aspects of the way the vowels are produced.

	Jones (1956)	Gimson (1962)	Trager & Smith (1951)	Kenyon & Knott (1935)
seat	iː	iː	iy	i
sit	i	ɪ	i	ɪ
set	e	e	e	ɛ
sat	æ	æ	æ	æ
cut	ə	ʌ	ə	ʌ
cart	ɑ	ɑː	a	ɑ
cot	ɔ	ɒ	a	ɑ
caught	ɔː	ɔː	ɔh	ɔ
curt	əː	ɜː	ər	ɜˑ
full	u	ʊ	u	u
fool	uː	uː	uw	u

This encyclopedia uses Gimson's system, with the substitution of [a] for [æ].

Daniel Jones

A. C. Gimson

THINGS THAT CAN HAPPEN TO VOWELS

Vowel qualities can be much influenced by articulatory movements elsewhere in the vocal tract, especially at the back of the mouth and in the throat. The possibilities include the following.

Nasalization
The soft palate is lowered, allowing some of the air stream to escape through the nose – an important feature of many vowels in French and Portuguese, for example. The diacritic for nasalization is ~.

Widening
In some languages, variations in the size of the pharynx (§22) affect vowel quality. 'Wide' vowels are produced when the tongue root is pulled forward and the larynx is lowered, thus enlarging the pharynx. Vowels where this does not take place are then termed 'narrow'. The West African language, Twi, illustrates this kind of contrast.

Rhoticization
In some languages, vowels are articulated with an additional feature: *r-colouring*, or *rhoticization*. These vowels are usually articulated with the tip or front of the tongue raised, as would be the case for a retroflex [ɽ] (p. 157). They are widely used in American and British English dialects in words where *r* follows the vowel, as in *sir, word*. The phonetic symbol for a rhoticized vowel is ˑ, as in [ɑˑ], though sometimes special symbols are used, such as [ɚ].

The Cardinal Vowel system

The first widely used system for classifying vowels was devised by the British phonetician, Daniel Jones (1881–1976). The *Cardinal Vowel* diagram (or quadrilateral) is a set of standard reference points based on a combination of articulatory and auditory judgments. The front, centre, and back of the tongue are distinguished, as are four levels of tongue height:

- the highest position the tongue can achieve without producing audible friction;
- the lowest position the tongue can achieve; and
- two intermediate levels, dividing the intervening space into auditorily equidistant areas.

The grid provides a basis for vowel classification, along with information about the accompanying position of

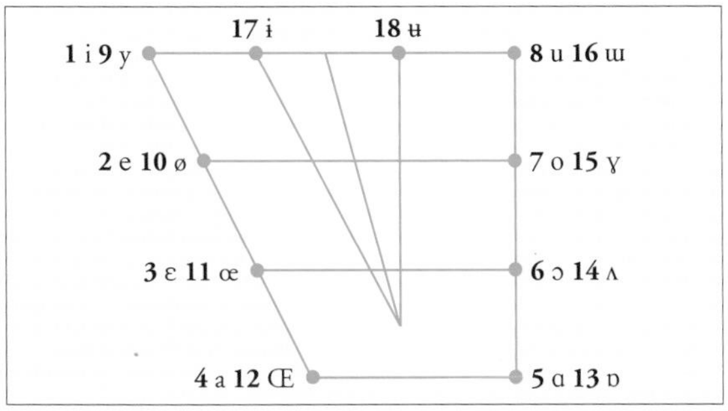

the lips. Jones gave the main vowel-points numbers, distinguishing a *primary* series (1–8) from a *secondary* series (9–16), and adding two further points (17–18). Each of these vowel-points was also given a phonetic symbol. The distinction between primary and secondary cardinal vowels is based on lip position. The first five primary vowels are all unrounded: front [i], [e], [ɛ], and [a], and back [ɑ]. The remaining three back vowels are rounded: [ɔ], [o], and [u]. In the secondary series, the lip position is reversed: the first five are rounded: front [y], [ø], [œ], and [ɶ], and back [ɒ]. The remaining three back vowels are unrounded: [ʌ], [ɤ], and [ɯ]. The two other vowels represent the high points achieved by the centre of the tongue: they are unrounded [ɨ] and rounded [ʉ].

Several other proposals have been made about ways of dividing up the vowel area that reflect articulatory movements (as established from a study of X-ray photographs) more accurately; but Jones's diagram continues to be widely used, especially in Europe. It should be emphasized that the cardinal vowels are not real vowels: they are invariable reference points (available on record) that have to be learned by rote. Once phoneticians have learned them, they can be used to locate the position of the vowels in any speaker. For more precise descriptions of vowels occurring within a broad area of the diagram, it is possible to use diacritic marks along with the vowel symbol, as shown on p. 155, and above right.

USING THE CARDINAL VOWEL DIAGRAM

Once the cardinal vowel values have been learned (a matter of auditory practice), it is possible to place the vowels of a speaker of any language onto the chart in a fairly precise way – if necessary, confirming the auditory judgments by acoustic measurements. In this way, typical articulations in different languages can be compared – the five-vowel system (p. 169) of Spanish, alongside that of Japanese, for example. The two systems are very similar, but most of the Japanese vowels are articulated in slightly more open positions than the Spanish; the close back vowel also shows a difference in lip rounding. (It is standard practice to use the nearest (rounded or unrounded) cardinal vowel symbols, when locating 'real' vowels on the chart.)

English has a more complex vowel system, as can be seen from the following chart (the accent represented is Received Pronunciation, p. 39).

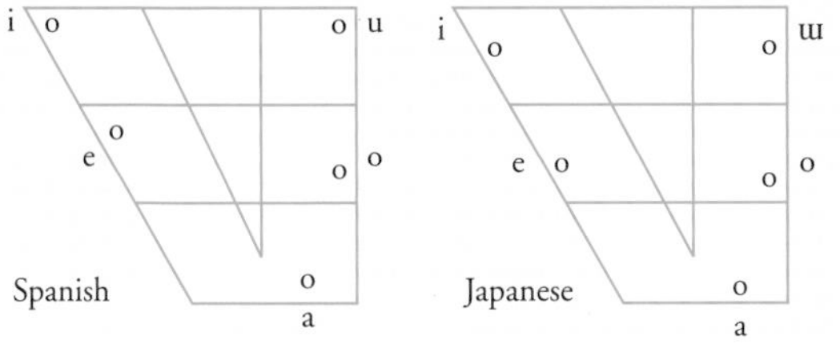

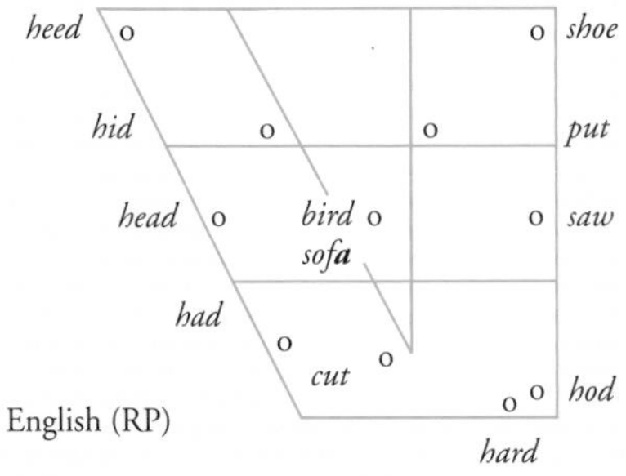

VOWEL GLIDES

Languages frequently make use of a distinction between vowels where the quality remains constant throughout the articulation (*pure* or *monophthong* vowels) and those where there is an audible change of quality. The latter are known as vowel *glides*. If a single movement of the tongue is involved, the glides are called *diphthongs*; a double movement produces *triphthongs*. Diphthongal glides in English can be heard in such words as *say, fine, cow, boy,* and *so*. Triphthongal glides are found in certain pronunciations of such words as *fire, power,* and *sure*.

The tongue movements of several diphthongs, represented by arrows, are drawn on the Cardinal Vowel diagram. The accent is Midwestern American.

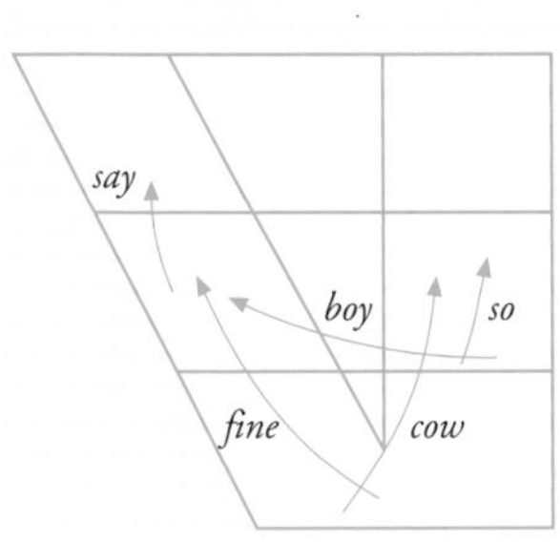

THE MAIN VOWEL DIACRITICS

Symbol ˔ or ˕
articulation lower than cardinal value, e.g. e̞, e˕

Symbol ˔ or ˔
articulation higher than cardinal value, e.g. e̝, e̝.

Symbol ⁺ or ₊
articulation further forward than cardinal value, e.g. o⁺, o̟

Symbol ⁻ or ₋
articulation further back than cardinal value, e.g. i⁻, i̠

Symbol ~
nasalized vowel, e.g. ã

Symbol ¨
centralized vowel, e.g. ë

Symbol ː
long vowel, e.g. iː

Symbol ˑ
half-long vowel, e.g. iˑ

Symbol ˒
vowel more rounded than normal, e.g. ɔ˒

Symbol ˓
vowel less rounded than normal, e.g. ɔ˓

CONSONANTS

Consonants are normally described with reference to six criteria.

- The source of the air stream – whether from the lungs (*pulmonic*) or from some other source (*non-pulmonic*) (pp. 124–7).
- The direction of the air stream – whether moving outwards (*egressive*) or inwards (*ingressive*) (pp. 126–7).
- The state of vibration of the vocal folds – whether vibrating (*voiced*) or not (*voiceless*) (p. 128).

- The position of the soft palate – whether raised (*oral*) or lowered (*nasal*) (p. 130).
- The place of articulation in the vocal tract.
- The manner of the articulation.

Sounds using non-pulmonic and ingressive air streams (clicks, ejectives, and implosives) are described on pp. 126–7. The present section therefore deals largely with pulmonic egressive sounds, which in fact constitute the vast majority of the sounds of speech. Within the remaining criteria, place and manner of articulation provide the main possibilities for consonant variation.

PLACE OF ARTICULATION

Two reference points are involved in defining consonantal places of articulation: the part of the vocal tract that moves (the 'active' articulator) and the part with which it makes contact (the 'passive' articulator) (p. 130). Eleven possible places are used in speech, as indicated in the figure. (A full list of phonetic symbols is given on p. 161 and in Appendix II.)

1. Bilabial. Both lips are involved in the articulation, e.g. [p], [b], [m].

2. Labio-dental. The lower lip articulates with the upper teeth, e.g. [f], [v].

3. Dental. The tongue tip and rims articulate with the upper teeth, e.g. [θ], [ð], as in *thin* and *this* respectively.

4. Alveolar. The blade (and sometimes the tip) of the tongue articulates with the alveolar ridge (p. 130), e.g. [t], [s]. Sounds articulated at the rear of this ridge (e.g. [ɹ],

as in some pronunciations of *red*) are sometimes classified separately as *post-alveolar*.

5. Retroflex. The tip of the tongue is curled back to articulate with the area between the rear of the alveolar ridge and the front of the hard palate, e.g. [ʈ], [ɖ], as heard in many Indian English accents.

6. Palato-alveolar. The blade (and sometimes the tip) of the tongue articulates with the alveolar ridge, with a simultaneous raising of the front of the tongue towards

the hard palate, e.g. [ʃ], [ʒ], as in *shoe* and French *je* respectively.

7. Palatal. The front of the tongue articulates with the hard palate, e.g. [ç], [j], as in German *ich* and *ja* respectively.

8. Velar. The back of the tongue articulates with the soft palate, e.g. [k], [g].

9. Uvular. The back of the tongue articulates with the uvula, e.g. [ʀ], as in French *rue* (certain accents).

10. Pharyngeal. The front wall of the pharynx (in the region of the epiglottis) articulates with the back wall, e.g. [ħ], [ʕ], both found in Arabic.

11. Glottal. The vocal folds come together to cause a closure or friction, e.g. [h], [ʔ] (the glottal stop, p. 128) – a rather different method of articulation from any of the other consonants.

Other ways of describing articulation, in the context of phonology, are discussed in §28.

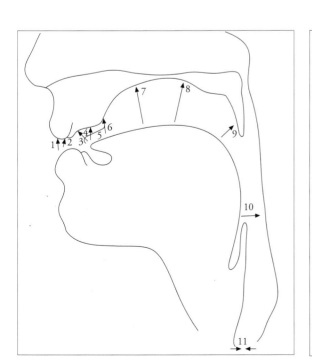

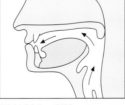

SOME CONSONANT PLACES OF ARTICULATION

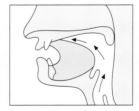

Bilabial [p] and [b]

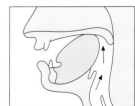

Alveolar [t] and [d]

Velar [k] and [g], when followed by an [i] vowel

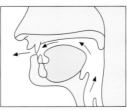

Labio-dental [f] and [v]

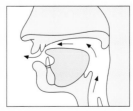

Dental [θ] and [ð]

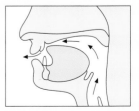

Alveolar [s] and [z]

Coarticulation

The vocal organs do not move from sound to sound in a series of separate steps. Speech is a continuously varying process (p. 137), and sounds continually show the influence of their neighbours. For example, if a nasal consonant (such as [m]) precedes an oral vowel (such as [a]), some of the nasality will carry forward, so that the onset of the vowel will have a somewhat nasal quality. The reason is simply that it takes time for the soft palate to move from its lowered position (required for [m]) to the raised position (required for [a]). It is still in the process of moving after the articulation of [a] has begun. Similarly, if [a] were followed by [m], the soft palate would begin to lower during the articulation of the vowel, to be ready for the following nasal consonant.

When sounds involve overlapping or simultaneous articulations in this way, the process is known as *coarticulation*. If the sound becomes more like a following sound (its 'target'), we are dealing with *anticipatory* coarticulation; if the sound displays the influence of the preceding sound, we are dealing with *perseverative* coarticulation. Anticipatory effects are far more common: a typical example in English is the way vowel lip position affects a preceding [s], in such words as *see* (where the [s] is pronounced with spread lips) and *sue* (where [s] is pronounced with rounded lips).

SECONDARY ARTICULATIONS

Often a consonant is produced using two points of articulation, one closure (the 'primary' articulation) being more marked than the other (the 'secondary' articulation). There are four main kinds of secondary articulation.

Labialization   The lips are rounded at the same time as the primary articulation is made, as in the initial consonants of *sue* and *shoe*. A labialized consonant is indicated by [ʷ] placed beneath the main symbol, or [ʷ] placed after it, as in [s̫], [sʷ].

Palatalization   The tongue is raised to a high front position at the same times as the primary articulation is made. An [i] vowel resonance is added to the consonant, and is symbolized by a small raised [ʲ]. Palatalized consonants are found, for example, in Slavonic languages – as in the contrast between Russian palatalized [tʲ] (e.g. [bratʲ] 'to take') and non-palatalized [t] (e.g. [brat] 'brother').

Velarization   The tongue is raised to a high back position at the same time as the primary articulation is made. An [ɯ] vowel resonance is added to the consonant, and is symbolized by a small raised [ɣ] or by the sign [~] through the consonant symbol. A velarized [ɫ] can be heard in English, as in *pool*. A series of velarized sounds occurs in Arabic.

Pharyngealization   The pharynx is narrowed at the same time as the primary articulation is made. An [ɑ] vowel resonance is added to the consonant, and is symbolized by a small raised [ʕ] or by the [~] diacritic – the same as for velarization, but as no language is known to contrast these articulations, there is no ambiguity. Pharyngealized consonants are found, for example, in Arabic.

MEASURING COARTICULATION

It is possible to measure the degree of overlap between consonant articulations. In one study, subjects pronounced words containing the adjacent consonants [kt] (as in *cocktail*), and [tk] (as in *Watkins*), and the sequence of articulations was plotted using an electropalatograph (p. 141). It might be expected that the [k] closure at the end of *cock* would be completely released before the [t] closure for *tail* was begun; but this does not happen in normal speech. In the case of [tk], one subject made an almost simultaneous closure of the two sounds, as can be seen from this palatograph print-out of the middle portion of the word *Watkins*.

(Each circle represents a point of contact between tongue and palate. The velar area is at the top of each diagram; the alveolar area is at the bottom. Frames are at intervals of 10 msec (From W. J. Hardcastle & P. Roach, 1977, p. 39).)

```
      401              402              403              404
oo.......o       ooo...oooo       oooo.ooooo       oooooooooo
o........        oo.....o         ooo..ooo         ooo.oooo
o........        o.......         oo...ooo         ooo..ooo
.........        .........        ooo....o         ooo...oo
.........        .........        ooo...oo         ooo...oo
.........        oo......         ooooooo          ooooooo
......           ......           oo....           ooooo

      405              406              407              408              409
oooooooooo       oooooooooo       oooooooooo       oooooooooo       oooooooooo
oooooooo         oooooooo         oooooooo         oooooooo         ooooooooo
ooo..ooo         ooo..ooo         ooo..ooo         ooo..ooo         ooo.oooo
oo....oo         ooo...oo         ooo...oo         ooo..ooo         ooo..ooo
ooo....o         ooo....o         ooo....oo        ooo....o         ooo...oo
ooo...oo         ooo...oo         ooo...oo         ooo...oo         ooo...oo
oooooooo         oooooooo         oooooooo         oooooooo         ooooooooo
oooooo           oooooo           oooooo           oooooo           oooooo

      410              411              412              413              414
oooooooooo       oooooooooo       oooooooooo       oooooooooo       oooooooooo
oooooooo         oooooooo         oooooooo         oooooooo         ooooooooo
oooooooo         oooooooo         oooooooo         oooooooo         oooooooo
ooo..ooo         ooo.oooo         ooooooo          oooooooo         ooo...oo
ooo...oo         ooo...oo         ooo...oo         ooo...oo         ooo...oo
ooo...oo         oooo.ooo         oooo.ooo         ooo..ooo         ooo....o
oooooooo         oooooooo         oooo.ooo         oooo..oo         ......
ooo...           oo....           oo....           o.....

      415              416              417              418              419
oooooooooo       oooooooooo       oooooooooo       oooo.ooooo       oooo...ooo
oooooooo         oooooooo         oooooooo         ooo..ooo         ooo..ooo
oooooooo         oooooooo         oooooooo         ooo..ooo         ooo.oooo
ooo..ooo         ooo..ooo         ooo...oo         oo...oo          oo....oo
ooo...oo         ooo....o         oo.....o         oo...oo          o......
ooo....o         oo......         oo.....o         oo.....          o......
......           ......           o.......         .........        .........
                                                   ......           ......
```

PARAMETRIC PHONETICS

The notion of coarticulation applies to every articulatory component involved in the production of a stretch of speech. This can be seen if the functioning of each component is plotted separately, to show the relative movements of the articulators over time. The diagram shows seven parameters representing the action of the lungs, vocal folds, soft palate, front and back of the tongue, jaw, and lips during the articulation of the word *horse* (after L. F. Brosnahan & B. Malmberg, 1970, p. 70).

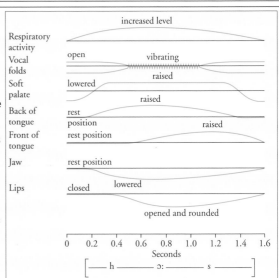

MANNER OF ARTICULATION

There are four main kinds of constriction made by the articulators in producing consonants, and these are used to provide a further dimension of classification. (The full range of phonetic symbols is given on p. 161.)

TOTAL CLOSURE

Plosive A complete closure is made at some point in the vocal tract; the soft palate is raised. Air pressure thus builds up behind the closure, which is then released explosively, as in [p] and [b]. The broader category of *stop* includes closures produced by other air streams (pp. 126–7), as well as plosives.

Nasal A complete closure is made at some point in the mouth; the soft palate is lowered, so that air escapes through the nose, as in [m] and [n]. Voiceless nasals are shown with the diacritic [̥], as in [m̥].

Affricate A complete closure is made at some point in the mouth; the soft palate is raised. Air pressure builds up behind the closure, and is then released relatively slowly (compared to a plosive release). The first element of the sound has a sharp plosive character, but this is followed by an element of audible friction, as in [tʃ] and [dʒ] (heard in English *church* and *judge* respectively).

INTERMITTENT CLOSURE

Roll or **Trill** One articulator taps rapidly against another – typically the tongue tip against the alveolar ridge or the tongue back against the uvula, in the different kinds of trilled *r*, heard for example in many English, French, and German accents.

Flap A single tap is made by one articulator against another, as in some pronunciations of the *r* in *very*, or the *d* in *ladder*, where the tongue tip taps once against the alveolar ridge. In Spanish, a contrast is made between a trilled and a flapped *r*, as in *perro* [pero] 'dog' and *pero* [peɾo] 'but'.

PARTIAL CLOSURE

Lateral A partial closure is made at some point in the mouth, in such a way that the air stream is allowed to escape around the sides of the closure. Various kinds of *l* sound are the result.

NARROWING

Fricative Two vocal organs come so close together that the movement of air between them causes audible friction, as in [f], [z], [h]. Some fricatives have a sharper sound than others, because of the greater intensity of their high frequencies (p. 137): [s], [z], [ʃ] (as in *shoe*), and [ʒ] (as in French *je*). These are known as *sibilants*.

Linguistic range

The above descriptions give only a limited impression of the range of sounds found in the languages of the world. A more accurate impression emerges when we examine some of the possibilities of articulation within a single category of consonant. Several kinds of stop consonant, for example, are illustrated in the following list (which does not show details of vowel quality). (After P. Ladefoged, 1982.)

VOWEL-LIKE CONSONANTS

Certain consonants have some of the phonetic properties of vowels: two alveolar sounds, [l] and [ɹ], the bilabial [w], and the palatal [j]. They are usually referred to as *approximants* (or *frictionless continuants*), though the latter two are commonly called *semi-vowels*, as they have exactly the same articulation as vowel glides. Although phonetically vowel-like, these sounds are usually classified along with consonants on functional grounds (p. 154).

Description	Symbol	Example	Language
Manner			
voiced	b	bənu	Sindhi 'forest'
voiceless unaspirated	p	pənu	Sindhi 'leaf'
aspirated	pʰ	pʰənu	Sindhi 'snake hood'
murmured (breathy)	bʱ	bʱənə̪nu	Sindhi 'lamentation'
implosive	ɓ	ɓəni	Sindhi 'curse'
laryngealized (creaky)	b̰	báábè	Hausa 'quarrel' (verb)
ejective	k'	k'ààkà	Hausa 'how'
nasal release	dn	dno	Russian 'bottom'
prenasalized	nd	ndizi	Swahili 'banana'
lateral release	tɬ	tɬàh	Navaho 'oil'
ejective lateral release	tɬ'	tɬ'éeʔ	Navaho 'night'
affricate	ts	tsait	German 'time'
ejective affricate	ts'	ts'áal	Navaho 'cradle'
Place			
bilabial	p b	pig	English
dental	t̪ d̪	mut̪t̪u	Malayalam 'pearl'
alveolar	t d	muttu	Malayalam 'density'
retroflex	ʈ ɖ	muʈʈu	Malayalam 'knee'
palatal	c ɟ	ciri	Quechua 'cold'
velar	k g	kara	Quechua 'expensive'
uvular	q ɢ	qara	Quechua 'skin'
glottal	ʔ	ʔalla	Arabic 'God'
labio-velar	k͡p g͡b	akpá	Yoruba 'arm'

L'ASSOCIATION PHONÉTIQUE INTERNATIONALE (INTERNATIONAL PHONETIC ASSOCIATION)

This Association was inaugurated in 1886 by a small group of language teachers in France who had found the practice of phonetics useful in their work and wished to popularize the methods. It was first known as The Phonetic Teachers' Association, changing to its present title in 1897.

One of the first activities of the Association was to produce a journal in which the contents were printed entirely in phonetic transcription. The idea of establishing a phonetic alphabet was first proposed by Otto Jespersen (1869–1943) in 1886, and the first version of the International Phonetic Alphabet (IPA) was published in August 1888. Its main principles were that there should be a separate letter for each distinctive sound, and that the same symbol should be used for that sound in any language in which it appears. The alphabet was to consist of as many roman alphabet letters as possible, using new letters and diacritics only when absolutely necessary. These principles continue to be followed today.

The IPA has been modified and extended several times, and is now widely used in dictionaries and textbooks throughout the world. Some of its special letters have even been accepted as part of the new orthographies devised for previously unwritten languages, such as in certain parts of Africa.

Paul Passy, founder of the International Phonetic Association

---

ðə laːst m.f.

əz membəz wɪl nəu, ðɪs ɪz ðə laːst nʌmbər əv ði **m.f.** ɪn ɪts preznt fɔːm. aː dʒɜːnl wəz pʌblɪʃt fə ðə fɜːst taɪm ɪn 1889, ðəu priːvjəslɪ, frəm 1886, ɪt əd əpɪəd əz " ðə fənetɪk tiːtʃə ". ɪn 1889, aːr əsəusɪeɪʃn hæd 321 membəz ɪn 18 kʌntrɪz, ðə mədʒɒrətɪ kʌmɪŋ frəm *swiːdn, *dʒɜːmənɪ ən *fraːns. tədeɪ, wiː hæv mɔː ɒn 800 membəz ɪn əuvə 40 kʌntrɪz, ðə greɪt mədʒɒrətɪ kʌmɪŋ frəm ðə *junaɪtɪd steɪts ən *greɪt brɪtn.

nau ðət wiː əv dɪsaɪdɪd tə prɪnt aː njuː *Journal* ɪn ɔːθɒɡrəfɪ, fə ðə fɜːst taɪm ɪn dʒuːn 1971, ɪt ɪz həupt ðət ðə riːdəʃɪp wɪl bɪ ɪnlaːdʒd ən ðət kɒntrɪbjuːʃnz wɪl bɪ rɪsiːvd frəm ə waɪdə sɜːkl əv fəunɪtɪʃnz ən tiːtʃəz. məust əv aː membəz huː əv rɪplaɪd tə ðə sɜːkjələr ɪn ðə laːst **m.f.** həv sɪgnɪfaɪd ðət ðeɪ wɪʃ tə kəntɪnju tə səbskraɪb tə ðə njuː *Journal*. ðəuz huː əv nɒt jet ɪnfɔːmd əs əv ðɛər ɪntenʃnz ər ɜːdʒd tə duː səu wɪðaut dɪleɪ, sɪns aː faɪnænsɪz wɪl nɒt əlau əs tə send ðə *Journal* tə fɔːmə membəz huːz səbskrɪpʃnz ə nɒt rɪnjuːd.

wiː ɪkspekt ðə njuː *Journal* tə kənteɪn əbaut 50 peɪdʒɪz ət ði autset. fə ðɪs riːzn, ɪn ðə fɜːst nʌmbəz ət liːst, wiː wɪl lɪmɪt ðə leŋkθ əv kɒntrɪbjuːʃnz tʊ ə mæksɪməm əv əbaut 3,000 wɜːdz. ðə fɒləuɪŋ nəuts fə kəntrɪbjutəz gɪv ən ɪndɪkeɪʃn əv ðə rɪkwaɪəmənts əv preznteɪʃn fə ðə *Journal* ; ðeɪ wɪl ɪn fjuːtʃə bɪ prɪntɪd ɒn ðə *Journalz* kʌvə.

The contents page to the last number of *Le Maître Phonétique*, which appeared in 1970. The headings are in French, the official language of the Association. Each article has been written in a transcription that partly reflects the pronunciation of the author. For example, Soravia uses [ou] to represent the diphthong found in such words as *know* ([founetiks] = *phonetics*), whereas Lewis uses [əu] (as in [təunl] = *tonal*) and Fox uses [əɷ] ([təɷn] = *tone*). The asterisk is used before a word that is a proper name.

lə

meːtrə fɔnetik

organ də l asosjasjɔ̃ fonetik ɛ̃ternasjɔnal, 1970

tablə də matjeːr   paːʒ
2

1. artiklə də fɔ̃.
   səm rimaːks ɒn ðə founetiks əv ə dʒipsi daiəlekt (G. Soravia) · 4
   *rɔdʒə *kɪndənz tounmaːks ədæptid tə *frenʃ intouneiʃn   40
   (G. Dietrich)   6
   kɔreksjɔ̃ ·   9
   itæljən prənʌnsieiʃn (L. Canepari) ·   10
   ə nɔut ɒn "The North Wind and the Sun" pæsidʒ in   11
   *kæntəniːz (K. C. Leung) ·   28
   mɔːr əbaut ə fəgɒtn təun pætn (N. Hodek) ·   29
   ði 'ʌn'naun 'sɪtizn (J. W. Lewis) ·   31
   ðə laːst **m.f.** (A. C. G.) ·   36
   ðə fəgɒtn təun : ə rɪplaɪ (A. Fox) ·   37
   ðə təunl sɪstəm əv rimaut spitʃ (J. Windsor Lewis) ·   38
   ə sədʒestʃən fər ə nju: simbl (E. Stankova) ·
   ə nɔut ɒn ðə fonetik pəkjuːliæritiːz əv ə klaːs daiəlekt əv
   *mlʌja:lʌm (A. Chandrasekhar) ·
   ɪŋgliʃ : kɒkni (J. R. Hurford)

The Association Secretary's statement explaining the demise of *Le Maître Phonétique*.

The notice, which appeared in the 1970 issue, was headed 'The last m.f.': 'As members will know, this is the last number of the m.f. in its present form. Our journal was published for the first time in 1889, though previously, from 1886, it had appeared as 'The Phonetic Teacher'. In 1889, our association had 321 members in 18 countries, the majority coming from Sweden, Germany and France. Today, we have more than 800 members in over 40 countries, the great majority coming from the United States and Great Britain.

Now that we have decided to print our new *Journal* in orthography, for the first time in June 1971, it is hoped that the readership will be enlarged and that contributions will be received from a wider circle of phoneticians and teachers ...'

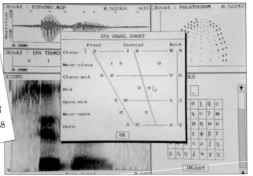

IPA on screen An IPA transcription tutorial, using a multimedia environment of the Computerized Speech Lab (p. 135). When students are unsure of a transcription, the vowel or consonant chart can be displayed, which speaks each phone and provides a spectrographic display with a click of the mouse.

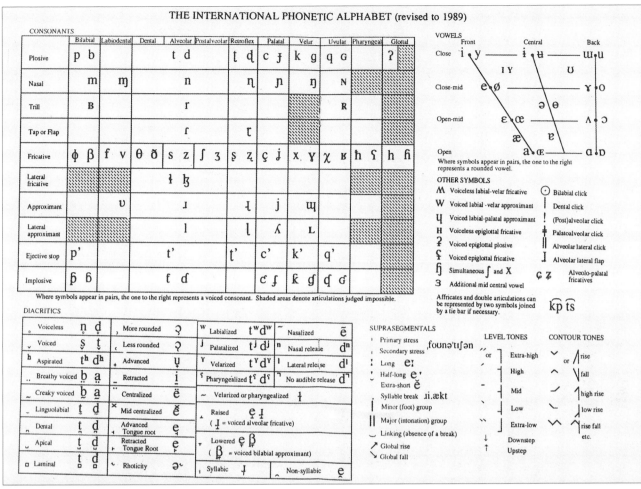

The International Phonetic Alphabet (1989 revision)

Category	Examples		
Place			
labiodentals (upper teeth to lower lip)			
plosives	p̪	b̪	
nasal	m̪		
dentolabials (lower teeth to upper lip)			
plosives	p̪	b̪	
nasal	m̪		
bidentals (teeth brought together)	h̪	ʉ̪	

Manner	
denasal	m̃
nasal escape	p̃
stronger articulation	f̬
weaker articulation	m̮
reiterated articulation	p\p\p
whistled articulation	s̩

Air stream	
ingressive (for a normally egressive segment)	p↓
egressive (for a normally ingressive segment)	!↑
silent articulation ('mouthing')	(ʃ)

Vocal fold activity	
pre-voicing (voicing starts earlier than normal)	ᵥb
post-voicing (voicing starts later)	zᵥ
partial voicing of a normally unvoiced segment	f₍ᵥ₎
pre-aspiration	ʰp

Phonatory settings	
breathy/whispery	v̤
whisper	ṿ
creak	v̰
falsetto	F̰

Pause	
short	(.)
medium	(..)
long	(...)

Degrees of indeterminacy	
segment perceived but no features can be identified	( ) or ○
segment is consonantal, but cannot be further specified	(C)
segment is a stop, but cannot further specified	(S)
segment sounds like the symbol noted, but transcriber is unsure	(t)
sound obscured by external noise	((2 syllables))
segment for which no symbol is provided	*

Left: A selection of the symbols devised by a British research team for transcribing disordered speech (after M. Duckworth, *et al.*, 1990); the diacritics are shown used with standard IPA symbols. Further symbols have been devised for other types of voice quality and features of connected speech. Note the section recommending symbols for use when the phonetician is unsure which sound has been used – a common problem when transcribing the unstable pronunciations of handicapped speakers.

Below: Some of the symbols used by an American research team for transcribing the speech of children (after C. Bush, *et al.*, 1973).

Workshop markers for fricatives
○ markedly spread lips, with orifice wide and shallow, [β]
⊕ protruded, labialized and rounded sounds, [f]; [v]
m̺ heavily dentalized, [f̺], [v̺]

Workshop markers for glides and liquids
ȣ Exceptionally rounded lips
⊕ Labially protruded [w]
ʃ A flapped [l]

Workshop markers for nasals and stops
⌒ snap release, e.g. m̑, n̑
⊕ heavily protruded lips, [p]

Phonetics is the study of how speech sounds are made, transmitted, and received (§27). It is a subject that requires as its source of data a human being with an intact auditory mechanism and a functioning set of vocal organs. The person's particular language background is not strictly relevant: phoneticians would draw the same conclusions about the production and reception of speech whether they were dealing with speakers of English, Hindi, or Chinese. Although the categories outlined in §27 can be used for the analysis of any language, that section provides no information about the way these categories are actually used, in the languages of the world.

By contrast, the primary aim of *phonology* is to discover the principles that govern the way sounds are organized in languages, and to explain the variations that occur. A common methodology is to begin by analysing an individual language, to determine which sound units are used and how they pattern – the language's 'phonological structure'. The properties of different sound systems are then compared, and hypotheses developed about the rules underlying the use of sounds in particular groups of languages, and ultimately in all languages ('phonological universals', §14).

The distinction between phonetics and phonology can be seen from a second point of view. The human vocal apparatus can produce a very wide range of sounds; but only a small number of these are used in a language to construct all of its words and sentences. Phonetics is the study of all possible speech sounds; phonology studies the way in which a language's speakers systematically use a selection of these sounds in order to express meaning.

There is a further way of drawing the distinction. No two speakers have anatomically identical vocal tracts, and thus no-one pronounces sounds in exactly the same way as anyone else (a motivation for the study of voiceprints, §6). There is even a considerable amount of variation in the sounds of a single speaker. Yet when using our language we are able to discount much of this variation, and focus on only those sounds, or properties of sound, that are important to the communication of meaning. We think of our fellow-speakers as using the 'same' sounds, even though acoustically they are not. Phonology is the study of how we find order within the apparent chaos of speech sounds.

In its search for significant generalizations about sound systems, phonology is continually looking beneath the 'surface' of speech, to determine its underlying regularities, and to establish how these relate to

other areas of language, notably syntax and morphology (§16). Much of present-day phonological theory is thus concerned with the various kinds of abstract representation it is necessary to set up in order to explain the range and distribution of phonetic segments found in languages. And in the context of generative linguistics (p. 413), there is an even more ambitious aim: to arrive at phonological analyses that have a demonstrable mental reality for the language users (p. 163).

PHONEMES

Phonological analysis relies on the principle that certain sounds cause changes in the meaning of a word or phrase, whereas other sounds do not. An early approach to the subject used a simple methodology to demonstrate this. It would take a word, replace one sound by another, and see whether a different meaning resulted. For example, we hear *pig* in English as consisting of three separate sounds, each of which can be given a symbol in a phonetic transcription, [pɪg]. If we replace [p] by, say, [b], a different word results: *big*. [p] and [b] are thus important sounds in English, because they enable us to distinguish between *pig* and *big*, *pan* and *ban*, and many more word pairs.

In a similar way, [ɪ] and [e] can be shown to be important units, because they distinguish between *pig* and *peg*, *pin* and *pen*, and many other pairs. And so we could continue, using this technique – the 'minimal pairs' test – to find out which sound substitutions cause differences of meaning. The technique has its limitations (it is not always possible to find pairs of words illustrating a particular distinction in a language), but it works quite well for English, where it leads to the identification of over 40 important units. In the earliest approach to phonological analysis, these 'important units' are called *phonemes*.

Phonemes are transcribed using the normal set of phonetic symbols (p. 161), but within slant lines, not square brackets – /p/, /b/, /ɪ/, etc. This shows that the units are being seen as part of a language, and not just as physical sounds.

Allophones

In working out the inventory of phonemes in a language, using this approach, we soon come across sounds that do not change the meaning when we make a substitution. For example, the consonants at the beginning of *shoe* and *she* have very different sound qualities (p. 158). For *shoe*, the lips are rounded, because of the influence of the following [u] vowel; for

SOME MINIMAL PAIRS FOR ENGLISH PHONEMES (SOUTHERN BRITISH)

Vowels

/iː/ – /ɪ/	seat – sit
/ɪ/ – /e/	sit – set
/e/ – /a/	set – sat
/a/ – /ʌ/	cat – cut
/ʌ/ – /ɑː/	cut – cart
/ɑː/ – /ɒ/	cart – cot
/ɒ/ – /ɔː/	cot – caught
/ɔː/ – /ʊ/	cord – could
/ʊ/ – /uː/	pull – pool
/uː/ – /ɜː/	pool – pearl
/ɜː/ – /eɪ/	pearl – pale
/eɪ/ – /aɪ/	day – die
/aɪ/ – /ɔɪ/	buy – boy
/ɔɪ/ – /əʊ/	toy – toe
/əʊ/ – /aʊ/	hoe – how
/aʊ/ – /ɪə/	now – near
/ɪə/ – /ɛə/	tear (noun) – tear (verb)
/ɛə/ – /ʊə/	tear – tour
/ʊə/ – /iː/	sure – she
/ə/ – zero	wait<u>e</u>r – wait

Consonants

/p/ – /b/	pig – big
/b/ – /t/	bee – tea
/t/ – /d/	tin – din
/d/ – /k/	din – kin
/k/ – /g/	cap – gap
/g/ – /h/	gag – hag
/h/ – /m/	hen – men
/m/ – /n/	map – nap
/n/ – /ŋ/	sin – sing
/ŋ/ – /l/	sink – silk
/l/ – /r/	lid – rid
/r/ – /w/	red – wed
/w/ – /j/	well – yell
/j/ – /tʃ/	you – chew
/tʃ/ – /dʒ/	chin – gin
/dʒ/ – /f/	large – laugh
/f/ – /v/	fat – vat
/v/ – /θ/	heave – heath
/θ/ – /ð/	wreath – wreathe
/ð/ – /s/	though – so
/s/ – /z/	bus – buzz
/z/ – /ʃ/	zoo – shoe
/ʃ/ – /ʒ/	Confucian – confusion
/ʒ/ – /t/	beige - bait

she, the lips are spread. If we now substitute one of these sounds for the other, we do not get a change of meaning – only a rather strange-sounding pronunciation. There is only one phoneme here – the voiceless palato-alveolar phoneme /ʃ/ (p. 157) – but it turns up in two different phonetic 'shapes', or variant forms, in these two words. These phonetic variants of a phoneme are known as *allophones*.

When we study a new language, it is important to pay careful attention to the phonetic variations which occur, to ensure that we make the right decisions about which sounds count as phonemes and which count as allophones. We do not know this information in advance; we have to work it out. And in doing so we have to be ready to cope with differences between the way sounds work in different languages. For example, English does not distinguish the meanings of words using a contrast between [ʃʷ] and [ʃ], but some other languages do (e.g. Lak). Sound differences that separate allophones in English may separate phonemes in another language, and vice versa – a principle that is clearly illustrated by the *l* sounds of such words as *leaf* and *pool*. The first *l* ('clear' *l*) is articulated much further forward in the mouth than the second ('dark' *l*) – as can be felt, if the sounds are said slowly to oneself. In English, these are allophones of a single /l/ phoneme. In Russian, however, they are different phonemes.

BEYOND THE SEGMENT

Several approaches to phonology have assumed that a language's sound system can best be analysed in terms of a series of individual segments ([b], [a], [s], etc.). But there are a number of phonological characteristics which affect units that are much larger than the individual segment, such as syllables, words, phrases, and sentences.

Several segments in a word or phrase may display the same phonetic feature – for example, they may all be lip-rounded or nasalized (p. 155). In particular, languages often display cases of *harmony* between consonants or vowels. In certain kinds of 'vowel harmony', for example, all the vowels within a word have to be of the same general type. Turkish is such a case, where words contain (with certain exceptions) only front vowels or back vowels. Thus we find [verdim] 'I gave' with front vowels, and [tʃodʒuk] 'child' with back vowels. But no words are formed with front + back combinations, such as [e] + [o] – a situation quite unlike English, where the sequence of vowels in a polysyllabic word is not predictable in this way.

The analysis of phonological features in terms of units larger than the segment is a preoccupation of several current theories, such as 'prosodic' phonology and 'autosegmental' phonology. Patterns of pitch, loudness, tempo, rhythm, and tone of voice provide another set of data which cannot be analysed with reference to single segments. These aspects of phonology are usually studied under a heading that well reflects this different emphasis: 'suprasegmental' phonology (§29). A specific approach that emphasizes the relationship between segments and syllabic sequences of rhythm and stress is known as 'metrical' phonology.

GROUPING SOUNDS INTO PHONEMES

In the phonemic approach to phonology, linguists faced with an array of sounds usually use three criteria in deciding whether these sounds belong to the same phoneme.
Complementary distribution The sounds must complement each other, in terms of where they occur in words. For example, in the case of the two /ʃ/ sounds in *shoe* and *she*, the rounded variety occurs only before rounded vowels, and the spread variety only before non-rounded vowels. Where we find the one, we do *not* find the other: they are mutually exclusive, never occurring in the same phonetic environment. Such sounds are said to be in 'complementary distribution'.
Free variation If the sounds do occur in the same place in a word, then they can belong to the same phoneme only if they do not change the meaning of the word. For example,

voiceless plosive sounds at the end of words are sometimes articulated in a relaxed way, and sometimes are pronounced quite strongly. The /p/ of *cup* might be heard with a tiny amount of audible breath ('aspiration') following its release, or a relatively large amount. But the different amounts of aspiration do not affect the meaning of the word: replacing weakly aspirated [pʰ] by strongly aspirated [pʰ] does not thereby change *cup* into some other word. Such sounds are said to be in 'free variation' – though whether the variation is in fact genuinely free, and not conditioned by such factors as social class or regional background, is an interesting question (p. 334).
Phonetic similarity To belong to the same phoneme, sounds ought to display a reasonable amount of physical similarity. The two kinds of /ʃ/ or the two kinds of /p/, in the

above examples, satisfy this criterion, as the variants in each case have a great deal in common – the /ʃ/s are both voiceless palato-alveolar fricatives, and the /p/s are both voiceless bilabial plosives. However, it is sometimes possible to find sounds in complementary distribution that are *not* phonetically similar, and in these cases analysts would be reluctant to treat them as members of the same phoneme. A case in point is English [h] and [ŋ]: the former occurs at the beginning or in the middle of words; the latter only in the middle or at the end. They therefore rarely contrast. Could they, then, be taken as allophones of a single phoneme? No, because they have nothing phonetically in common, apart from both being consonants – [h] is a voiceless glottal fricative; [ŋ] is a voiced nasal continuant.

HOW MANY MINIMAL PAIRS *ARE* THERE?

A convenient way of displaying a language's phonemic substitutions is to construct a chart of possible words or syllables. Below is part of a chart adapted from Denyse Rockey's *Phonetic Lexicon* (1973, pp. 56–7). It shows some of the 117 monosyllables in English that end with /b/ (though this figure includes several obsolete, dialect, and technical words). The initial sounds of these words are listed verti-

cally on the left, and the vowel sounds are listed horizontally across the top.

Charts of this kind have all kinds of practical applications. They can help language teachers and speech therapists in pronunciation work. They can be a source of information to budding poets and Scrabble-masters (p. 64). Linguists can compare the use a language makes of individual combinations of phonemes and

thus calculate the amount of work a phoneme has to do in a language. For example, English does not use final consonants with equal frequency, as can be seen from the following list, which is derived from Rockey's data. Each figure refers to the number of monosyllabic words ending with the consonant listed. It shows, for instance, that over twice as many monosyllables end in /k/ as end in /g/.

	i	ɪ	ɛ	æ	ɒ(+r)	ɒ/ɑ	ɔ(+r)
–	.	.	ebb	abb	.	ob	orb
p	.	.	.	.	.	.	.
b	.	bib	.	.	barb	bob	.
t	.	Tib	.	tab	.	.	.
d	dieb	dib	deb	dab	.	Dob	daub
k	.	.	keb	cab	.	cob	corbe
g	.	gib	.	gab	garb	gob	gaub
f	.	fib	.	.	.	fob	.
v	.	.	.	.	.	.	.
θ	.	.	.	.	.	.	.
ð	.	.	.	.	.	.	.
s	.	.	sib	.	sab	sob	sorb
z	.	.	.	.	.	.	.
ʃ	.	.	.	.	.	.	.
ʒ	.	.	.	.	.	.	.
h	.	.	.	.	.	hob	.
tʃ	.	.	.	.	.	.	.
dʒ	.	jib	.	jab	.	job	.

/-d/	429
/-z/	383
/-t/	376
/-n/	330
/-l/	313
/-k/	304
/-m/	240
/-p/	223
/-s/	212
/-f/	153
/-g/	138
/-tʃ/	132
/-v/	122
/-b/	117
/-ʃ/	105
/-θ/	104
/-ŋ/	87
/-dʒ/	84
/-ð/	32

DISTINCTIVE FEATURES

In a phonemic analysis, it is necessary to recognize smaller units than the segment, in order to explain how sets of sounds are related. This can be seen by comparing any two contrasting segments, using the articulatory criteria introduced in §27.

- English /p/ and /b/ differ in one respect only: /p/ is voiceless, and /b/ is voiced. In other respects, they are the same: they are both bilabial, plosive, oral, and pulmonic egressive.
- /p/ and /g/ differ in two respects: there is a contrast of voicing, and there is also a contrast in the place of articulation – bilabial vs velar.
- /p/ and /z/ differ in three respects: this time, there is a contrast in the manner of articulation (plosive vs fricative), alongside the contrasts in voicing and place.

All segments in a language can be analysed in this way, either from an articulatory or an acoustic (p. 146) point of view, and the result is a set of contrasting components known as *distinctive features*. The English segment /p/, for example, is a combination of the features of 'voicelessness', 'plosiveness', and 'bilabiality'. In early versions of distinctive feature theory, these features are given two values, symbolized by the signs + and –, as in [±voice], [±nasal]. For example, [n] is both [+nasal] and [+voice]; [p] is [–nasal] and [–voice]. A small set of these contrasts is worked out and applied to all the sounds that turn up in a language. Results may be presented in the form of a matrix, in which the presence or absence of each feature is noted (see below).

In phonological theory since the 1980s, features have become a focus of attention in their own right, and are widely viewed as the basic unit of phonological representation. The merits of *unary* (single-valued) as opposed to *binary* analyses have been presented by some models. In addition to questions of feature identification and definition, however, recent research has focused on the way features are organized within phonological representations, as part of non-linear phonology. In particular, *feature geometry* looks especially at the non-linear relationship between features, and at the way they can be grouped into a hierarchical array of functional classes.

Distinctive feature theory has been primarily used by *generative* approaches to linguistics (§65), where the aim is to provide an account of phonology that can be integrated within a theory of grammar (§16). It is argued that distinctive features are the important facts to take into account when carrying out a phonological analysis, as they reveal more about the way in which the sounds of a language are organized, and more readily permit generalized statements within and between languages, than do descriptions based on phonemes and allophones. A particular advantage is that the same set of terms can be used for describing both vowels and consonants – something traditional articulatory descriptions were unable to do (as can be seen from the diverse, 'two-mouth' terminology of §27).

DISTINCTIVE-FEATURE MATRICES

The features are listed on the left of each matrix, and the segments are listed along the top. Each segment is analysed in terms of all features. The terminology used in these particular matrices relates to the traditional articulatory terms used in §27 in the following way (V = vowel, C = consonant):

+ compact	low V
– compact	high and mid V
+ consonantal	obstruction in vocal tract
– consonantal	no vocal tract obstruction
+ continuant	fricative / approximant C
– continuant	stop / affricate C
+ diffuse	high V; labial / dental / alveolar C
– diffuse	low V; palatal / velar / back C
+ flat	rounded V
– flat	unrounded V
+ grave	back V; labial / velar / back C
– grave	front V; dental / alveolar / palatal C
+ nasal	nasal C
– nasal	oral C
+ strident	fricative / affricate C with high-frequency noise
– strident	C with low-frequency noise
+ vocalic	glottal vibration with free passage of air through vocal tract
– vocalic	no glottal vibration or free passage of air
+ voice	voiced C
– voice	voiceless C

(After R. Jakobson & M. Halle, 1956.)

English consonant matrix

	p	b	f	v	m	t	d	θ	ð	s	z	n	tʃ	dʒ	ʃ	ʒ	k	g	l	r	w	j	h	ŋ
consonantal	+	+	+	+	+	+	+	+	+	+	+	+	+	+	+	+	+	+	+	+	–	–	–	+
vocalic	–	–	–	–	–	–	–	–	–	–	–	–	–	–	–	–	–	–	+	+	–	–	–	–
diffuse	+	+	+	+	+	+	+	+	+	+	+	+	–	–	–	–	–	–	+	+	–	–	–	–
compact	–	–	–	–	–	–	–	–	–	–	–	–	–	–	–	–	–	–	–	–	–	–	–	–
grave	+	+	+	+	+	–	–	–	–	–	–	–	–	–	–	–	+	+	–	–	+	–	+	+
flat	–	–	–	–	–	–	–	–	–	–	–	–	–	–	–	–	–	–	–	–	+	–	–	–
voice	–	+	–	+	+	–	+	–	+	–	+	+	–	+	–	+	–	+	+	+	+	+	–	+
continuant	–	–	+	+	–	–	–	+	+	+	+	–	–	–	+	+	–	–	+	+	+	+	+	–
strident	–	–	+	+	–	–	–	–	–	+	+	–	+	+	+	+	–	–	–	–	–	–	–	–
nasal	–	–	–	–	+	–	–	–	–	–	–	+	–	–	–	–	–	–	–	–	–	–	–	+

Matrix for a seven-vowel system

	i	e	a	u	o	ɔ	ɑ
consonantal	–	–	–	–	–	–	–
vocalic	+	+	+	+	+	+	+
diffuse	+	–	–	+	–	–	–
compact	–	–	+	–	–	+	+
grave	–	–	–	+	+	+	+
flat	–	–	–	+	+	+	–
voice	+	+	+	+	+	+	+
continuant	+	+	+	+	+	+	+
strident	–	–	–	–	–	–	–
nasal	–	–	–	–	–	–	–

PHONOLOGICAL RULES

In traditional accounts of phonology, a sound is described as occurring in a particular position within a syllable or word, and that is all. No reference is made to our knowledge of the relationships that exist between the various types of sound in different contexts. Yet this information is essential if we are to understand the way sounds systematically relate to each other and to the grammar and lexicon of a language.

To illustrate this point, we may consider such pairs of words as *telegraph* and *telegraphy*. A phonological analysis of these words is not complete simply by giving each a phonemic transcription: /teləgrɑːf/ vs /təleɡrəfɪ/. We also need to show that, despite the different patterns of strong and weak vowels within them, the pronunciations are systematically related, with other pairs of words in the language displaying the same kind of relationship (such as *microscope / microscopy*). In recent years, relationships of this kind have become a major focus of phonological investigation. And one of the main techniques for demonstrating such regularities in the sound patterns of language has been through the use of *phonological rules.*

Phonological rules are general statements about the relationships between sounds, or classes of sound. They summarize what happens when sounds occur in particular grammatical or phonetic contexts. In English, for example, [b] is used at the beginning and at the end of words, but especially in the latter position it loses some of its voicing: we say [dʒab̥] (*jab*), with a 'devoiced' sound. This observation can be summarized in the form of a rule: '[b] becomes [b̥] at the end of a word.' The validity of the rule can then be tested against other examples, to see if there are exceptions.

Phonological rules are expressed in a special notation to make the description as clear and succinct as possible and (according to some analysts) to identify the essential theoretical properties of sound systems. The above rule could be written as follows (the symbol '→' means 'becomes'; '/' means 'in the context of'; and '#' means 'word boundary'):

$$[b] \rightarrow [b̥] \;/ - \#$$

In generative phonology, such rules would be written using a distinctive feature notation:

$$\begin{bmatrix} + \text{ consonantal} \\ - \text{ nasal} \\ + \text{ voice} \end{bmatrix} \rightarrow \begin{bmatrix} + \text{ consonantal} \\ - \text{ nasal} \\ - \text{ voice} \end{bmatrix} \;/ - \#$$

(or, 'voiced oral consonants become voiceless oral consonants before a word boundary'). Several such notational conventions have been devised in order to cope with all the types of phonetic relationship that have been observed.

There are many kinds of phonological rule. Some rules, such as the above, change the distinctive features of segments. A further example, from the domain of connected speech, would be the change of [n] to [m] in the phrase *ten boys*, because of the influence of the following [b]. Here, the rule would summarize the fact that 'an alveolar nasal becomes bilabial before a following bilabial consonant'.

Other rules add or delete segments. An addition rule accounts for the way in which some English accents add vowels between certain consonant segments, as in the pronunciation of *film* as [filəm]. A deletion rule occurs when vowel segments are regularly omitted from such phrases as *I am* (→ *I'm*) in certain grammatical contexts. There are also rules that combine two segments as one, as when *would* + *you* become [wʊdʒuː] (p. 166).

Phonological rules are not restricted to making statements about the sound patterns of a particular language. They are also used to demonstrate the similarities and differences between the sound systems of different languages. Is the rule about consonant devoicing at the ends of words found only in English, or does it apply to a larger group of languages, or possibly to all languages? The formulation of phonological rules is thus seen as an important step towards the phonologist's goal of discovering the universal principles governing the use of sound in language.

ABSTRACT OR CONCRETE?

In order to arrive at satisfactory generalizations, phonologists have often introduced abstract underlying forms into their rules from which several pronunciations can be derived. For example, the words *impossible*, *indecisive*, and *inconclusive* all begin with the same prefix, meaning 'not', but the pronunciations differ. In the first case, it is [ɪm] (because of the following bilabial); in the second case it is [ɪn] (before the alveolar consonant); and in the third case, for many speakers, it is [ɪŋ] (before the velar consonant). How can this variation be explained?

It is not very convincing to suggest that one form is more important than the others, and set up a rule in which two of these forms are derived from the third. It is more plausible to say that all three are 'equal', and to derive them from a single 'underlying form'. One such representation would be [ɪN], where 'N' stands for a nasal feature.

This solution seems reasonable, as 'N' is clearly related to the three pronunciations, each of which is nasal. But what happens if we extend the example to include such forms as *irregular* and *illiberal*? Again, the prefix means 'not'; and the differences seem to result from the following sounds. Should we therefore group [l] and [r] along with [m], [n], and [ŋ], and have a single rule for all five possibilities?

If we do, we must set up an underlying form from which all can plausibly be derived. [ɪN] no longer seems appropriate, as two of the sounds are not nasal. [ɪC] (where 'C' stands for 'consonant') would be too general, as not all consonants are used as part of the set of negative prefixes. Some intermediate category needs to be devised, which is sufficiently abstract to enable all the sounds to be grouped together, yet sufficiently concrete (that is, phonetically real) to provide a meaningful explanation about what is taking place. It would be possible to invent a category [X] (where 'X' = [m, n, ŋ, l, r]), but this seems an arbitrary solution, which lacks clear phonetic motivation. Moreover, it is not immediately obvious how this category would be useful in describing other areas of the language.

Problems of this kind have attracted a great deal of discussion in phonological theory in recent years. There is much disagreement about the extent to which phonological analyses of this kind do or should express psychological reality – that is, represent the native speaker's intuitions about the way the sound system works (p. 413). And the degree of abstractness that should be allowed into an analysis is especially controversial. Some approaches permit the use of symbols in the underlying representations that have no phonetic reality at all. Other (so-called 'natural') approaches require that all symbols introduced into an analysis bear a clear relationship to the physically real processes of articulation.

SYLLABLES

The syllable is of considerable relevance to the task of phonetic and phonological description. It is a notion that people intuitively recognize ('Shall I put it in words of one syllable?') and there are several writing systems in which each syllable is represented by a symbol (p. 203). But it is by no means easy to define what syllables are or to identify them consistently. Do such words as *fire*, *meal*, and *schism* have one syllable or two? Do *meteor* and *neonate* have two syllables or three?

A syllable is a unit that is larger than a single segment and smaller than a word. However, this characterization can be seen from both a phonetic and a phonological point of view. In phonetics, some have attempted to identify syllables on the basis of the amount of articulatory effort needed to produce them. The psychologist R. H. Stetson (1892–1950) was one who argued that each syllable corresponds to an increase in air pressure, air from the lungs being released as a series of chest pulses – the *pulse* or *motor* theory of syllable production. These pulses can often be readily felt and measured, especially when people speak emphatically. The main objection to the theory is that the pulses are sometimes very difficult to detect – for example, in adjacent syllables when two vowels co–occur (as in the word *doing*, which is two syllables, but usually spoken with a single muscular effort).

The linguist Otto Jespersen (1860–1943) presented an alternative phonetic approach, known as the *prominence* theory. This defines the syllable in auditory terms, arguing that some sounds (vowels) are intrinsically more sonorous than others (p. 134), and that each peak of sonority corresponds to the centre of a syllable. The problem with this view is that other factors than sonority enter into the definition of prominence (such as the pitch level of a sound), making the notion difficult to define objectively. Also, prominence theory does not always give a clear indication of where the boundary between syllables falls. In such words as *master*, should the syllable division be *ma-ster*, *mas-ter*, or *mast-er*? We are left with this problem, even though in each case the relative sonority of the sounds is the same.

A phonological approach

Phonological views of the syllable focus on the way sounds combine in a language to produce typical sequences. Two classes of sound are established: sounds that can occur on their own, or are at the centre of a sequence of sounds (*vowels* (V)); and those that cannot occur on their own, or are at the edge of a sequence (*consonants* (C)) (p. 154). Typical sequences include CV *see*, CVC *hat*, CCVC *stop*, etc. In this way the range of syllable types used in a language can be identified and different languages compared. For example, some languages use only V or CV syllables (e.g. Hawaiian); others use several consonants before and after the vowel (e.g. English can have as many as three before and four after – CCCVCCCC, as in some pronunciations of *strengths*).

The syllable, in this view, takes its place as an important abstract unit in explaining the way vowels and consonants are organized within a sound system. There is, moreover, empirical evidence for the psychological reality of syllables, from the study of speech errors and related phenomena. In 'slips of the tongue', for example, the kinds of substitutions generally display the influence of syllabic structure: initial consonants tend to replace each other, as do final consonants. Thus one study reports many reversals of the types 'feak and weeble' (for *weak and feeble*) or 'tof shelp' (for *top shelf*), but there are few reversals that mix up places in syllable structure (p. 264).

POSSIBLE SYLLABLES

The number of possible syllables (i.e. combinations of different consonants and vowels) varies greatly from language to language. Totals from the UPSID survey (p. 167) include:

Hawaiian	162
Rotokas	350
Yoruba	582
Tsou	968
Gã	2,331
Cantonese	3,456
Quechua	4,068
Vietnamese	14,430
Thai	23,638

JUNCTURE

Phonetic boundaries used to demarcate words or other grammatical units are known as *junctures*. There are several phrases in English that are distinguishable in this way:

that stuff	vs that's tough
an aim	a name
I scream	ice cream
nitrate	night rate

In the first case, for example, the [s] of *stuff* is stronger; and the [t] of *tough* is aspirated. It is not always easy to hear the differences when the phrases are said side-by-side; but the acoustic changes can be readily observed in a spectrogram (p. 136).

CONNECTED SPEECH

When words combine into connected speech, several things can happen to the pronunciation of their individual segments. The speed and rhythm can cause some segments to adopt a weaker articulation, some to drop out, some to be put in, and some to change character altogether.

Strong and weak

Words sometimes have both strong ('accented') and weak ('unaccented') forms, depending on whether they are pronounced with force. Words that express grammatical relationships in a language are particularly affected. In the following selection from English, the pronunciations on the left are heard when the words are said in isolation, or with emphasis; on the right, when they are said in normal conversation.

a	/eɪ/	/ə/
and	/and/	/ənd, ən, n/
could	/kʊd/	/kəd, kd/
had	/had/	/əd, d/
him	/hɪm/	/ɪm/
is	/ɪz/	/s, z/
not	/nɒt/	/nt, n/

Elision

In rapid speech, sounds may be left out, or *elided*, especially when they occur as part of a cluster of consonants. In English, alveolar consonants are commonly lost, especially at the ends of words, e.g. the final alveolar plosive would normally be dropped in such phrases as *next day*, *mashed potatoes*, *stopped speaking*, or *got to go* (= 'gotta go'). The initial weak vowel may elide in such phrases as *go away* and *try again*.

Liaison

A sound may be introduced between words. Liaison is a notable feature of French, e.g. the final *t* of *c'est* is pronounced when followed by a vowel. It can also be illustrated from English Received Pronunciation (p. 39). In this accent, the final *r* is not sounded in such words as *four* and *father*, when they are pronounced in isolation, or at the end of a sentence; but when followed by words that begin with a vowel, a 'linking /r/' is regularly used, as in *four o'clock* or *father and mother*.

Assimilation

In connected speech, adjacent sounds frequently influence each other so that they become more alike, or *assimilate*. There are three main kinds of assimilation:

regressive (or *anticipatory*), in which a sound is influenced by a following sound, e.g. *ten bikes* being pronounced as /tem baɪks/.

progressive, in which a sound is influenced by a preceding sound, e.g. *lunch score* becomes /lʌnʃ ʃkɔː/.

coalescent (or *reciprocal*), in which there is mutual influence or 'fusion', e.g. *don't you* becomes /dəʊntʃu/.

These effects partly illustrate the role of phonetic coarticulation (p. 158), but they are also partly phonological in character, as the rules differ from language to language.

COMPARATIVE PHONOLOGY

Given that the human vocal tract is capable of articulating such a wide range of sounds (§27), several questions naturally arise. Which sounds turn up most frequently in the languages of the world? Are there any sounds that occur in all languages? What patterns of sound can be found in different languages, and are there any similarities between the patterns that occur?

Questions about language universals and tendencies (§14) cannot be answered in an impressionistic way, nor even by comparing the language studies of several authors, whose methodology is likely to differ. Answers require a systematic survey of a representative sample of languages, in which the same analytic methods are used in each case, and which is sufficiently large to enable some statistical conclusions to be drawn. The findings presented in the following pages are based on an American survey known as UPSID (The *U*niversity of California, Los Angeles *P*honological *S*egment *I*nventory *D*atabase). The inventories of 317 languages were included, with one language being selected from each family grouping recognized (e.g. one from West Germanic, one from East Germanic, and so on (§50)). The segments were analysed as phonemes (p. 162), each unit being represented by its most characteristic variant. (After I. Maddieson, 1984.)

Number of segments

It is not yet known whether there is an upper limit on the number of segments that can be efficiently distinguished in speech, or a lower limit set by the smallest number of segments needed to build up a vocabulary. The smallest inventories in the UPSID sample contained only 11 segments: Rotokas (Indo-Pacific) and Mura (Chibchan). Several Polynesian languages are known to have very small inventories. By contrast, the largest inventory belonged to !Xũ (Khoisan), with 141 segments, with several other languages of this family displaying comparably large totals. Between these extremes, 70% of the languages in the sample had between 20 and 37 segments.

When the inventories are analysed into types of sound, consonants emerge as being far more common than vowels. The number of consonants (C) in an inventory varies between 6 and 95 (a mean of 22.8); the number of vowels (V) varies between 3 and 46 (a mean of 8.7). If we divide V by C, the resulting ratio varies between 0.065 and 1.308. It is possible to say that the 'typical' language has over twice as many Cs as Vs. Larger inventories tend to have a higher proportion of Cs. However, several languages do not conform to these trends, such as Haida (Amerindian), with 46C but only 3V, and Pawaian (Indo-Pacific), which actually has more V (12) than C (10).

Dependencies

Several important dependencies can be observed between the sounds that are used in languages. These take the form of 'implicational' statements, of the type: 'If X occurs, then Y will occur.' For example, there are only four exceptions in the UPSID sample to the statement that if a language contains /p/, it will also contain /k/. There is only one exception (Hawaiian) to the statement that if /k/ occurs, then /t/ will occur (though /t/ can in fact be heard in some Hawaiian varieties). Similarly, if there is /g/, there will be /d/; if /d/, then /b/; and if /m/, then /n/.

More generally, nasals do not occur unless stops occur at the same place of articulation (five exceptions); voiceless nasals and approximants (p. 159) do not occur unless the language has their voiced counterparts; and mid-vowels do not occur unless there are high and low vowels (two exceptions).

Areal statements

The UPSID survey selects single languages from the main language families. There is also a need for detailed phonological studies of all the languages spoken within a geographical area, to determine the nature of any preferences for certain types of sound. Such *areal* studies (p. 33) would draw attention to such features as the prevalence of click consonants in South Africa (and also in certain East African languages), pharyngeals and glottals in Afro-Asiatic languages, retroflex consonants in South Asia, or implosives and labio-velar coarticulation (p. 158) in African languages. Historical evidence is sometimes available to explain the development of an areal phonological feature, but all too often the reasons are lost.

FAVOURITE CONSONANTS

What would a language look like, if it included only the most common consonant segments? The 20 most frequent consonants were extracted from the UPSID file, to display the following system (alveolar and dental phones are grouped together):

p, b   t, d   tʃ   k, g   ʔ
f   s   ʃ
m   n   ɲ   ŋ
w   l, r   j   h

Most languages have between 14 and 16 of these segments. No language has exactly this system, but some are very close to it, e.g. Bambara (Niger-Congo), which lacks [ʔ], and includes [z] and [dʒ].

The UPSID survey shows the typical range of consonant segments to be between five and 11 stops, one and four fricatives, two and four nasals, and four others. No one segment is found in all languages. (After I. Maddieson, 1984.)

Why did the click sounds spread from the Khoisan languages into other parts of South and East Africa? One theory is that Zulu and Xhosa women borrowed the clicks so as to disguise words that would be taboo in their own languages.

A group of brides in a Zulu village.

STOPS

All languages in the UPSID survey have stop consonants (p. 159), with voiceless segments occurring much more commonly than voiced (92% vs 67%). Other types of stop are much less common, such as aspirated (29%), voiceless ejectives (16%), and voiced implosives (11%). Most languages have two types of stop, but the number varies between one and six. Languages with very complex sets of stops include Igbo (Niger-Congo) and !Xū (Khoisan), each with six types. The Igbo inventory, for example, is as follows:

5 voiceless unaspirated plosives   5 voiceless aspirated plosives
5 voiced plosives   5 breathy voiced plosives
2 voiceless implosives   1 voiced implosive

Similarly, most languages have stops at three or four places of articulation (excluding glottal stops). Over 99% have bilabial, dental/alveolar, and velar stops. A few have only two places of articulation (e.g. Hawaiian). Some (mainly Australian languages) have as many as six, with stops in bilabial, dental, alveolar, retroflex, palatal, and velar positions.

FRICATIVES

At least one fricative (excluding /h/) is found in 93% of the UPSID languages; most of the cases where fricatives are absent are Australian. As can be seen from the following graph, the majority of languages have up to four fricatives, but some have 12 or more.

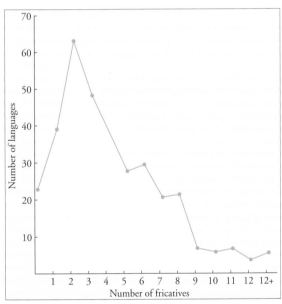

The most frequent fricative is a dental/alveolar sibilant: 83% of the languages have some form of /s/. Next comes /ʃ/ and /f/, then /z/, /x/, /v/, and /ʒ/, in that order. The asymmetry between /s/ and /z/ is worth noting: the latter is found in only a third as many languages. /h/, when analysed as a fricative (as opposed to a kind of breathy vowel), is found in 63% of the languages.

The largest set of fricatives is found in Kabardian (Caucasian), where there are 22 in all, grouped into eight types:

7 voiceless non-sibilant   7 voiced non-sibilant
2 voiceless sibilant   2 voiced sibilant
1 voiceless non-sibilant ejective   1 voiceless sibilant ejective
1 voiceless lateral   1 voiced lateral

NASALS

Almost all UPSID languages (97%) have at least one phoneme whose main allophone is a voiced nasal, and this is usually /n/ (in 96% of cases). If there is a second nasal, it will usually be /m/. Languages with two, three, or four nasals are common; the maximum seems to be six. Only four languages in the whole sample have no nasal segments at all (such as Rotokas (Indo-Pacific)).

The majority of nasal consonants are voiced: 93%. Fewer than 4% are voiceless. The most common nasal segments are dental/alveolar, followed by bilabial, velar, and palatal.

LIQUIDS AND APPROXIMANTS

The UPSID analysis distinguishes between 'liquid' sounds (/l/ and /r/) and 'approximant' sounds (/j/ and /w/) (p. 158). Most languages (96%) have at least one liquid; 72% have more than one. /l/ segments are somewhat more common than /r/ segments. Irish Gaelic has the largest number of liquids: 10 (2 voiced flaps, 2 voiceless flaps, 4 voiced laterals, and 2 voiceless laterals). At the other extreme, several languages have none, such as Nootka (Amerindian). The majority of liquids are voiced (83%); 87% of them are dental/alveolar. The most common /r/ segments are also voiced (97%), and involve rapid tongue-tip movements (trills, taps, and flaps – 86%). Uvular [ʀ]. found in French and German, is not a common segment.

The approximants are also widely used. A /j/ segment is found in 86% of the languages; a /w/ segment in 76%.

GLOTTALICS

Ejectives are the most common consonant to use a glottalic air stream (pp. 126–7). They are typically voiceless (99%) and are commonly stops (60%). Two-thirds of all ejectives are found in Amerindian languages, especially from North America. In 100% of cases, if a language has a single ejective, it is /k'/. Some languages have as many as five ejective consonants, e.g. bilabial, dental/alveolar, palatal, velar, and uvular.

The majority of implosives are found in African languages. These are typically voiced (97%). If a language has a single implosive, it is usually /ɓ/. Some languages have as many as four such segments: bilabial, dental/alveolar, palatal, and velar or uvular.

SEGMENT FREQUENCY WITHIN A LANGUAGE

In southern British English, an analysis of the frequency of vowels and consonants in conversation produced the following totals (after D. B. Fry, 1947).

Consonants %		Vowels %	
n	7.58	ə	10.74
t	6.42	ɪ	8.33
d	5.14	e	2.97
s	4.81	aɪ	1.83
l	3.66	ʌ	1.75
ð	3.56	eɪ	1.71
r	3.51	iː	1.65
m	3.22	əʊ	1.51
k	3.09	a	1.45
w	2.81	ɒ	1.37
z	2.46	ɔː	1.24
v	2.00	uː	1.13
b	1.97	ʊ	0.86
f	1.79	ɑː	0.79
p	1.78	aʊ	0.61
h	1.46	ɜː	0.52
ŋ	1.15	ɛə	0.34
g	1.05	ɪə	0.21
ʃ	0.96	ɔɪ	0.14
dʒ	0.60	ʊə	0.06
tʃ	0.41		
θ	0.37		
ʒ	0.10		

VOWELS

The 2,549 vowel segments in the UPSID data can be classified on the basis of place and manner of articulation as follows:

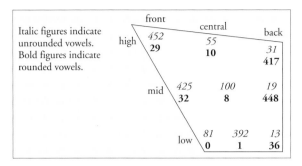

	front	central	back
Italic figures indicate unrounded vowels. Bold figures indicate rounded vowels.			
high	*452* **29**	*55* **10**	*31* **417**
mid	*425* **32**	*100* **8**	*19* **448**
low	*81* **0**	*392* **1**	*13* **36**

It can be seen that front vowels are usually unrounded (94%), and back vowels are usually rounded (93.5%). Low vowels are usually central (75%), and central vowels are usually low (69%). High front vowels are much more common than high back vowels.

The smallest vowel systems turn out to have three members (fewer than 6% of UPSID languages). Some languages have been analysed as having fewer than this (such as Kabardian (Caucasian)), but the analysis depends on how much of the phonetic contrasts observed can be attributed to the consonant system. There seem to be no clear cases of 1-vowel languages. By contrast, the largest number of vowel segments is 24 (!Xū (Khoisan)). Most languages have between 5 and 7 vowels – a point that can cause some surprise to speakers of Indo-European languages, which have many more. German and Norwegian both have 15 vowel-quality contrasts (disregarding length) – the largest totals in the survey.

The more vowel qualities there are in a language, the more likely that language is to show length contrasts – though in fact only 20% of the languages have both long and short vowel segments. Similarly, only 22% of the languages contrast oral and nasal vowels.

There are only 83 clear cases of diphthongal phonemes in the whole UPSID sample, found in only 23 languages. Over a quarter of these occur in just one language, !Xū, which has four series of diphthongs: oral, nasalized, pharyngealized oral, and pharyngealized nasal.

VOWEL SYSTEMS

Phonologists usually describe vowel systems with reference to the articulatory space they occupy, as represented by such models as the Cardinal Vowel diagram (p. 156). About 86% of the languages in the UPSID survey have their vowels evenly and widely distributed within this space (the principle of 'vowel dispersion'), and it thus becomes possible to talk about vowel arrangements using an analogy with basic geometrical shapes. Most vowel systems are 'triangular' in shape, especially based on a 3- or 5- vowel pattern. Fewer than 10% of the languages have 'square' or 'rectangular' systems. (Diphthongs are not taken into account in the systems illustrated right.)

3-vowel systems

i   u
  a

Aranda (Australian)
Greenlandic
(Eskimo-Aleut)

e   o
  a

Amuesha (Andean-
Equatorial)

4-vowel systems

i ɨ u
  a

Rukai (Austronesian)

i
e   o
  a

Klamath (Penutian)

5-vowel systems

i   u
 e   o
   a

Spanish (Indo-European)

i   ɯ
 ɛ   ɔ
   a

Japanese (Isolate)

i   ɷ
    o
 ɛ
   a

Hebrew (Afro-Asiatic)

i   u
    ɔ
 æ
   a

Taishan (Sino-Tibetan)

6-vowel systems

i ɨ u
 e   o
   a

Lappish (Uralic)

i   u
 e ə o
   a

Kanakuru (Afro-Asiatic)

i   u
 e   o
   ə
   a

Malay (Austronesian)

i   u
 e   o
 æ a

Chamorro (Austronesian)

7-vowel systems

i   u
 e   o
  ɛ ɔ

Katcha (Niger-Congo)

i   u
 ɪ   ɷ
 e   o
   a

Kunama (Nilo-Saharan)

8-vowel systems

i y   u ɯ
     o
  ɛ œ

Osmanli (Ural-Altaic)

i   u
 e   o
   ə
  ɛ ɔ
   a

Javanese (Austronesian)

9-vowel system

i   u
 ɪ   ɷ
 e   o
  ɛ ɔ
   a

Masai (Nilo-Saharan)

12-vowel system

iː   uː
 ɪ   ɷ
     ɜː
 e ə ɔː
 æ ʌ ɒɑ

English (Indo-European)

14-vowel systems

i ĩ   u ũ
 e ẽ   o õ
 ɛ ɛ̃ ɔ ɔ̃
  a ã

Bambara (Niger-Congo)

iː uː i   u
e: o: e ø
 ɛ: ɔ: ɛ ɔ
  a: a

Wolof (Niger-Congo)

20-vowel system

i   u ĩ   ũ
 ɪ   ɷ   ĩ̃   ũ̃
 e ə o   ẽ ɔ̃ õ
 æ a ɒ   æ̃ ã ɒ̃

Panjabi (Indo-European)

FROM ONE EXTREME TO THE OTHER

The remarkable differences between the phonological systems of the world's languages is nowhere better illustrated than by a comparison of the smallest and largest consonant inventories in the UPSID survey (some phonetic symbols have been changed in the 1989 IPA revision, p. 161).

ROTOKAS (Indo-Pacific)

Consonants	Bilabial	Alveolar	Velar
Voiceless plosive	p	t	k
Voiced plosive			g
Voiced non-sibilant fricative	β		
Voiced tap		D	

!XŨ (Khoisan)

Consonants — Non-clicks (47)	Bilabial	Alveolar	Alveolar velarized	Palato-alveolar	Palato-alveolar velarized	Palatal	Velar	Velar pharyngealized	Variable place	Labial-velar
Voiceless plosive	p	t	ƫ				k			
Voiceless aspirated plosive	pʰ	tʰ					kʰ			
Voiced plosive	b	d	ɖ				g			
Breathy voiced plosive							g̤			
Voiceless ejective stop		t'					k'			
Voiced ejective stop	b'	d'					g'			
Voiceless sibilant affricate		ts	ʦ	tʃ	ƭ					
Voiceless aspirated sibilant affricate		tˢʰ		tʃʰ						
Voiced sibilant affricate			dz		dʒ					
Voiceless sibilant ejective affricate		ts'		tʃ'						
Breathy voiced sibilant affricate		dz̤		dʒ̤						
Voiced sibilant ejective affricate		dz'		dʒ'						
Voiceless non-sibilant fricative							x			
Voiced non-sibilant fricative									ɦ	
Voiceless sibilant fricative		s		ʃ						
Voiced sibilant fricative		z		ʒ						
Voiced nasal	m	n					ŋ	ŋˤ		
Long voiced nasal		m:								
Breathy voiced nasal	m̤									
Laryngealized voiced nasal	m̰									
Voiced flap		ɾ								
Voiced central approximant						j				w

Clicks (48)	Dental	Dental nasalized	Dental nasalized and velarized	Dental velarized	Alveolar	Alveolar nasalized	Alveolar nasalized and velarized	Alveolar velarized	Palatal	Palatal nasalized	Palatal nasalized and velarized	Palatal velarized
Voiceless					ǃ			ǂ	ʗ			Ꞓ
Voiceless aspirated					ǃʰ	ŋ̊ǃʰ			ʗʰ	ŋ̊ʗʰ		
Glottalized voiceless						ŋǃˀ	ŋǂˀ			ŋʗˀ	ŋꞒˀ	
Voiced					ɡǃ	ŋǃ		ɡǂ	ɡʗ	ŋʗ		ɡꞒ
Breathy voiced					ɡǃ̤	ŋǃ			ɡʗ	ŋʗ		
Glottalized voiced								ɡǂˀ				ɡꞒˀ
Voiceless affricated	ǀˢ			ǁˢ								
Voiceless aspirated affricated	ǀˢʰ	ŋǀˢʰ										
Glottalized voiceless affricated		ŋǀˢˀ	ŋǀˢʰ									
Voiced affricated	ɡǀˢ	ŋǀˢ		ɡǁˢ								
Breathy voiced affricated	ɡǀˢ	ŋǀˢ										
Glottalized voiced affricated				ɡǁˢˀ								
Voiceless lateral affricated									ʗˡ			Ꞓˡ
Voiceless aspirated lateral affricated									ʗˡʰ	ŋʗˡʰ		
Glottalized voiceless lateral affricated										ŋʗˡˀ	ŋꞒˡˀ	
Voiced lateral affricated									ɡʗˡ	ŋʗˡ		ɡꞒˡ
Glottalized voiced lateral affricated												ɡꞒˡˀ
Breathy voiced lateral affricated									ɡʗˡ	ŋʗˡ		

'It ain't what you say, but the way that you say it.' This familiar comment, immortalized in song, is the time-honoured way of briefly indicating what 'suprasegmental' analysis is all about. The 'segments' of spoken language are the vowels and consonants, which combine to produce syllables, words, and sentences – the 'verbal' aspect of speech (§§27–8). But at the same time as we articulate these segments, our pronunciation varies in other respects. We make use of a wide range of tones of voice, which change the meaning of what we say in a variety of different ways. It is these effects that provide the data of suprasegmental analysis.

PROSODIC FEATURES

The basic psycho-acoustic properties of sound are the source of the main linguistic effects: pitch and loudness (§§23, 25). These effects, along with those arising out of the distinctive use of speed and rhythm, are collectively known as the *prosodic features* of language – a broader sense of *prosody* than that found in the study of literature, where it refers to the metrical patterns found in lines of poetry (§12).

The most important suprasegmental effects in a language are provided by the linguistic use of pitch, or melody – the *intonation* system. Different levels of pitch (*tones*) are used in particular sequences (*contours*, or *tunes*) to express a wide range of meanings. For example, all languages seem to make use of the difference between a falling and a rising pitch pattern, and this is widely interpreted as expressing a contrast between 'stating' and 'questioning'. In English orthography, the contrast is signalled by the use of punctuation (p. 207), as in *They're waiting.* vs *They're waiting?* In speech, a much wider range of tones is available to express various nuances and degrees of emphasis (cf. the extra emotion suggested by *They're waiting*??!).

Another important prosodic feature is loudness, which is used to convey gross differences of meaning, such as the increased volume usually associated with anger, as well as the fine contrasts heard on the different syllables in a word (p. 166). Syllabic loudness is usually referred to as *stress*, the syllables being referred to as 'stressed' or 'unstressed'; but the term *accent* is also often used ('accented' vs 'unaccented'), referring to the way the prominence of a syllable is frequently due to the use of pitch as well as loudness (p. 173).

Variations in tempo provide a third suprasegmental parameter. It is possible to speed up or slow down the rate at which syllables, words, and sentences are produced, to convey several kinds of meaning. In many languages, a sentence spoken with extra speed conveys urgency; slower speed, deliberation or emphasis. A rapid, clipped single syllable may convey irritation; a slowly drawled syllable, greater personal involvement. Compare:

'Shall I leave now?' asked Janet. 'Yes,' snapped John rudely.
'Shall I leave now?' asked Janet. 'Ye-e-s,' replied John, thoughtfully stroking his beard.

Pitch, loudness, and tempo together enter into a language's expression of *rhythm*. Languages vary greatly in the way in which rhythmical contrasts are made. English makes use of stressed syllables produced at roughly regular intervals of time (in fluent speech) and separated by unstressed syllables – a 'stress-timed' (or *isochronous*) rhythm. In French, the syllables are produced in a steady flow, resulting in a 'machine-gun' effect – a 'syllable-timed' rhythm. Loudness is the basis of rhythmical effects in English (as shown by the way it is possible to tap out a sentence in a 'te-*tum*, te-*tum*' way). By contrast, the length of a syllable (whether long or short) was the crucial feature of rhythm in Latin; and pitch height (high vs low) is a central feature of the rhythm of many oriental languages.

PARALINGUISTIC FEATURES

Apart from the contrasts signalled by pitch, loudness, tempo, and rhythm, languages make use of several other distinctive vocal effects, using the range of articulatory possibilities available in the vocal tract (§22). The laryngeal, pharyngeal, oral, and nasal cavities can all be used to produce 'tones of voice' which alter the meaning of what is said. These effects are sometimes referred to as effects of 'timbre' or 'voice quality', and studied under the heading of vocal *paralanguage* – a term intended to convey the less central role played by these features in the communication of meaning, compared with that of prosodic features.

One of the clearest examples of a paralinguistic feature is whispered speech, used in many languages to add 'conspiratorial' meaning to what is said. Another is the marked lip-rounding which is widely used as a tone of voice when adults talk to babies or animals. But few of these effects are truly universal. For example, a 'breathy' or 'husky' tone of voice conveys deep emotion or sexual desire in many languages; but in Japanese, it is routinely used as a way of conveying respect or submission. A 'creaky' or 'gravelly' tone of voice is often used in English to convey unimportance or disparagement; but in Finnish, it is a normal feature of many voice qualities, and would not have this connotation. And there is no equivalent in English to the use of strongly nasalized speech to convey a range of emotional nuances in Portuguese.

ROAD HOGS AND HOT POTATOES

Why do people sometimes introduce bursts of speed into their speech? This question was addressed as part of a linguistic analysis of a psychiatric interview. (The results were published in a book called *The First Five Minutes* – so called, because the microscopic nature of the analysis made it impracticable to publish more than five minutes' worth of material!)

The authors concluded that there were six main conditions that led people to speak more quickly than usual.

• *Road hogs* Speakers think they are about to be interrupted, so they speed up in order to forestall it.

• *Hot potatoes* Speakers realize that what they are saying is unpleasant, so they speed up to get it over with as quickly as possible.

• *Getaways* Speakers realize that they have said something unpleasant or threatening, so they speed up to put as much 'ground' as possible between themselves and the distasteful topic.

• *Smokescreens* Speakers realize that what they have said might be taken in the wrong way, so they speed up, presenting new material that will capture the attention of their listeners.

• *Greener pastures* Speakers, while speaking, think of something more interesting to say, so they speed up to get to the new topic as quickly as possible.

• *Rebounds* Speakers perceive that their speed of speaking is inappropriately slow, and in correcting this they end up speaking more quickly than they had intended.

(After R. E. Pittenger, C. F. Hockett & J. J. Danehy, 1960.)

TRANSCRIBING INTONATION

The first scientific attempt to transcribe the patterns of English intonation was made by Joshua Steele in *An essay towards establishing the melody and measure of speech* in 1775. It had been prompted by remarks made in an essay by James Burnet the previous year. Burnet had claimed that there was no such thing as intonation in English. The music of our language, he argued, is 'nothing better than the music of a drum, in which we perceive no difference except that of louder or softer'.

Steele rebutted this point of view in an original manner. He pasted a piece of paper to the finger-board of a bass viol next to the fourth string, and marked the notes on it that corresponded to the various frets. He then imitated the inflection of the voice by sliding his finger up and down the string, and found that the beginnings and ends of these inflections could usually be located in the intervals between the frets. He then devised a transcription which represented these observations – the first systematic transcription of English intonation.

In Steele's transcription of a line of poetry, as spoken by himself, the accent marks are to be interpreted as musical notes. The vertical symbols mark length, on a scale from longest to shortest (꟭, ı, î, ĭ). Three degrees of emphasis are indicated by the symbols △, ∴, and .. (from heavy to light). Pauses are also marked, using a system of rests, as in music. The symbols underneath the text indicate an increased level of loudness.

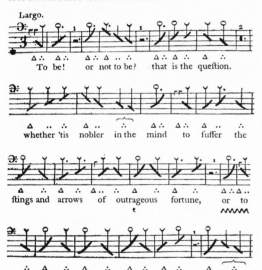

Above: The first few lines of Steele's transcription

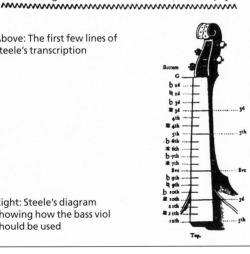

Right: Steele's diagram showing how the bass viol should be used

MODERN TRANSCRIPTIONS

Contemporary transcriptions of intonation vary greatly, as they reflect different theoretical views of the nature of the subject. Some approaches attempt to provide a faithful phonetic record of melodic movement; others are more phonological in character (§28), including only those aspects of melody which seem to be crucial for expressing contrasts in meaning. Some phonetic studies rely on auditory judgments alone; others use a combination of auditory and acoustic analysis. Within the phonological studies, there is difference of opinion over the extent to which pitch contrasts are capable of being analysed using the procedures of phonemic analysis, and over the extent to which grammatical and semantic considerations (§§16–17) should be allowed to influence the nature of a transcription. As a consequence, several competing descriptive frameworks are in present-day use.

PHONETIC APPROACHES

Right: The widely used interlinear system The lines represent the upper and lower limits of pitch range. Size of dot indicates relative loudness of each syllable, and the dot with a tail marks the most prominent syllable. The method has been nicknamed the 'tadpole' transcription. The language in this example is Italian.

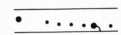

Quando ci rivedremo?

Let me have a look at that stethoscope.

35. (i) 'AM I' Hilda SAID 'PREGNANT?'

The typography in these cases provides an accurate reflection of the phonetic changes in the melody. (From D. L. Bolinger, 1964, pp. 282ff, and, for the version with prominence represented by capitals, R. P. Stockwell, 1972, p. 107.)

Three ways of using musical notation. The first description (top) follows the musical model very closely. The language is Hungarian. (From I. Fónagy & K. Magdics, 1963.) The second (bottom left) shows four pitch levels more impressionistically drawn against an unspecified musical stave, the duration of each tone being represented by the length of the marks. The numerals refer to toneme levels (p. 174). The language is Chinese. (From N-C. Chang, 1958.) The third (bottom right) gives a very approximate pitch movement against an unspecified stave. The language is French. (From P. Delattre, 1966.)

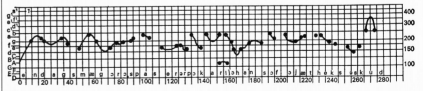

The information derived from a spectrographic analysis (p. 136). The language is Norwegian. (From E. Haugen & M. Joos, 1952, p. 47.)

'Come ,on. ‖ 'Let's get ,going.

One of the widely used 'tonetic' systems of transcription. The accents represent pitch directions, placed before the word to which they apply. The double line indicates the boundary between the two intonation units; the raised vertical line marks a stressed syllable. (After J. D. O'Connor & G. F. Arnold, 1973.)

the | man is 'eating a ↑bowl of PÒRRidge |

In this system, a range of phonological symbols is used within the line of print. The most prominent syllable is printed in small capitals, with an accent representing the direction of pitch movement above the vowel. The remaining symbols represent other features of pitch and stress, placed before the syllable to which they apply. Note that sentence-initial capitals and punctuation marks are not used. (After D. Crystal, 1969.)

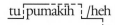

Pitch The movement of pitch is shown here by the direction of the solid and broken lines. Three main pitch levels (high, mid, low) are represented. The language is Kunimaipa (New Guinea). (From A. Pence, 1964.)

// 4 well they / may do at / <u>A</u> level //

Five main tones are recognized in this system, tone 4 (which is falling–rising in pitch) being shown here. The main melodic contours are identified by //, and smaller rhythm units by /. The main emphasis within a unit is underlined. (After M. A. K. Halliday, 1967.)

The 'man in the 'street is
3–   °2–3 3–   °2–3 3–
'selling 'apples 'quickly.
°2–3   °2–3   °2––4

There are four pitch levels, numbered from 1 (high) to 4 (low). The small circle marks the beginning of each pitch movement. (After K. L. Pike, 1945.)

THE FUNCTIONS OF INTONATION

Intonation, and the other suprasegmental features of language, perform a variety of different functions.

Emotional The most obvious function is to express a wide range of attitudinal meanings – excitement, boredom, surprise, friendliness, reserve, and many hundreds more. Here, intonation works along with other prosodic and paralinguistic features to provide the basis of all kinds of vocal emotional expression.

Grammatical Intonation plays an important role in the marking of grammatical contrasts. The identification of such major units as clause and sentence (§16) often depends on the way pitch contours break up an utterance; and several specific contrasts, such as question and statement, or positive and negative, may rely on intonation. Many languages make the important conversational distinction between 'asking' and 'telling' in this way, e.g. *She's here, isn't she?* (where a rising pitch is the spoken equivalent of the question mark) vs *She's here, isn't she!* (where a falling pitch expresses the exclamation mark).

Information structure Intonation conveys a great deal about what is new and what is already known in the meaning of an utterance – what is referred to as the 'information structure' of the utterance. If someone says *I saw a BLUE car*, with maximum intonational prominence on *blue*, this pronunciation presupposes that someone has previously queried the colour; whereas if the emphasis is on *I*, it presupposes a previous question about which person is involved. It would be very odd for someone to ask *Who saw a blue car?*, and for the reply to be *I saw a BLUE car!*

Textual Intonation is not only used to mark the structure of sentences; it is also an important element in the construction of larger stretches of discourse (§20). Prosodic coherence is well illustrated in the way paragraphs of information are given a distinctive melodic shape in radio news-reading. As the news-reader moves from one item of news to the next, the pitch level jumps up, then gradually descends, until by the end of the item the voice reaches a relatively low level.

Psychological Intonation can help to organize language into units that are more easily perceived and memorized. Learning a long sequence of numbers, for example, proves easier if the sequence is divided into rhythmical 'chunks'. The ability to organize speech into intonational units is also an important feature of normal language acquisition – a feature that is often absent in cases of language disorder (§§40, 46).

Indexical Suprasegmental features also have a significant function as markers of personal identity – an 'indexical' function. In particular, they help to identify people as belonging to different social groups and occupations (such as preachers, street vendors, army sergeants) (§§6–12).

The most neutral tone; a simple statement of fact; detached.

Emotionally involved; the higher the falling tone, the more involved the speaker. The choice of emotion (e.g. surprise, excitement, irritation) depends largely on context and facial expression.

A routine, uncommitted comment; often used as a conversational 'noise' while someone else is talking.

Context and facial expression are important factors here. With a 'pleasant' face, the tone is sympathetic and friendly, asking the speaker to carry on; with an 'unpleasant' face, it is guarded or grim.

Disbelief or shock – the extent of the emotion depending on the width of the tone.

Mild query or puzzlement; a tone often used in echoing what has just been said.

Bored, sarcastic, routine.

Accompanied by a 'negative' face, a tone of uncertainty, doubt, or tentativeness; if a 'positive' face, a tone of encouragement or urgency.

A tone of emotional involvement, expressing great emphasis. Depending on the face and the context, so the attitude might be impressed, challenging, or complacent.

TONE LANGUAGES

In well over half the languages of the world, it is possible to change the meaning of a word simply by changing the pitch level at which it is spoken. Languages that allow this are known as *tone languages*, and the distinctive pitch levels are known as *tones* or *tonemes*.

The number of distinctive tones in a language varies. The simplest systems have only two tones, high vs low (e.g. Zulu); Yoruba has three (high, mid, low); Lushai has four (extra-high, high, mid, low); Thai has five (low, mid, and high-falling, high-rising, low-falling-rising); Cantonese Chinese has six (mid- and low-level, high- and low-falling, and high- and low-rising).

Tonal differences may affect either the vocabulary or the grammar of a language. Probably the most widely known case of lexical contrast is Mandarin Chinese, which has four tones, each of which has been given a 'tone letter', and also a number, in systems of transcription.

Tone	Letter	Example	Meaning
high-level	˥	ma¹	mother
high-rising	˧	ma²	hemp
low-falling-rising	˩	ma³	horse
high-falling	˥˩	ma⁴	scold

Many tongue-twisters have been devised based on this feature of the language, such as:

Mama¹ qi ma³. Ma³ man. Mama¹ ma⁴ ma³.
'Mother rides horse. Horse slow. Mother scolds horse.'

Grammatical uses of tone are also common. In several languages of West Africa (e.g. Twi, Bini), a change of tone signals the difference between certain tense forms. In Bini, for instance, a low tone is used for present tense, and a high or high-low tone for past tense.

The tones themselves are of two kinds: some stay at a single pitch level; others involve a change of pitch level ('gliding' tones). Tone languages are usually classified into those that use gliding tones (*contour* tone languages) and those that do not (*register* tone languages). Thai and Mandarin Chinese illustrate the first type; Zulu and Hausa illustrate the second.

When a sequence of tones is uttered, adjacent tones tend to influence each other in much the same way as segments do (p. 166). Such assimilations are known as *tone sandhi*. For example, a low tone preceded by a high tone will usually begin with a downward pitch movement. In particular, the intonation system of the language can cause changes in the pitch level of tones. In a sentence where there is a gradually falling intonation contour, the tones towards the beginning of the sentence will be spoken at a higher level than the tones towards the end. This gradual lowering of tones in an utterance is known as *downdrift*. It may even result in a high tone at the end of a sentence having the same absolute pitch level as a low tone at the beginning!

Accent

Tone languages have to be distinguished from *pitch-accent* languages (e.g. Swedish, Japanese, Serbo-Croat), in which a particular syllable in a word is pronounced with a certain tone, or 'accent'. For example, Japanese /sòra/ 'sky' has a falling accent on the first syllable, whereas /kawà/ 'river' has a rising accent on the second. A language may also contain minimal pairs that contrast only in word accent. In Swedish, the sentence *Den här tomten är bra* means either 'This site is fine' or 'This goblin is fine', depending on the accentual pattern of *tomten*.

These languages must be distinguished from those where each word has a fixed place for the point of maximum prominence, though there is no restriction over which tone is used. 'Accent', in such cases, is synonymous with 'stress'. In Czech or Finnish, for example, the main accent generally falls on the first syllable of a word; in Persian or Turkish, on the last; in Polish or Welsh, on the penultimate syllable. English and Russian are different again: in these languages, the accentual pattern of any given word is fixed, but there is no single pattern used throughout the language.

SILENCE

An important feature of speech transcriptions is the marking of pauses. Pauses are used to demarcate linguistic units, to signal the cognitive activity of the speaker, and to help structure speech interactions. They may be silent, or filled with a vocalization (such as English *er(m)*).

Silence can also communicate a meaning in its own right, as shown by the many descriptive phrases for kinds of silence – 'threatening', 'thoughtful', and so on. Here, silence is far more than the absence of speech. Sometimes, pauses can be quite specific in intention – such as the didactic function used in teaching ('It's called a –?') or the social function of avoiding a taboo (such as a host's 'Do you need to –?'). Equally, expectations of silence may be imposed by a social group (as in meetings), or have an institutionalized value, as in churches, libraries, and theatres.

Cross-cultural differences are common over when to talk and when to remain silent, or what a particular instance of silence means (p. 38). In response to the question 'Will you marry me?', silence in English would be interpreted as uncertainty; in Japanese it would be acceptance. In Igbo, it would be considered a denial if the woman were to continue to stand there, and an acceptance if she ran away.

ENGLISH STRESS

In English words, each syllable is pronounced with a certain level of loudness, or *stress*. Usually, three levels of stress are recognized: *primary* or *main* stress; *secondary* stress; and *unstressed*.

The main stress patterns can be seen in the following list (ˈprimary; ˌsecondary; unstressed syllables unmarked):

two syllables
ˈfinish ˈfemale ˈunder
beˈhind Chiˈnese maˈchine

three syllables
ˌunderˈstand ˌafterˈnoon
ˈyesterday ˈconsequence
ˈphotoˌgraph imˈportant

four syllables
reˈmarkable ˌunimˈportant
ˈcaterpillar ˈheliˌcopter

five syllables
conˌsiderˈation
ˌsatisˈfactory
adˈminiˌstrative

six syllables
deˌsiraˈbility
ˌmeteoroˈlogical

seven syllables
ˌuniˈlateralism ˌunreˌliaˈbility

eight syllables
ˌinterˌnationalizˈation

Compound words also need to be identified in terms of stress, for example:

ˈwindˌscreen ˈgreenˌfly
ˌbroken-ˈhearted

Some interesting contrasts occur when the stress pattern of compounds differs from that of phrases (units consisting of separate words). Compare:

ˈwhite ˈhouse (any building)
ˈWhite ˌHouse (the President's house)
ˈlightˈhousework (at home)
ˈlighthouse ˌwork (at sea)

Advertising slogan writers (and linguists) enjoy playing with these forms. One sign outside a New York kiosk read: 'Even hot dogs enjoy our hot dogs' – a sentence any linguist would be proud of.

SPEECH AND MUSIC

Intonation has often been called the 'melody' or 'music' of speech, and musical notation has sometimes been used in the transcription of intonation (p. 172). But the analogy is not really a good one. There are two main differences. Music, typically, is composed to be repeated; speech, typically, is not. And, if we examine modern western music, we find tones that have been given absolute values, whereas those of speech are relative.

The consequences of this second point are far reaching. Notes have fixed frequencies (e.g. middle C now has a frequency of 264 Hz), and instruments can be tuned to ensure that their notes are compatible. But speech is not like this. Men, women, and children use tones with the same linguistic function (for stating, asking, etc.), yet produce them at widely differing frequencies. Moreover, two people of the same sex may both use the 'same' rising tone to ask a question, but one may produce it with a higher frequency range than the other. And even within a single speaker, the pitch at which a tone is produced may vary from one moment to the next, without this affecting the meaning of what is said. Language is not affected by these biological or random variations. The tones of intonation are relative, not absolute. People are not instruments. They do not speak out of tune.

On the other hand, the evident similarities between speech and music have led to several fruitful developments in both subjects. Some linguists have borrowed terminology from music in their search for clear ways of describing suprasegmental effects; and certain composers and music analysts have, in turn, looked to suprasegmental studies for ideas about the attributes and range of the voice.

MUSIC → SPEECH

There is no traditional terminology in phonetics for describing the many variations of pitch, loudness, and tempo which can be found in connected speech. One sequence of studies therefore looked to music for its descriptive terminology, and proposed analogous categories for the analysis of the suprasegmental effects that can be heard on stretches of utterance. These included such notions as:

piano / pianissimo decreased levels of loudness
forte / fortissimo increased levels of loudness
diminuendo gradually decreasing loudness
crescendo gradually increasing loudness
allegro / allegrissimo increased tempo of speech
lento / lentissimo decreased tempo of speech
accelerando gradually increasing tempo
rallentando gradually decreasing tempo

The following extract from the beginning of a sermon illustrates the way some of these effects combine to produce the overall tone of voice associated with this variety. Parts of the text correspond to certain prosodic effects, as shown. (Certain other prosodic effects of pitch range are also noted, but several details of the transcription have been omitted.)

high
the 'book of the 'prophet isÁiah | – 'thirtieth CHÁPter | –

diminuendo
the 'fifteenth 'verse of the CHÁPter | –

crescendo
isÁiah | chapter 'thirty 'verse fiftÈEn |– –

resonant
in re'turning and RÈST | – ye 'shall be SÀVED | – –

piano
in 'quietness – and in CÒNfi-dence | – 'shall 'be your STRÈNGTH | –

allegro diminuendo
in re'turning and 'rest ye shall be SÀVED | in 'quietness and in CÒNfidence | – 'shall be 'your STRÈNGTH |
(After D. Crystal & D. Davy, 1969.)

SPEECH → MUSIC

In recent years several composers, such as Luciano Berio (1925–) and Karl-heinz Stockhausen (1928–), have been experimenting with ways of displaying the voice in all its possible modes of expression, in association with new techniques of composition involving electronic devices.

Various procedures are used (after I. Anhalt, 1972):
• The virtuoso performance of a live monody, part speech, part song, with emphasis on the prosody and paralanguage.
• The use of a tape recording of a person's voice, carefully chosen in terms of language, dialect, age, voice quality, and so on.
• Autopolyphony – several layers of the same person's utterances superimposed through multiple recordings.
• Polyphonies of small groups of voices, with structures saturated by certain phonemic, prosodic, or paralinguistic features. Special attention is paid to the use of consonants – a feature without precedent in western music, where the emphasis has traditionally been on vowels – and to non-periodic rhythms.
• Polyphonies of large groups, representing such situations as the cocktail party, mass responses, the sound of a mob, and so on.
• The complementation of vocal sound by percussive, electronic, and other effects.

For example, in *Cento*, by Istvan Anhalt (1919–), a live choir of 12 voices is accompanied by vocal and instrumental sounds pre-recorded on tape. The text is a collage of fragments of a poem, some words being split and other elements recombined.

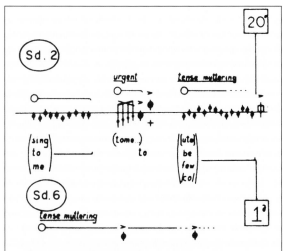

Berio's *Sequenza III* (1958) In this piece, lasting 8′ 40″, a woman presents a sequence of disturbing vocal behaviours, reflecting a range of bizarre moods. The extract illustrates just a few of the composer's uses of vocal labels, and clearly displays the combination of linguistic and musical notation that is the hallmark of the work.

Throughout the piece, alongside periods of sustained singing, we find such effects as: muttering, breathy whispering, whimpering, humming, laughter, and the use of narrow and wide pitch range; variations in pause; a range of 'vocal tics' such as clicks, coughs, and gasps; various trills and tremolos (e.g. striking the hand against the mouth, or using the hand over the mouth as a mute); and there are several semantic labels, such as tense, witty, joyful, excited, and frantic.

Some of the notational conventions used in the work include: *Sd.* subdivision; ⌑ tongue click; ♦ brief sung note; ⌔ cough; ↘ sigh; ⁊ whine; ⁙ gasp; ⌁ finger snap.

STYLIZED TUNES

Some kinds of intonation pattern have a very close relationship to music – in particular the stylized tunes, or chants, used by street vendors, auctioneers (p. 53), blues performers, train conductors, and so on. These are often produced with values

which are near absolute.

Stereotyped tunes can also be heard in everyday speech, such as the sing-song 'calling' intonation of 'Come and ↑ get ↓ it!' or '↑ Mi ↓ chael!', where the levels are about a minor third apart. This tune is also common with warnings or reminders of a routine or cajoling kind, as in 'It's on the ↑ ta ↓ ble' (i.e. 'I've told you a million times!'). Children, too, have their stylized tunes – notably, in cat-calling (shown on the stave above).

It is an accepted principle of phonetic study that individual sounds do not have meanings: it does not make sense to ask what [p] or [a] 'mean'. The smallest units of language that are meaningful are the elements of grammar known as morphemes (p. 90), such as *un-* and *-ness*. However, this ignores the existence of an interesting (though limited) tendency in language to develop forms that speakers feel *do* have a close relationship to objects or states in the outside world. In such cases, individual sounds are thought to reflect, or symbolize, properties of the world, and thus to 'have meaning'. This phenomenon is known as *sound symbolism*, though in literary contexts it is more commonly referred to as *onomatopoeia* (p. 74).

Sound-symbolic forms are usually considered to be features only of literary expression (of poetry, in particular) or of such restricted areas as child language (*bow-wow*) or the language of comic strips (*Zap!*, *Pow!*). In fact, several everyday lexical items are onomatopoeic, even though the sound symbolism may not be immediately obvious. In English, for example, there are a number of items that can be given a phonetic classification in this way. They can be grouped on the basis of their initial consonants, vowels, or final consonants, as when words beginning with /sl-/ are said to convey unpleasant associations (*slime, slither, slug, sloppy*, etc.), or words containing high front vowels associations of smallness (*teeny weeny, wee*, etc.). Final consonants also present an interesting basis of classification. Examples include:

/-p/	lap, clip, rip
/-k/	crack, creak, click, cluck, flick, whack
/-b/	blob, glob, jab, rub
/-l/	bubble, trickle, rustle
/-z/	ooze, wheeze
/-ʃ/	smash, crash, crush, splash, slash, lash
/-f/	puff, gruff, biff, cough, woof

But English, and Indo-European languages generally, are not good exemplars of the use of sound symbolism. To see the importance of this feature, we must look elsewhere. Korean, for instance, has over a thousand words that are sound-symbolic in character; and a correspondingly large onomatopoeic vocabulary also occurs in Japanese.

JAPANESE ONOMATOPOEIA

Japanese has over three times as many onomatopoeic expressions as English, and uses them to express a wider-ranging set of linguistic distinctions. Sound imitation (*giseigo*) is used to reflect physical, audible noises relating to the actions or movements of people, animals, and things. Manner imitation (*gitaigo*) refers to feelings and figurative expressions about objects and natural surroundings, in which sounds play no part.

The most popular forms are reduplications – patterns of consonants and vowels that occur twice in immediate succession. These are used far more than in English, which prefers simple forms to reduplications: compare such uncommon forms as *pitter-patter* and *ding-dong* alongside the common *bang, splash*, and *plop*. In Japanese, reduplicated forms occur normally in everyday conversation. Their range can be illustrated from the following examples (after H. Kakehi, *et al.*, 1981).

giseigo:	*gachagacha*	rattle
	chirinchirin	tinkle
	kasakasa	rustle
gitaigo:	*tobotobo*	plod
	furafura	roam
	kirakira	twinkle
	betabeta	stick to
	dabudabu	baggy, loose

Not all onomatopoeias are reduplicative:

gisshiri	packed full, crowded
shikkari	firmly, strongly

Very often, more than one level of meaning is expressed. For example, *barabara* refers to very strong rain ('pelting down'); but it may also refer to things that have been broken up, scattered, or disorganized. It could be used in such contexts as: 'The family is *split up*', 'The queue is *not straight*', or 'We left as a group, but came home *separately*.' *Gorogoro* is used for sounds, such as the purring of a cat, or for rumbling noises (such as thunder, or heavy objects); but it is also used to express manner, such as a state of discomfort caused by a lump, the way in which things are strewn around in abundance, or the state of being idle.

There are also several grammatical factors that must be taken into account. For instance, the particle *to* is used to indicate that the preceding expression is a quotation: *Inu ga wanwan to naku* 'The dog goes bow-wow' – something which in English would be more naturally expressed by a single lexical item, 'The dog is *barking*.' Also, certain forms are typically used in the expression of grammatical meanings, such as the use of *gungun* (steadily, rapidly) and *dondon* (at a great rate) in progressive contexts (as in *gungun ookikunatte* 'went on growing and growing').

Some of the sound-symbolic forms encountered during a comic-book fight. The example comes from *Asterix y Galiad*, a Welsh translation of *Asterix the Gaul*. However, the representation of these non-verbal sound effects would work in either language.

TYPES OF SYMBOLIC MEANING

Several attempts have been made to find specific correspondences between sounds and meanings. For example, in several languages an association has been suggested between close vowels (especially [i]) and smallness, and open vowels (especially [a]) and largeness, as in English *teeny, little, bit, slim, -ling* vs *large, vast, grand*, French *petit* vs *grand*. On the other hand, there are several counter-examples to this tendency – most obviously, English *big* vs *small*.

To be convincing, evidence of fundamental links between sound and meaning needs to be provided from a large number of languages. The same pattern must be found in languages of very different types and be confirmed by experiments into speakers' intuitions. A certain amount of descriptive work has been carried out; but corresponding psycholinguistic studies (p. 418) have not. The American linguist, Morris Swadesh (1909–67), brought together several such descriptive observations. For instance, he drew attention to the use of [i]-type vowels to express nearness (this) and [a]- or [u]-type vowels to express distance ('that/you') in many languages:

	'this' ([i])	*'that/you'* ([a/u])
Chinook	-i-	-u-
Klamath	ke-	ho-, ha
Tsimshian	gwii-	gwa
Guaraní	tyé	tuvicha
Maya	li'	la', lo'
Binga	ti	ta
Fur	in	illa
Didinga	ici	ica
Tamil	idɨ	adɨ
Thai	nii	nan
Burmese	dii	thoo

Sometimes some quite specific correspondences have been noted, such as the tendency for languages to express 'mother' with a nasal, and 'father' with an oral front consonant.

	'mother'	*'father'*
Dakota	ena	ate
Nahuatl	naan	ta'
Tiv	ng	ter
Luo	mama	baba
Hebrew	ima, em	aba, av
French	mère, mama	père, papa
Tamil	ammaa	appa
Yucatec	nan	tat
Greenlandic	anaana(q)	ataataq

Again, the pattern is not universal. In Georgian, *máma* means 'father'; and in a number of South Asian languages (e.g. Tamil, Telugu), *mama* means 'mother's brother'.

UNIVERSAL MEANINGS?

There is certainly limited evidence of a few broad sound/meaning correspondences in language. But there are many exceptions to the correlations that have been proposed, and when individual features are studied across a wide range of languages, a variety of divergent meanings emerge. The use of phonological reduplication within a word is widespread, but meanings vary greatly, as some of these examples show (M. Swadesh, 1972).

CONCLUSIONS

The examples of sound-symbolism are fascinating, but in the absence of frequency information about the phonological and lexical patterns in the various languages, it is not possible to arrive at a definitive interpretation. The cross-linguistic similarities may indeed have evolved separately, indicating a basic human propensity to use certain sounds in certain ways, or they may simply be the result of language contact over a long period of time. In the absence of historical data, drawing conclusions from sound symbolism about the origins of language would be premature (§49). Far more descriptive data are needed, accompanied by experimental investigation of the speakers' intuitions about the relationship between sounds and meanings.

NONSENSE VERSE

The semantic value of sounds is nowhere better illustrated than in successful nonsense verse, the most famous example of which is the first verse of Lewis Carroll's *Jabberwocky*.

'Twas brillig, and the slithy toves
Did gyre and gimble in the wabe:
All mimsy were the borogoves,
And the mome raths outgrabe.

Carroll also provided interpretations of some of the nonsense words, such as *slithy* = 'lithe and slimy', *mimsy* = 'flimsy and miserable', *mome* = 'from home', and *outgrabe* = 'something between bellowing and whistling, with a kind of sneeze in the middle'.

The poem has also been translated. The extent to which the effects carry over into foreign languages can be judged from these extracts:

Le Jaseroque
Il brilgue: les tôves lubricilleux
Se gyrent en vrillant dans le guave.
Enmimés sont les gougebosqueux,
Et le momerade horsgrave.
(F. L. Warrin, 1931)

Der Jammerwoch
Es brillig war. Die schlichte Toven
Wirrten und wimmelten in Waben;
Und aller-mümsige Burggoven
Die mohmen Räth' ausgraben.
(R. Scott, 1872)

Meaning of reduplication	Language	Examples
Plural	Bella Coola	*s-tn* 'tree', *s-tntn* 'trees'
	Hausa	*suna* 'name', *sunana-ki* 'names'
	Tsimshian	*am* 'good', *am'am* 'several are good'
Repetition	Karok	*páchup* 'kiss', *pachúpchup* 'kiss a lot'
Intensity	Karok	*go* 'see', *go-go* 'look at carefully'
Scattered distribution	Nootka	*mah'tii* 'house', *maamah'ti* 'dispersed houses'
Space	Somali	*fen* 'gnaw at', *fen-fen* 'gnaw at on all sides'
Continuation	Nahuatl	*kweyooni* 'flashes once', *kwe'kweyooka* 'is flashing'
Smallness	Nez Percé	*q'eyex* 'club', *q'eyexq'eyex* 'small club'
Diminutiveness	Sahaptin	*pshwa'* 'rock', *pswa'pswa* 'pebble'
Past tense	Greek	*leipo* 'I leave', *léloipa* 'I have left'
Adjective marker	Nez Percé	*sik'em* 'horse', *sik'eemsik'em* 'mean'

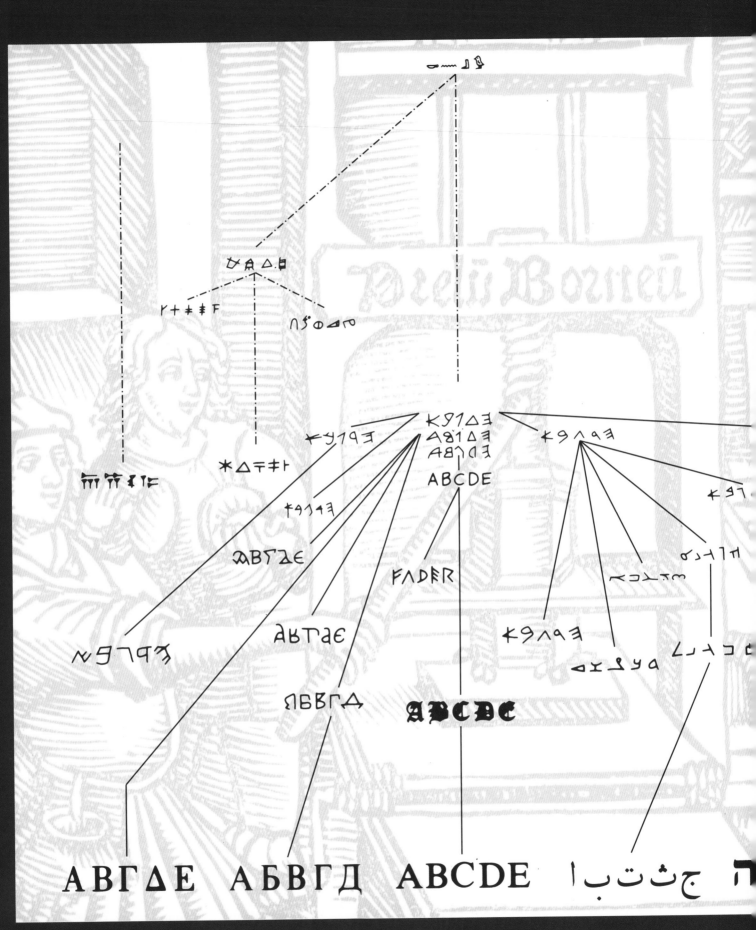

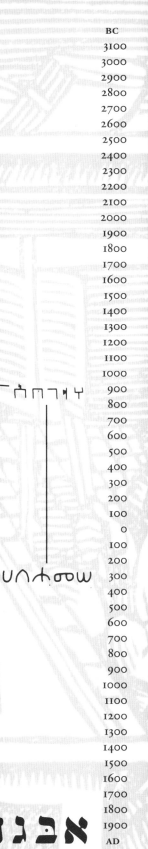

The medium of language: writing and reading

PART V

There is a curious ambiguity about the study of written language: certain aspects, such as the history of the alphabet, have been meticulously investigated by generations of scholars; others, such as the psychological processes underlying the tasks of reading, writing, and spelling, have attracted serious study only in the last decade or so. From a scientific viewpoint, we know far less about the written language than we do about the spoken, largely because of the 20th-century bias in linguistic studies towards the analysis of speech – a bias which is only nowadays beginning to be corrected. Part V therefore has to be shorter than Part IV – at least, for the present.

There are two underlying themes to this Part. First it is emphasized that writing and speech are different and equal manifestations of language. Writing should not be seen as merely 'transcribed speech', because its formal characteristics, and its strategies of production and comprehension, are quite unlike those encountered in speech. Secondly, the notion of 'written language' is shown to be extremely broad and multifaceted, subsuming any kind of visual realization of language (such as manuscript, typescript, and print).

We begin by examining the similarities and differences between written and spoken language.

A contrast is drawn between the study of the physical properties of the graphic medium (graphetics) and of the linguistic system which makes use of that medium (graphology). We explore the many facets of graphic expression, as found in handwriting, printing, and the electronic media. Several traditions of study are described, such as palaeography, epigraphy, and calligraphy. The writing systems of the world are introduced through a historical perspective: we look at the precursors of writing, and then at pictographic, ideographic, logographic, syllabic, and alphabetic systems. Separate accounts are given of several individual systems, from ancient hieroglyphic to modern shorthand.

The variety of writing systems, and the historical emergence of the alphabet, raises many theoretical questions – not least the question of how the process of reading and writing actually takes place in the brain. We review the main psychological models of reading that have been proposed, and look briefly at the more poorly researched fields of writing and spelling. Part V then concludes with a review of the issues involved in the many proposals for spelling reform.

A tiny sample of the world's alphabets over the centuries. The picture in the background dates from 1511 and shows the Flemish press of Jodocus Bardius ('Ascensius').

WRITING SUPREME

The history of language study illustrates widely divergent attitudes concerning the relationship between writing and speech. For several centuries, the written language held a preeminent place. It was the medium of literature, and, thus, a source of standards of linguistic excellence. It was felt to provide language with permanence and authority. The rules of grammar were, accordingly, illustrated exclusively from written texts.

The everyday spoken language, by contrast, was ignored or condemned as an object unworthy of study, demonstrating only lack of care and organization. It was said to have no rules, and speakers were left under no illusion that, in order to 'speak properly', it was necessary to follow the 'correct' norms, as laid down in the recognized grammar books and manuals of written style. Even pronunciation could be made to follow the standard written form, as in recommendations to 'say your *h's* and not to 'drop your *g's* (p. 32). The written language, in short, was the main plank on which the prescriptive tradition rested (§1).

SPEECH SUPREME

There was sporadic criticism of this viewpoint throughout the 19th century, but it was not until the present century that an alternative approach became widespread. This approach pointed out that speech is many thousands of years older than writing (§49); that it develops naturally in children (whereas writing has to be artificially taught); and that writing systems are derivative — mostly based on the sounds of speech. 'Writing is not language', insisted the American linguist, Leonard Bloomfield (1887–1949), 'but merely a way of recording language by means of visible marks.'

It was also argued that, as speech is the primary medium of communication among all peoples, it should therefore be the primary object of linguistic study. In the majority of the world's cultures, in fact, there would be no choice in the matter, as the languages have never been written down. Early linguistics and anthropology therefore stressed the urgency of providing techniques for the analysis of spoken language — especially in cases where the cultures were fast disappearing and languages were dying out. 'When we think of writing as more important than speech,' wrote Robert Hall (1911–) in a popular paperback, *Leave Your Language Alone* (1950), 'we are putting the cart before the horse in every respect.'

Because of this emphasis on the spoken language, it was now the turn of writing to fall into disrepute. Many linguists came to think of written language as a tool of secondary importance — an optional, special skill, used only for sophisticated purposes (as in scientific and literary expression) by a minority of communities. It was needed in order to have access to the early history of language (philology, §50), but this was felt to be a woefully inadequate substitute for the study of the 'real' thing, speech. Writing, seen as a mere 'reflection' of spoken language, thus came to be excluded from the primary subject matter of linguistic science. The pendulum swung to the opposite extreme in the new generation of grammars, many of which presented an account of speech alone.

COMPROMISE

It is understandable but regrettable that writing and speech should have been allowed to confront each other in this way. There is no sense in the view that one medium of communication is intrinsically 'better' than the other. Whatever their historical relationship, the fact remains that modern society makes available to its members two very different systems of communication, each of which has developed to fulfil a particular set of communicative needs, and now offers capabilities of expression denied to the other. Writing cannot substitute for speech, nor speech for writing, without serious disservice being done. The scientific study of speech in its own right is now a well-developed subject (Part IV). The analogous study of the written language is less advanced, but has just as promising a future.

The wheel turns full circle. Nowadays greetings cards are available that sing when you open them.

THE DIFFERENCES BETWEEN WRITING AND SPEECH

Writing and speech are now seen as alternative, 'equal' systems of linguistic expression, and research has begun to investigate the nature and extent of the differences between them. Most obviously, they contrast in physical form: speech uses 'phonic substance', typically in the form of air-pressure movements (§23); writing uses 'graphic substance', typically in the form of marks on a surface. But of far greater interest are the differences in structure and function that follow from this basic observation.

These differences are much greater than people usually think. The contrast is greatest when written texts are compared with informal conversation; but even in fairly formal and prepared speech settings, such as a teacher addressing a class, the structure of the language that is spoken bears very little similarity to that found in writing. It is something that is immediately apparent if a stretch of speech is tape recorded and transcribed. Even a fluent speaker produces utterances that do not read well when written down (p. 94).

The differences of structure and use between spoken and written language are inevitable, because they are the product of radically different kinds of communicative situation. Speech is time-bound, dynamic, transient – part of an interaction in which, typically, both participants are present, and the speaker has a specific addressee (or group of addressees) in mind. Writing is space-bound, static, permanent – the result of a situation in which, typically, the producer is distant from the recipient – and, often, may not even know who the recipient is (as with most literature). Writing can only occasionally be thought of as an 'interaction', in the same way as speech (exceptions include personal correspondence and, more important, the growing field of computer-based interaction, such as e-mail). It is therefore not surprising to find differences emerging very quickly when languages first come to be written down, as has been observed in such cases as Basque and Tok Pisin.

Points of contrast

• The permanence of writing allows repeated reading and close analysis. It promotes the development of careful organization and more compact, intricately structured expression. Units of discourse, such as sentences and paragraphs, are clearly identified through layout and punctuation. By contrast, the spontaneity and rapidity of speech minimizes the chance of complex preplanning, and promotes features that assist speakers to 'think standing up' – looser construction, repetition, rephrasing, filler phrases (such as *you know, you see*), and the use of intonation and pause to divide utterances into manageable chunks (p. 52, §29).

• The participants in written interaction cannot usually see each other, and they thus cannot rely on the context to help make clear what they mean, as they would when speaking. As a consequence, writing avoids words where the meaning relies on the situation (*deictic* expressions, such as *this one, over there*, p. 106). Writers also have to anticipate the effects of the time-lag between production and reception, and the problems posed by having their language read and interpreted by many recipients in a diversity of settings. In the absence of immediate feedback, available in most speech interaction, care needs to be taken to minimize the effects of vagueness and ambiguity.

• Written language displays several unique features, such as punctuation, capitalization, spatial organization, colour, and other graphic effects (§32). There is little in speech that corresponds, apart from the occasional prosodic feature (§29): for example, question marks may be expressed by rising intonation; exclamation marks or underlining may increase loudness; and parentheses may lower tempo, loudness, and pitch. But the majority of graphic features present a system of contrasts that has no spoken-language equivalent. As a result, there are many genres of written language whose structure cannot in any way be conveyed by reading aloud, such as timetables, graphs, and complex formulae.

• Grammatical and lexical differences are also important. Some constructions may be found only in writing, as in the case of the French simple past tense (the *passé simple*). Certain items of vocabulary are rarely or never spoken, such as many polysyllabic chemical terms, or the more arcane legal terms. Conversely, certain items of spoken vocabulary are not normally written, such as *whatchamacallit* (with no standard spelling), and certain slang or obscene expressions.

• Written language tends to be more formal than spoken language and is more likely to provide the standard that society values. It also has a special status, mainly deriving from its permanence. Written formulations, such as contracts, are usually required to make agreements legally binding (p. 390). Sacred writings are used as part of the identity and authority of a religious tradition (p. 388).

Mutual influence

Despite these differences, there are many respects in which the written language can influence the spoken. Soon after learning to read, children use the written medium as a means of extending their spoken vocabulary – as indeed do many adults. Some words may be known only in written form. Loan words may come into a language through the written medium. Sometimes the whole of a language may be known only from writing (as with Latin, or certain cases of foreign language learning, §62). And an old written language can be the source of a modern spoken one (as in Hebrew). Writing systems may derive from speech, in a historical sense, but in modern society the dependence is mutual.

NEWSPEAK

The written language is amusingly used to point up the idiosyncrasies of a speech style, in this 1963 *Guardian* editorial:

The BBC has introduced a. New method of disseminating the spoken word at any rate we think it is new because we don't. Remember hearing it until a week or two ago it consists of. Putting the fullstops in the middle of sentences instead of at the end as we were. Taught at school as a corollary to this new sentences are run on without a break readers will say we are in. No position to talk but this appears to be a deliberate policy on the part of the BBC whereas our. Misprints are accidental.

The practice seems to have started as a. Means of enlivening the reports of otherwise tedious football matches on a. Saturday afternoon now it has spread to the. News columns as it were and the effect is to make the subject matter. Confusing the interest of the listener is directed to the. Manner of delivery rather than the. Events recounted we tried to discover whether the ellipses or hiatuses followed a. Definite pattern or whether the breaks were made. Arbitrarily a pattern did emerge it seems that most of the breaks come after the. Definite or indefinite article or after a. Preposition sometimes they follow. Verbs but they always come when you. Least expect them and they constitute an outrage on what. We in the trade call the. Genius of the language.

PORTRAYING THE SOUND OF SPEECH

The differences between speech and writing are most clearly displayed when people attempt to portray the sound of the former using the graphic properties of the latter. The most complex and ingenious ways of doing this are to be found in written literature, where authors are continually battling to put sounds into words.

The graphic conventions authors use have received little study, especially from a cross-linguistic viewpoint. Different languages do not display the same range of written language conventions for the portrayal of speech. In English, for example, emphatic speech is not usually printed in a heavy typeface, but this is common in Chinese fiction. And the use of repeated letters (as in *ye-e-es*) can have a range of interpretations, such as emphasis and hesitation, in different languages. This can lead to ambiguity, especially when texts are translated. For example, a character in the English translation of Alexander Solzhenitsyn's *Cancer Ward* is recorded as saying 'No-o'. The use of this convention in the original Russian would convey an emphatic negative; but the English version is far more likely to signal a hesitant one. Italics, likewise, can be ambiguous, both within and between languages, being used variously as a marker of foreign words, technical terms, book titles, emphasis, and several other effects.

The way the written language conveys the effects of sound is now beginning to be studied more systematically. Some of the graphic effects in widespread use are illustrated below (after R. Chapman, 1984).

VERBAL DESCRIPTION

Probably the most common technique is to make use of descriptive words and phrases. Some authors take great pains to make their descriptions vivid, precise, and meaningful.

> ... a note of menace pierced through his voice.
> (James Joyce, *Dubliners*)

> 'Undoubtedly, undoubtedly,' broke in Mr Verloc in a deep deferential bass of an oratorical quality ...
> (Joseph Conrad, *The Secret Agent*)

> His voice lifted into the whine of virtuous recrimination.
> (William Golding, *Lord of the Flies*)

> 'But my darling,' he protested in the cajoling tone of one who implores a child to behave reasonably.
> (Aldous Huxley, *Point Counter Point*)

> ... a soft, greasy voice, made up of pretence, politeness and saliva.
> (Anthony Trollope, *Ralph the Heir*)

PUNCTUATION

The punctuation system can be altered or expanded, or certain features used with unexpected frequency.

> These two – they're twins, Sam 'n Eric. Which is Eric – ? You? No – you're Sam –
> (William Golding, *Lord of the Flies*)

> Tiens, Zazie ... regarde!! le Métro!!! (Here, Zazie ... look!! the Metro!!!)
> (Raymond Queneau, *Zazie dans le Métro*)

Sometimes the author may go so far as to explain:

> – Oh¡¡ (¡¡ c'est le point d'indignation) (Oh¡¡ (¡¡ is the indignation mark))
> (Raymond Queneau, *Le Chiendent*)

SPELLING

The spelling can be altered, to convey the impression of regional accent, personality, or other effects (p. 77).

> The family name depends wery much upon you, Samivel, and I hope you'll do wot's right by it.
> (Charles Dickens, *Pickwick Papers*)

> Aw knaow you. Youre the one that took away maw girl. Youre the one that set er agen me. Well, I'm gowin to ev er aht.
> (G. B. Shaw, *Major Barbara*)

> Oh, there you are steward. Ole man dlunk, bline dlunk. Purrimabed.
> (G. B. Shaw, *Major Barbara*)

> An' they're always speshully savidge when they haven't any tusks.
> (Richmal Crompton, *William the Bad*)

A Germanic pronunciation of French is portrayed in this extract:

> Eh! pien, si ces tames feulent fus dennit gombagnie, dit Nucingen, che fus laiserai sèle, gar chai drop manché. (= Eh! bien, ci ses dames veulent vous tenir compagnie ... je vous laisserai seul, car j'ai trop mangé. 'Well if these ladies want to keep you company, I will leave you alone, because I have eaten too much.')
> (Honoré de Balzac, *Splendeurs et misères des courtisanes*)

CAPITALIZATION

Varying the use of capital letters can convey loudness, special significance, and several other effects.

> 'At such times as when your sister is on the Ram-page, Pip,' Joe sank his voice to a whisper and glanced at the door, 'candour compels fur to admit that she is a Buster.'
> Joe pronounced this word, as if it began with at least twelve capital B's.
> (Charles Dickens, *Great Expectations*)

Extended capitalization usually expresses loudness.

> 'MISS JEMIMA!' exclaimed Miss Pinkerton, in the largest capitals.
> (William Makepeace Thackeray, *Vanity Fair*)

> Heedless of grammar, they all cried, 'THAT'S HIM!'
> (R. H. Barham, *The Jackdaw of Rheims*)

PORTRAYING THE SOUND OF SILENCE

Graphic devices are often used to express reactions when no words are spoken at all.

'We might go in your umbrella,' said Pooh.
'?'
'We might go in your umbrella,' said Pooh.
'? ?'
'We might go in your umbrella,' said Pooh.
'!!!!!!'
For suddenly Christopher Robin saw that they might.
(A. A. Milne, *Winnie the Pooh*)

These frames from Hergé's adventures of Tintin show the way comic strips use contrasting punctuation marks in isolation to identify dramatic action and character reaction.

TYPE SPACING AND SIZE

Variations in type size and spacing provide a wide range of possible effects (§32).

Alice couldn't see who was sitting beyond the Beetle, but a hoarse voice spoke next. 'Change engines –' it said, and there it choked and was obliged to leave off.

'It sounds like a horse,' Alice thought to herself. And an extremely small voice, close to her ear, said,

'You might make a joke on that – something about "horse" and "hoarse", you know.'
(Lewis Carroll, *Through the Looking Glass*)

Once on the bridge, every other feeling would have gone down before the necessity – then n e c e s s i t y – for making my way to your side and getting what you wanted.
(G. B. Shaw, *The Man of Destiny*)

LETTER REPETITION

The repetition of letters and hyphens generally shows extra spoken emphasis, but other effects are also sometimes conveyed by this technique.

And I've lost you, lost myself,
Lost all-l-l-l-   (Robert Browning, *Men and Women*)

What a beautiful, *byoo-ootiful* song that was you sang last night.   (William Makepeace Thackeray, *Vanity Fair*)

'Shhhhhhhhhhh! Shhhhhhhhhhhhhhh! 'they said.
(William Faulkner, *Dry September*)

Fuego ... fueeego! (Fire ... Fire!)
(V. B. Ibañez, *Sangre y arena*)

Tout à coup, très bas, mais la bouche grand ouverte, il psalmodie 'vaaaaaaache' et sa tête retombe.
(Suddenly, very quietly, but with his mouth wide open, he chants 'coooooooow' and his head falls back.)
(Raymond Queneau, *Le Chiendent*)

ITALICS

The use of italics is found in a variety of contexts, conveying loudness and other tones of special significance.

'Hel-*lo*!' said my aunt as I appeared.
(H. G. Wells, *Tono Bungay*)

'What *can* you mean by talking in this way to *me*?' thundered Heathcliffe with savage vehemence.
(Emily Brontë, *Wuthering Heights*)

Chicago will be ours! *Chicago will be ours!*
(Upton Sinclair, *The Jungle*)

'I'm desperately fond of Shirley.'
'*Desperately* fond – you small simpleton! You don't know what you say.'
'I *am desperately* fond of her: she is the light of my eyes.'
(Charlotte Brontë, *Shirley*)

SCIENCE FICTION

The genre of science fiction often experiments with the written language, in its attempts to characterize the communicative habits of future times and alien beings. In Alfred Bester's *The Demolished Man* (1953), a group of gifted telepathic people meet at a cocktail party, and all begin to communicate at once. The result is a pattern of interlinked thoughts, so complex that it evokes a comment from one of the participants. The comment itself illustrates two other graphic features, neither of which has a spoken language counterpart: the experimental use of a logogram in the proper name, and the use of an ironic question-mark.

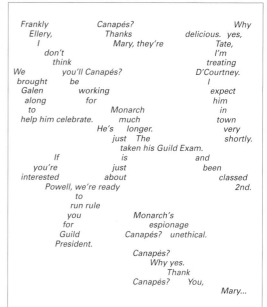

Frankly   Canapés?   Why
  Ellery,   Thanks   delicious. yes,
  I   Mary, they're   Tate,
    don't   I'm
      think   treating
We   you'll Canapés?   D'Courtney.
brought   be   I
  Galen   working   expect
    along   for   him
      to   Monarch   in
  help him celebrate.   much   town
                    He's   longer.   very
                      just The   shortly.
                        taken his Guild Exam.
      If   is   and
    you're   just   been
  interested   about   classed
    Powell, we're ready   2nd.
      to
      run rule
      you   Monarch's
      for   espionage
      Guild   Canapés? unethical.
      President.
                  Canapés?
                    Why yes.
                    Thank
                  Canapés? You,
                            Mary...

'@kins! Chervil! Tate! Have a heart! Will you people take a look at the pattern (?) we've been weaving...'

UGH! AARGH! HA HA!

Non-verbal vocalizations are among the most difficult of sounds to represent in written form. Even a 'straightforward' event, such as a laugh, can be shown in several ways. A selection from various authors brings to light:
Ha! ha! ha!
Ha, ha!
Ha, ha, ha!
Ha-ha-ha!
Ha-ha, ha-ha!
Ha ha!

He! he! he!
He, he!
He, hee, hee, hee!
Ho, ho, ho!
Haw-haw!
HA! HA! HA! HO! HO! HO!
The vowel variations indicate different types of laugh – normal (a), giggle (e), and hearty (o). They may also express different characters:
'Ho-ho-ho!' laughed dark Cat.
'Hee-hee-hee!' laughed the

tippling bride ...
'Heu-heu-heu!' laughed dark Cat's mother ...
(T. Hardy, *Tess of the D'Urbervilles*)
· In languages that lack initial aspiration, the convention may look quite different.
– Mi fate proprio ridere, scusate, ah, ah, ah. (You really make me laugh, excuse me, ha, ha, ha.)
(I. Silone, *Il seme sotto la neve*)

Sometimes an entire story can be told non-verbally.

32 · GRAPHIC EXPRESSION

It is traditional in language study to distinguish 'spoken' from 'written' language; but the latter term does not capture the range of expression that the visual medium makes available. 'Written' implies, first and foremost, 'handwritten' – but plainly there are many other ways of presenting written language, using such technologies as the printing press, the typewriter, and the video display unit. The term 'graphic' subsumes all these modes, and we shall therefore use it throughout this section, to emphasize the importance of adopting a broad framework for the study of the way language is visually presented. We shall not, however, use the phrase 'graphic language', as found in such fields as typography, because it applies to a much wider class of phenomena than that dealt with in this encyclopedia – including the use of pictures, graphs, musical notation, and so on.

The different varieties of graphic expression seem to have no parallel in spoken language. Speech belongs to individuals, and is not split between two people (apart from such special cases as foreign language interpreting). There is nothing in speech that corresponds to what happens when someone dictates a letter, and then allows a typist to present the message in graphic form. There are no spoken language equivalents to the specialist scribe, editor, draughtsman, cartographer, or graphic designer – though certain parallels can be found in the work of the barrister and actor.

The properties of graphic expression are not widely appreciated. A few graphic conventions are introduced in schools as prescriptions (such as how to lay out a letter, address an envelope, and set out a science experiment or a mathematics problem); but attention is not directed to the learning of general principles of visual language organization that would apply in different times, situations, and technologies. Most conventions are ignored, and as a result people have only fragmentary skills in producing and interpreting the range of forms which are available for linguistic expression – something they discover to their cost, when they are faced with such tasks as preparing posters or handouts for general use, and find that they are unable to convey the effect they require.

By contrast, there are several professions that have studied aspects of graphic expression in great detail. In particular, there has been minute analysis of the letters of the alphabet, and the thousands of forms these letters take (in the different styles of handwriting, typewriting, print, and electronic text). The specialists involved include typographers, type designers and manufacturers, historians of printing, historians of inscriptions (epigraphers) and handwriting (palaeographers, p. 189)), art historians, forensic scientists, and many others interested in both the aesthetic properties of graphic expression and its utilitarian functions (in publishing, advertising, cartography, etc.). However, these diverse approaches have not resulted in an agreed descriptive apparatus or terminology, and several important aspects of the subject continue to be neglected – not least, the analysis of the *effects* conveyed by graphic communication.

MODES OF GRAPHIC EXPRESSION

The several modes of graphic expression are identified in this diagram, in relation to the study of other kinds of human visual communication and to the linguists' use of the terms 'spoken' and 'written' language. The classification is based on an analysis by the British typographer, Michael Twyman (1934–), who subsumes all graphic effects under the heading of 'graphic language'.

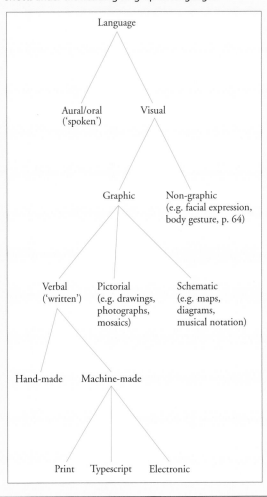

WRITING THE DATE

The graphic expression of dates is one of the conventions universally taught in schools. But it is difficult for schools to keep up with contemporary typographic practice, and to distinguish between the many social usages. These are some of the graphic conventions which have been used to express the date in English.

31 January 1996
31st January 1996
31st January, 1996
31st January. 1996
January 31 1996
January 31, 1996
January 31st 1996
January 31st, 1996
January 31st. 1996
31.1.96   1.31.96
31/1/96   1/31/96
31-1-96   1-31-96
31.i.96
31 Jan 1996
31 Jan 96
31 Jan. '96
1996-01-31
1996 January 31

The main distinction is whether the day precedes the month, as in British and Continental practice, or follows it, as in American practice. Thus, 6/7/41 would refer to 6 July in the former case, and to 7 June in the latter. The mixing of Arabic and Roman numerals is also a British convention.

The use of these conventions varies over time. The current fashion is not to use suffixes or punctuation (e.g. *31 January 1996*), although older styles are still often taught in school (e.g. *January 31st, 1996*). The styles also vary in terms of social situation. Abbreviations are more likely to be used in informal letters than in formal correspondence; and the use of the suffix commonly appears in literature for special occasions, such as wedding invitations. In works on astronomy or geophysics, the order year–month–day is usual (*1996 January 31*), and this is also the order recommended by the International Organization for Standardization when numbers only are used (1996-1-31).

TYPES OF GRAPHIC EXPRESSION

Verbal graphic expression is so enormously varied that it defies any simple system of classification. One approach, which analyses texts in terms of the reading strategies they imply, is presented below (after M. Twyman, 1982, which deals, in addition, with pictorial and schematic configurations of graphic communication).

PURE LINEAR

Nothing in graphic expression really corresponds to the uninterrupted linearity which is so typical of speech. Word spaces, line endings, and pages are normal graphic conventions, which it is usually impractical to disregard.

The spiral of characters on the two sides of the Phaistos disc illustrates a continuously linear form. This terracotta tablet, about 16 cm in diameter, was found in Crete in 1908. Several characters are recognizable (such as parts of the body, animals, and tools), and interpretations of some sequences have been proposed, but the disc as a whole has not been deciphered.

INTERRUPTED LINEAR

This is the normal convention used in continuous text. The spaces occur between linguistic units (words), and line breaks usually occur between words or syllables (using the hyphen).

The present page illustrates two line-break principles in operation. The larger size of text has a justified right-hand margin, with irregular spaces between words, and occasional hyphens at graphic syllable boundaries. The present paragraph has an unjustified ('ragged-edge') right-hand margin, with regular spaces between words, and many fewer word divisions. In both cases, line endings do not correspond to units of meaning. In contrast, the example to the right is taken from a series of books designed for slow readers, in which most of the line endings have been made to coincide with the boundary of a grammatical unit, such as a sentence, clause, or clause element (§16).
(From D. Crystal & J. Foster, 1983, p.7.)

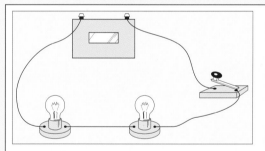

Electric circuits

The complete path along which an electric current flows, from its start to its finish, is called an *electric circuit*.
The diagram shows a simple electric circuit.
The electric current comes out of a battery,
goes through a switch and two light bulbs,
and then back to the battery again.
When the switch is on, the circuit is complete
and the light bulbs work.
When the switch is off, the circuit is said to be *broken*,
and the light bulbs do not work.

Different types of electric current

The current produced by a battery flows in the same direction all the time. Electricity that goes
only in one direction is known as *direct current*, or D.C.
The current made in power stations flows very rapidly in one direction round a circuit and then in the other direction. An electric current that changes direction in this way is known as an *alternating current*, or A.C.
An alternating current, passing through the filament of a light bulb, flows backwards and forwards
50 times a second.

LISTS

A list is an ordered series of lines, visually arranged one beneath the other, each acting as a semantic unit. They range from short sequences of single words (as in shopping lists) to lengthy arrays of technical description, as can be found in collectors' catalogues and restaurant menus.

LES PLATS DU SAVOY GRILL

... HORS D'ŒUVRE ...

Le Carpaccio de Boeuf aux Truffes £15.85
(Thinly sliced marinated beef with celery and truffle)

La Salade César £9.75
(Caesar Salad)

La Salade de Tomates et Mozzarella "Jacqueline" £9.50
(Roasted mozzarella and tomato salad with black olives, red pepper and pesto)

Le Saumon Fumé et Crabe Moscovite £15.25
(Smoked salmon parcel with potato salad and caviar)

Le Pâté de Foie de Canard £19.50
(Duck liver pâté with an orange scented brioche)

... LES POTAGES ...

Le Potage de Maïs et Moules £9.75
(Corn chowder, mussels and vegetables)

Le Potage de Panais et Pommes au Curry £8.50
(Cream of parsnip and apple soup, with curry spice)

... LES FARINEUX ...

Le Risotto de Crabe, Gratiné aux Artichauts £15.15
(Crab risotto, with artichoke and herb crust)

Les Tagliatelles à l'Aiglefin Fumé et Ail £15.75
(Fresh noodles with smoked haddock and garlic)

... LES POISSONS ...

Les Filets de Sole Pochés "Doria" £19.50
(Lightly poached fillets of sole with cucumber relish and cubed potatoes)

Le Rouget Sauté à la Purée de Fenouil et Poivrons Rouges £16.85
(Pan-fried red mullet with creamed fennel and red pepper sauce)

Le Mille-Feuille de Homard et Escargots de Bourgogne £23.00
(Lobster and Burgundy snails layered with seasonal vegetables)

Le Turbot Rôti à la Crème de Morilles £23.00
(Roast turbot with creamed morels and a celery and carrot frit)

MATRICES

A matrix is an arrangement of linguistic, numerical, or other information in rows and columns, designed to be scanned vertically and horizontally. Matrices are widely used in technical publications, but several everyday topics are also conventionally treated in matrix form, such as this football league table.

F.A. Carling Premiership

| | | <—HOME—> | | | | <—AWAY—> | | | | | |
	Plyd	W	D	L	For	Agt	W	D	L	For	Agt	GD	Pts
1) Newc. U.	7	4	0	0	9	1	2	0	1	5	2	+11	18
2) Man. U.	7	3	0	0	8	2	2	1	1	6	6	+6	16
3) L'pool	7	4	0	0	10	2	1	0	2	3	3	+8	15
4) Arsenal	7	2	2	0	7	4	2	1	0	3	0	+6	15
5) Aston Villa	7	3	1	0	7	4	2	1	1	2	3	+4	14
6) Leeds U.	7	2	0	1	4	3	2	1	1	8	6	+3	13
7) Midd'bro	7	2	1	0	4	1	1	2	1	3	3	+3	12
8) Notts F.	7	1	2	0	4	3	1	3	0	7	6	+2	11
9) Spurs	7	1	0	2	3	5	2	2	0	8	5	+1	11
10) Wimb'n	7	2	1	1	8	8	1	0	2	4	5	–1	10
11) Chelsea	7	1	2	0	5	2	1	1	2	3	5	+1	9
12) Sheff. W.	7	1	1	2	3	6	1	1	1	5	3	–1	8
13) Blackb'n R.	7	2	1	1	8	4	0	0	3	2	7	–1	7
14) Everton	7	1	0	2	4	5	1	1	2	5	5	–1	7
15) QPR	7	1	0	3	3	9	1	0	2	3	3	–6	6
16) Coventry	7	1	2	0	3	2	0	1	3	4	12	–7	6
17) West Ham	7	1	1	2	5	7	0	1	2	2	4	–4	5
18) S'hmpton	7	1	1	1	5	5	0	1	3	2	9	–7	5
19) Bolton W.	7	1	1	1	4	5	0	0	4	4	12	–9	4
20) Man. C.	7	0	1	3	1	5	0	0	3	2	6	–8	1

LINEAR BRANCHING

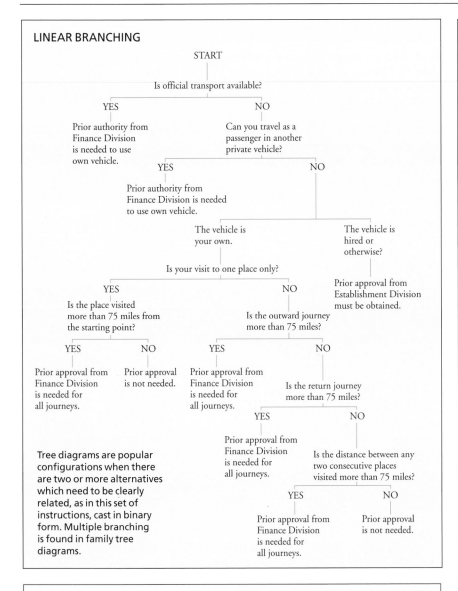

START

Is official transport available?

YES — Prior authority from Finance Division is needed to use own vehicle.

NO — Can you travel as a passenger in another private vehicle?

YES — Prior authority from Finance Division is needed to use own vehicle.

NO —

The vehicle is your own.

The vehicle is hired or otherwise?

Prior approval from Establishment Division must be obtained.

Is your visit to one place only?

YES — Is the place visited more than 75 miles from the starting point?

YES Prior approval from Finance Division is needed for all journeys.

NO Prior approval is not needed.

NO — Is the outward journey more than 75 miles?

YES Prior approval from Finance Division is needed for all journeys.

NO — Is the return journey more than 75 miles?

YES Prior approval from Finance Division is needed for all journeys.

NO — Is the distance between any two consecutive places visited more than 75 miles?

YES Prior approval from Finance Division is needed for all journeys.

NO Prior approval is not needed.

Tree diagrams are popular configurations when there are two or more alternatives which need to be clearly related, as in this set of instructions, cast in binary form. Multiple branching is found in family tree diagrams.

NON-LINEAR VIEWING

In this form of presentation, the lines are not read in sequence. The typography directs the reader's attention to different parts of the text, which may or may not be read in detail. Initial reading may proceed in any direction (even vertically upwards). These conventions are standard in advertising (p. 394), popular journalism (p. 392), and some forms of poetry (p. 75).

GRAPHIC SYMBOLISM

Like sound symbolism (§30), graphic properties can be used to represent the extralinguistic world in a direct manner. The illustrations show this principle at work in the worlds of business, education, and humour.

The distinctive typographic design used by the fashion firm Streets of London How are the effects to be interpreted? The account of the firm's policy, printed on the inside cover of one of their catalogues (from the mid-1980s), provides the clue.

Out on its own. A style all its own. *Streets* veers off the beaten track. Exploring new trends. Going beyond the norm. Bringing the remote within reach with a look of solitary refinement. Distant. Different. And desirable. Break away and break the monotony.

OF LONDON

Learning to read This is one of a series of animated letters devised to help teach sound–letter relationships to children (From L. Wendon, 1985, p. 28).

SAMMY SNAKE
This snake slithers and slides along making a soft hissing sound in words, like this 'sssss'.

Graphic humour Cartoonist Edward McLachlan has ingeniously exploited the graphic nature of these words.

GRAPHETICS AND GRAPHOLOGY

The writing system of a language can be studied from two points of view, which relate to each other in the same way that phonetics and phonology do for the study of speech (§§27–28). *Graphetics*, a term coined on analogy with *phonetics*, is the study of the physical properties of the symbols that constitute writing systems. *Graphology*, coined on analogy with *phonology*, is the study of the linguistic contrasts that writing systems convey. Very little research into these domains has been carried out within the field of linguistics (§65); in particular, the notion of graphetics is not widely employed. In such fields as typography, chirography (handwriting), and psychology, however, aspects of these topics have now received considerable study, especially in relation to the teaching of reading and writing, and the task of visual perception (§§34, 44).

GRAPHETIC ISSUES

A properly developed theory of graphetic science would deal with the range of implements and associated human skills required for the production and reception (reading) of linguistic marks on surfaces, screens, and other backgrounds, in any language. This would primarily involve the study of motor control and coordination of hands and eyes (cf. the use of the vocal organs for speech, §22), and of the psychological processes involved when these marks are perceived and remembered by the reader (cf. the field of speech reception, §25).

There is great scope for the development of graphetic studies, when we consider the range of variation in graphic practice displayed by modern languages, and throughout the history of writing. Most noticeably, languages vary in the direction in which they are written – left-to-right, right-to-left (e.g. Arabic), top-to-bottom (e.g. traditional Japanese), and the uncommon bottom-to-top (e.g. some forms of Ancient Greek). More than one direction may be involved, as in the *boustrophedon* method of writing lines in alternate directions, used in several early systems (see right). A language may use several different conventions simultaneously – such as the common use of vertical arrangement in neon signs and on book spines.

The nature of the writing implement and surface will have some influence on the kind of system that develops. The history of graphic expression shows a variety of implements, including the use of reeds, quills, brushes, steel points, fountain pens, pencils, ball-point pens, fibre-tipped pens, chalks, crayons, typewriters, laser printers, photocomposing systems, and word processors. The implements rely on a range of natural and synthetic products, from the early use of blood and plant juices to the modern range of coloured inks, photochemicals, lights, and electrical charges. Many surfaces have been involved, such as animal bone, rock, clay, wax, pottery, cloth, papyrus, parchment, paper, film, and electronic display screens. Often, techniques have to be devised for special functions, such as architectural drawing, record keeping, laundry marking, security coding, writing on glass, wood, or film, and writing that can be read electronically, as in department store check-outs and libraries.

The three main eras of graphic expression – handwriting, printing, and electronic – share many graphetic properties; but they have developed separate traditions and disciplines of study, and they will therefore be reviewed separately in the following pages. Graphology, in the linguistic sense, will be discussed separately in §33.

THREE KINDS OF OX-WRITING

There are several examples of *boustrophedon* in the history of writing. In particular, it was used in a transitional period of early Greek writing. The Greek name means 'ox-turning', referring to the way the ox would pull a plough, moving first in one direction, then the other.

In theory, there are three possible ways of writing boustrophedon. In (a), the lines reverse but the words do not. In (b), the words reverse as well as the lines. In (c) the letters reverse as well as words and lines.

(a) This is an illustration of writing of way possible one in a boustrophedon style. The but ⸢direction reverse lines the words do not.

(b) This is another illustration nl .gnitirw nodehportsuob fo this case, both the lines and .desrever era sdrow eht

(c) The third illustration shows wʰat happens when letters are reversed as well as words and lines.

This drawing of an early Greek treaty (6th–5th century BC) is of the third kind, as can be seen most clearly from the reversed *E*'s.

Boustrophedon writing has also been found in many other parts of the world. Several inscriptions have been found in the countries in and around the Mediterranean Sea – in Crete, Cyprus, Italy (both in Etruscan and in the Italic languages), Asia Minor (Hittite), and ancient South Arabia. But there are also inscriptions much further afield, in India, Central America, Easter Island, and northern Europe (in the early runic alphabet).

An unlikely – but effective – mode of graphic expression: smoke in air, lasting for only a matter of minutes.

HANDWRITING

The many forms and styles of handwriting (or *chirography*) have attracted a wide range of aesthetic, psychological, and scientific studies, each with its own aims and procedures. Moreover, each of the main families of writing systems (European, Semitic, East Asian) has its own complex history of handwriting styles. No universally agreed system of classification exists, and there is considerable controversy over approach and nomenclature. All that can be done in this section, therefore, is to present a few of the categories and descriptions that are widely recognized, using the European writing tradition as the domain of illustration. (For other traditions, see p. 190.)

Book hand   This is a professional form of writing, found in many different styles, used mainly for copying literature. It was formalized, clear, and regular, displaying little scribal idiosyncrasy.

Documentary hand   This form consists of a range of hands used by officials and private individuals as part of daily routine. It is generally found as a rapidly produced cursive, often very irregular and difficult to read.

Majuscule   Several forms of writing consist of letters broadly contained within a single pair of horizontal lines: they are usually referred to as *capital* letters. The Greek and Latin alphabets were originally written in this way. The chiselled inscriptions of ancient Greek served as the model of writing on papyrus rolls (which survive from around 300 BC). The Latin form used throughout the Roman Empire from the 1st century AD is known as *rustic* capitals (in contrast with the more formal square capitals chiselled on stone in Roman inscriptions).

Early Roman rustic capitals

Minuscule   Several forms of writing consist of letters whose parts extend above and below a pair of horizontal lines. They are usually known as *small* letters. Minuscule writing was a gradual development, in regular use for Greek by the 7th–8th century AD. The original form ('pure minuscule') was later modified, as uncials and other features (such as Greek accents) were added.

The Gospels of Stoudion – the earliest dated true minuscule (AD 835)

Uncial   This form of writing was especially used in Greek and Latin manuscripts from the 4th to the 8th century AD. It consists of large (the etymological meaning of the term is 'inch-high') rounded letters. A later development, *half uncial*, prepared the way for modern small letters.

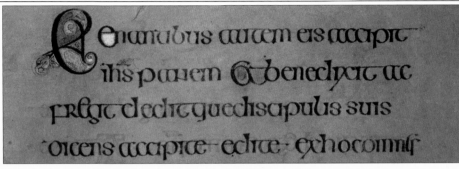

Insular half-uncial writing, as found in the Irish Book of Kells, c. AD 800

Cursive   In this form of writing, the characters are joined in a series of rounded, flowing strokes, which promotes ease and speed (etymologically, cursive = 'running'). It is found in general use from around the 4th century BC, and in time replaced uncial and half-uncial writing as a handwriting norm.

Insular   This form of writing was developed in Ireland from around the 5th century AD. It was brought to England by Irish monks, where it was used alongside uncial writing, which it ultimately supplanted.

Carolingian minuscule   This form of writing was named after Emperor Charlemagne (742–814), who promoted it throughout Europe. It was widely acclaimed for its clarity and attractiveness, and exercised great influence on subsequent handwriting styles. It is from this period that we find the development of the 'dual alphabet' – the combination of capital letters and small letters in a single system.

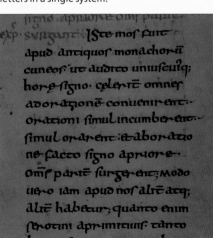

An example of late 8th-century Carolingian minuscule.

Black letter   This was a development of Carolingian minuscule, widely used in many variations between the 11th and 15th centuries. The rounded strokes became straighter, bolder, and more pointed. Often referred to as *Gothic* script, it became the earliest model for printer's type in Germany.

A Gothic book hand of the 14th century.

Humanistic (Roman)   This form of writing, also based on the Carolingian, was devised in Italy by Poggio (1380–1459) as an alternative to black-letter writing. it was originally known as Antiqua, reflecting the concern of the humanist movement of the period to return to ancient Latin sources. It subsequently became the basis for roman letters in printing.

The prototype roman script of Poggio.

Humanistic (cursive, or informal)   This form of sloped cursive lettering was developed by the Italian scribe Niccolò Niccoli (1364–1437). In due course, it led to the development of what are now called *italic* letters in printing.

The prototype italic script of Niccoli.

PALAEOGRAPHY

Palaeographers study ancient and medieval handwriting in order to establish the provenance, date, and correct form of a text. The subject principally involves the study of writing on papyrus, parchment (vellum), or paper, though it does not exclude other forms (such as graffiti). Most palaeographic research has been into manuscripts within the Greek/Latin tradition.

There are innumerable problems facing the palaeographer. In olden times, few books were dated, and title pages are a late medieval development. The absence of spaces between words in preclassical and classical texts can lead to ambiguity. Also, variant texts have to be brought together, to determine which is the original reading.

The problem of textual error is particularly serious. It is not surprising, given the 'routine' nature of the task, that copyists would introduce errors as they worked – errors which would be compounded as further copies of a manuscript were made. Indeed, in some cases, the scribes did not know the language or dialect of the manuscript they were copying. There are even cases on record of scribes copying right across a two-column text, producing a totally unintelligible version.

Another big problem arises out of the use of abbreviations, especially common in Roman times. Letters at the end of a word would be replaced by a point or other sign (*suspension*, e.g. *imp.* = *imperator* 'emperor'); and letters would be omitted within words (*contraction*, as in the shortened forms of Jewish or Christian holy names). Whole words were sometimes replaced by shorthand signs, e.g. Latin *et* = 7, *est* = ÷. By the end of the middle ages, over 13,000 abbreviations and signs were in use.

Palaeographic detective work is assisted by a detailed knowledge of the language, the historical events of the period, the contemporary use of writing materials, the mannerisms of the scribes, and especially the history of handwriting styles. In modern times, such techniques as the use of ultraviolet light (to bring out faded handwriting) have proved invaluable.

EPIGRAPHY

Epigraphy is the study of ancient inscriptions – texts that have been made on hard, durable material, such as stone, marble, metal, clay, pottery, wood, and wax, using such techniques as engraving, carving, embossing, and painting. Its aim is to ascertain the nature of the original records of ancient civilizations, thereby providing the primary data for historical and philological enquiry. In this process, it provides considerable insight into the early development of writing systems.

Several kinds of ancient inscriptions exist. Many are found on or within large monuments, such as the Egyptian pyramids, or the Persian rock carving at Bīsitūn (p. 303). Memorial inscriptions are also frequent on such objects as seals, rings, medals, and coins (the separate study of the latter being known as *numismatics*).

Large numbers of clay and papyrus inscriptions have survived throughout the Near East containing information about historical events and daily business activities. And there are thousands of inscriptions of a more classical nature, such as graffiti. Illustrations of ancient inscriptions are shown on pp. 307, 319, and 329.

DIPLOMATICS

Diplomatics, from the Greek *diploma* (folded), is the study of legal and administrative documents of all kinds. Most attention has been paid to the public documents of monarchs, emperors, and popes, which are usually classified separately from the many varieties of private document that exist.

One of the main aims of the subject is the identification of genuine documents as distinct from drafts, copies, or forgeries. Particular attention is paid to the materials and inks used, as well as to the handwriting style, the forms of seal or signature, and the linguistic features of the text (such as the choice of language, the way information is structured, and the kind of dating system employed).

ANGLO-SAXON ORIGINALS

In an early Anglo-Saxon technique, it was possible to make more than one 'equally original' version of a document. The text would be written out two or more times on a single sheet of parchment. The space between the texts would then be filled in by various words or symbols – often the word *chyrographum* ('handwriting') – and the sheet would be cut irregularly through this writing. To prove that the texts were genuine was then a simple matter: only the original texts would exactly match when reassembled.

MINIM CONFUSION

In some medieval styles of handwriting, several letters were formed by a series of joined vertical strokes ('minims'), without further distinction. Sequences of *m*, *n*, *v* (written as *u*) and *i* (which lacked a distinguishing dot) would thus appear identical. A six-stroke sequence could be interpreted as *ium*, *miu*, *iniu*, *niui*, and many other possibilities, giving rise to major problems of interpretation.

MAGNA CARTA

This important document was validated by a seal (below), not a signature. Seals have had the function of validation since Classical times. King John would have had to rely on them as a signal of identity for – like many medieval monarchs – he could not write.

CALLIGRAPHY

The art of penmanship, or handwriting at its most formal, is known today as *calligraphy*. It is a major art form in eastern Asia, China, Korea, Japan, and in Arabic-speaking countries. In Europe and America, it has been less widely practised, though there has been a strong revival of interest since the end of the 19th century, and especially in North America in the latter part of the 20th century. The artistic effect depends on a combination of factors – good-quality materials, the selection of an appropriate and effective writing instrument, the correct formation of the symbols according to an accepted style of writing, the placing of these symbols in an elegant sequence, and the harmonious layout of the text on the page. There have been several famous schools of calligraphy, and the subject has attracted a great deal of historical study in which specialists identify the different styles of writing and how they have evolved.

Right: A fine example of 18th-century calligraphy.

Above: A handwritten English alphabet (top: round hand) compared with Italic print (middle) and Roman print (bottom).

Right: An elegant Arabic script, taken from an illuminated manuscript of the Qur'an, made in 1789.

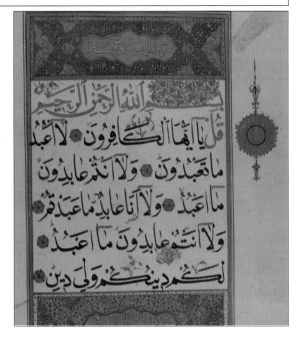

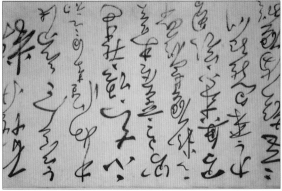

Above: Two examples of Chinese calligraphy, both ink on paper. The lower illustration is from Huai-su (born 725), a monk during the T'ang dynasty, who became noted for a rapid cursive style in which all the strokes are connected. The forms are often so simplified that they are capable of being read only by calligraphers. The primary interest lies in the way shapes and spaces can be created to produce a harmonious and meaningful whole. The upper illustration, of a very different cursive style, is from Mi Fu (1051–1107), who lived during the Sung dynasty, and who was a major influence on literary calligraphy.

GRAPHOLOGY (PSYCHOLOGICAL)

A person's handwritten mark or signature holds a special place in society. It is required for legal agreements, and it forgery can be illegal. Likewise, a person's general handwriting conveys identity: no two people's writing is the same in every respect (cf. voiceprints, §6).

It is a short step from here to the view that handwriting conveys information about a person's character and personality – the subject of *graphology*. Although speculation about this relationship has existed since Roman times, popular interest is quite recent, with the term itself being introduced towards the end of the 19th century by the French abbot, Jean Hippolyte Michon (1806–81). This sense of graphology, it should be emphasized, must be clearly distinguished from the linguistic use of the term found on p. 187.

Graphologists study handwriting variation using several parameters, notably:

Size   whether large or small, wide or broad, constant or varying, and including the relative size of individual letters or letter elements (e.g. the length of the cross stroke of a *t*).

Layout   the arrangement of writing on the page, including the size of margins and the distance between lines (narrow or wide, constant or varying).

Line direction   whether straight, sloping upwards or downwards, or curved.

Connection   whether a sequence of letters is joined or separate, and how the upstrokes and downstrokes interconnect (curved, angular, with various flourishes).

Temporal features   whether the speed of writing is rapid or slow – in rapid writing, for example, *t* cross strokes and *i* dots may be misplaced, and strokes may appear between adjacent words.

Regularity   whether the size, angle of writing, and distance between strokes is constant or varying, and whether there is an even or disjointed appearance to stretches of writing.

Letterforms   whether simplified or elaborated, involving different degrees of legibility.

Angle   whether letters are upright, or slanting to the right or left to different degrees, and whether this is constant or varying.

Shading   the thickness or thinness of different strokes.

Handwriting characteristics have been studied with reference to all kinds of normal and pathological psychological and physiological states. Most of the early publications dealt with the writing of monarchs, criminals, authors, politicians, and other professionals, but more recent works have examined the writing of the general population – sometimes, from quite specific points of view (such as to determine someone's suitability for employment).

Some examples of graphological interpretation are given below. The analyses sometimes convey an initial intuitive plausibility, but there are many individual differences, and there still need to be controlled empirical investigations into the personality generalizations that have been proposed. There are also many differences of opinion among practitioners about the analyses (such as whether meaning is best located within the different elements of a letter, or within the letters and words as wholes). At present, we lack the scientific evidence required to demonstrate the accuracy or reliability of graphological procedures and conclusions.

LETTER INTERPRETATIONS

Extracts from Eric Singer's *A Manual of Graphology* (1953), showing the kinds of relationship postulated between forms and personality traits. The drawings are by Gertrude Elias.

Different kinds of *t* cross

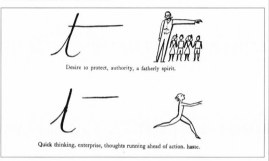

Desire to protect, authority, a fatherly spirit.

Quick thinking, enterprise, thoughts running ahead of action. haste.

Angles of writing

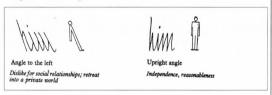

Angle to the left
Dislike for social relationships; retreat into a private world

Upright angle
Independence, reasonableness

The meanings of *D/d*

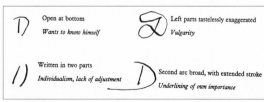

Open at bottom
Wants to know himself

Left parts tastelessly exaggerated
Vulgarity

Written in two parts
Individualism, lack of adjustment

Second arc broad, with extended stroke
Underlining of own importance

A quiz question

'There are two writings [below], the upper one by a gentleman, the lower one by a lady. If you were asked whether you think this couple would make a good match in marriage, what would you say?'

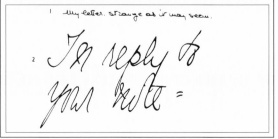

SIGNATURE INTERPRETATIONS

Rosa Baughan's *Character Indicated by Handwriting: a practical treatise in support of the assertion that the handwriting of a person is an infallible guide to his character* is one of many books on graphology that appeared at the end of the 19th century. It includes copies of many famous signatures, with personality interpretations.

Napoleon Bonaparte
'There is the dominant will in the strongly marked "t", and in the hard, thick line which terminates the flourish; his egotism and self-assertion are evidenced in this flourish, his originality in the peculiar form of the capital letter "B"; but ambition is here "still the lord of all".'

Alexander Pope
'An elegant signature, perfectly free from pretentiousness. The simple form of the two capital letters shows culture and refinement of a high order, and the liaison of the capital letter "A" to the name shows deductiveness and logical power, of which no poet ever had more.'

Mozart
'Sensuous tenderness in the sloping movement and the downstrokes of the letters ...'

(*Answer*: 'A marriage between these two people would be a failure from the start. They are too different. Look at size and spacing, at the angle of writing and at the form of connection. Their personal experiences of space, their social inclinations, their personal ways of adjustment to life and society are completely incompatible, and will never agree together.')

PRINT

The selection and organization of letterforms and other graphic features of documents is the concern of *typography*. Traditionally, the design of books was the main concern of typographers. The 19th-century information explosion meant that other printed documents (e.g. leaflets) vied for the reader's attention. Today, typography is concerned with the organization of documents of all kinds – including databases of information distributed electronically (p. 195). Typographers deal with all matters relating to the appearance and effectiveness of documents: the shapes and sizes of letters and other symbols; the spaces between letters, words, and lines; the length of lines and size of margins; the extent and location of illustrations; the use of colour; and all other matters of spatial organization, or 'configuration'. In addition, typographers need to be involved in such matters as the choice of paper and method of printing, aspects of software use in the preparation and delivery of documents, and the means of electronic distribution of non-printed texts. These issues must all be evaluated in their own right, as part of an overall judgement about the appropriateness of the design for its intended use.

The design of individual letters is traditionally the main concern of specialists called 'type designers'. Originally, in the western tradition, letterforms were devised to reflect the properties of the main 15th-century manuscript hands – the roman, cursive, and black-letter styles (p. 188). Since then, there has been a remarkable proliferation of styles, especially in recent years since the technology required to design type has been available on personal computers. It has been estimated that well over 30,000 typefaces have been designed since the invention of printing – a variety that has so far prevented the development of any system of classification.

ABCDEFGHIJKLMNOPQRSTUVWXYZ
abcdefghijklmnopqrstuvwxyz
0123456789 & @ £ $ % ( ) [ ] { }

Punctuation

. , ; : ' " ! ? / _ – — … " " ' ' « » ‹ › ¿ ¡ ·

Orthographic and phonetic variants

fi fl æ Æ œ Œ Á Â Å Ç È Ê Ë Í Î Ï å ç ø Ø ß ı ª º

Diacritical marks

` ´ ^ ¨ ` ^ ~ ˇ ˙ ˚ (xH)

Mathematical symbols

÷ ≠ ≈ < > ≤ ≥ ° √ ± ƒ ¡ ¬ ∫ ‰ / ∞ ∏ ∑ ∂

Greek letters   Other symbols

Δ Ω μ π   * † ‡ § ¶ • ® © ™ ¤ ¥ ¢ # ◊

Left: The set of characters in a typical typeface that can be accessed from the keyboard of a personal computer – usually around 180.

Below Left: In 1916, L. A. Legros & J. C. Grant (in their survey, *Typographical Printing-Surfaces*) suggested that 275 characters could form the basic set for printing in Latin-based languages. They showed many additional special characters, including these to aid the printing of scribal abbreviations.

SCRIBAL ABBREVIATIONS.

ã ā ꞇꞗ ƀ b̄ c̃ c̄ ꝯ ꝏ d̄ ꝺ ē ē ꝟ ꝭ ꝼ ꝼ g̃ g̃ ꞗ h̄
ī ij ꝁ t̄ ꞁ Ꞁ ꝳ ḿ m̄ ꝳ m̄ ñ ñ ꝴ õ ō
ꝑ ꝑ ꝑ ꝑ ꝑ ꝗ ꝗ ꝗꝑ ꝶ r̄ š š ꞇ t̄ ꞇ ꞇ
ū ū ū ṽ ꝟ ŵ x̄ x̄ ȳ ȳ z̄ ꝣ
& ℮ ꝴ ꝰ ſſ ꝫ ꝙ ꞎ ꝭ ℮⟩
Ā Ꝺ Ē Ī Ō Ṁ Ᵽ Ᵽ Ᵽ Ꞃ V̄

TYPOGRAPHIC MEASUREMENT

TYPOGRAPHIC MEASUREMENT

A wide range of typographic terminology has developed to handle the many kinds of typeface and setting, but this continues to be subject to professional scrutiny. It is argued that several terms and concepts originally devised for use with metal type are no longer clearly applicable in the context of digital typography (e.g. the *point* size of pieces of type, or the notion of *leading* – the spacing between lines of type).

Several proposals have been made for alternative systems of measurement based on the characteristics of the printed image (as produced by any method) rather than on the characteristics of the 'body size' of the traditional piece of type, but these have proved to be controversial. Draft proposals for an international standard were drawn up in the late 1970s, based on the height of capital letters, but no agreement proved possible.

A more recent approach argues that any new system should be based on the height of small letters, which predominate in most printed text. It proposes a four-level system, using the notions of 'x height' (the height of the small letter *x*), 'ascenders' (a part of a letter that extends above the height of the letter *x*, as in *h*) and 'descenders' (a part which extends below the *x*, as in *p*). The approach is in principle applicable to other (non-roman) writing systems. Greek and Cyrillic require no modification. The mean height of Arabic, Hebrew, and Indian scripts can be aligned with the roman *x* height. And Chinese, Korean, and other oriental scripts can be aligned with capital height. (From S. Ó Brógáin, 1983.)

Typography

A ▸
B ▸
C ▸
D ▸

Τυπογραφία
Greek

B ▸
C ▸

Τипография
Cyrillic (Russian)

B ▸
C ▸

לַדְּפִיסוּן
Hebrew

B ▸
C ▸

طباعة
Arabic

A ▸
C ▸

印刷
Chinese

B ▸
C ▸

उसकी पूजा
Devanāgarī (Hindi)

A Capital line	1 'Body' size
B Mean line	2 Ascender height
C Base line	3 *x* height
D Descender line	4 Ascender-descender height

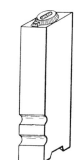

Metal type Traditionally the surface of the type would be inked and the ink transferred to paper by applied pressure.

Modern digital type has no 'body'. Letters are mathematically stored (as a series of outline co-ordinates and control points) as digital data. The letters are not seen until output by a device (e.g. a laser printer) capable of interpreting the digital data. A typical data format is PostScript (p. 195).

A selection of modern typefaces

FF Kosmik

abcdefghijklmnopqrstuvwxyz
ABCDEFGHIJKLMNOPQRSTUVWXYZ
1234567890 .,;:'"«»&!?

Pajamas

ABCDEFGHIJKLMN
OPQRSTUVWXYZ
1234567890 .,;"'?!?

The importance of typographic design

Lack of thought in this area can often lead to unsatisfactory results. The width of the table on this page of an early typing manual (A. E. Morton, *Modern Typewriting and Manual of Office Procedure*, 1929) has led to its being printed sideways ('landscape'). The result is that, when the book is held in the normal way, some of the headings appear upside down.

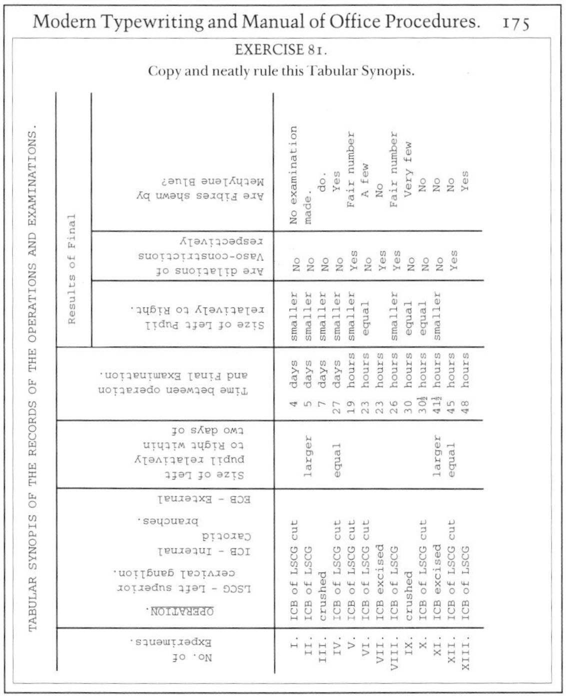

Modern Typewriting and Manual of Office Procedures.   175

EXERCISE 81.
Copy and neatly rule this Tabular Synopsis.

[table printed sideways]

Lack of thought can also lead to misleading results. Are the recipients of this form supposed to fill in their details by writing on the line above or below the prompts?

Please provide your contact details below:

First name   Family name

Company

Address

Post town   Postcode

COMPLEX EXPLANATIONS

It is not difficult to find attempts at written explanation that fail to communicate because of unnecessarily complex language (§63). An important application of typographic research involves presenting readers with alternative typographic versions of the same message, to see whether their performance is helped or hindered. Some versions, it seems, are much easier to read and understand.

However, there is no such thing as a 'best' way of displaying information typographically. The background and experience of the reader, as well as the subject matter and the circumstances of use, have also to be taken into account. This was shown by a study that looked at various ways of presenting the complex information that might be put out by a space-age travel agency (a). Someone who has to sort out this situation for the first time will find it helpful to have the information set out as a logical tree (b), because the format helps the reader to distinguish between relevant and irrelevant factors. On the other hand, an experienced person, familiar with the various alternatives, could find this format too unwieldy, and might prefer the more compact, tabular presentation (c). A further alternative is given (d). (After P. Wright, 1977.)

(a) When time is limited, travel by Rocket, unless cost is also limited, in which case go by Space Ship. When only cost is limited an Astrobus should be used for journeys of less than 10 orbs, and a Satellite for longer journeys. Cosmocars are recommended, when there are no constraints on time or cost, unless the distance to be travelled exceeds 10 orbs. For journeys longer than 10 orbs, when time and cost are not important, journeys should be made by Super Star.

(b)

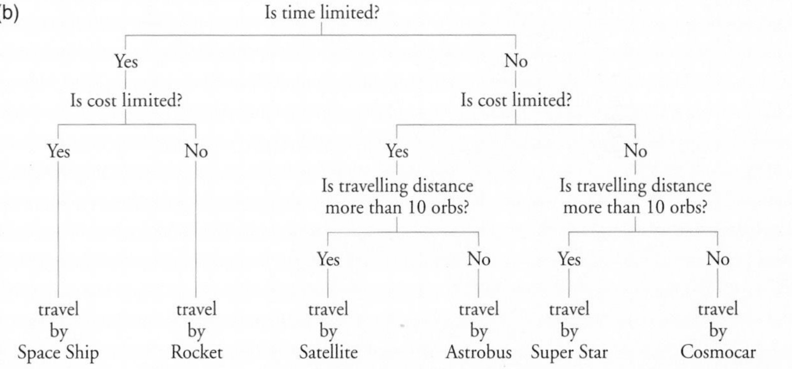

Is time limited?
— Yes — Is cost limited?
  — Yes → travel by Space Ship
  — No → travel by Rocket
— No — Is cost limited?
  — Yes — Is travelling distance more than 10 orbs?
    — Yes → travel by Satellite
    — No → travel by Astrobus
  — No — Is travelling distance more than 10 orbs?
    — Yes → travel by Super Star
    — No → travel by Cosmocar

(c)

	If journey less than 10 orbs	If journey more than 10 orbs
Where only time is limited	travel by Rocket	travel by Rocket
Where only cost is limited	travel by Astrobus	travel by Satellite
Where time and cost are not limited	travel by Cosmocar	travel by Super Star
Where both time and cost are limited	travel by Space Ship	travel by Space Ship

(d) *Where only time is limited*
     travel by rocket.

   Where only cost is limited
     travel by satellite if journey more than 10 orbs.
     travel by astrobus if journey less than 10 orbs.

   Where both time and cost are limited
     travel by space ship.

   Where time and cost are not limited
     travel by super star if journey more than 10 orbs.
     travel by cosmocar if journey less than 10 orbs.

Printing

There are two main dimensions to the invention of printing: the use of a relief surface to make copies of an image, and the development of movable type. The first of these is known to have been used in China from at least around the 7th century AD: the earliest known book, *The Diamond Sutra,* was printed using inked wooden blocks, in 868. The second dimension emerged during the 11th century, when movable blocks, carved with individual characters, came to be used. By the beginning of the 15th century, in Korea, the process had developed to the extent that printers were manufacturing bronze sets of type containing 100,000 pieces. But none of these discoveries became known in the West, and they had no influence on the subsequent history of printing.

In Europe, the main step forward came in the mid-15th century, with the invention in Germany of movable metal type in association with the hand-operated printing press – developments that are generally credited to Johannes Gutenberg (1390s–1468). Metal type was set by hand until the introduction of various systems of mechanized typesetting in the 19th century. The Linotype machine was introduced towards the end of the century, and became standard in newspaper offices. Techniques of photocomposition became a commercial reality in the 1950s. The latest development, computerized digital typesetting, has been in use since the late 1960s.

William Caxton (c. 1422–1491) An engraving of William Caxton demonstrating the working of his press, on the occasion of a royal visit.

Gutenberg's printing press In fact, we do not know what Gutenberg's original printing press looked like. This imaginative reconstruction is on display in the Gutenberg Museum, Mainz.

Gutenberg's 42-line Bible, set in Gothic type, was completed in 1456. The text is St Jerome's Latin version. Its design is as close as possible to the style of manuscript books, and in some copies illuminations were added by hand. There are no page numbers, title page, or other identifying marks of its printing provenance. Title pages were not common until the end of the 15th century.

TYPING

The idea for a typewriter had been considered in the 18th century, but the prototype of modern machines was not constructed until 1867 (by the American inventor, Christopher Latham Sholes (1819–90)).

Typewriters have the advantage over everyday handwriting, in terms of clarity and speed, but they lack the range of typographic variants available in printing (e.g. differences in type size and shape, justified setting (p. 185), or the provision of many special symbols). However, modern word processors, electronic typewriters, and personal computers have overcome some of these disadvantages, offering a range of typographical options.

The standard QWERTYUIOP keyboard arrangement dates from the first machines. Its design has attracted generations of criticism, on ergonomic grounds. Although most typists are right-handed, this keyboard makes the left hand do 56% of the work. Of all movements for successive letters, 48% use only one hand instead of two – most noticeable when typing such words as *addressed*. Finger dexterity is not linked to letter frequency – for example, the two strongest fingers of the right hand are used for two of the least frequent letters, *j* and *k*.

Why this arrangement was chosen is not clear. Some letter separations are motivated by the need to avoid key jamming (e.g. *q* and *u*). But there is no simple principle. The second line has a largely alphabetical arrangement. The top line, according to one story, contains the letters of the word *typewriter*, so that sales staff could find them easily when demonstrating early machines!

As a result, many alternative keyboards have been designed, to try to improve speed and efficiency. Most are based on statistical counts of letter frequency. But all attempts to reform the keyboard have failed because of the vast cost of machine replacement and typist retraining. The old layout is now standard in computer and word processor keyboards, and seems likely to remain so.

ELECTRONIC MEDIA

The development of computing and communications technology in the 1970s made it possible to transmit graphic data from a central source to remote televisions, using a system known as *teletext*. This system became a mainline source of news, weather, and other up-to-date information for consumers with teletext-equipped television receivers. More advanced services, known as *viewdata*, were then developed – *Prestel* being the tradename of the service started by British Telecom in 1979 – which allowed consumers to 'talk back' using the telephone network. This meant that certain shopping and booking transactions could be carried out from home. However, the systems were slow, and take-up was poor.

Attention shifted to the capabilities of personal computers (PCs). The 1980s experienced a revolution in computer technology which continues to have far-reaching consequences for the preparation and delivery of information. The Macintosh computer, launched by Apple Computer Inc in 1985, allowed users to carry out operations by moving a connected 'mouse' across the desk (whose movements were mirrored by a pointer on the computer screen), and by clicking a button on the mouse to indicate requests or responses. Options available to users were listed in menus which 'dropped down' as the user clicked; items available to users were represented on screen by icons; and opened documents were represented in on-screen 'windows'. This so-called *graphical user interface* (GUI), brought computer access to people who were previously uninterested in learning obscure computer programming languages.

DESKTOP PUBLISHING

Third party software allowed users to create documents, integrating pictures and text, using a wide range of typefaces, with large character sets, in many sizes. *PageMaker*, developed by Aldus Corporation, was the first widely available software of this kind. As documents were created on-screen, the system recorded the user's requirements as *PostScript* descriptions of finished pages. (PostScript is a page-description language developed by Adobe Systems – capable of recording whole pages of text and images of all kinds – and it soon became a standard means of page description.) Apple also manufactured a laser printer which efficiently output pages on receiving PostScript instructions from the computer. Aldus Corporation's Paul Brainerd thus coined the term 'desktop publishing'.

The combination of PC, system software, page-description language, and laser printer revolutionized the publishing industries: professional publishers started using these systems because they gave individuals more control over the appearance of documents, and over the supply of complete documents to their printers and manufacturers; and non-professionals started to produce complex documents themselves now that high-quality publishing tools were affordable and accessible. (However, those without typographic expertise did not necessarily obtain high-quality results!) GUI operation was quickly made available on other PCs, the most widely-used software of this kind being Microsoft Corporation's *Windows*.

NEW MEDIA

Also at this time, the presentation, storage, and manipulation of images, moving images, and sound on PCs was significantly improved; and the technology of storing digital data on compact discs (CDs) allowed large amounts of data to be distributed. New publishing media have evolved from a combination of these developments: huge databases of information can be published on CD with powerful access software; and so-called *multimedia* publications on CD integrate text, still and moving images, and sound into products with which consumers can interact on their PC. This has led to a significant increase in the use of PCs at home, since many multimedia titles are valuable educational tools.

Throughout the 1970s, computers at important US (and later international) research centres were connected to form a network to speed up communication. In the 1980s commercial services started to allow access to this network, now widely known as the *Internet*, by any computer users with a modem to interface between their computer, the telephone network, and the service-provider's computer. In the 1990s complex documents, integrating text and images, were made available to any computer user with access to the Internet. The system is fully interactive because it depends on the telecommunications network, which has been significantly improved since the early Prestel offerings. And, since film and music can now be delivered 'on-demand' across telecommunications networks, the technologies of computer and television are rapidly converging. New battle-lines are also being drawn, as businesses in the electronics industry compete over the best means of delivering interactive facilities to rapidly increasing numbers of enthusiastic consumers.

GRAPHIC TRANSLATABILITY

The typographic implications of electronic media technologies are far reaching. Computer and television screens are still not capable of the flexibility of presentation of traditional printing systems. The problem has been identified as one of 'graphic translatability' – the conversion of graphic expression from a medium with one range of resources into another in which the range is different.

This printed reference makes use of subtle typeface contrast and spatial variation to identify the levels and kinds of information. Also, the design software can automatically make suitable word-breaks at line endings.

1749

McGee, C. E.
'SHAKESPEARE IN CANADA: THE STRATFORD SEASON. 1989'
Shakespeare Quarterly 41 (1990): 114-20. 1990
Review-article on the Stratford (Ontario) Festival's 1989 productions: Richard Monette's *Comedy of Errors*, Jeannette Lambermont's *Titus Andronicus*, Michael Langham and Brian Bedford's *Merchant of Venice*, John Wood's *Henry V*, Richard Ouzounian's *Midsummer Night's Dream*, and Bernard Hopkins's *Love's Labor's Lost (World Shakespeare Bibliography* for 1989, Items 2138, 4233, 3217, 2636, 3433, and 2919).

This electronic (CD-based) version of the same reference has had to use much larger type because of the physical constraints of the computer screen on which the text will be displayed and read. Only one size of type is used in order to reduce the time taken to generate the image on screen. Spatial variation is cruder, and the typography makes use of colour in place of subtle typographic distinction.

World Shakespeare Bibl., 4 - xref

1749. McGee, C. E.
'Shakespeare in Canada: The Stratford Season. 1989.'
Shakespeare Quarterly
41 (1990): 114-20. 1990
[Review-article on the Stratford (Ontario) Festival's 1989 productions: Richard Monette's *Comedy of Errors*, Jeannette Lambermont's *Titus Andronicus*, Michael Langham and Brian Bedford's *Merchant of Venice*, John Wood's *Henry V*, Richard Ouzounian's *Midsummer Night's Dream*, and Bernard Hopkins's *Love's Labor's Lost (World Shakespeare Bibliography* for 1989, Items 2138, 4233, 3217, 2636, 3433, and 2912.]

33 · GRAPHOLOGY

Graphology, in its linguistic sense, is the study of the systems of symbols that have been devised to communicate language in written form. It must be clearly distinguished from the psychological sense of the term, which refers to the study of handwriting as a guide to character and personality (p. 191). It also needs to be seen in contrast with *graphetics*, the study of the physical properties of manuscript, print, and other forms of graphic expression (§32). Linguistic graphology is an abstract study (as is its counterpart in the study of speech, *phonology*, §28), dealing with the kind of elements used in a language's writing system, the number of elements there are and how they interrelate, and the rules governing the way these elements combine in written texts.

GRAPHEMES
The term *graphology* was coined on analogy with *phonology*, and several of the phonological notions used in the study of speech have also been applied to the study of written language. In particular, the idea of a *grapheme* has been developed, analogous to *phoneme* (p. 162). Graphemes are the smallest units in a writing system capable of causing a contrast in meaning. In the English alphabet, the switch from *cat* to *bat* introduces a meaning change; therefore, *c* and *b* represent different graphemes. It is usual to transcribe graphemes within angle brackets, to show their special status: <c>, <b>. The main graphemes of English are the 26 units that make up the alphabet. Other graphemes include the various marks of punctuation: <.>, <;>, etc., and such special symbols as <@>, <&>, and <£>.

Graphemes are abstract units, which may adopt a variety of forms. The grapheme <a>, for example, may appear as *A, a, a*, or in other forms, depending on the handwriting style or typeface chosen. Each of these possible forms is known as a *graph* (cf. *phone* in speech). There is a vast amount of physical variation in the shapes of graphs that does not affect the underlying identity of the grapheme. Whether a word is printed *cat, CAT, cat*, or even *caT* or *cAt*, we still recognize it as a sequence of three graphemes <c>, <a>, <t>.

Variants and features
When graphs are analysed as variants of a grapheme, they are known as *allographs* (analogous to *allophones*, p. 162). It is sometimes possible to work out the rules governing the use of particular allographs: in English, for example, we find 'capital letters' (*upper case*) at the beginning of a sentence or proper name and in a few other contexts; otherwise, 'small letters' (*lower case*) are

used. However, the choice of most allographs seems to be dictated by factors that are little understood, such as fashion, prominence, elegance, or personality (§32).

Graphology also makes use of the notion of *distinctive features* (p. 164). A grapheme is perceived as a single configuration, or *gestalt*, and not as a set of lines and dots; but it is nonetheless possible to analyse the shapes into their components, to determine what the salient parameters of contrast are – curve vs straight line, presence vs absence of dot, left-facing vs right-facing curve, and so on. In French, accents are contrastive (as in <é>, <ê>, and <è>). In Chinese and Japanese, the contrasts are carried by the strokes that constitute the characters. However, no general typology of distinctive graphological features has yet been established.

Functional differences
The analogy between graphology and phonology is important, but there is no identity of function (§31). Graphemes may signal phonemes, but they may also signal words or word parts (as with the numerals, where each grapheme <1>, <2>, etc. is spoken as a word that varies from language to language). Graphemes of punctuation show links and boundaries between units of grammar that may have nothing to do with the sound of speech (notably, the use of the hyphen (p. 207)). And several of the morphological relationships between words (p. 90) are conveyed by graphology more clearly than phonology: for example, the link between *sign* and *signature* is closer in writing than in speech (where the *g* is pronounced in the second word, but not in the first), and the same applies to such sets as *telegraph / telegraphy / telegraphic*, where there are several stress and vowel changes in speech, but none in writing.

LANGUAGE DIFFERENCES

Languages sometimes differ in their choice of allographs to mark linguistic units.

Word classes
There are several differences between the personal pronouns:
English *I, you.*
German *ich* (I), *Sie* (you).
French *je* (I), *vous* (you).
Spanish *yo* (I), *Vd.* (= usted), *Vds.* (= ustedes) (singular and plural forms of 'you').

Nouns in German all begin with a capital letter:
English *the lamp, a hammer*
German *die Lampe, ein Hammer*

Days and months
English *Monday, Tuesday…*
French *lundi, mardi…*
Spanish *lunes, martes…*
English *January, February…*
German *Januar, Februar…*
Spanish *enero, febrero…*
French *janvier, février…*

Language names
English *I speak Portuguese.*
Portuguese *Falo português.*

Questions and exclamations
In Spanish, question marks and exclamation marks are used both at the beginning and at the end of a sentence, the first one being inverted:
¿Como se llama este pueblo?
'What is this village called?'
¡Qué día! 'What a day!'

SPECIAL WRITING SYSTEMS

Graphological studies have a functional as well as a formal dimension. Within a language, several kinds of system may be invented in order to perform a specialized set of functions. One classification recognizes five types, differentiated according to the purpose for which they were devised (after J. Mountford, 1973):

Orthography The writing system in standard everyday use, which consequently attracts most study.

Stenography A system that enables writing to take place at speed, as in the many systems of shorthand (p. 208).

Cryptography A system devised to keep a written message secret (p. 58).

Paedography A system devised to help children to read, as in such alphabets as i.t.a. (p. 219).

Technography A system that enables a specialized field to perform its function, such as phonetic transcription (p. 160), chemical notation, cartography, or computer coding.

GRAPHOLOGY AT BREAKFAST

A comparative study of writing systems usually deals with different languages; but it is important to remember that different systems may coexist within a single language. Runic and Latin alphabets are both found in Old English. In Chinese, there is now the use of the romanized alphabet *pin-yin* alongside the use of characters (p. 314). In Japan, however, four writing systems are in regular daily use (five, if arabic numbers are counted as a separate system), as can be seen from the back of this 1995 cornflakes packet:

• The English alphabet is noticeable in the brand names and international product design, including (on the side of the packet) the slogan 'Best to you every morning' (advertising is a variety in which English script and loan words are very common, p. 394).

• The more complex-looking characters are *kanji* logograms (p. 202), derived from Chinese. For example, the statement mid-right contains the characters for 'nature' (*shizen*) and 'mercy' (*megumi*).

• Several graphemes from the rounded *hiragana* syllabic script can be seen on the page. They are used for various particles that express grammatical distinctions. The translation of *Kellogg's* is itself interesting: [top right] the English word is retained, but the 's

particle is reinforced by the hiragana symbol の *no*, expressing possession; [mid right] *Kellogg* is a loan word in Japanese, so it is in katakana (*ke-ro-g-gu*); a *no* particle might have been used here, but in this instance is not.

• Loan words (from languages other than Chinese) are expressed in the angular *katakana* syllabic script (p. 203). For example *cornflake* emerges [mid right] as *ko·n·fu·re·ku* (with two uses of ‾ showing long vowels). The final word in the sentence [mid right], *tappuri*, is an unusual use of katakana to emphasize a native Japanese word.

no (possessive)
= 'Kellogg's Quality Guarantee'

arabic numerals

ke·ro·g·gu
= kellogg

ケロッグ keroggu ('Kellogg') *katakana*

コーンフレーク kōnfurēku ('Cornflake') *katakana*

には ni wa (particles) *hiragana*

自然 shizen ('nature') *kanji*

の no (particle) *hiragana*

恵み megumi ('Mercy') *kanji*

タップリ tappuri ('full of') *katakana*

= 'Kellogg's Cornflakes are full of nature's mercy' (i.e. 'nourishment')

Punctuation marks

THE SOMALI PROBLEM

One of the stated aims of the 1969 revolution in Somalia was to solve the problem of which writing system to use for the country's main language, Somali.

For several years, the question had been highly controversial, with the merits of Latin, Arabic, and Osmanian scripts all being advocated. The last of these was named after its early 20th-century inventor, Osman Yusuf, and shows an interesting mixture of Arabic, Italian, and Ethiopic elements. It is drawn (right)

with accompanying Latin equivalents (from D. Diringer, 1968).

The role of Latin script, mainly deriving from Italian influence in the area, is evident in the way vowels as well as consonants are symbolized (unlike in Arabic), and also in the left-to-right direction of the writing. Some letter shapes are taken over from the Latin alphabet, though they are not given the same phonetic values; others are arbitrary inventions, displaying the general influence of

Ethiopic scripts. Arabic influence is found in the order of the letters, and in the ways of representing long vowels (not shown here).

The Osmanian alphabet was not successful. In January 1973 a Latin script was

finally adopted, and given official status.

’ b t g̣ ḥ ḥ d r s ṣ d g̣ f
q k l m n w h i u o a e

THE HISTORY OF WRITING

Myths and legends of the supernatural shroud the early history of writing, as they do of speech (§§3, 49). Archaeological discoveries provide enthralling pinholes of illumination along with frustrating problems of interpretation. An account of the early history of writing has gradually emerged, but it contains many gaps and ambiguities.

The matter is complicated by the fact that, in this early period, it is by no means easy to decide whether a piece of graphic expression should be counted as an artistic image or as a symbol of primitive writing. In principle, the difference is clear: the former convey personal and subjective meanings, and do not combine into a system of recurring symbols with accepted values; by contrast, the latter is conventional and institutionalized, capable of being understood in the same way by all who are using the system. When the product is a rock carving or painting of an animal, there is little doubt that its purpose is non-linguistic (though whether it has an aesthetic, religious, or other function is debatable). However, when the product is a series of apparent geometrical shapes or tiny characters, the distinction between art and writing becomes less obvious. The languages may even reflect the problem: in early Greek, and in Egyptian, the same word was used for both 'write' and 'draw'.

One point, at least, is fairly clear. It now seems most likely that writing systems evolved independently of each other at different times in several parts of the world – in Mesopotamia, China, Meso-America, and elsewhere. There is nothing to support a theory of common origin. There are of course similarities between these systems, but these are not altogether surprising, given the limited ways of devising a system of written communication.

Precursors

The earliest examples of a conventional use of written symbols are on clay tablets discovered in various parts of the Middle East and south-east Europe from around 3500 BC. Large numbers of tablets made by the Sumerians have been found in sites around the Rivers Tigris and Euphrates in present day Iraq and Iran. For example, on tablets from the city-state of Uruk, about 1,500 symbols have been listed, most of them abstract in character. They seem to have recorded such matters as land sales, business transactions, and tax accounts.

Several correspondences have been noted between the symbols used on these tablets and the clay tokens that were used throughout the area for several thousand years before the advent of writing. These tokens, of several distinctive shapes, seem to have been used as a system of accounting from at least the 9th millennium BC. A selection of tokens from Susa, dating from the end of the 4th millennium BC, is shown right. The adjacent diagram shows the relationship between some of the tokens and the incised characters that appear in the earliest Sumerian tablet inscriptions (not all of which can be interpreted). The similarity between the three-dimensional tokens and the two-dimensional inscriptions is striking. (After D. Schmandt-Besserat, 1978.)

PRIMITIVE PICTURE-WRITING

Exploration has revealed many primitive pictures and signs that resemble writing, but that lack the systematization we expect of a writing system. Human figures, geometric signs, and other shapes have been found carved or painted above and below ground on rocks ('petroglyphs'), buildings, tombs, pottery, and other objects in many parts of the world. Their significance is generally unknown. (From D. Diringer, 1968.)

(i) Coloured river pebbles from the Azilian culture of southern France

(ii)   Geometric signs on stones found in Spain

(iii)   Various patterns found in California

CLAY TOKENS

These tokens from Susa, dating from around 3000 BC, appear in many different shapes. Some of the commonest shapes are here compared with the incised characters in the earliest Sumerian inscriptions (only some of which have been interpreted.)

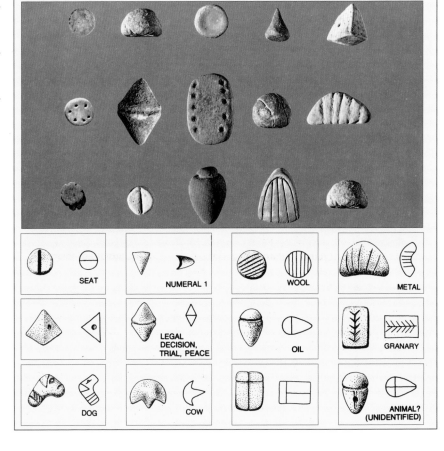

SEAT

NUMERAL 1

WOOL

METAL

LEGAL DECISION, TRIAL, PEACE

OIL

GRANARY

DOG

COW

ANIMAL? (UNIDENTIFIED)

TYPES OF WRITING SYSTEM

It is possible to talk about writing systems on the basis of such graphetic factors (§32) as the size, style, and configuration of the symbols, or the direction in which they are written; but this does not help us to understand what the graphemes are and how they are used. In principle, any of the systems to be described below could be written in almost any set of graphetic conventions. Sometimes, for example, several directions are used during the history of a language, as in early Greek, which at different periods was written right-to-left, left-to-right, and even using alternate directions (in *boustrophedon* writing, p. 187).

A more useful approach to writing systems is to classify them into cases that show a clear relationship between the symbols and sounds of the language (*phonological* systems) and those that do not (*non-phonological* systems). The vast majority of present-day systems are phonological; the non-phonological systems are mainly found in the early history of writing, which is where we begin.

NON-PHONOLOGICAL SYSTEMS
PICTOGRAPHIC

In this system, the graphemes (often referred to as *pictographs* or *pictograms*) provide a recognizable picture of entities as they exist in the world. For example, a set of wavy lines might represent the sea or a river, and outlines of people and animals represent their living counterparts. There is no intention to draw the reality artistically or exactly, but the symbols must be sufficiently clear and simple to enable them to be immediately recognized and reproduced, as occasion demands, as part of a narrative.

To 'read' such a script, it is enough only to recognize the symbols, and the sequence may then be verbally described in a variety of ways, in whatever language one happens to speak. There is thus a great deal of possible ambiguity when it comes to reading sequences of pictograms, and many of these scripts have proved difficult or impossible to decipher. The problem can be illustrated with a modern pictogram, such as the road sign (right). Without knowing the context, the sign could be 'read' in all kinds of ways – someone has been/will be/is digging/clearing/stopping a landslide – or even (as was discovered in a competition to find the most absurd road-sign interpretation) struggling to put up an umbrella on a windy day! Modern drivers know the likely context, so ambiguity is uncommon. When we are studying 5,000-year-old pictograms, the likely context may not be known. The many undeciphered or partly-deciphered pictographic scripts of ancient Crete illustrate the size of the problem (cf. the Phaistos disc, p. 185).

Pictograms constitute the earliest system of writing and are found in many parts of the world where the remains of early people have been discovered. They have been discovered in Egypt and Mesopotamia from around 3000 BC, and in China from around 1500 BC.

PICTOGRAPHIC SYMBOLS

Below: Some of the pictographic symbols used on seals and tablets in the early Minoan period in Crete (from D. Diringer, 1968). Over 100 symbols represent human figures, body parts, animals, and other everyday objects. Not everything is immediately recognizable, showing that there has been some development towards an ideographic system.

Below: A drawing of one of the wooden tablets carved with symbols, found on Easter Island (from D. Diringer, 1968). The direction of writing alternates (boustrophedon, p. 187), with the alternate rows inverted: the reader has to turn the tablet upside down at the end of each line. The pictographic character of many symbols is clear (e.g. birds, fish), but others cannot be interpreted. The script as a whole has not been deciphered.

Below: Drawing of a Zapotec inscription from the old city of Monte Albán in south-western Mexico (from J. Marcus, 1980). Four visitors to the city are being met by a Zapotec ruler. Their names (indicated by the shaded sections) are (a) '13 Knot', (b) '9 Monkey', (c) '1 Owl', and (d) 'Treble Scroll'. In front of the latter is a place name, (e) 'Hill of 1 Jaguar', and (f) the name of the Zapotec ruler, which is not fully decipherable.

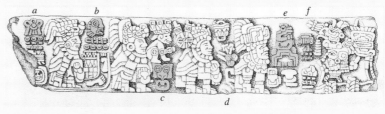

Below: Some modern pictographic road signs, alongside an Indian rock drawing from New Mexico. The parallel between the two cultures is instructive. In the one case, the road leads to water, and vehicles should take care; in the other, the rocky trail is safe for the mountain goat, but not for the rider. The parallel would have been even closer, if the modern sign had contained a fish!

IDEOGRAPHIC

Ideographic writing is usually distinguished as a later development of pictographic. *Ideograms*, or *ideographs*, have an abstract or conventional meaning, no longer displaying a clear pictorial link with external reality. Two factors account for this. The shape of an ideogram may so alter that it is no longer recognizable as a pictorial representation of an object; and its original meaning may extend to include notions that lack any clear pictorial form. In early Sumerian writing, for example, the picture of a starry sky came to mean 'night', 'dark', or 'black'; a foot came to represent 'go', 'stand', and other such notions.

It is rare to find a 'pure' ideographic writing system – that is, one in which the symbols refer directly to notions or things. Most systems that have been called ideographic in fact contain linguistic elements. The symbols stand for words in the language, or parts of the symbols represent sounds. The Sumerian, Egyptian, Hittite, and other scripts of the early period were all mixtures of pictographic, ideographic, and linguistic elements.

CUNEIFORM

The cuneiform method of writing dates from the 4th millennium BC, and was used to express both non-phonological and phonological writing systems in several languages. The name derives from the Latin, meaning 'wedge-shaped', and refers to the technique used to make the symbols. A stylus was pressed into a tablet of soft clay to make a sequence of short straight strokes. In later periods, harder materials were used. The strokes are thickest at the top and to the left, reflecting the direction of writing: at first, symbols were written from top to bottom; later, they were turned onto their sides, and written from left to right.

The earliest cuneiform was a development of pictographic symbols. Subsequently, the script was used to write words and syllables, and to mark phonetic elements. It was used for over 3,000 years throughout the Near East by such cultures as the Sumerians, Babylonians, Assyrians, and Hittites, finally dying out as the Christian era approached. The latest cuneiform tablets date from the 1st century BC. The script could not be read until the 19th century, when several of the languages it represented were finally deciphered.

The columns right show a series of original pictograms, first vertically, then in the altered position used by later cuneiform. Two versions of cuneiform are shown – an illustration from the early period, and one from the later period, when simplified symbols were introduced by the Assyrians (after D. Diringer, 1968).

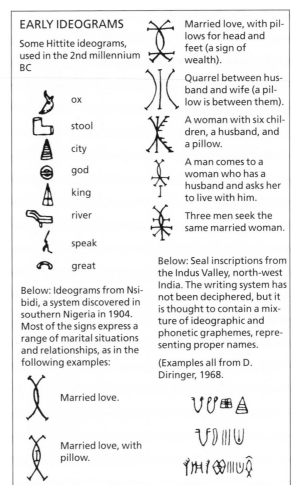

EARLY IDEOGRAMS

Some Hittite ideograms, used in the 2nd millennium BC

ox
stool
city
god
king
river
speak
great

Married love, with pillows for head and feet (a sign of wealth).

Quarrel between husband and wife (a pillow is between them).

A woman with six children, a husband, and a pillow.

A man comes to a woman who has a husband and asks her to live with him.

Three men seek the same married woman.

Below: Ideograms from Nsibidi, a system discovered in southern Nigeria in 1904. Most of the signs express a range of marital situations and relationships, as in the following examples:

Married love.

Married love, with pillow.

Below: Seal inscriptions from the Indus Valley, north-west India. The writing system has not been deciphered, but it is thought to contain a mixture of ideographic and phonetic graphemes, representing proper names.

(Examples all from D. Diringer, 1968.

TODAY'S IDEOGRAMS

Modern signs are frequently ideographic, as with the diagonal lines used to express prohibition (e.g. no right turn). Signs such as 'no dogs allowed' and 'do not iron' mix pictograms and ideograms.

The Black Obelisk of Shalmanazer III (858–824 BC), discovered at Nimrud. The monument is carved with scenes showing tribute bearers and Assyrian cuneiform texts.

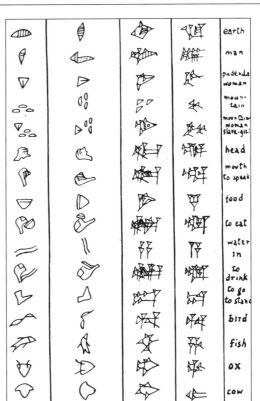

				earth
				man
				pudenda woman
				mountain
				mountain woman slave-girl
				head
				mouth to speak
				food
				to eat
				water in
				to drink
				to go to stand
				bird
				fish
				ox
				cow

EGYPTIAN HIEROGLYPHIC

In Egypt, a form of pictography developed around 3000 BC, which came to be called *hieroglyphic* (from the Greek 'sacred carving'), because of its prominent use in temples, tombs, and other special places. The term has also come to be used for scripts of a similar character from other cultures, such as the Hittite, Mayan, or Indus Valley; but the most fully developed system of hieroglyphic writing is undoubtedly the Egyptian. The system continued in use for three millennia, until it was finally replaced by the Coptic-based script of the early Christian era.

The units of the writing system are known as *hieroglyphs*. They tend to be written from right to left, with the symbols generally facing the beginning of a row; but vertical rows are also found, following the line of a building. The script gives the general impression of being pictorial, but in fact it contains three types of symbol that together represent words:

- Some symbols are used as ideograms, representing real-world entities or notions:

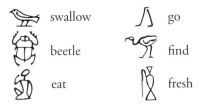

swallow

go

beetle

find

eat

fresh

- Some symbols (*phonograms*) stand for one or more consonants, in much the same way as the *rebus* system is used in present-day children's games (p. 65). For example, in English we might use a picture of a bee followed by the letter (phonogram) *R* to represent the word *beer*, or followed by *K* to represent the word *beak*. In hieroglyphic, this convention was used to express two-consonant sequences as well as single consonants.

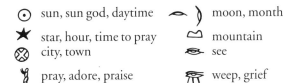

m-n   m-s   n

- *Determinative* symbols are signs that have no phonetic value but are placed next to other symbols to tell the reader what kind of meaning a word has. Words that would otherwise appear to be identical could thus be differentiated. An analogy might again be drawn with a word game in English that could distinguish the two senses of the word *table* by adding a chair (for the item of furniture) and an eye (for the typographical arrangement). Egyptian symbols that were commonly used as determinatives included the following:

sun, sun god, daytime   moon, month

star, hour, time to pray   mountain

city, town   see

pray, adore, praise   weep, grief

A combined example

The hieroglyph ⟨image⟩ is composed of two elements: ⟨image⟩ which is the ideographic symbol for 'wood', and ⟨image⟩ and ⟨image⟩, which are the phonetic symbols for *h and t* respectively. Combined, these would represent the word *htì*. However, *htì* had two meanings: 'carve' and 'retreat'. These are therefore distinguished by the addition of a determinative: the addition of a knife symbol produces ⟨image⟩ 'carve', and the addition of a pair of legs walking backwards produces ⟨image⟩ 'retreat' (after H. Brunner, 1975).

ROYAL NAMES

Two Egyptian royal names in hieroglyphic, showing (a) the royal-divine names, (b) the personal names.

Amen-em-het I (reigned 1991–1962 BC)

Below: Alexander the Great (356–323 BC).

The names are surrounded by a ring, or *cartouche*, which was intended to protect the bearer of the name from harm. (From D. Diringer, 1968.)

A hieroglyphic inscription from Thebes, 18th Dynasty (c. 1490 BC). The statue is of Sennefer, Chancellor and Superintendent of the Palace at the time of Hatshepsut or Tuthmosis III. The inscription consists of a prayer to Osiris, a list of Sennefer's positions and achievements, and a request for a happy afterlife. The statue, of black granite, is 87 cm high.

THE ROSETTA STONE

Egyptian hieroglyphic remained undeciphered until the 19th century. Members of Napoleon's Egyptian expedition of 1799 discovered a black basalt stone, measuring 114 x 72 cm, at Rashid (Rosetta). The stone was carved with three different scripts: hieroglyphic, the derived *demotic* script, used for everyday purposes, and Greek.

The Greek version could of course be translated, and this provided the key to the other texts. The stone commemorates the accession of Ptolemy V Epiphanes (205–180 BC). It thus contains several royal names, whose phonetic values could be related to those of the names in Greek. The text was finally published in 1822 by the French Egyptologist Jean-François Champollion (1790–1832). The Rosetta stone is now in the British Museum.

LOGOGRAPHIC

Logographic writing systems are those where the graphemes represent words. The best-known cases are Chinese, and its derivative script, Japanese *kanji* (pp. 197, 315). The symbols are variously referred to as *logographs*, *logograms*, or – in the case of oriental languages – *characters*. But there are two terminological complications. First, because Chinese writing derives from an ideographic script, with several pictographic elements, the characters are commonly referred to as ideographs. However, this term is really not appropriate, as the characters refer to linguistic units, and not directly to concepts or things. Secondly, the characters in fact often represent *parts* of words (morphemes, p. 90) as well as whole words, so that even the term 'logographic' is somewhat misleading; but in the absence of a more appropriate term (such as 'morphographic'), it continues to be used.

Several thousand graphemes are involved in a logographic system. The great Chinese dictionary of Kāngxī (1662–1722) contains nearly 50,000 characters, but most of these are archaic or highly specialized. In the modern language, basic literacy requires knowledge of some 2,000 characters. Similarly, in Japanese, 1,850 characters are prescribed by the Japanese Ministry of Education and adopted by law as those most essential for everyday use. Of these, 881 are taught during the six years of elementary school.

Most languages make use of some logograms: a selection of widely used graphemes is given below.

Right: Chinese and Japanese characters are classified on the basis of the number of strokes used to write them. The increasing order of graphic complexity can be seen in this list of 300 primary characters in Chinese, which may be used individually or as part of compound forms. (From D. Diringer, 1968.)

MODERN LOGOGRAMS

These symbols are widely used in modern written languages. Their spoken equivalents, of course, vary from language to language. The most developed logographic systems are found in scientific notations, such as in logic and mathematics (p. 385).

$$+ \quad - \quad \times$$
$$= \quad \div \quad \pm \quad \circ \quad \approx$$
$$> \quad < \quad \geq \quad \leq \quad \sqrt{}$$
$$\infty \quad ♀ \quad ♂$$

$$f(z) = \int_{-1}^{1-\eta} e^{zt}\varphi(t)\,dt + \int_{1-\eta}^{1} e^{zt}\varphi(t)\,dt = l_1 + l_2$$

CHINESE CHARACTERS

Traditionally, Chinese characters are divided into six types (*liùshū* 'six scripts').

• *xíngshēng* Most characters are of this type, containing two elements. There is a semantic element, known as a 'radical' (similar to the 'determinatives' of hieroglyphic, p. 201). This is combined with a phonetic element, whose function is to remind the reader of how the word is to be pronounced.

For example, the word 'mother' *mā* is expressed by the semantic element 'woman' 女 followed by a phonetic indicator *mǎ* 馬. The word for 'scold' is also *mà* (with a different tone, p. 174), and this is expressed by the semantic element 'mouth' 口 (repeated) followed by the same phonetic indicator. The meaning of the *ma* character when used alone ('horse') is disregarded.

媽 'mother'   罵 'scold'

• *zhǐshì* These characters represent abstract ideas and are closest to ideograms, e.g.

Character	English
中	'middle'
大	'large'
小	'small'
一	'one'

• *huìyì* Compound characters in which the elements have a semantic connection, e.g.
'sun' + 'moon' = 'bright' 明
'woman' + 'woman' = 'quarrel' 奻
'man' + 'man' + 'man' = 'crowd' 众

• *zhuǎnzhù* Characters formed by modifying the shape or orientation of a character to produce a word of related meaning, e.g. the character for 'corpse' 尸 derives from that for 'man' 人.

• *jiǎjiè* Characters that were borrowed from others of similar pronunciation, e.g. 萬 *wàn* 'ten thousand' derives from the use of this character for *wàn* 'scorpion'.

• *xiàngxíng* A small group of characters that retain a close connection with original pictograms, e.g. the forms for (a) 'sun', 'day' (*rì*), (b) 'mountain' (*shān*) and (c) 'field' (*tián*).

	Ancient form	Modern form
(a)	⊙	日
(b)	⋀	山
(c)	⊞	田

一 1	匕 31	尢 61	子 91	斤 121	弗 151	缶 181	兆 211	亞 241	垂 271
丨 2	冫 32	叉 62	中 92	戶 122	冊 152	至 182	放 212	金 242	芙 272
丿 3	刀 33	廾 63	心 93	午 123	皿 153	辛 183	众 213	來 243	旁 273
丶 4	力 34	开 64	止 94	牛 124	且 154	衣 184	谷 214	兔 244	寅 274
乀 5	勹 35	才 65	丐 95	令 125	目 155	交 185	豆 215	弟 245	魚 275
乙 6	乃 36	广 66	氏 96	不 126	自 156	亥 186	呂 216	易 246	鳥 276
乚 7	又 37	弋 67	丑 97	木 127	巨 157	糸 187	克 217	炙 247	鹿 277
亅 8	乂 38	丸 68	互 98	开 128	四 158	虫 188	臣 218	函 248	翌 278
乛 9	乄 39	凡 69	云 99	水 129	只 159	束 189	囧 219	甾 249	率 279
亅 10	卩 40	凡 70	无 100	火 130	民 160	未 190	酉 220	果 250	离 280
𠃌 11	卜 41	毛 71	丹 101	犬 131	凸 161	虍 191	卵 221	俐 251	殳 281
二 12	丩 42	口 72	丹 102	爪 132	丙 162	舟 192	臼 222	肃 252	壺 282
十 13	丁 43	囗 73	卂 103	天 133	自 163	自 193	角 223	癸 253	象 283
人 14	万 44	回 74	亢 104	壬 134	尤 164	自 194	囟 224	非 254	咼 284
入 15	厂 45	尸 75	六 105	凶 135	禾 165	耳 195	豸 225	面 255	馬 285
入 16	三 46	己 76	文 106	日 136	禾 166	臣 196	采 226	革 256	舀 286
八 17	彡 47	巳 77	方 107	日 137	矛 167	而 197	幺 227	肩 257	為 287
八 18	巛 48	弓 78	万 108	月 138	永 168	因 198	弟 228	盾 258	巢 288
儿 19	彳 49	马 79	勿 109	巴 139	瓜 169	而 199	串 229	卤 259	樂 289
九 20	个 50	幺 80	欠 110	玉 140	戊 170	西 200	華 230	录 260	鼠 290
九 21	厶 51	小 81	气 111	主 141	矢 171	西 201	車 231	鹵 261	蜀 291
十 22	勺 52	巾 82	毛 112	玄 142	冬 172	丏 202	貝 232	癸 262	齊 292
七 23	久 53	山 83	手 113	白 143	正 173	肉 203	百 233	泉 263	壽 293
冂 24	久 54	屮 84	丰 114	囟 144	皮 174	臼 204	身 234	者 264	齒 294
冖 25	夂 55	山 85	丰 115	瓦 145	穴 175	甘 205	艮 235	畏 265	睪 295
凵 26	夕 56	巾 86	斗 116	田 146	它 176	囟 206	辰 236	乘 266	龍 296
厶 27	女 57	土 87	卝 117	由 147	宁 177	由 207	長 237	飛 267	龜 297
厶 28	乩 58	工 88	爿 118	甲 148	米 178	曲 208	重 238	馬 268	燕 298
大 29	大 59	干 89	牙 119	用 149	羊 179	羽 209	隹 239	高 269	翻 299
匚 30	大 60	也 90	于 120	甶 150	矣 180	兆 210	隹 240	羋 270	爵 300

PHONOLOGICAL SYSTEMS
SYLLABIC

In a system of syllabic writing (a *syllabary*), each grapheme corresponds to a spoken syllable, usually a consonant-vowel pair. Such systems have been found from earliest times (e.g. Mycenean Greek) and in modern times can be seen in Amharic, Cherokee, and Japanese *kana*. The number of graphemes in a syllabary varies – from around 50 to several hundred.

CYPRIOT

The clearest example of a syllabic script in classical times comes from Cyprus, where it was used from about the 6th to the 3rd century BC. Typical symbols are shown below, along with an interpretation of the sound values (from O. Masson, 1961).

The Cypriot (or Cypriote) syllabary was deciphered towards the end of the 19th century; the inscriptions are mostly in Greek, though the script seems to have been designed for a different language. There is no way of indicating vowel length, several Greek sounds cannot be distinguished, and syllables containing two consonants have to be expanded as two syllables (e.g. *ptolin → po-to-li-ne*), much as modern Japanese has to do with foreign loan words. The script is mainly written from right to left. The system may be distantly related to the early linear script known as Linear B (p. 303), which was also largely syllabic in character.

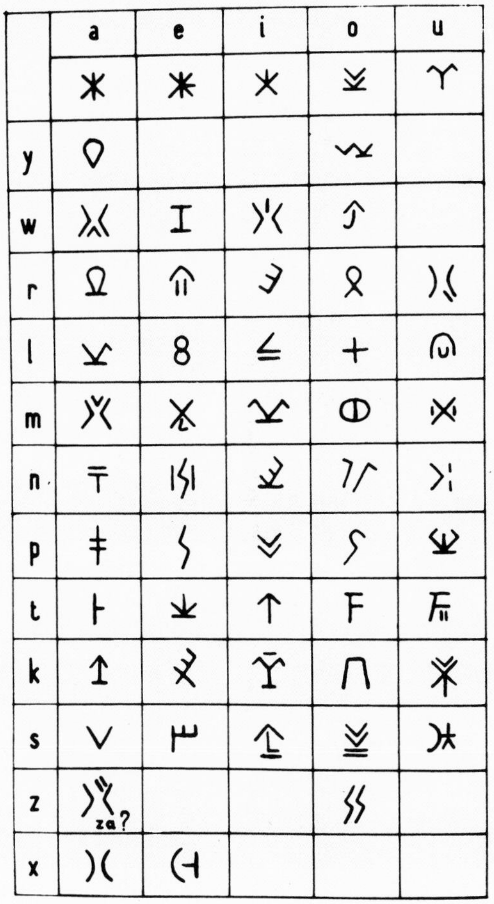

	a	e	i	o	u
	✳	✳	✕		Υ
y					
w					
r					
l					
m					
n					
p					
t					
k					
s					
z	za?				
x					

KATAKANA

The Japanese *katakana* syllabary contains 75 graphemes, three of which enter into combinations to produce a further 36 forms.

The system contains a few phonetic features, such as the regular use of   to mark the voiced element in a contrast. The system is used mainly to write foreign words which have come to be used in Japanese (other than those of Chinese origin):

アメリカ
America

オーストラリア
Australia

コーヒー
coffee

ジャズ
jazz

ジャンボジェット
jumbo jet

テレビ
television

ア a	カ ka	ガ ga	サ sa	ザ za	タ ta	ダ da	ナ na	ハ ha	バ ba	パ pa	マ ma	ラ ra	ワ wa	ファ fa	ン n
イ i	キ ki	ギ gi	シ shi	ジ ji	チ chi	ヂ ji	ニ ni	ヒ hi	ビ bi	ピ pi	ミ mi	リ ri		フィ fi	
ウ u	ク ku	グ gu	ス su	ズ zu	ツ tsu	ヅ zu	ヌ nu	フ fu	ブ bu	プ pu	ム mu	ル ru			
エ e	ケ ke	ゲ ge	セ se	ゼ ze	テ te	デ de	ネ ne	ヘ he	ベ be	ペ pe	メ me	レ re		フェ fe	
オ o	コ ko	ゴ go	ソ so	ゾ zo	ト to	ド do	ノ no	ホ ho	ボ bo	ポ po	モ mo	ロ ro		フォ fo	ヲ o
ヤ ya	キャ kya	ギャ gya	シャ sha	ジャ ja	チャ cha	ヂャ ja	ニャ nya	ヒャ hya	ビャ bya	ピャ pya	ミャ mya	リャ rya			
ユ yu	キュ kyu	ギュ gyu	シュ shu	ジュ ju	チュ chu	ヂュ ju	ニュ nyu	ヒュ hyu	ビュ byu	ピュ pyu	ミュ myu	リュ ryu			
ヨ yo	キョ kyo	ギョ gyo	ショ sho	ジョ jo	チョ cho	ヂョ jo	ニョ nyo	ヒョ hyo	ビョ byo	ピョ pyo	ミョ myo	リョ ryo			

CHEROKEE

This syllabary was invented in 1821 by a half-Cherokee Indian named Sequoya, and came to be used by the people and missionaries for many years. Its 85 symbols show the strong influence of the Latin alphabet, but the Latinate symbols are not used with their original sounds. (From H. A. Gleason, 1955.)

D a	R e	T i	Ꮠ o	O u	i ʌ		
f ga	Ꮞ ge	Ꭹ gi	A go	J gu	E gʌ		
Ꮼ ha	Ꭿ he	Ꭲ hi	Ꮏ ho	Γ hu	Ꮩ hʌ	Ꭶ ka	
W la	Ꮣ le	Ꭴ li	G lo	M lu	Ꮄ lʌ	Ꮏ hna	
Ꮜ ma	Ꭻ me	H mi	З mo	Ꭹ mu		G nah	
Θ na	Ꮑ ne	Ꮒ ni	Z no	Ꮔ nu	Ꮕ nʌ	s	
I gwa	Ꮰ gwe	Ꭼ gwi	Ꮬ gwo	Ꮙ gwu	Ꭱ gwʌ	Ꮮ ta	
Ꭴ sa	4 se	b si	Ꮗ so	Ꭸ su	R sʌ	Ꮬ ti	
Ꮭ da	Ꮬ de	Ꭵ di	Ꭺ do	S du	Ꭾ dʌ	Ꮮ tla	
Ꮎ dla	L dle	C dli	Ꮸ dlo	Ꮏ dlu	P dlʌ	Ꮬ te	
Ꮐ dza	Ꮺ dze	Ꮯ dzi	K dzo	Ꮶ dzu	Ꮓ dzʌ		
Ꮹ wa	Ꮤ we	Ꮻ wi	Ꮴ wo	Ꮽ wu	Ꮗ wʌ		
Ꮿ ya	Ᏸ ye	Ᏹ yi	Ꮖ yo	Ꮆ yu	B yʌ		

ALPHABETIC

With alphabetic writing, there is a direct correspondence between graphemes and phonemes, which makes it the most economic and adaptable of all the writing systems. Instead of several thousand logograms, or several dozen syllables, the system needs only a relatively small number of units, which it then proves easy to adapt to a wide range of languages. Most alphabets contain 20–30 symbols, but the relative complexity of the sound system (§28) leads to alphabets of varying size. The smallest alphabet seems to be Rotokas, used in the Solomon Islands, with 11 letters. The largest is Khmer, with 74 letters.

In a perfectly regular system, as in some of the alphabets that have been devised by linguists to record previously unwritten languages, there is one grapheme for each phoneme. However, most alphabets in present-day use fail to meet this criterion, to some degree, either because the writing system has not kept pace with changes in pronunciation, or because the language is using an alphabet not originally designed for it. Languages very greatly in their graphemic/phonemic regularity. At one extreme we find such languages as Spanish and Finnish, which have a very regular system; at the other, we find such cases as English and Gaelic, where there is a marked degree of irregularity. The extent to which there is a lack of correspondence between graphemes and phonemes is inevitably reflected in the number of arbitrary 'spelling rules' that children have to learn (p. 215).

There are also many alphabets where only certain phonemes are represented graphemically. These are the 'consonantal' alphabets, such as Aramaic, Hebrew, and Arabic, where the marking of vowels (using diacritics) is optional. There are also cases, such as the alphabets of India, where diacritics are used for vowels, but the marking is obligatory, with the diacritics being attached to the consonantal letters.

The earliest-known alphabet was the North Semitic, which developed around 1700 BC in Palestine and Syria. It consisted of 22 consonant letters. The Hebrew, Arabic, and Phoenician alphabets were based on this model. Then, around 1000 BC, the Phoenician alphabet was itself used as a model by the Greeks, who added letters for vowels. Greek in turn became the model for Etruscan (c. 800 BC), whence came the letters of the ancient Roman alphabet, and ultimately all western alphabets.

NEW ALPHABETS FROM OLD

The development of the early alphabet, and five modern alphabets.

Modern Roman		Arabic			Greek			Hebrew			Cyrillic (Russian)	
Letter		Letter	Name	Transliteration	Letter	Name	Transliteration	Letter	Name	Transliteration	Letter	Transliteration
A	a	ا	alif	' ,'[1]	A α	alpha	a	א	aleph	- or '	А а	a
B	b	ب	ba	b	B β	beta	b	ב	beth	b, v	Б б	b
C	c	ت	ta	t	Γ γ	gamma	g	ג	gimel	g	В в	v
D	d	ث	th	th	Δ δ	delta	d	ד	daleth	d	Г г	g
E	e	ج	jim	j	E ε	epsilon	e	ה	he	h	Д д	d
F	f	ح	ha	h	Z ζ	zeta	z	ו	vav, waw	v, w	Е е	e, ye
G	g	خ	kha	kh	H η	eta	e, ē	ז	zayin	z	Ж ж	zh
H	h	د	dal	d	Θ θ	theta	th	ח	heth	ḥ	З з	z
I	i	ذ	dhal	dh	I ι	iota	i	ט	teth	ṭ	И и	i
J	j	ر	ra	r	K κ	kappa	k	י	yod	y, j, i	Й й	ĭ, i
K	k	ز	zay	z	Λ λ	lambda	l	כך[1]	kaph	k, kh	К к	k
L	l	س	sin	s	M μ	mu	m	ל	lamed	l	Л л	l
M	m	ش	shin	sh	N ν	nu	n	מם[1]	mem	m	М м	m
N	n	ص	ṣad	ṣ	Ξ ξ	xi	x	נן[1]	nun	n	Н н	n
O	o	ض	ḍad	ḍ	O o	omicron	o	ס	samekh	s	О о	o
P	p	ط	ṭa	t	Π π	pi	p	ע	ayin	ʻ	П п	p
Q	q	ظ	ẓa	z				פף[1]	pe	p, f	Р р	r
R	r	ع	ain	' [2]	P ρ	rho	r				С с	s
S	s	غ	ghain	gh	Σ σ,s[1]	sigma	s	צץ[1]	sade	ṣ	Т т	t
T	t	ف	fa	f	T τ	tau	t	ק	qoph	ḳ	У у	u
U	u	ق	qaf	q	Y υ	upsilon	y	ר	resh	r	Ф ф	f
V	v	ك	kaf	k	Φ φ	phi	ph	ש	shin	sh, š	Х х	kh, x
W	w	ل	lam	l	X χ	chi	ch, kh	שׂ	śin	ś	Ц ц	ts, c
X	x	م	mim	m	Ψ ψ	psi	ps	ת	tav, taw	t	Ч ч	ch, č
Y	y	ن	nun	n	Ω ω	omega	o, ō				Ш ш	sh, š
Z	z	ه	ha	h							Щ щ	shch, šč
		و	waw	w							Ъ ъ	''[1]
		ي	ya	y							Ы ы	i
											Ь ь	'[2]
											Э э	e
											Ю ю	yu, ju
											Я я	ya, ja

¹ glottal stop
² voiced pharyngeal fricative

¹ at end of word

¹ at end of word

¹ palatalization ('soft') sign
² non palatalization ('hard') sign

North Semitic	𐤀	𐤁	𐤂	𐤃	𐤄	𐤅	IZ	𐤇𐤇	⊕	𐤆	𐤋	𐤌𐤌	𐤍	𐤎	O	𐤐	𐤓	99	𐤗	w	†x			
Late Phoenician	𐤀	𐤁	𐤂	𐤃	𐤄	𐤅	𐤆	𐤇𐤇	⊙	𐤈𐤈	𐤋	𐤌𐤌	𐤍	𐤎	O	𐤐	𐤓	𐤒	𐤗	𐤈𐤈				⊙
Early Greek	ΔΔΛ	𐊡𐊡Β	𐊚𐊚	ΔΔ	𐊟𐊠	𐌅𐌅𐌅	I	𐊧𐊧	⊕⊙	𐊰𐊰	𐊧𐊧	𐌌𐌌	𐌍𐌍	𐊴𐊴	O	𐌂𐌂	𐌐𐌐	99	𐊻𐊻	𐌔	T			
Classical Greek	A	B	Γ	Δ	E	Y	IZ	H	Θ	I	K	Λ	M	N	Ξ	O	Π		P	Σ	T	Φ	X	Ψ	Ω

ALPHABETIC SCRIPTS

The range of the world's alphabetic scripts can be seen in this selection of extracts from Biblical texts. Other examples are found on pp. 190, 305. (From E. Gunnemark & D. Kenrick, 1985.)

Armenian

Balinese

Buginese

Burmese

Coptic

Devanagari

Ethiopic

Georgian

Gujarati

Javanese

Kannada

Khmer

Malayalam

Maldivian

Sinhalese

Syriac

Tamil

Telugu

Thai

Tibetan

ANGLO-SAXON TIMES

The earliest English alphabet was devised by missionaries in Britain, who used the Irish forms of the Latin alphabet to present the sounds of Anglo-Saxon as phonetically as possible. But they ran into difficulties when they encountered four sounds which had no counterpart in Latin.

• /w/ came to be written with a runic symbol P, known as 'wynn'. It was replaced by uu or w in Middle English and is rarely found after 1300.

• /θ/ and /ð/ (as in modern English thin and this) came to be written by a runic symbol, known as 'thorn', þ. Later a further symbol, ð, was devised by drawing a line through the Latin d; this came to be called 'eth'. However, the two new letters were not used to separate the two sounds, and in the Middle English periods they were replaced by th. Curiously, þ has survived to the present day, in such artificial forms as 'Ye Olde English Tea Shoppe', where the Y really stands for a badly made þ.

• /a/ (as in modern English hat) was pronounced quite high in the mouth, almost with the quality of [e] (p. 156). This quality was represented by using the Latin digraph æ, which came to be called 'ash', after the name of the runic symbol that represented the same sound. By the Middle English period it had fallen out of use, probably because sound changes (§54) had made it no longer needed.

RUNES

The runic alphabet was used in north-west Europe, mainly in Scandinavia and the British Isles, and has been preserved in about 4,000 inscriptions and a few manuscripts. It dates from around the 3rd century AD and continued to be used on charms and monuments until the 17th century. The common runic alphabet (given at right) consisted of 24 letters, and is usually known as the 'futhork' or 'futhark', from the names of its first six letters. Several variant shapes of the letters exist. The version found in Britain used extra letters to cope with the range of Anglo-Saxon sounds. No-one knows where the alphabet came from but it is probably derived from the Roman alphabet; there were many trade contacts between Roman and Germanic peoples in the Rhine area during the first centuries of our era.

Below: One side of the Franks Casket, an 8th-century AD carved box, with a narrative inscribed in runes.

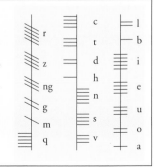

OGHAM

The origins of the ogham (or ogam) alphabet are unknown, though links have been proposed with both runic and Etruscan. It was used for writing Irish and Pictish from around the 4th century AD. There are about 500 inscriptions, mainly on stone monuments in southern Ireland. The alphabet has 20 letters, divided into four sets of five letters. The letters were simple strokes or notches cut into the edge of a stone. They are usually read from bottom to top, or from right to left.

GRAPHOLOGICAL CONTRASTS

Once a writing system has been devised, it can be used to convey a wide range of graphological contrasts. These are best illustrated from the range of possibilities available in alphabetic systems.

Spelling The essential identity of words is conveyed by the correct selection and sequence of graphemes – the spelling rules of the language. This is the main component of any graphological description. It is a study that needs to include, not only the 'normal' rules that have to be learned in order to read and write, but any dialectal, stylistic, or 'free' variations. Dialectal variation is illustrated by American–British differences such as *color / colour* or the use of *thru* for *through*. Stylistic variation can be illustrated by the way authors adapt the spelling system to reflect or suggest the pronunciation of non-standard speech (p. 182). An interesting example is the use of *shuvvle* for *shovel*, in portrayals of Cockney speech: the two forms have identical pronunciations, in fact, but the former manages to convey the impression of a non-standard accent. Free variations (p. 163) include such alternatives as *judgment / judgement* and *-ise / -ize*.

Special symbols A large number of symbols are available to express frequently occurring meanings in an economical way. Most of these are logograms (p. 202), such as +, @, £; but some do not relate to individual words, such as ✂, used to mark the place where paper may be cut; ☛, which indicates a direction; ☎, marking a telephone number; and the dagger (†), showing that a person is dead. Special symbols may also be used to help organize a written text (such as asterisks or superscript numbers relating to footnotes) or to draw attention to part of it (such as a large star before a name in an advertisement). An important use of the asterisk has been to show omitted letters, especially in taboo words (p. 61).

Abbreviations Shortened forms of words are a major feature of written language, as in the use of titular contractions and abbreviations such as *Mr*, *Dr*, *Ms*, *Lt*, and *Capt*, or the use of acronyms, such as *COD*, *VIP*, and *NATO*. The abbreviations may even come from a different language, and the full form may not be known, e.g. *e.g.* (= *exempli gratia*), *i.e.* (= *id est*), and *etc.* Some abbreviations are spoken as words (e.g. *NATO* is usually /ˈneɪtəʊ/); some are spelled out (e.g. *VIP* is always /ˈviː ˈaɪ ˈpiː/); some are automatically expanded (e.g. *Mr* is /ˈmɪstə/); and some permit a choice (e.g. *viz.* spoken as /vɪz/ or as *namely*).

Graphic contrasts Italic, boldface, capitalization, colour, and other graphic variations are major ways of expressing semantic contrasts, some of which are illus-

trated on pp. 182–3 and in §32. The size of the graphemes, for example, is a major way of conveying the relative importance of parts of a message, such as in advertisements or invitations. The switch from Roman to Gothic type may convey an 'old world' connotation, as in many Christmas cards and shop signs. However, it should be noted that not all languages have the same set of possibilities – for example, there is no use of italics or capitalization in Hebrew.

Capitalization Initial capital letters mark both lexical and grammatical units (p. 196), usually sentences or words. A single graphic contrast is involved: big vs small. The graphic contrast between large and small capital letters (A vs ᴀ) conveys no conventional meaning difference. Also, capitalization does not apply to numbers: if 33 were to appear at the beginning of a sentence, it would not be written ³3.

Spatial organization

The general disposition of symbols on a page (or other format) can itself convey semantic contrasts. This is something newspaper editors are very much aware of when they juxtapose stories on the same page – in one case, a story about the Ethiopian famine of 1984 was placed next to a story about the mountains of food being stored in Europe. If the stories had been on different pages, the effect would have been lost. Other examples of contrastive layout include the use of captions under pictures (particularly noticeable when the caption is placed under the wrong picture), the placing of headlines or titles, the layout of headings and subheadings in a script or report, and the layout of literary texts, especially poetry (pp. 72, 392).

DEVIANT SPELLING

The use of abnormal spelling to make a point is more common than we might think. It is sometimes used as an economical way of expressing a contrast in poetry, or identifying a personality in a story. And it is a commonly used device in the world of advertising, where it can make the name of a product or shop stand out and be remembered, or provide the basis for a legal trade mark. (After S. Jacobson, 1966.)

Bar-B-Q
EZ Lern (*U.S. driving school*)
Fetherwate

Firetuf
Hyway Inn
Kilzum (*insect spray*)
Koffee Kake

Kwik Koin Wash
Loc-tite
Masqit
No-glu
Resistoyl

Rol-it-on
Savmor (*discount store*)
Strippit
Tini-plugs
Wundertowl

PUNCTUATION

The punctuation system of a language has two functions. Its primary purpose is to enable stretches of written language to be read in a coherent way; its secondary role is to give an indication of the rhythm and colour of speech (though never consistently). It roughly corresponds to the use of suprasegmental features (§29), but it differs from speech in that its contrasts are to some extent taught in schools, and norms of punctuation are conventionally laid down by publishing houses in their style manuals.

Features that separate

Punctuation is mainly used to separate units of grammar (sentences, clauses, phrases, words, §16) from each other. The various marks are organized in a broadly hierarchical manner: some identify large units of writing, such as paragraphs; others identify small units of intermediate size or complexity. The main English-language conventions are as follows:

- *space:* separates words; identifies paragraphs – the first sentence begins a new line, with the first word usually indented; extra space may also be inserted between paragraphs, especially to mark a break in the discourse.
- *period (full stop):* identifies the end of a sentence, along with question and exclamation marks; sometimes followed by a wider space than is usual between words (printing and typing conventions differ); also used to mark abbreviations (though practice varies); a sequence of (usually three) periods indicates that the text is incomplete.
- *semi-colon:* identifies the coordinate parts of a complex sentence, or separates complex points in a list (as in the previous paragraph).
- *colon:* used mainly to show that what follows it is an amplification or explanation of what precedes it – as in the present sentence.
- *comma:* a wide range of uses, such as marking a sequence of grammatical units, or a unit used inside another; displays a great deal of personal variation (such as whether it should be used before *and* in such lists as *apples, pears, and plums*).
- *parentheses* ( ) and *brackets* [ ]: used as an alternative to commas to mark the inclusion of a grammatical unit in the middle or at the end of a sentence.
- *dash:* used in pairs with the same function as parentheses or brackets; used singly to separate a comment or afterthought occurring at the end of a sentence or to express an incomplete utterance; in informal writing, often replaces other punctuation marks.

THE SEMANTICS OF LAYOUT

The importance of layout for semantic effect can be seen in this poem of José Paulo Paes (translated by Edwin Morgan). The spacing between the words gives time for the reader (who knows Descartes' famous dictum) to build up an expectation that the last word is going to be *sum.* The effect would be lost if the poem had been printed in a single line.

The Suicide, or Descartes à Rebours

cogito

ergo

boom

- *quotation marks (inverted commas):* identify the beginning and end of an extract of speech, a title, a citation, or the 'special' use of a word. The choice of single vs double quotes is variable: the latter are more common in handwritten and typed material, and in American printing.
- *hyphen:* marks two kinds of divisions within a word – to show that a word has been split in two because of the end of a line (a feature that has no spoken counterpart), and to relate the parts of a phrase or compound word to each other (as in *pickled-herring merchant –* vs *pickled herring-merchant –* and *washing-machine*); practice varies greatly in the latter use, with British English using hyphens in many contexts where American English would omit them.

Features that convey meaning

Some punctuation features express a meaning in their own right, regardless of the grammatical context in which they occur. (Special symbols of this kind are illustrated on the facing page.)

- *Question mark:* usually expresses a question, but occasionally found with other functions, such as marking silence (p. 182) or uncertainty (e.g. *this is an interesting* (?) *point*).
- *Exclamation mark:* shows varying degrees of exclamatory force (e.g. *!!!*); also, some special uses (e.g. *John* (!) *was there*).
- *Apostrophe:* most commonly used to mark the genitive singular or plural (*cat's, cats'*), and grammatical contractions (*I'm, won't*); found also in certain words (*o'clock, fish 'n' chips*); subject to a great deal of usage variation (*St Johns* or *St John's*? *Harrods* or *Harrod's*?) and uncertainty (**ice cream cone's, *todays bargains*).

SHORTHAND

Shorthand is a method of writing at speed using special symbols or abbreviations for the usual letters and words of speech. It is a system intended for a limited readership (usually only one person, the writer) and for short-term preservation (apart from the occasional literary or scientific diary). It is therefore prone to idiosyncratic use: it is quite common for secretaries trained in the same system to be unable to read each other's shorthand.

The practice of shorthand writing is variously known as stenography ('narrow writing'), tachygraphy ('quick writing'), and brachygraphy ('short writing'). It is best known from its use in press reporting and in clerical and secretarial work – mainly the verbatim recording of legal proceedings and the dictation of business correspondence – though in recent years the advent of voice-recording equipment has somewhat reduced the demand for professional shorthand skills.

Shorthand was well known in Ancient Greece and Rome – the earliest recorded instance is the system used by the historian Xenophon to write the memoirs of Socrates. In 63 BC, a Roman freeman, Marcus Tullius Tiro invented a system for recording the speeches of Cicero – a system that continued in use for over 1,000 years. Julius Caesar was one of many in this early period who learned the use of shorthand.

The use of shorthand died out in the middle ages because of its imagined association with witchcraft. The 16th century saw a revival, and produced the first printed manual in English: Timothy Bright's *Characterie: An Arte of Shorte, Swifte, and Secrete Writing by Character* (1588). Shorthand became extremely popular in 17th-century England, especially in relation to the aims of the movement to find a universal language (§58). Several systems were invented – notably, those of John Willis, Thomas Shelton, Jeremiah Rich, and William Mason. It came to be studied in school. In church, sermons would be written down and taken home for later study. In the 18th century, the demands of the Industrial Revolution promoted the use of shorthand in business administration, and its popularity grew in Europe. Finally, the 19th century saw the invention of the main shorthand systems that are still in present-day use.

There is a variety of methods of writing shorthand. Some abbreviate the normal spelling of words; others are based on ways of representing the sounds of speech; still others require the user to learn a list of arbitrary symbols; and there are several combinations of these approaches. The result is that over 400 shorthand systems have been devised for the English language alone.

SAMUEL PEPYS'S DIARY

A page from Samuel Pepys's original shorthand diary. The diary was written between 1660 and 1669, when Pepys was forced to stop writing because of failing eyesight. It consists of six small volumes, totalling over 3,000 pages, written in a system devised by the early 17th-century translator, Thomas Shelton. The system contains reduced forms of letters, dots for vowels, abbreviated words, and 265 arbitrary symbols, such as *2* for *to*, a larger *2* for *two*, *5* for *because*, *6* for *us*, etc. There are also several 'empty' symbols, used presumably to foster the secrecy of the work, and several of the more censorable passages are written in various foreign languages.

The diary remained unread for several decades, as Pepys left no key to the system, and it was not deciphered until the beginning of the 19th century. It was first published in 1825.

Samuel Pepys (1633–1703)

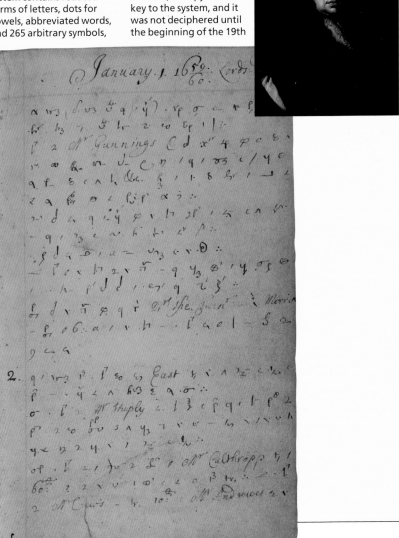

GENERAL BERTRAND'S DIARY

N. so. le mat. en cal: il déj. bi. se. trv. un. peu fat ...

This is part of an entry (for 20 January 1821) from the diary of General Henri-Gatien Bertrand, who was companion to Napoleon during his exile on the island of Saint Helena. The diary is written in such an abbreviated style that it is tantamount to a shorthand system. This kind of private shorthand is probably quite widespread among diarists. An interpretation of the passage reads: *Napoléon sort le matin en calèche: il déjeune bien, se trouve un peu fatigué* ('Napoleon goes out in the morning in a carriage: he lunches well, finds himself a little tired').

ISAAC PITMAN (1813–97)

Pitman's *Stenographic Sound Hand*, published in 1837, was based on the sounds of English. The system uses a combination of straight lines, curves, dots, and dashes, as well as a contrast in positioning and shading (heavy vs light). Several of the graphic contrasts relate systematically to the sound system (§27); for example, all stop consonants are shown by straight lines; all labial consonants slope backwards; and the distinction between voiced and voiceless sounds is indicated by line thickness. Most vowels are omitted.

Pitman's is the main system in use in Britain, and is widely used in other English-speaking countries. The phonetic principles of the approach also make it relatively easy to adapt for use with other languages.

JOHN ROBERT GREGG (1867–1948)

Gregg devised an alternative to Pitman which avoided the latter's reliance on shading and positioning. His approach uses separate symbols for consonants and vowels, and all symbols are written on a single line in the same thickness. His symbols also make more use of loops and circles, compared with Pitman's angular system, and the line of writing more closely resembles a longhand script. It is now the main system in use in the USA, and has been adapted to several other languages.

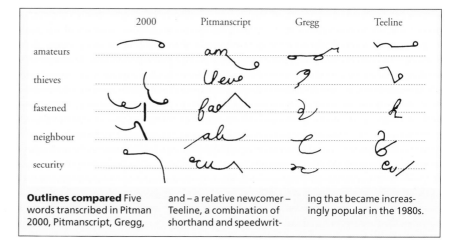

	2000	Pitmanscript	Gregg	Teeline
amateurs				
thieves				
fastened				
neighbour				
security				

Outlines compared Five words transcribed in Pitman 2000, Pitmanscript, Gregg, and – a relative newcomer – Teeline, a combination of shorthand and speedwriting that became increasingly popular in the 1980s.

SHORTHAND BY MACHINE

A stenotype machine, invented in 1906 by W. S. Ireland, an American court-reporter. It is mainly used to record the verbatim proceedings of law courts and legislative meetings.

It is a small machine, with a keyboard of 22 keys that the operator strikes using both hands simultaneously. The left-hand fingers type consonants occurring before vowels, and these are printed on the left of the paper; the right hand fingers type consonants occurring after vowels, and these appear on the right. The thumbs type the vowels, which appear in the centre. The sequences of letters are then printed (without noise) on a roll of paper. The printout looks strange, because some words are abbreviated, and some letters have to be typed using combinations of other letters.

An experienced stenotype operator has no difficulty keeping up with normal conversational speed (p. 271). The system is standard, so that the output of different operators is mutually intelligible (not always the case with pen shorthand). However, the expense of the machines, and the training of operators, has limited the application of the approach.

The inset shows a stenographer at work in court, in a scene from *Airplane II*.

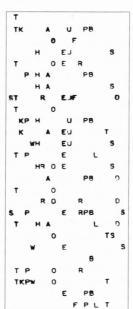

A sample of stenotype shorthand

READING

It might have been thought desirable, before beginning the account of written language, to present an anatomical and physiological description of the visual and manual systems in human beings, in much the same way as the articulatory/auditory systems were presented for speech in Part IV. However, this is not usually done in linguistic discussions of reading and writing because there is so little that can be said in our present state of knowledge. The study of what happens when language is visually perceived and processed is very recent, and while a certain amount is now known about the likely processing operations involved, the neuroanatomical correlations of these processes remain obscure. Moreover, there is perhaps little in principle that *can* be said, given that the structures of the eye and hand do not seem to be biologically adapted for written language in the way that the vocal organs are for speech (though, given the relatively recent development of writing, §33, this is hardly surprising). As a result, the bulk of the enquiries are carried out by psychologists concerned less with the structure and function of the eyes, and more with models of the 'deeper' ways in which the brain works when it processes written language.

Eye movements

One physiological topic has attracted considerable attention, however: the nature of eye movements. These movements can be recorded using various techniques, such as by attaching a mirror to a contact lens placed on the cornea; it is then possible to film a beam of light reflected off the mirror. (See also the computational technique described below.) Using such methods, researchers have shown that the eyes work together, and that when searching for an object they move in a series of rapid jerks, known as *saccades* (from French, 'the flick of a sail'). Between each movement there is a period of relative stability, known as a *fixation*. During reading, the eyes do not follow lines of print in a smooth linear manner, but proceed in a series of saccades and fixations. We usually make 3–4 fixations a second, though rate and duration can be affected by the content of what is read, and there are some interlanguage variations.

What happens during a fixation is of particular importance in studying the process of reading. The nerve cells that convert light into electrical pulses are located in the *retina*, at the back of the eye. The central region of the retina, where these receptor cells are packed closely together, is known as the *fovea*. It extends

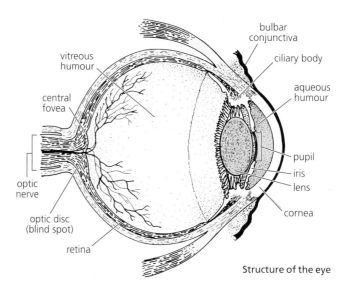

Structure of the eye

for some 2° of visual angle, and is the area that gives the best visual detail, such as is required for identifying graphic forms. The further a stimulus is from the fovea, the poorer our ability to discriminate. The *parafoveal* area surrounds the fovea, and this in turn is surrounded by the *periphery*. These areas are less involved in the act of reading, but they do have some relevance in the detection of larger visual patterns in a text.

Perceptual span

How much linguistic material can be seen during a fixation? Most information about visual perceptual span comes from using a tachistoscope: subjects are presented with a briefly flashed sequence of letters or words, and are then tested to see how many they recall. In a single exposure of 1/100 sec, it is usually possible to recall 3–4 isolated letters or 2–4 short words. Several factors affect subjects' performances, such as the distance of the stimuli from the eyes, or whether the letters or words are linguistically connected.

However, this approach does not replicate what actually happens in reading, where people make several fixations a second and do not have to name what they have seen. Accordingly, several other methods of studying perceptual span have been tried. One sophisticated study involved the use of computer technology

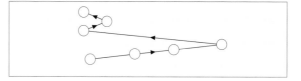

A SEQUENCE OF EYE MOVEMENTS

Fixations are shown as circles, and the order of movement is shown by arrows; information about the duration of each fixation is not given. In the fixations for the sentence 'The vehicle almost flattened a pedestrian' given here, the reader spends most of the time at the beginning of the sentence. Note (i) that the word *a* does not receive a separate fixation (and possibly nor does *the*); (ii) the first part of the sentence is looked at three times. Effects of this kind require a complex explanation, in which physical features of a text (such as word length) interact with its semantic properties.

(K. Rayner & G. W. McConkie, 1977). An eye-movement monitor illuminated the eye with invisible infrared light, and measured the amount of light reflected from certain parts of the eye's surface. A computer was then attached to this equipment and programmed to check the eye position 60 times a second, keeping a record of where the person was looking and how long each movement or fixation took. The text to be read was displayed on a screen, also under the control of the computer, thus enabling the researchers to make changes in the display during the period of an eye movement.

In one experiment, a piece of text was 'mutilated' by replacing each letter with an *x*. When subjects looked at this display, the computer automatically replaced the *x*'s within a certain region around their point of central vision with the letters from the original passage. This created a 'window' of normal text in the subject's foveal region for that fixation. When the subject's eyes moved, the old window was replaced by *x*'s and a new window was created. The size of the window was under the control of the researcher: in the table (see right), a window of 17 characters is shown. Subjects had no difficulty reading under these conditions, unless the window became too small.

By using different window sizes and mutilating the text in different ways, it was possible to draw various conclusions about perceptual span. Reducing the window size slowed the subjects' reading speeds, but it did not affect their ability to comprehend the text (even if all the reader could see was nine letters – little more than a word at a time). The study suggested that subjects were using letter information no further than 10 or 11 positions from their centre of vision, though information about word-length and general shape could be obtained from further away. A follow-up study also showed that these regions were not symmetrical around the centre of vision: on the left side, the area used during a fixation was restricted to four letter positions.

It is possible to conclude that, when looking at a text of average type size about 30 cm away, readers do not usually identify more than two or three short words (about 10 letters) on each fixation. Larger units cannot be seen 'all at once'.

THEORIES OF HOW WE READ

Following a fixation during reading, a visual pattern of graphic features is conveyed to the retina, and then transmitted via the optic nerve for interpretation by the brain (§45). The stages involved in this process are not well understood, and several different theories have been proposed to explain what happens when fluent readers read. One reason why the field is so controversial is that it is extremely difficult to obtain precise information about the events that take place when people read. In fact, very little actually seems to happen, apart from the eye movements – and these do not

begin to explain *how* the reader is managing to draw meaning out of the graphic symbols. Similarly, if people are tested after they have read something, we may find out something about *what* they have read, but not about how they read it. Nor are experimental situations necessarily convincing, because they make readers do abnormal things. And analysing the behaviour of people with reading handicaps may produce results that do not apply to healthy readers (p. 261).

Given the difficulties, the field of reading research would not seem to be a particularly promising or attractive one. It is, however, an area that has attracted many investigators, partly by virtue of its very complexity, and partly because any solutions to the problem of how we read would have immediate application in areas of high social concern. A large number of children have great difficulty in learning to read, and many never read well. Estimates suggest that between 10% and 20% of the U.S. population, for example, are functionally illiterate (p. 274). Such figures thus bring a sense of urgency to reading research.

'Reading' in all of this does not mean simply 'reading aloud', which might be done by a suitably equipped automatic machine that would not know what it was saying. 'Reading' crucially involves appreciating the sense of what is written: we read for meaning. It is this link – between graphology (§33) and semantics (§17) – that has to be explained by any theory of reading.

JOINT READING

Smith has taught himself to read Russian letters, but he hasn't had time to learn the language. Bronski was brought up speaking Russian, but he never learned to read. One day, Bronski gets a letter in Russian from a relative. He cannot read it. He shows it to Smith. Smith cannot understand it. But all is well: Smith reads the words aloud; Bronski recognizes them, and interprets them. He is happy. But who is 'reading'?

FIXATION WINDOWS

A line of text on four successive fixations, using Rayner and McConkie's technique. Each window area is 17 letters wide – that is, eight letter positions to the left of fixation (marked with a dot) and eight to the right.

Fixation number	Text
1	Xxxxhology means perxxxxxxxx xxxxxxxxx xxxx xxxx xxxxxxx Xxxx xx x
2	Xxxxxxxxxx xxxxs personality diaxxxxxx xxxx xxxx xxxxxxx. Xxxx xx x
3	Xxxxxxxxxx xxxxx xxxxxxxxxx xiagnosis. from hanx xxxxxxx. Xxxx xx x
4	Xxxxxxxxxx xxxxx xxxxxxxxxx xxxxxxxxx xxxm hand writing. Xxxx xx x

GRAPHIC TYPOGRAPHY

One of several typographic systems designed for research in visual pattern identification. The general aim of such research is to see whether, by varying visual form, words can be made more discriminable and pronunciation features more salient. The typography, which enhances the main graphic features of letters, makes the visual shape of a word stand out more clearly than it does when printed in a conventional way. It should be noted that each letter is the same whenever it occurs. Certain morphemes (p. 90) are separated with dashes, and a few pronunciation cues are added; for example, *l* and *r* are shaded, and vowels are darker. (From L. Brooks, 1977.)

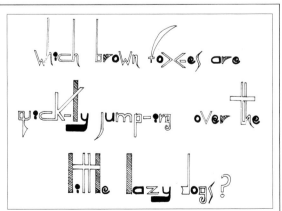

READING BY EAR OR BY EYE?

Most people have encountered the struggle that takes place as a child is learning to read. A major feature of this task is that words and letters are 'sounded out'. It is as if reading is possible only if the symbols are heard – reading 'by ear'. One theory of reading therefore argues that a phonic or phonological step is an essential feature of the process – a theory of 'phonic mediation'. The view implies that reading is a serial or linear process, taking place letter-by-letter, with larger units gradually being built up.

The alternative view argues that there is a direct relationship between the graphology and the semantics, and that a phonological bridge is unnecessary (though it is available for use when reading aloud). Words are read as wholes, without being broken down into a linear sequence of letters and sounded out – reading 'by eye'. Readers use their peripheral vision to guide the eye to the most likely informative part of the page. Their knowledge of the language and general experience helps them to identify critical letters or words in a section of text. This initial sampling gives them an expectation about the way the text should be read, and they use their background knowledge to 'guess' the remainder of the text and fill in the gaps. In this view, a text is like a problem that has to be solved using hypotheses about its meaning and structure.

The arguments for and against these views are complex and multifaceted, deriving from the results of a vast number of experiments on aspects of reading behaviour. Some of the points that have been raised are summarized below.

Support for the ear
• Associating graphemes and phonemes is a natural process, which cannot be avoided when first learning to read.
• Letter recognition is very rapid – about 10–20 msec per letter – which is enough to account for average reading speeds (around 250 words per minute). These speeds are similar for both silent and oral reading (though the latter is slightly slower, presumably for articulatory reasons), and are close to the norms for spontaneous speech (p. 125).
• Statistical studies of word frequency (§15) show that most words in a text are of very low frequency, several occurring only once over long periods; some will be completely new to a reader. Readers can therefore have few expectancies about such material and will need to decode it phonologically. It is an everyday experience to break new long words up into phonemes or (more usually) syllables: try *picomalesefeso,* and see.
• When people read difficult material, they often move their lips, as if the phonology is needed in order to help comprehension. There may be other sub-vocal movements not so far observed.
• It is difficult to see how the 'eye' theory can handle the many variations in type and handwriting. Yet we

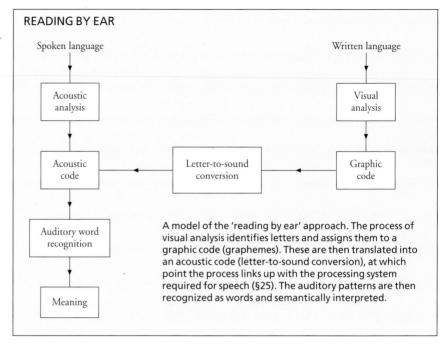

READING BY EAR

A model of the 'reading by ear' approach. The process of visual analysis identifies letters and assigns them to a graphic code (graphemes). These are then translated into an acoustic code (letter-to-sound conversion), at which point the process links up with the processing system required for speech (§25). The auditory patterns are then recognized as words and semantically interpreted.

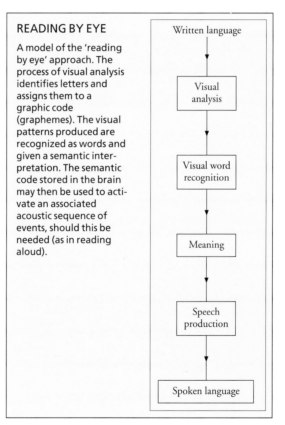

READING BY EYE
A model of the 'reading by eye' approach. The process of visual analysis identifies letters and assigns them to a graphic code (graphemes). The visual patterns produced are recognized as words and given a semantic interpretation. The semantic code stored in the brain may then be used to activate an associated acoustic sequence of events, should this be needed (as in reading aloud).

are able to read these variations quite rapidly, even in experimental situations (using such forms as *BoAt*).
• Reading by eye would be a very complex matter. Each word would have to be given a separate orthographic representation in the brain, along with a separate retrieval process. This is not a parsimonious explanation.

Support for the eye

• Fluent readers are not confused by such homophones as *two* and *too*. Phonology cannot help in such cases. Moreover in words like *tear*, there is no way of deciding which pronunciation is involved (/tɪə/ or /tɛə/) until *after* the reader has selected a meaning.

• In one type of reading disorder ('phonological dyslexia', p. 274), people lose the ability to convert isolated letters into sounds; they are unable to pronounce even simple nonsense words, e.g. *pob*). But they *are* able to read real words, showing that a non-phonological route from print to meaning must exist.

• The 'ear' theory does not explain how some people can read at very rapid speeds, which can be in excess of 500 words per minute. The eyes can take in only so many letters at a time. Rapid reading poses less of a problem for the 'eye' theory, as it simply requires that readers increase their sampling as they speed up.

• In brief exposure experiments, people identify whole words more rapidly than isolated letters. For example, if subjects are shown BAG, BIG, A, I, IBG, etc., and asked whether they have just seen A or I, they perform best with the familiar words. This is the 'word superiority' effect.

• The fact that different sounds are written identically, and different letters can have the same pronunciation, complicates a phonological view. Also, some orthographic rules seem totally unrelated to the phonology, e.g. *skr-* is acceptable in English speech, but does not occur in normal writing.

• Some higher-order processing must be involved in reading, because of several observed effects. Experiments have shown that it is easier to recognize letters in real words than in nonsense words. Typographic errors are often not noticed when reading through a text (the proof-corrector's problem). Errors made by fluent readers while reading aloud are usually syntactically or semantically appropriate; they make few phonologically induced errors (cf. the findings of speech perception, p. 147).

Compromise?

It is evident that neither approach explains all aspects of reading behaviour; it is likely that people make use of both strategies at various stages in learning and in handling different kinds of reading problem. The 'ear' approach (sometimes referred to as a 'bottom-up' or 'Phoenician' theory, because of its reliance on basic letter units) is evidently very important during the initial stages. Perhaps after several exposures to a word, a direct print–meaning pathway comes to be built up. But the 'eye' approach (sometimes referred to as a 'top-down' or 'Chinese' theory, because of its reliance on whole-word units) is certainly needed in order to explain most of what goes on in fluent adult reading.

It should be noted that some of the arguments that come to mind, in relation to this issue, do not clearly support either theory. For example, it has been argued

that people who have been profoundly deaf since birth, and who subsequently learn to read, provide clear support for the 'eye' theory; in their cases a phonological bridge cannot be available. However, the fact that such people do have great difficulty in learning to read could be interpreted to show the importance of phonological mediation after all. Similarly, the existence of Chinese and Japanese *kanji* (pp. 197, 202) is sometimes proposed in support of the view that a phonological stage is unnecessary. But here too the evidence is ambiguous. Logographic systems seem to be difficult to learn, with few users mastering more than about 4,000 symbols out of the 50,000 or so which exist. On the other hand, very little is known about the orders of difficulty that are encountered in learning *kanji* symbols, and the degrees of expertise that exist in using logographic systems.

As with most major theoretical oppositions, elements of both approaches are required to explain the experimental findings. As a consequence, several 'compromise' models have been devised, which integrate the main features of both 'ear' and 'eye' theories. Some of these models are extremely complex, postulating a large number of components and pathways, but this is only to be expected. Despite the clear visual signals provided by the written medium, learning to read is a complex process, and only an appropriately sophisticated theory will explain it.

A COMBINED MODEL

This incorporates some of the findings from the experimental work referred to in this section. It is based on the approach of the British psychologist John Morton (1933–), but it ignores several detailed features of that model (especially on the output side) and does not use his distinctive terminology, in which the units of word recognition and production are referred to as *logogens*.
1. Familiar words are visually analysed, recognized, and assigned a meaning. Their spoken form may be retrieved from the speech-production system, which may be activated by the meaning (reading with understanding) or by the visual patterns directly (reading without understanding).
2. Unfamiliar words are visually analysed and may then be analysed phonologically (letter-to-sound conversion). The resulting sound pattern can be referred back to the auditory word-recognition system, to see whether it 'rings a bell'.

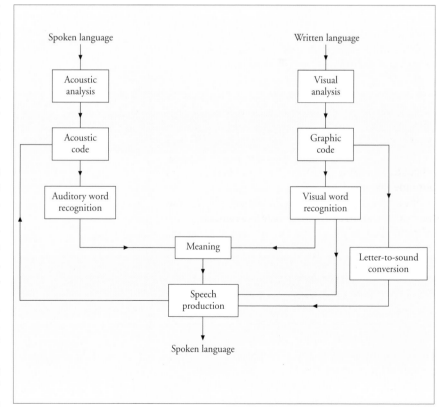

WRITING

It is extremely difficult to discover what happens when people compose a written text. Few satisfactory experimental techniques have been devised. Direct observation of the handwritten product gives very limited information, for it fails to preserve the order in which revisions are made. Direct observation of people engaged in writing tells us little about what is going on 'beneath the surface'. And introspection is of little value, for as we think about our writing activity, so we destroy its naturalness. Fluent writers are in any case unaware of what they do when they put pen to paper.

Only the most general of accounts can be given of what is involved in the writing process, therefore. Models of this process recognize at least three factors.

• There must be a planning stage, in which thoughts are organized, and a lexical/grammatical outline prepared. This involves writers working out what their readers need to know, in order for their message to be understood. In particular, they must anticipate the effect their words will have (§21).

• Writers need to be aware of the linguistic and social conventions affecting their use of written language. These include such general considerations as the need to make handwriting legible, to stay within the constraints of a single writing system, and to follow the normal conventions of graphic expression (such as writing in the expected direction) as well as the specific requirement to follow the rules of spelling and punctuation (§33).

• Writers need to choose a specific medium of expression, such as handwriting, typing, or word processing, and this requires a consideration of motor-control abilities. Several factors are involved, such as hand–eye coordination, hand grip or position, position of the body, and so on. Many people have a slow handwriting speed, or have difficulty holding an implement or working a machine (most noticeable in the case of physical handicap, p. 282). The result is not simply that a message takes longer to write. The attention and memory may be so taken up with controlling the motor activity that linguistic content and structure may be affected. People can forget what they wanted to write, even after they have begun to write it.

However, these three factors are not the whole story. For example, they do not allow for the fact that a great deal of written composition is *rewriting*. Any model must take into account the act of revision – from the first stages of making notes, jottings, and headings, through various drafts, to the final version. This is a promising field of research – the self-corrections and errors introduced while composing written language. How do writers ensure that their work is legible, readable, and lucid? How do they detect problems in these respects? How do they identify the problems? How do they correct them? Are the corrections appropriate? Many such questions await answers.

A model of written composition must also allow for the fact that what people see when they write may affect the way they think. Authors' comments are illuminating: 'It doesn't look right now I've written it down', 'That's not what I'm trying to say.' Meaning does not always exist prior to writing; often the process operates in reverse. A typical comment is Edward Albee's: 'I write to find out what I'm thinking about' (§5). Such remarks emphasize the main lesson to be learned from the study of the process of writing: it is not a merely mechanical task, a simple matter of putting speech down on paper. It is an exploration in the use of the graphic potential of a language – a creative process, an act of discovery.

TIME TO THINK

An extract from a video study describing the writing behaviour of some high-school boys. The length of the writer's pauses between words is marked in seconds. In line 5, for example, he paused for 16.6 secs; he then changed the period to a colon, and paused again before continuing.

'Pause' refers only to the ceasing of the writer's pen movement. During these pauses, other kinds of body activity may be taking place: the eyes may scan the text or look away, and the hand may move away from the text (presumably reflecting major decision-making) or stay close to it (suggesting that the writer expects to resolve the problem quickly).

The evidence suggests that pauses reflect the occurrence of mental planning and provide clues to the difficulty of the writing task. Variations in pause length may thus convey information about the process of writing, especially when considered along with other temporal aspects of writing. (From A. Matsuhashi, 1982.)

1 Truly.6successful1.1person.5-to.8-person2.3communi-
2 1.8cation3.5is1.9difficult1.3because6.9people.6in.9general1.1are.9poor
3 1.0listeners.7.0They1.0would.7rather1.4listen.5to.9themselves1.9speaking
4 2.1than.4someone.7else.5. 4.7It.9is.7my.7feeling1.9that9.7this.8occurs
5 1.6because1.1of1.2a.8basic2.7self-centeredness.16.6. 5.5people4.8tend1.2to
6 1.9be.6more.5interested.7in.7their.9own.7lives1.5to1.2bother1.0exposing
7 1.3themselves.7to.5how.7others.8live.

SOME THINGS THAT WRITERS DO

A piece of handwritten text, showing four of the things that writers do while composing:
Deletion: elimination of false starts, and unnecessary or wrongly chosen words.
Rearrangement: separating or bringing together material; changing logic or word order.
Consolidation: making the text more compact or streamlined, while retaining the content.
Differentiation: adding or expanding material.

Note that the changes give no information about the sequence of events that occurred while the text was being written.

SPELLING

Reading and writing have long been thought of as complementary skills: to read is to recognize and interpret language that has been written; to write is to plan and produce language so that it can be read. It is therefore widely assumed that being able to read implies being able to write – or, at least, being able to spell. Often, children are taught to read but given no formal tuition in spelling; it is felt that spelling will be 'picked up'. The attitude has its counterpart in the methods of 200 years ago, when teachers carefully taught spelling, and assumed that reading would follow automatically.

Recent research into spelling errors and 'slips of the pen' has begun to show that matters are not so simple. There is no necessary link between reading and writing: good readers do not always make good writers. Nor is there any necessary link between reading and spelling: there are many people who have no difficulty in reading, but who have a major persistent handicap in spelling – some researchers have estimated that this may be as many as 2% of the population. There seems moreover to be a neuro-anatomical basis for the distinction, as shown by brain-damaged adults who can read but not spell, and vice-versa (p. 274).

With children, too, there is evidence that knowledge of reading does not automatically transfer to spelling. If there were a close relationship, children should be able to read and spell the same words; but this is not so. It is commonplace to find children who can read far better than they can spell. More surprisingly, the reverse happens with some children in the early stages of reading. One study gave children the same list of words to read and to spell: several actually spelled more words correctly than they were able to read correctly.

Why so difficult?

Why should reading and spelling be so different? It is partly a matter of active, production skills being more difficult than passive, receptive ones. Spelling is a more conscious, deliberate process, which requires awareness of linguistic structure, and a good visual memory, to handle the exceptions to the regular patterns. It is possible to read by attending selectively to the cues in a text, recognizing just a few letters, and guessing the rest. It is not possible to spell in this way: spellers have to reproduce all the letters.

Also, more things can go wrong while spelling: there are far more graphemic alternatives for a phoneme than there are phonemic alternatives for a grapheme. For example, *sheep* has really only one possible pronunciation, /ʃiːp/; whereas the form /ʃiːp/ could be written in at least three different ways – *sheep, sheap, shepe*. One study worked out that in English there are 13.7 spellings per sound, but only 3.5 sounds per letter (G. Dewey, 1971).

However, the differences between reading and spelling cannot be explained simply by arguing that spelling is 'more difficult', for this would not explain such facts as children who can spell better than they read. Rather, the two skills seem to involve different learning strategies. Whereas reading is largely a matter of developing direct links between graphic expression and meaning (p. 213), spelling seems to involve an obligatory phonological component from the very outset. The study of spelling errors shows that we learn to spell by making associations between graphemes and phonemes, and not simply on the basis of how grapheme sequences 'look'. Visual strategies *can* be important; for example, with irregular words, where a phonological strategy could not work, people do sometimes write down alternative spellings to see which 'looks right'. But for the most part, it is the signs of phonological activity that are the most noticeable – as when we see beginners painfully writing C-A-T and saying the letter names of sounds as they write, or adult writers sounding out words (especially long words) while writing them down.

Why is there this preference for phonology? Perhaps because spelling involves a conscious ability to form linear sequences of letters – an ability that is routinely required for processing the linear phoneme-strings of speech, but that is not found in visual pattern recognition (as is required for whole word reading). To be a good speller, we need to have both this phonological awareness (to cope with the regular spelling patterns) and a good visual awareness (to cope with the exceptions). Poor spellers, it seems, lack this double skill.

SPELLING MISTAKES

Spelling mistakes are not very common in adult hand-written texts – descriptive studies suggest that, on average, about 1% of letters are affected, and 1–1.5% of words. One study classified errors into four formal types: omissions (*buton*), additions (*hopefull*), substitutions (*attendence*), and inversions (*tabel*). Other possibilities are rare. The diagram shows which kind of error occurs in different letter positions in a word. There is very little difference in the first letter. Insertion errors are much more likely towards the end of a word, whereas the other types are more likely towards the beginning. Substitutions and omissions seem to go together. (After A. M. Wing & A. D. Baddeley, 1980.)

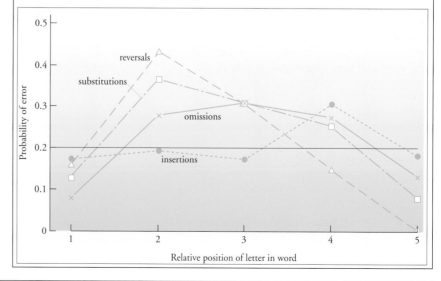

HOW IRREGULAR IS ENGLISH SPELLING?

The widespread impression that English spelling is 'chaotic' and 'unpredictable' is based on such famous sentences as 'Though the rough cough and hiccough plough me through, I ought to cross the lough.' However, descriptive studies show that this kind of thing is the exception, not the rule. It is difficult to arrive at a firm figure for the amount of spelling irregularity in a language, because people differ over which words to include in the study. Should proper names be included, for example? Should the estimates be based on word types or tokens (§15)? In one USA study, a computer analysis of 17,000 English words showed that 84% were spelled according to a regular pattern, and that only 3% were so unpredictable that they would have to be learned totally by rote (P. R. Hanna, *et al.*, 1971). A widely cited figure is that English is about 75% regular. On the other hand, the 400 or so irregular spellings are largely among the most frequently used words in the language, and this promotes a strong impression of irregularity.

Where does the irregularity come from?

The history of the language provides many reasons for the irregularities of English spelling.

• The basic fact is that, in the Anglo-Saxon period, an alphabet of 24 graphemes (the Latin alphabet, plus four new symbols) had to cope with a sound system of nearly 40 phonemes. Later, *i/j* and *u/v* were distinguished, and *w* was added, but many sounds still had to be signalled by combinations of letters.

• After the Norman conquest, French scribes respelled a great deal of the language, introducing such conventions as *qu* for *cw* (*queen*), *gh* for *h* (*night*), and *c* before *e* or *i* in such words as *circle* and *cell*.

• The printing process caused complications. Many early printers were foreign (especially from Holland), and they used their own spelling norms. Also, until the 16th century, line justification (p. 185) was often achieved by abbreviating and contracting words, and also by adding extra letters (usually an *e*) to words, rather than extra space.

• Especially after printing, the writing system did not keep pace with the sound changes that were affecting the language (§54). The 'Great Vowel Shift' of the 15th century was the main reason for the diversity of vowel spellings in such words as *name, sweet, ride, way, house*. Similarly, letters that were sounded in Anglo-Saxon became 'silent', e.g. the *k* of *know* and *knight*, or the final *e* in *stone, love*, etc.

• In the 16th century, there was a fashion to make spelling reflect Latin or Greek etymology (p. 332), e.g. the *g* was added in *reign* (from *regno*), and the *b* in *debt* (from *debitum*). Unfortunately, many false forms were concocted: for example, the *s* of *island* was added because the word was thought to come from Latin *insula*, whereas in fact it is Anglo-Saxon in origin.

• In the late 16th and early 17th centuries, many new loan words entered English from such languages as French, Latin, Greek, Spanish, Italian, and Portuguese. In the following list of words from this period, it is not difficult to see some of the new patterns of spelling (e.g. *-que, -zz-, -ll-*) that would make learning to spell consistently a much more complex matter, especially in longer words.

anonymous	epitome	idiosyncrasy
armadillo	excrescence	inclemency
balcony	exhilarate	intrigue
bizarre	galleon	moustache
brusque	gazette	piazza
canoe	genteel	pneumonia
caustic	grotesque	potato
chaos	grotto	system
cocoa	harass	vogue

The result is a system that is an amalgam of different traditions: Anglo-Saxon, French, and Classical spelling patterns are all used. The system is basically a phonemic one, but the phonemes are represented by letter *patterns* as well as single letters. In addition, the spelling preserves a great deal of information about the relationships between words (e.g. *author/authority, sign/signature*), and enables us to see links with other languages, which have many similarly spelled words. Foreigners who have only a reading knowledge of English are much helped by this similarity. But the task facing the child learner remains considerable.

A page from John Hart's *A Methode or Comfortable Beginning for all Unlearned, Whereby They May Bee Taught to Read English, in a Very Short Time, With Pleasure* (1570)

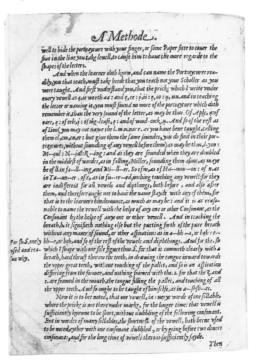

THE GHOTI PHENOMENON

A famous comment by G. B. Shaw has promoted the view that English spelling is highly irregular. He observed that *fish* could be written as *ghoti* – *f* as in 'cough', *i* as in 'women', and *sh* as in 'nation'. But joining together exceptional spellings proves nothing about the basic system of the language. An even more bizarre example is G. Dewey's (1971) spelling of *taken* as *phtheighchound* (as in 'phthisic', 'weigh', 'school', 'glamour', 'handsome').

SPELLING REFORM

A desire to eradicate irregular spelling can be traced back to the 16th century. In 1551, John Hart (d. 1574) complained of the 'vices' of English writing, which cause it to be 'learned hard and evil to read'. In the following centuries, several experimental orthographies were published. By the 19th century, the view that English needed a more consistent orthography had attracted widespread British and American support. A landmark was the publication in 1844 of an augmented Roman alphabet known as 'Phonotypy' by Isaac Pitman (1813–97). Soon after, in 1876, the Spelling Reform Association was founded in the USA, followed by the Simplified Spelling Board (1906), and the Simplified Spelling Society (1908) in Britain. A system of 'Nue Spelling' was devised and widely promulgated, and this was followed by many other proposals in the first half of this century.

Systems of spelling reform are of several kinds. Some, such as Nue Spelling (p. 218), are *standardizing* systems: they aim for a more regular use of the familiar letters; no new symbols are invented. Others, such as i.t.a. (p. 219) are *augmenting* or *supplementing* systems, which add new symbols to those of the regular alphabet. Occasionally, *supplanting* systems are devised, in which all the letters are new: an example is Shaw's Proposed British Alphabet (p. 218).

THE PROS AND CONS OF SPELLING REFORM

Advantages

• Children would save an enormous amount of time and emotional effort in learning to read.
• It would be of great help to children with learning difficulties.
• Because fewer letters would be used (an estimated saving of 15%), there would be a great saving in writers' time, and in the time and costs of typing, printing, and associated matters (paper, ink, storage, transport, etc.).
• There would be considerable benefits to foreign learners of English, and thus to the spread of English throughout the world.

Disadvantages

• There would be a major break in continuity between old and new spelling, especially in the more radical schemes. The period of transition would present major problems. It is difficult to see how a programme of spelling reform could be implemented in a practical or realistic way.

• All who have learned old spelling have a vested interest in it, and few would be willing to learn an alternative system, or wish to have their children learn one. The problem of inertia and conservatism is probably insuperable.
• The saving in costs might be outweighed by the need to reprint important works in new spelling.
• As a phonetic principle came to be intuitively recognized, differences between accents might promote diversity of spellings.
• There seems to be no agreement amongst the various groups of reformers about an optimum system. Also, the arguments are often presented in an evangelistic manner, which many find unappealing.

The history of the spelling reform movement indicates that the disadvantages are generally felt to outweigh the advantages. The problems, it would seem, are too great to be overcome. But the enthusiasm of spelling-reform bodies all over the world continues unabated.

PARLIAMENTARY PROPOSALS

The Simplified Spelling Society's publication *New Spelling* was presented to Parliament in 1949. The new system was to be introduced in three stages.

1. It would first be introduced into the primary schools; after five years, old spelling would cease to be taught.
2. During the next five years, new spelling would be compulsory in films, advertisements, and public announcements.
3. After ten years, it would be compulsory in all legal documents, records, etc. New literature would not be granted copyright unless it was printed in new spelling.

The bill was rejected, but by only 87 votes to 84! A subsequent bill, in 1953, in fact passed its first stage, though later opposition by the Ministry of Education forced it to be withdrawn.

Some irregular English spellings

all	course	listen	shoulder
although	debt	move	some
among	do	none	sugar
answer	does	of	sure
are	done	once	talk
aunt	dough	one	two
Autumn	early	only	was
blood	eye	own	water
build	folk	people	were
busy	friend	pretty	what
castle	gone	quay	where
clerk	great	receive	who
climb	have	rough	whole
colour	hour	said	women
comb	island	salt	you
come	journey	says	young
cough	key	scarce	
could	lamb	shoe	

SOUND–SPELLING CORRESPONDENCES

A U.S. spelling study (p. 216) plotted the correspondences between English vowels and their spellings. A selection of their results illustrates the way some of these relationships are highly regular, whereas others are much less so. The spelling of /a/ was entirely regular in their sample (though a few rare exceptions do exist, e.g. *plait*). On the other hand, the spelling of /ɪ/ is split between *i* and *y*, and there are many exceptions (using all vowel letters, as in *women*, *busy*, and *village*).

Sound	Spelling	%	Example
/iː/	e	72	me
	ee	10	see
	ea	10	meat
/eɪ/	a	80	late
	ai	9	sail
	ay	6	say
/aɪ/	i...e	74	side
	y	14	shy
	igh	6	high
/əʊ/	o...e	87	hope
	oa	5	boat
	ow	5	low
/uː/	u...e	90	rune
	ew	3	few
/ɪ/	i	73	bid
	y	23	happy
/e/	e	93	set
	ea	4	stealth
/a/	a	100	cat
/ʌ/	u	88	hut
	o	10	son
/ɒ/	o	95	cot
	a	5	wash

SOME SPECIFIC PROPOSALS

World English Spelling

Forskor and seven yeerz agoe our faathers braut forthh on this kontinent a nue naeshon, konseevd in liberti, and dedikaeted to the propozishon that aul men ar kreeaeted eekwal. Nou wee ar en.gaejd in a graet sivil wor, testing whether that naeshon, or eni naeshon soe konseevd and soe dedikaeted, kan long enduer. Wee ar met on a graet batlfeeld ov that wor.

Regularized English

Regularized Inglish iz a system ov spelling which lays down definit rules ov pronunciation which wood make it eazier for aull children to lern to read and write. In aull probability it wood lead to a saving ov at least wun year's wurk for aull schoolchildren. It wood aulso contribute very largely towaurdz abolition ov the existing amount ov illiteracy and backwardness in reading.

New Spelling

Forskor and seven yeerz agoe our faadherz braut forth on dhis kontinent a nue naeshon, konseevd in liberti, and dedikaeted to dhe propozishon dhat aul men ar kreeaeted eekwal. Nou we ar en.gaejd in a graet sivil wor, testing whedher dhat naeshon or eni naeshon soe konseevd and soe dedikaeted, kan long enduer. We ar met on a graet batlfeeld ov dhat wor.

Simpler Spelling Association

forskor and sevn yɛrz əgo aur faɦərz brɔt forɦ. ɒn his kɒntinənt ə niu naʃən, kənsɛvd in libərti, and dedikɑted tu ƀ prɒpəziʃən ɦat ɔl men ɑr krɛɑted ɛkwəl.

nɑɪ we ɑr engɑjd in ə grɑt sivil wɔr, testiŋ hwehər ɦat naʃən ɔr eni naʃən so kənsɛvd and so dedikɑted, kan lɔŋ endiur. we ar met ɒn ə grɑt batl-fɛld ɒv ɦat wɔr.

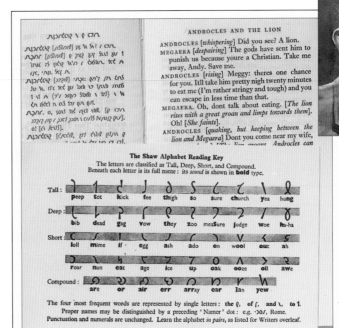

THE SHAW ALPHABET FOR WRITERS

One of the most recent alphabet inventions was inspired by George Bernard Shaw (1856–1950); it is often referred to as 'Shavian'. As a writer, Shaw felt there was an enormous waste of time and effort involved in English spelling, and he was a vigorous campaigner for a new alphabet. He himself always wrote in Pitman's Shorthand, which was then transcribed by a secretary.

In his will, Shaw appointed the Public Trustee to seek and publish an alphabet of at least 40 letters to enable English to be written without indicating single sounds by groups of letters or by diacritical marks. He termed this the 'Proposed British Alphabet'. There was a competition, and in due course Kingsley Read's design was adjudged the winner.

The alphabet follows the normal basic conventions of English, being read from left to right, and using word spaces. Punctuation and numerals are unchanged. There are four types of letter: *shorts*, *talls* (letters with ascending strokes), *deeps* (letters with descending strokes), and *compounds*.

Several phonetic principles are used; e.g. voiceless and voiced consonants (§27) are related by reversed shapes. Capitals are not distinguished. Proper names are identified by a raised 'namer' dot. The four words *the*, *of*, *and*, and *to*, are given separate symbols: , , , and respectively. In the diagram above, the letter names are given below the symbols: the sound of each letter is given in bold type.

ARGUING THE CASE

The flavour of the arguments surrounding spelling reform is well captured in this extract from a letter written by Shaw to the periodical *Tit-Bits* (22 March 1946). He is reacting to an earlier proposal from the reformer, Mont Follick:

Everything that Dr Follick says about our spelling is true; but it was said by Alexander J. Ellis a hundred years ago, and has been repeated again and again by the most eminent phoneticians without producing the smallest effect. The reason is that as so presented the change has seemed enormously expensive and the phonetically spelt texts ridiculous and even sometimes obscure.

What is needed is a new alphabet of not less than 42 letters, which is the lowest number sufficient to represent all the sounds of spoken English recognizable by a single symbol each. Dr Follick, by confining himself to 22 letters of the present alphabet, is compelled to represent single sounds by several letters, and has landed himself in such monstrosities as 'ei tscheir' to spell 'a chair'; 9 letters for 3 sounds! I can write 'a chair' 12 times in a minute, and 'ei tscheir' only 9 times. The number of minutes in a day is 1,440. In a year 525,600!!!

To realize the annual difference in favour of a forty-two letter phonetic alphabet as against Dr Follick's Ootomatik alphabet you must multiply by the number of minutes in the year, the number of people in the world who are continuously writing English words, casting types, manufacturing printing and writing machines, by which time the total figure will have become so astronomical that you will realize that the cost of spelling even one sound with two letters has cost us centuries of unnecessary labour. A new British 42 letter alphabet would pay for itself a million times over not only in hours but in moments. When this is grasped, all the useless twaddle about enough and cough and laugh and simplified spelling will be dropped, and the economists and statisticians will be set to work to gather in the orthographic Golconda.

	Traditional column				*Augmented column*		
	NAME	CHARACTER	EXAMPLE		NAME	CHARACTER	EXAMPLE
1.	ae	æ	ænjel				
2.	bee	b	beetl	25.	zess	ʒ	houseʒ
3.	kee	c	curly	26.	whae	wh	whether
4.	dee	d	didn't	27.	chae	ch	chicken
5.	ee	ee	eeven	28.	ith	th	thicken
6.	ef	f	færly	29.	thee	th	therfor
7.	gae	g	given	30.	ish	ʃh	ʃhwdn't
8.	hae	h	hasn't	31.	zhee	ʒ	uezueal
9.	ie	ie	ievory	32.	ing	ŋ	thinkiŋ
10.	jae	j	jeneral				
11.	kae	k	kwickly	33.	ur	r	absurd
12.	el	l	lieon				
13.	em	m	mœtor	34.	ah	a	farther
14.	en	n	never	35.	aw	au	aufœl
15.	oe	œ	œnly	36.	at	a	atlas
16.	pee	p	prievæt	37.	et	e	ended
17.	rae	r	rythm	38.	it	i	idiot
18.	ess	s	sudden	39.	ot	o	offis
19.	tee	t	tueba	40.	ut	u	uther
20.	ue	ue	uesfœl	41.	oot	ω	wωdn't
21.	vee	v	very	42.	oo	(ω)	tatt(ω)
22.	wae	w	wether	43.	ow	ou	allou
23.	yae	y	yuŋster	44.	oi	oi	annoi
24.	zee	z	zombi				

little red hen

Wuns upon a tiem
little red hen
livd in a barn with her fiev chicks.
a pig, a cat and a duck mæd
ther hœm in the sæm barn.
eech dæ little red hen
led her chicks out
tω lωk for fωd.
but the pig, the cat and the duck
wωd not lωk for fωd.

i.t.a. The Initial Teaching Alphabet, devised in 1959 by James Pitman (1901–85), was a system of 44 lower-case letters, each corresponding to a single phoneme (§28). Extra symbols were introduced to handle contrasts not systematically represented by traditional orthography – hence its characterization as an 'augmented' Roman alphabet. The 24 tradi-tional letters were retained. Capitals were larger versions of the lower-case letters.

The i.t.a. was not a proposal for the permanent reform of English spelling, but a system intended to assist children in their first encounter with reading. Irregularities were not eliminated, simply post-poned. The main aim was to design a system that closely resembled traditional orthography, to ensure an easy trans-fer to normal spelling in due course. As a result, certain fea-tures often eliminated in spelling-reform proposals were retained on the grounds that they would aid this tran-sition; for example, the system kept double letters, as in *appl*, and vowels in unstressed sylla-bles were not all reduced to one. The system was a com-promise between simplifica-tion and familiarity.

The i.t.a. was not a 'method' for teaching reading (p. 252); but it could be used in relation to several such meth-ods. For example, phonic approaches might be aided by the consistent links between graphemes and phonemes; and look-and-say approaches might find the appearance of each letter in only one form helpful, because it would remove variations in the visual patterns of words.

At its peak, i.t.a. was being used in several countries, including some where English was being taught as a second language (§62). In the 1980s, however, its popularity drasti-cally declined.

A SUCCESSFUL REFORM

The differences between British and Ameri-can spelling show that changes can be intro-duced if circumstances are right. The changes derive from the rules introduced by Noah Webster (1758–1843), such as the use of -*or* for -*our* and -*er* for -*re*. In his later writings, Webster came to advocate spelling reform.

Examples of the spelling differences include the following (*indicates a rule that applies to many other words of the same type).

U.S.	*Britain*
catalog	catalogue
cruelest	cruellest*
gray	grey
honor	honour*
license (noun)	licence
liter	litre*
program	programme (except in computing)

U.S.	*Britain*
theater	theatre*
traveler	traveller*
worshiping	worshipping

Several spellings have come to be used in both countries, but there are still strong usage preferences:

U.S.	*Britain*
encyclopedia	encyclopaedia*
jail	gaol
leaped	leapt*
omelet	omelette
practice (verb)	practise

Right: The title page of Webster's success-ful 'Blue-backed Speller' (1783)

A
Grammatical Inſtitute,
OF THE
ENGLISH LANGUAGE,
COMPRISING,
An eaſy, conciſe, and ſyſtematic Method of
EDUCATION,
Deſigned for the Uſe of Engliſh Schools
IN AMERICA.
IN THREE PARTS.
PART I.
CONTAINING,
A new and accurate Standard of Pronunciation.
BY NOAH WEBSTER, A. M.
Uſus eſt Norma Loquendi. CICERO.
HARTFORD:
PRINTED BY HUDSON & GOODWIN,
FOR THE AUTHOR.

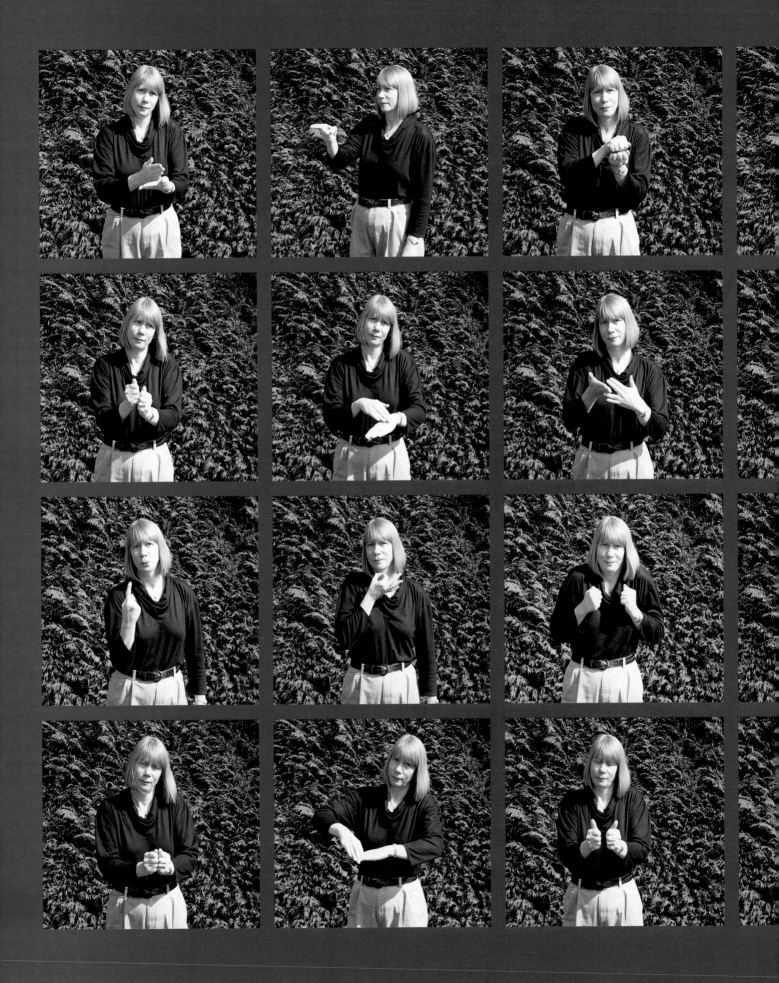

The medium of language: signing and seeing

PART VI

In recent years, the study of spoken and written language has been supplemented by interest in a third means of linguistic communication – sign language, or simply, 'sign'. This mode of behaviour is of particular importance because, like speech (and unlike writing, and other codes), several of its manifestations have a natural, biological basis. Most of this interest is directed at the various natural sign languages used by the deaf population (§46), but any survey must also take into account the nature of the artificially constructed sign languages and systems that have been devised to help hearing people communicate with the deaf. Other kinds of signing behaviour used by the hearing population are more restricted in character; these are described in relation to nonverbal communication in §64.

Sign is one of the most neglected aspects of communication study, as is reflected in the regrettably small extent of this part of the encyclopedia. The neglect is due to several factors – not least the widespread popular as well as scholarly reluctance to accept the possibility that sign could be a real language, worthy of systematic study. Researchers

in the field face several difficulties. The number of people for whom signing is their natural, everyday language is relatively small, and it is not always easy to find people who are able to communicate in a fluent and unselfconscious way. Moreover, it is only since the 1970s that film and video techniques have become sufficiently routine to enable the basic data to be recorded for analysis. But recording the data is only a first step: special ways of analysing and transcribing the data have to be devised, to enable appropriately detailed descriptions to be made. As a result, the true complexity of this medium of visual communication has begun to be appreciated only in recent years.

Part VI therefore begins with a consideration of several popular fallacies about sign language, in particular stressing the importance of seeing sign as a language in its own right. The study of sign language structure is then introduced with reference to American Sign Language, which has attracted most of the linguistic research since the 1960s. Part VI concludes by looking at some of the other signing systems that have been developed for use with the hearing-impaired population.

A filmed sequence of signs from British Sign Language, used as part of an experiment into the way deaf people remember signs. The signs, in sequence are: (top row) true, you, worth, car; (line 2) milk, blue, through, new; (line 3) who, few, cold, paper; (line 4) agree, wash, brother, break. The static nature of these pictures means that it is possible to read in other interpretations in some cases.

MYTHS AND REALITY

The first step in considering the nature of sign language is to eradicate traditional misconceptions about its structure and function. Popular opinions about the matter are quite plain: sign language is not a real language but little more than a system of sophisticated gesturing; signs are simply pictorial representations of external reality; and because of this, there is just one sign language, which can be understood all over the world. It is now clear, from the results of the first research studies of this subject, dating from the 1960s, that all of these opinions are wrong.

A clear distinction must be drawn, first of all, between sign language and gesture. To sign is to use the hands in a conscious, 'verbal' manner, to express the same range of meaning as would be achieved by speech (especially by grammar, §16). By contrast, gesturing is far less systematic and comprehensive; there are in fact very few hand gestures (§64), and these are used in *ad hoc* way to express a small number of basic notions. Everyone can gesture; but few have learned to sign. (A similar point can be made about facial expressions and body movements.)

Some of the hand movements of sign language can be plausibly interpreted by non-signers because they reflect properties of the external world (they are *iconic*); but the vast majority of signs are not. It is possible that many of the signs were iconic when they were first devised, but little information is available about this point in the past, which some have speculated may be as early as the origins of human language (§49). In any case, whatever the original situation, the iconicity has been lost in most instances because of the influence of linguistic change, which affects sign as it does spoken language (§54).

As a result of linguistic change, and because of independent creation in different parts of the world, no single sign language exists. There are many such languages (American, French, Danish ...), and they are not mutually intelligible. They use different signs and different rules of sign formation and sentence structure. Even within an area that uses the same spoken language, the differences may be so great as to preclude mutual comprehension – as happens, for example, between British and American Sign Language (BSL and ASL).

Sign languages have a structure of comparable complexity to spoken and written language and perform a similar range of functions. There are rules governing

COMPARING SIGN LANGUAGES

When a comparison is made of different sign languages, structural differences clearly emerge. In a study of Chinese Sign Language (CSL) and American Sign Language (ASL), for example, it proved possible to identify several systematic differences in the use of hand shapes and movements.

• There are signs in both languages that have the same form, but different meaning: for example, ASL signers recognize the CSL sign for *father*, but interpret it as the ASL sign *secret*; CSL *help* is equivalent to ASL *push*.

• Some CSL signs use sign shapes or movements which are not possible formations in the ASL system, such as the signs for *Wednesday* and *introduce*.

• Some CSL signs have the form of possible signs in ASL, but are not in fact actually used in ASL; for example, elements of the CSL sign for *distracted* are like the ASL signs for *yellow* and *separate*, but the particular CSL combination is not an ASL sign.
(After E. Klima & U. Bellugi, 1979.)

CSL *distracted*

CSL *father*, like ASL *secret*

CSL *Wednesday*

ASL *yellow*

CSL *help*, like ASL *push*

CSL *introduce*

ASL *separate*

ICONIC SIGNS?

The signs of sign language are often deceptively iconic. After its meaning has been revealed, a sign may appear 'obvious'; but it proves not so easy to predict the meaning from the shape of the sign alone. This can be seen even in a sign language which aims for maximum iconicity. The pictures are of Gestuno, a system adopted by the Unification of Signs Commission of the World Federation of the Deaf in 1975. Once one is told that these are animal signs, it becomes possible to make reasonable guesses at what they mean – but even so, the guesses are often wrong (glosses are given at the foot of the page).

1: hen   2: horse   3: lion
4: monkey

the way signs are formed, and how they are sequenced – rules that have to be learned either as children (e.g. from deaf parents, §46) or as adults (e.g. when working with the deaf). There are a large number of signs available within a sign language (around 4,000 have been recorded in ASL), and these are used to convey a considerable range of meaning. When two fluent signers communicate, they provide impressive evidence of the creative potential of sign, and of its social and psychological reality as a language.

MODERN DEVELOPMENTS

Very little information is available about the early history of sign languages. References to deaf signing are found in Greek and Roman writings, but there are no details. In recent times, the study of signing is dated from the work of the French educator, Abbé Charles Michel de l'Epée (1712–89), who in 1775 developed a sign language for use in a school for the deaf in Paris. The origins of his system are obscure: several of his signs were modifications of those used by the French native deaf population, but he also made some use of the Spanish manual alphabet (p. 227), and he may have incorporated some of the signs used by the Spanish Benedictine monks. Several foreign educators studied at his school, and the influence of this system spread to many parts of the world, including Russia, Ireland, and America. For example, the American educator Thomas Gallaudet (1787–1851), together with Laurent Clerc (1785–1869), a teacher of the deaf, brought the signs to the USA, where they came to be used alongside those already in use by the American deaf population. Modern American Sign Language (ASL, or Ameslan) derives from this system.

When a sign language becomes widely used, it develops the same kind of dialects and varieties as occur in spoken language. This kind of variation can be seen in ASL, which is now used by over half a million deaf people – by many, as a native language. Some varieties are regional in origin (§8), but others are due to the age at which the sign language is learned, and to social factors, such as the home environment (whether the parents are deaf) and the educational background of the signer. A further important variable is the extent to which the sign language has been influenced by the spoken language of the community. A dialect continuum (p. 25) seems to exist among the American deaf, and this is probably a universal phenomenon. The continuum ranges from ASL varieties that show no influence of spoken language to those that have been markedly shaped by properties of English – by word order, in particular. Several pidgin varieties of signing exist along this continuum (§55).

An important stage in the history of sign language analysis took place in the 1960s, when the term *cherology* was coined on analogy with *phonology* (§28) to refer to the study of the contrastive units (*cheremes*) that occur in a sign language. The structural analyses subsequently made provided a valuable indication of the difficulty researchers face as they try to 'capture' the dynamic, multi-dimensional properties of sign.

In this approach, three classes of cheremes are identified (after W. C. Stokoe *et al.* 1965):
• *tab* (*tabula*) the location in the sign space where a sign is made;
• *dez* (*designator*) the active hand configuration used to make the sign; and
• *sig* (*signation*) the action of the active hand. Signs are described as simultaneously occurring combinations of tab, dez, and sig.

Various constraints affect the use of these contrasts. Not all possible combinations occur. Some are physically impossible. Some are not used by convention – for example, signs are not made from head to shoulder but from head to chest. There is a strong tendency towards hand symmetry: if a sign requires two active hands, both hands will have identical shapes and orientations. Several such constraints govern the structure of a sign language, and a major focus of recent research has been to discover the rules governing sign formation, and the contexts (such as poetry, irony, or humour) where departures from these rules are tolerated.

TRANSCRIBING SIGNS

A series of signs with their tab and dez elements transcribed (see below). Sig actions cannot be clearly shown without moving film. The pictures show the right hand as dez and the left, when used, as tab. Left-handed signers often use the left hand as dez. The triple mark above the V shows that the sign is made with the fingers bent.

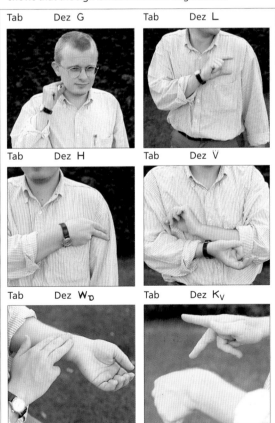

Tab	Dez G	Tab	Dez L
Tab	Dez H	Tab	Dez V̈́
Tab	Dez W_ᴅ	Tab	Dez K_V

SOME ASL SIGN SYMBOLS

Tab

ᴨ	neck
[ ]	trunk
\	upper arm
⌐	elbow, forearm
⍺	wrist, arm on its back
ᴅ	wrist, arm face down

Dez

5	spread hand
G	index finger points from fist
H	index and second finger, side by side, extended
I	little finger extended from compact hand
K	index finger points from fist, and thumb touches middle of second finger
L	thumb and index finger at right angles, others usually bent into palm
O	fingers curved and squeezed together over thumb
V	index and second fingers extended/spread ('victory')
W	thumb and little finger touch, other fingers extended/spread

Sig

∧	upward movement
∨	downward movement
>	rightward movement
⍺	palm-up rotation
ᴅ	palm-down rotation
#	closing action
℘	circular action
⊙	entering action

SOME ASL WORDS

O 5 ℘⊙#	included
O⊙ F ∧	soul, spirit(ual)
O⊙ F ℘	tea
O⊙ H⍺̂	resign, quit

Note: When two sig elements are placed horizontally, they are signed in sequence; when placed vertically, they are signed together.

A great deal is now known about the structure of natural signing, following several years of detailed study of American Sign Language (ASL). It has become clear that this language has a highly developed structure which needs to be described in its own terms. And as research continues on other sign languages, similar conclusions are beginning to emerge.

Describing sign language 'in its own terms' is, however, easier said than done. We are so used to thinking of language in terms of the structures of speech or writing that it is extremely difficult to grasp what is going on when a completely different medium in involved. This can be seen by considering the effect of a monologue in sign when it is given a fairly literal 'translation' into English. Here is an extract from one study (I. M. Schlesinger & L. Namir, 1978, p. 100):

Two children. One marry. Two grandchildren. Work close frat building. One still school. Mother gone. My aunt true me phone. Sorry can't funeral. Me work. Me awful cry. Come night.

This kind of transcription inevitably gives the impression of a reduced or simplified language – the grammar is highly telegraphic, there are no inflectional endings, and words are omitted. But this is to judge one language by the criterion of another – something that breaks a cardinal principle of modern language study (§2). A word-for-word translation from a foreign language (§57) would give just as odd a result. In omitting articles or the copula verb *be* (as in *man happy*), for example, ASL is no different from Russian. And, conversely, ASL makes use of many conventions that other languages lack – such as the simultaneous use of signals (e.g. hand signs plus facial expressions, eye movements, and shifts of the body), that literal translations cannot easily convey. Moreover, the speed of fluent signing – between one and two signs per second – produces a conversational rate that is comparable to that of speech. It usually takes longer to make a sign than to pronounce a word, but many signs express a meaning far more succinctly than the corresponding spoken output.

THE USE OF SIGN SPACE

The expressive potential of sign can be appreciated only by looking at signing behaviour in some detail. There is, first of all, a three-dimensional *sign space*: vertically, this consists of the distance just below the waist to the top of the head (signs are rarely made above the head, below the waist, or towards the back of the head or body); laterally, the space forms a 'bubble' which extends outwards in front of the signer from extreme right to extreme left. Within this space, there is room to make an indefinitely large number of signs, and it is possible to see several organizational principles operating. 'Locations' can be established that identify different sentence elements or semantic functions.

- Time relationships can be expressed by dividing the space into neutral (present), further forward (future), and further back (past) areas; these areas can then be used both for tense forms and for time adverbs (*then, now, next, last,* etc.).
- Several persons (pronouns) can be distinguished using different spatial areas: *you* is front-centre; one third-person form is signed to the right; another to the left; and others divide up the intervening space. Moreover, once a space is established for a given person, it is normally 'reserved' for that person for the remainder of the conversation.
- Questions can be signalled by an appropriate accompanying facial expression, such as raised eyebrows and backwards head tilt.
- Great use is made of reduplication (p. 177) to express such notions as plurality, aspect, degree, or emphasis; for example, such verbal meanings as continuity, repetition, or habituality can all be signed by repeating a verb sign with varying speed.
- The use of pause between signs or sign sequences is available to mark grammatical boundaries.
- The whole spatial area can be enlarged or confined to express 'louder' or 'quieter' signing.

The normal signing space

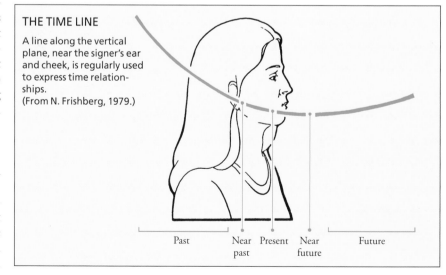

THE TIME LINE

A line along the vertical plane, near the signer's ear and cheek, is regularly used to express time relationships.
(From N. Frishberg, 1979.)

Past   Near past   Present   Near future   Future

ASPECT MODULATIONS

ASL makes use of a complex system of simultaneous sign 'modulations', analogous in function to the sequential inflections of spoken morphology (p. 90). These can be illustrated by the forms used to convey semantic contrasts of aspect (p. 93). In one study, the variations on the sign for *sick* were analysed, and several aspectual modulations were recognized. Eight of these are illustrated in the figure below. The horizontal dimension represents the relative length of the sign, and the vertical divisions show the number of repetitions of the movement. The blank sections represent the relative durations of 'holds' (i.e. points at which the hand is held steady). Muscular tension, accentuation, and certain other characteristics of the movements are not represented.
(After E. Klima & U. Bellugi, 1979.)

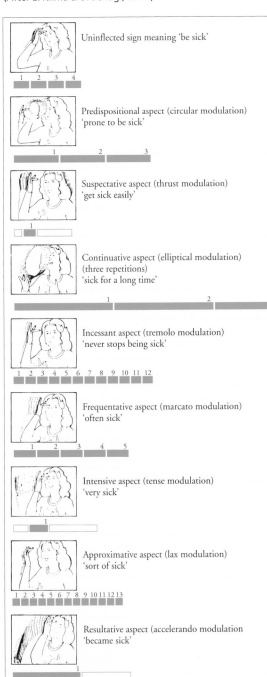

Uninflected sign meaning 'be sick'

Predispositional aspect (circular modulation) 'prone to be sick'

Suspectative aspect (thrust modulation) 'get sick easily'

Continuative aspect (elliptical modulation) (three repetitions) 'sick for a long time'

Incessant aspect (tremolo modulation) 'never stops being sick'

Frequentative aspect (marcato modulation) 'often sick'

Intensive aspect (tense modulation) 'very sick'

Approximative aspect (lax modulation) 'sort of sick'

Resultative aspect (accelerando modulation 'became sick'

Relative sign duration

STRUCTURE CONTRASTS

The non-manual activities which accompany a sequence of signs can have an important structural function in ASL.

(a) The sequence of signs 'woman-forget-purse' is used as a statement, *The woman forgot the purse* (the articles are not separately signed).

(b) The same sign sequence is accompanied by a forward movement of the head and shoulders, and the eyebrows are raised: this would express the yes-no question, *Did the woman forget the purse?*

(c) The same sequence is used as part of the sentence 'woman-forget-purse-recently-arrive' (*The woman who forgot the purse has just arrived*). Here, the relative clause section (*The woman who forgot the purse*) is signalled by having the brow and upper lip raised, and the head tilted back.
(After S. K. Liddell, 1980.)

Several sign languages may be in regular use within the boundaries of a particular speech community. The most widely used are the concept-based systems that have developed naturally among the deaf communities, and it is these that are most commonly referred to as 'sign language' – American Sign Language, British Sign Language, Danish Sign Language, etc. In addition, in recent years educators and linguists have devised several new kinds of signing systems. These are mainly taught to deaf children or adults, but they are also sometimes found being used with other handicapped populations.

The greatest proliferation of new signing systems has been within the English speech community. Most approaches involve modifications of ASL or BSL, with the aim of bringing the signing closer to spoken English. Several of these systems emerged in the late 1960s in the USA, notably Seeing Essential English (1966), and its two derivatives, Linguistics of Visual English (1971) and Signing Exact English(1972). Other systems were devised that closely followed the structure of speech, such as Signed English (1969) and Manual English (1972). Given the urgent need for progress in the educational domain, and the sincerity and enthusiasm of the creators, all of the systems have been put to valuable use in a range of teaching situations. However, objective techniques for evaluating their relative strengths and weaknesses have not so far been devised.

Each of these systems aims to reflect the structure of English, but they do this in different ways. All follow English word order, but they differ in the way they form signs, and in how much finger spelling (see below) they use. Many arbitrary decisions have to be made by the system's creator; for example, it is not obvious how to allocate signs to such forms as irregular nouns, verbs, or adjectives (§16). Should past-tense forms (*took, gone*, etc.) be signed with the same sign as past participle forms (*taken, went,* etc.) or with different signs? Should *took* be signed as '*take* + PAST', '*take* + *-ed*', '*take* + *e* + *d*', or '*t* + *o* + *o* + *k*'? There are many such possibilities, and different systems go in different directions, with varying degrees of consistency.

AMER-IND

Over the centuries, the North American Indians have spoken hundreds of languages from several different families (p. 322). It is not surprising, then, that they developed a form of signing as a means of communication between different tribes. Following early descriptions of this 'hand talk', an adaptation was made for use with the handicapped by Madge Skelly (1903–), an Indian-born speech pathologist. The system is conceived as a gestural code, rather than a language. It contains a limited number of signs, representing concrete meanings, and it has no grammatical structure apart from sequence. The signs are chosen so as to be immediately recognizable, so that the viewer can interpret without formal instruction, and regardless of language background. Four signs are illustrated below.

PAGET-GORMAN SIGN SYSTEM (PGSS)

The earliest proposal to be widely adopted in modern times was based on Richard Paget's *A Systematic Sign Language* (1951).

After his death in 1955, this system was developed in Britain by his widow, Grace Paget, and Pierre Gorman, at that time librarian of the Royal National Institute for the Deaf. It contains some 3,000 signs, representing the words and morphemes (p. 90) of spoken English. Sentences are signed following English word order. The system makes use of a set of 'basic' signs – semantic fields such as 'action', 'animal', 'colour', 'container', and 'food'. Different words belonging to each field are identified with reference to the same basic sign, plus an identifying sign.

Six of the PGSS basic signs

1 action 4 container
2 animal 5 thing
3 colour 6 think

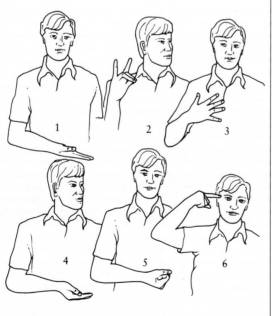

The different colour words, for example, are all derived from the basic sign above. To sign *blue*, one hand is held as for *colour*, while the first finger of the other hand is held pointing up, back outwards, in line with the signer's side (i.e. the colour of the sky). To sign *red*, the same basic sign is used, while the other hand makes the sign for *blood*.

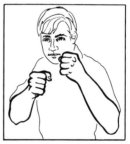

fight

heaven

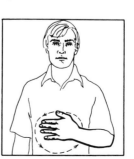

hungry

mirror

FINGER SPELLING

Finger spelling, or dactylology, is a signing system in which each letter of the ordinary alphabet is given its own sign. The principle can be applied to any language which has developed an alphabetic writing system. However, there are conventional differences: in particular, the British manual alphabet is formed using two hands, whereas the American and Swedish systems, for example, use only one.

The main strength of finger spelling is its great scope and flexibility. It is quick to learn and can then be used to sign an indefinite number of words. It is a particularly useful system for signing proper names, which are not given their own signs in other sign systems. However, it is a slow system to use, rarely exceeding 300 letters per minute (about 60 words). Moreover, it cannot be used at all unless one is able to spell (a problem for young children, who also have difficulty controlling the hand shapes required). From the receiver's point of view, it is difficult to distinguish the hand shapes at a distance, and, even close to, intelligibility can be a problem if the rate of signing speeds up, and the signer begins to omit letters.

Finger spelling is best thought of as an auxiliary signing system, a convenient bridge between spoken or written language and sign language proper. The use of the method has been documented from the 17th century. The philosopher George Dalgarno, for example, recommended its use by all members of a family whenever it contained a deaf child, arguing that the acquisition of spelled language would thereby be as natural as the acquisition of spoken language. In modern times, some educational approaches make a great deal of use of it – the 'Rochester' method in the U.S., for example, is based on a combination of finger spelling and speech, and it is reported that a Cyrillic manual alphabet is widely used in Russia.

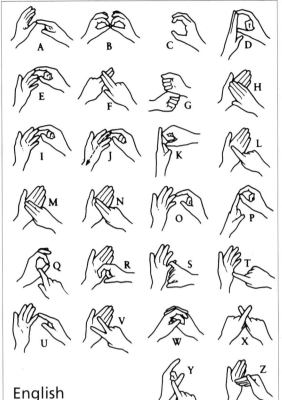

English

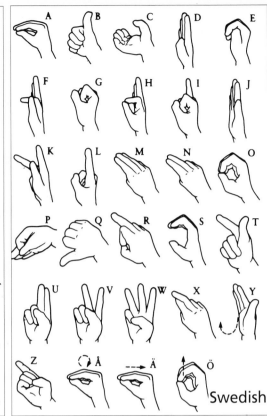

Swedish

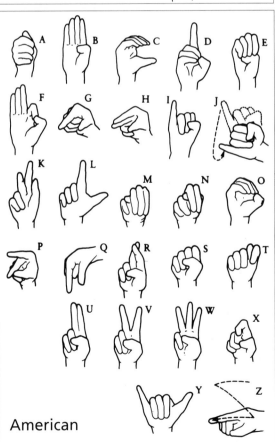

American

CUED SPEECH

Normal lip-reading techniques allow only certain sounds – those towards the front of the mouth – to be easily distinguished; and there are many sentences which lip readers find difficult to make out, especially when the context is unclear (such as *It is in the tin*, where the lip position is almost identical throughout). Cued Speech hopes to eliminate such difficulties by making it possible for a deaf person to 'see' the sounds of speech as they are spoken. It is a system of hand cues that are used alongside lip movements to draw attention to the phonemic (§28) contrasts of speech. The system was devised in 1966 by the American educator R. Orin Cornett (1913–), and it has since been adapted for use in 56 languages (as of 1995).

Below: The system uses 12 cues for help in clarifying the 44 English phonemes. Vowel cues are shown by the position of the hand. Four positions are recognized: at the side, throat, chin, and mouth. Each position signals a group of three vowels of different lip shapes; vowels with the same lip shape can then be readily distinguished by noting the accompanying hand position. Consonant cues are shown by the shape of the hand. There are eight hand shapes, each of which is associated with a group of consonants of different lip shapes; as with vowels, consonants with the same lip shape can then be distinguished by noting the accompanying hand shape.

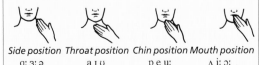

Side position Throat position Chin position Mouth position
ɑː ɜː ə   a ɪ ʊ   ɒ e uː   ʌ iː ɔː

PART VII

Child language acquisition

The study of how children learn to speak has proved to be one of the most fascinating, important, and complicated branches of language study in recent years. The fascination of the subject stems from the natural interest people take in the developing abilities of young children. Its importance lies in the way that language acquisition research can assist our understanding of language as a whole, and also in the many applications of this research – especially in the field of child language handicap (Part VIII). The complexity arises from the enormous difficulties that are encountered as soon as anyone attempts to establish and explain the facts of language development, especially in the very young child.

Part VII begins, therefore, with a discussion of some of the approaches and methods that have been used to find out about children's language – diaries, recordings, experiments, tests, profiles, and other procedures. The result of this enquiry has been an explosion of information about many details of language acquisition, and an increased awareness of such general issues as the nature of developmental stages, and the relationship between speech production and comprehension in the course of early learning. Several major theoretical accounts of child language acquisition have also been proposed in recent years, and these are reviewed in the final part of this section.

Following these general observations, sections 39–43 examine different aspects of the language acquisition process in somewhat greater detail. We begin with the early development of vocalization in infants during the first year of life, and the associated emergence of the skills of speech perception and speech interaction. Around 1 year of age, a more clearly defined linguistic ability is apparent, and it then proves possible to begin analysis in conventional linguistic terms, using the distinctions recognized in Parts III and IV. We look separately at phonological, grammatical, semantic, and pragmatic development, with particular reference to studies of preschool children.

Once children arrive in school, they meet a completely fresh range of factors that influence their language development. The final section of this Part therefore reviews recent and contemporary educational approaches to the question of how linguistic skills should be fostered in school. We begin with a discussion of the issues that arise in relation to spoken language (or 'oracy'), proceed to a review of the corresponding approaches that have been proposed in relation to the teaching of reading, and conclude with an account of current thinking about the most neglected area of all, the child's developing awareness of written language.

An ingenious way of fostering an early interest in words: a 'reading express' in a public library.

For over 200 years, scholars have shown an interest in the way children learn to speak and understand their first language. Several small-scale studies were carried out, especially towards the end of the 19th century, using data recorded in parental diaries. But detailed, systematic investigation did not begin until the middle decades of the 20th century, when the tape recorder came into routine use. This made it possible to keep a permanent record of samples of child speech, so that analysts could listen repeatedly to obscure extracts, and thus produce a detailed and accurate description. Since then, the subject has attracted enormous multi-disciplinary interest, notably from linguists and psychologists, who have used a variety of observational and experimental techniques to study the process of language acquisition in depth.

Central to the success of this rapidly emerging field lies the ability of researchers to devise satisfactory methods for eliciting linguistic data from children. The problems that have to be faced are quite different from those encountered when working with adults (p. 414). Many of the linguist's routine techniques of enquiry cannot be used with children. It is not possible to carry out certain kinds of experiments, because aspects of children's cognitive development – such as their ability to pay attention, or to remember instructions – may not be sufficiently advanced. Nor is it easy to get children to make systematic judgments about language – a task that is virtually impossible below the age of 3. And anyone who has tried to obtain even the most basic kind of data – a tape recording of a representative sample of a child's speech – knows how frustrating this can be. Some children, it seems, are innately programmed to switch off as soon as they notice a tape recorder being switched on.

Since the 1960s, however, several sophisticated recording techniques and experimental designs have been devised. Children can be observed and recorded through one-way-vision windows or using radio microphones, so that the effects of having an investigator in the same room as the child can be eliminated. Large-scale sampling programmes have been carried out, with children sometimes being recorded for several years. Particular attention has been paid to devising experimental techniques that fall well within a child's intellectual level and social experience. Even prelinguistic infants have been brought into the research: acoustic techniques are used to analyse their vocalizations, and their ability to perceive the world around them is monitored using special recording equipment (§39). The result has been a growing body of reliable data on the stages of language acquisition from birth until puberty.

ANCIENT QUESTIONS

Child language study has exercised its fascination on rulers and scholars alike for over 2,000 years, especially in relation to such questions as the origins and growth of language (§49). Many felt that the study of linguistic development in the child (language *ontogenesis*) would provide clues about the linguistic development of the human race (language *phylogenesis*). Some interesting similarities have been noted between the vocal tracts of infants and non-human primates (§49), but there is still a great gap between the emotional expression of infants and the propositional content of adult language, which studies of acquisition have not yet been able to bridge.

Someone who was remarkably modern in his views was the Mogul Emperor of India, Akbar the Great (1542–1605). He believed that speech arose from people listening to others, and that children who were isolated from human contact would not be able to speak. A contemporary Persian account, the *Akbarnama* of Abu'l-Fazl, takes up the story:

As some who heard this appeared to deny it, he, in order to convince them, had a *serai* [mansion] built in a place which civilized sounds did not reach. The newly born were put into that place of experience, and honest and active guards were put over them. For a time, tongue-tied wet-nurses were admitted there, As they had closed the door of speech, the place was commonly called the Gang Mahal (the dumb-house). On the 9th August 1582 he went out to hunt. That night he stayed in Faizabad, and next day he went with a few special attendants to the house of experiment. No cry came from that house of silence nor was any speech heard there. In spite of their four years, they had no part of the talisman of speech, and nothing came out except the noise of the dumb.
(From H. Beveridge, 1897–1910, pp. 581–2.)

Akbar the Great

PARENTAL DIARIES

The earliest approach to the study of child language was to keep a written diary of observations about one's own child. Several 19th-century scholars engaged in this task, including August Schleicher and Charles Darwin. The approach fell out of favour with the advent of audio- and video-recording techniques, which permitted a more systematic, objective, and comprehensive analysis. It has nonetheless occasionally been used with good effect in recent decades – notably in Werner Leopold's four-volume study of his daughter Hildegard, published between 1939 and 1949, *Speech Development of a Bilingual Child*.

Below are some extracts from the earliest known diary study, by the German philosopher Dietrich Tiedemann (1748–1803) about his son, Friedrich, kept between 1782 (when the child was 6 months) and 1784:

On February 10th he showed the first sign of surprise and approval; so far his only expressions of pain, anger, impatience, and pleasure had been crying, writhing, laughing. Now, when he saw something new and delightful, he greeted it with the exclamation 'ach!' – the natural sign of admiration...

After all manner of exercise in the production of tones, and after the acquisition of some skill in using the speech organs variously, he commenced, on the 14th of March, to articulate consciously and to repeat sounds. His mother said to him the syllable 'Ma'; he gazed attentively at her mouth, and attempted to imitate the syllable...

A few words he pronounced clearly on November 27th and knew also their meanings exactly; these were 'Papa' and 'Mama'...

On the 8th of March, at the sight of an object, he would repeat its name if he had frequently heard it, but he still found it hard to pronounce words of several syllables.

On the 30th of July he finally succeeded in uttering complete, though short sentences, for example: *There he stands, There he lies*...

[February 14, 1784] This is as far as my observations go. Other business prevented me from their continuation. I greatly desire that others may make similar ones; it will then be possible to determine various things by comparison, and that important branch of psychology, too little exploited as yet, which studies the development of human faculties – the foundation of pedagogy – will make appreciable progress thereby. (From C. Murchison & S. K. Langer, 1927.)

RESEARCH PARADIGMS

There is no single way of studying children's language. Linguistics and psychology has each brought its own approach to the subject, and many variations have been introduced to cope with the variety of activities in which children engage, and the great age range that they present. Two main research paradigms are found.

Naturalistic sampling   A sample of a child's spontaneous use of language is recorded in familiar and comfortable surroundings. One of the best places to make the recording is in the child's own home, but it is not always easy to maintain good acoustic quality, and the presence of the researcher or the recording equipment can be a distraction (especially if the proceedings are being filmed). Alternatively, the recording can be made in a special setting, such as a research centre, where the child is allowed to play freely with toys while talking to parents or other children, and the observers and their equipment are unobtrusive.

A good quality, representative, naturalistic sample is generally considered an ideal datum for child language study. However, the method has several limitations. These samples are informative about speech production, but they give little guidance about the way children understand what they hear around them. Moreover, samples cannot contain everything, and they can easily miss some important features of a child's linguistic ability. They may also not provide enough instances of a developing feature to enable the analyst to make a decision about the way the child is learning. For such reasons, the description of samples of child speech has to be supplemented by other methods.

Experimentation   The methods of experimental psychology have been widely applied to child language research. The investigator formulates a specific hypothesis about children's ability to use or understand an aspect of language, and devises a relevant task for a group of subjects to carry out. A statistical analysis is made of the subjects' behaviour, and the results provide evidence that supports or falsifies the original hypothesis – or, at least, suggest ways in which the experiment might be better designed next time!

Using this approach, as well as other methods of controlled observation, researchers have come up with many detailed findings about the production and comprehension of groups of children. However, it is not easy to generalize the findings of these studies. What may obtain in a carefully controlled setting may not apply in the rush of daily interaction. Different kinds of subjects, experimental situations, and statistical procedures may produce different results or interpretations. Experimental research is therefore a slow, painstaking business; it may take years before researchers are convinced that all variables have been considered and a finding is genuine.

Sampling: how much? how often?

Those who do research in child language are always being pulled in two directions, when they have to decide questions of sampling. They can choose to follow a single child, or a small group of children, in an intensive way, taking relatively large samples at frequent intervals. Or they can select a large number of children and take smaller samples at less frequent intervals. Both procedures have their strengths and limitations. The former enables the researcher to plot the gradual emergence of linguistic patterns from absence to acquisition; but it is unable to provide confident generalizations about these patterns, given the small number of children examined. The latter permits such generalizations, but is likely to miss points of significant progress that fall between the sampling intervals.

Depending on the method used, therefore, sampling intervals can range from every few days, especially when the children seem to be undergoing a period of rapid progress, to 3 months or more. The major research programme launched by the American psychologist Roger Brown (1925–) in the 1960s sampled three children for at least two hours a month – in one case, for half an hour a week. By contrast, a British programme of the 1970s, directed by the psycholinguist Gordon Wells (1935–), involved 128 children, and took a half-hour sample from each child every three months. Even larger numbers of children are sometimes used, but this restricts the research to the study of a very small set of linguistic features. It should be borne in mind, too, that large samples do not guarantee the occurrence of important features. In the Wells project, a search for passive verbs (e.g. *was kicked*) in 18,000 utterances from 60 children who were recorded three times between 3 and 3½ years of age, produced next to nothing: 12 children used such a verb a total of 19 times!

Half-hour samples are a popular measure, though often people use a sample consisting of a fixed number of utterances (e.g. 100 utterances taken from some point in a recording session). Whatever the length, samples need to be as representative as possible of the child's language, and researchers therefore need to anticipate the influence of such factors as time of day, the nature of the setting, and the presence of observers (p. 233).

(p. 233).

RESEARCH COOPERATION

Children do not always see the need to cooperate to the best of their ability in language acquisition research, as the following story shows:

Another week we noticed that Adam would sometimes pluralize nouns when they should have been pluralized and sometimes would not. We wondered if he could make grammatical judgments about the plural, if he could distinguish a correct form from an incorrect form. 'Adam', we asked, 'which is right, "two shoes" or "two shoe"?' His answer on that occasion, produced with explosive enthusiasm, was 'Pop goes the weasel!' The two-year old child does not make a perfectly docile experimental subject. (From R. Brown & U. Bellugi-Klima, 1964, p. 134.)

An audiotape recording of a playgroup presents its own special problems – not least, the difficulty of telling the children apart, and the question of how to determine what is being said when everyone is talking (or shouting) at once.

LONGITUDINAL VS CROSS-SECTIONAL

Studies that follow the progress of a set of variables over time in the same set of children are known as *longitudinal* studies. Most child language research is of this form. However, it is also possible to build up a 'composite' picture of language emergence, by studying a set of variables in a group of children of different ages, using different subjects at each age. This is known as a *cross-sectional* study. Combined designs are also possible.

TALKING DOLLS

How do we know when young children are able to recognize errors in what people say? One ingenious research technique made use of a doll that was able to 'talk'. A toy panda, about 75 cm tall, was brought into a nursery where children (aged between 3 and 5) were playing. They were told that this was a very special kind of panda, because he was learning to talk. He wanted the children to come and see him one at a time, and talk to him so that his speech would improve. They were all very willing to help.

In the test sessions, two experimenters were involved. One stayed in the room with the panda and the child, playing with various materials. The other was outside the room, observing the session through one-way-vision glass and speaking into a microphone linked to a loudspeaker in the panda's head. The chil-

dren were trained to press a bell when the panda said something they thought was right, and to press a buzzer when he was wrong. The panda would also ask the children why he was wrong, if they did not spontaneously give a reason.

The children adapted to this situation enthusiastically, and so the technique was used in several kinds of study. It proved to be a very good way of testing sentence comprehension and conversational skills. In one of the comprehension studies, for example, a car was placed in each of four garages, and a fifth car was left outside. The doll then said such sentences as 'all the garages have cars in them' (which was true) and 'all the cars are in the garages' (which was false). The children's reactions then showed how far they were able to grasp the distinction between the sentences.

The main reason for developing this method was to reduce the extent to which a child might be influenced by an adult experimenter, or overawed by an artificial test situation. It proved to be an extremely successful technique, and it

has since been used in studies of speech production as well as of comprehension and interaction. By putting the children 'in charge', researchers are able to elicit a natural speaking style, and to observe several structures (such as the use of com-

mands) that are often avoided when talking to adults. (After P. Lloyd & M. Donaldson, 1976.)

Chu-Chu and child exchanging names at the beginning of a session.

TASK EFFECTS

Setting up an experimental task so that it does not hinder a child's performance is never easy. Even the simplest tasks can hide snags that make it difficult or impossible to interpret a response correctly. Where the child is seated, how the toys are arranged, and how the experimenter gives the instructions can all cause problems. The apparently simple instruction to 'Put the car behind the lorry', to test knowledge of 'behind' illustrates some of the difficulties.

1. The child is sitting opposite the experimenter. Should she put the car behind the lorry from her own point of view, at X, or from the experimenter's, at Y, or should she use her knowledge of the real world, and place the car at the back end of the lorry, at Z, as it would appear when travelling along the road? A failure to respond, or a wrong placement, may reflect only her confusion, not her lack of knowledge

of what the preposition means.

2. Now the child is alongside the experimenter, but there is still a problem. The tail end of the lorry is facing her. So she is still faced with the problem of what the experimenter intends.

3. A ball does not have a front and a back end, so there should be no difficulties from

the real world here. Unfortunately, it has been placed near the back of the table, so that the child has difficulty reaching behind it. Also, she might think that the car will fall off the table if she places it so far away. Such factors could once again lead her to act indecisively, or to put the car somewhere else, thus giving a misleading impression about her linguistic knowledge.

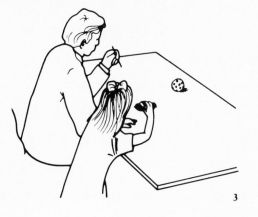

INDIVIDUAL DIFFERENCES

There has been a natural emphasis in language acquisition research on the universal characteristics of development. However, there are many individual differences which also need to be taken into account. Children may vary in their rate and strategies of learning for a variety of reasons, to do with such factors as sex, intelligence, personality, and social background (§§6–10). There are 'fast developers' and 'slow developers'. But it has not yet been possible to generalize about the way these variables affect the course of language development.

Popular notions nonetheless exist. For example, it is widely believed that girls learn to speak more rapidly than boys, and several researchers have noticed a trend for girls to be linguistically superior, at early ages. But there is negligible evidence for a definite effect. Samples tend to be very small, and measures selective. Such differences as are found seem to be due more to the effect of the different ways in which boys and girls are brought up, rather than to physiological or genetic factors. Parental style and expectations seem to be far more important.

Observer effects

The presence of research observers in a recording session may affect the mother more than the child! But it has taken some time for this point to be appreciated by researchers.

One of the first findings about maternal language concerned the presence of grammatical *expansions* when talking to a child. Mothers would often provide a gloss for their child's utterance which added elements that were not present:

CHILD: Go car.
MOTHER: Yes, daddy's going in his car.

In Brown's research project (p. 229), it was found that expansions appeared in nearly a third of mother's interactions, in early stages of learning. Their function seemed to be as a teaching aid for the child, in that the mothers were providing their children with a target that was slightly ahead of their performance. However, in Wells's project (p. 229), very few expansions were found. How is this discrepancy to be explained?

The main factor is thought to be the presence or absence of observers. In Brown's approach, there were always researchers present; in Wells's there were no researchers present, and the mother was alone with the child most of the time. Wells made use of radio microphones and a sampling programme in which 90-second recordings were made automatically at 20-minute intervals throughout the day, so that the parent would be unaware when a recording was taking place. With these parents, the frequency of expansions increased only when another adult was present. This suggests that the main function of expansions is to act as a gloss for the benefit of an observer, and not, as was first thought, solely to provide the child with extra grammatical information.

TECHNOLOGICAL REVOLUTIONS

The invention of the audio tape recorder led to the first revolution in child language research methodology. The invention of the video recorder may well prove to be a second. Each technique has its strengths and limitations.

The audio tape recorder is the more widely used means of obtaining child language data. Audio tapes and equipment cost less, and the technique is relatively unobtrusive. If radio microphones attached to the child's clothes are used, the actual recorder need not even be in the same room, and recordings of excellent quality can be made.

However, an audio recording gives no information about what a child is doing. Gestures and facial expressions, which are often used to supplement speech or show comprehension, are not available. It may not be possible to interpret sentences clearly: on an audio tape, *Put that over there* makes very little sense. It is possible to get round these problems to some extent, by having an observer present who makes notes on what is happening. But this is far inferior to a video record of the event, which can be viewed several times by different researchers.

With video, the tiniest features of non-verbal behaviour, and the role of the accompanying context, can be transcribed and analysed. It is thus a frequently used tool in modern child language research – especially in studies of comprehension and

parent–child interaction. But video studies are never straightforward: lighting, camera angles, sound recording, the intrusion of the camera, and other matters need to be carefully thought out if an informative picture is to be obtained.

'Fell down', says the child – a totally obscure utterance without the picture.

CHILDES

Modern methods of computational analysis and data processing could well revolutionize the study of language acquisition. One of the main problems facing the child language researcher is that the collection and transcription of data samples is extremely time-consuming. An hour of recorded conversational data can take 10 or more hours to transcribe, check, edit, and type. It has therefore been proposed that, once scholars have made their transcriptions, the data should be made available to the wider research community through the use of an

international computer network. This is the main aim of the Child Language Data Exchange System (CHILDES), which was established in 1984 by an international group of language acquisition researchers.

It is now possible to transcribe tape-recorded data directly into computer files, where the material can be edited, analysed, and duplicated. Files of data can thus be shared between researchers who have computer access to the central database, making a considerable saving of time and money. The process could also lead to a raising of

standards of data analysis, because errors can be readily checked and corrected, and extra analytical observations incorporated.

However, a sharing of resources is possible only if researchers can agree on a set of policies and standard conventions for obtaining, transcribing, and storing child language data in computerized form. These are currently under discussion. It will take some years before all the methodological problems can be solved, but the outlook for child language research is extremely promising.

PRODUCTION, COMPREHENSION, IMITATION

'Acquiring a language' involves two distinct skills: the ability to produce speech in a spontaneous way; and the ability to understand the speech of others. The former is relatively easy to study: all we have to do is turn a tape recorder on, and analyse what comes out. Research into speech comprehension is far more difficult because we need to take into account not only what is spoken to the child, but the situation in which it is uttered, and the child's prior knowledge of the world. In one study, a 2-year-old child was observed to respond correctly when his mother said, at bedtime, 'Go and get your pyjamas out of the drawer in your bedroom.' But it is not at all clear, without a careful investigation, which parts of this sentence the child had understood – it might simply be that the word *pyjamas*, said at bedtime, and coupled with the knowledge of where pyjamas are kept, was enough to produce the appropriate action.

What is the relationship between production and comprehension when it comes to language learning? There are three possibilities. The traditional, commonsense view is that comprehension always precedes production: children need to understand a word or grammatical construction before they use it. However, there is increasing evidence that this simple relationship does not always obtain. Production may precede comprehension, or the two processes may be so intimately connected that they develop in parallel. There is certainly a great deal of evidence to show that children produce a word or construction without having a full understanding of it. *Doggie*, says one young child, pointing to a cat. *He got hat on,* says another, and then later says *Take that hat on off* – as if *hat on* were a noun. This kind of thing happens frequently from around age 2 – and, indeed, it could be argued that our readiness to use linguistic forms we do not fully understand stays with us throughout life!

It has also been recognized that imitation is a distinct skill in language acquisition – many children spend a great deal of time imitating what their parents have just said. This is most noticeable when new sounds or vocabulary are being learned, but it has been shown that imitation may be important in the development of grammar too. Often, children imitate sentence patterns that they are unable to produce spontaneously, and then stop imitating these structures when they start to use them in their speech – suggesting that imitation is a kind of 'bridge' between comprehension and spontaneous production.

ELICITED IMITATION

The technique of 'elicited imitation' can be used to find out what a child knows about language. The experimenter reads out a sentence to be repeated. If the child makes any changes, these can indicate aspects of the language which are still being learned or not yet acquired. One 2¼-year-old child, 'Echo', gave the following imitations:

1. The owl eats candy and the owl runs fast.
Echo: Owl eat candy and he run fast.
2. The owl who eats candy runs fast.
Echo: Owl eat a candy and he run fast.

The first imitation suggests that Echo understands the meaning and structure of the coordinate sentence (p. 95). She uses the same strategy in the second case, which suggests that she cannot yet cope with the more difficult sentence containing a subordinate clause introduced by *who*, though she does follow its meaning. (After D. I. Slobin & C. A. Welsh, 1967.)

PLOTTING THE COURSE OF LANGUAGE DEVELOPMENT

A popular metaphor in child development is to talk of 'milestones' – the age at which a child takes a significant step forward in behaviour (such as sitting, crawling, standing). The metaphor does not work so well when it comes to language: too much happens too quickly. There is simultaneous development of sounds, grammar, meaning, and interaction skills; and significant progress can be made on several different fronts in a matter of days. It is thus no easy matter to quantify the amount of language learned by a child within a particular period (as we need to do in deciding what counts as 'normal' development, and in plotting departures from this norm (p. 281)).

Several attempts have been made to find important single measures of development, within particular linguistic levels (§13) – notably the notions of sentence length and vocabulary size, both of which steadily increase as children grow older. Such indices can provide general indications of progress, but they have serious limitations. Two sentences may consist of exactly the same number of words, morphemes, or syllables, and yet be very different in terms of their syntactic complexity: *I see a cat and a dog and a cow* is much simpler than *I see a cat that is next to a dog*, though both are the same length. Similarly, two children may both have vocabularies of 100 words, yet differ in the range of words used and in their meanings: one child may use *cold* to mean only 'cold weather', whereas the other may use it to apply to water, food, and grim facial expressions. In these circumstances, a single score, based on one developmental parameter, conceals more than it illuminates: it needs to be supplemented by a wider and more detailed series of measures that take into account the qualitative range of linguistic features used by the child.

After several years of acquisition research, in which many measures have been investigated, it is possible to isolate certain broad trends with some confidence, and these are the subject matter of §§39–43. It appears that most children do follow the same general path as they acquire sounds and grammatical structures, and several common trends are evident in the learning of vocabulary and pragmatics (§21) also. However, there seems to be considerable variation in rate of development, and there are many individual differences in the order of acquisition of specific features that have to be taken into account (p. 233). The study of these variations is a major emphasis of current child language research.

VOCABULARY SIZE

The average vocabulary size of ten samples of children between the ages of 1 and 6. (After M. E. Smith, 1926.) To interpret such totals, a great deal needs to be known about the method for defining 'words' used by the investigator (p. 104). Were *go, goes, going*, etc. counted as one word or several? Were words of radically different meaning (e.g. *bear* 'animal'/ 'carry') counted separately? Decisions of this kind have a major influence on the totals reached at in a word count.

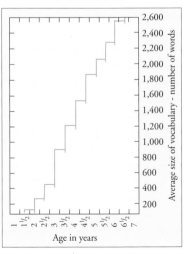

MLU

Measuring the mean length of utterance (MLU) has been one of the most widely practised indices of grammatical development in young children. The total number of utterances in a sample is divided by the total number of words (in some procedures) or morphemes (in others) (p. 90).

The best-known measure, which uses morphemes, was devised by Roger Brown (p. 231) in the 1960s. The diagram shows the way Brown's three subjects gradually increased their utterance length. Five stages of development are recognized, based on a division of the length continuum into intervals of 0.5 morphemes. There is a good correlation between MLU and age, but the relationship between MLU and the range of constructions found in a sample is less clear. Predicting the grammatical complexity of a speech sample from length alone is by no means straightforward, especially as length increases. (R. Brown, 1973.)

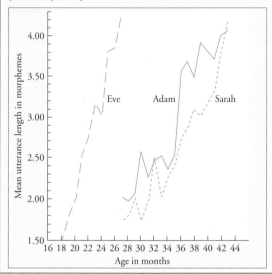

LANGUAGE TESTS

A language test takes a selection of linguistic features – for example, a set of consonants, grammatical constructions, or items of vocabulary – and establishes whether a child has knowledge of them, in either production or comprehension. The child's responses are scored, according to some predetermined criterion. As language ability progresses, higher scores are obtained.

Tests are widely used in the field of language handicap (§46), because they provide a convenient means of identifying children who require special teaching or therapy, and a way of moni-toring the success of intervention. But they are of limited value in fundamental research in child language, because they deal with only a fraction of the linguistic features being acquired. By their nature, tests have to be short and highly selective. They can give useful background information about a child's general level, but they cannot provide the detailed account of the emergence of linguistic skills that acquisition research requires.

A task from a language test is illustrated below. The *Screening Test of Spanish Grammar* is based on the language of the Mexican and Puerto Rican populations in the U.S. and is designed to identify Spanish-speaking children who do not demonstrate native syntactic proficiency commensurate with their age. In the comprehension part of the test, the examiner reads a sentence to the child, who has to point to the appropriate picture. The illustration shows four pictures used to test knowledge of a contrast involving two prepositions: *El perro está detrás de la silla* and *El perro está debajo de la silla* ('The dog is behind/underneath the chair'). The remaining two pictures are 'decoys'. (From A. S. Toronto, 1973.)

PROFILES

An extract from a profile of grammatical development used in the study of language handicap and based on a synthesis of findings from the study of normal language acquisition. The abbreviations in this procedure, known as LARSP (Language Assessment, Remediation and Screening Procedure) refer to different grammatical constructions, e.g.

SVO = 'Subject + Verb + Object'
PrN = 'Preposition + Noun' (§16).

The totals refer to the number of instances of a category used by a child in a sample of spontaneous speech.

Profiles permit a more detailed impression of the range of structures used than can be obtained from a test, and enable the analyst to plot emerging strengths and weaknesses in several areas of grammar simultaneously. In the present case, the child has begun to use constructions at Stage II (typically age 18 months–2 years), but there are several gaps, and he has not yet made much progress in Stage III. As the child in the sample had in fact reached the chronological age of 2 years 3 months, he would seem to be a somewhat slow developer, as far as the acquisition of grammar is concerned. (D. Crystal *et al.*, 1989.)

Stage I (0;9–1;6)	Minor	*Responses* 30			*Vocatives*	*Other*	*Problems*	
	Major	*Comm.*	*Quest.*	*Statement*				
		'V'	'Q'	'V' 6	'N' 8	Other	Problems	
Stage II (1;6–2;0)	Conn.		Clause			Phrase		Word
		V X	Q X	SV 3	A X 7	D N 11	V V 1	-ing 4
			2	SO	VO 4	Adj N 3	V part 2	pl 2
				SC 1	VC	NN	Int X	
				Neg X	Other	PrN 6	Other 1	
Stage III (2;0–2;6)		X + S:NP	X + V:VP	X + C:NP		X + O:NP 2	X + A:AP 1	-ed
		V X Y	Q X Y	SVC	VCA	D Adj N	Cop	-en
		let X Y		SVO 1	VOA	Adj Adj N	Aux^M_O	3s
		do X Y	VS (X)	SVA	VO$_d$O$_i$	Pr DN		gen
				Neg X Y	Other	Pron^P_O 4	Other	
Stage IV (2;6–3;0)		X Y + S:NP	X Y + V:VP	X Y + C:NP		X Y + O:NP	X Y + A:AP	n't
		+ S	QVS	SVOA	AA X Y	NP Pr NP	Neg V	'cop
			Q X Y +	SVCA	Other	Pr D Adj N	Neg X	'aux
		V X Y +	VS(X +)	SVO$_d$O$_i$		cX	2 Aux	
			tag	SVOC		XcX	Other	
Stage V (3;0–3;6)	*and*	Coord.	Coord.	Coord. 1	1 +	Postmod. 1 clause	1 +	-est
	c	Other	Other	Subord. A 1	1 +			-er
	s			S C	O	Postmod. 1 + phrase		-ly
	Other			Comparative				

THEORIES OF LANGUAGE ACQUISITION

IMITATION

Language acquisition has long been thought of as a process of imitation and reinforcement. Children learn to speak, in the popular view, by copying the utterances heard around them, and by having their responses strengthened by the repetitions, corrections, and other reactions that adults provide. In recent years, it has become clear that this principle will not explain all the facts of language development. Children do imitate a great deal, especially in learning sounds and vocabulary; but little of their grammatical ability can be explained in this way. Two kinds of evidence are commonly used in support of this criticism – one based on the kind of language children produce, the other on what they do not produce.

The first piece of evidence derives from the way children handle irregular grammatical patterns. When they encounter such irregular past-tense forms (p. 90) as *went* and *took*, or such plural forms as *mice* and *sheep*, there is a stage when they replace these by forms based on the regular patterns of the language. They say such things as *wented*, *taked*, *mices*, *mouses*, and *sheeps*. Evidently, children assume that grammatical usage is regular, and try to work out for themselves what the forms 'ought' to be – a reasoning process known as *analogy* (p. 332). They could not have learned these forms by a process of imitation. Adults do not go around saying such things as *wented* and *sheeps*!

The other kind of evidence is based on the way children seem unable to imitate adult grammatical constructions exactly, even when invited to do so ('elicited imitation', p. 234). The best-known demonstration of this principle in action is the dialogue reported by the American psycholinguist, David McNeill (1933–), where a child proved unable to use a pattern, even though the parent presented the correct adult model several times:

CHILD: Nobody don't like me.
MOTHER: No, say 'Nobody likes me.'
CHILD: Nobody don't like me.
(*Eight repetitions of this dialogue.*)
MOTHER: No, now listen carefully: say '*Nobody likes me.*'
CHILD: Oh! Nobody don't likes me.

The child, at this point in its learning of grammar, was clearly not ready to use the 'single negative' pattern found in this dialect of English. Such examples suggest that language acquisition is more a matter of maturation than of imitation.

INNATENESS

The limitations of an imitation/reinforcement view of acquisition led in the 1960s to an alternative proposal, arising out of the generative account of language (§65). It was argued that children must be born with an innate capacity for language development: the human brain is 'ready' for language, in the sense that when children are exposed to speech, certain general principles for discovering or structuring language automatically begin to operate. These principles constitute a child's 'language acquisition device' (LAD).

The child uses its LAD to make sense of the utterances heard around it, deriving from this 'primary linguistic data' hypotheses about the grammar of the language – what the sentences are, and how they are constructed. This knowledge is then used to produce sentences that, after a process of trial and error, correspond to those in adult speech: the child has learned a set of generalizations, or rules, governing the way in which sentences are formed. This sequence of events can be summarized in the following way:

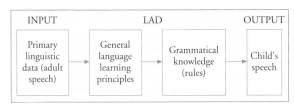

Jean Piaget (1896–1980)

There have been many differences of opinion over how best to characterize LAD. Some have argued that LAD provides children with a knowledge of linguistic universals (§14), such as the existence of word order and word classes; others, that it provides only general procedures for discovering how language is to be learned. But all of its supporters are agreed that some such notion is needed in order to explain the remarkable speed with which children learn to speak, and the considerable similarity in the way grammatical patterns are acquired across different children and languages. Adult speech, it is felt, cannot of itself provide a means of enabling children to work out the regularities of language for themselves, because it is too complex and disorganized (p. 52). However, it has proved difficult to formulate the detailed properties of LAD in an uncontroversial manner, in the light of the changes in generative linguistic theory that have taken place in recent years; and meanwhile, alternative accounts of the acquisition process have evolved.

COGNITION

The main alternative account argues that language acquisition must be viewed within the context of a child's intellectual development. Linguistic structures will emerge only if there is an already-established cognitive foundation – for example, before children can use structures of comparison (e.g. *This car is bigger than that*), they need first to have developed the conceptual ability to make relative judgments of size. Several early child language scholars maintained that such a relationship exists, but the most influential account stems from the model of cognitive development proposed by the Genevan psychologist Jean Piaget (1896–1980).

Several controlled studies have been carried out investigating the link between the stages of cognitive development proposed by Piaget and the emergence of linguistic skills. The links have been most clearly shown for the earliest period of language learning (up to 18 months), relating to the development of what Piaget called 'sensori-motor' intelligence, in which children construct a mental picture of a world of objects that have independent existence. For example, during the later part of this period, children develop a sense of object permanence – they will begin to search for objects that they have seen hidden – and some scholars have argued that the ability to name classes of objects (i.e. to give them a comparably 'permanent' linguistic status) depends on the prior development of this cognitive ability. However, it is difficult to show precise correlations between specific cognitive behaviours and linguistic features at this early age. The issue is a highly controversial one, which increases in complexity as children become linguistically – and cognitively – more advanced.

INPUT

For many years, in the wake of the innateness hypothesis, the importance of the language used by adults (especially mothers) to children was minimized. But studies of 'motherese', as it came to be called in the 1970s, showed that maternal input is by no means as complex and fragmentary as proponents of innateness theory claimed it to be. Many parents do not talk to their children in the same way as they talk to other adults. Rather, they seem capable of adapting their language to give the child maximum opportunity to interact and learn. Several of these adaptations have been noted (after C. A. Ferguson, 1977).

• The utterances are considerably simplified, especially with respect to their grammar and meaning. Sentences are shorter: one study showed that the average length of maternal sentences to 2-year-olds was less than four words – half that found when the mothers talked to other adults. There is a more restricted range of sentence patterns, and a frequent use of sentence 'frames', such as *Where's –?* or *That's a –*. The meanings are predominantly 'concrete', relating to the situation in which mother and child are acting.

• There are several features whose purpose seems to be clarification. Extra information is provided that would be considered unnecessary when talking to other adults. Sentences are expanded and paraphrased and may be repeated several times. The speed of speaking is much slower than that used to other adults.

• There is also an expressive, or affective, element in motherese, shown by the use of special words or sounds. Diminutive or reduplicative words (e.g. *doggie, choo-choo*) are common. English makes particular

use of a *y / ie* ending, and similar forms have been noted in several other languages, such as Japanese *-ko*, Gilyak *-k / -q*, Berber *-ʃ / -ʃtt*. Occasionally, totally different words will be used, e.g. *bunny* for 'rabbit'. There may be special use of individual sounds, such as the use of rounded lips in English, or special palatal sounds in Latvian and Marathi.

Some of these features also seem to function as ways of holding the child's attention, or of identifying particular words and sounds. This may well be the reason for the very common use of high, wide pitch-range in maternal speech. Mothers also devote a great deal of time to obtaining feedback from their children, especially in the first three years. Their speech contains a very high frequency of question forms, and many utterances have a high rising intonation (*yes?, all right?*).

These modifications are evidently important ways of establishing and maintaining meaningful communication with the child, as they can be found in the earliest mother–child interactions (§39). It has even been suggested that these features are universal, but this claim is premature in the absence of empirical studies, and there is already some counter-evidence from other cultures – several of these features are lacking in Samoan and Quiché Mayan, for instance. However, the highly structured character of maternal input is not in doubt, and its possible influence on the course of language acquisition is now taken very seriously.

Unfortunately, it is difficult to show correlations between the features of motherese and the subsequent emergence of these features in child speech, and even more problematic to move from talk about correlations to talk about causes. Some studies, searching for such relationships, have found very few; others have found occasional correlations between specific structures, though often with an appreciable time gap between the use of a feature by the mother and its subsequent use by the child; yet others argue that input structures are very closely tailored to the needs of the child (the 'fine tuning' hypothesis). The use of different research methodologies clouds the picture, but it is now plain that the nature and frequency of linguistic features in maternal input can no longer be neglected in devising theories of language acquisition.

CONCLUSIONS

It is not possible, in the present state of knowledge, to choose between these various approaches. The number of definite, general facts known about language acquisition is still very small. In particular, much more information is needed about the way children learn languages other than English. Doubtless imitative skills, a general language-learning-mechanism, cognitive awareness, and structured input all play their part in guiding the course of language acquisition. Unravelling the interdependence of these factors constitutes the main goal of future child language research.

MOTHERESE – OR OTHERESE?

The term 'motherese' seems a natural one, given the important role of mothers in early child development. However, it would be more accurate to refer to 'parentese', as fathers are also able to adapt their speech when talking to children, and use very similar strategies. Motherese and 'fatherese' are not identical, however. Fathers tend to be more intense and demanding in their communication, using more direct questions and a wider range of vocabulary.

But even 'parentese' is too specific a notion. Some of the characteristics of motherese can be found in other adults too – and even in 4-year-olds, when they talk 'down' to younger children. Moreover, in some non-Western cultures (e.g. Western Samoa), the primary caregivers may not be the parents at all, and the developing child may receive most of its linguistic stimulation from siblings, other adult relatives, or neighbouring families. A more neutral term, such as 'baby talk', is thus preferred by some researchers – though its ambiguity (speech *by* children or *to* children?) limits its usefulness. 'Caretaker speech' is also widely used.

Very little study of the nature of cultural differences has taken place. In the Samoan case, for example, many of the features of Anglo-American motherese (such as the use of simplified structure, expansions, and diminutives) were found to be absent. The turn-taking pattern was also different, often taking the form: child talks to mother → mother talks to older sibling → sibling attends to child. Such differences have important implications for the development of any theory of language acquisition in which motherese plays a part. (After E. Ochs, 1982.)

For many parents, a child's first words, uttered at around 1 year of age, mark the first real evidence of language development – the child has 'started to talk'. But this is to ignore a great deal of early progress during the first year, without which no first word would emerge at all. This progress has to be made in three main areas: sound production, speech perception, and speech interaction.

SOUND PRODUCTION

Between birth and 12 months, a vast change takes place in a baby's sound-producing abilities, and several stages of development have been proposed.

Stage I (0–8 weeks): Basic biological noises
Over the first few weeks of life, a baby's vocal sounds directly reflect its biological state and activities. States of hunger, pain, or discomfort that cause crying and fussing are known as *reflexive noises*. Breathing, eating, excreting, and other bodily actions concerned with survival cause a wide range of *vegetative* noises, such as sucking, swallowing, coughing, and burping. Infant reflexive cries have been studied in detail. The normal 'basic' cry consists of a series of 1-second pulses separated by brief pauses. The vocal folds (§22) vibrate strongly, and the pitch of the voice falls sharply with each pulse. The quality of the sound is similar to that of an [a] vowel.

It is not easy to attribute clearly different functions to cries at this age. Hunger and pain cries tend to merge into a single distress cry, though pain cries are often much tenser and have a different rhythm. Discomfort cries are usually much shorter ($\frac{1}{2}$ sec) and occur in brief sequences. Vegetative noises are even shorter ($\frac{1}{4}$ sec) and contain more consonant-like sounds.

There is nothing language-specific about these early sounds. However, they do have some features in common with later speech. An air-stream mechanism (§22) is being used to produce noise; there is rhythmical vocalization; the vocal folds are being used to produce pitch patterns: all of these are fundamental characteristics of later speech.

Stage II (8–20 weeks): Cooing and laughing
Between 6 and 8 weeks, the first cooing sounds are produced, generally when the baby is in a settled state. These sounds develop alongside crying, gradually becoming more frequent and more varied, as the child responds to the mother's smiles and speech. They are quieter, lower pitched, and more musical than crying, usually consisting of a short, vowel-like sound preceded by a consonant-like sound made towards the back of the mouth. Many have nasal quality.

Later in this period, cooing sounds are strung together - often 10 or more at a time. These strings are not pronounced in a rhythmical way; there are no clear intonational contours. However, some of the sequences (such as [ga] and [gu]) do begin to resemble the syllables of later speech. Then, at around 4 months, the first throaty chuckles and laughs emerge.

During the cooing stage, babies seem to be performing the first gross activities required for the production of speech. The tongue begins to move vertically and horizontally, and the vocal folds begin to be used in coordination with it. There is a great deal of lip movement and tongue thrusting, which it is thought may be a form of imitation.

Stage III (20–30 weeks): Vocal play
The sounds of vocal play are much steadier and longer than those of cooing. Most segments are over 1 second, and consist of consonant + vowel-like sequences that are frequently repeated. They are usually at a high pitch level, and involve wide glides from high to low. A considerable range of consonant and vowel qualities is apparent, including nasal and fricative sounds made in

GOOD TALKERS?

Frequent and varied vocal play and babbling is sometimes thought to be the sign of a good talker, or an indication of superior intelligence, memory, or personality. There is no evidence that any such correlations exist. There have been many quiet babies whose subsequent language development has been rapid; and, conversely, there are certain areas of mental subnormality (such as Down's syndrome) in which a good range of babbling can be heard. No-one has been able to discover a direct link between early vocalization and later intellectual or linguistic development (§7).

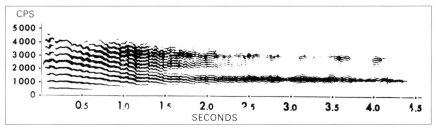

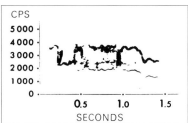

Acoustic analysis (p. 135) is essential in the analysis of early vocalizations. The upper trace (a) is a spectrogram of the first part of a pain cry (such as might be caused by an injection or other sudden stimulus) from a normal, healthy child: it shows a steady, full-bodied, falling pitch movement over some 4 seconds of expired breath. The infant then pauses for more air, and further expirations follow (not shown here).

Abnormal pain cries sound and look very different. Trace (b) is a cry from a baby born with a degree of brain damage: its main feature is a high-pitched, erratic phonation. Trace (c) is part of a long, strident cry (the expiration lasts for nearly 10 seconds) from a baby with meningitis. (After O. Wasz-Höckert, *et al*, 1968.)

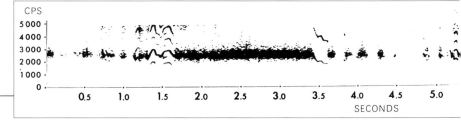

various parts of the mouth (§27). There are many individual differences in the order of emergence of these sounds, and several changes in the focus of the activity during the period – on some days uvular sounds may be the dominant sounds heard; on other days it may be labial sounds. In due course, the sounds combine into longer sequences, to produce the first babbled utterances.

There seems to be a strong element of practice in the activities of this period, but anyone who has observed it will recognize that it also provides a great deal of enjoyment for parent and child alike.

Stage IV (25–50 weeks): Babbling

Babbling is much less varied than the sounds of vocal play, in the early part of this period. A smaller set of sounds is used with greater frequency and stability, to produce the [bababa] and other sequences known as *reduplicated* babbling (because of the repeated use of the same consonant sound). About half-way through the period, this develops into *variegated* babbling, in which consonants and vowels change from one syllable to the next (e.g. [adu]). The rhythm of the utterance and the syllable length at this point are much closer to that found in speech. Babbled utterances seem to have no meaning, though some may resemble the words of later speech.

It used to be thought that there was no link between babbling and spoken language. The child was imagined to be trying out every possible sound in a random manner, and that babbling would stop before speech began. Recent studies have shown that this view does not hold. In many cases, babbling continues long after speech begins – sometimes as late as 18 months. Nor are the sounds of babbling a random selection: most of babbling consists of a small set of sounds very similar to those used in the early language to be spoken by the child. The brain seems to be controlling the development of babbling and early speech in a similar way, so that a set of well-practised sounds is available for use at the time when children become intellectually capable of using sound for the communication of meaning.

Stage V (9–18 months): Melodic utterance

Variations in melody, rhythm, and tone of voice (§29) become a major feature of child utterance towards the end of the first year. Parents begin to sense intentions behind these utterances, with their more well-defined shape, and often attribute meanings to them, such as questioning, calling, greeting, or wanting. Games and rituals may develop their own melodic contours. Individual syllables come to be used with a fixed melody, producing 'proto-words', where the sounds are clear, but it is not possible to be sure what they mean. These are the first real signs of language development, and children growing up in different language environments begin to sound increasingly unlike each other.

EARLY VOCALIZATION

Which consonant sounds (§27) do infants use most often in their early vocalizations? In the first six months, back (velar) consonants predominate. Then, between six and nine months, alveolar sounds become dominant. Labial sounds are never the most frequent. This pattern stabilizes at around nine months. Children seem to have the physical capability to produce the words of a language long before these sounds are used in speech. (After B. L. Smith & D. K. Oller, 1981.)

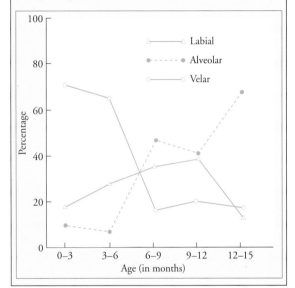

BABBLING IN DIFFERENT LANGUAGE ENVIRONMENTS

There is a considerable similarity in infant babbling patterns, whatever their language environment. The table below shows the occurrence of English or English-like consonant segments in the babbling of infants reared in 15 language environments. The consonants have been divided into two groups of 12: consonants which are heard frequently in English babbling (accounting in fact for about 95% of all consonants heard); and those which are heard infrequently. It can be seen that there is a very close correspondence between the different languages, though there is no identity. Only [m] and [b] turn up in all language environments.

The similarities are impressive. However, it should be noted that the numbers of children involved in these studies are very small – often only one child, and rarely more than five. The comparative picture may become more complex as the database increases. (After J. J. Locke, 1983.)

Environment	Age in months	Frequent English consonants											
		h	d	b	m	t	g	s	w	n	k	j	p
Afrikaans	11–12	*	*	*	*	*		*		*	*		*
Mayan	9	*	*	*	*	*			*				*
Luo	12	*	*	*	*		*			*		*	
Thai	10–11		*	*	*	*			*		*	*	*
Japanese	9–12		*	*	*	*		*		*			*
Hindi	9–10	*		*	*		*	*		*			*
Chinese	8–11	*		*	*	*	*		*	*	*	*	*
Slovenian	11		*	*	*	*	*		*	*			*
Dutch	11	*		*	*		*		*	*	*		*
Spanish	9	*	*	*	*	*			*	*			*
German	10–12		*	*	*	*			*	*	*	*	*
Arabic	6–10	*	*	*	*				*			*	*
Norwegian	0–12	*	*	*	*	*	*	*	*	*	*	*	*
Latvian	6–12	*	*	*	*		*		*	*	*		
English	1–15	*	*	*	*		*		*	*	*		

	Age in months	Infrequent English consonants											
		v	l	θ	z	f	ʃ	ð	ŋ	ʒ	r	tʃ	ʤ
Afrikaans	11–12		*				*				*		
Mayan	9												
Luo	12		*						*				
Thai	10–11												
Japanese	9–12	*											
Hindi	9–10												
Chinese	8–11								*				
Slovenian	11		*										
Dutch	11								*				
Spanish	9												
German	10–12											*	
Arabic	6–10	*			*								
Norwegian	0–12	*	*	*					*	*			
Latvian	6–12	*											
English	1–15	*	*			*							

SPEECH PERCEPTION

Very young babies present an extraordinary range of auditory abilities. There have been several experiments in which different sounds are played to babies, and their responses monitored. For example, day-old babies have been played their mother's voice speaking normally, the same voice speaking abnormally (in a monotone), and a stranger's voice: only the first caused them to attend. Other studies have shown how babies turn their heads towards the source of a sound within the first few days of life, and prefer human voices to non-human sounds as early as 2 weeks. Abilities of this kind are so apparent that some researchers have concluded that auditory training must begin within the womb.

The question of when babies learn to distinguish the sounds of speech is controversial. An auditory ability to discriminate certain pairs of consonants or vowels (e.g. [pa] vs [ba]) is present from around 4 weeks, and this ability to discriminate becomes increasingly sophisticated in subsequent months. An early finding was that infants seem able to perceive these distinctions in the same way as adults. Adults make a sharp, categorical distinction between such sounds as [pa] and [ba] in perception experiments (p. 147). When 1-month-old infants were presented with sets of sounds that also varied only in the degree of consonant voicing, they too made categorical distinctions (P. D. Eimas *et al.*, 1971). By careful monitoring of the babies' responses (see below), it was shown that presentations of two kinds of [pa] or two kinds of [ba] caused no reaction, whereas [pa] vs [ba] did.

On the basis of such findings, the investigators hypothesized that children's perceptual apparatus is in some way 'programmed' to discriminate speech sounds – that they are born with special 'feature detectors' that respond to the acoustic properties of speech. A great deal of research has since focused on this issue, in an attempt to determine whether the children are displaying a general auditory ability (which might be shared by certain other species – experiments on both chinchillas and rhesus monkeys have shown comparable responses), or whether it is a specific ability tuned to phonetic distinctive features. The amazingly early age at which infants begin to make auditory discriminations is now accepted, but the critical issue – how these basic perceptual capacities come to be affected by the infants' emerging experience of language – is not yet resolved.

Speech comprehension

Between 2 and 4 months, babies begin to respond to the meaning of different tones of voice, such as angry, soothing, or playful voices. From around 6 months, different utterances begin to be related to their situations, e.g. *Bye-bye*, *Clap hands*, or pointing in response to questions. Some individual words may be recognized, such as names of family members, or basic responses (e.g. *No*). Most children understand several words by the end of the first year. In one study of eight children, six showed clear evidence of understanding up to 20 words by the end of the first year, and one child understood as many as 60 (H. Benedict, 1979). In all cases, this comprehension ability was at least a month ahead of the appearance of the children's first words.

HABITUATION EXPERIMENTS

A widely used technique in infant speech perception is to play sounds to the baby through a pair of headphones or a loudspeaker, and then to monitor the baby's responses, such as the speed of its heart-beat. In this approach, a sound is played several times to the child, and the heart-rate is monitored. There is an initial 'orienting response' and a period of heart-rate deceleration, as the child gets used to the stimulus. This effect is known as 'habituation'. A second sound is then played. If the child notices the difference, there will be a new orienting response.

There are many methodological problems in this kind of research, especially with very young babies. Moreover, there is still some way to go before the findings about the perception of isolated syllables can be related to the perception of these syllables in connected speech. But the habituation paradigm has shown how it is possible to make a beginning in answering the difficult question: when are linguistic contrasts first perceived?

A 1-month-old infant sucking on a special nipple while listening to a recording of different syllables. The child's normal sucking rate is first established, then sequences of sounds are presented. As the child hears the first sound, the rate of sucking increases. During subsequent repetitions of the same sound, the sucking rate shows a gradual decrease. A new sound is then played to the child. If no distinction is perceived, the sucking rate will continue to decrease; but if a change is perceived, it will show a sudden increase.

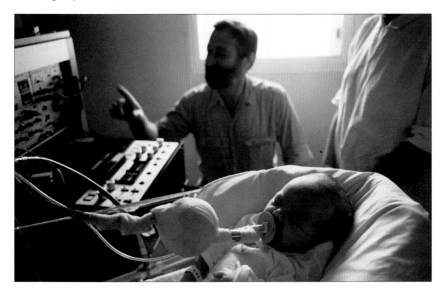

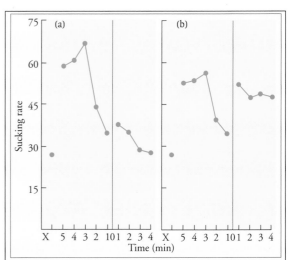

What happens when the difference between a pair of auditory stimuli is (a) ignored and (b) perceived by a group of children. The line at 0 represents the point when the sound stimulus is changed. The different presentations are shown at 1-minute intervals. X shows the normal sucking rate before the stimuli are presented. In the first case, two kinds of [ba] or two kinds of [pa] produce hardly any change in sucking rate. In the second case, the change from [pa] to [ba] (or vice versa) is clearly shown. (After P. D. Eimas *et al.*, 1971.)

SPEECH INTERACTION

From the moment a baby is born, a mother holds it in front of her, and talks to it – despite the fact that she knows it does not yet have any language! Mothers seem to have an instinct to promote communication as soon as possible, using the child's earliest biological noises (p. 238) as stimuli. Cries, burps, sneezes, and other vocalizations are seized upon and interpreted, as the extract (see box, right) shows. The mother is very ready to ascribe intentions to the baby's utterances and to build them into a conversation – something she does not do with its non-vocal activities, such as head movements or arm waving. The conversational pressure can be quite intense: in one study, over 100 questions, comments, and other utterances were used by a mother while attempting to elicit a burp from a 3-month-old: *Where is it?, Come on, come on, come on, You haven't got any, I don't believe you*, etc. (C. Snow, 1977).

It would seem that the foundations of conversation are being laid in these early interactions. The mother's behaviour is not random. She uses a large number of questions, followed by pauses, as if to show the baby that a response is expected and to provide an opportunity for it to respond. She continually greets the baby, even after very short periods of separation. Moreover, she talks to the child at length only when the child is (in principle) in a position to reply. While the baby is feeding, for example, mothers tend to remain silent, taking up the conversation only when the baby ceases to suck or needs to be winded. This cyclical pattern of speech and silence anticipates the fundamental structure of older conversations.

There are many changes in conversational style during the first year. At around 5 weeks, the exchanges become more emotive, as smiling develops. The mother's utterances change as the baby's vocalizations grow. At around 2 months, the emergence of cooing elicits a softer voice. Some time later, the baby begins to laugh, and the mother's voice becomes more varied in response. As the child starts to take interest in the environment and looks around, the mother speaks more loudly, drawing attention to different objects. Her intonation becomes more exaggerated, and she often repeats her sentences. Simple face-to-face games are played (such as peekaboo), promoting a great deal of communication.

After 6 months, the baby's more purposeful movements and explorations produce more extended commentaries by the mother. She no longer responds to every vocalization that is produced, but focuses special attention on those that are more structured in character – in particular, the first babbled utterances. Between 8 and 10 months, babies attempt to attract the attention of others by pointing. They begin to 'follow' adult conversations, looking first at one person, then at the other. By the time their first words appear, babies have learned a great deal, both from observation and from practice, about what a conversation is and how to participate within it.

ONE-SIDED CONVERSATIONS

Michael (3 months): (*Loud crying.*)

Mother: (*Enters room*) Oh my word, what a noise! What a noise! (*Picks up baby.*)

Michael: (*Sobs.*)

Mother: Oh dear, dear, dear. Didn't anybody come to see you? Let's have a look at you. (*Looks inside nappy.*) No, you're all right there, aren't you.

Michael: (*Spluttering noise.*)

Mother: Well, what is it, then? Are you hungry, is that it? Is it a long time since dinnertime?

Michael: (*Gurgles.*)

Mother: (*Nuzzles baby.*) Oh yes it is, a long long time.

Michael: (*Cooing noise.*)

Mother: Yes, I know. Let's go and get some lovely grub, then...

(D. Crystal, 1986, p. 51.)

A CONVERSATIONAL CYCLE AT AGE 10 WEEKS

1

2

3

4

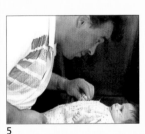
5

6

7

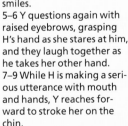
8

9

Conversational cycles involve fathers too. These stills from a documentary video are taken from a proto-conversation between a Turkish father Youssouf (Y) and his 10-week-old baby girl, Hande (H). The commentary is based on work by Colwyn Trevarthen (1993).

The sequence shows Y and H gazing into each other's eyes and trading expressions of sympathy in proto-conversation. They phrase their utterances, and take turns, clearly showing their interest in one another and their feelings for the other's changing states of assertion and apprehension, uttering and attending.

1 Y takes H in his arms, looks at her eyes and speaks to her, questioning with raised eyebrows. H, complaining, meets his eyes with intense concentration, knit brows and clenched hands.
2 Placed in front of him on the couch, H addresses Y, meeting his smile and gesturing with her right hand.
3–4 She watches his hand when he speaks, then closes her eyes, grimaces, and gestures again while he moves closer, watches her, and smiles.
5–6 Y questions again with raised eyebrows, grasping H's hand as she stares at him, and they laugh together as he takes her other hand.
7–9 While H is making a serious utterance with mouth and hands, Y reaches forward to stroke her on the chin.

By the time children are a year old, they have learned a great deal about the way adults use sounds to express differences in meaning (§28), but their own ability to produce these sounds lags some way behind. Some 1-year-olds can recognize several dozen words, involving a wide range of vowel and consonants, but their own ability to pronounce these words may be restricted to just two or three consonants and a single vowel. One child at 13 months could use only [b], [d], and [a], but he used these sounds to express a variety of words – for example, [ba] was used for *baby, bath, cup,* and *Peter.* By 15 months, he had added [m], [p], and [u] to his repertoire, and was thus able to distinguish a much larger number of words. He also began to use some of these consonants at the ends of words as well as at the beginning; for example, [pu] was used for a nasty smell, and [ʌp] was used for *up.* By age 2, he was using over a dozen consonants and vowels, and was able to pronounce over 200 words in an intelligible (though often immature) manner.

It is not possible, at present, to make precise predictions as to the order in which children come to use new sounds. Some children have 'favourite' sounds, which they introduce into many words, whether the sound is in the adult version or not; others 'avoid' sounds – for example, persistently dropping certain consonants at the ends of words. There may also be a great deal of variation in the way target sounds are produced - one child pronounced *blanket* as [bwati], [bati], [baki], and [batit], within a few hours of each other. Another produced ten different forms of *pen* within a single half-hour!

Nonetheless, as a result of several studies involving large numbers of children, certain general trends can be shown. For example, consonant sounds are more likely to be first used correctly at the beginnings of words; final consonants emerge later (though there are exceptions, such as the early use of final [f] and [s] in English). A 1971 survey of 100 English children showed that, during the second year, [p], [b], [k], [n], [f], [d], [g], [m], and [h] were commonly used word-initially; but only the first five of these sounds were developing word-finally (D. Olmsted, 1971). This survey also showed that at least eight vowels or diphthongs were usually in use by the end of the second year: [ɪ], [iː], [a], [ʊ], [ɒ], [ɔː], [ɑː], and [aɪ]. By age 4, all the vowels and diphthongs were in use, and only a few consonants were still posing problems – [θ], [ð], [dʒ], and [ʒ], and certain uses of [l], [ŋ], [t], and [z].

It is also possible to see trends in the way children change the sounds of the language, when they attempt to use them. These trends include:

- Fricative consonants (p. 159) tend to be replaced by stops, e.g. *see* is pronounced [tiː].
- Velar consonants (p. 157) tend to be replaced by alveolar consonants, e.g. *gone* is pronounced [dɒn].
- Consonant clusters are avoided, e.g. *sky* is pronounced [kaɪ].
- Consonants at the ends of words are often omitted, e.g. *hat* is pronounced [ha].
- Unstressed syllables are often dropped, e.g. *banana* becomes [nana].
- As words become longer, sounds in one part of a word can alter the pronunciation of sounds in other parts. This tendency for sounds to 'harmonize' (p. 163) is found with both consonants and vowels. Consonant harmony is found in such pronunciations of *dog* as [gɒg] or [dɒd], with identical (or near-identical) consonants. Vowel harmony would be heard if *window* were pronounced for example as [wʊʊwʊʊ] or [wada].
- There is a preference for [w] and [j] sounds to be used instead of [l] and [r], e.g. *leg* as [jeg].

THE 'FIS' PHENOMENON

Several studies have reported intriguing conversations between a young child and an adult, showing that there may be a big difference between what children hear and what they can say. The phenomenon was first reported in the following way:

One of us, for instance, spoke to a child who called his inflated plastic fish a *fis.* In imitation of the child's pronunciation, the observer said: 'This is your *fis?*' 'No,' said the child, 'my *fis.*' He continued to reject the adult's imitation until he was told, 'That is your fish.' 'Yes,' he said, 'my *fis.*' (J. Berko & R. Brown, 1960, p. 531.)

The effect has been referred to as the '*fis* phenomenon' ever since. Such reports indicate that children know far more about adult phonology than their own pronunciation suggests.

THE EMERGENCE OF CONSONANTS

Most English consonants begin to be acquired between 2 and 4 years of age. This diagram shows the order of emergence as found in a study which elicited pronunciations of words from 20 children, using photographs of familiar objects. The periods shown are averages, and the upper age-limit is based on a correct pronunciation by 90% of the children. The diagram also shows that some sounds were already being produced correctly by the majority of the children at age 2; and others were still not being said correctly at age 4. (After E. M. Prather *et al.,* 1975.)

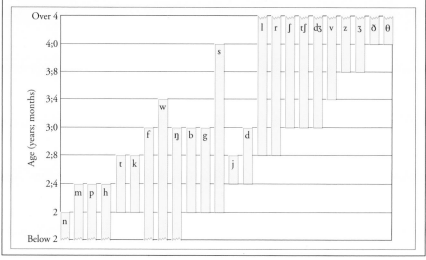

REDUPLICATION

During the second year, an effect known as *reduplication* (p. 177) is an important feature of children's phonologies: the different syllables of a word are pronounced in the same way. In one child, *water* was pronounced [wɔwɔ], *bottle* as [bubu], and *window* as [mumu]. Even monosyllabic words can be reduplicated, as when *ball* becomes [bɔbɔ].

Children do not all reduplicate to the same extent. With some children, most words are affected, and the process can be observed for several months. In other cases, there may be very few words involved, and the effect may last only a few days. The difference can be seen in the following word-lists, taken from two children, A and B. A is a reduplicator: the list contains ten complete reduplications and five items where there is only a small change between the syllables. B uses just one reduplicated word (*kitten*). (After R. G. Schwartz et al., 1980, p. 79.)

A:

Christmas	dʲɪdʲɪ
necklace	nɛkɛ
hungry	hʌːn
chip	tɪ
water	wɔwɔ
chicken	kɪkə
banana	mɪmɪ, mɪmɪ
thank you	dɛtɛː
sister	sɪsʌː
belly button	bebə
mouth	mɑmɑv
clock	kɑk
candy	keɪː
money	mɪmɪ
house	dɪdɪ

Tigger	tɪdɪ
scissors	dɪdɪ
take	kɛkɛ
Angie	næno

B:

Snoopy	supɪ, nupɪ
necklace	nɛkɪs
hungry	hʌŋkɪ
chip	tɪp
water	wɔt
chicken	tʃɪk
drop	dʌp
sock	ʃɑp
Francie	fæ⁓tɪ
hospital	pit
hair	heɪr
truck	tʌk
kitten	kɪkɪ
powder	pɑv
pencil	pɛtə
burger	bɜ˞gə
outside	aʊsaɪd
boat	bot
Eleanor	əno

The purpose of reduplication has been much discussed. It may be partly motivated simply by the need to play with sounds or to practise them. But it is more likely that the process helps children as they try to cope with the pronunciation of more complicated words. It has been argued that a word like *tiger*, with its changes of consonant and vowel, would be difficult for a 1½-year-old to learn at one go: reduplication would give the child a chance to master the pronunciation in stages, by first producing the word's syllable structure and stress, along with the most noticeable phonetic features. A more precise pronunciation would come later, after this phonetic outline had been learned.

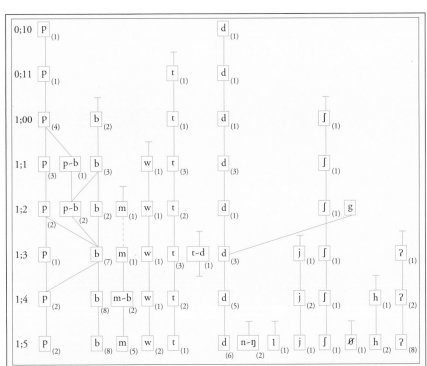

Phone trees So many things happen at once in a developing phonological system that it is always difficult to follow what is going on. 'Phone trees' are an attempt to visualize the emerging relationships between different types of phonetic segment, or *phone* (§27) over a period of time. The trees illustrated (above) show the initial consonant system of a child, *H*, between 10 months (0;10) and 17 months (1;5), based on a series of recorded samples. Development of different classes of phones over time is shown vertically, and the set of phones used by *H* at any one point is shown horizontally.

The procedure grouped together all *H*'s versions of a given word, as well as all *H*'s words that began with the same phones. Each class of phones is summarized within a box: for example, $\boxed{p}_{(4)}$ means that *H* used 4 tokens beginning with [p] in a given session; $\boxed{p \sim b}_{(2)}$ means that there were 2 cases of variation between [p] and [b]. If successive samples contained the same word, the boxes are joined by a solid vertical line; if a phone was being used in different words (e.g. *mama*, *milk*), they were linked by a dotted line. We can thus see how *H*'s phonological inventory increases over time, as well as the variation affecting individual words. (From C. A. Ferguson & C. B. Farwell, 1975.)

Diagrams of this kind have proved to be very useful in the study of phonological acquisition, as they clearly show the difficulty of making simple generalizations about how individual phonemes are learned.

INTONATION – EARLY AND LATE

Most children have begun to make some use of their language's intonation patterns (§29) before the end of the first year. Different tones of voice are used to express such meanings as questioning, demanding, calling, greeting, warning, recognition, and surprise. During the second year, as two-word sentences develop (p. 244), a wider range of attitudes is expressed, and prosody begins to signal differences in emphasis. At this point, it becomes possible to distinguish such general sentences as *Daddy gone* from the contrastive **Daddy** *gone* (i.e. not someone else).

As the child's grammatical and social abilities develop, so new uses of intonation emerge. For example, the contrast between rising and falling tones differentiates the two functions of a tag question in English ('asking', as in *He's outside, isn't he?*, and 'telling', as in *He's outside, isn't he!*), and this is learned during the third year, along with the grammar.

What is surprising is that the learning of intonation goes on for so long. Children seem to master the formal patterns of intonation quite early on, but their awareness of the range of meanings that these patterns convey is still developing as they approach their teens. This was first shown in a study of the way British radio and TV announcers read out football results (e.g. *Everton 3, Liverpool 3*). By listening to the intonation of the first part of the result, it is possible for adults to predict whether the score is going to be a draw, a home win, or an away win (p. 56). When this task was given to children aged 7 to 11, it was found that the youngest children were hardly able to do it, and even the oldest children did not reach the level of competence shown by the adults. In fact, only one child out of 28 got all the results right (A. Cruttenden, 1974).

The implications of this experiment go well beyond the world of football, for the intonation patterns used are to be found in everyday speech also. It seems that aspects of the intonation system are not only the first phonological features to be learned, but also some of the last. Even teenagers have been shown to have difficulty understanding the difference, signalled by intonation and pause, between such sentences as *she dressed, and fed the baby* (i.e. the person dressed herself, and then fed the baby) and *she dressed and fed the baby* (i.e. the baby is both dressed and fed). There can be few clearer examples of the differences that can exist between production and comprehension skills (p. 234).

SINGLE-WORD UTTERANCES

The earliest stage of grammatical development hardly seems like grammar at all, since only single words are involved – utterances such as *Gone, More, Dada,* and *Bye-bye.* Sometimes longer-sounding utterances are heard (such as *Allgone* or *All-fall-down*), but these are deceptive: they have been learned as whole phrases, and children use them as if they were single units.

Most of the words used at this stage (about 60%) seem to have a naming function and will develop into nouns. About 20% express actions. Many of these will develop into verbs, though not all. When a child says *In!*, holding a brick and gesturing violently at a container, we have to interpret this as an action utterance, even though the word class (p. 91) is a preposition. Other word classes are also found at this stage (such as adjectives and adverbs), along with several words that it is difficult to assign to any word class (such as *Bye-bye*).

The 'one-word' stage is usually most noticeable between 12 and 18 months. But to talk about it solely in terms of 'words' is misleading. In many respects, these early utterances function as if they were sentences (and they have been given capital letters above, to represent this interpretation). For example, one child used the word *dada* in three different ways: as he heard someone approach outside, he said *Dada?*, with a rising intonation; as he saw that it was indeed daddy, he said *Dada*, with a triumphant, falling intonation; and then he said *Da-da!*, with an insistent, level, intonation, with his arms outstretched. At a later stage in development, these three functions would be called 'question', 'statement', and 'command'. At this stage, these utterances do not have a distinctive grammatical form, but the use of prosody and gesture conveys the force of these sentence types nonetheless. In such cases, many scholars are happy to talk about 'one-word sentences', or *holophrases.*

TWO-WORD SENTENCES

Most people think of 'real' grammar as beginning when children string two or more words together, which takes place around 18 months. This tends not to happen abruptly. There is usually a transitional period, in which words are brought together, but the sequence is not uttered as a single, rhythmical unit, as in *Daddy. Gone.* Lengthy sequences of such words can often be heard: one child said *Daddy. Garden. See. Daddy. Daddy. Garden* in quick succession. But soon two-word sentences emerge with great confidence – and increasing frequency.

ON WUGS, AND OTHER THINGS

Languages often make use of a system of word endings to express grammatical meanings (§§16, 50). English has around a dozen such endings (*-ing, -s, -ed,* etc.). When do children learn about these morphological aspects of grammar?

One of the best-known early studies in child language investigated this question (J. Berko, 1958). The experimenter elicited from the children a series of forms which required different grammatical endings, such as plurals and past tenses. The instructions were all of the type illustrated in the picture (right), which was the first item in the study. The experimenter would show the child the picture and read out the text, leaving the child to supply the missing word in the sentence 'There are two-.' If the children said *wugs*, it was inferred that they had learned the plural ending. If they said *wug*, they had not.

It is important to use nonsense words in experiments of this kind, to guarantee a genuine response. If real words had been used (e.g. showing a picture of a cow, and asking for *cows*), a correct answer by a child would prove very little. The child might have learned the form *cows* by heart at some point, and might not really know that it was composed of *cow + -s.* Invented words get round this problem.

There have now been several studies of children's learning of English morphology. They show that some word endings (usually

This is a wug

Now there is another one. There are two of them. There are two _____

-ing and plural) first appear at around 18 months, but take several months to be used correctly. Other endings appear at intervals over the subsequent two years, and show a similarly gradual pattern of development. Many irregular inflectional patterns (e.g. comparative forms such as *worse*) may not be correctly used until the age of 8 or 9.

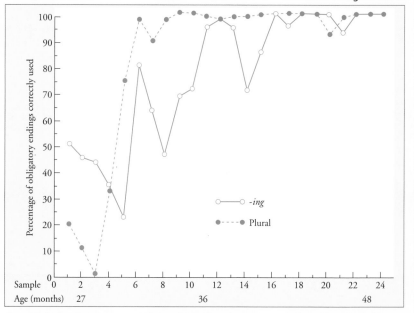

One child's development of the *-ing* and plural inflections between age 27 and 48 months. The diagram shows the gradual nature of morphological acquisition. The plural ending takes only a short time to reach the 90% level of correct use, whereas the *-ing* ending takes 16 months to get from a 50% level (at sample 1) to the 100% level (in sample 16). There are several dips in the child's performance, probably due to fluctuations in the number of instances that turned up in the various samples, but the general trend is rising. The curves start to flatten out at around the 90% level, which has led several investigators to conclude that this is the point when 'acquisition' of a feature can be confidently asserted. (After R. Brown, 1973.)

Several studies have been made of the meanings expressed by these two-word sentences. They include such sequences as the following:

an Actor performs an Action	*Daddy kick.*
an Action affects an Object	*Shut door.*
an Object is given a Location	*There teddy.*
an Object or Person is Described	*She cold.*

These sentences could also be described in more traditional grammatical terms. *Daddy kick*, for example, has the clause structure (p. 95) Subject + Verb; *She cold* could be analysed into Pronoun + Adjective word classes. However, not all sentences uttered by children at this stage are capable of a clear grammatical or semantic analysis. One child looked at a photograph of her father and said *Daddy Mummy*; another put a car in a garage and said *Car want*. We may hazard plausible meanings to such sequences, but definite interpretations are often out of the question.

SENTENCE STRUCTURE

At around 2 years of age, many children produce sentences that are three or four words in length (p. 235), and combine these words in several different ways to produce a variety of grammatical constructions. Typical sentences at this stage include *Man kick ball, Him got car, Where daddy going?*, and *Put that on there*. Questions and commands are being used as well as statements, and different clause patterns are now evident. By the end of the third year, clause structures of four or five elements can be heard, as in *You give me my car now*.

The 'telegraphic' character of early sentences has often been noted in many children – an impression derived from the omission of grammatical words (such as *the* and *is*) and word endings (such as *-ing*). By the end of the third year, this character has largely disappeared, and children's sentences more closely resemble their adult counterparts.

Towards the age of 3, there is a major grammatical advance, with the appearance of sentences containing more than one clause. A large proportion of these sentences are coordinate clauses (p. 95), linked mainly by *and* – a pattern which, once learned, produces utterances that go on and on:

Daddy have breaked the spade all up and – and – and it broken – and – he did hurt his hand on it and – and - and – it's gone all sore and...

Sentences involving subordination (p. 95) are also increasingly found at this age, using such words as '*cos, so, if, after, what,* and *when*:

I let go 'cos it hurted me.
Tell me what it's called.

A great deal of grammatical knowledge is required before these constructions are used correctly, and it is common to find errors and non-fluency as children attempt to handle longer sequences. For example, this child of 3 years 9 months gets into trouble with his sequence of tenses, as he tries to express a complicated thought:

If Father Christmas come down the chimney, and he will have presents when he came down, can I stay up to see him?

The sorting out of grammatical errors is a particular feature of 4-year-old speech. Many of the irregularities of syntax and morphology are being mastered around this age, though it can take several years before such errors as the following are eliminated:

You bettern't do that.
That's more better.
Are there much toys in the cupboard?
It just got brokened.
Are we going on the bus home?

The study of errors is important, because they show children breaking fresh grammatical ground. They provide the main evidence of how children go about actively learning new constructions.

More advanced grammatical constructions continue to be acquired throughout the early school years. Around the age of 7, more sophisticated forms of sentence connection begin to emerge, using such words as *really, though, anyway,* and (at later ages) *for instance, actually,* and *of course*. Children begin to distinguish different underlying meanings for sentences that look the same (e.g. *Ask John what time it is* vs *Tell John what time it is*). And they consolidate their awareness of the way sentences may have the same meaning even though they look very different – for example, the relationship between active and passive sentences (*The girl chased the boy* ↔ *The boy was chased by the girl*), which is not thoroughly sorted out until the ninth year. A popular impression of grammatical learning is that it is complete by age 5; but recent studies have shown that the acquisition of several types of construction is still taking place as children approach 10 or 11.

SAYING NO

Several studies have been made of the expression of negation by young children.

1. The first negative words emerge in the second year – usually *no* or *not* as a one-word sentence.

2. The negative words combine with other words to make two-word sentences: *No sit, Gone no, Not there.* Several different meanings can be expressed at this stage – in particular, non-existence, e.g. *No car* (while looking for a toy); rejection, e.g. *No drink* (while pushing a drink away); and denial, e.g. *Not mine* (pointing to someone else's coat). (L. M. Bloom, 1970.)

3. During the third year, negative words come to be used within constructions, e.g. *You no do that, Mummy not got it.* At the same time, such verbs as *can't* and *won't* appear.

4. The negative words and endings come to be used more accurately: *not* replaces *no*, and *n't* is used with more verbs, e.g. *You've not got one, She isn't going.* 'Double' negatives for emphasis (§1) are a normal development, e.g. *Nobody don't like to go in.*

5. A few advanced negative constructions are not acquired until the early school years, e.g. the use of *some* vs *any* (cf. *I've not got any* rather than **I've got any*), or the use of *hardly* and *scarcely*.

ASKING QUESTIONS

One of the first topics to be studied by child language researchers was how children learn to ask questions. Three main stages have been proposed for English, and similar developments have been noted in several other languages:
1. The earliest stage makes use of intonation (§29), e.g. *Daddy there?*, spoken with a high rising tone, in effect asks 'Is Daddy there?'
2. During the second year, children start to use question words. *What* and *where* are usually the first to be acquired, with *why, how,* and *who* coming later. These questions become more complex as the

third year approaches, e.g. *Where Daddy going?, What you doing in there?*
3. A major advance comes with the learning of the verb *to be*, and such auxiliary verbs as *have* and *do*. Children discover the apparently simple rule that turns statements into questions by changing the order of the Subject and Verb (e.g. *That is a car → Is that a car?*), and then learn that it is not so simple after all (e.g. it cannot be **Went he to town?*, but *Did he go to town?*). Sentences that use question words pose particular problems: *Where is Daddy going?* has in fact *two* forms indicating its status as a

question – the word *where* and the inversion *is Daddy*. Children often rely on the first alone, and for a while produce such sentences as *Where Daddy is going?*. (After R. Brown et al., 1968.)

The complexity of question formation can be seen from the following selection of errors, all made by 2-year-olds:
   Whose is that is?
   What are you did?
   What did you bought?
   Is it's my car?
   Don't he wanted it?
Despite this complexity, most of these difficulties are overcome before the age of 3.

The learning of vocabulary (§17) is the most noticeable feature of the early months of language acquisition. From the point when a child's 'first word' is identified, there is a steady lexical growth in both comprehension and production. An indication of the scope and speed of progress can be obtained from a study of American 1-year-olds: the average time it took eight children to get from 10 to 50 words in production was 4.8 months – about 10 new words a month. In comprehension, the children understood an average of 22 new words each month (H. Benedict, 1979). By 18 months, it is thought that most children can speak about 50 words and understand about five times as many.

THE CONTENT OF EARLY VOCABULARY

Young children talk about what is going on around them – the 'here and now' – and rapidly build a vocabulary in several semantic fields (p. 104).

- *People* mainly relatives and house visitors – *daddy, baba, grandma, man, postman*.
- *Actions* the way things move (*give, jump, kiss, gone*), and routine activities in the child's day (*bye-bye, hello*).
- *Food* occasions as well as products – *din-din, milk, juice, drink, apple*.
- *Body parts* usually facial words first (*mouth, nose*), then other areas (*toes, handie(s)*) and body functions (*wee-wee*).
- *Clothing* of all kinds – *nappy/diaper, shoes, coat*.
- *Animals* whether real, in pictures, or on TV – *doggie, cat, horse, lion*.
- *Vehicles* objects and their noises – *car, choo-choo, brrm*.
- *Toys and games* many possibilities – *ball, bricks, book, dolly, peep-bo*.
- *Household objects* all to do with daily routine – *cup, spoon, brush, clock, light*.
- *Locations* several general words – *there, look, in, up*.
- *Social words* response noises – *m, yes, no, ta*.
- *Describing words* early adjectives – *hot, pretty, big*.
- *Situational words* several 'pointing' words (deictics, p. 106) – *that, mine, them*.

HOW MUCH DO CHILDREN SAY IN A DAY?

Using radio microphones and tape recorders, it is now possible to make large-scale surveys of children's lexical usage. Large portions of a child's day can be recorded – in some cases, covering everything the child says between waking up and bedtime.

The table below gives the age of several German children recorded in one study, along with the length of the recording, and the number of word tokens (§15) used in the recording. As the recording times are not the same, the right-hand column gives a standardized total, based on an assumed 12-hour day.

Age (years; months)	Time (mins.)	Tokens	12-hr total
1;5	202	3,881	13,800
1;8	241	3,907	11,700
2;1	213	5,978	20,200
3;6	189	9,891	37,700
5;4	152	6,464	30,600
8;7	193	6,630	24,700
9;2	311	10,524	24,400
9;6	869	25,401	21,000
9;7	804	28,142	25,200

These results far exceeded the expectations of the researchers. No-one had imagined that children as young as 2 could produce in excess of 20,000 words in a day, or that a 3½-year-old could produce nearly twice that number!

The number of different words (word types, §15) used during the day was also much larger than had been expected. These ranged from a remarkable 1,860 (for the 1;5-year-old) to over 5,000 for an 11-year-old, with an average of 3,000 for the whole group. (After K. R. Wagner, 1985, p. 477.)

No corresponding survey has yet taken place for English. But as the children came from a variety of social backgrounds, and engaged in many kinds of activity during their day, it is likely that the figures will be fairly typical – in which case, traditional impressions of children's vocabulary growth (p. 234) will have to be radically revised, in an upward direction.

THE FIRST 50 WORDS

These are the first 50 words used by two American children between 11 and 16 months. There are very few items in common, and major differences in order (e.g. *mommy* is Sarah's second word, but Daniel's forty-third).

	Daniel		*Sarah*
1.	light	1.	baby
2.	uh-oh	2.	mommy
3.	what's that	3.	doggie
4.	wow	4.	juice
5.	banana	5.	bye-bye
6.	kitty	6.	daddy
7.	baby	7.	milk
8.	moo	8.	cracker
9.	quack	9.	done
10.	cookie	10.	ball
11.	nice	11.	shoe
12.	rock (noun)	12.	teddy
13.	clock	13.	book
14.	sock	14.	kitty
15.	woof-woof	15.	hi
16.	daddy	16.	Alex
17.	bubble	17.	no (-no)
18.	hi	18.	door
19.	shoe	19.	dolly
20.	up	20.	what's that?
21.	bye-bye	21.	cheese
22.	bottle	22.	oh wow
23.	no	23.	oh
24.	rock (verb)	24.	button
25.	eye	25.	eye
26.	nose	26.	apple
27.	fire	27.	nose
28.	hot	28.	bird
29.	yogurt	29.	alldone
30.	pee-pee	30.	orange
31.	juice	31.	bottle
32.	ball	32.	coat
33.	whack	33.	hot
34.	frog	34.	bib
35.	hello	35.	hat
36.	yuk	36.	more
37.	apple	37.	ear
38.	Big Bird	38.	night-night
39.	walk	39.	paper
40.	Ernie	40.	toast
41.	horse	41.	O'Toole
42.	more	42.	bath
43.	mommy	43.	down
44.	bunny	44.	duck
45.	my	45.	leaf
46.	nut	46.	cookie
47.	orange	47.	lake
48.	block	48.	car
49.	night-night	49.	rock (noun)
50.	milk	50.	box

(After C. Stoel-Gammon & J. A. Cooper, 1984, p. 264.)

THE MEANING OF EARLY WORDS

Children do not learn a word with its meaning 'ready made'. They have to work out for themselves what it must mean, and in so doing they make errors. Three types of error occur often during the second and third year.

1. *Overextension* A word is 'extended' to apply to other objects that share a certain feature, such as a common property of shape, colour, or size. *Dog* might be applied to other animals, or *moon* to other round objects.

2. *Underextension* In this case, the word is used with a narrower meaning than it has in the adult language. *Dog* might be applied only to the family dog, or *shoes* only to a child's own shoes.

3. *Mismatch* Here, there is no apparent basis for the wrong use of a word by the child, as when in one case a telephone was referred to as a *tractor*. There is usually no way of tracing back the association of ideas that has caused such misidentifications.

CUPS AND GLASSES

Children can take several years to learn the meaning of a word, especially when the word is used along with others to refer to objects or ideas that are not easy to distinguish. Even everyday objects may prove difficult to differentiate and label in a consistent way – such as the distinction between 'cups' and 'glasses'.

The uncertain boundary between these categories is well illustrated from the 25 drinking vessels drawn in the diagram below. For adults, some of these are clearly cups, some are clearly glasses, and some require a more complex kind of description. How long does it take children to become aware of these distinctions?

Children aged between 3½ and 12½ were shown this set of objects, and asked to carry out various tasks, such as naming, defining, and sorting. The youngest children used far fewer names to describe the objects, often overextending the word *cup* to apply to items which the 12-year-olds called *glass* (e.g. items 4 and 9 in the diagram). One 3-year-old went the other way, calling most things *glass*, and keeping *cup* for the smallest items.

Both *glass* and *mug* came to be used regularly by the 6-year-olds, who also added such labels as *dish* and *vase*. A still wider range of labels was used by the older children (e.g. *eggholder, can, measure*). During this period, also, there was an increasing use made of words reflecting the perceptual properties of the objects – especially their size, shape, and material (e.g. *big, round, paper*). However, between 6 and 9, the children's preferences showed a clear change: the older they became, the more they preferred to use attributes reflecting what they thought were the functional properties of the objects (e.g. *medicine cup, Martini glass*).

By age 9, some quite subtle distinctions were being made, with the names and definitions showing that the children were beginning to be aware that they were dealing with an area where boundaries are vague. This is most clearly shown from the definitions they gave, which contained qualifying words, such as *usually* or *could have*; for example 'a cup holds things to drink, and sometimes has a handle...', 'a glass is like a cup only it could be taller, doesn't have a handle, and could be plastic or glass'. It is age 12 before competence becomes close to that of an adult – nine years or more after the distinction is first introduced. (From E. S. Andersen, 1975.)

FOUR REPLIES

	Age 3	Age 6	Age 9	Age 12
1.	cup	glass	glass	fruit cup
2.	big cup	glass	glass	wine glass
3.	little cup	glass	a measure	cup for liqueur
4.	little cup	glass	glass	juice glass
5.	big cup	dish	little tiny dish	fruit cup
6.	big cup	glass	glass	glass
7.	cup	glass	cup	glass
8.	little cup	plastic cup	glass	medicine cup
9.	big cup	plastic cup	glass	glass
10.	cup	plastic cup	cup	outdoor cup
11.	Ron McDonald cup	plastic cup	glass	Ron McDonald happy cup
12.	little cup	plastic cup	cup	cup
13.	cup	glass	glass	cup
14.	big cup	cup	cup	coffee cup
15.	coffee cup	plastic cup	cup	sipper cup
16.	cup	cup	cup	coffee cup
17.	paper cup	paper cup	cup	Dixie cup
18.	big cup	cup	glass	glass
19.	orange cup	metal cup	measure for wine	measuring cup
20.	little cup	metal cup	cup	baby's metal cup
21.	coffee cup	mug	coffee mug	coffee cup
22.	coffee cup	glass cup	cup	beer mug
23.	coffee cup	glass (mug)	cup	mug
24.	cup	glass	cup	coffee cup
25.	cup	cup	cup	coffee cup

After the age of 18 months, very little precise information is available. By age 2, spoken vocabulary probably exceeds 200 words. But after this, estimates become extremely vague. A dramatic increase in the size and diversity of the lexicon takes place during the third year, so much so that it has not yet proved possible to make accurate calculations (especially about vocabulary comprehension), or work out any norms of spoken lexical frequency. What happens at older ages is largely guesswork, and vocabulary totals cited for these children should therefore be viewed with great caution.

Other issues

The study of semantic development takes in far more than vocabulary (p. 107). Grammatical constructions also need to be studied from a semantic point of view – for example, the way in which children master the complex conditional meaning of *if* constructions, or the causal meaning of *because, so,* or *since*. That there are problems here can be readily shown from the errors children make:

The man's fallen off the ladder because he's broken his leg.
I had one fish left, because its name was Bill.

Children aged 8 or 9 may have mastered the grammar of such constructions very well, but still be having difficulty with the meanings they encode. Auxiliary verbs such as *ought, must,* and *should* provide another problem area, as do subtle prepositional forms (e.g. *despite*) and verb contrasts (e.g. *ask* vs *tell, say* vs *promise*). The ability to use figurative expressions, and to see double meanings in language, also develops largely after the age of 6.

One of the most significant developments of this later period is the child's emerging ability to integrate several features of semantic knowledge into a single defining statement. Young children cannot define: in response to such questions as 'What's X?', they give empty, ambiguous, or idiosyncratic replies. *What's a shoe?* asked an adult. *That,* replied one young child, pointing. *And a sock,* replied another. *Mummy got a shoe* replied a third. Gradually, however, definitions become more sophisticated. A particular feature is singled out (*A knife is sharp*) or its function is specified (*A knife is when you cut with it*). But it is not until around age 8 or 9 that statements with something resembling an adult definitional form begin to be produced (*An apple is a sort of fruit, and it's round and red, and we eat it*). (B. Litowitz, 1977.)

Semantic development continues throughout the school years – and, indeed, throughout adult life. Unlike phonology and grammar, it is not largely over when children enter their teens. There is always new vocabulary to be learned, and new worlds of meaning to explore.

The task of language acquisition requires that children learn much more than patterns of sound, grammar, and vocabulary. They must also learn to use these patterns appropriately in a rapidly increasing range of everyday social situations. This developing *pragmatic* awareness (§21) has attracted a great deal of study in recent years, particularly in relation to the way children learn strategies of conversational interaction. It is not yet possible to talk about definite stages of development; but the very early age at which these strategies emerge is now clearly established.

CONVERSATIONAL SKILLS

Between the ages of 2 and 4, a remarkable development takes place in the ability of the child to participate in a conversation. At the earlier age, conversations are often very erratic and disjointed, with parents doing most of the 'work', and children using sequences of utterances, many of which are not obviously directed to any listener. The effect is a curious mixture of monologue and dialogue:

CHILD: Ball. Kick. Kick. Daddy kick.
MOTHER: That's right, you have to kick it, don't you.
CHILD: Mmm. Um. Um. Kick hard. Only kick hard.
   Our play that. On floor. Our play that on floor. Now.
   Our play that. On floor. Our play that on floor. No that.
   Now.
MOTHER: All right.
CHILD: Mummy, come on floor me.
MOTHER: Yes.
CHILD: You tip those out.
MOTHER: Mm. All right.
CHILD: That one broke.

(P. Fletcher, 1985, p. 64.)

The contrast with a 3-year-old's conversation is striking, with both parties very much involved with the detail of what each is saying:

CHILD: Hester be fast asleep, mummy.
MOTHER: She was tired.
CHILD: And why did her have two sweets, mummy?
MOTHER: Because you each had two, that's why.
   She had the same as you. Ooh dear, now what?
CHILD: Daddy didn't give me two in the end.
MOTHER: Yes, he did.
CHID: He didn't.
MOTHER: He did.
CHILD: Look he given one to – two to Hester, and two to us.
MOTHER: Yes, that's right.
CHILD: Why did he give?
MOTHER: 'Cos there were six sweets. That's two each.

(P. Fletcher, 1985, p. 91.)

By 3, it is plain that children have learned many aspects of conversational strategy. They are able to initiate a dialogue – the various ways of obtaining and holding a listener's attention. They can handle several of the conventions of turn-taking. They know a great deal about how to respond appropriately – for example, by providing clarification when requested to do so.

These skills develop greatly between 3 and 5. In particular, there is a major development in child awareness of the social factors that govern a successful conversation – such as the correct use of forms of address and markers of politeness (e.g. *please, sorry*), and how to make requests in an indirect way. They also learn to anticipate points of potential breakdown (carry out conversational 'repairs', p. 116), such as by repeating utterances that are unclear, or asking for clarification. In particular, they develop their ability to cope with situations where they do not have things all their own way. In one study of two 4-year-old children playing together, there were 576 sequences in which one child (*A*) requested the other (*B*) to perform an action; in 122 cases, *B* refused to comply. It was therefore necessary for *A* to adopt various persuasive tactics in order to gain compliance:

A: Say yes.
B: No.
A: I'll be your best friend if you say yes.

    ... ...

A: Change lunch boxes.
B: No.
A: You'll have a bigger one, so you will.

(M. McTear, 1985, p. 109.)

Some of these exchanges can be very lengthy. In the same study, *A*'s request for a pair of scissors was continued for over 60 turns before it was (reluctantly) complied with.

Studies of young children's conversations show that many adult interaction skills are already present well before school-age. There is still a great deal to learn, of course – for example, 5-year-olds do not make much use of such 'manipulating' devices as *you know* or *actually*, and they must learn the strategies associated with the more formal interactions that are part of educational learning and discussion (§44). But all of this will build on a foundation of conversational ability that in many children is already extremely sophisticated by the fifth year.

TALKING BACKWARDS

From around age 7, children develop a large creative repertoire of interactive linguistic skills, as they learn to tell jokes and riddles, insult each other, maintain group identity, and make up language games (p. 59). One of the most remarkable of these abilities is talking backwards.

A study of two 9-year-olds who were able to talk backwards showed two quite distinct styles. One child (*A*) reversed the sounds of each word and ignored the spelling. The second (*B*) reversed the spellings, sounding the letters out. The pronunciations which resulted were very different. *Size*, for example, would come out as [zaɪs], using *A*'s method, but would come out as [ezɪs] using *B*'s. Here is a selection of their reversed words:

	A	B
nine	naɪn	'ɛnɪn
guy	aɪg	jag
boil	lɔɪb	ljab
mouse	saʊm	'ɛsuam
continue	ujə'nɪtnak	'utənɪk
bomb	mab	bəmab
castle	lə'sæk	'ɛltsæk
axe	skæ	ksæ
bone	nob	'ɛnab
auto	oʹta	'otuwa
inhale	lɛ'nɪ	ɛlə'næ
elevate	'tevəlɛ	ˌɛtæ'levet

The sentence 'Please present an idea to the class' was translated by *B* as: [ɛsɛlp tənɛ'zɛp næʔəɛdə ʔʌt ʔɛt ʔɛ'sɛlk]. The words are not always perfectly accurate reversals; but there is clearly a system of rules governing their production.

Once someone learns to talk backwards, the ability seems to stay. Interviews with 27 adults who had been backward talkers as children showed that the ability was still present. Some were only able to do it slowly, or on short words, but three retained an impressive facility, reversing not only the order of sounds in words, but the order of words in sentences as well – and often at speeds very similar to those found in forwards speech! (After N. Cowan & L. Leavitt, 1982, pp 491, ff.)

TWINS

The language learning environment of twins is unique. During their early years, their linguistic experience differs greatly from that of single children. Singletons receive most of their language stimulation from adults or older children, whose utterances provide a more advanced learning 'target'. Twins, however, spend a great deal of time together, with each learning from a linguistic setting in which the other speaker is at the same developmental linguistic level. In such circumstances, it is hardly surprising to find many twins developing a private form of communication.

One study found a great deal of private language play in early-morning twin conversations. At 33 months, for example, there were dialogues in which each child responded to features of pronunciation it noticed in the other:

A: zæki su
B: (*laughing*) zæki su zæki (*both laugh*) æː
A: apiː
B: olp olt olt
A: opiː opiː
B: apiː apiː (*laughing*) api api api
A: ai ju
B: (*laughing*) ai ju api (*repeated several times*)
A: kaki (*repeated several times*)
B: ai iː oː
A: ai iː o oː

(E. O. Keenan, 1974, p. 171.)

To the outsider, this kind of dialogue might resemble a 'secret language', but it is no more than a form of phonetic play.

One of the most interesting features of twin language is the way in which they 'share' the response to an adult utterance:

MOTHER: What can you see in the picture?
TWIN A: A cat.
TWIN B: And a dog.

Observers have been struck by the intuitive way in which one twin is able to respond very rapidly to what the other has just said, and how the first twin is able to anticipate when to stop. They very seldom talk at the same time. Even very short utterances can be split in two:

MOTHER: What do you want me to read?
TWIN A: Puss.
TWIN B: In boots.

This kind of skill can only come from the frequent opportunities the twins have had to interact, in the early years. They know each other's rhythms, and each is able to predict a great deal of what the other is likely to say.

Perhaps because of this close dependence, twins are usually somewhat late in developing their individual language skills. When their language is formally assessed, during the third and fourth years, it is often found to be about 6 months behind the norm for singletons. On the other hand, there are certain aspects of their development that may be ahead of other children – notably, their ability to keep a conversation going, and to interact with adults. By age 7 or 8, the delay seems to have disappeared.

POTO AND CABENGA

GRACE: Cabenga, padem manibadu peeta.
VIRGINIA: Doan nee bada tengkmatt, Poto.

Reported extracts of this kind from a twin conversation achieved world-wide publicity in the late 1970s. They came from the Kennedy twins of San Diego, California, who at the age of 8 were still using their own private language. They called themselves by different names in this language: Grace became 'Poto' and Virginia became 'Cabenga' – names which were later used as the title of a film about their early years.

Their totally unintelligible speech for a while promoted the impression that the children were mentally retarded, but this proved not to be so. In due course, a detailed study of their language came to be made. This indicated that their speech was not as alien as its bizarre sound had led people to believe. It was basically a severely distorted form of English, with some features of German, several idiosyncratic grammatical characteristics, and a proportion of invented vocabulary. What made it so difficult to follow (and also to analyse!) was its extremely rapid speed of articulation and its staccato rhythm – features that later transferred to their English, when therapists began to work with them.

There are probably special reasons for the late retention of private speech in this case. The children, it seems, had very little opportunity to hear good models of English speech in their early years. They saw few other children in the area where they lived. Their parents were both working, and during the day they were cared for by their German grandmother who spoke no English. There was also an expectation that they might be retarded (because of a history of convulsions), which affected the style of the parents' interaction. Left to themselves, the twins would have had little alternative but to develop their own medium of communication.

SECRET LANGUAGES

Twins have often been observed to talk to each other in a way that is unintelligible to adults or other children. The phenomenon has been variously labelled 'cryptophasia', 'idioglossia', or 'autonomous speech'. Estimates of incidence are uncertain, but some have suggested that as many as 40% of twin pairs develop some form of private speech, especially in the second year.

There seems to be no basis for the view that a completely different 'language' is involved. The patterns heard can largely be explained with reference to the children's efforts to cope with the kind of language used around them, and to the kind of processes that take place in normal language acquisition. The twin situation promotes the continued use of immature and idiosyncratic patterns of sound, grammar, and vocabulary, and a personal style of interaction often characterized by abnormal intonation and rhythm. These patterns become particularly noticeable when the children continue to use them past the normal period of 'baby talk'. In the most dramatic cases, private speech has lasted until age 5 or more, when it often attracts a great deal of publicity.

When children arrive in school, they experience a different linguistic world. They meet for the first time children from unfamiliar regional, social, and ethnic backgrounds, whose linguistic norms differ greatly from their own. They encounter a social situation in which levels of formal and informal speech are carefully distinguished, and standards of correctness emphasized. The educational setting presents them with a variety of unfamiliar, subject-related styles of language. They have to learn a new range of linguistic skills – reading, writing, and spelling. And they find themselves having to talk about what they are doing, which requires that they learn a special technical vocabulary – a 'language for talking about language', or *metalanguage*.

In recent years, educationists have begun to recognize the complexity of the language demands being made on the young schoolchild, and to realize that progress in many areas of the curriculum is greatly dependent on a satisfactory foundation of linguistic skills. The traditional emphasis on *literacy*, the ability to read and write, has been supplemented by an emphasis on *oracy*, the ability to speak and listen. Teachers now pay increasing attention to a child's preschool linguistic experience, seeing this as a foundation on which they can build. Special efforts are made to relate different kinds of linguistic learning: the task of writing is being brought closer to the child's experience of reading; reading, in turn, is being brought into contact with the ability to use spoken language; and oral skills are being supplemented by work on listening comprehension. Above all, teachers have begun to stress that children's linguistic ability is a major factor influencing their success in the learning of other subject areas, such as science, mathematics, and history.

In the 1970s, this central, integrating role of language work promoted a host of new language schemes, materials, and approaches, and a philosophy which is best summarized in a phrase that became something of an educational slogan in Britain, following the UK government's publication of the 1975 report on the teaching of English in schools, *A Language for Life* ('The Bullock Report'): 'language across the curriculum'. Since then, other aspects of the role of language have come to be better appreciated – not least, the need for a corresponding emphasis on children's 'vertical' development, as they move between classes and schools and encounter different kinds of language experience in a variety of subject areas. From the children's point of view, a great deal of language work must seem fragmentary and inconsistent, as long as no effort is made to ensure a coherent frame of reference that will accompany them as they move through the educational system. Research into the best means of achieving a coherent linguistic approach is thus a major aim of the slowly developing field of *educational linguistics*. The whole perspective is now often summarized under the heading *KAL*, or 'knowledge about language'.

IMAGINATIVE SPEECH AND WRITING

Look at this strange animal on the blackboard (hard luck!). *What sounds would it make when it is: happy? hungry? ...*

This is a task taken from a course designed to foster children's ability to use speech and writing in a more imaginative way, aimed at children aged from around 7 to 12 (R. James & R. G. Gregory, 1966). It introduces elements of art, music, and drama, and stresses the enjoyment that can be obtained from the use of language. The various exercises try to make children more aware of the different qualities of sounds made by things, animals, and people, and to stimulate their imagination to use language themselves in a more personal and creative way.

What sounds do you make when: you are given an ice cream? somebody treads on your toe? you are in a haunted house and a door opens?

Make the sound of a clock. Now, instead of the sound, make the word that comes from the sound...

At more advanced stages, the children study the power of descriptive words and the sound effects conveyed by names:

NO TALKING!

The traditional emphasis in schools on the written language (§1) led language educationists in the 1970s to emphasize the important role of speech as part of children's development and learning. It was pointed out that talk was often discouraged, and that in almost every setting, teachers did most of the talking – filling up 70% of classroom time, according to one study.

A great deal was learned from the analysis of tape recordings of teacher–pupil dialogue. One study was able to draw attention to a hitherto unrecognized problem in the styles of questioning used by teachers. An example of the difficulty comes from a class on religious education, in which T(eacher) is asking two P(upil)s about life in New Testament Palestine.

T: How did they get the water from the well? ... Do you remember? ... Yes?
P1: They ... ran the bucket down ... er ... and it was fastened on to this bit of string and it ... [*some inaudibility*] ... other end to the water.
T: You might do it that way. ... Where did they put the water ... John?
P2: In a big ... er ... pitcher.
T: Good ... in a pitcher ... which they carried on their ...?
P2: Heads.
The first question is open-ended, and *P1* takes this to mean that an improvised answer would be appropriate. He does his best, but receives only the comment 'You might do it that way', spoken in a doubtful intonation. *P2*, perhaps noticing this, gives *T* a different kind of answer, the name of the object. This is evidently the answer *T* wants, and so *P2* gets the praise – even though we might think that *P1*'s response was not unworthy.

Having studied several cases of communicative difficulty of this kind, the author comments:

The teacher teaches within his frame of reference; the pupils learn in theirs, taking in his words, which 'mean' something different to them, and struggling to incorporate this meaning into their own frames of reference. The language which is an essential instrument to him is a barrier to them. (D. Barnes, 1969, pp. 29, 30.)

As a result of such studies, the spoken language of teachers and pupils became a major focus of interest in the 1970s.

STRUCTURE vs USE

There is considerable recognition these days of the need to develop a child's linguistic skills so that they will promote educational growth inside school as well as social and personal development outside school. However, there is much less agreement about the best way of achieving a competent and confident use of language in these domains. Since the 1950s, the controversy has focused on the competing claims of two approaches to language teaching – one based on 'structure', the other based on 'use'.

Parsing

The traditional structural approach stresses the importance of getting children to analyse grammar in a conscious way, and to learn the appropriate terminology. The technique, as traditionally practised, is known by such names as 'parsing', 'clause analysis', or 'diagramming' (p. 96). Sentences would be analysed into their constituent parts, the labels for the different parts of speech would be learned, and great stress would be laid on the mastery of formal rules (§§1, 62).

This is still the most widely practised approach to mother-tongue teaching in Europe, but during the 1960s it fell out of favour in most English-speaking countries. Parsing was felt to develop a mechanical, analytic set of skills that bore little relationship to children's everyday linguistic needs. Most children, it was argued, found such exercises dull and irrelevant, unrelated to the problems and practices of living English.

Language in use

In place of parsing, there developed various approaches to the study of language in use. Pupils and their teachers would collect samples of real linguistic situations, both spoken and written, and discuss the distinctive features of the language. Typical situations, used by one leading project of the 1970s for work with older secondary school children were: advertising, news reporting, operating instructions, being tactful, using technical terms, and projecting an image. Pupils would use tape recordings, collections of written material, role play, and other techniques that provided involvement and realism. By choosing situations that would be meaningful and motivating, educationists hoped that pupils would explore the nature of their experience when using or responding to language, and thus arrive at a fresh understanding of its meaning for them. In this way, it was felt that they would develop their awareness of what language is and how it is used, and by degrees extend their own competence in handling it. Similar ideas were introduced at junior levels using more elementary functional notions, such as asking questions, giving instructions, and providing explanations.

The 'language in use' approach is still widely practised, but it too has limitations. As teachers and pupils became more involved in language activities, the need to have available a more systematic way of analysing and talking about the language became increasingly apparent. However, the approach made no provision for a standard descriptive apparatus. Criticism therefore came from teachers who felt such an apparatus was necessary, in order to facilitate the understanding of texts, and to make comparisons between them. Other critics argued, with varying levels of cogency and emotion, that a return to 'older standards' was prerequisite for progress.

Current trends

The situation in the 1980s was unclear. At one extreme there were those who advocated a wholesale return to the principles and practices of traditional parsing. At the other, there were those who avoided anything that smacked of grammatical terminology. Fortunately, in the 1990s, several fruitful intermediate positions have begun to emerge – particularly in the UK, promoted by the principles underlying the new National Curriculum in English. There is now a healthy movement arguing for a general approach based on 'awareness of language', aimed particularly at the middle years of schooling. It aims to stimulate the child's curiosity about language, and to integrate the various elements of language training in school – both 'horizontally', in relation to the different language elements across the curriculum (English, foreign languages, minority languages, etc.), and 'vertically', as the child moves up through the school. Structural and functional elements are involved, and much of the appeal of the approach lies in the way in which pupils are invited to discover the importance of *both* these aspects of language work for themselves.

Contrasting covers of two school books reflect the change in attitude towards language teaching in recent years. The first is a grammar book intended for use in Brazilian primary schools: the children are shown happily holding a grammar book, and writing out a list of parts-of-speech labels. The second is a language awareness text for use with young senior-school pupils: it shows some of the varied topics, from smoke signals to television, that form its content.

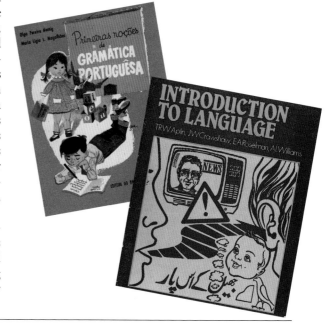

Jack and Jill
Steep huge slanted
Stamp stamp! CLIMB
Ah Well!
Stumble stumble
Clop OUCH!
O-oo-o crown

Trot Trot Trot
quick quick quick
Ah soothing
Cotton vinegar
Brown paper
Ow JILL! BED

An 11-year-old's 'poem', based on some of the work in the James & Gregory course.

What taste and what size would you give to sweets with these names? Cholly, Teenies, Wumps, Chooce, Jelloc, Quangles?

They study the stress patterns of phrases and sentences in prose and poetry; they begin to experiment with language, in the form of nonsense verse; and they look at how the effects are produced in a range of descriptive and atmospheric poetry. Here, this kind of approach links up with the traditional focus on written literature. But it is hoped that by grounding the study of literary language in the early experience of speech and sound, children will develop a more sensitive and creative approach to language work, not only in their imaginative reading and writing but also in their everyday speaking and listening.

LEARNING TO READ

Literacy has long been considered the main evidence of a child's educational progress. As a result, more attention has been paid to the nature of the task facing children as they learn to read than to any other area of the curriculum. Hundreds of reading schemes and philosophies have been devised in the past 200 years, and many have achieved a degree of success. However, it is usually an open question whether success is due to the properties of an approach or to the enthusiasm with which it is promoted by its adherents. Systematic research into the teaching of reading is relatively recent, and, although a currently fashionable field, there have as yet been few definitive findings into the nature of the child's reading process (discussed in §34) and the effectiveness of different teaching methods.

Many positions are advocated. Some recommend the initial use of a particular scheme or method to all children; others argue that there is no 'right way', and that a range of approaches should be available to suit the needs of individual children. For some, reading is essentially the skill of decoding written symbols; for others, it is a means of discovering the meaning 'behind' the symbols. In this deeper view, reading plays a fundamental role in promoting children's critical and imaginative thinking, and thus their intellectual and emotional development. A similar concern motivates the view that the teaching of reading should not be restricted to the classroom. In particular, several recent studies have indicated that regular parental reading aloud to children, accompanied by informal discussion of what is being read, may be the single most important factor in promoting reading ability.

In the afternoon, John visits a farm! He says hello to the [Farmer], who shows him around. They see some [Cows], some [Hens] and some [Pigs]. Then John and the farmer ride along a [Cornfield] on the [Tractor].

Active reading

There are two contemporary preoccupations. First, there is a focus on the need to motivate children to read by providing materials and activities that are interesting. It is pointed out that the content of traditional reading-scheme books is singularly uninspiring: children often view such reading as a dull, decoding task, and choose very different kinds of books ('real books') when they read by themselves for enjoyment. Today, this contrast is less apparent, with new schemes placing a greater emphasis on story-telling and more appealing visual design. The world of the child's own experience is also increasingly represented, though the use of familiar social situations and everyday visual language contexts, such as road signs, shop names, and vehicle labels (e.g. *taxi, police*).

A page from a lively modern sticker book – the *Rosie and Jim Sticker Book* (1992), illustrated by Joan Hickson, and based on a television series written by John Cunliffe. Some of the coloured stickers provided with the book have been placed in their positions on the page. In material of this kind, the pictures stand in for certain key words, thereby helping to reduce the reading load and to provide cues to meaning. The children get practice in recognizing the precise location of words in whole sentences, and this is reinforced by the action of sticking. However, mixing captions and maintext can raise possible teaching problems: if the caption words are shown with a captial letter, the children are exposed to a usage which conflicts with normal writing practice when the stickers are in place.

Breakthrough The active approach to reading is nowhere better illustrated than in the use of the word cards and sentence maker provided by the scheme *Breakthrough to Literacy* (D. Mackay *et al.*, 1970). Words are taken from a holder and placed on a sentence frame, to make sentences of a child's own choosing. The sentences can build on the children's personal experiences; they use words that reflect their spoken language; and they can be 'written' without the need to cope with the task of handwriting.

Syllabic teaching cards are part of a set designed to introduce children to reading through the use of syllables (as opposed to phonemes or whole words). The particular programme is known as the 'syllabary curriculum'. At the stage shown, pictures are being used to motivate a sequence of words in a sentence. Later stages involve techniques for the identification of sounds and the blending of syllables. (From P. Rozin & L. R. Gleitman, 1974.)

Secondly, there is an emphasis on training the cognitive skills that children need in order to read efficiently. Research has shown the relevance of such abilities as classifying, sequencing, and pattern matching; and new 'pre-reading' materials therefore provide practice in these areas, along with opportunities to draw, cut out, colour in, and so on. It is also evident that many children find their first encounter with the world of print confusing, so that a great deal of attention is now being paid to ways of providing an opportunity to think about what is involved in reading and writing (e.g. how are books made? what is writing for?), and a metalanguage for talking about these activities (e.g. *page, line, beginning, space*).

Much of this work involves an *active* approach to reading. When children encounter a word they cannot read, emphasis is now often laid on helping them to work out for themselves what it must be, by using such techniques as reading on to the end of the sentence, reading back to the sentence beginning, and checking any illustrations. In this approach, the intention is to make them rely less on the mechanical task of decoding letters, and to capitalize more on their linguistic experience and awareness of context so that they can *guess* what a word might be. Reading, according to the American researcher, Frank Smith (1928–) is a 'psycholinguistic guessing game'. This is not to say that accuracy in word decoding is unimportant. Rather, it is stressed that 'getting the words right' is a gradual process – as indeed it is in spoken language acquisition (§38).

In recent years, attention has also been drawn to the many different kinds of activity that are found under the heading of 'fluent reading'. At one extreme, there is the careful, complete, and vocal technique known as 'reading aloud'; at the other, there is the rapid, selective, and silent technique known as 'scanning' or 'skimming' – something widely practised by time-pressed adults as they work quickly through a report or read the morning newspaper. In between there are many other activities, such as critical reading (e.g. underlining sections of text, or adding marginal notes), proof-reading (checking one's own or someone else's text for errors), and reading for learning (if you suddenly discovered that as soon as you had read this page you would be asked questions on it, your reading strategy would alter immediately). Current thinking about reading draws attention to the importance of all these real-world skills.

SOME APPROACHES TO READING

It is not possible to make a neat classification of reading schemes into types, because many are based on a mixture of principles. However, some general comparisons can be made, as is illustrated below for three kinds of approach.

	Characteristics	Advantages	Disadvantages
'Basal reading' programmes	Widely used in the U.S.; a large-scale system of preparatory texts, graded readers, work books, tests, and other materials.	Comprehensive; graded; carefully planned; children get to know the characters, setting, etc.	Expensive; can be used inflexibly; does not promote an exploratory use of language outside the scheme.
Language experience programmes	Integrates work in listening, speaking, reading and writing, using a variety of materials and activities relating to the child's own world.	Caters for individual differences; promotes creativity, confidence, and meaningful activities.	Little grading of structure; difficult to evaluate progress; little motivation to read outside the child's immediate world.
Individualized programmes	Children select their own reading based on interests and ability, and read at their own pace; each child has its own programme, using checklists and charts, and discusses reading with the teacher.	Maintains interest; fosters independence and confidence; is flexible; makes no public distinction between good and bad readers.	Difficult to organize book availability, record-keeping, discussion time with teacher; no systematic development of skills.

ALPHABET DECODING

Several techniques have been proposed that try to facilitate the task of decoding the phonic basis of the writing system. Some, such as *Unifon* or *i.t.a.* (p. 219), introduce new symbols. Some make use of colours to highlight certain sound–letter combinations. Diacritics may also be added to letters, as in the following illustration of a system from the 1960s. (Silent letters are marked with a slash; long vowels have a bar over; digraphs have a bar under; schwa (see Appendix I) is marked with a dot; and an asterisk is used for exceptions.)

Ŏnce upon àtīm℘ à hen livℇd on à fạrm. Thè hen …

'PHONICS' VS 'WHOLE WORD'

Since the early 19th century, the relative merits of phonic and whole-word approaches have dominated educational debate about the teaching of reading. Schemes have been devised based largely on one principle or the other, and there have been several 'mixed' schemes, which attempt to integrate the strengths of each. In recent years, the debate has taken on a new dimension, in the light of the evidence accumulated by experimental psychology about the nature of the reading process (§34).

• *Phonic* approaches are based on the principle of identifying the regular sound-letter relationships in a writing system, and teaching the child to use these to construct or decode words. Phonic schemes have attracted a great deal of support, mainly because of the way they give children a rationale for 'sounding out' new words. On the other hand, they have also been severely criticized. The child's phonetic awareness is often not up to the task of phonic decoding. The task of blending isolated sounds into whole words is not easy: to get from *c* [kə] + *a* [a] + *t* [tə] to *cat* [kat], an actual change of pronunciation is involved, as the phonetic transcription shows. And first books have severe restrictions on their permitted vocabulary, which often results in artificial or bizarre sentences (e.g. *Pat and Dad ran*).

• *Whole-word* or *look-and-say* approaches are based on the principle of recognizing individual words as wholes, without breaking them down into constituent letters or sounds. The main aim is to avoid the use of strings of meaningless phonic syllables, and to permit access to longer and more meaningful sentences, through the use of frequently occurring words (*the, go, saw, little, my,* etc.) – and even much longer words, such as *aeroplane* and *doctor*. Whole-word approaches have been criticized for their lack of clear grading principles, and for the way words are often arbitrarily selected, unrelated to the child's experience.

LINE BREAKS

There is much that is not known about the factors that promote and hinder the process of reading in the young child. Even basic typographical questions remain unresolved, such as the optimum size of type or the distance between lines in the first texts. One such question relates to the necessity of line division. Is a child's reading ability affected by the way in which lines of text end? A completely arbitrary set of line breaks is bound to cause some difficulty – hyphenation, for example, would hardly be a help to young readers! But would their performance be facilitated if lines were made to end according to certain linguistic principles – for example, following a major semantic or syntactic boundary?

In a study of adult recall, it was found that the first of the following two sentences was much easier to learn than the second:

The very old man
was always sitting down
on one of the big chairs.

The very old
man was always sitting
down on one of the big
chairs.

The first set of line breaks occurs at major grammatical boundaries in the sentence, whereas the second does not. Would this kind of factor affect the reading ability of young children?

To obtain some evidence on this point, a recent study printed a story in several different ways, so that the line breaks were altered. A sample is given below: it shows the placement of *and* changed on three occasions, and *the* changed once. A text using justified right-hand margin setting (p. 185) was also prepared as a control. Groups of children read the stories aloud, and their performance was measured in terms of non-fluency, reading errors, and comprehension.

The results, although limited to given constructions, were clear. Breaks within grammatical phrases caused many more problems than breaks between phrases. Also, *and* at the beginning of a line caused more trouble than when it appeared at the end of the previous line. The small sample size makes these findings tentative, but they support the conclusion that line breaks are a possible hazard in early reading – a matter which should be borne in mind when designing texts for young readers or for those with a reading handicap (p. 274). (From B. Raban, 1981.)

Mr. West lived in a house with a monkey.	Mr. West lived in a house with a monkey.
One day, the monkey got up first.	One day, the monkey got up first.
He got up before Mr. West and	He got up before Mr. West
before the sun.	and before the sun.
He opened the window. The monkey	He opened the window. The
had a look down the street.	monkey had a look down the street.
There was no one about.	There was no one about.
"Mr. West is in bed and	"Mr. West is in bed
he is sleeping," he said.	and he is sleeping," he said.
"I'm going down the street	"I'm going down the street and
and into the park.	into the park
Mr. West can't stop me."	Mr. West can't stop me."

READABILITY FORMULAE

Over 50 procedures have been devised that claim to be able to compute how difficult a text is to read. The 'Fog Index' (1952), for example, is arrived at in four steps:

1. Select several 100-word samples from a text.

2. Calculate the average sentence length by dividing the number of words by the number of sentences. (Include only complete sentences.)

3. Obtain the percentage of long words in the entire sample: count the number of words containing three or more syllables and divide this total by the number of 100-word samples.

4. Add the results of 2 and 3, and multiply the total by 0.4. The product is the (American) grade level for which the text is appropriate, in terms of difficulty.

Several such formulae have been proposed, of varying levels of complexity. Most assume that difficulty can be measured simply in terms of the length of words and/or sentences. However, there is no neat correlation between sentence length and difficulty (p. 235); and not all long words are difficult to read. Factors such as the complexity of sentence construction and the nature of word meaning are far more important, but these issues the procedures usually ignore. Readability formulae have thus attracted a great deal of criticism, but in the absence of more sophisticated measures, they continue to attract widespread use, as a reasonably convenient way of predicting (though not explaining) reading difficulty.

READY TO READ?

m	R		this	33

(a) Circle each word.

F		ELEPHANT	to	b

(b) Circle each capital letter.

22	The plant grows.	blow snow flow	grows

(c) Circle each thing that is a sentence.

Sandy, Bruce and James ran home.

(d) Circle each full stop.

A series of tasks from one section of the LARR Test (*Linguistic Awareness in Reading Readiness*, 1983), which investigates young children's awareness of the features and functions of written language. The main aim is to see whether children have grasped the concepts that are required in order to recognize and talk about literacy skills. There is an important connection between children's awareness of the technical 'metalanguage' of literacy and their subsequent performance in reading and writing.

That there are 'errors' in this domain is readily illustrated from the replies some children give when asked about the form and function of language.

- 'Tell me a long word', an investigator asks some 3-year-olds. 'Train', replies one. 'Giraffe', replies another. Both are thinking of the length of the objects.

- 'Show me who's reading,' says an investigator, pointing to a set of pictures in which different people are reading, writing, drawing, and looking at photographs. The child points to the photographs.

Other kinds of difficulties are known: many children have problems in naming letters, or saying whether sequences of sounds are the 'same', or correlating short words in speech. There is little doubt that children need to have developed control over several metalinguistic notions before they are 'ready' to read and write.

However, the notion of 'readiness' has been somewhat controversial in recent years, and must be interpreted with caution. There is no single criterion for saying that a child is 'ready' to read. Several psychological factors are involved, such as concept development, memory, attention, intelligence, and left–right orientation. There should be several linguistic skills present, such as good sound discrimination, the ability to follow instructions, and a developing spoken language, as well as an ability to talk about language. Reading seems to presuppose a great deal.

But the exact requirements are by no means clear – as is shown by parents who have successfully taught their baby to read (usually through the use of words on cards, which are simultaneously shown and spoken for regular periods each day) – in some cases, starting as early as the first year. In such cases, the idea of a 'natural' stage of reading readiness becomes obscure.

(J. Downing *et al.*, 1983, Manual, pp 12–13)

LEARNING TO WRITE

A MOTOR SKILL

For many people, learning to write is primarily a matter of acquiring the motor skill of forming and sequencing letters in a fluent, automatic manner, and positioning them clearly on a page. But this involves far more than the correct formation of letter shapes: letter sizes, word spaces, spaces between lines, margins, and other matters of layout also need to be consistent, if a writing style is to be acceptable. These skills do not always come easily, and it is therefore necessary to determine the factors that promote or hinder the development of efficient handwriting. There have been few scientific studies, so that claims about the 'best' kind of handwriting to teach, and the 'best' way to teach it, tend to be impressionistic, subjective, and controversial.

Of the many issues raised, most attention has been paid to the question of 'writing posture' – the optimum position of the body for writing. It includes a consideration of such factors as hand position, finger grip, the angle of the body towards the paper, and the height of the writer's chair. Too low a chair, for example, can cause a twisted hand position, which inhibits finger movement, and thus prevents the formation of a free cursive (p. 188) style. In addition, simple management strategies need to be taught – such as the need to move the writing paper upwards as one nears the bottom of a page (rather than to move oneself, which is what some children do). The type of writing implement and the kind of paper need to be considered – a child may be unwilling to write with a certain kind of pen, or find it difficult. The question of when to introduce lined paper needs careful thought: lines help the child to control the direction and size of script, but they also constrain the spontaneity of a natural writing style. There may also be difficulty in transferring letter shapes from one visual plane (e.g. on a blackboard) to another (the page). And there may be problems of coordination between eye and hand movements, especially if there has been little experience of scribbling and drawing. It is easy to see why it can take children three years or more to develop a reasonably smooth, automatic writing technique.

HOLDING A PENCIL

The normal 'tripod' grip (top), widely recommended for everyday use, contrasted with a less efficient grip (bottom). Children often use even tighter grips – holding the pencil in a clenched fist, for example. This usually results in too much pressure on the paper, and an erratic writing style. It is also unnecessarily tiring.

POOR HANDWRITING?

One of the most widespread misconceptions is that poor handwriting in older children or adults indicates a careless or otherwise inadequate personality, or perhaps low intelligence (p. 191). The view has no basis in fact. Poor writing may be little more than the reflex of a busy or rushed lifestyle. It may even relate to high intelligence, where the writers are having difficulty keeping up with their thoughts.

Even in young children, it would not do to dismiss a piece of work simply because it looked messy. First impressions of the extract (right) cannot be good, but in fact it is part of an extremely impressive linguistic performance – a 34-page epic narrative in eight chapters, full of events and characters, written by Patrick, aged 5½. (From D. Mackay & J. Simo, 1976.)

CHAPTER SEVEN – IT was NOT. ROY TOLD MaRBELAR TO STOP THe AIRCRAFT a MINITe SO THeT HE CUDe GET HIS GUN, TO PLAY WITH IN THe PLANE

A MONTH'S PROGRESS

Although it takes a long time to control all the features of handwriting, monthly samples of a child's work will show several signs of progress. It is not difficult to see which of these two samples, taken a month apart from a 5-year-old girl, is the more advanced.

(a) Several letter shapes are made well, but there is a great deal of size variation (e, u, t), some contrasts are not clearly formed (g, u, c), word and line spaces are erratic, and the lines are not straight.

(b) Letters are of a more consistent size, and are better formed (there has been a notable advance in g);

word spaces are well used. Lines are steadier, but there is still need for improvement in the use of line spaces, and in the relative positions of letters on the line (e.g. in going, the second g is written on a level with the n, instead of descending below it).
(From D. Mackay & J. Simo, 1976.)

mummy went to the clinic instead of to school this morning.

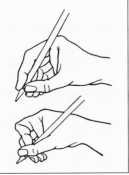

we are having a new car this afternoon and my grandma is going to have a ride in it.

A FUNCTIONAL SKILL

There is far more to writing than the automatic exercise of a motor skill – a point that has been emphasized in recent years, as researchers have begun to study the development of writing in relation to children's emerging cognitive, social, and linguistic abilities, and to the demands being made upon them by the curriculum. The unique role of written language as a means of enabling children to formulate their thoughts to themselves, and to reflect on what they mean, is now widely recognized. Writing is seen as an integral part of the process of learning, and not simply as an ancillary function – something to be used as a way of checking that learning has actually taken place (as in the traditional subject essay). This view requires a more sophisticated account of the nature of the writing process than has traditionally been available – in particular, it requires an appreciation that writing is used for a wide range of purposes and a variety of audiences (p. 214).

Why write?

The purpose of writing should never be taken for granted. One 5-year-old, returning from a nature ramble with his class, was asked by his teacher to 'write about it'. 'Why?' he replied. 'It's easier to tell you!' Adults tend to forget that the 'obvious' reasons for a community's use of writing (§31), may be quite obscure to the young child.

When the point is investigated, it quickly becomes apparent that writing is used for an indefinitely large number of purposes – to express feelings, tell stories, report events, complete forms, keep records, and much more (§4). Children have to learn about these purposes, and how the functional differences affect the nature of the language that is used. Several simple classifications of writing styles have been made, as a means of describing the nature and development of children's writing in school, and in order to give guidelines to teachers anxious to develop a balanced writing curriculum. One approach distinguishes three main styles: an 'expressive' style, close in style and content to the everyday use of speech, which focuses on the writer's personal feelings; a 'transactional' style, which focuses on reasoned, logical statement; and a 'poetic' style, which presents the reader with an imaginative experience. When this system is used to analyse the nature of traditional writing of older schoolchildren, it emerges that most of this writing is transactional, with expressive writing hardly being used at all. (After N. Martin *et al.*, 1976.)

Who is the child writing for?

The style and content of written language is much affected by the nature of the recipient (§31), and an important goal in working with children is thus to develop their 'sense of audience'. Several possible kinds of audience for child writing have been identified.

- Children may address themselves, as in diaries, notes, and first drafts.
- They may address their peers, as in writing an account of an event for their class, or writing a letter to a friend.
- They may address a trusted adult, using a very personal style of writing.
- They may address their teacher, seen as a partner in dialogue, in the expectation that they will receive help.
- They may address examiners, whether in routine class assessments or in formal examinations.
- They may address an unknown audience, as when they have to produce work for a public occasion, or write a letter of application for a job.

In the Martin, *et al.* study, it was found that half of all school writing had the examiner in mind – writing seemed to be used more as a means of testing than as a means of learning. In many settings, it was not being seen as *part* of the learning process, but as something that happened *after* learning was supposed to have taken place. Most of the other audience experiences were conspicuous by their absence. The research stressed the importance of giving children the opportunity of writing for a wide range of audiences, in view of the demands that would be placed upon them once they had left school, and pointed to the need to develop a balanced writing curriculum.

WRITING BLOCKS

All children (and adults) experience writing blocks at some time or other. Blocks arise for a variety of reasons: the writer may be unhappy about embarking on the writing task, be unsure how to express something, or simply not know what to say – the 'mind has gone blank'. In such cases, children need to be helped over the block. The 'Make-a-story' chart illustrates one way of helping children who are having difficulty with the development of a story. (From H. Cowie & H. Hanrott, 1984.)

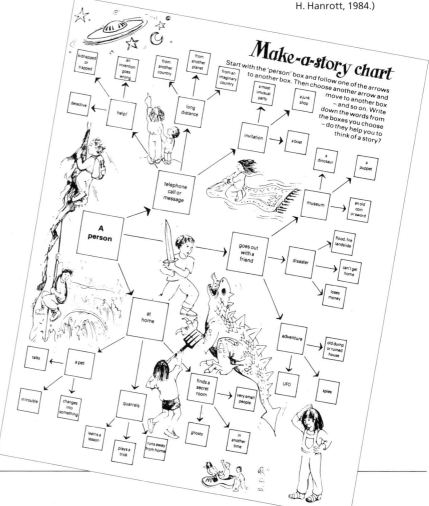

New approaches

Based upon such findings, several ways of fostering children's ability and enjoyment of writing have been suggested. New writing programmes encourage teachers to provide a variety of real audiences and functions for their pupils' work, so that children can see that their writing has a genuine purpose, and that it is not being done solely to be 'marked'. In addition to essays and experimental reports, there are now increasing opportunities to write in other styles for other audiences – such as magazine articles, or letters to the press. Many teachers have begun to keep a 'chart' of different kinds of writing produced by their pupils. And more attention is now paid to discussing samples of writing with the children, both in groups and individually. It has long been appreciated that writing arises out of talk, in the early years; perhaps the most important aspect of current thinking is the realization that the reverse process is just as important – to give children the opportunity to talk about what they write.

A LINGUISTIC SKILL

In addition to motor ability and functional awareness, young writers need to develop the ability to use the structures of language in an appropriate and mature manner. This ability takes several years to emerge. There have been few detailed longitudinal (p. 231) studies, so that analyses in terms of developmental stages tend to be very general or anecdotal; but a number of initial distinctions have been proposed. One scheme recognizes four stages of development (after B. M. Kroll, 1981):

1 A *preparatory* stage, when basic motor skills develop, and the principles of the spelling system are acquired.

2 A *consolidation* stage, usually from around the seventh year, when children begin to use the writing system to express what they can already say in speech. Writing at this stage closely reflects the patterns of the spoken language. There may be many colloquialisms, strings of clauses linked by *and*, unfinished sentences, and other features of the child's conversational experience.

3 A *differentiation* stage, from around the ninth year, in which writing begins to diverge from speech, and develops its own patterns and organization. Errors are common at first, as children learn new standards, and experiment with new structures found in their reading. Their written work becomes fuller and more diverse, as they encounter the need to produce different kinds of writing for different audiences and situations.

It is at this point that children most need guidance about the structures and functions of written language. In particular, they must learn that writing aids thinking in ways that speech cannot perform. Writing is a medium where there is time to reflect, to re-think, to use language as a way of shaping thought (§§31, 34).

Marking conventions

Recognizing the importance of writing has many consequences for the organization and practice of teaching. It is by no means easy to provide children with a range of audiences and purposes in the institutionalized setting of a school. Links need to be made with the outside community (e.g. local government, press, or employers). But creating such links is a slow and time-consuming process.

More important, new ways of responding to children's work need to be found, in order to recognize the strengths of different kinds of writing, and to provide the best kind of feedback. One of the problems of traditional marking practice is illustrated in this example of a story written by a young secondary-school boy. The 20 corrections give a general impression of failure, yet the mark given is 70% and the main comment is 'well done'. Whichever way the writer interprets the marking, there is a problem: if he notes the good mark, he must assume that the errors cannot be very important; if he notes the errors, he must assume that the teacher is giving him false praise.

In recent years there has been a great deal of discussion in educational circles about the need to develop more balanced and comprehensive kinds of assessment, in which interaction with the pupil plays a major part. But many theoretical and practical problems have to be faced before alternative philosophies and strategies of marking can be successfully implemented – not least, the constraints on the teacher's time. (From P. Gannon, 1985.)

They therefore need to see the importance of drafting, revising, and editing as essential ways of obtaining the best expression. From this point of view, such activities as crossing out have to be seen not simply as 'mistakes', to be criticized on grounds of haste or carelessness, but as an indispensable step in the search for the best expression of what children are trying to say.

4 The *integration* phase is found when writers have such a good command of language that they can vary their stylistic choices at will and develop a personal 'voice' – something which is rare before the middle teenage years, and which, in a sense, continues to develop throughout adult life.

PART VIII

Language, brain, and handicap

It has often been remarked that we come to appreciate the unique complexity and function of language only when it starts to go wrong. This happens daily in many small ways – when we detect ambiguity, express ourselves incoherently, or speak at cross-purposes. Less commonly, it happens in a dramatic and devastating manner, in the form of language handicap. Those who find it difficult or impossible to communicate, on account of some physical, psychological, or other disability, face a frustrating, isolated, and uncertain future, in which their handicap is often not recognized, and community support services may be inaccessible or absent. Drawing attention to the existence and extent of language handicap is thus an important role for any encyclopedia of language.

Most language handicaps involve a consideration of areas of the brain that may be impaired. Little is in fact known about the way the brain controls and processes language, and this provides the focus for a great deal of contemporary research, which is reviewed in the first section of this Part. We begin with a general account of brain structure and function, and look in particular at the main ideas about hemispheric

dominance and localization of function that have influenced thinking about language in the past 100 years. We then consider recent developments in the neurology of language, and refer to some of the fruitful ways in which we can make deductions about brain function from the study of human speech behaviour.

The section on language handicap opens with a general review of issues relating to incidence, causation, and classification, then looks at each major category of handicap individually. We begin with deafness, paying particular attention to recent technological advances in this field. This is followed by a discussion of the various handicaps of spoken and written language that can accompany damage to the language-processing areas of the brain – aphasia, dyslexia, and dysgraphia. The next sections consider the main kinds of 'output' problems – disorders of voice quality, articulation, and fluency – and the notion of language 'delay'. Part VIII then concludes with an examination of alternative communication systems and the rapidly developing field of communication aids, which involve the latest advances in information technology.

A 10-year-old physically handicapped child working with her speech and language therapist at Meldreth Manor School, Hertfordshire, UK. She is using an optical light pointer mounted on her head band to access her communication file, which consists of photographs and Rebus symbols (p.282).

The human brain consists of several anatomically distinct regions. The largest part is the *cerebrum*, which is divided into two great lobes of similar size – the left and right *cerebral hemispheres*. The hemispheres are connected to the spinal cord by the *brain stem*, which consists of the *mid-brain*, the *pons*, and the *medulla oblongata*. At the back of the pons is the *cerebellum*, which is responsible for the maintenance of body posture and the smooth coordination of all movements.

Most research has focused on the structure and function of the cerebrum, especially on its surface layer of grey matter (nerve cells), the cerebral *cortex*, which is the area primarily involved in the control of voluntary movement and intellectual functions, and in the decoding of information from the senses. Beneath the cortex is a body of white matter (fibre tracts), which transmits signals between the different parts of each hemisphere, and between the cortex and the brain stem. A notable feature is that the surface of the cortex is not smooth, but has folded in on itself, to produce a series of *convolutions*, or *gyri*, which are separated by *fissures*, or *sulci*.

The figure below shows the main anatomical features. Seen from above (a), the main feature is the *median longitudinal fissure* separating the hemispheres. It does not extend the whole way through the cerebrum: lower down, the hemispheres are joined by a thick bundle of nerve fibres, the *corpus callosum*. This is the means whereby information can be transmitted from one hemisphere to the other. Seen from the side (b), the main features are the *central sulcus* (the *fissure of Rolando*) and the *lateral sulcus* (the *Sylvian fissure*), which are used as criteria for dividing the brain into its four main lobes: *frontal, temporal, parietal*, and *occipital*.

One other important anatomical fact needs to be borne in mind when discussing brain functions: each hemisphere controls movement in and receives sensory input from the *opposite* side of the body. Many nerve fibres from the two hemispheres cross each other as they descend through the brain stem, so that the left hemisphere controls the movement of the right side of the body, and vice versa. That is why brain damage to one hemisphere is usually correlated with bodily effects (such as paralysis) on the opposite side. In the case of the ears, signals from each ear go to *both* hemispheres, but most information is transmitted to the opposite side – a fact that has led to an important technique for investigating brain function (p. 261). In the case of the eyes, the situation is yet more complex: the left half of the visual field of *each eye* transmits informa-

tion to the right hemisphere, and vice versa. Such sophisticated 'wiring', it has been suggested, enables us to make many more qualitative judgments about sounds and images (e.g. about their distance and location) than might otherwise be possible.

DOMINANCE

The functional relationship between the brain's two hemispheres has for over a century been a major focus of research in neuropsychology and clinical neurology. For some time, it was thought that one hemisphere (the left, in most people) was superior to the other in the control of most activities. Today, it is recognized that each has its own role, being more involved in the performance of some activities and less involved in others. A hemisphere is thus said to be the 'dominant' or 'leading' one for certain mental functions. The development of these functions within one or the other hemisphere is known as 'lateralization'.

Language and handedness have long been the two major factors in any discussion of cerebral dominance. The left hemisphere is dominant for language in most right-handed people (estimates are usually over 95%). This is most noticeable in cases of *aphasia* (p. 272), where damage to the left side of the brain may cause both language handicap and a right-sided paralysis. However, the

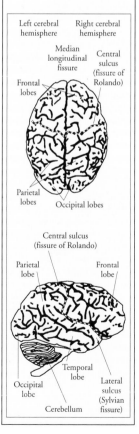

Below left: A section through the brain, showing the main anatomical areas.

Below: The brain seen from (top) above and (bottom) the side, showing the cerebral hemispheres and the four main lobes

Brain stem — Cerebrum

Pons Mid-brain

Medulla oblongata

Corpus callosum

Thalamus

Cerebellum

Spinal cord

Left cerebral hemisphere   Right cerebral hemisphere

Median longitudinal fissure

Central sulcus (fissure of Rolando)

Frontal lobes

Parietal lobes

Occipital lobes

Central sulcus (fissure of Rolando)

Parietal lobe

Frontal lobe

Temporal lobe

Occipital lobe

Cerebellum

Lateral sulcus (Sylvian fissure)

FINDING OUT ABOUT DOMINANCE

Brain abnormalities

- The traditional approach, used since the first systematic work on aphasia (p. 272) in the mid-19th century, is to identify the location of a specific area of brain damage (a 'lesion'), and see whether behaviour has been affected in any predictable way.
- It is sometimes necessary to remove the whole cortical area of a diseased hemisphere ('hemispherectomy'). The effects on behaviour can then be observed.
- It is possible to observe what happens to behaviour while one hemisphere is temporarily anaesthetized. The usual technique, often used before brain surgery, is to inject sodium-amytal into one of the carotid arteries (the 'Wada' technique); this paralyses a hemisphere for 2–3 minutes, during which time some of the patient's language or other abilities can be tested.
- A great deal of information has been obtained from the results of surgery which may be carried out in cases of severe epilepsy. The hemispheres are separated at the corpus callosum ('commisurotomy'). This enables the role of each side of the brain to be studied independently – the 'split brain' experiments.

These studies have shown that there are no major changes in intellect, personality, or everyday behaviour following the operation, but deficits are found in the ability of the two hemispheres to integrate their activities. The effect on language use is particularly dramatic. For example, when an object is presented to the right visual half-field, (right-handed) patients can talk about it: the visual information is relayed to the left hemisphere, where speech processing takes place. However, if the same object is presented to the left visual half-field, patients will be unable to talk about it, even though they have seen it: the visual information has gone to the right hemisphere, where no speech processing takes place.

Monitoring

- An established approach ('electroencephalography' (EEG)) uses electrodes placed on the surface of the scalp to monitor continuous cortical electricity activity – in particular, the amount of 'alpha' rhythm in the brain waves, which is reduced when an area of the brain is in active use.
- A related technique (the 'averaged evoked response') uses electrodes to monitor the activity in an area of the brain in response to repeated presentations of a stimulus.
- Techniques are also now available to monitor neuronal activity by observing changes in metabolic rate within a hemisphere. In particular, increases in cortical blood flow can be measured through radioactive tracers. There are also ways of showing different kinds of chemical action and temperature changes (p. 262).
- An area of the normal brain can be electrically stimulated, to see what effect this has on behaviour. This approach has mainly been used to establish areas of motor and sensory control (p. 262).

Experiments

The role of each hemisphere in processing a stimulus can be inferred from the different time it takes a person to react when stimuli are presented to each side of the body. In a 'dichotic listening' task, for example, different stimuli are simultaneously presented to each ear, and the subject has to report what is heard. When the signals to one ear prove to be more accurately or rapidly reported, it is concluded that the opposite hemisphere is more involved in their processing. In this way, for instance, a general right-ear advantage has been shown for linguistic signals, and a left-ear advantage for nonverbal signals, such as music and environmental sounds.

Problems

These approaches present many problems of principle and method. Although the imaging techniques now used in clinical neurology are a great step forward, they still convey very limited information about brain function. It is not always possible to be precise about the location of a lesion, which in any case is not usually a neatly defined area. Moreover, there is always a problem in generalizing from the performance of a diseased brain to that of a normal brain.

Studies using healthy brains also pose difficulties. There are problems with reaction-time experiments, where it is necessary to match competing stimuli in a very accurate way, and to control variations in subjects' responses (due to such factors as shifting attention). Also, the detailed data provided by monitoring devices (such as EEG) can as yet be given only a very general interpretation. However, technical progress, and associated computational analysis, suggest a promising future in this area.

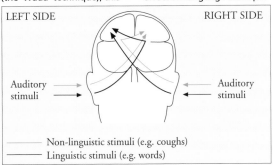

LEFT SIDE　　　　RIGHT SIDE

Auditory stimuli　　　　Auditory stimuli

——— Non-linguistic stimuli (e.g. coughs)
——— Linguistic stimuli (e.g. words)

The routes between ears and hemispheres, as shown by dichotic listening tasks.

relationship is not a symmetrical one: it does not automatically follow that the right hemisphere is dominant for language in left-handed people. Left-handers are by no means a homogeneous group, and in over 60% of cases the left hemisphere is either dominant for language or very much involved ('mixed' dominance). A pattern of mixed dominance throughout the body (for example, a person may be right-handed, left-footed, and right-eyed) further complicates the investigation.

The specialized intellectual functions of each hemisphere, and their neurophysiological bases, are only partly understood. There are important anatomical asymmetries between the hemispheres (for example, there are differences in the length and orientation of the Sylvian fissure, and there is often a larger left temporal plane (part of the temporal lobe)); but it is unclear how these relate to functional specializations. However, on the basis of various kinds of experimental and clinical evidence, several generalizations have been made. With right-handed people, the left hemisphere is found to be dominant in such activities as analytical tasks, categorization, calculation, logical organization, information sequencing, complex motor functions, and language.

The right is said to be dominant for the perception and matching of global patterns, part–whole relationships, spatial orientation, creative sensibility, musical patterns, and emotional expression or recognition.

These identifications must be made cautiously, avoiding an oversimplified contrast – such as is found when people talk about the left hemisphere as the 'analytic' or 'intellectual' part of the brain, and the right as the 'creative' or 'emotional' part. It is now known, for example, that the right hemisphere can handle certain nonverbal tasks that require intellectual capacity (such as spatial judgment), and that there is a limited capability for auditory analysis and comprehension. Moreover, it must not be forgotten that there are several activities that usually involve *both* hemispheres (such as face recognition, and the factors involved in attention and fatigue) – a fact that is currently attracting a great deal of research as scholars focus on the brain's integrating (rather than the lateralized) abilities. As with the studies of localization (p. 262), therefore, statements about the relationship between anatomical form and intellectual function, given our present state of knowledge, must remain extremely tentative.

LOCALIZATION

The idea that a single area of the brain can be related to a single behavioural ability, such as vision or speech, is known as the theory of cerebral 'localization'. Support for the theory came from the work of such neurologists as Paul Pierre Broca (1824–80) and Carl Wernicke (1848–1905), who had found that damage to specific areas of the brain correlated with the loss of certain kinds of linguistic ability in their patients (aphasia, p. 272). Damage to 'Broca's area' resulted in a reduced ability to speak, though comprehension remained relatively unimpaired. Damage to 'Wernicke's area' resulted in a reduced ability to comprehend speech, though the ability to speak was relatively unaffected.

From the outset, the theory was hotly contested by those who felt that other areas of the brain were involved in language processing. Several kinds of evidence were felt to go against a strict localizationist theory. Patients were found with apparently similar lesions, yet with very different linguistic abilities; and, conversely, similar linguistic difficulties could apparently result from lesions in widely different areas. There are now cases on record of patients whose Broca's and Wernicke's areas were unaffected by lesions, but whose linguistic ability was nonetheless seriously impaired; and conversely, there are cases of patients who have even had Broca's area surgically removed in both hemispheres, and who were still able to speak.

New techniques of neuroimaging (p. 261) have brought to light many such counter-examples to the localization hypothesis. When we add to this the facts that other symptoms (especially of a psychological kind) can result from so-called 'linguistic' lesions, and that it has so far been impossible to define specific brain areas in a precise way, we can readily understand such comments as that made by the British neurologist, John Hughlings Jackson (1835–1911): 'to locate the damage which destroys speech, and to locate speech, are two different things'. There may be many points within the neuronal network that, if damaged, could have the same effect on a person's linguistic processing ability. It does not much matter whether a telephone fault exists in the hand-set, along the line, or in the telephone exchange: the resulting deathly silence in the receiver is the same.

There is now little doubt that several other areas of the brain apart from the cortex are involved in linguistic processing. Neurolinguists and neuropsychologists postulate several kinds of subcortical connection, as well as connections between the hemispheres. The areas marginal to the classically located ones are of particular interest, in this respect; but research is also focusing on other parts of the brain, such as other parts of the frontal lobes, and the thalamus (p. 260). However, this direction of research does not support a theory of opposite extremes – that there is no localization at all in the brain, and that every region is equally involved in all activities (a theory of 'equipotentiality').

Despite the many exceptions, in the vast majority of cases where linguistic symptoms have been the result of brain damage, the lesion is in or around the areas originally identified by Broca and Wernicke. It seems that there may well be primary areas after all, but these have to be seen in the context of the brain as a whole, with other areas making a contribution to language skills. Determining the relationships between these areas is now a major goal of neurolinguistic research.

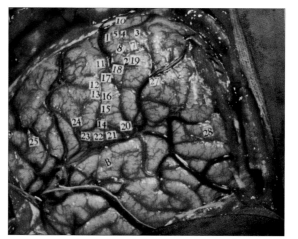

MAPPING THE CORTEX

The task of mapping the areas of the cortex involved in body activities was undertaken by a team of neurosurgeons in Montreal during the 1950s. Relationships were discovered by electrically stimulating different parts of the exposed brain in epileptic patients, in order to find out which areas were involved in seizures before proceeding to surgery. The brain contains no pain receptors, so the patients were not anaesthetized and could thus report their mental and physical sensations (such as a tingling sensation or a memory of some event). Muscle contractions at various points in the body could also be observed, as could sudden involuntary vocalizations and inabilities to speak.

The photograph shows the left hemisphere of a patient's brain with the places marked where responses were obtained. Most of the effects on language were disruptive. Stimulation of points 23 and 24 halted the patient's ability to articulate or caused speech to be slurred. Symptoms similar to aphasia resulted when points 26, 27, and 28 were stimulated. (From W. G. Penfield & L. Roberts, 1959.)

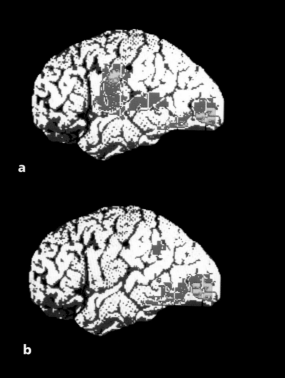

Cortical blood flow Two positron emission tomography scans of the left hemisphere, showing cerebral blood flow as active areas (colour-coded green and yellow). A tiny amount of a special chemical (^{133}Xe) is injected into the carotid artery, and the gamma radiation monitored. The distribution of blood is related to the activity of the nerve cells in different regions of the cortex. In (a) the subject is reading aloud. The main active areas of the brain are the visual cortex (green at right), the areas involved in speech production, including Broca's area (green at left), and the auditory area (green at centre), as the subject hears his own voice. In (b) the subject is reading silently. The only areas noticeably involved are to do with visual processing (green at right) and comprehension (green at left).

The homunculi Many of the results of this research were summarized in the shape of two 'homunculi' – a human form, drawn against the shape of the outer surface of the brain, in which the size of the parts of the body is made proportional to the extent of the brain area involved in their control. The large area of the brain devoted to the motor control of the vocal organs and the hand is clearly seen in the drawing of the 'motor homunculus' (right). A similar drawing was made to show the areas which receive input from the senses – the 'sensory homunculus' (far right). Once again, the large area devoted to the hands and vocal tract should be noted. (From W. G. Penfield & L. Roberts, 1959.)

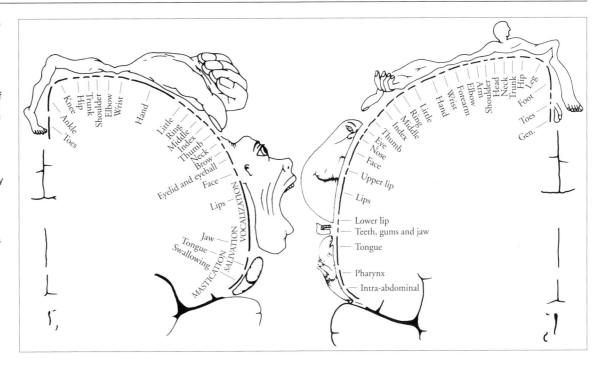

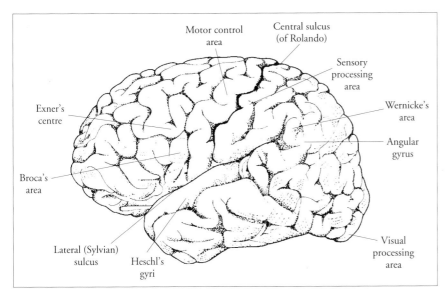

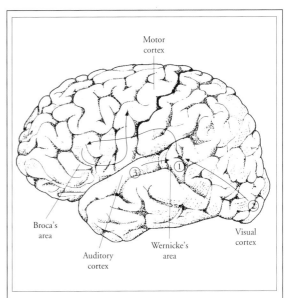

LANGUAGE AREAS

The areas which have been proposed for the processing of speaking, listening, reading, writing, and signing are mainly located at or around the Sylvian and Rolandic fissures (p. 260). Several specific areas have been identified.

• The front part of the parietal lobe, along the fissure of Rolando, is primarily involved in the processing of sensation, and may be connected with the speech and auditory areas at a deeper level.

• The area in front of the fissure of Rolando is mainly involved in motor functioning, and is thus relevant to the study of speaking and writing.

• An area in the upper back part of the temporal lobe, extending upwards into the parietal lobe, plays a major part in the comprehension of speech. This is 'Wernicke's area'.

• In the upper part of the temporal lobe is the main area involved in auditory reception, known as 'Heschl's gyri', after the Austrian pathologist R. L. Heschl (1824–81).

• The lower back part of the frontal lobe is primarily involved in the encoding of speech. This is 'Broca's area'.

• Another area towards the back of the frontal lobe may be involved in the motor control of writing. It is known as 'Exner's centre', after the German neurologist Sigmund Exner (1846–1926).

• Part of the left parietal region, close to Wernicke's area, is involved with the control of manual signing.

• The area at the back of the occipital lobe is used mainly for the processing of visual input.

NEUROLINGUISTIC PROCESSING

Some of the neural pathways that are considered to be involved in the processing of spoken language.

1. *Speech production*   The basic structure of the utterance is thought to be generated in Wernicke's area and is sent to Broca's area for encoding. The motor programme is then passed on to the adjacent motor area, which governs the articulatory organs.

2. *Reading aloud*   The written form is first received by the visual cortex, then transmitted via the angular gyrus to Wernicke's area, where it is thought to be associated with an auditory representation. The utterance structure is then sent on to Broca's area, as in (1).

3. *Speech comprehension*   The signals arrive in the auditory cortex from the ear (§25), and are transferred to the adjacent Wernicke's area, where they are interpreted.

NEUROPSYCHOLOGICAL MODELS OF LANGUAGE

In real life, a snatch of dialogue (*How are you?*, *Fine, thanks*) takes place so quickly that it is easy to forget the complexity of the neurological planning and execution involved in the process. Any model of the production and comprehension of language – whether spoken, written, or signed – involves several steps, each of which must have some kind of neural representation. Neuropsychological models of language attempt to delineate what these steps are and how they interrelate.

In speech production, for example, an initial intention to communicate is followed (or perhaps accompanied) by some kind of conceptualization of the message. There has also to be a point at which this conceptualization is encoded into the semantic and syntactic structure of the language used by the speaker (though it is not clear how far this stage can be separated from the preceding one). If the structure is to be spoken, it must first be given some sort of phonological representation (e.g. as syllables, phonemes, or distinctive features, §28). A motor-control programme must then be used, to coordinate the multiplicity of signals that have to be sent to the appropriate muscles controlling the different parts of the vocal tract (§27). While this activity takes place, it is being constantly self-monitored: feedback is being received from the ear, from the sense of touch, and from the internal sensations generated by the movement of parts of the body ('pro-prioceptive' feedback). Other kinds of internal monitoring, at 'higher' levels, may also take place. An analogous sequence of events would be involved if the structure were to be written or signed.

The nature of neurolinguistic programmes has attracted a great deal of research in recent years, especially in relation to speech production (§22). It is evident, for example, that the brain does not issue motor commands one segment at a time. A word such as *soup* is not neurologically transmitted as three separate steps – [s] + [u] + [p]. The articulation of [s] is lip-rounded, under the influence of the following vowel, which shows that the brain must be 'scanning ahead' while issuing commands for particular segments (coarticulation, p. 158). When we consider the whole range of factors that affect the timing of speech events (such as breathing rate, the movement and coordination of the articulators, the onset of vocal-fold vibration, the location of stress, and the placement and duration of pauses), it is evident that a highly sophisticated control system must be employed, otherwise speech would degenerate into an erratic, disorganized set of noises. It is now recognized that many areas of the brain are involved: in particular, the cerebellum and thalamus are known to assist the cortex in exercising this control (p. 260). But it is not yet possible to construct a detailed model of neurolinguistic operation that takes all speech-production variables into account.

A psycholinguistic model of speech production

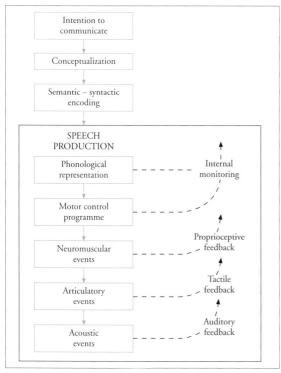

```
Intention to
communicate
     │
     ▼
Conceptualization
     │
     ▼
Semantic – syntactic
encoding
     │
     ▼
┌─────────────────────────────────────────────┐
│  SPEECH                                       │
│  PRODUCTION                                   │
│                                               │
│  Phonological          Internal               │
│  representation ─ ─ ─ ─ monitoring            │
│     │                                         │
│  Motor control                                │
│  programme                                    │
│     │                  Proprioceptive         │
│  Neuromuscular ─ ─ ─ ─  feedback              │
│  events                                       │
│     │                  Tactile                │
│  Articulatory  ─ ─ ─ ─  feedback              │
│  events                                       │
│     │                  Auditory               │
│  Acoustic     ─ ─ ─ ─   feedback              │
│  events                                       │
└─────────────────────────────────────────────┘
```

SLIPS OF THE TONGUE – OR BRAIN?

Tongue slips – involuntary departures from the speaker's intended production of a sequence of language units – are very common. Sounds, syllables, morphemes (p. 90), words, and sometimes larger units of grammar can be affected. Often, the deviant performance is immediately detected by the speaker (though not always consciously) and corrected.

Several large collections of tongue-slip data have now been made (see facing page, top right), and the errors analysed from a variety of viewpoints. Sigmund Freud, for example, saw tongue slips as symptoms of unconscious forces or mental conflict within an individual, which needed careful psychoanalytic interpretation. They have also been seen as providing insights into the mechanisms of language change and evolution (§54). But most recent research has studied these errors to see what light they throw on how the brain or mind works.

The main linguistic finding is that tongue slips are not random, but are largely explicable by reference to certain basic constraints. For example, the two words involved in a tongue slip (the word containing the slip and the word that influences it) are often found within the same syntactic constituent or intonation/rhythm unit (§§16, 29). Moreover, the influencing word is

William Archibald Spooner (1844–1930)
Spooner, an Anglican clergyman and Warden of New College Oxford, had a nervous manner that led him to produce many slips of the tongue – typically, involving reversals which led to unintentional comic effects. Several of the 'spoonerisms' attributed to him are famous, such as 'queer old dean' (for 'dear old queen').

often the most strongly stressed within the tone unit. And most tongue slips involve the symmetrical substitution within a syllable of one sound by another: for example, an initial segment in the influencing word replaces the initial segment in the slipped word.

Combining such constraints, it is possible to make predictions about the form tongue slips are likely to take when they occur. Given the intended sentence 'The car missed the *bike* / but hit the *wall*' (where / marks an intonation/rhythm boundary, and the strongly stressed words are italicized), the likely slips are going to include *bar* for *car* or *wit* for *hit*. Most unlikely would be *har* for *car* (showing the influence of a less prominent word in the second tone unit) or *lit* for *hit* (showing a final consonant replacing an initial one).

Tongue slips tell us a great deal about the neuropsychological processes that underlie speech. The different kinds of errors provide indirect evidence for some of the stages recognized by models of speech production, and suggest the kinds of linguistic unit that these models need to take into account. For example, if slips tend to occur inside rather than between intonation units, it suggests that this unit has a neuropsychological reality within which the events of articulation are serially organized and integrated.

TONGUE SLIPS CLASSIFIED

An enormous variety of tongue slips occurs in everyday speech. Here are examples of some of the most frequent categories found in a corpus of over 12,000 spontaneous slips (after V. A. Fromkin, 1973). The words affected are given in the second column. (For phonetics terminology, see §27.)

Initial consonant anticipated
a reading list → leading
it's a real mystery → meal
Initial consonant perseveration
black boxes → bloxes
gave the boy → goy
Consonant reversals
well made → mell wade
baked a cake → caked a bake
Final consonants
with a brush → wish
king, queen → king, quing
Consonant deletion
below the glottis → gottis

tumbled → tubbled
Consonant addition
optimal number → moptimal
kitchen sink → kinchen
Consonant movement
pinch hit → pitch hint
bacon and eggs → acon and begs
Consonant clusters
heater switch → sweeter hitch
damage claim → clamage dame
Consonant clusters divided
stick in the mud → smuck ... tid
fish grotto → frish gotto
Vowels
fill the pool → fool the pill
Bev and Bill → Biv and Bell
Vowel + r
foolish argument → farlish
fight very hard → fart ... hide
Single features
spell mother → smell bother
bang the nail → mang the mail
Errors within words
relevance → revelance
whisper → whisper

Stress changes
similarly → simil<u>a</u>rly
paying for it → pay f<u>o</u>ring it
Word reversals
a tank of gas → a gas of tank
a job for his wife → a wife for his job
Telescopic errors
Nixon witness → nitness
parking permit → parking pit
Derivational affixes (p. 90)
often → oftenly
flashing light → flasher
Blends
person/people → perple
draft/breeze → dreeze
Word substitution
I don't sleep very well in a single bed → ... speak very well ...
chamber music → chamber maid
Other grammatical errors
It looks as if → I look ...
the day when I was born → the day where ...

GENIE

The tragic case of 'Genie' bears directly on the critical period hypothesis. Genie was discovered in 1970, at the age of 13½, having been brought up in conditions of inhuman neglect and extreme isolation. She was severely disturbed and underdeveloped, and had been unable to learn language. In the course of her treatment and rehabilitation, great efforts were made to teach her to speak. She had received next to no linguistic stimulation between the ages of 2 and puberty, so the evidence of her language-learning ability would bear directly on the Lenneberg hypothesis (see right).

Analysis of the way Genie developed her linguistic skills showed several abnormalities, such as a marked gap between production and comprehension, variability in using rules, stereotyped speech, gaps in the acquisition of syntactic skills, and a generally retarded rate of development. After various psycholinguistic tests, it was concluded that Genie was using her right hemisphere for language (as well as for several other activities), and that this might have been the result of her beginning the task of language

learning after the critical period of left-hemisphere involvement. The case was thus thought to support Lenneberg's hypothesis, but only in a weak form. Genie was evidently able to acquire some language from exposure after puberty (she made great progress in vocabulary, for example, and continued to make gains in morphology and syntax), but she did not do so in a normal way. (For other 'lost' children, see §49.) (After S. Curtiss, 1977.)

A CRITICAL PERIOD FOR LANGUAGE?

The notion of a 'critical period' was first used by ethologists studying the origin of species-specific behaviour. It was found that with certain species (e.g. rats, goslings) there were periods in which a particular kind of stimulus had to be present if the baby was to develop normal behaviour.

The question was therefore raised whether there were critical periods in human maturation also. The American psycholinguist Eric Lenneberg (1921–75) argued that such a period existed in the case of language acquisition. The development of language was said to be the result of brain maturation: the hemispheres were equipotential at birth, with language gradually becoming lateralized in the left hemisphere (p. 262). The process began at around the age of 2 and ended at puberty, when the brain was fully developed, and lateralization was complete. At this point, there was no longer any neural 'plasticity' which would enable the right hemisphere to take over the language function if the left hemisphere was damaged.

The argument in favour of a critical period was based largely on claims about the

patterns of recovery in brain-damaged adults and children. If adults with left-hemisphere damage failed to recover language within a few months, it was argued, they would never do so. Children, however, showed an ability to recover over a longer period – and could make a complete recovery if they were very young at the time of the damage. In such cases, even total removal of the left hemisphere did not preclude the reacquisition of language.

Controversial evidence The critical-period hypothesis has been controversial. The pathological evidence is mixed, because comparisons of adult and child cases are extremely difficult to make, and paths of recovery have not been studied in a detailed linguistic way. It may be that aspects of child recovery are helped by the involvement of the right hemisphere; but there are also cases of left-hemisphere damage producing severe and long-lasting aphasia in children.

The evidence of normal language acquisition (Part VII) is also mixed. Aspects of phonological and grammatical acquisition do continue until around puberty; however,

most of these skills are well established before the age of 5, and some linguistic skills (in semantics and pragmatics) are still developing in teenage children and young adults.

The neuropsychological evidence generally fails to support the Lenneberg hypothesis, showing lateralization to be established long before puberty – some studies suggest this may even be as early as the third year. Cerebral anatomical asymmetries have been found at birth, and several functional asymmetries have been noted in infants (e.g. a preference for rightward turning and right-hand grasping). Certain dichotic listening advantages (p. 261) are also present from a very early age, including some related to speech perception.

On the other hand, lateralization plainly takes some years before it is firmly established, and this overlaps the main period of language acquisition in a way that is not yet understood. The relationship between lateralization and language is thus an extremely complex one, and presents a continuing research challenge in developmental neuropsychology and neurolinguistics.

Language handicap refers to any systematic deficiency in the way people speak, listen, read, write, or sign that interferes with their ability to communicate with their peers. At one extreme, the handicap may be quite mild, such as a minor impediment of pronunciation; at the other, there may be an almost total breakdown of all modes of communication, as in severe forms of brain damage. In every case, we see language to some degree ceasing to function in a natural, spontaneous, and unselfconscious way, and drawing attention to itself, thus becoming a barrier rather than a means to communication.

Because handicap exists in a continuum from mild to severe, it is very difficult to obtain accurate estimates of its prevalence (the number of cases in a population at any one time) or incidence (the number of new cases within a particular period). A British government survey of the 1970s indicated that about $\frac{1}{2}$% of the population were sufficiently seriously handicapped as to require the services of a speech therapist (see below), but accepted that this figure was vague and probably far too low. If other categories of the population are included, such as less seriously impaired people, or those who have an abnormal degree of difficulty with reading, writing, or spelling, the figure must approach 2–3%. And if a functional notion of handicap is used, to include the language problems faced by immigrants and other minority groups, the total increases dramatically to perhaps as many as 5% of the population. What is plain is that, however the problem is identified, several million people in the world suffer from an inability to communicate that limits their personal development, their social relationships, and their effective contribution to society. The main aim of research in this area is thus to understand the physical and linguistic basis of language handicap, and to devise therapeutic ways of alleviating the condition so that a handicapped person can achieve as full a life as possible.

THE CAUSES OF LANGUAGE HANDICAP

In about 40% of cases, a language handicap can be related to a clear physical cause. For example, many children are born with brain damage that causes a degree of mental or physical handicap, and linguistic skills are usually seriously impaired as a consequence. Deafness can have a crippling impact on the normal development of spoken language. Parts of the brain can be destroyed by illness, strokes, accidents, or acts of violence, to produce the many forms of aphasia (p. 272). Various kinds of abnormal growth may affect the functioning of the vocal folds, or may lead to the larynx having to be surgically removed. In such cases as these,

there is no doubt that the cause of the linguistic handicap lies in a person's abnormal physical condition.

However, in the majority of cases, it is not possible to find a clear organic cause, given the present state of medical knowledge. Thousands of children have a delayed language development, and in most of them there is nothing in their medical history that can account for the problem. There are many thousands of stutterers whose handicap, likewise, cannot be explained in any simple physical way. And a large number of people develop problems in the use of their voice that have no physical explanation. In such instances, we can search for 'functional' causes in a person's psychological, social, or linguistic background. A particular life-style, for example, may be the ultimate cause of a poor voice quality. A child's weak memory may explain a case of language delay. But in very many cases, even these dimensions of enquiry result in no clear cause being discovered.

Assessment of language handicap must also allow for the fact that many conditions have multiple causes. For example, the level of language achievement reached by a deaf child cannot be explained solely with reference to the child's degree of hearing loss: many other factors contribute – such as the child's personality and family background, and the kind and amount of exposure to spoken or signed language. Or again, an adult's voice disorder

NEED FOR SPEECH THERAPY

	Total population	% needing speech therapy	Numbers needing speech therapy
Adults			
Geriatric patients	40,000	9	3,600
Hospitalized stroke patients	16,000	33	5,000
Others (e.g. stutterers, voice disorders)	30,000	100	30,000
Children			
Preschool	2 million	3	60,000
Ordinary school	9 million	2	180,000
Educationally subnormal (moderate)	60,000	20	12,000
Educationally subnormal (severe)	35,000	50	17,500
Physically handicapped	12,000	25	3,000
		TOTAL	311,100

Estimates of numbers needing speech therapy in Britain cited in a government enquiry of the early 1970s. (Department of Education and Science, 1972.)

TERMINOLOGICAL HANDICAP

The field of language handicap is bedevilled by terminological difficulties. The problem of labelling individual handicaps will emerge at various places in this section; but even the most general of notions attracts a diversity of labels. Thus the heading to this section, 'handicap', might have used *disorder, disability, defect, disfunction,* or *impairment*. There is little to choose between such terms in a general account.

The professionals whose job it is to diagnose, assess, and treat language handicaps also vary in name from country to country, and even within countries. In the U.S., they are usually known as 'speech pathologists', though 'language pathologist' is also quite widespread. In Britain, the general term is 'speech and language therapist'. In Europe, the same tasks are carried out by 'orthophonists' (e.g. in France), 'logopaedists' (e.g. in Germany), and 'phoniatrists' (e.g. in the Czech and Slovak Republics). All attempts to standardize the name of the profession have so far failed.

The range of professional skills and qualifications found under these headings also varies – reflecting the fact that courses of study can range from just a few months to over four years. Some countries make a sharp distinction between those who specialize in language problems and those who look after more general kinds of learning handicap. Some make a distinction between problems of speech and those of hearing. Some have different kinds of specialists to deal with adults and children.

But one thing all countries share: a lack of financial resources being devoted to the study and treatment of what is probably the most neglected of all human handicaps.

might begin as hoarseness arising out of a straightforward disease, such as laryngitis; but anxiety over the continued use of the voice (if the person is a singer, for example) might promote the development of excessive strain while talking, with the result that the hoarseness continues long after the disease has disappeared. Similar combinations of organic and functional causative factors underlie most if not all language handicaps.

THE CLASSIFICATION OF LANGUAGE HANDICAPS

Studies of language handicap traditionally make use of a number of basic two-way distinctions as a means of imposing an initial organization on this complex field. Some of these distinctions provide a useful introductory perspective, but they must be used with great caution if their inevitable simplification is not mislead. The common classification of handicaps into 'organic' and 'functional' types (p. 266), for example, is well motivated in many cases, but ultimately breaks down when we encounter handicaps in which both elements play an important defining role. And a similar problem faces anyone wishing to make use of the most widely used primary classification of language handicap: production vs reception.

This way of looking at communicative breakdown, ultimately derived from information theory, is referred to in several different ways, such as motor/sensory, encoding/decoding, or executive/evaluative. A basic distinction is being drawn between handicaps of language production and handicaps of language reception. *Production* refers to the whole sequence of neurological, physiological, and anatomical steps required to encode a linguistic message and make it ready for transmission (p. 264). Any disruption to the normal chain of events would thus result in 'expressive' handicaps: a clear example would be a neurological complaint that led to slurred speech. *Reception* refers to the sequence of anatomical, physiological, and neurological steps required to decode such a message as it is being received. Disruptions here would result in

'receptive' handicaps: the clearest case is deafness.

There are however many kinds of handicap where problems of production and reception are simultaneously encountered. For example, aphasia (p. 272) is often classified into 'expressive' vs 'receptive' types, whereas it is usual to find both kinds of difficulty within the same patient, in varying proportions. Clinically, it is more accurate to talk of a patient being 'predominantly' expressive or receptive. And even the apparently 'straightforward' handicaps raise problems for the distinction. Deafness is patently a receptive handicap, but it often manifests itself in a highly disordered language production (p. 269). Cleft palate and stuttering are patently production handicaps, but in both cases problems of reception can be found: a significant proportion of cleft palate children have an additional hearing loss (p. 279); and stutterers may be so involved in the problems of fluency control that their ability to listen and comprehend may deteriorate. In all these cases, the simultaneous involvement of problems of production and reception warrants a more complex kind of analysis than the traditional binary account provides. Such handicaps are in fact more properly called 'syndromes', with several different elements contributing to their identification.

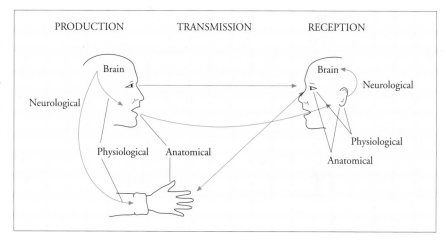

The communication chain
This is a widely used model for studying language handicap. Different steps within the processes of production and reception can be identified, and used to plot the primary 'location' of deficits, as when handicaps are said to be neurological ('central' vs 'peripheral'), physiological (e.g. muscular), or anatomical (e.g. cleft palate). However, the model does not show the importance of the various kinds of feedback (§§20, 25), nor the psychological, social, and other factors that can determine the seriousness of a language handicap.

LANGUAGE VS SPEECH

The term 'language', as used in this section, is a cover term for all modes of linguistic communication – whether by speech, hearing, reading, writing, or signing. (This, indeed, is its use throughout the encyclopedia.) In the traditional study of handicap, however, it is used in a more restricted way. A distinction is drawn between handicaps of 'language' and handicaps of 'speech'. The former refer only to the 'symbolic' aspects of communication, i.e. those concerned with the formulation and structuring of meaning – in modern terms,

primarily handicaps of grammar and semantics (Part III). The latter refer to the 'non-symbolic' aspects, that is, those concerned only with the use of sounds seen as a set of meaningless phonetic entities – as found in problems of voice quality, fluency, and articulation (Part IV).

Although this distinction is still widely used, it has begun to attract criticism in recent years. The term 'speech' is ambiguous, as it is often used in the sense of 'spoken language', which *includes* grammar and meaning (§31). Also, the focus on speech neglects the importance of other forms

of communicative handicap, such as those due to hearing and the visual modalities. Above all, the distinction leaves unclear the status of phonology (§28), which is concerned with both semantic and phonetic properties of language. For example, it is not obvious whether children who have failed to master the phonological system of their language should be classified as displaying a 'speech disorder' or a 'language disorder'. Alternative systems of classification are therefore required to solve the problems presented by the language/speech division.

Spoken language	Written language	Sign language
Phonetic handicaps (§27)	Graphetic handicaps (§32)	'Cheretic' handicaps (§36)
Phonological handicaps (§28)	Graphological handicaps (§33)	'Cherological' handicaps (§36)
Grammatical handicaps		
Semantic handicaps		

A linguistic classification of communication handicaps, using the model of structural levels (§13). Pragmatic handicaps are not shown. The terminology for signing handicaps is not a widely established usage.

DEAFNESS

About 1 in 1,000 children have a hearing loss that is present at birth, or acquired soon after, caused by pathology of the inner ear and its relationship to the auditory nerve (§25). Maternal rubella (German measles), meningitis, and several other diseases are known to be causative factors. Many more children have a hearing loss that they acquire in the preschool or early school period, because of pathology of the middle ear. Several middle-ear problems get better without intervention; but others recur, become chronic, and do not respond well to treatment. In such chronic cases, and in all cases of inner-ear deafness, there can be serious consequences for the development of speech comprehension and production.

Many adults – perhaps as many as a third of the population over 60 years of age – have an acquired hearing loss, which can noticeably affect their ability to comprehend and speak (the latter, because they are unable to use hearing to monitor what they are saying). Regular exposure to loud noise (at work, in discos, etc.) is a common cause. However, because language has been acquired before the onset of the deafness, these disorders are usually less serious.

The high incidence of the handicap is often not appreciated. It has been estimated that there are some 200,000 children (under 16) and 2 million adults suffering from some degree of hearing loss in Britain. In the USA, the figure is close to 20 million. Depending on the criterion of deafness used, estimates vary from 2% to 10% of the population. As many as 15 people in every 1,000 have a hearing loss in one ear.

TYPES OF DEAFNESS

There is no single, simple phenomenon of 'deafness' but a wide range of kinds and degrees of hearing impairment. The loss may affect only one ear (*unilateral*) or both ears (*bilateral*). At one extreme, there may be a slight inability to hear a few low-intensity frequencies (§23), which interferes only occasionally with normal communication; at the other extreme, a person may have no detectable response to any frequency, no matter how intense the sound. The latter is uncommon: most deaf people have some degree of 'residual' hearing. But a residual ability to hear amplified sound up to 500 Hz, for example, is of very limited value: at this level, people receive only about 10% of the information conveyed by the speech waveform.

The main classification of hearing loss is based on where the interference lies in the auditory pathway. *Conductive* deafness arises when there is interference with the transmission of sound to the inner ear, as when the middle ear becomes inflamed (*otitis media*) or the ear drum or ossicles are affected by disease or trauma. *Sensorineural* deafness arises when the source of interference lies within the inner ear, or along the auditory nerve to the brain. A case of sensorineural deafness is illustrated in the audiogram below of a child who was unable to respond to high frequency sounds such as [s] ('high tone' deafness).

Other forms of hearing impairment have been identified, such as *tinnitus* – a range of noises in the ear (ringing, hissing, pulsating, etc.) that can occur in acute, debilitating form. In the USA, for example, around 2 million people have this problem, to some degree. There is also the major problem of 'fluctuating' hearing loss, commonly related to persistent middle-ear infections, which can seriously affect young children's ability and motivation to attend to speech sounds, especially in noisy environments, and thus promote language delay and learning problems in school. There is also the little-understood *central* (or *cortical*) deafness, where there is loss of hearing sensitivity due to damage of the auditory nerve in the brain stem or in the hearing centres of the cortex. In this last case, of course, there is a problem of diagnosis, as if a person fails to respond, despite normal peripheral hearing, other factors (such as aphasia or mental handicap) may be involved.

THE AUDIOGRAM

This is the most widely used measure of hearing impairment. The horizontal dimension of the chart shows a range of sound frequencies up to 8,000 Hz; the vertical dimension shows a range of intensities of hearing loss up to 120 decibels. A person's ability to hear pure tones, presented at different frequencies and intensities, is plotted on the audiogram, and the curve compared with the normal minimal audibility curve (shown here as a straight line at 0). The sensitivity of each ear is separately measured using headphones, and marked by different symbols (o is here used for the right ear, and x for the left).

The audiogram below shows the responses of a 12½-year-old girl with a high-frequency loss in both ears, the loss being more severe in the left ear. A sample of her free writing is given on p. 269.

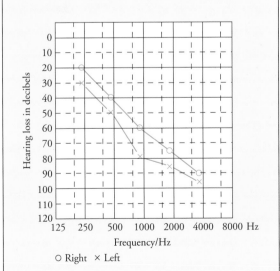

Right ◯   Left ✕

A sample of her free writing is given on p. 269.

WHO'S WHO

Otologists are doctors who have specialized in diseases of the ear.

Audiologists are clinicians who assess the nature and degree of hearing loss and conversation, and who advise on the rehabilitation of people with hearing impairment.

AUDIOMETRIC TESTS

Pure-tone audiometry

A specially calibrated machine generates pure tones (§23) at different frequencies and intensities. The tones are presented to one ear at a time through headphones (in an *air-conduction* test) or through the bones behind the ear (in a *bone-conduction* test). Any response to a sound is noted, and plotted as an audiogram.

The results of pure tone audiometry do not always correlate clearly with a person's ability to hear the complex tones of speech. Two people can have the same audiogram, yet display very different linguistic skills. It is therefore important to supplement such findings with the results of alternative tests, using speech stimuli.

Speech audiometry

The ability to respond to the sounds of speech is often assessed impressionistically, with the audiologist speaking at different levels and distances from the listener. A more precise estimate can be achieved by recording a series of words or sentences which have been carefully constructed so as to represent the different kinds of speech sound, and playing these to the listener at known intensities under various conditions. The kind and level of background noise, the characteristics of the room, and even the position of the listener's head can affect the response.

ORALISM vs MANUALISM

The issue of whether deaf children should be taught to sign (§35) has been hotly debated for over a century. There is strong opposition between those educators who support the primary role of signing ('manualists') and those who support the exclusive teaching of speech ('oralists'). There are also many who support a combined approach, in which speech and some kind of signing system are used simultaneously ('total communication') – an approach that has become particularly influential in recent years. The arguments are complex, and often emotional, because they raise questions of the identity of deaf people and the quality of their lives.

The main argument against manualism is that it is setting deaf people apart from all but their own small community, labelling them as 'deaf' and 'different', and making it difficult to communicate with the hearing world. The main argument against oralism is that its methods are often unsuccessful, with the deaf person becoming just as isolated, being left with speech that is limited and difficult to understand.

In support of manualism, it is argued that signing enables a deaf person to enjoy a wide range of communicative experience in the social and creative life of the deaf community. In support of oralism is the evidence that some methods have proved to be very successful, especially if a natural speaking environment is part of a child's early upbringing.

However, there are schools of thought within both approaches, which themselves give rise to fierce argument. In relation to oral approaches, there is controversy over the kind of oral language to teach the child – whether it should be natural conversation or a simplified input. Several 'structured' approaches are available under the latter heading. In relation to manual approaches, some educators think a 'pure' sign language, uninfluenced by speech, should be learned first, with other varieties coming later. Others think that this approach is sensible only for the small number of deaf children born to deaf parents. In cases where the parents have normal hearing, they argue, spoken language will be in use, and so a signing system related to speech might as well be used from the outset.

These controversies have been around, in some form, for over a century, promoted largely by the lack of objective data about the way deaf children learn. It is likely that, as research findings accumulate, some of these issues will be resolved. But there is little sign of this at present.

DEAF SIGNING – A NEW PERSPECTIVE

A deaf or hearing child born to deaf parents learns sign language as a 'mother tongue', producing a level of manual awareness and sophistication that is different from the deaf children of hearing parents or from hearing people who have learned to sign. Studies have begun to show stages of development in the way these 'native signers' learn to sign that can be related to the

stages of language acquisition found in hearing children (Part VII). This change of perspective is quite crucial: for these children, signing is not a handicap but a natural means of expression quite comparable to the expressive potential of spoken language. For them, learning to speak is the handicapping condition.

Contemporary society is gradually coming to give signing the recognition it requires, and deaf signers the opportunities they deserve – but it is an extremely slow process. In this encyclopedia, the linguistic status of signing is symbolized by treating it as a major section (Part VI), even though research has not yet advanced to a stage permitting a detailed treatment comparable to the sections on speaking and writing. In social, educational, and political life, too, progress is being made, with the image of the deaf signer as a handicapped person who displays bizarre behaviour slowly being eroded. In the USA, in particular, there is a strong movement to obtain recognition for the needs of the deaf, such as by providing interpreters in university classes, local government meetings, and television programmes.

DEAF – AND DUMB?

This widely used phrase is extremely misleading, and should be banned. It does not follow that, if someone is deaf, they will be unable to speak. Many deaf people achieve excellent levels of oral ability. Everything depends on such factors as family background, age of onset of deafness, and the kind of language education programme followed.

WRITTEN LANGUAGE

The following two samples of the free writing of deaf children have been chosen to illustrate the linguistic difficulties which can develop in deaf children's writing. The first (A) is from the 12½-year-old whose audiogram is given on p. 268. The story shows a very limited range of grammatical ability, with stereotyped sentence openings. The second (B) was written by a 16½-year-old boy with a loss of 90 db in both ears at low frequencies, and no response at all at higher frequencies. The highly deviant syntax results in a very low level of intelligibility.

A

There is a guinea pig. The guinea pig name is Funny. The guinea pig got black and white. The guinea pig got pink nose. The guinea pig is standing. The guinea pig is waiting the food. The guinea pig got pink ears. The guinea pig got four leg.

B

The Star Wars was the two spaceship a fighting opened door was coming the Men and Storm trooper guns carry on to Artoo Detoo and threepio at go the space. The Earth was not grass and tree but to the sand, R2D2 and C3PO at going look for R2D2 walk the sand people carry away Artoo Detoo sleep.

Gallaudet College, Washington, U.S.
The campus of Gallaudet University, with university president I. King Jordan addressing a graduating class. Gallaudet, established in 1864, is the world's only accredited liberal arts University for deaf and hard-of-hearing students.

TECHNOLOGICAL ADVANCES

There has been a considerable advance in the design of communication aids for the deaf in recent years, following progress in acoustics and instrumental phonetic research (§§23–4). Several approaches have been investigated in relation to the main sensory modalities. There have been experiments with vibro-tactile aids, for example, which represent speech frequencies by means of spatial vibration patterns applied to the fingers – a kind of audible braille (p. 282). But most technological aids fall into the two main categories of *auditory* ('hearing aids') and *visual*.

Hearing aids

It is thought that over 95% of babies born deaf have some degree of residual hearing, and therefore the earlier some kind of auditory training can be established, the better. A basic way of providing early help is to amplify sound to the child's ears through the use of a hearing aid. Similarly, hearing aids can be of great value with adults where hearing is deteriorating because of the natural process of aging (§6), as well as with those who have acquired a degree of hearing loss through disease or trauma. Hearing aids are therefore worn by many people: for example, it is estimated that nearly 2 million are currently in use in the USA.

However, hearing aids have their limitations – a fact that needs to be borne in mind when one faces the contemporary proliferation of firms offering a bewildering variety of aids. Hearing aids amplify, but do not necessarily clarify, speech. *All* sound in the environment of the aid is amplified – including background noise. Also, raising a listener's sensitivity may lead to discomfort with certain speech sounds and background noises – [s], for example, can become unpleasantly harsh. It is of course possible to reduce the output of an aid, but this can lead to the speech sounds becoming distorted. For such reasons, many hearing-impaired people have been known to reject their aids after a limited period of use: one report has suggested that as many as a half of all hearing aids purchased end up not being worn.

The problem is most marked when someone has a high-frequency hearing loss, which may remove many consonants and environmental noises (such as running water or a telephone bell). Here, it is essential to find an aid that selectively amplifies the frequencies that are most affected. However, if the loss is very severe, this approach will not help. An alternative is to use a type of aid that converts the high-frequency information in the sound wave into low frequencies that fall within the range of residual hearing – a procedure that is often beneficial, though the speech can end up very distorted in the process. Several other techniques have been devised in an attempt to cope with the many individual variations that exist.

Specialized audiological advice is essential in choosing a hearing aid. It is not easy to evaluate all the alternatives, and arrive at the one that is best suited to an individual's hearing problem and life-style. Nor is choosing an aid a once-and-for-all decision: technical advances are being made all the time, so that it is easy for a type of aid to become out of date. Also important is the need to maintain the aid so that it performs at peak efficiency – something that may seem obvious, but that is often disregarded, especially by old people.

Visual aids

The idea of a device that would make all the sounds of speech immediately visible to the deaf is over a century old, but only limited progress has been made towards this goal. Modern approaches to the task use techniques of acoustic analysis, and invoke the powerful display possibilities made available through computational electronics. Most of these approaches are at an early experimental stage, reflecting the state of the art in speech analysis and synthesis (§26), and commercial application is still a long way off; but the potential value of the research can be seen even in the basic displays that can currently be produced.

Most visual pattern displays aim to improve speech production as well as speech reception. To achieve this, the approaches present a speech target visually and store it on a display screen. The deaf person then attempts to pronounce the speech in such a way that the pattern produced matches the one already on the screen. The main advantage of this technique is that there is no delay in providing feedback about the success of the pronunciation. However, very little research has yet taken place into the relative efficiency of the various devices now available in promoting intelligible speech in young children.

Visual display devices that are routinely used in speech training programmes include the laryngograph (p. 141), which is used mainly for work on intonation, and several systems that train individual speech elements, such as fricatives and nasals, or distinctive features of sound, such as voicing (p. 128). Many are based on spectrographic displays (p. 136) or make use of some simpler form of spectral analysis.

Several other visual methods have been devised to assist the deaf, including the use of a palantypist (p. 209) to provide a simultaneous transcript of a conversation, and the provision of specially prepared subtitles for television programmes using the teletext service offered by some major networks (p. 195).

AUDITORY IMPLANTS

In some cases of almost total deafness, the damage seems to be located in the hair cells of the cochlea, with the auditory nerve to the brain remaining intact. In such cases, it proves possible to provide a sensation of hearing by direct electrical stimulation of the nerve endings, using tiny wires that are surgically implanted in or near the cochlea, and that pick up signals transmitted via a device placed in the outer ear.

Several kinds of implant have been devised. The basic type sends a single electrical impulse to the nerve fibres – based on either an amplified speech waveform or some kind of modified waveform (as in the case of hearing aids). More complex systems make use of a series of wires, each of which is capable of acting as an independent information channel carrying just one aspect of the speech signal (e.g. a formant, §23). These can be linked to the auditory nerve or directly into the cochlea ('cochlear implants' – see diagram below).

It is too soon to say how successful these implants can be. The basic sensations of sound that are produced using current techniques are apparently a long way from the sounds of normal speech, and the deaf person has to learn to decode these sensations. But on the principle that any auditory information is better than none, a great deal of interest is currently being shown in the development of the approach. It is however an operation that is used only on people who are permanently and profoundly deaf, as it is a complete substitute for normal hearing.

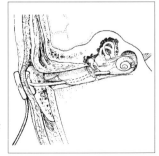

The audio signal is fed to an antenna coil (A) in the outer ear; it is picked up by the receiving coil (R) and sent to the electrode (E) in the cochlea. (From M. M. Merzenich, 1975.)

SPEECH SOUND PATTERNS

Six speech sound patterns, as produced on the Voice Visualizer (from W. Pronovost *et al.*, 1968).

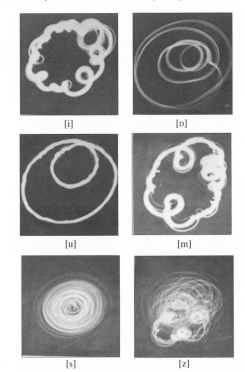

[i]   [ɒ]

[u]   [m]

[s]   [z]

SPEECH TRACES

In this experimental speech training system, features of place and type of articulation, and voicing, are shown as different kinds of traces varying in height, width, and colour, moving from left to right with time. (After G. J. Bristow & F. Fallside, 1979.)

SUBTITLES FOR THE DEAF

The invention of teletext as an additional service on the television signal allowed the broadcasting authorities in Britain (BBC and IBA) to introduce regular subtitling services from 1980 onwards. The aim is to help viewers who are deaf or hard of hearing to watch, at their own choice, subtitles that convey a soundtrack in written form. The viewer with a teletext receiver calls up the appropriate page number, and the subtitles automatically appear on the screen. Within a few years, each authority was providing up to 25 hours of teletext subtitling each week.

A sophisticated code has been developed so that the subtitles can best convey the information and feeling of the soundtrack. Speakers are identified either by the use of coloured text, or by placing the subtitle next to the person talking. Conventions have also been established to communicate any accent or tone of voice which the subtitler feels is germane to a viewer's grasp of the programme. Similarly, sound effects and music are described when relevant.

To allow viewers adequate time to read the subtitles and follow the pictures, the verbal soundtrack must be quite heavily edited. Most television programmes are prerecorded on videotape or film before transmission. A subtitler, working from a video cassette of the programme, and sometimes helped by a script, writes the subtitles onto a computer disk. This disk is then played into the television transmission system in synchrony with the programme.

Different techniques must be used with live programmes, such as news bulletins, sports coverage, or broadcasts of public events. In both Europe and the USA, systems have been developed using stenography or palantyping (p. 209). The output from the operator's machine is recognized by a computer containing a large phonetic dictionary, and this generates a written version as a subtitle. This system was first used to subtitle President Reagan's inaugural speech in 1981. However, in its early experimental days it was not error free, and the BBC later developed an alternative system, combining a number of different techniques, which depends on a closer relationship between the subtitling and the methods of television production. This system is called RECAP.

A subtitled exchange in the BBC word game 'Blankety Blank'. The word 'Bicycle' in the first line is spoken by the competitor. The remaining text is spoken by the host.

APHASIA

When an area of the brain involved in language processing is damaged (p. 263), the language disorder that results is known as *aphasia* or (especially in Britain) *dysphasia*. This terminological choice arises from a literal interpretation of the two prefixes: *a-phasia* suggests a 'total' lack of language; *dys-phasia* implies a 'partial' lack. However, the distinction has no clinical significance: all aphasic people have some residual language ability, even if this is only a minimal level of comprehension. It therefore makes no difference which prefix is used (as long as usage is consistent): we are dealing with a continuum of disability from very mild to very severe. The *a*-prefix is now more widespread, especially in the USA, and it has come to be used in the name of the research field, *aphasiology*.

A more important question relates to the nature of the behaviour affected. Aphasia is usually defined as a handicap of *language* comprehension and/or production caused by *specific* brain damage. It therefore clearly excludes language handicaps associated with other conditions, such as peripheral deafness (where there is no brain damage, p. 268) or senile dementia (where there is a more general deterioration of mental faculties). But it is more difficult to exclude handicaps that involve other aspects of symbolic expression and the associated cognitive skills – as when aphasic people display problems with understanding gestures, the symbolism of colours (as in traffic lights), performing arithmetical operations, remembering, or paying attention. Should these difficulties be considered as part of the disorder or separate from it? The focus of aphasic handicap is undoubtedly on problems of expression and comprehension in grammar and semantics, whether in speaking, listening, reading, writing, or signing; but these problems relate closely to difficulties of a pragmatic, cognitive, or perceptual kind, and a sharp boundary line cannot always be drawn.

CAUSES OF APHASIA

The brain is totally dependent on the oxygen conveyed by its blood supply; brain cells will die if deprived of oxygen for more than a few minutes. There are many *cerebro-vascular accidents* (CVAs, commonly known as 'strokes') that can cause this to happen, and these account for about 85% of all cases of aphasia. In adult western people, arteries can become 'furred up' with fatty cholesterol deposits, associated with such factors as smoking, diet, and lack of exercise: the deposits cause narrowing and obstruction of the arteries, and this may cause a stroke. Another possibility is for the arteries to become blocked by foreign matter that has entered the blood stream. Or they may haemorrhage in various ways. Whatever the reason, if these events take place in the areas of the brain that deal with language

processes (something that happens in about a third of all strokes), the result is likely to be aphasia. The other causes of aphasia include certain kinds of cerebral tumour, brain disease, and traumatic damage (head injuries due to traffic accidents, falls, acts of violence, etc.). About a quarter of all penetrating head injuries lead to aphasia. Altogether, the annual incidence of the handicap is about 0.6% of the population (1 in 200), with males more at risk.

About a quarter of all patients recover within three months. The rate of recovery then decreases, with full recovery increasingly unlikely after six months. A further 25% of patients are still severely affected after a year, with little subsequent improvement expected. The different communication modalities usually recover at different rates: generally, comprehension improves more rapidly than production. However, the process of recovery is little understood. It may be that cells close by the damaged area regain some of their function after a while, or perhaps other parts of the brain (such as the right hemisphere) may come to be used.

Samuel Johnson

Walter Scott

THE EFFECTS OF APHASIA

Samuel Johnson
From a letter written on 19 June 1783 three days after a stroke robbed him of speech:
I went to bed, and in a short time waked and sate up as has long been my custom, when I felt a confusion and indistinctness in my head which lasted, I supposed about half a minute: I was alarmed and prayed God, that however he might afflict my body, he would spare my understanding. This prayer, that I might try the integrity of my faculties I made in Latin verse. The lines were not very good, but I know them not to be very good. I made them easily, and concluded myself to be unimpaired in my faculties.

Soon after, I perceived that I had suffered a paralytick stroke, and that my Speech was taken from me. I had no pain and so little dejection in that dreadful state that I wondered at my own apathy...

In order to rouse the vocal organs I took two drams. Wine has been celebrated for the production of eloquence; I put myself into violent motion, and, I think, repeated it. But all was vain...

Walter Scott
From his diary, 5 January 1826:
Much alarmed. I had walked till 12 with Skene and Colonel Russell, and then sat down to my work. To my horror and surprise I could neither write not spell, but put down one word for another, and wrote nonsense. I was much overpower'd at the same time and could not conceive the reason. On waking my head was clearer... (W. E. K. Anderson, 1972, p. 55.)

(22 April 1830)
Anne would tell you of an awkward sort of fit I had on Monday last; it lasted about five minutes, during which I lost the power of articulation, or rather of speaking what I wished to say. I revived but submitted to be bled.
(S. G. Lockhart, 1900, p. 262.)

A more recent account
In 1960, Douglas Ritchie wrote a diary of his recovery from stroke. One year after the stroke he felt like this:
My speech? I might have had two or three stray words but I could not tell. In the Centre I rarely spoke to anyone. I had nothing to say

and I was embarrassed because I could not say anything. I read all the spare time I had. In the ambulance, where I used to spend upwards of two hours daily with four and five people week after week and where I was less embarrassed, I used sometimes to try different words. One week I was optimistic and the next there was nothing...

My writing was more depressing. I had only written 'Good luck, Clif' or a message like 'cigarretes' (spelt wrong – this might have aroused my suspicions, but it did not), and for the rest made the excuse that I did not write with my left hand. But it was my mother's birthday in May and I felt that I should write her a letter. I no sooner had the paper in front of me when every single word galloped out of sight. I was left staring at the blank sheet. Nearly half an hour passed; panic grew; this was nothing to do with my left hand. At length my wife came in and she dictated slowly, letter by letter, 'many happy returns...'. I managed to forget my panic for a time.
(D. Ritchie, 1960, pp. 96–7.)

TYPES OF APHASIA

There have been many different classifications of aphasia, reflecting the difficulty aphasiologists find in grouping patients together so that their medical and their behavioural symptoms coincide. A classification based on the site of the lesion(s) will make neurological sense, but may not result in a neat description in linguistic or psychological terms. Correspondingly, a behavioural classification usually cuts across some of the traditionally recognized neurological distinctions. There also may be some change in the aphasic symptoms, as the recovery period progresses. A few major categories have sufficient homogeneity, both medically and behaviourally, to stand the test of time, and these continue to be cited as 'classical' aphasic syndromes. These patients, however, may well be outnumbered by the many cases where the aphasic symptoms are 'mixed', to some degree, and where a classical diagnosis is unclear.

Broca's aphasia   The lesion is classically located in and around Broca's area, typically extending some way back along the Sylvian fissure (p. 262). The nature of the symptoms has led to its also being called *expressive* or *motor* aphasia. The language is usually characterized as markedly non-fluent – slow, laboured, hesitant, often one syllable at a time, with great difficulty in articulation, and disturbed suprasegmental features (§29). Sentences are short and reduced to a 'telegrammatic' style, with little use of the normal processes of grammatical construction (§16). Individual words are often repeated. Comprehension of everyday language is near-normal.

Wernicke's aphasia   The lesion is classically located in Wernicke's area (p. 262), though there is some variability. The nature of the symptoms has led to its also being called *receptive* or *sensory* aphasia. The language is characterized as fluent, often excessively so, with no articulatory difficulty, though there may be several erratic pauses. There is usually a severe disturbance of comprehension, though this is obscured by a normal intonation. The speech illustrates many stereotyped patterns, circumlocutions, unintelligible sequences (known as 'jargon'), errors in choosing words and phonemes (§28), and problems in retrieving words from memory.

Global aphasia   The symptoms are those of severe Broca's and Wernicke's aphasia combined. There is an almost total reduction of all aspects of spoken and written language. The patient's expressive abilities are minimal, and in most cases do not much improve over time. Comprehension of spoken language, initially very poor, shows limited recovery. The disorder is sometimes known as 'irreversible aphasia syndrome'.

EXPRESSIVE APHASIA

Several of the symptoms of Broca's aphasia can be seen from this French patient's description of the evolution of his disease (abnormal drops in pitch are marked by /):

Euh, hémiplégie, euh, fulgurant, euh, Hôpital Pasteur, Nice, Nice. Euh, Docteur Dupont. Euh, euh, examens/ enfin, examen, euh, enfin, un coma euh, un petit peu. Euh, un mois/ un mois, euh, pavillon F-3 /dy/ euh, Docteur Durand. Les reins. Euh, kinésithérapeute. Marche euh, euh, très bien, enfin, un peu, un peu.Euh, premier novembre, médica/ Le/ Giscard/ Docteur Giscard euh, rééducation. Euh, euh, oui, euh, kiné/ non, huit heures, kiné, euh, un quart d'heure …
(Uh, hemiplegia, uh, fulgurant, uh Pasteur Hospital, Nice, Nice. Uh, Doctor Dupont, uh, uh, examinations/ finally, examinations, uh, finally, a coma uh, a little bit. Uh, a month/ a month, uh, pavillon F-3 /dy/ uh, Doctor Durand. My kidneys. Uh, physiotherapist. Walk uh, uh, very well, a little, a little. Uh, November first, medica/ The/ Giscard/ Doctor Giscard uh, therapy. Uh, uh, yes, uh physio/ no, eight o'clock, physio, uh a quarter of an hour…)
(A. R. Lecours *et al.* 1983, p. 86)

RECEPTIVE APHASIA

Several of the symptoms of Wernicke's aphasia can be seen in this French patient's response to a question about his family (strong stresses are italicized):

Oui, j'ai une autre *femme* qui est restée depuis la /bœtʀe/ de l'enfant de *ma fils. Il a/* elle avait dix ans quand mon /fɛs/est mort. Et alors, elle est là maintenant. Elle va sur /syz/ ans. Elle va toujours à l'école, puisqu'elle se présente les/ Je l'avais envoyée à l'école puisque, moi, je travaillais bien dans les /syz/ I – euh – à la /faʀmid/ de/ de/ de /syz/, n'est-ce pas, de deux /ɛtmiʀ/. Et alors, je/ Cette /mwazɛ/ – la – euh, *Ginette*, elle s'appelle – elle/ elle /abil/… (Yes I have another *woman* who has remained since the /bœtʀe/ of the child of *my son. He is/* she was ten years old when my /fɛs/ died. And then, she is there now. She will soon be /syz/ years old. She is still going to school since she presents herself the/ I had sent her to school since I myself was indeed working in the /syz/ I – uh – at the /faʀmid/ of/ of /syz/ isn't it, of two /ɛtmiʀ/. And then, I/ This /mwazɛ/ – there uh, *Ginette* is her name – she/ she /abil/…)
(A. R. Lecours *et al.*, 1983, p. 94.)

OTHER SYMPTOMS

Aphasia is often accompanied by other symptoms which need to be taken into account when assessing the communication impairment as a whole.
• *Agnosia:* a difficulty in recognizing familiar sensory stimuli. When the disability relates to sounds, it is known as *auditory* agnosia; when it relates to pictures or shapes, it is known as *visual* agnosia.

• *Apraxia* (or *dyspraxia*): an often severe difficulty in controlling voluntary movements of limbs or vocal organs. In particular, there may be an inability to control sequences of sounds (*articulatory* or *verbal* apraxia) or gestures. The intention to communicate is present, but the patient cannot carry it out.
• *Anarthria* (or *dysarthria*): there is often an accompanying weakness or paralysis in the side of the body opposite the hemisphere which has been damaged (p. 260). When this affects the face or neck, the functioning of the vocal organs can be impaired, to produce a poorer quality of articulation. The effects range from mild to severe – from a slight slurring to total unintelligibility.

A group enjoying the atmosphere of a stroke club – one of many voluntary groups that have been set up to aid the process of rehabilitation in people who are impaired by the range of handicaps that follow a stroke – notably paralysis and aphasia.

DYSLEXIA AND DYSGRAPHIA

The onset of brain damage in adult life frequently leads to a disorder of reading or writing in people who have previously been literate. The handicap is usually accompanied by aphasic symptoms affecting spoken language (p. 272); occasionally, it is the only, or predominant, symptom. In all cases, the reading disorder is referred to as (*acquired*) *dyslexia* and the writing disorder as (*acquired*) *dysgraphia*. The *a-* prefix is also used, especially in Europe and North America (*alexia, agraphia*). The label 'acquired' distinguishes the handicap from the more widely known *developmental* kinds of dyslexia and dysgraphia that occur in young children where there is no evidence of any brain damage (see p. 275).

Neuropsychological studies of these handicaps have generally proceeded by classifying patients into types, based on a detailed description of the kinds of errors made. The process is a slow and difficult one, partly because of the large amounts of vocabulary that have to be analysed before an error pattern emerges, and partly because there are usually associated language symptoms that also need to be taken into account. Nonetheless, since the 1970s several types of acquired dyslexia and dysgraphia have been proposed, based on a small number of case studies.

TYPES OF ACQUIRED DYSLEXIA

Phonological dyslexia People with this problem are unable to read on the basis of the 'phonic' rules that relate graphemes to phonemes (§34). This means that they can manage to read familiar words, but they have great difficulty with new words (such as technical terms) or with simple nonsense words (such as *lak*).

Deep dyslexia Here too people are unable to read new or nonsense words, but in addition they make many semantic errors (e.g. reading *forest* as 'trees'). There are also several other types of difficulty, including visual errors (e.g. reading *signal* as 'single'), and errors that combine visual and semantic properties (e.g. reading *sympathy* as 'orchestra', presumably because of the link via *symphony*). Words with concrete (as opposed to abstract) meanings are easier to read. The table (right) gives further examples of this unusual syndrome.

Surface dyslexia People with this problem are very poor at recognizing words as wholes, and rely greatly on a process of 'sounding out' the possible relationship between graphemes and phonemes. Irregular words (such as *yacht*) pose particular difficulty. A wrongly pronounced word will be given a meaning on the basis of how it sounds, not how it looks (e.g. one person read *begin* as 'beggin', then added 'collecting money'). There is a problem with homophones (see Glossary, Appendix I) (e.g. one person understood *bury* as 'a kind of hat').

Several other types have been proposed. There is, for example, a visually based dyslexia, in which people fail to read the parts of a word correctly (e.g. one patient read 'night' when shown *near + light*), or confuse words of similar appearance (as when *met* was misread by one patient as 'meat', and *rib* as 'ride'). In such cases, the patient can often name the letters of the word correctly, but remains unable to identify the whole word. There are also several disorders of a neurologically more 'peripheral' kind, such as letter-by-letter reading, in which patients find it necessary to name all the letters of a word (aloud or subvocally) before they can identify it.

The search for 'pure' types of dyslexia is complicated by the occurrence of individual differences between patients, and by the existence of cases where symptoms are 'mixed'. Problems of interpretation are therefore considerable. Are deep dyslexic errors due to a partial impairment of the left hemisphere alone, or is the right hemisphere involved in some way? And, within the first of these possibilities, is the disorder the result of an impaired semantic system, or is that system intact, with the problems arising out of an impaired ability to make correspondences between graphemes and phonemes? Answers to such questions will only emerge once the database is enlarged by in-depth linguistic descriptions of many more cases.

TYPES OF ACQUIRED DYSGRAPHIA

Most work in this field has studied the disruption caused to spelling ability (p. 215). Three syndromes have been proposed, analogous to those proposed for acquired dyslexia.

Phonological dysgraphia People with this problem can spell real words but not nonsense words (though they can sometimes read many of them, and speak them aloud).

Deep dysgraphia Here too there is no ability to spell on a phonetic basis; if someone is asked to write a dictated nonsense word, for example, it is often replaced by a real word that is similar in sound (e.g. *blom* is written *flower*, presumably because of the word *bloom*). Errors seem to be semantically related (e.g. one person, asked to write *bun*, wrote *cake*). The spelling of words with concrete meaning is better than that of words with abstract meaning. The relationship to reading ability is unclear: one patient studied had normal reading ability, but most seem to have some deep dyslexic symptoms also.

Surface dysgraphia People with this problem can spell spoken nonsense words in a plausible way, but cannot spell irregular real words (e.g. one person wrote *biscuit* as *bisket*) – and even regular words may be affected. They seem dependent on using grapheme–phoneme conversion rules; whole-word spelling is impaired, though not entirely lost (e.g. one person spelled *yacht* as *yhagt*, showing some visual recall).

DEEP DYSLEXIA SYMPTOMS

The first patient providing evidence of a deep dyslexia syndrome was studied by a Medical Research Council team in Oxford in the 1960s – a person who had been a highly literate adult before his left-hemisphere injury. His reading errors were classified into five types (in each case the target word is on the left and the patient's version is on the right).

Semantic errors
act → play
close → shut
dinner → food
afternoon → tonight

Derivational errors (p. 90)
wise → wisdom
strange → stranger
pray → prayers
birth → born

Visual errors
stock → shock
quiz → queue
crocus → crocodile
saucer → sausage

Function words (p. 91)
for → and
his → she
the → yes
in → those

Non-words
wux → ('don't know')
wep → wet
dup → damp
nol → ('no idea')
(J. C. Marshall & F. Newcombe, 1980, pp. 1–3.)

DEEP DYSGRAPHIC ERRORS

Responses of one deep dysgraphic patient to part of a single-word dictation test.

Function words are particularly poor: some are not attempted; some bear little resemblance to the stimulus word. In three cases, he added content word homophones (1b, 4b, 9b), and was able to spell two of them. The content word list shows several visual errors (e.g. *why* for *way*), but none of the semantic errors that were also a feature of this person's handicap (e.g. writing *small* for *little*). (From F. M. Hatfield & K. E. Patterson, 1984, p. 189.)

STRING INSIDE MY HEAD

It was easy to talk about what I had seen in the park, or to sort out the ballet shoes, or to put books away neatly according to size, but to decipher the alphabet, or recognize C.A.T. and say what it spelt was almost impossible... When I was required to write, a strange feeling came over me, and I felt there was a long piece of string in my head.

My mother would say, 'C.A.T. spells cat. Susan, what does C.A.T. spell?

'I don't know, I don't know, Mrs Hampshire (as I called her at school), I don't know what it spells.'

The string inside my head stopped me from answering. It actually felt as though my skull housed a whole ball of string, with an end sticking out of my crown. I thought that if I pulled at this, I could get the string out, empty my head of it, unravel the tangle in my brain...

'Mummy, I can feel my string.'

'Don't be ridiculous, Susan.'

The page, the pencil, my mother's face, her slightly oily skin – not a line on it – her dark brown eyes compelling me to answer correctly, her nail polish half erased by the washing-up, all this I could see and remember – but I could not remember C.A.T. Probably the most difficult word in the world, C.A.T. If only the other children couldn't spell C.A.T.

'Stop looking in the mirror and think about how you spell cat.'

I couldn't. I just could not. I tried, but I couldn't. My head was empty – except for the string.
(From *Susan's Story* (1981, pp. 26–7), the autobiography of Susan Hampshire.)

Acquired dysgraphic patients are usually also dyslexic to some degree. Moreover, classification must allow for cases where there are specific motor or sensory impairments. For example, there are people who can speak, read, spell aloud, and type, yet who cannot produce the letter shapes or movements required for writing by hand. Letters are badly formed, misplaced, repeated, or omitted. In such cases, it is graphetic rather than graphological ability that is affected (p. 187).

DEVELOPMENTAL DYSLEXIA

Since the early years of this century, it has come to be widely recognized that there are children who, after a few years at school, are consistently seen to fail at the tasks of reading, writing, and spelling, despite normal intelligence, instruction, and opportunity to learn. No medical, cultural, or emotional reason is available to explain the discrepancy between their general intellectual and linguistic abilities and their level of achievement in handling written language. There is often a history of early language delay, but by age 9 or so, spoken language ability is apparently normal, whereas written language skills may remain at the level of a 5- or 6-year-old.

These are the children who have been called 'dyslexic', though alternative labels have been devised for the condition in an attempt to escape the originally medical connotations of this term (notably 'specific reading disability' and 'learning disability'). In fact there are around 40 different terms used for problems in this area, some of which retain a medical bias, such as 'minimal brain dysfunction' and (in parts of Europe) 'legasthenia'. Because the handicap is viewed as a problem with 'written language' in all its forms, the term 'dyslexia' usually subsumes the kind of difficulties referred to as 'dysgraphic' in the brain-damaged adult.

The blighted school career of such children, when no-one recognizes their handicap, has been well documented. Their ability to read, whether for information or pleasure, and their daily failure in their attempts at written work, has a devastating effect upon their ability and motivation to learn. There are often associated problems in coping with number symbols (in arithmetic), and in tasks requiring short-term memory, such as following instructions. Their poor writing and spelling tends to be viewed as a symptom of educational subnormality or lack of intelligence – or, if the child is known to be intelligent, leads to a charge of laziness or 'not trying', with subsequent punishment in school and increased family tension at home. As a result, it is not surprising to find that many such children become anxious, withdrawn, or aggressive – with deteriorating behaviour in some cases leading to them being described as maladjusted. Career prospects, in such cases, are minimal.

Questions of incidence and causation are discussed on pp. 276–7, along with a more detailed illustration of the range of dyslexic symptoms.

Incidence

The dyslexia problem is becoming increasingly recognized, with many countries now setting up organizations to draw attention to the handicap and to provide special help. In a very few countries, this help is guaranteed by legislation. It is however extremely difficult to arrive at an accurate estimate of incidence because there are no internationally accepted reading tests and criteria of handicap. In one survey of 16 countries, the mean percentage of non-retarded children with reading difficulties was 8% – but this covered a range that went from 1% (China) to 33% (Venezuela). Some estimates suggest that dyslexic boys outnumber girls in a ratio of around 3:1, others that it may be as many as 10:1.

The uncertainty derives from the fact that reading difficulty is a continuum from normal to abnormal, with the only criterion of handicap being that the children's ability is well below their age and intelligence. Everything therefore depends on how intelligence and reading achievement is measured, and what is considered to be 'well' below normal. For example, if the definition of dyslexia includes only those children who are retarded by at least two years in reading ability, the numbers affected will be appreciably greater than one which requires that they be retarded by at least three years. Such differences of method, even within a single country, make it virtually impossible to arrive at an agreed statement of incidence.

Causation

The question of causation has also promoted great controversy. Until recently, there was a widespread assumption that all dyslexics were fundamentally alike, and that a single cause of the handicap could be found. A large number of candidate 'causes' were therefore proposed, postulating any of several medical or psychological factors, such as visual perception, intersensory integration, memory, attention, eye movement, verbal processing, and hemispheric dominance (p. 260). There could be several possible approaches within any one of these headings. For example, under dominance it has been argued that dyslexia is the result of (a) a lack of dominance, (b) a lag in dominance development, (c) a specific left-hemisphere deficit, (d) right-hemisphere interference, or (e) a disintegration of functioning between the two hemispheres. The role of the left hemisphere is strongly implicated (as is suggested by associated spoken-language delays and errors, and problems of motor coordination), but its exact influence is unclear.

Recent reviews of what is now a vast experimental literature indicate that a unitary explanation for dyslexia is illusory. The modern focus on individual case studies (as opposed to the traditional use of group studies) is bringing to light the existence of a variety of dyslexic syndromes, reflecting several possible causes. A popular contemporary view is that there is a large set of

---

COPYING

Copying by three children, which shows some of the problems of the backward reader. The style of (b) is well behind that of (a), who is the same age, and in many respects it is not as well organized as that of the younger child (c).
(a) Normal reader, aged 9 years, 8 months.
(b) Backward reader, aged 9 years, 8 months, with a reading age of 6 years, 9 months.
(c) Normal reader, aged 6 years, 6 months, with a reading age of 6 years, 9 months. (From L. Bradley, 1983, p. 238.)

(a) *Then he went to sleep on the sand and this time nothing happened, and all was well and he slept till morning. The sun woke him up, and he had just had time to shake himself when he saw them coming across the sand.*

(b) *Then ne wen to sleernrthesen oonothis time nothno thinhand ollwos well anu neslepet ill morning Thesun wote hensself Upand nerenhen justhobtnemselt when nesewthenco nig gcross thesend*

(c) *Then he went to sleep on the sand and this time nothing happened and all was well and he slept till morning The sun woke him up and he had just had time to shake himself when he saw them coming across the sand.*

DYSLEXIC PROGRESS

(a) A sample of a dyslexic boy's free writing at 8 years of age. The sentence reads: 'My favourite hobby is art work and maths.'
(b) The same child's free writing at age 9 years, 8 months, after specialized help. The sentence reads: 'I was walking down the street and I heard a scream and I went into the house and I saw a man with a knife.'
(c) The same child's spelling at age 8. The words are: *see, cut, mat, in, ran, led, lot, hat, pen.*
(d) The same child's spelling of these words at age 9. (From M. Thomson, 1984, pp. 41–2.)

(a) *mI tan hah vshat wac atamas*

(b) *I was wocin don the stet andI hud a ssSrceem andI went in to the haws and I Sur a manuuif a knife*

(c) *Sam cbThan hi ham ban thn hat baa*

(d) *see cut mat in nan leg dot hat pen*

factors implicated in dyslexia, some sub-set of which turn up in individual cases. For example, in one group of children, there was clear evidence of an unstable eye dominance: the children had not established a stable 'leading' eye in their reading. Another group showed difficulties with making perceptual distinctions (e.g. distinguishing same/different letters). A further group displayed problems with short-term memory.

The main methodological problem in such research is to determine whether the weakness shown by dyslexics is the cause or the result of the handicap. For example, many of these children have faulty eye movements (shorter saccades, longer fixations, more regressions, §34), but it is an open question whether these form a constitutional problem that made it difficult for them to learn to read, or whether the poor movements began as a result of their difficulties with reading, or whether there is no functional relationship between them at all. If information is not available on what the children were like before they began to read, and on how they perform with non-reading tasks, it is difficult to interpret the results of such experiments.

The conflicting and ambiguous research findings, linked with ambitious claims about 'the' cause of dyslexia, have led to a great deal of scepticism about the condition, especially when the possibility of an underlying medical cause is being stressed. These doubts are slowly being resolved, but there is still a need for new research initiatives – in particular, devising individual development profiles, along the lines of the acquired dyslexia research, and relating findings more to the nature of reading development in normal children, in order to establish what counts as an 'abnormal' error. In such ways, it will be possible to devise better developmental classifications based on behavioural symptoms.

Acquired vs developmental?

The several similarities between the symptoms presented by the two kinds of dyslexia have led some scholars to argue that there is an underlying identity. Parallels have been proposed between developmental dyslexics and acquired deep dyslexics (p. 274) – for example, both groups have trouble in reading nonsense words, and are better at reading concrete words. However, so far there is little clear evidence that children display the kinds of semantic error that are crucial to the identity of the deep dyslexia syndrome. Similarly, there have been proposals that developmental dyslexia displays a parallel with acquired surface dyslexia (e.g. because of similarities in phonic reading ability) and with phonological dyslexia (e.g. because of similarities in direct visual word recognition). None of these positions has yet produced a substantial child database, however, and several differences between the adult and child populations remain – in particular, the greater variability of children's performance. There is, moreover, always the possibility that the brain mechanisms that underlie reading acquisition are different from those used to maintain reading skills in later life. The unity view thus provides us with a set of intriguing but at present largely speculative hypotheses.

COMMON FEATURES OF DYSLEXIA

A wide range of factors has been implicated in the search for a definition of dyslexia. The following features commonly recur, but it must be stressed that there is great variation between dyslexic children (and, of course, between those whose symptoms have continued into adult life). Probably no dyslexic child would display *all* of these features, but most display several.

Background features
• Sight normal.
• Hearing normal.
• IQ near-average or above.
• Health normal.
• Adequate first teaching.
• No previous emotional disturbance.
• No gross brain damage.

• No socio-cultural deprivation.
• No serious lack of schooling.

Psycholinguistic features
• Reading, spelling, and writing all below that expected for age and IQ.
• Persistent and often bizarre reading and spelling errors, e.g. letters reversed or out of order (confusion of *b*/*d*, *was*/*saw*, etc.).
• Confusion when labelling left and right, and generally poor directional ability.
• Difficulties in coding symbols and sounds, e.g. naming letters of the alphabet.
• Difficulties in sequencing, e.g. putting things in a series, remembering days of the week, keeping one's place.

• Poor short-term memory, e.g. remembering tables or instructions.
• A history of late language development.
• Some pronunciation difficulty, especially with long words.
• Non-fluency in speech.
• Poor auditory discrimination of speech sounds.
• Problems of visual perception.
• A history of motor clumsiness.
• Problems of finger differentiation.
• Mixed handedness or confused laterality.
• Poor concept of self.
• Sometimes good spatial skills, e.g. model making.

HYPERLEXIA

Reading-retarded children sometimes develop a surprising ability to read aloud – including the accurate production of quite advanced vocabulary, well beyond their level of comprehension. In one study, this remarkable skill was observed in a 7-year-old boy with an IQ of only 77, and a level of motor development equivalent to a 3½-year-old. He had learned nursery rhymes and television commercials as early as age 2, and learned to read soon after 4 with little help from his parents. By the time he was 5 years old, he was fluently reading aloud material that would be appropriate for a normal 10-year-old.

The ability such children have to read aloud goes well beyond their other cognitive abilities. They have great difficulty, for example, associating the words they read with objects or pictures. On the other hand, they have great facility in sounding out nonsense words. (After P. R. Huttenlocher & J. Huttenlocher, 1973.)

A serious directional problem illustrated in the writing of a 7-year-old girl. (From L. Tarnopol & M. Tarnopol, 1976, p. 283.)

VOICE DISORDERS

Many people develop an expressive handicap in which their voice has a markedly abnormal quality. The pitch, loudness, and timbre (§29) may be so inefficient that the message carried by the spoken language may be largely or wholly unintelligible. But even if the speech can be understood, the voice quality interferes with communication by calling attention to itself. The sound can be highly unpleasant – for example, the harsh hoarseness or highly nasal qualities that can be heard in some disorders. Alternatively, the voice quality may simply be inappropriate to the speaker or the needs of the situation – as when an older male teenager retains the high-pitched voice of a younger child.

Voice handicaps are classified into disorders of *phonation* (an abnormal kind of vibration in the vocal tract, as when the vocal folds fail to function normally) and disorders of *resonance* (abnormal modifications of the sound vibration as it passes through the cavities of the vocal tract, §22). The first type manifests itself mainly in abnormal qualities of pitch and loudness – such as very monotonous, high-pitched, or weak voices – and in a range of breathy, husky, and hoarse effects that are cumulatively labelled *dysphonia*. The second type is best illustrated from the many abnormal nasal resonances that can affect the voice – some excessively nasal (or 'twangy'), some with reduced nasality ('blocked nose' effects).

About a third of all voice handicaps have a clearly physical cause – an anatomical or neurophysiological abnormality in the vocal tract. Excessive friction between the vocal folds can cause *nodules* or *nodes* to form at their margins. Other interfering formations include polyps, contact ulcers, and various kinds of cancerous growth. Vocal-fold movement may become weak because of disease affecting the main nerve leading to the larynx. External damage, such as a blow to the neck, can easily affect larynx functioning.

The majority of voice disorders, however, have a non-physical, or 'functional' cause. For example, emotional stress can itself be sufficient for people to 'lose their voice', resulting in a range of psychological conditions that require lengthy and sympathetic investigation and therapy if they are to be resolved. Factors of this kind may also have physical consequences. Nodules and ulcers result from 'vocal abuse' – an excessive use of the voice, which in time causes chronic dysphonia. But the reasons for the abuse are functional, arising out of the life-style of the speakers: in particular, it is very common for nodules to form in those who live by their voice, such as singers and teachers, and who are regularly faced with vocally demanding situations.

LARYNGEAL ABNORMALITIES

The illustration shows some abnormal laryngeal conditions, all of which can cause dysphonia.
(a) Vocal nodules – inspiration followed by phonation. The vocal folds are prevented from closing properly along their midline.
(b) A large, broad-based polyp, which will interfere with the normal movement and closure of the vocal folds.
(c) Contact ulcers, formed at the point of maximum closure of the vocal folds.

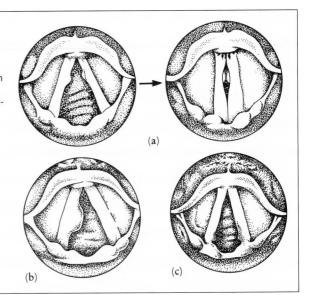

LARYNGECTOMY

Malignant growths in the throat, in the region of the vocal folds, can be treated with radiotherapy, but if this fails, it may be necessary to remove the larynx surgically, in an operation known as a *laryngectomy*. After this operation, the trachea (§22) cannot be rejoined to the pharynx, as food would spill into the lungs. The defect in the pharynx is therefore closed during the operation, and an alternative opening to the trachea is made at the front of the neck (a *tracheostomy*).

Patients who have had this operation are *laryngectomees*. Many learn to use the upper part of their pharynx and esophagus to initiate vibration, resulting in a throaty 'esophageal' voice quality. Alternatively, they may use an artificial larynx to provide a source of vibration – a device that emits a buzzing sound, and, when placed against the neck while they are 'mouthing' speech, provides a source of phonation.

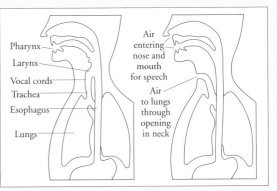

ARTIFICIAL LARYNX

The Nu Vois, from the US company Bivuna, one of a wide range of electronic larynxes now available for the laryngectomee. The larger item is held against the neck, at a point near where the larynx would be. The smaller item is an intra-oral adaptor: the tube is positioned within the mouth – an advantage for patients with tender neck muscles or who have difficulty holding the neck device in place.

CLEFT LIP AND PALATE

Between one and two out of every 1,000 children is born with cleft palate syndrome. A *cleft palate* is a congenital fissure along the midline of the palate (§22). It may extend throughout the whole palate (a) or affect only part of it (b). *Cleft lip* (an older label, 'hare lip', is nowadays felt to be demeaning) is the associated condition in which the upper lip is split. The lip may be only slightly notched, or the division may be complete (c), and include the upper teeth ridge behind (d). The split may be in the middle, on one side, or on both sides (e). Lip and palate may be simultaneously affected (f). There are also 'sub-mucous' clefts of the palate, in which the surface tissues have united, but the underlying structures have not.

Clefts of the lip or palate have very serious consequences because the condition affects not only the development of speech, but also the child's ability to eat. It is also extremely disfiguring, and a source of great emotional trauma to parents. Early surgical intervention is thus normal (lip operations are often within the first three months). Special prosthetic devices are sometimes used to cover the palatal gap, until the operation is performed, to aid the development of normal movement within the mouth.

Because of the early intervention, many cleft palate children develop fairly normal speech. However, problems of voice quality (often very nasal) and articulation can persist for several years, and there may be associated problems of language delay

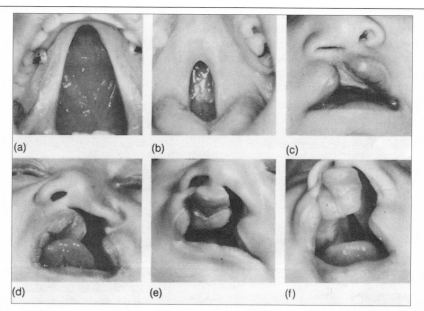

and hearing loss. A child who is making poor progress can still be largely unintelligible to all but the immediate family at the age of 3 or 4. The reasons governing lack of progress are not well understood, though a great deal must depend on the severity of the clefts and the extent to which the vocal organs have been able to grow in a normal way, after surgical closure, permitting flexible movement. The availability of intensive speech therapy is also a crucial factor.

ARTICULATION HANDICAPS

Traditionally, problems of articulation were studied solely from a phonetic point of view; today, there is also a phonological dimension to the analysis (§§27–8). An extremely wide range of difficulties is subsumed under the term. At one extreme, there are slight difficulties with pronunciation that hardly interfere with communication, but that cause some anxiety to the speaker (such as a lisp, or a 'weak' *r*). At the other, there are sound systems which are so misarticulated or disorganized that the person is largely unintelligible – something that is quite common in adults following acquired brain damage, when the motor control of speech can be severely disrupted (p. 273).

In children, many of the pronunciation problems that cause parental concern are due to a general delay in the ability to control movements of the vocal organs. Some children at age 4 or 5 are still pronouncing words in ways typical of a child of 2 or 3 – making immature omissions, substitutions, additions, or transpositions of sounds. (It should be added that the children's hearing may be perfectly normal, in such cases.) Others have more serious problems of incoordination, such as being unable to control the speed and direction of tongue movements, or to maintain consistent pressure between articulators. It takes only a slight lack of control to turn a plosive into an affricate or fricative (e.g. [p] becoming [pᶠ] or [f]), or a fricative into a plosive (e.g. [s] becoming [t]).

There are other articulation problems, however, that cannot be explained by such factors as language delay or poor motor coordination. In some cases, there is a difficulty in the perception of sounds (§25) – in particular, a failure to discriminate differences between related sounds (such as [p] vs [b]). In others, it proves impossible to detect any problems of an anatomical, neurophysiological, or sensory kind, and yet pronunciation may be considerably disordered. The explanation of such 'functional' articulation problems is unknown, though one must assume that something is wrong in the area of the brain involved in the control of phonological skills (both segmental and suprasegmental, §§28–9).

BREAKING THE CODE

One 4½-year-old girl produced the following pronunciations:

bees /biːt/	horse /hɔːt/
car /taː/	little /jɪt/
feather /tedʌ/	pen /pen/
finger /pɪnnʌ/	scissors /lɪkʌd/
five /paɪt/	seven /hebɪn/
girl /dɑʊ/	spoon /puːn/
cake /taɪ/	blue /bwuː/
train /braɪn/	boy /bɔɪ/
flower /pfɑʊə/	warm /wɔːm/
four /pɔː/	bird /bɜːd/

Her speech was generally difficult to understand, but her errors were usually not random. A detailed analysis shows some interesting trends, which would need to be confirmed by a much larger sample before a therapist would begin treatment.

• Vowels are generally correct, or nearly so.

• Fricatives (p. 159) are always replaced by plosives, except for two cases where [h] is involved, one case where [s] is omitted (in the consonant cluster, *spoon*), and one 'odd' case (*scissors*).

• Plosives are always articulated as plosives, but the child mixes up her place of articulation, substituting [t] for /k/ and [d] for /g/. She seems to have no problems with bilabial plosives, /p/ and /b/. Note that in all cases the contrast of voicing (p. 128) is maintained.

• There are evidently problems with /l/, which is omitted or replaced, and which turns up inexplicably in *scissors*.

• In no case is a consonant cluster used correctly, as in *blue*, *train*, and *flower*.

FLUENCY DISORDERS

A disorder of fluency, in the context of language, refers to a major lack of ability to communicate easily, rapidly, and continuously. The problem is most noticeable when people have difficulty in controlling the rhythm and timing of their speech, to produce the phenomenon of *stuttering* or (as it is more widely known in Britain) *stammering*.

Stuttering is difficult to summarize because it involves several kinds of non-fluency that vary considerably from speaker to speaker.

- The most widely recognized symptom is the abnormal amount of repetition of sounds, syllables, words, or phrases, e.g. *p-p-p-please, he's got a – got a – got a – car.*
- Sounds may be abnormally lengthened, e.g. *sssee*, where the initial [s] can last several seconds, often with an uncertain rhythm.
- The speaker prepares to articulate a sound, but is unable to release it. In severe cases, facial spasms and sudden body movements may be used in an effort to get over the 'block'.
- Extra words are introduced at points of difficulty, e.g. *oh, gosh*.
- Words show erratic stress patterns, and there is an abnormal intonation and speed of speech (§29).
- Words and phrases may be left unfinished.
- Speakers may avoid words and phrases that contain the sounds they find difficult, and replace these by circumlocutions. One stutterer, who had great difficulty with [p], would always replace *policeman* by 'officer of the law'.

A certain amount of 'normal non-fluency' is found in young children (especially around the age of 3), and indeed everyone is prone to hesitation, especially in situations where they have to speak under pressure. Stutterers too vary greatly in the control they have over their speech, and clinicians therefore look closely at the contexts that most promote a stutter when they are investigating the problem. It is very difficult to draw a clear line between normal speech and stuttering, though there is no mistaking the handicap in its severe form, with its uncontrolled, tense, and irregular speech, and the anxiety and embarrassment (for listener as well as speaker) that is invariably present.

Theories and treatment

Many theories of the origins of stuttering have been proposed, but there is no current consensus. Doubtless the many variations between stutterers obscure the existence of several contributing causative factors. Physical factors have often been implicated, such as mixed cerebral dominance (p. 260), a specific left-hemisphere deficit, or a defect in the feedback mechanism between ear and brain (which reduces a person's ability to monitor output efficiently). There have been several 'psychoneurotic' theories, which attempt to relate stuttering to the speaker's personality or emotional state (some tracing the problem back as far as infancy). 'Anxiety' theories stress the role that adverse listener reactions can play in promoting a stutter. A typical example is when parents prematurely correct their children for non-fluency, or become impatient when their child is non-fluent; this causes insecurity and anxiety, which in turn causes further growth in the non-fluency. It is difficult to choose between such theories, as so much of the relevant evidence is lacking (e.g. what happened when the stutterer was young?).

Many treatment methods and programmes are now available, all of which, in the absence of agreed theory, have had their successes and failures. Some methods focus on the feedback problem, such as by taking stutterers' attention away from their non-fluent speech (by playing specially generated noise into their ears while they speak). Others focus on altering the stutterer's breath control, or develop techniques in which speech comes more slowly or evenly than normal. Learning to relax is an essential feature of many methods, as is learning to interact with others (especially in the situations that cause particular tension). These days, particular attention is paid to helping the stutterer develop a style of behaviour which more closely resembles that of fluent people; many stutterers, it must be remembered, have become so isolated and withdrawn, on account of their stutter, that they may need to be taught a new way of life (or at least, way of looking at life) as therapy proceeds.

CLUTTERING

The main symptom of this well-known form of non-fluency is the excessive rapidity of speech. Clutterers seem unable to control their speech rate, and as a result introduce distortions of rhythm and articulation into their speech. Sounds become displaced, mispronounced, or omitted. Syllables telescope into each other. The utterance comes out in relatively short bursts, often interfering with syntax. The speed may increase as the utterance proceeds – a phenomenon known as 'festination'. Very often the resulting speech is largely unintelligible. What is surprising is that clutterers (unlike stutterers) are often unaware of the problems caused by their non-fluency.

There is no clear explanation for the handicap, though many researchers accept that it may well have a physical basis. Electrical recordings of brain activity often show significant abnormalities, for example. A possible theoretical explanation is an inadequate neural 'pacemaker' at the neurophysiological level in the motor control of speech (p. 264); but there is as yet no empirical support for this hypothesis.

DAF

The equipment used in a 'delayed auditory feedback' (DAF) system. The speaker talks into a microphone attached to a tape recorder. A device in the recorder delays the voice for a fraction of a second, and then plays it back through the headphones sufficiently loudly that it becomes the dominant sound to be heard. When this is done to normally fluent people, many of them start to stutter. The technique is sometimes used with stutterers, and in some cases it has a positive (but temporary) effect.

Why it should help is unclear: the stutterers may be benefitting from having their normal speech masked, or they may be being forced to speak more slowly, which itself helps to control a stutter. A great deal more research needs to be carried out into the variables involved (e.g. stuttering severity, delay time, feedback intensity) before clinicians will be in a position to say why some stutterers benefit, and others do not.

LANGUAGE DELAY

Most of the children seen in a speech therapy clinic show some kind of delay in their development of spoken language. In school, where there is usually an accompanying – and often more dramatic – delay in the acquisition of the written language (p. 276), estimates of prevalence vary from 2% to as much as 15%. Delays range from a barely noticeable few months to one of several years. In some conditions, teenage children and young adults may still be using a kind of spoken language equivalent to that found in 1- or 2-year-olds.

In about a third of cases, the reason for the delayed language development is known. Mentally handicapped children, for example, display some of the most marked delays. In a study of 1,381 severely subnormal children between the ages of 3 and 16, over 40% of the 16-year-olds were unable to use grammatical constructions; and $17\frac{1}{2}$% had not even reached the one-word stage (§41) (W. Swann & P. Mittler, 1976). Other groups where the language delay is part of a more general problem include those who are deaf, psychologically disturbed, autistic, or physically handicapped. Accidents, strokes, and other incidents result in acquired language problems (p. 272) for a small number of children.

In the majority of cases, however, there is no clear physical reason for the language delay. The children have no relevant medical history, are of normal intelligence, and are not socially deprived or emotionally disturbed. Nonetheless, their language is well behind that of their peers. In several instances, there are accompanying difficulties of a cognitive or social kind – such as a general auditory imperception, poor memory, poor concentration, or a reluctance to cooperate with others. However, not all delayed children display such problems: for many, the language difficulty is the primary or only symptom. And even when other problems are present, it is never easy to determine whether one factor (such as memory) is the 'cause' of the language delay.

'Aphasic' children

These are the children who are sometimes called 'developmentally aphasic' (or 'dysphasic') – labels that are somewhat controversial. The terms derive from an analogy with the linguistic symptoms of people who have suffered brain damage (p. 272), but they have been criticized on the grounds that the developmental condition raises quite different issues. Here, there is no evident brain damage, and the associated problems are best defined in psychological, social, and educational terms, and not neurologically. It has also been argued that the linguistic symptoms are different: language delay, typically, displays few usages that fall outside the range of normal language development; aphasic disturbance, typically, contains a great deal of abnormal, 'deviant' construction.

As with normal language acquisition, developmental language handicap needs to be investigated in terms of both production and comprehension: the children are regularly referred to as having predominantly 'expressive' or 'receptive' problems (pp. 234, 267), and of course there are many 'mixed' cases. Within each category, also, the problems may be located under any of the headings recognized in models of language structure and use (§13). Phonological handicaps manifest themselves in such areas as poor rhythmical ability, the persistence of immature processes of sound formation, and difficulties in auditory discrimination. Grammatical handicaps are shown by a restricted range of sentence constructions, uncertain control of word order, and the avoidance of particular features in morphology and syntax (e.g. omitting word endings on nouns and verbs, or forms of the verb *to be* in such sentences as *The man is happy*). Semantic handicaps are mainly noticeable in a limited vocabulary. And there are several kinds of pragmatic handicap (§21), whereby children fail to make use of norms of interaction appropriate to their age – for example, an inappropriate use of questions, or an inability to 'keep to the point'.

GRAMMATICAL HANDICAP

This $3\frac{1}{2}$-year-old boy (*C*) had several phonological problems, as can be seen from his unintelligible utterances (marked as *syllables*), but his main difficulties were a failure to develop a normal grammatical system. His short sentences are more typical of a $1\frac{1}{2}$- to 2-year-old. He also had some difficulty comprehending some of the therapist's (*A*) questions, and he hardly ever produced a sentence spontaneously.

A: What does the fire engine do?
C: *syllable*
A: Where does it go?
C: –
A: Hm?
C: *2 syllables*
A: Where does it go? Does it go to a fire?
C: Yes.
A: What does it do, when it gets to the fire?
C: Ladder.
A: There's a ladder, yes and what does the ladder do?
C: Go – up.
A: Goes up, yes. And then, when the ladder's up, what do the men do?
C: Water – out.
A: Oh. And what does the water do?
C: *4 syllables* Stop – fire.
A: It stops the fire.

C: Yes.
A: Mhm. And what do the men do?
C: On ladder here.
A: On the ladder.
C: Yes.
A: What do they do on the ladder?
C: Go up.
A: They go up, yes. And when they get to the top what do they do?
C: –
A: Hm?
C: –
A: Do they jump off?
C: Yes. No. Come down.
(D. Crystal *et al.*, 1976, p. 142.)

PRAGMATIC HANDICAP

This 10-year-old boy (*C*) has no real problems with segmental phonology or grammar, and he has a fairly good vocabulary. His main handicap is an inability to organize and maintain a conversation; his answers are often said to be 'bizarre' and his thinking 'confused', as illustrated by the following extract from a conversation with his speech

therapist (*A*) about a forthcoming sports day at his school.
A: Which race would you like to be in?
C: I like to be in X (= *a town several miles from the school*) in the sports day.
A: In X?
C: Yes.
A: What do you mean?
C: I mean something.
A: Is there a sports day in X?

C: There is not. There is a sports day in Y (= *his own school*).
A: Then what's X got to do with it?
C: Nothing.
A: Then why did you mention it?
C: Indeed I did mention it.
A: Why did you mention it?
C: I don't know.
(M. McTear, 1985, p. 246.)

ALTERNATIVE COMMUNICATION SYSTEMS

For many disabled people unable to make use of normal modes of communication, alternative systems have been devised. Some are designed to supplement normal language use ('augmentative' systems); others completely replace it ('alternative' systems). In the simplest cases, the letters of the written language are coded into a different medium, such as the use of braille by the blind. In other cases, the complex grammar and vocabulary of everyday language is simplified to meet the needs of the disabled person. Several new systems of manual signs (e.g. Amerind, §37), tokens, or pictorial symbols have now been invented with this consideration in mind.

The proliferation of systems, techniques, and aids reflects the range of handicapping conditions, and the existence of many individual differences. At one extreme, there are physically handicapped people with high intelligence and minimal motor skills (as with many of the cerebral palsied); at the other, there are mentally handicapped people with very low cognitive levels and normal motor skills. Most equipment has been designed with the needs of the former group in mind – people who may be able to control the movements of only one part of their body, such as their eyes. But far more is involved than the development of 'hardware'. The content of the system has to be sufficiently simple to permit easy learning, yet have enough potential to enable linguistic skills to develop. A difficult task is to decide exactly what vocabulary will be most useful to people at the outset (some selections are shown below), and how to display it (a particular problem with large communication boards, which may contain over 1,000 items).

Two basic techniques are employed. In 'direct selection', users type, touch, or point to the element of the message they wish to communicate, using any mobile body part to operate a variety of keyboards, keypads, switches, joysticks, and pointing devices (e.g. a stick attached to the head). For those who have some speech, voice-activated systems are also becoming available. The element is then displayed on a screen, printed out, or speech synthesized. In 'scanning', they wait while someone or something systematically scans a set of possible message elements (e.g. letters of the alphabet), and they indicate when the right element is reached. This can be a very slow process, but it can be speeded up in various ways, such as by using a two-stage scan, in which a group of elements is first identified, and the specific element in that group subsequently singled out.

The new 'information technology' promises to change the lives of many people who previously had negligible communicative ability. Microelectronic techniques make the new systems faster, more powerful, easier to use, and more portable.

BRAILLE

Braille is a system designed to facilitate the use of written language by blind people. It consists of a sequence of cells, each of which contains a 3 x 2 matrix of embossed dots. In Grade 1 braille, the cells represent letters, numbers, punctuation marks, and several short words and contractions. In Grade 2 braille, words are abbreviated using the symbols available from Grade 1 to produce a kind of shorthand system (p. 209).

Because of the time it takes to transcribe texts into braille, and because of the size of brailled books (often 20 times the size of a normal printed text), materials in this medium have been very limited. This situation is already changing with the advent of computer-assisted systems that turn text into braille. The text is typed on a standard typewriter keyboard, and is made available for editing before the final version is embossed. Other possibilities for speeding up the process of text preparation include the development of optical character recognition, which 'reads' an orthographic text, and converts it into a digital form capable of being used as input to a braille transcription system.

There are also several non-braille devices. With the Optacon, the fingers rest on a set of vibrating rods that provide a tactile 'image' of the text. The system permits a more faithful representation of the text than does braille, and can be used for all kinds of printed material.

It requires a considerable amount of training before it can be effectively used. However, there are now over 10,000 Optacons throughout the world, used on many writing systems – even including Japanese *kanji* (p. 202).

'Talking books' – texts recorded on audio cassettes – have been available to the blind for some time. A more recent development is the Kurzweil Reading Machine – a device that reads printed characters and converts them into synthesized speech using a system of phonological rules (§28). Many typefaces can be read at speeds of over 200 words a minute, which is only a little below average human reading speed (p. 212).

A B C D E F G H I J K L M N O P Q R

S T U V W X Y Z and for of the with

SYMBOL SYSTEMS

Several communication systems have been devised using pictures or objects of varying size, shape, and colour as logographic symbols (p. 202).
• Rebus symbols, used in some early writing systems, and widely known through their use in children's comics, are found in some approaches to early reading in mentally handicapped children. For example, a picture of a child eating ('eat') might be combined with the letter 'h' to produce the symbol for *heat* (p. 65).
• A system known as 'Non-SLIP' (= 'Non-Speech Language Initiation Program'), based on the work of David Premack (p. 402), was devised in the 1970s for use with the mentally handicapped. This made use of plastic symbols in various abstract shapes as a means of teaching syntactic sequences.
• Blissymbolics is a visual supplement to speech developed in the 1970s by Charles Bliss (1897–1985). Bliss, a chemical engineer, aimed to devise a set of symbols that could be 'translated' into any language (as could the symbols of chemistry). Some of these symbols are illustrated below on a standard chart, along with the written words. The approach has been used with a variety of clinical populations, including the cerebral palsied, mentally handicapped, and autistic.

Currently, a great deal of research is being devoted to investigating the strengths and weaknesses of the various systems, in relation to the needs of individual children at different stages of their communicative development.

 We all went to the zoo. We saw

 lions and tigers and giraffes and owls an...

 penguins and seals and koalas and hippos

 and monkeys and parrots.

+ AND we all had an icecream.

MODERN DEVELOPMENTS

Several systems use the latest electronic and computational technology to provide augmentative communication systems which can be adapted to a wide range of individual needs.

A Lightwriter, produced by Toby Churchill Ltd in the UK.

A computer version of the DynaVox 2c®, produced by Sentient Systems Technology Inc, USA, and distributed in the UK by Dynamic Abilities Ltd.

The Cameleon II, produced in 1997 by Cambridge Adaptive Communication, UK.

Putting systems to use

Two children share a joke using ORAC, a portable speech communication system produced by Mardis, UK.

This lady has called her pet and given him the command to sit, using the Speakeasy™ Voice Output Communication Aid produced by Ablenet® Inc, USA / Liberator, UK.

Two children with a Canon communicator, produced by Canon Inc, USA, a portable aid which prints messages out on a paper strip.

Stephen Hawking

One of the best-known users of an augmentative communication system is the theoretical physicist Professor Stephen Hawking of Cambridge University. He uses a Toshiba 1200XE computer placed in a box on the back of his wheel-chair, and powered by a battery under the chair. The screen is mounted on the arm on the chair. The system was put together for him by a local firm, Cambridge Adaptive Communications.

The computer runs a program called Equalizer™ (produced by Words+ Inc, USA) which moves a cursor across word-lists in the upper part of the screen. Hawking stops the movement by pressing a switch, and this selects words which are then printed on the lower part of the screen. When he has built up a sentence, he 'speaks' it by sending it to a synthesizer (made by Speech+, a division of Centigram Communications Corp, USA). A whole lecture can be delivered in this way, sentence by sentence.

Hawking can save what he writes on disk, and thus can produce books, papers, lectures, and other material. The program allows him to write equations in words, which are then translated into symbols and printed out appropriately.

Extra features have been added to the basic system in the 1990s . A mobile telephone allows Hawking to make and receive calls through the computer. He writes sentences using Equalizer™ and sends them to the synthesizer, which is connected to the phone. Separate commands tell the synthesizer to 'pick up' and 'put down' the phone. He is also now able to send and receive e-mail.

The languages of the world

PART IX

Aakwa, Anus, Bella Coola, Blood, Bok, Deerie, Gold, Grawadungalung, I, Kukukuku, Lule, Marraawarree, Mimika, Ngeq, Nupe, Ok, Ron, Santa, Shiriana, Tiini, Tzotzil, U, Yangman, Zyrian ... The litany of the world's lesser-known languages reads like a mixture of mad invention and poetic inspiration. Over 22,000 names of languages, dialects, and tribes have been collected, as part of the task of linguistic identification and classification. In the first sections of this Part, we look at the problems which would face anyone embarking on this task. How many languages are there? How many speakers do these languages have? Such questions are not easy to answer, and it is important to know why.

The multiplicity of languages leads naturally to a consideration of the reasons for the diversity. What are the origins of human language? In the next sections, we review the ancient speculations concerning the origins of language, and the attempts by scholars in the 20th century to say something sensible about the matter, using techniques borrowed from palaeontology and other sciences.

Comparative philology is the branch of language study which first looked as far back as possible into the history of language. Out of this study comes the basic classification of the world's languages into families. We describe the way in which families of languages are set up, and the alternative methods of classification that have been devised. We then outline the languages of the world, family by family, beginning with Indo-European, and ending with some of the languages which do not fit neatly into any of the families – the so-called 'isolates'.

When we try to account for linguistic diversity, it is the phenomenon of language change which is the central fact to be identified and explained. The remaining sections therefore describe the many ways in which language can change, and discuss the various reasons which have been proposed to account for this process. Finally, we look at some special cases which illustrate the ways in which social forces can promote new language growth – the world's pidgins and creoles.

The Tower of Babel by
Pieter Bruegel the Elder
(c. 1515-69).

There is no agreed total for the number of languages spoken in the world today. Most reference books give a figure of 5,000 to 6,000, but estimates have varied from 3,000 to 10,000. To see why there is such uncertainty, we need to consider the many problems facing those who wish to obtain accurate information, and also the reasons (linguistic, historical, and cultural) which preclude a simple answer to the question 'What counts as a language?'

DISCOVERIES

An obvious reason for the uncertainty over numbers is that even today new peoples, and therefore languages, continue to be discovered in the unexplored regions of the world – especially in the Amazon basin (as the Transamazonica road system is extended), Central Africa, and New Guinea. However, only a few languages are likely to be encountered in this way; and it is much more usual to find parts of the world where the people are known, but the languages spoken in their area are not. There are in fact many countries where linguistic surveys are incomplete or have not even begun. It is often assumed that the people speak one of the known languages in their area; or that they speak a dialect of one of these languages; but upon investigation their speech is found to be so different that it has to be recognized as a separate language.

ALIVE OR DEAD?

Against this steady increase in the world language total, there is a major factor which decreases it. For a language to count as 'living', there obviously have to be native speakers alive who use it. But in many parts of the world, it is by no means an easy matter to determine whether native speakers are still living – or, if they are, whether they still use their mother tongue regularly.

The speed with which a language can die in the smaller communities of the world is truly remarkable. The Amazonian explorations led to the discovery of many new languages, but they also led to their rapid death, as the Indians became swallowed up by the dominant western culture. Within a generation, all traces of a language can disappear. Political decisions force tribes to move or be split up. Economic prospects attract younger members away from the villages. New diseases take their toll. In 1962, Trumai, spoken in a single village on the lower Culuene River in Venezuela, was reduced by an influenza epidemic to a population of fewer than 10 speakers. In the 19th century, there were thought to be over 1,000 Indian languages in

Brazil; today, there are only 200. A quarter of the world's languages have fewer than 1,000 speakers; half have fewer than 10,000. It is likely that most of these languages will die out in the next 50 years.

LANGUAGE – OR DIALECT?

For most languages, the distinction between language and dialect is fairly clear-cut (p. 25). In the case of English, for example, even though regional vocabulary and local differences of pronunciation can make communication difficult at times, no-one disputes the existence of an underlying linguistic unity that all speakers identify as English, and which is confirmed by the use of a standard written language and a common literary heritage. But in hundreds of cases, considerations of this kind are in conflict with each other, or do not clearly apply.

The best-known conflicts occur when the criteria of national identity and mutual intelligibility do not coincide. The most common situation is one where two spoken varieties are mutually intelligible, but for political and historical reasons, they are referred to as different languages. For example, using just the intelligibility criterion, there are really only two Scandinavian languages: Continental (Swedish, Danish, and two standard varieties of Norwegian) and Insular (Icelandic, Faeroese). Swedes, Danes, and Norwegians can understand each other's speech, to a greater or lesser extent. But as soon as non-linguistic criteria are taken into account, we have to recognize at least five languages. To be Norwegian is to speak Norwegian; to be Danish is to speak Danish; and so on. In such cases, political and linguistic identity merge. And there are many other similar cases where political, ethnic, religious, literary, or other identities force a division where linguistically there is relatively little difference – Hindi vs Urdu, Bengali vs Assamese, Serbian vs Croatian, Twi vs Fante, Xhosa vs Zulu.

A new road cuts a swathe through the Brazilian rainforest.

NUMBER OF SPEAKERS

Number of speakers of the world's languages, based on the data provided in *the International Encyclopedia of Linguistics* (Bright, 1992). The total number of languages (including extinct ones) is 6,604. Most of the estimates were made during the 1980s, with some from the late 1970s. The world population total passed 5,000 million in July 1986, and had reached 5,111 million by mid-1988, which gives an indication of the order of magnitude unaccounted for in the final column.

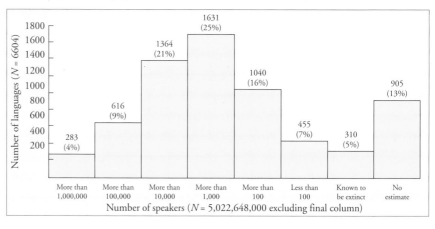

The opposite situation is also quite common. Here we find cases where spoken varieties are mutually *unintelligible*, but for political, historical, or cultural reasons they are nonetheless called varieties of the same language. The three main 'dialects' of Lapp fall into this category, for example. Chinese is a case where linguistic criteria alone are in conflict with each other. From the viewpoint of the spoken language, the many hundreds of dialects in China can be grouped into eight main types (p. 314), which are mutually unintelligible to various degrees. But speakers of all these dialects share the same written language tradition, and those who have learned the system of Chinese characters are able to communicate with each other. Despite the linguistic differences, therefore, Chinese is considered by its speakers to be a single language.

In the above cases, the languages in question have been well studied, and many speakers are involved. When languages have been little studied, or have very few speakers, it is much more difficult for linguists to interpret all the factors correctly. For example, when two languages are in close proximity, they often borrow words from each other – sometimes even sounds and grammar. On first acquaintance, therefore, the languages may seem more alike than they really are, and analysts may believe them to be dialects of the same language. This has proved to be a real problem in such parts of the world as South America, Africa, and South-east Asia, where whole groups of languages may be affected in this way. Similarly, decisions about how to analyse all cases of dialect continua (p. 25) will affect our final total of languages.

LANGUAGE NAMES

A big problem, in working on lesser-known language areas, is deciding what credence to give to a language name. This issue does not arise when discussing the main languages of the world, which are usually known by a single name that translates neatly into other languages – as in the case of *Deutsch, German, Tedesco, Nemetskiy,* and *Allemand,* for instance. But in many cases the situation is not so straightforward.

At one extreme, many communities have no specific name for their language. The name they use is the same as a common word or phrase in the language, such as the word for 'our language' or 'our people'. This is often so in Africa (where the name *Bantu,* which is given to a whole family of languages, means simply 'people'), and also in Meso- and South America. In the latter areas, we find such examples as *Carib* = 'people', *Tapuya* = 'enemy', and *Macu* = 'forest tribes'. Some tribes were called *chichimecatl* (= 'lineage of dogs'), *chontalli* (= 'foreigners') or *popoloca* (= 'barbarians'), and these labels led to the modern language names Chichimeca, Chontal, and Popoloca. Frequently, the name is the same as a river on which a tribe has been observed to live, as with the many groups of Land Dayak, in the West Indonesian family. In several Australian aboriginal languages, the name for the language

is the word for 'this': for example, the nine languages within the Yuulngu family are known as *Dhuwala, Dhuwal, Dhiyakuy, Dhangu, Dhay'yi, Djangu, Djinang, Djining,* and *Nhangu.* Asking native speakers what language they speak is of little practical help, in such circumstances, if they only answer 'this'!

At the other extreme, it is quite common to find a community whose language has too many names. A South American Indian tribe, for instance, may have several names. A tribe, first of all, will have a name for itself (see above). But adjacent tribes may give the people a different name (e.g. *Puelche* means 'people from the east' in Araucanian). The Spanish or Portuguese explorers may have given them a third name – perhaps a characteristic of their appearance (e.g. *Coroado* means 'crowned' in Portuguese). More recently, anthropologists and other investigators may have used another name, often based on the geographical location of the tribe (e.g. 'up-river' vs 'down-river'). And lastly, the same language may be spelled differently in Spanish, Portuguese, English, or in its own writing system (if one has been devised). For example, Machacali, spoken in Minas Gerais, Brazil, is sometimes spelled Maxakali, sometimes Maxakari. When the initial letters vary (as when the Peruvian language Candoshi is spelled Kandoshi), indexing is especially awkward.

There are further complications. Sometimes, the same name is applied to two different languages, as when *mexicano* is used in Mexico to refer to Spanish (otherwise known as *español* or *castellano*) and to the main Indian language (*nahuatl*). Sometimes, speakers from different backgrounds may disagree about whether their ways of speaking should be related at all. Speakers of Luri, spoken in south-west Iran, say that their speech is a dialect of Persian; speakers of Persian disagree. Asking the native speakers is evidently no solution, for their perceptions will be governed by non-linguistic considerations, especially of a religious, nationalistic, or socioeconomic kind.

TO CONCLUDE

When all these factors are taken into account, it is plain that there will be no single answer to the question 'How many languages?' In some parts of the world, there has been a tendency to over-estimate, by taking names too literally and not grouping dialects together sufficiently – the Malayo-Polynesian languages are often cited in this connection. In other places, the totals are likely to have been underestimated – Indonesian languages, for example. There are over 37,000 language names listed in the 12th edition of *Ethnologue* (Grimes, 1992), and these have been grouped into 6,528 living languages. The number listed in the Index to the *Atlas of the World's Languages* (Moseley & Asher, 1994) is 6,796. The *International Encyclopedia of Linguistics* (Bright, 1992) lists 6,604, but this includes some 300 extinct languages. These surveys generally use data from the 1970s and 1980s. A total of 6,000 would seem to be a safe estimate for the 1990s.

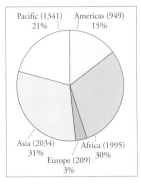

WHERE ARE MODERN LANGUAGES SPOKEN?

The geographical distribution of living languages, according to *Ethnologue* (Grimes, 1992), based on a total of 6,528 languages.

HOW MANY LANGUAGES HAVE THERE BEEN?

Based on what is known about the rate of language change at which new languages develop from a common origin (p. 331), it is possible to speculate about the number of languages which may have existed since the emergence of a human language faculty. Cautious estimates suggest 30,000; radical ones, over 500,000. A plausible 'middle of the road' figure is 150,000.

Estimating the number of speakers of a living language is, if anything, more complicated than estimating the number of languages. Any language which continues to be spoken in an area counts as 'one', in our language total. But the number of its speakers may vary wildly, from one decade to the next. A contemporary example is the Balkans, where the movements of population following civil wars in the countries of former Yugoslavia have led to dramatic differences, in both the totals of speakers, and the places they are to be found. Another example is the massive changes that affected people in Ethiopia and the surrounding regions during the famine of the early 1980s. The combined effects of large-scale loss of life, refugee migrations, and local government relocation policies mean that all estimates are now seriously out of date. It will be many years before accurate census information becomes available, and in the meantime, numerical data from the area must be viewed with extreme caution.

Trends in the world demographic situation will obviously be a major factor in any speaker estimates. The world population is currently increasing at a rate of about 1.6% per annum. In mid 1995, the number of people was estimated to be over 5,600 million. A UN projection to the year 2000 indicates a world population of well over 6,000 million. In these circumstances, any estimates of speakers, especially of the languages of the less-developed countries, are going to be well out of date as soon as they are printed. In the case of the many languages spoken within the Indian sub-continent, most of the available estimates were made in the 1970s; but as the population of India increased by 25% between 1971 and 1981, the figures need to be interpreted with a great deal of caution. All the estimates in Appendix III are subject to this proviso.

Even if a population is stable, it is rarely easy to obtain accurate information about the number of speakers. This is obviously a problem in the less accessible parts of the world. Less obviously, it is a problem which can affect any country, especially where minority groups are involved. The information might be obtained from a census, but not all census forms contain questions about linguistic background. Some countries do not think the matter important; others would like to know, but find it difficult to phrase the questions in such a way that they do not offend minority groups.

It is in any case difficult to use a questionnaire to establish the facts of language use (p. 26). In many of the more multilingual communities in the world, it is not even easy to answer the simple question, 'What is your mother tongue?' Nor is it easy to allow for such diverse cases as might be found in a British immigrant family from Pakistan, where in addition to their mother tongue, the mother's English might be poor, the father's moderate, and the teenage children's good, or even fluent. How does one cater for the situation in Scotland, where there is enormous variation in the fluency with which people command Gaelic? How does one cater for the situation in countries where English is an official language (e.g. India, Nigeria), but the population has achieved various levels of proficiency? How does one allow for people who have only a reading knowledge of a language, or who use a language only for special purposes (§63)? There are innumerable complications of this kind facing the linguistic demographer.

Moreover, how trustworthy is the information about language ability obtained through a census or other official report? There are many parts of the world where language estimates may be inflated, because people who may have relatively little command of a language claim they speak it, in order to support the cultural or political cause with which the language is associated (e.g. Breton,

An extract from the 1996 Canadian census form. The two language questions focus on speaking, but listening comprehension is implicit in the way question 9 is phrased.

By contrast, the 1991 census form used in England had no language question at all: respondents were asked to state their country of birth only.

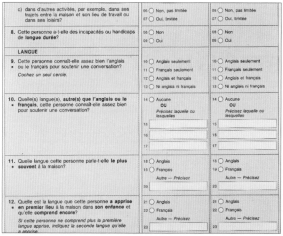

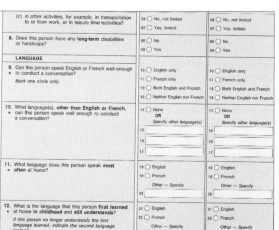

Welsh). Equally, there are many places where it has been unspoken government policy to underestimate the number of speakers of a minority language, in order to play down the political significance of that section of the community (e.g. Breton, Xhosa). Official figures, in such circumstances, should not be taken too literally.

Uncertainty over the name of a language does not help, and this is very common (p. 287). Often, the name of a dialect, the name of a language, and the name of a language family become confused – as if someone were to say 'He doesn't speak English; he speaks Cockney', or '…he speaks Germanic'. In a little-known area of the world, the reality of the situation may not be at all obvious. For example, Kru, Chin, Kachin, Dayak, Teso, Nuer, and Mongo-Nkundu are names that have been used both for single languages and for whole groups of languages, and speaker numbers are dramatically altered depending on which perspective one adopts. Mandara is a Chadic name which is sometimes used for a single language and sometimes for a group of related languages. If the former interpretation is taken, the speakers number some 30–40,000; if the latter, the total is nearly 2 million.

Approximations and uncertainties are thus the norm in language estimates, especially for those languages which are rapidly expanding, and those which are in a state of serious decline. In Appendix III, where speaker estimates are given for 1,000 languages, it has often not been possible to choose between conflicting totals; and in these cases, both upper and lower totals are listed.

Indo-European	386	2,500,000,000
Sino-Tibetan	272	1,088,000,000
Austronesian	1212	269,000,000
Afro-Asiatic	338	250,000,000
Niger-Congo	1354	206,000,000
Dravidian	70	165,000,000
Japanese	12	126,000,000
Altaic	60	115,000,000
Austro-Asiatic	173	75,000,000
Tai	61	75,000,000
Korean	1	60,000,000
Nilo-Saharan	186	28,000,000
Uralic	33	24,000,000
Amerindian (North, Central, South America)	985	22,400,000
Caucasian	38	7,800,000
Miao-Yao	15	5,600,000
Indo-Pacific	734	3,500,000
Khoisan	37	300,000
Australian aborigine	262	30,000
Palaeosiberian	8	18,000
Isolates	296	2,000,000

Family statistics Estimated numbers of languages (6,533) and speakers (5,002,648,000) in the main language families of the world in the late 1980s, based on the *International Encyclopedia of Linguistics* (Bright, 1992). The language totals include 310 extinct languages (p. 328). There are a further 71 pidgin/creole languages in this listing (p. 336), totalling some 2 million speakers, as well as 75 sign languages, where estimates of the number of users are unclear.

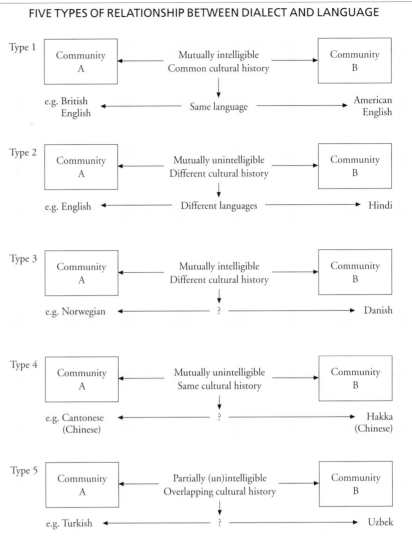

FIVE TYPES OF RELATIONSHIP BETWEEN DIALECT AND LANGUAGE

Type 1 — Community A — Mutually intelligible / Common cultural history — Community B
e.g. British English ← Same language → American English

Type 2 — Community A — Mutually unintelligible / Different cultural history — Community B
e.g. English ← Different languages → Hindi

Type 3 — Community A — Mutually intelligible / Different cultural history — Community B
e.g. Norwegian ← ? → Danish

Type 4 — Community A — Mutually unintelligible / Same cultural history — Community B
e.g. Cantonese (Chinese) ← ? → Hakka (Chinese)

Type 5 — Community A — Partially (un)intelligible / Overlapping cultural history — Community B
e.g. Turkish ← ? → Uzbek

THE TOP 40 LANGUAGES

1. Mandarin Chinese (726) (all Chinese languages, p. 314: 1071)
2. English (427) (cf. p. 361)
3. Spanish (266)
4. Hindi (182) (with Urdu: 223)
5. Arabic (181)
6. Portuguese (165)
7. Bengali (162)
8. Russian (158)
9. Japanese (124)
10. German (121)
11. French (116)
12. Javanese (75)
13. Korean (66)
14. Italian (65) (standard Italian only: 40)
15. Panjabi (60) (West and East)
16. Marathi (58)
17. Vietnamese (57)
18. Telugu (55)
19. Turkish (53)
20. Tamil (49)
21. Ukrainian (45)
22. Polish (42)
23. Bhojpuri (41)
24. Gujarati (36)
25. Malayalam (30)
26. Kannada (26)
   Sunda (26)
28. Hausa (24)
   Maithili (24)
30. Oriya (23)
31. Burmese (22)
32. Persian (22)
33. Thai (21)
   Dutch (21)
35. Awadhi (20)
   Yoruba (20)
37. Malay (19) (all varieties)
38. Nepali (18)
39. Uzbek (17)
40. Assamese (15)

Speaker estimates for the world's top 40 languages (given in millions). The estimates are based on the number of mother-tongue (first-language) speakers, as reported in Bright (1992) and Grimes (1992). Where there is a difference between these sources, a total is the average of the two estimates. The table does not include second-language totals, which in many cases are considerably higher (e.g. English > 800+ million, Spanish > 350+ million, Hindi > 350+ million, Russian > 290+ million), and some languages not in this table would enter it (e.g Bahasia Indonesia, 110+ million), if second-language totals were included.

For centuries, people have speculated over the origins of human language. What is the world's oldest spoken language? Have all languages developed from a single source? What was the language spoken in the Garden of Eden? How did words come to be, in the very beginning? These questions are fascinating, and have provoked experiments and discussion whose history dates back 3,000 years. The irony is that the quest is a fruitless one. Each generation asks the same questions, and reaches the same impasse – the absence of any evidence relating to the matter, given the vast, distant time-scale involved. We have no direct knowledge of the origins and early development of language, nor is it easy to imagine how such knowledge might ever be obtained. We can only speculate, arrive at our own conclusions, and remain dissatisfied. Indeed, so dissatisfied was one group of 19th-century scholars that they took drastic action: in 1866, the Linguistic Society of Paris published an edict banning discussion of the topic at their meetings. But the theorizing continues, and these days there is a resurgence of interest, as new archaeological finds and modern techniques of analysis provide fresh hints of what may once have been.

EARLY 'EXPERIMENTS'

The lengths to which some people have gone in order to throw light on the question are truly remarkable – if the accounts are to be believed. One of the best-known reports concerns the Egyptian king, Psamtik I, who reigned in the 7th century BC. According to the Greek historian, Herodotus, Psamtik wished to find out which of all the peoples of the world was the most ancient. His way of determining this was to discover the oldest language which, he thought, would be evidence of the oldest race. This is how Herodotus tells the story.

He gave two new-born babies of ordinary men to a shepherd, to nurture among his flocks after this manner. He charged him that none should utter any speech before them, but they should live by themselves in a solitary habitation; and at the due hours the shepherd should bring goats to them, and give them their fill of milk, and perform the other things needful. Thus Psammetichus did and commanded because he desired, when the babes should be past meaningless whimperings, to hear what tongue they would utter first.

And these things came to pass; for after the shepherd had wrought thus for a space of two years, when he opened the door and entered in, both the babes fell down before him, and cried *becos*, and stretched out their hands. Now when the shepherd heard it for the first time, he held his peace; but when this word was often-times spoken as he came to care for

them, then he told his lord, and brought the children into his presence when he commanded. And when Psammetichus had also heard it, he enquired which nation called anything *becos*; and enquiring, he found that the Phrygians call bread by this name. Thus the Egyptians, guided by this sign, confessed that the Phrygians were elder than they. That so it came to pass I heard of the priests of Hephaestus in Memphis.

Phrygian is now extinct, but at the time it was spoken in an area corresponding to the north-western part of modern Turkey.

Psamtik's conclusion was wrong, for we know from philological studies that Phrygian is but one of several languages which had developed in that period of history. So why did the children say *becos*? Doubtless they had begun to babble naturally and repetitively to each other, in a similar way to twins (see p. 249), and this was one of the 'snatches' that the shepherd recognized. Some commentators have even suggested that they were imitating the sound of the goats!

Whether the Psamtik experiment ever took place is open to question. Possibly the origins of the story lie in a fiction invented by someone to discredit the Egyptians. But whatever the reality, the initiative credited to Psamtik has apparently had its parallels in several later times and places. At least two similar experiments have been reported – though again, there are doubts as to their authenticity (see also p. 230).

Psamtik I of Egypt (663–610 BC)

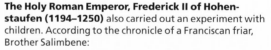

The Holy Roman Emperor, Frederick II of Hohenstaufen (1194–1250) also carried out an experiment with children. According to the chronicle of a Franciscan friar, Brother Salimbene:

He made linguistic experiments on the vile bodies of hapless infants, bidding foster-mothers and nurses to suckle and bathe and wash the children, but in no wise to prattle or speak with them; for he would have learnt whether they would speak the Hebrew language (which had been the first), or Greek, or Latin, or Arabic, or perchance the tongue of their parents of whom they had been born. But he laboured in vain, for the children could not live without clappings of the hands, and gestures, and gladness of countenance, and blandishments.

James IV of Scotland (1473–1513) is said to have carried out a similar experiment. The account given in the History of Robert Lindesay of Pitscottie runs as follows:

The king took a dumb woman and put her in Inchkeith, and gave her two young children in company with her, and furnished them of all necessary things pertaining to their nourishment, that is to say food, drink, fire and candle, clothes, with all other kinds of necessaries which is required to man or woman, desiring the effect hereof to come to know what language the children would speak when they came to lawful age. Some say they spoke good Hebrew, but as to myself I know not but by hearsay.

FIVE THEORIES OF THE ORIGINS OF LANGUAGE

The Danish linguist, Otto Jespersen (1860–1943), grouped commonly held theories about the origins of language into four types, and added a fifth of his own. They are often referred to by nicknames.

The 'bow-wow' theory

Speech arose through people imitating the sounds of the environment, especially animal calls. The main evidence would be the use of onomatopoeic words (p. 176), but as few of these exist in a language, and as languages vary so much in the way they represent natural sounds, the theory has little support.

The 'pooh-pooh' theory

Speech arose through people making instinctive sounds, caused by pain, anger, or other emotions. The main evidence would be the universal use of sounds as interjections (p. 91), but no language contains many of these, and in any case the clicks, intakes of breath, and other noises which are used in this way bear little relationship to the vowels and consonants found in phonology. The spelling is never a satisfactory guide.

The 'ding-dong' theory

Speech arose because people reacted to the stimuli in the world around them, and spontaneously produced sounds ('oral gestures') which in some way reflected or were in harmony with the environment. The main evidence would be the universal use of sounds for words of a certain meaning, but apart from a few cases of apparent sound symbolism (p. 176), the theory has nothing to commend it. Several fanciful examples have nonetheless been cited – *mama* is supposed to reflect the movement of the lips as the mouth approaches the breast, and *bye-bye* or *ta-ta* show the lips and tongue respectively 'waving' good-bye.

The 'yo-he-ho' theory

Speech arose because, as people worked together, their physical efforts produced communal, rhythmical grunts, which in due course developed into chants, and thus language. The main evidence would be the universal use of prosodic features (p. 171), especially of rhythm; but the gap between this kind of expression and what we find in language as a whole is so immense that an explanation for the latter would still have to be found.

The 'la–la' theory

Jespersen himself felt that, if any single factor was going to initiate human language, it would arise from the romantic side of life – sounds associated with love, play, poetic feeling, perhaps even song. But again, the gap between the emotional and the rational aspects of speech expression would still have to be accounted for.

CHILDREN OF THE WILD

For several hundred years, cases have been reported of children who have been reared in the wild by animals or kept isolated from all social contact. These cases are listed below, adapted from Lucien Malson's *Wolf Children* (1972). Sometimes the information is based on little more than a brief press report. At other times, the cases have been studied in detail – in particular, the stories of Victor, Kaspar Hauser, Amala and Kamala, and Genie.

The ideas of Psamtik I receive no support at all from these children. Only some of the reports say anything about the children's language abilities, and the picture is quite clear: none could speak at all, and most had no comprehension of speech. Most attempts to teach them to speak failed. The cases of 1694, 1731, and 1767 (Fraumark) are said to have learned some speech, and Tomko of Hungary (also 1767) is reputed to have learned both Slovak and German. The 1717 girl and the 19th-century Bankipur child are both said to have learned some sign language. But of the well-attested cases, the results are not impressive. Victor, the 'Wild Boy of Aveyron', remained unable to speak, though he could understand and read to some extent. Kamala of Midnapore learned some speech and sign. The two most successful cases on record are Kaspar Hauser, whose speech became quite advanced, and Genie (p. 265), who learned a few words immediately after discovery, and whose subsequent progress in speech was considerable.

Ramu the 'wolf-child' found near Lucknow, India. The magazine is dated 21 February 1954.

Peter the 'wild boy' found in a wood in Hanover and brought to England by King George II.

RECORDED CASES OF CHILD ISOLATION

	Date of discovery	Age at discovery		Date of discovery	Age at discovery
Wolf-child of Hesse	1344	7	Wolf-child of Sekandra	1872	6
Wolf-child of Wetteravia	1344	12	Child of Sekandra	1874	10
Bear-child of Lithuania	1661	12	Wolf-child of Kronstadt	?	23
Sheep-child of Ireland	1672	16	Child of Lucknow	1876	?
Calf-child of Bamberg	c1680	?	Child of Jalpaiguri	1892	8
Bear-child of Lithuania	1694	10	Child of Batsipur	1893	14
Bear-child of Lithuania	?	12	Child of Sultanpur	1895	?
Kidnapped Dutch girl	1717	19	Snow-hen of Justedal	?	12
Two boys of Pyrenees	1719	?	Amala of Midnapore	1920	2
Peter of Hanover	1724	13	Kamala of Midnapore	1920	8
Girl from Sogny	1731	10	Leopard-child of India	1920	?
Jean of Liège	?	21	Wolf-child of Maiwana	1927	?
Tomko of Hungary	1767	?	Wolf-child of Jhansi	1933	?
Bear-girl of Fraumark	1767	18	Leopard-child of Dihungi	?	8
Victor of Aveyron	1799	11	Child of Casamance	1930s	16
Kaspar Hauser of Nuremberg	1828	17	Assicia of Liberia	1930s	?
Sow-girl of Salzburg	?	22	Confined child of Pennsylvania	1938	6
Child of Husanpur	1843	?	Confined child of Ohio	1940	?
Child of Sultanpur	1843	?	Gazelle-child of Syria	1946	?
Child of Sultanpur	1848	?	Child of New Delhi	1954	12
Child of Chupra	?	?	Gazelle-child of Mauritania	1960	?
Child of Bankipur	?	?	Ape-child of Teheran	1961	14
Pig-boy of Holland	?	?	Genie, U.S.A.	1970	13½
Wolf-child of Holland	?	?			

SCIENTIFIC APPROACHES

By contrast with the informal discussion and speculation of preceding centuries, serious attempts have been made in recent years to see if modern science can throw any light on the question of the origins of language. The study is sometimes called *glossogenetics* – the study of the formation and development of human language, in both the child and the race. The main sciences involved are biology (especially sociobiology), anthropology, psychology, semiotics (p. 403), neurology (for the study of brain evolution), primatology, and linguistics.

THE EVIDENCE FROM PALAEONTOLOGY

Might it be possible to deduce, from the fossil record of early man, the point at which speech began? The matter has been well investigated, but the results are not conclusive.

It is possible to make plaster casts of the bony cavities within the skulls which have been found. It can be shown, for example, that both Neanderthal man and Cro-Magnon man (pre-30,000 BC) had similar brain sizes to that of modern man. But this information is of limited value. The relative size and shape of the brain can be established, but none of the more relevant detail (such as the orientation of the various furrows, or sulci (§45)). In any case, there is no direct correlation between the size of a brain and the use of language: in modern man, language is found in people with small brains, such as nanocephalic dwarfs, or children who have had large areas of brain removed – and some gorillas have a brain size close to these. It is plausible that an increase in the number of brain cells increases intellectual or linguistic capacity, but no correlation has been established.

Another way of looking at the problem is to ask whether primitive man had the physiological capacity to speak, and this has led to a great deal of interesting research. The problem is that only the shape of the jaws and the oral cavity are preserved in fossils; there is no direct information about the size and shape of the soft tissues of tongue, pharynx or larynx, nor about the ability to move these organs (§22). Most of the reasoning has therefore had to be based on reconstruction using plaster casts, and comparison with the physiology and vocalization of present-day primates and human infants.

It is possible to say with some conviction, using this kind of argument, that the older hominids did not possess speech; but the position of the more recent remains is unclear. It is unlikely that *Australopithecus* (who appeared around 4–5 million BC) could speak, but the evidence is ambiguous for Neanderthal man (70–35,000 BC). Linguists and anatomists have compared the reconstructed vocal tract of a Neanderthal skull with those of a newborn and an adult modern human. The newborn and Neanderthal vocal tracts are remarkably similar. Neanderthal man would have been able to utter only a few front consonant-like sounds and centralized vowel-like sounds, and may have been unable to make a contrast between nasal and oral sounds. This is well below what is found in the phonologies of the world's languages today (p. 167). It would have been possible to construct a linguistic code out of these limited sounds, but it would have required a level of intellectual ability apparently lacking at that evolutionary stage. On the other hand, these phonetic abilities are far ahead of modern primates. It has thus been concluded that Neanderthal man represents an intermediate stage in the gradual evolution of speech. Cro-Magnon man (35,000 BC), by contrast, had a skeletal structure much more like that of modern man.

PRIMATE VOCAL TRACTS

The vocal tracts of primates are very different from that of modern man. They have long, flat, thin tongues, which have less room to move. The larynx is higher, and there is little sign of a pharynx. There is no evidence of ability to change the configurations of the vocal tract, to produce the range of sounds required in speech. In the course of evolution, posture becomes erect, and the head moves forward. The larynx descends and a long, flexible pharyngeal cavity develops. (From V. E. Negus, 1949.)

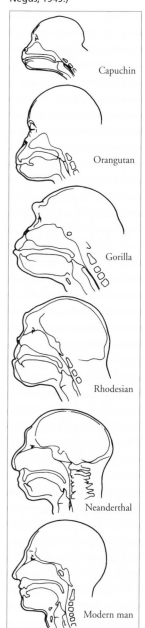

Capuchin

Orangutan

Gorilla

Rhodesian

Neanderthal

Modern man

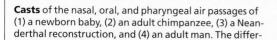

Casts of the nasal, oral, and pharyngeal air passages of (1) a newborn baby, (2) an adult chimpanzee, (3) a Neanderthal reconstruction, and (4) an adult man. The differences in dimensions can be clearly seen (below right) when the four tracts are drawn so that they are nearly equal in size. (After P. Lieberman, 1972.)

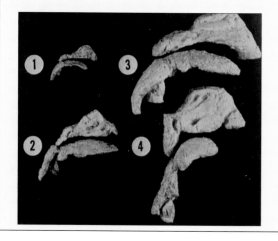

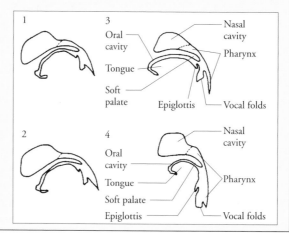

HOMO LOQUENS

It would seem that the human vocal tract evolved from a non-human primate form to enable fast and efficient communication to take place. Speech is not merely the incidental result of a system designed for breathing and eating. The changes that took place in the larynx, pharynx, and mouth came about at the cost of less efficient breathing, chewing, and swallowing. Modern man can choke from food lodged in the larynx; monkeys cannot. The survival value of speech must be considerable to compensate for such deficiencies. The human being, in short, seems to have evolved as a speaking animal – *homo loquens.*

Some hominids had a human-like vocal tract as far back as 200,000 BC, but they probably did not have a sufficiently developed nervous system to control it. There is general agreement on a time-scale from 100,000 to 20,000 BC for the development of speech. If the Neanderthal evidence is accepted, this scale narrows to 50–30,000 BC, in the latter part of the Upper Palaeolithic period.

This is the conclusion regarding speech. But the lack of physical similarities with modern man does not prove that there was no language in an abstract sense, or other modes of communication. At the time indicated above, cultural development was relatively advanced, and there must have been some efficient way of transmitting information about skills from one generation to the next. Any degree of social interdependence – as found in tribal grouping, religious activity, or group hunting techniques – would seem to require a communication system. Cave drawings of the period also suggest the existence of an intellectual capability such as would be required for language.

An elaborate gesture system is one possibility. The early development of language may well have been assisted by some kind of signing, which would have been the simplest way of communicating basic meanings – such as how to use tools. Hands were no longer necessary for locomotion, so they could be used for other activities. Perhaps primitive people who were skilful in using signs stood a better chance of survival. Natural selection could then have led to the development of the intellectual faculties prerequisite for speech.

Learning to use tools, and to pass the skills on, would be most efficiently done through language. It has even been suggested that learning to use tools and learning language are interrelated skills. They are localized in the same general area of the brain (§45); and both tool using and gesture require sophisticated use of the hands. However, some non-human primates can use tools, and it is unlikely that the hands could have been used for two such different purposes for long. Nonetheless, in an indirect way, tools could have promoted the development of speech. Sounds made at the same time as the gestures might have come to be associated with various activities. The idea has been pro-

posed that, as tools came to be used for more advanced purposes, food would be stored, so that there would be intervals between meals, and thus more time available for the mouth to be put to other uses – such as the development of spoken language.

We can only speculate about the link between oral and gestural language. Similarly, the gap between human language and the communication systems of the nearest primates remains vast, and there is no sign of a language-like increase in communicative skills as one moves from lower to higher mammals. Human language seems to have emerged within a relatively short space of time, perhaps as recently as 30,000 years ago. But that still leaves a gap of over 20,000 years before the first unequivocal evidence of written language (p. 198).

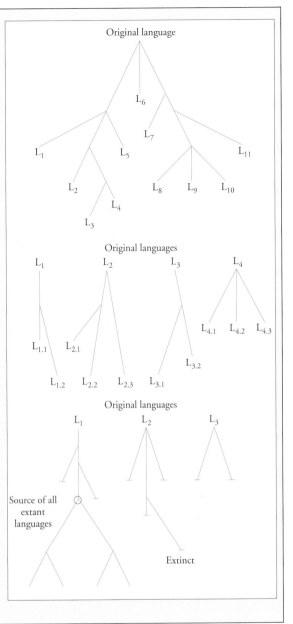

WAS THERE EVER AN ORIGINAL LANGUAGE?

Right: The view that all languages have diverged from a common source, the result of cultural evolution or divine intervention, is known as *monogenesis.* The existence of differences between languages is then explained as a result of people moving apart, in waves of migration around the world. In this view, language universals (§14) would be interpreted as evidence of common origin.

Centre: The opposite view, that language emerged more or less simultaneously in several places, is known as *polygenesis.* Language universals, and other similarities between languages, are then explained by pointing to the similar constraints which must have operated upon the early speakers (in terms of both their physiology and their environment), and by the likelihood that, as groups came into contact, their languages would influence each other – a process known as *convergence.*

Bottom: There is also a third possibility, given the vast time-scale involved. All of the languages that now exist may indeed have diverged from a common source, but this may have been just one line of descent from an earlier era when several independent languages emerged.

The first scientific attempts to discover the history of the world's languages were made at the end of the 18th century. Scholars began to compare groups of languages in a systematic and detailed way, to see whether there were correspondences between them. If these could be demonstrated, it could be assumed that the languages were related – in other words, that they developed from a common source, even though this might no longer exist.

Evidence of a common origin for groups of languages was readily available in Europe, in that French, Spanish, Italian, and other Romance languages (p. 303) were clearly descended from Latin – which in this case is known to have existed. The same reasoning was applied to larger groups of languages, and by the beginning of the 19th century, there was convincing evidence to support the hypothesis that there was once a language from which many of the languages of Eurasia have derived. This proto-language came to be called Proto-Indo-European (p. 298). Very quickly, other groups of languages were examined using the same techniques.

The main metaphor that is used to explain the historical relationships is that of the language family, or family tree. Within the Romance family, Latin is the 'parent' language, and French, Spanish, etc. are 'daughter' languages; French would then be called a 'sister' language to Spanish and the others. The same approach is used with larger groups. Within the Indo-European family, Proto-Indo-European is the parent language, and Latin, Greek, Sanskrit, and others are the daughter languages. In a large family, it will be necessary to distinguish various 'branches', each of which may contain several languages, or 'sub-families' of languages.

This way of talking must not be taken too literally. A 'parent' language does not live on after a 'daughter' language is 'born', nor do languages suddenly appear in the way implied by the metaphor of birth. Nor is it true that, once branches of a family begin to emerge, they develop quite independently, and are never afterwards in contact with each other. Languages converge as well as diverge. Furthermore, stages of linguistic development are not as clear-cut as the labels on a family tree suggest, with change operating smoothly and uniformly throughout. Linguistic change, we now know, is much more uneven, with different social groups responding to change in different ways (p. 330).

Since the 19th century, other classificatory terms have come into use. *Family* is still used as a general term for any group of languages where there is a likelihood of a historical relationship (and this is the way the terms is used in this encyclopedia). But in some classifications, a distinction is drawn in terms of how definite the relationship is. If there is clear linguistic evidence of a close relationship, the term *family* continues to be used; but where the relationship is less definite, or more remote, the grouping is referred to as a *phylum*. Sometimes the term *macro-phylum* is used for yet more general and less definite groupings. It is evident, for example, that all the Aboriginal languages of Australia (p. 326) are related, but as there is no clear-cut historical evidence which bears on the matter, and little typological work, scholars often refer to the Australian '(macro)phylum' rather than to the Australian 'family'.

THE COMPARATIVE METHOD

In historical linguistics, the *comparative method* is a way of systematically comparing a series of languages in order to prove a historical relationship between them. Scholars begin by identifying a set of formal similarities and differences between the languages, and try to work out (or 'reconstruct') an earlier stage of development from which all the forms could have derived. The process is known as *internal reconstruction*. When languages have been shown to have a common ancestor, they are said to be *cognate*.

The clearest cases are those where the parent language is known to exist. For example, on the basis of the various words for 'father' in the Romance languages, given below, it is possible to see how they all derived from the Latin word *pater*. If Latin no longer existed, it would be possible to reconstruct a great deal of its form, by comparing large numbers of words in this way. Exactly the same reasoning is used for cases where the parent language does not exist, as when the forms in Latin, Greek, Sanskrit, Welsh, etc. are compared to

August Schleicher (1821–68) The 'family tree' theory (*Stammbaumtheorie*) was introduced by the German linguist Schleicher, who thought of language as an organism which could grow and decay, and whose changes could be analysed using the methods of the natural sciences.

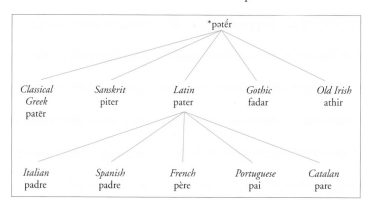

*pətḗr

Classical Greek	Sanskrit	Latin	Gothic	Old Irish
patēr	piter	pater	fadar	athir

Latin → pater

Italian	Spanish	French	Portuguese	Catalan
padre	padre	père	pai	pare

reconstruct the Indo-European form, *pəter. The asterisk in front of a form, in historical linguistics, shows that the form in question is a reconstruction which has not been attested in written records. Exactly how such reconstructed forms were pronounced is a matter of (at times fierce) debate: some scholars are happy to assign phonetic values to the forms, and pronounce them as if they were part of a real language; others argue that the forms are little more than abstract formulae, summarizing the sets of correspondences which have been noted (§54).

TYPES OF LINGUISTIC CLASSIFICATION

There are two main ways of classifying languages: the *genetic* (or *genealogical*) and the *typological* (§14). Both are used in contemporary language work, but the former has received far more investigation, and has the better developed procedures and frame of reference. A further approach (an *areal* classification) is reviewed in §8.

GENETIC CLASSIFICATION

This is a historical classification, based on the assumption that languages have diverged from a common ancestor. It uses early written remains as evidence, and when this is lacking, deductions are made using the comparative method to enable the form of the parent language to be reconstructed. The approach has been widely used, since its introduction at the end of the 18th century, and provides the framework within which all world-wide linguistic surveys to date have been carried out. The success of the approach in Eurasia, where copious written remains exist, is not matched in most other parts of the world, where a classification into families is usually highly tentative.

TYPOLOGICAL CLASSIFICATION

This is based on a comparison of the formal similarities which exist between languages. It is an attempt to group languages into structural types, on the basis of phonology, grammar, or vocabulary, rather than in terms of any real or assumed historical relationship. For example, it is possible to group languages in terms of how they use sounds – how many and what kinds of vowels they have, whether they use clicks, whether they use tones, and so on. Languages can also be classified in terms of whether their word order is fixed or free, and which order is favoured (p. 98). The earliest typologies, however, were in the field of morphology (p. 90). These, propounded by August von Schlegel (1767–1845) and others in the early 19th century, recognized three main linguistic types, on the basis of the way a language constructs its words.

Isolating, analytic, or root languages

All the words are invariable: there are no endings. Grammatical relationships are shown through the use of word order. Chinese, Vietnamese, and Samoan are clear cases. For example, 'I bought some oranges to eat' in Beijing Chinese would be:

Wǒ	mǎi júzi	chī
literally, I	buy orange	eat

Inflecting, synthetic, or fusional languages

Grammatical relationships are expressed by changing the internal structure of the words – typically by the use of inflectional endings (p. 90) which express several grammatical meanings at once. Latin, Greek, and Arabic are clear cases. For example, the *-o* ending of Latin *amo* 'I love' simultaneously expresses that the form is in the first person singular, present tense, active, and indicative.

Agglutinative or agglutinating languages

Words are built up out of a long sequence of units, with each unit expressing a particular grammatical meaning, in a clear one-to-one way. A sequence of five affixes might express the meaning of *amo*, for example – one for each category of person, number, tense, voice, and mood. Turkish, Finnish, Japanese, and Swahili form words in this way. 'He who gets water for me' in Swahili is *anayenipatia maji*, which can be analysed as:

a	– na –	ye	– ni	– pat	– i	– a	(maji)
he	PRESENT TENSE	who	me	gets	for		(water)

Polysynthetic or incorporating languages

Words are often very long and complex, containing a mixture of agglutinating and inflectional features, as in Eskimo, Mohawk, and Australian languages. For example, the aboriginal language Tiwi expresses 'I kept on eating' as *ngirruunthingapukani,* which is analysable as:

ngi	– rru –	unthing	– apu	– kani
I	PAST TENSE	for some time	eat	repeatedly

Some linguists, however, do not regard this as a separate typological category.

PHILOLOGIST – OR LINGUIST?

People who study the history of languages are sometimes called *comparative philologists* (or just 'philologists') and sometimes *historical linguists*. The difference lies partly in the training, partly in the subject matter. The philological tradition is one of painstaking textual analysis, often related to literary history, and using a fairly traditional descriptive framework. The newer, linguistic approach tends to study historical data more selectively, as part of the discussion of broader issues in linguistic theory, in the process using the conceptual apparatus of modern linguistics. Needless to say, proponents of the two approaches do not always see eye to eye. Philologists are often still sceptical of the new science, remembering the days when linguists considered historical topics to be of secondary importance (§65). Historical linguists, similarly, are often impatient with the philologist's reluctance to develop general explanatory theories of language change. But nowadays there are many signs that the skills of these two categories of scholar are being seen as complementary, not in opposition.

WHAT SORT OF LANGUAGE IS ENGLISH?

English is a Germanic language, according to the genetic method of classification. But from other points of view, the picture alters. Culturally, it displays many similarities with Romance, in view of the large number of loan words (p. 332) it has taken in from French and Italian, and the way these languages have even exercised some influence on grammar (e.g. *chicken supreme*) and phonology (e.g. the use of final /ʒ/ in words like *garage*). If we consider the place names of North America, then we have to allow a relationship with Amerindian languages (*Chappaquiddick, Susquehanna*). From a typological viewpoint, English is in fact more similar to an isolating language like Chinese than Latin: there are few inflectional endings, and word-order changes are the basis of the grammar.

Three-in-one
Isolating: The boy will ask the girl.
The girl will ask the boy.
Inflecting: The biggest boys have been asking.
Agglutinating: anti-dis-establish-ment-arian-ism.

THE PROBLEM OF CLASSIFICATION

These days, typological questions are of undoubted interest – especially in relation to the search for language universals (§14). But some of the early classifications have been severely criticized because of the way they were interpreted. No one would now follow the early tendency of typologists, under the influence of Darwin, to evaluate languages as if they were points on an evolutionary scale – that isolating languages are 'not as well developed' as inflecting languages, for example. Nor is there any evidence that languages of a particular type are inevitably associated with particular geographical areas, or with people of a particular ethnic or cultural group. It must also be appreciated that there is no such thing as a 'pure' instance of one of the above types. Languages seem to have these characteristics to various degrees.

Is a typological classification possible therefore? Everything depends on how we evaluate the variables which provide the basis of the classification. Morphology is only one variable. When we take into account *all* the features of language – syntax, phonology, discourse, and language use (§13) – the nature of the problem is evident. There are a vast number of possible classifications, and how should we decide which criteria are the most important? If two languages are 90% similar in phonology and 50% similar in grammar, are they more or less closely related than two languages which are 50% similar in phonology and 90% in grammar? Linguistic theory has hardly begun to answer such questions.

Both typological and genetic classifications ignore the relevance of cultural links between languages – the fact that languages influence each other by contact, such as by borrowing words from each other. Sometimes languages that have no historical relationship can converge so that they seem to be members of the same family. Conversely, related languages can be influenced by other languages so much that the differences become more striking than the similarities. The role of cultural contact is a real problem in studying many language families, where it is often totally unclear whether two languages are similar because they share a common origin, or because they have borrowed from each other (p. 332).

Some linguists have tried to move away from a classification into general types, proposing instead to rank languages in terms of individual structural criteria. One criterion could be the number of morphemes (p. 90) per word in a language (an 'index of synthesis'). In the sentence, 'The boys saw the girls', there are 5 words but 8 morphemes, producing a synthetic index of 1.6. Using this criterion, according to one study, the average for English was 1.68, compared with 1.06 for Annamese and 3.72 for Eskimo. There are several other grammatical ratios which could be investigated in this way.

THE LANGUAGE FAMILIES OF THE WORLD

NETH.	THE NETHERLANDS
BELG.	BELGIUM
LUX.	LUXEMBOURG
SWITZ.	SWITZERLAND
ANDR.	ANDORRA
1	SLOVENIA
2	CROATIA
3	BOSNIA-HERZEGOVINA
4	YUGOSLAVIA
5	MACEDONIA
6	ALBANIA
7	ARMENIA
8	AZERBAIJAN

Afro-Asiatic
Algonquian
Altaic
Andean-Equatorial
Australian Aboriginal
Austro-Asiatic

Austronesian
Caucasian
Dravidian
Eskimo-Aleut
Formosan
Gê-Pano-Carib

Hokan
Indo-European
Indo-Pacific
Iroquoian
Japanese
Khoisan

Remaining areas contain isolated, unclassified or unknown languages – or no speakers at all

GREENLAND

ALASKA

CANADA

UNITED STATES
OF AMERICA

PACIFIC   OCEAN

ATLANTIC

OCEAN

MEXICO

NORTH KOREA
SOUTH
KOREA

JAPAN

CUBA

DOMINICAN REP

TAIWAN

BELIZE
JAMAICA HAITI
GUATEMALA HONDURAS
EL SALVADOR NICARAGUA
COSTA RICA
PANAMA

PHILIPPINES

HAWAII

MARSHALL
ISLANDS

GUYANA
VENEZUELA   SURINAME
FRENCH GUIANA
COLOMBIA

CUBA

ECUADOR

PAPUA NEW GUINEA

NDONESIA

SOLOMON
ISLANDS

KIRIBATI

PERU

BRAZIL

MELANESIA

TUVALU

WESTERN
SAMOA

SOCIETY ISLANDS

BOLIVIA

VANUATU

FIJI

TONGA

FRENCH POLYNESIA

PARAGUAY

AUSTRALIA

EASTER ISLAND

CHILE

ARGENTINA

URUGUAY

TASMANIA

NEW ZEALAND

	an		Oto-Manguean		Uralic
	ro) Chibchan		Paleosiberian		Uto-Aztecan
	kogean		Penutian		
	ené		Sino-Tibetan		
	r-Congo		Siouan		
	Saharan		Tai		

'Indo-European' is the name scholars have given to the family of languages that first spread throughout Europe and many parts of southern Asia, and which are now found, as a result of colonialism, in every part of the world. The parent language, generally known as 'Proto-Indo-European', is thought to have been spoken before 3000 BC, and to have split up into different languages during the subsequent millennium. The differences were well-established between 2000 and 1000 BC, when the Greek, Anatolian, and Indo-Iranian languages are first attested.

WHO WERE THE INDO-EUROPEANS?

Archaeological evidence shows the existence of a semi-nomadic population living in the steppe region of southern Russia around 4000 BC, who began to spread into the Danube area of Europe and beyond from around 3500 BC. The people are known as the Kurgans, because of their burial practices (*kurgan* being the Russian for 'burial mound'). Kurgan culture seems to have arrived in the Adriatic region before 2000 BC, and this coincides well with the kind of time-scale needed to produce large amounts of linguistic change. The ancestors of the Kurgans are not known, though there are several similarities between Proto-Indo-European and the Uralic family of languages (p. 306), spoken further east, and these may well have had a common parent, several thousand years before.

By comparing the similar vocabulary of the extant Indo-European languages, it is possible to draw some conclusions about the geographical origins and life-style of the people. For instance, many family words (such as 'mother', 'husband', 'brother') can be reconstructed for Proto-Indo-European. These include several words for 'in-laws', which seem to have been used solely with reference to the bride. Evidence of this kind suggests that it was the wife who was given a position within the husband's family, rather than the other way round, and that the society must therefore have been patriarchal in character.

The reconstructed language has words for horses, dogs, sheep, pigs, and other animals; there is a word for some kind of vehicle, and this vehicle definitely had wheels; there are many words for parts of the body; there are several words relating to farming, and a few words relating to tools and weapons; many abstract notions are attested, relating to such fields as law, religious belief, and social status; numerals went to at least 100. Words relating to fauna and flora are of particular interest, for they can provide clues as to the place of origin of the people. There are no words for 'palm tree' or 'vine', for example, which sug-gests, independently of any archaeological evidence, that the migrations did not begin in the Mediterranean area. But other clues often seem contradictory. The word for 'beech tree' is widely attested, and, as this tree does not grow in Asia, it has been suggested that the Indo-Europeans must have originated in north-central Europe. On the other hand, there is little evidence of a common word for 'oak', which is also a European tree, and if this word was not known to the Indo-Europeans, the view is supported that their migration must have begun in Asia after all. Indo-European philology (§50) raises many fascinating questions of this kind.

THE DISCOVERY OF PROTO-INDO-EUROPEAN

It was not possible to deduce the existence of this family of languages until scholars became aware of the systematic resemblances which can be found between European languages and Sanskrit, the oldest-attested language of the Indian sub-continent. When these were first noticed, in the 16th century, many people thought that Sanskrit was the parent of the European languages; but towards the end of the 18th century the systematic studies began which showed conclusively that this was not the case.

Following an early statement of the common origin hypothesis in 1786, by Sir William Jones, the early 19th century produced several major works which laid the foundation of Indo-European philology. In 1816, the German philologist Franz Bopp published a study, whose scope is well illustrated by its title (translated): *On the conjugation system of the Sanskrit language, in comparison with those of the Greek, Latin, Persian and Germanic languages*. The relationship of Germanic to Latin, Greek, Slavic, and Baltic was demonstrated in a work written in 1814 by the Danish linguist, Rasmus Rask, but not published until 1818: *Investigation on the Origin of the Old Norse or Icelandic Language*. Further philological treatises followed, mainly written by Germans, such as Jakob Grimm and August Schleicher. In 1833, Bopp began the publication of the first major Indo-European gram-mar: *Comparative Grammar of Sanskrit, Zend, Greek, Latin, Lithuanian, Old Slavic, Gothic, and German*. It took 19 years to complete, and by its third edition incorporated Celtic and Albanian. In due course, this work and its contemporaries became out of date, as a result of the vast amount of philological study undertaken in the second half of the 19th century. A further publishing landmark was Karl Brugmann's *Outline of Comparative Indo-European Grammar* (1897–1916). A new *Indo-European Grammar*, the outcome of a project directed by the Polish linguist, Jerzy Kuryłowicz, commenced publication in 1968.

William Jones (1746–94)
British orientalist and jurist, whose presidential address to the Bengal Asiatic Society in 1786 contained the following observation, generally quoted as the first clear statement asserting the existence of Indo-European:

The Sanskrit language, whatever be its antiquity, is of a wonderful structure; more perfect than the Greek, more copious than the Latin, and more exquisitely refined than either, yet bearing to both of them a stronger affinity, both in the roots of verbs, and in the forms of grammar, than could possibly have been produced by accident; so strong, indeed, that no philologer could examine them all three, without believing them to have sprung from some common source, which, perhaps, no longer exists.

Jacob Grimm (1785–1863)
Well known to children
everywhere for the collection
of fairy tales and songs which
he compiled with his brother.
To linguists and philologists,
he is also remembered for his
major works in Germanic
philology, especially his
explanation of how the consonants of different Indo-
European languages relate
to each other. There is, for
example, a regular relationship between words begin-
ning with *p* in Latin and *f* in
Germanic languages (as in
pater and *father*), or
between initial *t* in Greek
and initial *th* in English (as in
treis and *three*). The rules
governing these sound shifts
became known as 'Grimm's
law' (p. 330).

WHAT DID PROTO-INDO-EUROPEAN SOUND LIKE?

There are no written records relating to this period. The Kurgans must have been illiterate – unlike the people of Egypt and Mesopotamia of the time. So the entire character of Proto-Indo-European has been the result of painstaking reconstruction on the part of philologists, using the methods outlined on p. 294.

There is general agreement about the number of contrasts in the consonant system (p. 167), though the status of some of the less well-attested sounds (such as /b/) is disputed. This system seems largely to have been composed of plosives (p. 159), organized into three series: voiceless, voiced, and (less definitely) voiced aspirate. Four main places of articulation were used: labial, dental, palatal or velar, and labio-velar. There was a single fricative, which was voiced or voiceless according to context. In addition, there were probably one or more laryngeal consonants (see below). There were two nasals, two continuants, and two semi-consonants (p. 154), all of which could occur at the centres of syllables as well as at syllable edges. This system may be summarized as follows:

	Labial	Dental	Palatal/Velar	Labio-velar
Plosives				
Voiceless	p	t	k	k^w
Voiced	b	d	g	g^w
Voiced aspirate	bh	dh	gh	g^wh
Fricatives		s(z)		
Nasals	m	n		
Continuants		l	r	
Semi-consonants	w		j	

There is more disagreement over the vowel system – vowels, as always (p. 169), being more difficult to analyse. Four main contrasts are generally recognized: mid-front, mid-back, open, and central, the first three occurring both in long and short forms (though how far these were independent contrasts, as opposed to laryngeally controlled variants, is unclear). In addition, some scholars recognize two further contrasts in close position, /i/ and /u/, but the overlap with the use of these sounds as semi-consonants makes this analysis less certain also. The possible vowel system can thus be summarized as follows:

(i)		(u)
e/e:	ə	o/o:
	a/a:	

THE LARYNGEAL THEORY

Towards the end of the 19th century, the Swiss linguist Ferdinand de Saussure (p. 411) put forward the view that, in order to explain various anomalies in early Indo-European forms, an extra set of sounds would have to be postulated as occurring in Proto-Indo-European. Saussure did not suggest any phonetic details for these sounds, but later they came to be called *laryngeals*, a term taken from the study of Semitic languages (p. 318), where consonants in the region of the larynx were known to occur. Laryngeal consonants did not occur in any Indo-European language known at the time, but the previous existence of some kind of sound, it was argued, was indicated by the way they had caused the changes to take place in adjacent vowels (altering their length and quality) that had long been noticed in the extant languages.

The laryngeal theory was immediately controversial, and received little support for many years. But attitudes changed after 1927, when it was found that Hittite (discovered several years after the theory was postulated) had a sound, represented by *h*, that occurred in some of the places where Saussure had predicted the laryngeals should be. However, the phonetic character of these laryngeals is still quite unclear, and philologists disagree on how many laryngeal sounds there were, whether their phonetic properties can (or should) be defined, and whether better analyses can be found. It is generally recognized that there must have been three (some say four) types, pronounced somewhere in the back part of the mouth, probably as fricatives or glottal stops (p. 159). They are usually symbolized by H or schwa (ə), and numbered with subscripts (H_1, H_2, etc. or $ə_1$, $ə_2$, etc.) Alternative analyses which postulate an earlier vowel, rather than a laryngeal, have also been proposed.

Laryngeal theory can be illustrated in this way. Most Proto-Indo-European basic forms (or 'roots') had a structure of Consonant–Vowel–Consonant (CVC, which is often written as CeC, when discussing this language), e.g. **bher-* 'bring', **med-*, 'measure'. But several forms had only one consonant, e.g. **es-* 'be', **dō-* 'give'. It is argued that these roots can be reconstructed as having the regular CVC structure, by postulating a laryngeal as the 'missing' consonant, e.g. **Hes-*, **doH-*. In roots such as **doH-*, with a preceding vowel, when the laryngeal finally disappeared, it caused the vowel to lengthen, as is attested in Latin *dōnum* 'gift', and elsewhere. Using these techniques, it is possible to show that almost all the roots of the proto-language (there are still a few exceptions, such as numerals) had a CVC structure.

SOME GRAMMATICAL FEATURES

People often think that the oldest languages must have been simpler than their modern counterparts (§49). The noun inflections of Proto-Indo-European clearly show this not to be so. It is possible to reconstruct three genders (masculine, feminine, and neuter) and up to eight cases (nominative, vocative, accusative, genitive, dative, ablative, locative, instrumental). Adjectives agreed in case, number, and gender with the noun. The verb system was also rich in inflections, used for aspect, mood, tense, voice, person, and number (p. 93). Different grammatical forms of a word were often related by the feature of *ablaut*, or *vowel gradation*: the root vowel would change systematically to express such differences as singular and plural, or past and present tense, as is still the case in English *foot/feet* or *take/took*.

55 INDO-EUROPEAN VARIETIES

Our father, who art in
Heaven...

Celtic
Ein Tad, yr hwn wyt yn y
nefoedd (Welsh)
Ár n-atheir, atá ar neamh
(Irish Gaelic)
Ar n-athair a tha air nèamh
(Scottish Gaelic)
Ayr ain, t' ayns niau (Manx)
Agan tas ny, us yn nef (Cornish)

Germanic
Unser Vater, der Du bist im
Himmel (German)
Undzer voter, vos bist im himl
(Yiddish)
Fæder ūre, þū þe eart on
heofonum (Old English)
Onze vader, die in de heme-
len zijt (Dutch)
Fader vår, du som er i himme-
len (Norwegian)
Fader vår, som är i himmelen
(Swedish)
Vor Fader, du som er i himlene
(Danish)

Italic
Pater noster, qui es in caelis
(Latin)
Notre père, qui es aux cieux
(French)
Padre nuestro, que estás en
los cielos (Spanish)
Pai nosso, que estás nos céus
(Portuguese)
Pare nostre, que estau en lo
cel (Catalan)

Albanian
Ati ynë që je në qiell

Greek
Páter 'ēmōn, 'o en toīs
ouranoīs (New Testament)
Patéra mas, poù eīsai stoùs
ouranoús (Modern)

Baltic
Teve mūsų, kurs esi danguje
(Lithuanian)
Mūsu tēvs debesīs (Latvian)
Tāwa noūson, kas tu essei en
dangon (Old Prussian)

Slavic
Otīče našī iže jesi na
nebesīchū (Old Church
Slavonic)
Ótče naš, súščij na nebesách
(Russian)
Ojča naš, katory jěść u nebe
(Belorussian)
Otče naš, ščo na nebi
(Ukrainian)

Ojcze nasz, któryś jest w
niebiesiech (Polish)
Otče náš kterýž jsi v nebesích
(Czech)
Otče náš, ktorý si v nebesiach
(Slovak)

Oče naš, što si na neboto
(Macedonian)
Oče naš, koji si na nebesima
(Serbo-Croat)
Otče naš, kojto si na nebe-
sata (Bulgarian)
Oče naš, ki si na nebesih
(Slovene)

Armenian
Mer hayr or erknk'umn (East)
Ov hayr mer or erkink'n es
(West)

Iranian
Max fyd, kæcy dæ ærvty
midæg (Ossetic)
Yā bāwk-ī ēma, ka la āsmān-
ā-y (Kurdish)
Ei pedar-e-mā, ke dar āsmān
hasti (Persian)
Phiṭh manī, ki bihishtā asti
(Baluchi)
Aj jmuǧplāra, če pa āsmān
kx̌e ye (Pashto)

Indo-Aryan
Bho asmākham svargastha
pitaḥ (Sanskrit)
Saggaṭha no pitā (Pali)
He hamāre svargbāsī pitā
(Hindi)

He sāḍe pitā, jihṛā surg vic hai
(Panjabi)
E asān-jā piu, jo āsmāna men
āhe (Sindhi)
Ai sāni māli, yus asmānas
paṭh chu (Kashmiri)
He hāmrā svargavāsī pitā
(Nepali)

O ākāśamānnā amārā bāpa
(Gujarati)
He āmacya svargātila pityā
(Marathi)
Svargayehi väḍasiṭina
apagēpiyāṇeni (Sinhalese)

He āmār svargat thakā pitri
(Assamese)
He āmāder svargastha pitā
(Bengali)
He āmbhamānañka svar-
gasha pitā (Oriya)

Dáde amaré, kaj isién k'o
devlé (Romani)

GEOGRAPHICAL DISTRIBUTION OF THE INDO-EUROPEAN FAMILY OF LANGUAGES

AZ.   AZERBAIJAN
BELG.   BELGUIM
LUX.   LUXEMBOURG
SWITZ.   SWITZERLAND
SLO.   SLOVENIA
CRO.   CROATIA
B-H.   BOSNIA-HERZEGOVINA
YUGO.   YUGOSLAVIA
MAC.   MACEDONIA
ALB.   ALBANIA

THE INDO-EUROPEAN FAMILY TREE, REFLECTING GEOGRAPHICAL DISTRIBUTION

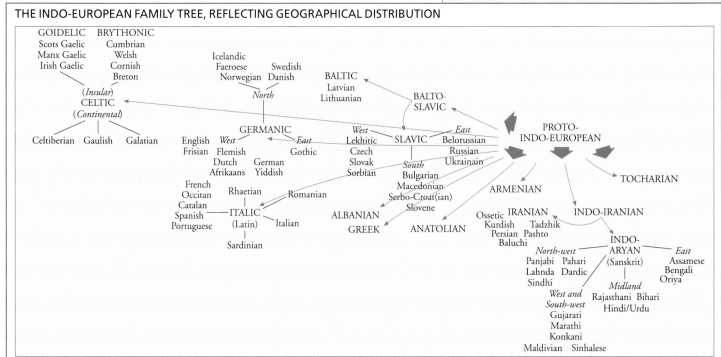

THE INDO-EUROPEAN FAMILY

ALBANIAN

This language forms a single branch of the Indo-European family, spoken by nearly 6 million people in Albania, and nearby parts of the Balkans, Greece, Turkey, and in Italy. Albanian has two main dialects, known as Gheg (in the north) and Tosk (in the south), but these contain many further dialect divisions, not all of which are mutually intelligible. The history of the language is obscure, and it is not possible to demonstrate a clear relationship with any other Indo-European group. This is partly because of the many loan words which have shaped the modern language, and partly because so few written remains of earlier times exist, dating only from the 15th century, largely on religious themes. An official alphabet was not introduced until 1909, using roman characters. Since the Second World War, the official language has been based on the Tosk dialect.

ANATOLIAN

A group of languages, now extinct, spoken from around 2000 BC in parts of present-day Turkey and Syria. The main Anatolian language is Hittite, shown to be Indo-European only as recently as 1915. Its written remains, consisting of tablets inscribed with cuneiform writing (p. 200), date from the 17th century BC. The earliest forms of Hittite ('Old Hittite') are the oldest Indo-European texts so far discovered. Most of the texts have religious themes, but they also contain a great deal of historical and social information. Other languages of the group are Palaic, Lydian, Lycian, and Luwian (represented in cuneiform and hieroglyphic systems). Also grouped under this heading are certain languages which do not belong to the Indo-European family (Hurrian, Urartian) or where the relationship is not certain (Phrygian).

ARMENIAN

This branch of Indo-European consists of a single language, spoken in many dialects by between 5 and 6 million people in the Armenian republic and Turkey, and (through emigration) in parts of the Middle East, Europe, and the United States. The spoken language may have been established soon after 1000 BC, but there was no written form until after the introduction of Christianity. Classical Armenian, or *Grabar*, is the language of the older literature, and the liturgical language of the Armenian church today. The oldest writings date from the 5th century, and the 38-letter alphabet, invented by St Mesrop, is still widely used. Modern literary Armenian exists in two standard varieties: East Armenian is the official language of Armenia; West Armenian is the dominant variety elsewhere. Because of the large numbers of loan words (see p. 332) which have come into the language, its basic Indo-European character is often obscured.

BALTO-SLAVIC

Baltic languages and Slavonic languages are often placed together as a single branch of Indo-European, because of their similarities, though there is some dispute over whether these constitute evidence of common origin rather than of more recent mutual influence. Taken together, these languages are spoken by about 300 million people, more than half of whom speak Russian.

The main *Baltic* languages are Latvian (also known as Lettish) and Lithuanian, with written texts dating from the 14th century. There are around 4 million speakers in the Baltic area, with a further million abroad, mainly in the United States. Both languages have standard forms, and many dialects. Several other languages of this group are now extinct, though there are a few written remains of Old Prussian.

The *Slavonic* (or *Slavic*) languages are more numerous, and are usually divided into three groups: *South Slavonic*, found in Bulgaria, the countries of former Yugoslavia, and parts of Greece, includes Bulgarian, Macedonian, Serbian, Croatian, and Slovene; *West Slavonic*, found in the Czech and Slovak republics, Poland, and eastern areas of Germany, includes Czech, Slovak, Sorbian, and Polish; *East Slavonic*, found in the countries which replaced the USSR, includes Russian, Belorussian, and Ukrainian. The name *Lekhitic* is sometimes given to a group of West Slavonic languages originally spoken along the Baltic between the Vistula and the Oder, including Polish, Kashubian, Polabian (died out in the 18th century), and Slovincian. Each of the main Slavonic languages has an official status as a standard (pp. 38, 366); but there are numerous dialect differences within these groupings. Old Church Slavonic is evidenced in texts dating from the 9th century, and its later form (Church Slavonic) is still used as a liturgical language in the Eastern Orthodox Church. The distinctive Cyrillic alphabet (p. 204), attributed to Saints Cyril and Methodius in the late 9th century, is still used for writing Bulgarian, Serbian, Macedonian, and all the East Slavonic languages. In modified forms, it is also used for about 100 non-Slavonic minority languages of Russia.

GERMANIC

The various branches of the Germanic family of languages derive from the migrations of the Germanic tribes who lived in northern Europe during the 1st millennium BC. Some Germanic words are recorded by Latin authors, and Scandinavian inscriptions in the runic alphabet (p. 205) are recorded from the 3rd century AD. The earliest main texts is the Gothic Bible of Bishop Ulfilas (or Wulfila), translated around AD 350, using an alphabet of his own devising (the Gothic alphabet: p. 188). Anglo-Saxon and Old High German are recorded from the 8th century, and the oldest forms of Scandinavian languages from the 12th century.

A bilingual tablet in Hittite and Luwian, dating from around 1400 BC, on which is written a ritual against the plague. The tablet was found in Hattusas, modern Bogazköy, Turkey. Inscriptions from this area provided some of the earliest evidence for the classification of Hittite as an Indo-European language.

A page from the Codex Argenteus, a 5th- or 6th-century copy of the Bible from Ulfilas; its name derives from the lettering, which is in gold and silver on a purple parchment. It is kept at Uppsala, in Sweden, not far from the Goths' homeland.

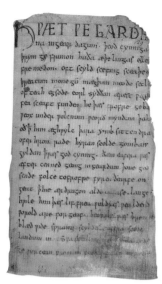

A page from the oldest epic poem in English, *Beowulf* The work was probably composed in the 8th century, but the only surviving manuscript dates from around AD 1000. It tells the story of a Scandinavian hero, Beowulf, who fights and kills a monster, Grendel, in Denmark. He is later made king of the Geats, in southern Sweden, where, as an old man, he kills a dragon, in a fight that leads to his own death.

This inscription, carved in an almost impossible position at the top of a steep cliff in Behistun (modern Bisitun), Iran, recounts the feats of King Darius the Great of Persia (522–486 BC). It is in three languages, Old Persian, Akkadian, and Elamite, and proved to be of particular value in deciphering the cuneiform writing system.

Germanic languages are used as a first language by over 550 million people, largely because of the world-wide role of English (§59). They are usually classified into three groups. *East Germanic* languages are all extinct, and only Gothic is preserved in manuscript to any extent – most recently, in a few words recorded in the Crimea in the 16th century. *North Germanic* includes the Scandinavian languages of Swedish and Danish (*East Scandinavian*), Norwegian, Icelandic, and Faeroese (*West Scandinavian*), and the older states of these languages, most notably the literary variety of Old Icelandic known as Old Norse – the language of the Icelandic sagas. *West Germanic* comprises English and Frisian (often grouped as Anglo-Frisian), and German, Yiddish, Netherlandic or Dutch (including local, Flemish dialects in Belgium), and Afrikaans (often grouped as Netherlandic–German). Dialect similarities often blur the distinctions suggested by these labels (§§8, 47).

GREEK

The branch of Indo-European consists of a single language, represented in many dialects, and attested from around the 14th century BC. The earliest evidence of the language is found in the inscriptions discovered at Knossos and other centres in Crete, written mainly on clay tablets in a syllabic script known as Linear B, and discovered to be Greek only as recently as 1952 (p. 203). This period of the language is referred to as Mycenaean Greek, to be distinguished from the later, classical Greek, dating from the 8th century BC, when texts came to be written in the Greek alphabet (p. 204) – notably the epic poems, *Iliad* and *Odyssey*. The great period of classical drama, history, philosophy, and poetry ended in the 4th century BC. A later variety of Greek, known as *koine* (or 'common') Greek, was spoken throughout the eastern Mediterranean from around the 4th century BC for nearly a thousand years. In its written form, it was the language of the New Testament (p. 388). The modern varieties of Greek, now spoken by over 11 million people in Greece, Cyprus, Turkey, the United States, and other localities, derive from this *koine* (p. 43).

INDO-IRANIAN

This branch of Indo-European comprises two large groups, known as Indo-Aryan (or Indic) and Iranian. There are over 200 Indo-Aryan languages, spoken by over 825 million people in the northern and central parts of the Indian subcontinent. They may be divided into several groups, on a broadly geographical basis: the *Midland* group mainly includes Hindu/Urdu (p. 286), the Bihari languages, and the Rajasthani languages; the *Eastern* group includes Assamese, Bengali, and Oriya; the *West* and *South-west* groups include Gujarati, Konkani, Maldivian, Marathi, and Sinhalese; and the *North-west* group includes Panjabi, Sindhi, Lahnda, the Dardic languages, and the Pahari languages. The Romani languages of the gypsies is also a member of Indo-Iranian. The early forms of Indo-Aryan, dating from around 1000 BC, are collectively referred to as Sanskrit – the language in which the Vedas, the oldest sacred texts, are written (p. 388). Later forms, the Prakrits, lasted 1,000 years, and were the medium of Buddhist and Jain literature.

During the same period, the Iranian languages were being spoken in an area centred on modern Afghanistan and Iran – especially Old Persian and Avestan (the sacred language of the Zoroastrians), both of which have texts dating from the 6th century BC. The group has over 70 languages spoken by over 75 million people, but many of these languages, and innumerable dialects, have not received a definite classification. Major languages include the closely related Persian (or Farsi) and Tadzhik, as well as Pashto, Ossetic, Kurdish, and Baluchi.

ITALIC

The main language of this family is Latin, the language of Rome and of its surrounding provinces, preserved in inscriptions from the 6th century BC, and most systematically in literature from the 3rd century BC. Other languages of the period include Faliscan, Oscan, Umbrian, and Venetic, spoken in and to the north-east of modern Italy. From the spoken, or 'vulgar' form of Latin, used throughout the Roman empire, developed the *Romance* languages – French, Spanish, Portuguese, Italian, Romanian, Sardinian, Occitan (in southern France), Rhaetian (various dialects in northern Italy and Switzerland), Galician (in north-west Spain), and Catalan (predominantly in north-east Spain). A Romance language known as Dalmatian, spoken along the Croatian coast, became extinct when its last known speaker died in 1898. But the main Romance languages have spread, as a result of colonialism, throughout the world, so that today around 650 million people speak a Romance language, or one of the creoles based on French, Spanish, or Portuguese (pp. 336–41).

TOCHARIAN

This language, now extinct, was spoken in the northern part of Chinese Turkistan during the 1st millennium AD. The first evidence of Tocharian was discovered only in the 1890s, in the form of various commercial and Buddhist religious documents, dating from around the 7th century, and on the basis of these discoveries two dialects were established – an eastern variety, from the Turfan region, which was labelled Tocharian A, and a western variety, from the Kucha region, which was labelled Tocharian B. The functions of these dialects, and the identity of their speakers, have been sources of controversy in comparative philology, as has the very name of the language (based on that of the Tochari people, who lived further east, and who were probably speakers of an Iranian language). But the status of Tocharian as an independent Indo-European language is not in doubt.

For Celtic, see pp. 304–5

THE HISTORY OF ONE INDO-EUROPEAN FAMILY: CELTIC

EARLY CELTIC

The Celts were the first Indo-European people to spread across Europe. Known to the Greeks as *Keltoi*, they emerged in south-central Europe around the 5th century BC, speaking a language which has been reconstructed under the name of Common (or Proto-) Celtic. In a series of waves they spread throughout most of Europe, reaching as far as the Black Sea and Asia Minor, south-west Spain, central Italy, and the whole of Britain. Their culture is known as La Tène (after the Swiss archaeological site of that name).

The main migration was by the Galli, or Gauls, into France, northern Italy, and the north of Europe. Evidence of the Gaulish language is found throughout this area in place names and inscriptions. In other places, the language goes under different names. The Celts who went into the Balkans and Asia Minor were called *Galatae* by the Greeks, and Galatian remained in use until around the 5th century AD. The Celts who went into Spain were known as *Celtiberi*, and Celtiberian is found in inscriptions (only partly decipherable), especially in the north and east. Some 2nd-century BC inscriptions in Switzerland are often referred to as Lepontic.

The range of Celtic dialects spoken on the Continent of Europe has been labelled Continental Celtic. Insular Celtic refers to the dialects which came to be spoken in the British Isles and Brittany, and almost all our information about the Celtic languages comes from this area. There seem to have been two waves of invasion: the first, into Ireland in the 4th century BC, led to a type of Celtic known as Goidelic (or Gaelic) which later reached Scotland and the Isle of Man; the second, into southern England and Wales, and later over to Brittany, produced a type of Celtic known as Brythonic (or, simply British). Linguistically, the first language group is known as Q-Celtic, because it retained the /kw-/ sound of Proto-Indo-European, writing it as *q*, later *c*; the second group is referred to as P-Celtic, because /kw-/ developed into /p-/. The contrast can be seen in such pairs of words as modern Irish Gaelic *ceathair*, Welsh *pedwar* 'four'.

THE FORTUNES OF INSULAR CELTIC

The Anglo-Saxon invasions in the 5th century AD pushed the British Celts westward and northward, so that the various dialects quickly became distinct. In the area now known as Cornwall and Devon, the language developed into Cornish; in Wales, into Welsh; and in Cumbria and parts of Scotland into Cumbric. There was a movement into Brittany from southern England, around the 5th century AD, which led to the development of Breton. In its early period, Breton was very similar to Cornish, and it is said that the two languages were mutually intelligible until the 15th century.

The movement of Goidelic peoples continued from Ireland into the Isle of Man, and by the 10th century they were also found throughout Scotland. The geographical boundaries led quickly to distinct dialects of the original languages, known as (Common) Gaelic. From about the 10th century, there is evidence of the distinction between Irish and Scottish Gaelic (until recently often called Erse), and doubtless Manx Gaelic began to diverge at this time too. It is not clear how long these dialects stayed mutually intelligible, but the development of different cultural and literary traditions in the middle ages persuades most writers to take them as different languages from this time.

In recent times, Celtic languages have spread outside Britain on two occasions. In 1865, 150 Welsh settled in Patagonia (in Argentina) and by the early 1900s their numbers had increased so that there were nearly 3,000 speakers of Patagonian Welsh. Nowadays, the language has largely disappeared, under the influence of Spanish. In the 18th century, many Gaels emigrated to Cape Breton Island, Nova Scotia; there were an estimated 30,000 speakers of Cape Breton Gaelic in the 1930s, but only a few are left today.

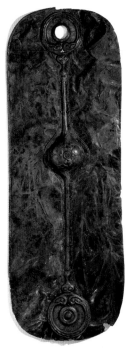

This bronze shield is a product of the La Tène culture of the 3rd century BC. Its height is 1.13m.

CELTIC MOVEMENTS IN EUROPE, AND THEIR MAIN LINGUISTIC CONSEQUENCES

In Europe, the most noticeable modern characteristic of this language family is its dramatic decline, under the influence of its powerful linguistic neighbours, English and French. But equally dramatic is the 20th-century revival of interest in Celtic languages, as symbols of nationalistic unity, and as keys to earlier periods of cultural and literary brilliance. Today, over 1.2 million people speak a Celtic language.

PERIODS OF DEVELOPMENT

Early (5th–9th c)
A few names and inscriptions in Irish Gaelic, Welsh, Breton, and Cornish. The language of the early Irish period is preserved in a writing system known as Ogam (p. 205).

Old (9th–12th c)
Old Welsh, Cornish, and Breton can be distinguished, on the basis of glosses and vocabulary lists. Because of the work of Christian missionaries, there is far more available for Old Irish, and it is difficult to draw a line between Irish literature of the Old and Middle periods,

Middle (12th–15th c)
An extensive literature in Welsh and Irish, several plays in Cornish, and verse fragments and plays in Breton. There is no Scots Gaelic literature, as the earliest Scots Gaels wrote in Irish.

Modern (16th–20th c)
Cornish   Little further development, the language dying out at the beginning of the 19th century. A recent revival of interest is based on the Middle Cornish period.

Manx   A largely religious literature (the Book of Common Prayer was translated in the early 17th century), some ballads, and carols. The Isle of Man was wholly Manx-speaking until the 18th century, and the laws of the island are still promulgated in Manx. There were still some 5,000 speakers at the beginning of the 20th century, but the last mother-tongue speakers died in the late 1940s.

Breton   A major period of growth, from the mid-17th century, led to a new orthography, several grammars, and a large literature of plays, legends, and ballads. A strong nationalistic movement began in the 1890s, and Breton was recognized as a school subject in the 1950s. There are no official figures, but it has been suggested that there were around a million speakers in the 1940s and that this figure is now more than halved.

Irish Gaelic   Ireland was wholly Gaelic-speaking until the 17th century, but the dominance of English, and the effects of the 19th-century famine and emigration, led to a sharp decline. According to census fig-

ceʊo
mìle
fàilte

Traditional Gaelic script
A semi-uncial form of medieval writing (p. 188). The sign expresses the traditional greeting: 'a hundred thousand welcomes'.

ures, some 5,000 people claim to be monolingual in Irish, and over a million to be speakers of Irish and English (without specifying level of proficiency). The constitution makes Irish the first official language. Gaelic has been taught in schools since 1922, and a standard grammar has been developed, along with a movement for reform of the complex spelling system. There is now a marked resurgence of interest in the language and its literature.

Scottish Gaelic   There was a major period of poetic literature in the 18th century, but a standard written language did not develop until the Bible translation of 1801. It is still spoken in the west, especially in the Isles and parts of the Highlands, and it now attracts a strong nationalistic interest; but the decline in numbers has been steady in the present century (from over 250,000 in 1891 to fewer than 80,000 in the 1990s).

Welsh   Wales was monoglot until the 16th century, when the Act of Union with England (1536) led to a rapid decline in numbers of Welsh speakers. Revivals in the 18th and 19th centuries led to Welsh being taught in schools, and the present century has seen this revival continue on an unprecedented scale, with the language now given official status. It is too soon to say whether this interest has come too late to stem the steady decline in the number of speakers – from just under a million in 1900 to around half a million in the 1981 census – but fresh factors are now operative, not least in the form of a Welsh-speaking television channel, and the total remained stable in 1991.

Sign of the times Road signs in Wales are these days printed in both Welsh and English – a policy which does not satisfy some nationalists.

URALIC

The Uralic family consists of over 30 languages which have descended from an ancestor, called Proto-Uralic, spoken in the region of the north Ural Mountains in Russia over 7,000 years ago. Uralic languages are attested in written form from the 13th century. The most noticeable trend in the 20th century has been the decline of many of the languages, under the influence of dominant neighbours, especially Russian. Also, several of these languages have more than one name – an earlier derogatory name, used by outsiders, has often been replaced by a form more acceptable to the people.

Two main branches of the family are represented today: *Finno-Ugric* and *Samoyedic*. The Finno-Ugric group of languages is found in one part of central Europe, and in those northern territories where Europe and Asia meet. In the north, the 'Finnic' branch of the family is located in the region between northern Norway and the White Sea, the whole of Finland, and parts of adjacent Soviet territory. The main language of the group is Finnish, with over 5.5 million speakers in Finland, Sweden, Russia, and (through emigration) the USA. Estonian has over 1 million, mainly in Estonia. There are only around 25,000 speakers of the Sami group of languages (formerly known as Lappish), but they are spread throughout the whole of the north.

Curiously isolated from the rest of the family is the main language of the 'Ugric' branch – Hungarian (or Magyar). This is spoken by nearly 11 million people as a national language in Hungary, and by a further 3 million in surrounding areas, and through emigration in many parts of the world. Two other Ugric languages are found to the east of the Urals, around the River Ob, and are known as Ob-Ugric. They are Khanty (or Ostyak), with over 13,000 speakers, and Mansi (or Vogul), with around 3,000.

The remaining Finno-Ugric languages are spoken within Russia. One group is found in the Kola Peninsula in the north, and southwards towards the Gulf of Riga. Some of these languages (Ingrian, Livonian, and Votic) have very few speakers, and may not survive for long. Karelian, the most widespread, has over 100,000 speakers. Vepsian has only some 2,000. A second group is found further into the Soviet Union, scattered around the central Volga. The most widely used languages are Mordvin (or Erza), with over 800,000 speakers; Mari (or Cheremis), with over 600,000; Udmurt (or Votyak), with over 500,000; and Komi (or Zyryan), with around 250,000.

The other branch of the Uralic family is spoken by the Samoyeds – fewer than 30,000 people scattered throughout a vast area in Siberia and Arctic Russia, whose economy is largely based on reindeer hunting and breeding. The most widely spoken language is Nenets (or Yurak), with around 27,000 speakers. Selkup (or Ostyak Samoyed) has around 1,700. The other languages still spoken are Nganasan (Tavgi, or Aram), with around 1,000 speakers, and Enets (or Yenisey), which had less than 100 speakers in 1989. The last of a group of languages once spoken in the Sayan Mountain area seems to have recently died out.

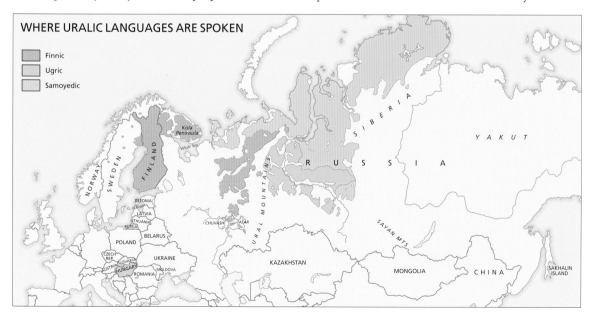

WHERE URALIC LANGUAGES ARE SPOKEN

Finnic
Ugric
Samoyedic

WHERE CAUCASIAN LANGUAGES ARE SPOKEN

North-west
North-central
North-east
Southern

The inscription on this fragment of an engraved cross is written in Khutsuri, an ecclesiastical script of 38 letters used in Old Georgian. The palaeographic evidence (p. 189) suggests that the date is 11th century. The cross is preserved in the grounds of the new Church of the Transfiguration in Akhalaki, some 30 miles north-west of Tiflis.

CAUCASIAN

The area between the Black Sea and the Caspian Sea, surrounding the Caucasus Mountains, is relatively small and compact – not quite twice the size of the United Kingdom – but it contains one of the highest concentrations of languages in the world. Leaving aside the Indo-European, Semitic, and Altaic languages which have infiltrated the area in the past 3,000 years, there are nearly 40 languages which are recognized as belonging to a single Caucasian family (see also, p. 333). They are classified into four regionally based types: the *North-West Caucasian*, or *Abkhazo-Adyghian* group; the *North-Central Caucasian* group; the *North-East Caucasian* group; and the *Southern Caucasian* (or *Kartvelian*) group.

The family as a whole is represented by nearly 8 million speakers, almost all to be found in the Caucasus region. Over 4 million of these live in Georgia, speaking a Kartvelian language – mainly one of the dialects of Georgian, which is the state language, used throughout the area. Other languages of the south are Zan (including Mingrelian and Laz) and Svan. Only Georgian has a written form, which dates from the 5th century AD.

In the north-west, the main languages are Kabardian (or Circassian), with over 350,000 speakers, Adyghe (over 250,000) and Abkhaz (around 90,000). There are around 45,000 speakers of Abaza. In the 1980s, only one person was known to speak Ubykh – a language whose large number of consonants (80) illustrates the special place of this family in phonological studies (pp. 168–9).

Most of the languages of the north-east belong to the Dagestanian group. The main languages are Avar (over 450,000), Lezghian or Kuri (around 350,000), Dargwa or Khjurkili (over 250,000), Lak (over 90,000), and Tabassaran (over 70,000). Several other languages are spoken by 10,000 or fewer. Also in the north-east, the Nakh group of languages comprises Chechen (over 900,000), Ingush (over 190,000) and Bats (around 3,000), found in a single village in Georgia. The linguistic profile of this area is complicated by the difficulty of drawing a clear line between language and dialect (p. 286), and this has led to several different estimates of the number of languages in the Caucasian family.

Several of the northern languages have a written form, based on the Cyrillic alphabet (p. 204), and are used as state languages. There is much evidence of the influence of previous periods of contact with adjacent families (such as Arabic and Persian). Today, the most noticeable influence on the family, especially in the area of vocabulary, is Russian.

PALAEOSIBERIAN

The once-extensive Palaeosiberian culture is now represented by only a few thousand people scattered throughout north-eastern Siberia. The languages they speak have been classified into four groups, and since the 19th century these have been studied together under the 'Palaeosiberian' heading; but the groups are not genetically related to each other, and therefore they do *not* constitute a family in the linguistic sense. Nor are the links with other families any clearer, though several attempts have been made to trace connections with other families found in the region.

The *Luorawetlan* group is the best-represented, in the far north-east, consisting of Chukchi (about 11,000), Koryak (or Nymylan, 5,000), and Kamchadal (or Itelmen), Aliutor and Kerek, with only a few hundred speakers between them. To the west, the *Yukaghir* group is now represented by just a single language (Yukaghir, or Odul), spoken by around 150 people. Further west again, along the Yenisey River, about 900 people speak the only surviving member of the *Yeniseian* group – Ket (or Yenisey-Ostyak). And to the south, about 400 speak Gilyak (or Nivkhi), which has no known relatives. Since the earlier part of this century, each of these languages has been given a written form, based on the Cyrillic alphabet (p. 204).

KOREAN AND JAPANESE

Korean There are evident similarities between the Korean language and the Altaic family, but it is not clear whether these can best be explained by a hypothesis of common descent or one of influence through contact. Thus in some classifications the language is placed within the Altaic family, and in others it is left isolated. A relationship with Japanese has also been suggested.

Korean is spoken by over 60 million people in North and South Korea (where it is an official language), China, Japan, and Russia. The language has been much influenced by Chinese: more than half its vocabulary is of Chinese origin, and the earliest records of the language, dating from before the 12th century, are written in Chinese characters.

Japanese The genetic relationship between Japanese and other languages has not been clearly established. It is most often considered to be a member of the Altaic family, but resemblances with other language families of the region have also been noted. There are several varieties, those in the south (and especially in the Ryukyu Islands) displaying major differences from the standard language based on the Tokyo dialect.

Japanese is spoken by around 121 million people on the islands of Japan, and by a further 5 million in other parts of the world, especially in Brazil and the United States. Apart from a few isolated forms, the first written records of Japanese date from the early 8th century, using Chinese characters, or *kanji* (p. 315).

SAKHALIN
ISLAND

Y A K U T

A

*Chukchi
Peninsula*

*Kamchatka
Peninsula*

NORTH
KOREA

JAPAN

SOUTH
KOREA

▨	Korean
▢	Japanese
▨	Altaic
▨	Luorawetlan
▨	Yukaghir
▨	Yeniseian
▨	Gilyak

WHERE JAPANESE, KOREAN,
PALAEOSIBERIAN, AND ALTAIC ARE SPOKEN

Japan is one of the world's
leading publishers of books,
magazines and, especially,
newspapers. The major
papers appear in morning
and evening editions. Daily
circulation in 1994 was over
71 million, the second highest (after Russia) in the
world. It has been estimated
that on average each
Japanese household reads
two papers a day. Bookshops
and newspaper stalls attract
many browsers, who often
stay for considerable periods
of time.

ALTAIC

The Altaic family of languages cover a vast area, from
the Balkan peninsula to the north-east of Asia – an area
which includes the Altai mountain region of central
Asia, from which the family receives its name. It comprises about 60 languages, classified into three groups:
Turkic, Mongolian, and *Tungusic*. The common ancestry of these groups is maintained by many scholars; but
this hypothesis is contested by those who feel that the
linguistic similarities could be explained in other ways
– such as the mutual influences displayed when languages are in contact with each other (p. 33).

Over half of the Altaic languages belong to the Turkic group, whose best-known member is Turkish, spoken by around 50 million people in Turkey and
surrounding territories. Other main languages of the
south-west are Azerbaijani (14 million) and Turkmen
(around 3 million), both spoken mainly in Russia,
Iran, and Afghanistan. In the south-east, there is

Uzbek (over 15 million), spoken mainly in Uzbekistan, and Uighur (around 7 million), mainly found in
China (Xinjiang) and nearby Russia. In the north-
west, the main languages are Tatar (over 5 million),
Kazakh (over 7 million), Kirghiz (over 2 million), and
Bashkir (around 1 million), found largely in Kazakhstan, Kirghizstan, and Russia, with some speakers in
China and nearby territories. In the north-east, languages are spoken by smaller numbers. There are over
300,000 speakers of the geographically isolated language, Yakut, and 190,000 speakers of Tuva (or
Tuvinian), but other languages number only tens of
thousands (including one named Altai – formerly,
Oirot – which should not be confused with Altaic, the
name of the family as a whole). Chuvash, spoken by
over 1.5 million in the middle Volga region, is usually
listed along with other Turkic languages, but many
consider it to be a separate branch within the Altaic
family.

The main Mongolian language is known as Mongol
(or Khalka), spoken in two main varieties by over 4
million people in the Mongolian People's Republic
and nearby China. Related languages in the same
region are Buryat (around 300,000), Dongziang or
Santa (around 280,000), Dagur, and Tu or Monguor
(both fewer than 100,000). Further west, the group is
represented by Oirat, Kalmyk (both over 270,000),
and Mogol (around 50,000). There are many uncertainties of classification in this area, due principally to
problems of applying the distinction between language
and dialect (p. 286).

The Tungusic (or Manchu-Tungus) group is spoken
in a large number of dialects over a wide area. Evenki
(formerly Tungus) may have as many as 20,000 speakers; but the other languages have fewer than 10,000 –
Lamut (or Even), Nanai, and Manchu. The Manchu
people of north-east China number over 4 million, but
less than 1,000 now speak the once important Manchu
language – a lingua franca between China and the outside world for over 200 years.

There is little evidence of the early development of
the Altaic family. Written remains of Turkic are found
in a runic script dating from the 8th century AD; but
Mongolian script dates only from the 13th century;
and the earliest Manchu records are even more recent –
mid-17th century. Several writing systems seem to
have been used throughout the early period.

In the 20th century, the most notable developments
have come from the major political changes which
have affected the area since the First World War. There
has been a considerable effort to modernize the languages, especially by promoting fresh vocabulary. Several new literary languages have emerged, based on
local languages (as in the case of Uzbek), and some of
the older written languages have been reformed (seen
most dramatically in the case of Turkish, which in
1929 replaced Arabic by Latin script).

DRAVIDIAN

The Dravidian family is a group of over 25 languages, most of which are found close together in the southern and eastern areas of India – though one language (Brahui) is curiously isolated, being spoken 1,000 miles away from the main family, in the north of Pakistan. Through emigration, speakers of the main Dravidian languages are today found throughout South-east Asia, in eastern and southern regions of Africa, and in cities in many parts of the world.

The name given to the family comes from a Sanskrit word, *drāvida*, which is used in an early text, with apparent reference to one of the languages, Tamil. Tamil has the oldest written records of this family, dating from the 3rd century BC, and scholars believe it to be close to the ancestor language, known as Proto-Dravidian. But, despite the historical records and associated reconstruction, there is little agreement about the origins of the language, or its speakers. One tradition speaks of migration from lands to the south, now submerged; other views suggest a movement from Asia, via the north-west, perhaps around 4000 BC. A relationship has been proposed with both the Uralic and the Altaic language families, but the hypothesis is controversial. There is, however, strong support for the view that Dravidian languages were once spoken in the north of India, and were gradually displaced by the arrival of the Indo-European invaders (§51).

The four main languages of the family are Telugu, Tamil (both with over 50 million speakers), Kannada (also known as Kanarese), and Malayalam (both with over 26 million speakers). Each language can be identified with a state in southern India – Andhra Pradesh, Tamil Nadu, Mysore, and Kerala, respectively. Of the four, Tamil has the greatest geographical spread, including several million speakers in Sri Lanka, Malaysia, Indonesia, Vietnam, parts of East and South Africa, and many islands in the Indian and South Pacific Oceans. The other languages are not so widely used outside India, though both Telugu and Malayalam have some currency. Written records date from the 5th century AD for Kannada, the 7th century for Telugu, and the 9th century for Malayalam.

Other languages with over a million speakers include Gondi (nearly 2 million), Brahui (1.7 million), Kurukhi (or Oraoni), and Tulu. Kui has around half a million. Malto, isolated from the other languages in the northeast, is spoken by around 90,000 people. The remaining languages of the family have many fewer speakers, sometimes numbering only a few thousand – but it is not always obvious how to draw the line between language and dialect (p. 286). New languages continue to be reported – Naiki, Pengo, and Manda have been identified only since the early 1960s – and there are some 45 other languages which are often listed along with the Dravidian family, though lacking clear genetic affiliation.

WHERE DRAVIDIAN LANGUAGES ARE SPOKEN

The fight for independence

Soon after Indian independence, Dravidian language militants began to fight for a political structure in which their separate languages would be represented. In 1948, the report of the Linguistic Provinces Commission opposed any change, largely on the grounds that 'sub-nations' would be a major obstacle to the spread of national consciousness in the new India. Further pressure led to a second committee of enquiry, which reached the same conclusion, but accepted that, if the demand continued to be insistent, the matter should be reopened. Many people saw in this the first real chance of success, and from 1949 the campaign intensified, especially among the Telugu speakers in Madras. The climax came in December 1952, with the death of Potti Sriramulu, who had chosen a hunger strike, the time-honoured method of Gandhi, to make his point. Prime Minister Nehru backed down, and the first of the language-based states, Andhra Pradesh (for Telugu) was inaugurated in October 1953. Three years later, the whole of south India was reorganized on the basis of linguistic regions.

The introduction of news bulletins in Urdu caused a Hindu/Moslem language conflict in Karnataka (formely Mysore) in October 1994. Rioting in Bangalore caused considerable damage and 25 deaths.

AUSTRO-ASIATIC

Most of the languages of this family are spoken in South-east Asia, in the countries between China and Indonesia; but a few are found further west, in the Nicobar Islands and in parts of India. The membership of the family, and its main subdivisions, are not entirely clear. Few of the languages have a written history, and classification has been based on other methods (p. 295). Links between this and other families (in particular, the Austronesian family) have been proposed, but are uncertain.

Three main branches of the family are generally recognized. The largest branch is the *Mon-Khmer* group of languages, spoken throughout the south-eastern mainland, mainly in North and South Vietnam, Laos, Cambodia, and parts of Myanmar (Burma) and Malaysia. It has three main languages. Mon (or Talaing) is spoken in Myanmar and Thailand by nearly half a million; Khmer (or Cambodian), the official language of Cambodia, is spoken by over 7 million people. Inscriptions in both languages date from the 6th–7th centuries AD.

The main language of the group, Vietnamese, poses something of a problem. This language is spoken by around 55 million people in North and South Vietnam, Laos, and Cambodia, and in recent years small groups of emigrants have taken it to many parts of the world. Its status in the Mon-Khmer group has, however, been disputed: some scholars see it as a marginal member, while

some relate it to the Tai family (p. 312). Its early history is obscured by the use of Chinese throughout South-east Asia – the result of over 1,000 years of rule by China, which lasted until the 10th century AD. The modern Latin-based alphabet, known as Quoc-ngu ('national language'), was introduced only in the 17th century.

The other two language groups are clearly separated geographically from the Mon-Khmer. The *Munda* group of languages is spoken in several parts of India, mainly in the north-east, but also in a few central areas. Mundari (around 800 thousand) and Santali (around 4 million) are the most widely used languages. Lastly, a tiny group of languages is spoken by around 20,000 people on the Nicobar Islands in the Bay of Bengal. These have been considered a separate, *Nicobarese* branch of the Austro-Asiatic family, but there is some evidence to suggest that they are a branch of Mon-Khmer.

There are over 170 Austro-Asiatic languages, spoken by over 75 million people. Exactly how many depends on the distinction drawn between language and dialect (p. 286), and on the criteria used to demonstrate structural similarities (p. 295). A few other languages spoken in Malaysia and India have at times been proposed as members of the family. Nothing is known about the early movements of the peoples involved. It is possible that the various groups of languages which make up the Mon-Khmer branch began to split up in the second millennium BC, but where the Austro-Asiatic peoples came from, and when they migrated, remains pure guesswork.

A group of Vietnamese children learning English.

WHERE AUSTRO-ASIATIC LANGUAGES ARE SPOKEN

TAI

The Tai family of languages are all found in South-east Asia, in an area centred on Thailand, and extending north-eastwards into Laos, North Vietnam, and China, and north-westwards into Myanmar (Burma) and India. The spelling 'Tai' is used to avoid confusion with the main language of the family, Thai (or Siamese), which is the official language of Thailand.

The 60 or so Tai languages are usually divided into three groups: *south-western*, *central*, and *northern*. Most speakers belong to the south-western group, which includes Thai, spoken by over 20 million people in a wide range of dialects, and Lao (or Laotian), widely spoken in Thailand, and the official language of Laos (3 million). Isan (Thailand) has some 15 million; the two varieties of Zhuang (China) have over 12 million; Lanna or Yuan (Thailand) has over 6 million; and Shan, Tho, Buyi, Dong, and Nung each have over a million. But in this part of the world, such estimates are very approximate.

The relationship between the Tai family and other languages is unclear. Written remains of the south-western group date from around the 13th century. Links have been proposed both with the Sino-Tibetan and the Austronesian families. In particular, several languages of south-west China, belonging to the Kadai and Kam-Sui groups, display interesting similarities to Tai.

SINO-TIBETAN

The membership and classification of the Sino-Tibetan family of languages is highly controversial. The 'Sinitic' part of the name refers to the various Chinese languages (often, misleadingly, referred to as 'dialects'); the 'Tibetan' part refers to several languages found mainly in Tibet, Myanmar (Burma), and nearby territories. But as there are notable similarities with many other languages of the region, some scholars – notably in China – adopt a much broader view of the family, so as to include the Tai and Miao-Yao groups (p. 313).

The *Sinitic* languages (see p. 314) are spoken by over 1,000 million people. The vast majority of these are in China (over 980 million) and Taiwan (19 million), but substantial numbers are to be found throughout the whole of South-east Asia, especially in Hong Kong, Indonesia, Malaysia, Thailand, and Singapore. Important Chinese-speaking communities are also found in many other parts of the world, especially in the USA.

There are some 275 languages in the *Tibeto-Burman* family, and these have been classified in several different ways. It is possible to identify 'clusters' of languages which have certain features in common, such as the 45 or so Lolo languages, spoken by around 3 million people in parts of Myanmar, Thailand, Vietnam, Laos,

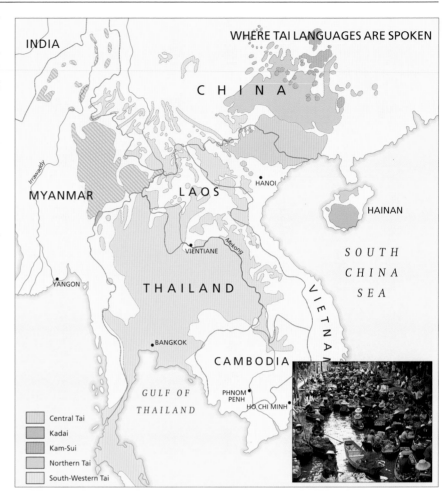

WHERE TAI LANGUAGES ARE SPOKEN

Central Tai
Kadai
Kam-Sui
Northern Tai
South-Western Tai

WHERE SINO-TIBETAN LANGUAGES ARE SPOKEN (INCLUDING MIAO-YAO)

Miao-Yao
Sinitic
Tibeto-Burman

Biggest book Two views of the Kuthodaw Pagoda in Myanmar (Burma). The whole Buddhist canon is carved on stone slabs housed in 729 stupas in the Pagoda. The achievement, sometimes called the 'world's largest book', was created by King Mindon in 1872, with the help of 2,400 monks.

Facing page (inset): Thai traders in Bangkok's Floating Market.

and China. The 50 or so Naga, Kuki, and Chin languages, spoken in Myanmar and India, comprise another group. But groupings of this kind display many differences as well as similarities, and it has not yet proved possible to find a neat way of classifying these, and the other groups thought to belong to the same family, into two or three types. It is by no means clear, for example, whether the small group of Karen languages, spoken by around 4 million people in Myanmar and Thailand, should be included or excluded from the Sino-Tibetan family.

After Chinese, the two main languages of this family are Burmese and Tibetan. Burmese is spoken by around 22 million people in Myanmar as a mother tongue, and several million more use it as a second language throughout the region. It has written records dating from the 11th century. Speaker estimates for Tibetan are very uncertain, largely because of the influence of Chinese in recent years; but a figure of 4 million seems likely, chiefly in China and Nepal. There are several major dialects, which are sometimes viewed as separate languages. Written records date from the 8th century AD, treating largely of Buddhist religious subjects. The alphabet of this period, which reflects the pronunciation of the time, is still in use today, with the result that there is considerable divergence between spelling and modern Tibetan speech.

MIAO-YAO

This is a small group of about 15 languages, also called Hmong-Mien, spoken in southern China and adjacent parts of South-east Asia - especially northern Laos, Thailand, and Vietnam. The two chief languages, which give the group its name, are Miao (also called Hmong), spoken in several varieties by 4.5 million people, and Yao (also called Mien), spoken by nearly a million. The sub-classification of the group into languages and dialects is controversial, as indeed is its status as a separate language family. Links with Tai, Mon-Khmer, and Sino-Tibetan have been suggested, and it is within the latter family that Miao-Yao languages are most often placed.

THE LANGUAGES OF CHINA

Because there has long been a single method for writing Chinese, and a common literary and cultural history, a tradition has grown up of referring to the eight main varieties of speech in China as 'dialects'. But in fact they are as different from each other (mainly in pronunciation and vocabulary) as French or Spanish is from Italian, the dialects of the south-east being linguistically the furthest apart. The mutual unintelligibility of the varieties is the main ground for referring to them as separate languages. However, it must also be recognized that every variety consists of a large number of dialects, many of which may themselves be referred to as languages. The boundaries between one so-called language and the next are not always easy to define.

The Chinese refer to themselves and their language, in any of the forms below, as *Han* – a name which derives from the Han dynasty (202 BC–AD 220). Han Chinese is thus to be distinguished from the non-Han minority languages used in China. There are over 150 of these languages (such as Tibetan, Russian, Uighur, Kazakh, Mongolian, and Korean), spoken by around 9% of the population.

THE CHINESE LINGUISTIC REVOLUTION

The 20th-century movement for language reform in China has resulted in the most ambitious programme of language planning (§61) the world has ever seen. The programme has three aims:

(i) to simplify the characters of classical written Chinese, by cutting down on their number, and reducing the number of strokes it takes to write a character;

(ii) to provide a single means of spoken communication throughout the whole of China, by popularizing the Beijing-based variety, which has been chosen as a standard;

An oracle bone This remnant of China's Bronze Age, from the Shang dynasty of the 2nd millennium BC, was found in the Anyang district of Henan. Shang kings had questions inscribed on polished ox bones or tortoise shells. A pattern of holes was drilled in them, and they were then heated until they cracked. The pattern of cracks produced by this process was interpreted as the ancestral spirits' way of answering the questions. Thousands of oracle bones have now been discovered, and the study of their inscriptions has now become a new branch of Chinese linguistic studies, known as *jiǎ gǔ shū*.

(iii) to introduce a phonetic alphabet, which would gradually replace the Chinese characters in everyday use.

There have been moves to reform the language from as early as the 2nd century BC, but there has been nothing to equal the complexity of the present-day programme, in which frequent reference is made to the names of several different varieties of the Chinese language.

Wényán ('literary speech' or 'body of classical writing'). The cultivated literary language, recorded from around 1500 BC, and the traditional unifying medium for all varieties of Chinese. Its complex system of characters is explained on p. 202. It differs greatly from everyday speech, especially in its terse grammatical style and specialized literary vocabulary. It is now less widely used, because of the success of the current reform movement for written Chinese.

'Dialect'	Where spoken
Cantonese (Yùe)	In the south, mainly Guangdong, southern Guangxi, Macau, Hong Kong. (46 million)
Gan	Shanxi and south-west Hebei. (21 million)
Hakka	Widespread, especially between Fujian and Guangxi. (26 million)
Mandarin	A wide range of dialects in the northern, central, and western regions. North Mandarin, as found in Beijing, is the basis of the modern standard language. (720 million)
Northern Min (Mǐnběi)	North-west Fujian. (10 million)
Southern Min (Mǐnnán)	The south-east, mainly in parts of Zhejiang, Fujian, Hainan Island and Taiwan. (26 million)
Wu	Parts of Anhui, Zhejiang, and Jiangsu. (77 million)
Xiāng (Hunan)	South central region, in Hunan. (36 million)

WHERE THE MAIN CHINESE 'DIALECTS' ARE SPOKEN

- Cantonese
- Gan
- Hakka
- Xiang
- Mandarin
- Min Bei
- Min Nan
- Wu

Báihuà ('colloquial language'). A simplified, vernacular style of writing, introduced by the literary reformer Hu Shih in 1917, to make the language more widely known to the public, and to permit the expression of new ideas. A style of writing which reflected everyday speech had developed as early as the Sung dynasty (AD 960–1279), but had made little impact on the dominant *wényán*. However, the 'May Fourth Movement' which originated in political demonstrations on 4 May 1919 after the Paris Peace Conference) adopted Hu Shih's ideas, and *báihuà* was recognized as the national language in 1922.

Pǔtōnghuà ('common language'). The variety later chosen as a standard for the whole of China, and widely promulgated under this name after the establishment of the People's Republic of China in 1949. (In Taiwan, it goes under the name of *guóyǔ*, or 'national speech'; in the West, it is generally referred to simply as 'Mandarin'.) It embodies the pronunciation of Beijing, the grammar of the Mandarin dialects, and the vocabulary of colloquial Chinese literature. In 1956, it became the medium of instruction in all schools, and a policy of promoting its use began (p. 367). It is now the most widely used form of spoken Chinese, and is the normal written medium for almost all kinds of publication.

Pīnyīn ('phonetic spelling'). After several previous attempts to write Chinese using the letters of the roman alphabet, this writing system was finally adopted in 1958. Its main aims are to facilitate the spread of *pǔtōnghuà*, and the learning of Chinese characters. *Hànyǔ Pīnyīn* is now in widespread use; it has the 26 roman letters, plus *ü* and four diacritics for tones. In the 1970s, for example, a new map of China was published using the alphabet, and a list of standard spellings for Chinese place names was compiled. New codes were devised for such diverse uses as telegraphy, flag signals, braille, and deaf finger-spelling (p. 227).

The future of the reform programme is not entirely clear. It may be that *pīnyīn* will ultimately supplant the general use of characters, or there may be a reaction to preserve the traditional written language. With

Chinese typewriter
This Chinese typewriter, made in Japan in the late 1970s, came complete with six cases of Chinese characters, a type tray, lay-out charts and type tweezers. The typists would first align the tray, then press a key, which would make an arm pick up the required character and strike it against the paper. The machine could type vertically and horizontally. It was a slow process, with good typists averaging at most 20 characters a minute. The word processor has now made this technology obsolete.

pǔtōnghuà, new varieties of regional pronunciation are certain to develop (for instance, Máo Zédōng spoke it with a marked Hunan accent), which may lead to problems of intelligibility. And if *pǔtōnghuà* is to succeed as a popular means of communication, it needs to anticipate the potential conflict with local regional dialects (for example, whether local words should be used). Much will depend on how flexibly the authorities interpret the notion of standard, and whether they are able to achieve a balance between the competing pressures of respecting popular usage (where there is a strong case for variety) and the need for national communication (which could lead to a form of centralized laying down of prescriptive linguistic rules).

ROMANIZING CHINESE

Several systems of romanization for Chinese have been invented. The oldest in current use is known as Wade–Giles, introduced by Sir Thomas Wade in 1859, and developed by his successor in Chinese Studies at Cambridge University, Herbert Giles. This is the system which is most familiar to western eyes. In the 1930s, a system known as *gwoyeu romatzyh* ('national romanization') was devised by Lin Yu-t'ang and Chao Yuen-ren. During the Second World War, Yale University introduced an intensive programme of Chinese training for Air Force pilots, and introduced a new system, related more clearly to American pronunciation. But *pīnyīn* has now become the dominant system. The name for China illustrates some of the differences between these systems:

中 國

Chinese characters
Wade–Giles	Chūngkuo
Gwoyeu romatzyh	Jonggwo
Yale	Jūnggwo
Pīnyīn	Zhōngguó

Some familiar spellings, with their pīnyīn equivalents:

Peking	Běijīng
Canton	Guǎngzhōu
Mao Tse-tung	Máo Zédōng

'TIGERS DO NOT BREED DOGS'

These phrases, usually of four characters, illustrate the telegraphic literary style of *wényán*. The nearest equivalent to this proverb in English is perhaps 'Like father, like son.' Mao Zédōng was particularly adept at incorporating classical features of this kind into his political speeches.

'CALAMITIES DO NOT OCCUR SINGLY'

The equivalent phrase in English is 'It never rains but it pours.'

虎	父	無	犬	子	禍	不	單	行
hǔ	fù	wú	quǎn	zǐ	huò	bù	dān	xing
(tiger)	(father)	(no)	(dog)	(son)	(calamity)	(no)	(single)	(act)

THE LANGUAGES OF AFRICA

Africa contains more languages than any other continent – some 2,000, spoken by over 480 million people. The language total is uncertain, because many areas are inaccessible, and many dialect groups have not been well investigated, but it is probably an underestimate. Very few of these languages are spoken by large numbers: less than 5% have more than a million speakers. As a consequence, Africa is a continent of lingua francas. Arabic is used throughout the north and northeast; Swahili is used throughout most of East Africa; English and French are widespread, often as official languages, in former colonial territories; and, especially in West and Central Africa, several languages have come to be used as ways of fostering communication between different tribes (such as Hausa, Bambara-Malinka, Wolof, Kongo, Lingala, and various pidgins and creoles, such as Pidgin English, Krio, and Sango).

The most widely accepted classification of African languages, made by Joseph Greenberg (1915–) in the 1960s, recognizes four main families, though there is considerable difference of opinion about the boundaries between them, and about several of the language groups which they subsume. There is little historical evidence available to aid classification. Written records of most African languages have existed only since missionary activities began on the continent, less than 150 years ago. As a consequence, the field of African languages has proved to be one of the most controversial areas within the domain of comparative linguistics.

NIGER-CONGO

This is the largest African family, with around 1,350 languages, and several thousand dialects, whose status is often difficult to determine. The family spreads across the whole of sub-Saharan Africa, west of the River Nile, and extends along the eastern half of the continent as far north as the Horn of Africa. It is divided into several groups of languages, which are estimated to have diverged well over 5,000 years ago, though the order and rate of divergence is controversial. There are also several isolated languages (p. 328). Accurate statistics are impossible in some areas, especially those affected by civil war (in the 1990s, notably Rwanda).

The largest group is the *Benue-Congo* – around 800 languages spoken by about 150 million people throughout central and southern Africa, over half of them (spoken by two-thirds of these people) belonging to the Bantu sub-group. The main Bantu languages are Yoruba (20 million), Igbo (12 million), Lingala and Luba (both 8 million), Shona and Rwanda (both 7 million), Xhosa and Zulu (sometimes considered dialects of the same language, but considered by their speakers to be different languages – both over 6 million), and Kongo and Makua (both 5 million). Swahili also has 5

million native speakers, but is additionally used by around 30 million speakers as a lingua franca in parts of East Africa. Some classifications include Yoruba and Igbo as members of the Kwa family. The largest non-Bantu languages are found in Nigeria: Efik (4 million, chiefly as a second language), and Tiv (2 million).

The *Kwa* group of over 75 languages is spoken by about 14 million in the southern part of the bulge of West Africa. Major languages are Akan (7 million), and Ewe (2 million). Ijọ is now thought to be part of a separate branch (Ijoid), spoken by about 1.5 million. English or French are official languages in the area.

The *Adamawa-Ubangi* group of around 180 languages is spoken by about 6 million people in the remote, northern part of central Africa, between Nigeria and Sudan. Its main members are Sango, a creolized language used throughout the Central African Republic and nearby areas (about 5 million, including second language speakers) and Gbaya (850,000). Several pidgins and creoles are spoken in the area.

The *Gur* group consists of over 80 languages spoken by about 11 million people in a broad area around the Upper Volta River, between Mali and Nigeria. Its main member is Mooré (or Mossi), spoken by around 4 million.

The *Atlantic* (or *West Atlantic)* group, as its name suggests, consists of over 60 languages spoken in the extreme western part of the African bulge. Fula (or Fulfulde) is the most widespread language, spoken in most West African states by around 13 million in several varieties, some mutually unintelligible. Other languages include Wolof and Fuuta Jalon, both spoken by over 2 million.

The *Mande* group of over 45 languages is also spoken by over 12 million in the western part of the bulge. Its main members are Bambara (2 million), Malinka (3 million), Dyula, and Mende (each over 1 million).

About 30 *Kordofanian* languages are spoken in the Nuba Mts area of central Sudan by less than half a million people.

NILO-SAHARAN

The major group of languages in this family is spoken in two areas around the upper parts of the Chari and Nile rivers, and is generally referred to by the name *Chari-Nile*. It contains around 180 languages, whose sub-classification has given rise to much controversy. In particular, scholars have argued for over 100 years about the best way of classifying the languages spoken along the Nile, in Sudan, Uganda, and nearby territories (the so-called *Nilotic* group). An Eastern Sudanic group includes such languages as Luo (3.2 million), Dinka (spoken in several varieties by over 2 million), Kalenjin and Teso (both 1.4 million), Acholi, Alur, Bari, Lango, Maasai, and Nuer (all with over half a million speakers). A Central Sudanic group includes Lugbara (nearly 1 million), Lendu, Mangbetu, and Ngambai (all over half a million). Nile Nubian, or Dongolawi, is spoken in Sudan and Egypt by around a

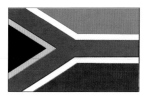

THE NEW SOUTH AFRICA

The 1993 constitution of the Republic of South Africa recognizes the following languages at national level: Afrikaans, English, Ndebele, Sesotho sa Leboa, Sesotho, Swati, Xitsonga, Setswana, Tshivenda, Xhosa, and Zulu. It proclaims that conditions are to be created for their development, and for the promotion of their equal use (p. 371). At the same time, provision is to be made for the establishment of an indepent Pan South African Language Board, which would implement these aims, and also be responsible for promoting respect for other languages used by South African communities. Specifically named in the constitution are German, Greek, Gujerati, Hindi, Portuguese, Tamil, Telugu, Urdu, and (for religious purposes) Arabic, Hebrew, and Sanskrit.

Old Nubian documents from Qasr Ibrim, Egypt

WHERE AFRICAN LANGUAGES ARE SPOKEN

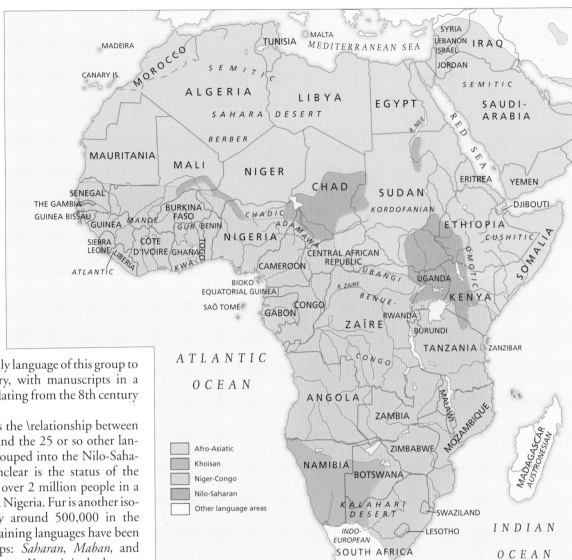

Afro-Asiatic
Khoisan
Niger-Congo
Nilo-Saharan
Other language areas

million speakers. It is the only language of this group to have a long written history, with manuscripts in a modified Coptic alphabet dating from the 8th century AD (Old Nubian).

Argument also surrounds the \relationship between the Chari-Nile languages and the 25 or so other languages which have been grouped into the Nilo-Saharan family. Particularly unclear is the status of the Songhai group, spoken by over 2 million people in a wide area between Mali and Nigeria. Fur is another isolated language, spoken by around 500,000 in the Sudan and Chad. The remaining languages have been classified into small groups: *Saharan, Maban,* and *Komuz.* The Saharan language, Kanuri, is the largest, with around 4 million speakers.

KHOISAN

This is the smallest language family in Africa, consisting of fewer than 40 languages, spoken by about 300,000 people; but they are a well-known group because of their use of click consonants (p. 126). They are spoken in the southern part of Africa, in an area around the Kalahari Desert extending from Angola to South Africa, though two click languages are spoken as far north as Tanzania (Sandawe and Hatsa). 'Khoisan' derives from the name of the largest Hottentot group (the Khoi-Khoin) and that of the Bushmen in the Nama region of Namibia (San). Only about a third of these languages have over 1,000 speakers. Nama (spoken chiefly in Namibia) may have as many as 150,000; Sandawe (spoken in Tanzania) has about 70,000. The numbers are diminishing, and several languages are known to have become extinct. About half of the languages have been given a written form by missionaries and others.

There is often no clear correlation between language groups and racial or cultural groups in Africa. The Pygmies, who live in the central forests, have no single language, but use the languages of neighbouring peoples. By contrast, the Khoisan of South Africa do form a homogeneous linguistic and racial group. The picture shows a village in Botswana.

AFRO-ASIATIC

This family, formerly known as Hamito-Semitic, is the major family to be found in North Africa, the eastern horn of Africa and south-west Asia. It contains over 300 languages, spoken by nearly 250 million people. There are five (in some classifications, six)major divisions which are thought to have derived from a parent language that existed around the 7th millennium BC.

The *Semitic* languages have the longest history and the largest number of speakers. They are found throughout south-west Asia, including the whole of the Saudi Arabian peninsula, and across the whole of North Africa, from the Atlantic to the Red Sea. The oldest languages of the group, now extinct, date from the 3rd millennium BC; they include Akkadian, Amorite, Moabite, and Phoenician, all once spoken in and around the Middle East. There was a vast literature in Akkadian, written in cuneiform script (p. 200). Hebrew dates from the 2nd millennium BC; its classical form was preserved as the written language of Judaism; its modern spoken and written form is used by over 3 million people in Israel and a further million throughout the world. Old Aramaic, the language of Jesus and the Apostles, also dates from this period. Syriac, a variety of Late Aramaic, was the literary and religious language of Christians throughout the Middle East for several centuries. Aramaic dialects are still spoken by some 200,000 people in tiny groups in the region.

The major language of the group is Arabic, spoken in eight major varieties by over 180 million people as a mother tongue, and used by several million more as a second language. It exists in both classical and colloquial forms. Classical (or literary) Arabic is the sacred language of Islam, and is used as a lingua franca of educated people throughout the Arabic-speaking world. Colloquial Arabic exists in many modern varieties, not all of which are mutually intelligible – they include Algerian, Moroccan, Egyptian, Syrian, Iraqian, and several dialects of Arabia and the Sahara. Maltese, spoken by over 300,000 people on the island of Malta, is also a development from Arabic.

In the south of the region, in Ethiopia, there are several Semitic languages, notably Tigrinya (4 million), Amharic (the official language of Ethiopia, used by around 14 million), and varieties of Gurage (around 1 million).

The remaining branches are less widespread. *Egyptian* is now extinct: its history dates from before the 3rd millennium BC, preserved in many hieroglyphic inscriptions and papyrus manuscripts (p. 201). Around the 2nd century AD, it developed into a language known as Coptic. Coptic may still have been used as late as the early 19th century, and is still used as a religious language by Monophysite Christians in Egypt.

There are over 30 *Berber* languages spoken throughout North Africa by around 10 million people, mainly in Algeria and Morocco. They include Riff, Kabyle, Shluh, and Tamashek, the widely scattered language of the Tuareg nomads. There are about 50 *Cushitic* languages, spoken by around 24 million people. The largest is Oromo (or Galla), several varieties of which are spoken in Ethiopia and Kenya by over 10 million people; and Somali, spoken in Ethiopia, Somalia, and Kenya by over 5 million. There are over 160 *Chadic* languages, whose status within the Afro-Asiatic family is less clear. These languages are spoken by over 28 million people in an area extending from northern Ghana to the Central African Republic. Hausa is undoubtedly the most important language of this group, spoken by around 25 million people as a mother tongue, and by several million more as a second language throughout the region. It is the only Chadic language to have a written form – a roman alphabet now being used in place of the Arabic script introduced in the 16th century.

Lastly, there are over 20 *Omotic* languages, spoken by nearly 3 million people in western Ethiopia and northern Kenya. About two-thirds of these are speakers of Wolaytta. Omotic is sometimes classified as a separate branch of Afro-Asiatic, and sometimes as a western branch of Cushitic.

Tifinagh Below left: The Tuareg tribesmen have preserved a unique form of writing, known as *tifinagh* ('characters'). It derives from Numidian, an ancient Libyan script used in Roman times. The system consisted only of consonants, usually written right to left.

Below: Maltese is the only form of Arabic to be written in the Latin alphabet. It is related to the western Arabic dialects, but it also shows the marked influence of the Romance languages (via Sicily). This holiday advertisement shows some of the symbols needed to cope with the Semitic sounds.

AUSTRONESIAN

The Austronesian language family covers a vast geographical area, from Madagascar to Easter Island, and from Taiwan and Hawaii to New Zealand – a territorial range which is reflected in an alternative name sometimes given to the family: Malayo-Polynesian. It is one of the largest families, in terms of both number of speakers (around 270 million) and number of languages (over 1,200).

In this part of the world, it is particularly difficult to establish language identities. Apart from the usual problems of distinguishing dialects from languages (p. 286), several different names may be used with reference to the speakers in an area, and it is never obvious whether these names refer to different languages, or are simply alternative names for the same languages. For example, over 70 names have been recorded for the various dialects of the Dayak language of north-western Borneo and south Sarawak, but it is possible that research will show several of these to be so different that they could legitimately be counted as distinct languages. The linguistic picture is also complicated by the existence of many pidgins and creoles (§55) which have grown up as the result of trade contacts in the area. Moreover, several languages have come to be extensively used as lingua francas – notably Bahasa Indonesia, Bazaar Malay, Chinese, English, and French.

The classification of the languages of the Austronesian family is controversial. One influential approach distinguishes a *Formosan* group of about 20 languages, spoken in Taiwan by some 300,000 people, from the rest, which are collectively called Malayo-Polynesian (in a slightly narrower sense than that used above). The latter group is then divided into three branches. The *Western* branch contains over 500 languages, spoken in Madagascar, Malaysia, the Indonesian Islands, the Philippines, parts of Vietnam and Cambodia, and the western end of New Guinea. Two languages of Micronesia (Chamorro and Palauan) are also included. The *Central* branch of 150 languages is spoken by about 4.5 million people in the central islands of Indonesia, such as Timor, Flores, and Maluku (the Moluccas). The *Eastern* branch of over 500 languages is spoken over most of New Guinea, and throughout the 10,000 or more islands of Melanesia, Micronesia, and Polynesia. Most of them form a family usually referred to as *Oceanic*. Despite its geographical and linguistic diversity, only a small minority of speakers (about 2.5 million) belongs to the eastern branch.

Because of the many structural differences between the languages, it is estimated that the Austronesian family has a history of development of over 4,000 years, with archaeological and linguistic evidence suggesting a probable geographical origin in the New Guinea area. But despite extensive research into Austronesian languages in recent years, the early history of this family remains obscure and controversial, and several competing linguistic sub-classifications have been proposed.

INDO-PACIFIC

There are over 650 languages spoken in New Guinea, which do not belong to the Austronesian family, and about a further 100 spoken in the islands to the immediate east and west. Two small language groups lie much further away from those spoken in the New Guinea region, and some scholars believe that there is enough evidence to justify their placement within this group: Andamanese, from the Andaman Islands in the Bay of Bengal; and Tasmanian, now extinct, from the island of Tasmania, to the south of Australia (p. 321). About 3.5 million speakers are involved.

Over half of the Indo-Pacific languages have been shown to be related, especially many of those in central New Guinea. But the linguistic picture is by no means certain: in the more inaccessible parts of New Guinea, there are still tribes who have not been contacted, and whose languages are not known; and data are sparse on many others, which may have only tens or hundreds of speakers. Many different classifications have been proposed, some of which recognize over 100 sub-families. Other names for the family, such as *Papuan*, are also in use. There is no clear genetic basis for the Indo-Pacific grouping: it is a convenience, bringing together the languages of the New Guinea region which are not Austronesian.

There is nowhere to compare with the multilingual diversity of New Guinea – so many languages crammed into a land area of only 300,000 square miles, and containing a total population of only around 6 million. A sense of this complexity can be obtained by 'translating' these figures into British terms: Britain, one third of the size, would find itself containing nearly 200 languages, separated from each other by distances of only 20 miles.

A map of the area covered by the Indo-Pacific and Austronesian families, and more detailed information about some of the languages, is provided on pp. 320–21.

The Easter Island inscriptions (illustrated here on a carved wooden gorget) are pictures with magical significance, and not a form of writing. The literature of Oceania is oral, consisting of many memorized passages for use in social events, and also lengthy myths about events and places, which would be formally recited. The language was held in special esteem: the recitation of a myth belonging to some other clan was considered theft.

Andamanese A tiny number of people speak various dialects of Andamanese, on the Andaman Islands in the Bay of Bengal. There were around 500 speakers in the 1950s, but this figure had been more than halved by the early 1980s. The language is not clearly related to any of the others in the region, but a tentative placement alongside other Indo-Pacific languages has been proposed.

Pilipino Pilipino is the name given to the national language of the Philippines, when the country became independent in 1946. It is a standardized form of Tagalog, an indigenous Austronesian language spoken in central and south-western parts of the island of Luzon, which includes the capital, Manila. There are around 11 million native speakers of Tagalog, but some 40 million now speak Pilipino, which along with English is the medium of instruction in schools. There is an extensive literature of folklore and mythology in Tagalog, and also in the other major indigenous languages of the Philippines, Cebuano (about 12 million speakers throughout the south) and Ilocano (over 5 million speakers in the north). A movement for a new national language, Filipino, began in the 1970s.

Malay Malay, an Austronesian language, is extensively spoken throughout Malaysia and Indonesia as a second language, and is the mother tongue for around 17 million people. The dialect of the south Malay Peninsula has become the standard language, and under the name of Bahasa Indonesia (*bahasa* = 'language') has been the official language of Indonesia since 1949; it is often referred to simply as Indonesian. A pidginized form of Malay, known as Bazaar Malay, is widely used as a lingua franca throughout the Indonesian archipelago. Its use long predates the time of contact with European languages, in the 17th century. Another form, known as Baba Malay, is used by Chinese communities in Malaysia. Written records of Malay date from the 7th century AD, consisting of various inscriptions found on Sumatra. The modern standard language alphabet is now different from that of the older, literary Malay, because of the introduction of spelling reforms.

Malagasy Indonesian traders migrated to the uninhabited island of Madagascar during the 1st millennium AD, the linguistic differences with other Austronesian languages suggesting that the separation took place towards the beginning of the period. Despite its closeness to Africa, the language shows only the occasional influence of African languages and Arabic. There are now around 10 million speakers. The standard language is based on the dialect of the largest ethnic group, the Merina ('elevated people' – those who lived on the plateau), who were dominant in the 19th century. Various dialects of Malagasy are also used on several of the islands in the region around Madagascar.

Tok Pisin This English-based pidgin language is widely used within Papua New Guinea, especially in the north of the country. It is spoken by over 2 million people – by 50,000 or so as a mother tongue (§55).

Sundanese There are around 25 million speakers of Sundanese, an Austronesian language found throughout the western part of Java. Written records date from the 14th century.

Javanese Javanese, an Austronesian language, has the largest number of mother-tongue speakers in the area – over 75 million. It is spoken throughout the island of Java, and to some extent in Malaysia. It has a strong written literary tradition, dating from the 8th century, which continues to flourish, although somewhat eclipsed these days by the influence of the standard language, Bahasa Indonesia.

Shadow-puppet plays are found in many parts of South-east Asia, originating in Java 1,000 years ago. Carved or leather puppets, fixed on sticks, represent mythological figures. Light from a flame lamp passes through holes in the puppets onto a cloth screen, to produce a spectacle of flickering shadows which symbolize a mystical world. The narrator follows a basic scenario, using stock phrases to introduce heroes and events; but there is much improvization, adding music, satire, and local details, and introducing many voice qualities. The plays often last all night long.

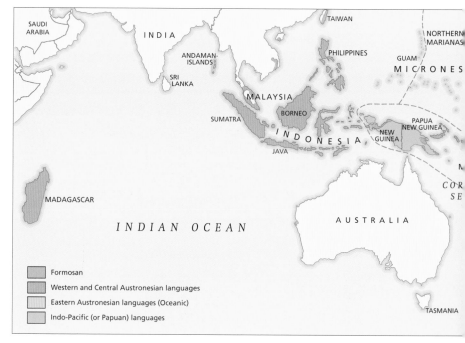

Motu Motu, an Austronesian language, is spoken by around 15,000 in the central part of Papua New Guinea. A pidginized variety (once known as Police Motu, because it became the language of the multilingual police force) developed as a trade language between speakers of Austronesian and Indo-Pacific languages; it is now called Hiri Motu. It is spoken by around 150,000 throughout the country, where it has official status.

The Mahabarata Legend in Barong dance, Bali.

Chamorro One of the two languages in Micronesia (the other being Palauan) which belong to the western branch of Austronesian. It is spoken by around 75,000 people, mainly on the island of Guam, where the official language is English.

Tasmanian There were five main dialects spoken in Tasmania, and these have now been classified as two languages. There is little information available about them: the last known speakers died towards the end of the 19th century. Tasmanian is not clearly related to any other language, but some scholars feel that a placement within the Indo-Pacific family is justified.

Maori The Maori population has been steadily increasing during the 20th century, and there has been a revival in the language and culture. Maori, an eastern Austronesian language, is now an optional second language in schools. There are around 100,000 speakers, all of whom are bilingual in English. Maori is heard often in the form of songs, speeches, and ritual challenges, at special gatherings, and when official visitors to New Zealand are being formally received (p. 49).

Gilbertese This has the largest number of speakers of all the languages of the eastern Austronesian branch in Micronesia. It is spoken on the 16 coral atolls which constitute the Gilbert Islands, named after the Englishman Thomas Gilbert, who arrived there in 1788.

Tahitian Tahitian is widely used as a lingua franca throughout French Polynesia, and is the native language of the Society Islands. There are some 125,000 speakers in all. It is an official regional language in Tahiti.

Tongan This is the national language of the Kingdom of Tonga, also known as the Friendly Islands. It is spoken by over 100,000 people.

Samoan There are over 325,000 speakers of Samoan in Western Samoa (where it is an official language, along with English) and American Samoa. Several sizeable communities now live in New Zealand and the USA.

Fijian About 350,000 people speak Fijian as a first or second language of the Fiji Islands. This is less than half the population of the islands, the remainder being Indian, Chinese, and other immigrants. The standard form, based on the Bauan dialect, is used in broadcasting and in the press, along with Hindi and English.

Easter Island One of the first islands to be settled in Polynesia. Only a small number of its tiny population of 1,800 speak the language, which is also known as Rapanui or Pascuanese.

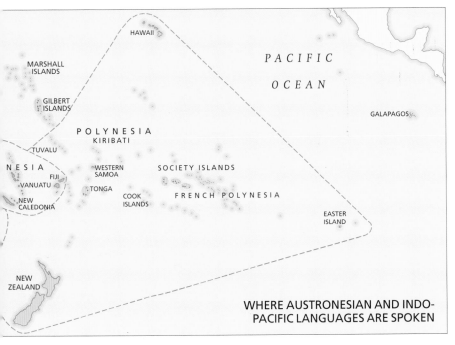

WHERE AUSTRONESIAN AND INDO-PACIFIC LANGUAGES ARE SPOKEN

THE LANGUAGES OF THE AMERICAS

NORTH AMERICAN INDIAN LANGUAGES

There were originally around 300 languages spoken by the indigenous American Indian (or Amerindian) tribes, but this number had more than halved by the 1970s. Many of the languages are now spoken by only a few old people. Only about 50 of the languages have more than 1,000 speakers; only a handful have more than 10,000. In the mid-1980s, the total number of speakers was estimated at around 500,000.

The Amerindian languages have been classified into over 50 families, showing many kinds and degrees of interrelationship. However, this allows a great deal of scope for further classification, and Amerindian linguistics has thus proved to be a controversial field, generating many proposals about the links between and within families (see further, p. 324). It is not known whether the languages have a common origin. The peoples are thought to have migrated from Asia across the Bering Strait, perhaps in a series of waves, but the only North American languages which show any clear links with Asian languages are those belonging to the Eskimo-Aleut family.

Eskimo-Aleut is the name given to a small group of languages spoken in the far north, in Alaska, Canada, and Greenland, and stretching along the Aleutian Islands into Siberia. Eskimo is the main language, spoken in many varieties by around 60,000. Its two main branches – Yupik in Alaska and Siberia, Inupiaq (Inuit, or Inuktitut) elsewhere – are sometimes classified as separate languages. Greenlandic Eskimo has official status in Greenland, alongside Danish. A standard written form dates from the mid-19th century. There are also a few hundred speakers remaining of Aleut.

Further south, the *Na-Dené* group consists of about 50 languages, spoken in two main areas: Alaska and north-west Canada, and south-west-central USA. Most of the languages belong to the Athabaskan family, whose best-known member is Navajo, with around 130,000 speakers – one of the few Amerindian languages which has actually increased in size in recent years. The various dialects of Apache are closely related to Navajo.

The *Algonquian* (or *Algonkian*) family is geographically the most widespread, with over 30 languages covering a broad area across central and eastern Canada, and down through central and southern USA. Many well-known tribes are represented – the Arapaho, Blackfoot, Cheyenne, Cree, Fox, Micmac, Mohican, Ojibwa, Potawatomi, and Shawnee – though only Cree and Ojibwa have substantial numbers of speakers (each around 35,000).

The remaining languages defy easy classification. Some scholars have proposed genetic links between the 20 or so Siouan languages (which include Crow and Dakota, or Sioux), the 15 or so Iroquoian languages (which include Mohawk and Cherokee), and other small groups, but the relationships are controversial. There are many isolates (p. 328).

FROM NORTH TO SOUTH

The main linguistic bridge between North and South America is formed by the (Macro-) *Penutian* group, which in its broadest interpretation consists of over 60 languages (many of these grouped into smaller families), spoken from south-west Canada down through the western states of the USA, throughout Mexico and Central America, and into south-west South America. In a narrower interpretation, only the 25 or so North

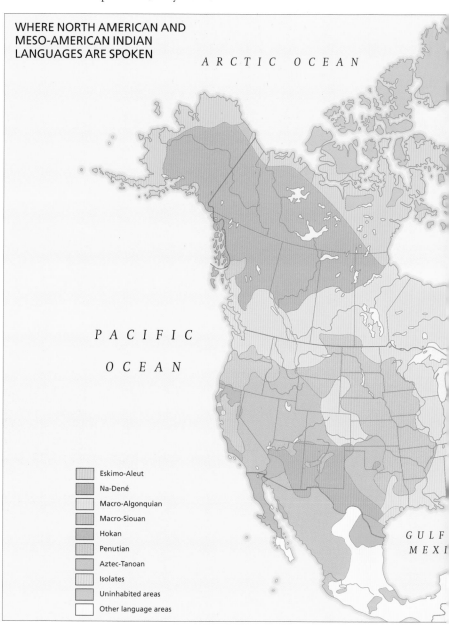

WHERE NORTH AMERICAN AND MESO-AMERICAN INDIAN LANGUAGES ARE SPOKEN

ARCTIC OCEAN

PACIFIC OCEAN

GULF
MEXI

Eskimo-Aleut
Na-Dené
Macro-Algonquian
Macro-Siouan
Hokan
Penutian
Aztec-Tanoan
Isolates
Uninhabited areas
Other language areas

Zapotec Indians from Juchitán, southern Mexico.

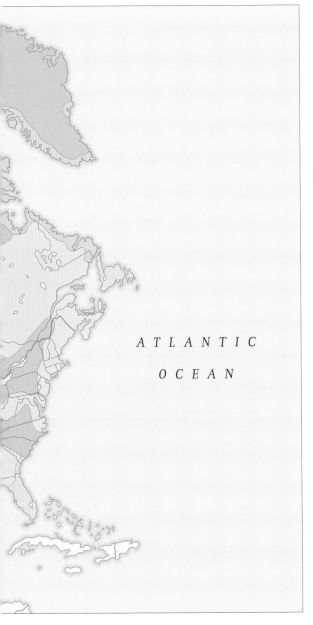

ATLANTIC

OCEAN

American languages, none of which has many speakers, are subsumed under this heading.

The broader interpretation includes the languages of the Mayan family – about 30 languages, some in several mutually unintelligible varieties, spoken by over 3 million people in Mexico and Central America. They include Yucatec and the many varieties of Quiché, both with over half a million speakers, and Mam, Kekchi, and Cakchiquel, each with over a quarter of a million. In South America, the main candidate for membership of Penutian is Mapudungan (or Araucano), spoken mainly in Chile by around 400,000. Chipayan and Uru (spoken by a few hundred people in Bolivia) have also been proposed as belonging to Penutian.

The *Hokan* group of around 20 languages is spoken by small numbers in parts of western and south-west USA, and eastern Mexico. Similarly, most of the 50 or so languages which belong to the *Uto-Aztecan* group have few speakers today. The group, which is distantly related to the Tanoan languages (a proposed *Aztec-Tanoan* family), includes the languages of such well-known tribes as the Comanche, Paiute, Shoshone – and also the Hopi (p. 15). Three Uto-Aztecan languages are still widely spoken (in several varieties) in Mexico: Nahuatl (around a million speakers), Tarahumar (over 50,000), and Pima-Papago (around 15,000).

ISOLATES

There are over 30 languages whose relationship to the main language groups in North America has not so far been determined. About 20 of these are the Salish languages, spoken along the Canadian/USA Pacific coastline, and some way inland. They include Bella Coola, Okanogan, Shuswap, and Squamish. These days, the numbers of speakers are very small – mostly fewer than 1,000 and in several cases fewer than 10. Pentlach, spoken on Vancouver Island, was already extinct in the 1970s. The five languages of the Wakashan family, spoken on the British Columbia coast (notably, Nootka and Kwakiutl) constitute another isolated group.

An early Aztec manuscript with place-name glyphs, listing taxes collected from various towns in Mexico.

The Pueblo Indians of Arizona and New Mexico are linguistically very diverse – about 25,000 people speak languages belonging to no fewer than four families. In the east, they mainly speak Tewa (a member of the Tanoan family) and Keresan (a language isolate); in the west, they speak Keresan Zuñi (a Penutian language) and Hopi (a Uto-Aztecan language). The picture shows part of a pow-wow ceremony in New Mexico.

CENTRAL AMERICA

The indigenous languages of Central America are generally known as Meso-American (or Middle American) Indian languages. In an area extending from Mexico to Nicaragua, there are some 250 languages which some approaches have classified into about 10 families, spoken by around 7 million people. Several of the languages belong to one of the North American families (Penutian, Hokan, Aztec-Tanoan); some belong to South American families (grouped under Macro-Chibchan). The only group which is restricted to this region is *Oto-Manguean*. Almost all Oto-Manguean languages are spoken within a small area centred on the state of Oaxaca, Mexico. The main languages (all spoken in several varieties, some mutually unintelligible), are Zapotec (about half a million speakers), Otomí, and Mixtec (each about a quarter of a million).

SOUTH AMERICAN INDIAN LANGUAGES

Indigenous Indian languages are used throughout the whole of the continent of South America, including the southern part of Central America and the Antilles group of islands. They are spoken by over 11 million people. In former times, as many as 2,000 languages may have been spoken in the area, but only 400–500 of these have been attested. Despite the considerable efforts of ethnographers and missionaries, especially in the present century, few languages have been completely described. Many tribes consist of small numbers living in extremely remote jungle areas. Even in the more accessible cases, there is considerable uncertainty over the identity of the languages, and what kind of language/dialect boundaries operate (p. 286). Many are under threat of extinction as western civilization (in the linguistic shape of Spanish and Portuguese) opens up the area. It seems likely that over 1,000 tribes have become extinct before their languages could be recorded.

In spite of this decline, South America remains one of the most linguistically diversified areas of the world. Some accounts suggest that there are more than 100 language families on the continent. However, because of the difficulties in obtaining accurate information, classifications of the languages have tended to be very general, and there are many differences among the subgroupings which have been proposed. At the most general level, three major groups have been suggested.

The *Chibchan* group is one of the most widespread, being found in Central America, Columbia, Venezuela, and south into Bolivia and Brazil. There are over 20 languages in the group, but only a few, such as Guaymi (45,000), Kuna or Cuna (35,000), and Waika (16,000), have reasonably large numbers of speakers, and several are on the verge of extinction. Several other languages have been proposed as part of a *Macro-Chibchan* group.

The *Gê-Pano-Carib* group of nearly 200 languages is spoken east of the Andes along most of the length of the continent and along the Brazilian Amazon basin. It has a very small number of speakers (perhaps a million) for such a vast area. The *Macro-Gê* family has over 30 languages, spoken mainly in eastern Brazil. *Panoan* is a family of about 30 languages spoken from Peru and Bolivia eastward to Brazil, and southward to Paraguay and Argentina. The *Carib* family, also within this group, is one of the largest in South America, containing over 30 languages spoken by tiny numbers throughout the whole northern region. Several other small langue families have been associated with this group.

The *Andean-Equatorial* group consists of about 250 languages, and contains many sub-divisions. Within the Equatorial division, for example, there is the Arawakan group of nearly 70 languages, which once extended into North America, and is still widespread, being spoken by about 350,000 from Central America to southern Brazil, and from the Andes to the east coast. Goajiro (over 120,000), Black Carib (100,000), and Campa (50,000) make up 80% of the speakers of this group. Within the Andean division, the Quechumaran group is preeminent in the Andes highlands between Colombia and Argentina. Aymará was once a major language throughout the central Andes, but is now restricted to around 600,000 speakers in Bolivia and Peru. Quechua, the official language of the Incas, is now spoken in over 30 varieties by nearly 7 million from Colombia to Chile. It is widely used as a lingua franca, and its literary history dates from the 17th century. In the south, in Paraguay, the Indian language of Guaraní (a member of the Tupian family of about 60 languages) is spoken by over 3 million people (mainly non-Indians), and is the majority language of that country – the only Indian language to achieve such a status. By contrast, over a dozen Tupian languages have become extinct in the first half of this century.

The South American Indians migrated from the north, but hardly any of the languages of the area are plausibly related to the language families of North and Middle America. The only links which have attracted support are under the heading of Penutian, where some scholars have placed Araucanian, Chipayan, and Uru. Others, however, see these languages as part of the Andean-Equatorial group.

A LARGER PERSPECTIVE

In a fresh classification presented in 1985 by the American linguist Joseph Greenberg (1915–), *all* the languages of the New World are brought together, and grouped into three main families: Na Dené, Eskimo-Aleut, and Amerind. Eskimo-Aleut is seen as part of a 'Euroasiatic' family, whose other members include Indo-European, Altaic, Japanese, Korean, and several other languages. Amerind is an extremely large family, comprising 11 sub-families and, at a lower level of classification, nearly 200 groups of languages (a reanalysis of the languages included in the families listed on pp. 322–5). It covers the whole of North, Central, and South America, and incorporates several languages previously thought to be isolates (§53).

An extract from a youth education section of an Asunción newspaper (3 October 1995), showing part of a programme for fostering awareness of Guaraní, with translations in Spanish.

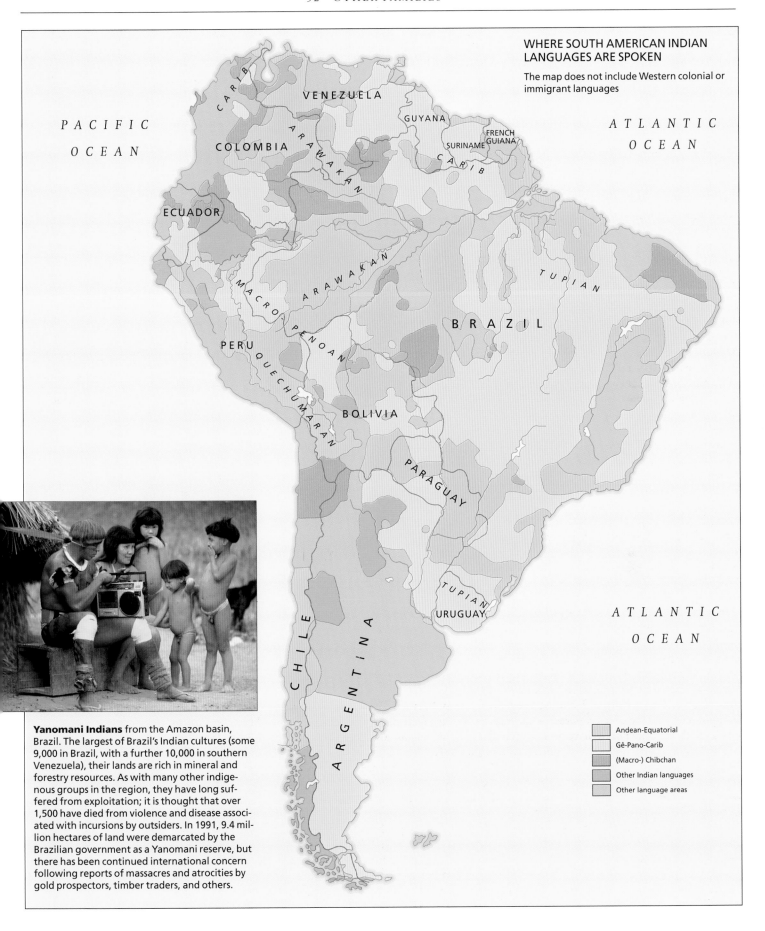

WHERE SOUTH AMERICAN INDIAN
LANGUAGES ARE SPOKEN

The map does not include Western colonial or
immigrant languages

PACIFIC
OCEAN

ATLANTIC
OCEAN

VENEZUELA

GUYANA

SURINAME

FRENCH
GUIANA

CARIB

COLOMBIA

ARAWAKAN

ECUADOR

MACRO–PENOAN

ARAWAKAN

TUPIAN

B R A Z I L

PERU

QUECHUMARAN

BOLIVIA

PARAGUAY

TUPIAN
URUGUAY

ATLANTIC
OCEAN

CHILE

ARGENTINA

Andean-Equatorial

Gê-Pano-Carib

(Macro-) Chibchan

Other Indian languages

Other language areas

Yanomani Indians from the Amazon basin,
Brazil. The largest of Brazil's Indian cultures (some
9,000 in Brazil, with a further 10,000 in southern
Venezuela), their lands are rich in mineral and
forestry resources. As with many other indigenous groups in the region, they have long suffered from exploitation; it is thought that over
1,500 have died from violence and disease associated with incursions by outsiders. In 1991, 9.4 million hectares of land were demarcated by the
Brazilian government as a Yanomani reserve, but
there has been continued international concern
following reports of massacres and atrocities by
gold prospectors, timber traders, and others.

AUSTRALIAN ABORIGINAL LANGUAGES

No clear relationship has yet been found between Aboriginal languages and the rest of the world's languages. With no written records, historical discussion is largely speculation. In the 18th century, there may have been over 500 Aboriginal languages in Australia, spoken by over 300,000 people. Today, about 250 languages are documented from many parts of Australia (but excluding Tasmania: see p. 321). Only five languages have more than 1,000 speakers; most have very few; and at least half are nearly extinct.

A frequently cited estimate is that fewer than 30,000 people speak the languages today, with different levels of ability. But, for many reasons, population estimates are difficult. Aboriginal people often live in isolated areas; most are bilingual to differing degrees; and it is not always easy to obtain accurate information from the speakers themselves, many of whom overestimate or underestimate their ability to use the language, for social or political reasons. By the same token, scepticism is sometimes expressed about the results of national surveys, which might be used as evidence for or against the provision of educational or social facilities for Aboriginal groups.

Aboriginal languages have been grouped into 28 families, all of which are thought to be related. All but one of these are found in the northern parts of Western Australia, Northern Territory, and Queensland, in an area comprising no more than one-eighth of the continent. Arnhem Land in particular shows a high concentration of these languages. By contrast, a single family, Pama-Nyungan, covers the remainder of the continent; about 175 languages once belonged to this family, but fewer than 50 are spoken today, most of these surviving in the north-west.

The languages with the largest number of speakers are Tiwi, Walmatjari, Warlpiri, Aranda, Mabuyag, and Western Desert – all but the first belonging to the Pama-Nyungan family. Several of the languages have come to be used as lingua francas. Gunwinygu is used in this way in much of north-east Arnhem Land, and Pitjantjatjara in much of northern Western Australia, partly as a church language. Warlpiri is one of the most vigorous of these languages, spoken in many central and southern parts of Northern Territory. Several pidgins and creoles (§55), related to English, have also developed in northern areas.

The future of Aboriginal languages is uncertain, but several of the languages now have a written form, and bilingual school programmes have been devised. Organizations such as the Australian Institute of Aboriginal Studies promote the study of these languages, their history, and their contemporary social and political status. It therefore seems likely that a small number of these languages will remain vigorous for some time to come.

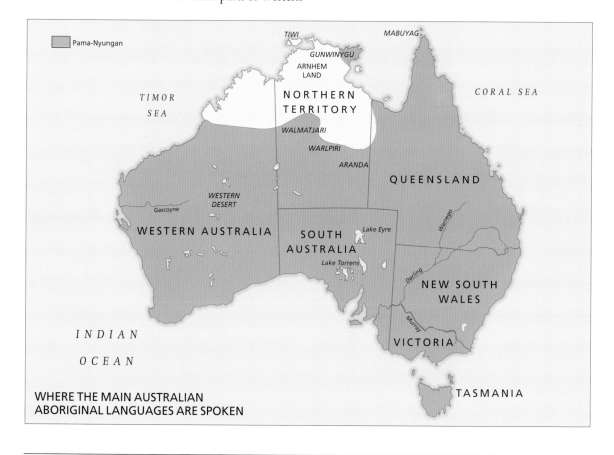

WHERE THE MAIN AUSTRALIAN ABORIGINAL LANGUAGES ARE SPOKEN

Below: Aboriginal carvings at Wilpena sacred canyon (left) and paintings from Yourambulla cave (right), Flinders, South Australia.

Above: A march through Melbourne, organized by NAIDOC (National Aborigines' and Islanders' Day Observance Committee). Most of the people are Aborigines from southern Australia, and the banners show different tribal names in Victoria. The banner at the back says 'Pay the rent, you're on Koorie land' (*Koorie* being a label used by Aboriginal people for themselves). The black, yellow, and red flag is the Australian Aboriginal flag.

THE DREAMING

No-one knows how long Aboriginal peoples have been in Australia, but estimates of at least 40,000 years have been made. According to traditional belief, life began during a mythological period known as the 'Dreaming' – a period which had a beginning but no end. During that beginning, the Aboriginal world was formed by spirit beings, both animal and human in form. They moved across the land, which was believed to have been soft and malleable, creating the shape of the territory as they went, and thus leaving signs of their spiritual presence. Many physical features of the landscape were thought to be formed by these beings, and the sites are consequently held to be sacred.

Several of these sites are rocks, caves, and trees, often marked by carvings or paintings. Motifs include animal tracks, artefacts, humans, kangaroos, and other mammals. There are also many kinds of geometrical shapes, often in combinations. These are not an attempt at written language, but seem to be symbols representing the significant places in the landscape. On the other hand, several sets of parallel lines have been found which seem to have been made by a finger dipped in an ochre paste. They are sometimes referred to as 'tally marks', because of the possibility that they may have been a register of people, periods of time, or events.

Aborigines thus see themselves as having a very close spiritual (as well as economic) relationship to the land, and to particular places in it. But today, many of the sacred sites are in danger – partly from natural erosion, but more particularly from industrial development and vandalism. Legislation is now available to protect them, but conflicts of interest can still occur. As one Nyungar Aborigine, Ken Colbung, put it: 'I am sure that people who are not of Aboriginal descent are unaware of the strong emotional feeling we have for a particular place. We see it as part of our spiritual background; and that is what is being consistently undermined. The problem is not simply one of mining and the royalties which, at least in part, should come to us. It is one of *land*.'

A language isolate is a language which has no known structural or historical relationship to any other language (p. 295). Most of the world's languages can be grouped into families using comparative linguistic techniques. But occasionally one encounters a language where resemblances to other languages are few or non-existent. Sometimes, the few points of contact are sufficient to motivate a tentative classification – thus some scholars place the Scots language Pictish within Celtic, the African languages Fur and Songhai within the Nilo-Saharan group, the Mexican language Huave within Penutian, and Tasmanian and Andamanese within Indo-Pacific. However, others see the differences as more important than the points of similarity, and list these languages as isolates.

Many languages have been classified as isolates simply because little is known about them, linguistically or historically. For example, preliminary research into South American Indian languages has brought to light several possible isolates, but further study may well indicate relationships with other languages – provided the cultures survive long enough for these studies to be carried out (p. 324). Examples are Callahuaya in Bolivia, and Aricapu, Baenna, Hixkaryana, Juma, and Natu in Brazil. Then, from a historical point of view, there are several languages of ancient Asia Minor which are known only from passing references to them in classical Greek literature, or occasional place names and inscriptions – examples include Bithynian, Cappadocian, Carian, Cataonian, Cilician, Gergito-Salymean, Hattic, Isaurian, Lycaonian, Myriandynian, Ördek-Burnu, Paphlagonian, Pisidian, Pontic, and Sidetic. It is unlikely that their affiliations will ever be known.

The diagram gives some information about several of the languages which have been proposed as isolates. It includes languages which remain undeciphered, languages where there is insufficient material available to establish a family relationship, and languages where, despite a great deal of data, the relationship is undetermined. Two of the best-known isolated languages, Korean and Japanese, are discussed on p. 308.

1) Iberian This language was spoken in parts of southern and eastern Spain, especially around the Ebro River, in pre-Roman times. It may formerly have been used throughout a much wider area of western Europe. It is known mainly through inscriptions on stones and artefacts of the period, few of which can be interpreted. Its 28-letter alphabet shows the influence of both the Greek and the Phoenician alphabets, but for the most part its history is unclear.

2) Basque is the only language remaining of those which must have been spoken in south-west Europe before the advent of the Indo-European invasions. Estimates of the number of speakers vary, from 500,000 to over 700,000. Most Basques live in a 4,000-square-mile area of northern Spain and south-west France, but many went into exile in the USA after the Spanish Civil War. Attempts have been made to show a relationship with Caucasian languages (p. 307), with North African languages, and also with Iberian, the now extinct language of many inscriptions found along the Mediterranean coasts; but none has been convincing. The written history of the language can be traced to Roman times, through various inscriptions. There is now intensive local concern to develop the language, and introduce it into primary education; but for many abroad, the language and culture are more associated with the violence of the political separatist movement, Euzkadi ta Azkatasuna (ETA). (*Euskara* is the Basque word for their language (p. 34).)

3) Etruscan The area of Tuscany in modern Italy is the site of the ancient country of Etruria, where the Etruscan civilization was at its height in the 6th century BC. The language is known from about 10,000 inscriptions, mainly short epitaphs and dedications, written in an alphabet probably derived from the Greek, and from which in due course came the Latin alphabet. The language may still have been spoken as late as the 4th century AD.

Only a few words of the language have been deciphered: no contemporary translations seem to have survived, and little progress has been made using philological methods, because Etruscan seems to bear no relationship to any other language. There is no extant literature or historical record of the civilization. Why this should be so remains one of the great unanswered questions of classical studies.

4) Linear A This is the name given to a Cretan script used in the middle of the 2nd century BC. It has still not been deciphered, and the language it represents is therefore not known, though some believe it to be Minoan (or Eteocretan). The name refers to the way the script is written in lines, probably from left to right – a contrast with previous hieroglyphic writing. The label 'A' distinguishes the script from Linear B, which was used to write Greek later in the same millennium (p. 303).

5) Sumerian This is the oldest known language to be preserved in written form. Inscriptions date from around 3100 BC, written in cuneiform script (p. 200). The existence of Sumerian was not recognized until cuneiform was deciphered in the 19th century, when it was realized that this language was quite different from others written in the same script. Sumerian was spoken in southern Mesopotamia (part of modern Iraq) until the 2nd millennium BC. It was then supplanted by a Semitic language (Akkadian) – though the written form of Sumerian continued to be used for nearly 2,000 years. There are many records of the language – business, legal, religious, administrative, and private texts and inscriptions. Literary work is preserved from the later period, in a range of forms including hymns, rituals, proverbs, and myths. Several dialect forms are known. Attempts have been made to relate the language to many other families, including Altaic and Dravidian, but none has been successful.

A Sumerian account listing the amount of grain paid to officials and servants of the temple of Baal, c. 2400 BC.

Mohenjo-Daro

6) Elamite This extinct language was spoken in the ancient country of Elam – an area now corresponding to Khuzistan in south-west Iran. The oldest writings are in the form of pictographic inscriptions from the 3rd millennium BC. Later writing is in cuneiform script. The language was still in use in the 1st millennium AD. A relationship with Dravidian has been proposed.

An Elamite inscription stamped on a baked clay brick, dating from the 12th century BC. It describes the rebuilding of the temple of the 'Great King' by King Shil-hak-Inshushinak I.

7) Mohenjo-Daro The name (which means 'the mound of the dead') refers to a group of mounds on the bank of the Indus River in Pakistan. Excavations at the site since the 1920s have brought to light the remains of a major city, dating from the 3rd millennium BC. The many finds contain evidence of a script, which so far is undeciphered.

8) Burushaski This language is spoken in north-west Kashmir, India, and in a small part of adjoining Pakistan, by over 50,000 people belonging to the Burusho tribe. It has no written form.

9) Nahali About 5,000 people speak this language in a small area in south-west Madhya Pradesh, in India. Some scholars have related the language to the Munda group of Austro-Asiatic (p. 311), but most view it as independent.

10) Gilyak This language is spoken by some 400 people in north-east Russia, on the island of Sakhalin and on parts of the mainland opposite. Gilyak (or Nivkhi, the name used by the people themselves) is often listed along with the neighbouring Palaeosiberian languages (p. 308), but proposed links with these and other languages of the area (especially Korean

and the Altaic languages (p. 309)) have not been accepted.

11) Ainu About 16,000 Ainu tribespeople live in Hokkaido, Japan, and in the Sakhalin and Kuril Islands, but in recent years, the culture as well as the language has lost ground to the Japanese, and there are now probably no native speakers left. The traditional Ainu are unlike the Japanese

An Ainu tribesman

in physical appearance, and it is thought that they may be descendants of Caucasoid peoples who were once spread throughout north Asia.

12) Kutenai There are many spellings and names for this language – Kootenay, Cootenais, Skalzi, Arc-a-plat, and Flatbow are some of those recorded. It is spoken by a North American Indian tribe, mainly in south-east British Columbia and Alberta, but also in northern parts of Idaho, Washington, and Montana. Their numbers are decreasing–fewer than 200 in the 1980s. Some scholars have postulated relationships with other Amerindian languages (p. 322), but none of the proposals is generally accepted.

13) Keres Also known as Keresan, or Queres, this language is spoken in two main varieties by 8,000 speakers in the 1980s. Originally thought to be a member of the Hokan-Siouan family, it is now considered an isolate.

14) Tarasca This language was spoken by around 60,000 in the late 1960s, in parts of south-west-central Mexico. It goes under several names and spellings, including Tarascan, Porepecha, and Mechoacan. A relationship to other languages of the area has been proposed (under the general heading of Penutian, p. 322), but is unclear. In recent years, the number of speakers has been decreasing, with many Tarascan Indians becoming assimilated within the mixed European culture dominant in Mexico.

15) Het This South American Indian language, also known as Chechehet, became extinct at the end of the 18th century. It was spoken in Argentina, and is known from only a few words and place names.

16) Karankawa This language, also known as Clamcoets, was spoken by Indian tribes living along the Texan coastline in the 18th century. They seem to have died out by the mid-19th century, with the influx of white settlers into the area.

17) Calusa An extinct tribe of American Indians who lived in the south-west part of Florida until the end of the 18th century, and perhaps later. Many families emigrated to Cuba, to escape from the invasions of other tribes, and, ultimately, the British.

18) Beothuk This language, spoken by an Indian tribe on the island of Newfoundland, is now extinct. Its last known speaker died in 1829. Some scholars have argued that it should be classified as an Algonquian language, but the opinion is controversial. The Beothuk rubbed red ochre on their bodies – a practice which may well be the reason for the European name 'Red Indians'.

54 · LANGUAGE CHANGE

Languages are always in a state of flux. Change affects the way people speak as inevitably as it does any other area of human life. Language purists do not welcome it (p. 5), but they can do very little about it. Language would stand still only if society did. A world of unchanging linguistic excellence, based on the brilliance of earlier literary forms, exists only in fantasy.

During the greater part of the 19th century, linguistic scholarship used the comparative method (p. 294) to establish the facts of language change. What features of language have changed in the past? When did they change? How did they change? During the present century, especially as a consequence of recent trends in sociolinguistics (p. 335), the emphasis has shifted towards a search for explanations. *Why* do languages change?

WHAT CHANGES?

All aspects of language structure and use are subject to changes, but the most noticeable and frequent changes affect pronunciation and vocabulary, and it is these which have attracted most study. The science of comparative philology was at first entirely devoted to the study of sound change, and contemporary sociolinguistic studies have a similar emphasis.

SOUND CHANGE

From the earliest days of comparative philology, it was noted that the sounds of related languages corresponded to each other in apparently systematic ways – what were referred to as 'sound shifts'. Later, on the basis of several studies, it was concluded that these shifts operated in such a regular manner that they could be seen as sound 'laws'. The first and most famous of these laws was worked out by Jacob Grimm in 1822, in his Germanic grammar, and it has since become known as 'Grimm's law'.

Grimm noticed that where a word in Sanskrit, Latin, or Greek began with [p], the Germanic languages usually used [f], as in:

| *Latin* | pater | *English* | father |
| | piscis | | fish |

In a similar way, words beginning with [t] usually had [θ], as in:

| *Latin* | tres | *English* | three |

Altogether, nine sets of correspondences were noted, which fell into a clear phonetic pattern, suggesting that Germanic languages had diverged from Indo-European in a regular way. It was not possible to say exactly when the changes took place, but they were complete by the time the earliest Germanic texts came to be written (4th century AD Gothic).

However, Grimm's law did not explain all the differences between Germanic and the other languages. There seemed to be several exceptions. For example, the word for 'daughter' was *dauhtar* in Gothic and *duhitā́* in Sanskrit; but according to Grimm's law, the Sanskrit form should have been **dhuhitā́*. Or again, the word for 'father' was *fadar* in Gothic and *pitā́* in Sanskrit. The change from [p] to [f] was regular, but why did the [t] become [d], when according to Grimm's law it should have been [θ]?

Grimm's law

Indo-European	Germanic
	Voiced plosives
Voiced aspirates*	(unaspirated)
bh ⟶	b
dh ⟶	d
gh ⟶	g
Voiced plosives (unaspirated)	Voiceless plosives
b ⟶	p
d ⟶	t
g ⟶	k
Voiceless plosives	Voiceless aspirates*
p ⟶	f
t ⟶	θ
k ⟶	x

The 'circular' relationship between the correspondences is its major feature:

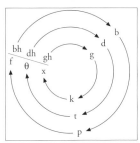

*Grimm's term includes both aspirated plosives and fricatives (p. 159).

Verner's law

Germanic Voiceless fricatives	Germanic Voiced fricatives (arising from Grimm's law)	Later forms
f ⟶	v ⟶	b
θ ⟶	ð ⟶	d
x ⟶	ɣ ⟶	g

if
(i) the consonant is not initial
(ii) the preceding and following sounds are voiced
(iii) the preceding vowel is unstressed

TYPES OF SOUND CHANGE

The processes which affect sound change are many and various. This list illustrates some of the types which regularly occur.

Assimilation. Probably the most important type of change, in which one sound is influenced by the pronunciation of a neighbouring sound (p. 166).
Example: Latin *noctem* (*night*), which became *notte* in Italian, the /k/ being assimilated to the following /t/.

Dissimilation. A sound moves away from the pronunciation of a neighbouring sound.
Example: German *Kartoffel* (*potato*), earlier *Tartuffeln*, where the /k/ dissimilated from /t/ in the 17th century.

Merger or **coalescence.** Two sounds become one. Example: Old English /e:/ and /æ:/, which became Modern English /i:/, as in *sweet* (OE *swēte*) and *clean* (OE *clǣne*),

Split. One sound becomes two.
Example: Old English /s/, which was realized as [z] only between voiced sounds, as in *thousand* (OE *thūsend*); in Modern English, /z/ has split off from /s/, becoming a phoneme in its own right.

Loss. A sound disappears from the language.
Example: Old English velar fricative [x], which was a variant of /h/, as in *eahta* (*eight*); this sound had disappeared by early Modern English.

Haplology. The loss of a sound, because of its similarity to a neighbouring sound.
Example: Modern English *England*, from Old English *Englalond* (land of the Angles).

Metathesis. Two sounds change places.
Example: English *third*, from Anglo-Saxon *ðridda*.

Syncope. The loss of medial sounds.

Example: Latin *domina* becoming Italian *donna* (*lady*).

Apocope. The loss of final sounds.
Example: Modern English *help*, from Old English *helpe*.

Prothesis. The introduction of an extra initial sound.
Example: Latin *schola* (*school*) becoming Spanish *escuela*, Old French *escole*, etc.

Epenthesis. The introduction of an extra medial sound.
Example: Old Icelandic *ofn*, alongside Old English *ofen*, Modern English *oven*.

There were several discrepancies of this kind. Many of them came to be resolved by examining the phonetic contexts in which the sounds occur. The German philologist, Hermann Grassmann (1809–77), worked out an explanation for the kind of case illustrated by *dhuhitā. He argued that these forms all had a sequence of two aspirates in Indo-European, and that this was enough to block the application of Grimm's law. His formulation became known as 'Grassmann's law'. The Danish linguist, Karl Verner (1846–96), discovered a reason for cases such as pitā. He found that Grimm's law worked well whenever the stress fell on the root syllable of the Sanskrit word; but when it fell on another syllable, the consonants behaved differently. A further change took place: [p, t, k] did not stay as [f, θ, x], but became [b, d, g]. The precise formulation of this regularity became known as 'Verner's law'.

As a result of such explanations, philologists in the later part of the 19th century began to feel that *all* exceptions to sound laws could be explained, as long as proper attention was paid to the phonetic environment and to such matters as stress. The view was highly controversial, but it exercised a great deal of influence on the subsequent development of the comparative method, and of linguistic theory.

HOW DO WE KNOW WHAT OLD LANGUAGES SOUNDED LIKE?

Contemporary accounts

Writers sometimes give an account of contemporary pronunciation features – often indirectly, in the form of a satirical comment or passage about a certain style of speech. For example, in *The Merry Wives of Windsor*, Falstaff reacts to the speech of the parson, Sir Hugh Evans, who has tried to pronounce the words *cheese* and *butter*: '"Seese" and "putter"? Have I lived to stand at the taunt of one that makes fritters of English?'. But more direct evidence comes from the detailed accounts made by *orthoepists*, specialists in the study of pronunciation. In 17th-century England, there were many such writers, including Bishop John Wilkins (1614–72) and the mathematician John Wallis (1616–1703). In the *Orthographie* of John Hart (d. 1574), for instance, which was published in 1569, we find detailed descriptions of the organs of speech and of the sounds of 16th-century English.

Poetic evidence

The way in which early poets made words rhyme, or gave their lines a particular metrical pattern, provides a great deal of evidence about where the stress fell in a word, and the way vowels were pronounced. Puns, too, draw our attention to points of similarity between sounds. For example, we can infer from the way Chaucer rhymes *was* with the French *par cas* that its pronunciation must have been something like 'wass'. Such comparisons do not tell us exactly how the words were pronounced, nor whether these were normal pronunciations of the time; but they do provide the historical linguist with valuable clues.

Alphabetic evidence

When European languages first came to be written down, those who devised the alphabets borrowed symbols from alphabets already in use elsewhere – usually Latin. They would then modify or add to these symbols whenever they came across sounds which the older alphabet could not cope with. It is thus possible to use these changes as evidence of differences in the way the two languages were spoken. For example, when the Latin alphabet was used for Anglo-Saxon, the symbol æ was added – presumably because the missionaries felt that Latin *a* and *e* were inadequate to represent the sound they heard.

Comparative reconstruction

This procedure works backwards from languages whose pronunciations are known, using the comparative method to reconstruct earlier forms (p. 294). Most of our information about the oldest states of languages derives from this method. But the further back in history we travel, the less certain our phonetic deductions are likely to be. It may be clear that an early language contrasted two sounds, but quite unclear as to how this contrast was actually realized in speech.

Tape recordings

Historical linguists of the future will be able to rely on the records and tapes made in the present century, as the clearest evidence of all for linguistic change.

WHY DOES JAQUES LAUGH FOR AN HOUR?

In *As You Like It*, the courtier Jaques reports meeting the court jester, Touchstone, in the forest.

And then he drew a dial from his poke,
And, looking on it with lack-lustre eye,
Says very wisely 'It is ten o'clock;
Thus we may see' quoth he 'how the world wags;
'Tis but an hour ago since it was nine;
And after one hour more 'twill be eleven;
And so, from hour to hour, we ripe and ripe,
And then, from hour to hour, we rot and rot;
And thereby hangs a tale.'
When I did hear
The motley fool thus moral on the time,
My lungs began to crow like chanticleer
That fools should be so deep contemplative;
And I did laugh sans intermission
An hour by this dial.

What was it that made Jaques laugh a whole hour? The bawdy pun involved can be appreciated only when we realize that *hour* and *whore* were pronounced alike, at that time.

THE NEOGRAMMARIANS

This is the name given to the group of German philologists who claimed in the 1870s that 'sound laws have no exceptions'. They were called *Junggrammatiker*, somewhat scornfully, by their older colleagues, and this name, translated as 'neogrammarians', has continued to be used for them. The group included such men as August Leskien (1840–1916), who coined the above slogan, and Karl Brugmann (1849–1919). Brugmann's five-volume comparative grammar of Indo-Germanic (i.e. Indo-European) languages (published in an enlarged second edition between 1897 and 1916) remains unsurpassed in its comprehensive coverage of the field.

'THEY HAVE BEEN AT A GREAT FEAST OF LANGUAGES AND STOL'N THE SCRAPS'

This is Moth, in *Love's Labour's Lost*, talking about a conversation between Holofernes, the schoolmaster (here shown played by Frank Middlemass), and Sir Nathaniel, the curate (John Rogan). Between the lines of Holofernes' description of Don Armado's pronunciation, valuable hints about contemporary speech styles and attitudes can be gleaned.

He draweth out the thread of his verbosity finer than the staple of his argument. I abhor such fanatical phantasimes, such insociable and point-devise companions; such rackers of orthography, as to speak 'dout' fine, when he should say 'doubt'; 'det' when he should pronounce 'debt' – d, e, b, t, not d, e, t. He clepeth a calf 'cauf', half 'hauf'; neighbour vocatur 'nebour'; neigh abbreviated 'ne'. This is abhominable – which he would call 'abbominable'. It insinuateth me of insanie: ne intelligis, domine? to make frantic, lunatic.

GRAMMATICAL CHANGE

The most noticeable way in which grammatical systems change is known as *analogy*. In this process, irregular grammatical patterns are changed in accordance with the regular patterns which already exist in the language.

A well-studied case is the verb system in the history of English. Several of the irregular verbs of Anglo-Saxon have fallen under the influence of the regular verbs in the past 1,000 years. For example, *helpan* (help) had *healp* as a past tense and *holpen* as a past participle; but by the 14th century, the verb had become regular, using the normal *-ed* ending – *helped*. During the early Middle English period, over 40 other verbs (including *walk, climb, burn,* and *step*) were influenced in the same way. Social factors, such as the development of the standard language, and the growth of printing, slowed the change down, so that present-day English still has many irregular verbs. But the force of analogy can still be heard, when people use non-standard forms (such as *knowed*), or when children, learning the language, experiment with such forms as *goned*. The tension between regular and irregular forms is also illustrated by problems of modern usage, such as the choice of *strove* vs *strived*, *chid* vs *chided*, or *sown* vs *sowed*.

Analogy does not operate only in word forms. Syntactic constructions can also be affected. In Anglo-Saxon, for example, the Subject–Verb–Object pattern applied only to main clauses; in subordinate clauses, the object preceded the verb. In Modern English, both clause types show the same order (§14).

Analogy does not create new grammatical patterns: it simply extends the range of a pattern which already exists in the language. Other processes of change have a more radical role, creating new patterns and eliminating old ones. For example, in Latin, the relationship between subject and object was shown by inflectional endings, and the order of the elements was not important; but in the modern Romance languages, these relations are expressed by word order. In early Indo-European, there were three grammatical genders for nouns – masculine, feminine, and neuter; these have been retained in modern German and Greek, but are reduced to two in modern Swedish (common vs neuter) and French (masculine vs feminine), and have been completely lost in modern English.

SEMANTIC CHANGE

This is perhaps the most obvious area of linguistic change, and the one which many people find the most fascinating. Semantic change is profoundly connected with the life, literature, and culture of a community. Innumerable examples can be found in the pages of old books, or simply by careful watching and listening to everyday usage. But plotting the history of the changes in the form, meaning, and use of words and morphemes is difficult work, because the evidence is often lacking.

To find out about lexical history, or *etymology*, the best source of information is a dictionary which has been written on historical principles, such as the *Oxford English Dictionary*. Many languages also have specialized etymological dictionaries.

New words and old

The two most obvious factors in semantic change are the arrival of new words and the loss of old ones. In most languages, the vast majority of new words are in fact *borrowings* from other languages – though this term is not a very appropriate one, as new words are not given back at a later stage! Borrowing proceeds in all directions. *Weekend* and *parking* have been borrowed by French from English; *chic* and *savoir-faire* have been borrowed by English from French. Some languages have borrowed so extensively that native words are in a minority.

A special type of borrowing is known as a *loan translation* or *calque*. In this process, a word is not borrowed whole, but its parts are translated separately and a new word formed – as when German produced the equivalent of English *telephone* in *Fernsprecher* (literally, *fern* 'distant' + *sprecher* 'speaker').

When a word or sense ceases to be used, it is said to be *obsolescent* or *obsolete*. This often happens because an object or concept is no longer of value to a community (other than to the historian or literary scholar); but a word or sense may become obsolescent if it develops unpleasant associations, or is replaced by another word which is felt to be more modern. *Wight* (person), *leman* (sweetheart), and *hie* (hasten), are examples from Elizabethan English which are now no longer used; *humour* (= 'temperament') and *conceit* (= 'idea') illustrate obsolete senses from the same period.

SOME TYPES OF SEMANTIC CHANGE

Extension. A word widens its meaning.
Example: In Latin, *virtue* was a male quality (cf. *vir* 'man'); today, it applies to both sexes.

Narrowing. A word becomes more specialized in meaning.
Example: In Old English, *mete* referred to food in general (a sense which is retained in *sweetmeat*); today, it refers to only one kind of food.

Shift. A word moves from one set of circumstances to another.
Example: *Navigator* once applied only to ships, but it now applies to planes, and even to cars.

Figurative use. A shift in meaning based on an analogy or likeness between things.
Example: *Crane*, a bird with a long neck, has led to the use of *crane* as a piece of equipment for lifting weights.

Amelioration. A word loses an original sense of disapproval.
Example: *Mischievous* has lost its strong sense of 'disastrous', and now means the milder 'playfully annoying'.

Pejoration. A word develops a sense of disapproval.
Example: *Notorious* once meant 'widely known', and now means 'widely and unfavourably known'.

SOME SURPRISING ETYMOLOGIES

The words in the left-hand column once had the meaning given on the right.

treacle	← wild animal
villain	← farm labourer
taxation	← fault finding
bonnet	← a man's hat
furniture	← equipment
pretty	← ingenious
cheater	← rent collector
naughty	← worth nothing
vulgar	← ordinary
sly	← wise
publican	← public servant
orchard	← garden (without fruit trees)

SOME SOURCES OF ENGLISH WORDS

ballot	Italian
banshee	Scots Gaelic
chow mein	Chinese
garage	French
gong	Javanese
goulash	Hungarian
junta	Spanish
kiosk	Turkish
llama	Quechua
marmalade	Portuguese
robot	Czech
schmaltz	Yiddish
slim	Dutch
sofa	Arabic
tomato	Nahuatl
tycoon	Japanese
veranda	Hindi
window	Old Icelandic
yen (= 'desire')	Chinese

BOYFRIENDS AND GIRLFRIENDS

Whether a language will borrow a word whole, or translate its parts, is never predictable. As the words *girlfriend* and *boyfriend* spread from the west to the east, they were handled differently. The Chinese loan-translated the words as *nan pengyou* (male friend) and *nü pengyou* (female friend). The Japanese, however, borrowed the words as wholes, adapting them to their sound system: the result was *bōifurendo* and *gārufurendo*.

LEXICOSTATISTICAL GLOTTOCHRONOLOGY

This is an approach, devised by the American linguists Morris Swadesh (1909–67) and Robert Lees (1922–) in the late 1940s, which determines the rate at which a language has changed, over the centuries. It aims to work out the length of time which has elapsed since two related languages (or two languages thought to be related) began to diverge. *Glottochronology* is the name of the study; *lexicostatistics* is the name of the technique it uses (but some authors use the two terms synonymously).

A sample of vocabulary is taken from the languages, using the basic word-list given right, and the number of similar words between the languages is counted, allowing for the effect of phonetic change. Thus, Italian *padre* and Portuguese *pai* would be accepted as equivalent, or *cognate*, words for 'father', because the relationship is explicable (p. 294), whereas there is no reasonable phonetic explanation which could relate either of these to, say, the Eskimo word for 'father', *ataataq*. The word-list tries to avoid geographically or culturally biased words, such as the names of plants or animals, which would vary greatly from one part of the world to another.

Glottochronologists assume that the lower the number of vocabulary agreements between the two samples, the longer the languages have been separated. Two languages which have 60% vocabulary in common would be thought to have diverged longer ago than two languages which have 80% in common. Swadesh and Lees took several languages where the period of time-change is known, and worked out a correlation between the percentage of common vocabulary and the interval of time (or 'time-depth') which has elapsed since they diverged (as in the case of the Romance languages, which have diverged from Latin since the early Christian era). They found that on average two languages would have 86% in common after 1,000 years of separation.

Working backwards, on this basis, they constructed a table of historical divergence, extracts from which are given below. Using this kind of table, estimates have been given for the possible point of divergence of the languages in many of the world's families. The Caucasian family (p. 307) is outlined, as an illustration.

CRITICISMS

The approach is a controversial one for several reasons. The method itself has been attacked on the ground that it is impossible to construct a word-list that shows no cultural bias – *sun* and *moon*, for example, have great religious significance in some cultures. It is also argued that the rate of change may not be the same for all languages, and that far more known language histories would need to be analysed before the 86% figure was truly convincing. The method becomes less definite the further back in history it goes, and the slightest of errors in the compilation of the word sample could result in great inaccuracy: for instance, after 70 centuries of divergence, there would be only 12% of cognates left, so that if just one cognate was misanalysed, the result would be three centuries in error. There are all kinds of problems which arise relating to whether words from different languages are indeed 'the same' – in meaning as well as in form. And often, not enough information is available about a language (especially for older states) for a complete sample to be drawn up.

Swadesh was fully aware of the limitations of the procedure. But he argued that there must be a balance between the forces which maintain uniformity in language and those which encourage fluctuation, and pointed out that it is possible to obtain ancillary evidence from the dating methods used in archaeology. Certainly, the approach has generated many interesting hypotheses about early language states and the relative chronology of modern languages, and several scholars still use it in their work – if only because no alternative technique has been devised.

THE BASIC WORD-LIST

I	horn	lie
you	tail	sit
we	feather	stand
this	hair	give
that	head	say
who	ear	sun
what	eye	moon
not	nose	star
all	mouth	water
many	tooth	rain
one	tongue	stone
two	claw	sand
big	foot	earth
long	knee	cloud
small	hand	smoke
woman	belly	fire
man	neck	ash
person	breasts	burn
fish	heart	path
bird	liver	mountain
dog	drink	red
louse	eat	green
tree	bite	yellow
seed	see	white
leaf	hear	black
root	know	night
bark	sleep	hot
skin	die	cold
flesh	kill	full
blood	swim	new
bone	fly	good
grease	walk	round
egg	come	dry
		name

GLOTTOCHRONOLOGICAL ESTIMATES OF THE TIME DEPTH OF LANGUAGES

For example, if two languages spoken today have 60% cognates, they diverged 16.9 centuries ago – around 300 AD. The scale stops at 25,000 years ago.

Percentage of divergence between two languages	Minimum number of centuries of divergence
100	0
95	1.7
90	3.5
85	5.4
80	7.4
75	9.5
70	11.8
65	14.3
60	16.9
55	19.8
50	22.9
45	26.5
40	30.3
35	34.8
30	39.9
25	45.9
20	56.6
15	75.6
10	102.6
5	148.4
1	255.0

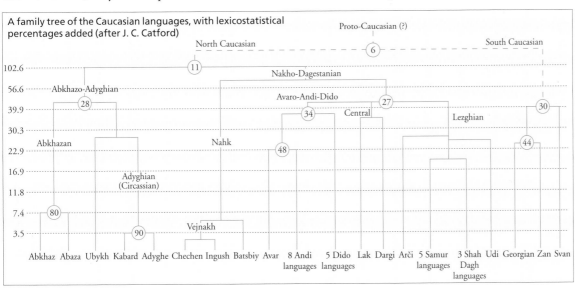

A family tree of the Caucasian languages, with lexicostatistical percentages added (after J. C. Catford)

HOW DOES LANGUAGE CHANGE?

During the later part of the 19th century, it was believed that a sound change affected the whole of a language simultaneously: one sound system would smoothly develop into the next, and all words which contained a particular sound would be affected in the same way.

We now know that linguistic change does not operate in such an 'across-the-board' manner. Some speakers introduce the change into their speech before others; some use it more frequently and consistently than others; and some words are affected before others. A more accurate view is to think of a change gradually spreading through the words of a language – a view that is known as *lexical diffusion*. At first just a few people use the change sporadically in a few words (commonly occurring words are influenced very quickly); then a large number of words are affected, with the sound gradually being used more consistently; then the majority of the words take up the change.

CHANGE FROM ABOVE

Three New York department stores were the setting for the first major sociolinguistic investigation of language change in English, carried out by William Labov in the early 1970s. Labov wanted to find out why New Yorkers do not always pronounce the final /r/ in words like *car* – a fluctuation which had previously been considered a case of 'free' (i.e. random) variation. Using data obtained from the salespeople at these stores, he was able to show that the variation was systematic – a matter of social status.

The stores represented the top, middle, and bottom of the shopping range. Saks is on Fifth Avenue, a fashionable shopping area. Macy's is a middle-class store, in the middle of the price range. Klein's is near the Lower East Side, dealing in low-priced goods. Labov worked on the assumption that the sales-people's accents would reflect those of their customers, and that the use of /r/ would vary from store to store.

The research technique involved visiting each store, and asking staff questions about where certain goods were located – always requiring the answer that they were on the 'fourth' floor. An interviewer on the fourth floor would ask simply, 'Which floor is this?' By pretending not to hear the answer, the interviewer was able to obtain a second response, more emphatic than the first. All pronunciations of *fourth* were noted, along with background data about the interviewees (sex, approximate age, etc.). In each store, there were 264 interviews.

Labov found that the use of /r/ was highest in Saks, next highest in Macy's, and lowest in Klein's. In other words, the higher the socioeconomic group, the more likely speakers are to use /r/. Moreover, speakers in Klein's used /r/ much more often in their emphatic responses, which were more carefully pronounced that their first, casual reply. This was confirmed in other studies, which showed the incidence of /r/ to increase still further in yet more careful speech, during reading aloud. Labov interpreted this to mean that these speakers were manifesting a linguistic change in progress: /r/ had been unconsciously recognized as a marker of high prestige, and was beginning to be used in careful lower-class speech. The direction of change was 'from above'.

The evidence for this kind of process has largely come from sociolinguistic studies of contemporary linguistic variation. Pioneered by William Labov (1927–), these studies proceed on the assumption that the variation in language use which is found in any community (and which fuels the debates over linguistic identity and acceptability (pp. 2–5)) is evidence of change in progress in a language. Detailed observations are made of the way in which different kinds of people speak in different social settings. The parameters along which these differences can be plotted are known as *linguistic variables* (p. 32). By examining the frequency with which different people used a variable, Labov was able to draw conclusions about the motivation, direction, and rate of linguistic change.

These are small-scale studies, but they have large-scale implications. It is likely that the same gradual process of change affects whole languages as well as dialects. This process is not very accurately represented using the family-tree model (§50), with its clean splitting off of branches, and several proposals have been made for a more dynamic and sociolinguistically real alternative. The metaphor of a 'wave' has proved particularly attractive since the late 19th century: a change spreads through a language in much the same way as a stone sends ripples across a pool. But even this implies too regular a movement to account for the reality of sociolinguistic variation.

CHANGE FROM BELOW

Martha's Vineyard is a small island off the east coast of Massachusetts. Here, Labov studied the way in which the diphthongs (p. 156) [ai] and [au] seemed to be changing. Traditionally, the first element of these diphthongs was a vowel sound which resembled the *a* in far. But now, many people were pronouncing this vowel with a central quality, resembling the *er* of *butter* ([əi] and [əu]). Could this change be explained?

To establish the nature of the variation, Labov interviewed several islanders, and obtained examples of words containing these diphthongs. The results were analysed in terms of such factors as age, location, and occupation. He found that the change was most noticeable in the speech of people aged 30–45, and was least in evidence in the oldest group (over 75). The change was also more common in the western part of the island, especially in the Chilmark area, where the fishing trade is centred. The fishermen used more of the centralized diphthongs than did people of any other occupation – indeed, the pronunciation had long been around in their speech, but in a less marked form. This suggested that the change had begun with the fishermen in the west, and spread from there.

But why should the fishermen have initiated this change? Labov's explanation relates to the way the island is used during the summer as a tourist centre: its 6,000 permanent residents are increased by over 40,000 [ai]- or [au]-using visitors. The local fishermen (especially the oldest) reacted against this invasion in many ways, one of which was the subconscious exaggeration of speech features which made them sound different. Other islanders came to imitate the way the fishermen were speaking, because (again subconsciously) they admired their traditional character and way of life. In due course, the change spread throughout the island – a change 'from below'.

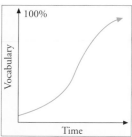

Rates of change The rate at which a change spreads through a language can be drawn as a curve with a characteristic S-shape. There is a slow start, with few words affected; a period of rapid expansion, with most words affected; and a slow conclusion (after M. Chen, 1972).

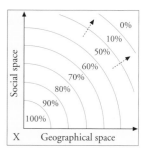

A wave model of linguistic change A change starts at point X, and moves simultaneously through a geographical area (shown horizontally) and through the strata of society (shown vertically). The further it travels, the less effect the change has. If many changes were taking place at once, the speakers furthest away from X would gradually lose their linguistic identity with those at X. They would become different dialects, and in due course perhaps even different languages (after C.-J. Bailey, 1973).

Sunset at Menemsha, Martha's Vineyard

WHY DOES LANGUAGE CHANGE?

It is easy to recognize a change in language – but only after it has taken place. It is not difficult to reflect on how people spoke several years ago, to point to a new word which has recently entered the language, or to express an opinion about the emergence of a cliché. What is almost impossible is to predict a language change. Which sounds, words, or grammatical constructions *will* change in the next 10, 20 ... years?

It is just as difficult to be precise about the origins of a change in language. Who first used the new form? Where was it used? And when, exactly? Historical dictionaries always give an approximate date of entry for a new word or meaning – but these dates invariably reflect the earliest known use of that word in the *written* language. The first use of the word in speech is always an unknown number of years previously.

To obtain answers to these questions, we need to know more about why language changes. If we understood the causes of change, we could begin to make predictions about when a change was likely to take place, and observe it while it was happening. There has long been imaginative speculation on the matter, with suggested causes coming from fields as far apart as theology (that change is a consequence of human arrogance, as manifested in the Tower of Babel) and climatology (that change is the consequence of human physical location – the mountain-dweller having a physiologically different capacity for speech compared with the valley-dweller). Some scholars have adopted a highly pessimistic view, feeling that the causes can never be found.

These days, the speculation and pessimism are being replaced by an increasing amount of scientific research, which has shown that there is no single reason for language change. Several factors turn out to be implicated, some to do with the nature of language structure, and some with the nature of society.

SPUTNIK

Only rarely can we give an exact date of entry for a new word into a language – a modern example being the international use of the word *sputnik*, following the launch of the first artificial satellite on 4 October 1957. On 3 October, the word was unknown. By the evening of 4 October, it had entered hundreds of languages.

THE NATURE OF SOCIETY

Geography When people move away from each other, their language will diverge. The two groups will have different experiences, and at the very least their vocabulary will change. Similarly, when people come into contact with each other, their language will converge. The sounds, grammar, and vocabulary of one group are likely to exercise some influence on the other. These days, the increased mobility of people, within and between countries (p. 36), makes this a major factor.

New vs old New objects and ideas are continually being created, and language changes to take account of them. At the same time, old objects and ideas fall out of daily use, and the language becomes obsolete.

Imperfect learning According to one view, children could be the initiators of language change. They might learn the adult forms imperfectly, and a new standard could gradually emerge. There are indeed similarities between the processes of language acquisition (§38) and historical change, but it is unlikely that there is a causal connection. Children imitate society, rather than the reverse.

According to another view, change is the result of one population imperfectly learning the language of another. This is a common occurrence, as illustrated by many immigrant groups, or the levels of bilingualism found in contact areas (§60). The minority language forms a 'substratum' which in the long term influences majority usage. For example several varieties of American English display the influence of the West African linguistic background of its black population.

Social prestige People come to talk like those they identify with or admire (p. 51). The process may be conscious or subconscious. Conscious change can be observed in those cases where people go out of their way to use or avoid a certain feature in their spoken or written language – such as *whom* or intrusive /r/

(§1). Subconscious change, where people are not aware of the direction in which their speech is moving, is less noticeable, but far more common. The movement may be towards a favoured accent or dialect (one which has 'positive prestige'), or away from one which is held in low esteem ('negative prestige'). The speakers are usually aware of the existence of linguistic differences (e.g. 'I don't like the way those people talk'), but unaware of any trend in their own speech related to their attitude.

Recent research in sociolinguistics has shown the way in which patterns of change relate to social prestige. For example, the work of Labov and others has

shown that conscious change in American and British English is usually in the direction of those linguistic forms which are widely and openly recognized as prestigious (they have 'overt prestige', as in the case of standard English). This kind of change is often initiated by people from the lower middle-class or upper working-class – especially women, who seem to be more aware of these factors than men. By contrast, subconscious change is usually in the opposite direction, away from overt prestige. It is often initiated by working-class men, and associated with such attributes as toughness and virility, which carry 'covert prestige'.

THE NATURE OF LANGUAGE

Social factors can motivate people to change their language, but is there anything in language itself which, so to speak, 'welcomes' a change?

Ease of articulation In the 19th century, it was widely felt that sounds changed because speakers would want to speak using as little effort as possible. On this basis, sounds and sound systems should become simpler over long periods of time. Some types of sound change do provide evidence for this view – such as the trend in many languages to weaken or drop final consonants, or to allow adjacent sounds to influence each other, as in the case of assimilation (p. 166). But there are also many cases where articulatory complexity is unaffected by a sound change –

and even cases where it seems to have increased. Only a small part of language change can be explained by a principle of least articulatory effort.

Analogy Irregular features in the grammar of a language are often influenced by its regular patterns: the exceptions are made to conform to the rule (p. 236). This trend towards 'neat-

ness' has a parallel in phonology, where many changes have led to the development of a more symmetrical sound system (p. 167).

Randomness Might language change have no systematic explanation? It has been proposed that change might be essentially unpredictable – the result of arbitrary changes in fashion or

chance errors in articulation. Certainly, many changes in vocabulary are isolated and arbitrary; but there is no strong case for randomness in phonology or grammar. On the contrary, similar processes of change have been found in unrelated languages all over the world.

PIDGIN LANGUAGES

A pidgin is a system of communication which has grown up among people who do not share a common language, but who want to talk to each other, for trading or other reasons. Pidgins have been variously called 'makeshift', 'marginal', or 'mixed' languages. They have a limited vocabulary, a reduced grammatical structure, and a much narrower range of functions, compared to the languages which gave rise to them. They are the native language of no-one, but they are nonetheless a main means of communication for millions of people, and a major focus of interest to those who study the way languages change.

It is essential to avoid the stereotype of a pidgin language, as perpetrated over the years in generations of children's comics and films. The 'Me Tarzan, you Jane' image is far from the reality. A pidgin is not a language which has broken down; nor is it the result of baby talk, laziness, corruption, primitive thought processes, or mental deficiency. On the contrary: pidgins are demonstrably creative adaptations of natural languages, with a structure and rules of their own. Along with creoles (p. 338), they are evidence of a fundamental process of linguistic change, as languages come into contact with each other, producing new varieties whose structures and uses contract and expand. They provide the clearest evidence of language being created and shaped by society for its own ends, as people adapt to new social circumstances. This emphasis on processes of change is reflected in the terms *pidginization* and *creolization*.

Most pidgins are based on European languages – English, French, Spanish, Dutch, and Portuguese – reflecting the history of colonialism. However, this observation may be the result only of our ignorance of the languages used in parts of Africa, South America, or South-east Asia, where situations of language contact are frequent. One of the best-known non-European pidgins is Chinook Jargon, once used for trading by American Indians in north-west USA. Another is Sango, a pidginized variety of Ngbandi, spoken widely in west-central Africa.

Because of their limited function, pidgin languages usually do not last for very long – sometimes for only a few years, and rarely for more than a century. They die when the original reason for communication diminishes or disappears, as communities move apart, or one community learns the language of the other. (Alternatively, the pidgin may develop into a creole.) The pidgin French which was used in Vietnam all but disappeared when the French left; similarly, the pidgin English which appeared during the American Vietnam campaign virtually disappeared as soon as the war was over. But there are exceptions. The pidgin known as Mediterranean Lingua Franca, or Sabir, began in the middle ages and lasted until the 20th century.

Some pidgins have become so useful as a means of communication between languages that they have developed a more formal role, as regular auxiliary languages. They may even be given official status by a community, as lingua francas. These cases are known as 'expanded pidgins', because of the way in which they have added extra forms to cope with the needs of their users, and have come to be used in a much wider range of situations than previously. In time, these languages may come to be used on the radio, in the press, and may even develop a literature of their own. Some of the most widely used expanded pidgins are Krio (in Sierra Leone), Nigerian Pidgin English, and Bislama (in Vanuatu). In Papua New Guinea, the local pidgin (Tok Pisin) is the most widely used language in the country.

An extract from a glossary of political terms listed in a Tok Pisin booklet on government and independence. It was produced by the Political Education Committee in Port Moresby, Papua New Guinea, in August 1972.

GAVMAN
NA
INDEPENDENS

Port E. Gwainobuo—Lento canito

Right: The front page of *Wantok* ('Friend'), a Papua New Guinea weekly newspaper written entirely in pidgin (Tok Pisin) (with an English sports section).

Right, below: A street poster from Freetown, Sierra Leone, written in Krio: 'Electricity has no legs: it's Kabelmetal cable that carries it.'

GAVMAN	Em i dispela lain man i save lukautim kantri. Ol pipel yet i makim dispela lain long mekim dispela wok.
GRUP	Em i olsem sampela pipel ol i gat wanpela kain sindaun na wanpela laik.
HAUS OV ASEMBLI	Em i wanpela lain memba ol pipel i putim long foapela yia, na ol i save bung long Pot Mosbi long wokim ol lo, na painimaut ol gutpela rot long lukautim Papua Nu Gini.
INKAM TAKIS	Em i wanpela takis Gavman i save tekewe long pe bilong olgeta man, sapos pe bilong ol inap. Dispela takis ol i kolim inkam takis na dispela ol takis mani i go long Gavman.
INDEPENDENS	Em i taim long ol pipel bilong Papua Nu Gini bai i lukautim kantri bilong ol.
KING	Em i wanpela man i bosim kantri.
OL LO	Gavman i kamapim ol lo long alivim olgeta pipel. Dispela ol lo i save karamapim olgeta pipel, na olsem, ol i mas bihainim, na ol i no ken kotim o kalabusim wanpela man sapos i no brukim dispela ol lo.
LEGISLETIV KAUNSIL	Em i wanpela bikpela Kaunsil i kirap long 1951. Bikpela lain memba Gavman i makim, na liklik lain memba ol pipel i makim. Long 1964 Haus ov Asembli i kirap na senisim Legisletiv Kaunsil.
LAIBEL	Giaman samting man i raitim long pas o pepa long bagarapim nem bilong narapela man.
LOKAL GAVMAN	Em i wanpela liklik Gavman i gat memba ol pipel i makim. Dispela Gavman i lukautim sampela lain pipel ol i stap long sampela hap. Dispela liklik Gavman em i ken wokim ol lo o rul bilong warem bikpela o nesanel gavman i orait long en i wokim.
MINISTA	Em i wanpela man i bosim wanpela Dipamen bilong Gavman, na tu em i memba bilong Kabinet.

GOVERNMENT This is a group [line] of people who look after [look out for] a country. All the people elect this group in order to do this work.
GROUP It is a number of people who share the same activities [one kind sit down] and the same interests.
HOUSE OF ASSEMBLY It is a group of members that the people put in every four years, and they regularly meet [know how to meet] in Port Moresby to make [work] the laws and to find out the best ways [the good roads] of looking after Papua New Guinea.
INKAM TAKIS It is a tax that the government takes from the pay of every person whose pay is of a certain level. This tax is called income tax and the money goes to the government.
INDEPENDENS It is the time when the people of Papua New Guinea will look after their own country.
KING He is a man who rules a country.

WANTOK

NIUSPEPA BILONG YUMI OL PAPUA NIUGINI STRET · 26 YIA NAU

32 pes · Namba 1,138 · Wik i stat long Fonde, April 18, 1996 · 50 toea

Robinson Crusoe muvi bai kamaut long Ogas

— William Takaku (raithat) wantaim Pierce Brosnan long dispela muvi nem bilong em 'Robinson Crusoe.' Brosnan em wanpela ekta husat i save ektim dispela James Bond muvi *Goldeneye*. Takaku na Brosnan i wokim dispela muvi long Madang long 1994. Muvi ya i soim wei bilong ol waitman na wei bilong ol blek man na long wanem wei tupela i kam kamap long wanpela tingting long traim long save gut long wei na pasin bilong tupela yet. Dispela muvi nau bai kam aut long 23 Ogus long dispela yia. LUKIM STORI LONG PES 16.
Poto: William Takaku.

Pablik Solisita laik Ombusu i mas fri

VERONICA HATUTASI i raitim.

Kot bin givim 'death penalty' long em

LOYA bilong Charles Ombusu, Danajo Koeget bilong Pablik Solisita i laikim kot long larim Ombusu i go olsem fri man. Dispela em bikos i nogat witnes long em i kilim man na bagarapim meri.

Ombusu wantaim 21 krismas bilong Oro provins em i namba wan man long Papua Niugini husat Suprim kot i bin laik kilim em long sas bilong kilim dai man na tu bagarapim pikinini meri bilong man ya long las yia.

Loya Koeget i laikim Ombusu long go fri bikos suprim kot i no gat witnes long kotim Ombusu long mekim ol dispela pasin.

Narapela samting tu em Mista Koeget i tok planti ripot na nius i bin kamap pinis long redio, telivisen na ol niuspepa long dispela samting. Na ol pablik i ting Ombusu tasol i bin wokim dispela rong. Olsem na dispela i no gutpela long pulim kot long dispela samting i go yet. Insait long ripot bilong em, em i askim kot long stapim kot long dispela mak nau bikos apil bilong em i orait pinis.

Ombusu i bin apil egensim olpela disisen bilong Nesenel Kot long kilim em bikos em (Ombusu)

i kilim man na tu kisim 5-pela krismas long bagarapim meri.

Suprim Kot i bin oraitim dispela apil bilong Ombusu bikos Nesenel Kot i bin sasim Ombusu long tupela sas wantaim insait long wanpela kot. Suprim Kot i ting kot bilong Ombusu i no gutpela long pulim kot long dispela samting i go yet. Insait long ripot bilong em, em i askim kot long stapim kot long dispela mak nau bikos apil bilong em i orait pinis.

Pablik Prosekyuta, Panuel Mogish, long wankain taim tu i strong olsem kot bilong Ombusu i mas kamap gen long Nesenel Kot gen.

Belo na Kanage wantaim sampela wanwok bilong em i go baim buai long tupela meri Manus long 3 Mail insait long Mosbi sta na wok long kaikai buai na paitim tokpisin wantaim tupela meri ya i stap.

Ol i tokpisin i stap na tripela yangpela meri i wokabaut i kam na abrusim ol na i go. Em nau wanpela bilong dispela tupela meri Manus ya i kirap na tokim Kanage wantaim ol wanwok bilong em: Ol olsem yet, olgeta belo ol i save painim kam i go olsem.

Wanpela wanwok bilong Kanage kirap na askim dispela meri Manus: Ol i save painim wanem samting? Arapela meri Manus ya kirap na tokim dispela wanwok bilong Kanage: Olsem nau tasol mama karim yu na yu no save na askim.

Wanwok bilong Kanage kirap na tokim meri wansolwara bilong em: Nogat wantaim samting ol i save kolim samting...olgeta samting i gat nem ya.

Meri kramsel ya lukluk long wanwok bilong Kanage na tokim em: Ol i painim sosis na not dok.

Kanage sanap isi tru na kaikai buai bilong em pinis na laitim wanpela smok na putim long maus. Na em i pulim strengpela win pinis na tok: Kain pasin bilong dabolim dabolim na popelesen bilong Papua Niugini i wok long bikpela hariap.

Joke Boss MOSBI

INSAIT

4-PES RAGBI LIG NIUS

I go moa long pes 2.

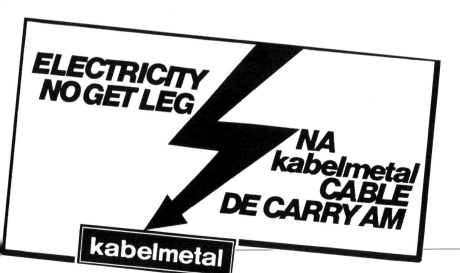

TOYOTA LAND CRUISER

SAPOS ROT IBAGARAP NA YU PAINIM HAT LONG IGO... GO WANTAIM 4WD LAND CRUISER!

LUKIM MIPELA NAU LONG ELA MOTORS
ISTAP OLGETA HAP LONG PAPUA NIUGINI!

Ela Motors

TOYOTA

SHAKESPEARE IN PIDGIN

The range of pidgin English is well illustrated by the translations which have been made of such works as the Bible and Shakespeare. Here is an extract from *Julius Caesar* (Act III, Scene 2), translated into Krio pidgin and Tok Pisin.

Friends, Romans, countrymen, lend me your ears;
I come to bury Caesar, not to praise him.
The evil that men do lives after them;
The good is oft interred with their bones;
So let it be with Caesar. The noble Brutus
Hath told you Caesar was ambitious.
If it were so, it was a grievous fault;
And grievously hath Caesar answer'd it.
Here, under leave of Brutus and the rest –
For Brutus is an honourable man;
So are they all, all honourable men –
Come I to speak in Caesar's funeral.

Krio

Padi dem, kohntri, una ohl wey dey na Rom. Meyk una ohl kak una yeys. A kam ber Siza, a noh kam preyz am. Dem kin memba bad wey pohsin kin du lohng tem afta di pohsin kin dohn dai. Boht plenti tem di gud wey pohsin du kin ber wit im bon dem. Meyk i bi so wit Siza. Bra Brutohs dohn tel una sey Siza na bin man wey want pas mak. It i tohk tru, na badbad ting dis ya. En Siza dohn get im bad pey foh dat. A tayk pamishohn frohm Bra Brutohs dem foh kam tohk na Bra Siza im berin. En Bra Brutohs na ohnareybul O! Dem ohda wan sef na ohnareybul.
(From T. Decker, 1965, p. 74.)

Tok Pisin

Pren, man bolong Rom, Wantok, harim nau. Mi kam tasol long plantim Kaesar. Mi noken beiten longen. Sopos sampela wok bolong wampela man i stret; sampela i no stret; na man i dai; ol i wallis long wok i no stret tasol. Gutpela wok bolongen i slip; i lus nating long giraun wantaim long Kalopa. Fesin bolong yumi man. Maski Kaesar tu, gutpela wok i slip.

Brutus ia tokim yu long Kaesar i mangal. Sopos olosem, bikpela pekato tru. Tasol Kaesar Kalopa bekim pinis long virua belongen. Tru Brutus, na ol pren bolongen, gutpela man. I orait. Ol i gipim mi orait long mi toktok sore hia long Kaesar.
(From J. J. Murphy, 1966, pp. 19–20.)

A page from a New Guinea road safety handbook *Rot Sefti Long Niugini* (1972), with instructions in English (top), Tok Pisin (middle), and Hiri Motu (bottom).

If you have an accident, get the other driver's number, if possible his name and address and report it to the police. Do not fight him or abuse him.

Sapos yu kisim bagarap kisim namba bilong narapela draiva, sapos yu ken, kisim naim bilong em na adres tu, na tokim polis longen. Noken paitem em o tok nogut long em.

Bema kerere davaria neganai, taraka o motuka taria tauna ena ladana oi abia bona ena noho o gaukara gabuna danu abia. Taraka o motuka ena naba danu abia vadaeni Police hamaoroa. Oi heai bona hereva dika lasi.

CREOLE LANGUAGES

A creole is a pidgin language which has become the mother tongue of a community – a definition which emphasizes that pidgins and creoles are two stages in a single process of linguistic development. First, within a community, increasing numbers of people begin to use pidgin as their principal means of communication. As a consequence, their children hear it more than any other language, and gradually it takes on the status of a mother tongue for them. Within a generation or two, native language use becomes consolidated and widespread. The result is a creole, or 'creolized' language.

The switch from pidgin to creole involves a major expansion in the structural linguistic resources available – especially in vocabulary, grammar, and style, which now have to cope with the everyday demands made upon a mother tongue by its speakers. There is also a highly significant shift in the overall patterns of language use found in the community. Pidgins are by their nature auxiliary languages (§58), learned alongside vernacular languages which are much more developed in structure and use. Creoles, by contrast, are vernaculars in their own right. When a creole language develops, it is usually at the expense of other languages spoken in the area. But then it too can come under attack.

The main source of conflict is likely to be with the standard form of the language from which it derives, and with which it usually co-exists. The standard language has the status which comes with social prestige, education, and wealth; the creole has no such status, its roots lying in a history of subservience and slavery. Inevitably, creole speakers find themselves under great pressure to change their speech in the direction of the standard – a process known as *decreolization*.

One consequence of this is the emergence of a continuum of several varieties of creole speech, at varying degrees of linguistic 'distance' from the standard – what has been called the 'post-creole continuum'. Another consequence is an aggressive reaction against the standard language on the part of creole speakers, who assert the superior status of their creole, and the need to recognize the ethnic identity of their community. Such a reaction can lead to a marked change in speech habits, as the speakers focus on what they see to be the 'pure' form of creole – a process known as *hypercreolization*. This whole movement, from creolization to decreolization to hypercreolization, can be seen at work in the recent history of African-American English in the USA.

The term *creole* comes from Portuguese *crioulo*, and originally meant a person of European descent who had been born and brought up in a colonial territory. Later, it came to be applied to other people who were native to these areas, and then to the kind of language they spoke. Creoles are now usually classified as 'English based', 'French based', and so on – though the genetic relationship of a creole to its dominant linguistic ancestor is never straightforward, as the creole may display the influences of several contact languages in its sounds, vocabulary, and structure.

Today, the study of creole languages, and of the pidgins which gave rise to them, attracts considerable interest among linguists and social historians. To the former, the cycle of linguistic reduction and expansion which they demonstrate, within such a short time-scale, provides fascinating evidence of the nature of language change. To the latter, their development is seen to reflect the process of exploration, trade, and conquest which has played such a major part in European history over the past 400 years.

Members of Radio Nous Mêmes ('Ourselves Radio'), a local radio station in the Maroni River area of French Guiana.

French	Guianese Créole	Krio	English
Mangez	Mãʒe	Chop	Eat
J'ai mangé	Mo mãʒe	A chop	I ate
Il/Elle a mangé	Li mãʒe	I chop	He/She ate
Je mange/Je suis en train de manger	Mo ka mãʒe	A de chop	I am eating
J'avais mangé	Mo te mãʒe	A bin chop	I ate/had eaten
Je mangeais	Mo te ka mãʒe	A bin de chop	I was eating
Je mangerai	Mo ke mãʒe	A go chop	I shall eat
Il/Elle est plus grand que vous	Li gros pas u	I big pas yu	He/She/It is bigger than you

CREOLES COMPARED

The similarities between European-based creoles are striking, as can be seen from this comparison of the verb phrase in the French-based creole of Guiana and the English-based Krio of Sierra Leone (after L. Todd, 1984, p. 24).

WHERE DO PIDGINS AND CREOLES COME FROM?

The world's pidgins and creoles display many obvious differences in sounds, grammar, and vocabulary, but they have a remarkable amount in common. Two opposed theories have attempted to explain these differences.

MANY SOURCES?

A long-standing view is that every creole is a unique, independent development, the product of a fortuitous contact between two languages. On the surface, this 'polygenetic' view is quite plausible. It seems unlikely that the pidgins which developed in South-east Asia should have anything in common with those which developed in the Caribbean. And it is a general experience that these varieties come into use in an apparently spontaneous way – as any tourist knows who has faced a souvenir seller. Would not the restricted features of the contact situations (such as the basic sentence patterns and vocabulary needed in order to trade) be enough to explain the linguistic similarities around the world?

The view is tempting, but there are several grounds for criticism. In particular, it does not explain the *extent* of the similarities between these varieties. Common features such as the reduction of noun and pronoun inflec-

Saturday Market, Freetown, Sierra Leone.

tions, the use of particles to replace tenses, and the use of repeated forms to intensify adjectives and adverbs are too great to be the result of coincidence. Why, then, should the pidginized forms of French, Dutch, German, Italian, and other languages all display the same kind of modifications? Why, for example, should the English-based creoles of the Caribbean have so much in common with the Spanish-based creoles of the Philippines? How could uniformity come from such diversity?

ONE SOURCE?

The opposite view argues that the similarities between the world's pidgins and creoles can be explained only by postulating that they had a common origin (i.e. are 'monogenetic'), notwithstanding the distance which exists between them. Moreover, a clear candidate for a 'proto'-language has been found – a 15th-century Portuguese pidgin, which may in turn have descended from the Mediterranean lingua franca known as Sabir (p. 340). The Portuguese are thought to have used this pidgin during their explorations in Africa, Asia, and the Americas. Later, it is argued, as other nations came to these areas, the simple grammar of this pidgin came to be retained, but the original Portuguese vocabulary was replaced by words taken from their own languages. This view is known as the *relexification* hypothesis.

There is a great deal of evidence to support the theory, deriving from historical accounts of the Portuguese explorations, and from modern analyses of the languages. For instance, every English-based pidgin and creole has a few Portuguese words, such as *savi* 'know', *pikin* 'child', and *palava* 'trouble'. In Saramaccan, an English-based creole of Suriname, 38% of the core vocabulary is from Portuguese. Early accounts of Chinese pidgin refer to a mixed dialect of English and Portuguese. And on general grounds, relexification of a single 'proto'-pidgin seems a more plausible hypothesis than one which insists on a radical parallel restructuring of several languages.

The shift in approach, implicit in the relexification theory, is fundamental: it is not the case that English, and the other languages, were 'creolized', but that an original (Portuguese) creole was 'Anglicized'. However, not all the facts can be explained in this way. Pitcairnese creole has no Portuguese influence, and yet has much in common with other varieties. What accounts for those similarities? Then there are several pidgins and creoles which have developed with little or no historical contact with European languages – Sango and Chinook, for instance. And there seem to be many structural differences between European and non-European pidgins and creoles, which the common origin hypothesis finds difficult to explain.

The evidence is mixed. Disentangling the structural similarities and differences between these varieties is a difficult task, and the evidence could be taken to support either a monogenetic or a polygenetic theory. Far more descriptive studies are needed before we rule out one view or the other.

Meanwhile, other theories have been proposed, in an attempt to explain these similarities and differences. Other forms of simplified speech have been noted, such as that used by children (§41), in telegrams and headlines, and in talking to foreigners (p. 377). It is possible that the processes underlying pidgins and creoles reflect certain basic preferences in human language (such as fixed word order, or the avoidance of inflections). In this connection, these languages provide fresh and intriguing evidence in the search for linguistic universals (§14).

Street scene in Port-au-Prince, Haiti.

PIDGINS COMPARED

Lexical similarities and differences between pidgins are clearly illustrated in this list of items collected by F. G. Cassidy in the 1960s, taken from the set of 'basic words' used in glottochronology (p. 333). The English element predominates in Tok Pisin and Chinese Pidgin; in Sango, the vast majority of the words are African; in Chinook, most words are from Chinook or other Amerindian languages (but note the influence of both French and English). French names for parts of the body have emerged in Sango and Chinook. Though there is no historical connection between the languages, note also the coincidences of thought which have produced the figurative phrases for *feather* (grass-of-bird (Tok Pisin), hair-of-bird (Sango), and leaf-of-bird (Chinook)), and the words for *heart* in Tok Pisin and Chinook, both of which stress the notion of heartbeat.

English	Tok Pisin	Chinese Pidgin	Sango	Chinook Jargon
bell	bɛl	bell	ngbéréná	tíntin
big	bɪgfɛlə	big	kótá	hyás
bird	pɪgɪn	bird(ee)	ndɛkɛ	kalákala
bite	kajkajɪm	bitee	tɛ	múckamuck
black	blækfɛlə	black	(zo)vɔkɔ́	klale
blood	blʊt	blood	méné	pilpil
cold	kilfɛlə	colo	dé	cole, tshis
come	kəm	li	ga	chahko
die	daj	dielo	kúi	mémaloost
dog	dɔg	doggee	mbo	kámooks
drink	drɪŋk	dlinkee, haw	yç	muckamuck
ear	ir	ear	mé	kwolánn
earth	grawn	glound	sése	illahie
eat	kajkaj	chowchow	kóbe, tɛ	múckamuck
fat	gris	fat, glease	mafuta	glease
feather	gras bɪlɔŋ pɪgɪn	fedder	kɔ́á tí ndɛkɛ	kalákala yaka túpso
fish	fiʃ	fishee	susu	pish
give	gɪvɪm	pay	fú	pótlatch
green	grinfɛlə	gleen, lu	vɔkɔ́ kété	pechúgh
hair	gras bɪlɔŋ hɛd	hair	kɔ́á	yákso
hand	hæn	hand, sho	mabɔ́kɔ	le mah
head	hɛd	headee	li	la tet
heart	klak	heart	coeur	túmtum
know	save	savvy	hínga	kumtuks
man	mæn	man	kɔ́lî	man
no	no	na	non	wake
nose	nos	peedza	hɔ̃	nose
one	wənfɛlə	one piecee	ɔ́kɔ́	ikt
small	lɪklɪk	likki	kété	ténas
sun	sən	sun	lá	sun, ótelagh
talk	tɔk	talkee	tɛnɛ	wáuwau
two	tufɛlə	two	óse	mokst
warm	hɔtfɛlə	warm	wá	waum

100 PIDGINS AND CREOLES

(After Ian F. Hancock, 1971)

1 Hawaiian Pidgin/Creole
English-based, with influence of Chinese, Japanese, Hawaiian, Portuguese, and Philippine languages; about 500,000 speakers, many as a first language.

2 Pitcairnese Creole English
Descendents of the mutineers from HMS *Bounty*, who settled here in 1790. English-based with a little Tahitian influence; about 45 speakers.

3 Chinook Jargon
Chinook-based, with influence of English, French, Nootka, and Salishan dialects. Now nearly extinct.

4 Pidgin Eskimo
Eskimo-based pidgins used in trading with whites and with Athabaskan Indians.

5 Pachuco (Pochismo)
Spanish–English contact language in limited use in Arizona and parts of southern California.

6 Trader Navaho
Navaho-based, used by traders to the Indians.

7 Franco-Amerindian
Used in the 17th century between French settlers and Indians, around Montreal.

8 Souriquoien
Used in the 17th century between French fishermen and people in Nova Scotia.

9 New Jersey Amerindian
Once used between English and Dutch traders and New Jersey Indians. A largely Algonquian vocabulary.

10 Mobilian
Choctaw-based pidgin, formerly used by many Indian tribes along the Gulf Coast and Mississippi River.

11 Amerindian Pidgin English
English-based pidgin once used widely in the USA between traders and Indians. First recorded in 1641.

12 Sea Islands Creole English (Gullah)
English-based creole used along the USA south-east coast. Many features in common with West African varieties. Estimates vary, 125,000.

13 Louisiana Creole French
A French-based creole still used in parts of eastern Louisiana by about 40,000, but diminishing in use.

14 Belize Creole English
Used as a lingua franca in rural areas; as a first language in mainly urban areas; over 100,000.

15 Meskito Coast Creole
A pidginized form of some of the Caribbean creole dialects used along the Meskito Coast area of Nicaragua.

16 Nahuati–Spanish Creole
Used in Nicaragua from the 16th century, and now probably extinct.

17 Papiamentu (Papiamento)
A Spanish creole, derived from a Portuguese pidgin, with Dutch vocabulary influence. Used in Curaçao, Bonaire, and Aruba by over 250,000 speakers.

18 Pidgin Spanish
A Spanish-based trading language used mainly by two Indian tribes in Venezuela.

19 Spanish Creole
Several varieties used by Indians in Colombia, such as Palenquero (about 3,000).

20 Caribbean Creole English
Around 30 English-based creoles found throughout the Caribbean and locally in Central America, some in several varieties. The largest is Jamaican Creole, with some 2 million speakers (and cf. 27).

21 Haitian French Creole
Used in three main varieties in Haiti by over 6 million speakers.

22 Virgin Islands Dutch Creole
Widely used in the 19th century (a New Testament translation was produced in 1818), but now nearly extinct.

23 Antilles Creole
French-based varieties spoken by over a million in such islands as Grenada, Guadaloupe, Dominica, Martinique, Saint Lucia, Trinidad, and Tobago.

24 Sranan
English-based creole of coastal Suriname and other coastal ports. A widely used lingua franca, and a first language of over 100,000 speakers. Saramaccan is used in central

regions by about 25,000.

25 Aukaans (English Bush Negro)
English-based creole varieties used in Suriname by about 20,000. Djuka is the only creole to have developed a syllabic writing system. Pidgin Djuka is used between the Bush Negroes and the Trio Indians.

26 French Guiana Creole
French-based creole, with some Portuguese influence, used in Cayenne and along the coast; about 50,000 speakers.

27 Trinidad and Tobago Creole
French-, Spanish-, and English-based varieties are used in these islands. The influence of immigrant languages, such as Hindi, is apparent.

28 Guyanese Creole/ Creolese
English-based creole used in Guyana, with influences from other creoles, such as Barbados and Sierra Leone; about 700,000.

29 Nikari Karu Pidgin
A Portuguese-based pidgin, used in Guyana near Brazil.

30 Guyana Dutch Pidgin
This variety is reported to have been used on inland rivers in Guyana, in the 19th century. A creolized form is still used in the Berbice River area.

31 Portuguese Bush Negro
Portuguese-based dialects used in Suriname, with English and African vocabulary influence.

32 Brazilian Creole Portuguese
Used by Brazilians of African ancestry in rural areas. An Italian–Negro variety known as Fazandeiro exists in São Paulo, and other creoles are known in the region.

33 Lingoa Gêral
A Tupí–Guaraní-based pidgin used in Brazil; now losing ground to Portuguese.

34 Cocoliche
A variety of Italianized Spanish used around Buenos Aires.

35 Franco-Spanish Pidgin
A contact language with limited use in Buenos Aires – also referred to as 'Fragnol'.

36 Russenorsk
A contact language, derived from Russian and Norwegian, now nearly extinct.

37 Anglo–Romani
A creolized variety, derived from Romani and English, used by Gypsies in Britain.

38 Sheldru (Shelta)
An Anglo-Irish creole, used mainly by Irish travellers and their descendents in England, USA, and elsewhere; based on English grammar with Irish vocabulary.

39 Inglés de Escalerilla
A Spanish–English-based pidgin used in some Mediterranean ports, such as Malaga and La Linea.

40 North African Pidgin French
A French-based pidgin, also known as 'Petit Mauresque'.

41 Sabir
A pidginized variety of Provençal, used in many Mediterranean ports (and in the Middle East, during the Crusades). Now extinct.

42 Cape Verde Creole
A Portuguese-based creole, used in two main dialects in the Cape Verde Islands; spoken by groups descended from 19th-century immigrants in Massachusetts and California.

43 Kryôl
A Portuguese-based creole, used in Senegal; about 57,000 speakers.

44 Gambian Krio (Aku)
An English-based creole used in the Gambia; widely used as a second language, with limited use as a first language. Gradually being ousted by English and pidginized Wolof.

45 Crioulo
A Portuguese-based creole used in Guinea, widely used as a lingua franca; about 400,000.

46 Krio
An English-based creole of an area based on Freetown in Sierra Leone; about 350,000 speakers as a first language, and widely used (over 3 million) as a second. An old-fashioned variety is also found in Liberia.

47 (A)Merico (Settler English)
An English-based creole used along the Liberian coast.

48 Liberian Pidgin English
An English-based pidgin used by over 1.5 million throughout Liberia. Kru English is a pidgin used by Kru fishermen in Liberia and along the coast.

49 Petit-Nègre
A French-based pidgin used mainly by soldiers in the Côte d'Ivoire and other former French possessions along the West African coast.

50 West African Pidgin English
A mutually intelligible chain of English-based pidgins and creoles is found throughout West Africa.

51 Gulf of Guinea Portuguese
A group of creoles used on the islands of Annobon, São Tomé, and Principe.

52 Cameroon Pidgin English
An English-based pidgin, creolized in some urban areas, used in Cameroon as a second language by about 2 million speakers.

53 Ewondo Populaire
An African-based pidgin used as a trade language in the Cameroon.

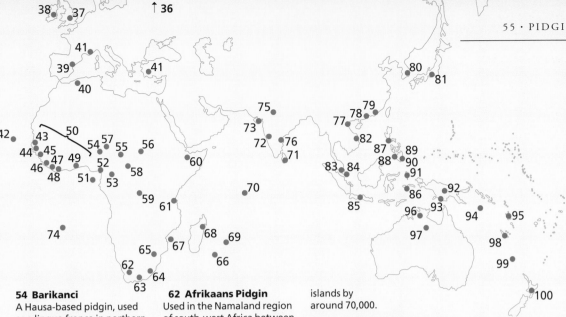

later by the Chinese in Davao, the Philippines.

91 Ternateño
A language once used in Ternate, the Moluccas, between Spanish Mexican soldiers and local Portuguese.

92 Tok Pisin (Neo-Melanesian)
An English-based pidgin, influenced by local Papuan languages, widely used in Papua New Guinea by around 2 million people (about 50,000 as a first language).

93 Hiri Motu
A pidginized variety of Motu, formerly often called 'Police Motu', much influenced by English vocabulary, widely used as a trade language for over 100 years in the Port Moresby area of Papua New Guinea; about 250,000.

94 Solomon Islands Pidgin
An English-based pidgin used in and around the Solomon Islands; becoming creolized in urban centres (about 1,000 speakers); about 100,000 as a second language.

95 Bislama (Beach-la-Mar)
An English-based pidgin, the national language of Vanuatu, and used in surrounding areas as a lingua franca (about 130,000); some first-language use.

96 Bagot Creole English
An English-based variety deriving from Australian Pidgin, used on the Bagot Aboriginal Reserve near Darwin.

97 Australian Pidgin
An English-based pidgin which may have developed out of Neo-Melanesian. Torres Strait Pidgin/Creole, spoken by over 10,000 in the Torres Strait Islands, Queensland, is also English- (Tok Pisin-) based.

98 New Caledonia Pidgin (Kaldosh)
A French-based pidgin used in New Caledonia, in the south-west Pacific.

99 Norfolkese
An English-based creole which developed from Pitcairnese, used by settlers who moved to Norfolk Island in the 19th century; about 500.

100 Maori Pidgin
An English-based pidgin used during the early years of colonization in New Zealand; no longer spoken.

---

54 Barikanci
A Hausa-based pidgin, used as a lingua franca in northern Nigeria. Pidginized Hausa is also found in northern Cameroon, and on the desert route to Mecca.

55 Tekrur
An Arabic-based pidgin, widely used as a lingua franca near Lake Chad, and in the Bodélé depression.

56 Juba Arabic (Sudanese Creole Arabic)
An Arabic-based creole which developed in the southern Sudan around the end of the 19th century; about 20,000 as a first language; 50,000 as a second.

57 Galgaliya
An Arabic-based pidgin used by the Kalamáfi tribe in north-eastern Nigeria.

58 Sango
A pidginized variety of Ngbandi, with French vocabulary influence, used widely in the Central African Republic by about 200,000 as a first language and 5 million as a second.

59 Congo Pidgins
Many pidginized varieties of local African languages in the Congo, such as Kituba (derived from Kikongo) and Lingala (pidginized Ngala). Kituba has around 4 million speakers as a second language; Munukutuba has over 1 million.

60 Asmara Pidgin Italian
An Italian-based pidgin still used in Eritrea.

61 Swahili Pidgins
Several varieties of pidginized Swahili are used in eastern Africa, such as Kisettla, spoken in Kenya between Europeans and Africans. Creolized in some areas.

62 Afrikaans Pidgin
Used in the Namaland region of south-west Africa between tribespeople and Afrikaners. Creolized in some areas.

63 Cape Dutch (Taal Dutch)
Afrikaans-based varieties used in the South African Cape; the label 'Cape Coloured Afrikaans' is also used.

64 Fanagaló
A Xhosa-based English pidgin used mainly by African mineworkers around Johannesburg, and in Zimbabwe and Namibia. It is known by many names, such as Mine Kaffir and Kitchen Kaffir.

65 Zambia Pidgins
Several African-language-based pidgins are used in the Zambian copper belt, such as Town Bemba and Settla.

66 Réunionnais
A French-based creole used in Réunion by over 500,000 people.

67 Barracoon
A language used in the 19th century in the Mozambique ports, containing elements from many languages, such as Arabic, Swahili, Portuguese, and Malagasy.

68 Mauritian French Creole
Used by most of the population of Mauritius, and by some in Madagascar and the Comoros Islands; increasingly influenced by English.

69 Morisyen
A French-based creole, used in Mauritius by around 600,000 people as a first language; a separate dialect (Rodrigues Creole) is used on nearby Rodrigues Island.

70 Seychellois (Seselwa)
A French-based creole, used in the Seychelles and other islands by around 70,000.

71 Sri Lankan Portuguese
A Portuguese-based creole formerly used by Indo-Portuguese Christian immigrants, and still spoken in parts of Sri Lanka. About 50,000 speak Sri Lankan Creole Malay.

72 Goanese
A Portuguese-based creole in Goa; probably extinct.

73 Indian Portuguese
Several pidgin and creole varieties used along the Indian coast, now largely extinct.

74 St Helena Creole
An English-based creole used on the island of St Helena; has some use as a pidgin.

75 Bazaar Hindustani
A Hindi-based pidgin, used as a lingua franca in urban centres in northern India.

76 Madras Pidgin
An English-based pidgin, much influenced by Dravidian languages, used during British rule in India, and still found.

77 Tay Boy
A French-based pidgin, widely used in Vietnam during the period of French control; now extinct.

78 Makista (Macauenho, Macanese)
A Portuguese-based creole, influenced by Chinese vocabulary, formerly used in Macao, and still in Hong Kong.

79 China Coast Pidgin
An English-based pidgin, formerly in widespread use in coastal China and Hong Kong; now almost extinct.

80 Bamboo English
An English-based pidgin used in Korea, especially during the Korean War; almost extinct.

81 Japanese Pidgin
An English-based pidgin widely used in Japanese ports in the late 19th century, and also in areas which saw American occupation in the 1940s; no longer used.

82 Vietnam Pidgin
An English-based pidgin used in Vietnam between local people and American service personnel; now extinct.

83 Malacca Portuguese
A Portuguese-based creole used in western Malaysia by about 3,000 people.

84 Singapore Portuguese
A Portuguese-based creole, with some Malay and English influence, used in Singapore.

85 Jakarta Portuguese
A Portuguese-based creole, formerly spoken in Jakarta, and now probably extinct.

86 Bazaar Malay
A pidginized variety of standard Malay, widely used in Malaysia and Indonesia. Also in this area, Baba Malay (a pidginized variety influenced by Chinese) and Betawi.

87 Caviteño and Ermitaño
Spanish-based creoles used in the area around Manila, in the Philippines.

88 Chavacano
A Spanish-based creole, with influences from Tagalog and Cebuano, used chiefly in Zamboanga, the Philippines, by about 280,000.

89 Davaueño
A Spanish-based creole, used in Davao, the Philippines.

90 Bamboo Spanish
A Spanish-based pidgin, used first by the Japanese and

The linguistic variety in the modern world can be seen on sale daily at any international news-stand.

PART X

Language in the world

Language is the main means whereby people communicate. It is also, ironically, the main means whereby people fail to communicate. These simple facts motivate the content and organization of Part x of the encyclopedia. We need to examine the problem from both international and intranational points of view. In the former case, we are dealing with the difficulties posed by the existence of so many languages in the world, and the solutions that have been proposed to alleviate them. In the latter case, we need to consider the consequences for mutual understanding that stem from the existence of so many specialized varieties within a language.

We begin by considering the way foreign languages can act as a barrier to international communication and the various methods that have been proposed to reduce or eliminate the problem. One possible solution lies in translating and interpreting – a field whose future will be much affected by progress in computer applications. Another is to create an international auxiliary language (such as Esperanto) or to simplify an existing language for international use (such as Basic English). A third solution is to promote the development of an existing language as a world language – something that currently seems to be happening to English. A fourth is to foster the growth of multilingualism in individuals and societies, either through the natural course of events, as people come into contact, or through the promotion of special educational procedures for teaching languages. Each of these approaches is given separate discussion and illustration. A focus is provided by the branch of sociolinguistics known as 'language planning' – an area that has attracted increasing attention in recent years.

Within a language, the co-existence of many specialized varieties presents a further area of enquiry. Fields such as science, medicine, law, religion, and mass communications have developed styles of language that require careful study if they are to be understood. Popular attitudes to specialized language also need to be taken into account – notably, in the work of the various campaigns for 'plain English'. We examine the background to several of these varieties, illustrating the kinds of linguistic features they display. Part x then concludes by considering the impact of the 'information explosion', which presents us daily with a mass of linguistic data, only a fraction of which can be assimilated, and which, as it accumulates, makes for increasing difficulties of organization and retrieval.

The discovery that language can be a barrier to communication is quickly made by all who travel, study, govern, or sell. Whether the activity is tourism, research, government, policing, business, or data dissemination, the lack of a common language can severely impede progress and can halt it altogether. 'Common language' here usually means a foreign language; but the same point applies in principle to any encounter with unfamiliar dialects or styles within a single language. 'They don't talk the same language' has a major metaphorical meaning alongside its literal one (§63).

Although communication problems of this kind must happen thousands of times each day, very few become public knowledge. Publicity comes only when a failure to communicate has major consequences, such as strikes, lost orders, legal problems, or fatal accidents – even, at times, war. A reported instance of communication failure took place in 1970, when several Americans ate a species of poisonous mushroom. No remedy was known, and two of the people died within days. A radio report of the case was heard by a chemist

who knew of a treatment that had been successfully used in 1959 and published in 1963. Why had the American doctors not heard of it, seven years later? Presumably because the report of the treatment had been published only in journals written in European languages – other than English. (After D. A. E. Shephard, 1973.)

Several comparable cases have been reported. But isolated examples do not give an impression of the size of the problem – something that can come only from

EU BABEL

The European Commission building in Brussels. Nowhere does the foreign language barrier exist so markedly as in the offices of the European Union. In 1994, the Joint Interpreting and Conference Service in Brussels, which serves many agencies and institutions of the EU, was providing 120,000 interpreter days (at a cost of 70 million ecu), and with 400 full-time staff and about 300 free-lancers had become the largest interpreting service in the world. From 1995 the task increased again, with member states using 11 official languages in their work, and presenting a translation problem involving a theoretical 110 language pairs. In the 9-language days of the early 1990s, EU institutions were already translating over 3 million words a day.

It is impossible to find expert interpreters for all language pairs, or to provide maximum coverage on all occasions. If interpretation into and out of all 11 languages were to be provided, it would require at least 33 interpreters (using the JICS system of three interpreters per booth, when more than six languages are spoken at a meeting). Pragmatic solutions therefore have to be found. One is the use of a relay system: if there is no Finnish/Portuguese interpreter, for example, English might be used as an intermediary language. Also, every effort is made to find interpreters who each know three or four languages. But there is always a shortage of trained interpreters.

More radical solutions have been proposed, such as the reduction of the number of working languages to five or six (as in the UN), but these suggestions are highly controversial. No country would be comfortable about giving up its linguistic status. The long-term problem nonetheless has to be confronted: as EU membership grows (to a theoretical maximum of nearly 30 languages), the case for a single relay language is bound to become increasingly persuasive. (See further, §57.)

CRITICAL LANGUAGES

In 1985, the U.S. Department of Education published a list of 169 languages which the U.S. Government considered to be 'critical', in the sense that knowledge of them would promote important scientific research or security interests of a national or economic kind. The aim, supported by special funding, was to help counter what the *Washington Post* called the nation's 'language illiteracy'. (Spellings have been made to conform to those used in Appendix III.)

	Albanian	Eskimo	Kikuyu	Nēwāri	Swedish
	Amharic	Estonian	Kirghiz	Ngala	Tagalog
	Arabic	Ewe-Fon	Kongo	Norwegian	Tajik
	Armenian	Fijian	Korean	Nyanja	Tamil
	Assamese	Finnish	Kpelle	Oriya	Tatar
	Aymará	French	Krio	Oromo	Telugu
	Azerbaijani	Fulani	Kumauni	Panjabi	Temen
	Bahasa	Gã	Kurdish	Papiamento	Thai-Lao
	Indonesia	Ganda	Lahnda	Pashto	Tibetan
	Balinese	Gbaya	Lamani	Persian	Tigrinya
	Baluchi	Georgian	Latvian	Polish	Tiv
	Bamileke	German	Lithuanian	Polynesian	Toba Batak
	Bashkir	Greek	Luba	Portuguese	Tsonga
	Basa (Kru)	Guaraní	Macedonian	Quechua	Tungus
	Belorussian	Gujarati	Madurese	Rappang	Turkish
	Bemba	Haitian Creole	Maithili	Romanian	Turkmen
	Bengali	Hausa	Malagasy	Romani	Tuvinian
	Berber	Hebrew	Malayalam	Rundi	Uighur
	Bhojpuri	Hindi	Manchu	Russian	Ukrainian
	Bikol	Hmong	Mandekan	Rwanda	Urdu
	Bulgarian	Hungarian	Manipuri	Sango	Uzbek
	Burmese	Iban (Malay)	Marathi	Santali	Vietnamese
	Buryat	Icelandic	Maya	Serbo-Croatian	Visayan
	Cambodian	Igbo	Mende	Shona	Wolof
	Catalan	Ilocano	Minangkabau	Sindhi	Yakut
	Chinese	Irish	Mixtec	Sinhalese	Yao
	Chuvash	Italian	Mongolian	Slovak	Yiddish
	Ciokwe	Japanese	Mordvin	Slovene	Yoruba
	Czech	Javanese	More	Somali	Yucatec
	Danish	Kamba	Mundari-Ho	Songhai	Zapotec
Achinese	Dari	Kannada	Nahuatl	Sotho	Zulu-Xhosa
Acholi	Dinka	Kanuri	Neo-	Spanish	
Afrikaans	Dutch	Kashmiri	Melanesian	Sundanese	
Akan	Efik	Kazakh	Nepali	Swahili	

studies of the use or avoidance of foreign-language materials and contacts in different communicative situations. In the English-speaking scientific world, for example, surveys of books and documents consulted in libraries and other information agencies have shown that very little foreign-language material is ever consulted. In one study, an analysis of over 60,000 British Library requests in the field of science and technology showed that only 13% were for foreign-language periodicals (C. A. Bower, 1976). Studies of the sources cited in publications ('citation analysis') leads to a similar conclusion: the use of foreign-language sources is often found to be as little as 10%. Likewise, in the non-English-speaking world, there is also a marked reliance on native-language material – though here the special influence of English must be considered (sometimes accounting for over half the requests made or sources used (§59)).

There are several ways of getting around the foreign-language barrier, but none is simple, nor has any as yet been entirely successful.

1. Increase the number and availability of translating and interpreting services (§57).
2. Develop an auxiliary language that everyone will understand (§58).
3. Develop an existing language as a world language that everyone will understand (§59).
4. Provide increased motivation and opportunity to learn foreign languages (§§60, 62).

THE BUSINESS WORLD

The language barrier presents itself in stark form to firms who wish to market their products in other countries. British and American industry in particular has in recent decades often been criticized for its linguistic insularity – for its assumption that foreign buyers will be happy to communicate in English, and that awareness of other languages is therefore not a priority. In the 1960s, over two-thirds of British firms dealing with non-English-speaking customers were using English for outgoing correspondence; many had their sales literature only in English; and as many as 40% employed no-one qualified to communicate in the customers' languages. A similar problem was identified in other English-speaking countries. And non-English-speaking countries were by no means exempt – though the widespread use of English as an alternative language made them less open to the charge of insularity.

The criticism and publicity given to this problem since the 1960s seems to have greatly improved the situation. Industrial training schemes have promoted an increase in linguistic and cultural awareness – for example, programmes of industrial visits abroad, temporary exchanges of junior managers, or the appointment of overseas agents. Many firms developed their own translation service or international telephone service; to take just one example from Britain, Rowntree

Mackintosh began to publish their documents in six languages (English, French, German, Dutch, Italian, and Xhosa). Some firms run part-time courses in the language with which they are most involved; some produce their own glossaries of technical terms, to ensure consistency when material is being translated. It is now much more readily appreciated that marketing efforts can be delayed, damaged, or disrupted by a failure to take account of the linguistic needs of the customer, or to look after one's own linguistic interests abroad (in such areas as patenting and trade-mark control).

The changes in awareness have been most marked in English-speaking countries, where the realization has gradually dawned that by no means everyone in the world knows English well enough to negotiate in it (§59), and that this is especially a problem when English is not an official language of public administration, as in most parts of the Far East, Russia, Eastern Europe, the Arabic world, Latin America, and French-speaking Africa (p. 357). Even in cases where foreign customers can speak English quite well, it is often forgotten that they may not be able to understand it to the required level – bearing in mind the regional and social variation which permeates speech (Part II) and which can cause major problems of listening comprehension. In securing understanding, how 'we' speak to 'them' is just as important, it appears, as how 'they' speak to 'us'.

A class of foreign students at the Bell Language School in Cambridge. There are over 600 such schools in Britain – though less than a third of these are officially recognized by a professional body. In the early 1990s, they were dealing with over 20,000 students each year, and generating an annual turnover of over £300 million. Many schools throughout the world now put on courses geared to the special needs of specific groups of foreigners, such as doctors, bankers, lawyers, or industrialists.

Expolangues This annual linguistic 'motor show', with around 500 languages represented, has been held in Paris since 1983. The exhibits reflect ongoing language-related activities in commerce, technology, culture, education, publishing, and several other fields.

BIENVENUE - HOSGELDINIZ
WELCOME - BENVENUTI
BEM VINDOS
受付 - WILLKOMMEN
ΚΑΛΩΣ ΗΛΘΑΤΕ

57 · TRANSLATING AND INTERPRETING

When people are faced with a foreign-language barrier, the usual way round it is to find someone to interpret or translate for them. The term 'translation' is the neutral term used for all tasks where the meaning of expressions in one language (the 'source' language) is turned into the meaning of another (the 'target' language), whether the medium is spoken, written, or signed. In specific professional contexts, however, a distinction is drawn between people who work with the spoken or signed language (*interpreters*), and those who work with the written language (*translators*). There are certain tasks that blur this distinction, as when source speech is turned into target writing (for example, in monitoring foreign-language broadcasts, or in writing sub-titles for foreign films). But usually the two roles are seen as quite distinct, and it is unusual to find one person who is equally happy with both occupations. Some writers on translation, indeed, consider the interpreting task to be more suitable for extrovert personalities, and the translating task for introverts!

TRANSLATING

It is sometimes said that there is no task more complex than translation – a claim that can be readily believed when all the variables involved are taken into account. Translators not only need to know their source language well; they must also have a thorough understanding of the field of knowledge covered by the source text, and of any social, cultural, or emotional connotations that need to be specified in the target language if the intended effect is to be conveyed. The same special awareness needs to be present for the target language, so that points of special phrasing, contemporary fashions or taboos in expression, local (e.g. regional) expectations, and so on, can all be taken into account. On the whole, translators work *into* their mother tongue (or language of habitual use), to ensure a result that sounds as natural as possible – though some translators have argued that, for certain types of text (e.g. scientific material) where translation accuracy is more crucial than naturalness, it makes sense for translators to be more fluent in the source language.

THE PROBLEM OF TRANSLATION

The aim of translation is to provide semantic equivalence between source and target language. This is what makes translation different from other kinds of linguistic activity, such as adapting, *précis* writing, and abstracting. However, there are many problems hidden within this apparently simple statement, all to do with what standards of 'equivalence' should be expected and accepted.

Exact equivalence is of course impossible: no translator could provide a translation that was a perfect parallel to the source text, in such respects as rhythm, sound symbolism (§30), puns, and cultural allusions. Such a parallel is not even possible when paraphrasing within a single language: there is always some loss of information.

On the other hand, there are many kinds of inexact equivalence, any of which can be successful at a certain level of practical functioning. It therefore follows that there is no such thing as a 'best' translation. The success of a translation depends on the purpose for which it was made, which in turn reflects the needs of the people for whom it was made. An inelegant, rough-and-ready translation of a letter can suffice to inform a firm of the nature of an enquiry. A translation of a scientific article requires careful attention to meaning, but little attention to aesthetic form. The provision of a dubbed film script will warrant scrupulous care over the synchronization of lip movements, often at the expense of content (p. 396). Literary work requires a sensitive consideration of form as well as content, and may prompt several translations, each of which emphasizes a different aspect of the original. It is easy

LEVELS OF TRANSLATION

• *Word-for-word* Each word (or occasionally morpheme, p. 90) in the source language is translated by a word (or morpheme) in the target language. The result often makes no sense, especially when idiomatic constructions are used:

It's raining cats and dogs.
Il est pleuvant chats et chiens.

• *Literal translation* The linguistic structure of the source text is followed, but is normalized according to the rules of the target language:

It's raining cats and dogs.
Il pleut des chats et des chiens.

• *Free translation* The linguistic structure of the source language is ignored, and an equivalent is found based on the meaning it conveys:

It's raining cats and dogs.
Il pleut à verse.

PAS OP VOOR
"GOUD"-VERKOPERS

ATTENTION !
VENDEURS "D'OR" !

BEWARE OF
"GOLD" SELLERS

HÜTEN SIE SICH VOR
"GOLD" VERKÄUFERN

ART. 337 W.v.STR.
A.P.V. 46

Free translation in practice

to see that what might be 'best' for one set of circumstances may be entirely unsuitable for another.

Several different kinds of translation have been proposed, to allow for this range of possibilities. In a *pragmatic* translation, the emphasis is entirely on accuracy and knowledge of the subject, as required for instructional manuals and much scientific research (§21). In an *aesthetic* translation, important for literary material, the focus is on preserving the emotional as well as the cognitive content of the work, and on maintaining some level of stylistic equivalence (§12). *Ethnographic* or *sociolinguistic* translations aim to pay full attention to the cultural backgrounds of the authors and the recipients, and to take into account differences between source and target language, as when Christian religious traditions based in the Middle East are 'translated' into the cultural norms of Central Africa or modern-day America (§§9–10). And there are various kinds of *linguistic* translation, where the aim is to convey the structural flavour of the original text, often in a quite literal manner, emphasizing such features as archaisms, dialectisms, and levels of formality (§§8, 10). Most translations, of course, are mixtures of these theoretical types, reflecting the complex reality of language in use, where 'pure' varieties are conspicuously absent.

PROFESSIONALISM

Translators aim to produce a text that is as faithful to the original as circumstances require or permit, and yet that reads as if it were written originally in the target language. They aim to be 'invisible people' – transferring content without drawing attention to the considerable artistic and technical skills involved in the process. The complexity of the task is apparent, but its importance is often underestimated, and its practitioners' social status and legal rights undervalued. Some countries view translation as a menial, clerical task, and pay their translators accordingly. Others (such as the Japanese) regard it as a major intellectual discipline in its own right. The question of status is currently much debated, especially in Europe, where demand for translators is rocketing, especially in relation to the EU.

Since the 19th century the important role of the professional translator has come increasingly to be recognized. Some hold full-time jobs in translation agencies or in government or commercial organizations, where they provide an in-house service; but there is also a large cadre of free-lance translators, usually working from home. The field now has its own training courses, examinations, career structure, and professional organizations – such as the American Translators' Association, the Translators' Guild of the (British) Institute of Linguists, and the Fédération Internationale des Traducteurs. The European Union of Associations of Translation Companies was formed in 1994.

The number of translations made is certainly on the increase, fuelled by a growing number of specialized multilingual publications (such as journals that publish editions in more than one language or provide issues specially devoted to translations of foreign scientific material). As a consequence, several central organizations have now developed to coordinate information about the availability of translations and to facilitate their accessibility, once they are made – notably the International Translations Centre at Delft (The Netherlands) and the National Translations Center in Chicago. In this domain, of course, the advent of computational techniques of information storage and retrieval has been a blessing – although one that is not yet as widely shared as it might be. In a 1971 study, over 90% of a sample of academic staff had never used any translation indexes; and other reports indicate that perhaps as many as 80% of scientists are not even aware of their existence (J. A. Large, 1983).

Great claims have been made for translation. It has been called the key to international understanding. The Japanese see it as a key to learning. Western Europe, it has been said, 'owes its civilization to translators' (L. G. Kelly, 1979). It is all probably so.

HOW FAST CAN TRANSLATORS WORK?

The only satisfactory answer is: it depends – upon such factors as the translators' experience, their familiarity with the subject matter, and whether they dictate the translation or have to type it themselves. The difficulty of the text is a crucial factor: a translator may be able to achieve 1,000 words per hour for popular writing, but only 400 for technical material. The linguistic relationship between source and target language is also relevant: languages which share structural and cultural patterns will be easier to relate than those which are widely different. And the direction of translation can also affect speed: some translators are almost twice as fast in working from language A into B as they are from B into A.

Assuming a continuous text, with familiar subject matter, self-typing, and an aim of producing a 'polished' translation, estimates of translator output vary from between 2,000 and 8,000 words a day, with most people producing about 3,000. Estimates of the gain in speed from using machine translation (p. 352) are not yet clear: the need for human editing of the machine-translated text has to be taken into account, and this can still be considerable at present.

THE BARRIER IN OPERATION

The translation literature is full of anecdotes about errors which illustrate the foreign-language barrier in operation (§56). Some errors are simply funny; others can provoke a diplomatic incident.

• *L'Afrique n'érige plus des autels aux dieux* ('Africa no longer erects altars to the gods'), said one UN delegate. The sentence was misheard as...*hôtels odieux* and translated as 'Africa no longer builds horrible hotels'.

• During a television interview in the United States, Soviet premier Khrushchev was told he was 'barking up the wrong tree'. However, this was translated into Russian as 'baying like a hound' – a highly insulting expression.

• Many problems occur during Bible translation. In a translation into an Indian language of Latin America, *ass* was translated as 'a small long-eared animal'. The effect was to suggest that Jesus entered Jerusalem riding on something which closely resembled a rabbit.

• In tone languages (§29), it is almost impossible to adapt the words to a western melody and preserve the meaning. In one Latin American tone language, as a consequence, the missionaries found that a sung translation about 'sinners' was in fact about 'fat people'.

• The slogan 'Come alive with Pepsi' was once translated in a Chinese newspaper (in Taiwan) as 'Pepsi brings your ancestors back from the grave'!

Language of publication	Language of citations %			
	English	German	French	Other
PSYCHOLOGY				
English	92.5	5.2	0.7	1.6
German	2.7	91.1	6.2	0.0
French	25.6	7.4	64.0	3.0
CHEMISTRY				
English	79.4	11.9	4.7	4.0
German	22.8	64.0	6.2	7.0
French	36.7	27.9	29.1	6.3
PHYSICS				
English	86.2	5.9	2.0	5.9
German	35.3	58.1	1.4	5.2
French	49.8	15.3	30.7	4.2

Language sources Scientists tend to use material published in their own language before they use foreign-language sources. This analysis of citations is taken from an early study of English, French, and German journals in three fields during 1952. German authors cited German sources almost as much as English authors cited English sources. French authors used a wider range of sources – perhaps because there are fewer scientific publications in this language – but they still cited French work more frequently than did either of the other groups. Similar results have since been found in citation analyses of several other languages. (After C. M. Louttit, 1957.)

THREE WAYS OF TESTING THE QUALITY OF A TRANSLATION

- In *back-translation*, one translates a text from language A into language B; a different translator then turns the B text back into A, and the resulting A text is compared with the original A text. If the texts are virtually identical, it is strong evidence that the original translation was of high quality (though not incontrovertible evidence, because the second translator might have improved upon the work of the first in the reverse process).
- In *knowledge testing*, speakers of language B are tested about the content of the translation (e.g. using a questionnaire), and the same questions are put to speakers of A. If the results correspond, the translation must be efficient.
- In *performance testing*, speakers of language B are asked to carry out actions based on the text (e.g. in a repair manual), as are speakers of A. The results can then be compared to determine translation efficiency. This is a very time-consuming process, however, and requires expert supervision if clear results are to be obtained.

A good back-translation...

Original: Leaks occurring beyond relief valve could cause some indication of low oil pressure.

Back-translation: If oil is leaking at the outside of the pressure relief valve, it can activate the warning of oil low pressure.

... and a bad one

Original: Troubleshooting precautions.

Back-translation: Preventions while repairing. (R. W. Brislin, 1976, p. 10.)

TWAIN'S BACK-TRANSLATION

Mark Twain once complained that his sketch 'The Celebrated Jumping Frog of Calaveras County' had been unsuccessful in France because of a bad translation. He therefore carried out his own back-translation of the French text to prove his point.

Twain's original

'"Now, if you're ready, set him alongside of Dan'l, with his fore paws just even with Dan'l's, and I'll give the word." Then he says, "One – two – three – git!" and him and the feller touched up the frogs from behind, and the new frog hopped off lively, but Dan'l give a heave, and hysted up his shoulders – so – like a Frenchman, but it warn't no use.'

Twain's back-translation

'"Now if you be ready, put him all against Daniel, with their before-feet upon the same line, and I give the signal" – then he added: "One, two, three – advance!" Him and the individual touched their frogs by behind, and the frog new put to jump smartly, but Daniel himself lifted ponderously, exalted the shoulders thus, like a Frenchman – to what good?'

TRANSLITERATION

When the source language is written in a different script from the target language (§33), it is often necessary to provide a *transliteration* of an original word, rather than a translation – something commonly done with the names of people, places, institutions, and inventions. Here, each character of the source language is converted into a character of the target language; for example, Russian спутник 'companion, satellite' becomes *sputnik*.

Transliteration needs to be distinguished from *transcription*, in which the *sounds* of the source words are conveyed by letters in the target language. For example, an English transcription of Soviet premier Gorbachev's name would have to be *Gorbachoff*, to reflect the way it is pronounced in Russian. This approach is often unavoidable with languages that use partial alphabetic scripts (e.g. Arabic, p. 204), where transliteration would be very difficult, or logographic scripts (e.g. Japanese *kanji*, p. 202), where it would be impossible.

Both approaches have their problems. With transcriptions, the target equivalents are likely to differ when the words are converted into different languages, as in English *Tchaikovsky*, Dutch *Tsjaikowskij*, Hungarian *Csajkovszkij*. With transliterations, there is often the problem of there being insufficient symbols in the target language (so that diacritics have to be added) or too many symbols (in which case arbitrary choices have to be made). Arbitrariness is most noticeable when there is no close correspondence between the sounds of the source and target languages.

As a result, there are often several transliteration systems available, as has happened with Chinese (p. 314) and Russian (where, for example, the familiar form Khrushchev could appear as Xruščev, or in several other ways). In the absence of an internationally agreed scheme, it is often very difficult to trace terms and names in international indexes. A Russian name beginning with я might be transliterated into *ia*, *ja*, or *ya*, with major retrieval problems unless the conversion system is known.

ONLY A NAME...

Transliteration makes especial sense with foreign personal or brand names, where unfortunate consequences can result if a translation is used. For example, it would be risky to translate the name of the British chain of chemists, *Boots*, into some equivalent word for footwear in a foreign language, in case the connotations were harmful. The same risk applies in reverse, as when we encounter 'iceberg' as the name for certain textiles, or 'east wind' as the name of farm machinery – both examples of translations from Chinese. Hilarity or embarrassment accompanies names when they have taboo or risqué associations, such as Kräpp toilet tissue from Scandinavia, or Bimbo bread from Spain.

The problem is further complicated when western names are turned into logographic languages (p. 202). First the name has to be given a phonetic equivalent in the language. *Crystal*, for example, has been turned into Japanese as *Kuri-su-taru*. Each syllable, however, can be rendered by several characters, each with a different meaning. Several 'translations' of the name are therefore possible – some of which might be flattering, others insulting. (One meaning of *Crystal*, it seems, is 'chestnut-celebration-barrel'!) There are dictionaries which give lists of 'safe' equivalents for western names – usually by choosing rare characters, which prompt a phonetic rather than a semantic interpretation.

TRANSLITERATING RUSSIAN

One system of English equivalents for Russian letters. Over a third have alternatives.

Russian alphabet	English transliteration
а	a
б	b
в	v
г	g
д	d
е (ё)	e (ё)
ж	ž *or* zh
з	z
и	i
й	j *or* ĭ
к	k
л	l
м	m
н	n
о	o
п	p
р	r
с	s
т	t
у	u
ф	f
х	h *or* kh
ц	c *or* ts
ч	č *or* ch
ш	š *or* sh
щ	šč *or* shch
ъ	" *or* "
ы	y
ь	' *or* '
э	ė *or* é
ю	ju *or* yu
я	ja *or* ya

TERM BANKS

One of the most urgent contemporary needs is the international unification of terminology. If people are not to be perpetually at cross purposes, the terms used in instructional manuals, codes of practice, scientific research, government meetings, and many other situations need to be correlated and standardized. Scientific research, especially in rapidly developing areas such as medicine and computing, is particularly at risk, where work could easily be duplicated. Several efforts have therefore been made to organize data banks of terminology in various fields, using computational techniques of information storage and retrieval. For example, the European Union (EU) term bank, EURODICAUTOM (European Automatic Dictionary), is now publicly accessible on-line via Euronet, and containing terms in the official languages of the Community. Each term or abbreviation is listed along with a contextual example, equivalent items in other EU languages, a definition, and bibliographical references.

```
DO TERM
% P001 -DLL V-26
PRESS L FOR TERMINOLOGY OR X FOR ABBREVIATION
*L
TYPE CODE OF SOURCE LANGUAGE
DG GERMAN      DK DANISH      EG ENGLISH     FG FRENCH
IT ITALIAN     NG DUTCH       PT PORTUGUESE  SP SPANISH
*EG
TYPE CODE(S) OF TARGET LANGUAGE(S) WITH SINGLE SPACE BETWEEN
(FOR EXAMPLE: DG NG) OR A FOR ANY LANGUAGES
*A
SOURCE LANGUAGE     :EG
TARGET LANGUAGE(S) :DG IT FG NG DK SP PT
SUBJECT CODE        :
 PRESS Q OR ANOTHER COMMAND
*Q
TYPE YOUR QUESTION
*INFLATION
                                        DOC =    1 PAGE =   1
BE= BTM    TY= TFI74  NI= 0038128  DATE = 750220  CF= 4
     CM  EC4 ECB
EG VE  INFLATION
    PH  PRICE INFLATION IS MOST LIKELY TO OCCUR WHEN DEMAND
        INCREASES WHILE THE LABOUR SUPPLY IS TIGHT AND THE
        INDUSTRIAL CAPACITY IS FULLY UTILIZED...WHEN SOURCES OF
        SUPPLY DRY UP..
FG VE  INFLATION
    PH  EXCES DE POUVOIR D'ACHAT OU EXCES DES MOYENS DE PAIEMENT.
        ON LA CONFOND SOUVENT...AVEC LA SIMPLE HAUSSE DES PRIX.
        OR CELLE-CI EST LA CONSEQUENCE DE L'INFLATION ET NON DE
        L'INFLATION ELLE-MEME.
        PRESS C TO CONTINUE OR GIVE ANOTHER COMMAND
```

The result of an on-line search for the term *inflation* in EURODICAUTOM. Several steps are involved.
1. Does the enquirer require a term or an abbreviation (L or X)?
2. Which source and target languages are involved? (In the example, the source language was English, and all other EU languages were requested as targets.)
3. Is there a subject code, e.g. medicine, nuclear science? (None, in this case.)
4. The term is then typed in, and any listings are printed out (in this case, only an English and a French listing are available). The printout gives various details of sources, and the last occasion when the record was updated (date 750220, i.e. 20 February 1975). There is also a reliability code (CF) using a scale from 0 to 5.

FALSE FRIENDS

Words that look the same in two languages often do not mean the same thing. They are known as *faux amis* ('false friends'). Here are some French–English examples (* = wrong meaning).

abusif   *abusive/incorrect, excessive
achever   *achieve/finish (off)
avertissement *advertisement/warning
bande   *band/gang
carpette   *carpet/rug
demander   *demand/request
éventuel   *eventual/possible
fastidieux   *fastidious/tiresome
idiome   *idiom/language (of a group)
incohérent   *incoherent/inconsistent
inconvénient *inconvenient/drawback
information *information/news
lard   *lard/bacon
libeller   *libel/make out a cheque
partition   *partition/musical score
pétulant   *petulant/lively
phrase   *phrase/sentence
pourpre   *purple/crimson
prétendre   *pretend/claim
prune   *prune/plum
résumer   *resume/summarize
rogue   *roguish/arrogant
sensible   *sensible/sensitive
sommaire   *summary/contents list
starter (car) *starter/choke
sympathique *sympathetic/agreeable
truculent   *truculent/realistic
verbe   *verb/word
veste   *vest/jacket
vivace   *vivacious/hard-wearing
(P. Thody & H. Evans, 1985.)

And a few others...
German *also* = therefore
Spanish *constipado* = having a head cold
Danish *øl* = beer
Italian *caldo* = warm
Polish *karawan* = funeral procession

TRANSLATION SHIFTS

The French definite article, *le/la/l'/les* is usually thought of as the equivalent of the English definite article *the*. However, there are many exceptions to this rule, where the translation 'shifts' from one form to another. *La* is translated by 'a' in *Il a la jambe cassée* 'He has a broken leg' and *l'* can become zero in *l'amour* 'love'. In a study of French articles found in French texts with English translations, the various possible equivalences were worked out. The table shows that *le* is equivalent to *the* in only 64.6% of all cases. *Du* 'of the' is translated by zero (no article at all) more than half the time. *Un* 'a' has the best rating, with 70%. (After R. Huddleston, in J. C. Catford, 1965, p. 81.)

French	English				
	zero	the	some	a	(other)
zero	**67.7**	6.1	0.3	11.2	14.6
le	14.2	**64.6**	–	2.4	18.9
du	**51.3**	9.5	11.0	5.9	22.4
un	6.7	5.8	2.2	**70.2**	15.1

BEST TRANSLATIONS?

A great deal can be learned about the art and craft of translating by comparing cases where different people have translated the same text. The following versions of the opening verse of Baudelaire's *L'Albatros* shows the different attention paid to form and content in the varying treatment of rhyme, rhythm, word order, and lexical choice.

Souvent, pour s'amuser, les hommes d'équipage
Prennent des albatros, vastes oiseaux des mers,
Qui suivent, indolents compagnons de voyage,
Le navire glissant sur les gouffres amers.

Often to amuse themselves, the men of the crew trap albatrosses, the great sea-birds, that follow the ship slipping over the bitter deeps, like idle travelling companions.

(A. Hartley)

Often, for their amusement, sailors catch albatross, those vast birds of the sea, indolent companion of their voyages, that follow the ship gliding across the bitter depths.

(F. Scarfe)

In order to amuse themselves, the members of the crew often catch albatrosses, those huge sea-birds which, as indolent companions on the voyage, follow the ship gliding over the bitter depths.

(I. F. Finlay)

Sometimes, sailors to amuse themselves
catch albatrosses, great birds of the sea,
which as companions follow indolently
the vessel gliding over bitter gulfs.

(C. F. MacIntyre)

Sometimes for sport the men of loafing crews
Snare the great albatrosses of the deep,
The indolent companions of their cruise
As through the bitter vastitudes they sweep.

(R. Campbell)

In sport a vessel's crew will often take
The mighty albatross, who on the breeze
Doth idly sail and follow in the wake
Of ships that glide upon the bitter seas.

(A. Conder)

Often, as an amusement, crewmen
Catch albatrosses, huge birds of the sea,
Who follow, indolent companions of the voyage,
The ship gliding over the salty deeps.

(W. Fowlie)

(From I. F. Finlay, 1971, pp. 129–32.)

TRANSLATING NAMES

Mari, Mary, Marie, Marenka, Marinka, Marienka, Maruska, Mara, Mana, Maruse, Marka, Marena ...

The problem facing the literary translator is well illustrated by this list of names, which are just some of the ways of translating 'Mary' in Czech, each expressing its own mood and level of intimacy. English has no such range of expressions; the nearest, Marie and Maria, are thought of as different names. For everyday translational purposes, it may not be important to convey such exact distinctions in an English version; but in translating literary texts, nuances of this kind often need close attention.

WHEN FOREIGN IS BEST

Sometimes it pays *not* to translate, as the business world has long known. Sales can benefit if a product is given a foreign name. In 1960 a Finnish firm distributed tinned coffee for the home market using Finnish labels. Sales were poor. The firm then had new labels made with a text in English on the same tins, and sales rocketed. Similarly, English marketing firms and other businesses make use of foreign languages to convey special effects – such as the use of French for the names of restaurants, night-clubs, and perfumes. In one page of a British telephone directory, under 'Restaurants', nearly half the names were in a language other than English – *La Bella Napoli, Le Patron, Les Deux R, Les Quatre Saisons, Mamma Mia, Maison Romano, Que Pasa, Rendez-vouz, Roma, Santa Lucia, Shangri-La...*

The culture that seems to make most use of foreign languages as a part of business enterprise is Japanese. Here, a wide variety of foreign names is used, depending on the particular quality of the product the manufacturer wishes to stress. In the field of car names, for example, English is used in order to convey an impression of good quality and reliability (e.g 'Crown'). If elegance is to be stressed, a French name is chosen (e.g. 'Ballade'). A sports car often has an Italian name (e.g. 'Leone').

The linguistic effects are most noticeable in television commercials, where appropriate American, French, etc. settings are used along with the foreign language (without translation). Japan is the only monolingual country to make frequent use of foreign languages (primarily English and French) in its commercials. The viewer usually does not understand them, but the connotations of prestige associated with these languages are enough to warrant their use. The purpose of the language (§4) is not to communicate ideas, but to appeal to the sensibilities of the Japanese viewer, who the manufacturers believe is much influenced by the values of modern cosmopolitan society.

FOREIGN ELEMENTS IN JAPANESE COMMERCIALS

English
Terrific, everybody, new, life, now, healthy, power, big, sale, open, happy, nice, beautiful, night, extra.

French
Plaisir 'pleasure', *image* 'image', *café* 'coffee', *printemps* 'spring', *chocolat* 'chocolate', *accessoire* 'accessory'.

German
Auslese 'selection', *schick* 'chic', *schön* 'beautiful', *Sahne* 'cream', *Wagen* 'car'.

Italian
Carina 'sweetheart', *manifesto* 'manifest', *buongiorno* 'good morning'.

Spanish
Olé 'hey', *domingo* 'Sunday', *bonita* 'pretty'.

Combinations of words are also common, such as *high quality, happy smoking time, light and smooth, quick and overnight service, la mesure d'élégance* 'the standard of elegance', *nouvel coloris* 'new shade'. Whole sentences may be used, such as *Je suis une femme qui aime la vie* 'I am a woman who loves life' (spoken by a Japanese woman), *We want you to win, Get action on your car.* There may even be combinations of English and French (e.g. *bon shop, santé soft*) or a foreign language plus Japanese (e.g. *soft kapuseru* 'soft capsule', *auto wakkusu* 'auto wax', p. 197). (After H. Haarman, 1984.)

SOME JAPANESE CAR NAMES

Daihatsu	*Nissan*	*Toyota*
Domino	Bluebird	Camry
Charade	Cherry	Carina
Charmant	Laurel	Celica
	Micra	Corolla
	Patrol	Corona
	Prairie	Cressida
	Silvia	Starlet
	Stanza	Tercel
	Sunny	
	Violet	

INTERPRETING

Interpreting is today widely known from its use in international political life (p. 344). When senior ministers from different language backgrounds meet, the television record invariably shows a pair of interpreters hovering in the background. At major conferences, such as the United Nations General Assembly, the presence of headphones is a clear indication that a major linguistic exercise is taking place. In everyday circumstances, too, interpreters are frequently needed, especially in cosmopolitan societies formed by new generations of immigrants and *Gastarbeiter* (§9). Often, the business of law courts, hospitals, local health clinics, classrooms, or industrial tribunals cannot be carried on without the presence of an interpreter. Given the importance and frequency of this task, therefore, it is remarkable that so little study has been made of what actually happens when interpreting takes place, and of how successful an exercise it is.

Doubtless the recency of developments in the field partly explains this neglect. One procedure, known as *consecutive* interpreting, is very old – and presumably dates from the Tower of Babel! Here, the interpreter translates after the speaker has finished speaking (either in short bursts, or at the very end of a discourse). This approach is widely practised in informal situations, as well as in committees and small conferences. In larger and more formal settings, however, it has been generally replaced by *simultaneous* interpreting – a recent development that arose from the availability of modern audiological equipment and the advent of increased international interaction following the Second World War.

Of the two procedures, it is the second that has attracted most interest, because of the complexity of the task and the remarkable skills required. In no other context of human communication is anyone routinely required to listen and speak at the same time, preserving an exact semantic correspondence between the two modes. Moreover, there is invariably a delay of a few words between the stimulus and the response, because of the time it takes to assimilate what is being said in the source language and to translate it into an acceptable form in the target language. This 'ear–voice span' (p. 147) is usually about 2 or 3 seconds, but it may be as much as 10 seconds or so, if the text is complex. The brain has to remember what has just been said, attend to what is currently being said, and anticipate the construction of what is about to be said. As one writer has put it:

As you start a sentence you are taking a leap in the dark, you are mortgaging your grammatical future; the original sentence may suddenly be turned in such a way that your translation of its end cannot easily be reconciled with your translation of its start. Great nimbleness is called for to guide the mind through this syntactical maze, whilst at the same time it is engaged upon the work of word-translation.
(R. Glemet, in D. Gerver, 1976, p. 168)

How it is all done is not at all clear. That it is done at all is a source of some wonder, given the often lengthy periods of interpreting required, the confined environment of an interpreting booth, the presence of background noise, and the awareness that major decisions may depend upon the accuracy of the work. Research projects have now begun to look at these factors – to determine, for example, how far successful interpreting is affected by poor listening conditions, or the speed at which the source language is spoken. It seems that an input speed of between 100 and 120 words per minute is a comfortable rate for interpreting, with an upper limit of around 200 w.p.m. But even small increases in speed can dramatically affect the accuracy of output. In one controlled study, when speeds were gradually increased in a series of stages from 95 to 164 w.p.m., the ear–voice span also increased with each stage, and the amount correctly interpreted showed a clear decline (D. Gerver, 1969). Also, as the translating load increases, not only are there more errors of commission (mistranslations, cases of vagueness replacing precision), there are also more errors of omission, as words and segments of meaning are filtered out. These are important findings, given the need for accuracy in international communication. What is needed is a more detailed identification of the problem areas, and of the strategies speakers, listeners, and interpreters use to solve them. There is urgent need to expand what has so far been one of the most neglected fields of communication research.

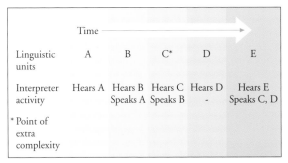

	Time →				
Linguistic units	A	B	C*	D	E
Interpreter activity	Hears A	Hears B Speaks A	Hears C Speaks B	Hears D -	Hears E Speaks C, D
* Point of extra complexity					

THE EAR–VOICE SPAN

When the input language is straightforward, the interpreter will be a regular 2 or 3 seconds behind the speaker. But when an unexpected textual difficulty emerges, or the speaker suddenly speeds up, the delay may increase, with a consequential 'knock-on' effect that may take some time to resolve. During this period, when the ear–voice span is several seconds long, the interpreter's cognitive linguistic processing abilities are under great pressure.

A common linguistic reason for interpreting delay occurs when translating from a language where the verb occurs at the end of the sentence (SOV languages, §14) into a language where the verb occurs in the middle (SVO languages). The interpreter often has to wait until the speaker gets to the end of the sentence before it is possible to translate the intervening material. The problem occurs in the case of translating Japanese into English, and, notoriously, in translating German subordinate clauses.

MACHINE TRANSLATION

The idea of using machines to provide translations between natural languages has been recognized since the 1930s, but an appropriate climate for development did not arise until the years following the Second World War. At that time, the rise of information theory, the success of advanced code-breaking techniques (p. 58), and the invention of the electronic computer all indicated that machine translation (MT) could be a reality. Warren Weaver, a founder of the field, caught the optimism in a 1947 memorandum: 'One naturally wonders if the problem of translation could conceivably be treated as a problem of cryptography. When I look at an article in Russian, I say: "This is really written in English, but it has been coded in some strange symbols. I will now proceed to decode." ' As a result, several groups began research programmes into MT during the 1950s, and great claims were made for the future of the subject (W. Weaver, 1955).

However, initial results were not encouraging. The systems proved to be very limited in the kind of data they could handle. Translations were crude, full of errors, and required so much human post-editing that they proved to be more expensive than having a human translator carry out the whole task in the first place. The main reason was the lack of a sufficiently sophisticated linguistic theory to provide a frame of reference for the tasks that MT needed to undertake. The earliest MT system did little more than look for equivalences between the words in each language – in effect, they acted as an automatic bilingual dictionary. After several decades of linguistic research, it is easy to see why these approaches could not have worked. They ignored the problem posed by the grammatical dimension of language analysis – the different levels of syntactic organization (§16), and the absence of straightforward formal correspondences between units of grammar (such as is illustrated by the use of the definite article, p. 349). They also ignored the different ways in which languages structure meaning: word-for-word translation is often not possible and usually not desirable (p. 346). Nor was there any way of distinguishing between the different senses of words or deciding whether a group of words was an idiom. Many ambiguities can be resolved only by using an analysis in terms of semantics (§17) or of real-world knowledge, and such analyses were not available at that time. There was evidently a great deal more to MT than 'code breaking'.

The dissatisfaction was summarized in a US report of 1966 by the Automatic Language Processing Advisory Committee (ALPAC), which concluded that human translating was faster, more accurate, and less expensive than MT, and that no further support for the latter should be provided. As a consequence, only a minimal amount of MT research was carried on in subsequent years, either in the USA or in Europe (though continued support was provided in the Soviet Union).

A NEW MOOD

The pendulum has begun to swing back again in recent years, following the major intellectual and technological developments of the 1970s in linguistics (§65) and computing. A new mood is abroad, promoted by the promising practical achievements of new commercial MT projects, by the great potential of the new research programmes in artificial intelligence, and by an increased theoretical awareness of the translation task which has come from progress in linguistics. There is also a greater realism concerning what MT can and cannot do, and a recognition of the need to devise techniques of human/machine collaboration, in order to get the best results from both. The main developments have been to provide systems of analysis that allow for grammatical and semantic complexity. The first steps were in devising automatic procedures ('algorithms') for parsing the syntactic structure of a sentence, and for carrying out an

A PRE-EDITED TRANSLATION

The extract below speaks for itself. It has been pre-edited in Hong Kong on the Chinese University Language Translator (CULT), a system used for the automatic translation of Chinese journal papers in mathematics and physics into English. There are very few places where further editing is necessary – but this has to be balanced against the amount of pre-editing time involved. There is also the point that the amount of pre-editing will vary, depending on the structural similarity between the languages.

A fixed set of pre-editing rules must therefore be formulated to enable inexperienced and even monolingual people to transform quickly the input into machine-translatable form. With this arrangement, post-editing can be kept to a minimum, if not all together eliminated. Given time and better programming techniques, these pre-editing rules will gradually be reduced so that the computer will eventually take up this routine work. Pre-editing can therefore solve many of the present linguistic problems that are otherwise dependent on further research in natural language, computational linguistics and transformation mathematics. In other words, models that are much more comprehensive and sophisticated than the present ones have to be designed. These models may take years to perfect and, at present, pre-editing is absolutely essential in order to achieve the goal. In present stage of our development, very complex sentences can be translated with the aid of pre-editing. A sentence which has a complicated structure can be analysed by the existing program if it is broken up into simpler sentences which are then readily translated by the computer. Sentences in Chinese are often without verbs or subjects and pre-editing can add the verbs or subjects so that these sentences can thus be analysed and translated. (S. C. Loh, 1976, p. 108.)

SYSTRAN

One of the best-known first-generation MT systems, SYSTRAN, was developed in the U.S. with particular reference to Russian–English translation – for example, it was used to translate Russian into English during the Apollo–Soyuz space project. It later came to be used by the EEC for a limited range of purposes (such as abstract searches) with certain languages (mainly French). Its future status is unclear, in view of the emergence of more powerful, second-generation systems, such as EUROTRA.

Russian-English
An extract follows, showing the kind of output produced by SYSTRAN, and the kind of post-editing required to produce an acceptable translation. The numbers in the Russian transliteration have been inserted by the computer to represent Cyrillic letters not found in the computer's (Latin-based) character set.

Original
Sovremenny1 a3roport predstavl4et sobo1 slojny1 kompleks injenernyx sooru-

jeni1, texniceskix sredstv, dl4 razme5eni4 kotorogo trebuets4 territori4, izmer4ema4 v otdel6nyx sluca4x tys4cami gektarov (naprimer moskovski1 a3roport Domodedovo, H6h-1orkski1 a3roport Kennedi).

Raw SYSTRAN output
A contemporary airport is the involved complex of engineer constructions and techniques, for arrangement of which the territory, measured sometimes is required by thousands of hectares (for example the

Moscow Airport Domodedovo, Kennedy's New York Airport).

Revised output
The modern airport is an elaborate complex of engineering structures and technical devices requiring a large territory, which, in some cases, measures thousands of hectares (for instance, Domodedovo Airport in Moscow or Kennedy Airport in New York). (F. Knowles, 1979, p. 130.)

analysis of word-structure. An automatic morphological analysis (p. 90) was particularly necessary to enable the computer to find words in its dictionary memory: *cats*, for example, would have to have its ending removed, in order to locate the base form *cat*. The problem is not very great for English, which uses few endings, but it is a major issue for languages that rely more on inflections.

Later developments have begun to introduce semantic information into the procedure, and to use artificial intelligence techniques to simulate human thought processes ('knowledge-based MT'). If the computer is given enough data on the meaning of words and about the context of a sentence, it is argued, it should be able to work out for itself what analysis to make in cases where individual words or sentences are ambiguous. The computer, like the human reader, should be able to use inference routines, and look back at the preceding discourse in order to check its interpretation of a point. The principle is undeniable, but it has proved extremely difficult so far to write programs that can handle more than fragments of discourse and take account of such matters as pronoun cross-reference (p. 119). The advent of special programming languages, designed to handle the properties of natural language in a more direct way, will facilitate the task; but it will take many years before the pure research results in routine commercial applications. Research in natural language processing (p. 416) and the development of large corpus descriptions (p. 415) will also add a new dimension to MT research, allowing a much more detailed and extensive application of MT methods than has previously been possible.

In the meantime, increasing use is being made of 'interactive' systems of MT, in which human beings pre-edit or postedit the text that the computer processes. In pre-editing, a natural language source text is rewritten, using a controlled syntax and vocabulary, to produce a version that the computer can handle with relative ease. This procedure is practicable only in restricted situations (such as scientific abstracting), because of the large expenditure of time and training required to prepare the input; but it has produced successful translations in several cases. In postediting, 'raw' machine-produced data in the target language is edited into an error-free text – also a time-consuming procedure, and one that is often tedious and time wasting (because the human translator may have to duplicate a great deal of the computer's work in order to eliminate an error). However, there are several levels of quality possible in postediting, ranging from a basic 'threshold' level of intelligibility to a highly polished style. If the most basic editing steps only are undertaken, the gains in translation speed can be very great. But the choice, of speed vs quality, is not always an easy one to make.

THE FUTURE

It is unlikely that machines will replace human translators in the forseeable future; but they can already help to take a great deal of the drudgery out of routine translation work, and enable far more material to be processed than would otherwise be the case. Firms such as Automated Language Processing Systems (ALPS) or Weidner Communications now have systems that can process quantities of scientific text in certain areas at rates of up to 14,000 words per hour – which, even after editing, produces a rate of over 1,000 w.p.h., several times faster than is possible 'by hand'. There is also the rapidly developing world of 'machine-aided translation' – the use of computationally organized data banks and all kinds of peripheral equipment to help translators in their work. A word processor can save enormously on the production of translation drafts, for example; and a great deal of time can be saved if the translator has on-line access to a term bank (p. 349) to discover the 'best' equivalent for a source-language word (instead of having to engage in a slow hunt for it through dated dictionaries). More and more people are finding that the benefits outweigh the disadvantages, and this in turn adds to the mood of optimism that pervades current MT debate. New techniques are being established, such as: incorporating the results of post-editing experience into the system; using inductive techniques of pattern-matching and probability to provide an MT system with a knowledge-base derived from real texts; and devising 'sublanguages', with reduced syntax and lexicon, so that texts can be prepared which will work within the constraints of a system (cf. the notions of restricted language and Nuclear English, pp. 56, 360). For many years the MT world has been quite a small one, with few research programmes and commercial organizations involved. This situation is now dramatically changing.

TELEPHONE TRANSLATION

The automatic translation of telephone conversations, using fifth-generation computers, should be a reality by AD 2000, according to proposals made by the Japanese Ministry of Posts and Telecommunications in 1985. If Japan were to undertake the development alone, it was estimated to take about 15 years at a cost of 400 million dollars. Japan has therefore suggested joint development proposals with several countries, in the interests of saving time and money, the first agreement (with France) being reached in 1985.

MT output These extracts use a German–English system marketed by the Logos Corporation in the Federal Republic of Germany. The original, taken from a construction contract, is shown along with the raw MT output and the post-edited output.

Post-edited output:
Stair repair work.
Repair main entrance step at all buildings as follows:
1. Carefully remove complete shoe scraper frames.
2. Repair damages which have resulted from removal of shoe scraper with epoxy cement mortar.
3. Scrape out cracks in step and repair with epoxy cement mortar.
4. Scrape out cracks between step and building approx. 1 cm–5 cm wide, and repair with epoxy cement mortar.

Raw MT output:
Stair repair work.
Main entrance step at all buildings such as follows repair:
1. Carefully completely expand door mat frame.
2. Repair damages which have resulted by developing the door mat with epoxy cement mortar.
3. Scrape rents in the level and repair with epoxy cement mortar.
4. Approximately scrape rents between level and building one CM broadly to 5 CM and repair with epoxy cement mortar.

Original text:
Treppenreparaturarbeiten.
Haupteingangsstufe an allen Gebäuden wie folgt reparieren:
1. Fußabstreiferrahmen sorgfältig komplett ausbauen.
2. Beschädigungen, die durch den Ausbau des Fußabstreifers entstanden sind, mit kunststoffvergütetem Zementmörtel ausbessern.
3. Risse in der Stufe auskratzen und mit kunstsoffvergütetem Zementmörtel ausbessern.
4. Risse zwischen Stufe and Gebäude ca. 1 cm bis 5 cm breit auskratzen und mit kunststoffvergütetem Zementmörtel ausbessern.

Many people believe that the foreign-language barrier can be surmounted through the use of an 'artificial' language (AL) – a language which has been specially invented to facilitate international communication. The term 'auxiliary language' is often preferred, especially by AL supporters who find the connotations of 'artificial' too limiting. In particular, Esperantists (p. 356) feel that their language is highly developed in the range of functions it can perform, and is also natural, to the extent that these days several children have had it introduced to them as a mother tongue. However, 'auxiliary' is by no means restricted to ALs; it is also used to refer to natural languages that have been chosen to aid communication within a special domain (e.g. the use of English or French at international conferences). 'Artificial' thus continues to be a widely used designation.

ALs are commonly divided into two types (though several projects in fact display features of both). The first type uses an invented set of elements – often numbers or special symbols – that stand for basic concepts; these are then grouped into a logical (and supposedly universal) classification, based on scientific or philosophical principles. These *a priori* languages were particularly common in the 17th century, but proposals along these lines have continued to be made at intervals ever since. By contrast, *a posteriori* languages are based on elements drawn from natural languages – invariably from one or more of the languages of Western Europe. Most ALs that have been devised in the last century belong to this second type. A further division is also sometimes made, within the latter category, between those ALs that do not allow for exceptions (e.g. Esperanto) and those that are closer to existing natural languages, permitting some degree of irregularity (e.g. Occidental).

HISTORICAL BACKGROUND

Several hundred ALs have been recorded, and new ones continue to be devised. The desire for a universal language can be traced back to Classical times, but the idea began to flourish only in the 17th century, when world exploration brought to light many new languages, and Latin began to fall from favour as a universal medium. Francis Bacon (1561–1626) was one of the first to ask whether things could be represented by 'real characters' that would be understood regardless of language, instead of the usual letters or sounds. Detailed systems were devised by Wilkins, Dalgarno, Leibniz, Comenius, and several others. It was an age when symbol systems of all kinds stimulated curiosity, especially those that seemed to express concepts directly – music, numerals, ideograms (§33), shorthand (p. 208), and cryptography (p. 58). However, all

An extract from *An essay towards a real character and a philosophical language* (1668) by Bishop John Wilkins (1614–72). Wilkins's approach classified all ideas and things into 40 basic types, or genera (e.g. herbs, fish, sickness). Each genus was symbolized by a consonant and vowel (for speech) and by a written sign. Different items within a genus were then identified through the use of extra consonants or vowels or by additional written strokes.

An extract from the first universal language scheme, Francis Lodwick's *A Common Writing: whereby two, although not understanding one the others language, yet by the helpe thereof, may communicate their minds one to another* (1647). A basic set of 'radical' words was selected (e.g. *drink*), and each assigned a character. Related words were shown by the addition of special marks.

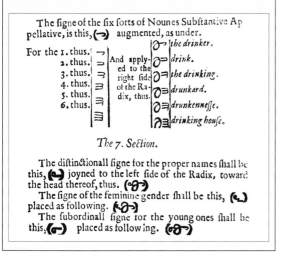

The 7. Section.

The Lords Prayer.

Hai coba ૪૪ ia ril dad, ha babi io fஅymta, ha falba io velca, ha talbi io vemg૪, m૪ ril dady me ril dad io velpi ral ai ril i poto hai faba vaty, na io fᖆeldy૪s lal ai hai balgas me ai ia fᖆeldy૪s lal ei ૪૪ ia valgas rᖆ ai na mi io velco ai, ral bedodl૪ nil io cᖆalbo ai lal vagasie, nor ai falba, na ai tado, na ai tadala ia ha pi૪by૪ ꝚꞀ m૪ io.

the invented systems, though simple, logical, and plausible at the outset, became extremely arbitrary and complicated as they were developed. As the illustrations show, the learner was presented with a virtually impossible memory load, and a rigid classification within which it proved difficult to incorporate new knowledge.

For such reasons, *a priori* schemes fell out of favour at the end of the 17th century. They had a revival a century later, with the rise of the 'general grammar' movement (p. 84), which aimed to discover universal principles of thought behind the variety of grammatical forms in language. There was much more at stake here than international communication: it was felt that a good philosophy of signs, or 'ideology', would help to eliminate vagueness and ambiguity from language, provide a better vehicle for thought, and be a more efficient means of spreading knowledge. But the resurgence of interest was short-lived. By the mid-19th century, there was little active support, and since then the vast majority of AL proposals have been *a posteriori* in character.

In the last quarter of the 19th century, there was another flurry of enthusiasm, with several AL proposals competing with each other for public support. The first large-scale movement was Volapük, followed closely by Esperanto, Idiom Neutral, Ido, and several dozen other systems. In 1924, the International Auxiliary Language Association was formed in New York, focusing on the promotion of common vocabulary between the various systems. Most of the proposals have had very short lives, but some, such as Esperanto, have achieved an impressive international use.

Since the turn of the century, an enormous amount of time, energy, money, and ingenuity has been expended on the invention and dissemination of AL proposals. In the early years they were usually seen by their supporters as a key to a world of mutual understanding, clearer thinking, and peaceful coexistence. The use of a common language does not guarantee peace, however, as is plain from terrorist activity in many parts of the world. In recent years, therefore, there has been a tendency to adopt less ambitious goals, and there have been several local successes, with different countries and organizations (especially on the Continent of Europe) being persuaded to introduce an AL dimension into aspects of their daily life – in hotels, telephone boxes, telegrams, advertisements, and timetables. Even with the most successful of these movements, however, very limited progress has been made towards the goal of an internationally recognized and universally used auxiliary language.

A CENTURY OF ARTIFICIAL LANGUAGES

Language	Inventor	Date	Comment
Volapük ('World Language')	Johann Martin Schleyer	1880	8 vowels, 20 consonants; based largely on English and German (p. 302).
Esperanto ('Lingvo Internacia')	Ludwig Lazarus Zamenhof	1887	5 vowels, 23 consonants, mainly West European lexicon; Slavonic influence on syntax and spelling (p. 302).
Idiom Neutral	V. K. Rosenberger	1902	A former supporter of Volapük; strongly influenced by Romance (p. 303).
Latino Sine Flexione (Interlingua)	Giuseppe Peano	1903	Latin without inflections; vocabulary mainly from Latin words.
Ido	Louis de Beaufront or Louis Couturat	1907	A modified version of Esperanto (the name means 'derived from' in Esperanto).
Occidental	Edgar von Wahl	1922	Devised for the western world only; largely based on Romance.
Novial	Otto Jespersen	1928	Mainly Ido vocabulary and Occidental grammar. Novial = New + *I*nternational *A*uxiliary *L*anguage.
Interglossa	Lancelot Hogben	1943	Published only in draft form.
Interlingua	International Auxiliary Language Association	1951	A Romance-based grammar, with a standardized vocabulary based on the main Western European languages.
Glosa	W. Ashby and R. Clark	1981	A modified version of Interglossa. Contains a basic 1,000-word vocabulary, derived from Latin and Greek roots.

And a selection of other projects

Perio (1904), Lingua Internacional (1905), Ekselsioro (1906), Ulla (1906), Mondlingvo (1906), Lingwo Internaciona (Antido) (1907), Mez-Voio (1908), Romanizat (1908), Romanal (1909), Latin-Esperanto (1911), Europeo (1914), Nepo (1915), Hom Idyomo (1921), Espido (1923), Néo (1937), Esperantuisho (1955), Globaqo (1956), Modern Esperanto (1958), Delmondo (1960), Utoki (1962), Eurolengo (1972), Uropi (1986).

SOLRESOL

This remarkable language was the invention of a French music master, Jean François Sudre, at the beginning of the 19th century. Solresol, or 'Langue Musicale Universelle', was based on the principle that the tones of music, as named in the seven-note diatonic scale (do, re, mi, fa, sol, la, si), could be used as the elemental syllables of a universal language.

Two-note combinations were used for grammatical words, e.g. *si* 'yes', *do* 'no', *re* 'and', *dore* 'I', *domi* 'you'. Common words used three-note combinations, e.g. *doredo* 'time', *doremi* 'day', *dorefa* 'week', *doresol* 'month', *dorela* 'year', *doresi* 'century'. Four-note combinations were divided into different classes (or 'keys'), each one being based on a particular note. 'La', for example, was used for the field of industry and commerce. Over 9,000 five-note combinations were used for the names of animals, vegetables, and minerals. Semantic opposites were often expressed by reversing the order of syllables, e.g. *misol* 'good' vs *solmi* 'evil'.

The unique feature of this AL is that it could be played, whistled, or sung, as well as spoken! It became very popular in the mid-19th century, and won several prizes. As with all *a priori* languages, it was difficult to learn, and, with so few sounds permitted, it must have sounded extremely monotonous. However, it still had some supporters at the beginning of the present century, and thus proved to be one of the longest surviving artificial languages.

KLINGON

tlhIngan Hol Dojatlh'a'
(Do you speak Klingon?)

The official language of the Klingon Empire, and the only known intergalactic language, invented by Marc Okrand for the 1984 film, Star Trek III. There is now a Klingon dictionary of 1,500 words, an outline grammar (it is an OVS language, p. 98), conversational course material, and a growing body of enthusiasts on the Internet.

ESPERANTO

The best-known of all ALs, Esperanto, was the invention of a Polish oculist, Ludwig Lazarus Zamenhof (1859–1917). The scheme was first published in Russian in 1887 under the title *Mezhdunarodny yazyk* ('An international language') using the pseudonym 'Doktoro Esperanto' ('Doctor Hopeful'). The language was called 'Lingvo Internacia', but the name 'Esperanto' quickly caught on, and in due course became the official title. The first Esperanto journal (*La Esperantisto*) was published in 1889, and the First Universal Congress of Esperanto was held in 1905, bringing together nearly 700 delegates from 20 countries. That year also saw the publication of the *Fundamento de Esperanto*, an authoritative statement of the language's structure and vocabulary, which was to be the 'obligatory basis for Esperantists of all time'.

Today Esperanto is frequently encountered at international conferences. Several journals and newspapers are published in the language, and there is a large translated literature, including the Bible and the Qur'an. There is extensive original work in the language, and several countries transmit radio broadcasts in Esperanto. In the 1970s, it was said to be taught in over 600 schools and 31 universities around the world. Estimates vary greatly about the number of fluent speakers (as with any language (§48)), from less than 1 million to over 15 million, almost all being second-language speakers, at various levels of proficiency. By 1972, there were over 60 states with a national association, and over 1,250 local societies. However, membership is often low, and usually does not provide a clear guide to the number of speakers. In 1979, the World Esperanto Association had around 31,000 members, most being in Eastern Europe (especially Bulgaria, Poland, the Czech and Slovak Republics, and Hungary). Japan is the main non-European country with Esperanto speakers.

Esperanto has still to achieve official status as an international language. A proposal to the United Nations in 1966 was signed by nearly a million people from 74 countries, but was not accepted. There is a great deal of opposition from those who favour English as a world language, and from supporters of other ALs. There are also objections on political grounds, because of the language's East European background and the present-day trend by many organizations (of varying political or religious views) to use Esperanto as a language of international propaganda. However, it was used in 1994 by such diverse public figures as the Pope (in his Easter message) and pop-star Michael Jackson (in a video launching a new CD), and several politicians have come to support its use as a 'bridge' language (p. 344).

La Reĝa Pavilono. La konstruaĵo estas aktuale restaŭrata, tiel ke parto de la ekstero povas esti kaŝita kaj kelkaj salonoj povas esti provizore fermitaj.

Brighton kaj Hove

Brighton kaj Hove estas la ĉefa feriurbo de Britujo. Ĝi situas nur unu horon for de Londono, kaj pro sia pozicio, sia historio, sia marbordo, sia kulturo, kaj siaj modernaj distraĵoj estas ideala kiel loko por ferio en Anglujo, aŭ kiel centro por rondvojaĝo tra Britujo kaj Eŭropo, ne gravas en kiu sezono de la jaro. Ĉiam ĝia situacio estis la ŝlosilo de ĝia reputacio kaj prospero. Situanta ĉe la suda marbordo, kun vetero inter la plej bela de Britujo, ĝi rigardas en unu direkto al la maro kaj al Francujo (distanca kvar horojn per ŝipo) kaj en la alia direkto al Londono (distanca nur unu horon per ŝoseo aŭ per fervojo). Jam ducent jarojn ĝi estas la brituja centro de distriĝo, modo, kaj bona stilo ĉemara.

La Princo-Regento estis persono ekstravaganca, kies ekscesojn senkulpigis lia facila ĉarmo kaj bela konduto. Li konstruigis en la urbo eksterordinaran somerpalacon, kiu fariĝis centro de distriĝo, eleganto kaj bona tono, ecoj pro kiuj Brajtono estas de tiam daŭre konata. Liaj amikoj kaj kortego sekvis, kaj granda proporcio de la bela tiuepoka arkitekturo de la urbo rezultis el ilia amo de Brajtono. Ili difinis stilon kaj etoson, kies influo restas ĝis la hodiaŭo – etoson, kiun tiuj perceptos la vizitanto.

La Reĝa Pavilono, la propra palaco de la Princo-Regento, estis kompletigita en 1823. Kreite je tre alta kosto, ĝi prezentas unike imponajn historiajn asociojn, per kiuj hindaj kaj orientaj influoj estas fanditaj kun la forta brita tradicio. Multaj el la mebloj tie videblaj venas el la rezidejo de la Reĝino, Palaco Buckingham kaj Kastelo Windsor. Ankaŭ aliloke, tra la tuta Brighton kaj Hove, la grandiozo de la Regenta periodo (la frua 19-a jarcento) estas ĝaluze konservata en belegaj krescentoj (stratoj en formo de lunarko) kaj avenuoj, ĉirkaŭitaj de parkoj kaj ĝardenoj, kiujn admiras vizitantoj el la tuta mondo.

Supera stilo

Brighton (Brajtono) origine estis malgranda fiŝista vilaĝo kun la nomo Brighthelmstone. Ek de ĉirkaŭ la jaro 1750 estis rekonataj la sanigaj kvalitoj de ĝia maravko. Fariĝis laŭmode ĝin viziti, ĉar ĝi estis facile atingebla per kaleŝo el Londono. Ĝia prospero estis certigita kiam la Princo-Regento, la estonta Reĝo Georgo IV, enamiĝis al la urbo.

Part of a tourist information brochure about Brighton, England, published by the British Tourist Authority.

Ludwig Zamenhof Zamenhof's first drafts of an international language were made when he was 15. His own language background was very mixed: Russian was used at home, with Yiddish, Polish, and Hebrew (in the synagogue) outside, and French, German, Latin, Greek, and English taught in school. In his later life, he advocated a world religion, which he called *Homaranismo* ('member of the human race'), dedicated to peace, tolerance, and the unity of peoples. Ironically, this ideal was the cause of a split within the Esperantist movement, many members wishing to stress the practical value of the language rather than its religious significance.

THE STRUCTURE OF ESPERANTO

Sixteen grammatical rules (§16) have been explicitly laid down.
1. *La* is the only article.
2. All nouns end in -*o*; plurals add -*j*. There are two cases, nominative and objective – the latter ending in -*n*. Other meanings are expressed by prepositions.
3. All adjectives end in -*a*, and agree with the noun.
4. Numerals do not change their forms.
5. The pronouns are *mi, vi, li / ŝi / ĝi, ni, vi, and ili* ('I, you, he / she / it, we, you, they' respectively).
6. Verbs have the same ending throughout a tense form. There are present, past, and future tenses; imperative, infinitive, and subjunctive moods, and five participle forms.
7. Adverbs add an -*e* ending to the root.
8. Prepositions govern the nominative case.
9. There are no silent letters.
10. The accent falls on the penultimate syllable.
11. Compound words can be formed by combining roots.
12. Only one negative word in a clause is allowed.
13. The objective case is used when nouns reply to *where?*
14. An indefinite preposition, *je*, is used when the choice of another preposition would be unclear.
15. Loan words follow the system of orthography.
16. The *a* of the article, and the *o* of nouns, may be dropped for reasons of euphony.

There are only about 15,000 roots in the language, but these can be combined in various ways to produce a large vocabulary. In particular, great use is made of prefixes and suffixes to form complex words.

Several criticisms have been made of the language. Within the grammar, the use of the objective case (not found in several modern languages) has been particularly controversial, as has the use of agreement between noun and adjective. Languages that do not fit the Latinate use of tenses or prepositions find particular problems. In vocabulary, several formations have been criticized for not using the form common in modern languages. Some words are thus not easy to recognize; for example, *hospital* is *malsanulejo* (the root *sana* 'health' plus affixes). There are also several *faux amis* (p. 349), such as *foresto* = 'absence'.

The Slavonic bias to the pronunciation system has been a further source of contention: not all languages share Esperanto's reliance on diphthongs and sibilants (§27). Similarly, use of circumflexed letters is often considered cumbersome, especially in typing and computational setting (though the substitution of *h* for ^ is permitted).

The language is relatively straightforward to learn to read, as can be judged from a glance at any illustrative text. As always with language learning, however, passive competence is much easier to achieve than active use, and a great deal of memory work is still needed before fluency is acquired.

AN IDEAL ARTIFICIAL LANGUAGE

Several criteria have been proposed for an 'ideal' international artificial language, some of which are rather more achievable than others.

Easy to learn   This is usually taken to mean that the grammar has to be regular and simple, compared to that of natural languages; the semantic formation of words has to be based on clear principles; the spelling should be phonetic; and there should be no difficult sounds.

Relatable to mother tongues   It should be possible to translate into and out of any natural language with comparable ease; its structure would be flexible, capable of reflecting the idiom of the speaker's own language; it would display many universal features of language, and use word roots that have a history of international use.

A rich range of functions   It must be able to fulfil the ordinary needs of everyday speech and writing, as well as the specialized needs of science, religion, trade, sport, politics, etc. It must also be capable of being used in international communications media, such as telegrams, radio, and television.

Standardized   There should be no dialectal variation, in order to avoid the risk of reduced intelligibility. An authoritative body would monitor all proposals for new forms.

Neutral   It must be politically and linguistically unaligned, and therefore equally acceptable to all countries. Many AL supporters see this as an indispensable step towards the unity of mankind and a world of peace.

Providing insight   Several AL supporters see international communication as only one aim. They also hope that the greater regularity and clarity of these languages will enable people to think more logically or rationally, and thus establish a deeper understanding of the nature of reality. This search for a philosophical language, in which words and ideas would be logically linked without ambiguity or irregularity, was particularly common in 17th-century ALs, which were generally in the form of taxonomies of concepts expressed in a complex notation.

THE PROBLEMS

The international acceptance of an AL is a long uphill battle for its supporters, who have to overcome problems of a social, linguistic, and political kind.

Motivation   How is the inventor of an AL to persuade people to learn it, when no-one else knows it? To avoid this problem, there has to be a massive period of simultaneous learning, which is extremely difficult to organize. Zamenhof was one who saw this as a crucial factor. His solution was to include promissory forms at the end of his introductory book that read: 'I, the undersigned, promise to learn the international language proposed by Dr Esperanto, if it appears that 10 million people have publicly given the same promise.' He planned to publish a book that would contain all their names and addresses – something that it has never been possible to do (though there is a register of Esperanto translators).

Identity   One of the chief functions of language is to express identity, and this explains a large number of linguistic differences (Part II). ALs do not permit these differences. They are therefore in conflict with the aspirations of movements where there is a desire to retain and express national, regional, or social identities. The growth of nationalism, in particular, stopped the expansion of ALs in the late 18th century – a time when linguistic divisions were seen as an asset and source of pride – and it has had a marked effect on the AL movement since the First World War.

Linguistic bias   It is not as easy to develop a simple and common language as is claimed. Most ALs are based on western Indo-European languages, and this acts as a barrier to speakers of other languages. There is still a marked linguistic parochialism among ALs, which tend to underestimate the diversity of the world's languages (Part IX).

Semantic differences   Insufficient attention is paid to the semantic differences that exist between languages: words do no have meanings that can be neatly broken down into components (as some 17th-century systems tried to do), or that are exactly equivalent to each other. Speakers of different languages may translate their mother-tongue words into an AL, but this does not necessarily mean that they understand each other any better. The figurative, idiomatic, and connotative (p. 103) uses of words will differ: for example, American and Chinese attitudes to a word like *capitalism* will not alter simply because both sides agree to use the same AL label.

Antagonism   Many people who are sympathetic to the general idea of a universal language are put off by the great fervour with which proponents of ALs present their causes. Several AL organizations arrange public occasions with songs and hymns, each displaying a faith in the efficacy of its own AL which reaches evangelical proportions. Some ALs have been censured because the authorities associate them with political movements. Esperanto, in particular, has been frequently persecuted – notably in Germany and the Soviet Union in the 1930s, when the organization was suppressed and many of its members arrested or shot.

FIVE EXAMPLES

English
For, of the things that mankind possesses in common, nothing is so truly universal and international as science.

Esperanto (using *h* for accents)
Char el la komunaj posedajhoj de la homaro, neniu estas tiel vere ghenerala kaj internacia kiel la scienco.

Ido
Nam del kozi, quin la homaro posedas komune, nula es tam vere universala ed internaciona kam la cienco.

Novial
Den ek li coses kel li homaro posese comunim, nuli is tam verim general e international kam li scientie.

Occidental
Nam de omni comun possedages del homanité niun es tam vermen general e international quam scientie.

Latino Sine Flexione
Nam, de commune possesiones de genere humano, nihil es tam generale et internationale quam scientia.

And a test in Interlingua
Translate!
Tote le membros del communitate de linguas occidental son in un certe senso dialectos individual que devia plus o minus de un *patrono commun*. De iste facto son derivate tote le principios methodic supportante le compilation del *Dictionario Interlingua–Anglese*. Le termine *interlingua* es solmente un synonymo plus technic de *lingua de patrono*. Illo representa un lingua que es international proque su elementos existe de facto o potentialmente in un gruppo de linguas national.

Crib (if required)
All the members of the western community of languages are in a sense individual dialects which deviate more or less from a *common pattern*. From this fact are derived all the working principles underlying the compilation of the *Interlingua–English Dictionary*. The term *interlingua* is merely a more technical synonym of *pattern language*. It stands for a language that is international because it elements exist actually or potentially in a group of national languages.

MODIFIED NATURAL LANGUAGES

The language barrier has also been attacked by several proposals to simplify the structure of a natural language, usually by reducing the complexity of its grammar or the size of its vocabulary. All the main Western European languages have been modified in this way, the most famous approach being that of Charles Kay Ogden (1889–1957), known as *Basic English* (1930). BASIC is an acronym for 'British American Scientific International Commercial'. It consists of 850 words selected to cover everyday needs: 400 general nouns, 200 picturable objects, 100 general qualities, 50 opposites, and 100 operations (adverbs, particles, etc.). The working principle is that all words not on this list can be replaced by those that are (permitting several inflectional varia-

tions). The basic vocabulary is supplemented by several international and scientific words (e.g. *radio*, *geography*, *radium*, names of countries and currencies). The operation of the system is illustrated below.

The system was strongly supported in the 1940s by such people as Churchill and Roosevelt, but there were also many criticisms. The simplification of the vocabulary is achieved at the expense of a more complex grammar and a greater reliance on idiomatic construction. The replacement forms are often unwieldy, involving lengthy circumlocutions. And although BASIC proved easy to learn to read, it proved very difficult to write in the language in such a way that meaning was clearly preserved. The system is now largely of historical interest, though analogous principles can be found in several spheres of foreign and remedial language teaching (e.g. the concept of a restricted defining vocabulary in some contemporary dictionaries).

A SECTION FROM THE *BASIC* DICTIONARY

(C. K. Ogden, 1932.)

A TRANSLATION INTO *BASIC*

Below is a section of an economics text, followed by Ogden's own translation of it into BASIC:

Narrow dispersions, skewed negatively, signify deliberate human restriction of output. Skewed positively, after the introduction of selection of employees by test or examination, a narrow dispersion indicates a successful system of selection.

The tendency to a common level of output being more frequent, is a sign that output is being consciously kept inside a certain limit. When the lowest outputs are most frequent and the output of workers not widely different and generally high, after selection of workers by test has come into use, the tendency may be taken as a sign of the efficiency of the system of selection.
(C. K. Ogden, 1983, p. 146.)

Charles Kay Ogden

BASIC ENGLISH

OPERATIONS 100 ETC.	THINGS — 400 General				THINGS — 200 Picturable		QUALITIES — 100 General	QUALITIES — 50 Opposites	EXAMPLES OF WORD ORDER
COME	ACCOUNT	EDUCATION	METAL	SENSE	ANGLE	KNEE	ABLE	AWAKE	
GET	ACT	EFFECT	MIDDLE	SERVANT	ANT	KNIFE	ACID	BAD	THE
GIVE	ADDITION	END	MILK	SEX	APPLE	KNOT	ANGRY	BENT	CAMERA
GO	ADJUSTMENT	ERROR	MIND	SHADE	ARCH	LEAF	AUTOMATIC	BITTER	MAN
KEEP	ADVERTISEMENT	EVENT	MINE	SHAKE	ARM	LEG	BEAUTIFUL	BLUE	WHO
LET	AGREEMENT	EXAMPLE	MINUTE	SHAME	ARMY	LIBRARY	BLACK	CERTAIN	MADE
MAKE	AIR	EXCHANGE	MIST	SHOCK	BABY	LIKE	BOILING	COLD	AN
PUT	AMOUNT	EXISTENCE	MONEY	SIDE	BAG	LIP	BRIGHT	COMPLETE	ATTEMPT
SEEM	AMUSEMENT	EXPANSION	MONTH	SIGN	BALL	LOCK	BROKEN	CRUEL	TO
TAKE	ANIMAL	EXPERIENCE	MORNING	SILK	BAND	MAP	BROWN	DARK	TAKE
BE	ANSWER	EXPERT	MOTHER	SILVER	BASIN	MATCH	CHEAP	DEAD	A
DO	APPARATUS	FACT	MOTION	SISTER	BASKET	MONKEY	CHIEF	DEAR	MOVING
HAVE	APPROVAL	FALL	MOUNTAIN	SIZE	BATH	MOON	CHEMICAL	DELICATE	PICTURE
SAY	ARGUMENT	FAMILY	MOVE	SKY	BED	MOUTH	CLEAN	DIFFERENT	OF
SEE	ART	FATHER	MUSIC	SLEEP	BEE	MUSCLE	CLEAR	DIRTY	THE
SEND	ATTACK	FEAR	NAME	SLIP	BELL	NAIL	COMMON	DRY	SOCIETY
MAY	ATTEMPT	FEELING	NATION	SLOPE	BERRY	NECK	COMPLEX	FALSE	WOMEN,
WILL	ATTENTION	FICTION	NEED	SMASH	BIRD	NEEDLE	CONSCIOUS	FEEBLE	BEFORE
ABOUT	ATTRACTION	FIELD	NEWS	SMELL	BLADE	NERVE	CUT	FEMALE	THEY
ACROSS	AUTHORITY	FIGHT	NIGHT	SMILE	BOARD	NET	DEEP	FOOLISH	GOT
AFTER	BACK	FIRE	NOISE	SMOKE	BOAT	NOSE	DEPENDENT	FUTURE	THERE
AGAINST	BALANCE	FLAME	NOTE	SNEEZE	BONE	NUT	EARLY	GREEN	HATS
AMONG	BASE	FLIGHT	NUMBER	SNOW	BOOK	OFFICE	ELASTIC	ILL	OFF,
AT	BEHAVIOUR	FLOWER	OBSERVATION	SOAP	BOOT	ORANGE	ELECTRIC	LAST	DID,
BEFORE	BELIEF	FOLD	OFFER	SOCIETY	BOTTLE	OVEN	EQUAL	LATE	NOT
BETWEEN	BIRTH	FOOD	OIL	SON	BOX	PARCEL	FAT	LEFT	GET
BY	BIT	FORCE	OPERATION	SONG	BOY	PEN	FERTILE	LOOSE	OFF
DOWN	BITE	FORM	OPINION	SORT	BRAIN	PENCIL	FIRST	LOUD	THE
FROM	BLOOD	FRIEND	ORDER	SOUND	BRAKE	PICTURE	FIXED	LOW	SHIP
IN	BLOW	FRONT	ORGANIZATION	SOUP	BRANCH	PIG	FLAT	MIXED	TILL
OFF	BODY	FRUIT	ORNAMENT	SPACE	BRICK	PIN	FREE	NARROW	HE
ON	BRASS	GLASS	OWNER	STAGE	BRIDGE	PIPE	FREQUENT	OLD	WAS
OVER	BREAD	GOLD	PAGE	START	BRUSH	PLANE	FULL	OPPOSITE	QUESTIONED
THROUGH	BREATH	GOVERNMENT	PAIN	STATEMENT	BUCKET	PLATE	GENERAL	PUBLIC	BY
TO	BROTHER	GRAIN	PAINT	STEAM	BULB	PLOUGH	GOOD	ROUGH	THE
UNDER	BUILDING	GRASS	PAPER	STEEL	BUTTON	POCKET	GREAT	SAD	POLICE.'
UP	BURN	GRIP	PART	STEP	CAKE	POT	GREY	SAFE	
WITH	BURST	GROUP	PASTE	STITCH	CAMERA	POTATO	HANGING	SECRET	WE
AS	BUSINESS	GROWTH	PAYMENT	STONE	CARD	PRISON	HAPPY	SHORT	WILL
FOR	BUTTER	GUIDE	PEACE	STOP	CART	PUMP	HARD	SHUT	GIVE
OF	CANVAS	HARBOUR	PERSON	STORY	CARRIAGE	RAIL	HEALTHY	SIMPLE	SIMPLE
TILL	CARE	HARMONY	PLACE	STRETCH	CAT	RAT	HIGH	SLOW	RULES
THAN	CAUSE	HATE	PLANT	STRUCTURE	CHAIN	RECEIPT	HOLLOW	SMALL	TO
A	CHALK	HEARING	PLAY	SUBSTANCE	CHEESE	RING	IMPORTANT	SOFT	YOU
THE	CHANCE	HEAT	PLEASURE	SUGAR	CHEST	ROD	KIND	SOLID	NOW.
ALL	CHANGE	HELP	POINT	SUGGESTION	CHIN	ROOF	LIKE	SPECIAL	
ANY	CLOTH	HISTORY	POISON	SUMMER	CHURCH	ROOT	LIVING	STRANGE	
EVERY	COAL	HOLE	POLISH	SUPPORT	CIRCLE	SAIL	LONG	THIN	
NO	COLOUR	HOPE	PORTER	SURPRISE	CLOCK	SCHOOL	MALE	WHITE	
OTHER	COMFORT	HOUR	POSITION	SWIM	CLOUD	SCISSORS	MARRIED	WRONG	SUMMARY
SOME	COMMITTEE	HUMOUR	POWDER	SYSTEM	COAT	SCREW	MATERIAL		OF
SUCH	COMPANY	ICE	POWER	TALK	COLLAR	SEED	MEDICAL	NO VERBS	RULES
THAT	COMPARISON	IDEA	PRICE	TASTE	COMB	SHEEP	MILITARY		
THIS	COMPETITION	IMPULSE	PRINT	TAX	CORD	SHELF	NATURAL	IT	PLURALS
I	CONDITION	INCREASE	PROCESS	TEACHING	COW	SHIP	NECESSARY	IS	IN 'S'.
HE	CONNECTION	INDUSTRY	PRODUCE	TENDENCY	CUP	SHIRT	NEW	POSSIBLE	
YOU	CONTROL	INK	PROFIT	TEST	CURTAIN	SHOE	NORMAL	TO	DERIVATIVES
WHO	COOK	INSECT	PROPERTY	THEORY	CUSHION	SKIN	OPEN	GET	IN 'ER','ING','ED'
AND	COPPER	INSTRUMENT	PROSE	THING	DOG	SKIRT	PARALLEL	ALL	FROM 300 NOUNS.
BECAUSE	COPY	INSURANCE	PROTEST	THOUGHT	DOOR	SNAKE	PAST	THESE	
BUT	CORK	INTEREST	PULL	THUNDER	DRAIN	SOCK	PHYSICAL	WORDS	
OR	COTTON	INVENTION	PUNISHMENT	TIME	DRAWER	SPADE	POLITICAL	ON	
IF	COUGH	IRON	PURPOSE	TIN	DRESS	SPONGE	POOR	THE	ADVERBS
THOUGH	COUNTRY	JELLY	PUSH	TOP	DROP	SPOON	POSSIBLE	BACK	IN 'LY'
WHILE	COVER	JOIN	QUALITY	TOUCH	EAR	SPRING	PRESENT	OF	FROM
HOW	CRACK	JOURNEY	QUESTION	TRADE	EGG	SQUARE	PRIVATE	A	QUALIFIERS.
WHEN	CREDIT	JUDGE	RAIN	TRANSPORT	ENGINE	STAMP	PROBABLE	BIT	
WHERE	CRIME	JUMP	RANGE	TRICK	EYE	STAR	QUICK	OF	DEGREE
WHY	CRUSH	KICK	RATE	TROUBLE	FACE	STATION	QUIET	NOTEPAPER	WITH
AGAIN	CRY	KISS	RAY	TURN	FARM	STEM	READY	BECAUSE	'MORE' AND 'MOST'
EVER	CURRENT	KNOWLEDGE	REACTION	TWIST	FEATHER	STICK	RED	THERE	
FAR	CURVE	LAND	READING	UNIT	FINGER	STOCKING	REGULAR	ARE	QUESTIONS
FORWARD	DAMAGE	LANGUAGE	REASON	USE	FISH	STOMACH	RESPONSIBLE	NO	BY INVERSION
HERE	DANGER	LAUGH	RECORD	VALUE	FLAG	STORE	RIGHT	VERBS	AND 'DO'.
NEAR	DAUGHTER	LAW	REGRET	VERSE	FLOOR	STREET	ROUND	IN	
NOW	DAY	LEAD	RELATION	VESSEL	FLY	SUN	SAME	BASIC	OPERATORS
OUT	DEATH	LEARNING	RELIGION	VIEW	FOOT	TABLE	SECOND	ENGLISH.	AND
STILL	DEBT	LEATHER	REPRESENTATIVE	VOICE	FORK	TAIL	SEPARATE		PRONOUNS
THEN	DECISION	LETTER	REQUEST	WALK	FOWL	THREAD	SERIOUS	A	CONJUGATE
THERE	DEGREE	LEVEL	RESPECT	WAR	FRAME	THROAT	SHARP	WEEK	IN FULL.
TOGETHER	DESIGN	LIFT	REST	WASH	GARDEN	THUMB	SMOOTH	OR	
WELL	DESIRE	LIGHT	REWARD	WASTE	GIRL	TICKET	STICKY	TWO	MEASUREMENT
ALMOST	DESTRUCTION	LIMIT	RHYTHM	WATER	GLOVE	TOE	STIFF	WITH	NUMERALS,
ENOUGH	DETAIL	LINEN	RICE	WAVE	GOAT	TONGUE	STRAIGHT	THE	CURRENCY,
EVEN	DEVELOPMENT	LIQUID	RIVER	WAX	GUN	TOOTH	STRONG	RULES	CALENDAR,
LITTLE	DIGESTION	LIST	ROAD	WAY	HAIR	TOWN	SUDDEN	AND	AND
MUCH	DIRECTION	LOOK	ROLL	WEATHER	HAMMER	TRAIN	SWEET	THE	INTERNATIONAL
NOT	DISCOVERY	LOSS	ROOM	WEEK	HAND	TRAY	TALL	SPECIAL	TERMS
ONLY	DISCUSSION	LOVE	RUB	WEIGHT	HAT	TREE	THICK	GRAMOPHONE	IN ENGLISH
QUITE	DISEASE	MACHINE	RULE	WIND	HEAD	TROUSERS	TIGHT	RECORDS	FORM.
SO	DISGUST	MAN	RUN	WINE	HEART	UMBRELLA	TIRED	GIVES	
VERY	DISTANCE	MANAGER	SALT	WINTER	HOOK	WALL	TRUE	COMPLETE	
TOMORROW	DISTRIBUTION	MARK	SAND	WOMAN	HORN	WATCH	VIOLENT	KNOWLEDGE	
YESTERDAY	DIVISION	MARKET	SCALE	WOOD	HORSE	WHEEL	WAITING	OF	
NORTH	DOUBT	MASS	SCIENCE	WOOL	HOSPITAL	WHIP	WARM	THE	THE
SOUTH	DRINK	MEAL	SEA	WORD	HOUSE	WHISTLE	WET	SYSTEM	ORTHOLOGICAL
EAST	DRIVING	MEASURE	SEAT	WORK	ISLAND	WINDOW	WIDE	FOR	INSTITUTE,
WEST	DUST	MEAT	SECRETARY	WOUND	JEWEL	WING	WISE	READING	TO
PLEASE	EARTH	MEETING	SELECTION	WRITING	KETTLE	WIRE	YELLOW	OR	KING'S PARADE
YES	EDGE	MEMORY	SELF	YEAR	KEY	WORM	YOUNG	WRITING	CAMBRIDGE, ENGLAND.

The original Basic English vocabulary, as it was printed in the early publications.

Many people feel that the only realistic chance of breaking the foreign-language barrier is to use a natural language as a world lingua franca. The history of ideas already provides precedents, with Latin used as a medium of education in western Europe throughout the middle ages, and French used as the language of international diplomacy from the 17th to the 20th centuries. Today, English is the main contender for the position of world lingua franca (p. 360).

There are few competitors. Several other languages have an important local role as a lingua franca but no comparable international level of use, such as Russian in eastern Europe, or Spanish in South and Central America. More people in the world speak Chinese than any other language (§48), but Chinese is too unfamiliar in the West to be a serious contender. French is still widely used, but far less than it was a century ago.

Many factors contribute to the gradual spread of a language – chiefly political and military might, economic power, and religious influence (all of which artificial languages lack, §58). These same factors mean that the development of a world language is not viewed with enthusiasm by those who would have to learn it. Such a language, it can be argued, would give its originating culture an unprecedented influence in world affairs and scientific research. For example, scientists who used it as a mother tongue would be in a privileged position: they would not have to spend time learning it and would more easily assimilate ideas expressed in it. Furthermore, it is thought, a world language would inevitably erode the status of minority languages and pose a threat to the identity of nations (§9). Many people thus view the current progress of English towards world-language status with concern and often with antagonism (p. 361).

Ironically, the main danger to the growth of a world language comes from within. As the language becomes used in all corners of the world, by people from all walks of life, so it begins to develop new spoken varieties which are used by local people as symbols of their identity (Part II). In the course of time, these new varieties might become mutually unintelligible. How far this diversification will affect English cannot be predicted (p. 361). It is not easy to weigh the trend towards diversity against the trend towards unity that results from increased modern contacts through travel and communications. A hundred years ago, predictions were being made that British and American English would by now be mutually unintelligible. Linguistic predictions have a habit of being wrong.

LANGUAGES WITH SPECIAL STATUS IN 175 COUNTRIES

Afghanistan Dari, Pashto
Albania Albanian
Algeria Arabic
Angola Portuguese
Antigua and *Barbuda* English
Argentina Spanish
Armenia Armenian
Australia English
Austria German
Bahrain Arabic
Bangladesh Bengali
Barbados English
Belarus Belarussian
Belgium Dutch, French, German
Benin French
Bermuda English
Bhutan Dzongkha
Bolivia Spanish, Aymara, Quechua
Bosnia and Herzegovina Serbo-Croatian
Botswana English, Tswana
Brazil Portuguese
Brunei Malay, English
Bulgaria Bulgarian
Burkina Faso French
Burundi Rundi, French
Cambodia Khmer
Cameroon English, French
Canada English, French
Cape Verde Portuguese
Central African Republic French, Sango
Chad Arabic, French
Chile Spanish
China Mandarin Chinese
Colombia Spanish
Comoros Comorian, Arabic, French
Congo French
Costa Rica Spanish
Côte d'Ivoire French
Croatia Croatian
Cuba Spanish
Cyprus Greek, Turkish
Czech Republic Czech
Denmark Danish
Djibouti French, Arabic
Dominica English
Dominican Republic Spanish
Ecuador Spanish
Egypt Arabic
El Salvador Spanish
Equatorial Guinea Spanish
Estonia Estonian
Fiji English
Finland Finnish, Swedish
France French
Gabon French
Gambia English
Georgia Georgian
Germany German
Ghana English

Greece Greek
Guadeloupe French
Guatemala Spanish
Guinea French
Guinea-Bissau Portuguese
Guyana English
Haiti French, Haitian Creole
Honduras Spanish
Hungary Hungarian (Magyar)
Iceland Icelandic
India Hindi, English, 14 regional languages
Indonesia Bahasa Indonesia
Iran Farsi (Persian)
Iraq Arabic
Irish Republic Irish, English
Israel Hebrew, Arabic
Italy Italian
Jamaica English
Japan Japanese
Jordan Arabic
Kazakhstan Kazakh
Kenya Swahili, English
Kiribati English
Kirghizstan Kirghiz, Russian
Korea (N. and S.) Korean
Kuwait Arabic
Laos Lao
Latvia Latvian
Lebanon Arabic
Lesotho Sotho, English
Liberia English
Libya Arabic
Liechtenstein German
Lithuania Lithuanian
Luxembourg French, German, Letzebuergesch
Macedonia Macedonian
Madagascar French, Malagasy
Malawi English, Nyanja
Malaysia Malay
Maldives Divehi (Maldivian)
Mali French
Malta Maltese, English
Martinique French
Mauritania Arabic
Mauritius English
Mexico Spanish
Moldova Romanian
Mongolia Khalka
Morocco Arabic
Mozambique Portuguese
Myanmar Burmese
Namibia English
Nepal Nepali
Netherlands Dutch
New Zealand English, Maori
Nicaragua Spanish
Niger French
Nigeria English
Norway Norwegian
Oman Arabic
Pakistan Urdu
Panama Spanish

Papua New Guinea Tok Pisin, Hiri Motu, English
Paraguay Spanish, Guaraní
Peru Spanish, Quechua, Aymara
Philippines Pilipino, English
Poland Polish
Portugal Portuguese
Puerto Rico Spanish, English
Qatar Arabic
Réunion French
Romania Romanian
Russia Russian
Rwanda Rwanda, French, English
São Tomé and Principe Portuguese
Saudi Arabia Arabic
Senegal French
Seychelles English, French, Creole
Sierra Leone English
Singapore Chinese, Malay, Tamil, English
Slovakia Slovak
Slovenia Slovene
Somalia Somali, Arabic
South Africa Afrikaans, English, 9 regional languages
Spain Spanish (Catalan, Basque, Galician)
Sri Lanka Sinhala, Tamil
Sudan Arabic
Suriname Dutch
Swaziland Swati, English
Sweden Swedish
Switzerland French, German, Italian, Romansch
Syria Arabic
Taiwan Mandarin Chinese
Tajikistan Tajik
Tanzania Swahili, English
Thailand Thai
Togo French
Trinidad and Tobago English
Tunisia Arabic
Turkey Turkish
Turkmenistan Turkmen
Uganda English, Swahili
Ukraine Ukrainian
United Arab Emirates Arabic
United Kingdom English
USA English
Uruguay Spanish
Uzbekistan Uzbek
Vanuatu Bislama, French, English
Venezuela Spanish
Vietnam Vietnamese
Yemen Arabic
Yugoslavia Serbo-Croatian
Zaire French
Zambia English
Zimbabwe English

WORLD ENGLISH

In the minds of many people, there is no longer an issue. They argue that English has already become a world language, by virtue of the political and economic progress made by English-speaking nations in the past 200 years, and is likely to remain so, gradually consolidating its position.

An impressive variety of facts about usage support this view. According to conservative estimates, mother-tongue speakers have now reached around 400 million; a further 350 million use English as a second language (p. 372); and a further 100 million use it fluently as a foreign language. This is an increase of over 40% since the 1950s. More radical estimates, which include speakers with a lower level of language fluency and awareness, have suggested that the overall total is these days well in excess of 1,000 million. The variation results largely from a lack of precise data about English language use in such areas as the Indian sub-continent, where the historical impact of the language exercises a continuing influence on many of its 900 million people, and China, where there has been a burst of enthusiasm for English language studies, with over 100 million people watching the BBC television English series *Follow Me*. One visitor, returning to China in 1979 after a gap of 20 years, wrote: 'In 1959, everyone was carrying a book of the thoughts of Chairman Mao; today, everyone is carrying a book of elementary English.' Even if only 10% of these learners become fluent, the effect on totals is dramatic: the number of foreign learners is immediately doubled.

Surveys of range of use carried out by UNESCO and other world organizations reinforce the general statistical impression. English is used as an official or semi-official language in over 60 countries, and has a prominent place in a further 20. It is either dominant or well established in all six continents. It is the main language of books, newspapers, airports and air-traffic control, international business and academic conferences, science, technology, medicine, diplomacy, sports, international competitions, pop music, and advertising. Over two-thirds of the world's scientists write in English. Three-quarters of the world's mail is written in English. Of all the information in the world's electronic retrieval systems, 80% is stored in English. People communicate on the Internet largely in English. English radio programmes are received by over 150 million in 120 countries. Over 50 million children study English as an additional language at primary level; over 80 million study it at secondary level (these figures exclude China). In any one year, the British Council helps over a quarter of a million foreign students to learn English, in various parts of the world. Half as many again learn English in the USA.

It would be possible to continue with such statistics for several pages, but their significance can be illustrated more succinctly by comments made by foreign learners themselves:

- 'When I finish learn English, my pay as secretary will be increase by nearly ten times.'

    (Egyptian trainee secretary.)

- 'My company plans big deals with Arabic world. None of us speak Arabic, and they do not know Japanese. All our plans and meetings are in English.'

    (Japanese businessman.)

- 'After I learned English, I felt I was in touch with the international world for the very first time.'

    (Nigerian teacher.)

- 'If I want to keep up to date with the latest techniques and products. I must certainly maintain my English very strongly.'

    (Indian doctor.)

- 'Nearly everyone in Denmark speaks English. If we didn't, there wouldn't be anyone to talk to.'

    (Danish university student.)

Russian children learning English in a kindergarten language laboratory, Moscow.

Opposition to English The influence of English within a country has often been bitterly condemned. France has issued laws banning its use in certain public domains (p. 4). In French-speaking Québec, English advertisements, shop names, and traffic signs have been changed, in an effort to stop the advance of English in the province. There have been anti-English movements in Spain, Germany, Mexico, Myanmar, India, and several other countries; but for the most part they have had little effect.

INTERNATIONAL VARIETIES

Some people think they already see signs of the break-up of the language when they find difficulty in understanding the English used in India, West Africa, or other parts of the world – even, at times, within Great Britain and North America (§8). Variation can also be seen in the written language, mainly in a distinctive regional lexicon. An English edition of an Indian newspaper, for example, might refer routinely to *roti*, *kapra*, and *makan* ('bread, clothing, and dwelling'), a *rail roko* (railway strike), and to such quantities as a *crore* ('10 million') or *lakh* ('100,000'). In some international varieties of English, the local standard vocabulary (including words for local food, fauna, or flora) may run to thousands of items.

This variation raises a question mark against the notion of 'world' English. With so many varieties, which one should be used as the international medium? Should it be American, British, Indian, Australian...? Teachers in particular are faced with a conflict of aims: should they teach British or American English? both? or neither, focusing on the variety found in their own country? What effect will their decision have on the ability of their students to communicate at an international level?

Nuclear English

These problems are of recent origin, and are now attracting considerable discussion. One proposal, made by the British linguist Randolph Quirk (1920–), argues that the problem of variety would be avoided if the language were specially adapted to produce a 'nuclear' English for international use. 'Nuclear English' would provide a core of structure and vocabulary from within the range of acceptable English. It would eliminate all features that are 'dispensable', in the sense that the language has an alternative means available for their expression. Examples of omissible structures include the range of tag questions (*isn't it?*, *aren't they?*, etc.), which might be reduced to a single form (such as (*isn't that right?*); or one of the indirect object constructions (English has both *I gave the man a book* and *I gave a book to the man*). When all such options are removed, in both grammar and vocabulary, we are left with the obligatory minimum of the language, its communicative nucleus.

To be successful, Nuclear English would have to be easier to learn than any variety of 'full' English; it would have to meet the communicative needs of its users; and it would have to be capable of development into an 'expanded' form, for more advanced uses. It is too soon to say how far such proposals can be taken; but there is no doubt that the possibilities of linguistic *adaptation* provide an interesting theoretical alternative to proposals of outright *adoption*, which have so far been the focus of attention, and the source of much controversy. (After R. Quirk, 1982.)

ESTIMATES OF THE NUMBER OF ENGLISH SPEAKERS IN THE WORLD

The first column of data gives figures for those who speak English as a mother tongue or first language. The second gives recent total population figures (usually 1990) for those countries where English has special status as a medium of communication, including those where people learn it, usually in school, as a second language. These totals bear little correlation with the real use of English in the area. There are no figures available for people who have learned English as a foreign language, in countries where the language has no official status. The question mark is used for cases where no-one knows how many first-language speakers there are (the estimate given on p. 289 suggests there may be as many as 50 million in this category).

Country	First-language speakers of English	Country population	Country	First-language speakers of English	Country population	Country	First-language speakers of English	Country population
American Samoa	?	39,700	Ireland	3,334,000	3,509,000	St Lucia	27,000	151,000
Antigua and Barbuda	76,600	80,600	Jamaica	2,319,000	2,391,000	St Vincent and the		
Australia	15,366,000	17,073,000	Kenya	?	24,872,000	Grenadines	115,000	115,000
Bahamas	228,000	253,000	Kiribati	?	71,100	Seychelles	2,000	68,700
Bangladesh	?	107,992,000	Lesotho	?	1,760,000	Sierra Leone	?	4,151,000
Barbados	257,000	257,000	Liberia	?	2,595,000	Singapore	?	2,718,000
Belize	123,000	189,000	Malawi	?	8,830,000	Solomon Is	?	319,000
Bermuda	56,300	59,300	Malaysia	358,000	17,886,000	South Africa	3,080,000	30,797,000
Bhutan	?	1,442,000	Malta	70,600	353,000	Sri Lanka	?	17,103,000
Botswana	?	1,295,000	Marshall Is	?	45,600	Suriname	?	411,000
British Virgin Is	11,600	12,200	Mauritius	?	1,080,000	Swaziland	?	770,000
Brunei	10,400	259,000	Micronesia	?	108,000	Tanzania	?	24,403,000
Cameroon	?	11,900,000	Montserrat	12,000	12,000	Tonga	?	96,300
Canada	15,972,000	26,620,000	Namibia	130,000	1,300,000	Trinidad and Tobago	616,500	1,233,000
Cayman Is	26,000	26,000	Nauru	600	9,000	Tuvalu	?	9,100
Cook Is	?	19,300	Nepal	?	18,910,000	Uganda	?	16,928,000
Dominica	3,300	82,200	New Zealand	3,152,000	3,389,000	U.K.	56,236,000	57,384,000
Fiji	?	740,000	Nigeria	?	88,500,000	U.K. islands	201,500	201,500
Gambia	?	860,000	N Marianas	40,500	45,000	U.S.	221,227,000	251,394,000
Ghana	?	15,020,000	Pakistan	?	122,600,000	U.S. Virgin Is	86,000	107,000
Gibraltar	10,800	30,800	Palau	?	14,300	Vanuatu	?	147,000
Grenada	101,000	101,000	Papua New Guinea	?	3,671,000	Western Samoa	?	186,000
Guam	28,000	132,000	Philippines	?	61,480,000	Zambia	?	8,456,000
Guyana	567,000	756,000	Puerto Rico	?	3,336,000	Zimbabwe	?	9,370,000
Hong Kong	117,000	5,841,000	St Chrisopher			Other depen-		
India	?	844,000,000	and Nevis	44,100	44,100	dencies	19,800	33,000
						TOTALS	324,025,600	1,828,442,800

The spread of English as a world language   This map shows the growing use of English, both in those countries where it is a mother tongue, and in those where it has official or semi-official status. The main countries of the world have been shown larger or smaller than their actual size, to reflect their relative share of the world's population. The role of the Indian sub-continent in the population estimates for English is obvious. There are over 900 million people in that area, but estimates of those who are fluent in the language have been as low as 3%. (From R. W. Bailey & M. Görlach, 1982.) (The country names in this map reflect 1982 usage.)

60 · MULTILINGUALISM

People brought up within a western society often think that the monolingualism that forms a routine part of their existence is the normal way of life for all but a few 'special' people. They are wrong. Multilingualism is the natural way of life for hundreds of millions all over the world. There are no official statistics, but with around 5,000 languages co-existing in fewer than 200 countries (§§47, 59) it is obvious that an enormous amount of language contact must be taking place; and the inevitable result of languages in contact is *multilingualism,* which is most commonly found in an individual speaker as *bilingualism.*

The widespread impression that multilingualism is uncommon is promoted by government policies: less than a quarter of the world's nations give official recognition to two languages, according to the list on p. 359, and only six recognize three or more. However, when we look at what is taking place within each country, studying the speakers rather than the national policies, a very different picture emerges. It has been argued, in fact, that there is no such thing as a totally monolingual country. Even in countries that have a single language used by the majority of the population (e.g. Britain, USA, France, Germany, Japan), there exist sizeable groups that use other languages. In the USA, around 10% of the population regularly speak a language other than English. In Britain, over 100 minority languages are in routine use. In Japan, one of the most monolingual of countries, there are substantial groups of Chinese and Korean speakers. In Ghana, Nigeria, and many other African countries that have a single official language, as many as 90% of the population may be regularly using more than one language. It is an interesting irony that there may be more bilingual people in an officially monolingual country than in an officially bilingual one, because in the latter case there tends to be territorial separation between the groups (as in Belgium, Switzerland, or the countries of former Yugoslavia).

MAINTENANCE, SHIFT, AND DEATH

It is impossible to generalize about the way multilingualism manifests itself around the world; there are vast differences in social and cultural situations. Often the majority of a population is bilingual (e.g. the widespread use of Spanish and Guaraní in Paraguay, where the former is used as the official language, and the latter as the national language); often only a small minority may be affected (e.g. Gaelic speakers in Scot-

land). The majority of the bilingual speakers may be concentrated in the cities, or they may be found throughout the country, with focal points in those rural areas where languages are in contact. The bilingualism may be due to a long-standing co-existence of different groups (as in Belgium) or to a more recent and shifting co-existence (as with the many *Gastarbeiter* groups in Europe, p. 36). We need to examine many such situations in individual detail, in order to arrive at valid conclusions about the social antecedents and consequences of multilingualism.

An important characteristic of these situations is their fluidity. It is rare to find a setting where the languages are stable and balanced, and where social controversy over government policy is not a major issue (Paraguay is one such exception). Usually the language balance is changing, either spontaneously or because of government pressure. In some areas, the level of bilingualism is increasing (e.g. Sweden since the Second World War); in others it is decreasing, with second- and third-generation immigrants becoming increasingly monolingual (e.g. the USA).

A distinction is commonly drawn between cases where one language is holding its own despite the influence of powerful neighbours (language *maintenance*) and cases where a language has yielded to this influence, and speakers have assimilated to the dominant culture (language *shift*). Other possibilities include extensive vocabulary borrowing by one of the languages, or the emergence of a new 'hybrid' as a result of the contact, as with pidgins and creoles (§55). Lastly, as shown by the history of the Celtic languages (p. 304), the contact can lead to a language being completely eliminated (language *death*).

LANGUAGE DEATH

It is unusual to see the death of a language commemorated – but in this particular case the judgment may have been premature. In recent years an enthusiastic revivalist campaign has been launched to breathe new life into the Cornish language (p. 305).

WHAT CAUSES MULTILINGUALISM?

A multilingual situation can develop for reasons which may be difficult to disentangle because of their obscure historical origins. Often the situation is of the people's own choosing; but it may also be forced upon them by other circumstances.

• *Politics* Annexation, resettlement, and other political or military acts can have immediate linguistic effects. People may become refugees, and have to learn the language of their new homes. After a successful military invasion, the indigenous population may have to learn the invader's language in order to prosper.

• *Religion* People may wish to live in a country because of its religious significance, or to leave a country because of its religious oppression. In either case, a new language may have to be learned.

• *Culture* A desire to identify with a particular ethnic culture or social group usually means learning the language of that group. Nationalistic factors are particularly important (§9).

• *Education* Learning another language may be the only means of obtaining access to knowledge. This factor led to the universal use of Latin in the Middle Ages, and today motivates the international use of English (§59).

• *Economy* Very large numbers of people have migrated to find work and to improve their standard of living. This factor alone accounts for most of the linguistic diversity of the U.S., and an increasing proportion of the bilingualism in present-day Europe.

• *Natural disaster* Floods, volcanic eruptions, famine, and other such events can be the cause of major movements of population. New language contact situations then emerge as people are resettled.

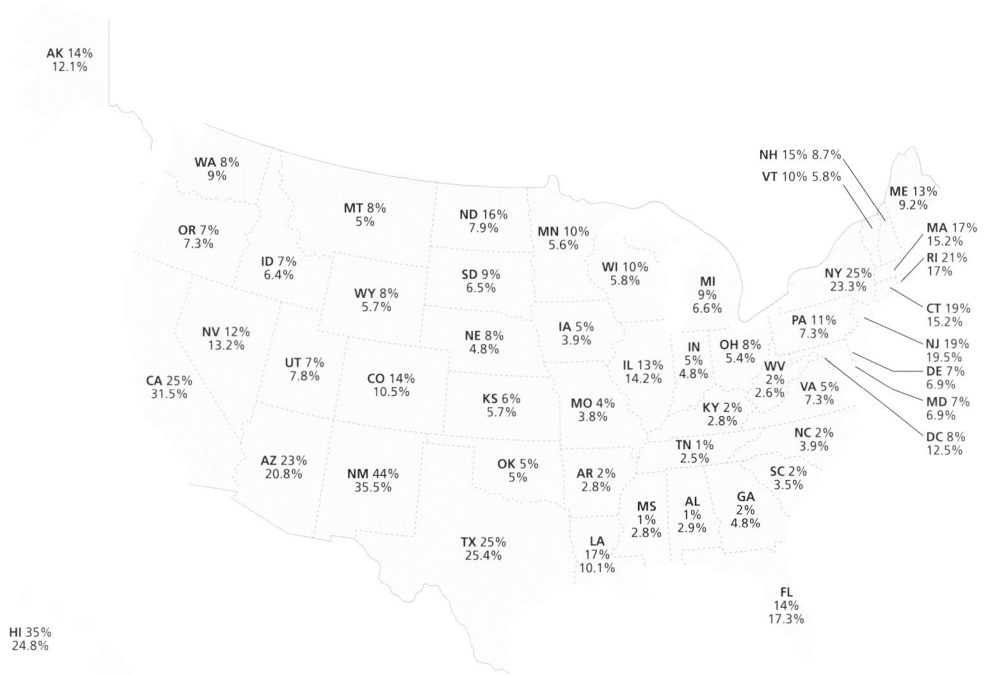

AK 14% 12.1%
WA 8% 9%
OR 7% 7.3%
CA 25% 31.5%
NV 12% 13.2%
ID 7% 6.4%
MT 8% 5%
WY 8% 5.7%
UT 7% 7.8%
AZ 23% 20.8%
CO 14% 10.5%
NM 44% 35.5%
ND 16% 7.9%
SD 9% 6.5%
NE 8% 4.8%
KS 6% 5.7%
OK 5% 5%
TX 25% 25.4%
MN 10% 5.6%
IA 5% 3.9%
MO 4% 3.8%
AR 2% 2.8%
LA 17% 10.1%
WI 10% 5.8%
IL 13% 14.2%
MI 9% 6.6%
IN 5% 4.8%
OH 8% 5.4%
KY 2% 2.8%
TN 1% 2.5%
MS 1% 2.8%
AL 1% 2.9%
GA 2% 4.8%
FL 14% 17.3%
SC 2% 3.5%
NC 2% 3.9%
VA 5% 7.3%
WV 2% 2.6%
PA 11% 7.3%
NY 25% 23.3%
NH 15% 8.7%
VT 10% 5.8%
ME 13% 9.2%
MA 17% 15.2%
RI 21% 17%
CT 19% 15.2%
NJ 19% 19.5%
DE 7% 6.9%
MD 7% 6.9%
DC 8% 12.5%
HI 35% 24.8%

The estimated percentage of people with a non-English background in the U.S. The first figure is based on a 1976 Survey of Income and Education (after F. Grosjean, 1982); the second is based on the 1990 census. The highest figures are in the northeast (around New York and its hinterland) and in the southwest (where the main influx of Spanish speakers has taken place). The past 20 years has seen a steady increase in the states of the south and along the west coast, most dramatically in California and Florida (Louisiana is the only southern state where the trend is in the opposite direction); most other states show stability or a decrease.

AK ALASKA
AR ARKANSAS
AZ ARIZONA
CA CALIFORNIA
CO COLORADO
CT CONNECTICUT
DC DISTRICT OF COLUMBIA
DE DELAWARE
FL FLORIDA
GA GEORGIA
HI HAWAII
IA IOWA
ID IDAHO
IL ILLINOIS
IN INDIANA
KS KANSAS
KY KENTUCKY
LA LOUISIANA
MA MASSACHUSETTS
MD MARYLAND
ME MAINE
MI MICHIGAN
MN MINNESOTA
MO MISSOURI
MS MISSISSIPPI
MT MONTANA
NC NORTH CAROLINA
ND NORTH DAKOTA
NE NEBRASKA
NH NEW HAMPSHIRE
NJ NEW JERSEY
NM NEW MEXICO
NV NEVADA
NY NEW YORK
OH OHIO
OK OKLAHOMA
OR OREGON
PA PENNSYLVANIA
RI RHODE ISLAND
SC SOUTH CAROLINA
SD SOUTH DAKOTA
TN TENNESSEE
TX TEXAS
UT UTAH
VA VIRGINIA
VT VERMONT
WA WASHINGTON
WI WISCONSIN
WV WEST VIRGINIA
WY WYOMING

A JOURNEY TO WORK

'My French friend had been brought up with the erroneous idea that the United States was a monolingual English-speaking country with a few, fast-disappearing linguistic minorities. One day I took him to work with me by a roundabout route to show him the great linguistic diversity that can be found in an American city – in this case, Boston.

As we walked to the bus stop, we passed a group of Haitian children playing ball and shouting at each other in Haitian Creole. On the bus to Cambridge we sat next to an Armenian American from Waltham reading one of the two daily Armenian newspapers published in the Boston area. Walking down Cambridge Street, we found ourselves for a short while in a little Portugal – the people around us spoke Portuguese, the stores sold Portuguese goods, the restaurants offered Portuguese specialities, and the children in the area were off to their bilingual programs in school.

We continued on our tour and went to Boston's North End for breakfast. Now we were in Italy. A procession in honor of a saint was getting under way, a group of elderly Italian-speaking people was playing cards in the shade of a tree, and storekeepers were setting up their displays of Italian cold cuts and cheeses. Notices posted on the walls were in Italian, and as we entered a pastry shop the customers were all speaking Italian to one another.

From the North End we walked a few blocks to Chinatown, with its Chinese-speaking inhabitants, street signs in Chinese and English, bilingual school, and Chinese stores, clubs, and temples. Because time was getting short we decided not to visit Dorchester with its large Creole-speaking Haitian population, and we quickly passed through South Boston, where many Hispanic Americans live. We did have time, however, to buy the local bilingual Spanish–English paper and check the times at the local cinema that shows only Spanish films.

We then arrived at my university, which welcomes, in addition to its American student population, students from thirty foreign countries. In the laboratory we set about our day's work on a research project concerning yet one more language actively used in the United States, American Sign Language, the manual–visual language of many deaf Americans.'
(F. Grosjean, 1982, pp. 42–3.)

Di Paola
CAFFE
CAPPUCCINO
ICE CREAM
SPUMONI · FRAPPE

A corner of 'Little Italy'

BEING BILINGUAL

Research into bilingualism usually distinguishes between large-scale analyses of multilingual societies ('societal' bilingualism, p. 362) and small scale analyses of the settings in which bilingual speakers interact ('individual' bilingualism). Several fundamental questions have to be dealt with under the latter heading – in particular, how bilingualism is to be identified and defined, and what its purpose is within the speech community. Both questions have 'obvious' answers, neither of which is adequate.

WHAT IS A BILINGUAL?

The obvious answer is: someone who speaks two languages. But this answer will not suffice. It does not allow for those who make irregular use of one or other language, or those who have not used the language at all for many years (so-called 'dormant' bilinguals). Nor does it allow for the many people who have developed a considerable skill in comprehending a foreign language, but who do not speak it; or those who have learned to read in another language, but who cannot speak or write it. It leaves unclear the relationship between different languages and different dialects, styles, or levels of the same language (as in the case of diglossia, p. 43). And above all, this definition says nothing about the level of proficiency that has to be attained before speakers can legitimately claim to be bilingual.

The notion of proficiency raises some very complex issues. Again, the 'obvious' answer is to say that people are bilingual when they achieve native-like fluency in each language. But this criterion is far too strong. People who have 'perfect' fluency in two languages do exist, but they are the exception, not the rule. The vast majority of bilinguals do not have an equal command of their two languages: one language is more fluent than the other, interferes with the other, imposes its accent on the other, or simply is the preferred language in certain situations. For example, a child of French/English parents went to school and university in France. She became a geography teacher, married a British doctor, and came to live in England, where she had her first child. In general conversation, she could cope with ease in either language; but she found herself unable to teach geography in English, and she was extremely reluctant to discuss baby care in French. In each case she knew the slang, jargon, and phrasing which is naturally assimilated when learning a new skill – but this was available in only one of her languages. Her linguistic competence certainly did not resemble that of monolingual teacher-mothers.

This situation seems to be typical. Studies of bilingual interaction have brought to light several differences in linguistic proficiency, both within and between individuals. Many bilinguals fail to achieve a native-like fluency in either language. Some achieve it in one (their 'preferred' or 'dominant' language), but not the other. For such reasons, scholars now tend to think of bilingual ability as a continuum: bilingual people will find themselves at different points on this continuum, with a minority approaching the theoretical ideal of perfect, balanced control of both languages, but most being some way from it, and some having very limited ability indeed. However, the notion is a difficult one to make precise, because so many different abilities are involved – in speaking, listening, reading, and writing, as well as in phonology, grammar, vocabulary, and pragmatics (Parts III–V).

WHY USE TWO LANGUAGES?

Here, the 'obvious' answer is: to communicate with people of different language backgrounds. And once again, the obvious answer will not account for the remarkable range of linguistic behaviour that can be observed in adult bilinguals. The 'easy' cases are those where a bilingual meets different monolingual people within a multilingual society, and changes from one language to the other in order to communicate with them. Somewhat more complex are cases where a bilingual chooses to use one language knowing that the listener would prefer the other (for example, electing to be tried in the language of a minority group, in order to embarrass the authorities). Here, language choice is a symbol of national identity.

But such bilingual/monolingual interactions and confrontations account for only a minority of cases. More often, in a multilingual society, bilinguals interact with other bilinguals, and opt to use their different languages in a complex network of interaction that proves extremely difficult to describe and explain. The choice of language will vary depending on the type of person addressed (e.g. members of the family, schoolmates, colleagues, superiors, friends, shopkeepers, officials, transport personnel, neighbours), and on the location or social setting (e.g. a family may vary their language use depending on whether they are at home, in the street, or in church; at the office, someone may talk to a colleague in language X, but over lunch talk to the same person using language Y). Even more complex, and not well understood, are the many cases when a bilingual talks to another bilingual with the same language background, and yet changes from one language to another in the course of the conversation – a phenomenon known variously as 'language mixing', 'language switching', or simply 'code switching'.

DORMANT LANGUAGES

There is no clear indication as to whether there is a limit to human multilingual ability. Cardinal Giuseppe Mezzofanti (1774–1849), librarian at the Vatican, is reputed to have been able to speak 50 languages (most with great fluency), to understand a further 20, and to translate 114. The Victorian diplomat Sir John Bowring (1792–1872) was said to have spoken 100 languages and read another 100. Unfortunately, there is no way of knowing exactly what proficiency level was achieved by these remarkable language learners.

It is in fact highly unusual to maintain proficiency in more than two or three languages at a time. Most multilinguals have a single dominant language, others being 'dormant' to varying degrees. The typical situation can be illustrated by a case study that was made in the field of aphasia (p. 272). It emerged that the person had learned seven languages during his life, but five had become dormant. His mother tongue had been Hungarian. At the age of 4, he moved to Poland, learned Polish, and stopped using Hungarian. When he was 6 he returned to Hungary, and had to relearn Hungarian. At the age of 10, he moved to Romania, using Romanian in school and Yiddish socially. Two years later he returned to Hungary, where in school he learned German, English, and Hebrew. This was followed by six years in Germany, during which time German became his dominant language. At 25, he moved to the U.S., where English became dominant. At the time of the study, only English and Hungarian were regularly used (his wife is Hungarian). The others were dormant, and in some cases almost forgotten. (L. Galloway, 1978.)

Cardinal Giueseppe Mezzofanti

Language switching

Switching between languages is extremely common and takes many forms. A long narrative may switch from one language to the other. Sentences may alternate. A sentence may begin in one language, and finish in another. Or phrases from both languages may succeed each other in apparently random order (though in fact grammatical constraints are frequently involved). Such behaviour can be explained only by postulating a range of linguistic or social factors such as the following.

• Speakers cannot express themselves adequately in one language, so switch to the other to make good the deficiency. This may trigger a speaker to continue in the other language for a while. An example from a Spanish/English study (G. Valdés Fallis, 1976): *Porque alli hay cashews. You don't like them?* (Because here are some cashews...'). This tends to happen a great deal when the speaker is upset, tired, or otherwise distracted.

• Switching to a minority language is very common as a means of expressing solidarity with a social group. The language change signals to the listener that the speaker is from a certain background; if the listener responds with a similar switch, a degree of rapport is established. The same switch may of course also be used to exclude other people, who do not know the language, from the group.

• The switch between languages can signal the speaker's attitude towards the listener – friendly, irritated, distant, ironic, jocular, and so on. Monolinguals can communicate these effects to some extent by varying the level of formality of their speech; bilinguals can do it by language switching. If two bilinguals normally talk to each other in language X, the choice of Y is bound to create a special effect. A common example is for a mother to tell her child to do something in one language, and then, if the child fails to obey, to switch to another language, thereby showing her stronger emphasis or displeasure.

These are but some of the sociolinguistic functions that language switching can perform. The phenomenon is evidently a complex and subtle one, with speakers usually being totally unaware of the extent to which they have been switching in a conversation. If interrupted, they may even be unable to say which language they were using in their last sentence. Monolinguals often dismiss or satirize language switching, using such pejorative labels as 'Franglais', 'Spanglish', or 'Tex-Mex'. Perhaps because of this kind of criticism, many bilingual people come to be very self-conscious about their switching, and try to avoid it in talking to strangers or on formal occasions. But in informal speech, it is a natural and powerful communicative feature of bilingual interaction, which presents linguists with one of their most intriguing analytical challenges.

BILINGUAL VERBAL STRATEGIES

Language switching is a major feature of this conversation between two native Americans of Mexican ancestry. *E* is a university teacher, who is working as a volunteer in a day care centre where *M* is a social worker. The Spanish passages are translated in parentheses.

E: What do you dream in?
M: I don't think I ever have any conversations in my dreams. I just dream. Ha. I don' hear people talking: I jus' see pictures.
E: Oh, they're old-fashioned, then. They're not talkies yet, huh?
M: They're old-fashioned. No, they're not talkies yet. No, I'm tryin' to think. Yeah, there too have been talkies. Different. In Spanish and English both. An' I wouldn't be too surprised if I even had some in Chinese. (*Laughter*) Yeah, Ed. Deveras. ('Really') (*M offers E a cigarette which is refused*)

Tu no fumas, verdad? Yo tampoco. Deje de fumar ('You don't smoke, do you? I don't either. I stopped smoking') and I'm back to it again.

...

M: An' – an' – an' they tell me, 'How did you quit, Mary? I di'n' quit. I – I just stopped. I mean it wasn't an effort that I made. Que voy a dejar de fumar porque me hace daño o ('That I'm going to stop smoking because it's harmful to me, or') this or tha', uh-uh. It just – that – eh – I used to pull butts out of the – the wastepaper basket. Yeah (*Laughter*) I used to go look in the (*unclear speech*). Se me acababan los cigarros en la noche ('My cigarettes would run out on me at night'). I'd get desperate, y ahi voy al basurero a buscar, a sacar, you know? ('And there I go to the wastebasket to look for some, to get some, you know?')

(*Laughter*) Ayer los (*unclear speech*) no había que no traia cigarros Camille, no traia Helen, no traia yo, el Sr. de Leon ('Yesterday the – there weren't any. Camille didn't have any, Helen, I, Mr. de Leon didn't have any') and I saw Dixie's bag crumpled up, so I figures she didn't have any, y ahi ando en los ceniceros buscando a ver onde estaba la – ('And there I am in the ashtrays looking to see where there was the –') I din' care whose they were.

The authors of this study point out that *M*'s language switching is not random. *M* is ambivalent about her smoking, and she signals this through her choice of language. Spanish sentences in this conversation reflect her embarrassment and personal involvement; English is used for more general or detached statements.
(J. Gumperz, 1970.)

BILINGUAL ACQUISITION

There is a widespread popular impression that the children of bilingual parents are linguistically at risk. It is said that their brains will not be able to cope, and that they will grow up 'semilingual', confused, or retarded. There is no justification for this pessimism, as is evident from the confident fluency displayed by millions of bilingual and trilingual children all over the world. By the time these children arrive in school, the vast majority will have reached the same stage of linguistic development as have their monolingual peers.

But the process of learning two languages is not exactly the same as the process of learning one (Part VII). Three main stages of development have been noted:
1. The child builds up a list of words, as does a monolingual child, but the list contains words from both languages. It is rare for these words to be translation equivalents of each other.

2. When sentences begin to contain two or more elements, words from both languages are used within the same sentence, e.g. (from a 2-year-old German/English child) *ein* ('a') *big cow, from up in Himmel* ('sky'). The amount of mixing rapidly declines. In one study, at the beginning of the third year, nearly 30% of the sentences contained mixed vocabulary; by the end of the year, it was less than 5%.
3. As vocabulary grows in each language, translation equivalents develop. But the acquisition of separate sets of grammatical rules takes longer. For a while, a single system of rules seems to be used for both languages, until finally the two grammars diverge.

When bilingual children reach this stage, usually in the fourth year, they have become aware that the two languages are not the same. They typically use each language to the parent who speaks it, and not to the other. Indeed, if one parent uses the language of the other to the child, there may be quite a reaction. The child may be surprised, embarrassed, fail to understand, think it funny, or become upset. An extract from a recent bilingual-acquisition study illustrates this last reaction. Lisa (nearly 4 years old) has an Italian father and a German mother. The father uses a short German sentence to her, to which she replies:
Lisa: No, non puoi. ('No, you can't')
Father: Ich auch – spreche Deutsch. ('I also speak German.')
Lisa: No, tu non puoi! ('No, you cannot.')
(V. Volterra & T. Taeschner, 1978.)

Not surprisingly, it is at this age that children try to play their parents off against each other. One child would always switch into French when he saw his English father approach him purposefully at bedtime!

Language, sooner or later, proves to be a thorn in the flesh of all who govern, whether at national or local level. Different social groups wish to see their linguistic identities and interests maintained, and may actively – and often violently – campaign for recognition (§9). Governments have to react to these differences, officially or unofficially: they may wish to reconcile them, or try to eliminate them. With the pace of change increasing, and countries becoming more heterogeneous, cosmopolitan, and internationally aware, it is not possible to rely on the slow course of natural linguistic evolution to resolve the many pressures and conflicts that arise. Many governments, accordingly, try to solve their problems by engaging in conscious, principled 'language planning', or 'linguistic engineering'.

Language planning involves the creation and implementation of an official policy about how the languages and linguistic varieties of a country are to be used. Decisions of a fundamental nature may need to be made, especially in the developing countries. But planning issues are to be found in all countries, as people debate such topics as the place of minority languages, the role of an academy in safeguarding standards (§1), the influence of the media on usage (p. 396), the value of spelling reform (p. 217), the avoidance of sexist language (p. 46), the modernization of religious language (p. 388), the need for plain English (p. 382), stylistic standards in publishing (p. 392), and the maintenance of oracy and literacy levels in school (§44).

Language planning is carried out by a variety of government departments and agencies, academies, committees, popular societies, and individuals. Activities range from the political and judicial, at one extreme, to the unofficial and illegal, at the other. Popular attitudes towards planning proposals include everything from complete support, through partial approval, general indifference, and mild antagonism, to total antipathy. Historical, political, economic, religious, educational, judicial, and social factors all have to be disentangled. As a consequence, it is hardly surprising that those who study this subject have not yet reached the stage when they can explain why some planning proposals succeed, whereas others fail. The field of language planning, which dates only from the 1960s, is still largely at the stage of descriptive enquiry, with a continuing need for detailed case studies of the widely differing situations in individual countries; few general theoretical principles have been proposed. However, the area continues to attract a great deal of interest, for both applied and theoretical reasons.

Most obviously, its findings and analyses may assist those (politicians, educators, lawyers, etc.) whose responsibility it is to make decisions about the development of languages in society, many of whom have no specialized knowledge of linguistic issues. But it also presents a fresh perspective for our understanding of linguistic change (§54). Many linguists have held the view that language change is a natural, spontaneous phenomenon, the result of underlying social and/or linguistic forces that it is impossible or undesirable to tamper with. We should 'leave our language alone' (p. 180). However, language planning studies have shown that it is quite possible for social groups to alter the course of a language, and that the question of desirability is a highly controversial one. It is still unclear how far languages can be permanently influenced by social manipulation, but there is now strong evidence that such factors must be taken seriously when considering historical linguistic matters.

TWO KINDS OF LANGUAGE PLANNING

Many analysts recognize a binary classification of language-planning activities, based on whether the changes affect primarily linguistic structure or linguistic use (§13). In *corpus planning*, the changes are introduced into the structure (or 'corpus') of a language/variety – as when changes are proposed in spelling, pronunciation, grammar, or vocabulary. In *status planning*, changes are proposed in the way a language/variety is to be used in society (thus altering its status) – as when it is permitted for the first time in law courts or in official publications. The distinction is not clear-cut, because not all kinds of planning activity can be neatly classified in this way, but it is widely encountered in language planning research.

PLANNING IN PRACTICE

Selecting the norm
If several languages are spoken within a country, it is usually necessary to choose a single language as a norm for official, educational, and other purposes. It may prove possible to use one of the indigenous languages, but intergroup rivalry may make it necessary to introduce a language from elsewhere as a lingua franca (e.g. Hindi in India, English in Ghana), in which case the relative merits of these languages will need to be debated. In addition, it may be necessary to choose a particular variety of a language (Part II), or to construct a new variety, taking into account such factors as formality, social class, regional dialect, and previous literary use.

Codification
If an indigenous language is chosen, it will need to be developed to meet the demands placed upon it as a medium of national or international communication. If the language has previously existed only in spoken form, or in an unusual writing system, an alphabet will have to be devised, along with rules of spelling and punctuation. An early aim will be the codification of the pronunciation, grammar, and vocabulary to provide a set of norms for standard use, especially if there is a great deal of local variation.

Modernization
The vocabulary will need to be modernized, to enable foreign material (in such areas as science, medicine, or the consumer society) to be translated in a consistent way. Principles will have to be agreed for the introduction of new terms; for example, should they be loan words, or coinages based on native roots? New styles of discourse may need to be developed, for use on radio or in the press. Decisions will need to be made about new or uncertain usages, especially in technical contexts (e.g. how to abbreviate scientific terms).

Implementation
The chosen standard will need to be officially implemented, by using it for government publications, in the media, and in schools. Inevitably, it will come to be viewed as the 'best' form of language in the speech community (§1), because it will be associated with educational progress and social status. It will also provide the norm for literary style, and may be associated with factors of a nationalistic, cultural, or religious kind. In due course, it is likely to be promulgated as a norm through an official body, such as an academy, or through prescriptive grammars, dictionaries, and manuals of usage.

INVENTING AN ALPHABET

One of the first tasks facing explorers, missionaries, and administrators, when they encounter a new language, is to devise a means of writing it down. The basic linguistic task is to ensure that each phoneme is represented by a grapheme (§§28, 33). But there are hundreds of possible graphemic shapes: /tʃ/, for example, could be written as *c, č, ć, ch, ts, tch,* and in many other ways. The choice between them involves factors of a psychological, historical, social, and educational kind. Language-planning principles thus need to be borne in

mind from the outset.

Political, religious, and other considerations may affect the choice of which kind of alphabet to adopt. A community may wish to 'align' with countries that use Roman, Cyrillic, Arabic, or other alphabets. It may also be important to choose a set of characters that can be used by all the languages throughout an area (as in the case of the All-India Alphabet). Written uniformity is often a powerful political symbol. It is also an economical measure, as it reduces the costs of printing and word processing.

For a language where there

are many new sounds, a decision has to be made about whether to invent new letters, combine letters into digraphs, or go in for diacritics (such as accents). If the first path is taken, there is still the question of whether the new forms should be adaptations of familiar letters, or totally fresh inventions (as in the use of some phonetic symbols).

Many other questions need to be considered. For example, if some features of a language are only occasionally used to contrast meanings (as often happens with the tones of a tone language, p. 174), should they be systematically repre-

sented by some form of symbol, or can they be ignored? Should grammatical differences be represented in the spelling (as in the case of English *find* vs *fined*)? And how should loan words, with their distinctive phonology, be written down? Even a well-established writing system can be faced with problems of this kind, as in the continuing debate over whether French loans in English should keep their accents (*rôle, cliché, résumé,* etc.).

A PLANNING MYTH

Probably the best-known myth in the history of language planning is the story that German nearly became the national language of the U.S. in the 19th century, losing to English by only one vote in the legislature (the 'Muhlenberg' legend). In fact, all that was involved was a request, made by a group of Virginia Germans, to have certain laws issued in German *as well as* in English. The proposal was rejected by one vote, apparently cast by a German-speaking Lutheran clergyman, Frederick Muhlenberg (1750–1801). But the general status of English as the major language was never in doubt. (After S. B. Heath & F. Mandabach, 1983.)

Chinese language planning Some of the most ambitious programmes of language planning ever conceived have taken place in China since the 1950s, with hundreds of millions of people affected. The two main developments have been the provision of a romanized alphabet (*pīn-yīn*), and the promotion of a common spoken language, *pŭtónghuà*, to provide a means of communication between the various regional languages (p. 314). Reports of early progress in the campaign are illustrated by Datian county in Fujian province, which has over a dozen dialects, and where it was said that 'people separated by a blade of grass could not understand each other'. A group of officials from the north on one occasion needed as many as seven interpreters to make a speech to the people in this area. But after an active teaching campaign, officials using *pŭtónghuà* were able to address large crowds without any interpreter being needed. The picture shows a *pīn-yīn* class taking place in an experimental school in Ningwu County, Shanxi.

ALPHABETS IN CONFLICT

The Roman alphabet has been so successful that it has begun to threaten the status of other alphabets. A question mark hangs over the future of Chinese characters, now that the romanized system known as *pin-yin* has been brought into use (p. 315). And in India, there is a body known as Roman Lipi Parishad (RLP) campaigning for the adoption of the Roman alphabet for the main languages of the country.

The arguments are complex ones, as can be seen from the situation in India.

• The RLP argue that the country cannot afford the luxury of making machines for each of the alphabetic scripts used in India (p. 205). Already, some 70% of mechanical typewriters in India are made for English, and the rest for all the

other scripts. Electronic typewriters are made only for English.
• The RLP point to the need to anticipate the use of computers, in relation to the country's economy. The Roman script is easier to adapt to electronic screens and keyboards than the various Devanagari scripts. A larger dot-matrix system (p. 195) would be needed, to cope with the diacritics that are used above, below, preceding, and following the Devanagari letters.
• It is claimed that there is a greater demand for material in the Roman alphabet. In Bombay, for example, there was an experiment in which telephone directories were printed using both the English and Devanagari alphabets. There was a demand of 300,000 for the former; but less than 50% of the 5,000 Devanagari copies were sold.

• On the other hand, the Roman script is not accepted as an alternative by any of the 22 Indian languages recognized by the Sahitya Akadami, the highest body devoted to literature.
• The cultural identity of the main groups in India is very much bound up with the use of an individual alphabet.

Opponents therefore argue that the adoption of Roman script would diminish one of the most important symbols of identity (§§9–10), and perhaps be the thin end of the wedge towards the eventual supplanting of indigenous scripts. These are highly emotive issues, and it remains to be seen whether the economic arguments will be able to make much progress, given the highly charged atmosphere of linguistic debate in present-day India.

CAPITALS IN FRISIAN?

Frisian, spoken in several dialects in the northern part of Schleswig-Holstein, provides a good example of the way the invention of spelling rules can reflect social forces. In devising an orthography for the language, the question arose as to whether nouns should

be written with a capital letter, as in German, or with a lower-case letter, as in other languages. Support for the capital letter proposal came from those who wished to see Frisian's ties with Germany strengthened. Opposition came from those who wished to

see a more autonomous future for Frisian. The issue remains unresolved, with both groups arguing the relative merits of each position, and producing publications that follow their favoured orthographic principle. (After A. Walker, 1984.)

EDUCATIONAL POLICY

One of the most important ways in which a country's language policy manifests itself is in the kind of provision it makes for the linguistic education of children. Which languages and language varieties are to be taught in schools, from what age, and for how long? These questions are only partly answerable with reference to the field of foreign-language learning and teaching (§62); far more fundamental are factors arising out of government policy and popular opinion, where a wide range of positions is found. Languages can be actively promoted, passively tolerated, deliberately ignored, positively discouraged, and even banned.

The results of active promotion are most clearly shown by the progress of English towards world-language status (§59). Many countries encourage the teaching of English in school, often at the expense of other languages: a recent case is Spain, where the early 1980s saw the widespread replacement of French by English as the first foreign language. At the other extreme, there are many examples of languages receiving official disapproval: a clear case is the reluctance of several countries to teach German since the Second World War (e.g. in France, Italy, Israel).

The fortunes of minority languages are closely bound up with the political aspirations of their speakers, and the extent to which the government of the day perceives these to be a threat. Again, the whole gamut of official attitudes can be found. There may be a strong local government policy of language maintenance (p. 362), as happens with the teaching of Welsh in Wales. On the other hand, there are many instances of languages being discouraged (e.g. Gaelic in 16th-century Ireland) or banned (e.g. Catalan in Franco's Spain).

Official attitudes today are generally sympathetic, with an increasing number of countries supporting (at least in principle) a bilingual or multilingual educational policy. In Europe, an early EEC Council Directive asked member states to promote the 'teaching of the mother tongue and culture of the country of origin' to all immigrants (p. 374). Progress varies greatly from country to country, however, with some countries (such as Britain) providing immigrants with relatively little by way of mother-tongue education, and others (such as Sweden) providing a great deal (p. 37). Conflict is never far away, as progress towards linguistic recognition inevitably proves to be too slow for some people, and too rapid for others. Vocal and vigorous objections to educational linguistic policies are thus commonly encountered all over the world. Regrettably, only the most violent tend to attract international attention.

BILINGUAL PROGRAMMES

There has been an extremely rapid growth in bilingual education programmes, with reference to minority languages, in recent years. Over $1,000 million have been spent in this area in the USA alone. However, the reasons for introducing such programmes vary greatly. In some countries, the aim is to find a single language capable of unifying the nation (e.g. Bahasa Indonesia). In Russia, the teaching of Russian to speakers of regional languages has promoted ideological assimilation and national solidarity. The teaching of English in many African countries ensures greater access to world opportunities. The teaching of local African languages to minority groups in South Africa during the 1950s and 1960s was felt to be a way of consolidating the divisions within that society in relation to the Homelands policy of that time. In the USA, the primary concern is to guarantee the civil rights and equal opportunities of minority groups – rights that have been confirmed several times in the US Supreme Court since the 1970s. In all cases, it should be stressed, bilingual education is not simply a matter of *language* learning: it involves the acquisition of all the knowledge and skills that identify the minority culture.

Maintenance vs transitional

Bilingual programmes have always attracted controversy. Two main views are argued (with many variant positions). On the one hand, maintaining the mother tongue is said to develop a desirable cultural diversity, foster ethnic identity, permit social adaptability, add to the psychological security of the child, and promote linguistic (and perhaps even cognitive) sensitivity. To achieve this, bilingual instruction needs to be retained throughout the whole of a child's school career. On the other hand, it is pointed out that a permanent dual-language policy may foster social divisions and narrowness of outlook (through ethnocentric churches, media, schools, etc.); the children may become 'trapped' in their mother tongue, and fail to achieve in the majority language, thus reducing their access to prosperity; and where there is inadequate teacher preparation, timetabling, and materials, they may fail to achieve in their mother tongue also. They should therefore be educated in their mother tongue only until they are able to continue in the majority language. Although many bilingual programmes subscribe in principle to the former, 'maintenance' view of bilingual education, in practice the majority (in the USA and Britain, at least) are of the latter, 'transitional' type – though often accompanied by maintenance elements (e.g. in literature, music, dance) in a continuing parallel teaching programme.

POSITIVE POLICIES

In 1982, the Commission of the European Communities to the Council of Europe asked each EC member country to report on the progress it had made in providing education for the children of migrant workers. Several signs of progress were apparent. Special reception classes were being created in many countries, and a number of types of provision existed at primary level (there was much less at secondary level). In France, for example, the language and culture of origin was being taught to immigrant primary school children for three hours each week, under the heading of 'environmental studies', as long as they came from countries with which France had a bilateral agreement. In Belgium, when the number of immigrant children in a nursery exceeded 30%, the number of these children would be multiplied by two in order to establish the quota of nursery teachers required. (See also pp. 37, 371.)

The 7.44 from Mons to Brussels

Belgium has also taken up an idea first tried out on a commuter train from Brighton to London – language learning by train. In May 1984 the last carriage of the 7.44 a.m. Intercity train from Mons to Brussels (a French-speaking area) was reserved for passengers who wished to learn Dutch or English. They paid their normal fare plus a small fee for the tuition, given by teachers trained by the Belgian Centre d'Animation en Langues. The venture was at first extremely successful, and within a few years, there were four 'language trains' in operation. However, enthusiasm waned, and the venture did not survive into the 1990s.

These views about the nature of bilingual education continue to be emotionally debated, for they reflect fundamentally different conceptions of the kind of nation people want to see around them. Maintenance views anticipate a society that is characterized by cultural pluralism and linguistic diversity; transitional views look towards a culturally homogeneous society, characterized by minority assimilation and language 'shift' (p. 362). However, the issues are more complex than this simple opposition suggests, for there are many kinds and degrees of support for both positions, and compromise views have also been proposed.

Case studies show that the notion of 'language loyalty' is never a simple one. For example, within an immigrant group, some members may wish (with varying degrees of conviction) to have their children retain their linguistic identity; others may wish them to 'shift' to the majority language as quickly as possible in order to participate fully in the new society; and yet others may wish to have them use their new language in public, but to retain their mother tongue for a range of private occasions (e.g. home, church, club). There are many further possible positions, reflecting the different influences of racial, geographical, political, cultural, economic, religious, and other factors. Given the emotional and volatile state of mind with which people approach the problem, it is impossible to say whether a genuine 'integrated pluralism' can be achieved in modern educational programmes. But the need to counter this inherent subjectivity makes it even more desirable to carry out detailed and objective studies of linguistic attitudes, within the field of language planning.

LANGUAGE IMMERSION

In Quebec, in the 1960s, a new kind of bilingual education programme was introduced, which has since proved to be popular and successful. The proposal came from the English-speaking minority, who wished to make their children proficient in a second language, French, in order to cope with a society where the role of French was becoming increasingly dominant. The idea was to arrange for the whole of their children's first encounter with schooling to be in the second language (§62) – a programme of 'immersion'. The children would speak in their mother tongue to a bilingual teacher, who would reply in the second language. Gradually, the children would come to use the second language themselves. Then, at a later stage, English would be introduced into the classroom.

After several years of experimentation, two patterns have come to be established. 'Primary' immersion starts at kindergarten, entirely in French. Gradually an element of English is introduced, until by mid-primary level the children are taught 60% in English and 40% in French. 'Secondary' immersion usually starts in the first year of secondary school with a booster year in which all teaching is done in French. This is followed by a 'post-immersion' teaching programme which follows the proportions of the primary school.

The approach continues to attract support. The children acquire a much higher level of competence than they would through traditional teaching methods (though this is still a long way from native-like proficiency, and doubts have been expressed over how effective the children's linguistic skills are outside of school). Their attitudes towards French-Canadian people tend to be more positive (though evidence is mixed on this point). And their mother-tongue abilities do not seem to suffer from the experience, but may even improve in certain respects. However, for this last outcome to be certain, there needs to be a supportive and strong first-language environment in the community. With speakers of minority languages where the home linguistic situation is weak or unstable, an immersion programme would be unlikely to result in maintenance, but would probably hasten the process of assimilation to the majority language.

A French immersion class taking place at a junior school in Montreal.

ENDANGERED LANGUAGES

Recent estimates of language populations (p. 286) suggest that half of the world's languages will become extinct in the 21st century, and that only 1,000 or so languages may remain by the 22nd. The speed of this decline is largely a consequence of the political and economic pressures which are motivating people to replace their traditional language by one which gives them access to the languages of more powerful cultures.

The publication in the early 1990s of major surveys of the world's languages (p. 287) has placed the facts before an increasingly concerned public. Bodies such as the UNESCO Committee on Language Endangerment, the Foundation for Endangered Languages (established in the UK in 1995), and the Linguistic Society of America's Committee on Endangered Languages and their Preservation are already handling many enquiries and fostering research initiatives. Information is gradually becoming available on the Internet - such as through the World Wide Web site of the Summer Institute of Linguistics. And a clearing-house for the world's endangered languages was established in 1995, at the request of UNESCO, in the University of Tokyo.

There are two aspects to the current concern. On the one hand, many communities are anxious to revive, maintain, and if possible enhance their endangered language. Progress here depends on recognizing the vast differences between the political and cultural situations - as illustrated by Welsh, Gaelic, Maori, Quechua, and the American Indian and Australian Aboriginal languages - which demand very different solutions. At the same time, progress also depends on collaboration between minority groups, such as those who form the European Bureau for Lesser Used Languages. There is then a real chance of influencing international policies.

On the other hand, it is evident that most of the endangered languages of the world are beyond practical help. In many cases, such as the hundreds of languages of New Guinea, there are only a few elderly speakers left, and only a small number of concerned outsiders. Given the difficulty there has been in achieving language rights for such well-known communities as the Welsh or the Bretons, the likelihood of attracting world interest in these cases is remote. The linguistic plight of the 20 or so reported speakers of Usku in Irian Jaya or of Pipil in El Salvador has a low international priority. In these circumstances, linguists are concerned to determine the urgency of the need in such situations, document what is already known about the languages, extend the knowledge-base as much as possible, and thus make a contribution to preserving the languages, if only in archive form.

MAJOR ISSUES

This kind of work raises major intellectual, political, and economic issues. Obviously, the cost of the required fieldwork on a world scale, with some 3,000 languages at risk, is immense. But there are more profound questions which have received little discussion. What exactly are we doing when we try to keep a small language alive? What is the value of a language (and the cultural heritage it expresses) to the world, and what does the world gain by preservation? Does loss of linguistic diversity present civilization with a problem in any way analogous to the loss of species in biology? Then, at a more practical level, what are realistic and unrealistic goals in working with endangered languages? At what point do the linguistic issues become swallowed up in larger political considerations? For example, which countries are antagonistic – whether passively or actively – to preserving the identity of their minority groups?

Such questions presume a public awareness of linguistic issues, especially relating to multilingualism, which is widely lacking in strongly monolingual western environments such as Britain and the USA. New international initiatives, such as those reported on the facing page, are beginning to make an impact, but the task is an uphill one. The concept of a language as a 'national treasure' is still one which takes many people by surprise – and even English has no national linguistic archive. In the meantime, while initiatives slowly grow, languages steadily die – currently, one every two weeks or so.

THE EUROPEAN BUREAU OF LESSER USED LANGUAGES

The aim of the Bureau is to conserve and promote the lesser-used autochthonous languages of the European Union, together with their associated cultures. It is an independent body, with its head office in Dublin, which works in close cooperation with the European Commission, the European Parliament, their member state institutions, and other European bodies. It came into being in 1982, when members of a Brussels colloquium representing the various 'small peoples' of Europe voted to support an organization which would act on their behalf at an international level. The Bureau has since received formal recognition for its role, and is often referred to in resolutions of the European bodies. Its bulletin, *Contact*, is published three times a year.

THE VALLÉE D'AOSTE

A French-speaking enclave in north-west Italy, on the borders of France and Switzerland. Here, French is a minority language, and the right of the inhabitants to receive a bilingual education in French and Italian is recognized by statute. The area is also notable for its 'minority within a minority': three small communities in the Lys Valley form a Germanic, Walser-speaking island, dating from the 18th century. Their rights, too, are protected by statute.

Words, words, words ...

There is no specific reference to minorities in the U.N. Charter or the Universal Declaration of Human Rights, but since the 1980s a number of statements by leading international bodies have produced a contemporary climate of opinion in which linguistic minorities are receiving, at least in principle, a long overdue measure of recognition. Extracts from some of these statements are reproduced below.

Resolution on the languages and cultures of regional and ethnic minorities in the European Community (1987)

The European Parliament ...
2. Points out again the need for the Member States to recognize their linguistic minorities in their laws and thus to create the basic conditions for the preservation and development of regional and minority cultures and languages ...
[and recommends that]
5. they carry out educational measures including:
– arranging for pre-school to university education and continuing education to be officially conducted [in these languages] on an equal footing with instruction in the national languages ...
6. that they carry out administrative and legal measures including:
– providing a direct legal basis for the use of regional and minority languages ...
– reviewing national provisions and practices that discriminate against minority languages ...
– requiring decentralized central government services also to use the national, regional and minority languages ...
– officially recognizing surnames and place-names expressed in a regional or minority language,
– accepting place names and indications on electoral lists in a regional or minority language;

7. they take measures in respect of the mass media, including:
– granting and making possible access to local, regional and central public and commercial broadcasting systems in such a way as to guarantee the continuity and effectiveness of broadcasts in regional and minority languages ...
8. they take measures in respect of the cultural infrastructure including:
– ensuring that representatives of groups that use regional or minority languages are able to participate directly in cultural facilities and activities,
– the creation of foundations or institutes for the study of regional and minority languages ...
– the development of dubbing and subtitling techniques to encourage audiovisual productions in the regional and minority languages ...
9. they take social and economic measures including:
– providing for the use of the regional and minority languages in public concerns (postal services etc),
– recognition of the use of the regional and minority languages in the payments sector (giro cheques and banking),
– providing for consumer information and product labelling in regional and minority languages,
– providing for the use of regional languages for road and other public sign and street names ...

European Commission for Democracy through Law (1993)

1. The international protection of ethnic, linguistic and religious minorities must be a fundamental component of the international protection of Human Rights, and as such falls within the scope of inter-State co-operation. It represents a basic element of peace and stability in Europe. ...
4. For the purposes of this text, 'minority' shall mean a group which is smaller in number than the rest of the population of a State, whose members, although nationals of that State, have ethnic, religious, or linguistic features different from those of the rest of the population, and are guided by the will to safeguard their culture, traditions, religion or language ...

United Nations Declaration on the Rights of Persons Belonging to National or Ethnic Religious and Linguistic Minorities (1992)

Resolution 47/135
Article 1
1. States shall protect the existence and the national or ethnic, cultural, religious and linguistic identity of minorities within their respective territories, and shall encourage conditions for the promotion of that identity ...
Article 2
1. Persons belonging to [minorities] have the right to enjoy their own culture, to profess and practise their own religion, and to use their own language, in private and in public, freely and without interference or any form of discrimination. ...

Article 4
3. States should take appropriate measures so that, wherever possible, persons belonging to minorities have adequate opportunities to learn their mother tongue or have instruction in their mother tongue.
4. States should, where appropriate, take measures in the field of education, in order to encourage knowledge of the history, traditions, language and culture of the minorities existing within their territory ...

Resolution on Linguistic and Cultural Minorities in the European Community (1994)

The European Parliament ...
B. declaring the need for a European linguistic culture and recognizing that its scope also includes protection of the linguistic heritage, the overcoming of the language barrier, the promotion of lesser-used languages and the safeguarding of minority languages ...
H. whereas the Community should encourage action by the Member States in cases where the protection of such languages and cultures is inadequate or non-existent ...

M. whereas many lesser-used languages are endangered, with a rapid drop in the number of speakers, and whereas this endangers the well-being of specific population groups and greatly diminishes Europe's creative potential as a whole ...
2. Points out again the need for Member States to recognize their linguistic minorities and to make the necessary legal and administrative provisions for them to create the basic conditions for the preservation and development of these languages ...

62 · FOREIGN LANGUAGE LEARNING AND TEACHING

To many people, the most obvious way of reducing some of the power of the language barrier (§56) is to promote the teaching and learning of foreign languages in a variety of child and adult educational settings. This widely practised approach is undoubtedly very successful, as can be judged by the millions who succeed in mastering a foreign language, even to levels that are comparable to those achieved by 'natural' bilinguals (§60). English-speaking monoglots often express amazement at the linguistic proficiency displayed by foreigners – not least, the standards routinely achieved in English – and conclude that foreigners must have a 'gift' for language learning, which they lack, or that English must be a particularly easy language to learn. There is no basis for these suggestions. A few gifted language learners do exist (p. 364), but most people arrive at their fluency only as a result of hard work, expended over a considerable period of time.

On the other hand, there is also a great deal of educational failure and lack of achievement in the language-learning field, which also requires explanation. Many people, from a variety of linguistic backgrounds, are actually embarrassed by their linguistic inadequacy when travelling abroad, and wish to overcome it. Many have tried to learn a foreign language, but have made little progress in it. 'I was never very good at languages in school' is a widely heard complaint. It is therefore important to study the factors that govern success or failure in this field – such as the soundness of teaching methods, the attitudes and motivation of the learner, the availability of time and opportunities to learn, the adequacy of resources, and the chance to put the language to active use. It is evidently a complex situation which, in view of the enormous amounts of time and money expended within the foreign language 'industry' all over the world, warrants careful investigation. And in recent years, the subject of foreign language teaching and learning has in fact developed to become today the largest domain of enquiry within applied linguistics (§65).

TEACHING AND LEARNING

The use of two headings for this section, *foreign language teaching* (FLT) and *foreign language learning* (FLL), reflects an important development in the modern study of the subject. FLT was at one time thought to be exclusively a matter of teaching techniques; it was felt that, if teaching was above a certain minimum level of efficiency, learning would automatically follow. Teaching was the active skill; learning, the passive one. Today, the active role of the learner is an established principle. It is recognized that there are important individual differences among learners, especially in personality and motivation, that can directly influence the teaching outcome. In this view, people are seen to be largely responsible for their own progress. Research is therefore now directed not only at the way teachers teach, but also at the way learners learn.

The term 'acquisition' (Part VII) is sometimes used to replace 'learning' in this context, when the emphasis is on the natural, unconscious way in which a learner can assimilate a foreign language (as in bilingual contexts, or when using one of the 'natural' approaches to FLT, p. 377). In several approaches, however, 'acquisition' and 'learning' are carefully distinguished: the former is then restricted to what takes place in 'natural' learning situations; the latter to what takes place in classrooms when following a structured course with a teacher.

FOREIGN AND SECOND

Several terminological distinctions are drawn within this field. A person's 'mother tongue' or 'first language' (L1) is distinguished from any further languages that may be acquired (L2, L3, etc.). The term 'foreign language' is popularly used to refer to any language that is not a native language in a country; and 'second language' is also commonly used in this way, especially in the U.S. (a usage which is increasing worldwide). But many linguists distinguish between 'foreign' and 'second' language use, recognizing major differences in the learning aims, teaching methods, and achievement levels involved.

A *foreign* language (FL), in this more restricted sense, is a non-native language taught in school that has no status as a routine medium of communication in that country. A *second* language (SL) is a non-native language that is widely used for purposes of communication, usually as a medium of education, government, or business. In this usage, English, for example, has foreign language status in Japan, but second lan-

BOULANGERIE = BAKERY?

At a purely linguistic level, French *boulangerie* translates into English as *bakery*. However, there is no cultural equivalence between the two notions: in many French villages, the bakery acts as a social centre in ways its English counterpart does not.

LANGUAGE – AND CULTURE

Today, learning a foreign language is likely to mean learning a great deal about the foreign civilization and culture at the same time. Books and materials increasingly incorporate information about such matters as the physical geography, economy, history, politics, religion, social institutions, educational system, literature, art, music, science, technology, media, and sport, as well as about daily life-style, popular beliefs, folk customs, and social values. The material is inevitably very selective; but it helps the learner to become more fully aware of differing ways of behaviour, and reduces the risks of culture shock, foreigner stereotyping, and intolerance.

A cultural frame of reference becomes increasingly important the greater the 'distance' between languages. To succeed in an oriental language, for example, a westerner needs the support of several of the above studies. But a cultural perspective is needed even with 'nearby' languages, in order to grasp the social significance of a linguistic feature (e.g. slang, accents, or terms of address, p. 44) or to follow the subject matter of daily conversation. For example, in every country, knowing the names of the most famous men and women of a culture, whether they are political figures, folk heroes, or media stars, is a major factor in really understanding the meaning of a newspaper report, a debate on television, or the course of conversation.

At the same time, there are risks in adopting a cultural perspective. Some learners want to learn a language *without* having to take on board all its cultural 'baggage'. British textbooks, for example, are often edited to remove features which are perceived to betray a British cultural bias, in view of the sensitivity which some countries display about this matter.

guage status in Nigeria. The latter term is also used with reference to immigrants and indigenous groups whose L1 is a minority language: in the USA, for example, English is a second language for millions of immigrants from a wide range of language backgrounds (p. 363) as well as for speakers of American Indian languages.

WHY LEARN FOREIGN LANGUAGES?

The question requires an answer, in a world where we frequently find indifference or hostility expressed towards foreign languages and foreign people, where teaching resources are limited, and where other subjects clamour for extra slots within the school timetable. The criticisms come mainly from within the English-speaking world, where FLT has often been attacked on the grounds that the time would be better spent on science, mathematics, or the mother tongue. Many people think that FLT is unnecessary in a world where an increasing number of people understand English (§59).

Moreover, even in places where FL instruction is provided, the use of traditional teaching methods has meant that many pupils find FL work boring and difficult. In British secondary schools, for example, 60% drop their FL after three years, and even those who pass their exams are often unable to use the language for everyday purposes. Such facts fuel the arguments of those who think that FLT should become a minority subject or even be dropped from the curriculum altogether.

Arguments of this kind are rarely encountered in non-English-speaking countries, where there is a great demand for FL courses. In German secondary schools, for example, all pupils take a foreign language to an advanced level. In France the figure is around 85%. In Britain, the figures are much lower, but the climate is slowly changing. In the 1960s, only 20% of schoolchildren took a foreign language; in the early 1980s, well over 80% were taking one for up to three years. In the USA, a Commission on Foreign Language and International Studies was set up in 1978 to consider the FL situation: it concluded that American incompetence in FLL had reached the stage where it threatened national security and economic development (e.g. only 2% of American scientists could understand material published in Russian). Several recommendations have since been made to improve the status and facilities for FL work, at both school and college levels. Extra funding has been allocated, both federally and privately. Some states (e.g. Michigan) have already mandated an FL component as part of high school certification.

In Europe, the Committee of Ministers of the Council of Europe has recommended that FLT in schools should be increased and diversified, that children should learn more than one foreign language if possible, that they should start as early as possible, and that facilities should be made longer-term. There should be a single language policy for a school, in which all language work (L1 and L2) should be integrated. In the 1980s, several languages associations and committees have reiterated this plea, though limited funding has led to limited implementation.

WHICH LANGUAGE?

In most non-English-speaking countries, English is first choice (§59). In English-speaking countries, this position is usually taken by French, which has a highly prestigious literature and culture, and which has been used as an international lingua franca since the 18th century (e.g. the official languages of the Council of Europe are English and French). In Britain, the proximity of France and numerous points of historical connection have led to the concentration on French in schools and, once a subject is established, the need to provide continuity of teaching makes it difficult to displace.

After French, Spanish and German both have substantial followings in schools, the former especially in the U.S. because of the proximity of Spanish-speaking countries and the high level of immigration from these areas. Each language has considerable international status. Spanish is the world's third international language, being used in over 20 countries. German is an important lingua franca throughout much of Eastern Europe.

It is extremely difficult to predict which languages children will need most in adult life. Patterns of language choice in the various settings of adult education are quite different from those found in school. A recent BBC TV Italian series was watched by 1.8 million people, and a Russian series by about 1 million people, though neither language is much taught in British schools. Japanese and Chinese are now being offered by several centres of further education in the U.K. Trade and tourism seem to be particularly influential factors.

ANSWERING THE CRITICS

The FLT world has not been slow to meet the challenge of the critics. An enormous outpouring of intellectual and practical effort has been devoted to overhauling the traditional machinery of language teaching. At the same time, the rationale for FLL has come to be publicly defended.

• FLL is no longer a luxury, in an international world. It is a necessity, if a country is to exercise a role in world affairs. Especially in Europe, it is seen as a criterion of responsible international citizenship. It is a strength to be able to meet people from other countries on equal linguistic terms.

• FLL has an essential role in preparing children to cope with the new perspectives brought about by a rapidly changing society – not only abroad, but within their own community. It can help overcome their insecurity and develop their confidence as they face up to the demands of social and personal relationships not usually encountered in a mother-tongue context.

• There is no doubt that language is prerequisite for full mutual understanding and cooperation between nations. FLL promotes understanding, tolerance, and respect for the cultural identity, rights, and values of others, whether abroad, or at home in minority groups. People become less ethnocentric, as they come to see themselves and their society in the eyes of the rest of the world, and encounter other ways of thinking about things. Language learning, as well as travel, broadens the mind.

• Success in the international world of commerce and industry is becoming more and more dependent on FLL (§56). Young people now find they have more career opportunities when they know a foreign language and are increasingly moving to localities where some degree of FL competence is required of them. This mobility is no longer something that affects only executives but is found with all grades and categories of personnel, such as marketing staff, legal specialists, secretaries, and technicians.

• FLL is becoming increasingly important as unemployment and reduced working hours add to people's leisure time. Tourist travel is a major motivation, but many have come to find FLL a satisfying leisure activity in its own right, enabling them to have direct access to the world of foreign cinema, radio and television, vocal music, literature, and the history of ideas.

• FLL provides a valuable perspective for those whose interest is primarily in the mother tongue. Ultimately, the only way to appreciate the unique identity and power of a language is by contrasting it with others.

• FLL is a primary educational right, which should be made available to all people, whether they avail themselves of it or not.

THE COUNCIL OF EUROPE

Recommendation R (82) 18 of the Committee of Ministers of the Council of Europe, adopted in September 1982, is a clear statement of the issues involved in the teaching and learning of modern languages. The statement recognizes three general premises, following these by a set of general and specific recommendations to do with language learning in schools and higher education, language learning by migrants and their families, initial and further teacher training, and measures of international cooperation. The premises, and the statement of general measures to be implemented, are given below.

The Committee of Ministers...

Considering that the rich heritage of diverse languages and cultures in Europe is a valuable common resource to be protected and developed, and that a major educational effort is needed to convert that diversity from a barrier to communication into a source of mutual enrichment and understanding;

Considering that it is only through a better knowledge of European modern languages that it will be possible to facilitate communication and interaction among Europeans of different mother tongues in order to promote European mobility, mutual understanding and co-operation, and overcome prejudice and discrimination;

Considering that member states, when adopting or developing national policies in the field of modern language learning and teaching, may achieve greater convergence at the European level, by means of appropriate arrangements for ongoing co-operation and co-ordination of policies;

Recommends the governments of member states, in the framework of their national educational policies and systems, and national cultural development policies, to implement by all available means and within the limits of available resources, the measures set out in the appendix to the present recommendation.

Measures to be implemented concerning the learning and teaching of modern languages

General measures

1. To ensure, as far as possible, that all sections of their populations have access to effective means of acquiring a knowledge of the languages of other member states (or of other communities within their own country) as well as the skills in the use of those languages that will enable them to satisfy their communicative needs and in particular:

   1.1. to deal with the business of everyday life in another country, and to help foreigners staying in their own country to do so:

   1.2 to exchange information and ideas with young people and adults who speak a different language and to communicate their thoughts and feelings to them;

   1.3 to achieve a wider and deeper understanding of the way of life and forms of thought of other peoples and of their cultural heritage.

2. To promote, encourage and support the efforts of teachers and learners at all levels to apply in their own situation the principles of the construction of language-learning systems (as these are progressively developed within the Council of Europe 'Modern languages' programme):

   2.1 by basing language teaching and learning on the needs, motivations, and characteristics and resources of learners;

   2.2 by defining worthwhile and realistic objectives as explicitly as possible;

   2.3 by developing appropriate methods and materials;

   2.4 by developing suitable forms and instruments for the evaluation of learning programmes.

3. To promote research and development programmes leading to the introduction, at all educational levels, of methods and materials best suited to enabling different classes and types of student to acquire a communicative proficiency appropriate to their specific needs.

The Committee of Ministers of the Council of Europe meeting in Strasbourg

SUCCESSFUL LANGUAGE LEARNING

There is as yet no single theory that can account for the diversity of FLL behaviour, and explain why some learners succeed in their task, whereas others fail. A hint of the complexity of the task facing researchers can be obtained from the résumé of relevant factors on this page.

• It is unclear how far there may be a genuine *aptitude* for FLL. Given sufficient motivation, intelligence, and opportunity, anyone can learn a language; but the task is likely to be less onerous if certain general personal qualities are present. Among these, it has been suggested, are empathy and adaptability, assertiveness and independence, with good drive and powers of application. People need to be capable of assimilating knowledge in difficult conditions. They should have a good memory, and be good at finding patterns in samples of data (non-linguistic as well as linguistic). Of particular importance is an ability to detect phonetic differences (e.g. of stress, melody, vowel quality) – something which can manifest itself in other domains, such as drama or music.

• Motivation is a central factor. Students need to see that foreign languages are taken seriously by those whom they respect, especially in the community at large (encouragement from local employers, civic interest in town twinning, etc.). It is critical to take the lan-guage out of the classroom, so that students see its use in a native community. Parental support seems to be a critical factor with younger children. Moreover, motivation applies to teacher as well as student: it is difficult to teach enthusiastically if it is known that most of the class are going to drop their language at the earliest opportunity, or that society places little store by it.

• Attitude towards the foreign language is important. If a student perceives a country or culture to be unpleasant, for whatever reason (e.g. its politics, religion, eating habits), the negative attitude is likely to influence language learning achievement – and conversely.

• Students can benefit from being taught to 'learn how to learn' foreign languages – useful strategies, such as silent rehearsal, techniques of memorization, and alternative ways of expressing what they want to say (paraphrase). They may also benefit from training in the kinds of basic skills involved in FLL, such as those identified above.

• Exposure to (and practice in) the foreign language needs to be regular – a problem which particularly affects FLT in schools, where timetable pressure, examinations, and holidays may lead to discontinuities. Whenever possible, the aim should be to teach 'little and often'. Too much exposure at any one time can be as ineffective as too little, readily leading to fatigue and superficial assimilation ('quickly learned is quickly forgotten').

• Exposure to native users of the foreign language is a real benefit, through the use of authentic materials (e.g. audio tape, video tape, newspaper library) and, in school, foreign language teaching assistants. A parallel emphasis on output, as well as input, is desirable: 'practice makes perfect'. An important dimension is the use of educational visits abroad – but these need to be properly prepared and followed up in class, and the experience should enable children to be genuinely integrated within the FL environment. Out-of-school activities should be encouraged, such as pen friends, private exchanges, and weekend culture simulation courses.

• Teaching objectives need to be carefully selected and graded, to permit realistic progress with underachievers, as well as with the gifted. Different kinds of objectives should be explored. Are all four linguistic modes to be introduced (speaking, listening, reading, writing), and if so, in which order? Might limited competence in two languages be better than an excellent command of one? Should the learners be exposed to only certain varieties (§11) of the foreign language? Should the focus be on communicative skills or on formal techniques (such as translation) (p. 378)? How far should L1 input be used in L2 teaching?

• Teaching methods need to be flexible to suit the needs of individual children (e.g. their interests and cognitive skills) and to make best use of classroom design and resources (e.g. the availability of audio-visual aids). There is no single 'formula' for successful FLT (p. 378). There should be opportunities for teachers to interact with children in groups, pairs, and individually, and for pupils to interact with each other. If classes are too big, it will be impossible to obtain genuine participation and practice.

• There should be an opportunity to take more than one foreign language in school, to follow them to an advanced level, and to continue with them after school. Special arrangements may need to be made, involving interschool and local government cooperation. New combinations of subjects, more suited to the needs of modern society, should be introduced, such as FL + science, FL + economics.

• Teacher training needs to continue at in-service as well as initial levels. Teachers need to be technically competent, that is they are able to teach *in* the foreign language, if required. They need to keep themselves up-to-date with the latest research into their language and society, as well as in FLT techniques.

WHEN SHOULD L2s BE TAUGHT?

Traditionally, L2s have been introduced at a relatively late stage of development – usually around the age of 10 or 11. In recent decades, the benefits of an early start have been urged, given the natural way in which young children learn language (cf. critical periods, p. 265), the positive results of some immersion programmes (p. 369), and the likelihood that they can devote more time to the task. Several experimental FL programmes have been tried out in primary school, and their effectiveness evaluated.

The results have been mixed. FLT with young children can work well, but only if learning conditions are optimal. The teaching objectives need to be limited, graded, and clearly defined. Specialist teachers need to be available. Methods need to be devised that are appropriate to the interests and cognitive level of the children. And the transition to secondary school needs to be borne in mind, because a lack of continuity can negate previous work. Unfortunately, these conditions do not often obtain, and many early FLT projects have achieved disappointing results (the greatest success coming in second language situations, such as in Africa). Children who start at age 11, it seems, soon catch up on their 8-year-old peers.

However, even if formal FLT is not introduced, it is still possible to develop young children's general language awareness – to sensitize them towards the existence and variety of the languages of others as well as of their own language – and to foster the enjoyment that can come from being in contact with foreign languages. Children can learn FL games, songs, rhymes, sayings, everyday greetings, and many basic notions (e.g. counting, parts of the body, telling the time). In particular, if pupils from other language backgrounds are present, the multilingual setting can be used to generate a mutual linguistic and cultural interest. The experience can provide a valuable foundation for the systematic study of foreign languages at later ages. In the 1990s, an increasing number of countries are introducing a foreign language at an early age.

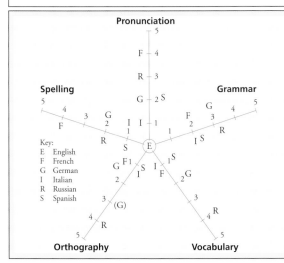

Key:
E English
F French
G German
I Italian
R Russian
S Spanish

Interlingual distance The structural closeness of languages to each other has often been thought to be an important factor in FLL. If the L2 is structurally similar to the L1, it is claimed, learning should be easier than in cases where the L2 is very different. However, it is not possible to correlate linguistic difference and learning difficulty in any straightforward way (p. 376), and even the basic task of quantifying linguistic difference proves to be highly complex, because of the many variables involved.

The diagram shows one analyst's informal estimate of the structural distance between English and several other languages. Pronunciation, spelling, choice of alphabet (orthography), grammar, and vocabulary are each rated separately, using a scale from 1 (least distance) to 5 (greatest distance). On this basis, Italian comes closest to English (scoring 6), followed by Spanish (7), German (10), French (12), and Russian (15). German would score higher if Gothic script were taken into account (3 rather than 1 along the orthography scale). (After C. V. James, 1979.)

THEORIES OF LANGUAGE LEARNING

As with the study of first language acquisition (p. 236), several theories of the nature of the FLL process have been propounded, with similar issues being addressed. Indeed, comparisons are frequently made with the way children learn their first language (L1), as a means of providing hypotheses to guide FL research.

THE BEHAVIOURIST VIEW

A great deal of language learning and teaching in the 1950s and 1960s was influenced by the tenets of behaviourism (pp. 236, 412). In this view, FLL is seen as a process of imitation and reinforcement: learners attempt to copy what they hear, and by regular practice they establish a set of acceptable habits in the new language. Properties of the L1 are thought to exercise an influence on the course of L2 learning: learners 'transfer' sounds, structures, and usages from one language to the other. A widely used typology distinguishes two kinds of transfer. Similarities between the two languages cause 'positive transfer': it proves acceptable to use the L1 habits in the L2 setting (e.g. the assumption that the subject goes before the verb satisfactorily transfers from English to French). Differences cause 'negative transfer', generally known as 'interference': the L1 habits cause errors in the L2 (e.g. the same assumption about subject–verb order does not satisfactorily transfer into Welsh). Typical interference errors include: *I wait here since 3 hours* (from French) and *How long must my hand in plaster stay?* (from German). Problems of negative transfer are thought to provide a major source of FLL difficulty. The main aim of behaviourist teaching is thus to form new, correct linguistic habits through intensive practice, eliminating interference errors in the process.

There are several problems presented by this account of FLL. Imitation alone does not provide a means of identifying the task facing learners, who are continually confronted with the need to create and recognize novel utterances that go beyond the limitations of the model sentences they may have practised. Nor does imitation suffice as an explanation of the way learners behave: not many of the errors that are theoretically predicted by the differences between L1 and L2 in fact occur in the language of learners; and conversely, other errors are found that seem unrelated to the L1. In a frequently-cited early study (H. C. Dulay & M. K. Burt, 1973), 145 Spanish-speaking children aged 5 to 8 were observed while learning English. Six structures were selected and the error patterns analysed. It emerged that interference errors (such as *They have hunger* from *Ellos tienen hambre*) accounted for only 3% of the errors made. The majority of the errors (85%, with a further 12% unclear) were thought to resemble those that appear in the course of L1 acquisition (e.g. *They*

hungry). Analyses of this kind have proved to be controversial (largely because of difficulties in validating the error analysis – see below), but their general conclusion is widely supported. The systematic comparison of L1 and L2, in order to predict areas of greatest learning difficulty – a procedure known as *contrastive analysis* – explains only a small part of what goes on in FLL.

THE COGNITIVE VIEW

The main alternative to the behaviourist approach sees as central the role of cognitive factors in language learning (pp. 236–7). In this view, learners are credited with using their cognitive abilities in a creative way to work out hypotheses about the structure of the FL. They construct rules, try them out, and alter them if they prove to be inadequate. Language learning, in this account, proceeds in a series of transitional stages, as learners acquire more knowledge of the L2. At each stage, they are in control of a language system that is equivalent to neither the L1 nor the L2 – an *interlanguage* (L. Selinker, 1972).

Error analysis plays a central role in this approach. Errors are likely to emerge when learners make the wrong deductions about the nature of the L2, such as assuming that a pattern is general, when in fact there are exceptions. The errors provide positive evidence about the nature of the learning process, as the learner gradually works out what the FL system is. For example, learners who say *vous disez* instead of *vous dites* 'you say' have assumed, wrongly, that the *-ez* ending found after *vous* in most other French verbs (*marchez, donnez,* etc.) also applies to *dire* 'say'. The error in this case indicates that a faulty generalization (or analogy, p. 236) has been made.

Since the 1970s, cognitive approaches to FLL have been in the ascendant, and error analysis in particular has attracted a great deal of attention. However, the analysis of errors turns out to be a highly complex matter, involving other factors than the cognitive. Some errors are due to the influence of the mother tongue, as contrastive analysis claims. Some come from external influences, such as inadequate teaching or materials. Some arise out of the need to make oneself understood by whatever means possible (e.g. replacing words by

TWO MODELS OF FOREIGN LANGUAGE LEARNING

Behaviourist	Cognitive
L2 input obtained from controlled, formal, instruction	Exposure to authentic use of L2 in near-natural situations
↓	↓
Imitation and reinforcement (conscious) strategies	Input processed using natural (universal, unconscious) strategies
↓	↓
L2 habits established	Transitional stages of learning (interlanguage)
↓	↓
L2 output	L2 output

THE MONITOR MODEL

In the 1970s, an influential view of the relationship between acquisition and learning was propounded by the American linguist, Stephen Krashen (1941–). This account recognizes a subconscious, natural process ('acquisition'), which is the primary force behind FL fluency. 'Learning' is seen as a conscious process that monitors, or edits, the progress of acquisition and guides the performance of the speaker. Its role is – or should be – minor, being used only to correct errors in speech or to give speech a more 'polished' appearance.

The emphasis on acquisition leads Krashen to propose an 'input hypothesis', which suggests that teachers should try to replicate in the classroom the conditions which occur in L1 acquisition. The parallel is drawn between the input of teacher to student and that from mother (or caretaker) to child (see facing page).

In fact, traditional FLT provides learners with a great deal of conscious knowledge of linguistic rules. As a result, they may come to rely too much on this knowledge, so that it actually gets in the way of their ability to communicate. People who worry too much about making a mistake, and who thus are reluctant to use their FL ability, are in this view 'overusing' their monitor.

Theories of this kind are inevitably controversial, given our limited knowledge of the psychological processes involved in speech production. There is plainly a need to take into account the distinction between conscious and subconscious awareness in language processing, and between formal and informal settings, but the way these variables interact, it has been argued, is more complex than anything which has so far been proposed.

In particular, since the 1980s, attention has been focused on applying a psycholinguistic perspective to FLL, in which the varying demands of information processing by the brain are used as an explanation for variability of errors. The student who can say *Mrs Brown lives in Reading* but **Mrs Brown who live in Reading has just won the lottery* makes the error because of the extra load involved in processing the subordinate clause.

gestures). Moreover, not all errors are equally systematic, disruptive, or unacceptable. Errors of vocabulary, for example, are less general and predictable than errors of grammar, but they are usually more disruptive of communication. Some errors, indeed, become so acceptable that they do not disappear: they become 'fossilized' – tolerated by learners (insofar as they are conscious of them) because they do not cause major problems of communication (e.g. the pronunciation errors that constitute a foreign accent).

Above all, error analysis is complicated by the fact that it is often unclear what the learner intended to say, and thus how to identify the error that has been made. For example, does *The lady eat it* display an error of the noun (*ladies*) or verb – and if the latter, should the correct form be *eats*, *is eating*, *ate*, or some other variant? And even if we assume that the speaker intended to say *eats*, we are still left with the question of whether the error is one of pronunciation (the speaker having difficulty with the [ts] cluster) or grammar – and, within the latter heading, whether the difficulty is one of morphology (lack of awareness of the ending) or syntax (lack of awareness of number agreement between subject and verb) (§16).

Despite the difficulties, research into errors continues to provide a fruitful way of investigating the processes underlying FL acquisition. However, as with contrastive analysis, the approach cannot provide a complete explanation. Most FLL settings do not constitute the kind of 'pure', natural linguistic situation that is presupposed by the cognitive approach, but contain elements of formal teaching, in which learners are systematically introduced to fragments of the L2 (e.g. one tense at a time). To understand the way languages come to be learned in these 'mixed' settings, it is thus proving necessary to devise more sophisticated models, which focus on the relationship between the processes of natural acquisition and those of formal learning, and which pay adequate attention to the needs and aims of the students, and to the nature of the social setting in which FLL interaction takes place.

There is something in the poetry of
Wordsworth which ~~is~~ *will* always ~~to~~ live. He

ERRORS IN LANGUAGE LEARNING

The error in this sentence, written by a Swedish student, seems straightforward, but it is not easy to say exactly what the error is, why it was made, and whether the teacher has made the best correction. Is the student confusing *be to* and *will*? Or has he learned the past tense use of *be to* in this context (as in *There was something in the poetry which was to live forever*), and assumed that the present tense would work in the same way? If so, is there not an additional error in the position of *always*? And would not *forever* be a more idiomatic word? The corresponding construction in Swedish is *som alltid skall leva*, but this will not explain all that is going on.

THE NATURAL ORDER HYPOTHESIS

During the 1970s, several studies drew attention to the fact that different FL learners make similar errors, regardless of their language background. Such errors as *I going* and *this a book* were observed in Spanish, Russian, Japanese, and several other learners of English. The conclusion was drawn that there must be a universal creative process at work; learners were said to be following a natural 'internal syllabus' (as opposed to the 'external' syllabus of the classroom). Several of the errors closely resembled those made by children learning their mother tongue. Analogies were therefore drawn with the 'language acquisition device' postulated by some child-language analysts (p. 234), and a parallel was proposed between the natural order of L1 acquisition and the way people acquired a foreign language.

Particular attention was focused on the way in which foreign learners of English used a set of grammatical morphemes (§16), such as *-ing*, *-ed*, and plural *-s*, which L1 studies had already found to be acquired in a certain order (p. 244). The errors learners made with each item were counted, and the morphemes were ranked on the basis of how accurately they were used. This ranking was then assumed to reflect the order in which the learners were acquiring these morphemes. Similar orders were found in several different FLL contexts, in both spoken and written language, thus supporting the idea of a natural, universal sequence of acquisition that was independent of the influence of the learner's first language.

If natural order exists, there would be major implications for external syllabuses, which would presumably be modified in that direction. However, criticisms have been made of this kind of approach. Order of acquisition as based on a cross-sectional study of speech samples may not correspond to the order of acquisition that would emerge from a longitudinal study (p. 231). The findings are of limited generality: only a very small number of grammatical items have been analysed, and there have been very few studies (most of which to date have focused on English, so that it is unclear how genuine the claimed universals are). And differences in acquisition order have already begun to emerge, casting doubt on the universality of the natural order hypothesis.

CHILD VS ADULT ACQUISITION

The similarities between L1 and L2 acquisition errors are striking, but there are many differences between the two kinds of learning situation (over and above issues of neurological development, p. 265), which makes it difficult to see a parallel between adult foreign language learners and young children acquiring their mother tongue.

• The adult has a set of formed cognitive skills and strategies that should make the FLL task easier (e.g. the ability to memorize, imitate, and use dictionaries). A major asset is the ability of most adults to read and write.

• Adults already have a language, and this inevitably reduces their motivation to learn another beyond minimal levels. Migrants, for example, generally learn only enough to enable them to survive in their new country.

• There are several emotional differences between adults and children when it comes to learning. In particular, adults are more self-conscious about FLL, and are less able to assimilate cultural differences.

• Adults meet a greater variety of L2 situations than do children learning their L1. Children's needs are also very different (e.g. they need language for play and emotional expression). Accordingly, the range of teaching objectives will differ in each case.

• The adult has less time and opportunity than the child for FLL. Some estimates suggest that it takes well over a year to accumulate as much L2 experience as a young child gets from the L1 in a month.

• Adults invariably find themselves in a less natural learning environment than children. It is rarely possible to devise a teaching situation which closely resembles that encountered by the L1 child, with its one-to-one interaction and strong emotional (caregiver) support.

• There is an uncertain parallel between the way in which mothers talk to their children and the way in which people talk to adults using a foreign language ('foreigner talk'). Certainly, adult L1 speakers adapt to learners, and (often unconsciously) try to help them by speaking slower and louder, repeating words, simplifying their grammar, and using stereotyped expressions (of which pidgin *savvy* is probably the most famous). They also ignore many errors. But it is unclear how universal or how systematic these input strategies are.

• Similarly, it is unclear how far teacher language displays correspondences with motherese (p. 237); the differences, at present, are more striking than the similarities. To facilitate learning, in the early stages, teachers need to keep their input relatively simple, interesting, comprehensible, relevant to the learning task, sufficiently repetitive to enable patterns to be perceived, and capable of providing appropriate feedback. Generalization proves difficult, given the great variation that exists among teaching methods (p. 378).

TEACHING METHODS

In the long search for the best way of teaching a foreign language, hundreds of different approaches, or *methods*, have been devised. Each method is based on a particular view of language learning, and usually recommends the use of a specific set of techniques and materials, which may have to be implemented in a fixed sequence. Ambitious claims are often made for a new teaching method, but none has yet been shown to be intrinsically superior. The contemporary attitude is flexible and utilitarian: it is recognized that there are several ways of reaching the goal of FL competence, and that teachers need to be aware of a range of methods, in order to find the one most appropriate to the learner's needs and circumstances, and to the objectives of the course. It is frequently necessary to introduce an eclectic approach, in which aspects of different methods are selected to meet the demands of particular teaching situations.

Several classifications of teaching methods have been made, in an attempt to impose some degree of order on what is a highly diverse and idiosyncratic field. Some analysts make use of the fundamental distinction between language structure (form) and language use (function) (§13). Under the first heading, they include those methods that focus on the teaching of formal rules and categories, and that emphasize the importance of accurate written translation and the understanding of literature. Under the second heading, they include methods that lay stress on the teaching of active participation in natural and realistic spoken language settings, and where the emphasis is on communicative success rather than on formal accuracy. Many approaches are biased in one or the other direction, though it is also common to find approaches that claim to integrate the strengths of both positions.

Certain methods are widely recognized because of their influential role in the history of ideas surrounding this subject.

Easy listening New FLT methods are invented every day. Many claim to provide remarkable progress – at a price. This advertisement, taken from a South American newspaper in 1984, is typical of its genre. What makes it especially intriguing is its proposed integration of behaviourist and mentalist linguistic theories (p. 412)!

SPANISH GERMAN FRENCH
MASTER IT WITH NO COURSE OR TEACHER
UNBELIEVABLE?
BUT TRUE
A successful application of B.F. Skinner's and Noam Chomsky's Theories has resulted in a system that makes it possible. And to top it all, you'll do it in less than 90 days and no more than 200 hours. By appointment only. Please call us, Tel: ** ** **. and ask for Mrs. ****. We'll gladly show you how it works at no cost.

The grammar translation method This method derives from the traditional approach to the teaching of Latin and Greek, which was particularly influential in the 19th century. It is based on the meticulous analysis of the written language, in which translation exercises, reading comprehension, and the written imitation of texts play a primary role. Learning mainly involves the mastery of grammatical rules and memorization of long lists of literary vocabulary, related to texts which are chosen more for their prestigious content than for their interest or level of linguistic difficulty. There is little emphasis laid on the activities of listening or speaking.

This approach dominated early work in modern language teaching. A minority still find its intellectual discipline appealing; but the vast majority of teachers now recognize that the approach does little to meet the spoken language needs and interests of today's language students.

The direct method This approach, also known as the *oral* or *natural* method, is based on the active involvement of the learner in speaking and listening to the foreign language in realistic everyday situations. No use is made of the learner's mother tongue; learners are encouraged to think in the foreign language, and not to translate into or out of it. A great deal of emphasis is placed on good pronunciation, often introducing students to phonetic transcription (§27) before they see the standard orthography. Formal grammatical rules and terminology are avoided.

The direct method continues to attract interest and enthusiasm, but it is not an easy approach to use in school. In the artificial environment of the classroom, it is difficult to generate natural learning situations and to provide everyone with sufficient practice. Several variants of the method have thus evolved. In particular, teachers often permit some degree of mother-tongue explanation and grammatical statement to avoid learners developing inaccurate fluency ('school pidgin').

The audio-lingual method Also known as the *aural–oral* method, this approach derives from the intensive training in spoken languages given to American military personnel during the Second World War, which resulted in a high degree of listening and speaking skill being achieved in a relatively short time-span. The emphasis is on everyday spoken conversation, with particular attention being paid to natural pronunciation. Language is seen as a process of habit formation (p. 376): structural patterns in dialogues about everyday situations are imitated and drilled (first in choral speech, then individually) until the learner's responses become automatic. There is a special focus on areas of structural contrast between L1 and L2. There is little discussion of grammatical rules. Language work is first heard, then practised orally, before being seen and used in written form.

COMMUNICATIVE TEACHING

During the 1970s, there was a widespread reaction, in both L1 and L2 teaching (§44), against methods that stressed the teaching of grammatical forms and paid little or no attention to the way language is used in everyday situations. A concern developed to make FLT 'communicative' by focusing on learners' knowledge of the functions of language, and on their ability to select appropriate kinds of language for use in specific situations.

Increased interest was shown in the situations themselves, and in the kind of language the learner would be likely to meet (e.g. at a bank, eating out). 'Situational syllabuses' aimed to recreate these situations, and to teach the various linguistic activities involved, such as requesting, thanking, complaining, and instructing.

'Notional' (or 'functional') syllabuses provided a major alternative to the emphases of formal language teaching. Here, the content of a course is organized in terms of the meanings ('notions') learners require in order to communicate in particular functional contexts. Major communicative notions include the linguistic expression of time, duration, frequency, sequence, quantity, location, and motion. Major communicative functions include evaluation, persuasion, emotional expression, and the marking of social relations.

Communicative methods have attracted universal interest, and much influenced the practice of modern FLT. But there has also been a critical reaction, as linguists and teachers encounter problems in providing a principled basis for interrelating the proposed notions and functions. Of particular importance is the need to provide learners with principles that will enable them to make a 'bridge' between functional aspects of language and the correct use of formal structures. Proponents of the approach have recognized these problems, and there has been considerable discussion of the way communicative teaching might develop in the future. (After K. Johnson & D. Porter, 1983.)

The approach can instil considerable conversational fluency in a learner, and was widely used, especially in the 1950s and 1960s. Its reliance on drills and habit-formation makes it less popular today, especially with learners who wish for a wider range of linguistic experience, and who feel the need for more creative work in speech production.

New methods

During the 1960s, several fresh approaches to FLL were devised, aiming to provide a radical alternative to traditional methods, which their proponents believe have failed. They drew attention to the success with which people acquire more than one language all over the world (§60), and contrasted this with the limited achievements of the classroom situation, and the partial accounts of learning presented by the various theories (p. 376). If FLL could be made more natural, and the learner made more receptive to the task, it was argued, more efficient learning would result.

The effectiveness of the different methods remains to be thoroughly evaluated; but each has its reported successes, and some (especially the first three in the list (right)), have come to be widely practised. The following outlines (with the originator's name in parentheses) indicate the thrust of each approach, but they convey nothing of the emotional atmosphere and sense of involvement promoted by these methods, which are central to their claims of success.

Since the 1980s, the emphasis has moved away from the devising of new methods to a concern over evaluation. The focus is more on devising principles and procedures which can be applied to demonstrate how well a teaching method, technique, test, textbook, etc. works. Contemporary FLT is less concerned with new lamps than with polishing (and assessing) the old.

Learning by hypnosis   An unorthodox method of foreign language learning – 'I am learning English while sleeping,' says the notice.

HUMANISTIC APPROACHES

Suggestopedia (Georgi Lozanov) An approach based on suggestology, the science of suggestion. Devised by a Bulgarian psychiatrist, it was originally used as a general teaching method in that country's primary schools; elsewhere, it has mainly been applied in the field of adult FLT. The method is based on the view that the brain (especially the right hemisphere, §45) has great unused potential, which can be exploited through the power of suggestion. Language learning can be promoted by drawing on the reserve capacities of the unconscious mind. Blocks to learning are removed (using 'desuggestion' techniques), and a positive attitude towards language learning developed ('resuggestion').

In their opening lesson (or 'concert'), learners are presented with large amounts of the foreign language. The text is translated, then it is read aloud in a dramatic way against a background of classical music. The aim is to provide an atmosphere of total relaxation and enjoyment, in which learning is incidental. After a session, there should be a sense of euphoria, reminiscent of the feelings that follow a visit to a health spa (the 'spa effect'). By using a large amount of linguistic material, the suggestion is conveyed that language learning is easy and natural. In a later session, students use the material in various communicative activities. The emphasis, then is wholly on informal communication; no attention is drawn to grammatical errors. Learners, it is claimed, assimilate far more from such an 'immersion' than would traditionally be expected.

The silent way (Caleb Gattegno) This approach aims to provide an environment which keeps the amount of teaching to a minimum and encourages learners to develop their own ways of using the language elements introduced. In the first lesson, the teacher introduces a small L2 vocabulary to talk about a set of coloured rods, using a few verbs (equivalent to 'take', 'give', 'pick up', and 'put'), adjectives, pronouns, etc., and gradually extending the length of the sentence (e.g. 'Take the green rod and give it to Michael'). The aim is to help the learners to become self-reliant – to select their own sentences and be in control of them, with good intonation and rhythm. The teacher does not repeat the material or provide sentences for students to imitate; and no use is made of the learners' L1. Charts containing vocabulary and colour-coded guides to pronunciation are made available to enable the teacher to guide the student's learning while saying as little as possible. As students say more to each other, so the teacher says less – hence the 'silent' way.

Total physical response (James J. Asher) This method stresses the importance of aural comprehension as an exclusive aim in the early months of learning. The name derives from the emphasis on the actions that learners have to make, as they are given simple commands (e.g. 'stand', 'sit', 'stop'). More advanced language is introduced by building up chains of actions, using either spoken or written commands.

Community language learning (Charles A. Curran) This approach builds on the kind of 'whole person' relationship found in counselling therapy. The main aim is to foster strong personal links between the teacher/counsellor and the learners, and thus to eliminate whatever is found threatening in the FLL situation. There is no prepared material. The learners talk naturally in their L1, and seek from the teacher FL equivalents for what they want to say. The teacher provides the translation, and the students repeat it. Each session is tape recorded, and is followed by a discussion with the teacher of what went on.

Natural approach (Tracy D. Terrell) This method emphasizes the role of 'natural' language acquisition, and underscores the parallels between L2 and L1. It stresses the importance of emotional rather than cognitive factors in learning, and of mastering vocabulary rather than grammatical rules. There is no formal correction. The aim is to establish an ability to understand the basic content of a communication in informal settings. Learners use their L1 while their L2 comprehension is developing.

Language from within (Beverly Galyean) This method encourages learners to be introspective about their own needs, interests, values, and 'here and now' activities, and to talk about these emotional responses to others. All material comes from the students, as they become more self-aware, and build up a close relationship with each other. The aim is to enable the cognitive, affective, and interactive elements in learning to 'flow together' – hence the alternative name for this approach, 'confluent' teaching.

Delayed oral practice (Valerian A. Postovsky) This approach, often known as the 'comprehension approach', is based on the principle that it is far easier for learners to achieve competence in recognizing language, whether in speech or writing, than in producing it. A basic receptive competence is established, and this is used as a foundation for work involving retrieval skills.

MATERIALS

The days are long gone when FLT materials consisted only of a grammar book and a dictionary. Today, there is a vast variety of printed materials – course books, workbooks, readers, programmed courses, collections of facsimile material, simplified literature, cue cards, charts, newspapers, magazines, posters, picture cards, cut-outs, and much more. These are supplemented by a range of materials using other media, such as CDs, records, audio tapes, slides, transparencies, filmstrips, video tapes, toys, games, and puppets. The advent of computer technology introduces a further potentially inexhaustible domain of ancillary equipment and a wide range of new interaction techniques. In modern foreign language teaching and learning, materials design and implementation is a major enterprise – the area where the principles of applied linguistic theory, the demands of classroom practice, and the realities of commercial production lie uneasily together.

ra

Hiragana: ら

kirai	dislike
rampu	lamp
torakku	truck
	(K–39)

ru

Hiragana: る

aruku	to walk
rusui	care-taker (during one's absence)
taoru	towel
	(K–41)

A selection of *kana* cards (left), providing Japanese learners with practice in recognizing the symbols of the *katakana* and *hiragana* alphabets (p. 203). On one side, the symbol is given with three examples of its use; on the other side, there is the name of the symbol, a romanized version of each word, a translation, arrows showing how to write the symbol, and the equivalent symbol in the other *kana* system.

Right: A page from Book 1, Lesson 1, of a popular 1930s German course, *Deutsches Leben*. The exercise drills questions and answers, and introduces the three forms of the definite article, *der*, *die*, and *das*.

(Seite zwei)   FRAGE UND ANTWORT

Das ist das Papier. Was ist das ?   Das ist das Papier.

Das ist die Tafel.
Was ist das ?
Das ist die Tafel.

Das ist die Tür.
Was ist das ?
Das ist die Tür.

Das ist das Fenster.
Was ist das ?
Das ist das Fenster.

Das ist der Fussboden.
Was ist das ?
Das ist der Fussboden.

Das ist die Decke. Was ist das ?   Das ist die Decke.

Das ist die Wand.
Was ist das ?
Das ist die Wand.

Das ist das D...

Below: An ingenious way of providing practice in present-tense sentence patterns – part of a unit from Book 1 of *The Cambridge English Course* (M. Swan & C. Walter, 1984).

NOTES AND VOCABULARY

Abbreviated words are given in full on their first occurrence.

petite mécanique light engineering
la formation training
la rentabilité profitability
avantages (*m*) **sociaux** fringe benefits (restaurant, expenses, *etc.*)
Curriculum Vitae
prétentions (*f*) salary required
Publicité (*f*) advertising
transmettra forward
un adjoint assistant
commerciaux
organisation (*f*)
un fichier card index, record

Some authentic written language materials. The materials are accompanied by lexical glosses for the less familiar items – one of the items in a textbook anthology for advanced students of French (D. E. Ager, 1970).

B **The Swan-Walter Universal Holiday Postcard Machine**

1 It's easy to write holiday postcards! Write one now and send it to a friend.

Dear ...N...
Well, here we are in ...T... ...W..., and we are having a/an ...A... time. I am sitting / lying ...Pr... ...Pl..., writing postcards, drinking ...D... and looking at ...L... ...N... is ...V..., and ...PN... are ...V... ...Pr... ...Pl... Tomorrow we are going to ...T... I'm sure it will be ...A...
Wish you were here,
Love, ...N...

POSTCARD DICTIONARY

N (name)	T (town, city, village)	W (weather)	A (adjective)		Pr (preposition)
John	Rome	The sun is shining	wonderful	terrible	in
Mary	Manchester	It is raining	beautiful	awful	on
Alexandra	Honolulu	It is snowing	lovely	horrible	at
Mother	etc.	There is a hurricane	exciting	catastrophic	under
etc.		etc.	interesting	boring	by
			magnificent	etc.	near
					opposite
					etc.

Pl (place)	D (drink)	L (things to look at)	V (verb)	PN (plural noun)
my room	coffee	the sea	shopping	the children
their room	beer	the mountains	sightseeing	Mummy and Daddy
the bar	wine	the rain	sleeping	George and Sue
the beach	etc.	the sheep	drinking beer	etc.
a café		etc.	dancing	
a tree			playing cards	
a mountain			having a bath	
etc.			etc.	

THE LANGUAGE LABORATORY

The best-known technological aid in FLT is undoubtedly the language laboratory – a room, usually divided into booths, where students can listen individually to tape recordings of FL material, and where they may record and play back their own responses, while being monitored by a teacher.

When these laboratories were first introduced, they were heralded as a technique that would vastly improve the rate and quality of FLL. They would take the burden of repetitive drills away from the teacher, provide more opportunities for learners to practise listening and speaking, and enable them to develop at their own rates and monitor their own progress. Many schools were quick to install expensive laboratory equipment. However, within a few years, it became apparent that there would be no breakthrough. The expected improvements did not emerge, and the popularity of the 'language lab' showed a marked decline.

There were several reasons for the failure to live up to expectations. The taped materials were often poorly designed, leading to student frustration and boredom. The published programmes failed to reflect the kind of work the student was doing in class. Few modern languages staff had received training in materials design or laboratory use. And it proved difficult to maintain the equipment once it had been installed.

Today, the strengths and limitations of the laboratory are better realized, and the vastly increased potential of modern electronic hardware has led to a certain revival. There is now considerable interest in *language learning laboratories*, which contain much more than the traditional systems – in particular, the introduction of interactive computational aids and video materials has proved to be extremely popular.

It is now clear that, when used properly, laboratories can provide a valuable extra dimension to FLT. For example, the taped material can provide a variety of authentic and well-recorded models for the training of listening comprehension. And laboratories can be used as resource centres, or libraries, giving learners extra opportunities to practise at their chosen level.

At the same time, the limitations of laboratories must be borne in mind. Their value will always depend on the development of appropriate teaching materials which reinforce what has been taught in class and provide opportunities for creative use; and here there is an urgent need for research into the efficacy of the different approaches which have been devised. Laboratory software, it seems, has some way to go before it can compare in sophistication with the hardware.

A language laboratory that incorporates computer-assisted language learning (CALL) work stations. Microcomputers, used as word processors, complement the audio facilities, enabling interactive teaching of written language skills. Several kinds of FLT exercise can be computationally controlled, such as sentence restructuring, checking of translation or dictation tasks, and cloze testing (see below) using texts displayed on the screen. These days, increasingly ingenious and motivating interactive games are available, using computational techniques. In *Storyboard*, for example, learners are given a passage of blanks; they have to 'buy' words and complete the passage before their supply of money runs out.

	A		C	
Master track	The man is running. The men?	BLANK	The men are running.	BLANK
Learner track	BLANK	The men is running.	BLANK	The men are running.
		B		D

A typical sequence of events on a language laboratory tape. In this illustration, the tape is double-track, enabling the foreign model to be recorded on one track, and the learner's voice on the other. An example of one kind of drill is given. Learners first hear a sample sentence, and are given a stimulus to respond to (A). They then record their response (B), hear the correct version (C), and have an opportunity to repeat it (D).

TESTING

Teachers need to test student performance, or enter them for formal examinations. Test results are critical, not only because they affect careers, but because of the influence they exercise on motivation to learn.

It is now widely appreciated that tests perform a variety of functions. Four main types are usually recognized.
• *Proficiency tests* determine how much of the L2 a learner has mastered, regardless of the course of study followed, as in national examinations, and the international Test of English as a Foreign Language.
• *Achievement tests* determine how much of a particular course of study has been mastered. These are com-

monly used at the end of school terms.
• *Diagnostic tests* aim to find out what a student still has to learn in a language. The results provide feedback for the teacher, by displaying the learner's strengths and weaknesses. Although they are very different from achievement tests (e.g. they are not always given marks or graded), students often fail to see the difference.
• *Prognostic* (or *aptitude*) *tests* try to predict how well a person will succeed in learning an L2. These tests focus on specific kinds of activity (e.g. sound imitation, pattern matching), and provide data about individual difficulties.

Testing can focus on any

linguistic skill (speaking, listening, reading, writing) and on any linguistic component (e.g. vocabulary, pronunciation, grammar, spelling). Many ways of eliciting information have been devised; such as asking students to make a translation, carry out an action, or give a paraphrase. Anticipating the effects of a task is not easy, however; a question may be unnecessarily difficult, or an answer may require information that has not been taught. It is therefore always necessary to look critically at test procedures, and to aim for improvements in test design, selection, and administration.

Anyway, Susie said that there were no (1) — things as fairies, elves, this that and (2) — other. Well, the night she put her (3) — under the pillow we forgot to put (4) — money there and take it away – we (5) — all about it. (C *laughs*) So she got up (6) — the morning, 'My tooth's all gone and (7) — no money.' Dave said, 'Well, there you (8) — you see. You said you didn't believe (9) — fairies so how can you expect the (10) — to come and see you if...'. Oh (11) — I do believe in fairies (D *laughs*), you know (12) — really do.' (C *laughs*). So Dave said, 'Well, try (13) — tonight.' So that night, thank goodness, we (14) — (C *laughs*) So the next morning she gets up (15) — happy. 'Oh, they've been, they've been...

Cloze testing   In this kind of language test, every *n*th word is omitted from a passage (the gaps are usually between five and seven words apart), and the student has to complete (or 'close') the gaps. This form of testing is widely used: it is good at establishing whether a student has a 'feel' for the language, and for testing awareness of points of detail. Several types of cloze test exist; for example, students can be given the omitted words below the passage, or they can be given an initial letter as a clue. In the example above, taken from a workbook on conversational English, there are no clues: the student must fill in any appropriate word, bearing in mind the informal style of the passage. (K. Morrow, 1978, p. 49.)

'They don't seem to be talking the same language.' This common observation acts as a reminder that barriers to communication exist, and indeed are commonplace, even within a langua.e. Linguistic difficulties are inevitable when there is interaction between people from different racial, regional, cultural, social, or occupational backgrounds – something that is increasingly common in modern society as people become more mobile and come into contact with diverse forms of linguistic behaviour. A major aim of linguistic studies, accordingly, is to investigate the factors that promote and maintain the existence of varieties within a language (Part II), and to provide descriptions of their use. These studies have an intrinsic intellectual interest, as they provide a means of observing change in contemporary culture and civilization. But they can also be of practical assistance, by clarifying the reasons for the use of unfamiliar language, and thus providing a perspective that may help to resolve cases of linguistic conflict.

There is no theoretical limit to the number of special purposes to which language can be put. As society develops new facets, so language is devised to express them. In recent times, whole new areas of expression have emerged, in relation to such domains as computing, broadcasting, commercial advertising, and popular music. Over a longer time-scale, special styles have developed associated with religion, law, politics, commerce, the press, medicine, and science. A detailed linguistic account of any one of these areas would itself require an encyclopedia, as the analysis of the language used would require an exposition of the conceptual system that gave rise to it. The following illustrations of linguistic varieties and attitudes are inevitably highly selective, therefore, in both range and depth of treatment. But they do provide a hint of the extensive resources that language makes available to meet the special needs of developing societies, and of the complications that arise as people slowly come to terms with them.

PLAIN ENGLISH CAMPAIGNS

Popular anxiety over special uses of language is most markedly seen in the campaigns to promote 'plain' speaking and writing – notably, the Plain English movements of Britain and the USA. The main aim of these campaigns is to attack the use of unnecessarily complicated language ('gobbledegook') by governments, businesses, and other authorities whose role puts them in linguistic contact with the general public. The campaigners argue that such language, whether spoken or written, should be replaced by clearer forms of expression.

The movements took shape only in the late 1970s, so it is too soon to ascertain their long-term influence on the characteristics of language varieties. But they have certainly played a major part in promoting public awareness of the existence of communication problems, and have influenced many organizations to do something about it. In Britain, the campaign was launched in 1979 by a ritual shredding of government forms in Parliament Square, London. By 1982, the government had published a report telling departments to improve the design of forms, and to abolish those that were unnecessary. By 1985, around 15,700 forms had disappeared and 21,300 had been revised. In the USA, President Carter's Executive Order of March 1978 required regulations to be written in plain English, and although this was revoked by President Reagan in 1981, it promoted a great deal of legislation throughout the country, and an increase in plain English usage among corporations and consumers.

Today the Plain English campaigns continue to grow, focusing especially on such everyday consumer products as forms, official letters, licences, leases, contracts, insurance policies, and guarantees. In Britain, annual publicity is given to the Plain English Awards competition, which gives trophies to organizations

Cartoon taken from the *Quarterly Review of Doublespeak* (January 1996), published by the National Council of Teachers of English in Urbana, Illinois.

A GOLDEN BULL WINNER

One of the winners of the British Golden Bull awards in 1982 was a written decision made by a government insurance officer, which opened in the following way:

As insurance officer I have decided to review the decision dated 19.9.83 for the following reasons: that by its decision of 31.1.84 the medical board varied the assessment of disablement resulting from the relevant loss of faculty and this constitutes a revision of a decision on a special question.

My revised decision is as follows: A disablement gratuity of £21.50 based on an assessment of 3% per week from 8.6.83 to 22.11.83 and £11.12 per week from 23.11.83 to 6.12.83 based upon an assessment of 20% for the period 8.6.83 to 1.12.83 and a disablement gratuity of £52.75 based upon an assessment of 3% from 2.12.83 to 1.6.84 are awarded for the same accident for which a disablement gratuity of £21.50 based upon an assessment of 3% from 24.3.83 to 7.6.83 and a disablement pension of £10.72 per week from 8.6.83 to 22.11.83 and £11.12 per week from 23.11.83 to 13.12.83 (total £290.64) was awarded and paid... (Quoted in C. Maher & M. Cutts, 1986, p. 12.)

that have produced the clearest documents, and booby prizes (the Golden Bull Awards) to those whose materials are least intelligible. In the USA, similar interest is shown in the annual Doublespeak Awards, awarded by the National Council of Teachers of English to 'American public figures who have perpetrated language that is grossly unfactual, deceptive, evasive, euphemistic, confusing, or self-contradictory'.

In these cost-conscious days, it is stressed that clear language not only avoids anxiety on the part of the recipient, it also saves time and money. The campaigns have large dossiers of problem cases. In one case, an official government letter provoked so many complaints and questions that a second letter had to be sent to explain the first. In another, an application form was wrongly filled in by 50% of the applicants, which resulted in a considerable outlay of effort in returning and reprocessing the form. On the positive side, there are cases of businesses revising their literature to avoid legal jargon, and benefiting from increased sales.

Particular concern is expressed about the ambiguities and omissions found in medical labels. For example, in one pharmaceutical survey, the instruction to 'use sparingly' was found to be misunderstood by 33% of patients. The instruction to 'take two tablets four hourly' received a variety of interpretations (e.g. to take eight tablets an hour). Related areas of concern include the use of warning labels on household goods (such as disinfectants) and on toys for children.

The instructions accompanying do-it-yourself products are also regularly cited as a source of unnecessary expense or frustration. Few companies seem to test their instructions by having them followed by a first-time user. Often, essential background information is omitted, steps in the construction process are taken for granted, and some degree of special knowledge is assumed. This is especially worrying in fields where any failure to follow correct procedures can be dangerous.

Objections to material in plain English have come mainly from the legal profession. Lawyers point to the risk of ambiguity inherent in the use of everyday language for legal or official documents, and draw attention to the need for confidence in legal formulations, which can come only from using language that has been tested in courts over the course of centuries (p. 390). The campaigners point out that there has been no sudden increase in litigation as a consequence of the increase in plain English materials. Similarly, professionals in several specialized fields have defended their use of technical and complex language as being the most precise means of expressing technical and complex ideas. This is undoubtedly true: scientists, doctors, bankers, and others need their jargon, in order to communicate with each other succinctly and unambiguously. But when it comes to addressing the non-specialist consumer, the plain English campaigners argue, different criteria must apply.

WHAT IS PLAIN ENGLISH?

It is not easy to devise precise, consistent, and acceptable guidelines for those who wish to write in plain English. One proponent of the Plain English movement in the USA makes the following recommendations concerning readability and design. (For other views, see pp. 2, 254.)

Readability

• Prefer the shorter word to the longer one. Use simple, everyday words rather than fancy ones. Prefer verbs over nouns and adjectives. Prefer the specific word to the general.

• Write short sentences with an average of no more than 20 words. Use the active voice rather than the passive. Be a miser with compound and complex sentences and a spendthrift with simple sentences.

• Write short paragraphs with an average of about 75 words. Avoid paragraphs that exceed five typed lines for business letters and ten lines for longer compositions.

• Write with the ear. A sentence may look correct on paper but its cadence may be jarring. Listen to your sentences in your head as you write, and do not write anything that you could not comfortably say.

Design

Write for the eye as well as the mind. Prepare an overall design, positioning understandable headings, subheadings, and captions for each segment, showing the organization of the text. Make the whole document visually appealing.

• Use appropriate underlining, ink colour that contrasts sharply with the paper, lists, boxes or panels, bold or other typefaces to emphasize key points.

• Use 'white space' in margins, and between sections, paragraphs, and lines, to make the document look good.

(J. Y. Dayananda, 1986, p. 13.)

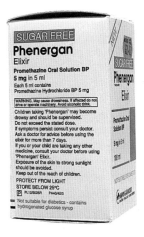

BEFORE AND AFTER

An illustration of plain English in action can be seen from the British campaign's version of a contract for moving goods from one house to another.

(Quoted in C. Maher & M. Cutts, 1986, p. 12.)

Original version
GENERAL LIEN – The contractor shall have a general lien upon all goods in his possession for all monies due to him from the customer or for liabilities incurred by him and for monies paid on behalf of the customer, and if part of the goods shall have been delivered, removed or despatched or sold the general lien shall apply in respect of such goods as remain in the Contractor's possession. The Contractor shall be entitled to charge a storage charge and all other expenses during which a lien on the goods is being asserted and all these conditions shall continue to apply thereto.

Plain English version
OUR RIGHT TO HOLD THE GOODS – We have a right to hold some or all of the goods until you have paid all our charges and other payments due under this contract. These include charges, taxes or levies that we have paid to any other removal or storage business, carrier or official body. While we hold the goods and wait for payment you will have to pay storage charges and all other necessary expenses. This contract will apply to the goods held in this way.

Men of science In previous centuries, scientists from different subject areas were keen to follow each other's progress. Ideas and findings were exchanged and debated in scientific societies, as depicted in this print of an early meeting of the Royal Institution, London.

THE LANGUAGE OF SCIENCE

The aim of science is to determine the principles governing the physical universe. Progress towards this end, however, is to a large extent dependent on the use of language. The knowledge base of a subject, upon which all scientists depend, is accessible only if previous generations have managed to express their findings in a precise and unambiguous manner. Similarly, present-day scientists, hoping to make their own contribution to this knowledge base, must satisfy the same linguistic constraints if their work is to be correctly interpreted and accepted by their peers. Research findings are of limited value, until they are written up and published.

The methodology of science, with its demand for objectivity, systematic investigation, and exact measurement, has several linguistic consequences. There is an overriding concern for impersonal statement, logical exposition, and precise description. Emotional comment, humour, figurative expression, and other aspects of personal language are avoided (except in writing intended for a lay audience). The mathematical expression of relationships promotes an extensive use of numerals, operators, letters, and other special symbols, which are frequently used in word-like and sentence-like combinations (as formulae, equations, etc.). Lengthy sequences of text can be written in logographic form (p. 202), thus giving the language of science its highly valued status as a universal medium of expression.

Vocabulary and grammar

In addition to this distinctive graphology (§33), scientific language illustrates several important features of vocabulary and grammar. The large technical vocabulary is undoubtedly its most characteristic feature, reflecting the specialized subject matter of scientific domains of enquiry. Everyday words are too vague for many scientific purposes, so new ones have to be invented. This novel vocabulary is largely based on borrowings from Latin and Greek, showing the influence of Classical languages during the period of scientific discovery following the Renaissance. It contains many compound expressions, some of which (in such fields as chemistry) can be extremely long and unpronounceable, requiring abbreviation for prac-tical use (a familiar example is *TNT*, short for *trinitrotoluene*). At the other extreme, some fields delight in using everyday words to identify new hypotheses and discoveries – notably, in contemporary particle physics, where we find such technical terms as *strangeness*, *flavour*, *colour*, and *charm*.

Moreover, scientific vocabulary requires continual updating in the light of the process of discovery. Science is in fact the main birthplace for new words in a language: in a comprehensive English dictionary (§18), the vast majority of the words would be scientific (or technological) terms. More than 750,000 species of insect have been discovered, for example; and if all their names were incorporated into the largest available dictionaries, the books would immediately double in size.

The grammar of scientific language also contains several distinctive features. Sentences are often long and have a complex internal structure. The complexity is centred on the noun phrases (§16) rather than the verb phrases, as can be seen from the illustration below. But probably the best-known grammatical feature is the use of the passive construction: *The mixture was poured ...*

SCIENTIFIC VOCABULARY

(Dates given are of the first recorded appearance in the *Oxford English Dictionary*)

16th century

1533	catarrh
1527	cornea
1543	cranium
1551	genus
1578	glottis
1598	mumps
1551	species
1531	temperature
1548	tibia
1550	vacuum

17th century

1626	acid
1605	acoustic
1628	apparatus
1694	axis
1601	cardiac
1638	formula
1641	gravity
1605	laboratory
1615	logarithm
1656	microscope
1626	pedicle
1693	pharynx
1601	rheumatism
1668	stamen

18th century

1751	antiseptic
1791	carbonic
1791	etiolate
1771	fauna
1791	hydrogen
1794	molecule
1759	nectary
1776	neurosis
1794	nitrogen
1704	nucleus
1790	oxygen
1726	thyroid

19th century

1849	allotropy
1867	aphasia
1865	barograph
1812	centigrade
1890	chromosome
1839	cirrhosis
1832	cretaceous
1882	dynamo
1856	gyroscope
1822	laryngitis
1878	metabolism
1892	micron

20th century

1913	allergy
1946	cybernetics
1901	genetics
1951	laser
1912	millibar
1929	penicillin
1934	positron
1910	quantum
1942	radar
1912	vitamin

instead of *We poured the mixture ...* The intention behind this usage is straightforward: as in this example, it enables a description to be made impersonally, without an agent being expressed (contrasting with the use of a personal pronoun in the corresponding active construction). However, the overuse of complex passive sentences in scientific writing has attracted considerable criticism in recent years, and there is now a marked tendency to avoid them. The *Handbook for Chemical Society Authors* (1961), for example, recommends: 'Before the final typing every paper should be scrutinised to see whether it cannot be improved by eliminating abstract words and passive voices.' But the weight of traditional usage is not easy to throw off, as illustrated by this very recommendation, which itself uses two passives!

Intelligibility gap

The gap between scientific and everyday language is a large one, which it is difficult to bridge. Scientists are often unable to express themselves in terms the lay person can understand, or are too busy to bother. There is frequently a need to maintain secrecy, in such areas as national security or industrial invention. Not surprisingly, therefore, there is a widespread mistrust of scientific language, which is only partly alleviated through popular science publications and radio or television programmes. It is still the exception to find popularizations of science that maintain intelligibility while avoiding oversimplification, and that come to be acclaimed by specialist and lay person alike.

AN EXAMPLE

This short extract (G. H. Williams, 1960, pp. 252–3) illustrates well the nominal bias of scientific language. In the final sentence of the paragraph, for example, 16 of the 24 words are part of noun phrases: *Smaller quantities of tarry products ... the reported yields of diaryls ... the diazo- and azo-compounds discussed above.* By contrast, verb phrases are extremely short, and use a restricted range of items: in the whole extract we have *provide, be* (four times), *add, effect, obtain,* and *discuss* – typical of the 'manipulatory' meanings that the majority of the verbs in scientific language express (*adjust, align, arrange, begin, boil, bring, continue,* etc.). Note also the inverted commas, to identify the use of a vague word from everyday discourse.

(a)   Preparative Use of Diacyl Peroxides
The thermal decomposition of diacyl peroxides provides what is undoubtedly the "cleanest", and, provided the required peroxide is readily available, most convenient source of aryl radicals for the arylation of aromatic substrates. The purified peroxide, which is generally crystalline, is added to the aromatic solvent, and the decomposition is effected by heating, usually to about 70–80°. Smaller quantities of tarry products are obtained, and the reported yields of diaryls are generally higher than with the diazo- and azo-compounds discussed above.

NONVERBAL EXPRESSION

A large part of scientific expression consists of representations that are wholly or partly non-linguistic in character – such as physical models, charts, pictures, maps, graphs, and diagrams. The immediacy and economy of presentation achieved by these methods is self-evident. It would be impossible to provide a coherent account in words of all the interrelationships found on a map, graph, or tree diagram, for example, and verbal descriptions of formulae and equations are often highly complex and ambiguous (§33). On the other hand, linguistic and non-linguistic modes of expression are never totally independent of each other: verbal language is always needed in order to interpret and amplify the meaning or use of nonverbal representations.

ALTERNATIVE 'LANGUAGES'

Chemists have four ways in which they can describe the substances they study: they can use a verbal label, write a formula, draw a structural diagram, or build a structural model. Each has its strengths and weaknesses. Verbal labels are basic, but their length (often several dozen morphemes, p. 90) can make them unusable. Formulae are shorter; but whereas these can display the elements of a substance, they do not show their physical relationship. The internal structure of a substance can be shown using a structural diagram; but this is restricted to two dimensions. Only structural models provide a three-dimensional picture.

Label: METHANE
Formula: CH_4
Structural diagram:
$$H-\overset{\displaystyle H}{\underset{\displaystyle H}{C}}-H$$
Structural model:

EXPLAIN THIS!

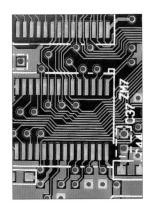

It would be possible to provide a verbal description for this electronic circuit, but it would be so long and complex as to be unintelligible. On the other hand, the verbal description of the elements of such circuits is an essential feature of training programmes in the subject.

MATHEMATICAL EXPRESSIONS

$$\sqrt{\frac{250}{3}} + 7$$

This simple mathematical expression is unambiguous, in its non-verbal form, with all elements simultaneously present. But as soon as we attempt to read it aloud, in a serial way, complications arise. The verbal version would be: 'the square root of two hundred and fifty divided by three plus seven'. But this written formulation could be interpreted in several ways, such as:

or $\dfrac{\sqrt{250}}{3} + 7$

or $\dfrac{\sqrt{250}}{3+7}$

or $\sqrt{200 + \dfrac{50}{3}} + 7$

or $\sqrt{200 + \dfrac{50}{3+7}}$

In speech, careful use of intonation and rhythm could distinguish some of these interpretations, but the risk of ambiguity would always be present.

THE LANGUAGE OF MEDICINE

The field of medicine, more than any other, forces a confrontation between scientific and everyday language. Outside the world of the research laboratory and clinic, there exists the daily routine of medical practice – a communication situation in which a doctor attempts to understand the problems of a patient, and the patient attempts to understand the doctor's diagnosis. Language is involved at all points in the medical consultation. The initial statement of symptoms is of critical significance, as it guides the doctor's search for the clinical signs of the condition. Similarly, the doctor's explanation of a problem, and the recommendations for treatment, need to be clear and complete if the patient is to understand and follow the correct course of action (p. 383).

Communication problems

The need for careful listening and expression by both parties should be self-evident in a field as sensitive and serious as health. In practice, many problems arise. Patients worried about their health are often uncertain or confused in their accounts. Busy doctors will not have the time to take up every point the patient has alluded to. Moreover, there is a tradition of medical interviewing which hinders the development of a genuine communicative interaction. One study of ten major medical journals in the 1960s found general agreement about the following characteristics of doctor–patient communication (after S. B. Heath, 1979):

1 Topics of conversation should be restricted to those dealing with the patient's body and conditions contributing to disease.
2 Conversation should only be with the patients, not with relatives or friends.
3 It is the task of the doctor, not the patient, to ask questions.
4 The doctor should avoid telling all the truth, and discourage the elaboration of information from other sources.
5 Patients should be told that they are ultimately responsible for the improvement of their own health, which will occur only if they follow the doctor's advice.

This tradition is still widely encountered, though it has attracted criticism from both within and outside the medical profession in recent years.

Studies of medical communication have brought to light several types of situation in which there has been a breakdown of communication, and where the consultation has had an unsatisfactory outcome. Regional, social, and cultural differences between doctor and patient can all be sources of linguistic difficulty (especially in the case of immigrant patients). Even age can intervene. In one American study, the problem was so serious that it was found helpful to devise a questionnaire phrased in appropriate slang to enable older doctors to communicate with inner city teenage patients (C. C. Levine, 1970).

The careful analysis of medical interviews, using audio- or video-recorded samples, has brought to light many instances of these difficulties. Some people are naturally taciturn in formal situations, because their social or cultural background has developed in them a sense of 'knowing their place'. Some find it necessary to talk at length about unrelated topics as a preliminary to introducing their symptoms. Some play down the importance of these symptoms, because they have been brought up 'not to make a fuss'. Each type of case presents doctors with a problem of communication analysis.

But linguistic problems continue to occur even when doctor and patient share the same social background. Doctors need to be alert to pick up the linguistic cues that may express the patient's real reason for coming to the surgery ('By the way, doctor...') or the issue that is causing most subconscious worry (such as repeatedly referring to the heart during the conversation). They also need to anticipate points of potential misunderstanding – such as the common patient interpretation of the word *growth* ('You have a small growth here') to mean 'cancer', or *thrombosis* to mean 'heart disease'. Some disease names convey major negative connotations, because of the fear attached to the disease in a pre-scientific era, and this motivates change: *leprosy*, for example, is now the focus of a campaign for replacement by *Hansen's disease*.

Medical communication researchers have also drawn attention to several areas where medical staff could promote their own communicative skills – for example, by providing explanations of what they are doing to a patient while they are doing it, by welcoming questions from patients (rather than fostering the 'Doctor knows best' attitude), and by avoiding patronising or discourteous language (e.g. 'Drink it down like a good girl', said to an older female hospital patient).

Above all, medical staff need to be aware of the many functions that language can perform (§4), and in particular that language may be used to signal the desire for social contact, and need not be taken literally. For example, in one study, 40 hospital patients who asked for relief from pain were given either routine nursing attention or a visit from a nurse specially trained in communication skills: only two of the former group obtained immediate relief from their 'pain', whereas 14 of the latter group did so; and all of the former group required analgesics, compared with only six of the latter (M. B. Tarasuk *et al.*, 1965). Such findings illustrate the need for a perspective on communication to be a routine part of medical training.

SYMPTOMS OF BREAKDOWN

Several studies have collected data that indicate the kinds of communication problem that frequently arise in hospitals. Typical quotations include:

• I didn't like to ask; perhaps it's just me; I felt they might think I was prying or being nosey.
• I was strung up when the doctors were there, and forgot things.
• They would give you pills and if you asked what they were for you were told to take it and never mind. You were treated like a child, as if it was nothing to do with you if the medicine was changed. There was no reason given.
• They leave you in the dark too much. If only they treated you as if you could understand something.
• I feel better knowing. You always imagine things are worse than they are.

Many hospitals now give patients an information booklet telling them what they need to know in advance. Several researchers believe that a paragraph about communication should be a routine feature of such literature. One suggestion reads as follows:

Don't be afraid to ask the doctors or the nursing staff any questions you want to ask about your illness or its treatment or about anything else that worries you. Some people find it difficult to remember all they want to ask when the doctor or sister comes round. You may find it helpful, and it will help them, if you make a list of your questions to show them when they visit you. (C. M. Fletcher, 1973.)

The final breakdown

Nowhere has this communication gap been greater than in the management of the terminally ill patient. According to one (1970) estimate, 80% of dying patients know that they are dying and want to talk about it; whereas 80% of doctors deny this, and believe that the patient should not be told. Fortunately, the present-day climate of medical opinion seems to be changing, slowly, for the better. (W. A. Cramond, 1970.)

NAMING OF PARTS

A diagram of the muscles of the neck, taken from one of the classical accounts of human anatomy, *Gray's Anatomy*, and showing the traditional use of Latin nomenclature. Most people identify medical language with this kind of terminology, or its vernacular equivalent; and indeed, the labels of anatomy and physiology do form the core of the subject. However, the kinds of conversation that take place in hospitals and clinics introduce a wide range of additional terminology. People, locations, routine objects, and daily activities all have their special labels, idioms, or abbreviations, e.g. *intern, registrar, SRN, ENT, path lab, sluice, day room, theatre, medical records, op, scrub up, draw-sheet, sample, drainage tube*. It is not difficult to hear sentences that are unintelligible, save to the initiated, e.g. *Staff wants you to do the TPRs on the four hourlies* (i.e. 'The staff nurse wants you to take the temperatures, pulses, and respirations of those patients who need this information recorded every four hours').

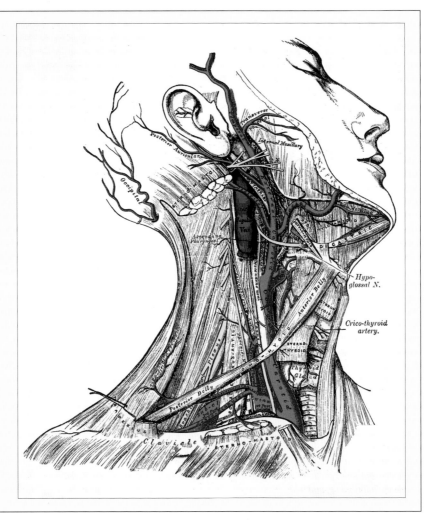

CONSULTATION STYLES

Analyses of the language used in consultations have brought to light great differences in styles of interaction. In one study, patient comments of the type 'I'm feeling run down. I've got a pain in my back, and I feel tired all day' were found to elicit a wide variety of responses, such as:

- Mmmm. Right, just go into the next room and get undressed. I'll be along in a minute.
- Tell me. Just where is this pain?
- When do you feel tired? In the morning when you get up or in the afternoon?
- Do you have headaches and pains behind the eyes?
- I think you're depressed. How do you feel about that?
- What sort of pain is it?
- What do you mean by 'I feel tired all day'?
- Yes go on.
- You look very pale.

(P. S. Byrne & B. E. L. Long, 1976, pp. 22–3.)

The responses vary enormously. At one extreme the doctor's mind seems already made up; at the other, the doctor is ready to enter into a long discussion about further symptoms.

Computer-aided diagnosis
Computers now play an essential role in many diagnostic investigations, as in this display and analysis of a brain section using a CT scanner. Moreover, the range of medical conditions is now so vast, and the doctor's time so limited, that several clinical centres have begun to introduce computer-assisted diagnostic systems. In an extension of this procedure, it is even possible in some centres for patients to begin the diagnostic process by themselves. They are presented with a series of questions about their medical history and symptoms on a computer screen. They are given sets of possible answers, and they make their selection by pressing buttons on their console. There is no time constraint, and they may change their answers at any time, or simply leave questions blank. The answers are then stored in the computer, to be printed out when the doctor is ready to analyse them.

LANGUAGE AND RELIGION

IN THE BEGINNING

The close relationship between language and religious belief pervades cultural history. Often, a divine being is said to have invented speech, or writing, and given it as a gift to mankind. One of the first things Adam has to do, according to the Book of Genesis, is name the acts of creation:

And the Lord God having formed out of the ground all the beasts of the earth, and all the fowls of the air, brought them to Adam to see what he would call them: for whatsoever Adam called any living creature the same is its name...

Many other cultures have a similar story. In Egyptian mythology, the god Thoth is the creator of speech and writing. It is Brahma who gives the knowledge of writing to the Hindu people. Odin is the inventor of runic script, according to the Icelandic sagas. A heaven-sent water turtle, with marks on its back, brings writing to the Chinese. All over the world, the supernatural provides a powerful set of beliefs about the origins of language (§49).

Religious associations are particularly strong in relation to written language, because writing is an effective means of guarding and transmitting sacred knowledge. Literacy was available only to an elite, in which priests figured prominently. Echoes of this link reverberate in English vocabulary still, through such connections as *scripture* and *script*, or the reference to *scripture* as *Holy Writ*. And there are widespread sanctions for human action expressed authoritatively in phrases of the form: 'for it is written'.

Sacred writings

At the centre of all the world's main religions lies a body of sacred writing, revered by believers. Scrupulous attention is paid to identifying or preserving the linguistic features of the original texts. Often, the texts are accompanied by a long tradition of commentary, which may itself take on special religious significance.

Buddhism   The Pali Canon, based on oral tradition, containing the teaching of the Buddha. Pali became the canonical language for Buddhists from many countries, but comparable texts came to exist in other languages, such as Chinese and Japanese, as the religion evolved.

Christianity   The Bible, consisting of the 39 books of the Old Testament, written in Hebrew, and the 27 books of the New Testament, written in Greek. Several other writings, known collectively as the Apocrypha, and preserved only in Greek, have controversial status. A Latin translation of the Bible, known as the Vulgate, is prominent in the Roman Catholic tradition.

Hinduism   The Vedas, a wide range of texts, written in Sanskrit, and preserved largely through a meticulous oral tradition, which takes particular care over accuracy of pronunciation (p. 409).

Islam   The Qur'an, or Koran, which Muslims believe was dictated to the Prophet Mohammed by Allah through the angel Jibreel (Gabriel) beginning in the month Ramadan. The whole revelation took place during a period of over 20 years. It is written in classical Arabic, in a style which is considered miraculous, beyond ability to imitate. The memorization of the text in childhood acts simultaneously as an introduction to literacy.

Judaism   The Hebrew Bible, or Old Testament, especially as found in its first five books, traditionally said to be written by Moses. Later varieties of Hebrew, and some Aramaic, form the language of the large collection of oral and written commentaries on the Bible, known as the Talmud.

Literacy is often introduced into a community by the spread of a religion. As a result, the distribution of writing systems in the world today reflects the distribution of world religions far more clearly than it does the distribution of language families.

TRANSLATING THE WORD

Not all religions favour the translation of their sacred books. Judaism, Hinduism, and Islam stress the sacredness of the language itself and resist translation, whereas Buddhism, and especially Christianity, actively promote it. But ultimately, all major religious works are translated – either from one language into another, or from an older variety of language into a modern variety.

The formal process of religious translation is a long-term, painstaking and frustrating task, usually carried out by committee. Translators have to satisfy two criteria, which are always incompatible, because one looks backwards and the other forwards. First, the translation must be historically *accurate*, faithfully representing the meaning of the source, insofar as this can be known, and integrated within the religious tradition of which it is a part. Secondly, it must be *acceptable* to the intended users of the translation – which, in practice, means that it must be intelligible, aesthetically pleasing, and capable of relating to current trends in religious thought, social pressures, and language change. No translation can ever satisfy the demands of all these factors, and all translations are thus to some extent controversial (§57).

The linguistic issues involved may relate to major conflicts of cultural or historical interpretation, or be localized problems of style. A phrase such as 'Give us this day our daily bread' is not easy to translate into a language such as Eskimo, where the staple food is not bread; nor is it easy to handle the Biblical parable of the fig-tree, which refers to seasonal change, in a language where there are no words for seasons, such as Yucatec. But even

The Egyptian god, Thoth, represented with the head of an ibis, embracing King Seti I. As inventor of hieroglyphs, he was named 'lord of holy words'. He is said to have accomplished the work of creation by the sound of his voice alone. The Egyptian goddess of writing, Seshat, was Thoth's principal spouse.

subtle, apparently minor, linguistic differences can become major points of controversy. To address the divinity as *thou* will satisfy those who feel that religious language should adhere closely to tradition and be special, set apart from the everyday language; but *you* will be preferred by those who wish religious language to have an immediate contemporary meaning and application. The *thou/you* debate has rumbled on for decades in English – with echoes in other languages that use a second-person-pronoun distinction.

From the invention of printing until the mid-1990s, some or all of the Bible has been published in nearly 2,000 languages, with several hundred new translation projects ongoing; but a major language with a long literary tradition will itself contain many translations. Some English translations have proved to be specially influential, such as the Great Bible (Cranmer's Bible) of 1539, the Authorized Version (or King James Bible) of 1611, and the Douai Bible of 1609–10. The chief points of controversy then were partly doctrinal, partly stylistic, but both stemmed from the major changes in Christian belief taking place at the time in Europe – changes which led William Tyndale, for example, to claim that his translation, unlike previous ones, would enable the Bible to be understood by all, even by 'a boy that driveth the plough'.

Questions of level and accessibility remain central today. Nor can the religious translators ever rest, for at their shoulder is the demon of language change (§54). What might seem a 'safe' word today may be loaded with irrelevant meaning tomorrow. A contemporary example is *soul*, which has developed fresh meanings in African-American English, and which would require translators to look carefully at any version they produced in which the traditional senses of *soul* might seem misleading or laughable.

Before printing, Bibles had to be copied by hand – a vast undertaking for a work whose English translations generally contain over ¾ million words and 3½ million letters. This is a page from a 14th-century German Bible, possibly from Lüttich (Liège), showing the evangelist Matthew and a priest of the Teutonic Order.

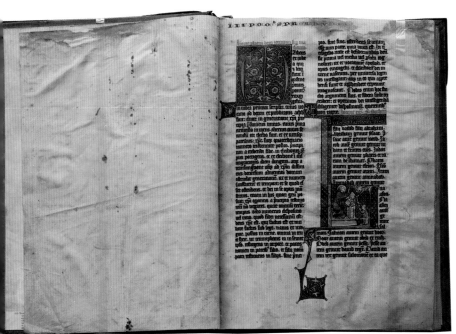

VARIETIES OF RELIGIOUS LANGUAGE

The most striking feature of a religious language is its heterogeneity, deriving from the wide range of activities involved in public and private worship, and the involvement of religion in all aspects of daily living and thinking. Several varieties, all distinctive in their use of linguistic structure, are widely encountered.

Liturgical forms both spoken and sung, produced by individuals and in unison, as monologue and dialogue, and including such acts as invocations, petitions, doxologies (statements of glory or praise), intercessions, thanksgivings, rosaries, litanies, chants, hymns, psalms, and canticles.

Preaching from formal written sermon to spontaneous monologues or even dialogues (as the congregation reacts), and sometimes involving elements of song or chant (as in African-American preaching, or the *hwyl* heard in Welsh).

Ritual forms used in relation to cultural or social practices, such as baptisms, funerals, confessions, meal-times, remembrance services, weddings, initiation ceremonies, circumcisions, invocations, meditations, cleansing rites, oaths, vows, exorcisms, and the blessing of people, objects, or places.

Readings from sacred texts, in an original language or in translation, and with varying degrees of literalness, formality, and modernity. The texts themselves will contain a wide range of varieties, such as parables, psalms, historical narrative, apocalyptic description, poetry, and paradox.

Doctrinal statements as expounded in official 'canonical' documents, creeds, articles of faith, sutras, expository pamphlets, courses of instruction, catechisms, and, these days, teach-ins on cable television. Closely associated with this, there is the dimension of theological language, as expounded by theologians, biblical scholars, and other religious professionals (p. 51).

Private affirmations of belief in supernatural beings, expressions of mystical power (such as the Hindu mantras), expressions of identity and conversion (such as glossolalia), ecstatic prayers, prophesying, oracles, spirit possession, and testimony giving.

Many communities use a totally different language for religious purposes – such as Ge'ez in the Ethiopian Church, or the traditional use of Latin in western Christianity. At the opposite extreme, there are those communities who recommend plain speaking, or even no speech at all. The distrust of earthly languages, and the power of silence in spiritual matters, is especially evident in 17th-century Quakerism: 'All languages are to me no more than dust', wrote George Fox in 1660, and repeated use was made of the exhortation from Ecclesiastes to 'let your words be few'.

THE LANGUAGE OF THE LAW

'The law is a profession of words'. This dictum opens David Mellinkoff's classic study *The Language of the Law* (1963), and it is not possible to find a more succinct way of introducing the present section. Whatever the legal domain – government legislation, courtroom activities, or the documentation that constrains our daily lives (contracts, conveyances, regulations, by-laws, etc.) – we are faced with this fundamental principle: the words of the law are, in fact, the law. There is no other variety where the users place such store on the nuances of meaning conveyed by language, where unstated intentions are so disregarded, and where the history of previous usage counts for so much.

The overriding concern for precise and consistent linguistic interpretation has, over the centuries, produced a highly distinctive style whose complexity is particularly apparent in the written language. This style has frequently been criticized by the lay public, on the ground that much of legal language is unnecessarily complex, and could be simplified without loss (p. 382). The point is, indeed, often made by lawyers themselves. Mellinkoff, a professor of law, considers his profession to display four linguistic 'mannerisms' that warrant criticism: wordiness, lack of clarity, pomposity, and dullness (see far right).

Historical factors explain the character of present-day legal language. Stylistic tradition is a major influence here, as with several other varieties (e.g. religious language, p. 388): *each and every, have and hold, null and void, rest residue and remainder*, and many other phrases can be traced back to Anglo-Saxon, Old French, or Medieval Latin. The repetition, alliteration, and rhythm of many expressions (e.g. *the truth, the whole truth...*) reflect the need, in an age before printing and general literacy, for the law to be remembered clearly, and passed on consistently. The use of tautologous expression in English documents is often due to the influence of different languages: for example, a French or Latin term used alongside an Anglo-Saxon one (e.g. *made and signed, breaking and entering, will and testament*) reflects the uncertainty of early draftsmen as to whether the two terms had the same meaning. In such cases, the safest course of action was to include both.

Historical explanation, however, does not stop the persistent call for change in legal language by eliminating archaic or Latinate expressions, simplifying grammatical structure, and adding punctuation. Those in favour of change argue that this would make legal language more intelligible to consumers, saving much time, anxiety, and money, and would also greatly simplify the job of lawyers themselves. Those who defend the complexity of legal language argue that its characteristics are the product of centuries of effort to devise an unambiguous, reliable, and authoritative means of regulating human society and resolving conflict. In their view, the need for consistency in legal interpretation, and for confidence in judgments (which, they argue, can save much time, anxiety, and money), far outweigh the gain that would come from an increase in popular understanding.

While many lawyers these days accept the desirability of some degree of simplification, there is a natural caution about leaving the safe, charted domain of traditional legal language, and entering into a world that may be hiding a host of undiscovered linguistic pitfalls. Doubtless a certain amount of planned change could be introduced without harm (simplified documents have in fact increased in currency in recent years); but this is inevitably a slow process, given the need to think through carefully the consequences of every change.

---

7. (1) MONEYS to be invested under this Settlement may be invested or otherwise applied on the security of or in the purchase or acquisition of real or personal property (including the purchase or acquisition of chattels and the effecting or maintaining of policies of insurance or assurance) rights or interests of whatsoever kind and wheresoever situate including any stocks funds shares securities or other investments of whatsoever nature and wheresoever whether producing income or not and whether involving liability or not or on personal loan with or without interest and with or without security to any person (other than the Settlor or any Spouse of the Settlor) anywhere in the world including loans to any member of the Specified Class and the Trustees may grant indulgence to or release any debtor (other than as aforesaid) with or without consideration and may enter into profit sharing agreements and give and take options with or without consideration and accept substitution of any security...

This extract illustrates the traditional style of legal language. An important feature is the distinctive graphology (§33). Certain conventions of layout and typography are present, but there is a total lack of punctuation.

The reasons for this distinctive feature of legal style are not entirely clear, but they probably have to do with the early use of punctuation as a graphic device to help people read texts aloud. Most legal documents are purely written records, so there would have been little need to punctuate them. When these documents came to be printed, compositors – doubtless influenced by the inconsistency of manuscript punctuation – developed the practice of printing texts without any punctuation at all. Gradually, the tradition grew that punctuation had no part to play in legal writing.

LEGAL 'MANNERISMS'

Wordiness
annul and set aside = annul
entirely and completely remove = remove
totally null and void = void
without let or hindrance = without hindrance

Lack of clarity
The use of lengthy sentences containing obscure words and awkward constructions: *Although the will itself was silent as to who would take if the son predeceased the mother, she not having at the time of the son's death remarried, and the son leaving issue at his death, which event occurred, this omission by itself, in the will only, cannot aid the son and defeat the testator's clear intention that the son should take only in the event he survived the death or remarriage of his mother...*

Pomposity
the people in their wisdom; in the discharge of that important duty; trifles with justice; the result will be to weaken or subvert what it conceives to be a principle of the fundamental law of the land.

Dullness
Partly due to the above features, but also a consequence of the tendency to go into the minutiae of a procedure, as part of its justification: *The reason for denying an appeal in the latter case is not because the order on the motion to vacate is not within the terms of section 963 of the code allowing appeals, for it may be, and indeed, an order refusing to vacate a final judgment is in its very nature a special order made after the judgment, but because it would be virtually allowing two appeals from the same ruling, and would, in some cases, have the effect of extending the time for appealing contrary to the intent of the statute.*
(After D. Mellinkoff, 1963, Ch. 3.)

SPOKEN LEGAL LANGUAGE

The language of the courtroom is familiar to millions (if only through the media of films and television), but only recently has there been any systematic research into the complex rules of linguistic behaviour that participants are expected to follow. Most lay people fail to grasp the extent of these rules until they have had the experience of acting as a witness. After the event, the almost universal reaction is frustration – of not being allowed to say what they wanted in the way they wanted. Once people are in court, they must follow its procedures, and use its language; if they do not, they may be held 'in contempt'.

There are several everyday functions of language that witnesses are not allowed to use. They must not report what other people have said ('hearsay'), evaluate other people or events ('opinion'), give their listeners extra context (i.e. they must simply 'respond to the question'), or show such emotions as humour. Similarly, the legal experts are subject to linguistic constraints, such as how to introduce evidence or cross-examine witnesses. Books have been written on court 'tactics' – how to manipulate witnesses, impress judges, and influence juries.

At a trial, language counts for everything. In terms of structural analysis (p. 79, §20), a trial is little more than a giant narrative, with a beginning (the opening statements), middle (the presentation of evidence), and end (the closing arguments and verdict). However, unlike most stories, this one is told by many people, including two 'official' story-tellers (counsel for the defence and for the prosecution), and exists in at least two conflicting versions. Resolving the conflict depends totally on the linguistic skills of all concerned.

THE CHARACTERISTICS OF LEGAL LANGUAGE

- Common words with uncommon meanings:
action = law suit
avoid = cancel
hand = signature
presents = this legal document
said = mentioned before
specialty = sealed contract

- Old and Middle English words no longer in general usage:
aforesaid   thenceforth
forthwith   thereby
hereafter   theretofore
heretofore   whereby
said (*adjective*)   witnesseth

- Latin words and phrases, including some that have become part of the language as a whole (e.g. *affidavit, alias, alibi*):
*corpus delicti   per stirpes
ejusdem generis   quasi
ex post facto   res gestae
in personam   retraxit
lex loci actus   sui juris
nolle prosequi   vis major*

- Words derived from French (many now in general use, e.g. *appeal, assault, counsel, crime, plaintiff, verdict*):
demurrer   fee simple
easement   lien
estoppel   tort

- Technical terms with precise and well-understood meanings ('terms of art'):

appeal   defendant
bail   felony
contributory   injunction
negligence   libel

- Less precise terms and idioms, in standard use in daily legal discussion (sometimes referred to as legal 'argot'):
alleged
issue of law
objection
order to show cause
strike from the record
superior court
without prejudice

- Formal or ceremonial words and constructions in written documents and in spoken courtroom language:
Signed, sealed, and delivered
Whereas... (in contracts)
You may approach the bench
Comes now the plaintiff
Your Honour
May it please the court
Hear ye, hear ye, hear ye
I do solemnly swear...
The truth, the whole truth, and nothing but the truth

- The conscious use of vague words and phrases to permit a degree of flexibility in interpretation:
adequate cause
as soon as possible
fair division
improper
malice

nominal sum
reasonable care
undue interference

- The use, conversely, of words and phrases to express precise meaning:
irrevocable
in perpetuity
nothing contained herein

This convention motivates the use of long lists of near synonyms in documents, as in these phrases from a standard form, in which a person is released:

from any and all manner of action or actions, cause and causes of action, suits, debts, dues, sums of money, accounts, reckonings, bonds, bills, specialities, covenants, contracts, controversies, agreements, promises, trespasses, damages, judgments, executions, claims, and demands whatsoever, in law or equity, which against him I have had, now have, or which my heirs, executors, or administrators, hereafter can, shall, or may have, for or by reason of any matter, cause, or thing whatsoever, from the beginning of the world to the day of the date of these presents...

Fairly comprehensive, one imagines!
(After D. Mellinkoff, 1963, Ch. 2.)

EFFECTIVE COURTROOM STRATEGIES

Lawyers

1. Vary the way in which you ask questions.
2. Give your own witnesses a chance to speak at length; restrict the opportunity of witnesses under cross-examination to short, direct answers to the specific questions asked.
3. Convey a sense of organization in your interviews of witnesses and your remarks to the jury.
4. Adopt different styles of questioning with different kinds of witnesses, e.g. women, the elderly, children, expert witnesses.

5. Remain poker-faced throughout; do not reveal surprise even when an answer is totally unexpected; save dramatic reactions for special occasions.
6. Rhythm and pace are important; do not bore the jury with slowness; use silence strategically.

7. Repetition can be useful for emphasis but it should be used with care so as not to bore the jury.
8. Avoid interrupting a witness, especially when being given a responsive answer; it gives the impression you want to hide some of the facts.

9. Use objections sparingly; they not only call attention to the material being objected to, but also convey an impression of attempting to conceal information.

Witnesses

1. Vary the way in which you give answers.
2. Give long answers wherever possible; make the opposition lawyer stop you frequently during cross-examination, to give the impression of reluctance to have your full story placed before the jury.
3. Try to confuse the organization that the opposition lawyer has planned for the cross-examination.
4. Adopt different styles of answering questions asked by different questioners (e.g. deference to the judge, no rehearsed answers while under direct examination, no hostility to the opposition lawyer).

5. Do not show surprise even when questions are unexpected; save dramatic reactions for special moments.
6. Use rhythm and pace to advantage. Upset the opposition lawyer's pace with variations in response timing (e.g. asking *Would you please repeat the question?* after an especially long or complex question).
7. React to a cross-examiner's repetition of material, e.g. by saying *Why do you keep asking me the same question?*
8. Interrupt the opposition lawyer by volunteering answers, as soon as you can see the drift. This gives the impression that you are cooperative and serves to confuse the lawyer's style.
9. Blurt out relevant facts and opinions on cross-examination, even though the opposition lawyer may attempt to limit your answer. These attempts will give the impression that the lawyer is trying to conceal some of your evidence.

(After W. M. O'Barr, 1982, Table 7.1.)

LANGUAGE AND THE PRESS

The world of modern newspaper and magazine publishing presents a wider range of linguistically distinctive varieties than any other domain of language study. Within the pages of a daily paper there will be juxtaposed such diverse categories as news reports, editorial comments, imaginative articles, reviews, letters, captions, headlines, sub-headings, announcements, television programme descriptions, lists of sports results, cartoon dialogues, competitions, crossword clues, and many kinds of advertising. Sunday papers in some countries are even more diversified, providing a variety of supplements on different topics.

With such a range of content, there is no likelihood of finding a single style of writing used throughout a paper, nor of finding linguistic characteristics that are shared by all papers. Although each paper has its distinctive visual 'house style' (p. 13) and follows a set of general norms laid down by its editorial staff, the idea that there is a homogeneous method of writing used by all journalists ('journalese') seems to have little foundation. 'Journalese', like 'jargon' and several other labels, is for many people no more than a loaded word, identifying a style of newspaper writing they dislike.

There are of course certain superficial similarities between newspaper styles arising out of the fundamental constraints of the medium. Information has to be compressed into a limited space, usually in columns, and without loss of legibility. Interest has to be focused, captured, and maintained through the use of large type, dramatic headlines, frequent sub-headings, short paragraphs, and succinct sentences. The occurrence of photographs, the recency of the information reported, and the need to maintain human interest will in various ways influence the choice of vocabulary and grammar. For example, most sentences will be narrative statements (rather than questions or exclamations); and the use of the past tense will dominate (except in headlines and captions). But within general constraints of this kind, stylistic preferences vary enormously.

In just a few instances, features of style have developed that are idiosyncratic to the genre of newspaper/magazine writing and are frequently used, thus giving credence to the notion of 'journalese'. Well-known examples from English are the altered order of subject and verb (e.g. ... *commented Dr Brown*), and the use of long lists of descriptive adjectives (e.g. *Tall, blue-eyed, 32-year-old publisher John Brown said* ...). The distinctive grammar of headlines provides a further illustration. But, on the whole, there are few linguistic features that are restricted to the world of journalistic writing.

If the weather's bad. . .
BLAME THE COMPUTER IN FUTURE

THAT big black cloud for ever hanging over the heads of Britain's weathermen has vanished.

Those "Yah, ha-ha-got-it-wrong-again" remarks from the weather-conscious public won't trouble them too much any more.

For should that "continuing dry" forecast develop into a depressing downpour they can blame the new member of the staff: Mr. Comet.

Mr. Comet—a £500,000 computer, joined the ranks of the Meteorological Office, Bracknell, Berkshire, yesterday.

He can scan half a million weather reports from all over the world—and come up with the answers in one and a half hours: Blow, blaze, or below freezing.

He requires an operating staff of three and another 50 processers to feed in weather statistics. But he can cope with 1 million calculations a second. And he is hardly ever wrong.

(*Daily Express* 3 November, 1965)

Weather Forecasting by Numbers
From Our Science Correspondent

Revolutions can begin quietly. One began yesterday at the Meteorological Office headquarters at Bracknell. For the first time in routine procedure an electronic computer contributed to the forecast chart published today on this page. To look at there is nothing special about the chart. The change for the forecaster was only that an extra aid was given him. As well as preparing his own forecast chart of pressure distribution—always the first step in forecasting—he received a second chart drawn from the computer-made calculations. For the issued chart he could make use of either or both as he pleased.

(*The Times*, 3 November, 1965)

Style wars   The contrast in newspaper styles is best seen when different papers deal with the same story. The opening lines of a 1965 news item, taken from two London papers – *Daily Express* (top) and *The Times* (bottom) – demonstrate the difficulty of arriving at satisfactory generalizations about 'newspaper language'.

HEADLINESE

Complaint on eggs upheld
Man finds girl in car

Most headlines differ from everyday language by omitting many of the less important words in a sentence, to produce an elliptical, 'tele-grammatic' construction. They also display a very restricted range of sentence structures. In recent decades, for example, the English press has made considerable use of *on* (in the sense of 'about') as part of 'headlinese':
Bishops disagree on divorce
Protest on rail cuts
New move on libraries

Concern on smoking
(Quoted in G. W. Turner, 1972.)

However, despite the syntactic restrictions, there is still an opportunity for variation, and in fact the style chosen for headlines and sub-headings often provides one of the most distinctive features of a newspaper. At one extreme we find such plain, unemotional wordings as *Christmas unemployment total at record level*. At the other, we find such dramatic (and, out of context, unintelligible) items as *Crash, bang, wallop!* or *Oh yes she is!* Several papers also add interest to their headlines by making a distinctive use of word play, such as these items taken from issues of *The Guardian* (London):
• *Plans for chess fight unchecked*
(Arrangements for a chess match are to go ahead)
• *Getting a true bill of fare*
(Foreigner who can't afford his fare home tries to be deported by deliberately not paying a restaurant bill)
• *Give us this way our daily bread*
(Article on breadmaking)
• *How to compose yourself*
(A young composer's attitude to life)

JERUSALEM

Chronicles

12 NISAN, 2060 (1700 B.C.E.)

NEWS OF THE PAST

VOL. I, NO. 1

SODOM AND GOMORRAH WIPED OUT IN WORST DISASTER SINCE FLOOD

Burning Sulphur, Violent Blasts, Flames Shooting Up to the Sky...

Sodom and Gomorrah, as well as a goodly portion of the Valley of Siddim, are visible from a height just east of Hebron (Elonei Mamrei). A few early risers were near this spot when the disaster struck, and it is from one of these eyewitnesses that we received the following account.

I was watching the sun rise behind the hills in the east when it happened. At first there was just the sound — a low, ominous rumble which, in a moment, turned into a deafening roar.

Seeking the source of the sound, I looked up to the heavens. But at that very moment I became aware that something was transpiring in the valley below. I looked — and this is what I saw:

Two Cities Ablaze

Sodom and Gomorrah were rapidly being devoured by a fiercely burning blaze that seemed to have sprung up from nowhere and was moving in a westerly or northwesterly direction.

(The spot where I was standing soon became a common vantage point for hundreds of Hebronites who had been awakened by the terrific noise and were hurrying to the hill top. Individually and in groups, they arrived and stared, wide-eyed, at the horror below.)

Many of the houses that lay in the path of the flames but had not yet been touched by them had already collapsed, indicating that a violent earthquake had preceded the fire. That also helped to account for the fact that no one was fleeing: The inhabitants of the two cities must all have been killed or trapped within a few minutes of the outbreak of the disaster.

Meanwhile, the nearby cities of Admah and Zevoim were rapidly being evacuated, their inhabitants fleeing toward the range of mountains which was serving as our lookout point.

It was difficult to make out what exactly was happening inside the cities, because of the heavy black smoke billowing upward toward the darkened sky. The sun had long since disappeared. Earth and sky seemed to have become one, and there were moments when it appeared that the flames were not shooting up to the sky but that, on the contrary, it was the heavens that were pouring fire down upon the earth.

Balls of Fire

This impression was heightened not only by the frequent flashes of lightning that streaked down into the valley and momentarily lit up the ghastly scene, but also by the appearance of great balls of fire that plunged earthward, exploded with a resounding boom, and then shot up again in the form of belching flames.

Judging from the pungent odour which now began to reach us on the mountain top, I would say that these fire-balls were globs of sulphur....

Further proof that an earthquake had taken place was provided for us shortly before noon, when — to our renewed amazement — we noticed that a large (*Continued on P. 2, Col. 5*)

LOT SAVED!

HEBRON, 11 Nisan (CNS). Judge Lot of Sodom and his daughters are safe, it was reliably reported early this evening. They are the only persons known to have come out of the holocaust of Sodom and Gomorrah alive.

The story of their miraculous escape is told by a Zoar man who fled to Hebron when his city was

Portion of Flooded Area

threatened by the waves of the Salt Sea late this afternoon.

At sunrise this morning, watchmen on the northern wall of Zoar noticed a group of people approaching the gates of the city in a half-run. As the figures came nearer, the watchmen recognized Abraham's nephew, Lot. The judge is a well-known figure in these parts. With him were his two beautiful daughters and two unidentified men.

Visit Unexplained

Asked who the strangers were, Lot replied that only he and his daughters sought entrance to the city, and so, without any further hesitation, the guards opened the gates of the city to their honoured and unexpected guests.

When Lot declined to state the reason for his sudden appearance at Zoar at this unearthly hour, it was supposed that there had been another dispute between him and the men of Sodom.

Speculation on the matter, however, was soon interrupted, as the great holocaust broke over Sodom and Gomorrah.

Jericho Reports Salt Sea Receding

(Chronicles News Service)

JERICHO, 11 Nisan.— The waters of the Salt Sea are slowly and steadily retreating southward, threatening to leave the port city of Beth Hoglah "high and dry".

The movement of the sea began early this afternoon. It was supposed at first that the strange phenomenon was merely a "freak low tide". But this hopeful supposition had gradually to be discarded, as it became increasingly evident that this was no movement of the tides — but, rather, a violent and fundamental change in the country's terrain:

The sea is receding, and the eye can actually follow its progress as it makes its way southward, leaving behind it dry land.

(At the moment, the waters of the Jordan are spreading over the vacated area; but, once the river will begin digging a new bed for itself, most of this land will be left dry, though local farmers say it is doubtful whether such salty soil is cultivable.)

Explanation Sought

It is believed now that the recession of the Salt Sea is somehow connected with the disturbance that took place this morning in the south, as evidenced by the heavy billows of smoke that have been rising from that sector since the early morning hours.

LARSA FALLS TO HAMMURABI

RIM-SIN FLEES SOUTH

(Euphrates News Agency)

LARSA, 4 Nisan.— Larsa, for decades the capital of King Rim-Sin, was captured today by the allied forces of Babylonia, Mari, and Eshnunna.

King Rim-Sin left the capital shortly before the enemy troops entered. He is fleeing in a southeasterly direction.

(For more details and an analysis of the situation in the East — see Page 4.)

HYKSOS TAKE EGYPTIAN CAPITAL

(Foreign News Service)

ZOAN.— Memphis, capital of northern Egypt and the last serious obstacle to the Hyksos' conquest of the entire country, surrendered to the invader yesterday, after a siege which lasted 7 months.

To all intents and purposes, the capture of Memphis marks the end of Egypt's 20-year resistance against the Hyksos. Thebes, capital of the southern zone, is not expected to make more than a token stand.

Population Starving

The destruction, during the early weeks of the siege, of the many waterways in the vicinity upon which Memphis depended for its water supply took a heavy toll among the city's inhabitants. Those who are not already dead are in a more or less advanced state of dying.

The starved and plague-ridden population of the long-besieged city must have presented a horrible sight to the conquerors, but it is doubtful whether they were very much disturbed by it, as they went about their systematic work of pillage and destruction.

By order of King Salitu, of the Hyksos, an image of the god Sutekh was set up today in the Temple of Ra, to take the place of the Egyptian deity as top god of the land. (The Egyptian equivalent of the god Sutekh is Seth.)

Mysterious Blaze-Quake Sweeps Valley of Siddim

(Chronicles News Service)

HEBRON, 11 Nisan.— Nature's four basic elements — earth, fire, wind, and water — combined today to bring terror and death to the twin-cities of Sodom and Gomorrah, in the worst catastrophe the world has seen since the Great Flood.

The disaster, a deadly combination of storm, earthquake, fire and flood, struck with a suddenness that provided no opportunity for escape. All the inhabitants of the two cities are believed to have been killed.

The earth tremors began at sunrise, mounting in force with such startling swiftness that a few minutes later there was not a house in either city that was not wrecked or damaged. Whatever was left alive or whole by the quake was quickly consumed by the raging blaze that followed in its wake, driven along its route of death and destruction by a stiff easterly wind.

Valley Sinks

The upheaval caused a sudden lowering of the earth's level throughout the Valley of Siddim, south of the Salt Sea. This, in turn, brought the waters of the Salt Sea down upon the valley and the burning cities.

As this is being written, the waters of the sea, having inundated Sodom and Gomorrah, as well as the neighbouring towns of Admah and Zevoim, are still advancing southward.

Reports from Jericho indicate fundamental changes in that sector, too.

(For further details, see eyewitness account on this page.)

'EXTRA' QUICKLY SOLD OUT

Copies of the Extra Edition put out by *Chronicles* last night on the Sodom-Gomorrah disaster were quickly snatched up by an eager populace. Our horse-back-riding messengers reached such distant places as Jericho, Shechem, Beth Shemesh, and Gezer.

Advancing Waters Threaten Zoar

(Chronicles News Service)

From Zoar, near the southern end of the Siddim Valley, comes word that the population is fleeing the city in panic, following the realization that the waves of the Salt Sea are bearing down on the city.

During most of the day the people remained calm, as, except for a few tremors early this morning, the city (formerly called Bela) had been spared in the general disaster that had overtaken the valley. Zoar was considered safe. A number of refugees from the stricken cities to the north came to Zoar in the course of the day, to seek a haven behind its walls.

Towards evening, however, there came a change for the worse.

The men at the lookout posts on the wall suddenly saw something that caused the blood to freeze in their veins:

The waters of the Salt Sea were advancing across the valley, along its entire width, and were rapidly bearing down on the city!

Among those fleeing the city are Lot and his daughters, first of the refugees — and the only ones from Sodom and Gomorrah — to reach Zoar this morning.

Most of the fugitives are seeking shelter for the night in caves in the mountains to the west.

PRIESTS CONFER ON DISASTER

(Chronicles News Service)

The priests of Hebron, Salem, and Jericho were called together this morning, in their respective cities, for emergency talks concerning the Sodom-Gomorrah disaster.

Details of the discussions are lacking, but it is believed that the hurried preparations of special sacrifices in all the temples come as a direct result of these discussions.

Announcements issued by the priests and circulated among all the towns and villages in the vicinity call upon every man to bring a sacrifice to the local or family deity, so as to appease the wrath of the gods.

Abraham, invited to the Hebron session of priests as the representative of his god, aroused the ire of the local populace by refusing to attend the discussions.

Scene of Disaster — Before and After

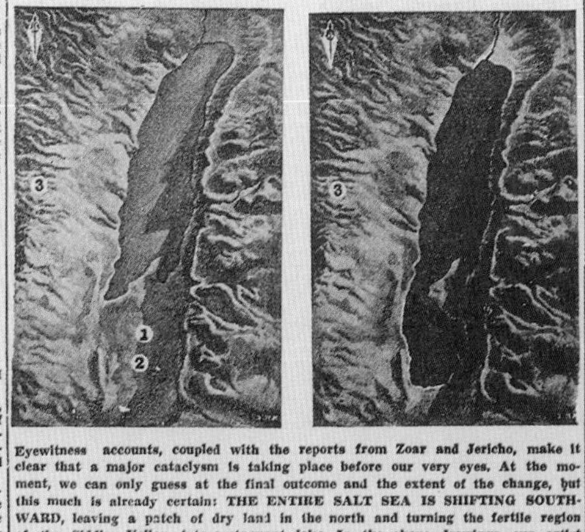

Eyewitness accounts, coupled with the reports from Zoar and Jericho, make it clear that a major cataclysm is taking place before our very eyes. At the moment, we can only guess at the final outcome and the extent of the change, but this much is already certain: THE ENTIRE SALT SEA IS SHIFTING SOUTHWARD, leaving a patch of dry land in the north and turning the fertile region of the Siddim Valley into a stagnant lake. In the above drawings, our artist gives us a bird's eye view of the entire district — before the disaster (left) and afterwards (right). The numbers 1 and 2 indicate Sodom and Gomorrah, while 3 shows the hilltop near Hebron from which the upheaval was observed.

Abraham's Conduct Arouses Suspicion Among Hebronites

By a Staff Writer

Among those who watched the progress of the catastrophe from the heights around Hebron was Abraham the son of Terach. Some of the other observers of the tragedy are quick to link the Hebrew's name with the disaster that struck the Siddim Valley with such unprecedented violence this morning.

While no one has been able to "put his finger" on any overt act on Abraham's part, several people seem to be convinced that he had something to do with the catastrophe — or, at any rate, knew about it beforehand. As evidence for their contention, they cite the following facts:

(1) Abraham was the first man on the hill from which the disaster was subsequently observed by hundreds of Hebronites. A man of 99, he could hardly have been quicker to reach the spot than the young men who hurried there as soon as they heard the first noises, at sunrise. Abraham must, therefore, have arrived at his vantage point some time before sunrise — and before anything had begun to happen in the valley below.

(2) Three strangers visited Abraham yesterday. Unusually tall in stature, and coming at the hour of noon — an unusual time for people to travel on such a hot day, the strangers aroused considerable attention among the people of Hebron. The men remained with Abraham for several hours.

(3) Towards evening, two of Abraham's guests were seen walking off in a southeasterly direction — towards the Valley of Siddim. What happened to the third man nobody knows.

Extra, extra! One of the clearest ways of identifying the salient features of a special use of language is to use the variety in an unexpected or incongruous context. The dramatic effect is evident in this illustration – from the front page of an issue of *Chronicles*, which reported the events of the Old Testament in the language and techniques of modern journalism. The paper was first published monthly in 1951 by the Reubeni Foundation in Israel, in the form of individual issues that sold as a normal newspaper. After 48 issues, covering a period of over 2,500 years, the papers were republished in book form.

THE LANGUAGE OF ADVERTISING

The aim of advertising is to draw attention to a product or service in order to sell it. Whether we are shopping, reading the paper, travelling to work, watching television, or simply lazing around, we cannot avoid seeing advertisements – probably, if we bothered to count, several hundred every day. They come in an extraordinary range of forms and contexts. The largest and most noticeable group belong to commercial consumer advertising; but there are also such categories as trade advertising (from manufacturers to retailers), retail advertising (from shops to customers), prestige advertising (e.g. by government departments), classified advertising (want ads, house sales, etc.), and direct mailing. The activities involve posters, signs, notices, showcards, samples, circulars, catalogues, labels, wrapping paper, price tags, tickets, footballers' shirts, and many other devices. The ears can be assailed as well as the eyes, with slogans, jingles, street cries, loudspeaker messages, and the range of auditory effects heard in radio and television advertising.

In most cases, it is the visual content and design of an ad that makes the initial impact and causes us to take note of it. But in order to get people to identify the product, remember its name (or at least make them feel that it is familiar), and persuade them that it is worth buying, ads rely almost totally on the use of language. Both elements, psychological and linguistic, are essential: they combine to produce a single 'brand image' of a product. However, little objective evidence is available to show how (or whether) ads succeed in their aims. A great deal of market research is carried out by firms and advertising agencies (e.g. asking people whether they can recall the content of an ad), but the link between language and sales remains unclear.

Analyses of advertising style by linguists and professional copywriters have drawn attention to several important features of this variety. Most obviously, the language is generally laudatory, positive, unreserved, and emphasizing the uniqueness of a product (*There's nothing like X...*). The vocabulary tends to be vivid and concrete. Figurative expressions are common (*eating sunshine* (cereals), *smiling colour* (hair shampoo)). Rhythm, rhyme, and other phonetic effects are noticeable (*Wot a lot I got*, *Milk has gotta lotta bottle*). There may be deviant spellings, especially in the brand names (*Rice Krispies*, p. 206). And considerable use is made of inexplicit grammatical constructions, which lend an air of vagueness – and thus safety – to the claims for the product: *X gets clothes cleaner* (than what?), *X costs less* (than what?), *Many people say ...* (who?), *X treats aches and pains* (all?).

The field of advertising is a controversial one, as people dispute the ethics and effects of 'hard' selling tactics, fraudulent claims, commercial sponsoring in sport, the intrusiveness of advertisements, and their effect on children. Its language therefore needs careful investigation and monitoring. But it is not an easy field to make generalizations about. Its boundaries blur with other forms of persuasive language, such as speeches, sermons, and public announcements. And within the genre, there is so much variation in subject matter that it is impossible to maintain a single attitude that will encompass everything. Whatever our view about advertisements for cigarettes, washing powders, or cough remedies, it is unlikely to be the same as the view we hold about advertisements dealing with the dangers of smoking, the sale of houses, or the needs of the Third World.

Poster pillars These advertisements for theatres, restaurants, political parties, and other local issues, are a common sight in several European countries.

An ad from a successful modern campaign, where the language counted for everything. The original slogan, launched by the lager firm, Heineken, read: 'Heineken refreshes the parts other beers cannot reach'. This slogan was so successful that it became possible for the firm, within a very short time, to assume everyone knew it, and to introduce a series of linguistic jokes based on the word *part*, e.g. 'Heineken refreshes the parrots other beers cannot reach', and the illustration below. This is an unusual use of language and an uncommon advertising technique. Anyone lacking a knowledge of the original version would find it very difficult to see the point of such sentences!

A theatre poster at Avenue Theatre, London, 1894. The densely packed text is typical of the time.

Heineken refreshes the pirates other beers cannot reach.

LAWFUL ADVERTISING

An illustration produced by the Equal Opportunities Commission of Britain, showing the force of the Sex Discrimination Act of 1975. This act states that it is unlawful to treat anyone, solely because of his or her sex, less favourably than anyone of the opposite sex. Apart from its relevance in employment, education, and training, the act applies to the public provision of goods, facilities, services, accommodation, and premises, and thus bears directly on advertising language.

In an advertisement checklist issued by the Commission, five guidelines are recommended:

• Watch out for words like Sales*man*, Store*man*. If these are used, make sure the ad also clearly offers the job to both sexes.

• Make sure that advertisements for jobs which have in the past been done mainly by men or women only (e.g. mechanic, typist) could not be understood to indicate a preference for one sex.

• If the ad contains words like *he, she, him, her*, make sure that they are used as alternatives, e.g. *he or she* or *him/her*, and are consistent throughout the advertisement.

• If your client does not agree, point out that, in one way or another, the ad must make clear that the vacancy is open to both men and women.

• Pictures can give a biased impression too. If they are used, ensure that men and women are shown fairly, in both numbers and prominence. Otherwise a bold disclaimer should be placed as close to the illustration as possible.

ADVERTISING COMPOUNDS

Novel compound words, used as adjectives, are probably the most noticeable feature of advertising language. Such compounds do occasionally become part of the everyday language, such as *top-quality, economy-size.*

day-in-day-out protection
satin-soft skin
craftsman-made furniture
top-quality bulbs
economy-size packet
feather-light flakes
creamy-mild soap
chocolate-flavoured cereal
relief-giving liquid
longer-lasting shave
coffee-pot fresh
all-purpose fertilizer
ready-to-eat cereal
up-to-the-minute styling
go-anywhere refrigerator
(After G. N. Leech, 1966.)

TELEVISION ADVERTISING

This form of advertising shares many of the linguistic features of consumer advertising in general, but there are certain important differences. Less use is made of written language, partly because of the limited size of screen, but also because there is no time for the viewer to read lengthy material. On the other hand, the medium makes available the infinite possibilities of the spoken language, with its reliance on voice qualities, spoken dialogues, adventure dramas, and many other kinds of interaction.

The simultaneous use of sound and vision can present problems, however. Most advertisements use speech to make their main linguistic claims, and use writing to reinforce what is said, or to add any disclaimers (e.g. *Battery not included, While supplies last*). But it is easy to ignore the 'small print' on the screen. It is not there for long, and the viewer may turn away at the crucial moment. Also, the fact that television advertising takes place in real time can lead to difficulties of comprehension and evaluation. In printed advertising, there is always time to reread the material, and thus to analyse what the ad actually says. On television, this opportunity is lacking, and there is thus little chance of evaluating the nature of the claims that are made. Some analysts have argued that these issues pose a particular problem when considering the kind of advertising that is aimed at children (M. L. Geis, 1982).

The daily barrage of advertising in London's Piccadilly Circus. A walk through the centre of any city places us in contact with thousands of advertisements, in the form of posters, physical models, and neon signs. But it is unlikely that we 'see' (that is, consciously register) more than a tiny fraction.

TOP TWENTIES

In a study of the vocabulary used in television advertising, the 20 most common adjectives and verbs, in order of frequency, were:

Adjectives	Verbs
1 new	1 make
2 good/better/best	2 get
3 free	3 give
4 fresh	4 have
5 delicious	5 see
6 full	6 buy
7 sure	7 come
8 clean	8 go
9 wonderful	9 know
10 special	10 keep
11 crisp	11 look
12 fine	12 need
13 big	13 love
14 great	14 use
15 real	15 feel
16 easy	16 like
17 bright	17 choose
18 extra	18 take
19 safe	19 start
20 rich	20 taste

Good and *new* were over twice as popular as any other adjective. The verbs seem unremarkable, until we recall the special contexts in which they are used in this variety, e.g.
Made by Smith's.
Get XXX today.
X gives you everything.
When you have an X...
(After G. N. Leech, 1966.)

THE LANGUAGE OF BROADCASTING

Broadcasting, as a national medium, has existed only since the 1920s; but its popularity and power have been so great that it has already given language several new varieties. People now take for granted such styles as newsreading, weather reporting, programme announcing, disc-jockey patter, and sports commentary, and they can easily forget that these styles are only about two generations old. The medium has also greatly increased popular awareness of linguistic diversity. An evening's listening or viewing provides an encounter with many regional accents, social dialects, and occupational uses of language (Part II). Only the seasoned traveller would have encountered such a linguistic range a century ago.

There is, accordingly, no such thing as a single homogeneous 'language' of broadcasting. In aiming to inform, educate, and entertain, the medium reflects all aspects of contemporary society and incorporates most of its language. The result is a range of linguistic variety that exceeds even the heterogeneity of the press (p. 392): discussions, news reports, soap operas, situation comedies, games, popular science, cartoons, plays, children's programmes, and much more – including, of course, a considerable proportion of recent cinema output.

The uniqueness of radio

Because we can see speakers and context, the language used in television programmes plays a less prominent role than it does on the radio. Here, speech is everything. Sound effects, music, and silence are of course important; but radio is *par excellence* the speaker's medium. Nowhere else does the human voice receive such undivided attention. And as a consequence, great care is needed both to maximize its effects (especially through a lively use of prosody, §29) and to avoid idiosyncrasies (which radio tends to exaggerate). Above all, broadcasters have to pay special attention to the problem of how much listeners can hear and take in at a time. There is no opportunity for immediate playback if something is misunderstood. As far as possible, therefore, broadcasting language has to be clearly organized, and make use of sentences that are relatively short and uncomplicated.

For the linguist, radio has uniquely interesting features. It is person-to-person communication that is mouth-to-ear, but not face-to-face, and where direct feedback is not possible. The totally auditory world of disembodied sound can involve the emotions and imagination of the listener in ways that have no parallel. Its simultaneous reception by millions promotes the language it uses as a standard (e.g. 'BBC English') and gives it an unequalled status and authority within a community (§61). The question of the kind of language professional broadcasters should use is therefore a controversial one, and in several countries the relative merits of standard vs regional and formal vs informal usage continue to be debated.

EDITING

Much of the professional 'finish' of many radio and television programmes is achieved by tape editing. Even spontaneous interviews and talks can be 'cleaned up' before being broadcast by removing major non-fluencies (such as too many 'ers and ums' – a technique sometimes called 'de-umming').

In films, *dubbing* is another much-used technique – modifying or adding to the soundtrack. When a change of language is involved, this is one of the most complex linguistic operations imaginable. Accents have to be matched to convey similar social effects, and words have to be found that look like the originals. One writer clearly illustrates the extent of the problem:

Yes can easily become *ja*, especially when the speaker is a slack-lipped American, but it is hard to turn it into *igen* or *kyllä* or *naam* or *ne* or *evet*. A cowboy saying *yah* or *yeah* might just about be saying *ouais*, if not *oui*, but Sir John Gielgud affirming with precise actor's diction in close-up is excruciating to dub. (Anthony Burgess, 1980, p. 302.)

A BBC newsreader of the 1950s, dressed in a suit for the occasion, spoke in a correspondingly formal style. But the old order changeth... Fashions of radio language (and, indeed, of clothing) have altered, just as in other areas of language use. In Britain, these changes have been particularly noticeable in recent years, where there has been a strong trend towards the introduction of regional and informal speech. However, the new styles have not gone unnoticed by those who see themselves as defenders of traditional linguistic values. The BBC continues to receive a large postbag from people complaining about what they see as a decline in linguistic standards (§1).

SCREENPLAYS

Broadcasting language has its written side too, in the form of the scripts that provide the basis of the programmes. These display several interesting linguistic features of layout and terminology, as can be seen from this extract from a script by Dennis Spooner for a TV series (*Jason King*). This is one of several possible formats in current use, but several of its conventions are standard. Each shot is numbered and headed: *Ext.* ('Exterior') vs *Int.* ('Interior'), the scene location, *Night* vs *Day*, the type of set, and the time it should last. The change of shot is indicated by *cut to* (vs *dissolve*). Camera positions and movements are identified using such phrases as *another angle*, *on ...*, and *POV* ('point of view', i.e. the scene is shot as it would be seen by the character). Directions are in capitals. (After M. Hulke, 1982, p. 205.)

| 13. *INT. HOTEL CORRIDOR. NIGHT. STUDIO. (0.10)* | 13. |

REYNOLDS IS RAPPING AT KING'S DOOR, OBVIOUSLY NOT FOR THE FIRST TIME. HE WAITS, LISTENS AT THE DOOR, AND THEN, DECIDING THAT KING MUST BE ASLEEP, HE TAKES A PLASTIC CARD, OR AN IMPLEMENT, FROM HIS PERSON, AND UNLOCKS THE DOOR.

CUT TO:

| 14. *INT. KING'S HOTEL ROOM. NIGHT. STUDIO. (0.20)* | 14. |

REYNOLDS MOVES INTO KING'S ROOM, AND CLOSES THE DOOR BEHIND HIM. HE LOOKS AROUND THE ROOM.

ANOTHER ANGLE

REYNOLDS MOVES ACROSS THE LIVING ROOM, PART OF THE SUITE, AND OPENS A DOOR THAT LEADS INTO THE BEDROOM.

ON REYNOLDS

AS HE LOOKS INTO THE (UNSEEN) BEDROOM, AND NOTES THAT KING IS NOT THERE. HE CLOSES THE DOOR, AND TURNS AWAY.

ANOTHER ANGLE

REYNOLDS CROSSES TO THE DESK, LOOKING FOR A CLUE AS TO WHERE KING HAS GONE. AT THE DESK, WHICH IS BY THE WINDOW, HE HEARS THE MURMUR OF VOICES BELOW. REYNOLDS TURNS TO THE WINDOW. WE ARE ON HIM AS HE LOOKS OUT.

CUT TO:

| 15. *EXT. LONDON HOTEL. NIGHT. LOCATION. (0.05)* | 15. |

REYNOLD'S P.O.V.

WE SEE KING BELOW, MOVING AWAY, AND GIVING A SALUTORY WAVE TO THE COMMISSIONAIRE, WE HEAR, IN MUFFLED TONES:

KING:

. . . A walk round the Park might help me sleep. . .

AND KING TURNS, AND MOVES AWAY.

THE POWER OF LANGUAGE

A recurrent theme of the present section has been the concern and controversy that can arise when people encounter the powerful influence of language in special settings. Between professionals, of course, there is no problem: whether the subject matter is medicine, science, or baseball, the ability to use a specialized variety of language is a necessary part of professional competence. The difficulties arise only when others come into contact with it, by accident or design, and find themselves threatened by its lack of familiarity or clarity – as happens so often in such fields as science, medicine, religion, and the law. Proposed solutions are complex, and range from large-scale recommendations for reform to proposals that accept the linguistic complexity, and introduce children to these varieties while at school.

In the case of the mass media, the issues are somewhat different. Here the chief anxiety relates to the use of language to convey the truth. Whether we are faced with a newspaper editorial, a radio news report, a film documentary, or a piece of television advertising, we are confronted with the results of language selection: someone has made a decision about what shall be communicated and what withheld. Inevitably, then, questions arise about the reasoning used, and the form of its linguistic expression. Suspicion about motives is universal: 'Don't believe everything you read/hear.'

These issues vary in seriousness, depending on the subject matter, and the kind of society in which they are raised. There is an extensive everyday terminology that illustrates the many ways in which the abuse of linguistic power shows itself. At one extreme we are faced with such 'mild' notions as sales rhetoric, exaggerated claims, and sensationalism; at the other we find a wide range of strongly pejorative labels, such as bias, prejudice, propaganda, misinformation, censorship, indoctrination, brain-washing, and psychological (which usually means linguistic) warfare. These words are used in all kinds of social situations where people are in conflict – most commonly when the conflicts are 'organized', as in politics, religion, and trade union negotiations. However, it is impossible to agree about their meaning, as they often function only as emotional 'snarl words'.

Ironically, there is a far less extensive vocabulary available to express the various kinds of freedom and openness of expression that people aspire to. In a democratic society, there are of course many kinds of activities that represent freedom in action, such as public enquiries, opinion polls, and press conferences. But the concept of openness in public debate and dissemination seems not to have motivated a corresponding supply of 'purr words' for everyday use.

GENERAL SEMANTICS

Alfred Korzybski (1879–1950) A Polish–U.S. scientist and philosopher whose system of linguistic philosophy, known as *general semantics,* attracted considerable popular interest in the 1930s and 1940s (notably through his book *Science and Sanity* (1933) and the popularizations that ensued). It still has a certain following, especially in the U.S., though its emphasis on word meaning (rather than on sentences or contexts) has not made the approach appeal to modern semanticists (§17).

General semantics looks critically at the way people use words without carefully considering what they mean. It recommends the analysis of meaning as a way of promoting mutual understanding, both between individuals and across generations. Words are seen as deceptively stable entities, which obscure the variety of meanings that people give to them. People continue to use the same word even though there may have been a major change in the reality to which it once referred. One proposed solution is the indexing of verbal labels: different senses can be distinguished by numbering (e.g. *fascism₁* and *fascism₂*) or dating (e.g. $Hitler_{1930}$ vs $Hitler_{1939}$), to distinguish exactly which aspect of a notion is being referred to.

Several attempts to apply these ideas followed, in such fields as psychotherapy and language teaching. One of Korzybski's popularizers, Stuart Chase, illustrated the kind of practical level of analysis involved. In *The Tyranny of Words* (1938), he investigated the way nearly 100 people used the word *Fascism*: everyone he asked disliked it (it was a 'snarl' word), but there was little agreement as to what it meant, as can be seen from the following selection of comments:

A dictator suppressing all opposition.
One-party government.
Obtaining one's desires by sacrifice of human lives.
Hitler and Mussolini.
War. Concentration camps.
Empiricism, forced control, quackery.
Same thing as communism.
Exaggerated nationalism.
Lawlessness.
Terrorism, religious intolerance, bigotry.
A large Florida rattlesnake in summer.

Chase found 15 distinct concepts in the answers. He comments: 'Multiply the sample by ten million and picture if you can the aggregate mental chaos. Yet this is the word which is soberly treated as a definite thing by newspapers, authors, orators, statesmen, talkers, the world over.' He concludes that only a programme of semantic training can help people to control their reliance on words at the expense of realities. 'What the semantic discipline does is to blow ghosts out of the picture and create a new picture as close to reality as one can get... The probability of better judgments is greatly improved, for [a person] is now swayed more by happenings in the outside world than by reverberations within his skull.' (S. Chase, 1938, pp. 129–30, 141.)

CRITICAL LANGUAGE STUDY

In the late 1980s, the factors which underlie social interaction, and especially the relationship between language and power, began to receive systematic investigation in a new branch of linguistics which has come to be called *critical language study. Critical* is here used in an idiosyncratic sense, referrring to a desire to show up the connections between language, power, and ideology which are often hidden beneath the forms of language that people use. There are many contexts, such as interviewing, teaching, training, news reporting, informing (e.g. by a bureaucracy), and announcing (e.g. by governments), in which hidden agendas can be shown to operate. A critical approach aims to reveal what these agendas are, and thus promote an awareness of the issues which - over and above its intrinsic interest - can be of value to those for whom domination and oppression are real issues.

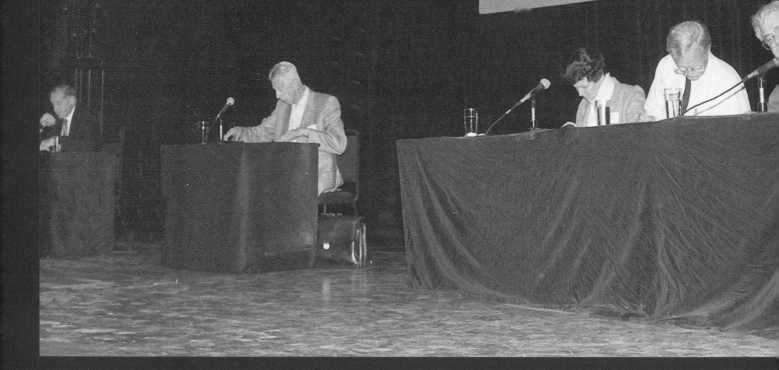

Language and communication

In this final Part, the aim is to place the study of language in a broader intellectual perspective. This is done, first of all, by showing how language relates to other modes of communication, within the more general heading of semiotics. The main 'design features' of human language are reviewed, and compared with the properties displayed by animal communication. There seems to be little in common: the creativity and structural complexity of language cannot be found in the natural communicative behaviour of other species (though the extent to which language can be taught to chimpanzees requires our separate consideration). There is a clear contrast, also, with the various domains of nonverbal expression. We look at such areas as facial expression, bodily gesture, and tactile communication, as well as at some of the language-based codes and surrogates that are in use around the world. By noting the similarities and differences between language and these other areas, we can more easily identify the subject's boundaries – though the search for a clear definition of 'language' seems no nearer as a result.

The second and final section outlines the development and current scope of linguistics, the science of language study. The opening perspective is historical, dealing with the emergence of systematic ideas about the nature of language among the scholars of Ancient Greece, Rome, and India, and tracing the persistent interest in language through the Middle Ages and the Renaissance to modern times. The most rapid period of development has been the 20th century, where we find unprecedented progress in linguistic scholarship. A brief account is given of the history of ideas from the pioneering statements of Ferdinand de Saussure to the present day, in particular recognizing the influential role played by Noam Chomsky in giving direction to the modern subject. A separate section deals with the nature of linguistic data, and with contemporary methods of handling it computationally. Part XI then concludes with a summary of the main branches of linguistics, and of the various points of contact the subject has with other academic fields.

A plenary session at the XV International Congress of Linguists, held in Quebec in 1992.

64 · LANGUAGE AND OTHER COMMUNICATION SYSTEMS

A widely recognized problem with the term 'language' is the great range of its application. This word has prompted innumerable definitions. Some focus on the general concept of 'language', some on the more specific notion of 'a language'. Some draw attention to the formal features of phonology (or graphology), grammar, and semantics (Parts III–VI). Some emphasize the range of functions that language performs (Parts I, II). Some stress the differences between language and other forms of human, animal, or machine communication (see below). Some point to the similarities. At one extreme, there are definitions that are highly technical in character; at the other, there are extremely general statements, reflecting the way in which the notion has been applied figuratively to all forms of human behaviour, such as the 'language' of music, cookery, or the cinema.

Most textbooks in the subject avoid the problem, preferring to characterize the notion of language rather than define it. They recognize that the question of identifying an individual language has no single, simple answer, because formal and social criteria are often in conflict (§47). Similarly, they note the correspondingly complex problems that arise when attempting to construct a definition of language in general that makes a precise and comprehensive statement about formal and functional universal properties. The set of definitions given below exemplifies the way different writers have attempted to tackle the problem, and illustrates some of the difficulties involved. There seems little to be gained by trying to summarize the content of the present volume in a single sentence – unless it is the banal observation that 'language' is what this encyclopedia is about!

A more useful approach to language, and one used by most modern linguists, is to identify the various properties that are thought to be its essential defining characteristics. The aim is to determine what 'counts' as a human language, as opposed to some other system of communication. Two main kinds of enquiry have been used. One focuses upon identifying the universal structural properties of language, and this is discussed in Part III (§§13–15). The other is to contrast language with non-human forms of communication and with other forms of human communication.

DESIGN FEATURES OF COMMUNICATION

The most widely acknowledged comparative approach has been that proposed by the American linguist Charles F. Hockett (1916–), who used a zoological mode of enquiry to identify the main points of connection between language and other systems of communication, especially those found in animals. His set of 13 design features of communication using spoken language were as follows:

- *Auditory–vocal channel* Sound is used between mouth and ear, as opposed to a visual, tactile, or other means (pp. 405–7).
- *Broadcast transmission and directional reception* A signal can be heard by any auditory system within earshot, and the source can be located using the ears' direction-finding ability (p. 142).
- *Rapid fading* Auditory signals are transitory, and do not await the hearer's convenience (unlike animal tracks, or writing, §31).

Charles F. Hockett

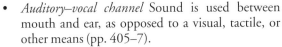

LANGUAGE DEFINITIONS

'Language is a purely human and non-instinctive method of communicating ideas, emotions and desires by means of voluntarily produced symbols.' (E. Sapir, 1921.)
'A language is a system of arbitrary vocal symbols by means of which the members of a society interact in terms of their total culture.' (G. Trager, 1949.)
A language is 'a set (finite or infinite) of sentences, each finite in length and constructed out of a finite set of elements'. (A. N.

Chomsky, 1957.)
Language is 'the institution whereby humans communicate and interact with each other by means of habitually used oral–auditory arbitrary symbols'. (R. A. Hall, 1964.)

A dictionary definition
1. the words, their pronunciation, and the methods of combining them used and understood by a considerable community and established by long usage.
2a. audible, articulate, meaningful sound as produced by the action of the vocal organs.
2b. a systematic means of communicating ideas or feelings by the use of conventionalized signs, sounds, gestures, or marks having understood meanings.
2c. an artificially constructed primarily formal system of signs and symbols (as symbolic logic) including rules for the formation of admissible expressions and for their transformation.
2d. the means by which animals communicate or

are thought to communicate with each other.
3. the faculty of verbal expression and the use of words in human intercourse ... significant communication.
4. a special manner or use of expression.
(*Webster's Third New International Dictionary*, 1961.)

And a comment
'The question "What is language?" is comparable with – and, some would say, hardly less profound than –

"What is life?", the presuppositions of which circumscribe and unify the biological sciences ... it is not so much the question itself as the particular interpretation that the biologist puts upon it and the unravelling of its more detailed implications within some currently accepted theoretical framework that nourish the biologist's day-to-day speculations and research. So it is for the linguist in relation to the question "What is language?"'
(J. Lyons, 1981, p. 1.)

- *Interchangeability* Speakers of a language can reproduce any linguistic message they can understand (unlike the differing courtship behaviour of males and females in several species).
- *Total feedback* Speakers hear and can reflect upon everything that they say (unlike the visual displays often used in animal courtship, which are not visible to the displayer).
- *Specialization* The sound waves of speech have no function other than to signal meaning (unlike the audible panting of dogs, which has a biological purpose).
- *Semanticity* The elements of the signal convey meaning through their stable association with real-world situations (unlike dog panting, which does not 'mean' a dog is hot; it is 'part of' being hot).
- *Arbitrariness* There is no dependence of the element of the signal on the nature of the reality to which it refers (unlike the speed of bee 'dancing', which directly reflects the distance of the nectar from the hive).
- *Discreteness* Speech uses a small set of sound elements that clearly contrast with each other (unlike growling, and other emotional noises, where there are continuous scales of variation in strength).

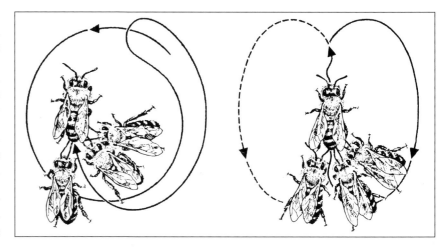

- *Displacement* It is possible to talk about events remote in space or time from the situation of the speaker (unlike most animal cries, which reflect immediate environmental stimuli).
- *Productivity* There is an infinite capacity to express and understand meaning, by using old sentence elements to produce new sentences (unlike the limited, fixed set of calls used by animals).
- *Traditional transmission* Language is transmitted from one generation to the next primarily by a process of teaching and learning (unlike the bee's ability to communicate the source of nectar, which is passed on genetically).
- *Duality of patterning* The sounds of language have no intrinsic meaning, but combine in different ways to form elements (such as words) that do convey meaning (unlike animal calls, which cannot be analysed into two such levels of structure).

The applicability of the 13 design features to six systems of communication (after C. F. Hockett, 1960, pp. 10–11). The music column refers only to western music since the time of Bach. A question mark indicates that it is unclear or unknown whether a system has a particular feature. A blank space indicates that a feature cannot be determined because other information is lacking.

The 'language' of bees
One of the most closely investigated forms of animal communication is the 'dance' performed by a honey bee when it returns to the hive, which conveys precise information about the source and amount of food it has discovered. Several kinds of movement pattern have been observed. In the 'round dance' (above, left) used when the food source is close to the hive, the bee moves in circles alternately to left and right. In the 'tail-wagging dance' (above, right), used when the source is further away, the bee moves in a straight line while wagging her abdomen from side to side, then returns to her starting point. The straight line points in the direction of the food, the liveliness of the dance indicates how rich a source it is, and the tempo of the dance provides information about its distance. For example, in one study, an experimental feeding dish 330 metres from the hive was indicated by 15 complete runs through the pattern in 30 seconds, whereas when the dish was moved to 700 metres distance, only 11 runs were carried out in that time. No other animal communication system seems able to provide such a quantity of precise information – except human language. (After K. von Frisch, 1962.)

	Bee dancing	Stickleback courtship	Western meadowlark song	Gibbon calls	Language	Instrumental music
The vocal-auditory channel	no	no	yes	yes	yes	auditory, not vocal
Broadcast transmission and directional reception	yes	yes	yes	yes	yes	yes
Rapid fading	?	?	yes	yes, repeated	yes	yes
Interchangeability	limited	no	?	yes	yes	?
Total feedback	?	no	yes	yes	yes	yes
Specialization	?	in part	yes?	yes	yes	yes
Semanticity	yes	no	in part?	yes	yes	no (in general)
Arbitrariness	no		if semantic, yes	yes	yes	
Discreteness	no	?	?	yes	yes	in part
Displacement	yes, always		?	no	yes, often	
Productivity	yes	no	?	no	yes	yes
Traditional transmission	probably not	no?	?	?	yes	yes
Duality of patterning	no		?	no	yes	

CHIMP COMMUNICATION

The formal and functional complexity of language is such a distinctive human trait that many scholars think the designation *homo loquens* ('speaking man') to be a better way of identifying the species than any other single criterion that has been suggested (such as tool using) (p. 293). This is not to disregard the complex patterns that have been observed in the natural communicative systems of birds, insects, apes, and other animals (the subject matter of the field of *zöosemiotics*). But no animal system remotely compares with the level of sophistication found in human language. The evolutionary gap is very wide. Only the recent experiments in teaching language to chimpanzees have suggested that this gap may be somewhat narrower than has traditionally been assumed.

Early experiments to teach chimpanzees to communicate with their voices failed because of the insufficiencies of the animals' vocal organs (p. 292). However, when attempts were made to communicate with them using the hands, by teaching a selection of signs from American Sign Language (ASL, see Part VI), dramatic progress was claimed. The first subject was a female chimpanzee named Washoe, whose training began in 1966 when she was less than a year old. It took her just over four years to acquire 132 ASL signs, many of which bore striking similarities to the general word meanings observed in child language acquisition (Part VII). She also began to put signs together to express a small set of meaning relations, which resembled some of the early sentences of young children, such as *want berry, time drink, there shoe* (B. T. & R. A. Gardner, 1975).

Since then, several other chimpanzees (and also gorillas) have acquired a vocabulary of signs, and alternative teaching procedures have been tried. For example, in the case of the chimps Moja and Pili, sign language teaching began soon after birth, and training was carried out by native signers. Both chimps began to sign when they were about 3 months old, and had over a dozen signs by the age of 6 months – a marked contrast with Washoe, who had only 2 signs after 6 months of training.

A quite different way of proceeding was introduced in the case of a 5-year-old chimpanzee called Sarah, in a research programme that began in 1954 (D. & A. J. Premack, 1983). She (and, later, several others) was taught a form of written language – to arrange and respond to vertical sequences of plastic tokens on a magnetic board. Each token represented a word, e.g. small blue triangle = *apple*, small pink square = *banana*. In due course, the trainer was able to teach Sarah to respond correctly to several basic semantic sequences (e.g. 'give Mary apple'), including a number of more abstract notions, such as 'same/different' and 'if/then' (e.g. ? *apple different banana*).

Chimp language research attracted considerable media publicity in its early years, with reporters focusing on the implications of the work. What would chimps say if they could use language? What would they think of the human race? Would they claim civil rights? Such speculations were wholly premature, given the limited findings of the research to date. These findings are in any case controversial, receiving a range of reactions extending from total support to total antipathy. A variety of interpretations seems possible. It is evident that chimps can learn to imitate signs, combine them into sequences, and use them in different contexts, but the explanation of this behaviour is less clear. Many scholars believe that the chimps' behaviour can be explained as a sophisticated imitation ability rather than as evidence for some form of linguistic processing, and they argue the need for fuller accounts to be provided of chimp behaviour, and of the training methods used, in order to evaluate the claims being made about learning. More systematic data have begun to be collected, but it will be some time before these questions can be resolved.

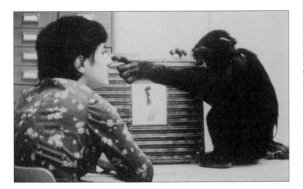

'Peony nose touch' Peony, one of the 'second generation' of chimps trained in the Premack study, carries out this instruction, which her trainer has placed on the magnetic board. (D. Premack & A. J. Premack, 1983, p. 29.)

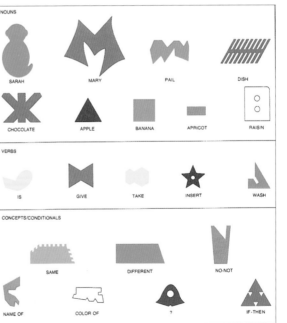

WASHOE'S WORDS

Washoe's typical vocabulary can be seen from the signs she used in a study of her responses to 500 questions. The signs were grouped by the authors into 13 general types (it should be noted that an idiosyncratically broad notion of 'noun' is used, including such items as *dirty* and *listen*):

Proper names (her companions)
Don, Dr G, Greg, Roger, Linn, Mrs G, Susan, Washoe

Pronouns
me, we, you

Common nouns

baby	dirty	nut
bath	drink	pants
bed	flower	pencil
berry	food	purse
bird	fruit	ride
blanket	gun	shoe
book	hammer	smoke
brush	hat	spoon
bug	ice	swallow
car	key	sweet
cereal	leaf	tree
chair	listen	water
cheese	lollipop	window
clothes	look	wiper
comb	man	woman
cow	meat	

Possessives
mine, yours

Traits
funny, good, hungry, stupid

Colours
black, white, green, red

Temporal
time

Negative
can't, enough, no

Imperative
gimme, help

Appetitive
please, want

Quantitative
hurry, more

Verbs
bite, catch, cry, go, hug, open, peekaboo, smile, tickle

Locatives
in, out, up, there

Typical sequences
Me Washoe   Food fruit
You me out   Time drink
Susan bite there   Good me

Sarah's symbols (left) Symbols used in communicating with Sarah and the other chimps. (From D. Premack & A. J. Premack, 1983, p. 21.)

SEMIOTICS

Language can also be studied as part of a much wider domain of enquiry: *semiology*, or *semiotics* - a subject which owes a great deal to US philosopher Charles Sanders Peirce (1839–1914), as well as to the work of Ferdinand de Saussure (p. 411). This field investigates the structure of all possible sign systems, and the role these play in the way we create and perceive patterns (or 'meanings') in sociocultural behaviour. The subject is all-inclusive, therefore, dealing with patterned human communication in all its modes (sound, sight, touch, smell, and taste) and in all contexts (e.g. dance, film, politics, eating, clothing). The subject matter of the present book would form but a small section of any proposed encyclopedia of semiotics.

AUDITORY-VOCAL

The diagram below shows the relationship between language, as identified in Parts III–VI, and other aspects of human communication. The structured use of the *auditory–vocal* mode, or channel (p. 404), results in the primary manifestation of language: speech. But non-linguistic uses of the vocal tract are also possible: physiological reflexes, such as coughing and snoring; musical effects, such as whistling; and the communication of identity, in the form of voice quality (§6). The suprasegmental aspects of vocal expression (§29) are usually included within the study of language, though it is difficult to draw a clear-cut boundary line between some of these effects (those placed under the heading of 'paralanguage', such as giggling and whispering) and those that clearly fall outside language.

VISUAL

The visual mode is used for a variety of purposes, some linguistic, some not. The primary way in which visual effects have a linguistic use is in the various deaf sign languages (Part VI). In addition, there is the historically derivative use of the visual mode that resulted in the development of written language. Further writing-based codes, such as semaphore and morse, would also be included here. Non-linguistic forms of visual communication include the systems of facial expression and bodily gesture, which are the subject matter of *kinesics* (p. 406).

TACTILE

Tactile communication has very limited linguistic function, apart from its use in deaf–blind communication and in various secret codes based on spoken or written language (p. 58). Its main uses are non-linguistic, in the form of the various ways in which bodily contact and physical distance between people can signal contrasts of meaning – the subject matter of *proxemics* (p. 401).

The communicative use of the visual and tactile modes is often referred to as 'nonverbal communication', especially in academic discussion. In everyday terms, it is the area of 'body language'.

OLFACTORY AND GUSTATORY

There seems to be little active role for the olfactory and gustatory modes in human communication (a marked contrast with the important use of these senses for communicative purposes in the animal kingdom). However, they do play an important part in our reception of information about the outside world (e.g. in smelling and tasting food). The communicative use of body odour seems to have a mainly sexual role in human society; but there are several anecdotes of its use in other domains. One linguist even claimed to be able to tell when his informants (p. 414) were under strain (and perhaps therefore were being less reliable) by the different body odour they exuded!

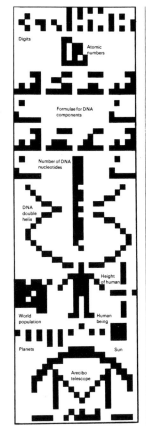

Other modes? This is the pictographic message transmitted into space by the Arecibo radio telescope in Puerto Rico in 1974. The signal was aimed at the cluster of 300,000 stars, known as M13, in the Hercules constellation.

The message consists of a series of radio pulses which can be arranged into a pictogram. It includes data on the chemical basis of life on earth, the human form, and the solar system. It assumes, of course, that the communicative system of the receiving species is capable of responding to the same semiotic contrasts as are displayed in the pictogram (shape, length, etc.). If the entity receiving the signal happens to have a communicative system based on, say, heat, the astronomers will have wasted their time!

The Hercules target is 24,000 light years away – which means that, if any one or thing is there to receive it, and chooses to reply, the response should arrive in about 50,000 years' time.

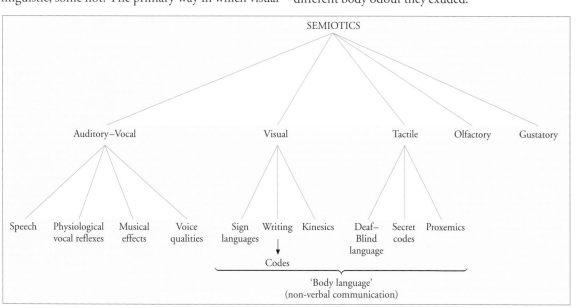

AUDITORY–VOCAL EFFECTS

The main systems of communication using the auditory–vocal channel have been described elsewhere in this volume (Part IV). However, from time to time linguists have reported types of auditory communication that fall outside the normal use of the vocal apparatus – notably, the whistled speech of several rural populations. This is found in some Central and South American tribes, as well as in the occasional European community (e.g. in Turkey and the Canary Islands, based on Turkish and Spanish respectively).

Whistled speech

Eusebio Martinez was observed one day standing in front of his hut, whistling to a man a considerable distance away. The man was passing on the trail below, going to market to sell a load of corn leaves which he was carrying. The man answered Eusebio's whistle with a whistle. The interchange was repeated several times with different whistles. Finally the man turned around, retraced his steps a short way and came up the footpath to Eusebio's hut. Without saying a word he dumped his load on the ground. Eusebio looked the load over, went into his hut, returned with some money, and paid the man his price. The man turned and left. Not a word had been spoken. They had talked, bargained over the price, and come to an agreement satisfactory to both parties – using only whistles as a medium of communication. (G. M. Cowan, 1948, p. 280.)

This conversation took place between Mazateco speakers, members of a tribe that lives in and around the State of Oaxaca, Mexico. The whistled conversations closely correspond to patterns of spoken language, as has been shown by having the whistlers translate their tunes into speech. It is thus quite unlike the unstructured whistling patterns used as attention signals (e.g. 'wolf-whistling') in Euro-American culture. For example, in the following sequence of whistled utterances (where the tones are classified from 1 (high) to 4 (low), and glides between tones are marked by a dash), quite specific meanings are signalled, as the following transcription of Mazateco shows:

1,1,3,3,2,4 *hme¹ čʔa¹ šī³ kī³-čʔaí²-ve⁴*
'What did you bring there?'
1,4,1,1 *čʔa¹na⁴ hme¹-ni¹*
'It is a load of corn.'
1,3,3,4,3 *hnā¹ tī³-ʔmī³ koaí⁴-ʔnī³*
'Well where are you going with it?'
3,2,4,2,3,4 *te³ na²nko⁴ tī²-vhī³ koa⁴*
'I am taking it to Tenango.'
3,3,3,3,2,3,2–4,3 *ʔa³-tī³-ʔmī³ ka³ te² na³-ni²⁻⁴ʔnī³*
'Are you going to sell it then?'
2,3,3,2,2–3 *tī²-vhī³ ka³ te² na²⁻³*
'I am going to sell it.'
1,1,3,2,4,4,2,3,1–3,4 *ho¹ thī¹ čʔaí³-ʔnī²*
ʔī⁴-ta⁴ te² na³-naí¹⁻³-vi⁴
'How much will you take then? Sell it to me here.'

4–3,4,3,3,3,2,4 *ka⁴⁻³ tą ǫ⁴ kʔoa³ nka³ hnko³ ka² šá⁴*
'I will take $2.50 a box.'
(G. M. Cowan, 1948, pp. 284–5.)

The whistled tunes are based on the patterns of tone and rhythm used in the spoken language, and can convey precise distinctions. With very few exceptions, each 'syllable' of whistle corresponds to a syllable of speech. Ambiguity is uncommon, because the topic of the conversation is usually something evident in the situation of the speakers. However, it is important for both speakers to use the same musical key, otherwise confusion may arise.

Whistled dialogues tend to contain a small number of exchanges, and the utterances are short. They are most commonly heard when people are at a distance from each other (e.g. when working the land), but they can also be found in a variety of informal settings. Although women are able to understand whistled speech, it is normally used only by and between males.

Nuba (Sudan) musicians prepare for a tribal gathering.

DRUM SIGNALLING

In several parts of the world – notably Africa, the Americas, and the Pacific – drums, gongs, horns, and other musical instruments have been used to simulate selected features of speech (primarily, tones and rhythms). In Africa, drums are the usual instruments involved, and quite elaborate systems of communication have developed.

One system, used among the Jabo tribe of Eastern Liberia, makes use of a wooden signal 'drum' (actually, more like a bell, as it has no skin covering) – a hollowed tree trunk, often over 2 metres in length. This has a longitudinal slit with lips varying in thickness, thus allowing several different tones to be produced. Two straight sticks are used for beating, and further tonal variations can be made by altering the way these sticks hit the drum. Other types of drum are also used for different purposes (such as dancing).

The drummer, an official of the town's law-enforcing authority, controls the way meetings take place, using special signals to do such things as call for order, summon people, and end the meeting. These signals consist mainly of fixed formulae, with a few variations and additions. The Jabo rarely use these drums for communicating with other villages (unlike the drum signalling found in many other parts of Africa).

The words and syllables of Jabo are tonal (§29): there are four basic tones, which are often linked by glides, and these interact with aspects of the vowel and consonant system. There is also considerable variation in the length of these tonal contrasts, which accounts for several of the drum patterns used. Some examples of these signals, with a transcription in Jabo, are given below. (From G. Herzog, 1945.)

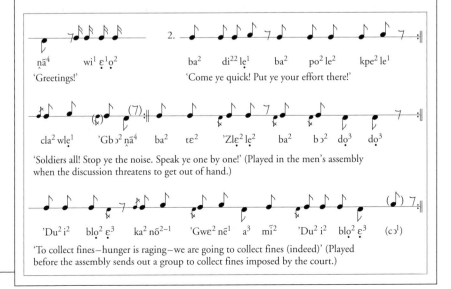

nā̃⁴ wi¹ ɛ¹o²
'Greetings!'

ba² di²² le¹ ba² po²le² kpe² le¹
'Come ye quick! Put ye your effort there!'

cla² wle¹ 'Gb ɔ² nā̃⁴ ba² tɛ² 'Zle² le² ba² b ɔ² do² do³
'Soldiers all! Stop ye the noise. Speak ye one by one!' (Played in the men's assembly when the discussion threatens to get out of hand.)

'Du² i² blo² ɛ³ ka² nō²⁻¹ 'Gwe² nē̃¹ a³ mī² i² 'Du² i² blo² ɛ³ (c ɔ¹)
'To collect fines – hunger is raging – we are going to collect fines (indeed)' (Played before the assembly sends out a group to collect fines imposed by the court.)

TACTILE EFFECTS

The communicative use of touching behaviour, proxemics, has in recent years attracted a great deal of research by psychologists, sociologists, and anthropologists. A very wide range of activities is involved, as is suggested by this small selection of terms expressing bodily contact:

embrace	lay on (hands)	punch
guide	link (arms)	shake (hands)
hold	nudge	slap
kick	pat	spank
kiss	pinch	tickle

The communicative value of tactile activities is usually fairly clear within a culture, as they comprise some of the most primitive kinds of social interaction (several of the activities are found between animals). They express such 'meanings' as affection, aggression (both real and pretend), sexual attraction, greeting and leave taking, congratulation, gratitude, and the signalling of attention. They operate within a complex system of social constraints: some of the acts tend to be found only in private (notably, sexual touching); some are specialized in function (e.g. the tactile activities carried on by doctors, dentists, hairdressers, or tailors); and some are restricted to certain ceremonies (e.g. weddings, graduation, healing). Everyone has a subjective impression about how these activities take place, and what they mean. But there are many differences in behaviour between individuals and groups, and it is not easy to make accurate generalizations about society as a whole.

It is difficult to study tactile activity in an objective way: a basic problem is how to obtain clear recordings in which the participants are unaware of the observer (especially if the behaviour is being filmed). There are thus few detailed accounts of the range of communicative tactile acts in a society, and of the factors governing their use. It is evident, however, that some societies are much more tolerant of touching than others, so much so that a distinction has been proposed between 'contact' and 'non-contact' societies – those that favour touching (such as Arabs and Latin Americans), and those that avoid it (such as North Europeans and Indians). In one study of couples sitting together in cafés, it was found that in Puerto Rico the people touched each other on average 180 times an hour; in Paris it was 110 times an hour; whereas in London there was no touching at all (S. M. Jourard, 1963).

The distance people stand from each other, and the way they hold their bodies when interacting, are other important facets of proxemic behaviour. There are norms of proximity and orientation within a culture that communicate information about the social relationship between the participants. A common research procedure is to observe the point at which people are made to feel uncomfortable when others invade their 'body space', by moving too close to them (e.g. in a queue, outside a cinema, on a beach). Any cultural variations can easily lead to conflict and misinterpretations. Latin Americans, for example, prefer to stand much closer to each other than North Europeans, so that when the former and the latter converse, there may be a problem. The present author recalls one such conflict during a conversation with a student from Brazil, who came and stood before him at some 45 cm distance – a normal interaction distance for her, but much too close for him. He instinctively moved back to the distance he found most comfortable – nearer 1 metre. However, as he did so, the student moved forward, unconsciously maintaining her own norm. He retreated further, not wishing to be so close to the student. After both had circled the desk several times, he capitulated, and asked her to sit down!

TADOMA COMMUNICATION

Tadoma is a method of tactile speech communication that has evolved between people who are both deaf and blind. Speech is perceived by placing a hand against the face of the speaker and monitoring the articulatory movements involved. Usually, the thumb is used to sense the movements of the lips, and the fingers fan out over the side of the face and neck. Devised in Norway in the 1890s, it got its name from its first use in the U.S. with two deaf–blind children, Tad Chapman and Oma Simpson (R. Vivian, 1966.)

Several other tactile methods of communication are used with the handicapped, such as braille (p. 282). It is also possible to 'translate' such codes as morse and finger spelling (p. 227) into tactile form.

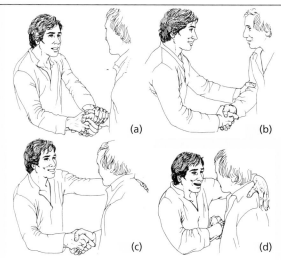

THE AMPLIFIED HAND-SHAKE

In a culture where hand-shaking is a normal formality, extra warmth can be expressed only by extra activity, such as increased firmness, longer duration, and more vigorous vertical movements. The second hand may also be brought into play, as shown in the diagrams, which illustrate increasing warmth: (a) hand clasping, (b) arm clasping, (c) shoulder clasping, and (d) shoulder embracing. (From D. Morris, 1977, p. 93.)

DISTANCE ZONES

An American study suggests that there may be four proximity zones when people interact:
- *Intimate*   Less than 45 cm, used for intimate relationships.
- *Personal*   Between 45 cm and 1.3 metres, for reasonably close relationships.
- *Social consultative* Between 3 and 4 metres, for more impersonal relationships.
- *Public*   Above 4 metres, for public figures and public occasions.
(E. T. Hall, 1959.)

The rules of Indian caste (p. 38) illustrate the point even more precisely. According to tradition in one part of India, members of each caste may not approach each other within the following distances:

Brahmins – Nayars: 2 metres
Nayars – Iravans: 8 metres
Iravans – Cherumans: 10 metres
Cherumans – Nayadis: 20 metres

The rules, which are still followed in some areas, work in an additive way: thus, a Nayadi may not come closer to a Brahmin than 40 metres (M. Argyle, 1975).

VISUAL EFFECTS

The field of non-verbal visual communication, kinesics, can be broken down into several components: facial expression, eye contact, gesture, and body posture. Each component performs a variety of functions. Movements of the face and body can give clues to a person's personality and emotional state. The face, in particular, signals a wide range of emotions, such as fear, happiness, sadness, anger, surprise, interest, and disgust, many of the expressions varying in meaning from culture to culture. In addition, the face and body send signals about the way a social interaction is proceeding: patterns of eye contact show who is talking to whom; facial expression provides feedback to the speaker, expressing such meanings as puzzlement or disbelief; and body posture conveys a person's attitude towards the interaction (e.g. relaxation, interest, boredom). Several kinds of social context are associated with specific facial or body behaviours (e.g. waving while taking leave). Ritual or official occasions are often primarily marked by such factors as kneeling, standing, bowing, or blessing.

Visual effects interact very specifically with speech. Gestures and head movements tend to coincide with points of emphasis. Hand movements in particular can be used to add visual meaning to what has been said ('drawing pictures in the air'). Patterns of gaze distinguish the participants in a conversation: a listener looks at a speaker nearly twice as often as the speaker looks at the listener. They also assist in marking the structure of a conversation (§20): for example, speakers tend to look up towards the ends of their utterances, thus giving their listeners a cue that an opportunity to speak is approaching.

Several visual effects may well be universal, but the focus of interest in recent years has been on the cultural differences that can be observed in face and body movements. Some societies use many gestures and facial expressions (e.g. Italian); others use very few (e.g. Japanese). Moreover, a visual effect may seem to be shared between societies, but in fact convey very different meaning. Thus, in France, using a finger to pull down the eyelid means that the speaker is aware of something going on, whereas in Italy the same gesture means that the listener must *become* aware. Cultural variations in visual effects are among the first things a foreigner notices, but it can be very difficult working out what they mean, and even more difficult deciding whether one is permitted to use them.

EYEBROW FLASHING

When people greet each other at a distance, wishing to show that they are ready to make social contact, they raise their eyebrows with a rapid movement, keeping them raised for about one-sixth of a second. The behaviour has been noted in many parts of the world, and is considered universal (though some cultures suppress it, e.g. the Japanese, who consider it indecent). We are not usually aware that we use this signal, but it evokes a strong response in a greeting situation, and is often reciprocated. To receive an eyebrow flash from someone we do not know is uncomfortable, embarrassing, or even threatening. (After I. Eibl-Eibesfeldt, 1972.) Below: an eyebrow flash made by a Samoan (left) and a Waika Indian (right).

BODY TRANSCRIPTION

Some of the symbols, or *kinegraphs*, which have been used in order to transcribe the various movements of face and body. Different sets of symbols have been devised for different areas of the body: head, face, trunk, shoulder/arm/wrist, hand/fingers, hip/leg/ankle, foot activity, and neck. The symbols below are from the set for facial activities. (From R. L. Birdwhistell, 1952.)

Symbol	Meaning	Symbol	Meaning
— ⬭ —	Blank-faced	ϕ ϕ	Slitted eyes
— ⌢	Single raised brow (⌢ indicates brow raised)	⊙ ⊙	Eyes upward
— ⌣	Lowered brow	-⊙ ⊙-	Shifty eyes
＼/	Medial brow contraction	＂⊙ ⊙＂	Glare
∴∵	Medial brow nods	⊃	Tongue in cheek
⌢ ⌢	Raised brows	⌢	Pout
○ ○	Wide eyed	+++	Clenched teeth
— ○	Wink	⊌	Toothy smile
⊚ ⊚	Sidewise look	⊞	Square smile
୬ ୧	Focus on auditor	◎	Open mouth
⊗ ⊗	Stare	S◎L	Slow lick–lips
◉ ◉	Rolled eyes	Q◎L	Quick lick–lips
		∞	Moistening lips
		⬭	Lip biting

COME HERE?

Beckoning can be carried out with the palm of the hand facing up or down. People used to the former could interpret the latter to mean 'Go away'! The chart shows the preferred pattern in countries between Britain and North Africa. (After D. Morris *et al.*, 1978.)

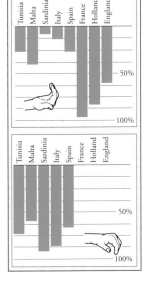

BEING HUMBLE

Points of similarity as well as difference can be seen in the expression of an attitude among various cultures. In one early study, the communication of humility was found to make use of such body postures as the following:

• Join hands over head and bow (China).
• Extend or lower arms (Europe).
• Stretch arms towards person and strike them together (Congo).
• Crouch (Fiji, Tahiti).
• Crawl and shuffle forward; walk on all fours (Dahomey).
• Bend body downward (Samoa).
• Permit someone to place a foot on one's head (Fundah, Tonga).
• Prostrate oneself, face down (Polynesia).
• Bow, extend right arm, then move it down, up to head, and down again (Turkey, Persia).
• Throw oneself on the back, roll from side to side, and slap outside of the thighs (Batokas).
(After M. H. Krout, 1942.)

Sign 'language'

Many gestural systems have evolved to facilitate communication in particular situations. They are often
referred to as 'sign languages', but few have developed
any degree of structural complexity or communicative
range, and it is therefore important to distinguish them
from 'sign language proper' – the natural signing
behaviour of the deaf (Part VI). Several might properly
be described as 'restricted languages' (p. 56).

In many parts of the world, such as India, Thailand,
and Japan, pantomime and dance have come to use
complex systems of symbolic hand gestures in association with facial expressions and body movements. The
events of a story, its deeper meaning, and the emotional states of the characters may all be conveyed in
this way. For example, in the *Bhārata Nātya-śāstra*
('principles of dramatic art'), the 6th-century BC manual of Hindu dance, there are over 4,000 picture patterns for the hands (*mudrās*).

• Religious or quasi-religious groups and secret societies often develop ritual signing systems so that
members can recognize and communicate with
each other. Such signs are used in Freemasonry,
practised by some 6 million people mainly in the
USA and Britain, and in many of the secret societies of the Far East, such as the Hung Society.

• Several monastic orders developed signing systems
of some complexity, especially if their members
were vowed to silence, as in the case of the Trappist
monks, a development of the medieval Cistercian
order.

• Simple signing systems are found in a wide range of
professions:

sports   players or officials can signal the state of play,
or an intention to act in a certain way.

entertainment   a group of performers can coordinate their activities, such as acrobats, musicians.

theatres/cinemas   ushers can signal the number and
location of seats.

casinos   officials can report on the state of play, or
indicate problems that might affect the participants in
a game.

sales/auctions   auctioneers can convey the type and
amount of selling and buying.

aviation marshalling   ground staff can send information about the position of an aircraft, the state of its
engines, and its desired position.

radio/television direction   producers and directors
can signal to performers the amount of time available,
instructions about level of loudness or speed of speaking, and information about faults and corrections.

diving   divers can communicate depth, direction,
time, and the nature of any difficulties they have
encountered.

truck driving   drivers can exchange courtesy signals,
give information about the state of the road, or show
they are in trouble.

heavy equipment drivers   people controlling cranes,
hoists, and other equipment can signal the direction
and extent of movement.

fire service   fire-officers can send directions about
the supply of water, water pressures, and the use of
equipment.

bookmaking   bookies send signals about the number of a race or horse, and its price (see left).

noisy conditions   environmental noise may make
verbal communication impossible (e.g. in cotton
mills) and a signing system may result.

TICK-TACK TALK

One of the most intriguing sights at
dog tracks and racecourses in Britain
is the system of tick-tack signing
used to circulate information about
the way bets are being placed. A
signer acts as an agent for a group of
bookmakers who have bought his
'twist card', on which the dogs or
horses are given different numbers
to those on the official race card.
The same set of tick-tack signs is
used by all signers, identifying the
amount of a bet, a horse or dog
number, and the number of a race;
but only those who have an individual signer's twist card will be able to
interpret what a number refers to.

Number signs
1   right hand on top of hat
2   right hand on nose
3   right hand under chin
4   right hand sweeps a curve
5   right hand on shoulder
6   sign 5 then 1
7   sign 5 then 2
8   sign 5 then 3
9   sign 5 then 4
10   clap hands
£5   right hand held up, palm
outwards, fingers spread
£10   both arms held up with fingers spread
£50   clenched fists held together
£100   left hand held up with fingers spread
£500   hands outline a circle
£1,000   hands play imaginary piano
('grand piano' = 'a grand' =
£1,000)

Some signs for odds
Evens   arms held in front, moving up
and down
11/10   hands together, forming a
pyramid
6/4   one right finger in the left
ear-hole

No bet. 'I don't want it'   Horse number two   Each movement outwards
from the crossed position
denotes £100

Nine to four against   Evens   I want to pay to lose

Language has been an object of fascination and a subject of serious enquiry for over 2,000 years. Often, the observations have been subjective and anecdotal, as people reflected on such topics as the nature of meaning, ideals of correctness, and the origins of language (§§1, 49). But from the earliest periods, there has also been an objective approach, with scholars investigating aspects of grammar, vocabulary, and pronunciation in a detailed and organized way. At the end of the 18th century, the subject attracted an increasing number of specialists (§50), so much so that it rapidly became possible to see the emergence of a new field of scientific research with language analysis as its focus. This approach, first known as *philology*, dealt exclusively with the historical development of language. In the present century, the subject has broadened to include the whole range of subject matter represented in this book, and it is now generally called *linguistics* (or *linguistic science*). Linguistics today is a widely practised academic discipline, with several domains of application (p. 412).

EARLY HISTORY

A religious or philosophical awareness of language can be found in many early civilizations (p. 388). In particular, several of the important issues of language analysis were addressed by the grammarians and philosophers of Ancient Greece, Rome, and India.

THE GREEKS

The earliest surviving linguistic debate is found in the pages of Plato (c. 427–347 BC). *Cratylus* is a dialogue about the origins of language and the nature of meaning – first between Socrates and Hermogenes, then between Socrates and Cratylus. Hermogenes holds the view that language originated as a product of convention, so that the relationship between words and things is arbitrary: 'for nothing has its name by nature, but only by usage and custom'. Cratylus holds the opposite position, that language came into being naturally, and therefore an intrinsic relationship exists between words and things: 'there is a correctness of name existing by nature for everything: a name is not simply that which a number of people jointly agree to call a thing.' The debate is continued at length, but no firm conclusion is reached.

The latter position is more fully presented, with divine origin being invoked in support: 'a power greater than that of man assigned the first names to things, so that they must of necessity be in a correct state.' By contrast, Aristotle (384–322 BC) in his essay *De interpretatione* ('On interpretation') supported the former viewpoint. He saw the reality of a name to lie in its formal properties or shape, its relationship to the real world being secondary and indirect: 'no name exists by nature, but only by becoming a symbol.'

These first ideas developed into two schools of philosophical thought, which have since been labelled *conventionalist*, and *naturalistic*. Modern linguists have pointed out that, in their extreme forms, neither view is valid (p. 101). However, various modified and intermediate positions were also argued at the time, much of the debate inspiring a profound interest in the Greek language.

Another theoretical question was discussed in ancient Greece: whether regularity (*analogy*) or irregularity (*anomaly*) was a better explanation for the linguistic facts of Greek. In the former view, language was seen to be essentially regular, displaying symmetries in its rules, paradigms, and meanings. In the latter, attention was focused on the many exceptions to these rules, such as the existence of irregular verbs or the lack of correspondence between gender and sex (p. 93). Modern linguistics does not oppose the two principles in this way: languages are analysed with reference to both rules and exceptions, the aim being to understand the relationship between the two rather than to deny the importance of either one. The historical significance of the debate is the stimulus it provided for detailed studies of Greek and Latin grammar.

In the 3rd century BC, the Stoics established more formally the basic grammatical notions that have since, via Latin, become traditional in western thought. They grouped words into parts of speech, organized their variant forms into paradigms, and devised names for them (e.g. the cases of the noun). Dionysius Thrax (c. 100 BC) wrote the first formal grammar of Greek – a work that became a standard for over 1,000 years.

The focus throughout the period was entirely on the written language. The word *grammar* (Greek: *grammatike*) in fact originally meant 'the art of writing'. Some attention was paid to basic notions concerning the articulation of speech, and accent marks were added to writing as a guide to pronunciation. But the main interests were in the fields of grammar and etymology, rather than phonetics. A doctrine of correctness and stylistic excellence emerged: linguistic standards were set by comparison with the language of the ancient writers (e.g. Homer). And as spoken Greek (the *koine*) increasingly diverged from the literary standard, we also find the first arguments about the undesirable nature of linguistic change (§1): the language had to be preserved from corruption.

Plato (c. 427–c. 347 BC)
Luna marble head, 1st century AD.

Aristotle (384–322 BC)
In this 14th-century picture by Francesco Traini (in the church of St Catherine, Pisa), St Thomas Aquinas is being shown a book by Aristotle. Plato sits on the other side of St Thomas.

THE ROMANS

Roman writers largely followed Greek precedents and introduced a speculative approach to language. On the whole, in their descriptive work on Latin, they used Greek categories and terminology with little change. However, the most influential work of the Roman period proved to be an exception to this trend: the codification of Latin grammar by Marcus Terentius Varro (116–27 BC) under the headings of etymology, morphology, and syntax. *De lingua latina* ('On the Latin language') consisted of 26 books, though less than a quarter of these survive. Varro's work takes into account several differences between Latin and Greek (e.g. the absence of the definite article in the former). He also held the view (which is remarkably modern) that language is first and foremost a social phenomenon with a communicative purpose; only secondarily is it a tool for logical and philosophical enquiry.

Especially towards the end of the millennium, several authors wrote major works in the fields of grammar and rhetoric (§12) – notably, Cicero (106–43 BC) on style, and Quintilian (1st century AD) on usage and public speaking. Julius Caesar wrote on grammatical regularity – it is said, while crossing the Alps on a military campaign. Aelius Donatus (4th century AD) wrote a Latin grammar (*Ars maior*) that was used right into the Middle Ages, its popularity evidenced by the fact that it was the first to be printed in wooden type, and had a shorter edition for children (the *Ars minor*). In the 6th century, Priscian's *Institutiones grammaticae* ('Grammatical categories') was another influential work that continued to be used during the Middle Ages: it contains 18 books, and remains the most complete grammar of the age that we have.

The main result of the Roman period was a model of grammatical description that was handed down through many writers in Europe, and that ultimately became the basis of language teaching in the Middle Ages and the Renaissance. In due course, this model became the 'traditional' approach to grammar, which continues to exercise its influence on the teaching of English and other modern languages (§§ 1, 62).

THE INDIANS

During the above period, techniques of minute descriptive analysis were being devised by Indian linguists, which could have been of great influence had these descriptions reached the western world (something that did not take place until the 19th century). The motivation for the Indian work was quite different from the speculative matters that attracted Greek and Roman thinkers (though they did not ignore those topics). The Hindu priests were aware that their language had diverged from that of their oldest sacred texts, the Vedas (p. 388), in both pronunciation and grammar. An important part of their belief was that certain religious ceremonies, to be successful, needed to reproduce accurately the original form of these texts. Change was not corruption, as in Greece, but profanation. Several ancillary disciplines (*Vedānga*, 'limbs of the Vedas'), including phonetics, etymology, grammar, and metrics, grew up to overcome this problem.

Their solution was to establish the facts of the old language clearly and systematically and thus to produce an authoritative text. The earliest evidence we have of this feat is the work carried out by the grammarian Pāṇini, sometime between the 5th and 7th centuries BC, in the form of a set of 4,000 aphoristic statements known as *sūtras* ('threads'). The *Aṣṭādhyāyī* ('Eight books'), dealing mainly with rules of word formation, are composed in such a condensed style that they have required extensive commentary, and a major descriptive tradition has since been established. The work is remarkable for its detailed phonetic descriptions: for example, places of articulation are clearly described, the concept of voicing is introduced, and the influence of sounds on each other in connected speech is recognized (the notion of *sandhi*). Several concepts of modern linguistics derive from this tradition.

A page from the Aṣṭādhyāyī, Pāṇini's compilation of Sanskrit grammar, in an early 19th-century printing. The script is Devanagari.

Far left: **Cicero**, in an engraving of 1584

Below: **Varro**, in an engraving of 1584

THE MIDDLE AGES

Very little is known about the development of linguistic ideas in Europe during the 'Dark Ages', though it is evident that Latin, as the language of education, provided a continuity of tradition between classical and medieval periods. Medieval learning was founded on seven 'arts', of which three – grammar, dialectic, and rhetoric – formed one division, known as the *trivium*. Grammar (mainly using Priscian and Donatus) was seen as the foundation for the whole of learning. A tradition of 'speculative' grammars developed in the 13th and 14th centuries, in which grammatical notions were reinterpreted within the framework of scholastic philosophy. The authors (the 'Modistae') looked to philosophy for the ultimate explanation of the rules of grammar. A famous quotation from the period states that it is not the grammarian but 'the philosopher [who] discovers grammar' (*philosophus grammaticam invenit*). The differences between languages were thought to be superficial, hiding the existence of a universal grammar (§14).

The Middle Ages also saw the development of western lexicography (§18) and progress in the field of translation, as Christian missionary activity increased. In the East, Byzantine writers continued to expound the ideas of the Greek authors. There was a strong tradition of Arabic language work related to the Qur'an (which was not to be translated, p. 388). From around the 8th century, several major grammars and dictionaries were produced, as well as descriptive works on Arabic pronunciation. For a long time, these remained unknown in Western Europe. Opportunities for contact with the Greek, Arabic, and Hebrew linguistic traditions only came later, as a result of the Crusades.

THE RENAISSANCE

The rediscovery of the Classical world that came with the 'revival of learning', as well as the discoveries of the New World, transformed the field of language study. Missionary work produced a large quantity of linguistic material, especially from the Far East. The Chinese linguistic traditions were discovered. Arabic and Hebrew studies progressed, the latter especially in relation to the Bible. In the 16th century, several grammars of exotic languages came to be written (e.g. Quechua in 1560). There was a more systematic study of European languages, especially of the Romance family. The first grammars of Italian and Spanish date from the 15th century. Major dictionary projects were launched in many languages. Academies came into being (p. 4). The availability of printing led to the rapid dissemination of ideas and materials.

As we approach modern times, fresh philosophical issues emerged. The 18th century is characterized by the arguments between 'rationalists' and 'empiricists' over the role of innate ideas in the development of thought and language. Such ideas provided the basis of certainty in knowledge, according to Cartesian philosophy, but their existence was denied by philosophers (such as Locke, Hume, and Berkeley) for whom knowledge derived from the way the mind operated upon external sense impressions. The issue was to resurface in the 20th century (p. 413).

Several other important trends have been noted during the 17th and 18th centuries: the breakdown of Latin as a universal medium of communication, and its replacement by modern languages (§59); the many proposals for universal languages, shorthand systems, and secret codes (§§33, 58); the beginnings of a systematic approach to phonetics (§27); the development of 'general' grammars, based on universal principles, such as the 17th-century grammar of Port Royal (§14); and the major elaborations of traditional grammar in schools (§1). Then, as the 19th century approached, the first statement about the historical relationship between Sanskrit, Greek, and Latin was made, ushering in the science of comparative philology (§50).

Part of the opening leaf of the First Grammatical Treatise. The drawing of Snorri Sturluson [above right] is by an Icelandic artist Kjurfan Guðjónsson (1921).

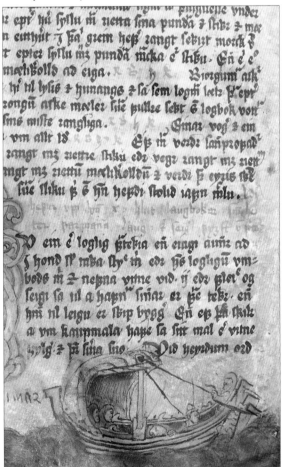

THE 'FIRST GRAMMARIAN'

The *Prose Edda* is a 13th-century textbook on poetic style and construction, written by the Icelandic chief, Snorri Sturluson. Appended to the manuscript are four treatises on grammar, written in the mid-12th century, the first of which has attracted special attention because of the originality of its thought. The authorship of this 'First Grammatical Treatise' is unknown, but the writer has come to be known as the 'first grammarian'.

This early exercise in spelling reform (p. 217) summarizes and illustrates the principles needed to improve the use of the Latin alphabet for writing Old Icelandic. It is the only work of this period to draw attention to the problems involved in applying Latin letters to a vernacular language. It contains several acute phonetic observations, and, in its emphasis on finding symbols to express sound contrasts, anticipates the basis of 20th-century phonological theory (§28).

A translation of part of the opening page (E. Haugen, 1972):

I have written an alphabet for us Icelanders also, in order that it might become easier to write and read... I have used all the Latin letters that seemed to fit our language well and could be rightly pronounced, as well as some other letters that seemed needful to me, while those were taken out that did not suit the sounds of our language. Some of the consonants of the Latin alphabet were rejected, and some new ones added. No vowels were rejected, but a good many were added, since our language has the greatest number of vowel sounds.

TWENTIETH-CENTURY LINGUISTICS

The growth of modern linguistics, from the end of the 18th century to the present day, has in large part already been summarized in earlier sections of this volume. The majority of the concepts used in the discussion of language history, acquisition, structure, substance, and use stem from this perspective (reflecting the background of the author). However, there remain several loose ends of a historical and theoretical nature that need to be drawn together in this final part of the book.

EUROPE AND AMERICA

Two main approaches to language study, one European, one American, unite to form the modern subject of linguistics. The first arises out of the aims and methods of 19th-century comparative philology (§50), with its focus on written records, and its interest in historical analysis and interpretation. The beginning of the 20th century saw a sharp change of emphasis, with the study of the principles governing the structure of living languages being introduced by the Genevan linguist, Ferdinand de Saussure (1857–1913). Saussure's early work was in philology, but he is mainly remembered for his theoretical ideas, as summarized in the *Cours de linguistique générale* ('Course in general linguistics'), which is widely held to be the foundation of the modern subject. This book was in fact published posthumously in 1916, and consists of a reconstruction by two of Saussure's students of his lecture notes and other materials.

The second approach arose from the interests and preoccupations of American anthropologists, who were concerned to establish good descriptions of the American Indian languages and cultures before they disappeared. Here, there were no written records to rely on, hence historical analysis was ruled out. Also, these languages presented very different kinds of structure from those encountered in the European tradition. The approach was therefore to provide a careful account of the speech patterns of the living languages. A pioneer in this field was Franz Boas (1858–1942), who published the first volume of the *Handbook of American Indian Languages* in 1911. Ten years later, another anthropologically oriented book appeared: *Language* by Edward Sapir (1884–1939). These works proved to be a formative influence on the early development of linguistics in America. The new direction is forcefully stated by Boas (p. 60): 'we must insist that a command of the language is an indispensable means of obtaining accurate and thorough knowledge, because much information can be gained by listening to conversations of the natives and by taking part in their daily life, which, to the observer who has no command of the language, will remain entirely inaccessible'.

SAUSSUREAN PRINCIPLES

Some of Saussure's most central ideas were expressed in the form of pairs of concepts:

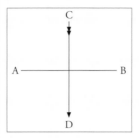

Diachrony vs synchrony
He sharply distinguished historical ('diachronic') and non-historical ('synchronic') approaches to language study. The former sees language as a continually changing medium; the latter sees it as a living whole, existing as a 'state' at a particular moment in time. In his diagram, AB represents a synchronic 'axis of simultaneities' – a language state at some point in time; CD is a diachronic 'axis of successions' – the historical path the language has travelled.

In this view, it is always necessary to carry out some degree of synchronic work before making a diachronic study: before we can say how a language has changed from state X to state Y, we need to know something about X and Y. Correspondingly, a synchronic analysis can be made without referring to history. Saussure illustrates this point using an analogy with a game of chess: if we walk into a room while a chess game is being played, it is possible to assess the state of the game by studying the position of the pieces on the board.

Langage vs langue vs parole
The many senses of the word 'language' prompted Saussure to introduce a threefold set of terms, the last two of which were central to his thinking. *Langage* is the faculty of speech present in all normal human beings due to heredity – our ability to talk to each other. This faculty is composed of two aspects: *langue* (the language system) and *parole* (the act of speaking). The former is the totality of a language, which we could in theory discover by examining the memories of all the language users: 'the sum of word-images stored in the minds of individuals'. *Parole* is the actual, concrete act of speaking on the part of a person – a dynamic, social activity in a particular time and place.

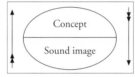

Signifiant vs signifié
Saussure recognized two sides to the study of meaning, but emphasized that the relationship between the two is arbitrary (p. 408). His labels for the two sides are *signifiant* ('the thing that signifies', or 'sound image') and *signifié* ('the thing signified', or 'concept'). This relationship of signified to signifier Saussure calls a linguistic *sign*. The sign is the basic unit of communication within a community: *langue* is seen as a 'system of signs'.

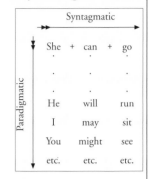

Syntagmatic and associative (or paradigmatic)
A sentence is a sequence of signs, each sign contributing something to the meaning of the whole. When the signs are seen as a linear sequence, the relationship between them is called *syntagmatic*, as in *She + can + go*. When a sign that is present is seen as contrasting with other signs in the language, the relationship is called *associative* (in later studies, *paradigmatic*), as in *She* vs *He*, *can* vs *will*, *go* vs *run* in the above sentence. These two dimensions of structure can be applied to phonology, vocabulary, or any other aspect of language. The result is a conception of language as a vast network of interrelated structures and mutually defining entities – a linguistic *system*.

Ferdinand de Saussure (1857–1913)

Edward Sapir (1884–1939)

LATER DEVELOPMENTS

Both European and American approaches developed rapidly. In Europe, Saussure's ideas were taken up by several groups of scholars (especially in Switzerland, Czechoslovakia, France, and Denmark), and schools of thought emerged based on Saussurean principles (notably, the Linguistic Circle of Prague, which was founded in 1926). The field of phonology (§28) was the first to develop, with later progress coming in such areas as grammar and style. Saussure's influence continues to be strong today, with his notion of a language 'system' becoming the foundation of much work in semiotics and structuralism (pp. 79, 403).

In America, the development of detailed procedures for the study of spoken language also led to progress in phonetics and phonology, and especial attention was paid to the distinctive morphology and syntax (§16) of the American Indian languages. The first major statement synthesizing the theory and practice of linguistic analysis was *Language* by Leonard Bloomfield (1887–1949), which appeared in 1933. This book dominated linguistic thinking for over 20 years, and stimulated many descriptive studies of grammar and phonology. In due course, the Bloomfieldian approach came to be called 'structuralist', because of the various kinds of technique it employed to identify and classify features of sentence structure (in particular, the analysis of sentences into their constituent parts, p. 96). It also represented a behaviourist view of linguistics, notably in its approach to the study of meaning (p. 101). However, its appeal diminished in the 1950s, when there was a sharp reaction against the limitations of structural linguistic methods, especially in the area of grammar (p. 96).

This extract from an obituary of Bloomfield, written by Bernard Bloch in the journal *Language* in 1949 (p. 93), summarizes this scholar's achievement:

There can be no doubt that Bloomfield's greatest contribution to the study of language was to make a science of it. Others before him had worked scientifically in linguistics; but no one had so uncompromisingly rejected all prescientific methods, or had been so consistently careful, in writing about language, to use terms that would imply no tacit reliance on factors beyond the range of observation ... It was Bloomfield who taught us the necessity of speaking about language in the style that every scientist uses when he speaks about the object of his research: impersonally, precisely, and in terms that assume no more than actual observation discloses to him.

Bloomfield's opposition to unscientific impressionism in language studies is neatly summarized by the wry comment he made on one occasion: 'If you want to compare two languages, it helps to know one of them!'

SCHOOLS OF THOUGHT

Many different approaches to linguistics emerged in the middle decades of this century, some of which have attracted a great deal of support. The distinguishing feature of five of these approaches is outlined below. (For corresponding developments within the field of generative linguistics, which has been dominant since the 1960s, see p. 413.)

Functional sentence perspective
An approach used by the Prague School of linguists to analyse utterances in terms of their information content, and still widely used in the Czech Republic and other countries of eastern Europe. The semantic contribution of each major element in a sentence is rated with respect to the 'dynamic' role it plays in communication.

Dependency grammar
A type of formal grammar developed in the 1950s, notably by the French linguist, Lucien Tesnière (1893–1954). It explains grammatical relationships by setting up 'dependencies' (or 'valencies') between the elements of a construction.

Tagmemics
A theory developed since the 1950s by the American linguist, K. L. Pike (1912–), which focuses particularly on the need to relate linguistic 'forms' and 'functions'. A central notion is the contrast between the 'emic' units, which are functionally contrastive in a language (such as phoneme and morpheme), and the 'etic' units that give them physical shape (cf. phonetics, §28).

Stratificational grammar
A theory devised by the American linguist S. M. Lamb (1929–) in the 1960s that views language as a system of related layers ('strata') of structure.

Systemic linguistics
A theory developed since the 1960s by the British linguist M. A. K. Halliday (1925–) in which grammar is seen as a network of 'systems' of interrelated contrasts; particular attention is paid to the semantic and pragmatic aspects of analysis (§§17, 21) and also to the way intonation is used in the expression of meaning (§29).

John Rupert Firth (1890–1960) (below, left) J. R. Firth, Professor of General Linguistics in the University of London from 1944 to 1956, was a key figure in the development of British linguistics. A central notion in his approach is that the patterns of language that appear at a particular level of description (§13) cannot be explained using a single analytic system. Different systems may need to be set up at different places, in order to handle the range of contrasts involved (an approach known as *polysystemicism*).

Leonard Bloomfield

Roman Jakobson (1896–1982) Jakobson was one of the founders of the Prague School of linguistics and a major contributor to many fields of study in Slavonic languages and general linguistics. In 1941 he moved to America, where he held professorial posts at Columbia and Harvard between 1946 and 1967.

Louis Hjelmslev (1899–1965) The leading theoretician of the Copenhagen School of linguistics, Hjelmslev propounded a formal approach to language study in the 1930s known as *glossematics*.

Daniel Jones (1881–1967) The leading British phonetician in the first half of this century, Jones was Professor of Phonetics at the University of London from 1921 to 1949.

CHOMSKY

In 1957, Avram Noam Chomsky, Professor of Linguistics at the Massachusetts Institute of Technology (1928–), published *Syntactic Structures*, which proved to be a turning point in 20th-century linguistics. In this and subsequent publications, he developed the conception of a *generative grammar* (p. 97), which departed radically from the structuralism and behaviourism of the previous decades. Earlier analyses of sentences were shown to be inadequate in various respects, mainly because they failed to take into account the difference between 'surface' and 'deep' levels of grammatical structure. At a surface level, such sentences as *John is eager to please* and *John is easy to please* can be analysed in an identical way; but from the point of view of their underlying meaning, the two sentences diverge: in the first, John wants to please someone else; in the second, someone else is involved in pleasing John. A major aim of generative grammar was to provide a means of analysing sentences that took account of this underlying level of structure.

To achieve this aim, Chomsky drew a fundamental distinction (similar to Saussure's *langue* and *parole*) between a person's knowledge of the rules of a language and the actual use of that language in real situations. The first he referred to as *competence*; the second as *performance*. Linguistics, he argued, should be concerned with the study of competence, and not restrict itself to performance – something that was characteristic of previous linguistic studies in their reliance on samples (or 'corpora') of speech (e.g. in the form of a collection of tape recordings). Such samples were inadequate because they could provide only a tiny fraction of the sentences it is possible to say in a language; they also contained many non-fluencies, changes of plan, and other errors of performance. Speakers use their competence to go far beyond the limitations of any corpus, by being able to create and recognize novel sentences, and to identify performance errors. The description of the rules governing the structure of this competence was thus the more important goal.

Chomsky's proposals were intended to discover the mental realities underlying the way people use language: competence is seen as an aspect of our general psychological capacity. Linguistics was thus envisaged as a mentalistic discipline – a view that contrasted with the behavioural bias of previous 20th-century work in the subject, and connected with the aims of several earlier linguists (such as the Port-Royal grammarians, p. 84). It was also argued that linguistics should not simply limit itself to the description of competence. In the long term, there was a still more powerful target: to provide a grammar capable of evaluating the adequacy of different accounts of competence, and of going beyond the study of individual languages to the nature of human language as a whole (by discovering 'linguistic universals', (§§14, 38). In this way, it was hoped, linguistics would be able to make a contribution to our understanding of the nature of the human mind.

The essence of the approach is summarized by Chomsky in a 1986 book (*Knowledge of Language*, p. xxvi) as providing an answer to the question 'How comes it that human beings, whose contacts with the world are brief and personal and limited, are nevertheless able to know as much as they do know?' By studying the human language faculty, it should be possible to show how a person constructs a knowledge system out of everyday experience, and thus move some way towards solving this problem.

A major feature of Chomsky's approach was the technical apparatus he devised to make the notion of competence explicit – the system of rules and symbols that provides a formal representation of the underlying syntactic, semantic, and phonological structure of sentences (aspects of this apparatus have been referred to in earlier sections, pp. 97, 107, 164). A primary notion – the transformational rule (p. 97) – led to the approach being commonly referred to as *transformational grammar* (or *TG*). Since the 1950s, much of linguistics has been taken up with proposals to develop the form of generative grammars, and the original theory has been reformulated several times. During the same period, also, there have been several proposals for alternative models of grammatical analysis to those expounded by Chomsky and his associates, some of which have attracted considerable support. As a consequence, linguistic theory, the core of scientific language study, is now a lively and controversial field.

Noam Chomsky

SOME THEORETICAL CONSEQUENCES OF GENERATIVE THEORY

Since the 1960s, several fresh theoretical approaches to grammatical analysis have emerged, most of which can be seen as a development of Chomsky's proposals – or as a reaction against them.

Case grammar
The American linguist, Charles Fillmore (1929–), devised a theory which focuses on the semantic roles (or 'cases') played by elements of sentence structure.

Relational grammar
This approach views grammatical relations (e.g. 'subject', 'object') as central, rather than the formal categories (e.g. 'noun phrase', 'verb phrase') of earlier generative theory (§16).

X-bar (X̄) theory
The theory provides an alternative account of phrase structure within a generative grammar. Further levels of phrase structure are recognized, and distinguished using different numbers of bar symbols.

Montague grammar
This approach derives from the work of the American logician Richard Montague (1930–70), and is based on the study of logical languages. A close correspondence is set up between the categories of syntax and semantics.

Generalized phrase structure grammar
This theory does not recognize the role of transformations in a generative grammar. Instead, it focuses on developing the phrase structure dimension to grammatical analysis (p. 96).

Functional grammar
Several approaches look for alternatives to an abstract, formal approach to grammar. This particular theory adopts a pragmatic view of language as social interaction (§21), and sets up 'functional' units of a pragmatic and syntactic kind within sentence structure.

Realistic grammar
Grammatical analyses should be 'psychologically real', according to this approach. Formal patterns should be related to the psychological factors that underlie linguistic behaviour, such as comprehension and memory.

Network grammar
This kind of grammar has developed out of research into artificial intelligence, aiming to simulate the way in which people understand the sentences of a language.

OBTAINING LINGUISTIC DATA

Many procedures are available for obtaining data about a language. They range from a carefully planned intensive field investigation in a foreign country to casual introspection about one's mother tongue carried out in an armchair at home.

Informants

In all cases, someone has to act as a source of language data – an *informant,* or *consultant.* Informants are (ideally) native speakers of a language who provide utterances for analysis and other kinds of information about the language (e.g. translations, comments about correctness, or judgments on usage). Often, when studying their mother tongue, linguists act as their own informants, judging the ambiguity, acceptability, or other properties of utterances against their own intuitions. The convenience of this approach makes it widely used, and it is considered a primary datum in the generative approach to linguistics (p. 413). But a linguist's personal judgments are often uncertain, or disagree with the judgments of other linguists, at which point recourse is needed to more objective methods of enquiry, using non-linguists as informants. The latter procedure is unavoidable when working on foreign languages, or in such mother-tongue fields as child speech (§38) or language variation (§§8–12).

Many factors must be considered when selecting informants – whether one is working with single speakers (a common situation when languages have not been described before), two people interacting, small groups, or large-scale samples. Age, sex, social background, and other aspects of identity are important, as these factors are known to influence the kind of language used (Part II). The topic of the conversation and the characteristics of the social setting (e.g. the level of formality) are also highly relevant, as are the personal qualities of the informants (e.g. their fluency and consistency). For larger studies, scrupulous attention has to be paid to the sampling theory employed. And in all cases decisions have to be made about the best investigative techniques to use.

Recording

Today, data from an informant are often tape recorded. This enables the linguist's claims about the language to be checked, and provides a way of making those claims more accurate ('difficult' pieces of speech can be listened to repeatedly). But obtaining naturalistic, good-quality data is never easy. People talk abnormally when they know they are being recorded, and sound quality can be poor. A variety of tape-recording procedures have thus been devised to minimize the effects of the 'observer's paradox' (how to observe the behaviour of people when they are not being observed). Some recordings are made without the speakers being aware

of the fact – a procedure that obtains very natural data, though ethical objections must be anticipated. Alternatively, attempts can be made to make the speaker forget about the recording, such as by keeping the tape recorder out of sight, or using radio microphones. A useful technique is to introduce a topic that quickly involves the speaker, and stimulates a natural language style (e.g. asking older informants to talk about how times have changed in their locality).

An audio tape recording does not solve all the linguist's problems, however. Speech is often unclear or ambiguous. Where possible, therefore, the recording has to be supplemented by the observer's notes about the non-verbal behaviour of the participants, and about the context in general. A facial expression, for example, can dramatically alter the meaning of what is said (p. 406). Video recordings avoid these problems to a large extent, but even they have limitations (the camera can be highly intrusive, and cannot be everywhere), and transcriptions always benefit from any additional commentary provided by an observer (p. 233).

Elicitation

Linguists also make great use of structured sessions, in which they systematically ask their informants for utterances that describe certain actions, objects, or behaviours. With a bilingual informant, or through the use of an interpreter, it is possible to use translation techniques ('How do you say *table* in your language?', 'What does *gua* mean?'). A large number of points can be covered in a short time, using interview worksheets and questionnaires. Often, the researcher wishes to obtain information about just a single variable, in which case a restricted set of questions may be used: a particular feature of pronunciation, for example, can be elicited by asking the informant to say a restricted set of words. There are also several indirect methods of elicitation, such as asking informants to fill the blanks in a substitution frame (e.g. *I – see a car*), or feeding them the wrong stimulus for correction ('Is it possible to say *I no can see?*').

Corpora

A representative sample of language, compiled for the purpose of linguistic analysis, is known as a *corpus.* A corpus enables the linguist to make objective statements about frequency of usage, and it provides accessible data for the use of different researchers. Its range and size are variable. Some corpora attempt to cover the language as a whole, taking extracts from many kinds of text; others are extremely selective, providing a collection of material that deals only with a particular linguistic feature. The size of a corpus depends on practical factors, such as the time available to collect, process, and store the data: it can take up to several hours to provide an accurate transcription of a few minutes of speech (p. 233). Sometimes a small sample of data will be enough to decide a linguistic hypothesis;

A CAUTIONARY TALE

The informant arrived and we started our work. 'How do you say *I run* in your language?' The Indian was quiet for a while. First he looked down; then he looked out. Suddenly his face lit up as if struck by a sudden flash of inspiration. He spoke very rapidly. If I had been able to transcribe what he said, it would have spread across the page several times. I gulped and bravely started to write; but after a few syllables, I was already hopelessly bogged down. 'How did you say that?' With his repetition I added two more syllables, then bogged down again. When I asked for the third repetition, the informant began to waver and finally to change his story, and so I had to give up entirely. To my self-justifying and half self-accusing 'But that surely doesn't all mean just *I run*', he said, 'Why of course not. It means I was sitting here with you; then I looked out of the door and saw a deer, so I quickly grabbed my spear and now I am running after it.' Then, almost philosophically, he added to himself, 'Only a fool would run for nothing.'
(J. A. Loewen, 1964, p. 189.)

A reverse lexicon
An extract from the Brown University Corpus listing words in reverse alphabetical order.

REDEMPTION
EXEMPTION
GUMPTION
RESUMPTION
PRESUMPTION
CONSUMPTION
ASSUMPTION
OPTION
ADOPTION
SORPTION
ABSORPTION
ERUPTION
INTERRUPTION
CORRUPTION
DISRUPTION
DESERTION
INSERTION
ASSERTION
EXERTION
ABORTION
PORTION
PROPORTION

COMPUTER CORPORA

A 'standard' corpus is a large collection of data available for use by many researchers. In English linguistics, there are now three standard computer corpora, all in machine-readable form, and thus, in principle, available anywhere in the world.

The London–Lund Corpus of Spoken English This corpus of educated spoken British English consists of the spoken material collected as part of the Survey of English Usage (see below right). The data consist of 87 texts of 5,000 words each. It was transferred to computer tape in the 1970s at the Survey of Spoken English, University of Lund, and is also partly available in printed form. In addition to the running text, a lexical concordance has been compiled.

The Brown University Corpus of American English This corpus is drawn from U.S. printed sources published in 1961. It comprises 500 samples of about 2,000 words each representing 15 main varieties of the language. It is available via computer tape, printout, and microfiche. Apart from the running text, there are lexical concordances, word frequency lists, and a reverse alphabetical list.

The Lancaster–Oslo/Bergen Corpus of British English This is the British equivalent of the Brown corpus. It was compiled by researchers in the Universities of Lancaster and Oslo, and prepared for computer analysis at the Norwegian Computing Centre for the Humanities in Bergen. Facilities are available similar to those provided by the Brown corpus.

ICAME There is now a clearing centre for storing and distributing information on corpus studies in English: the International Computer Archive of Modern English (ICAME), based at Bergen University. Its aims are to compile an archive of English-language material available for computer processing, and to collect and distribute information on research that uses this material.

by contrast, corpora in major research projects can total millions of running words. An important principle is that all corpora, whatever their size, are inevitably limited in their coverage, and always need to be supplemented by data derived from the intuitions of native speakers of the language, through either introspection or experimentation.

Experiments

Experimental techniques are widely used in linguistics, especially in those fields that have been influenced by the methods of sciences where experimentation is routine. Phonetics (§24) is the subject most involved in this approach, but experimental testing is also common in several other areas, such as child language acquisition (§38) and language pathology (§46). In grammar and semantics, experimental studies usually take the form of controlled methods for eliciting judgments about sentences or the elements they contain. Informants can be asked to identify errors, to rate the acceptability of sentences, to make judgments of perception or comprehension, and to carry out a variety of analytical procedures.

Reconstruction

The limiting case of linguistic study, one might imagine, is when no data are available at all – as in the case of the historical study of language where written records are lacking. But it is possible to break through even this apparent barrier, by using the 'reconstruction' techniques of comparative philology (§50). The forms of Proto-Indo-European and other reconstructed languages may be totally hypothetical in status, but they have nonetheless become a major field of linguistic enquiry.

THE SURVEY OF ENGLISH USAGE

This survey, begun in London in 1960 by the British linguist Randolph Quirk (1920–), aims to describe the grammatical repertoire of adult educated native speakers of British English. The corpus comprises 200 texts of spoken or written material, classified as follows (figures refer to the number of texts of each type):

Origin in writing (100)
Printed (46)
Learned arts (6)
Learned sciences (7)
Instructional (6)
Press: general news (4)
Press: specific reporting (4)
Administrative/official (4)
Legal and statutory (3)
Persuasive writing (5)
Prose fiction (7)

Non-printed (36)
Continuous writing: imaginative (5), informative (6)
Social letters: intimate (6), equal (3), distant (4)
Non-social letters: equal (4), distant (4)
Personal journals (4)

As spoken (18)
Drama (4)
Formal scripted oration (3)
Broadcast news (3)
Talks: informative (4), imaginative (2)
Stories (2)

Origin in speech (100)
Monologue (24)
Prepared (but unscripted) oration (6)
Spontaneous oration (10)
Spontaneous commentary: sport (4), non-sport (4)

Dialogue (76)
Surreptitious: intimate (24), distant (10)
Non-surreptitious: intimate (20), distant (6)
Telephone: intimate (10), distant (6)

TAGGING A TEXT

Many of the operations that a computer can perform on a corpus are linguistically trivial, though they save an enormous amount of time (e.g. listing of words in frequency of use or alphabetical order). More interesting is the possibility of automatically analysing the structure of the corpus, from a grammatical, semantic, or phonological point of view (§26). This is the aim of several current research programmes.

A first step is to provide an automatic means of 'tagging' each word in the corpus with a label that indicates its word class (§16). This enables the user to distinguish between such superficially identical items as *bear* (animal) and *bear* (action), or the many different syntactic functions of *that*. Larger constructions (such as different kinds of clause, p. 95) can also be tagged, to facilitate the retrieval of grammatical information.

Two tagged sentences from the London–Lund corpus are given (from J. Svartvik *et al.*, 1982, p. 57). Abbreviations are as follows (other symbols refer to suprasegmental features of pronunciation, §29):

CD	*that* used as subordinator
NP	proper noun
RA	personal pronoun, subject
RN	personal pronoun, object
VA + D	main verb, past tense
VA + G	main verb, *-ing* form
VA + N	main verb, past participle
VB + 5	*was* form of *to be*
*VH + O	contracted form of *have*, present tense
VA + O	main verb, base form

(See further, J. Svartvik & R. Quirk, 1980, from which the classification of Survey of English Usage texts (right) has been taken.)

0101000563 B	I⟨RA⟩ ‖ knew ⟨VA + D⟩ that ⟨CD⟩ he ⟨RA⟩ was ⟨VB + 5⟩ c*oming■ ⟨VA + G⟩
0101000564 B	I've ⟨RA★VH + O⟩ ‖ heard ⟨VA + N⟩ Stan ⟨NP⟩ !Carter ⟨NP⟩ m*ention ⟨VA + O⟩ him■ ⟨RB⟩

THE COMPUTER AGE

The use of the computer to foster corpus analysis (p. 415) is but one of many ways in which the study of language is changing in response to the availability of computational techniques. In addition to the 'routine' use of computers in such areas as numerical counting, statistical analysis, and pattern matching, linguistics provides a range of opportunities for the manipulation of non-numerical data, using natural language texts. Some of these tasks are fairly elementary, such as indexing and concordancing. Others are far more complex, such as the computational perspective required to facilitate speech recognition and synthesis (§26), machine translation (p. 352), and language learning (p. 381).

Since the 1980s, the chief focus of computational linguistic research has been in the area known as *natural language processing* (NLP). Here, the aim is to devise techniques which will automatically analyse large quantities of spoken (transcribed) or written text in ways broadly parallel to what happens when humans carry out this task. NLP deals with the computational processing of text - both its understanding and its generation - in natural human languages. It thus forms a major part of the domain of computational linguistics; but it is not to be identified with it, as computers can also be used for many other purposes in linguistics,

such as the processing of statistical data in authorship studies (p. 68).

The field of NLP emerged out of machine translation in the 1950s (p. 352), and was later much influenced by work on artificial intelligence. There was a focus on devising 'intelligent programs' (or 'expert systems') which aimed to simulate aspects of human behaviour, such as the way people can infer meaning from what has been said, or use their knowledge of the world to reach a conclusion (p. 353). A more specifically linguistic contribution has since been in evidence, involving detailed syntactic and semantic analyses, often on a much larger scale than hitherto, and using a variety of linguistic theories. Most recently, particular attention has been paid to the nature of discourse (in the sense of text beyond the sentence) and there has been a confrontation with the vast size of the lexicon, using the large amounts of lexical data now available in machine-readable form from commercial dictionary projects.

Progress has been considerable, but successful programs are still experimental in character, largely dealing with restricted tasks in well-defined settings. There is still a long way to go before computer systems can get anywhere near the flexible and creative world of real conversation, with its often figurative expression and ill-formed construction. As we approach 2001, the world of *2001* is still a long way off.

COMPUTER CONVERSATIONS

SHRDLU

SHRDLU (a name based on the second half of the 12 most frequent letters in the alphabet, according to Morse, p. 86) was written in 1972 by Terry Winograd. It shows some of the features of conversation which can be simulated on a computer. This system operated in a very small world – a box, a table, blocks, and pyramids – which could be manipulated according to the human speaker's (H) instructions. The computer (S) could answer questions about its actions and could assimilate new information, but it could not change the topic.

H: Pick up a red block.
s: OK.
H: Grasp the pyramid.
s: I don't understand which pyramid you mean.
H: Find a block which is taller than the one you are holding and put it in the box.
s: By 'it' I assume you mean the block which is taller than the one I am holding. OK.
H: What does the box contain?
s: The blue pyramid and the blue block.

The second exchange identifies a problem, as there were three pyramids in the scene, and it was not obvious which one H meant. The third exchange shows that SHRDLU detected a possible ambiguity in the word *it*.

(After M. McTear, 1987.)

ELIZA

By contrast, Eliza, devised by J Weizenbaum in 1966, and named afer the heroine of *Pygmalion*, was programmed to converse about any subject – albeit by pragmatically cheating. The extract is from a mock psychotherapeutic interview, in which the computer has the part of the doctor. The system asks apparently relevant questions, but this is a false impression. The program has merely analyzed H's input sentence, and used this to randomly trigger a prompt from a small range of potentially relevant responses, often using various lexical relations – *computer* relates to *machine*, for example. 'Empty' utterances provoke equally 'empty' responses.

The performance is nonetheless convincing, as a simulation – and people have sometimes reacted to it in unexpected ways. The author reports that his secretary once asked him to leave the room so that she could talk with ELIZA in private! And Robin Dempsey, in David Lodge's *Small World*, uses it as a confidante.

E: Good day. What is your problem?
H: I am having trouble with the computer.
E: Do machines worry you?
H: This one does...
E: Earlier you said you were having trouble with the computer.
H: That's right, and it hasn't got any better.
E: What does that suggest to you?
H: That computers are no use.
E: How would you react if machines took over?
H: I think it would be a disaster.
E: Does anyone else think it would be a disaster?
H: Yes. Quite a lot of people.
E: Quite a lot of people.
H: That's right.
E: Are you prepared to elaborate?
H: No. I have to go.
E: What do you really think about me?
H: Not much.
E: Why not much?
H: Because you are just a silly computer program.
E: Perhaps the real reason is hard to talk about.
H: Well, you have a point.

"HELLO," Robin typed on the keyboard.

"HELLO, HOW ARE YOU FEELING?" replied ELIZA, the printed words appearing instantly on the VDU.

"I'M FEELING TERRIBLE," Robin replied.

"WHAT DO YOU MEAN BY THAT PRECISELY?"

"I'M FEELING DEPRESSED."

"WHY DO YOU THINK YOU ARE DEPRESSED?"

"BECAUSE I'M LONELY."

"DO YOU LIVE WITH YOUR FAMILY?"

"NO."

"DO YOU HAVE ANY FRIENDS?"

"NOT REALLY."

"WHY IS THAT?"

Robin Dempsey paused for some considerable time before he typed in his reply: "I DON'T KNOW."

"DO YOU REALLY NOT KNOW OR ARE YOU JUST AVOIDING THE QUESTION?"

Robin Dempsey flushed and typed rapidly: "I USED TO HAVE FRIENDS ONCE."

"WHEN WAS THAT?"

"BEFORE I WAS MARRIED."

"YOU DIDN'T TELL ME YOU WERE MARRIED."

"I'M DIVORCED."

"TELL ME ABOUT YOUR DIVORCE."

Robin Dempsey typed rapidly for fifteen minutes without stopping ...

(David Lodge, *Small World*, 1984, III.1.)

BOOKING A FLIGHT

GUS (the Genial Understander System) is a system devised by D. G. Bobrow and others in 1977 which uses frames to structure the discourse. A frame is a knowledge structure which represents a situation which is predictable, or stereotyped. It consists of a series of slots, which in turn consist of a very restricted set of possible responses. This type of approach can be used when a dialogue is fairly predictable, and there are few options to take – such as booking a flight through a travel agent, where there are only so many slots (point of departure, date of departure, method of travel, etc.) and types of filler (1 to 31 for date, 1 to 12 months, etc.).

G: Hello. My name is Gus. I can help you plan a simple trip by air. Where do you want to go?
H: I want to go to San Diego on May 28.
G: What time do you want to leave?
H: I must be in San Diego before 10 am.
G: Would you like PSA flight 102 that arrives at 9.15?
H: What is the next flight?
G: Air California flight 310 that leaves at 8.30 am and arrives at 10.00 am.
H: I'll take the first one. ...

G: What date do you want to return on?
H: On Friday in the evening…

GUS is continually making assumptions about what the enquirer means, based on the knowledge about the world which has been built into the system. The first exchange is interpreted as a request for a reservation, even though no such request is made directly ('Will you make me a reservation for San Diego on May 28?'). It also assumes the request is for a flight, not a journey by rail, road, or sea. Then in the second exchange, it infers from the response a likely departure time. H has not answered G's question about the time of leaving in a

straightforward way ('I want to leave at 8 o'clock'). Another possible ambiguity which Gus resolves is the interpretation of the 'on Friday', which must mean the Friday after the departure, and not, for example, the Friday after this conversation (as in 'I want to go to San Diego on Friday'). Features such as these, which we take for granted in everyday conversation, have to be thought out and carefully programmed, if a human–machine interaction is to be successful.

(After D. G. Bobrow, *et al*, 1977.)

PRIMITIVE DISCOURSE

Anyone who uses a card to obtain money from a bank teller machine is engaging in a primitive kind of human–computer interaction. The bank computer does most of the 'talking'; the recipient has only to punch in some basic numerical information and respond to the prompts. Usually only the most elementary information exchange is present. Politeness is minimal - perhaps a brief word of welcome or the use of *please*. Only the more advanced machines dare to say such things as *Good morning*, preferring to avoid the complications of working out what time of the day it actually is.

HELLO, DAVE …

[Bowman's] movement in the field of view must have triggered something in the unfathomable mind that was now ruling over the ship; for suddenly, Hal spoke.
'… Too bad about Frank, isn't it?'
'Yes,' Bowman answered, after a long pause. 'It is.'
'I suppose you're pretty broken up about it?'
'What do you expect?'
HAL processed this answer for ages of computer-time; it was a full five seconds before he continued: 'He was an excellent crew member.'

Many people have an image of human-machine linguistic interaction which has been permanently coloured by an encounter with a talking science-fiction computer - such as Deep Thought in Douglas Adams' *The Hitch-hiker's Guide to the Galaxy*, or HAL (the Heuristically controlled ALgorithmic computer) in Arthur C Clarke's *2001*. HAL not only carried out the control tasks on the space mission, he could also talk, think, empathize – and plot. The above extract from his conversation with flight commander Dave Bowman is indistinguishable from any human–human interaction. Even the processing delay is appropriate, as a response to such a curt rhetorical question. By comparison, the conversational powers of 20th-century computer systems are still in the electronic stone age.

THE DOMAIN OF LINGUISTICS

The development of linguistics, the science of language, has been particularly marked in recent decades. There has been an increased popular interest in the role of language in relation to human beliefs and behaviour (§§1, 63), and an accompanying awareness of the need for a separate academic discipline to deal adequately with the range and complexity of linguistic phenomena. The university teaching of linguistics emerged during the 1960s, and since then, several branches of linguistic enquiry have been established.

The subject has now developed a clear identity – notwithstanding occasional uncertainty over its name and coverage. *Linguistics* is the usual designation, with *linguistic science* often used as a paraphrase. The field of *phonetics* (§27) is sometimes considered to be a separate discipline, because of its emphasis on the 'pre-linguistic' aspects of speech analysis; but it is more commonly included within the coverage of linguistics, as many see it as an indispensable foundation for language research. Also, the label for the person who practises general linguistics has caused some concern: 'linguistician' is sometimes used, but it is not popular among students of the subject, who normally refer to themselves as 'linguists'. There is thus occasional ambiguity with the general use of the term 'linguist' meaning 'fluent in many languages'.

Different dimensions of the subject can be distinguished, depending on the focus and interests of the linguist. *Diachronic* (or *historical*) and *synchronic linguistics* have developed as a result of the distinction introduced by Saussure (p. 411): the former is the study of language change (§54); the latter the study of language states, regardless of their history. When linguists try to establish general principles for the study of all languages, they are said to be practising *theoretical* (or *general*) *linguistics*. When they concentrate on establishing the facts of a particular language system, they practise *descriptive linguistics*. And when the focus is on the similarities and differences between languages, the subject is often referred to as *comparative* (or *typological*) *linguistics* (§§14, 50).

Linguistics shares with other sciences a concern to be objective, systematic, consistent, and explicit in its account of language. Like other sciences, it aims to collect data, test hypotheses, devise models, and construct theories. Its subject matter, however, is unique: at one extreme, it overlaps with such 'hard' sciences as physics and anatomy; at the other, it involves such traditional 'arts' subjects as philosophy and literary criticism. The field of linguistics includes both science and the humanities, and offers a breadth of coverage that, for many aspiring students of the subject, is the primary source of its appeal.

INTERDISCIPLINARY FIELDS

Anthropological linguistics
The study of language variation and use in relation to the cultural patterns and beliefs of the human race, as investigated using the theories and methods of anthropology (§§2–5).

Applied linguistics
The application of linguistic theories, methods, and findings to the elucidation of language problems that have arisen in other domains. The term is especially used with reference to the field of foreign language learning and teaching (§62), but it applies equally to several other fields, such as stylistics (§12), lexicography (§18), translation (§57), and language planning (§61), as well as to the clinical and educational fields below.

Biological linguistics
The study of the biological conditions for language development and use in human beings, with reference both to the history of language in the human race and to child development (§§45, 49).

Clinical linguistics
The application of linguistic theories and methods to the analysis of disorders of spoken, written, or signed language (§46).

Computational linguistics
The study of language using the techniques and concepts of computer science, especially with reference to the problems posed by the fields of machine translation (p. 352), information retrieval, and artificial intelligence (§26).

Educational linguistics
The application of linguistic theories and methods to the study of the teaching and learning of a language (especially a first language) in schools and other educational settings (§§44, 62).

Ethnolinguistics
The study of language in relation to ethnic types and behaviour, especially with reference to the way social interaction proceeds (§9).

Geographical linguistics
The study of the regional distribution of languages and dialects, seen in relation to geographical factors in the environment (§8).

Mathematical linguistics
The study of the mathematical properties of language, using concepts from such fields as algebra, computer science, and statistics (§15).

Neurolinguistics
The study of the neurological basis of language development and use in human beings, especially of the brain's control over the processes of speech and understanding (§45).

Philosophical linguistics
The study of the role of language in the elucidation of philosophical concepts, and of the philosophical status of linguistic theories, methods, and observations (§§5, 17).

Psycholinguistics
The study of the relationship between linguistic behaviour and the psychological processes (e.g. memory, attention) thought to underlie it (§§7, 38).

Sociolinguistics
The study of the interaction between language and the structure and functioning of society (§§10–12, 60–3).

Statistical linguistics
The study of the statistical or quantitative properties of language (§15).

Theolinguistics
The study of language used by biblical scholars, theologians, and others involved in the theory and practice of religious belief (§63).

ENVOI

Linguistics has provided the conceptual framework within which this encyclopedia has been written. Little reference has therefore been made to the other academic traditions of language study mentioned on this page. It has occasionally been possible to acknowledge them; but there has been no attempt to give a systematic account, as they operate within a quite different intellectual perspective, and use radically different procedures of study.

An integrated account of the history of ideas in language scholarship is beyond the scope of the present volume. In philosophy alone, for example, there is a major academic tradition, focusing on the study of ordinary language, which to treat responsibly would include the consideration of a large number of authors, including Ludwig Wittgenstein, A. J. Ayer, and Gilbert Ryle – a major enterprise in its own right. Similarly, many eminent psychologists, such as A. R. Luria, L. S. Vygotsky, and Jean Piaget, have written at length on language, and there is a long tradition of experimental psychological enquiry into linguistic behaviour, which would have to be carefully considered. Issues of similar standing would have to be faced in the language historiography of other fields, such as anthropology, sociology, and mathematics.

The absence of systematic reference to these other major traditions is thus the main limitation of the present volume. At the same time, by restricting the book to a single perspective, it has been possible to give more numerous, detailed, and systematic illustrations of the use and structure of language than would otherwise have been the case. It has enabled the emphasis to be more on the diverse patterns of language structure and the variety of language functions, and less on the many approaches and methods that have been devised to analyse these matters, and the various controversies which accompany them. A comprehensive history of linguistic thought, paying proper attention to the contribution of all these academic issues and traditions is long overdue. But that will have to be left for some other encyclopedia...

I GLOSSARY

This glossary contains a brief definition of all the specialized language terms used in the text of this encyclopedia, along with some of the associated linguistic terminology likely to be encountered by the general reader. The glossary excludes four types of term:
(i) words in everyday use that do not raise any particular problem of meaning (such as the names of punctuation marks); (ii) names of different theories and approaches (as in linguistics and language teaching); (iii) the very detailed terminology of grammatical description and particular schools of thought; and (iv) background terms from related disciplines, such as anatomy, acoustics, or medicine. Names of languages, language families, dialects, and scripts are given in Appendix VI. A selection of more specialized dictionaries of linguistic terms is given at the end of Appendix IV.

Glossary conventions

- The alphabetical arrangement of the glossary is letter by letter.
- Each head-word is followed in parentheses by an abbreviated indication of the main sub-field to which it belongs (e.g. *sem* = *semantics*). The abbreviations used are given to the right.
- Within entries, words or phrases that are themselves defined elsewhere in the glossary are preceded by †. Superscript numerals are used when it is important to distinguish a particular sense within cross-references (e.g. grammar[1]).
- Synonymous terms are given in bold type, preceded by the word 'also'.

- Most entries lack exemplification, as this can be found within the body of the encyclopedia; in a few cases, where the main text does not provide sufficient illustration, examples are given in parentheses, without the use of 'e.g.'.
- At the end of each entry, there is a page reference to a section of the encyclopedia where related subject matter may be found.

Abbreviations used

acou	acoustics	Lat.	Latin
anat	anatomy	*ling*	general linguistics
app	applied linguistics	*neuro*	neurolinguistics
clin	clinical	*phonet*	phonetics
E.	English	*phonol*	phonology
esp.	especially	*phys*	physiology
Fr.	French	*poet*	poetics
gen	general application	*prag*	pragmatics
Ger.	German	*psycho*	psycholinguistics
gram	grammar	*rhet*	rhetoric
graph	graphetics/graphology	*sem*	semantics
hist.	historical linguistics	*semiot*	semiotics
It.	Italian	*socio*	sociolinguistics
J.	Japanese	*styl*	stylistics

abessive (*gram*) An †inflection[1] that typically expresses the meaning of 'without'. 92

ablative (*gram*) An †inflection[1] that typically expresses such meanings as 'by/with/from'. 92

ablaut (*hist*) A †vowel change that gives a word a new grammatical function (*drink → drank*); also, **gradation**. 299

abstract *see* **concrete**

accent 1 (*phonet*) Features of pronunciation that signal regional or social identity; cf. †dialect. 24 2 (*phonol*) A type of emphasis given to a spoken word or syllable. 166 3 (*graph*) A mark above a letter, showing its pronunciation. 196

acceptable (*ling*) Said of any usage that †native speakers feel is possible in a language. 414

accidence (*gram*) Changes in the †form[2] of words signalling different grammatical functions (*walking/walked...*); cf. †morphology. 90

accommodation (*socio*) Adjustments that people make to their speech, influenced by the speech of those they are talking to. 51

accusative (*gram*) An †inflection[1] that typically identifies the †object of a †verb; also, **objective**. 92

acoustic phonetics (*phonet*) The branch of †phonetics that studies the physical properties of speech sounds. 132

acquired (*clin*) Said of any linguistic disorder that results from injury or disease; cf. †developmental. 273

acquisition *see* **language acquisition**

acrolect (*socio*) In †creole studies, the most prestigious †variety of a language, seen in contrast with other varieties. 24

acronym (*gen*) A word made up out of the initial letters of a phrase (*laser*). 90

acrostic (*gen*) A poem or other text in which certain letters in each line make a word. 64

active 1 (*gen*) Said of language that a person actually uses – as opposed to language that is known but not used (**passive** knowledge). 378 2 (*phonet*) Said of an †articulator that moves (towards an immobile, **passive**, articulator). 130

active voice *see* **voice**

acuity (*phonet*) The ability to detect and discriminate sound. 145

adessive (*gram*) An †inflection[1] that typically expresses the meaning of 'on' a place. 92

adjacency pair (*socio*) A single sequence of stimulus-utterance †response-utterance by two different speakers, e.g. question + answer. 118

adjective (*gram*) A type of word identifying an attribute of a †noun (*a **red** chair*), in many languages showing †degree contrasts. 91

adjunct (*gram*) A less important or omissible element in a grammatical construction (*She ran **quickly***). 95

adnominal (*gram*) Any element in a †noun phrase that is a †modification[1] of the noun. 95

adverb (*gram*) A word whose main function is to specify the kind of action expressed by a †verb (*He spoke **angrily***); other functions include acting as †intensifier (**very** *big*) and as a †sentence connector (***Moreover**, they laughed*). 91

adverbial (*gram*) Said of †words, †phrases, or †clauses that function as †adverbs. 95

aerometry (*phonet*) The measurement of air flow during speech. 139

affective (*sem*) Said of the emotional or attitudinal meaning of an utterance. 103

affirmative (*gram*) A †sentence or †verb that has no marker of †negation (*He's running*). 95

affix (*gram*) A meaningful form that is attached to another form, to make a more complex †word (***un-** + *kind* + ***-ness***); cf. †infix, †prefix, †suffix. 90

affixing language (*ling*) A language that uses †affixes as its main way of expressing grammatical relationships. 295

affricate (*phonet*) Said of a †consonant in which a complete †closure of the †vocal tract is gradually released (ʧ, Ger. *pfennig*). 159

agent(ive) (*sem*) A linguistic form expressing who or what is responsible for an action (*The **man** laughed*, *farmer* 'one who farms'). 93

agglutinative/agglutinating language (*ling*) A type of language in which †words consist of lengthy strings of forms. 295

agnosia (*clin*) Loss of ability to interpret sensory information: **auditory agnosia**, affecting speech sounds. 273

agrammatism (*clin*) A language disorder that produces speech of a typically †telegrammatic quality (*man see ball*). 273

agraphia *see* **dysgraphia**

agreement *see* **concord**

air-stream mechanism (*phonet*) An arrangement of parts of the †vocal tract that acts as a source of energy for speech sound production. 124

alaryngeal (*clin*) Said of speech without the †larynx. 278

alexia *see* **dyslexia**

alienable (*gram*) Applied to relationships where a possessed item is seen as having a temporary or non-essential dependence on a possessor (*the* *man's car*); cf. **inalienable**, where the dependence is permanent or necessary (*the man's brain*). 93

allative (*gram*) An ⁺inflection[1] that typically expresses the meaning of 'to' a place. 92

alliteration (*poet*) A sequence of words beginning with the same sound, especially as used in poetry. 74

allo- (*ling*) A variation in the ⁺form[2] of a linguistic unit that does not alter its basic identity, e.g. **allophones** (variants of a ⁺phoneme), **allomorphs** (variants of a ⁺morpheme), **allographs** (variants of a ⁺grapheme). 90, 162, 196

allograph *see* **allo-**

allomorph *see* **allo-**

allonym (*gen*) A name an author assumes that belongs to someone else; cf. ⁺pseudonym. 112

allophone *see* **allo-**

alphabet (*gen*) A writing system in which a set of symbols ('letters') represents the ⁺phonemes of a language; cf. ⁺dual alphabet. 204

alphabetism (*gram*) A word made of initial letters, each being pronounced (*VIP*). 90

alternation (*ling*) The relationship between the different ⁺forms[2] of a linguistic unit, usually symbolized by ~ (*cat ~ cats*). 90

alveolar (*phonet*) Said of a ⁺consonant in which the tongue makes contact with the bony prominence behind the upper teeth (ŧ, ɳ). 157

ambilingual (*gen*) Someone who can speak two languages with equal facility; also, **balanced bilingual**. 364

amelioration (*hist*) A change of meaning in which a word loses an originally unpleasant reference; cf. ⁺deterioration. 332

amplitude (*acou*) The intensity of a sound. 134

anacoluthon (*gram, rhet*) An unexpected break in a ⁺sentence (*John might – Are you listening?*). 52

anacusis (*clin*) Total deafness. 268

anagram (*gen*) A word or phrase formed by changing the order of letters in another word or phrase. 65

analects (*gen*) A selection of passages taken from an author. 66

analogy (*ling*) A change that affects a language when ⁺regular forms begin to influence less regular forms. 236, 332

analytic **1** (*gram*) *see* **isolating** **2** (*sem*) Said of sentences expressing a ⁺tautology (*Bachelors are unmarried*); contrasts with **synthetic**. 107

ananym (*gen*) A name that has been written backwards. 112

anap(a)est (*poet*) A unit of ⁺metre consisting of two light beats followed by a heavy beat. 74

anaphora (*gram*) A feature of grammatical structure referring back to something already expressed; the ⁺pronoun in *When Mary saw John, she waved* is 'anaphoric'; cf. ⁺cataphora, ⁺exophoric. 119

anarthria *see* **dysarthria**

animate (*gram*) Said of words (esp. ⁺nouns) that refer to living things, and not to objects or concepts (**inanimates**). 91

anomia (*clin*) A ⁺language[4] disorder in which the primary symptom is difficulty in remembering the names of things. 273

antecedent (*gram*) A part of a ⁺sentence to which some other part grammatically refers (*This is the cat that chased the rat*). 119

anthropological linguistics (*ling*) The study of (esp. non-western) languages in relation to social or cultural patterns and beliefs. 418

anthroponomastics (*sem*) The study of personal names. 112

anthropophonics (*phonet*) The study of the human potential for vocal sound. 18

anticipatory *see* **regressive**

antonym (*sem*) A word that is opposite in meaning to another word (*good/bad, single/married*). 105

aorist (*gram*) A form of the ⁺verb in some ⁺inflecting languages, esp. referring to an action without any particular completion, duration, or repetition. 93

aperiodic *see* **periodic**

apex (*phonet*) The tip of the tongue. 131

aphasia (*clin*) A ⁺language[4] disorder resulting from brain damage, which affects a person's ability to produce or understand ⁺grammatical and ⁺semantic structure; also, **dysphasia**. 272

aphasiology (*clin*) The study of ⁺aphasia. 272

aphesis (*hist*) The loss of an ⁺unstressed ⁺vowel from the beginning of a word ('*mongst*). 330

aphonia *see* **dysphonia**

aphorism (*gen*) A succinct statement expressing a general truth (*More haste, less speed*). 53

apico- (*phonet*) Said of a sound using the tip (or ⁺apex) of the tongue, e.g. 'apico-dental'. 157

apocope (*hist*) The omission of a final ⁺syllable, sound, or letter in a word. 330

apostrophe (*rhet*) A ⁺figurative expression in which an idea, inanimate object, or absent person is addressed as if present. 70

appellative (*sem*) A personal name used as an everyday word (*a sandwich*). 112

applied linguistics (*ling*) The application of the theories, methods, or findings of ⁺linguistics to the solution of practical problems. 418

apposition (*gram*) A series of ⁺nouns or ⁺noun phrases with the same meaning and grammatical status (*Mr Jones, the baker*). 95

appropriate (*ling*) Said of any use of language considered to be compatible with a given social situation; cf. ⁺correctness. 2

approximant (*phonet*) A ⁺consonant in which the organs of ⁺articulation approach each other, but without ⁺closure or audible friction ({ɭ, {j}); also, **frictionless continuant**. 159

approximative system *see* **interlanguage**

apraxia (*clin*) Loss of ability to carry out voluntary muscular movements for the production of speech; also, **dyspraxia**. 273

aprosody *see* **dysprosody**

aptitude (*app*) A person's natural ability to learn a language; evaluated using an **aptitude test**; also, **prognostic test**. 375

aptronym (*gen*) A name that fits a person's nature or occupation (*Mr Clever, Mr Smith*). 112

arbitrariness (*ling*) The absence of any physical correspondence between linguistic signals and the entities to which they refer; cf. ⁺iconic. 401

archaism (*gen*) An old word or phrase no longer in general spoken or written use. 332

area (*ling*) A geographical region identified on the basis of its linguistic characteristics. 33

areal linguistics (*ling*) The study of geographical regions which are characterized by shared linguistic properties; cf. **geographical linguistics**. 33

argot (*gen*) Special vocabulary used by a secretive social group, e.g. gypsies. 58

article (*gram*) A word that specifies whether a ⁺noun is ⁺definite or indefinite (*the/a*). 91

articulation (*phonet*) The physiological movements involved in modifying a flow of air to produce speech sounds. 130

articulator (*phonet*) A ⁺vocal organ involved in the production of a speech sound. 130

articulatory phonetics (*phonet*) The branch of ⁺phonetics that studies the way speech sounds are produced by the ⁺vocal organs. 124

artificial language (*gen*) **1** An invented language used to facilitate international communication; also, **auxiliary language**. 354 **2** An invented language used in computer programming, e.g. BASIC. 353

artificial larynx (*clin*) A portable device that provides a source of vibration for speech, for people who have no ⁺larynx. 278

artificial speech (*phonet*) The output of a ⁺speech synthesizer. 149

ascender (*graph*) A part of a letter that extends above the height of the letter *x*. 192

aspect (*gram*) The duration or type of temporal activity denoted by a ⁺verb, e.g. completion or non-completion of an action; cf. ⁺perfective. 93

aspiration (*phonet*) Audible breath that may accompany the ⁺articulation of a sound (E. *pen* ɓʰen). 163

assimilation (*phonol*) The influence exercised by one sound upon the ⁺articulation of another, so that the sounds become more alike. 166

associative meaning (*sem*) The sense associations that are not part of a word's basic meaning (*birthday* → presents, party, etc.). 103

assonance (*poet*) The repeated use of ⁺vowels to achieve a special effect. 74

asterisked form **1** (*ling*) A usage that is not ⁺acceptable or not ⁺grammatical[2] (**do have gone*). 88 **2** (*hist*) A form in linguistic history for which there is no written evidence (Indo-European **penkʷe* 'five'). 294

asyndeton (*rhet*) The omission of ⁺conjunctions to achieve an economical form of expression (*They ran with haste, with fear*). 91

atelic *see* **telic**

attested (*ling*) Said of linguistic forms where there is evidence of present or past usage. 294

attribute **1** (*phonet*) An identifiable feature of sound sensation, e.g. ⁺pitch, ⁺loudness. 144 **2** (*sem*) A defining property of the meaning of a word (*round* is an attribute of *ball*). 107

attributive (*gram*)   Said of ⁺adjectives or other forms that are ⁺modifiers of a ⁺noun within the ⁺noun phrase (*the big table*); contrasts with predicative uses (*The table is big*). 95

audiogram (*clin*)   A graph used to record a person's ability to hear ⁺pure tones. 268

audiolingual (*app*)   Said of a language-teaching method based on the use of drills and dialogues for speaking and listening; also, **aural–oral**. 378

audiology (*clin*)   The study of hearing and hearing disorders, esp. their diagnosis, assessment, and treatment. 268

audiometer (*clin*)   An electronic instrument that measures the sensitivity of hearing. 268

auditory agnosia   *see* **agnosia**

auditory discrimination (*phonet*)   The process of distinguishing between (esp. speech) sounds. 145

auditory phonetics (*phonet*)   A branch of ⁺phonetics that studies the way people perceive sound. 142

aural-oral   *see* **audiolingual**

automatic translation   *see* **machine translation**

autonomous speech   *see* **idioglossia**

autosegmental (*phonol*)   An approach to ⁺phonology that includes the study of features of sound that extend beyond individual ⁺segments. 163

auxiliary language   **1** (*socio*)   A language adopted by different speech communities for purposes of communication. 354   **2** (*gen*)   *see* **artificial language**

auxiliary verb (*gram*)   A ⁺verb used along with a ⁺lexical verb to make grammatical distinctions (*She is going/might go*). 91

baby talk (*gen*)   **1** A simplified speech style used by adults to children. 237   **2** An immature form of speech used by children. 246

back (*phonet*)   Said of sounds made in the back part of the mouth (⟨ɑ⟩) or with the back part of the tongue (⟨k⟩, ⟨ɡ⟩). 131

back-formation (*hist*)   A process of ⁺word formation where a new word is formed by removing an imagined ⁺affix from another word (*editor → edit*). 332

back slang (*gen*)   A secret language in which words are said backwards. 59

balanced bilingual   *see* **ambilingual**

basal readers (*app*)   The first textbooks used in a graded reading programme. 253

base (*ling*)   A component of a ⁺transformational grammar, in which the basic sentence patterns of a language are ⁺generated. 97

basilect (*socio*)   In ⁺creole studies, a language ⁺variety furthest away from the one that carries most prestige (the ⁺acrolect). 24

behaviourism (*gen*)   The study of observable and measurable behaviour (here, of the linguistic stimuli and responses made by participants in speech situations). 412

bel (*acou*)   Unit for the measurement of acoustic intensity; cf. ⁺decibel. 134

bidialectal (*socio*)   Applied to someone who is proficient in the use of two ⁺dialects. 24

bidialectism (*socio*)   An educational policy that recommends the teaching of a non-standard ⁺dialect along with a ⁺standard one. 26

bilabial (*phonet*)   Said of a ⁺consonant made with both lips (⟨p⟩, ⟨m⟩). 157

bilingual (*gen*)   Said of an individual or a community that regularly uses two languages; cf. ⁺ambilingual. 362

binary (*ling*)   Said of any linguistic analysis that sets up an opposition between two alternatives. 79

binary feature (*phonol*)   Any ⁺phonetic variable that enables sounds to be classified into two mutually-exclusive possibilities, e.g. ⁺voice¹ ('voiced' vs 'voiceless'). 164

binaural (*phonet*)   Using both ears. 142

biolinguistics (*ling*)   The study of the biological preconditions for language development and use in human beings, both as individuals and as a race; also, **biological linguistics**. 418

bisyllable (*phonet*)   A word with two ⁺syllables. 166

blade (*phonet*)   The part of the tongue between the ⁺apex and the ⁺centre; also, **lamina**. 131

blend (*gram*)   The result of two elements fusing to form a new word or construction (*breakfast + lunch = brunch*); cf. ⁺coinage. 90

block (*clin*)   In ⁺stuttering, an obstruction experienced by the speaker that prevents the production of speech. 280

body language (*semiot*)   Communication using body movement and appearance, as opposed to speaking, writing, or ⁺sign³. 403

body size (*graph*)   The size of a piece of type. 192

borrow (*hist*)   To introduce a word (or some other linguistic feature) from one language or ⁺dialect into another; vocabulary borrowings are usually known as **loan words**. 332

bound form (*gram*)   A ⁺morpheme that cannot occur on its own as a ⁺word (E. *de-*, *-tion*). 90

boustrophedon (*graph*)   Writing in which lines run in alternate directions. 187

brachygraphy (*graph*)   Shorthand writing. 208

bracketing (*ling*)   A way of showing the internal structure of a string of elements ((*The girl*) (*ate*) (*a cake*)). 97

breaking   *see* **voice mutation**

breath group (*phonet*)   A stretch of utterance produced within a single breath expiration. 124

breathy (*phonet*)   A ⁺voice quality that involves the use of audible breath. 128

broad (*phonet*)   Said of a ⁺transcription of speech that shows only the major ⁺phonetic contrasts; cf. ⁺narrow, ⁺phonemic transcription. 160

Broca's area (*neuro*)   An area of the brain that controls the expression of spoken language; cf. ⁺Wernicke's area. 262

buccal (*phonet*)   Applied to sounds made in or near the ⁺cavity of the cheek. 127

cacography (*gen*)   Bad handwriting or spelling. 276

cacology (*gen*)   Unacceptable pronunciation or use of language. 2

cacophony (*gen*)   Unpleasant, harsh sounds, esp. of speech. 2

caesura (*poet*)   A break in the ⁺rhythm of a line of poetry. 74

calligraphy (*gen*)   The art of beautiful handwriting. 190

calque (*hist*)   A ⁺borrowed item in which the parts are translated separately into the new language (E. *superman* from Ger. *Übermensch*); also, **loan translation**. 332

cant (*gen*)   The special speech of a group with low social standing, e.g. thieves. 58

cardinal number (*gram*)   The basic form of a numeral (*one*, etc.); cf. ⁺ordinal. 99

cardinal vowels (*phonet*)   A set of reference points, based on auditory and articulatory criteria, used to identify ⁺vowels. 156

caretaker speech (*psycho*)   The speech of adults when they talk to children; also, **motherese**. 238

case (*gram*)   In an ⁺inflecting language, the form of a ⁺noun, ⁺adjective, or ⁺pronoun, showing its grammatical relationship to other words. 93

catachresis   *see* **malapropism**

catalect (*gen*)   Any part of an author's literary work seen as separate from the rest. 66

cataphora (*gram*)   A feature of grammatical structure that refers forward to another unit; (in *John said this*, the ⁺pronoun is 'cataphoric'); cf. ⁺anaphora and ⁺exophoric. 119

catenation (*ling*)   The linking together of a series of linguistic forms, e.g. sounds or words. 95

catenative (*gram*)   A ⁺lexical verb that governs another lexical verb (*try to run*). 91

causative (*gram*)   A linguistic element that expresses the notion of 'cause' (the causative verb *kill* = 'cause to die'). 93

cavity (*phonet*)   An anatomically defined chamber in the ⁺vocal tract, e.g. oral, nasal. 124

central   *see* **centre**

centre (*phonet*)   The top part of the tongue, between ⁺front and ⁺back; involved in **central** sounds. 131

centum language (*hist*)   An Indo-European language that kept the sound ⟨k⟩ in such words as *centum* ('hundred'); cf. ⁺satem language. 330

channel (*gen*)   A medium selected for communication (e.g. speech, writing). 48

character (*graph*)   A graphic sign used in a writing system, esp. one that is not part of an ⁺alphabet. 202

chereme (*ling*)   The smallest contrastive unit in a ⁺sign language. 223

cherology (*ling*)   The study of ⁺sign language. 223

chest pulse (*phonet*)   A contraction of the chest muscles that forces air into the ⁺vocal tract. 166

chiasmus (*rhet*)   A balanced pattern in which the main elements are reversed. 70

chirography (*graph*)   The study of handwriting forms and styles. 188

chrestomathy (*gen*)   An anthology of passages usually used for learning a language. 378

chroneme (*phonol*)   An abstract unit that accounts for differences in the ⁺duration of speech sounds, e.g. long vs short ⁺consonants. 412

chronogram (*gen*)   A phrase or sentence in which letters that are also Roman numerals (e.g. C, X) combine to form a date. 64

chunking (*psycho*)   Dividing an utterance into parts, e.g. to make it easier to remember. 173

cipher (*gen*)   A secret ⁺code¹ in which letters are transposed or substituted. 58

circumlocution (*gen*)   The use of more words than is necessary to express a meaning. 2

class   *see* **word class**

classifier (*gram*)   A ⁺morpheme which indicates that a word belongs to a particular ⁺semantic class, e.g. animates, large objects. 91

clause (*gram*)   A structural unit smaller than the ⁺sentence but larger than ⁺phrases or ⁺words; cf. ⁺dependent, ⁺main clause. 95

clavicular breathing (*clin*)   A way of breathing, in which inhalation comes from using the neck muscles to raise the collar bones. 125

cleft palate (*clin*)   A congenital fissure in the middle of the ⁺palate, often found along with a split in the upper lip (**cleft lip**, also 'hare lip') and teeth ridge. 279

cleft sentence (*gram*)   A sentence in which a single ⁺clause has been split into two sections, each with its own ⁺verb (*It was Mary who arrived*). 95

cliche (*gen*)   An expression which has become so overused that it no longer conveys much meaning, and is criticized (*a fate worse than death*). 2

click (*phonet*)   A sound produced using the ⁺velaric ⁺air-stream mechanism (E. {!} 'tut'). 126

clinical linguistics (*ling*)   The application of linguistics to the analysis of disorders of spoken, written, or ⁺sign language. 418

clipping (*gram*)   A process of ⁺word formation in which a new word is produced by shortening (*examination → exam*); also, **reduction**. 90

clitic (*gram*)   A form that resembles a ⁺word but that cannot stand on its own as a normal utterance because it is structurally dependent on a neighbouring word (Fr. *je*). 91

close (*phonet*)   Said of a ⁺vowel made with the tongue in the highest position possible without causing audible friction (e.g. {i}, {u}); vowels a degree lower are **half/mid-close**; cf. ⁺open³. 153

closed   1 (*gram*)   Said of any ⁺word class whose membership is limited to a small number of items, e.g. ⁺pronouns, ⁺conjunctions; cf. ⁺open¹. 91   2 (*phonol*)   Said of a ⁺syllable ending in a ⁺consonant; cf. ⁺open². 166

closure (*phonet*)   A contact made between ⁺vocal organs in order to produce a speech sound. 159

cloze procedure (*app*)   A technique used in the teaching and testing of reading, in which readers guess words omitted at intervals from a text. 381

cluster (*phonol*)   A series of adjacent ⁺consonants occurring at the beginning or end of a ⁺syllable (*stray, books*). 166

cluttering (*clin*)   A ⁺speech disorder in which utterances are produced in an excessively rapid and unrhythmical way. 280

coalescence (*hist*)   The fusing of originally distinct linguistic units. 330

coarticulation (*phonet*)   An ⁺articulation involving the simultaneous or overlapping use of more than one point in the ⁺vocal tract ({ɡb}, {ŋm}). 158

cochlea (*anat*)   The part of the inner ear that contains the organ of hearing. 143

code   1 (*gen*)   Any system of signals used for sending messages, often in secret form. 58   2 (*socio*)   A language, or ⁺variety of language. 48

code switching (*socio*)   Changing from the use of one language or ⁺variety to another; also, **language mixing**. 365

codify (*app*)   To provide a systematic account of a language (esp. its ⁺grammar¹ and vocabulary). 366

cognate (*hist*)   A language or linguistic form that is historically derived from the same source as another, e.g. Spanish and French are 'cognate languages', both deriving from Latin. 294

cognitive meaning   *see* **denotation**

coherence (*ling*)   The underlying logical connectedness of a use of language. 119

cohesion (*ling*)   The ⁺formal¹ linkage between the elements of a ⁺discourse or ⁺text (the ⁺pronoun is 'cohesive' in *The man left. He...*). 119

coinage (*gen*)   The creation of a new word out of existing elements (*postperson*); cf. ⁺blend. 90

collective noun (*gram*)   A ⁺noun that denotes a group of entities (*army, government*). 91

collocation (*sem*)   The habitual co-occurrence (or mutual **selection**) of ⁺lexical items. 105

coloratura (*gen*)   A soprano singer with a high vocal range. 18

comitative (*gram*)   An ⁺inflection¹ that typically expresses the meaning 'with'. 92

command (*gen*)   A type of ⁺sentence in which someone is told to do (or not do) something. 121

comment (*ling*)   Part of a ⁺sentence that says something further about the sentence ⁺topic (*The car was in the garage*); also, **new** information. 94

comment clause (*gram*)   A ⁺clause that adds a parenthetic remark to another clause (*The answer, you see, is complicated*). 52

common noun (*gram*)   A ⁺noun that refers to a class of objects or concepts (*chair, beauty*); cf. ⁺proper noun. 91

communicative approach (*app*)   An approach to language teaching that focuses on language ⁺functions² and ⁺communicative competence, and not on ⁺grammatical¹ structure. 378

communicative competence (*ling*)   A person's awareness of the ⁺rules¹ governing the ⁺appropriate use of language in social situations. 48

comparative   *see* **degree**

comparative linguistics (*ling*)   A branch of ⁺linguistics that relates the characteristics of different languages or ⁺varieties. 84

comparative method (*hist*)   A technique that compares forms taken from ⁺cognate languages to see if they are historically related. 294

comparative philology (*hist*)   The study of the historical relationship between languages. 294

compensation (*phonet*)   An alternative ⁺articulation that counteracts the effect of some abnormality in the ⁺vocal organs. 18

competence (*ling*)   Unconscious knowledge of the system of ⁺grammatical¹ ⁺rules¹ in a language; cf. ⁺communicative competence, ⁺performance. 413

complement (*gram*)   A ⁺clause element that completes what is said about some other element, such as the ⁺subject (*That book looks nice*). 95

complementarity (*sem*)   A type of oppositeness of meaning; two words are **complementaries** if to assert one denies the other (*single/married*). 105

complementary distribution (*phonol*)   A property of sounds that cannot appear in the same ⁺phonetic ⁺environment¹ (E. {tʰ} and {t}). 163

complex sentence (*gram*)   A ⁺sentence consisting of more than one ⁺clause (esp. including a ⁺dependent clause). 95

complex tone (*acou*)   A sound wave consisting of two or more ⁺pure tones. 133

component   1 (*ling*)   The major sections of a ⁺generative grammar. 82   2 (*sem*)   A basic feature of word meaning (*girl* = human, female, etc.). 107

componential analysis (*sem*)   The analysis of vocabulary into a finite set of basic elements (⁺components²). 107

compound   1 (*ling*)   Said of a linguistic unit composed of elements that can function separately elsewhere, e.g. a compound ⁺word/⁺sentence. 90   2 (*socio*)   Said of ⁺bilinguals who are thought to have a single meaning system underlying their use of words in both languages; cf. ⁺coordinate². 364

comprehension (*gen*)   The ability to understand and interpret language; cf. ⁺production. 263

compressed speech (*phonet*)   Speech that has been acoustically altered so that it uses a smaller range of ⁺frequencies than normal. 138

computational linguistics (*ling*)   The application of the concepts and techniques of computer science to the analysis of language. 418

computer language   *see* **language²**

concatenation   *see* **catenation**

concord (*gram*)   A ⁺grammatical¹ relationship in which the ⁺form² of one element requires the corresponding form of another (*She eats*). 95

concordance (*gen*)   An ordered list of the words used in a particular text or ⁺corpus. 415

concrete   1 (*gram*)   Said of ⁺nouns that refer to physical entities (*book, train*); contrasts with **abstract**. 91   2 (*phonol*)   Said of analyses that emphasize the ⁺phonetic reality of speech sounds; contrasts with **abstract**. 165

conditional (*gram*)   1 Said of a ⁺clause that expresses a hypothesis or condition (*If it rains, you'll get wet*). 95   2 Said of a ⁺verb form that expresses hypothetical meaning (Fr. 'conditional tense' *je marcherais* 'I would walk'). 93

conditioning (*ling*)   The influence of linguistic ⁺context¹ on a ⁺form² (E. *a → an* when followed by a ⁺vowel). 166

conductive (*clin*)   Said of a hearing loss where sound fails to reach the ⁺cochlea. 268

conjugation (*gram*)   The set of ⁺verbs that occur in the same forms in an ⁺inflecting language. 295

conjunction (*gram*)   A word that connects words or other constructions (*cat and dog*). 91

connective/connector (*gram*)   An item whose function is to link linguistic units, e.g. ⁺conjunctions, certain ⁺adverbs (*however*). 91

connotation (*sem*)   The personal associations aroused by words; cf. ⁺denotation. 103

consonance (*poet*)   The repetition of sounds in the same position in a sequence of words. 74

consonant (*phonol*)   A speech sound that functions at the ⁺margins of ⁺syllables, produced when the ⁺vocal tract is either blocked or so restricted that there is audible friction (⟨k⟩, ⟨s⟩, etc.); cf. ⁺vowel, ⁺semi-vowel. 157

constative (*ling*)   An utterance that is a descriptive statement, analysable into truth values (*The table is red*); cf. ⁺performative. 121

constituent (*gram*)   A linguistic unit that is a component of a larger construction. 96

constituent analysis (*gram*)   A process of analysing a construction into its major components (**immediate constituents**), each component being further analysed until a set of irreducible elements is left (**ultimate constituents**). 96

constriction (*phonet*)   A narrowing in the ⁺vocal tract, in order to produce a speech sound. 159

contact (*socio*)   Said of languages or ⁺dialects in close geographical or social proximity, which thus influence each other. 33

content word (*gram*)   A type of word that has an independent, 'dictionary' meaning (*chair, run*); cf. ⁺function word. 91

context (*ling*)   **1** The linguistic environment of an element. 82   **2** The non-linguistic situation in which language is used. 100

continuant (*phonet*)   A speech sound made with an incomplete ⁺closure of the ⁺vocal tract. 159

continuous   *see* **progressive**[1]

contoid (*phonet*)   A ⁺consonant defined solely in ⁺phonetic terms. 153

contour (*phonol*)   **1** A distinctive sequence of ⁺prosodic features (esp. ⁺tones[1]). 169   **2** Said of a ⁺tone language that uses ⁺gliding tones. 174

contraction 1 (*gram*)   A shortened linguistic ⁺form[2] attached to an adjacent form (*I'm*), or a ⁺fusion of forms (Fr. *de le → du*). 166   **2** (*poet*) The ⁺elision of ⁺syllables to keep a line's ⁺metre regular. 74

contradictory   *see* **complementarity**

contrary   *see* **antonym**

contrast (*ling*)   Any ⁺formal[1] difference that serves to distinguish meanings in a language; **contrastive** differences are also known as **distinctive, functional, significant**. 162

contrastive   *see* **contrast**

contrastive analysis (*app*)   The identification of structural differences between languages, seen as points of potential learning difficulty. 376

contrastive stress (*phonol*)   Extra emphasis given to a word, in order to draw attention to its meaning (*John bought a red car*). 171

convention (*gen*)   The tacit agreement of speakers to use the same ⁺rules[1] in order to communicate. 408

conventionalism (*sem*)   The view that there is a

relationship of ⁺arbitrariness between words and things; also, **nominalism**; cf. naturalism. 408

convergence (*socio*)   A process of linguistic change in which ⁺dialects or ⁺accents[1] become more like each other; contrasts with **divergence**. 51

conversational implicature (*prag*)   An implication deduced from an utterance, using the ⁺cooperative principles that govern the efficiency of conversations (*A bus!* = 'We must run'). 117

conversational maxims (*prag*)   General principles thought to underlie the efficient use of language, e.g. speakers should be relevant and clear. 117

conversation analysis (*ling*)   A method of studying the structure of conversations using the techniques of ⁺ethnomethodology. 116

converseness (*sem*)   A type of oppositeness of meaning, such that one word presupposes the other (*buy/sell*). 105

conversion (*gram*)   A type of ⁺word formation in which an item changes its ⁺word class without the addition of an ⁺affix (*smell* = verb/noun). 90

cooperative principle (*prag*)   A tacit agreement between speakers to follow the same set of ⁺conventions ('maxims') when communicating. 117

coordinate 1 (*gram*)   Said of ⁺clauses displaying ⁺coordination. 95   **2** (*socio*) Said of ⁺bilinguals who are thought to have different meanings for the corresponding words in their two languages. 364

coordination (*gram*)   The linking of linguistic units that have the same grammatical status, e.g. two ⁺noun phrases (**the cat and the dog**). 95

coordinator (*gram*)   A ⁺conjunction used in ⁺coordination (*and, but*). 95

coprolalia (*clin*)   Uncontrolled use of obscene language. 266

copula (*gram*)   A ⁺verb whose main role is to link other elements of the ⁺clause (*It is ready*). 95

coreference (*sem*)   The use of elements that can be interpreted only by referring to another element in a text. 119

coronal (*phonet*)   Said of sounds where the ⁺blade of the tongue is raised to the hard ⁺palate. 157

corpus (*ling*)   A collection of language data brought together for linguistic analysis. 415

correctness (*gen*)   An absolute standard of language use deriving from the rules of institutions (e.g. language academies) or respected publications (e.g. dictionaries); cf. ⁺appropriate. 2

correlative (*gram*)   Said of constructions using a pair of connecting words (*either/or*). 95

countability   *see* **countable**

countable (*gram*)   Said of ⁺nouns denoting separable entities, as shown by their use with such forms as *a* (*dog, chair*); **count(able)** nouns contrast with **uncountable/non-count** (⁺mass) nouns. 91

creaky (*phonet*)   A ⁺voice quality produced by very slow vibration of the ⁺vocal folds. 128

creativity (*ling*)   A characteristic of language that enables speakers to produce and understand an indefinitely large number of sentences. 401

creole (*socio*)   A ⁺pidgin that has become the mother tongue of a speech community (through a process of **creolization**). 338

critical period (*psycho*)   A period of time in child development during which language is thought to be most easily learned. 265

cross-sectional (*gen*)   Said of studies that sample the language of a group of individuals at a single point in time; cf. ⁺longitudinal. 231

cryptanalysis (*gen*)   The process of ⁺deciphering or ⁺decoding secret messages (**cryptograms**). 58

cryptograms   *see* **cryptanalysis, cryptography**

cryptography (*gen*)   The preparation of secret messages (**cryptograms**), using ⁺codes[1] and ⁺ciphers. 58

cryptology (*gen*)   The study of ⁺cryptography and ⁺cryptanalysis. 58

cryptophasia   *see* **idioglossia**

cued speech (*clin*)   A method of ⁺speech-reading in which manual cues help to distinguish sounds. 227

cuneiform (*graph*)   An ancient writing system that used wedge-shaped characters. 200

cursive (*gen*)   A form of handwriting in which separate characters in a sequence have been joined. 188

cycle (*acou*)   A single complete vibration, forming part of a ⁺sound wave. 133

dactyl (*poet*)   A unit of rhythm in poetic ⁺metre, consisting of one heavy beat followed by two light beats. 74

dactylology (*clin*)   Signing in which each letter of the alphabet is given its own sign; also, **finger spelling**. 227

dative (*gram*)   An ⁺inflection[1] that typically expresses an ⁺indirect object relationship (Lat. *Dedi epistolam puellae* 'I gave the letter to the girl'). 93

daughter language   *see* **parent language**

decibel (*phonet*)   A unit for measuring the relative ⁺intensity of sounds, esp. in the assessment of hearing loss. 134

decipher (*gen*)   To work out the meaning of a message in ⁺code[1] (esp. in ⁺cipher). 58

declarative (*gram*)   A grammatical construction used in expressing a ⁺statement (*The dog barked*). 121

declension (*gram*)   A set of ⁺nouns, ⁺adjectives, or ⁺pro-nouns that show the same ⁺inflections[1] (**decline**). 93

decline   *see* **declension**

decode (*gen*)   **1** To use the brain to interpret an incoming linguistic signal. 264   **2** To convert a secret message into intelligible language. 58

deconstruction (*styl*)   An approach to literary theory that aims to show the contradiction in ⁺structuralist principles of textual analysis. 79

decreolization (*socio*)   Change in a ⁺creole that makes it more like the ⁺standard language of an area. 338

deep grammar/structure (*ling*)   An underlying level of grammatical organization that specifies how sentences should be interpreted; cf. ⁺surface grammar/structure. 98

defective **1** (*gram*)   Applied to words that do not follow all the rules of the class to which they belong (E. †auxiliary verbs, which lack the usual verb †inflections[1]). 91   **2** (*graph*)   A writing system consisting only of †consonant symbols. 204

defining   *see* **restrictive**

defining vocabulary (*app*)   A core set of words used to define other words. 111

definite (*gram, sem*)   Said of a specific, identifiable entity or class of entities (*the car*); contrasts with **indefinite** (*a car*). 91

degree (*gram*)   A contrast of comparison in †adverbs or †adjectives; usually identified as **positive** (*big*), **comparative** (*bigger*), and **superlative** (*biggest*). 92

deixis (*ling*)   Features of language that refer directly to the personal, temporal, or locational characteristics of the situation (**deictic forms**) (*you, now, here*). 106

deletion (*ling*)   Omitting an element of sentence structure (*that* in *I said he was ready*). 97

demonstrative (*gram*)   Applied to forms whose function is to distinguish one item from other members of the same class (*this/that*). 99

denasal **1** (*phonet*)   Said of sounds whose †nasality has been reduced or removed. 130   **2** (*clin*)   Said of a †voice quality with poor nasal †resonance. 278

denotation (*sem*)   The objective ('dictionary') relationship between a word and the reality to which it refers; also, **cognitive/referential** meaning; cf. †connotation. 100

dental (*phonet*)   Said of a †consonant made by the †apex and rims of the tongue against the teeth. 157

dependent (*gram*)   Said of any element whose †form[2] or †function[1] is determined by another part of the sentence (in *the red car*, the †article and †adjective depend on the †noun); also, **subordinate**. 95

derivation **1** (*gram*)   A major process of †word formation, esp. using †affixes to produce new words (*act → action*); cf. †inflection[1]. 90   **2** (*gram*)   The set of analytical steps required to †generate a sentence. 97   **3** (*hist*)   The origins or historical development of a language or form. 294

descender (*graph*)   A part of a letter that extends below the depth of the letter *x*. 192

description (*ling*)   An objective and systematic account of the patterns and use of a language or †variety; cf. †prescription. 2

deterioration (*hist*)   A change of meaning in which a word acquires a negative evaluation; also, **pejoration**; cf. †amelioration. 332

determinative (*graph*)   A part of a †logogram that indicates its †semantic content; also, **radical**; cf. †phonetic. 201

determiner (*gram*)   An item that co-occurs with a †noun to express such meanings as number or quantity (*the, some, each*). 96

determinism   *see* **linguistic relativity**

developmental (*clin*)   Said of any linguistic disorder that arises out of an abnormal process of development in the child, e.g. 'developmental †aphasia'; cf. †acquired. 273

developmental (psycho)linguistics (*ling*)   The study of the acquisition of language in children. 228

deviance (*ling*)   Failure to conform to the †rules[1] of the language. 88

devoiced (*phonet*)   Said of a sound in which the normal amount of †vocal fold vibration (†voice[1]) has been reduced. 165

diachronic   *see* **historical, synchronic**

diacritic (*graph*)   A mark added to a symbol to alter its value, e.g. an †accent[3]. 156

diadochokinesis (*clin*)   The ability to carry out rapid repetitive movements of the †vocal organs. 273

diagnostic test (*app*)   A test to show what a language learner knows and does not know. 381

diagramming   *see* **parsing**

dialect (*ling*)   A language †variety in which the use of grammar and vocabulary identifies the regional or social background of the user; cf. †accent[1]. 24

dialect continuum (*socio*)   A chain of dialects whose end-points are not mutually intelligible. 25

dialectology (*ling*)   The study of (esp. regional) dialects; also, **dialect geography**. 26

dialinguistics (*ling*)   The study of the range of †dialects and languages in a speech community. 26

dichotic listening (*psycho*)   A technique for determining which half of the brain is primarily involved in processing auditory effects. 261

diction (*gen*)   The effective choice of words, esp. the vocabulary used by a poet or other writer. 73

diglossia (*socio*)   The use of two †varieties of a language throughout a †speech community, each with a distinct set of social functions. 43

digraph (*graph*)   **1** A †graphic unit in which two symbols have combined to function as one (*encyclopædia*). 367   **2** Any sequence of two letters pronounced as a single sound (*ship, wood*). 367

dimeter (*poet*)   A line of verse containing two units of rhythm (†foot). 74

diminutive (*gram*)   An †affix with the general meaning of 'little' (It. *-ino*). 90

diphthong (*phonet*)   A †vowel in which there is a perceptible change in quality during a †syllable (*time, road*); cf. †monophthong, †triphthong. 156

diplomatics (*graph*)   The study of legal and administrative documents. 189

directive (*prag*)   An utterance intended to get other people to do (or not do) something (*Sit down*); also, **command**. 121

direct method (*app*)   A method of language teaching that emphasizes speaking in the †target[2] language and avoids the conscious learning of †grammar[1]. 378

direct object (*gram*)   A †clause element immediately affected by the action of the †verb (*She hit him*); contrasts with a less directly affected (indirect) object (*I gave John a letter*). 95

direct speech (*gen*)   The actual utterance spoken by a person; cf. †indirect (or reported) speech. 77

discontinuous (*gram*)   The splitting of a grammatical construction by the insertion of another unit (*switch the light on*). 95

discourse (*ling*)   A continuous stretch of (esp. spoken) language larger than a †sentence. 116

discourse analysis (*ling*)   The study of patterns of linguistic organization in †discourses. 116

discovery procedure (*ling*)   A set of techniques automatically applicable to a sample of language to produce a correct †grammatical[2] analysis. 412

discrete (*ling*)   Said of linguistic elements that have clearly defined boundaries. 401

disjunction (*sem*)   An alternative or contrastive relationship between elements in a sentence (*Either we're early or the bus is late*). 107

displacement (*semiot*)   The ability of language to refer to contexts removed from the speaker's immediate situation (*I was angry yesterday*). 401

dissimilation (*phonol*)   The influence sound segments have on each other, so that they become less alike. 330

dissonance (*gen*)   The use of sounds to convey unpleasant effects. 74

distinctive (*phonol*)   Said of a feature capable of making a difference of meaning between otherwise identical forms, e.g. †vocal fold vibration; cf. †contrast. 162

distribution (*ling*)   The total set of linguistic †environments[1] in which an item can occur. 163

disyllable (*phonol*)   A word of two †syllables. 166

ditransitive (*gram*)   Said of †verbs that take two †objects (*give, show*). 95

divergence   *see* **convergence**

dominant language (*socio*)   **1** The most important language in a †multilingual speech community. 362   **2** The language a †bilingual knows best. 364

dorsal (*phonet*)   Said of sounds made with the †back ('dorsum') of the tongue ([k], [g]). 131

doublet (*gen*)   A type of word game in which a series of single-letter substitutions links pairs of words. 65

downdrift (*phonol*)   A gradual lowering of †tones throughout an utterance in a †tone language. 174

drift (*hist*)   A gradual series of related changes in the historical development of a language. 330

dual (*gram*)   A †grammatical[1] contrast of †number in some languages, referring to 'two of'. 92

dual alphabet (*graph*)   The use of capital and small letters in a single system. 188

dualism (*sem*)   A theory that postulates a direct, two-way relationship between linguistic forms and the entities to which they refer. 100

duality of structure (*ling*)   The structural organization of language into two abstract †levels[1]: meaningful units (e.g. words) and meaningless segments (sounds, letters). 401

duration (*phonet*)   The length of time involved in the †articulation of a sound or †syllable. 171

dynamic **1** (*gram*)   Type of †verb that expresses activities and changes of state, allowing such forms as the †progressive[1] (*He's running*); cf. †stative. 93   **2** (*socio*)   Said of language analyses that take account of temporal change. 330

dyne (*acou*)   A unit of measurement for sound pressure. 134

dysarthria (*clin*)   A motor speech disorder that leaves someone unable to articulate speech sounds; in severe form, also, **anarthria**. 273

dysfluency (*clin*)   The loss of ability to control the smooth flow of ⁺speech production, resulting in hesitancy, poor ⁺rhythm, ⁺stuttering, etc. 280

dysgraphia (*clin*)   A ⁺language⁴ disorder that primarily affects the ability to write; also, **agraphia**. 274

dyslalia (*clin*)   A disorder of ⁺articulation that has no clear physical cause. 279

dyslexia (*clin*)   A ⁺language⁴ disorder that affects the ability to read; also, **alexia**, **word blindness**. 274

dysnomia   *see* **anomia**

dysphasia   *see* **aphasia**

dysphemism (*rhet*)   A use of language that emphasizes unpleasantness (*a horrible dirty day*); cf. ⁺euphemism. 61

dysphonia (*clin*)   The loss of ability to use the ⁺vocal folds to produce normal ⁺voice¹; in severe form, **aphonia**. 278

dyspraxia   *see* **apraxia**

dysprosody (*clin*)   The loss of ability to produce speech with a normal ⁺intonation. 278

dysrhythmia (*clin*)   The loss of ability to produce normal ⁺rhythm in ⁺speech production. 280

ear training (*phonet*)   A technique in ⁺phonetics to train the ability to identify speech sounds. 160

echolalia (*clin*)   The automatic repetition of all or part of what someone has said. 273

economy (*ling*)   The use of the smallest possible number of ⁺rules¹ and symbols in carrying out a linguistic analysis. 165

educational linguistics (*ling*)   The application of ⁺linguistics to language teaching and learning in schools and other educational settings. 250

egocentric speech (*psycho*)   Speech that does not take account of the needs of the listener. 237

egressive (*phonet*)   Said of sounds produced using an outwards-moving ⁺air-stream mechanism. 125

ejective (*phonet*)   A ⁺consonant produced using the ⁺glottalic ⁺air-stream mechanism. 126

elaborated code (*socio*)   A relatively formal, educated language use involving a wide range of linguistic structures; cf. ⁺restricted code. 40

elative (*gram*)   An ⁺inflection¹ that typically expresses the meaning 'out of' a place. 92

electroaerometer (*phonet*)   An instrument that records air flow during speech. 139

electrokymograph (*phonet*)   An instrument that records the changes in the air flow from mouth and nose during speech. 139

electrolaryngograph (*phonet*)   An instrument that records ⁺vocal fold vibration. 141

electromyograph (*phonet*)   An instrument that records muscular contractions during speech. 139

electropalatograph (*phonet*)   An instrument that makes a continuous record of the contacts between tongue and ⁺palate during speech. 140

elicit (*ling*)   To obtain utterances or linguistic judgments from ⁺informants. 414

elision (*phonol, poet*)   The omission of sounds in connected speech (*bacon 'n' eggs*). 166

ellipsis (*gram, rhet*)   The omission of part of a sentence (e.g. for economy, emphasis), where the missing element is understood from the ⁺context¹ (*A: Where's the book? B: On the table*). 94

elocution (*gen*)   The art of speech training to produce effective public speaking. 70

embedding (*gram*)   Inserting one ⁺grammatical¹ unit within another (*The man **who left** was my uncle*). 95

emic (*phonol*)   An approach to speech analysis that sets up a system of abstract ⁺contrastive units, esp. ⁺phonemes; cf. ⁺etic. 412

emotive meaning (*sem*)   The emotional content of a use of language. 10

empty word (*gram*)   A meaningless word that expresses a grammatical relationship (*It's today he goes*); also, **prop word**; cf. ⁺content word. 91

encipher (*gen*)   To write a message using a ⁺cipher. 58

enclitic (*gram*)   An ⁺unstressed form attached to a preceding word (*cannot*). 91

encode (*gen*)   To give linguistic shape to a meaning, as part of communication. 264   **2** To convert a message from one system of signals into another (esp. for secrecy); cf. ⁺decode². 58

endocentric (*gram*)   Said of a construction where there is a ⁺grammatical¹ ⁺head (*the tall men*); cf. ⁺exocentric, which lacks a head (*People left early*). 95

endophoric (*gram*)   Said of the relationships of ⁺cohesion that help to define the structure of a ⁺text; cf. ⁺exophoric. 119

enjamb(e)ment (*poet*)   The running on of a sentence between two couplets of verse without pause. 74

environment 1 (*ling*)   The parts of an ⁺utterance or ⁺text that are adjacent to an item of language. 165   **2** (*socio*)   The social or cultural situation in which a particular use of language takes place. 48

epenthesis (*phonol*)   The insertion of an extra (**epenthetic**) sound in the middle of a word. 330

epicene (*gram*)   A ⁺noun that can refer to either sex without changing its form (*teacher*). 47

epiglottis (*anat*)   A structure that closes over the ⁺larynx during swallowing. 124

epigram (*gen*)   A short, witty statement, in verse or prose. 53

epigraph (*gen*)   **1** An inscription on stone, buildings, coins, etc. 189   **2** A phrase or quotation above a section in a book or on the title page. 53

epigraphy (*gen*)   The study of inscriptions, esp. their interpretation in ancient times. 189

epithet (*gen*)   Any item that characterizes a ⁺noun and is regularly associated with it (*Ethelred **the Unready***). 105

eponym (*gen*)   The name of a person after whom something, e.g. a place, a book title, is named (*Washington, Hamlet*). 112

equative (*gram*)   Applied to a ⁺clause which relates two elements that are identical in meaning (*Mr Jones is a butcher*). 95

ergative (*gram*)   Applied to a construction in some languages where the ⁺object of a ⁺transitive verb and the ⁺subject of an ⁺intransitive one are in the same ⁺case. 93

error 1 (*neuro*)   An inaccuracy in the spontaneous use of language attributable to a malfunctioning of the neuromuscular commands from the brain. 264   **2** (*app*)   A language learner's systematic use of a linguistic item that does not conform to the ⁺rules¹ of the target² language, because knowledge of these rules is incomplete; contrasts with unsystematic, ⁺performance faults (**mistakes**). 376

error analysis (*app*)   The systematic interpretation of the unacceptable forms used by someone learning a language. 376

esophageal   *see* **oesophageal**

essive (*gram*)   An ⁺inflection¹ that typically expresses the meaning 'at' a place. 92

état de langue (*ling*)   The 'state of a language' seen at a particular time, regardless of its antecedents or subsequent history. 411

ethnography of communication (*socio*)   The study of language in relation to the social and cultural variables that influence human interaction. 48

ethnolinguistics (*ling*)   The study of language in relation to ethnic groups and behaviour. 418

ethnomethodology (*socio*)   The detailed study of the techniques used during linguistic interaction. 116

etic (*phonet*)   The analysis of the physical patterns of speech without reference to their function within the language; cf. ⁺emic. 412

etymological fallacy (*hist*)   The view that an earlier (or the oldest) meaning of a word is the correct one. 332

etymology (*hist*)   The study of the origins and history of the ⁺form¹ and meaning of words. 332

etymon (*hist*)   The ⁺form¹ from which a later form derives (Lat. *mater* → Fr. *mère*). 332

euphemism (*gen*)   The use of a vague or indirect expression in place of one that is unpleasant or offensive (*pass away* for *die*). 61

euphony (*gen*)   A pleasing sequence of sounds. 74

exclamation (*gram*)   An emotional expression marked by strong ⁺intonation in speech or by an exclamation point in writing (*Good grief!*); cf. ⁺command, ⁺question, ⁺statement. 121

exclusive (*gram*)   Said of a first-⁺person ⁺pronoun (*we*) that does not include the person being addressed; cf. ⁺inclusive. 92

excrescent (*ling*)   Said of a sound added to a word to make the pronunciation easier. 330

exegesis (*gen*)   An interpretation of a text, esp. of a biblical kind. 389

existential (*gram*)   A sentence emphasizing the idea of existence (*There is a book on the table*). 95

exocentric   *see* **endocentric**

exophoric (*gram*)   Said of a linguistic unit that refers directly to the ⁺extralinguistic situation (*there, her*); cf. ⁺endophoric. 119

expansion 1 (*gram*) The process of adding new elements to a construction, without its basic structure being affected. 95 2 (*psycho*) An adult response to a child which adds grammatical elements that the child has omitted. 233

experimental phonetics (*phonet*) The use of instrumentation and experimental techniques to investigate the properties of speech sounds; also, **instrumental phonetics**. 138

expletive (*gen*) An exclamatory word or phrase, usually obscene or profane. 61

expression (*ling*) 1 Any string of elements treated as a unit for analysis, e.g. a ⁺sentence, ⁺idiom. 95 2 All aspects of linguistic ⁺form¹ (as opposed to meaning). 82

expressive 1 (*gen*) Said of a use of language that displays or affects a person's emotions. 10 2 (*clin*) Said of disorders of language ⁺production, e.g. 'expressive aphasia'. 267

extension 1 (*sem*) The class of entities to which a word is correctly applied, e.g. the extension of *flower* is *rose, daffodil*, etc.; cf. ⁺intension. 107 2 (*hist*) Widening the meaning of a word. 332

extralinguistic (*ling*) Said of anything (other than language) to which language can relate. 82

extraposition (*gram*) Moving an element to a position at one end of a ⁺sentence (*Working here is nice → It's nice working here*). 95

extrinsic (*anat*) Said of sets of muscles that control the gross movements of certain ⁺vocal organs, e.g. tongue, ⁺larynx. 131

eye dialect (*gen*) A way of spelling words that suggests a regional or social way of talking (*Thankee koindly, zur*). 182

eye rhyme (*poet*) A pair of words that seem to rhyme from the spelling, but have different pronunciations (*come/home*). 74

false friends (*app*) Words in different languages that resemble each other in ⁺form¹, but express dissimilar meanings (Fr. *demander* = 'request', not 'demand'); also, **faux amis, false cognates**. 349

false vocal folds *see* **ventricular folds**

family (*hist*) A set of languages that derive from a common ancestor (⁺parent) language, and are represented as a **family tree**. 294

feature (*ling*) Any typical, noticeable, or ⁺contrastive property of a ⁺level¹ of language. 82

feedback 1 (*prag*) The ongoing reaction speakers receive from their listeners, which helps them to evaluate the efficiency of their communication. 118 2 (*phonet*) The information speakers obtain by monitoring their own speech activity. 264

felicity conditions (*prag*) The criteria that must be satisfied if a ⁺speech act is to achieve its purpose. 121

feminine *see* **gender**

festination (*clin*) Abnormal increase of speed while speaking. 280

field *see* **semantic field**

fieldwork (*ling*) The principles and procedures of obtaining linguistic data from ⁺informants, esp. in their home environment. 414

figurative (*gen*) Said of an expressive use of language when words are used in a non-literal way to suggest illuminating comparisons and resemblances (**figures of speech**). 70

filled pause (*ling*) A vocal hesitation (*erm*). 174

filter (*acou*) A device used to separate the ⁺frequency components of a ⁺sound wave. 133

filtered speech (*phonet*) Speech passed through ⁺filters to alter its acoustic characteristics. 133

finger spelling *see* **dactylology**

finite (*gram*) A form of a ⁺verb that can occur on its own in a ⁺main clause and permits variations in ⁺tense, ⁺number, and ⁺mood (*They ran, She is running*); contrasts with **non-finite**. 93

finite-state grammar (*ling*) A simple kind of ⁺generative device that is able to process only a very limited range of sentences. 97

first language (*gen*) The language first acquired as a child (**mother tongue, native language**), or preferred in a ⁺multilingual situation. 372

first person *see* **person**

'fis' phenomenon (*psycho*) A child's refusal to accept an adult imitation of what it has just said. 242

fixation (*graph*) A period of relative stability between rapid eye movements. 210

flap (*phonet*) A ⁺consonant produced by a single rapid contact between two organs of articulation, e.g. the tongue tip movement [ɾ] in *very*. 159

flexion *see* **inflection**

fluency (*gen*) Smooth, rapid, effortless use of language; cf. ⁺dysfluency. 280

flyting (*poet*) An exchange of curses or personal abuse in verse form. 60

focal area (*socio*) A region where ⁺dialect forms are relatively homogeneous and tend to influence the forms used in adjoining areas. 28

focus (*gram*) An element in a sentence to which the speaker wishes to draw special attention (*It was John who wrote to me*). 107

folk etymology (*hist*) Altering an unfamiliar word to make it more familiar (*asparagus → sparrow-grass*); also, **popular etymology**. 332

foot (*phonol, poet*) A basic unit of ⁺rhythm, esp. used in describing poetic ⁺metre. 74

foregrounding (*poet*) Any departure from a linguistic or socially accepted norm, esp. in literary language. 71

foreign language (*app*) A non-native language, esp. one that has no official status in a country; cf. ⁺second language. 344

forensic linguistics (*ling*) The use of linguistic techniques to investigate crimes in which language data constitute part of the evidence. 69

form 1 (*ling*) The outward appearance or structure of language, as opposed to its function, meaning, or social use (**formal** vs ⁺notional¹). 82 2 (*gram*) The variations in which a linguistic unit can appear (the 'forms' *walk, walks*, etc.). 91

formal 1 *see* **form**¹ 2 *see* **formality**

formalist (*styl*) Said of an approach that studies the structural (⁺formal¹) basis for literary effects in great detail. 78

formality (*socio*) A scale of language use, relating to situations that are socially careful or correct (**formal**) or otherwise (**informal**). 40

formal universal (*ling*) An obligatory feature of ⁺grammar² construction; cf. ⁺substantive universal. 85

formant (*acou*) A concentration of acoustic energy, esp. distinctive in ⁺vowels¹ and ⁺voiced sounds. 135

formative (*gram*) An irreducible grammatical element that enters into the construction of larger linguistic units. 90

form class (*gram*) A set of items that display similar or identical grammatical features. 91

formulaic (*ling*) Said of a sentence that does not permit the usual range of grammatical variation (*Many happy returns*); also, **fossilized** or **stereotyped** sentences, or **routines**. 52

form word *see* **function word**

fortis (*phonet*) Said of ⁺consonants made with relatively strong muscular effort and breath force ([f], [p]); cf. ⁺lenis. 159

fossilized (*ling*) Said of any construction that lacks ⁺productivity, e.g. ⁺idioms (*spick and span*), ⁺formulaic utterances (*So be it!*). 52

frame (*gram*) A specific ⁺structural² ⁺context within which a class of items can be used. 95

free form (*gram*) A minimal grammatical unit that can be used as a ⁺word without additional elements; also known as a free ⁺morpheme; cf. ⁺bound form. 90

free translation (*gen*) A ⁺translation expressing the meaning rather than the ⁺form¹ of the ⁺source language; contrasts with **literal** (word-for-word) translation. 346

free variation (*phonol*) The substitution of one sound for another without causing any change of meaning. 163

frequency (*acou*) The number of ⁺sound waves per second produced by a source of vibration. 133

fricative (*phonet*) Said of a ⁺consonant made when two ⁺vocal organs come so close together that the air moving between them produces audible friction ([f],[z]); also, **spirant**. 159

frictionless continuant *see* **approximant**

front (*phonet*) Said of sounds made in the front part of the mouth or by the front part (⁺blade) of the tongue ([i], [t]); cf. ⁺back, ⁺centre. 131

fronting 1 (*phonol*) ⁺Articulation of a sound further forward in the mouth than is normal. 157 2 (*gram*) Moving a ⁺constituent from the middle or end of a ⁺sentence to the front (*Smith his name was*). 95

full verb *see* **lexical verb**

full word *see* **content word**

function (*ling*) 1 The relationship between a linguistic form and the other elements of the system in which it is used, e.g. a ⁺noun as ⁺subject or ⁺object of a ⁺clause. 95 2 The role language plays in communication (e.g. to express ideas, attitudes) or in particular social situations (e.g. religious, legal). 10

functional 1 (*ling*) Said of linguistic approaches that treat the notion of ⁺function as central, esp.

to show ⁺grammar communicating meaning in social interaction. 413 **2** (*clin*) Said of a linguistic disorder that has no apparent physical cause. 266 **3** (*ling*) *see* **contrastive**

functional change **1** (*hist*) An alteration in the role of a linguistic feature in historical development. 330 **2** (*gram*) The use of a ⁺word in different grammatical roles (***round the corner, a round table***). 92

functional load/yield (*phonol*) The use a language makes of a ⁺contrast in ⁺phonology (E. /p/ /b/ has a 'high' functional load, often distinguishing pairs of words). 163

function word (*gram*) A word whose role is largely or wholly to express a grammatical relationship (*to, a*); also, **form/grammatical/structural word**. 91

functor *see* **function word**

fundamental frequency (*acou*) The lowest-⁺frequency component in a complex ⁺sound wave, of particular importance in determining a sound's ⁺pitch. 133

fusion (*ling*) The merging of distinct linguistic elements (Lat. *-us* + noun ending simultaneously signals ⁺number, ⁺gender, and ⁺case). 295

fusional language *see* **inflecting language**

futhork (*graph*) The runic alphabet; also, **futhark**. 205

geminate (*phonol*) A sequence of identical adjacent sounds in one ⁺morpheme (It. *notte* 'night'). 162

gender (*gram*) A way of grouping words into different ⁺formal¹ classes, using such labels as **masculine, feminine, neuter, animate**. 93

genealogical *see* **genetic classification**

generalization (*psycho*) A process in ⁺language acquisition in which a first use of a linguistic feature is extended to a class of items (⁺plural *-s* on E. regular ⁺nouns); cf. ⁺overgeneralization. 236

generate *see* **generative**

generative (*ling*) Said of a ⁺grammar² that uses a set of ⁺formal¹ ⁺rules¹ to define the membership of (**generate**) the infinite set of ⁺grammatical¹ ⁺sentences in a language. 97

generic (*gram*) A word or sentence that refers to a class of entities (*the Chinese, the rich*). 91

genetic classification (*hist*) The grouping of languages into ⁺families based on their historical relationships; also, **genealogical classification**. 295

genitive (*gram*) An ⁺inflection¹ that expresses such meanings as possession and origin (*girl's bag, man's story*); also applied to related structures (*the cover of the book*). 93

genre (*gen*) An identifiable category of artistic (here, literary) composition, e.g. the novel. 52

geolinguistics (*ling*) The study of the geographical distribution of the languages and dialects of the world, with reference to their political, economic, and cultural status; also called **geographical linguistics**; cf. **areal linguistics**. 33

gerund (*gram*) A ⁺noun derived from a ⁺verb (a 'verbal noun'), esp. as found in Latin grammar, or

in grammars based on Latin (*amandum* 'loving'). 91

gerundive (*gram*) An ⁺adjective derived from a ⁺verb (a 'verbal adjective'), esp. as found in Latin grammar, or in grammars based on Latin (*amandus* 'lovable'). 91

ghost form (*hist*) A word originating in an error during the copying, analysing, or learning of a language, which does not exist in the original language. 189

given *see* **topic**

glide (*phonet*) **1** A transitional sound made as the ⁺vocal organs move towards (**on-glide**) or away from (**off-glide**) an ⁺articulation ([j] in *puny* [pʲuːni]). 137 **2** A ⁺vowel¹ where there is an audible change of quality (⁺diphthong, ⁺triphthong). 156 **3** A ⁺tone¹ involving a change of ⁺pitch level. 174

gliding *see* **glide³**

global aphasia (*clin*) ⁺Aphasia involving a severe disorder of ⁺production and ⁺comprehension. 273

glossal (*anat*) Pertaining to the tongue. 131

glossary (*gen*) An alphabetical list of the terms used in a special field. 111

glossogenetics (*ling*) The study of the origins and development of language. 292

glossograph (*phonet*) An instrument that records the movements of the tongue during speech. 140

glossolalia (*gen*) Speaking in tongues, as practised by certain religious groups. 11

glottal (*phonet*) Said of sounds made in the ⁺larynx resulting from the ⁺closure or narrowing of the ⁺glottis, e.g. ⁺whisper, ⁺creaky. 157

glottalic (*phonet*) Said of the ⁺air-stream mechanism that used the ⁺glottis as the source of vibration for ⁺ejective and ⁺implosive sounds. 126

glottalization (*phonet*) An ⁺articulation involving a simultaneous ⁺glottal ⁺constriction. 126

glottal stop (*phonet*) The audible release of a ⁺closure at the ⁺glottis; (*bottle* as [bɒʔl]). 128

glottis (*anat*) The aperture between the ⁺vocal folds. 128

glottochronology (*hist*) An approach to language history in which a statistical technique (⁺lexicostatistics) is used to quantify how far languages have diverged from a common source. 333

glottograph (*phonet*) An instrument that monitors the extent of ⁺glottal opening, using a light source. 141

goal (*sem*) The entity affected by the action of a ⁺verb (*The man kicked the ball*); also, **patient, recipient**. 95

govern *see* **government**

government (*gram*) A type of grammatical linkage in which one word requires a specific ⁺form² of another (Lat. *ad.* 'governs' the ⁺accusative form: *ad Romam* 'to Rome'). 95

gradable (*gram, sem*) Said of a word (esp. an ⁺adjective) that can be compared or intensified (*big → very big, bigger*). 105

gradation *see* **ablaut**

gradience (*gram*) A pattern of gradually increasing irregularity at the boundary of a ⁺word class. 92

grammar (*ling*) **1** The study of ⁺sentence structure, esp. with reference to ⁺syntax and ⁺morphology, often presented as a textbook or manual. 88 **2** A systematic account of the ⁺rules¹ governing language in general, or specific languages, including ⁺semantics, ⁺phonology, and often ⁺pragmatics. 82

grammatical (*gram*) **1** Pertaining to ⁺grammar¹. 88 **2** Said of constructions that conform to the ⁺rules¹ of a grammar²; those that do not are **ungrammatical**. 88

grammatical word *see* **function word**

graph (*graph*) The smallest ⁺discrete segment in a stretch of writing or print (t, T, *t*, etc.). 196

grapheme (*graph*) The smallest ⁺contrastive unit in the writing system of a language (*t, e, ;, ?*). 196

graphemics (*graph*) The study of ⁺graphemes. 196

graphetics (*graph*) The study of the visual properties of written or printed language. 187

graphic *see* **graph**

graphology (*graph*) **1** The (study of the) writing system of a language. 196 **2** The analysis of handwriting to discover the writer's character. 191

groove (*phonet*) A type of ⁺fricative ⁺consonant produced when the tongue is slightly hollowed along its central line ([s], [ʃ], etc.). 159

group *see* **phrase**

habitual (*gram*) Said of a form (esp. a ⁺verb or ⁺adverb) expressing repetition of an action (*often*). 93

half-close/-open *see* **close, open**

hapax legomenon (*styl*) A word that occurs only once in a text, author, or language. 67

haplography (*graph*) An omission made in a sequence of identical letters (*occurrence →* *ocurrence*). 215

haplology (*phonol*) The omission of sounds in a sequence of similar ⁺articulations (*probably →* /prɒblɪ/). 330

hard contact (*clin*) A very ⁺tense² articulation heard in ⁺stuttering when the speaker attempts a difficult word. 280

hard palate *see* **palate**

hare lip *see* **cleft palate**

harmonic (*acou*) A ⁺frequency of sound vibration that is a multiple of the ⁺fundamental frequency; also, **overtone**. 133

harmony (*phonol*) Similarity of ⁺articulation between sounds in the same word or phrase; occurs as **consonant harmony** and **vowel harmony**. 161

head (*gram*) The main element in a ⁺phrase on which other elements depend, and which controls the function of the phrase as a whole (*All the new **books** from the library are on the table*). 95

headword (*app*) The item that occurs at the beginning of a ⁺dictionary entry. 108

hertz (*acou*) The unit for measuring vibration; once known as 'cycles per second'. 133

heterographs (*gen*) Words that have the same meaning or pronunciation, but differ in spelling (*bear* vs *bare*). 106

heteronyms (*gen*) Words that differ in meaning but are identical in either pronunciation or spelling (*threw* vs *through*). 106

heterophemy (*gen*) An unintentional error in spoken or written language. 166

heterotopy (*gen*) A misplaced sound during (esp. fast) speech. 280

hexameter (*poet*) A line of verse containing six units of rhythm (+foot). 74

hiatus 1 (*phonet*) The use of adjacent +vowels[1] in different +syllables. 166 2 (*gen*) A break in a +sentence that leaves it incomplete. 52

hierarchy (*ling*) A classification of linguistic units into a series of successively subordinate +levels[3], esp. an analysis of +sentences into +clauses, +phrases, +words, and +morphemes. 82, 95

hieroglyphic (*graph*) A writing system using mainly pictorial symbols; esp. applied to Egyptian. 201

high (*phonet, phonol*) 1 Said of +vowels[1] (and sometimes +consonants) made by raising the tongue towards the roof of the mouth ([i], [k]). 153 2 Said of +tones[1] that use a relatively high level of +pitch range. 174 3 (*socio*) Said of the more prestigious +variety in +diglossia. 43

hiragana *see* **kana**

historical linguistics (*ling*) The study of development of language and languages over time; also, **diachronic linguistics** or (with different emphasis) **comparative philology**. 411

hold (*phonet*) To maintain a single position of the +vocal organs for a period of time. 159

holograph (*gen*) A document that is entirely written in the handwriting of its author. 189

holophrase (*psycho*) A grammatically unstructured utterance, usually consisting of a single word, typical of the earliest stage of language learning in children (*dada, allgone*). 244

homographs (*gen*) Words with the same spelling but different meanings (*wind* = 'air' vs *wind* = 'turn'). 106

homonyms (*gen*) Words with the same +form[1] but different meanings (*ear* = 'corn' vs *ear* = 'body part'). 106

homophones (*gen*) Words with the same pronunciation but different meanings (*rode/rowed*). 106

homorganic (*phonet*) Said of sounds made at the same place of +articulation ([p], [b], [m]). 159

honorific (*socio*) A use of language (esp. of grammar[1]) to express levels of politeness or respect. 99

hybrid (*gram*) A +word composed of elements from different languages (*television*, from Greek and Latin). 90

hydronymy (*gen*) The study of the names of rivers, lakes, etc. 114

hyperacusis (*clin*) An extremely acute ability to hear and distinguish sounds. 142

hyperbole (*gen, rhet*) Emphatic exaggeration (*There were millions of people in the cinema*). 70

hypercorrection (*socio*) A linguistic +form[1] that goes beyond the norm of a +target[2] +variety, because of the speaker's desire to be correct; also, **hyper-urbanism, overcorrection**. 2

hypercreolization (*socio*) The development of a kind of +creole that is a reaction away from the +standard language. 338

hypernasality (*clin*) Excessive +nasal +resonance in speech. 278

hyper-urbanism *see* **hypercorrection**

hyp(o)acusis (*clin*) An impairment of ability to hear and distinguish sounds. 268

hypocoristic (*gen*) A pet name (*Bill, honey*). 112

hyponasality (*clin*) Lack of normal +nasal +resonance in speech. 278

hyponymy (*sem*) The relationship between specific and general words, where the former is included in the latter (*cat* is a **hyponym** of *animal*). 105

hypostatize (*gen*) To speak of an abstract quality as if it were human. 70

hypotaxis (*gram*) The linking of a +dependent (**hypotactic**) clause to another part of the sentence using +conjunctions (*The boy left when the bell rang*); cf. +parataxis. 95

hysterical (*clin*) Said of disorders of +voice[1] or hearing that are psychological in origin. 278

iamb (*poet*) A unit of +metre consisting of an unstressed +syllable followed by a +stressed syllable ('*To be/ or not/ to be*'). 74

iconic (*sem*) Said of signals whose physical form corresponds to features of the entities to which they refer (as in +onomatopoeia, e.g. *cuckoo*). 222

ictus (*poet*) The +stressed +syllable in a unit of +metre. 74

idealization (*ling*) The ignoring of certain kinds of variability in linguistic data, in order to reach general conclusions. 413

ideation (*psycho*) The cognitive process of forming ideas and relationships of meaning, prior to their formulation in language. 264

ideational function (*ling*) The use of language to refer to the people, events, etc. in the world; cf. +interpersonal, +textual functions. 10

ideogram (*graph*) A symbol used in a writing system to represent a whole word or concept; also, **ideograph**. 200

ideograph *see* **ideogram**

idioglossia (*gen*) An invented form of speech whose meaning is known only to the inventor, e.g. the language sometimes used by twins; also, **autonomous speech, cryptophasia**. 249

idiolect (*ling*) The linguistic system of an individual speaker. 24

idiom (*sem*) A sequence of words that is a unit of meaning (*kick the bucket* = 'die'). 105

illative (*gram*) An +inflection[1] that typically expresses the meaning of 'into' a place. 92

ill formed (*gram*) Said of any +ungrammatical[1] sentence; cf. +well formed. 88

illocutionary act (*prag*) A +speech act involving a

+performative verb (baptize, promise, request, etc.); cf. +locutionary/+perlocutionary act. 121

imagery 1 (*gen*) The use of +metaphor, +simile, and other +figurative language, esp. in a literary context. 70 2 (*psycho*) Language that produces clear or vivid mental pictures. 103

imitation (*psycho*) The copying of linguistic behaviour, esp. while learning a language; cf. +comprehension, +production. 236

immediate constituent *see* **constituent**

immersion (*app*) Said of a +bilingual programme in which +monolingual children attend a school where another language is the medium of instruction. 369

imperative (*gram*) A grammatical +mood expressing a +command (*Look!*). 93

imperfect (*gram*) A +tense[1] form expressing such meanings as past duration and continuity (Lat. *amabam* 'I was loving/used to love'). 93

imperfective *see* **perfective**

impersonal (*gram*) Said of constructions or +verbs with an unspecified +agent (*It's raining*). 95

implicational universal (*ling*) A type of +universal statement that takes the form 'If a language has X, then it also has Y.' 85

implicature *see* **conversational implicature**

implosive (*phonet*) A +consonant made using the +glottalic +air-stream mechanism with inwards-flowing air ([ɓ], [ɗ]). 126

inalienable *see* **alienable**

inanimate *see* **animate**

incapsulating language *see* **polysynthetic language**

inceptive (*gram*) Said of a +verb form that specifies the beginning of an action ('be about to'), e.g. Lat. *-escere*; also, **inchoative**. 92

inchoative *see* **inceptive**

inclusive (*gram*) Said of a first-+person +pronoun that refers to both the speaker and someone else, as when *we* means 'me and you'; cf. +exclusive. 92

incompatibility (*sem*) A feature of mutually-defining items where the choice of one excludes the use of the others (*The ink is red/blue*). 105

incorporating language *see* **polysynthetic language**

indefinite *see* **definite**

indefinite vowel *see* **schwa**

independent clause *see* **main clause**

indexical 1 (*ling*) Said of features of speech or writing (esp. +voice quality) that reveal the personal characteristics of the user, e.g. age, sex. 173 2 (*sem*) *see* **deixis**

indicative (*gram*) A grammatical +mood that expresses objective statements (*My car is new*). 93

indirect object *see* **direct object**

indirect question (*gram*) A +question as expressed in +indirect speech (*He asked if she was in*). 77

indirect speech (*gram*) A construction in which the speaker's words are made +subordinate to a +verb of 'saying' (*She replied that she had*); also, **reported speech**; cf. +direct speech. 77

indirect speech act (*prag*) An utterance whose

linguistic +form[1] does not directly reflect its communicative purpose (using *It's cold in here* to mean 'Close the window'). 121

inessive (*gram*) An +inflection[1] that typically expresses location or position within a place. 92

infinitive (*gram*) A +non-finite form of the +verb, which in many languages acts as the basic form (E. *run*, Fr. *donner* 'to give'). 93

infix (*gram*) An +affix added within a +root[1]. 90

inflecting/inflected/inflectional language (*ling*) A language in which +words express grammatical relationships by using +inflections[1]; also, **synthetic/fusional** language. 295

inflection/inflexion **1** (*gram*) An +affix that signals a grammatical relationship, e.g. +case, +tense[1] (*girl's, walked*). 90 **2** (*phonet*) Change in voice +pitch during speech. 171

informal *see* **formality**

informant (*ling*) Someone who acts as a source of data for linguistic analysis. 414

information (*ling*) The way a message content is structured, e.g. into **given** and **new**. 120

ingressive (*phonet*) Said of all sounds produced with an inwards-moving air stream. 125

inhalation *see* **inspiration**

initiator (*phonet*) The +vocal organs that are the source of air movement, e.g. lungs. 124

innateness hypothesis (*psycho*) The view that a child is born with a biological predisposition to learn language, involving a knowledge of its +universal structural principles; also, **nativism**. 236

inner ear (*anat*) The part of the ear containing the +cochlea. 143

inspiration (*phys*) The act of drawing air into the lungs; also, **inhalation**. 124

institutional linguistics (*ling*) The study of the problems involved in +language planning. 366

instructive (*gram*) An +inflection[1] that typically expresses the meaning 'by'. 92

instrumental (*gram*) An +inflection[1] that typically expresses the meaning 'by means of'. 92

instrumental phonetics *see* **experimental phonetics**

intensifier (*gram*) A word or phrase that adds force or emphasis (**very** *good*, **awfully** *pretty*). 91

intension (*sem*) The set of defining properties that determines how a term is to be used (*table* → 'legs', 'flat surface', etc.). 107

intensity (*acou*) The power transmitted along a +sound wave. 134

interchangeability (*semiot*) The ability of a signalling system to be mutually transmitted and received by members of the same species. 400

interdental (*phonet*) A +consonant made by the +apex of the tongue between the teeth ([θ], [ð]). 157

interference *see* **transfer**

interjection (*gram*) A class of +words with +emotive meaning, which do not form grammatical relationships with other classes (*Gosh!, Yuk!*). 91

interlanguage (*app*) The language system used at an intermediate stage of foreign language learning. 374

intermediate vowel (*phonet*) A +vowel[1] that falls between two adjacent +cardinal vowels. 156

internal evidence (*hist*) Linguistic features in a text that indicate when the work was written. 189

internal rhyme (*poet*) The rhyming of words within lines of verse. 74

interpersonal function (*ling*) The use of language to establish and maintain social relations; cf. +ideational function, +textual function. 10

interpret (*gen*) To make an oral +translation[1]. 351

interrogative (*gram*) A type of +sentence or +verb form used in the expression of +questions (*Who is he?, Are they there?*); cf. +declarative. 95

interrogative word (*gram*) A word used at the beginning of a +clause to mark it as a +question (***Who*** *is here?*). 95

intervocalic (*phonet*) A +consonant used between two +vowels[1] (/p/ in *apart*). 166

intonation (*phonol*) The +contrastive use of +pitch in speech. 171

intonation contour *see* **tone unit**

intransitive (*gram*) Said of a +verb or +sentence that cannot take a +direct object (*She's going*); cf. +transitive. 95

intraoral pressure (*phonet*) The build-up of air inside the mouth needed to produce certain speech sounds, e.g. +plosives. 124

intrinsic (*anat*) Said of sets of muscles that control the fine movements of certain +vocal organs, e.g. tongue, +larynx. 131

intrusion (*phonet*) The use of sounds in connected speech that do not appear when the words or +syllables are heard in isolation, e.g. 'intrusive *r*' between +vowels[1] (as in *law(r) and order*). 166

intuition (*gen*) A person's instinctive knowledge of language, which decides whether +sentences are acceptable and how they can be interrelated. 414

invariable word (*gram*) A word that does not undergo any change in structure (*under, but*); cf. +variable word. 91

inversion (*gram*) A reversed sequence of elements (*He is going* → *Is he going?*). 245

irony (*gen*) Language that expresses a meaning other than that literally conveyed by the words (*That's marvellous*, said of poor work). 70

irregular (*gen*) Said of a linguistic +form[1] that is an exception to a pattern stated in a rule[1]. 408

isochrony/isochronism (*phonet*) A rhythmic pattern in which +stressed +syllables fall at roughly regular intervals throughout an utterance. 171

isogloss (*socio*) A line on a map showing the boundary of an area in which a linguistic feature is used; the lines mark such features as vocabulary (**isolex**), +morphology (**isomorph**), +phonology (**isophone**), +semantics (**isoseme**), or socio-cultural use (**isopleth**). 28

isolating language (*ling*) A language in which +words are +invariable and grammatical relations are shown mainly by +word order, e.g. Chinese; also, **analytic/root** language. 295

iterative (*gram*) A +form[1] that expresses the repetition of an action (*frequently*), esp. as part of the +aspect system. 93

jargon **1** (*gen*) The technical language of a special field. 56 **2** (*gen*) The obscure use of specialized language. 383 **3** (*psycho*) Unintelligible utterance with good +intonation, used by young children when learning to talk. 239 **4** (*clin*) Unintelligible speech in some +language disorders. 273

juncture (*phonol*) +Phonetic boundary features that demarcate units of grammar, e.g. certain features of +pitch, +duration, pause. 166

kana (*graph*) Either of the two Japanese +syllabic[2] writing systems, **hiragana** and **katakana**. 197

katakana *see* **kana**

kernel (*gram*) A basic type of +sentence structure, as used in early +generative grammar. 97

kin(a)esthesis (*phys*) Awareness of the movements and positions of the +vocal organs during speech; also, **kin(a)esthetic feedback**. 124

kineme (*semiot*) The smallest +contrastive unit of body expression. 406

kinesics (*semiot*) The systematic use of facial expression and bodily gestures/movements to communicate meaning. 403

koine (*socio*) The spoken language of a locality that has become a +standard language. 43

kymograph (*phonet*) An early device for recording information about +vocal organ movements. 138

labial (*phonet*) The active use of one or both lips in the +articulation of a sound ([f], [u]). 157

labialization (*phonet*) +Rounding the lips while making a speech sound. 158

labio-dental (*phonet*) Said of a +consonant in which one lip actively contacts the teeth ([f], [v]). 157

labio-velar (*phonet*) A speech sound made at the +velum with simultaneous lip +rounding ([w], [u]). 157

laminal (*phonet*) Said of a +consonant made with the +blade (or lamina) of the tongue in contact with the upper lip, teeth, or +alveolar ridge ([s], [t̪]). 159

langage (*ling*) The human faculty of speech. 411

language (*gen*) **1** The systematic, conventional use of sounds, signs, or written symbols in a human society for communication and self-expression. 400 **2** A specially devised system of symbols for programming and interacting with computers. 400 **3** The means animals use to communicate. 401 **4** (*clin*) The symbolic aspects of language[1], excluding +phonetics (and often +phonology). 267

language acquisition **1** (*psycho*) The process of learning a +first language in children. 228 **2** (*app*) The analogous process of gaining a +foreign or +second language. 370

language acquisition device (*psycho*) The innate capacity that enables children to learn their mother tongue; often, **LAD**. 236

language attitudes (*socio*) The feelings people have about their own language or the language(s) of others. 1

language centre/center (*neuro*) A brain area controlling †production or †comprehension. 262

language change (*hist*) Change within a language over a period of time; cf. †language shift. 330

language contact (*socio*) A situation of prolonged association between the speakers of different languages. 362

language disorder (*clin*) A serious abnormality in the system underlying the use of language. 266

language laboratory (*app*) A classroom that uses tape-recorder booths to enable students to listen and respond to foreign utterances. 381

language loss 1 (*socio*) The gradual loss of ability to use a language, e.g. in immigrant situations. 362 **2** (*clin*) The sudden loss of language as a result of brain damage. 272

language loyalty (*socio*) The personal attachment to a language that leads to its continued use in a country where other languages are †dominant. 369

language maintenance (*socio*) The continued use of and support for a language in a †bilingual or †multilingual community. 362

language pathologist/pathology *see* **speech pathologist/pathology**

language planning (*socio*) Official intentions and policies affecting language use in a country. 366

language shift (*socio*) A permanent change in a person's choice of language for everyday purposes (esp. as a result of immigrant movement). 362

language therapist *see* **speech pathologist**

langue (*ling*) The language system shared by a †speech community; cf. †*parole*. 411

laryngeal (*phonet*) A speech sound made in the †larynx. 128

laryngectomee (*clin*) Someone who has had a †laryngectomy. 278

laryngectomy (*clin*) The surgical removal of some or all of the †larynx. 278

laryngology (*clin*) The study of the anatomy, physiology, and diseases of the †larynx. 128

laryngopharynx (*anat*) The lower part of the †pharynx, between †larynx and †oropharynx. 130

laryngoscope (*clin*) A device inserted into the mouth to enable the †larynx to be seen. 129

larynx (*anat*) The part of the †trachea containing the †vocal folds. 128

lateral (*phonet*) Said of a †consonant in which air escapes around one or both sides of a †closure made in the mouth, as in the various kinds of *l* sound. 159

lateralization/laterality (*neuro*) The primary involvement of one hemisphere of the brain in the exercise of a bodily function, e.g. language. 260

latinate (*gram*) Applied to any †grammar¹ that is based on the terms and categories used in classical Latin grammar. 2

law (*hist*) A statement of the predictable relationships (esp. in the use of sounds) between different languages or states of a language. 330

lax *see* **tension**

leading (*graph*) The spacing between lines of type. 192

lect (*socio*) A collection of linguistic phenomena that has a functional identity within a speech community, e.g. a regional or social †variety. 24

length *see* **duration**

lenis (*phonet*) Said of †consonants made with a relatively weak degree of muscular effort and breath force ([b], [v]); cf. †fortis. 159

lenition (*phonet*) A relaxation of muscular effort during †articulation. 159

lento (*phonet*) Said of speech produced slowly or with careful †articulation. 171

lesion (*clin*) An abnormal change in body tissue due to injury or disease. 261

level 1 (*ling*) A major dimension of the structural organization of language, capable of independent study, e.g. †phonology, †syntax. 82 **2** (*gram*) A kind of representation recognized within the †derivation² of a sentence, e.g. †deep vs †surface grammar. 413 **3** (*gram*) One of a series of structural layers within a †sentence (†clause, †phrase, †word, etc.); also, **rank**. 95 **4** (*phonol*) A degree of †pitch height or †loudness during speech. 172 **5** (*socio*) A mode of expression felt to suit a type of social situation (formal, intimate, etc.). 40

lexeme (*sem*) The smallest †contrastive unit in a †semantic system (*run, cat, switch on*); also, **lexical item**. 104

lexical diffusion (*socio*) The gradual spread of a linguistic change through a language. 334

lexical item *see* **lexeme**

lexical field *see* **semantic field**

lexical verb (*gram*) A †verb expressing an action, event, or state; also, **full-/main** verb; cf. †auxiliary verb. 91

lexical word *see* **content word**

lexicography (*gen*) The art and science of dictionary-making (by **lexicographers**). 108

lexicology (*sem*) The study of the history and present state of a language's vocabulary. 108

lexicon (*sem*) The vocabulary of a language, esp. in dictionary form; also, **lexis**. 108

lexicostatistics (*hist*) A method for comparing the rates of change in sets of words in hypothetically related languages; cf. †glottochronology. 333

lexis *see* **lexicon**

liaison (*phonol*) The pronunciation of a †consonant at the end of a word when the next word begins with a †vowel (Fr. *C'est un ...* 'It is a ...'); cf. †linking. 166

ligature (*graph*) A character in which two or more letters have been joined together (æ, œ). 196

linear (*graph*) Said of †scripts using simply drawn characters instead of pictorial writing. 185

lingua franca (*gen*) A medium of communication for people who speak different †first languages. 359

lingual/linguo- (*phonet*) Said of any sound made with the tongue. 131

linguist 1 (*gen*) Someone who is proficient in several languages. 418 **2** (*ling*) A student or practitioner of the subject of †linguistics; also, **linguistician**. 418

linguistic 1 (*gen*) Pertaining to †language¹. **2** (*ling*) Pertaining to †linguistics. 418

linguistic atlas (*ling*) A set of maps showing the geographical distribution of linguistic items; also, **dialect atlas**. 30

linguistic change *see* **language change**

linguistic geography *see* **geographical linguistics**

linguistician *see* **linguist²**

linguistic relativity/determinism (*ling*) The hypothesis that a language's structure governs the way in which its speakers view the world. 15

linguistics (*ling*) The science of language. 408

linguistic science(s) *see* **linguistics**

linking (*phonol*) A sound introduced between two †syllables or †words, for ease of pronunciation (E. 'linking /r/' of *car and ...*); cf. †liaison. 166

linking verb *see* **copula**

lipogram (*gen*) A text from which a specific letter has been omitted throughout. 65

lip reading *see* **speech reading**

liquid (*phonet*) [l]- or [r]-type †consonants. 168

lisp (*clin*) An abnormal †articulation of a †sibilant †consonant, esp. [s]. 279

literal (*gen*) The usual meaning of a word or phrase; cf. †figurative. 70

literal translation *see* **free translation**

loan translation *see* **calque**

loan word *see* **borrow**

localization (*neuro*) The control of a specific kind of behaviour, e.g. speech, by a specific area of the brain. 262

locative (*gram*) A form that expresses location (*at the corner*). 93

locutionary act (*prag*) The †speech act of making a meaningful utterance; cf. †illocutionary act. 121

logocentrism (*styl*) A language- or word-centred view of literature or other behaviour. 79

logogram (*graph*) A symbol that represents a †word (as in Chinese); also, **logograph**. 202

logograph *see* **logogram**

logogriph (*gen*) A word puzzle using †anagrams. 65

logop(a)edics *see* **speech pathology**

logop(a)edist *see* **speech pathologist**

logorrhoea (*gen, clin*) Excessive, uncontrolled, incoherent speech. 273

long (*phonol*) Said of a †phoneme that †contrasts because of its greater †duration (the †vowel¹ of *beat* compared with *bit*). 153

longitudinal (*gen*) Said of studies that follow †language acquisition over a period of time; cf. †cross-sectional. 231

look-and-say (*app*) A method of teaching reading that focuses on the recognition of whole words; also, **whole word**; cf. †phonics. 253

loudness (*phonet*) The auditory sensation that primarily relates to a sound's intensity; also, **volume**. 44

low (*phonet, phonol*) **1** Said of †vowels¹ made with the tongue in the bottom area of the mouth ([a], [ɑ]). 153 **2** Said of †tones¹ that use a relatively low level of +pitch range. 174   **3** (*socio*) Said of the less prestigious +variety in +diglossia. 43

machine translation (*gen*)   The use of a computer to carry out the task of +translation; also, **automatic translation**. 352

macrolinguistics (*ling*)   A broad conception of linguistic enquiry, including psychological, cultural, etc. factors. 408

main clause (*gram*)   A +clause that does not depend on any other part of a +sentence (***The man arrived*** *after the bus left*); also, **independent clause**; cf. +subordination. 95

maintenance   *see* **language maintenance**

main verb   *see* **lexical verb**

majuscule (*graph*)   A form of writing consisting of capital letters; cf. +minuscule. 188

malapropism (*gen*)   An inappropriate word, used because of its similarity in sound to the intended word (*a paradigm of virtue*). 77

malformation (*gen*)   An unacceptable +word formation due to a wrong +analogy (*gooses* for *geese*). 332

manner   **1** (*phonet*)   The specific process of +articulation used in a sound's +production (+plosive, etc.). 159   **2** (*gram*)   An +adverbial answering the question 'how?' (*quickly*). 91

manual alphabet   *see* **dactylology**

manualism (*clin*)   The teaching of +sign³ to the deaf, to the exclusion of speech; cf. +oralism. 269

margins (*phonet*)   Sound +segments that form the boundaries of a +syllable ([k], [p] in *cup*). 166

marking/markedness (*ling*)   The presence/absence of a particular +contrastive feature in a language or languages. 85

masculine   *see* **gender**

mass (*gram*)   Said of +nouns that typically express general concepts and lack an indefinite +article or +plural (*information*); cf. +countable. 91

matched guise (*socio*)   Recording two languages or +dialects by the same speaker, in order to elicit listener +language attitudes. 23

mathematical linguistics (*ling*)   The study of the mathematical properties of language, esp. using statistical or algebraic concepts. 418

matronymic (*sem*)   A name derived from that of a person's mother (*Marjorison*); also, **metronymic**. 112

maxims   *see* **conversational maxims**

measure   *see* **metre**

mechanical translation   *see* **automatic translation**

medium (*gen*)   A dimension of message transmission, esp. speech, writing, +sign³. 123

mel (*acou*)   A unit of measurement for +pitch. 144

mentalistic (*ling*)   Said of the study of language through introspection rather than through the description of behaviour; cf. +behaviourism. 413

merger (*hist*)   The coming together of linguistic units that were originally distinguishable. 330

mesolect (*socio*)   In +creole studies, a +variety between +acrolect and +basilect. 338

metalanguage (*ling*)   A language used for talking about language. 250

metanalysis (*hist*)   A word deriving from a word-boundary error (E. *a naddre* → *an adder*). 330

metaphor (*gen*)   A +figurative expression in which one notion is described in terms usually associated with another (*launch an idea*). 70

metathesis (*ling*)   Alteration in a normal sequence of elements, esp. sounds (*aks* for *ask*). 330

metonymy (*hist*)   A +semantic change where an attribute is used for the whole (*crown = king*). 70

metre/meter (*poet*)   A rhythmical verse pattern; also, **measure**. 74

metrics (*poet*)   The study of metrical structure. 74

metronymic   *see* **matronymic**

microlinguistic (*ling*)   Said of highly detailed studies of language data. 408

mid (*phonet*)   Said of a +vowel¹ +articulated between +high¹ and +low¹ tongue positions ([e], [ʌ]); cf. +close, +open³. 156

middle ear (*anat*)   Part of the ear between the ear drum and the +inner ear. 142

minim (*graph*)   A single downstroke of the pen. 189

minimal pair (*phonol*)   Words that differ in meaning when only one sound is changed. 162

minuscule (*graph*)   A form of writing consisting of small letters; cf. +majuscule. 188

miscue (*app*)   An error made by someone learning to read; studied by **miscue analysis**. 252

mismatch (*psycho*)   A child's +semantically inappropriate use of a word, where there is no apparent basis for the error. 246

mistake   *see* **error²**

mixing   *see* **code-switching**

modal (*gram*)   A +verb that signals contrasts in speaker attitude (+mood), e.g. *may, can*. 93

modality   **1** (*semiot*)   A +medium of communication. 400   **2** (*gram*)   The system of +modal expression. 93

mode (*semiot*)   A +medium of communication. 400

modelling (*app*)   Providing language examples for a learner to follow. 372

modification   **1** (*gram*)   The structural dependence of one element (a **modifier**) upon another. 95   **2** (*phonet*)   Movement that affects the air flow in the +vocal tract. 130   **3** (*hist*) Any of several kinds of +formal¹ change in a word (*man* → *men*). 330

modifier   *see* **modification**

monaural (*phonet*)   Using one ear; cf. +binaural. 142

monitoring (*app*)   Critical self-listening. 374

monogenesis (*hist*)   The view that all languages come from an original language; cf. +polygenesis. 293

monoglot   *see* **monolingual**

monolingual (*gen*)   Said of a person/community with only one language; also, **unilingual**; cf. +bilingual, +multilingual. 362

monologue (*gen*)   Speech by an individual person. 48

monometer (*poet*)   A line of verse containing a single unit of rhythm (+foot). 74

monomorphemic (*gram*)   Said of a +word consisting of a single +morpheme. 90

monophthong (*phonet*)   A +vowel¹ with no detectable change in quality during a +syllable (*car*). 156

monosyllabic (*phonol*)   Said of a +word consisting of a single +syllable. 86

mood (*gram*)   Attitudes of fact, wish, possibility, etc. conveyed by a +verb (a +modal) or +clause, e.g. +indicative, +subjunctive. 93

mora (*phonol*)   A minimal unit of rhythmical time equivalent to a short +syllable. 74

morph (*gram*)   The physical form of a +morpheme. 90

morpheme (*gram*)   The smallest +contrastive unit of +grammar (*man, de-, -tion, -s,* etc.); cf. +bound form, +free form. 90

morphemics (*gram*)   The study of +morphemes. 90

morphology (*gram*)   The study of +word structure, esp. in terms of +morphemes. 90

morphophonemics   *see* **morphophonology**

morphophonology (*gram*)   The study of the relations between +morphology and +phonology. 90

morphosyntactic (*gram*)   Said of a category whose definition involves both +morphology and +syntax, e.g. +number. 90

morphotactics (*gram*)   The arrangement of +morphemes in a linear sequence. 90

motherese   *see* **caretaker speech**

mother tongue   *see* **first language**

motor phonetics   *see* **articulation**

move (*prag*)   A unit of speech in a +discourse. 116

multilingual (*gen*)   Said of a person/community with several languages; cf. +monolingual. 362

mutation (*gram, hist*)   A sound change in a word due to the influence of adjacent +morphemes or +words (Welsh *pen* 'head' → *fy mhen* 'my head'). 90

mutism (*clin*)   Involuntary inability to speak. 266

mytheme (*styl*)   The smallest contrastive unit of structure found in mythical narratives. 79

narrow (*phonet*)   Said of a +transcription that shows many +phonetic details; cf. +broad. 160

nasal   *see* **nasality**

nasality (*phonet*)   Sound made with the soft +palate lowered, thus allowing air to resonate in the nose (**nasals**), e.g. [m], [n], or **nasalized** sounds, e.g. [ã]. 130

nasopharynx (*anat*)   The part of the +pharynx adjoining the nasal +cavity. 130

native language   *see* **first language**

native speaker (*gen*)   A person whose language is a +first language or 'mother tongue'. 372

nativism   *see* **innateness hypothesis**

naturalism (*sem*)   The view that there is a close, 'natural' connection between words and things; cf. +conventionalism. 408

natural language (*gen*)   A language with ⁺native speakers; cf. ⁺auxiliary language², ⁺language². 354

negation (*gram*)   A process expressing the denial or contradiction of some or all of the meaning of a sentence; **negative** forms (**negators**) include *not*, *un-*, etc.; cf. ⁺affirmative. 245

negative, negator   *see* **negation**

neologism (*gen*)   A new or invented word or expression (*linguistified*). 73

neurolinguistics (*ling*)   The study of brain structure and function in relation to language use, acquisition, and disorder. 263

neuter   *see* **gender**

neutralization (*phonol*)   The loss of a ⁺contrast between two ⁺phonemes in a particular ⁺environment¹ (/t/ vs /d/ is 'neutralized' in *stop*). 163

neutral vowel   *see* **schwa**

new   *see* **comment**

node   *see* **nodule**

nodule (*clin*)   A small localized swelling ('node'), esp. on the ⁺vocal folds. 278

noise (*acou*)   A complex ⁺sound wave with irregular vibrations. 137

nomenclature (*gen*)   A system of terms used in a specialized field. 384

nominal (*gram*)   A ⁺noun or noun-like item. 91

nominalism   *see* **conventionalism**

nominalization (*gram*)   Forming a ⁺noun from some other ⁺word class (*redness, my answering ...*). 91

nominative (*gram*)   An ⁺inflection¹ that typically identifies the ⁺subject of a ⁺verb (Ger. ***Der Mann seht den Mann*** 'The man sees the man'). 93

nonce formation (*ling*)   An invented or accidental linguistic form, used once only (*brillig*). 90

non-count   *see* **countable**

non-defining   *see* **restrictive**

non-finite   *see* **finite**

non-restrictive   *see* **restrictive**

non-standard   *see* **standard**

non-verbal (*semiot*)   Said of communication that does not use words, e.g. gestural. 403

normative   *see* **prescription**

notation   *see* **transcription**

notional   **1** (*gram*)   Said of a grammar whose terms rely on ⁺extralinguistic notions, e.g. action, duration, time; cf. ⁺formal¹. 91   **2** (*app*)   Said of a syllabus based on an analysis of sentence meanings and functions; cf. ⁺communicative approach. 378

noun (*gram*)   A ⁺word class with a naming function, typically showing contrasts of ⁺countability and ⁺number, and capable of acting as ⁺subject or ⁺object of a ⁺clause. 91

noun phrase (*gram*)   A ⁺phrase with a ⁺noun as ⁺head (*the tall man in a hat*). 95

nuclear   *see* **nucleus**

nucleus (*phonol*)   The ⁺syllable in a ⁺tone group that carries maximum ⁺pitch prominence (**nuclear tone, tonic**) (*She went to **London***). 172

number (*gram*)   The grammatical category that

expresses such contrasts as '⁺singular/⁺plural/⁺dual' (*cat/cats, she is/they are*). 93

object (*gram*)   A ⁺clause element that expresses the result of an action (cf. ⁺direct/⁺indirect object). 95

objective   *see* **accusative**

object language (*ling*)   A language that is the object of analysis (using a ⁺metalanguage). 82

oblique (*gram*)   Said of any ⁺case form of a ⁺word except the ⁺nominative. 93

obsolescent (*gen*)   Said of a word or sense no longer used. 332

obstruent (*phonet*)   Sounds made with a constriction (⁺plosives, ⁺fricatives, ⁺affricates). 159

obviative (*gram*)   A fourth-⁺person form used in some languages, typically contrasting with the third person to mean 'someone/something else'. 92

occlusion (*phonet*)   The length of the ⁺closure during the ⁺articulation of a ⁺stop ⁺consonant. 159

oesophageal/esophageal (*phonet*)   Said of sounds or ⁺voice¹ produced in the upper part of the oesophagus, esp. after ⁺laryngectomy. 278

off-glide, on-glide   *see* **glide**

onomasiology (*sem*)   The study of sets of associated concepts in relation to their linguistic forms. 100

onomastics (*sem*)   The study of the ⁺etymology and use of ⁺proper names. 112

onomatology   *see* **onomastics**

onomatopoeia (*sem, poet*)   Words that imitate the sounds of the world (*splash, murmur*). 176

ontogeny (*ling*)   Growth and decay (here, of language) in the individual; cf. ⁺phylogeny. 230

open   **1** (*gram*)   Said of a ⁺word class with unlimited membership (⁺noun, ⁺adjective, ⁺adverb, ⁺verb); cf. ⁺closed¹. 91   **2** (*phonol*) Said of a ⁺syllable that ends in a ⁺vowel¹; cf. ⁺closed². 166   **3** (*phonet*)   Said of ⁺vowels¹ made with the tongue in the lowest possible position ([a], [ɑ]); ⁺vowels a degree higher are **half-/mid-open**. 153

opposition (*phonol*)   A linguistically important contrast between sounds. 162

optative (*gram*)   A ⁺mood of the ⁺verb, in some languages expressing desire or wish. 93

oracy (*app*)   Ability in speaking and listening. 250

oral (*phonet*)   Said of sounds made in the mouth (as opposed to the nose, ⁺nasal). 152

oralism (*clin*)   The teaching of speech to the deaf, to the exclusion of ⁺sign³; cf. ⁺manualism. 269

ordinal (*gram*)   A class of numerals (*first*, etc.); cf. ⁺cardinal number. 99

oropharynx (*anat*)   The part of the ⁺pharynx adjacent to the oral cavity. 130

orthoepy (*gen*)   The study of correct pronunciation, esp. as practised in the 17th/18th centuries. 331

orthography (*gen*)   The study of the use of letters and the rules of spelling in a language. 196

orthophonist   *see* **speech pathologist**

oscillograph (*acou*)   An instrument that provides a graphic representation of ⁺sound waves (an **oscillogram**). 138

oscilloscope (*acou*)   An instrument for the visual display of ⁺sound waves. 138

ossicles (*anat*)   The bones of the ⁺middle ear. 143

otology (*clin*)   The study of diseases of the ear. 268

oto(rhino)laryngology (*clin*)   The study of diseases of the ear, nose, and throat. 268

overcorrection   *see* **hypercorrection**

overextension   *see* **overgeneralization**

overgeneralization (*psycho*)   A learner's extension of a word meaning or grammatical ⁺rule¹ beyond its normal use (*men → mens*); also, **overextension**. 246

overtone   *see* **harmonic**

oxymoron (*rhet*)   A ⁺figurative combination of incongruous or contradictory words. 70

oxytone (*gen*)   A word with heavy ⁺stress on the final ⁺syllable (*represent*). 171

paedography (*graph*)   A writing system devised to help children to read. 196

palaeography (*graph*)   The study of ancient writings and inscriptions. 189

palatal (*phonet*)   Said of sounds made in the area of the hard ⁺palate ([ç], [j]). 157

palatalization (*phonet*)   An ⁺articulation in which the tongue moves towards the hard ⁺palate while another sound is being made. 158

palate (*anat*)   The arched bony structure that forms the roof of the mouth; divided into the **hard palate** and **soft palate** (**velum**). 124

palato-alveolar (*phonet*)   Said of a ⁺consonant made between the ⁺alveolar ridge and the hard ⁺palate ([ʃ]). 157

palatography (*phonet*)   The instrumental study of tongue contact with the ⁺palate, displayed as a **palatogram**. 140

palilalia (*clin*)   Involuntary repetition of words or phrases. 272

palilology (*rhet*)   Word repetition for emphasis. 70

palindrome (*gen*)   Words or expressions that read the same backwards or forwards. 65

pangram (*gen*)   A sentence that contains every letter of the alphabet. 65

paracusis (*clin*)   Any hearing abnormality. 268

paradigm (*gram*)   The set of ⁺inflectional¹ ⁺forms¹ of a word (Lat. *amo/amas/amat...*). 90

paradigmatic (*ling*)   The relationship of ⁺substitution between a linguistic unit and other units at a particular place in a ⁺structure². 411

paradox (*gen*)   An apparent contradiction that contains a truth. 70

paragram (*gen*)   A play on words by altering a letter, esp. in humour. 63

paralanguage (*ling*)   Features of speech or ⁺body language considered to be marginal to language; studied by **paralinguistics**. 171

paralinguistics   *see* **paralanguage**

parallelism (*styl*)   The use of paired sounds, words, or constructions. 60

paraphasia (*clin*)   An involuntary error in the production of words or phrases. 272

paraphrase (*gen*)   An alternative version of a sentence that does not change its meaning. 107

pararhyme (*poet*)   The repetition of the same initial and final consonants in different words (*tail/tall*). 74

parataxis (*gram*)   Constructions joined without the use of ⁺conjunctions (*I had tea, eggs...*); cf. ⁺hypotaxis. 95

parent language (*hist*)   A language from which other languages descend, e.g. Latin is the parent of **daughter** languages French, Spanish, etc., which are thus **sister** languages to each other. 294

parole (*ling*)   The concrete utterances of a speaker; cf. ⁺langue. 411

paronomasia (*gen*)   A play on words, or pun. 63

paronym (*hist*)   A word that comes from the same ⁺root² as another (*wise/wisdom*). 90

paroxytone (*phonol*)   A word with heavy ⁺stress on the penultimate syllable (*telegraphic*). 171

parsing (*gram*)   Analysing and labelling the grammatical elements of a ⁺sentence; also, **diagramming**. 251

participle (*gram*)   A word derived from a ⁺verb and used as an ⁺adjective (*a smiling face*). 91

particle (*gram*)   An ⁺invariable word with a ⁺grammatical¹ function (*to go, not*). 91

partitive (*gram*)   A form that refers to a part or quantity (*some, piece, ounce*). 92

part of speech   *see* **word class**

pasigraphy (*gen*)   The use of a system of symbols understood between languages (*1, 2, ⁺, £*). 202

passive   *see* **active, voice²**

patient   *see* **goal**

patois (*gen*)   A provincial ⁺dialect. 24

patronymic (*gen*)   A name derived from that of a person's father (*Peterson*). 112

pejoration   *see* **deterioration**

pejorative (*gen*)   Said of a linguistic form that expresses a disparaging meaning (*goodish*). 332

pentameter/pentametre (*poet*)   A line of verse containing five units of rhythm (⁺foot). 74

perfect (*gram*)   A ⁺tense¹ form typically referring to a past action that has present relevance (*I have asked*); cf. ⁺pluperfect. 93

perfective (*gram*)   A ⁺verb ⁺aspect typically stressing the completion of an action; contrasts with **imperfective**. 93

performance (*ling*)   The language actually used by people in speaking or writing; cf. ⁺competence. 413

performative (*prag*)   An ⁺utterance or ⁺verb that performs an action (*promise, baptise*). 121

periodic (*acou*)   Said of a ⁺waveform that involves a repeated pattern of vibration; contrasts with **aperiodic** (random) vibration. 133

periphrasis   **1** (*gram*)   The use of separate ⁺words instead of ⁺inflections¹ to express a ⁺grammatical¹ relationship (**periphrastic**) (*more happy* for *happier*). 92   **2** *see* **circumlocution**

perlocutionary act (*prag*)   A ⁺speech act that achieves a particular effect on a listener (frightens, persuades); cf. ⁺locutionary act. 121

perseveration (*clin*)   Involuntary continued use of a linguistic form. 273

person (*gram*)   A grammatical form (esp. a ⁺pronoun or ⁺verb) referring directly to the speaker ('first person'), addressee ('second person'), or others involved in an interaction (esp. 'third person'). 93

personal pronoun   *see* **person**

personification (*poet, rhet*)   The ⁺figurative attribution of human qualities to non-human notions. 70

petroglyph (*gen*)   An ancient stone inscription; also, **petrogram**. 198

petrogram   *see* **petroglyph**

pharyngeal (*phonet*)   Said of sounds made in the ⁺pharynx ([ħ], [ʕ]). 157

pharyngealization (*phonet*)   Narrowing of the ⁺pharynx while another speech sound is being made. 158

pharynx (*anat*)   The part of the throat above the ⁺larynx. 130

phatic (*ling*)   Said of language used to establish atmosphere or maintain social contact. 10

philology   *see* **comparative philology**

philosophical linguistics (*ling*)   The study of language in relation to philosophical concepts. 418

phon (*acou*)   Unit of measurement for the ⁺loudness level of sound. 144

phon(a)esthenia (*clin*)   An abnormally weak ⁺voice quality¹. 278

phon(a)esthetics (*phonet*)   The study of the aesthetic or symbolic properties of sound. 176

phonation (*phonet*)   The production of ⁺voice¹ through the use of the ⁺vocal folds. 128

phone (*phonet*)   The smallest perceptible ⁺discrete ⁺segment of speech sound. 152

phoneme (*phonol*)   The smallest ⁺contrastive unit in the sound system of a language. 162

phonemics (*phonol*)   The analysis of ⁺phonemes. 162

phonemic transcription (*phonol*)   A ⁺transcription of the ⁺phonemes in an utterance. 162

phonetic   **1** (*phonet*)   Pertaining to phonetics. 152   **2** (*graph*)   Part of a ⁺logogram that indicates its pronunciation; cf. ⁺determinative. 202

phonetic alphabet   *see* **phonetic transcription**

phonetician (*phonet*)   A ⁺phonetics specialist. 152

phonetics (*phonet*)   The science of speech sounds, esp. of their production, transmission, and reception ('⁺acoustic/⁺articulatory/⁺auditory phonetics'). 152

phonetic spelling (*gen*)   A spelling system that represents speech sounds in a one-to-one way. 215

phonetic transcription (*phonet*)   A ⁺transcription of all distinguishable phones in an utterance, using special symbols (a **phonetic alphabet**). 160

phoniatrics (*clin*)   Study of pathologies affecting ⁺voice quality¹ and pronunciation. 266

phonics (*app*)   A method of teaching reading that trains recognition of the sound values of individual letters; cf. ⁺look-and-say. 253

phonogram (*graph*)   A symbol representing a speech sound; cf. ⁺logogram. 201

phonography (*graph*)   A writing system that represents individual speech sounds. 199

phonologist (*phonol*)   A ⁺phonology specialist. 162

phonology (*phonol*)   The study of the sound systems of languages. 162

phonostylistics (*poet*)   The study of the expressive use of sound, esp. in poetry. 74

phonotactics (*phonol*)   The specific sequences of sounds that occur in a language. 162

phrasal verb (*gram*)   A ⁺verb consisting of a lexical element and ⁺particle(s) (*get up*). 91

phrase (*gram*)   A group of words smaller than a ⁺clause, forming a ⁺grammatical¹ unit (*in a box*). 95

phrase marker (*gram*)   A structural representation of a sentence in ⁺generative grammar, usually in the form of a ⁺tree diagram. 96

phrase-structure grammar (*gram*)   A ⁺generative grammar that provides an analysis of sentences into ⁺constituent elements. 96

phylogeny (*hist*)   Historical development (here, of language) in communities or in the human race as a whole; cf. ⁺ontogeny. 330

physiological phonetics   *see* **articulatory phonetics**

pictogram/pictograph (*graph*)   A symbol used in picture writing. 199

pidgin (*socio*)   A language with a reduced range of structure and use, with no ⁺native speakers. 336

pidginize (*socio*)   To develop into a ⁺pidgin. 336

pitch (*phonet*)   The auditory sensation of the height of a sound. 133

place of articulation (*phonet*)   The anatomical point in the ⁺vocal tract where a speech sound is produced (⁺labial, ⁺dental, etc.). 157

pleonasm (*gen*)   The unnecessary use of words (*in this present day and age*). 2

plethysmograph (*phonet*)   An instrument that records changes in air volume during speech. 125

plosive (*phonet*)   Said of a ⁺consonant made by the sudden release of a complete ⁺closure in the ⁺vocal tract ([p], [k]). 159

pluperfect (*gram*)   A ⁺verb form that typically expresses completion of an action before a specific past time (*I had jumped*); also, **past perfect**. 93

plural (*gram*)   A ⁺word form typically expressing 'more than one' in ⁺number (*cats, them*). 93

plurilingualism   *see* **multilingualism**

plurisegmental   *see* **suprasegmental**

pneumograph (*phonet*)   An instrument that measures chest movements during breathing. 139

pneumotachograph (*phonet*)   An instrument that measures air flow from nose and mouth. 139

poetics (*poet*)   The linguistic analysis of poetry (and sometimes of other creative language use). 73

point size (*graph*)   A system for measuring the size of pieces of type. 192

polarity (*gram*)   The system of contrast between ⁺affirmative and ⁺negative in a language. 93

polyalphabetic (*gen*)   Said of a ⁺cipher that makes use of many letter transformations. 58

polygenesis (*hist*)   The view that languages come from several original sources; cf. ⁺monogenesis. 293

polyglot/polylingual   *see* **multilingual**

polysemia/polysemy (*sem*)   Several meanings of a word (*plain* = 'dull/obvious/...'). 106

polysemic/polysemous (*sem*)   Showing ⁺polysemy. 106

polysyllabic (*phonet*)   Having more than one ⁺syllable. 87

polysynthetic (*ling*)   Said of a language that uses long ⁺word forms with a complex ⁺morphology; also, **incorporating, incapsulating**. 295

polysystemic (*ling*)   Said of an analysis that sets up different linguistic systems at different places in ⁺structure². 412

popular etymology   *see* **folk etymology**

portmanteau (*gram*)   A ⁺morph that can be analysed into more than one ⁺morpheme (Fr. *au* = *à le*). 90

positive   *see* **affirmative, degree, polarity**

possessive (*gram*)   A linguistic form that indicates possession (*my, mine, Mary's*). 93

postalveolar (*phonet*)   Said of a ⁺consonant made at the rear of the ⁺alveolar ridge. 157

postcreole continuum (*socio*)   A related series of ⁺varieties that develops when ⁺creole speakers are taught in the ⁺standard language. 338

postmodification (*gram*)   Items that occur within a ⁺phrase after the ⁺head (*the man in a suit*). 95

postposition (*gram*)   A ⁺particle that follows the ⁺noun it ⁺governs (Jap. *X kara Y made* 'from X to Y'); cf. ⁺preposition. 92

post-structuralism (*styl*)   A reaction to the ⁺structuralist analysis of literary texts. 79

postvocalic (*phonet*)   Following a ⁺vowel¹. 166

pragmatics (*prag*)   The study of the factors influencing a person's choice of language¹. 120

predicate (*gram*)   The ⁺clause element that gives information about the ⁺subject (*She saw a dog*). 94

predicative   *see* **attributive**

prefix (*gram*)   An ⁺affix added initially to a ⁺root¹ (*unhappy*). 90

prelinguistic (*psycho*)   Said of child utterance before the emergence of language. 230

preliterate (*hist*)   Said of a language before a writing system has developed. 198

premodification (*gram*)   Items that occur within a ⁺phrase before the ⁺head (*the funny clown*). 95

preposition (*gram*)   Items that ⁺govern and typically precede ⁺nouns, ⁺pronouns, and certain other forms (*in the box, to me, by running*). 91

presby(a)cusis (*clin*)   Gradual loss of the ability to hear and distinguish sounds as a result of old age. 268

prescription (*gen*)   An authoritarian (**prescriptive** or **normative**) statement about the correctness of a particular use of language; cf. ⁺description. 2

prescriptive   *see* **prescription**

presupposition (*sem*)   The information that a speaker assumes to be already known; cf. ⁺focus. 120

preterite (*gram*)   The ⁺simple¹ past ⁺tense form of a ⁺verb (*I saw*). 93

prevocalic (*phonet*)   Preceding a ⁺vowel¹. 166

principal parts (*gram*)   The ⁺forms² of a verb required to determine its ⁺conjugation (Lat. *amo/amare/amavi/amatum*). 91

proclitic (*gram*)   An unstressed word that depends on and is pronounced with a following word (*an*). cf. ⁺enclitic. 91

production (*ling*)   The active use of language; cf. ⁺comprehension. 263

productivity (*ling*)   The creative capacity of language users to produce and understand an indefinitely large number of sentences. 401

proficiency test (*app*)   A test that measures how much of a language someone knows. 381

pro-form (*gram*)   An item that substitutes for another item or construction (*so does John*). 119

prognostic test   *see* **aptitude test**

progressive 1 (*gram*)   A ⁺verb form that typically expresses duration or incompleteness (*He is running*); also, **continuous**; cf. ⁺simple. 93 **2** (*phonol*) Said of an ⁺assimilation when one sound causes a change in the following sound ([ʃ] → [tʃ] in *did she*). 166

prolongation (*clin*)   The abnormal or controlled lengthening of a sound in ⁺stuttering. 280

prominence (*phonet*)   The degree to which an element stands out from others in its ⁺environment¹. 171

pronominal (*gram*)   An item that functions as a ⁺pronoun. 91

pronoun (*gram*)   An item that can substitute for a ⁺noun or ⁺noun phrase (*it, who, himself*). 91

proper name/noun (*gram*)   A ⁺noun that labels a unique place, person, animal, etc. and lacks the grammatical forms of a ⁺common noun. 112

proposition (*sem*)   A unit of meaning in ⁺statement form that is asserted to be true or false (*The cat is asleep*). 107

prop word   *see* **empty word**

proscriptive (*ling*)   Said of ⁺prescriptive ⁺rules² that forbid a usage, e.g. criticism of *very unique*. 2

prosodic features   *see* **prosody¹**

prosody 1 (*phonol*)   The linguistic use of ⁺pitch, ⁺loudness, ⁺tempo, and ⁺rhythm. 171 **2** (*poet*) The study of versification. 74

pro(s)thesis (*phonol*)   The insertion of an extra sound at the beginning of a word. 330

proto-language 1 (*hist*)   A hypothetical ancestor language or form ('Proto-Indo-European'). 294 **2** (*psycho*) A stage before the emergence of a recognized linguistic form (**proto-word**). 239

proto-word   *see* **proto-language**

proverb (*gen*)   A short, pithy, rhythmical saying expressing a general belief. 53

proxemics (*semiot*)   The study of the communicative function of body distance, posture, etc. 403

pseudepigraphy (*gen*)   The false ascription of an author's name to a written work. 189

pseudolinguistic (*gen*)   Said of vocal behaviour with a superficial resemblance to language. 11

pseudonym (*gen*)   A fictitious name, esp. of an author. 112

psittacism (*gen*)   Meaningless repetitive ('parrot-like') speech. 272

psycholinguistics (*psycho*)   The study of language in relation to psychological processes. 418

pulmonic (*phonet*)   Pertaining to the lungs. 125

pure tone (*acou*)   A ⁺sound wave of a single ⁺frequency; cf. ⁺complex tone. 132

pure vowel (*phonet*)   A ⁺vowel¹ that does not change in quality during a ⁺syllable; cf. ⁺diphthong. 156

purism (*gen*)   The view that a language needs to preserve traditional standards of correctness and be protected from foreign influence. 2

qualifier (*gram*)   A word or phrase that limits the meaning of another element (**red car**). 95

quality (*phonet*)   The characteristic ⁺resonance, or ⁺timbre, of a sound. 133

quantifier (*sem*)   An item expressing amount (*all, some, each*). 91

quantitative linguistics   *see* **mathematical linguistics**

quantity (*phonol*)   The relative ⁺duration of ⁺contrastive sounds and syllables. 171

question (*gram*)   A sentence that asks for information or a response. 121

radical   *see* **determinative**

rank   *see* **level³**

readability formula (*app*)   A measure of the ease with which a written text can be read. 254

realization (*phonol*)   The physical expression of an abstract linguistic unit. 82

rebus (*gen*)   A combination of letters, pictures, and pictograms to make words and sentences. 65

received pronunciation (*phonol*)   The regionally neutral, prestige accent of British English. 39

receptive aphasia (*clin*)   A disorder of language⁴ ⁺comprehension caused by brain damage; cf. ⁺expressive². 272

recipient   *see* **goal**

reciprocal 1 (*gram*)   An item that expresses the meaning of mutual relationship (*each other*). 91 **2** (*phonol*)   A type of ⁺assimilation in which sounds influence each other. 166

reconstruction (*hist*)   The ⁺comparative linguistic analysis of extant texts to work out an earlier, non-extant state of a language. 294

recursive (*gram*)   Said of a ⁺grammatical¹ ⁺rule¹ that is capable of repeated application. 97

reduction 1 (*gram*)   The lack of one or more of the normal ⁺constituents in a construction (*gone to town*); cf. ⁺ellipsis. 95 **2** (*phonol*)   A ⁺vowel¹ that becomes ⁺central when a word is ⁺unstressed

([a] → [ə] as in *she can* → *she c'n go*). 166
3 (*hist*) A narrowing of meaning. 332
4 *see* **clipping.**

redundant (*ling*) Said of a feature that is unnecessary for the identification or maintenance of a linguistic ⁺contrast. 146

reduplication (*gram*) **1** A ⁺form² involving a repeated element (Lat. *curro* 'run' → *cucurri* 'ran'). 177 **2** A type of ⁺compound¹ word using repeated elements (*helter-skelter*). 90

reference (*sem*) The relationship between linguistic forms and entities in the world (**referents**). 102

referent   *see* **reference**

referential   *see* **denotation, reference**

reflexive (*gram*) A construction or ⁺verb in which ⁺subject and ⁺object relate to the same entity (*She washed herself*). 93

reflexiveness (*semiot*) The capability of language to 'talk about' itself; cf. ⁺metalanguage. 401

regional dialect   *see* **dialect**

register **1** (*phonet*) A physiologically determined range of the human ⁺voice¹, e.g. falsetto. 18 **2** (*socio*) A socially defined ⁺variety of language, e.g. scientific, legal, etc. 52 **3** (*phonol*) Said of a ⁺tone language that does not use ⁺gliding tones. 174

regression (*psycho*) A backward eye movement while reading a line of print. 210

regressive (*phonol*) Said of an ⁺assimilation when one sound causes a change in the preceding sound ([t] → [p] in *hot pig*); also, **anticipatory.** 166

regular (*ling*) Said of a linguistic form that conforms to the ⁺rules¹ of the language. 408

related (*hist*) Said of languages or forms that share a common origin. 294

relative clause   *see* **relative pronoun**

relative pronoun (*gram*) The item that introduces a ⁺dependent ⁺clause (**relative clause**) in a ⁺noun phrase, referring back to the ⁺noun (*the car **which** was sold...*). 95

relativity   *see* **linguistic relativity**

release (*phonet*) ⁺Vocal organ movement away from a point of ⁺articulation, esp. in ⁺plosives. 159

relexification (*socio*) A process in the development of ⁺pidgins in which original Portuguese vocabulary is replaced by native language words. 339

relic area (*socio*) A ⁺dialect area that preserves linguistic features from an earlier period. 28

repair (*prag*) The correction of a misunderstanding or error made during a conversation. 116

repertoire (*socio*) The range of languages or ⁺varieties that a speaker has available. 48

reported speech   *see* **indirect speech**

resonance (*phonet*) Air vibrations in the ⁺vocal tract that are set in motion by ⁺phonation. 130

respiration (*phys*) The act of breathing. 124

restricted code (*socio*) An informal ⁺variety of language thought to display a reduced range of structures; cf. ⁺elaborated code. 40

restricted language (*socio*) A highly reduced linguistic system found in narrowly defined settings, e.g. heraldry, weather reporting. 56

restrictive (*gram*) Said of a ⁺modifier that is an essential part of the identity of another element (*my brother **who's abroad***); also, **defining**; contrasts with **non-restrictive** or **non-defining**, where the modification is not essential (*my brother, **who's abroad***). 95

retracted (*phonet*) Said of the backwards movement of an ⁺articulator, e.g. the ⁺apex of the tongue. 157

retroflex (*phonet*) Said of sounds made when the ⁺apex of the tongue is curled back in the direction of the hard ⁺palate ([ʈ], [ʈ]). 157

rewrite rule (*gram*) A ⁺rule¹ in ⁺generative grammar of the form 'X → Y' (= 'replace X by Y'). 97

rheme (*ling*) The new information conveyed in a sentence; cf. ⁺theme. 120

rhetoric (*rhet*) The study of effective speaking and writing. 70

rhetorical question (*gram*) A ⁺question to which no answer is expected. 121

rhinolalia/rhinophonia (*clin*) ⁺Nasal resonance. 278

rhotacism (*clin*) A defective use of [r]. 279

rhotic area (*socio*) A ⁺dialect area in which /r/ is pronounced following a ⁺vowel (*car*). 28

rhoticization (*phonet*) The ⁺articulation of ⁺vowels¹ with *r*-colouring. 153

rhyme (*poet*) A correspondence of ⁺syllables, esp. at the ends of poetic lines. 74

rhythm (*phonol*) The perceived regularity of prominent units in speech. 171

roll   *see* **trill**

romanization (*graph*) The use of the Latin alphabet to transcribe non-Latin writing systems. 315

root **1** (*gram*) The basic form of a word, from which other words derive (*meaningfulness*); cf. ⁺stem. 90 **2** (*hist*) The earliest form of a word. 332 **3** (*phonet*) The furthest-back part of the tongue. 131 **4** *see* **isolating language**

rounded   *see* **rounding**

rounding (*phonet*) The visual appearance of the lips, permitting ⁺contrasts of **rounded** ([u]) and **unrounded** ([i]). 152

routine   *see* **formulaic**

rule (*gram*) **1** A generalization about linguistic structure. 97 **2** A ⁺prescriptive recommendation about correct usage. 3

saccades (*psycho*) Rapid eye movements used when searching for an object. 210

salience (*phonet, psycho*) The perceptual prominence of a sound. 145

sandhi (*gram*) A sound change affecting a word used in a specific grammatical ⁺context¹ (*do* → *don't*). 409

satem language (*hist*) An Indo-European language that replaced [k] by [s] in such words as *centum* ('hundred'); cf. ⁺centum language. 330

scansion (*poet*) The analysis of ⁺metre. 74

scheme (*rhet*) A ⁺figurative effect, e.g. ⁺rhyme, that changes the structure of language without affecting its meaning; cf. ⁺trope. 70

schwa/shwa (*phonet*) An ⁺unstressed ⁺vowel¹ [ə] made in the centre of the mouth, heard at the end of such words as *after* and *the*. 153

script (*graph*) Any system of written signs. 196

secondary articulation (*phonet*) The lesser point of ⁺stricture in a sound involving two points of ⁺articulation, e.g. lip ⁺rounding. 158

second language (*app*) A non-native language, esp. one that has an official role in a country. 372

second person   *see* **person**

segment (*phonet*) A ⁺discrete unit that can be identified in the stream of speech. 163

segmental phonology (*phonol*) The analysis of speech into ⁺phones or ⁺phonemes; cf. ⁺suprasegmental phonology. 162

segmentation (*phonet, gram*) The process of analysing speech into ⁺segments. 96, 162

selection(al) features   *see* **collocation**

semantic   *see* **semantics**

semantic component (*sem*) An element of a word's meaning (*girl* → young, female, human). 107

semantic differential (*psycho*) A technique for measuring the emotional associations of words. 103

semantic feature   *see* **semantic component**

semantic field (*sem*) An area of meaning identified by a set of mutually defining words (colour, furniture, etc.). 104

semantic relations (*sem*) The ⁺sense relations that exist between words, e.g. ⁺hyponymy. 105

semantics (*sem*) The study of linguistic meaning; also, semasiology, sematology, semology. 100

semasiology/sematology   *see* **semantics**

semi-consonant   *see* **semi-vowel**

semiology   *see* **semiotics**

semiotics (*semiot*) The study of the properties of signs and signalling systems, esp. as found in all forms of human communication; also, **semiology, significs.** 403

semi-vowel (*phonet*) A sound that displays certain properties of both ⁺consonants and ⁺vowels¹ ([l], [j]); also, **semi-consonant.** 153

semology   *see* **semantics**

sense relations (*sem*) The meaning relations between words, as identified by the use of ⁺synonyms, ⁺antonyms, etc.; cf. ⁺reference. 102

sensorineural (*clin*) Said of hearing loss due to damage to the ⁺inner ear. 268

sentence (*gram*) The largest structural unit that displays stateable ⁺grammatical¹ relationships, not ⁺dependent on any other ⁺structure². 94

sequencing **1** (*psycho*) Psychological processing of a series of linguistic elements. 277 **2** (*app*) The order in which a graded series of items is given to a learner. 378 **3** (*prag*) The rule-governed succession of utterances in a ⁺discourse. 120

shwa   *see* **schwa**

sibilant (*phonet*) A ⁺fricative made with a groove-like ⁺stricture in the front part of the tongue, to produce a hissing sound ([s], [ʃ]). 159

sight vocabulary (*app*) Words that can be recognized as wholes by someone learning to read. 252

sigmatism 1 (*clin*) Abnormal pronunciation of [s], esp. as a ⁺lisp. 279 **2** (*poet*) The repetitive use of [s] for effect. 74

sign 1 (*semiot*) A feature of language or behaviour that conveys meaning, esp. as used conventionally in a system; also, **symbol**. 411 **2** (*graph*) A mark used as an element in a writing system; also, **symbol**. 196 **3** (*ling*) Deaf ⁺sign language. 222

significant (*sem*) That which signifies; contrasts with *signifié*, that which is signified. 411

significant *see* **contrastive**

signification (*sem*) The relationship between signs and the things or concepts to which they refer. 100

significs *see* **semiotics**

signifié *see* **significant**

sign language (*ling*) A system of manual communication, esp. one used by the deaf. 222

simile (*rhet*) A ⁺figurative expression that makes an explicit comparison (*as tall as a tower*). 70

simple (*gram*) **1** Said of a ⁺tense¹ form that has no ⁺auxiliary verb ('simple present' *He runs*, etc.); cf. ⁺progressive¹. 93 **2** Said of a ⁺sentence containing one ⁺clause; cf. ⁺complex sentence, ⁺compound¹. 95

sine wave (*acou*) A simple ⁺waveform that produces a ⁺pure tone. 132

singular (*gram*) A form that typically expresses 'one of' in ⁺number (*dog, It is*). 93

sister language *see* **parent language**

situation (*ling*) The ⁺extralinguistic setting in which a use of language takes place. 48

slang (*gen*) **1** Informal, ⁺non-standard vocabulary. 53 **2** The ⁺jargon¹ of a special group. 56

slot (*gram*) A place in a construction where a class of items can be inserted (*the – car*). 95

social dialect *see* **dialect**

sociolect (*socio*) A social ⁺dialect. 38

sociolinguistics (*socio*) The study of the relationship between language and society. 418

soft palate *see* **palate**

solecism (*gen*) A minor deviation from what is considered to be linguistically correct. 2

sonagram/sonagraph (*phonet*) *see* **spectrograph**

sonant (*phonet*) A ⁺voiced sound. 128

sone (*acou*) Unit of measurement of ⁺loudness. 144

sonorant (*phonet*) A ⁺voiced sound made with a relatively free passage of air ([a], [l], [n]). 159

sonority (*phonet*) The relative prominence or 'carrying power' of a sound. 166

sound change (*hist*) A change in the sound system of a language, over a period of time. 330

sound law (*hist*) A regular, predictable series of ⁺sound changes. 330

sound pressure level (*acou*) The level of a sound as measured in ⁺decibels. 134

sound shift (*hist*) A series of related ⁺sound changes. 330

sound symbolism (*phonet*) A direct association between the sounds of language and the properties of the external world. 176

sound system (*phonol*) The network of ⁺phonetic ⁺contrasts comprising a language's ⁺phonology. 167

sound wave (*acou*) A wave-like air disturbance from a vibrating body, which transmits sound. 132

source language (*ling*) A language from which a word or text is taken. 346

spectrograph (*phonet*) An instrument that gives a visual representation of the acoustic features of speech sounds, in the form of a **spectrogram**; also, **sonagraph/sonagram**. 136

spectrum (*acou*) The range of ⁺frequencies that comprise a ⁺sound wave. 135

speculative grammar (*ling*) A type of grammatical treatise written in the middle ages. 410

speech 1 (*gen*) The oral medium of transmission for language (**spoken language**). 123 **2** (*clin*) The ⁺phonetic ⁺level¹ of communication (where disorder can occur); cf. ⁺language⁴. 267

speech act (*ling*) An ⁺utterance defined in terms of the intentions of the speaker and the effect it has on the listener, e.g. a ⁺directive. 121

speech and language therapist/therapy *see* **speech pathologist/pathology**

speech community (*socio*) A group of people, identified regionally or socially, who share at least one language or ⁺variety. 48

speech defect (*clin*) A regular, involuntary deviation from the norms of speech. 266

speech disorder (*clin*) A serious abnormality in the system underlying the use of spoken language. 266

speech event (*prag*) A specific act or exchange of speech (greeting, sermon, conversation, etc.) 48

speech impairment *see* **speech defect**

speech pathologist (*clin*) A person trained to diagnose, assess, and treat ⁺speech disorders; also, **language pathologist/therapist, logop(a)edist, orthophonist, speech and language therapist**. 266

speech pathology (*clin*) The study of all forms of involuntary, abnormal linguistic behaviour; also, **language pathology, logop(a)edics, speech and language therapy**. 266

speech perception (*psycho*) The reception and recognition of speech by the brain. 145

speech processing (*psycho*) The stages involved in the perception and production of speech. 264

speech production (*psycho*) The planning and execution of acts of speaking. 264

speech reading (*gen*) A method of interpreting a speaker who cannot be heard by following the movement of the mouth; also, **lip reading**. 227

speech reception *see* **speech recognition**

speech recognition (*psycho*) The initial stage of the ⁺decoding¹ process in ⁺speech perception. 149

speech science(s) (*ling*) The study of all factors involved in ⁺speech production and reception. 123

speech stretcher (*phonet*) A device that presents a slowed but undistorted recording of speech. 138

speech surrogate (*ling*) A communication system that replaces the use of speech (as in drum- or whistle-languages). 404

speech synthesizer (*phonet*) A device that simulates the ⁺speech-production process. 146

spelling pronunciation (*gen*) The pronunciation of a word based on its spelling (*says* as /seɪz/). 182

spelling reform (*gen*) A movement to make spelling more regular in its relation to speech. 217

spirant *see* **fricative**

spirometer (*phys*) An instrument for measuring the air capacity of the lungs. 125

split infinitive (*gram*) The insertion of a word between *to* and the ⁺infinitive form of the ⁺verb in English (*to boldly go*). 2

splitting (*hist*) One ⁺phoneme becoming two as a result of ⁺sound change. 330

spondee (*poet*) A unit of ⁺rhythm in poetic ⁺metre, consisting of two ⁺stressed ⁺syllables. 74

spoonerism (*gen*) The transposition of sounds between words, which gives a new meaning (*queer old dean* for *dear old queen*). 264

spread (*phonet*) Said of sounds made with lips stretched sideways ([i]). 152

stammering *see* **stuttering**

standard (*socio*) A prestige ⁺variety, used as an institutionalized norm in a community; forms or varieties not conforming to this norm are **non-standard** or (pejoratively) **sub-standard**. 24

standardization (*socio*) Making a ⁺form² or ⁺usage conform to the ⁺standard language. 366

starred form *see* **asterisked form**

state *see* **stative**

statement (*gram*) A sentence that asserts or reports information (*The dog saw the cat*). 121

static *see* **stative**

statistical linguistics (*ling*) The study of the statistical properties of language(s). 86

stative (*gram*) Said of ⁺verbs that express states of affairs rather than actions (*know, seem*); also, **static/state** verbs; cf. ⁺dynamic¹. 93

steganography (*gen*) The use of techniques to conceal the existence of a message. 58

stem (*gram*) The element in a word to which ⁺affixes are attached; cf. ⁺root¹. 90

stenography (*graph*) Shorthand writing. 208

stereotyped *see* **formulaic**

stop (*phonet*) A ⁺consonant made by a complete ⁺closure in the ⁺vocal tract ([p], [b]). 159

stratification (*ling*) A model of language as a system of related layers, or **strata**. 83

stress (*phonet*) The degree of force with which a ⁺syllable is uttered; syllables may be **stressed** or **unstressed** in various degrees (heavy, weak, etc.). 171

stressed   *see* **stress**

stress-timing   *see* **isochrony**

stricture (*phonet*)   An [+]articulation in which the air stream is restricted to some degree. 159

string (*ling*)   A linear sequence of linguistic elements. 95

strong form (*phonol*)   A [+]stressed [+]word form. 171

strong verb (*gram*)   A [+]verb that changes its [+]root[1] [+]vowel when changing its [+]tense (*sing/sang*). 91

structural   *see* **structure**

structuralism (*ling*)   An approach that analyses language (or any human institution or behaviour) into a set of [+]structures[1]. 79

structural(ist) linguistics (*ling*)   The study of a language's system of [+]formal[1] patterning (esp. in [+]grammar and [+]phonology), rather than of the meaning the patterns convey. 412

structural semantics (*sem*)   The study of the [+]sense relations between words. 105

structural word   *see* **function word**

structure (*ling*)   1 A system of interrelated elements, which derive their (**structural**) meaning from the relations that hold between them. 96 2 A sequential pattern of linguistic elements, at some analytical [+]level[2,3]; cf. [+]deep/surface structure. 98

stuttering (*clin*)   A disorder of speech [+]fluency marked by hesitancy, [+]blocks, sound repetitions, etc.; also, **stammering**. 280

stylistics (*ling*)   The study of systematic variation in language use (**style**) characteristic of individuals or groups; also, **stylolinguistics**. 66

stylolinguistics   *see* **stylistics**

stylometrics   *see* **stylostatistics**

stylostatistics (*ling*)   The quantification of [+]stylistic patterns; also, **stylometrics**. 67

subject (*gram*)   The [+]clause [+]constituent about which something is stated (in the [+]predicate) (***The books** are on the table*). 94

subjective   *see* **nominative**

subjunctive (*gram*)   A grammatical [+]mood used in some [+]dependent [+]clauses to express doubt, tentativeness, etc. (***Were** he here...*); cf. [+]imperative, [+]indicative. 93

subordinate   *see* **dependent**

subordination (*gram*)   The dependence of one grammatical unit upon another, as in **subordinate clauses** (*They left **after the show ended***). 95

subordinator (*gram*)   A [+]conjunction used in [+]subordination (*since, because*). 95

sub-standard   *see* **standard**

substantive (*gram*)   A [+]noun or noun-like item. 91

substantive universal (*ling*)   Basic elements that a [+]grammar[2] requires to analyse language data. 85

substitution (*ling*)   The replacement of one element by another at a specific place in a [+]structure[2]. 119

substitution frame (*gram*)   A specific [+]structure[2] in which a [+]substitution takes place (*a – cat*). 95

substrate/substratum (*hist, socio*)   A [+]variety that has influenced the structure or use of a more

dominant variety or language (the **superstratum**) in a community. 335

suffix (*gram*)   An [+]affix that follows a [+]stem. 90

superfix (*phonol*)   A vocal effect that extends over more than one [+]segment, e.g. [+]stress. 171

superlative   *see* **degree**

superstratum   *see* **substratum**

suppletion (*gram*)   The use of an unrelated form to complete a [+]paradigm (*go/goes/going/gone/**went***). 90

suprasegmental (*phonol*)   A vocal effect extending over more than one [+]segment, e.g. [+]pitch; also, **plurisegmental**. 171

surface grammar/structure (*ling*)   A [+]syntactic representation of a [+]sentence that comes closest to how the sentence is actually pronounced. 98

switching   *see* **code switching**

syllabary (*graph*)   A writing system in which the symbols represent [+]syllables. 203

syllabic 1 (*phonol*)   Said of a [+]consonant that can be used alone as a syllable (/l/ in *bottle*). 166 2 (*graph*)   Said of a writing system in which the symbols represent [+]syllables. 203

syllabification (*phonol*)   The division of a [+]word into [+]syllables. 166

syllable (*phonol*)   An element of speech that acts as a unit of [+]rhythm, consisting of a [+]vowel, [+]syllabic[1], or vowel/[+]consonant combination. 164

syllable-timed (*phonol*)   Said of languages in which the [+]syllables occur at regular time intervals; cf. [+]isochrony. 171

symbol   *see* **sign**[1,2]

syn(a)esthesia (*sem*)   A direct association between [+]form[1] and meaning (*sl-* in *slimy, slug*, etc.). 176

synchronic (*ling*)   Said of an approach that studies language at a theoretical 'point' in time; contrasts with **diachronic**. 411

syncope (*hist*)   The loss of sounds or letters from the middle of a word (*bo'sun*). 330

syncretism (*hist*)   The merging of [+]forms[2] originally distinguished by [+]inflection[1]. 330

syndeton (*gram*)   The use of [+]conjunctions to link constructions. 95

synonym (*sem*)   A word that has the same meaning (in a particular [+]context[1]) as another word (*a nice range/selection of flowers*). 105

syntactic (*gram*)   Pertaining to [+]syntax. 94

syntactics   *see* **syntax**

syntagm(a) (*gram*)   A string of elements forming a unit in [+]syntax. 94

syntagmatic (*ling*)   Said of the linear relationship between elements in a word or construction. 411

syntax (*gram*)   1 The study of [+]word combinations; also, **syntactics**; cf. [+]morphology. 2 The study of [+]sentence structure (including word structure). 94

synthesis   *see* **speech synthesis**

synthetic 1 *see* **inflecting language** 2 *see* **analytic**[2]

systematic phonology (*phonol*)   An approach that represents the speaker's knowledge of the [+]phonological relations between words (*telegraph/telegraphy*, etc.). 162

systemic (*ling*)   Said of an approach that analyses language into systems of [+]contrasts, and studies their functional use in social communication. 411

T (*socio*)   Said of a linguistic form (esp. a [+]pronoun) used to express social closeness or familiarity; cf. [+]V. 45

taboo (*gen*)   Said of a linguistic form whose use is avoided in a society. 61

tachistoscope (*psycho*)   A device used in reading research that gives a very brief exposure to a visual image, e.g. a letter. 210

tachygraphy (*graph*)   Shorthand writing. 208

tactics (*ling*)   The systematic arrangements of linguistic units in linear sequence. 82

tag (*gram*)   An element attached to the end of an utterance, esp. a **tag question** (*...isn't it?*). 173

tagmeme (*gram*)   A grammatical unit that relates an item's [+]form[1] and [+]syntactic [+]function[1]; the central notion in **tagmemic** analysis. 412

tambre, tamber   *see* **timbre**

tap (*phonet*)   A [+]consonant made by a single rapid tongue contact against the roof of the mouth (as sometimes heard in the /t/ of *writer*). 168

target 1 (*phonet*)   The theoretical position adopted by the [+]vocal organs during the [+]articulation of a sound. 137 2 (*app*)   The language or [+]variety that is the goal of an activity, e.g. into which a [+]translation is being made. 346

tautology (*gen*)   An unnecessary repetition of a word or idea. 390

taxonomic (*ling*)   Said of a linguistic approach that is mainly concerned with classification. 412

technography (*graph*)   A writing system devised for a specialized field. 196

teknonymic (*sem*)   A parent's name that derives from that of a child. 112

telegrammatic/telegraphic (*psycho*)   Said of speech that omits [+]function words and [+]dependent [+]content words (*Man kick ball*). 245

telescoped word   *see* **blend**

telestich (*gen*)   An [+]acrostic based on the last letters of words or lines. 64

teletex(t) (*gen*)   The transmission of [+]graphic data from a central source to a television screen. 195

telic (*gram*)   Said of a [+]verb when the activity has a clear terminal point (*kick*); contrasts with **atelic** verbs (*play*). 93

tempo (*phonol*)   Relative rate of speech. 171

tense 1 (*gram*)   A change in the [+]form[2] of a [+]verb to mark the time at which an action takes place (past, present, etc.). 93 2 *see* **tension**

tension (*phonet*)   The muscular force used in making a sound, analysed as strong (**tense**), weak (**lax**), etc. 159

tetrameter/tetrametre (*poet*)   A line of verse containing four units of rhythm ([+]foot). 74

text (*ling*)   A stretch of spoken or written language with a definable communicative function (news report, poem, road sign, etc.). 116

textlinguistics (*ling*)   The study of the linguistic [+]structure[1] of [+]texts. 116

textual function (*ling*)   The use of language to identify ⁺texts. 119

thematization (*ling*)   Moving an element to the front of a sentence, to act as the ⁺theme (*Smith his name is*); also, **topicalization**. 120

theme (*ling*)   The element at the beginning of a sentence that expresses what is being talked about (**The cat** *was in the garden*); cf. ⁺rheme. 120

theography (*styl*)   The study of the language people use to talk about God. 51

thesaurus (*gen*)   A book of words grouped on the basis of their meaning. 104

third person   *see* **person**

timbre (*phonet*)   A sound's tonal quality, or 'colour', which differentiates sounds of the same ⁺pitch, ⁺loudness, and ⁺duration. 133

tip   *see* **apex**

tmesis (*rhet*)   The insertion of a word or phrase within another (*absobloominglutely*). 70

tone   **1** (*phonol*)   The distinctive ⁺pitch level of a ⁺syllable. 171   **2** *see* **pure tone**

tone group/unit (*phonol*)   A distinctive sequence (or ⁺contour¹) of ⁺tones¹ in an utterance. 171

tone language (*ling*)   A language in which word meanings or ⁺grammatical¹ ⁺contrasts are conveyed by variations in ⁺tone. 174

toneme (*phonol*)   A ⁺contrastive ⁺tone¹. 174

tonetics (*phonet*)   The study of the ⁺phonetic properties of ⁺tones¹. 172

tone unit   *see* **tone group**

tonic   *see* **nucleus**

tonicity (*phonol*)   The placement of ⁺nuclear syllables in an utterance. 173

topic (*ling*)   The subject about which something is said (*The pen is red*); also, **given** information; cf. ⁺comment. 94

topicalization   *see* **thematization**

toponomasiology, toponomastics, toponomatology *see* **toponymy**

toponymy (*gen*)   The study of place names. 112

trachea (*anat*)   The passage between lungs and ⁺larynx. 124

trade language (*socio*)   A ⁺pidgin used to facilitate communication while trading. 336

traditional (*gram*)   Said of the attitudes and analyses found in language studies that antedate ⁺linguistic science. 3

transcription (*phonet*)   A method of writing speech sounds in a systematic and consistent way, from a particular point of view (⁺phonetic/⁺phonemic transcription, ⁺narrow/⁺broad); also, **notation**, **script**. 160

transfer (*app*)   The influence of a foreign learner's ⁺mother tongue upon the ⁺target² language; **positive transfer** facilitates learning, whereas **negative transfer** (**interference**) hinders it. 374

transform(ation) (*ling*)   A ⁺formal¹ linguistic operation (a **transformational rule**) that shows a correspondence between two structures, e.g. active and passive ⁺voice² sentences. 97

tranformational grammar (*ling*)   A ⁺grammar² that uses ⁺transformations. 413

transition   **1** (*phonol*)   The way adjacent sounds are linked (⁺glide, ⁺liaison, etc.). 166   **2** (*acou*) An acoustic change reflecting the movement of the ⁺vocal organs towards or away from a ⁺consonant (esp. ⁺plosive) ⁺articulation. 137   **3** (*socio*)   Said of a geographical region (a **transition area**) where there is no clear boundary between adjacent ⁺dialects. 28

transitive (*gram*)   Said of a ⁺verb taking a ⁺direct object (*She saw a dog*); cf. ⁺intransitive. 93

translation (*gen*)   **1** Conversion from one language into another.   **2** Conversion of written texts from one language into another; cf. ⁺interpret. 346

translative (*gram*)   An ⁺inflection¹ that typically expresses the meaning of change from one place to another. 93

transliteration (*gen*)   Conversion of one writing system into another. 348

tree diagram (*gram*)   A diagram used in ⁺generative grammar to show the hierarchical ⁺structure¹ of a ⁺sentence. 96

tremor (*clin*)   Involuntary shaking of the voice. 19

trial (*gram*)   A grammatical contrast of ⁺number in some languages, referring to 'three of'. 92

trigraph (*graph*)   Three written symbols representing one speech sound (*manoeuvre*). 215

trill (*phonet*)   A ⁺consonant made by the rapid tapping of one ⁺vocal organ against another (**trilled** /r/); also, **roll**. 159

trimeter (*poet*)   A line of verse containing three units of rhythm (⁺foot). 74

triphthong (*phonet*)   A ⁺vowel¹ containing three distinct qualities (*tower* /taʊə/). 156

trisyllable (*phonol*)   A word containing three ⁺syllables. 166

trivium (*gen*)   The medieval study of grammar, rhetoric, and logic. 410

trochee (*poet*)   A unit of rhythm in poetic ⁺metre, consisting of a ⁺stressed followed by an unstressed ⁺syllable. 74

trope (*rhet*)   A ⁺figurative effect, e.g. ⁺metaphor, that changes the meaning of language; cf. ⁺scheme. 70

turn (*prag*)   A single contribution of a speaker to a conversation (a **conversational turn**). 118

typography (*graph*)   The study of the graphic features of the printed page. 192

typological linguistics (*ling*)   The study of the structural similarities among languages, regardless of their history. 84

ultimate constituent   *see* **constituent**

umlaut (*hist*)   A ⁺sound change in which a ⁺vowel¹ is influenced by the vowel in the following ⁺syllable (**gosi* → *geese*). 330

uncial (*graph*)   A form of writing consisting of large, rounded letters. 188

uncountable   *see* **countable**

underextension (*psycho*)   The use of a word to refer to only part of its normal meaning, e.g. a child's use of *shoe* to mean only 'own shoe'. 246

underlying structure   *see* **deep grammar/structure**

ungrammatical   *see* **grammatical**

unilingual   *see* **monolingual**

universal (*ling*)   A property found in the analysis of all languages; cf. ⁺formal/⁺substantive universal. 84

universal grammar (*ling*)   A ⁺grammar² specifying the possible form a language's grammar can take. 84

univocalic (*gen*)   A written composition that uses only one ⁺vowel². 65

unmarked   *see* **marked**

unproductive (*ling*)   Said of a linguistic feature that is no longer used in the creation of new forms (the -*th* of *length, width*, etc.). 90

unrounded   *see* **rounding**

unstressed   *see* **stress**

unvoiced   *see* **voiceless**

urban dialectology (*socio*)   The study of the speech patterns used within a modern city community. 32

usage (*gen*)   The speech and writing habits of a community, esp. when there is a choice between alternative forms (**divided usage**). 2

utterance (*ling*)   A physically identifiable stretch of speech lacking any grammatical definition; cf. ⁺sentence. 94

uvula (*anat*)   The small lobe hanging from the bottom of the soft ⁺palate. 130

uvular (*phonet*)   Said of a ⁺consonant made by the ⁺back of the tongue against the uvula ([ʀ]). 157

V (*socio*)   Said of a linguistic ⁺form² (esp. a ⁺pronoun) used to express politeness or distance; cf. ⁺T. 45

valency (*gram*)   The number and type of bonds that ⁺syntactic elements may form with each other. 412

variable rule (*socio*)   A ⁺rule¹ that specifies the ⁺extralinguistic conditions governing the use of a linguistic feature (or variable). 32, 334

variable word (*gram*)   A ⁺word that expresses ⁺grammatical¹ relationships by changing its ⁺form² (*walk/walks/walking*); cf. ⁺invariable word. 91

variant (*ling*)   A linguistic ⁺form² that is one of a set of alternatives in a given ⁺context¹ (E. plural /s/, /z/, /ɪz/). 90

variety (*socio*)   A situationally distinctive system of linguistic expression (legal, formal, etc.). 48

velar (*phonet*)   Said of ⁺consonants made by the ⁺back of the tongue against the soft ⁺palate, or **velum** ([k]). 157

velaric (*phonet*)   Said of sounds, e.g. ⁺clicks, when the air has been set in motion by a ⁺closure at the soft ⁺palate. 126

velarization (*phonet*)   An ⁺articulation in which the tongue moves towards the soft ⁺palate while another sound is being made. 158

velopharyngeal (*anat*)   Said of the area between the soft ⁺palate and the back wall of the ⁺pharynx, which separates oral and nasal ⁺cavities. 130

velum   *see* **palate**

ventricular folds (*anat*)   Bands of tissue that lie above the ⁺vocal folds. 128

verb (*gram*)   A ⁺word class displaying such contrasts as ⁺tense¹, ⁺aspect, ⁺voice², ⁺mood, and typically used to express an action, event, or state (*run, know, want*). 91

verbal group   *see* **verb phrase**

verb phrase (*gram*)   **1** A group of words that have the same grammatical function as a single ⁺verb (*has been running*); also, **verbal group**. 95   **2** In ⁺generative grammar, the whole of a sentence apart from the first ⁺noun phrase. 96

verbless (*gram*)   A construction that omits a ⁺verb (*Although angry, they...*). 95

vernacular (*socio*)   The indigenous language or ⁺dialect of a community. 35

viewdata (*gen*)   The interactive transmission of data between a central source and a local television set. 195

vocal abuse (*clin*)   Overuse of the voice, resulting in a ⁺voice disorder. 278

vocal folds (*phonet*)   Two muscular folds in the ⁺larynx that vibrate as a source of sound; also known as **vocal cords/lips/bands**. 128

vocalic (*phonet*)   Pertaining to a ⁺vowel¹. 153

vocalization (*phonet*)   Any sound or utterance produced by the ⁺vocal organs. 124

vocal nodules   *see* **nodules**

vocal organs (*phonet*)   The parts of the body involved in the production of speech sounds. 124

vocal tract (*phonet*)   The whole of the air passage above the ⁺larynx. 124

vocative (*gram*)   A form (esp. a ⁺noun) used to address a person, animal, etc. (*Excuse me, sir*); in some languages identified by an ⁺inflection¹. 93

vocoid (*phonet*)   A speech sound lacking ⁺closure or audible friction; includes ⁺vowels¹ and vowel-like sounds ([l], [j]). 153

voice   **1** (*phonet*)   The auditory result of ⁺vocal fold vibration (**voiced** sounds, [b], [z], [e]); cf.

⁺voiceless, ⁺devoiced. 128   **2** (*gram*)   A grammatical system varying the relationship between ⁺subject and ⁺object of the ⁺verb, esp. contrasting **active** and **passive** voices (*The cat saw the dog* vs *The dog was seen by the cat*). 93

voiced   *see* **voice**¹

voice disorder (*clin*)   An involuntary, abnormal ⁺voice quality¹ that interferes with communication; cf. ⁺dysphonia. 278

voiceless (*phonet*)   Said of sounds made without ⁺vocal fold vibration ([f]), [p]); also, **unvoiced**. 152

voice mutation (*phonet*)   The development of an adult ⁺voice quality¹ after puberty; also, **breaking**. 19

voice onset time (*phonet*)   The point when ⁺vocal fold vibration starts relative to the release of a ⁺closure. 137

voiceprint (*phonet*)   A ⁺spectrographic display of the acoustic structure of a person's voice. 20

voice quality (*phonet*)   **1** The permanent, background, person-identifying feature of speech. 129   **2** A specific tone of voice. 171

volume   *see* **loudness**

vowel (*phonet, phonol*)   **1** A sound made without ⁺closure or audible friction, which can function as the centre of a ⁺syllable ([e], [i]). 153   **2** (*graph*) The analogous sign in a writing system. 204

wave   *see* **sound wave**

waveform (*acou*)   A graph of the movement of air particles in a ⁺sound wave. 132

wavelength (*acou*)   The distance travelled by a ⁺sound wave during a single ⁺cycle of vibration. 133

weak form (*phonol*)   The ⁺unstressed form of a ⁺word in connected speech (*of* → [ə] in *cup of tea*). 166

weak verb (*gram*)   A ⁺verb that forms its past ⁺tense¹ by adding an ⁺inflection¹ (*walk* → *walked*); cf. ⁺strong verb. 90

well formed (*ling*)   Said of a sentence that can be ⁺generated by the ⁺rules¹ of a ⁺grammar²; cf. ⁺ill formed. 88

Wernicke's area (*anat*)   An area of the brain that controls language ⁺comprehension; cf. ⁺Broca's area. 262

whisper (*phonet*)   Speech produced without ⁺vocal fold vibration. 128

whistled speech (*ling*)   A form of communication in which whistling substitutes for the ⁺tones¹ of normal speech. 404

whole word   *see* **look-and-say**

widening (*phonet*)   Enlarging the ⁺pharynx to produce a different ⁺vowel¹ quality. 153

word (*gram*)   The smallest unit of ⁺grammar that can stand alone as a complete utterance, separated by spaces in written language and potentially by pauses in speech. 91

word blindness   *see* **dyslexia**

word class (*gram*)   A set of words that display the same ⁺formal¹ properties, esp. their ⁺inflections¹ and ⁺distribution (⁺verb, ⁺noun, etc.); also known as **part of speech**. 91

word ending (*gram*)   An ⁺inflection¹ used at the end of a word (*horses, walking*). 90

word-finding problem (*clin*)   Inability to retrieve a desired word, symptomatic of ⁺aphasia. 273

word formation (*gram*)   The process of creating words out of sequences of ⁺morphemes. 90

word order (*gram*)   The sequential arrangement of ⁺words in a language. 98

x height (*graph*)   The height of the small letter *x*. 192

zero (*ling*)   An abstract unit used in an analysis that has no physical realization in speech. 90

zoösemiotics (*semiot*)   The study of the properties of animal communication. 402

II SPECIAL SYMBOLS AND ABBREVIATIONS

Non-phonetic symbols and abbreviations

All non-phonetic symbols and abbreviations used in this encyclopedia are listed in alphabetical order below. Page references are given when different sources cited use the same symbol with different meanings.

a	adjective (p. 108)
a	article (p. 86)
A	adverbial
adj	adjective
adv	adverb
ae	affected entity
AL	artificial language
ALPAC	Automatic Language Processing Advisory Committee
ALPS	Automated Language Processing Systems
Ameslan	American Sign Language
Anat	anatomy usage
AS	Anglo-Saxon
ASL	American Sign Language
at	attribute of
Aux	auxiliary
BASIC	British American Scientific International Commercial
BBC	British Broadcasting Corporation
BEV	Black English Vernacular
C	complement (p. 95)
C	sound velocity (p. 133)
C	consonant (p. 152)
CALL	computer-assisted language learning
CB	citizen band
CD	subordinate *that*
CHILDES	Child Language Data Exchange System
co	containment of
cps	cycles per second
CSL	Chinese Sign Language
CULT	Chinese University Language Translator
D	past tense
DAF	delayed auditory feedback
dB	decibel
DET	determiner
dez	designator
E	extrinsic muscles
-ed	past tense form
EEG	electroencephalography
EMG	electromyography
-en	past participle form
EURALEX	European Association for Lexicography
EURODICAUTOM	European Automatic Dictionary
excl	exclusive pronoun
EXT	exterior
f	feminine
F	feedback (p. 118)
F	frequency (p. 133)
F_0	fundamental frequency
F_1	first formant

F_2	second formant
F_x	fundamental frequency
FL	foreign language
FLL	foreign-language learning
FLT	foreign-language teaching
FN	first name
fr	from
Fr	French
G	*-ing* form of verb
I	initiating utterance (p. 118)
I	intrinsic muscles (p. 131)
ICAME	International Computer Archive of Modern English
incl	inclusive pronoun
INT	interior
IPA	International Phonetic Alphabet
H	high variety
Hz	hertz
IC	immediate constituent
ita	initial teaching alphabet
L	low variety (p. 43)
L	Latin (p. 108)
L_x	laryngeal waveform
L1	first language
L2	second language
L3	third language
LAD	language-acquisition device
LARSP	Language Assessment, Remediation, and Screening Procedure
LL	Late Latin
l/m	litres per minute
LN	last name
lo	location of
m	masculine
m	million
MLU	mean length of utterance
msec	milliseconds
MT	machine translation
n	noun
N	noun (p. 96)
N	nasal feature (p. 165)
N	past participle (p. 415)
NLP	natural language processing
Non-SLIP	Non-speech Language Initiation Program
NP	noun phrase (p. 96)
NP	proper noun (p. 415)
O	object
OED	Oxford English Dictionary
p	pronoun
P	pupil (p. 250)
P	phrase (p. 96)
Pathol	pathology usage
PGSS	Paget-Gorman Sign System
pl	plural

POV	point of view
PSG	phrase structure grammar
pu	purpose of
qu	quantity of
r	spoken response
R	non-linguistic response (p. 101)
R	response utterance (p. 118)
RA	personal pronoun, subject
RB	personal pronoun, object
RLP	Roman Lipi Parishad
RP	received pronunciation
s	speech stimulus (p. 101)
s	substantive (p. 358)
S	subject (p. 95)
S	non-linguistic stimulus (p. 101)
sg	singular
sig	signation
SL	second language
sp	specification of
SPL	sound pressure level
st	state of
su	substance of
T	*tu* (familiar) pronoun (p. 45)
T	teacher (p. 250)
tab	tabula
TG	transformational grammar
TLN	title with last name
UPSID	University of California, Los Angeles, Phonological Segment Inventory Database
v	verb
V	*vos* (polite) pronoun (p. 45)
V	verb (p. 95)
V	vowel (p. 152)
VA	main verb
VB	verb *be*
VH	verb *have*
VHF	very high frequency
VOT	voice onset time
VP	verb phrase
wph	words per hour
X	invented category
λ	wavelength
?	usage of doubtful acceptability/grammaticality
*	unacceptable or ungrammatical usage
( )	enclose optional grammatical elements (p. 97)
( )	enclose linguistic variables (p. 32)
+	semantic component applicable
–	semantic component inapplicable
0	base form of verb
5	*was* form of be
§	section cross-reference

Phonetic symbols

This list comprises all the phonetic symbols illustrated in this book, with the addition of several variant forms.

a open front unrounded vowel
æ front unrounded vowel between mid-open and open
ɐ central unrounded vowel between mid-open and open
ɑ open back unrounded vowel
ɒ open back rounded vowel
b voiced bilabial plosive
ƀ voiced bilabial fricative (esp. US)
ɓ bilabial implosive
bbb voiced bilabial trill
ʙ voiced lingualabial plosive
c voiceless palatal plosive
č voiceless palato-alveolar affricate (esp. US)
ç voiceless palatal fricative
ɕ voiceless alveolo-palatal fricative
d voiced alveolar plosive
đ voiced alveolar fricative (esp. US)
ɖ voiced retroflex plosive
ɗ alveolar implosive
ʤ voiced palato-alveolar affricate
ɽ voiced alveolar tap
e mid-close front unrounded vowel
ə or ɜ central unrounded vowel
ɚ or ɝ r-coloured central vowel
ɵ central rounded vowel
f voiceless labio-dental fricative
g voiced velar plosive
ɣ voiced velar fricative (esp. US)
ɠ velar implosive
ɢ voiced uvular plosive
h voiceless glottal fricative
ħ voiceless pharyngeal fricative
ɦ voiced glottal fricative
ɧ simultaneous ɦ and x
i close front unrounded vowel
ɨ close central unrounded vowel
ɪ or ɩ central front unrounded vowel between mid-close and close
j voiced palatal fricative/approximant
j or ɟ voiced palatal plosive
ǰ voiced palato-alveolar affricate (esp. US)
k voiceless velar plosive
l voiced lateral approximant
ɬ voiceless lateral fricative (esp. US)
ɫ voiceless lateral fricative
ɮ voiced lateral fricative
ɭ voiced retroflex lateral
ɺ voiced alveolar lateral flap
ʟ voiced lingualabial lateral
m voiced bilabial nasal
ɱ voiced labio-dental nasal
м voiced lingualabial nasal
n voiced alveolar nasal
ñ voiced palatal nasal (esp. US)
ɳ voiced retroflex nasal
ɲ voiced palatal nasal
ŋ voiced velar nasal
ɴ voiced uvular nasal
o mid-close back rounded vowel
ø mid-close front rounded vowel
œ mid-open front rounded vowel
Œ open front rounded vowel
ɔ mid-open back rounded vowel

p voiceless bilabial plosive
ppp voiceless bilabial trill
ƥ voiceless lingualabial plosive
q voiceless uvular plosive
r voiced alveolar trill
ɾ voiced alveolar tap/flap
ɹ voiced postalveolar fricative
ɻ voiced retroflex tap/flap
ɻ voiced retroflex approximant
ɽ voiced alveolar fricative trill
ʀ voiced uvular trill/tap/flap
ʁ voiced uvular fricative
s voiceless alveolar fricative
š voiceless palato-alveolar fricative (esp. US)
ʂ voiceless retroflex fricative
t voiceless alveolar plosive
ʈ voiceless retroflex plosive
ʧ voiceless palato-alveolar affricate
u close back rounded vowel
ʉ close central rounded vowel
ɯ close back unrounded vowel
u or ɷ or ʊ centralized back rounded vowel between mid-close and close
v voiced labio-dental fricative
ʋ voiced labio-dental approximant
ʌ mid-open back unrounded vowel
w voiced labio-velar approximant
ʍ voiceless labio-velar fricative
x voiceless velar fricative
y close front rounded vowel
y voiced palatal fricative/approximant (esp. US)
ʏ centralized front rounded vowel between mid-close and close
z voiced alveolar fricative
ž voiced palato-alveolar fricative (esp. US)
ʐ voiced retroflex fricative
ʑ voiced alveolo-palatal fricative
β voiced bilabial fricative
ɣ voiced velar fricative
ɛ mid-open front unrounded vowel
θ voiceless dental fricative
ð voiced dental fricative
ʎ voiced palatal lateral
ɸ voiceless bilabial fricative
χ voiceless uvular fricative
ʃ voiceless palato-alveolar fricative
ʄ palatalized voiceless palato-alveolar fricative
ʒ voiced palato-alveolar fricative
ʓ palatalized voiced palato-alveolar fricative
ɥ voiced labio-palatal approximant
ɰ voiced velar approximant
ʕ voiced pharyngeal fricative
ʔ or ? glottal plosive
ʘ bilabial click
ǀ dental click
ǃ postalveolar click
ǁ lateral click
ɤ mid-close back unrounded vowel

Diacritic and other conventions

Example of use

○ uncertain segment — m̃
← pulmonic ingressive — s̼
̥ voiceless — b̥
̬ voiced — s̬
ʼ ejective — pʼ
ʰ aspirated — pʰ
⁼ unaspirated — p⁼
.. breathy-voiced/murmured — b̤
◌̪ dental — t̪
◌ bidental — h̪
, or . retroflex — ṭ t.
◌ reverse labiodental — b̺
̫ labialized — t̫
ʸ or ⱼ palatalized — tʸ tⱼ tⁱ
or ⁱ
. or ~ velarized/pharyngealized — ɫ ł
~ laryngealized — b̰
ꟳ nasal fricative — mꟳ
„ tense articulation — f„
‿ lax articulation — m̺
◡ very short articulation — m̆
⁓ reiterated articulation — p-p-p
¬ non-audible release — b¬
( ) enclose a mouthed articulation — (f)
ˌ syllabic — n̩
⌢ or ⌣ simultaneous — k͡p
, or . raised — ẹ or e̝
, or . lowered — ẹ or e̞
+ advanced — u+ or u̟
- retracted — i̱ i-
◌̈ centralized — ë
~ nasalized — ã
ˡ or ʶ r-coloured — oˡ oʶ
: long — iː
· half-long — iˑ
◡ non-syllabic — ŭ
ₒ or ʷ rounding — f̫ fʷ
˒ more rounded — ɔ˒
˓ less rounded — y˓
ˈ primary stress — ˈma
ˌ secondary stress — ˌma
˜ high level tone — ˉma
_ low level tone — ˍma
ˊ high rising tone — ˊma
ˏ low rising tone — ˏma
ˋ high falling tone — ˋma
ˎ low falling tone — ˎma
ˆ rising-falling tone — ˆma
ˇ falling-rising tone — ˇma
. brief pause — .
- short pause — -
- - long pause — - -
- - - extra-long pause — - - -
/ or | or ‖ tone-unit boundary
or #
↑ step-up in pitch
° or | onset of pitch movement
/ boundary of foot
1 high pitch level
2 mid-high pitch level
3 mid-low pitch level
4 low pitch level
[ ] enclose phonetic units (phones or distinctive features)
/ / enclose phonological units (phonemes)

III TABLE OF THE WORLD'S LANGUAGES

Nearly 1,000 living languages are listed in alphabetical order in the following pages, along with information about the language family they belong to, where they are mainly spoken, and approximately how many speakers there are.

Only languages with over 100,000 speakers as a first language have been included, and only the main pidgins and creoles (see further, p. 340). All numbers are approximations, bearing in mind the problems of speaker-counting discussed in §48; estimates vary enormously in certain parts of the world. Regional varieties of major languages are not separately counted, even in cases where the differences are considerable: the totals in this Appendix will therefore sometimes be larger than those given in the earlier part of the book, where the focus was often on variety difference. If a language has widespread use as a second language, the estimated number of speakers is given in parenthesis.

Figures are given in thousands: 100 = 100,000 etc. Where millions of speakers are involved, the abbreviation *m* is used: 3m = 3 million, etc.

The level of classification used in specifying language families reflects the discussion in the body of the text (§§51–3). It should be noted that in some cases (mainly in Africa and the Americas) a very general classification is used –

far more abstract than in other cases (such as Indo-European). The question of levels is reviewed on p. 294.

The countries or areas listed are those where a language is mainly spoken. It is impracticable to list minority usage, which is often scattered over a wide area. Similarly, it is not possible to list all the alternative names given to some languages (see §47). For further details, and in all cases of omission from the following table, reference should be made to Bright (1992) or Grimes (1992): see Appendix IV.

Abbreviations

C	Central
E	East
I./Is.	Island(s)
L	Lake
N	North
R	River
Rep.	Republic
S	South
W	West

Name	Where spoken	Language family	How many (000)
Abron	Ghana, Côte d'Ivoire	Niger-Congo (Kwa)	572
Abung	Indonesia	Austronesian	500
Aceh	Indonesia	Austronesian	2.9m
Acholi (Akoli)	Uganda, Sudan	Nilo-Saharan	674
Adhola	Uganda, Kenya	Nilo-Saharan	235
Adi	India	Sino-Tibetan (Tibeto-Burman)	470
Adyghe (Adygei)	Russia, Middle East	Caucasian	260
Afar (Danakil)	Eritrea, Ethiopia, Djibouti	Afro-Asiatic (Cushitic)	700
Afrikaans	South Africa, Namibia	Indo-European (Germanic)	6m
Aimaq	Afghanisrtan, Iran	Indo-European (Iranian)	800
Aja-Gbe	Benin, Togo	Niger-Congo (Kwa)	250
Akan (Twi, Fante, Ashanti)	Ghana, Côte d'Ivoire	Niger-Congo (Kwa)	5.7m
Akoli *see* Acholi			
Akha	China, SE Asia	Sino-Tibetan (Tibeto-Burman)	260
Aklanon	Philippines	Austronesian	350
Albanian	Albania, Balkans	Indo-European (Albanian)	6m
Alur	Zaire, Uganda, Sudan	Nilo-Saharan	780
Amharic	Ethiopia	Afro-Asiatic (Semitic)	14m
Amis	Taiwan	Austronesian	130
Anaang	Nigeria	Niger-Congo (Benue-Congo)	246
Anga	India	Indo-European (Indo-Aryan)	424
Angas	Nigeria	Afro-Asiatic (Chadic)	100
Anglo-Romani	UK, N America	Indo-European (Germanic)	125
Anyin	Côte d'Ivoire, Ghana	Niger-Congo (Kwa)	432
Arabic	N Africa, Middle East, Arabian Peninsula	Afro-Asiatic (Semitic)	180m
Arakanese	Myanmar, Bangladesh	Sino-Tibetan (Tibeto-Burman)	650
Aramaic (Modern)	Middle East	Afro-Asiatic (Semitic)	167
Armenian	Armenia, Middle East	Indo-European (Armenian)	5.5m
Ashanti *see* Akan			
Assamese	India, Bangladesh	Indo-European (Indo-Aryan)	20m
Asu	Tanzania	Niger-Congo (Bantu)	315
Attié	Côte d'Ivoire	Niger-Congo (Kwa)	222

Name	Where spoken	Language family	How many (000)
Atuence	China	Sino-Tibetan (Tibeto-Burman)	520
Avar	Russia, Azerbaijan	Caucasian	483
Awadhi	India, Nepal	Indo-European (Indo-Aryan)	20.3
Awutu	Ghana	Niger-Congo (Kwa)	100
Aymará	Bolivia, Peru	South American (Jaqi)	2.1m
Azande *see* Zande			
Azerbaijani (Azeri)	Azerbaijan, Russia, Iraq	Altaic (Turkic)	14.1m
Aztec *see* Nahua(tl)			
Badaga	S India	Dravidian	105
Bade	Nigeria	Afro-Asiatic (Chadic)	100
Bagheli	India, Nepal	Indo-European (Indo-Aryan)	231
Bagri	India	Indo-European (Indo-Aryan)	1.2
Bahamas Creole English	Bahamas	Indo-European (Germanic)	225
Bahasa Indonesia *see* Indonesian			
Bai	China	Sino-Tibetan (Tibeto-Burman)	900
Balanta	Guinea-Bissau, Senegal	Niger-Congo (Adamawa-Ubangi)	304
Balinese	Indonesia (Bali)	Austronesian	3.8m
Balochi (Baluchi)	Pakistan, India	Indo-European (Iranian)	5.2m
Balti	Pakistan, India	Sino-Tibetan (Tibeto-Burman)	400
Bambara	W Africa	Niger-Congo (Mande)	1.5m
Bamendjou	Cameroon	Niger-Congo (Benue-Congo)	100
Bamun (Bamoun)	Cameroon	Niger-Congo (Benue-Congo)	215
Banda	Central Arab Rep., Sudan	Niger-Congo (Adamawa-Ubangi)	1m
Bandi	Guinea, Liberia	Niger-Congo (Mande)	126
Bangala	Zaire, Central Arab Rep.	Niger-Congo (Bantu)	3.5m
Bangaru	India	Indo-European (Indo-Aryan)	4m
Banggai	Indonesia	Austronesian	112
Bangubangu	Zaire	Niger-Congo (Bantu)	120

Name	Where spoken	Language family	How many (000)
Banjar	Indonesia, Malaysia	Austronesian	2.1m
Bareli	India	Indo-European (Indo-Aryan)	230
Bari	Sudan, Uganda, Zaire	Nilo-Saharan	340
Bariba	Benin, Nigeria	Niger-Congo (Gur)	250
Basaa	Cameroon	Niger-Congo (Bantu)	230
Bashkir	Russia	Altaic (Turkic)	1m
Basketto	Ethiopia	Afro-Asiatic (Omotic)	100
Basque	SW France, NW Spain	Isolate	700
Bassa	Liberia, Sierra Leone	Niger-Congo (Kru)	291
Batak	Indonesia	Austronesian	5.8m
Bathudi	India	Isolate	105
Baule	Côte d'Ivoire	Niger-Congo (Kwa)	1.5m
Beja	Sudan, Eritrea	Afro-Asiatic (Cushitic)	980
Belize Creole English	Belize	Indo-European (Germanic)	114
Belorussian	Belarus, Poland	Indo-European (Slavic)	7.2m
Bemba	Zambia, Zaire, Tanzania	Niger-Congo (Bantu)	1.9m
Bembe	Zaire	Niger-Congo (Bantu)	252
Bena	Tanzania	Niger-Congo (Bantu)	490
Bengali	Bangladesh, India	Indo-European (Indo-Aryan)	162m
Bera	Zaire	Niger-Congo (Bantu)	100
Bété	Côte d'Ivoire	Niger-Congo (Kru)	500
Bhatri	India	Indo-European (Indo-Aryan)	104
Bhilala	India	Indo-European (Indo-Aryan)	247
Bhili	India	Indo-European (Indo-Aryan)	1.6m
Bhojpuri	India, Nepal	Indo-European (Indo-Aryan)	41m
Bhumij	India	Austro-Asiatic (Munda)	220
Bicolano	Philippines	Austronesian	3.3m
Bilin	Eritrea	Afro-Asiatic (Cushitic)	105
Bima	Indonesia	Austronesian	500
Bingkokak	Indonesia	Isolate	150
Binukid	Philippines	Austronesian	100
Birom	Nigeria	Niger-Congo (Benue-Congo)	200
Bissa	Burkina Faso, Ghana, Côte d'Ivoire	Niger-Congo (Mande)	395
Biyo	China	Sino-Tibetan (Tibeto-Burman)	100
Blaan	Philippines	Austronesian	200
Bobo Fing	Burkina Faso, Mali	Niger-Congo (Mande)	160
Bodo	India, Nepal	Sino-Tibetan (Tibeto-Burman)	1m
Boomu	Mali, Burkina Faso	Niger-Congo (Gur)	300
Brahui	Pakistan, Afghanistan, Iran	Dravidian	1.7m
Braj Bhasha	India	Indo-European (Indo-Aryan)	11.5m
Breton	France (Brittany)	Indo-European (Celtic)	500
Brunei	Brunei, Malaysia	Austronesian	140
Budza	Zaire	Niger-Congo (Bantu)	226
Bugis	Indonesia	Austronesian	2.9m
Bukusu	Kenya	Niger-Congo (Bantu)	565
Bulgarian	Bulgaria and nearby areas	Indo-European (Slavic)	9m
Buli	Ghana, Burkina Faso	Niger-Congo (Gur)	157
Bulu	Cameroon	Niger-Congo (Bantu)	174
Bundeli	India	Indo-European (Indo-Aryan)	8m
Bura	Nigeria	Afro-Asiatic (Chadic)	250
Buriat	Russia	Altaic (Mongolian)	430
Burmese	Myanmar	Sino-Tibetan (Tibeto-Burman)	22m

Name	Where spoken	Language family	How many (000)
Busa-Boko	Benin, Nigeria	Niger-Congo (Mande)	100
Buyi	China	Tai	2m
Bwamu	Burkina Faso, Mali	Niger-Congo (Gur)	150
Cajun French	USA	Indo-European (Romance)	1m
Cakchiquel	Guatemala	Meso-American Indian (Mayan)	445
Cambodian *see* **Khmer**			
Cao Lan	Vietnam, China	Tai	100
Capiznon	Philippines	Austronesian	446
Carib, Black	C America	South American (Arawakan)	100
Caribbean Hindi	Suriname, Trinidad	Indo-European (Indo-Aryan)	150
Catalan	NE Spain, France (Rousillon), Andorra	Indo-European (Romance)	8.8m
Cebaara	Côte d'Ivoire	Niger-Congo (Gur)	459
Cebuano (Sebuano)	Philippines	Austronesian	12m
Chagga	Tanzania	Niger-Congo (Bantu)	800
Chakma	India, Bangladesh	Indo-European (Indo-Aryan)	513
Chaldean	Iraq	Afro-Asiatic (Semitic)	130
Cham	Cambodia, Vietnam, Malaysia	Austronesian	235
Chattisgarhi	India	Indo-European (Indo-Aryan)	6.7m
Chaungtha	Myanmar	Sino-Tibetan (Tibeto-Burman)	122
Chavacano	Philippines	Indo-European (Romance)	280
Chechen	Russia, Kazakhstan	Caucasian	900
Cheremis *see* **Mari**			
Chewa *see* **Nyanja**			
Chiga	Uganda	Niger-Congo (Bantu)	1m
Chin	Myanmar, India	Sino-Tibetan (Tibeto-Burman)	753
Chinese *see* **Gan, Hakka, Mandarin Chinese, Minbei, Minnan, Wu, Xiang, Yue**			
Chodri	India	Indo-European (Indo-Aryan)	150
Chokwe	Angola, Zambia, Zaire	Niger-Congo (Bantu)	1m
Chopí	Mozambique	Niger-Congo (Bantu)	333
Chuvash	Russia	Altaic (Turkic)	1.4m
Chwabo	Mozambique	Niger-Congo (Bantu)	665
Comorian	Comoros	Niger-Congo (Bantu)	300
Corsican	Corsica	Indo-European (Romance)	200
Crimean Turkish	Uzbekistan	Altaic (Turkic)	375
Crioulo	Guinea	Indo-European (Romance)	400
Czech	Czech Republic	Indo-European (Slavic)	11.7m
Dagaari	Burkina Faso	Niger-Congo (Gur)	500
Dagbani	Ghana, Togo	Niger-Congo (Gur)	400
Dai	China	Tai	840
Dan	Côte d'Ivoire, Liberia	Niger-Congo (Mande)	512
Danakil *see* **Afar**			
Dani	Indonesia	Indo-Pacific	300
Danish	Denmark, Germany, USA	Indo-European (Scandinavian)	5.3m
Dargwa	Russia	Caucasian	287
Dari	Afghanistan, Pakistan	Indo-European (Iranian)	6.6m
Datoga	Tanzania	Nilo-Saharan	400
Davaweño	Philippines	Austronesian	125
Dayak	Indonesia	Austronesian	520
Dhatki	Pakistan	Indo-European (Indo-Aryan)	200
Digo	Kenya, Tanzania	Niger-Congo (Bantu)	264
Dimli	Turkey	Indo-European (Iranian)	1m

Name	Where spoken	Language family	How many (000)
Dinka	Sudan	Nilo-Saharan	1.4m
Diola	Senegal, Guinea-Bissau	Niger-Congo (Adamawa-Ubangi)	390
Ditammari	Benin	Niger-Congo (Gur)	120
Dogon	Mali, Burkina Faso	Isolate	500
Dogri-Kangri	India	Indo-European (Indo-Aryan)	1.3m
Domari	Iran, Iraq, Turkey, Syria	Indo-European (Indo-Aryan)	500
Dong	China	Tai	1.4m
Dongolawi	Egypt, Sudan	Nilo-Saharan	875
Dongxiang	China	Altaic (Mongolian)	280
Dubla	India	Indo-European (Indo-Aryan)	202
Duruma	Kenya	Niger-Congo (Bantu)	189
Dusun	Malaysia	Austronesian	147
Dutch	Netherlands, Belgium, Suriname	Indo-European (Germanic)	20m
Dyerma	Niger, Nigeria	Nilo-Saharan	1.6m
Ebira	Nigeria	Niger-Congo (Benue-Congo)	500
Edo	Nigeria	Niger-Congo (Benue-Congo)	1m
Ekari	Indonesia	Indo-Pacific	100
Embu (Embo)	Kenya	Niger-Congo (Bantu)	242
Ende	Indonesia	Austronesian	170
Enga	Papua New Guinea	Indo-Pacific	165
English	USA, UK, Canada, UK, Ireland, Australia, New Zealand, South Africa, worldwide second language use	Indo-European	400m (900m–1500)
Erza	Russia	Uralic	857
Esan	Nigeria	Niger-Congo (Benue-Congo)	200
Estonian	Estonia	Uralic	1.1m
Etsako	Nigeria	Niger-Congo (Benue-Congo)	150
Ewe	Ghana, Togo	Niger-Congo (Kwa)	2m
Ewondo	NWC Africa	Niger-Congo (Bantu)	578
Fang	NWC Africa	Niger-Congo (Bantu)	526
Fante *see* Akan			
Farsi *see* Persian			
Fe'fe'	Cameroon	Niger-Congo (Benue-Congo)	124
Fijian	Fiji	Austronesian	337
Finnish	Finland, Sweden, Russia	Uralic	5.5m
Fon-Gbe	Benin, Togo	Niger-Congo (Kwa)	1m
French	France, Canada, Belgium, Switzerland, Luxembourg, Monaco, and widespread second language use	Indo-European (Romance)	109m (250m)
Frisian	Netherlands, Gemany, Denmark	Indo-European (Germanic)	750
Friulan	N Italy	Indo-European (Romance)	600
Fulacunda	Senegal, Gambia	Niger-Congo (Adamawa-Ubangi)	1.4m
Fulfulde	WC Africa	Niger-Congo (Adamawa-Ubangi)	1.8m
Fuliru	Zaire	Niger-Congo (Bantu)	266
Fur	Sudan, Chad	Nilo-Saharan	500
Fuuta Jalon	Guinea, Sierra Leone	Niger-Congo (Adamawa-Ubangi)	2.6m
Ga	Ghana, Togo	Niger-Congo (Kwa)	1m
Gaelic, Irish	Ireland	Indo-European (Celtic)	120
Gagauz	Moldova	Altaic (Turkic)	166
Galician	Spain, Portugal	Indo-European (Romance)	3.2m
Gamit	India	Indo-European (Indo-Aryan)	136
Gan	China	Sino-Tibetan (Chinese)	20.6m

Name	Where spoken	Language family	How many (000)
Ganda (Luganda)	Uganda, Tanzania	Niger-Congo (Bantu)	2.4m
Garhwali	India	Indo-European (Indo-Aryan)	1.3m
Garo	India, Bangladesh	Sino-Tibetan (Tibeto-Burman)	504
Gayo	Indonesia	Austronesian	180
Gbagyi	Nigeria	Niger-Congo (Benue-Congo)	250
Gbaya	WC Africa	Niger-Congo (Adamawa-Ubangi)	861
Gedeo	Ethiopia	Afro-Asiatic (Cushitic)	500
Gen-Gbe	Togo, Benin	Niger-Kongo (Kwa)	250
Georgian	Georgia	Caucasian	4m
German	Germany, Austria, Switzerland, E Europe, and widespread second language use	Indo-European (Germanic)	123m (200m)
Ghomala'	Cameroon	Niger-Congo (Benue-Congo)	260
Gikuyu	Kenya	Niger-Congo (Bantu)	4.4m
Gilaki	Iran	Indo-European (Iranian)	2m
Girasia	India	Indo-European (Indo-Aryan)	160
Giryama	Kenya	Niger-Congo (Bantu)	450
Gogo	Tanzania	Niger-Congo (Bantu)	1m
Gondi	India	Dravidian	2m
Gonja	Ghana	Niger-Congo (Kwa)	125
Gorontalo	Indonesia	Austronesian	900
Gourma	Burkina Faso, Togo	Niger-Congo (Gur)	393
Greek	Greece, Cyprus, Turkey, and surrounding areas	Indo-European (Greek)	11.5m
Gua	Ghana	Niger-Congo (Kwa)	120
Guajiro	Colombia, Venezuela	South American (Arawakan)	127
Guaraní	Paraguay	South American (Tupian)	3m
Guéré	Côte d'Ivoire	Niger-Congo (Kru)	197
Gujarati	India, Pakistan	Indo-European (Indo-Aryan)	33m
Gujuri	India, Pakistan	Indo-European (Indo-Aryan)	388
Gun-Gbe	Benin, Nigeria	Niger-Congo (Kwa)	173
Gurage	Ethiopia	Afro-Asiatic (Semitic)	842
Gurenne	Ghana, Burkina Faso	Niger-Congo (Gur)	525
Guro	Côte d'Ivoire	Niger-Congo (Mande)	206
Gusil	Kenya	Niger-Congo (Bantu)	1.4m
Guyanese Creole English	Guyana	Indo-European (Germanic)	700
Gwere	Uganda	Niger-Congo (Bantu)	250
Ha	Tanzania	Niger-Congo (Bantu)	725
Hadiyya	Ethiopia	Afro-Asiatic (Cushitic)	2m
Haitian Creole French	Haiti	Indo-European (Romance)	6m
Hakka (Kejia)	China	Sino-Tibetan (Chinese)	27.4m
Halbi	India	Indo-European (Indo-Aryan)	600
Hangaza	Tanzania	Niger-Congo (Bantu)	150
Hani	China, Vietnam	Sino-Tibetan (Tibeto-Burman)	520
Harauti	India	Indo-European (Indo-Aryan)	334
Hausa	Nigeria, Niger, and nearby areas	Afro-Asiatic (Chadic)	25m (40m)
Hawaii Creole English	Hawaii	Indo-European (Germanic)	500
Haya	Tanzania	Niger-Congo (Bantu)	1m
Hazaragi	Afghanistan	Indo-European (Iranian)	1.3m

Name	Where spoken	Language family	How many (000)
Hebrew	Israel, USA, Europe	Afro-Asiatic (Semitic)	2.7m
Hehe	Tanzania	Niger-Congo (Bantu)	630
Higi	Nigeria	Afro-Asiatic (Chadic)	180
Hiligaynon	Philippines	Austronesian	4.5m
Hindi	India, Fiji, Suriname, Guyanas, parts of Africa	Indo-European (Indo-Aryan)	182m (500m)
Hindko	Pakistan	Indo-European (Indo-Aryan)	4m
Hlai	China	Tai	750
Hmong	China, Thailand, Vietnam	Miao-Yao	4.5m
Ho	India, Bangladesh	Austro-Asiatic (Munda)	750
Honi	China	Sino-Tibetan (Tibeto-Burman)	100
Hrê	Vietnam	Austro-Asiatic (Mon-Khmer)	100
Hunde	Zaire	Niger-Congo (Bantu)	200
Hungarian (Magyar)	Hungary, Romania	Uralic	14.4m
Iban	Indonesia, Malaysia, Brunei	Austronesian	377
Ibanag	Philippines	Austronesian	500
Ibibio	Nigeria	Niger-Congo (Benue-Congo)	2m
Icelandic	Iceland	Indo-European (Scandinavian)	250
Idakho	Kenya	Niger-Congo (Bantu)	306
Idoma	Nigeria	Niger-Congo (Benue-Congo)	300
Ife	Togo, Benin	Niger-Congo (Benue-Congo)	100
Igala	Nigeria	Niger-Congo (Benue-Congo)	800
Igbo (Ibo)	Nigeria	Niger-Congo (Benue-Congo)	12m
Igede	Nigeria	Niger-Congo (Benue-Congo)	120
Ijo (Ijaw)	Nigeria	Niger-Congo (Ijoid)	410
Ikwere	Nigeria	Niger-Congo (Benue-Congo)	200
Ilocano	Philippines	Austronesian	5.3m
Indonesian	Indonesia	Austronesian	35m (125m)
Ingush	Russia	Caucasian	194
Intha	Myanmar	Sino-Tibetan (Tibeto-Burman)	141
Iraqw	Tanzania	Afro-Asiatic (Cushitic)	338
Isan	Thailand	Tai	15m
Isekiri	Nigeria	Niger-Congo (Benue-Congo)	500
Isoko	Nigeria	Niger-Congo (Benue-Congo)	300
Istro-Rumanian	Balkans	Indo-European (Romance)	147
Italian	Italy, San Marino, Switzerland, Sardinia, Slovenia, the Americas	Indo-European (Romance)	40m (65m)
Itawit	Philippines	Austronesian	106
Iu Mien	China	Miao-Yao	200
Izi	Nigeria	Niger-Congo (Benue-Congo)	593
Japanese	Japan, Brazil, USA	Isolate	126m
Jarai	Vietnam	Austronesian	200
Jarawa	Nigeria	Niger-Congo (Benue-Congo)	150
Javanese	Indonesia	Austronesian	75m
Jiarong	China	Sino-Tibetan (Tibeto-Burman)	100
Jingpho	Myanmar, China, India	Sino-Tibetan (Tibeto-Burman)	558

Name	Where spoken	Language family	How many (000)
Jita	Tanzania	Niger-Congo (Bantu)	217
Jju	Nigeria	Niger-Congo (Benue-Congo)	300
Judaeo-Spanish	Israel, Turkey	Indo-European (Romance)	160
Jula	Burkina Faso, Côte d'Ivoire	Niger-Congo (Mande)	1m
Kabardian	Russia	Caucasian	368
Kabiyé	Togo	Niger-Congo (Gur)	400
Kabyle	Algeria, France	Afro-Asiatic (Berber)	2.5m
Kachchi	India	Indo-European (Indo-Aryan)	471
Kado	Myanmar, China, Laos	Sino-Tibetan (Tibeto-Burman)	229
Kafa	Ethiopia	Afro-Asiatic (Omotic)	211
Kagulu	Tanzania	Niger-Congo (Bantu)	217
Kakwa	Uganda, Sudan, Zaire	Nilo-Saharan	148
Kalabari	Nigeria	Niger-Congo (Ijoid)	258
Kalanga	Botswana, Zimbabwe	Niger-Congo (Bantu)	220
Kalenjin	Kenya	Nilo-Saharan	1.4m
Kamba	Kenya	Niger-Congo (Bantu)	2.5m
Kambari	Nigeria	Niger-Congo (Benue-Congo)	100
Kambata	Ethiopia	Afro-Asiatic (Cushitic)	1m
Kami	Tanzania	Niger-Congo (Bantu)	315
Kanarese see Kannada			
Kanauji	India	Indo-European (Indo-Aryan)	6m
Kankanaey	Philippines	Austronesian	110
Kannada (Kanarese)	India	Dravidian	27m
Kanuri	Niger, Nigeria, Chad	Nilo-Saharan	4m
Kanyok	Zaire	Niger-Congo (Bantu)	200
Kaonde	Zambia, Zaire	Niger-Congo (Bantu)	217
Karachi-Balkar	Russia	Altaic (Turkic)	191
Karakalpak	Russia, Uzbekistan	Altaic (Turkic)	293
Karamojong	Uganda	Nilo-Saharan	294
Karelian	Russia, Finland	Uralic	118
Kashmiri	India, Pakistan	Indo-European (Indo-Aryan)	3m
Kashubian	Poland	Indo-European (Slavic)	200
Kayah	Myanmar, Thailand	Sino-Tibetan (Tibeto-Burman)	288
Kazakh	Kazakhstan, Russia, China	Altaic (Turkic)	7.6m
Kebumtamp	Bhutan	Sino-Tibetan (Tibeto-Burman)	400
Kejia see Hakka			
Kekchí	Guatemala, Belize	Meso-American Indian (Mayan)	277
Kela	Zaire	Niger-Congo (Bantu)	180
Kele	Zaire	Niger-Congo (Bantu)	160
Kendayan	Indonesia	Austronesian	150
Kerebe	Tanzania	Niger-Congo (Bantu)	100
Kerinci	Indonesia	Austronesian	300
Khandesi	India	Indo-European (Indo-Aryan)	147
Kharia	India	Austro-Asiatic (Munda)	135
Khasi	India, Bangladesh	Austro-Asiatic (Mon-Khmer)	535
Khmer (Cambodian)	SE Asia	Austro-Asiatic (Mon-Khmer)	8m
Khmu'	Laos, Thailand, Vietnam	Austro-Asiatic (Mon-Khmer)	340
Khorasani Turkish	Iran	Altaic (Turkic)	400
Khowar	Pakistan, India	Indo-European (Indo-Aryan)	250
Kilba	Nigeria	Afro-Asiatic (Chadic)	100
Kinaray	Philippines	Austronesian	288
Kirghiz	Kirghizstan, Russia, China	Altaic (Turkic)	2m

Name	Where spoken	Language family	How many (000)
Kissi	Guinea, Sierra Leone, Liberia	Niger-Congo (Adamawa-Ubangi)	441
Kituba	Congo	Niger-Congo (Kongo)	4.2m
Klao	Liberia, Sierra Leone	Niger-Congo (Kru)	161
Koho	Vietnam	Austro-Asiatic (Mon-Khmer)	100
Kok Borok	India, Bangladesh	Sino-Tibetan (Tibeto-Burman)	320
Koli	Pakistan	Indo-European (Indo-Aryan)	255
Kom	Cameroon	Niger-Congo (Benue-Congo)	127
Komering	Indonesia	Austronesian	700
Komi-Zyrian	Russia	Uralic	365
Komo	Zaire	Niger-Congo (Bantu)	150
Konde see Makonde			
Kongo	Zaire, Angola, Congo	Niger-Congo (Bantu)	4.7m
Konjo	Uganda	Niger-Congo (Bantu)	250
Konjo	Indonesia	Austronesian	325
Konkani	India	Indo-European (Indo-Aryan)	5m
Konkomba	Ghana, Togo	Niger-Congo (Gur)	340
Kono	Sierra Leone	Niger-Congo (Mande)	125
Konso	Ethiopia	Afro-Asiatic (Cushitic)	150
Korean	N and S Korea, Japan	Isolate	60m
Korku	India	Austro-Asiatic (Munda)	320
Koya	India	Dravidian	242
Kpelle	Guinea	Niger-Congo (Mande)	608
Krio	Sierra Leone	Indo-European (Germanic)	350
Kui	India	Dravidian	508
Kukna	India	Indo-European (Indo-Aryan)	153
Kulango	Côte d'Ivoire, Ghana	Niger-Congo (Gur)	116
Kului	India	Indo-European (Indo-Aryan)	172
Kuman	Uganda	Nilo-Saharan	147
Kumauni	India	Indo-European (Indo-Aryan)	1.2m
Kumyk	Russia	Altaic (Turkic)	189
Kunda	Zimbabwe, Zambia	Niger-Congo (Bantu)	100
Kuranko	Sierra Leone, Guinea	Niger-Congo (Mande)	250
Kurdi(sh)	Iraq, Iran, Turkey	Indo-European (Iranian)	6m
Kuria	Tanzania, Kenya	Niger-Congo (Bantu)	345
Kurmanji	Turkey, Syria, Iran, Russia	Indo-European (Iranian)	7.5m
Kurumba	India	Dravidian	700
Kurux	India	Dravidian	1.3m
Kusaal	Ghana	Niger-Congo (Gur)	198
Kuvi	India	Dravidian	300
Kuy	Cambodia, Thailand, Laos	Austro-Asiatic (Mon-Khmer)	650
Kwanyama	Angola, Namibia	Niger-Congo (Bantu)	150
Kwaya	Tanzania	Niger-Congo (Bantu)	102
Lahu	China, SE Asia	Sino-Tibetan (Tibeto-Burman)	580
Lala-Bisa	Zambia, Zaire	Niger-Congo (Bantu)	354
Lama	Togo, Benin	Niger-Congo (Gur)	140
Lamaholot	Indonesia	Austronesian	310
Lamani	India	Indo-European (Indo-Aryan)	1.5m
Lamba	Zambia, Zaire	Niger-Congo (Bantu)	170
Lamnso'	Cameroon	Niger-Congo (Benue-Congo)	125
Lampung	Indonesia	Austronesian	1.5m
Langi	Tanzania	Niger-Congo (Bantu)	275
Lango	Uganda, Sudan	Nilo-Saharan	843
Lanna	Thailand, Laos	Tai	6m

Name	Where spoken	Language family	How many (000)
Lao (Laotian)	Laos	Tai	3m
Latvian	Latvia	Indo-European (Baltic)	1.6m
Lauje	Indonesia	Austronesian	125
Lawangan	Indonesia	Austronesian	100
Ledo	Indonesia	Austronesian	130
Lega	Zaire	Niger-Congo (Bantu)	400
Lendu	Zaire	Nilo-Saharan	490
Lenje	Zambia	Niger-Congo (Bantu)	136
Lesser Antillean Creole English	Caribbean	Indo-European (Germanic)	192
Lesser Antillean Creole French	Caribbean	Indo-European (Romance)	1m
Letzebuergesch (Luxembourgeois)	Luxembourg, Belgium	Indo-European (Germanic)	336
Lezgi	Russia, Azerbaijan	Caucasian	350
Lhoba	India	Sino-Tibetan (Tibeto-Burman)	202
Li	China	Tai	750
Ligurian	Italy	Indo-European (Romance)	1.9m
Limba	Sierra Leone	Niger-Congo (Adamawa-Ubangi)	269
Limbu	Nepal, India	Sino-Tibetan (Tibeto-Burman)	200
Lingala	Zaire, Congo, Central African Rep.	Niger-Congo (Bantu)	8.4m
Lio	Indonesia	Austronesian	300
Lisu	China, Myanmar, Thailand	Sino-Tibetan (Tibeto-Burman)	635
Lithuanian	Lithuania	Indo-European (Baltic)	3.6m
Lobi	Burkina Faso, Côte d'Ivoire	Niger-Congo (Gur)	215
Logo	Zaire	Nilo-Saharan	210
Logooli	Kenya	Niger-Congo (Bantu)	197
Loko	Nigeria	Niger-Congo (Benue-Congo)	100
Loma	Liberia	Niger-Congo (Mande)	119
Lombard	Italy	Indo-European (Romance)	8.6m
Lomwe	Mozambique, Malawi	Niger-Congo (Bantu)	2m
Longandu	Zaire	Niger-Congo (Bantu)	121
Lozi	Zambia, Zimbabwe	Niger-Congo (Bantu)	450
Luba-Kasai	Zaire	Niger-Congo (Bantu)	6.3m
Luba-Shaba	Zaire	Niger-Congo (Bantu)	1.5m
Luchazi	Angola, Zambia	Niger-Congo (Bantu)	125
Lue	China, SE Asia	Tai	520
Luganda see Ganda			
Lugbara	Zaire, Uganda	Nilo-Saharan	920
Lunda	Zambia, Zaire, Angola	Niger-Congo (Bantu)	200
Luo	Kenya, Tanzania	Nilo-Saharan	3.2m
Luri	Iran	Indo-European (Iranian)	3m
Lushai	India, Myanmar	Sino-Tibetan (Tibeto-Burman)	344
Luvale	Angola, Zambia	Niger-Congo (Bantu)	600
Luxembourgeois see Letzebuergesch			
Luyia	Kenya, Uganda	Niger-Congo (Bantu)	2.9m
Ma(a)sai	Kenya, Tanzania	Nilo-Saharan	690
Maca	Mozambique	Niger-Congo (Bantu)	350
Macedonian	Macedonia, Greece	Indo-European (Slavic)	2m
Madi	Uganda, Sudan	Nilo-Saharan	233
Madurese	Indonesia	Austronesian	9m
Mafa	Cameroon, Nigeria	Afro-Asiatic (Chadic)	138
Magahi	India	Indo-European (Indo-Aryan)	10m
Magar	Nepal, India	Sino-Tibetan (Tibeto-Burman)	500
Magindanaon	Philippines	Austronesian	915
Magyar see Hungarian			
Maithili	India, Nepal	Indo-European (Indo-Aryan)	23.8m

Name	Where spoken	Language family	How many (000)
Makassar	Indonesia	Austronesian	1.6m
Makhuwa (Makua)	Mozambique, Tanzania	Niger-Congo (Bantu)	3.5m
Makonde (Konde)	Tanzania, Mozambique	Niger-Congo (Bantu)	1m
Makua *see* Makhuwa			
Malagasy	Madagasar	Austronesian	10m
Malay	Indonesia, Malaysia, Singapore, and nearby areas	Austronesian	19m (130m)
Malayalam	India	Dravidian	26m
Maldivian	Maldives	Indo-European (Indo-Aryan)	195
Malinke	Mali, Senegal	Niger-Congo (Mande)	800
Maltese	Malta	Afro-Asiatic (Semitic)	330
Malvi	India	Indo-European (Indo-Aryan)	644
Mam	Guatemala, Mexico	Meso-American Indian (Mayan)	260
Mamara	Mali	Niger-Congo (Gur)	300
Mambwe-Lungu	Zambia, Tanzania	Niger-Congo (Bantu)	307
Mampruli	Ghana, Togo	Niger-Congo (Gur)	167
Mandar	Indonesia	Austronesian	250
Mandarin Chinese	China, Taiwan, SE Asia	Sino-Tibetan (Chinese)	731m
Mandeali	India	Indo-European (Indo-Aryan)	226
Mandinka	Senegal, Gambia, Sierra Leone	Niger-Congo (Mande)	767
Mandyak	Guinea Bissau, Senegal	Niger-Congo (Adamawa-Ubangi)	163
Mangbetu	Zaire	Nilo-Saharan	650
Manggarai	Indonesia	Austronesian	500
Maninka	Guinea, Guinea Bissau, Liberia	Niger-Congo (Mande)	1.7m
Manja	Central African Rep., Cameroon	Niger-Congo (Adamawa-Ubangi)	136
Mano	Liberia, Guinea	Niger-Congo (Mande)	150
Manyika	Zimbabwe, Mozambique	Niger-Congo (Bantu)	450
Maori	New Zealand	Austronesian	100
Mapudungun	Chile, Argentina	South American (Araucanian)	440
Maranao	Philippines	Austronesian	603
Marathi	India	Indo-European (Indo-Aryan)	50m
Marba	Chad	Afro-Asiatic (Chadic)	100
Marendje	Mozambique	Niger-Congo (Bantu)	403
Margi	Nigeria	Afro-Asiatic (Chadic)	200
Mari (Cheremis)	Russia	Uralic	609
Marka	Burkina Faso	Niger-Congo (Mande)	100
Marwari	India, Pakistan	Indo-European (Indo-Aryan)	13.8m
Masa	Cameroon, Chad	Afro-Asiatic (Chadic)	183
Masaba	Uganda	Niger-Congo (Bantu)	500
Masai *see* Maasai			
Masalit	Sudan, Chad	Nilo-Saharan	200
Masbatenyo	Philippines	Austronesian	333
Masenrempulu	Indonesia	Austronesian	202
Matengo	Tanzania	Niger-Congo (Bantu)	150
Mazahua	Mexico	Meso-American Indian (Otopamean)	325
Mazandarani	Iran	Indo-European (Iranian)	2.1m
Mazatec(o)	Mexico	Meso-American Indian (Popolocan)	142
Mbai	Chad	Nilo-Saharan	100
Mbala	Zaire	Niger-Congo (Bantu)	200
Mbanza	Zaire	Niger-Congo (Adamawa-Ubangi)	200
Mbembe	Nigeria	Niger-Congo (Benue-Congo)	100
Mbole	Zaire	Niger-Congo (Bantu)	100

Name	Where spoken	Language family	How many (000)
Mbunda	Zambia, Angola	Niger-Congo (Bantu)	102
Mbundu	Angola	Niger-Congo (Bantu)	4.8m
Mbwela	Angola	Niger-Congo (Bantu)	100
Medumba	Cameroon	Niger-Congo (Benue-Congo)	210
Mende	Sierra Leone, Liberia	Niger-Congo (Mande)	1m
Meru	Kenya	Niger-Congo (Bantu)	1.2m
Mien	China, Laos, Thailand	Miao-Yao	884
Minbei	China, SE Asia	Sino-Tibetan (Chinese)	10.5m
Minnan	China, Taiwan, SE Asia	Sino-Tibetan (Chinese)	45.8m
Mina	India	Indo-European (Indo-Aryan)	765
Minangkabau	Indonesia	Austronesian	6m
Mingrelian	Georgia	Caucasian	500
Mískito	Nicaragua, Honduras	Meso-American Indian (Misumalpan)	160
Moba	Togo	Niger-Congo (Gur)	147
Moksha	Russia	Uralic	429
Mon	Myanmar, Thailand	Austro-Asiatic	920
Mongo-Nkundu	Zaire	Niger-Congo (Bantu)	216
Mongolian	China	Altaic (Mongolian)	4.6m
Mongondow	Indonesia	Austronesian	900
Mooré	Burkina Faso	Niger-Congo (Gur)	4m
Morisyen	Mauritius	Indo-European (Romance)	600
Mosi	Tanzania	Niger-Congo (Bantu)	240
Mpuono	Zaire	Niger-Congo (Bantu)	165
Mumuye	Nigeria	Niger-Congo (Adamawa-Ubangi)	400
Muna	Indonesia	Austronesian	200
Mundang	Cameroon, Chad	Niger-Congo (Adamawa-Ubangi)	100
Mundari	India, Nepal, Bangladesh	Austro-Asiatic (Munda)	850
Munukutuba	Congo	Niger-Congo (Kongo)	1.2m
Muong	Vietnam	Austro-Asiatic	767
Musey	Chad, Cameroon	Afro-Asiatic (Chadic)	120
Musi	Indonesia	Austronesian	150
Mwanga	Zambia, Tanzania	Niger-Congo (Bantu)	223
Mwera	Tanzania	Niger-Congo (Bantu)	345
Nahua(tl)	Mexico	Meso-American Indian (Uto-Aztecan)	1.2m
Nama	Namibia	Khoisan	146
Nandi	Zaire	Niger-Congo (Bantu)	903
Navajo	USA (Arizona, Utah, New Mexico)	N American Indian (Na-Dené)	130
Nawdm	Togo	Niger-Congo (Gur)	112
Naxi	China	Sino-Tibetan (Tibeto-Burman)	245
Ndali	Tanzania	Niger-Congo (Bantu)	150
Ndau	Zimbabwe, Mozambique	Niger-Congo (Bantu)	500
Ndebele	Zimbabwe	Niger-Congo (Bantu)	1.1m
Ndengereko	Tanzania	Niger-Congo (Bantu)	110
Ndonga	Namibia, Angola	Niger-Congo (Bantu)	240
Neapolitan-Calabrese	Italy	Indo-European (Romance)	7m
Nepali	Nepal, India, Bhutan	Indo-European (Indo-Aryan)	16m
Ngaju	Indonesia	Austronesian	250
Ngambai	Chad	Nilo-Saharan	600
Ngbaka	NWC Africa	Niger-Congo (Adamawa-Ubangi)	900
Ngbandi	Zaire, Central African Rep.	Niger-Congo (Adamawa-Ubangi)	210
Ngindo	Tanzania	Niger-Congo (Bantu)	220
Ngombe	Zaire	Niger-Congo (Bantu)	150
Ngoni	SEC Africa	Niger-Congo (Bantu)	205
Ngulu	Tanzania	Niger-Congo (Bantu)	132
Ngyemboon	Cameroon	Niger-Congo (Benue-Congo)	100

Name	Where spoken	Language family	How many (000)
Nhang	China, Vietnam	Tai	250
Nias	Indonesia	Austronesian	480
Nilamba	Tanzania	Niger-Congo (Bantu)	440
Nimadi	India	Indo-European (Indo-Aryan)	794
Norwegian	Norway, USA	Indo-European (Scandinavian)	5m
Nsenga	SE Africa	Niger-Congo (Bantu)	250
Ntomba	Zaire	Niger-Congo (Bantu)	100
Nuer	Sudan	Nilo-Saharan	840
Nung	Vietnam, China	Tai	1.5m
Nupe	Nigeria	Niger-Congo (Benue-Congo)	1m
Nyakyusa-Ngonde	Tanzania, Malawi	Niger-Congo (Bantu)	820
Nyamwezi	Tanzania	Niger-Congo (Bantu)	904
Nyanja (Chewa)	SE Africa	Niger-Congo (Bantu)	3.8m
Nyankole	Uganda	Niger-Congo (Bantu)	1.5m
Nyaturu	Tanzania	Niger-Congo (Bantu)	490
Nyemba	Angola	Niger-Congo (Bantu)	100
Nyiha	Tanzania, Zambia	Niger-Congo (Bantu)	306
Nyore	Uganda, Kenya	Niger-Congo (Bantu)	326
Nyoro	Uganda	Niger-Congo (Bantu)	911
Nyungwe	Mozambique	Niger-Congo (Bantu)	262
Nzema	Ghana, Côte d'Ivoire	Niger-Congo (Kwa)	242
Occitan	France	Indo-European (Romance)	10.2m
Ogan	Indonesia	Austronesian	300
Ogbia	Nigeria	Niger-Congo (Benue-Congo)	100
Oirat-Kalmyk	Russia	Altaic (Mongolian)	274
Okrika	Nigeria	Niger-Congo (Ijoid)	100
Ongbe	China	Tai	500
Oriya	India, Bangladesh	Indo-European (Indo-Aryan)	23.2m
Oromo	Ethiopia, Kenya	Afro-Asiatic (Cushitic)	10.6m
Osing	Indonesia	Austronesian	350
Ossete (Ossetic)	Russia	Indo-European (Iranian)	477
Otuho	Sudan	Nilo-Saharan	185
Palasi-Kohistani	Pakistan	Indo-European (Indo-Aryan)	220
Palaung	Myanmar, China, Thailand	Austro-Asiatic (Mon-Khmer)	543
Palembang	Indonesia	Austronesian	500
Pamona	Indonesia	Austronesian	106
Pampangan	Philippines	Austronesian	1.9m
Pangasinan	Philippines	Austronesian	1.6m
Pangwa	Tanzania	Niger-Congo (Bantu)	177
Panjabi (Punjabi)	Pakistan, India	Indo-European (Indo-Aryan)	78m
Pa'o	Myanmar	Sino-Tibetan (Tibeto-Burman)	561
Papiamentu	Caribbean	Indo-European (Portuguese)	262
Parauk	Myanmar, China	Austro-Asiatic (Mon-Khmer)	528
Pasemah	Indonesia	Austronesian	400
Pashayi	Afghanistan	Indo-European (Indo-Aryan)	108
Pashto	Afghanistan, Pakistan, Arabia	Indo-European (Iranian)	15.9m
Persian (Farsi)	Iran and nearby areas	Indo-European (Indo-Aryan)	20m (55m)
Pesisir	Indonesia	Austronesian	400
Phende	Zaire	Niger-Congo (Bantu)	420
Phu Tai	Laos, Thailand	Tai	150
Piemontese	Italy	Indo-European (Romance)	3m
Pilipino see Tagalog			
Plautdietsch	N America, Russia	Indo-European (Germanic)	306
Pogolo	Tanzania	Niger-Congo (Bantu)	185
Pökoot	Kenya, Uganda	Nilo-Saharan	170

Name	Where spoken	Language family	How many (000)
Polish	Poland and nearby areas	Indo-European (Slavic)	40m
Portuguese	Portugal, Brazil, parts of Africa	Indo-European (Romance)	154m
Pubian	Indonesia	Austronesian	400
Punjabi see Panjabi			
Purik	India	Sino-Tibetan (Tibeto-Burman)	142
Pwo	Myanmar, Thailand	Sino-Tibetan (Tibeto-Burman)	1.3m
Qashqai	Iran	Altaic (Turkic)	200
Qiang	China	Isolate	130
Quechua	Peru, Bolivia, Ecuador	S American (Quechuan)	8.4m
Quiché	Guatemala	Meso-American Indian (Mayan)	874
Rabha	India	Sino-Tibetan (Tibeto-Burman)	200
Rade	Vietnam	Austronesian	120
Rejang	Indonesia	Austronesian	1m
Réunion Creole French	Réunion	Indo-European (Romance)	555
Riang	India, Bangladesh	Sino-Tibetan (Tibeto-Burman)	100
Romani	Europe, Asia, USA	Indo-European (Indo-Aryan)	3m
Romanian (Rumanian)	Romania, Moldova	Indo-European (Romance)	23m
Romblomanon	Philippines	Austronesian	200
Ronga	Mozambique, South Africa	Niger-Congo (Bantu)	500
Roti	Indonesia	Austronesian	128
Rubassa	Nigeria	Niger-Congo (Benue-Congo)	100
Rufiji	Tanzania	Niger-Congo (Bantu)	200
Ruguru	Tanzania	Niger-Congo (Bantu)	506
Rumanian see Romanian			
Rundi	Burundi, Uganda	Niger-Congo (Bantu)	5m
Rungi	Tanzania	Isolate	166
Russian	Russia and nearby areas	Indo-European (Slavic)	155m (300m)
Ruund	Zaire, Angola	Niger-Congo (Bantu)	238
Rwanda	Rwanda, EC Africa	Niger-Congo (Bantu)	6.2m
Saamia	Kenya, Uganda	Niger-Congo (Bantu)	526
Sabaot	Kenya	Nilo-Saharan	100
Sadani	India	Indo-European (Indo-Aryan)	807
Safwa	Tanzania	Niger-Congo (Bantu)	158
Saharia	India	Indo-European (Indo-Aryan)	174
Saho	Eritrea, Ethiopia	Afro-Asiatic (Cushitic)	120
Sama	Philippines, Malaysia	Austronesian	271
Samo	Burkina Faso	Niger-Congo (Mande)	125
Samoan	Samoa, USA, New Zealand	Austronesian	328
Sanga	Zaire	Niger-Congo (Bantu)	431
Sangir	Indonesia	Austronesian	205
Sango	WC Africa	Niger-Congo (Ngbandi)	200
Santali	India, Bangladesh, Nepal	Austro-Asiatic (Munda)	3.8m
Sardinian	Sardinia	Indo-European (Romance)	1.5m
Sasak	Indonesia	Austronesian	2.1m
Sawu	Indonesia	Austronesian	100
Sea Islands Creole English (Gullah)	USA	Indo-European (Germanic)	125
Sebuano see Cebuano			
Sehwi	Côte d'Ivoire, Ghana	Niger-Congo (Kwa)	150
Selako	Indonesia	Austronesian	100
Semendo	Indonesia	Austronesian	105
Sena	Mozambique, Malawi	Niger-Congo (Bantu)	1.2m

Name	Where spoken	Language family	How many (000)
Serawai	Indonesia	Austronesian	150
Serbo-Croat(ian)	Balkans	Indo-European (Slavic)	19m
Serer-Sine	Senegal, Gambia	Niger-Congo (Adamawa-Ubangi)	650
Sgaw	Myanmar, Thailand	Sino-Tibetan (Tibeto-Burman)	2m
Shambala	Tanzania	Niger-Congo (Bantu)	485
Shan	Myanmar, Thailand	Tai	2.5m
Sharchagpakha	Bhutan	Sino-Tibetan (Tibeto-Burman)	400
Shawiya	Algeria	Afro-Asiatic (Berber)	150
Sherbro	Sierra Leone	Niger-Congo (Adamawa-Ubangi)	175
Shi	Zaire	Niger-Congo (Bantu)	654
Shilluk	Sudan	Nilo-Sharan	175
Shina	Pakistan, India	Indo-European (Indo-Aryan)	110
Shona	SE Africa	Niger-Congo (Bantu)	7m
Shubi	Tanzania	Niger-Congo (Bantu)	153
Sicilian	Italy	Indo-European (Romance)	4.7m
Sidamo	Ethiopia	Afro-Asiatic (Cushitic)	1.4m
Sikka	Indonesia	Austronesian	180
Simeulue	Indonesia	Austronesian	100
Sindhi	Pakistan, India	Indo-European (Indo-Aryan)	14m
Sinhala (Singhalese)	Sri Lanka	Indo-European (Indo-Aryan)	11.8m
Siraiki	Pakistan, India	Indo-European (Indo-Aryan)	15m
Slovak	Slovak Rep. and nearby areas	Indo-European (Slavic)	5.4m
Slovenian (Slovene)	Slovenia and nearby areas	Indo-European (Slavic)	2.2m
Sô	Laos, Thailand	Austro-Asiatic (Mon-Khmer)	130
Soga	Uganda	Niger-Congo (Bantu)	1.2m
Somali	NEC Africa	Afro-Asiatic (Cushitic)	5.6m
Songe	Zaire	Niger-Congo (Bantu)	938
Songhai	Mali, Niger, Burkina Faso	Nilo-Saharan	528
Soninke	W Africa	Niger-Congo (Mande)	972
Sora	India	Austro-Asiatic (Munda)	270
Sorsogon	Philippines	Austronesian	270
Sotho	South Africa	Niger-Congo (Bantu)	5.7m
Spanish	Spain, Americas	Indo-European (Romance)	266m (352m)
Sranan	Suriname	Indo-European (Germanic)	330
Sui	China	Tai	286
Sukuma	Tanzania	Niger-Congo (Bantu)	4m
Sumba	Indonesian	Austronesian	200
Sumbawa	Indonesia	Austronesian	300
Sumbwa	Tanzania	Niger-Congo (Bantu)	191
Sunda	Indonesia	Austronesian	25m
Susu	Guinea, Sierra Leone	Niger-Congo (Mande)	710
Swahili	EC Africa	Niger-Congo (Bantu)	1.3m (30m)
Swati (Swazi)	Swaziland, South Africa	Niger-Congo (Bantu)	1.6m
Swedish	Sweden, Finland, USA	Indo-European (Scandinavian)	10m
Sylhetti	Bangladesh	Indo-European (Indo-Aryan)	5m
Taabwa	Zaire, Zimbabwe	Niger-Congo (Bantu)	250
Tachelhit	Morocco, Algeria	Afro-Asiatic (Berber)	3m
Tadzhik *see* Tajiki			
Tagalog (Pilipino)	Philippines	Austronesian	10.5m (40m)
Tahitian	Society Is.	Austronesian	125
Tai Nüa	China, Myanmar	Tai	323

Name	Where spoken	Language family	How many (000)
Tai	Vietnam	Tai	785
Taita	Kenya	Niger-Congo (Bantu)	153
Tajiki	Tajikistan and nearby areas	Indo-European (Iranian)	2.9m
Takestani	Iran	Indo-European (Iranian)	220
Talishi	Russia, Iran	Indo-European (Iranian)	180
Tama	Chad, Sudan	Nilo-Saharan	105
Tamajeq (Tamashek)	Niger, Mali, Burkina Faso	Afro-Asiatic (Berber)	900
Tamang	Nepal	Sino-Tibetan (Tibeto-Burman)	536
Tamashek *see* Tamajeq			
Tamazight	Morocco, Algeria	Afro-Asiatic (Berber)	3m
Tamil	India, Sri Lanka, Vietnam	Dravidian	50m
Tangale	Nigeria	Afro-Asiatic (Chadic)	100
Tarifit	Morocco	Afro-Asiatic (Berber)	1m
Tarok	Nigeria	Niger-Congo (Benue-Congo)	140
Tatar	Russia	Altaic (Turkic)	5.5m
Tati, Jewish	Iran, Russia	Indo-European (Iranian)	262
Taungyo	Myanmar	Sino-Tibetan (Tibeto-Burman)	443
Tausug	Philippines	Austronesian	492
Teda	Chad, Niger, Libya	Nilo-Saharan	200
Telugu	India, SE Asia	Dravidian	54m
Tem	Togo, Benin	Niger-Congo (Gur)	300
Tengger	Indonesia	Austronesian	500
Teso	Uganda, Kenya	Nilo-Saharan	1.4m
Tetela	Zaire	Niger-Congo (Bantu)	750
Tetun	Indonesia	Austronesian	300
Thai	Thailand	Tai	24.6m (50m)
Tharaka	Kenya	Niger-Congo (Bantu)	100
Tharu	Nepal	Indo-European (Indo-Aryan)	530
Themne	Sierra Leone	Niger-Congo (Adamawa-Ubangi)	960
Tho	Vietnam	Tai	2m
Thuri	Sudan	Nilo-Saharan	154
Tibetan	China, Nepal	Sino-Tibetan (Tibeto-Burman)	4m
Ticinese	Switzerland	Indo-European (Romance)	780
Tigré	EC Africa	Afro-Asiatic (Semitic)	600
Tigrinya	Eritrea, Ethiopia	Afro-Asiatic (Semitic)	4m
Timor	Indonesia	Austronesian	650
Tiv	Nigeria	Niger-Congo (Benue-Congo)	1.5m
Tolaki	Indonesia	Austronesian	125
Toma	Guinea	Niger-Congo (Mande)	118
Tonga	Malawi	Niger-Congo (Bantu)	200
Tonga	Mozambique	Niger-Congo (Bantu)	225
Tonga	Zambia, Zimbabwe	Niger-Congo (Bantu)	880
Tongan	Tonga	Austronesian	108
Tontemboan	Indonesia	Austronesian	140
Toposa	Sudan, Ethiopia	Nilo-Saharan	105
Toraja-Sa'dan	Indonesia	Austronesian	500
Totonac	Mexico	Meso-American Indian (Totonacan)	261
Toucouleur	Senegal, Mauritania	Niger-Congo (Adamawa-Ubangi)	1.7m
Tsonga	South Africa, Mozambique	Niger-Congo (Bantu)	3.1m
Tswa	SE Africa	Niger-Congo (Bantu)	695
Tswana	SE Africa	Niger-Congo (Bantu)	3.3m
Tugen	Kenya	Nilo-Saharan	144
Tujia	China	Sino-Tibetan (Tibeto-Burman)	200
Tulu	India	Dravidian	1.2m
Tumbuka	SE Africa	Niger-Congo (Bantu)	1.5m

Name	Where spoken	Language family	How many (000)
Tupuri	Cameroon, Chad	Niger-Congo (Adamawa-Ubangi)	180
Turkana	Kenya,	Nilo-Saharan	250
Turkish	Turkey, Europe	Altaic (Turkic)	50m
Turkmen	Turkmenistan and nearby areas	Altaic (Turkic)	3.1m
Tuva	Russia, China	Altaic (Turkic)	191
Twi *see* Akan			
Udmurt	Russia	Uralic	550
Uighur	China, Russia	Altaic (Turkic)	6.8m
Ukrainian	Ukraine and nearby areas	Indo-European (Slavic)	45m
Ukwuani-Aboh	Nigeria	Niger-Congo (Benue-Congo)	150
Urdu	India, Pakistan	Indo-European (Indo-Aryan)	41m (85m)
Urhobo	Nigeria	Niger-Congo (Benue-Congo)	340
Uzbek	Uzbekistan and nearby areas	Altaic (Turkic)	16m
Vasavi	India	Indo-European (Indo-Aryan)	300
Venda	South Africa, Zimbabwe	Niger-Congo (Bantu)	600
Venetian	Italy	Indo-European (Romance)	2.1m
Vietnamese	Vietnam, Cambodia, Laos	Austro-Asiatic	55m
Waci-Gbe	Togo, Benin	Niger-Congo (Kwa)	280
Wagdi	India	Indo-European (Indo-Aryan)	757
Waray-Waray	Philippines	Austronesian	2.2m
Wasa	Ghana	Niger-Congo (Kwa)	150
Welsh	Wales	Indo-European (Celtic)	580
West Caribbean Creole English	Caribbean	Indo-European (Germanic)	2.2m
Wobe	Côte d'Ivoire	Niger-Congo (Kru)	150

Name	Where spoken	Language family	How many (000)
Wolaytta	Ethiopia	Afro-Asiatic (Omotic)	2m
Wolof	Senegal	Niger-Congo (Adamawa-Ubangi)	2.6m
Wu	China	Sino-Tibetan (Chinese)	77m
Xhosa	South Africa	Niger-Congo (Bantu)	6m
Xiang	China	Sino-Tibetan (Chinese)	36m
Yaka	Zaire, Angola	Niger-Congo (Bantu)	175
Yakut	Russia	Altaic (Turkic)	316
Yanadi	India	Dravidian	206
Yangbye	Myanmar	Sino-Tibetan (Tibeto-Burman)	810
Yao	SE Africa	Niger-Congo (Bantu)	1.2m
Yemba-Nwe	Cameroon	Niger-Congo (Benue-Congo)	350
Yi	China	Sino-Tibetan (Tibeto-Burman)	2.8m
Yiddish	USA, Russia, Israel	Indo-European (Germanic)	2m
Yoruba	Nigeria, Benin	Niger-Congo (Benue-Congo)	20m
Yucatec	Mexico, Belize	Meso-American Indian (Mayan)	500
Yue	China, SE Asia	Sino-Tibetan (Chinese)	54m
Zaghawa	Sudan, Chad	Nilo-Saharan	123
Zalamo	Tanzania	Niger-Congo (Bantu)	458
Zande (Azande)	WC Africa	Niger-Congo (Adamawa-Ubangi)	1.1m
Zapotec	Mexico	Meso-American Indian (Zapotecan)	485
Zhuang	China	Tai	12m
Zigula	Tanzania	Niger-Congo (Bantu)	336
Zinza	Tanzania	Niger-Congo (Bantu)	138
Zulu	South Africa	Niger-Congo (Bantu)	6m

IV   FURTHER READING

The order of references in this section follows the order of topics within each Part.

Part I
For a general discussion of attitudes to language, including the topics of magic and taboo, see O. Jespersen, *Mankind, nation and individual* (London: Allen & Unwin, 1946). Attitudes to the English language are discussed in R. Quirk, *The Use of English* (London: Longman, 2nd edn., 1968); see also R. Quirk & G. Stein, *English in use* (London: Longman, 1990); D. Cameron, *Verbal hygiene* (London: Routledge, 1995). A detailed account of the history of ideas relating to prescriptivism is found in J. & L Milroy, *Authority in language* (London: Routledge & Kegan Paul, 2nd edn., 1991). Orwell's views are related to the history of linguistic attitudes in W. F. Bolton, *The language of 1984* (Oxford: Blackwell, 1984). For popular attitudes to language change, see J. Aitchison, *Language change: progress or decay* (London: Fontana, 1981). Questions of linguistic excellence are reviewed in J. Edwards, *Language, society and identity* (Oxford: Blackwell, 1985). Glossolalia is discussed in W. J. Samarin, *Tongues of men and angels* (New York: Macmillan, 1972). The relationship of thought to language is the basis of Ch. 14 of H. H. Clark & E. V. Clark, *Psychology and language* (New York: Harcourt Brace Jovanovich, 1977). For Whorf's views see J. B. Carroll (ed.), *Language, thought and reality: selected writings of Benjamin Lee Whorf* (Cambridge, Mass.: M.I.T. Press, 1956), esp. the paper 'Science and linguistics'. For Sapir's views, see D. G. Mandelbaum (ed.), *Selected writings in language, culture and personality* (Berkeley & Los Angeles: University of California Press, 1949). For the cultural basis of language, see M. Agar, *Language shock: understanding the culture of conversation* (New York: William Morrow, 1994).

Part II
The speaking and singing voice is presented in detail in Part A of R. Luchsinger & G. E. Arnold, *Voice – speech – language* (Belmont, Ca.: Wadsworth, 1965). For

developments in old age, see D. S. Beasley & G. A. Davis (eds.), *Aging: communication processes and disorders* (New York: Grune & Stratton, 1981). On voiceprinting, see P. Ladefoged, *A course in phonetics* (New York: Harcourt Brace Jovanovich, 2nd edn., 1982), Ch. 8. The psychological background is discussed in D. S. Wright, et. al., *Introducing psychology: an experimental approach* (Harmondsworth: Penguin, 1970), esp. Chs. 18 and 19. On speech and personality, see K. R. Scherer, 'Personality markers in speech', in K. R. Scherer & H. Giles (eds.), *Social markers in speech* (Cambridge: C.U.P., 1979), pp. 147–209.

General introductions to dialectology, which cover all the matters raised in §8, are: J. K. Chambers & P. Trudgill, *Dialectology* (Cambridge: C.U.P., 1980) and K. M. Petyt, *Dialectology* (London: Deutsch, 1980). On geolinguistics, see R. J-L. Breton, *Géographie des langues* (Paris: Presses Universitaire de France., 2nd edn., 1983 – a volume in the *Que sais-je?* series). For linguistic variables, see W. Labov, *Sociolinguistic patterns* (Philadelphia: University of Pennsylvania Press, 1972). For ethnic and national identity, see J. Edwards, *Language, society and identity* (Oxford: Blackwell, 1985), and the papers in J. Edwards (ed.), *Linguistic minorities, policies, and pluralism* (London: Academic Press, 1984); also in P. Trudgill, *Sociolinguistics* (Harmondsworth: Penguin, 2nd edn., 1983), Chs. 3 and 7, where BEV is discussed.

For a general discussion of social identity and language, see P. Trudgill (*op. cit.*). The interaction of language and class is illustrated in detail in K. C. Phillipps, *Language and class in Victorian England* (Oxford: Blackwell, 1984); a historical dimension is provided by L. Mugglestone, '*Talking proper': the rise of accent as social symbol* (Oxford: Clarendon Press, 1995). For Bernstein's theory, see P. Atkinson, *Language structure and reproduction* (London: Methuen, 1986). For other case studies, see: J. J. Gumperz & D. Hymes (eds.), *Directions in sociolinguistics: the ethnography of communication* (New York: Holt, Rinehart & Winston, 1972); D. Hymes (ed.), *Language in culture and society* (New York: Harper & Row, 1964); J. A. Fishman (ed.), *Readings in the sociology of language* (The Hague: Mouton, 1968); R. Bauman & J. Sherzer (eds.), *Explorations in the ethnography of speaking* (Cambridge: C.U.P., 1974). Sexism is discussed in detail in P.

M. Smith, *Language, the sexes and society* (Oxford: Blackwell, 1985) and B Thorne, C. Kramarae & N. Henley (eds.), *Language, gender and society* (Rowley, Mass.: Newbury House, 1983).

For a theoretical discussion of contextual variables, see D. Hymes, *Foundations in sociolinguistics* (London: Tavistock, 1974). Several spoken and written varieties are illustrated in D. Crystal & D. Davy, *Investigating English style* (London: Longman, 1969); R. Quirk, *The use of English* (London: Longman, 2nd edn., 1968); R. Bauman & J. Sherzer (*ibid.*); and (for French) D. E. Ager, *Styles and registers in contemporary French* (London: University of London Press, 1970). Accommodation theory is discussed in H. Giles & R. St. Clair (eds.), *Language and social psychology* (Oxford: Blackwell, 1979), esp. Ch. 3. For slang, see E. Partridge, *Slang* (London: Barnes & Noble, 4th edn., 1970; for proverbs, see E. Strauss, *Dictionary of European proverbs* (London: Routledge, 1995, 3 vols); for swearing, G. Hughes, *Swearing: a social history of foul language, oaths and profanity in English* (Oxford: Blackwell, 1991). Seaspeak is introduced in *Seaspeak: essential English for international maritime use* (Oxford: Pergamon Press, 1983). Verbal art, hidden languages, and several other forms are discussed in B. Kirshenblatt-Gimblett (ed.), *Speech play* (Philadelphia: University of Pennsylvania Press, 1976). For cryptanalysis, see D. Kahn, *The codebreakers* (New York: Macmillan, 1967). Word games are thoroughly exemplified in T. Augarde, *The Oxford guide to word games* (Oxford: O.U.P., 1984), and puns are given separate treatment in W. Redfern, *Puns* (Oxford: Blackwell, 1984).

For general introductions to literary stylistics, see R. Chapman, *Linguistics and literature* (London: Edward Arnold, 1973) and *The language of English literature* (London: Edward Arnold, 1982); J. Haynes, *Introducing stylistics* (London: Routledge, 1993); and (with special reference to French) S. Ullmann, *Language and style* (Oxford: Blackwell, 1964). There are several important collections of papers, such as D. C. Freeman (ed.), *Linguistics and literary style* (New York: Holt, Rinehart & Winston, 1970) and S. Chatman (ed.), *Literary style: a symposium* (London: O.U.P., 1971). The language of poetry is discussed in G. N. Leech, *A linguistic guide to English poetry* (London: Longman, 1969); W. Nowottny, *The language poets use* (London: Athlone, 1962); and D. Attridge, *The rhythms of English poetry* (London: Longman, 1982). For the language of the novel, see G. N. Leech & M. H. Short, *Style in fiction: a linguistic introduction to fictional prose* (London: Longman, 1981); W. Nash, *Designs in prose: a study of compositional problems and methods* (London: Longman, 1980); R. Fowler, *Linguistics and the novel* (London: Methuen, 1977); and S. Ullmann, *Style in the French novel* (Oxford: O.U.P., 1957). For the language of individual novelists, see the various volumes in the Blackwell *Language Library*. For dramatic language, see D. Burton, *Dialogue and discourse* (London: Routledge & Kegan Paul, 1980). Authorship studies are discussed in C. B. Williams, *Style and vocabulary: numerical studies* (London: Griffin, 1970) and L. Doležel & R. W. Bailey (eds.), *Statistics and style* (New York: American Elsevier, 1969). For a historical account of linguistic stylistics, including stylostatistics, see N. E. Enkvist, *Linguistic stylistics* (The Hague: Mouton, 1973), and for a general bibliography, R. Bailey & D. M. Burton, *English stylistics: a bibliography* (Cambridge, Mass.: M.I.T. Press, 1968). For structuralism and related approaches, see R. Selden, *A reader's guide to contemporary literary theory* (Brighton: Harvester Press, 1985).

Part III

All linguistics textbooks contain a discussion of linguistic levels and associated matters of language structure: see references under Part XI. General questions of typology and universals are discussed in B. Comrie, *Language universals and linguistic typology* (Oxford: Blackwell, 1981). A range of typological approaches, including the notion of implicational universals, is presented in J. H. Greenberg (ed.), *Universals of language* (Cambridge, Mass.: M.I.T. Press, 1963). The distinction between formal and substantive universals is introduced in N. Chomsky, *Aspects of the theory of syntax* (Cambridge, Mass.: M.I.T. Press, 1965), and Chomsky's conception of the links between modern linguistics and early linguistic thought is presented in *Cartesian linguistics: a chapter in the history of rationalist thought* (New York: Harper & Row, 1966). The Port-Royal grammar is reprinted in facsimile by Scolar Press (Menston, Yorks, 1967). For an introduction to statistical issues in language, see G. A. Miller, *Language and communication* (New York: McGraw-Hill, 1951), Ch. 4, and C. Cherry, *On human communication* (New York: Science Editions, 1961), Ch. 5. For word-frequency information about English, see K. Hofland & S. Johansson, *Word frequencies in British and American English* (Bergen: Norwegian Computing Centre for the Humanities, 1982; also published by Longman). Zipf's approach is presented in G. K. Zipf, *The psycho-biology of language: an introduction to dynamic philology* (Cambridge, Mass.: M.I.T. Press).

For a general introduction to grammar, see F. R. Palmer, *Grammar* (Harmondsworth: Penguin, 2nd edn., 1984); N. Fabb, *Sentence structure* (London: Routledge, 1994). More detailed accounts are given in P. H. Matthews, *Morphology* (1974) and *Syntax* (1981), both Cambridge: C.U.P. For the original statement of generative grammar, see N. Chomsky, *Syntactic structures* (The Hague: Mouton, 1957). Note also the reference grammar by R. Quirk, S. Greenbaum, G. Leech & J. Svartvik, *A comprehensive grammar of the English language* (London: Longman, 1985). For general introductions to semantics, see F. R. Palmer, *Semantics* (Cambridge: C.U.P., 2nd edn., 1981); J. Lyons, *Language, meaning and context* (London: Fontana, 1981); J. R. Hurford & B. Heasley, *Semantics: a coursebook* (Cambridge: C.U.P., 1983); and S. Ullmann, *Semantics: an introduction to the study of meaning* (Oxford: Blackwell, 1962). For an advanced account, see J. Lyons, *Semantics*, Vols. 1 and 2 (Cambridge: C.U.P., 1977).

A wide-ranging collection of papers on dictionaries is: R. R. K. Hartmann (ed.), *Lexicography: principles and practice* (London: Academic Press, 1983). For the history of lexicography, see R. L. Collison, *A history of foreign-language dictionaries* (Oxford: Blackwell, 1982) and D. T. Starnes & G. E. Noyes, *The English dictionary from Cawdrey to Johnson* (Chapel Hill: University of North Carolina Press, 1946). For a more advanced discussion, see L. Zgusta, *Manual of lexicography* (The Hague: Mouton, 1971).

On general issues of naming, see E. Pulgram, *Theory of names* (1954). On personal names, see C. M. Matthews, *English surnames* (London: Weidenfeld & Nicolson, 1966) and R.M. Wilson & P.H. Reaney, *A dictionary of English surnames* (London: Routledge, 1991); L. Dunkling & W. Gosling, *Dictionary of first names* (London: Dent, 1983), which also contains several references to works on foreign names; and E. G. Withycombe, *The Oxford dictionary of English Christian names* (London: O.U.P., 1977). For an introduction to place-name studies, see K. Cameron, *English place names* (London: Batsford, 1961) and C. M. Matthews, *Place names of the English-speaking world* (London: Weidenfeld & Nicolson, 1972). A classic work on English place names is E. Ekwall, *The concise Oxford dictionary of English place-names* (Oxford, 4th edn., 1960). For detailed British studies, see the various county volumes of the English Place-Name Society (C.U.P.), published from the 1920s. For American place names, see G. R. Stewart, *American place-names* (New York: O.U.P., 1970).

For an introduction to discourse, see M. Stubbs, *Discourse analysis* (Oxford: Blackwell, 1983); G. Brown & G. Yule, *Discourse analysis* (Cambridge: C.U.P., 1983); and M. Coulthard, *An introduction to discourse analysis* (London: Longman, 1977). The study of text is introduced in R. de Beaugrande & W. Dressler, *Introduction to text linguistics* (London: Longman, 1981). An introductory account of pragmatic issues is R. Wardhaugh, *How conversation works* (Oxford: Blackwell, 1985). More technical discussions are G. N. Leech, *Principles of pragmatics* (London: Longman, 1983); S. Levinson, *Pragmatics* (Cambridge: C.U.P., 1983), and D. Sperber & D. Wilson, *Relevance* (Oxford: Blackwell, 1986).

Part IV

Any introduction to phonetics will provide an account of the relevant anatomy, physiology, and neurology of speech, but some books deal with these matters in more detail, such as: J. Laver, *Principles of phonetics* (Cambridge: C.U.P., 1994); G. J. Borden & K. S. Harris, *Speech science primer* (Baltimore: Williams & Wilkins, 2nd edn., 1984), Ch. 4; P. Lieberman & S.E. Blumstein, *Speech physiology, speech perception, and acoustic phonetics* (Cambridge: C.U.P., 1988); W. J. Hardcastle, *Physiology of speech production* (London: Academic Press, 1976); H. M. Kaplan, *Anatomy and physiology of speech* (New York: McGraw Hill, 2nd edn., 1971). For serious study, an anatomical atlas is recommended.

Acoustic analysis is introduced in D. B. Fry, *The physics of speech* (Cambridge: C.U.P., 1979); P. B. Denes & E. N. Pinson, *The speech chain* (New York: Doubleday, 1973); and also G. J. Borden & K. S. Harris (*ibid.*), Ch.3. A convenient collection of more advanced reading is D. B. Fry (ed.), *Acoustic phonetics* (Cambridge: C.U.P., 1976). Speech instrumentation is reviewed in G. J. Borden & K. S. Harris (*ibid.*), Ch. 6; C. Code & M. Ball (eds.), *Experimental clinical phonetics* (London: Croom Helm, 1984); and C. Painter, *An introduction to instrumental phonetics* (Baltimore: University Park Press, 1979). See also W. J. Hardcastle, 'Instrumental investigations of lingual activity in speech: a survey', *Phonetica* 29 (1974), pp. 129–57.

On the hearing mechanism, see J. L. Northern & M. P. Downs, *Hearing in children* (Baltimore: Williams & Wilkins, 1978), Chs. 2 and 3; P. B. Denes & E. N. Pinson (*ibid.*), Ch. 5; and G. J. Borden & K. S. Harris (*ibid.*), Ch. 5. For an introduction to speech perception in the context of auditory perception in general, see D. A. Sanders, A*uditory perception of speech* (Englewood Cliffs, N. J.: Prentice-Hall, 1977); in the context of psycholinguistics, see H. H. Clark & E. V. Clark, *Psychology and language* (New York: Harcourt Brace Jovanovich, 1977), Ch. 5.; in the context of deafness, see J. Bamford & E. Saunders, *Hearing impairment, auditory perception and language disability* (London: Whurr, 2nd edn., 1991). On speaker recognition, see F. Nolan, *The phonetic bases of speaker recognition* (Cambridge: C.U.P., 1983).

For a general account of phonetics, see J. D. O'Connor, *Phonetics* (Harmondsworth: Penguin, 1973) and P. Ladefoged, *A course in phonetics* (New York: Harcourt Brace Jovanovich, 2nd edn., 1982). A more advanced account is given in B. Malmberg (*ibid.*). A detailed introduction to English phonetics and phonology is A. C. Gimson, *An introduction to the pronunciation of English* (London: Edward Arnold, 5th edn., 1994). For a classical approach to phonology, see K. L. Pike, *Phonemics: a technique for reducing languages to writing* (Ann Arbor: University of Michigan, 1947). The pioneering monograph in the subject is N. Trubetskoy, *Principles of phonology* (trans. by C. M. Baltaxe of *Grundzüge der Phonologie*) (Berkeley & Los Angeles: University of California Press, 1939/1969). Modern introductions include R. Lass, *Phonology* (Cambridge: C.U.P., 1984); J. Clark & C. Yallop, *An introduction to phonetics and phonology* (Oxford: Blackwell, 1990). Generative phonology is introduced in L. M. Hyman, *Phonology: theory and analysis* (New York: Holt, Rinehart & Winston, 1975), metrical phonology in R. Hogg & C. B. McCully, *Metrical phonology: a course-book* (Cambridge: C.U.P., 1987). Suprasegmental features are introduced in E. Couper-Kuhlen, *An introduction to English prosody* (Tübingen: Niemeyer, 1986), A. Cruttenden, *Intonation* (Cambridge: C.U.P., 1985), and in D. L. Bolinger, *Intonation and its parts* (London: Edward Arnold, 1986). Most of the systems presented in the section are illustrated in D. L. Bolinger (ed.), *Intonation* (Harmondsworth: Penguin, 1972). Joshua Steele's *Melody and measure of speech* (1775) is available in facsimile from Scolar Press (Menston, Yorks., 1969). For pause, see D. Tannen & M. Saville-Troike (eds.), *Perspectives on silence* (Norwood, N. J.: Ablex, 1985). Vocal composition is discussed in I. Anhalt, *Alternative voices: essays on contemporary vocal and choral composition* (Toronto: University of Toronto Press, 1984). For a discussion of sound symbolism, see S. Ullmann, *Language and style* (Oxford: Blackwell, 1964). The full text of *Jabberwocky*, in three languages, will be found in M. Gardner (ed.), *The annotated Alice* (Harmondsworth: Penguin, 1965).

Part V

The relationship between speech and writing is discussed in many introductory textbooks on language study, such as R. Quirk, *The use of English* (London: Longman, 2nd edn., 1968). For a more advanced discussion, see D. Tannen (ed.), *Spoken and written language* (Norwood, N. J.: Ablex, 1982). For graphic expression, see M. Twyman, 'The graphic presentation of language', *Information Design Journal* 3 (1982), pp. 2–22. On the history of writing see R. Harris, *The origin of writing* (London: Duckworth, 1986), B. L. Ullman, *Ancient writing and its influence* (New York: Longman, 1963); on calligraphy, E. Johnston, *Writing and illuminating and lettering* (London: Pitman, 1925, 14th edn.), and the entry on calligraphy in the *Encyclopaedia Britannica* (15th edn.). Graphology (in the psychological sense) is introduced in E. Singer, *A manual of graphology* (London: Duckworth, 1953). On the development of printing see M. Twyman, *Printing 1770–1970* (London: Eyre & Spottiswoode, 1970); on typing, B. Bliven, *The wonderful writing machine* (New York: Random House, 1954).

Major texts on writing systems include D. Diringer, *The alphabet: a key to the history of mankind* (London: Hutchinson, 1948, 3rd edn., 1968), I. J. Gelb, *A study of writing* (Chicago: Chicago University Press, 1963), and P. T. Daniels & W. Bright (eds.), *The world's writing systems* (Oxford: Oxford University Press, 1995). See also W. Haas (ed.), *Writing without letters* (Manchester: Manchester University Press, 1976), F. Coulmas, *The writing systems of the world* (Oxford: Blackwell, 1989), and A. Robinson, *The story of writing* (London: Thames & Hudson, 1995). A more advanced theoretical discussion is J. Vachek, *Written language* (The Hague: Mouton, 1973). The English punctuation system is outlined in Appendix 3 to R. Quirk, et al., *A comprehensive grammar of the English language* (London: Longman, 1985). For shorthand, see H. Glatte, *Shorthand systems of the world* (London: Glatte, 1959).

The process of reading is introduced in A. W. Ellis, *Reading, writing and dyslexia: a cognitive analysis* (London: Erlbaum, 1984) and A. Kennedy, *The psychology of reading* (London & New York: Methuen, 1984). More specialized studies are to be found in A. S. Reber & D. L. Scarborough (eds.), *Toward a psychology of reading* (New York: Erlbaum, 1977) and J. F. Kavanagh & I. G. Mattingly, *Language by ear and by eye: the relationships between speech and reading* (Cambridge, Mass.: M.I.T. Press, 1972). On spelling, see U. Frith (ed.), *Cognitive processes in spelling* (London: Academic Press, 1980) and E. Carney, *A survey of English spelling* (London: Routledge, 1993). On writing see M. Nystrand (ed.), *What writers know: the language, process and structure of written discourse* (New York: Academic Press, 1982). On spelling reform, see W. Haas (ed.), *Alphabets for English* (Manchester: Manchester University Press, 1969) and G. Dewey, *English spelling: roadblock to reading* (New York: Teachers' College Press, 1971).

Part VI

For an introduction to sign, see E. Klima & U. Bellugi, *The signs of language* (Cambridge, Mass.: Harvard University Press, 1979) and J. G. Kyle & B. Woll, *Sign language* (Cambridge: C.U.P., 1985). Several aspects of sign language are introduced in R. L. Schiefelbusch (ed.), *Nonspeech language and communication: analysis and intervention* (Baltimore: University Park Press, 1980). A more advanced discussion of many aspects of sign is to be found in I. M. Schlesinger & L. Namir (eds.), *Sign language of the deaf: psychological, linguistic, and sociological perspectives* (New York: Academic Press, 1978), and W. C. Stokoe, *Semiotics and human sign languages* (The Hague: Mouton, 1972).

Part VII

An introductory account of child language is D. Crystal, *Listen to your child* (Harmondsworth: Penguin, 1986). See also P. & J. De Villiers, *Early language* (London: Fontana, 1979), J. Bruner, *Child's talk: learning to use language* (Oxford: O.U.P., 1983); C. Garvey, *Children's talk* (London: Fontana, 1984); G. Wells, *The meaning makers* (London: Hodder & Stoughton, 1987); and M. Donaldson, *Children's minds* (London: Fontana, 1978). For more detailed studies, see A. Cruttenden, *Language in infancy and childhood* (Manchester: Manchester University Press/St Martin's Press, 1979), P. Fletcher, *A child's learning of English* (Oxford: Blackwell, 1985), C. G. Wells, *Language development in the pre-school years* (Cambridge: C.U.P., 1985), and P. Fletcher & M. Garman (eds.), *Language acquisition* (Cambridge: C.U.P., 2nd edn., 1986). On phonological development, see J. L. Locke, *Phonological acquisition and change* (New York: Academic Press, 1983). On pragmatic development, see M. McTear, *Children's conversation* (Oxford: Blackwell, 1985) and the papers in E. Ochs & B. B. Schieffelin (eds.), *Developmental pragmatics* (New York: Academic Press, 1979). On twins, see S. Savić, *How twins learn to talk* (London: Academic Press, 1980).

On language awareness and the school curriculum, see E. Hawkins, *Awareness of language: an introduction* (Cambridge: C.U.P., 1984); C. Cazden, V. P. John & D. Hymes (eds.), *Functions of language in the classroom* (New York: Teachers College Press, 1972); D. Barnes, J. Britton & H. Rosen, *Language, the learner and the school* (Harmondsworth: Penguin, 1969, 3rd edn. by Barnes, Britton & M. Torbe, 1986); P. Doughty, J. Pearce & G. Thornton, *Language in use* (London: Edward Arnold, 1971);

and D. Crystal, *Child language, learning and linguistics* (London: Edward Arnold, 2nd edn., 1987), Ch. 3. On learning to read and write, see D. Mackay & J. Simo, *Help your child to read and write, and more* (Harmondsworth: Penguin, 1976); K. Perera, *Children's writing and reading: analysing classroom language* (Oxford: Blackwell, 1984); and H. Cowie (ed.), *The development of children's imaginative writing* (London: Croom Helm, 1984). On learning to read in general, see F. Smith, *Reading* (Cambridge: C.U.P., 1978) and E. Ferreiro & A. Teberosky, *Literacy before schooling* (London: Heinemann, 1983). On the teaching of reading, see R. Karlin, *Teaching elementary reading* (New York: Harcourt Brace Jovanovich, 3rd edn., 1980) and C. Matthes, *How children are taught to read* (Lincoln, Neb.: Professional Educators Publications, 1972). On handwriting, see C. Jarman, *The development of handwriting skills* (Oxford: Blackwell, 1979) and R. Sassoon, *The practical guide to children's handwriting* (London: Thames & Hudson, 1983).

Part VIII

The structure and function of the human brain is discussed in S. J. Dimond & J. G. Beaumont (eds.), *Hemispheric function in the human brain* (London: Elek Science, 1974) and with reference to language in E. H. Lenneberg, *Biological foundations of language* (New York: Wiley, 1967), where critical period theory is presented. Collections of papers on language and neurology include: S. J. Segalowitz & F. A. Gruber (eds.), *Language development and neurological theory* (New York: Academic Press, 1977) and S. J. Segalowitz (ed.), *Language functions and brain organization* (New York: Academic Press, 1983). Neurological models are the subject matter of M. A. Arbib, D. Caplan & J. C. Marshall (eds.), *Neural models of language processing* (New York: Academic Press, 1982). Slips of the tongue are discussed in V. A. Fromkin (ed.), *Speech errors as linguistic evidence* (The Hague: Mouton, 1973). Psycholinguistic issues are introduced in J. Aitchison, *The articulate mammal* (London: Routledge, 2nd edn., 1989); see also S. Pinker, *The language instinct* (New York: William Morrow, 1994; Harmondsworth: Penguin, 1994) and M. Garman, *Psycholinguistics* (Cambridge: C.U.P., 1990).

For a general introduction to language handicap, see D. Crystal, *Introduction to language pathology* (London: Whurr, 3rd edn. with R. Varley, 1993); W. H. Perkins, *Human perspectives in speech and language disorders* (Saint Louis: C. V. Mosby, 1978); G. H. Shames & E. H. Wiig, *Human communication disorders: an introduction* (Columbus: Merrill, 1982); and J. E. Nation & D. M. Aram, *Diagnosis of speech and language disorders* (San Diego: College-Hill Press, 2nd edn. 1984). On deafness, see E. D. Schubert, *Hearing: its function and dysfunction* (Vienna: Springer, 1980), J. L. Northern & M. P. Downs, *Hearing in children* (Baltimore: Williams & Wilkins, 2nd edn. 1978), and J. Bamford & E. Saunders, *Hearing impairment, auditory imperception and language disability* (London: Whurr, 2nd edn., 1991). On aphasia, see A. R. Lecours, F. Lhermitte & B. Bryans (eds.), *Aphasiology* (London: Baillière Tindal, 1983) and R. Lesser, *Linguistic investigations of aphasia* (London: Whurr, 2nd edn., 1989). On adult dyslexia, see M. Coltheart, K. Patterson & J. C. Marshall (eds.), *Deep dyslexia* (London: Routledge & Kegan Paul, 1980) and K. E. Patterson, J. C. Marshall & M. Coltheart (eds.), *Surface dyslexia* (London: Erlbaum, 1985); on child dyslexia, M. Thomson, *Developmental dyslexia* (London: Whurr, 2nd edn., 1989) and P. Bryant & L. Bradley, *Children's reading problems* (Oxford: Blackwell, 1985). For a general account, see A. W. Ellis, *Reading, writing and dyslexia: a cognitive analysis* (London & Hillsdale: Erlbaum, 1984).

On voice, see M. C. L. Greene, *The voice and its disorders* (London: Whurr, 5th edn. with L. Mathieson, 1989); on cleft palate, M. Edwards & A. C. H. Watson (eds.), *Advances in the management of cleft palate* (London: Churchill Livingstone, 1980); on articulation, M. Edwards, *Disorders of articulation* (Vienna: Springer, 1984); on fluency, P. Dalton & W. Hardcastle, *Disorders of fluency* (London: Whurr, 2nd edn., 1989); on language delay, C. T. Wren (ed.), *Language learning disabilities* (Rockville, Md.: Aspen, 1983). Alternative systems are discussed in R. L. Schiefelbusch (ed.), *Nonspeech language and communication: analysis and intervention* (Baltimore: University Park Press, 1980); technological aids in D. Hawkridge, T. Vincent & G. Hales, *New information technology in the education of disabled children and adults* (London: Croom Helm, 1985).

Part IX

On the languages of the world, see C. F. & F. M. Voegelin, *Classification and index of the world's languages* (New York: Elsevier, 1977); B. Comrie (ed.), *The world's major languages* (London: Routledge, 1987); E. Gunnemark & D. Kenrick, *A geolinguistic handbook* (Gothenburg: privately printed, 2nd edn., 1986); M. Ruhlen, *A guide to the languages of the world* (Stanford, 1976); K. Katzner, *The languages of the world* (London: Routledge, 3rd edn., 1994); G.L. Campbell, *Compendium of the world's languages* (London: Routledge, 1991; issued in concise form, 1995); B.F. Grimes (ed.), *Ethnologue: languages of the world* (Dallas: Summer Institute of Linguistics, 13th edn., 1996, with separate index); C. Moseley & R.E. Asher (eds.), *Atlas of the world's languages* (London: Routledge, 1993); and A. Meillet & M. Cohen, *Les langues du monde* (Paris: Champion, 1952). The most comprehensive account is in T. A. Sebeok (ed.), *Current trends in linguistics*, Vols 1–14 (The Hague: Mouton, 1963–76). On the origins of language, see O. Jespersen, *Language: its nature, development and origin* (London: Allen & Unwin, 1922). Lost children are discussed in L. Malson & J. Itard, *Wolf children* and *The wild boy of Aveyron* (London: N.L.B., 1972). The fossil evidence is reviewed in P. Lieberman, *The speech of primates* (The Hague: Mouton, 1972); see also his *On the origins of language* (New York: Macmillan, 1975).

For a general introduction to language change, see J. Aitchison, *Language change – progress or decay?* (London: Fontana, 1981). Historical linguistics is presented in W. P.

Lehmann, *Historical linguistics: an introduction* (London: Routledge, 2nd edn., 1993) and A. Arlotto, *Introduction to historical linguistics* (Boston: Houghton Mifflin, 1972). The history of English is detailed in B. M. H. Strang, *A history of English* (London: Methuen, 1970); a social perspective is found in D. Leith, *A social history of English* (London: Routledge & Kegan Paul, 1983). A general theoretical study is R. Lass, *On explaining language change* (Cambridge: C.U.P., 1980).

An introductory account of Indo-European linguistics is provided by W. B. Lockwood, *Indo-European philology* (London: Hutchinson, 1969), and the languages themselves are introduced and illustrated by several texts in the same author's *A panorama of Indo-European languages* (London: Hutchinson, 1972). Archaeological, cultural, and linguistic data are brought together in G. Cardona, H. M. Hoenigswald & A. Senn (eds.), *Indo-European and the Indo-Europeans* (Philadelphia: University of Pennsylvania Press, 1970). The debate over laryngeals is reviewed in W. Winter (ed.), *Evidence for laryngeals* (The Hague: Mouton, 1965). The Celtic languages are outlined and illustrated in W. B. Lockwood, *Languages of the British Isles: past and present* (London: Deutsch, 1975). Different families are covered in the series: *Routledge Language Family Descriptions* (London: Routledge, 1993–).

For a general account of pidgins and creoles, see L. Todd, *Pidgins and creoles* (London: Routledge, 2nd edn., 1990); for a detailed account of English-based varieties, with particular reference to Tok Pisin and Cameroon, see also her *Modern Englishes: pidgins and creoles* (Oxford: Blackwell, 1984). Specialized studies are included in D. Hymes (ed.), *Pidginization and creolization of languages* (Cambridge: C.U.P., 1971) and D. DeCamp & I. F. Hancock (eds.), *Pidgins and creoles: current trends and prospects* (Washington: Georgetown University Press, 1974).

Part X

The field is presented in J. A. Large, *The foreign-language barrier: problems in scientific communication* (Oxford: Blackwell, 1983). The commercial aspect is reviewed in D. Liston & N. Reeves, *Business studies, languages, and overseas trade: a study of education and training* (London: MacDonald & Evans/Institute of Export, 1985). Theoretical aspects of translation are presented in E.A. Nida, *Language structure and translation* (Stanford: Stanford University Press, 1975); J. C. Catford, *A linguistic theory of translation: an essay in applied linguistics* (London: O.U.P., 1965); and P. Newmark, *Approaches to translation* (Oxford: Pergamon Press, 1981). A practical account is I. F. Finlay, *Translating* (London: Teach Yourself Books, 1971). A historical account is L. Venuti, *The translator's invisibility* (London: Routledge, 1994). Both translation and interpreting are covered in R. W. Brislin (ed.), *Translation: applications and research* (New York: Gardner Press, 1976). A historical perspective is given in L. G. Kelly, *The true interpreter: a history of translation theory and practice in the West* (Oxford: Blackwell, 1979). On machine translation, see B. M. Snell (ed.), *Translating and the computer* (Amsterdam: North-Holland, 1979) and D. Arnold, L. Balkan, R. L. Humphreys, S. Meijer & L. Sadler, *Machine translation: an introductory guide* (Oxford: Blackwell, 1994).

Auxiliary languages are presented in J. A. Large, *The artificial language movement* (Oxford: Blackwell, 1985). Further general background is in M. Pei, *One language for the world* (New York: Devin-Adair, 1958). On Esperanto in particular, see P. G. Forster, *The Esperanto movement* (The Hague: Mouton, 1982). The theme of world English is discussed in detail in R. W. Bailey & M. Görlach (eds.), *English as a world language* (London: C.U.P., 1982), and J. A. Fishman, R. L. Cooper & A. W. Conrad (eds.), *The spread of English: the sociology of English as an additional language* (Rowley, Mass.: Newbury House, 1977). On the differences between regional standards, see P. Trudgill & J. Hannah, *International English* (London: Edward Arnold, 1982).

Bilingualism is introduced in F. Grosjean, *Life with two languages: an introduction to bilingualism* (Cambridge, Mass.: Harvard University Press, 1982); see also J. Edwards, *Multilingualism* (Lodnon: Routledge, 1994). Many issues of language planning are dealt with in J. Edwards, *Language, society and identity* (Oxford: Blackwell, 1985). A more specialized discussion is found in J. Edwards (ed.), *Linguistic minorities, policies and pluralism* (London: Academic Press, 1984) and J. Cobarrubias and J. A. Fishman (eds.), *Progress in language planning* (Berlin: Mouton, 1983). On endangered languages and related matters, see R.H. Robins & E.M. Uhlenbeck (eds.), *Endangered languages* (Oxford & New York: Berg, 1991).

Short introductions to foreign language learning are W. Littlewood, *Foreign and second language learning* (Cambridge: C.U.P., 1984) and D. A. Wilkins, *Second-language learning and teaching* (London: Edward Arnold, 1974). A detailed account is W. M. Rivers, *Teaching foreign-language skills* (Chicago & London: University of Chicago Press, 2nd edn., 1981). For a selection of texts illustrating new approaches see R. W. Blair (ed.), *Innovative approaches to language teaching* (Rowley, Mass.: Newbury House, 1982). Communicative language teaching is introduced in D. A. Wilkins, *Notional syllabuses* (London: O.U.P., 1976) and discussed in K. Johnson & D. Porter (eds.), *Perspectives in communicative language teaching* (London: Academic Press, 1983). See also C. James, *Contrastive analysis* (London: Longman, 1980), S. D. Krashen, *Principles*

and practice in second language acquisition (Oxford: Pergamon, 1982), and S. P. Corder, *Error analysis and interlanguage* (London: O.U.P., 1981). On laboratories, see P. S. Green (ed.), *The language laboratory in school* (Edinburgh: Oliver & Boyd, 1975). On testing, see A. Hughes & D. Porter (eds.), *Current developments in language testing* (London: Academic Press, 1983).

The various varieties of language reviewed in Ch. 63 are given further treatment in D. Crystal, *The Cambridge Encyclopedia of the English Language* (Cambridge: C.U.P., 1995). See also R. Carter & W. Nash, *Seeing through language: a guide to styles of English writing* (Oxford: Blackwell, 1990); A. Bell, *The language of news media* (Oxford: Blackwell, 1991); V.K. Bhatia, *Analysing genre: language use in professional settings* (London: Longman, 1993). On critical language study, see N. Fairclough, *Language and power* (London: Longman, 1989); N. Fairclough (ed.), *Critical language awareness* (London: Longman, 1992).

Part XI

Definitions of language are discussed in J. Lyons, *Language and linguistics* (Cambridge: C.U.P., 1981). On animal communication and non-verbal communication in human beings, see R. A. Hinde (ed.), *Non-verbal communication* (Cambridge: C.U.P., 1972). On teaching language to chimpanzees: E. Linden, *Apes, men, and language* (New York: Dutton, 1975/Penguin, 1976) and D. & A. J. Premack, *The mind of an ape* (New York: Norton, 1983). On language and communication generally, see W. S-Y. Wang, *Human communication: language and its psychobiological bases* (Readings from *Scientific American*) (San Francisco: Freeman, 1982). An account of most of the fields of this section is to be found in T. A. Sebeok (ed.), *Current Trends in Linguistics, Vol. 12: Linguistics and adjacent arts and sciences* (The Hague: Mouton, 1974), Part 2. Non-verbal communication is reviewed in M. Argyle, *Bodily communication* (London: Methuen, 1975) and D. Morris, *Manwatching* (London: Cape, 1977). For signing, see Part VI above.

Introductions to linguistics include D. Crystal, *Linguistics* (Harmondsworth: Penguin, 2nd edn., 1985); J. Lyons, *Language and linguistics* (Cambridge: C.U.P., 1981); V. Fromkin & R. Rodman, *An introduction to language* (New York: Holt, Rinehart & Winston, 3rd edn., 1983); D. L. Bolinger & D. A. Sears, *Aspects of language* (New York: Harcourt Brace Jovanovich, 3rd edn., 1981); R. H. Robins, *General linguistics: an introductory survey* (London: Longman, 3rd edn., 1980); R. Wardhaugh, *Investigating language: central problems in linguistics* (Oxford: Blackwell, 1993); R. L. Trask, *Language: the Basics* (London: Routledge, 1995). For a historical perspective, see G. C. Lepschy, *A survey of structural linguistics* (Oxford: Blackwell, 2nd edn., 1982), R. H. Robins, *A short history of linguistics* (London: Longman, 1967), and R. Harris & T. J. Taylor, *Landmarks in linguistic thought* (London: Routledge, 1988). On Chomsky, see J. Lyons, *Chomsky* (London: Fontana, 3rd edn., 1991); S. Modgil & C. Modgil (eds.), *Noam Chomsky: consensus and controversy* (Philadelphia & Lewes: Falmer, 1987); for a personal statement, see N. Chomsky, *Knowledge of language* (New York: Praeger, 1986). On linguistic methods, see W. J. Samarin, *Field linguistics* (New York: Holt, Rinehart & Winston, 1967); K. Ajmer & B. Altenberg, *English corpus linguistics* (London: Longman, 1991); P. Scholfield, *Quantifying language* (Clevedon: Multilingual Matters, 1995). On natural language processing, see M. McTear, *The articulate computer* (Oxford: Blackwell, 1987) and C. S. Butler (ed.), *Computers and written texts* (Oxford: Blackwell, 1992). See also the volumes in the Routledge *Language Workbooks* series (ed. R. Hudson, 1994–).

Other encyclopedias of language and linguistics are: N. E. Collinge (ed.), *An encyclopedia of language* (London: Routledge, 1989); W. Bright, *International encyclopedia of linguistics* (Oxford: O.U.P., 1992, 4 vols); K. Malmkjaer (ed.), *The linguistics encyclopedia* (London: Routledge, 1991); R. E. Asher, *et al.*(eds.), *The encyclopedia of language and linguistics* (Oxford: Pergamon, 1993, 10 vols); F.J. Newmeyer (ed.), Linguistics: the Cambridge survey (Cambridge: C.U.P., 4 vols, 1988. See also D. Crystal, *An encyclopedic dictionary of language and languages* (Oxford: Blackwell, 1992; Harmondsworth: Penguin, 1994) and *The Cambridge encyclopedia of the English language* (Cambridge: C.U.P., 1995).

More advanced terminology is introduced in D. Crystal, *A dictionary of linguistics and phonetics* (Oxford: Blackwell, 4th edn., 1996); L. Trask, *A dictionary of grammatical terms in linguistics* (London: Routledge, 1993) and *Dictionary of phonetics and phonology* (London: Routledge, 1995). Many general language terms can be found in R. R. K. Hartmann & F. C. Stork, *Dictionary of language and linguistics* (New York: Wiley, 1972). For applied fields, see J. Richards, J. Platt & H. Weber, *Longman dictionary of applied linguistics* (London: Longman, 1985). For clinical terms, see L. Nicolosi, E. Harryman & J. Kreshek, *Terminology of communication disorders* (Baltimore: Williams & Wilkins, 1978). For traditional rhetoric, see J. A. Cuddon, *A dictionary of literary terms* (London: Deutsch, 2nd edn., 1979), and R. A. Lanham, *A handlist of rhetorical terms* (Berkeley & Los Angeles: University of California Press, 1969). On communication generally, see J. Watson & A. Hill, *A dictionary of communication and media studies* (London: Edward Arnold, 1984).

V   REFERENCES

All works referred to in the body of the text are listed below.

Ager, D. E. 1970. *Styles and registers in contemporary French.* London: University of London Press.

Albert, E. M. 1964. 'Rhetoric', 'logic', and 'poetics' in Burundi: culture patterning of speech behaviour. *American Anthropologist* **66**, 35–54.

Alexejew, P. M., Kalinin, W. M. & Piotrowski, R. G. (eds.). 1968. *Sprachstatistik.* Munich: Fink.

Allport, G. W. & Odbert, H. S. 1936. Trait-names: a psycholexical study. *Psychological Monographs* 47 (211).

Andersen, E. S. 1975. Cups and glasses: learning that boundaries are vague. *Journal of Child Language* 2, 79–103.

Anderson, W. E. K. 1972. *The Journal of Sir Walter Scott.* Oxford Clarendon.

Anhalt, I. 1972. Composing with speech. In A. Rigault & R. Charbonneau (eds.), *Proceedings of the Seventh International Congress of Phonetic Sciences* (The Hague: Mouton), 447–51.

Argyle, M. 1975. *Bodily communication.* London: Methuen.

Bailey, C-J. 1973. *Variation and linguistic theory.* Arlington, Va.: Center for Applied Linguistics.

Bailey, R. W. & Görlach, M. (eds.) 1982. *English as a world language.* Cambridge: C.U.P.

Barnes, D. 1969. Language in the secondary classroom. In D. Barnes, J. Britton & H. Rosen, *Language, the learner and the school* (Harmondsworth: Penguin), 9–77.

Beaugrande, R. de & Dressler, W. 1981. *Introduction to text linguistics.* London: Longman.

Bell, A. 1984. Language style as audience design. *Language in Society* **13**, 145–204.

Benedict, H. 1979. Early lexical development: comprehension and production. *Journal of Child Language* 6, 183–200.

Berko, J. 1958. The child's learning of English morphology. *Word* 14, 150–77.

Berko, J. & Brown, R. 1960. Psycholinguistic research methods. In P. H. Mussen (ed.), *Handbook of research methods in child development* (New York: Wiley), 517–57.

Berlin, B. & Kay, P. 1969. *Basic color terms.* Berkeley: University of California Press.

Beveridge, H. 1897–1910. *The Akbarnama,* translation, 3 vols. Society of Bengal: Bibliotheca Indica.

Birdwhistell, R. L. 1952. *Introduction to kinesics: an annotation system for analysis of body motion and gesture.* Washington: Foreign Service Institute.

Bloom, L. M. 1970. *Language development: form and function in emerging grammars.* Cambridge, MA.: M.I.T. Press.

Bloomfield, L. 1933. *Language.* New York: Holt, Rinehart & Winston.

Bolinger, D. L. 1964. Around the edge of language: intonation. *Harvard Educational Review* 34, 282–96.

Bower, C. A. 1976. Patterns of use of the serial literature at the BLLD. *BLL Review* 4, 31–6.

Bradley, L. 1983. The organization of visual, phonological, and motor strategies in learning to read and to spell. In U. Kirk (ed.), *Neuropsychology of language, reading, and spelling* (New York: Academic Press), 235–54.

Bright, W. (ed.) 1992. *International encyclopedia of linguistics.* New York & Oxford: O.U.P.

Bright, W. & Ramanujan, A. K. 1964. Sociolinguistic variation and language change. In *Proceedings of the Ninth International Congress of Linguists* (The Hague: Mouton).

Brislin, R. W. 1976. Introduction. In R. W. Brislin (ed.), *Translation: applications and research* (New York: Gardner Press), 1–43.

Bristow, G. J. & Fallside, F. 1979. A hierarchically structured feature-based training system for the speech impaired. *University of Cambridge Department of Engineering Report* ELECT/TR 54.

Brooks, L. 1977. Visual pattern in fluent word identification. In A. S. Reber & D. L. Scarborough (eds.), *Toward a psychology of reading* (New York: Wiley), 143–81.

Brosnahan, L. F. 1961. *The sounds of language.* Cambridge: Heffer.

Brosnahan, L. F. & Malmberg, B. 1970. *Introduction to phonetics.* Cambridge: Heffer.

Brown, R. 1973. *A first language.* Cambridge, MA.: Harvard University Press.

Brown, R. & Bellugi-Klima, U. 1964. Three processes in the child's acquisition of syntax. *Harvard Educational Review* 34, 133–51.

Brown, R., Cazden, C. & Bellugi-Klima, U. 1968. The child's grammar from I to III. In J. P. Hill (ed.), *Minnesota Symposia on Child Development*, Vol. 2 (Minneapolis: University of Minnesota Press), 28–73.

Brown, R. & Gilman, A. 1968. The pronouns of power and solidarity. In J. A. Fishman (ed.), *Readings in the sociology of language* (The Hague: Mouton), 252–75.

Brunner, H. 1975. Hieroglyphic writing. *Encyclopaedia Britannica* (Macropaedia) Vol. **8**, 853–7.

Buren, P. van 1972. *The edges of language.* London: SCM Press.

Burgess, A. 1980. Dubbing. In L. Michaels & C. Ricks (eds.), *The state of the language* (Berkeley: University of California Press), 297–303.

Byrne, P. S. & Long, B. E. L. 1976. *Doctors talking to patients: a study of the verbal behaviour of general practitioners consulting in their surgeries.* London: H.M.S.O.

Cassidy, F. G. 1971. Tracing the pidgin element in Jamaican creole. In D. Hymes (ed.), *Pidginization and creolization of languages.* (Cambridge: C.U.P.), 203–21.

Catford, J. C. 1965. *A linguistic theory of translation.* Oxford: O.U.P.

Chambers, J. K. & Trudgill, P. 1980. *Dialectology.* Cambridge: C.U.P.

Chapman, R. 1984. *The treatment of sounds in language and literature.* Oxford: Blackwell.

Chase, S. 1938. *The tyranny of words.* London: Methuen.

Chen, M. 1972. The time dimension: contribution toward a theory of sound change. *Foundations of Language* 8, 457–98.

Chang, N-C. 1958. Tones and intonation in the Chengtu dialect. *Phonetica* 2, 59–84.

Chomsky, A. N. 1957. *Syntactic structures.* The Hague: Mouton.

Christopherson, P. 1939. *The articles: a study of their theory and use in English.* Copenhagen: Munksgaard.

Collison, R. L. 1982. *A history of foreign-language dictionaries.* Oxford: Blackwell.

Connor, W. 1978. A nation is a nation, is a state, is an ethnic group, is a … . *Ethnic and Racial Studies* 1, 377–400.

Cooper, R. L. 1984. The avoidance of androcentric generics. *International Journal of the Sociology of Language* 50, 5–20.

Cowan, G. M. 1948. Mazateco whistled speech. *Language* 24, 280–6.

Cowan, N. & Leavitt, L. 1982. Talking backward: exceptional speech play in late childhood. *Journal of Child Language* 9, 481–95.

Cowie, H. & Hanrott, H. 1984. The writing community: a case study of one junior school class. In H. Cowie (ed.), *The development of children's imaginative writing* (London: Croom Helm), 200–18.

Cramond, W. A. 1970. Psychotherapy of the dying patient. *British Medical Journal* 3, 389–93.

Cruttenden, A. 1974. An experiment involving comprehension of intonation in children from 7 to 10. *Journal of Child Language* 1, 221–31.

Crystal, D. 1969. *Prosodic systems and intonation in English.* Cambridge: C.U.P.

Crystal, D. 1986. *Listen to your child.* Harmondsworth: Penguin.

Crystal, D. & Davy, D. 1969. *Investigating English style.* London: Longman.

Crystal, D., Fletcher, P. & Garman, M. 1989. *The grammatical analysis of language disability: a procedure for assessment and remediation,* 2nd edn. London: Edward Arnold.

Crystal, D. & Foster, J. 1983. *Electricity.* London: Edward Arnold.

Curtiss, S. 1977. *Genie: a psycholinguistic study of a modern-day 'wild child'.* New York: Academic Press.

Dayananda, J. Y. 1986. Plain English in the United States. *English Today* 2 (1), 13–16.

Decker, T. 1965. Antony's speech from *Julius Caesar.* Reprinted in L. Todd, *Modern Englishes: pidgins and creoles.* Oxford: Blackwell, 1984.

Delattre, P. 1966. The distinctive function of intonation. In D. Bolinger (ed.), *Intonation* (Harmondsworth: Penguin), 159–74.

Department of Education and Science. 1972. *Speech therapy services.* ('The Quirk Report'). London: H.M.S.O.

Department of Education and Science. 1975. *A language for life.* ('The Bullock Report'). London: H.M.S.O.

Dewey, G. 1923. *Relative frequencies of English speech sounds.* Cambridge, MA.: Harvard University Press.

Dewey, G. 1971. *English spelling: roadblock to reading.* New York: Columbia University Press.

Diringer, D. 1968. *The alphabet,* 3rd edn. London: Hutchinson.

Downing, J., Ayers, D. & Schaefer, B. 1983. *Linguistic awareness in reading readiness (LARR) test.* Windsor: NFER-Nelson.

Duckworth, M., Allen, G., Hardcastle, W. & Ball, M. 1990. Extensions to the International Phonetic Alphabet for the transcription of atypical speech. Clinical Linguistics & Phonetics 4, 273–83.

Duffy, S. A. & Pisoni, D. B. 1992. Comprehension of syntactic speech produced by rule: a review and theoretical interpretation. *Language and Speech* 35, 351–89.

Dulay, H. C. & Burt, M. K. 1973. Should we teach children syntax? *Language Learning* 23, 245–57.

Dunkling, L. 1995. *The Guinness Book of Names,* 7th edn. London: Guinness Superlatives.

Duranti, A. 1983. Samoan speechmaking across social events: one genre in and out of a *fono. Language in Society* 12, 1–22.

Eibl-Eibesfeldt, I. 1972. Similarities and differences between cultures in expressive movements. In R. A. Hinde (ed.), *Non-verbal communication* (Cambridge: C.U.P.), 297–312.

Eimas, P. D., Siqueland, E. R., Jusczyk, P. & Vigorito, J. 1971. Speech perception in infants. *Science* **171**, 303–6.

Ellegård, A. 1962. *Who was Junius?* Stockholm: Almqvist & Wiksell.

Enkvist, N. E. 1978. Coherence, pseudo-coherence and non-coherence. In J-O.Ostman (ed.), *Cohesion and semantics* (Åbo: Åbo Akademi Foundation), 109–28.

Ervin-Tripp, S. 1972. On sociolinguistic rules: alternation and co-occurence. In J. J. Gumperz & D. Hymes (eds.), *Directions in sociolinguistics* (New York: Holt, Rinehart & Winston), 213–50.

Evans-Pritchard, E. E. 1948. Nuer modes of address. *The Uganda Journal* **12**, 166–71.

Fant, G. 1967. Auditory patterns of speech. In W. Wathen-Dunn (ed.), *Models for the perception of speech and visual form* (Cambridge, MA.: M.I.T. Press), 111–25.

Ferguson, C. A. 1976. The structure and use of politeness formulas. *Language in Society* **5**, 137–51.

Ferguson, C. A. 1977. Baby talk as a simplified register. In C. E. Snow & C. A. Ferguson (eds.), *Talking to children* (Cambridge: C.U.P.), 219–35.

Ferguson, C. A. 1983. Sports announcer talk: syntactic aspects of register variation. *Language in Society* **12**, 153–72.

Ferguson, C. A. & Farwell, C. B. 1975. Words and sounds in early language acquisition. *Language* **51**, 419–39.

Finlay, I. F. 1971. *Translating.* London: Teach Yourself Books.

Firth, J. R. 1957. A synopsis of linguistic theory, 1930–55. *Studies in Linguistic Analysis* (Oxford: Philological Society), 1–32.

Fishman, J. A. 1984. Mother tongue claiming in the United States since 1960: trends and correlates related to the 'revival of ethnicity'. *International Journal of the Sociology of Language* **50**, 21–99.

Fletcher, C. M. 1973. *Communication in medicine.* London: The Nuffield Provincial Hospitals Trust.

Fletcher, P. 1985. *A child's learning of English.* Oxford: Blackwell.

Fónagy, I. & Magdics, K. 1963. Emotional patterns in intonation and music. *Zeitschrift für Phonetik und allgemeine Sprachwissenschaft* **16**, 293–326.

Fox, J. J. 1974. 'Our ancestors spoke in pairs': Rotinese views of language, dialect, and code. In R. Bauman & J. Sherzer (eds.), *Explorations in the ethnography of speaking* (Cambridge: C.U.P.), 65–85.

French, N. R., Carter, C. W. & Koenig, W. 1930. The words and sounds of telephone conversation. *Bell Systems Technical Journal* **9**, 290–324.

Frisch, K. von. 1962. Dialects in the language of bees. *Scientific American* **207** (August).

Frishberg, N. 1979. Historical change: from iconic to arbitrary. Chapter 3 of E. Klima & U. Bellugi, *The signs of language* (Cambridge, MA.: Harvard University Press).

Fromkin, V. A. (ed.). 1973. *Speech errors as linguistic evidence.* The Hague: Mouton.

Fry, D. B. 1947. The frequency of occurrence of speech sounds in Southern English. *Archives Néerlandaises de Phonétique Expérimentale* **20**.

Fry, D. B. 1979. *The physics of speech.* Cambridge: C.U.P.

Galloway, L. 1978. Language impairment and recovery in polyglot aphasia: a case study of a hepta-lingual. In M. Paradis (ed.), *Aspects of bilingualism* (Columbia: Hornbeam Press), 121–30.

Gannon, P. 1985. *Assessing writing: principles and practice of marking written English.* London: Edward Arnold.

Gardner, B. T. & Gardner, R. A. 1975. Evidence for sentence constituents in the early utterances of child and chimpanzee. *Journal of Experimental Psychology* **104**, 244–62.

Geertz, C. 1968. Linguistic etiquette. In J. A. Fishman (ed.), *Readings in the sociology of language* (The Hague: Mouton), 282–95.

Geis, M. L. 1982. *The language of television advertising.* New York: Academic Press.

Gerver, D. 1969. The effects of source language presentation rate on the performance of simultaneous conference interpreters. In E. Foulke (ed.), *Proceedings of the 2nd Louisville Conference on Rate and/or Frequency Controlled Speech* (University of Louisville), 162–84.

Gerver, D. 1976. Empirical studies of simultaneous interpretation: a review and a model. In R. Brislin (ed.), *Translation* (New York: Wiley), 165–207.

Gimson, A. C. 1994. *An introduction to the pronunciation of English*, 5th edn. London: Edward Arnold.

Gleason, H. A. 1955. *An introduction to descriptive linguistics.* New York: Holt, Rinehart & Winston.

Godard, D. 1977. Same setting, different norms: phone call beginnings in France and the United States. *Language in Society* **6**, 209–19.

Gordon, D. P. 1983. Hospital slang for patients: crocks, gomers, gorks, and others. *Language in Society* **12**, 173–85.

Greenberg, J. 1985. *Language in the Americas.* Stanford: Stanford University Press.

Greimas, A. J. 1966. *Sémantique structurale.* Paris: Larousse.

Grenfell, M. 1977. *George – don't do that ...* (London: Macmillan).

Grice, H. P. 1975. Logic and conversation. In P. Cole & J. L. Morgan (eds.), *Speech acts* (New York: Academic Press), 41–58.

Grimes, B.F. (ed.) 1996. Ethnologue: languages of the world, 13th edn. Dallas: Summer Institute of Linguistics.

Grosjean, F. 1982. *Life with two languages.* Cambridge, MA.: Harvard University Press.

Gumperz, J. 1970. Verbal strategies in multilingual communication. In J. Alatis (ed.), *Bilingualism and language contact* (Washington: Georgetown University Press), 129–47.

Gunnemark, E. & Kenrick, D. 1985. *A geolinguistic handbook*, 2nd edn. Gothenburg: privately published.

Haarman, H. 1984. The role of ethnocultural stereotypes and foreign languages in Japanese commercials. *International Journal of the Sociology of Language* **50**, 101–21.

Haas, M. R. 1944. Men's and women's speech in Koasati. *Language* **20**, 142–9.

Hall, E. T. 1959. *The silent language.* New York: Doubleday.

Hall. R. A. 1964. *Introductory linguistics.* Philadelphia: Chilton.

Halliday, M. A. K. 1961. Categories of the theory of grammar. *Word* **17**, 241–92.

Halliday, M. A. K. 1967. *Intonation and grammar in British English.* The Hague: Mouton.

Halliday, M. A. K. & Hasan, R. 1976. *Cohesion in English.* London: Longman.

Hancock, I. F. 1971. A survey of the pidgins and creoles of the world. In D. Hymes (ed.), *Pidginization and creolization of languages* (Cambridge: C.U.P.), 509–23.

Hanna, P. R., Hodges, R. E. & Hanna, J. S. 1971. *Spelling: structure and strategies.* Boston: Houghton Mifflin.

Harada, S. I. 1976. Honorifics. In M. Shibatani (ed.), *Japanese generative grammar.* New York: Academic Press.

Hardcastle, W. J. & Morgan, R. A. 1982. An instrumental investigation of articulation disorders in children. *British Journal of Disorders of Communication* **17**, 47–65.

Hardcastle, W. J. & Roach, P. 1977. An instrumental investigation of coarticulation in stop consonant sequences. *Reading University Phonetics Laboratory Working Papers* **1**, 27–44.

Hatfield, F. M. & Patterson, K. E. 1984. Interpretation of spelling disorders in aphasia: impact of recent developments in cognitive psychology. In F. Clifford Rose (ed.), *Progress in aphasiology* (New York: Raven Press), 183–92.

Haugen, E. (ed.) 1972. *First grammatical treatise*, 2nd edn. London: Longman.

Haugen, E. & Joos, M. 1952. Tone and intonation in East Norwegian. *Acta Philologica Scandinavica* **22**, 41–64.

Haviland, J. B. 1979. Guugu Yimidhirr brother-in-law language. *Language in Society* **8**, 365–93.

Heath, S. B. 1979. The context of professional languages: an historical overview. In J. E. Alatis & G. R. Tucker (eds.), *Language in public life* (Washington: Georgetown University Press), 102–18.

Heath, S. B. & Mandabach, F. 1983. Language status decisions and the law in the United States. In J. Cobarrubias & J. A. Fishman (eds.), *Progress in language planning: international perspectives* (Berlin: Mouton), 87–105.

Hécaen, H. & Marcie, P. 1974. Disorders of written language following right hemisphere lesions: spatial dysgraphia. In S. J. Dimond & J. G. Beaumont (eds.), *Hemisphere function in the human brain* (London: Elek Science), 345–66.

Herzog, G. 1945. Drum signaling in a West African tribe. *Word* **1**, 217–38.

Hockett, C. F. 1958. *A course in modern linguistics.* New York: Macmillan.

Hockett, C. F. 1960. The origin of speech. *Scientific American* **203** (September).

Hulke, M. 1982. *Writing for television.* London: Black.

Huttenlocher, P. R. & Huttenlocher, J. 1973. A study of children with hyperlexia. *Neurology* **23**, 1107–16.

Irvine, J. T. 1974. Strategies of status manipulation in the Wolof greeting. In R. Bauman & J. Sherzer (eds.), *Explorations in the ethnography of speaking* (Cambridge: C.U.P.), 167–91.

Jackson, J. 1974. Language identity of the Vaupés Indians. In R. Bauman & J. Sherzer (eds.), *Explorations in the ethnography of speaking* (Cambridge: C.U.P.), 50–64.

Jacobson, S. 1966. *Unorthodox spelling in American trade marks.* Stockholm: Almqvist & Wiksell.

Jakobson, R. & Halle, M. 1956. *Fundamentals of language.* The Hague: Mouton.

James, C. V. 1979. Foreign languages in the school curriculum. In G. E. Perren (ed.), *Foreign languages in education* (London: CILT), 7–28.

James, R. & Gregory, R. G. 1966. *Imaginative speech and writing.* London: Nelson.

Johansson, S. & Hofland, K. 1989. *Frequency analysis of English vocabulary and grammar.* Oxford: Clarendon Press.

Johnson, K. & Porter, D. (eds.) 1983. *Perspectives in communicative language teaching.* London: Academic Press.

Jones, D. 1956. *An outline of English phonetics*, 8th edn. Cambridge: Heffer.

Jourard, S. M. 1963. An exploratory study of body-accessibility. *British Journal of Social and Clinical Psychology* **5**, 221–31.

Kaeding, F. W. 1989. *Häufigkeitswörterbuch der Deutschen Sprache.* Berlin: Mittler.

Kakehi, H., Mito, Y., Hayase, M., Tsuzuki, M. & Young, R. 1981. *Nichi-ei taishô onomatope jiten.* (A dictionary of Japanese onomatopes, with reference to English expressions). Tokyo: Gaku-shobô.

Karlsson, I. 1991. Female voices in speech synthesis. *Journal of Phonetics.* **19**, 111–20.

Keenan, E. 1974. Norm-makers, norm-breakers: uses of speech by men and women in a Malagasy community. In R. Bauman & J. Sherzer (eds.), *Explorations in the ethnography of speaking* (Cambridge: C.U.P.), 125–43.

Keenan, E. 1974. Conversational competence in children. *Journal of Child Language* **1**, 163–83.

Kelly, L. G. 1979. *The true interpreter: a history of translation theory and practice in the West.* Oxford: Blackwell.

Kent, R. D. & Burkard, R. 1981. Changes in the acoustic correlates of speech production. In D. S. Beasley & G. A. Davis (eds.), *Aging: communication processes and disorders* (New York: Grune & Stratton), 47–62.

Kenyon, J. S. & Knott, T. A. 1935. *The pronouncing dictionary of American English.* Springfield, MA.: Merriam.

Kersta, L. G. 1962. Voiceprint identification. *Nature* **196**, 1253–7.

Klima, E. & Bellugi, U. 1979. *The signs of language.* Cambridge, MA.: Harvard University Press.

Knowles, F. 1979. Error analysis of Systran output – a suggested criterion for the internal evaluation of translation quality and a possible corrective for system design. In B. M. Snell (ed.), *Translating and the computer* (Amsterdam: North Holland), 109–33.

Kroll, B. M. 1981. Developmental relationships between speaking and writing. In B. M. Kroll & R. J. Vann (eds.), *Exploring speaking-writing relationships: connections and contrasts.* Urbana: National Council of Teachers of English.

Krout, M. H. 1942. *Introduction to social psychology.* New York: Harper & Row.

Kuiper, K. & Haggo, D. 1984. Livestock auctions, oral poetry, and ordinary language. *Language in Society* **13**, 205–34.

Kurath, H. 1949. *Word geography of the Eastern United States.* Ann Arbor: University of Michigan Press.

Labov, W. 1982. Objectivity and commitment in linguistic science; the case of the Black English trial in Ann Arbor. *Language in Society* **11**, 165–201.

Ladefoged, P. 1982. *A course in phonetics*, 2nd edn. New York: Harcourt Brace Jovanovich.

Lamb, S. M. 1966. *Outline of stratificational grammar.* Washington: Georgetown University Press.

Lambert, W. E., Hodgson, R. C., Gardner, R. C. & Fillenbaum, S. 1960. Evaluational reactions to spoken language. *Journal of Abnormal and Social Psychology* **60**, 44–51.

Large, J. A. 1983. *The foreign-language barrier.* Oxford: Blackwell.

Lauder, A. 1965. *Let stalk Strine.* Sydney: Ure Smith.

Lecours, A. R. & Lhermitte, F. 1983. Clinical forms of aphasia. In A. R. Lecours, F. Lhermitte & B. Bryans (eds.), *Aphasiology* (London: Baillière Tindall), 76–108.

Leech, G. N. 1966. *English in advertising: a linguistic study of advertising in Great Britain.* London: Longman.

Leech, G. N. 1969. *A linguistic guide to English poetry.* London: Longman.

Legros, L. A. & Grant, J. C. 1916. *Typographical printing surfaces.* London: Longmans, Green.

Levine, C. C. 1970. Doctor–patient communication with the inner-city adolescent. *New England Medical Journal* **282**, 494–5.

Liberman, A. M., Harris, K. S., Hoffman, H. S. & Griffith, B. C. 1957. The discrimination of speech sounds within and across phoneme boundaries. *Journal of Experimental Psychology* **54**, 358–68.

Liddell, S. K. 1980. *American Sign Language syntax.* The Hague: Mouton.

Lieberman, P. 1972. *The speech of primates.* The Hague: Mouton.

Lisker, L. & Abramson, A. 1970. The voicing dimension: some experiments in comparative phonetics. In *Proceedings of the VIth International Congress of Phonetic Sciences* (Prague: Academia), 563–7.

Litowitz, B. 1977. Learning to make definitions. *Journal of Child Language* **4**, 289–304.

Lloyd, P. & Donaldson, M. 1976. On a method of eliciting true/false judgements from young children. *Journal of Child Language* **3**, 411–16.

Locke, J. L. 1983. *Phonological acquisition and change.* New York: Academic Press.

Loewen, J. A. 1964. Culture, meaning and translation. *The Bible Translator* **15**, 189–94.

Loh, S. C. 1976. Machine translation: past, present and future. *Bulletin of the Association for Literary and Linguistic Computing* **4**, 105–9.

Louttit, C. M. 1957. The use of foreign languages by psychologists, chemists and physicists. *American Journal of Psychology* **70**, 314–16.

Lyons, J. 1963. *Structural semantics.* Oxford: Blackwell.

Lyons, J. 1981. *Language and linguistics.* Cambridge: C.U.P.

Mackay, D. & Simo, J. 1976. *Help your child to read and write, and more.* Harmondsworth: Penguin.

Mackay, D., Thompson, B. & Schaub, P. 1970. *Breakthrough to literacy.* London: Longman.

Maclay, H. & Ware, E. E. 1961. Cross-cultural use of the semantic differential. *Behavioral Science* **6**, 185–90.

McTear, M. 1985. *Children's conversation.* Oxford: Blackwell.

McTear, M. 1987. *The articulate computer.* Oxford: Blackwell.

Maddieson, I. 1984. *Patterns of sounds.* Cambridge: C.U.P.

Maher, C. & Cutts, M. 1986. Plain English in the United Kingdom. *English Today* **2**, (1), 10–12.

Maltz, D. N. & Borker, R. A. 1982. A cultural approach to male–female miscommunication. In J. J. Gumperz (ed.), *Language and social identity* (Cambridge: C.U.P.), 195–216.

Marcus, J. 1980. Zapotec writing. In W. S-Y. Wang (ed.), *Human communication* (San Francisco: Freeman, 1982), 90–104.

Marshall, J. C. & Newcombe, F. 1980. The conceptual status of deep dyslexia: an historical perspective. In M. Coltheart, K. Patterson & J. C. Marshall (eds.), *Deep dyslexia* (London: Routledge & Kegan Paul), 1–21.

Martin, N., D'Arcy, P., Newton, B. & Parker, R. 1976. *Writing and learning across the curriculum* 11–16. (Schools Council Publications.) London: Ward Lock Educational.

Masson, O. 1961. *Les inscriptions chypriotes syllabiques.* Paris: Boccard.

Matsuhashi, A. 1982. Explorations in the real-time production of written discourse. In M. Nystrand (ed.), *What writers know* (New York: Academic Press), 269–90.

Mehrotra, R. R. 1977. *Sociology of secret languages.* Simla: Indian Institute of Advanced Study.

Mellinkoff, D. 1963. *The language of the law.* Boston: Little, Brown.

Merzenich, M. M. 1975. Studies on electrical stimulation of the auditory nerve in animals and man: cochlear implants. In D. B. Tower (ed.), *Human communication and its disorders* (New York: Raven Press).

Moerk, E. L. 1970. Quantitative analysis of writing styles. *Journal of Linguistics* **6**, 223–30.

Morris, D. 1977. *Manwatching.* London: Cape.

Morris, D., Collett, P., Marsh, P. & O'Shaughnessy, M. 1978. *Gesture maps.* London: Cape.

Morrow, K. 1978. *Advanced conversational English workbook.* London: Longman.

Moseley, C. & Asher, R.E. 1993. *Atlas of the world's languages.* London: Routledge.

Mountford, J. 1973. Writing-system: a datum in bibliographical description. In C. H. Rawski (ed.), *Toward a theory of librarianship* (Metuchen, N.J.: Scarecrow Press), 415–49.

Murchison, C. & Langer, S. K. 1927. Tiedemann's observations on the development of the mental faculties of children. *The Pedagogical Seminary and Journal of Genetic Psychology* **34**, 205–30.

Murphy, J. J. 1966. *The book of Pidgin English.* Brisbane: Smith & Patterson.

Nadoleczny, M. 1923. *Untersuchungen über den Kunstgesang.* Berlin: Springer.

Negus, V. E. 1949. *The comparative anatomy and physiology of the larynx.* New York: Hafner.

O'Barr, W. M. 1982. *Linguistic evidence: language, power, and strategy in the courtroom.* London: Academic Press.

Ó Brógáin, S. 1983. Typographic measurement: a critique and a proposal. *Professional Printer* **27**, 9–14.

Ochs, E. 1982. Talking to children in Western Samoa. *Language in Society* **11**, 77–104.

O'Connor, J. D. & Arnold, G. F. 1973. *Intonation of colloquial English*, 2nd edn. London: Longman.

Ogden, C. K. 1932. *The Basic dictionary.* London: Kegan Paul, Trench, Trubner.

Ogden, C. K. 1938. *Basic English.* London: Kegan Paul, Trench, Trubner.

Olmstead, D. 1971. *Out of the mouth of babes.* The Hague: Mouton.

Orton, H., Sanderson, S. & Widdowson, J. 1978. *The linguistic atlas of England.* London: Croom Helm; Atlantic Highlands, NJ: Humanities Press.

Osgood, C. E. 1952. The nature and measurement of meaning. *Psychological Bulletin* **49**, 197–237.

Pawley, A. & Syder, F. H. 1983. Two puzzles for linguistic theory: nativelike selection and nativelike fluency. In J. C. Richards & R. W. Schmidt (eds.), *Language and communication* (London: Longman).

Pear, T. H. 1931. *Voice and personality.* London: Chapman & Hall.

Pence, A. 1964. Intonation in Kunimaipa (New Guinea). *Linguistic Circle of Canberra Publications* **A3**, Australian National University.

Penfield, W. G. & Roberts, L. 1959. *Speech and brain mechanisms.* Princeton: Princeton University Press.

Pike, K. L. 1945. *The intonation of American English.* Ann Arbor: University of Michigan Press.

Pittenger, R. E., Hockett, C. F. & Danehy, J. J. 1960. *The first five minutes.* Ithaca: Martineau.

Potter, S. 1952. *One-upmanship.* London: Hart-Davis.

Prather, E. M., Hedrick, D. L. & Kern, C. A. 1975. Articulation development in children aged two to four years. *Journal of Speech and Hearing Disorders* **40**, 179–91.

Premack, D. & Premack, A. J. 1983. *The mind of an ape.* New York: Norton.

Pronovost, W., Yenkin, L., Anderson, D. C. & Lerner, R. 1968. The voice visualizer. *American Annals of the Deaf* **113** (March).

Quirk, R. 1982. International communication and the concept of Nuclear English. In R. Quirk, *Style and communication in the English language* (London: Edward Arnold), 37–53.

Raban, B. 1981. Line-breaks in texts for young readers. *Social Science Research Council Project* HR 6390/1. London: S.S.R.C.

Rayner, K. & McConkie, G. W. 1977. Perceptual processes in reading: the perceptual spans. In A. Reber & D. L. Scarborough (eds.), *Toward a psychology of reading* (New York: Wiley), 183–205.

Rips, L. J., Shoben, E. J. & Smith, E. E. 1973. Semantic distance and the verification of semantic relations. *Journal of Verbal Learning and Verbal Behavior* 12, 1–20.

Ritchie, D. 1960. *Stroke: the diary of a recovery.* London: Faber & Faber.

Rockey, D. 1973. *Phonetic lexicon.* London: Heyden.

Rosenberg, B. A. 1970. The formulaic quality of spontaneous sermons. *Journal of American Folklore* 83, 3–20.

Rozin, P. & Gleitman, L. R. 1974. *Syllabary: an introductory reading curriculum.* Washington: Curriculum Development Associates.

Salmond, A. 1974. Rituals of encounter among the Maori: sociolinguistic study of a scene. In R. Bauman & J. Sherzer (eds.), *Explorations in the ethnography of speaking* (Cambridge: C.U.P.), 192–212.

Sankoff, G. & Cedergren, H. 1971. Les contraintes linguistiques et sociales de l'élision du *l* chez les Montréalais. In M. Boudreault & F. Moehren (eds.), *Actes du XIIIe Congrès Internationale de Linguistique et de Phonologie Romanes.* Laval University Press.

Sapir, E. 1921. *Language.* New York: Harcourt Brace.

Schlesinger, I. M. & Namir, L. 1978. *Sign language of the deaf.* New York: Academic Press.

Schmandt-Besserat, D. 1978. The earliest precursor of writing. Repr. in W. S-Y. Wang (ed.), *Human communication* (San Francisco: Freeman, 1982), 80–9.

Schwartz, R. G., Leonard, L. B., Wilcox, M. J. & Folger, M. K. 1980. Again and again: reduplication in child phonology. *Journal of Child Language* 7, 75–87.

Scott, C. T. 1965. *Persian and Arabic riddles.* Bloomington: Indiana University.

Searle, J. R. 1976. A classification of illocutionary acts. *Language in Society* 5, 1–23.

Selinker, L. 1972. Interlanguage. *International Review of Applied Linguistics* 10, 201–31.

Shaw, F., Spiegl, F. & Kelly, S. 1966. *Lern yerself Scouse.* Liverpool: Scouse Press.

Shephard, D. A. E. 1973. Some effects of delay in publication of information in medical journals, and implications for the future. *IEEE Transactions on Professional Communication* PC-163, 143–7.

Sherwood Fox, W. 1919. Cursing as a fine art. *The Sewanee Review Quarterly* 27, 460–77.

Sherzer, J. 1974. *Namake, sunmakke, kormakke:* three types of Cuna speech event. In R. Bauman & J. Sherzer (eds.), *Explorations in the ethnography of speaking* (Cambridge: C.U.P.), 263–82.

Slobin, D. I. & Welsh, C. A. 1967. Elicited imitation as a research tool in developmental psycholinguistics. Center for Research on Language and Language Behavior, University of Michigan; repr. in C. S. Lauatelli (ed.), *Language training in early childhood education* (University of Illinois Press, 1971), 170–85.

Smith, B. L. & Oller, D. K. 1981. A comparative study of pre-meaningful vocalizations produced by normally developing and Down's syndrome infants. *Journal of Speech and Hearing Disorders* 46, 46–51.

Smith, M. E. 1926. An investigation of the development of the sentence and the extent of vocabulary in young children. *University of Iowa Studies in Child Welfare* 3 (5).

Snow, C. 1977. The development of conversation between mothers and babies. *Journal of Child Language* 4, 1–22.

Song, J. & Samouelian, A. 1993. A robust speaker-independent isolated word FIMM recognizer for operation over the telephone network. *Speech Communication* 13, 287–95.

Sperber, D. & Wilson, D. 1986. *Relevance.* Oxford: Blackwell.

Steiner, R. 1931. *Eurhythmy as visible speech.* New York: Anthroposophic Press.

Stockwell, R. P. 1972. The role of intonation. In D. L. Bolinger (ed.), *Intonation* (Harmondsworth: Penguin), 89–109.

Stoel-Gammon, C. & Cooper, J. A. 1984. Patterns of early lexical and phonological development. *Journal of Child Language* 11, 247–71.

Stokoe, W. C., Casterline, D. C. & Croneberg, C. G. 1965. *A dictionary of American Sign Language on linguistic principles.* Silver Spring, MD.: Linstok Press.

Stuhlman, O. 1952. *An introduction to biophysics.* New York: Wiley.

Svartvik, J. 1968. *The Evans statements: a case for forensic linguistics.* Stockholm: Almqvist & Wiksell.

Svartvik, J., Eeg-Olofsson, M., Forsheden, O., Oreström, B. & Thavenius, C. 1982. *Survey of spoken English.* Lund: Gleerup/Liber.

Svartvik, J. & Quirk, R. (eds.) 1980. *A corpus of English conversation.* Lund: Gleerup/Liber.

Swadesh, M. 1972. *The origin and diversification of language.* London: Routledge & Kegan Paul.

Swan, M. & Walter, C. 1984. *The Cambridge English Course 1.* Cambridge: C.U.P.

Swann, W. & Mittler, P. 1976. A survey of language abilities in ESN(S) children. *Special Education: Forward Trends* 3, 24–7.

Tannen, D. 1986. *That's not what I meant! How conversational style makes or breaks your relations with others.* New York: Morrow.

Tannen, D. 1990. *You just don't understand! Women and men in conversation.* New York: Morrow.

Tarasuk, M. B., Rhymes, J. P. & Leonard, R. C. 1965. An experimental test of the importance of communication skills for effective nursing. In J. K. Skipper & R. C. Leonard (eds.), *Social interaction and patient care* (Philadelphia: Lippincott).

Tarnopol, L. & Tarnopol, M. 1976. *Reading disabilities: an international perspective.* Baltimore: University Park Press.

Thody, P. & Evans, H. 1985. *Faux amis and key words.* London: Athlone Press.

Thomas, A. R. 1973. *The linguistic geography of Wales.* Cardiff: University of Wales Press.

Thomson, M. 1984. *Developmental dyslexia.* London: Edward Arnold.

Thorndyke, P. W. 1977. Cognitive structures in comprehension and memory of narrative discourse. *Cognitive Psychology* 9, 77–110.

Todd, L. 1984. *Modern Englishes: pidgins and creoles.* Oxford: Blackwell.

Toronto, A. S. 1973. *Screening test of Spanish grammar.* Evanston: Northwestern University Press.

Trager, G. 1949. *The field of linguistics.* Norman, OK.: Battenburg Press.

Trager, G. & Smith, H. L. 1951. *An outline of English structure.* Norman, OK.: Battenburg Press.

Trevarthen, C. 1993. The self born in intersubjectivity: the psychology of an infant communicating. In U. Neisser (ed.), *The perceived self* (Cambridge: C.U.P.), 121–173.

Trudgill, P. 1974. *The social differentiation of English in Norwich.* Cambridge: C.U.P.

Trudgill, P. 1983. *Sociolinguistics*, 2nd edn. Harmondsworth: Penguin.

Turner, G. W. 1972. The grammar of newspaper headlines containing the preposition *on* in the sense 'about'. *Linguistics* 87, 71–86.

Twyman, M. 1982. The graphic presentation of language. *Information Design Journal* 3, 1–22.

Ullmann, S. 1964. *Language and style.* Oxford: Blackwell.

Valdés Fallis, G. 1976. Social interaction and code-switching patterns: a case study of Spanish/English alternation. In G. Keller, R. Teschner & S. Viera (eds.), *Bilingualism in the bicentennial and beyond* (New York: Bilingual Press/Editorial Bilingüe).

Vivian, R. 1966. The Tadoma method: a tactual approach to speech and speech reading. *Volta Review* 68, 733–7.

Volterra, V. & Taeschner, T. 1978. The acquisition and development of language by bilingual children. *Journal of Child Language* 5, 311–26.

Wagner, K. R. 1985. How much do children say in a day? *Journal of Child Language* 12, 475–87.

Walker, A. 1984. Applied sociology of language: vernacular languages. In P. Trudgill (ed.), *Applied sociolinguistics* (London: Academic Press), 159–202.

Warren, R. M. & Warren, R. P. 1970. Auditory illusions and confusions. *Scientific American* 223, 30–6.

Wasz-Höckert, O., Lind, J., Vuorenkoski, V., Partanen, T. and Valanné, E. 1968. *The infant cry: a spectrographic and auditory analysis.* London: Heinemann/Spastics International Medical Publications.

Weaver, W. 1955. Translation. In W. N. Locke & A. D. Booth (eds.), *Machine translation of languages* (New York: Wiley), 15–23.

Webster's Third New International Dictionary. New York: Merriam-Webster.

Wells, J. C. 1962. A study of the formants of the pure vowels of British English. Unpublished MA Thesis, University of London.

Wendon, L. 1985. *The Pictogram System*, 9th edn. Barton, Cambridge: Pictogram Supplies.

Williams, C. B. 1970. *Style and vocabulary: numerical studies.* London: Griffin.

Williams, G. H. 1960. *Homolytic aromatic substitution.* Oxford: Pergamon.

Wing, A. M. & Baddeley, A. D. 1980. Spelling errors in handwriting: a corpus and distributional analysis. In U. Frith (ed.), *Cognitive processes in spelling* (London: Academic Press), 251–85.

Wright, J. 1898–1905. *English dialect dictionary.* London: Frowde.

Wright, P. 1977. Behavioural research and the technical communicator. *The Communicator of Scientific and Technical Information* 32, 3–13.

Zettersten, A. 1968. *A statistical study of the graphic system of present-day American English.* Lund: Studentlitteratur.

VI INDEX OF LANGUAGES, FAMILIES, DIALECTS, AND SCRIPTS

The index includes only those names cited in this book, excluding the Appendices. Major references are given in **bold** type.

Abaza 307, 333
Abkhaz 307, 333
Abkhazo-Adyghian 307, 333
Achinese 344
Acholi 344
Adamawa-Ubangi 316
Adyghe 307, 333
Afrikaans 239, 300, 303, 316, 341, 344, 359
  Pidgin 341
Afro-Asiatic 167, 169, 289, 297, **318**
Ainu 329
Akan 316, 344
Akkadian 303, 318, 328
Akoli 316
Aku 340
Albanian 33, 37, 298, 300, **302**, 344, 359
Aleut 322
Algonkin see Algonquian
Algonquian 92, 297, 322, 340
Aliutor 308
Alsatian 37
Altai 309
Altaic 289, 297, 307–8, **309**, 310, 324, 328, 329
Alur 316
Alyawarra 99
American Sign Language 222–7, 363, 402
Americo 340
Amerind 324
Amer-Ind 226
Amerindian 60, 112, 114, 126, 167–8, 226, 289, 295, **322**, 329, 339, 370, 411–12
  Pidgin English 340
Ameslan see American Sign Language
Amharic 91, 98, 112, 126, 203, 318, 344, 359
Amorite 318
Amuesha 169
Anatolian 298, 300, 302
Andamanese 99, 319, **320**, 328
Andean-Equatorial 169, 297, **324–5**
Andi 333
Angleutsch 4
Anglo-Frisian 303
Anglo-Romani 340
Anglo-Saxon 5, 60, 63,

110, 114–15, 189, 205, 216, 300, 302, 330, 332, 390–1
Annamese 296
  see also Vietnamese
Antido 355
Antilles Creole 340
Apache 117, 322
Apalai 98
Apurina 98
Arabic 3, 4, 7, 15, 23, 36, 43, 52, 61, 110–12, 120, 130, 157–9, 187, 190, 192, 197, 204, 239, 289, 295, 307, 309, 316, **318**, 320, 332, 341, 344, 348, 359–60, 367, 410
  Classical 7, 43, 111, 290, 318, 388
Aram 306
Aramaic 204, 318, 388
Aranda 169, 326
Arapaho 322
Araucanian 115, 287, 323, 324
Araucano see Araucanian
Arawakan 324–5
Arc-a-plat 329
Arči 333
Aricapu 328
Armenian 36, 205, 300, **302**, 344, 363
Asmara Pidgin English 341
Assamese 286, 300, 303, 344
Assyrian 200
Athabaskan 322, 340
Atlantic 316
Aukaans 340
Australian 8–9, 15, 168–9, 287, 289, 294–5, 297, **326–7**, 370
  Pidgin 341
Austro-Asiatic 289, 296, **311**, 329
Austronesian 169, 289, 296, 311–12, **319**
Avar 307, 333
Avaro-Ando-Dido 333
Avestan 303
Aymará 324, 344
Azerbaijani 309, 344
Aztec 15, 115, 323
Aztec-Tanoan 297, **323**, 324

Bacairi 98
Baenna 328
Bagot Creole English 341
Bahasa Indonesia 320, 344, 359, 368
Balinese 205, 344
Baltic 298, 300, 302

Balto-Slavic 300, 302
Baluchi 300, 303, 344
Bambara 167, 169, 316; see also Mandekan
Bamboo English 341
Bamboo Spanish 341
Bamileke 344
Bantu 33, 91, 287, 316
Bari 316
Barikanci 341
Barracoon 341
Basa 344
Bashkir 309, 344
Basque 33–4, 37, 42, 84, 181, 328, 359
Bats 307
Batsbiy 333
Bazaar-Hindustani 341
Beach-la-Mar 341
Belize Creole 340
Bella Coola 177, 323
Belorussian 300, 302, 344
Bemba 344
  Town 341
Bembe 10
Bengali 37, 52, 286, 289, 300, 303, 344, 359
Benue-Congo 316
Beothuk 329
Berber **84**, 237, 318, 344
Betawi 341
Bhojpuri 344
Bihari 289, 300, 303
Bikol 344
Bilin 90
Binga 177
Bini 174
Bislama 336, 341
Bithynian 328
Black Carib 324
Blackfoot 322
Bosnian 37
Brahui 310
Brazilian Creole Portuguese 340
Breton 37, 289, 300, 304–5, 370
British 304
British Sign Language 222, 226–7
Brythonic 304
Buginese 205, 344
Bulgarian 25, 33, 37, **300**, 302, 344, 359
Burmese 8, 84, 177, 205, 313, 344, 359
Burushaski 329
Buryat 309, 344
Buyi 312

Cakchiquel 323
Callahuaya 328
Calusa 329
Cambodian see Khmer

Cameroon Pidgin English 340
Campa 324
Candoshi 287
Cantonese 37
Cape Dutch 341
Cape Verde Creole 340
Cappadocian 328
Carian 328
Carib 21, 98, 115, 287, **324–5**
Caribbean Creole English 340
Catalan 25, 37, 294, 300, 303, 344, 368
Cataonian 328
Caucasian 126, 168–9, 289, 297, **307**, 328, 333
Caviteño 341
Cebuano see Sebuano
Celtiberian 300, 304
Celtic 34, 112, 114, 298, 300, **304–5**, 328, 362
Chavacano 341
Chadic 289, 318
Chamorro 169, 319, 321
Chari-Nile 317
Chechehet 329
Chechen 307, 333
Cheremis 306
Cherokee 203, 322
Chewa see Nyanja
Cheyenne 322
Chibcha 84
Chibchan (Macro-) 167, 297, **324–5**
Chichimeca 287
Chin 289, 312
China Coast Pidgin 341
Chinese 7–8, 36, 60, 99, 111–112, 162, 172, 182, 192, 196–7, 202–3, 213, 239, 287, 289, 295, 308, 311–13, **314–15**, 319, 332, 336, 340, 344, 347–8, 352, 359, 362–3, 367, 373, 388, 410
  Cantonese 166, 174, 314
  Classical 74, 110, 115, 190
  Hakka/Hsiang/Kan 314
  Mandarin **174**, 314–15, 359
  Min 314
  Pidgin 339
  Sign Language 222
  Wu 314
Chinook 177, 339
  Jargon 336, 339, **340**
Chipayan 323, 324
Chippewa 2
Choctaw 340
Chontal 287

Chukchi 21, 308
Chuvash 309, **344**
Cilician 328
Ciokwe 344
Circassian 307, 333
Clamcoets 329
Cocoliche 340
Comanche 323
Congo Pidgin 341
Cootenais 329
Coptic 201, 205, 317, 318
Cornish 300, 304–5, 362
Corsican 37
Cree 92, 322
Creek 8
Crioulo 340
Croatian 37, 286
Crow 322
Cumbrian/Cumbric 300, 304–5
Cuna 50, 59, 324
Cushitic 318
Cypriot(e) 203
Cyrillic 192, 204, 227, 302, 307–8, 367
Czech 25, 36–7, 174, 300, 302, 332, 344, 350, 359

Dagestanian 307
Dagur 309
Dakine 340
Dakota 177, 322
Dalmatian 303
Damin 127
Danish 7, 25, 33, 36–7, 117, 286, 300, 303, 322, 344, 349, 359
  Sign Language 222, 226
Dardic **300**, 303
Dargi 333
Dargwa 307
Dari see Persian
Davaueño 341
Dayak 289, 319
  Land 287
Delmondo 355
Devanagari 205, 367, 409
Dhimotiki 43
Dhangu 287
Dhay'yi 287
Dhiyakuy 287
Dhuwal 287
Dhuwala 287
Didinga 177
Dido 333
Dinka 316, 344
Djangu 287
Djinang 287
Djining 287
Djuka 340
  Pidgin 340
Dong 312

Dongolawi 316–17
Dongxiang 309
Dravidian 33, 85, 289, 297, **310**, 328–9, 341
Dutch 25, 33, 36–7, 93, 111, 114, 239, 300, 303, 340, 344–5, 348, 359, 368
  Creole/Pidgin 336, 339–41
Dyalnguy 42
Dyirbal 42
Dyula 316
Dzongkha 359

Efik 316, 344
Egyptian 189, 198, 200–1, 318
Ekselsioro 355
Elamite 303, 329
Enets 306
English 3–6, 10, 15, 21, 24, 33, 36–7, 42, 46–7, 50, 52–3, 56–7, 59, 61–3, 65, 67, 74, 84–99, 102, 105–8, 112, 114–20, 125–6, 130, 134, 154, 158–9, 162–6 169, 171, 174, 176–7, 182–3, 187, 196–7, 201, 204–5, 207–8, 213, 216–17, 226–7, 236–7, 239, 242–9, 251, 265, 269, 271, 274, 276, 279, 281, 286–9, 295, 298–9, 302–3, 305, 316, 319, 321, 330–2, 335–6, 339–11, 344–73, 375–81, 382–97, 409, 415
  American 8, 23, 31, 35, **44**, 53, 56, 112, 156, 334–5
  American vs British 7, 47, 109, 155, 184, 206–7, 360
  Australian 108
  Basic 358
  Black English Vernacular 23, **35**, 40, 60, 335, 338, 387
  British 23, 30, 32, 39, 48, 51, 53, 112, 120, 135, 156, 162, 166, 168, 173
  Canadian 23
  Cockney 53, 206, 289
  Creole 338–41
  Indian 157, 360
  Middle 71, 205, 332, 391
  New Zealand 50, 53
  Nuclear 360
  Old see Anglo-Saxon
  Pidgin 316, 336–41
  South African 108, 316
English Bush Negro 340
Ermitaño 341
Erse 304

Erza 306
Eskimo 15, 60, 90–1, 99, 294, 296, 322, 333, 344, 388
  Pidgin 340
Eskimo-Aleut 169, 297, **322**, 324
Esperanto 354–7
  Modern 355
Esperantuisho 355
Espido 355
Estonian 306, 344
Eteocretan 328
Ethiopic (scripts) 197, 205
Etruscan 187, 204–5, **328**
Euroasiatic 324
Eurolengo 355
Europeo 355
Euskera 34
Even 309
Evenki 309
Ewe 316, 344
Ewondo Populaire 340

Faeroese 286, 300, 303, 359
Faliscan 303
Fanagaló 341
Fante 286
Farsi see Persian
Fazandeiro 340
Fijian 321, 344
Filipino 320
Finnic 306
Finnish 24, 33, 36–7, 84, 92, 171, 174, 204, 295, 306, 344, 350, 359
Finno-Ugric 306
Flatbow 329
Flemish 25, 37, 51, 300, 303, 359
Fon 344
Fore 98
Formosan 319
Fox 92, 322
Fragnol 340
Franco-Amerindian 340
Franco-Spanish Pidgin 340
Franglais 4, 365
French 3–5, 7–8, 11, 21, 24–5, 33, 36–7, 42, 45, 48, 51–2, 55–6, 59, 63, 65, 71, 74, 85–7, 91, 95, 98–9, 105–6, 110–112, 114, 120, 127, 130, 155, 157, 159–60, 166, 168, 171–2, 177, 181, 182–3, 196, 216, 273, 289, 294–5, 300, 303, 305, 314, 316, 319, 332, 339–41, 344–50, 352, 354, 356, 359–60, 364–5, 367–73, 376, 380
  Canadian vs European 23
  Creole 36, 338, 340–41
  Norman 114, 330, 388–9

Pidgin 336, 339–41
  Sign Language 222
French Guiana Creole 340
Frisian 37, 300, 303, 367
Fula 316
Fulani 344
Fulfulde 316
Fur 177, 317, 328
Fuuta Jalon 316

Gã 166, 344
Gaelic 33, 50, 60, 93, 115, 204, **304-5**, 370
  Cape Breton 304
  Irish 168, 205, 294, 300, 304–5, 340, 344, 359, 362, 368
  Scottish 288, 300, 304–5, 332
Galatian 300, 304
Galgalīya 341
Galician 33, 37, 303, 359
Galla 318
Gambian Krio 340
Ganda 344
Gaulish 300, 304
Gbaya 316, 344
Ge'ez 389
Georgian 177, 205, 307, 333, 344
Gê, Macro 324
Gê-Pano-Carib 297, **324–5**
Gergito-Salymean 328
German 4, 7, 10, 21, 23, 25, 33, 36–7, 42, 45, 50, 71, 74, 86–7, 93, 98, 104–5, 110–112, 157, 159, 168, 169, 196, 239, 246, 249, 287, 291, 300, 302–3, 316, 330–32, 344–7, 349–51, 353, 355–6, 359, 364–5, 367–8, 373, 375–6, 380
  High vs Low 29, 37
  High vs Swiss 43
  Middle/Old High 104, 303
  Pidgin 339
Germanic 60, 67, 106, 112, 289, 295, 298–300, **302–3**, 330
Gestuno 222
Gheg 302
Gilbertese 321
Gilyak 237, 308, **329**
Globaqo 355
Glosa 355
Goajiro 324
Goanese 341
Goidelic 300, 304
Gondi 310
Gothic
  language 294, 298, 302, 330
  script 188, 194, 206, 302, 375
Grabar 302
Greek 294, 295, **303**, 384
  Classical 3, 7, 9, 61, 70,

91, 93, 101, 105, 110–12, 114–15, 188–9, 201, 203–4, 216, 290, 294, 298–9, 303, 328, 330, 355–6, 378, 408–10
  Modern 36–7, 43, 84, 177, 192, 204, 300, 303, 316, 344, 359
  Mycenean 187, 198–9, 203–4, 298, 303
  New Testament 300, 303, 384
Greenlandic 169, 177, 322, 359
Guaraní 42, 84, 177, 324, 340, 344, 359, 362
Guaymi 324
Gujarati 36, 37, 205, 300, 303, 316, 344
Gulf of Guinea Portuguese 340
Gullah 340
Gunwinygu 326
Gur 316
Gurage 318
Guugu-Yimidhirr 42
Guwal 42
Guyana Dutch Pidgin 340
Guianese Creole 338, 340

Haida 167
Haitian Creole 340, 344, 363
Hamitic 316
Hamito-Semitic 318
Han 314
Hanunóo 106
Hatsa 317
Hattic 328
Hausa 98, 126, 159, 174, 177, 316, 318, 341, 344
Hawaiian 166–8, 340
  Old 99
  Pidgin/Creole 340
Hebrew
  Classical 7–9, 59, 98, 181, 290, 318, 388, 410
  Modern 4, 23–4, 36, 84, 98, 105, 169, 177, 192, 204, 206, 316, 336, 344, 356, 359, 364
  Old 204
Het 329
Hindi 36, 58, 84, 162, 239, 286, 289, 300, 303, 316, 321, 332, 340, 341, 344, 359, 366
Hittite (Old) 187, 200, 299, 302
Hixkaryana 98, 328
Hmong 313, 344
Hmong-Mien 313
Ho 344
Hochdeutsch see German
Hokan 297, **323**, 324
Hokan-Siouan 329
Hom Idyomo 355
Hopi 15, 103, 323
Houailou 98

Huave 328
Hungarian 4, 24, 33, 36–7, 50, 106, 112, 172, 306, 332, 344, 348, 359, 364
Hurrian 302

Iban see Malay
Iberian 307, 328
Icelandic
  Modern 112, 286, 300, 303, 344, 359
  Old 11, 115, 298, 303, 330–32, 410
Idiom Neutral 355
Ido 355, 357
Igbo 12, 168, 174, 316, 344
Ijo 126, 316
Ilocano 320, 344
Ilongot 41
Indian Portuguese 341
Indo-Aryan (Indic) 300, 303
Indo-European 29, 33, 169, 176, 289, 297, **298–305**, 307, 324, 331, 357
Indo-Iranian 298, 300, 303
Indonesian 287, 320
  West 287
Indo-Pacific 85, 91, 167–8, 289, 297, **319**, 328
Inglés de Escalerilla 340
Ingrian 306
Ingush 333
  Interglossa 355
Interlingua 355, 357
Inuit 322
Inuktitut 322
Inupiac 322
Iranian 300, 302–3
Irish see Gaelic
Iroquoian 320
Isan 312
Isaurian 328
Israeli Sign Language 222
Italian 4, 7, 25, 33–4, 36–7, 45, 65, 71, 93, 111, 172, 183, 216, 289, 294–5, 300, 303, 314, 330, 332–3, 340, 344–5, 349–50, 359, 363, 365, 373, 375, 410
  Creole/Pidgin 339, 340–51
Italic 187, 303
Itelmen 308

Jabo 404
Jakarta Portuguese 341
Jamaican Creole 340
Jamamadi 98
Japanese 21, 36, 40, 56, 84, 92, 95, 98–9, 105–6, 111, 156, 169, 171, 174, 176, 187, 196–7, 202–3, 213, 237, 239, 282, 289, 295, 297, **308–9**, 324, 328, 332, 340, 344, 348, 350–61, 359–60, 373, 377, 380 388

Pidgin 341
Javanese 40, 59, 99, 169, 205, 289, **320**, 332, 344
Juma 328

Kabardian 168–9, 307, 333
Kabyle 318
Kachin 289
Kadai 312
Kaffir 341
Kaldosh 341
Kalenjin 316
Kalmyk 309
Kamba 344
Kamchadal 308
Kamsá 41
Kam-Sui 312
Kanakuru 169
Kanarese 310
Kandoshi 287
Kannada 103, 205, 310, 344
Kanuri 317, 344
Karankawa 329
Karelian 306
Karen 313
Karok 177
Kartvelian 307
Kashmiri 300, 344
Kashubian 302
Katcha 169
Katharevousa 43
Kazakh 309, 314, 344
Kekchi 323
Kerek 308
Keres(an) 323, 329
Ket 308
Khalka 309, 359
Khanty 306
Khjurkili 307
Khmer 204–5, 311, 344, 359
Khoikhoin 126, 317
Khoisan 33, 99, 126, 167–9, 289, 297, **317**
Khutsuri 307
Kikongo 341
Kikuyu 344
Kinyarwanda *see* Rwanda
Kirghiz 309, 344
Kirundi *see* Rundi
Kisettla 341
Kitchen Kaffir 341
Kituba 341
Klamath 169, 177
Klingon 355
Koasati 21
Komi 306
Komuz 317
Kongo 316, 344
Konkani 300, 303
Kootenay 329
Kordofanian 316
Korean 36, 40, 98–9, 112, 176, 192, 289, 297, **308**, 314, 324, 328, 329, 344, 359, 362
Koryak 308
Kpelle 344
Krio 316, 336–8, 340, 344

Kru 289, 344
English 340
Kryôl 340
Kui 310
Kuki 312
Kumauni 344
Kuna *see* Cuna
Kunama 169
Kunimaipa 173
Kurdish 300, 303, 344
Kuri 307
Kurukhi 310
Kutenai 329
Kwa 316
Kwakiutl 323

Lahnda 300, 303, 344
Lak 163, 307, 333
Lamani 344
Lamut 309
Lango 316
Lanna 312
Lao(tian) 312, 359
Lapp(ish) 8, 33, 37, 117, 169, 287, 306
Latin 3, 6–7, 41–2, 45, 53, 64, 70, 74, 84, 88–90, 92–3, 95, 98, 106, 110–15, 171, 181, 188–9, 194, 200, 203, 205, 216, 290, 294–5, 298–300, 302, **303**, 309, 311, 328, 330–33, 354–6, 359, 362, 378, 384, 387–9, 390-91, 408–10
Early 204
Medieval 390
Latin-Esperanto 355
Latino Sine Flexione 355
Latvian 237, 239, 300, 302, 344
Laz 307
Lekhitic 300, 302
Lendu 316
Lepontic 304
Letzebuergesch 37, 359
Lezghian 307, 333
Liberian Pidgin English 340
Linear A 328
Linear B 203, 303, 328
Lingala 316, 341
Lingoa Gêral 340
Lingua Internacional 355
Lingvo Internacia *see* Esperanto
Lingwo Internaciona 355
Lisu 98
Lithuanian 36, 298, 300, 302, 344
Livonian 306
Lolo 312
Lolo-Burmese 98
Losengo *see* Ngala
Louisiana Creole French 340
Luba 316, 344
Lugbara 316
Luo 179, 239, 316

Luorawetlan 308
Luri 287
Lushai 174
Luwian 302
Lycian 302
Lyconian 328
Lydian 302

Maasai 316
Maban 317
Mabuyag 326
Macanese 341
Macauenho 341
Macedonian 25, 33, 37, 300, 302, **344**, 359
Machacali 287
Macro- *see* individual languages
Macu 287
Madras Pidgin 341
Madurese 344
Magyar *see* Hungarian
Maithili 344
Makista 341
Makua 316
Makusi 98
Malacca Portuguese 341
Malagasy 10, 41, 98, **320**, 341, 344, 359
Malay 84, 106, 169, 289, **320**, 341, 344, 359
Baba/Bazaar 320, 341
Malayalam 159, 205, 310, 344
Malayo-Polynesian 287, **319**
Maldivian 205, 300, 303, 359
Malinka 316
Maltese 37, 318, 359
Malto 310
Mam 323
Manchu 309, 344
Manchu-Tungus 309
Manda 310
Mandara 289
Mande 316
Mandekan 344
Mangbetu 316
Manipuri 344
Mansi 306
Manus 63
Manx 300, 304–5
Maori 49, 52–3, 84, 115, **321**, 370
Pidgin 341
Mapudungan 323
Marathi 237, 289, 300, 303, 344
Mari 306
Masai 169, 316
Mauritian French Creole 341
Maxakali 287
Maya 177, 239, 344
see also Yucatec
Mayan 323
Mazateco 404
Mechoacan 329
Mediterranean Lingua Franca 336, 339

Mende 10, 316, 344
Menomini 93
Merico 340
Meskito Coast Creole 340
Meso-American 287, 324
Mexicano 287
Mez-Voio 355
Miao 63, 313
Miao-Yao 289, 312, **313**
Micmac 322
Mien 313
Min *see* Chinese
Minangkabau 344
Mine Kaffir 341
Mingrelian 307
Minoan 328
Mixtec 324, 344
Moabite 318
Mobilian 340
Mogol 309
Mohawk 295, 322
Mohenjo-Daro 329
Mohican 322
Mon 311
Mondlingvo 355
Mongol 309
Mongolian 309, 314 344
Mongo-Nkundu 289
Monguor 309
Mon-Khmer 36, 311, 313
Mooré 316
Mordvin(ian) 74, 306, 344
More 344
Morisyen 341
Mossi 316
Motu 321
Hiri/Police 321, 337, 341, 359
Munda 311, 329
Mundari 311
Munukutuba 341

Na-Dené 297, **322**, 324
Naga 312
Nahali 329
Nahua(tl) 60, 177, 323, 332, 344
-Spanish Creole 340
Naiki 310
Nakh 307, 333
Nakho-Dagestanian 307, 333
Nama 317
Nanai 309
Nandi 316
Natu 328
Nauruan 359
Navaho 6, 36, 98, 103, 106, 159, 322
Trader 340
Navajo *see* Navaho
Ndebele 316
Nenets 306
Néo 355
Neo-Melanesian *see* Tok Pisin
Nepali 300, 344, 359
Nepo 355
Netherlandic 303
Netherlandic-German 303

Nēwāri 344
New Caledonia Pidgin 341
New Jersey Amerindian 340
Nez Percé 177
Ngala 341, 344
Ngambai 316
Nganasan 306
Ngbandi 336, 341
Nhangu 287
Nicobarese 311
Niger-Congo 167–9, 289, 297, **316**, 332
Nigerian Pidgin English 336
Nikari Karu Pidgin 340
Nile Nubian 316–17
Nilo-Saharan 169, 289, 297, **316–17**, 328
Nilotic 316
Nivkhi 308, 329
Njamal 106
Nootka 6, 168, 177, 323, 340
Norfolkese 341
Norse, Old *see* Icelandic, Old
North African Pidgin French 340
Norwegian 25, 33, 36, 169, 172, 239, 286, 300, 303, 344, 359
Novial 355, 357
Nubian 316–17
Old 317
Nuer 44, 289, 316
Numidian 318
Nung 312
Nyanja 344, 359
Nymylan 308
Nyungar 327

Ob-Ugric 306
Occidental 354–5, 357
Occitan 37, 300, 303
Oceanic 319
Odul 308
Og(h)am 205, 305
Oirat 309
Oirot 309
Ojibwa 322
Okanogan 323
Omotic 318
Oraoni 310
Ordek-Burnu 328
Oriya 300, 303, 344
Oromo 318, 344
Oscan 303
Osmanian 197
Osmanli 169
Ossetic 300, 303
Ostyak (Samoyed) 306
Oto-Manguean 297, 324
Otomí 324

Pachuco 340
Pahari 300, 303
Paiute 323
Palaeosiberian 289, 297, **308**, 329

Palaic 302
Palauan 319, 321
Palenquero 340
Pali 300, 386
Pama-Nyungan 326
Panjabi 37, 169, 289, 300, 303, 344
Panoan 324–5
Paphlagonian 328
Papiamentu/o 340, 344
Papuan 319, 341
Pascuanese 321
Pashto 300, 344, 359
Pawaian 167
Pengo 310
Pentlach 323
Penutian 169, 297, **322–3**, 324–5, 328
Perio 355
Persian 36, 50, 63, 174, 287, 289, 298, 300, 303, 307, 344, 359
   Afghan (Dari) 344, 359
   Old 303
Petit Mauresque 340
Petit-Nègre 340
Phoenician 114, 204, 213, 318, 328
Phrygian 290, 302
Pictish 205, 328
Pilipino 320, 359
Pima-Papago 323
Pintupi 15
Pipil 370
Pisidian 328
Pitcairnese Creole 339, 340
Pitjantjatjara 102, 326
Pochismo 340
Polabian 302
Polish 25, 36–7, 174, 300, 302, 344, 349, 356, 359, 364
Polynesian 344
Pontic 328
Popoloca 287
Porepecha 329
Portuguese 7, 24–5, 36–7, 93, 112, 130, 155, 171, 196, 216, 251, 287, 289, 294, 300, 303, 316, 324, 332–3, 336, 338–9, 344, 359, 363
   Bush Negro 340
   Creole/Pidgin 336, 340–41
Potawatomi 92, 322
Proto-Dravidian 310
Proto-Indo-European 294, 298–9, 310, 330, 332, 413
Proto-Uralic 306
Provençal 340
Prussian, Old 300, 302
Puelche 287
Pukapuka 63

Quechua 98, 159, 166, 324, 332, 344, 370, 410
Quechumaran 324–5
Queres 329

Quiché 237, 323
Quoc-ngu 311

Rajasthani 300, 303
Rapanui 321
Rappang see Buginese
Réunionnais 341
Rhaetian 300, 303
Riff 318
Rodriguez Creole 341
Roman (script) 188, 197, 204–6, 367
Romanal 355
Romance 67, 106, 294–5, 318, 332–3, 355, 410
Romani 37, 300, 303, 340, 344
Romanian 33, 91, 300, 303, 344, 359, 364
Romanizat 355
Romansch 37, 359
Rotinese 60
Rotokas 166–8, 170, 204
Rukai 169
Rundi 11, 38, 344, 359
Russenorsk 340
Russian 3, 21, 25, 36–7, 93, 106, 111, 113, 158–9, 163, 174, 224, 289, 300, 302, 306–7, 314, 344, 348, 352, 359, 368, 373, 375, 377
   Sign Language 222
Rwanda 316, 344, 359

Sabir 336, 339, 340
Sahaptin 177
Saharan 317
Saint Helena Creole 341
Salishan 323, 340
Sami see Lapp
Samoan 40, 49, 53, 93, 237, 295, **321**
Samoyedic 306
Samur 333
San 126, 317
Sandawe 317
Sango 316, 336, 339, 341, 344
Sanskrit 7–8, 58, 71, 91, 111, 294, 298, 300, 303, 310, 316, 330 388, 409–10
Santa 309
Santali 311, 344
Saramaccan 339
Sardinian 37, 300, 303
Scandinavian 114, 286, 302–3, 348
Schweitzerdeutsch see German
Sea Islands Creole English 340
Sebuano 320, 341
Selkup 306
Semitic 188, 299, 307, **318**, 328
   North 204
Serbian 37, 286, 302
Serbo-Croat(ian) 36–7, 53,

93, 174, 300, 302, 344, 359
Seselwa 341
Sesotho 316
Sesotho sa Leboa 316
Setswana 316
Settla 341
Settler English 341
Seychellois 341
Shah Dagh 333
Shan 312
Shawnee 322
Sheldru (Shelta) 340
Shona 126, 316, 344
Shoshone 323
Shuswap 323
Siamese see Thai
Sidetic 328
Sindhi 159, 300, 303, 344
Singapore Portuguese 341
Sinhalese 205, 300, 303, 344, 359
Sinitic 312, 314–15
Sino-Tibetan 169, 289, 297, **312**, 313
Siouan 297, 322
Sioux 322
Skalzi 329
Slav(on)ic 33, 158, 298, 302, 355–6, 412
   Old Church 298, 300, 302
Slovak 25, 36–7, 291, 300, 302, 344, 359
Slovene (Slovenian) 37, 239, 300, 302, 344, 359
Slovincian 302
Solomon Islands Pidgin 341
Solresol 355
Somali 53, 177, 197, 318, 344, 359
Songhai 317, 328, 344
Sorbian 37, 300, 302
Sotho 344, 359
Souriquoien 340
Southern Paiute 6
Spanglish 4, 365
Spanish 4, 7, 25, 33, 36–7, 41–2, 59, 93, 111–12, 114–15, 130, 156, 159, 169, 183, 196, 204, 216, 223, 235, 239, 287, 289, 294, 300, 303, 314, 324, 330, 332, 340, 344, 349, 350, 359, 362–3, 365, 373, 375–7, 404, 410
   Creole/Pidgin 336, 339-41
Squamish 98, 323
Sranan 340
Sri Lankan Creole Malay 341
Sri Lankan Portuguese 341
Sudanese Creole Arabic 341
Sudanic 316
Sumerian 198, 200, **328**

Sundanese 40, 320, 344
Svan 307, 333
Swahili 84, 90, 91, 159, 295, 316, 341, 344, 359
   Pidgin 341
Swati 316, 359
Swedish 4, 24–5, 33, 36–7, 93, 106, 174, 227, 286, 300, 303, 332, 344, 359, 377
Swedlish 4, 377
Syriac 205, 318

Taal Dutch 341
Tabassaran 307
Tadzhik 300, 303, 344
Tagalog 36, 90, 98, 289, **320**, 341, 344
Tahitian 321, 340
Tai 289, 297, 311, **312**, 313
Taishan 169
Tajik see Tadzhik
Takelma 6
Talaing 311
Tamashek 318
Tamil 38, 177, 205, 289, 310, 316, 344, 359
Tanoan 323
Tapuya 287
Tarahumar 323
Tarasca(n) 329
Tasmanian 319, 321, 328
Tatar 37, 309, 344
Tavgi 306
Tay Boy 341
Tekrur 341
Telugu 177, 205, 289, 310, 316, 344
Temen 344
Ternateño 341
Teso 289, 316
Tewa 323
Tex-Mex 365
Thai 8, 21, 36, 58–9, 84, 166, 174, 177, 205, 239, 289, 312, 344, 359
Tho 312
Tibetan 40, 98–9, 205, 313, 314, 344
Tibeto-Burman 312
Tifinagh 318
Tigrinya 93, 318, 344
Tiv 177, 316, 344
Tiwi 295, 326
Toba Batak 344
Tocharian 300, 303
Tok Pisin 181, 320, 336–7, 339, **341**, 344, 359
Tongan 8, 10, 98, **321**
Torres Strait Pidgin/Creole 341
Tosk 302
Trinidad and Tobago Creole 340
Trumai 286
Tshivenda 316
Tsimshian 177
Tsonga 344
Tsou 166

Tswana 359
Tu 309
Tukano 42
Tulu 310
Tungus 309, 344
Tungusic 309
Tupian 324–5, 340
Turkic 309
Turkish 36–7, 60–1, 84, 90–1, 163, 174, 289, 295, 309, 332, 344, 359, 402
Turkmen 344
Tuva 309
Tuvinian 309, 344
Twi 155, 174, 286
Tzotzil 98

Ubykh 307, 333
Udi 333
Udmurt 306
Ugric 306
Uighur 309, 314, 344
Ukrainian 25, 36–7, 300, 302, 344
Ulla 355
Umbrian 303
Ural-Altaic 169
Uralic 169, 289, 297, 298, **306**, 310
Urartian 302
Urdu 37, 286, 289, 300, 303, 310, 316, 344, 359
Uru 323, 324
Usku 370
Uto-Aztecan 322–3
Utoki 355
Uzbek 309, 344

Vejnakh 333
Venetic 303
Vepsian 306
Vietnamese 36, 91, 98, 166, 289, 295, 311, 344, 359
   Pidgin 341
Virgin Islands Dutch Creole 340
Visayan 344; see also Sebuano
Vlaams 37
Vogul 306
Volapük 355
Votic 306
Votyak 306

Waika 324
Wakashan 323
Walmatjari 326
Warlpiri 326
Welsh
   Classical 106, 305
   Modern 31, 42, 45, 51, 53, 84, 91, 93, 98–9, 106, 112, 115, 174, 183, 289, 294, 300, 304–5, 368, 370, 376, 389
Patagonian 304

West African Pidgin 337, 340
West Atlantic 316
Western Desert 91, 326
Wishram 6
Wolaytta 318
Wolof 40, 52, 169, 316, 340, 344

Xhosa 33, 126, 167, 286, 289, 316, 344, 345
Xitsonga 316
!Xũ 126, 167–70

Yakut 8, 309, 344
Yana 6, 21
Yao 313, 344
Yayo 336

Yanomani 325
Yeniseian 308
Yenisey 306
Yenisey-Ostyak 308
Yiddish 36–7, 45, 300, 303, 332, 344, 356, 364
Yoruba 99, 159, 166, 174, 316, 344

Yuan 312
Yucatec 60, 177, 323, 344, 386
Yukaghir 308
Yupik 322
Yurak 306
Yuulngu 287

Zambia Pidgin 341

Zan 307, 333
Zapotec 84, 199, 323, 324, 344
Zend 298
Zhuang 312
Zulu 33, 167, 174, 286, 316, 344
Zuñi 8, 41, 103, 323
Zyryan 306

VII INDEX OF AUTHORS AND PERSONALITIES

Abramson, A. 147
Adams, Douglas 417
Adrian VI, Pope 9
Ager, D. E. 378
Akbar the Great 230
Albee, Edward 214
Albert, E. M. 38
Aldridge, John 71
Alexander the Great 201
Alexejew, P. M. 86
Alford, H. 5
Al-Khalil Ibn Aḥmad 111
Allport, G. W. 23
Amarasiṃha 111
Amen-em-het I 201
Andersen, E. S. 247
Anhalt, I. 175
Apollinaire, Guillaume 11, 75
Argyle, M. 405
Aristophanes of Byzantium 111
Aristotle 70, 100–1, 408
Armstrong, Louis 128
Arnauld, A. 84
Arnold, G. F. 173
Ascensius 179
Ashby, W. 355
Asher, J. J. 379
Asterix 176
Austen, Jane 78
Austin, J. L. 121
Ayer, A. J. 418

Bacon, Francis 354
Bacon, Roger 69
Baddeley, A. D. 215
Bailey, C-J. 334
Bailey, R. W. 361
Balzac, Honoré de 182
Barham, R. H. 183
Barnes, D. 250
Barthes, R. 79
Baudelaire 350
Baughan, R. 191
Beaufront, L.. de 355
Beaugrande, R. de 119
Becanus, J. G. 7
Beckett, Samuel 63
Békésy, G. von 144
Bell, A. 50
Bell, A. G. 134, 149
Bellugi(-Klima), U. 222, 225, 231
Benedict, H. 240, 246

Berio, Luciano 175
Berkeley, George 410
Berko, J. 242, 244
Berlaimont, N. de 111
Berlin, B. 106
Bernstein, B. 40
Bertrand, H-G. 208
Bester, Alfred 183
Betjeman, John 38
Bievre, Marquis de 63
Binet, A. 13
Bird, J. 20
Birdwhistell, R. L. 406
Bliss, C. 282
Bloch, B. 412
Bloom, L. M. 245
Bloomfield, L. 2, 29, 83, 91, 92, 94, 101, 180, 411–12
Boas, F. 411
Bobrow, D.G. 417
Bolinger, D. L. 172
Bombaugh, C. C. 65
Bonaparte, Napoleon 8, 191, 208
Bopp, F. 298
Borker, R. A. 118
Bower, C. A. 345
Bowring, J. 364
Bradley, L. 276
Brainerd, Paul 195
Bright, T. 208
Bright, W. 38
Brislin, R. W. 348
Bristow, G. J. 271
Broca, P. 262–3
Brockedon, W. 104
Brontë, Charlotte 183
Brontë, Emily 77–8, 183
Brooks, C. 78
Brooks, L. 211
Brosnahan, L. F. 18, 33, 158
Brown, R. 45, 231, 233, 235, 242, 244–5
Browning, Robert 74, 183
Brueghel (the Elder), Pieter 285
Brugmann, K. 298, 331
Brunner, H. 201
Buren, P. van 72
Burgess, Anthony 394
Burkard, R. 19
Burke, C. 51
Burnet, J. 172

Burt, M. K. 374
Byrne, P. S. 385

Caesar, Julius 68, 208, 409
Camden, W. 113
Campbell, R. 350
Carroll, Lewis 63, 65, 100, 177, 183
Carter, President J. 380
Cassidy, F. G. 339
Catford, J. C. 333, 349
Cawdrey, R. 109
Caxton, William 5, 194
Cedergren, H. 32
Chambers, J. K. 32
Champollion, J-F. 201
Chang, N-C 172
Chao, Y. 315
Chapman, R. 182
Charlemagne, Emperor 188
Charles v of Germany 7
Chase, S. 395
Chaucer, Geoffrey 194, 331
Chen, M. 334
Chomsky, A. N. 79, 84–5, 88, 97–8, 400, 413
Christie, J. 69
Christopherson, P. 88
Cicero 70, 409
Clark, R. 355
Clarke, Arthur C. 82, 417
Clerc, L. 223
Colbung, K. 327
Coleridge, Samuel Taylor 74
Collison, R. L. 111
Comenius, J. A. 354
Conder, A. 350
Connor, W. 34
Conrad, Joseph 182
Cooper, J. A. 246
Cooper, R. L. 47
Cornett, R. O. 227
Cortéz, H. 8
Corti, A. 143
Courtenay, J. B. de 19
Couturat, L. 355
Covarrubias y Horozco 111
Cowan, G. M. 404
Cowan, N. 250
Cowie, H. 256
Cramond, W. A. 384
Crompton, Richmal 182

Cruttenden, A. 243
Crystal, D. 173, 175, 185, 235, 241, 281
Cummings, E. E. 71–3, 75
Cunliffe, John 252
Curran, C. A. 379
Curtiss, S. 265
Cutts, M. 382
Cyril, St 302

Dalgarno, George 227, 354
Danehy, J. J. 171
Darius the Great 303
Darlington, C. D. 33
Darwin, Charles 230, 296
Davy, D. 175
Dayananda, J. Y. 383
Defoe, Daniel 4
Delattre, P. 172
Department of Education and Science 266
Derrida, J. 79
Dewey, G. 87, 215–16
Dickens, Charles 39, 71, 76–8, 182–3
Dieth, E. 30
Diodorus of Megara 101
Dionysius Thrax 408
Diringer, D. 197–200, 202
Donaldson, M. 232
Donatus 409–10
Donne, John 73
Downing, J. 254
Dressler, W. 119
Dryden, John 4, 63
Dulay, H. C. 376
Dunbar, William 60
Dunkling, L. 113
Duranti, A. 49

Edmont, E. 26
Eibl-Eibesfelt, I. 406
Eimas, P. D. 240
Elias, G. 191
Eliot, T. S. 71, 73, 74
Ellegård, A. 68
Emerson, Ralph Waldo 73
Empson, William 78
Enkvist, N. E. 119
Ervin-Tripp, S. 44
Estienne, R. 111
Eustachio, G. E. 142
Evans, H. 349
Evans, T. 69

Evans-Pritchard, E. E. 44
Exner, S. 263
Eysenck, H. 23

Fallside, F. 271
Fant, G. 148
Farwell, C. B. 243
Faulkner, William 183
Ferguson, C. A. 52, 56, 237, 243
Fichte, J. G. 7
Fielding, Henry 77
Fillmore, C. 413
Finlay, I. F. 350
Finlay, I. H. 75
Firth, J. R. 56, 83, 105, 412
Fishman, J. A. 36
Flaccus, Marcus Verrius 111
Fletcher, C. M. 386
Fletcher, P. 248
Follick, M. 218
Fónagy, I. 172
Foster, J. 185
Fowler, H. W. 88
Fowlie, W. 350
Fox, G. 389
Fox, J. J. 60
Francis, P. 68
Frederick II 290
French, N. R. 86
Freud, Sigmund 66, 264
Frisch, K. von 401
Frishberg, N. 224
Fromkin, V. A. 265
Fry, D. B. 134, 168

Gallaudet, T. 223
Galloway, L. 364
Galsworthy, John 39
Galyean, B. 379
Gannon, P. 257
Gardner, B. T. 402
Gardner, R. A. 402
Garman, M. 248
Gattegno, C. 379
Geertz, C. 40
Geis, M. L. 395
Genie 265, 301
Gerver, D. 351
Gilbert, T. 321
Giles, H. 315
Gilliéron, J. 26
Gilman, A. 45

Gimson, A. C. 155
Gissing, George 39
Gleason, H. A. 203
Gleitman, L. R. 252
Glemet, R. 351
Godard, D. 48
Golding, William 182
Gordon, D. P. 53
Gordon, R. K. 63
Görlach, M. 361
Gorman, P. 226
Gosling, W. 113
Grant, J. C. 192
Grassmann, H. 331
Graves, Robert 71
Gray, Thomas 73
Greenbaum, S. 88
Greenberg, J. 85, 316, 324
Gregg, J. R. 209
Gregory, R. G. 250
Greimas, A. J. 79
Grenfell, Joyce 119
Grice, H. P. 117
Grimm, Jacob 298, 330
Grosjean, F. 363
Grunwell, P. 161
Gumperz, J. 365
Gunnemark, E. 205
Gutenberg, Johannes 194
Guðjónsson, K. 410

Haarman, H. 350
Haas, M. R. 21
Haggo, D. 53
Hall, E. T. 405
Hall, R. A. 180, 400
Halle, M. 164
Halliday, M. A. K. 83, 119,
    173, 412
Hampshire, Susan 275
Hanna, P. R. 216
Hanrott, H. 256
Harada, S. I. 99
Hardcastle, W. J. 141, 158
Hardy, Thomas 39, 71, 183
Hart, J. 216–17, 331
Hartley, A. 350
Hasan, R. 119
Hatfield, F. M. 275
Haugen, E. 172, 410
Hauser, Kaspar 291
Haviland, J. B. 42
Hawking, S. 283
Haydon, B. R. 73
Heath, S. B. 367, 386
Hécaen, H. 275
Helmholtz, H. von 144
Hemingway, Ernest 77
Herbert, George 75
Herder, J. 7, 15
Hergé 182–3
Herodotus 68, 290
Hertz, H. R. 133
Herzog, G. 404
Heschl, R. L. 263
Hesychius of Alexandria
    111
Hickson, Joan 252
Higgins, Henry 24
Hjelmslev, L. 412

Hockett, C. F. 92, 171,
    400–1
Hogben, L. 355
Homer 110–11, 303
Hopkins, Gerard Manley
    73
Howitt, Peter 75
Hsü Shen 111
Huai-su 190
Huddleston, R. 349
Hulke, M. 396
Humboldt, W. von 15
Hume, David 410
Hu Shih 315
Huttenlocher, J. 277
Huttenlocher, P. R. 277
Huxley, Aldous 101, 182

Ibañez, V. B. 183
Inaudi, J. 13
Ireland, W. S. 209
Irvine, J. T. 40
Isidore of Seville 101

Jackson, J. 42
Jackson, J. H. 262
Jackson, Michael 357
Jacobson, S. 206
Jakobson, R. 78, 164, 412
James IV of Scotland 290
James, C. V. 375
James, Henry 77
James, R. 250
Januensis, J. B. 111
Jerome, St 194
Jespersen, O. 88, 160, 166,
    291, 355
Jodocus Bardius 179
John, King of England 189
John, Augustus 72
Johnson, K. 378
Johnson, Samuel 4, 108–9,
    111, 272
Jones, D. 155–6, 412
Jones, W. 298
Joos, M. 172
Jordan, I. K. 269
Joubert, J. 12
Jourard, S. M. 405
Joyce, James 72, 73, 77, 78,
    119, 182
Juanita 6
Junius 68

Kaeding, F. W. 87
Kakehi, H. 176
K'ang Hsi 202
Kay, P. 106
Keenan, E. 41, 249
Kelly, L. G. 347
Kelly, S. 27
Kempe, A. 7
Kempelen, W. von 149
Kennedy, President J. F. 20
Kenrick, D. 205
Kent, R. D. 19
Kenyon, J. S. 155
Kersta, L. G. 20
Klima, E., 222, 225
Knott, T. A. 155

Knowles, F. 352
Korzybski, A. 397
Krashen, S. 376
Kretschmer, E. 18
Kroll, B. M. 257
Krout, M. H. 406
Kuiper, K. 53
Kurath, H. 31
Kuryłowicz, J. 298

Labov, W. 40, 334–5
Ladefoged, P. 159
Lamb, S. M. 83, 412
Lambert, W. E. 23
Lancelot, C. 84
Langer, S. K. 230
Large, J. A. 347, 349
Lauder, A. 27
Lawrence, D. H. 8, 61
Leavitt, L. A. 248
Lecours, A. R. 273
Leech, G. N. 72, 88, 395
Lees, R. 333
Legros, L. A. 192
Leibniz, Gottfried Wilhelm
    354
Lenneberg, E. 265
Leopold, W. 230
L'Epée, C. M. de 223
Leskien, A. 331
Levine, C. C. 386
Lévi-Strauss, C. 79
Lhermitte, F. 273
Liberman, A. M. 146
Liddell, S. K. 225
Lieberman, P. 292
Lin, Y. 315
Lindesay, R. 290
Lisker, L. 147
Litowitz, B. 247
Livy 68
Lloyd, P. 232
Locke, John 410
Locke, J. L. 239
Lodge, David 416
Lodwick, F. 358
Loewen, J. A. 414
Loh, S. C. 352
Long, B. E. L. 387
Lonsdale, James 68
Louis XIII of France 65
Louttit, C. M. 347
Lowth, R. 3
Lozanov, G. 379
Luria, A. J. 416
Lyons, J. 105, 400

Macaulay, Thomas 7
McConkie, G. W. 210-11
McGoohan, P. 76
MacIntyre, C. F. 350
Mackay, D. 252, 255
McLachlan, E. 186
Maclay, H. 103
McNeill, D. 236
McTear, M. 248, 281, 416
Maddieson, I. 85, 167
Magdics, K. 172
Maher, C. 382
Makeba, Miriam 126

Malinowski, B. 10
Mallarmé, Stéphane 75
Malmberg, B. 158
Malory, Thomas 194
Malson, L. 291
Maltz, D. N. 118
Mandabach, F. 367
Mao Zedong 315
Marcie, P. 275
Marcus, J. 199
Marshall, J. C. 274
Martin, N. 256
Marx, Groucho 67
Mason, W. 208
Masson, O. 203
Matsuhashi, A. 214
Mayakovsky 75
Mehrotra, R. R. 58
Mellinkoff, D. 390-1
Melville, Herman 77
Mendenhall, T. C. 68, 69
Meredith, George 39
Merzenich, M. M. 270
Mesrop, St 302
Methodius, St 302
Mezzofanti, G. 364
Michon, J. H. 191
Mi Fu 190
Miller, Arthur 75
Milne, A. A. 183
Milton, John 73, 74
Minamoto no Shitago 111
Mindon, King 313
Mitford, Nancy 39
Mittins, W. H. 89
Mittler, P. 281
Moerk, E. L. 68
Moja 402
Molière 71
Montague, R. 413
Morgan, A. de 68
Morgan, E. 207
Morgan, R. A. 141
Morris, D. 405–6
Morrow, K. 401
Morse, Samuel 86
Morton, A. E. 193
Morton, J. 213
Motteux, P. 61
Mountford, J. 196
Mozart 191
Muhlenberg, F. 367
Murchison, C. 230
Murray, J. A. H. 109
Murray, L. 3

Nadoleczny, M. 19
Namir, L. 224
Napoleon   see Bonaparte
Negus, V. E. 292
Newcombe, F. 274
Newhart, Bob 117
Niccoli, N. 188
Nicot, J. 111

O'Barr, W. M. 391
Ó'Brógáin, S. 192
Ochs, E. 237
O'Connor, J. D. 173
Odbert, H. S. 23

Ogden, C. K. 100–1, 358
Okrand, M. 355
Oller, D. K. 239
Olmsted, D. 242
Opie, I. 11
Opie, P. 11
Orton, H. 30
Orwell, George 2
Osgood, C. E. 103
Osman Yusuf 197

Paes, José Paulo 207
Paget, G. 226
Paget, R. 226
Pāṇini 409
Partridge, Eric 53, 61, 62
Passy, P. 160
Patterson, K. E. 275
Pawley, A. 107
Peano, G. 355
Pear, T. H. 23
Peirce, C. S. 403
Pence, A. 173
Penfield, W. G. 262–3
Peony 402
Pepys, Samuel 208
Peter (wild-boy) 291
Philetos of Cos 111
Philip V of Spain 4
Piaget, J. 236–7, 418
Pike, K. L. 154–5, 173, 412
Pili 402
Pinter, Harold 75
Pitman, I. 209, 217–18
Pitman, J. 219
Pittenger, R. E. 171
Plato 9, 100–1, 408
Pleasence, Donald 75
Poggio 188
Pope, Alexander 191
Porter, D. 378
Postovsky, V. A. 379
Potter, S. 45
Pound, Ezra 74
Prather, E. M. 242
Premack, A. J. 402
Premack, D. 282, 402
Price, Vincent 128
Priestley, J. 2
Priscian 409–10
Pronovost, W. 271
Protagoras of Abdera 111
Psamtik I 290
Ptolemy V Epiphanes 201
Pythagoras 61

Queneau, Raymond 182–3
Quintilian 70, 409
Quirk, R. 88, 360, 415

Raban, B. 254
Rabelais 61
Ramanujan, A. K. 38
Ramu (wolf-child) 291
Rask, R. 298
Rasoherina, Queen 9
Rayner, K. 210–11
Read, K. 218
Reagan, President R. 13,
    382

Reid, E. 20
Reynolds, Joshua 109
Rich, J. 208
Richards, I. A. 78, 100–1
Richardson, Samuel 77
Richelieu, Cardinal 4
Rips, L. J. 103
Ritchie, D. 272
Roach, P. 158
Roberts, L. 262–3
Robinson, J. 51
Rockey, D. 163
Roget, P. M. 104
Rosenberg, B. A. 53
Rosenberger, V. K. 355
Ross, A. S. C. 39
Rozin, P. 252
Rubens 191
Rutherford, W. 144
Ryle, G. 418

Saintsbury, G. 74
Salimbene, Brother 290
Salmond, A. 49
Sanderson, S. 30
Sankoff, G. 32
Sapir, E. 6, 15, 400, 411
Sarah 402
Saussure, F. de 79, 299, 399, 403, 411–13, 418
Scarfe, F. 350
Schlegel, A. von 295
Schleicher, A. 230, 294, 298
Schlesinger, I. M. 224
Schleyer, J. M. 355
Schmandt-Besserat, D. 198
Schwartz, R. G. 243
Scott, C. T. 63
Scott, R. 177
Scott, Walter 272

Searle, J. R. 121
Selinker, L. 376
Sequoya 203
Seti I 388
Shakespeare 63, 69, 71, 73–6, 331, 337
Shalmanazer III 200
Shaw, F. 27
Shaw, George Bernard 24, 182–3, 216–18
Shelley, Percy Bysshe 14
Shelton, T. 208
Shephard, D. A. E. 344
Sherwood Fox, W. 65
Sherzer, J. 50, 59
Shilhak-Inshushinak I 329
Sholes, C. L. 194
Silone, I. 183
Simo, J. 255
Sinclair, Upton 183
Singer, E. 191
Skelly, M. 226
Slobin, D. I. 234
Smith, B. L. 239
Smith, F. 253
Smith, H. L. 155
Smith, M. E. 234
Snow, C. 241
Socrates 61
Solzhenitsyn, Alexander 78, 182
Southey, Robert 61
Spender, Stephen 73
Spiegl, F. 27
Spitzer, L. 78
Spock, Dr. Benjamin 47
Spooner, W. A. 264
Sriramulu, P. 310
Steele, J. 172
Steiner, Rudolf 407
Stetson, R. H. 166

Stine, H. 76
Stockhausen, Karlheinz 175
Stockwell, R. P. 172
Stoel-Gammon, C. 246
Stokoe, W. C. 223
Stoppard, Tom 76
Stuhlman, O. 144
Sturluson, Snorri 410
Suci, G. 103
Sudre, J. F. 355
Svartvik, J. 69, 88, 415
Swadesh, M. 177, 333
Swan, M. 380
Swann, W. 281
Swift, Jonathan 4, 65, 66
Syder, F. H. 107

Tacitus 68
Taeschner, T. 365
Tannenbaum, P. 103
Tarasuk, M. B. 386
Tarnopol, L. 277
Tarnopol, M. 277
Terrell, T. D. 379
Tesnière, L. 412
Thackeray, William Makepeace 183
Thody, P. 349
Thomas, A. R. 31
Thomas, D. M. 77
Thomas, Dylan 71, 72, 75, 76
Thomson, M. 276
Thorndyke, P. W. 119
Thucydides 68
Tiedemann, D. 230
Tin-Tin 182–3
Tiro, Marcus Tullius 208
Todd, L. 338
Todorov, T. 79

Toronto, A. S. 235
Torquemada 64
Trager, G. 155, 400
Trevarthen, C. 241
Trier, J. 104
Trollope, Anthony 182
Trudgill, P. 32, 39, 43
Tryphiodorus 65
Turner, G. W. 392
Twain, Mark 348
Twyman, M. 184–5, 193
Tyndale, William 389

Ulfilas, Bishop 302
Ullmann, S. 74

Valdés Fallis, G. 365
Valerius Harpocration 111
Varro, Marcus Terentius 409
Verlaine 73
Verner, K. 330–31
Vidler, M. 89
Vivian, R. 405
Voegelin, C. F. 287
Voegelin, F. M. 287
Volterra, V. 365
Vygotsky, L. S. 13, 418

Wade, T. 315
Wagner, K. R. 246
Wahl, E. von 355
Walker, A. 367
Wallis, J. 331
Walter, C. 380
Ware, E. E. 103
Warren, R. M. 147
Warren, R. P. 147
Warrin, F. L. 177
Washoe 402
Weaver, W. 352

Webster, Noah 109, 219
Weizenbaum, J. 416
Wells, G. 231, 233
Wells, H. G. 183
Wells, J. C. 135
Welsh, C. A. 234
Wendon, L. 186
Wenker, G. 26
Wernicke, C. 262–3
Wesley, Samuel 66
Wever, E. G. 144
Whorf, B. L. 15
Widdowson, J. 30
Wilkins, J. 331, 354
William I of England 12
Williams, C. B. 69
Williams, G. H. 385
Willis, J. 208
Wilson, Harold 20
Wing, A. M. 215
Winograd, T. 416
Wittgenstein, L. 102, 418
Wood, C. 64
Woolf, Virginia 77
Wordsworth, William 73
Wright, E. 65
Wright, J. 27
Wright, P. 193
Wulfila, Bishop 302
Wynne, A. 64

Xenophon 68, 208
Ximenes 64

Yeats, W. B. 66
Yule, G. U. 67

Zamenhof, L. L. 355–7
Zettersten, A. 86
Zipf, G. K. 87
Zizanii, L. 111

VIII INDEX OF TOPICS

The alphabetical arrangement of the index is letter by letter. Primary references are given in bold type. Appendices I–VII are not included.

abbreviations 44, 76, 87, 111, 184, 189, **206–7**, 216, 366, 384
abessive 92
ablative 92, 299
ablaut 299
aborigines (Australian) 326–7, 370
abstract meaning 6, 15, 274, 277
abstractness 82, 85, 165–6
Académie française 1, 4
academies **4**, 366, 410
Accademia della Crusca 4, 111
accent (speech variety)

dialect vs 24
foreign 35, 364, 377
judgments of 23, 39
regional 23, **24**, 39, 51, 126, 145, 149, 163, 182, 206, 217, 315, 396
accent (emphasis) see accentuation
accent (marks) 188, 196, 367, 408
accentuation 74, 166, **171**, 174, 356
acceptability 3, 5, 48, 334, 388–9, **414–15**
accessory nerve 131
accidence 90
accommodation 50–1
accuracy 388–9
accusative 92–3, 299, 356
achievement tests 381
Acoustical Society of America 20

acoustic cues 146, 150
acoustic nerve 131
acoustic reflex 143
acoustics 132–7, 270
acquisition 372, 377
see also child language, language learning
acronym **90**, 115, 206
acrostics 64
actio 70
active voice see voice (grammar)
activity 48, 52
Adam's apple 128
addition rules 165
additions 215, 265, 279
Addresses to the German Nation 7
address, modes of 44, 99
adessive 92
adjacency pairs 118
adjective 21, 71, 85, **91–3**,

244, 246, 299, 356, 392, 395
tense of 92
adjective phrase 95
Adobe Systems 195
adverbials 95
adverbs **91–3**, 244, 356
advertising 8, 63, 67, 174, 186, 197, 206, **394–5**
television 395
types of 394
aerometry 139
aesthetic translation 347
affective meaning 103
affirmations (religious) 389
affixation 41, **90–1**, 265, 283, 295
affricates 33, **159**, 279
Afghanistan 303, 309, 359
Africa 33–4, 53, 60, 63, 91, 126–7, 160, 167, 174, 287, 310, **316–17**, 320,

328, 340–1, 362
age **19**, 23, 40, 44, 99, 270, 334, 386
agglutinating/agglutinative languages 90, **295**
agnosia 273
ago 72
agraphia 274
agreement (grammatical) 95
air-conduction test 268
Airplane 2 209
air-stream mechanism **124–7**, 154, 157, 161, 238
Akbarnama 230
Albania 302, 359
Aldus Corporation 195
alexia 274
Algeria 318, 359
algorithms 352
allative 92
All-India Alphabet 367

alliteration 53, 70, 74, 390
allographs 196
allomorphs 90
allophones 162–3, 196
alphabet 8, 184, 196–7, **204–7**, 253, 302–3, 313, 331, 375
  augmented Roman 219
  cipher 58
  comic 62
  consonantal 204
  dual 188
  history of 204–5, 328
  invention of 366–7
  mystical 59
  reform 218–19
  symbolism of 407
  transliteration of 350
alphabetical order 59, 105, 108, 110
alphabetism 90
alternative communication 282–3
alveolar consonants *see* consonants
alveolar ridge 130, 141, **157–9**
Amazonian languages 286, 324–5
ambiguity 3, 57, 63, 89, 98, 181–82, 352–3, 355, 385, 404, 414, 417
amelioration 332
America 60, 322–5
  Central 187, 322–5
  North 295, **322**, 324, 329
  South 4, 98, 286–7, 322–3, **324–5**, 328
American Academy 4
American Dictionary of the English Language, An 109
Americanisms 5
American Journal of Education 3
American Library Association 47
American Name Society 115
American Samoa 361
American Translators' Association 347
Amerindian peoples 61, 199, 370
  see also Appendix VI
amplification 142–3, 270
amplitude 134
anagrams 64–5
analogy 236, **332**, 335, **408**
analysis by synthesis 148
analytic languages 295
anapaest 74
anaphora 119
anarthria 273
Andaman Is. 319–20
anechoic chamber 138
Anemerina tribe 9
Angola 317, 359
animals 8, 128, **400–3**
animateness 92–3
Ann Arbor trial 35

Annatom I. 92
anomaly 408
anthropological linguistics 418
anthropology 6, 10, 15, 107, 116, 180, 287, 292, 405, **411**, 418
anthroponomastics 112
anthropophonics 19
anthroposophy 407
anticipation (consonant) 265
Antigua and Barbuda 117, 359, 361
Antilles Is. 324
Antiqua 188
antonymy 105, 111, 355
anvil 143
anxiety theory (of stuttering) 280
aperiodic *see* periodicity
aphasia 81, 260, 262, 266, **272–7**, 364
  diary accounts of 272
  dysphasia vs 272
  recovery from 272–3
  types of 267, **273**, 281
aphasiology 272
apocope 330
Apocrypha 386
apostrophe (figurative) 70
apostrophe (punctuation) 207
apotropaic names 113
appetitive expression 400
Apple Computers Inc 195
approximants **159**, 167–8, 299
apraxia 273
aptitude (for languages) 375, 381
Arabia 187
Arabic academies 4
arbitrariness 101, 401
archaism 42, 49, 54, 56, 66, 73, 347, 390
archive, linguistic 370
areas (linguistic) 33, 167
Argentina 305, 324, 329, 340, 359
argot 58, 391
Aritama culture 11
Ars major/minor 409
article 67, **91**, 225, 356
  definite 33, 92, 349, 409
articulation 41, **130–1**, 135, 154-61, 165, 408–9
  abnormal 161, 267, 273, 279, 280
  ease of 166, 335
  manner of 154, 157, **159**, 161, 164
  place of 146, 154–5, **157**, 159, 161, 164, 279, 299, 409
  secondary 154, 158
articulators 130–1, 154-61
  active vs passive 130, 157
articulatory apraxia 273

artificial intelligence 116, 149, 352–3, 413, 416, 418
artificial languages 354–8
  a priori vs *a posteriori* 354
  ideal 357, 359
arytenoids 128
ascender 192
Asia 33, 36, 42, 94, 167, 177, 188, 190, 287, 322, **309–13**
Asia Minor 187, 328
aspect **93**, 176, 224, 299
aspirates 299, 330–1
aspiration 159, 161, **163**, 168
assimilation 145, **166**, 174, 330, 335
Association Phonétique Internationale 160
associative relations 411
assonance 74
Assyrians 200
Aṣṭādhyāyī 409
asterisk convention 88, 160, 206, 294–5
Asterix 183
athletic type 18
Atlas linguistique de la France 26, 29
attention 237, 272
attitude to languages 375
auctioneers 53, 175, 407
audibility threshold 134
audiogram 134, 268
audio-lingual method 378
audiology 268, 270
audiometry 268
audio-visual aids 375
auditory
  agnosia 273
  canal 142
  comprehension 149, 261
  discrimination **145**, 156, 240, 277, 279, 281
  feedback 280
  implants 270
  nerve 131
  perception **144–9**, 154, 166, 240, 263, 281
auditory-vocal channel 400–11, **403–4**
augmentative communication 282–3
augmenting system (spelling) 217
aural-oral method 378
auricle 142
Australia 8, 42, 319, **326–7**, 341, 359, 361, 370
Austria 50, 359
authentic materials 375, 381
authorship studies 68–9
autism 23, 281–82
Automated Language Processing Systems 353

Automatic Language Processing Advisory Committee 352
Automobile Association 15
autopolyphony 175
auxiliary languages 76, 336, 338, **354**
averaged evoked response 261
avoidance languages 8, 42
aygo-paygo speech 59
Azed 64
Azilian culture 198
Aztecs 8

babbling 22, 51, **238–9**, 241, 290
Babel, Tower of 7
Babylonians 200
baby talk 237
back slang 59
back-translation 348
backwards speech 248
Bahamas 361
Bahrain 359
bái-huà 315
Bali 321
Balkans 33, 36, 37
Bangladesh 359, 361
bank teller machine 417
Barbados 340, 359, 361
baritone 19
Barong dance 321
baseball, language of 56
Basic English 358
basilar membrane 143–4
bass voice 18–19
Battle of Maldon, The 60
BBC English 396
be (invariant) 35
beckoning 406
bee dancing 401
behavioural classification 273
behaviourism 101, 236, 376, 378, **412–13**
Behistun 303
Belgium 34, 37, 51, 359, 362, 368
Belize 340, 361
Benedictines 223
Benin 359
Beowulf 303
Bermuda 359, 361
Bernoulli effect 129
Bhārata nātya-śāstra 407
Bhutan 359, 361
Bible, the 7, 9, 42–3, 59, 63, 194, 302–3, 305, 340, **388**, 393, 410
  translation of 347, 356, **388–9**
bidentals 161
bilabials 137, **157**, 159, 161, 168, 279
bilateral hearing 142
bilingualism 23, 33–4, 37, 42, 50, 326, 335, **362–9**, 372, 414
  acquisition of 365

dormant 364
  maintenance vs transitional 368
  programmes for 368–9
  societal vs individual 364
binary analysis 79
biological capacity 84, 210, 221
biological linguistics 416
biological noises 238, 241
biology 292
Bīsitūn 189
black-letter writing 188
Blankety Blank 271
blasphemy 61
blend 90, 265
Blissymbolics 282
blocks (in stuttering) 280
Blue-backed speller 219
body language 50, 118, 224, **403–7**
body size (printing) 192
body types 18
Boggle 64
bold face type 195, 206
Bolivia 323, 325, 328, 359
bone-conduction test 268
book hand 188
bookmaking 407
Borneo 319
borrowing 4–5, 38, 41, 53, 99, 181, 197, 216, 287, 295–6, 302, **332**, 356, 362, 366–7
Botswana 317, 359, 361
boundaries (semantic) 247
boundaries (speech) 145, 185
bound morpheme 90
boustrophedon 187, 199
bow-wow theory 291
brachygraphy 208–9
brackets 97, 162, 207
Bradford accent 32
Brahma 388
Brahmin vs non-Brahmin speech 38
braille **282**, 315, 405
brain **259–65**, 292–3, 418
  damage to 215, 238, 261–2, 265–6 272, 274–5, 279, 281
  function of 260-1, 265, 379
  lobes of 143, 260, 263, 275
  slips of the 264–5
  split 261
brain-stem 260
brand image 394
Brazil 308, 324–5, 328, 340, 359
breaking (of voice) 19
Breakthrough to Literacy 252
breathing 124–5, 280
breathy voice 128, 159, 171
Britain 36, **37**, 56, 63, 113,

227, 304, 359, 361–62, 368, 373
  island dependencies 361
British Isles 205, 304, 340
British Virgin Islands 361
broadcasting 5, 43, 50, 56, 67, 195, **396**
  use of signs in 407
broadcast transmission 400–1
Broca's aphasia 273
Broca's area 262–3, 273
Brown University Corpus 415
Brunei 359, 361
buccal voice 127
Buddhism 303, 313, **388**
Bulgaria 302, 359
Bullock Report 250
Burkina Faso 359
Burma 311–13, 359
Burundi 11, 38, 359
Bushmen see Khoisan
business language 186, 345, 371
by-names 112

California 198
Calligrammes (1918) 11
calligraphy 190
calling intonation 175
call-signs 57
calque 332
calypso 60
Cambodia 311, 319, 359
Cambridge English Course, The 380
Cameleon II 283
Cameroon 340–41, 359, 361
Canada 23, 34, 288, 304, 322–3, 329, 340, 359, 361
Canon Communicator 283
cant 58
Cape Verde Is. 340
capitals (punctuation) 112, 183, **188**, 195–6, **206**, 218–19, 367
  rustic 188
captions 206
cardinal vowels 135, **156**, 169
caretaker speech 237
Caribbean 340
Carolingian minuscule 188
Cartesian thought 410
cartouche 201
case 3, 43, **92–3**, 98, 299, 356, 408
case grammar 413
caste **38**, 40, 405
cataphora 119
cat-calls 175
catch phrases 51, 67
categorical perception 147, 240
Catholicon 111
causative 93
Cayman Islands 361

CB slang 56
CDs 195
Ceefax 195
censorship 397
census 288, 305
Cento 175
Central African Republic 316, 318, 359
centre slang 59
cerebellum 260, 264
cerebral hemispheres **260–5**, 274, 276, 280, 379
cerebral palsy 282
cerebro-vascular accidents 272
cerebrum 260
cerumen 142
Chad 316, 341, 359
channel 48
chant 11, 41, 48–9, 60, 175
character (literary) 71, 77, 119
character (symbol) 202
Characterie 208
Character Indicated by Handwriting 191
chart recorder 138
cheremes 223
cheretic/cherological handicap 267
cherology 223
chiasmus 70
child language 9, 11, 14, 40, 51, 59, 62, 63, 173, 176, 180-1, 219, **229–57**, 265, 269, 332, 335, 354, 376–7, 418
  diaries of 230
  in school 250–57
  research on 230–5, 414–15
  theories of 236–7
Child Language Data Exchange System 233
children, wild/wolf 291
Chile 323, 324, 359
chimpanzees 292, **402**
China 43, 110, 190, 194, 198–9, 276, 308–9, 311–13, **314–15**, 341, 359–60, 388
Chinese box (in grammar) 96
Chinese typewriter 315
Chinese University Language Translator 352
Chinese vs Phoenician theories 213
chirography see handwriting
choice (stylistic) 66
Christianity 59, 64, 318, 347, **388–9**
Chronicles 393
chronogram 64
chunking 173, 181
cinefluorography 140
ciphers 58
circumlocution 8, 15, 99, 273, 280, 358

citation analysis 345
citations (dictionary) 111
clarification 237, 248, 270
clarity 382–3, 390, 397
class and language 23, 32, **38–40**, 42, 45, 71, 77, 120, 163, 334–5, 366
Classification and Index of the World's Languages 287
classifiers 33, 91
clause 68–9, **95**, 173, 245, 251, 332
clavicular breathing 125
clay tablets/tokens 198, 303
clearing house for endangered languages 370
cleft lip/palate 19, 140, 267, **279**
cliche 53, **147**
click sounds 33, **126**, 127, 154
click languages 126, 167, 317
climatology 335
clinical linguistics 418
clipping 90
closure, types of 159
cloze testing 381
cluttering 280
coalescence 166, **330**
coarticulation **158**, 166, 264
cochlea 143–4, 270
cochlear duct 143
cochlear implants 270
cocktail party phenomena 145, 147
code (language) **40**, 48, 59, 403
codes (secret) **58**, 352, 410
  touch 405
code-switching see switching
Codex Argenteus 302
Codex Sinaiticus 91
codification 2, **366**
cognates 294, 333
cognition 14–15
  adult vs child 377
  development of 22, 230, **236**–7, 252–3, 256, 277, 373–4
  deficiency in 40, 272, 281
coherence 119, 173
cohesion 119
co-hyponyms 105
coinage see neologism
collocation 72, **105**
Colombia 324, 340, 359
colon 207
colour (graphic use) 192, 195, 206
colour terms 106, 402
comic strips 176
comitative 92
comma 207
commands 245
commentary 72, 396
commercials (television) 350

Commission on Foreign Language and International Studies 373
commissives 121
commisurotomy 261
Committee on Endangered Languages and their Preservation 370
communication
  alternative/augmentative 282–3
  animal 400–2
  chain 267
  design features of 400–1
  language and 399–407
  mass 50, 70, 366, **397**
  problems in 344, 386
  theory of 87
  types of 403–7
  without dialogue 12
communicative needs 360, 375, 378, 409
communicative teaching 378
community language learning 379
compact discs 195
comparative method 294–5, 328, 330–1
comparison (grammatical) 84, 119
compensation 18
competence (language) 364, 375, **413**
competence (literary) 79
complement 95
complementary distribution 163
complementary terms 105
complexity 5–6, 22, 40, 55, 82, **95**, 234, 237, 245, 254, 336, 338–9, 355–8, 383–4, 390–2, 396, 399
  see also simplification
componential analysis 107
compounding **90**, 174, 356, 384, 395
comprehension see speech
comprehension approach 379
Comprehensive Grammar of the English Language, A 88
computational linguistics 415–18
computer, use of 20, 26, 68, 109, 111, 135–6, 138, 140–1, 194–5, 210–11, 216, 233, 261, 270–1, 282, 347, 349, 352–3, 356, 367, 380–1, 415, 416–19
computer age 416
computer-aided diagnosis 387
computer-assisted language learning 381
Computerized Speech

Laboratory 135, 138, 160
computer science 149, 349, 352, 418
concord 95
concordancing 416
concrete poetry 75
configuration 192, 206, 383
confluent teaching 379
Congo 341, 359
conjunction 57, 68, **91**, 95
conjunctive relations 119
connectivity 69, 77, **119**, 136–7, 146–7, 165, **166**, 175
connotations **103**, 346, 357, 386
consolidation (in writing) 214
consonants 74, **128–31**, **157**–9, 164, 175, 197, 209, 227, 238, 242, 265, 292, 404
  acoustics of 133, 135, 137, 154
  acquisition of 242–3
  alveolar 137, **157**, 159, 166, 168, 239, 242
  clusters of 166, 242, 265
  definition of 154
  dental 33, **157**, 159, 168, 299
  distribution of 166, 265
  English system of 162
  frequency of 167–9
  intensity of 134
  liquid 168
  palatal **157**, 159, 168, 237, 299
  perception of 146, 240, 242
  postalveolar 157
  retroflex 33, 155, **157**, 159, 167–8
  symbolism of 176–7
  semi- 155, **159**, 299
  tap 168
  uvular 33, **157**, 159, 168, 238
  velar 137, **157**, 159, 168, 239, 242, 299
consonant-vowel ratio 86, 167
constatives 121
constituents (syntactic) **96**, 251, 264, 412
consultant see informant
consumer society 366
Contact 370
contact/non-contact societies 405
contact ulcers 278
content words 275
context 40, 83, 98, 105, 173
contextual identity 48–65
continuants see approximants
contoid 155

contours 171–5
    stylized 175
contractions 189, 206, 216
contralto voice 18–19
contrastive analysis 374
contrastivity 66
conventionalism 101, 408
convergence 51, 293–6
conversation 43, 50, **52**,
    53, 60, 62–3, 71, 75,
    94, **116–21**, 181, 232,
    248–9, 378, 386, 414
    analysis 116, 406
    cross-sex 21
    exchanges 40, 48, 57,
    118, 241, 248–9
    handicaps in 281
    maxims of 117, 120
    repairs to 117, 248
    turns 57, **118**, 237, 248
converse terms 105
conversion (word) 90
convolutions 260
cooing 238
Cook Islands 361
cooperative principle 117
coordination 94–5, 245
Copenhagen School 412
copula 35
copying (writing) 276
coreference 119
corpora 47, 86, 88, 109,
    353, 413, **414–15**
    computer 415
corpus callosum 260
correctness **2**, 97, 250, 408
Corsica 34
cortex 260–3
cortical blood flow 261
Costa Rica 359
Council of Europe 368,
    373–4
counselling 379
Cours de linguistique générale
    411
courtesy expressions 52
courtroom 391
cranial nerves 131, 143
Cratylus 9, 408
creaky voice **128**, 159, 171
creativity 40, 58, 70, 73,
    79, 89, 214, 250–1,
    377–9, **399–400**
creoles 35, 303, 316,
    319–21, 326, 336,
    338–41, 362
creolization 336, 338
Crete 187, 199, 303, 328
cricoid cartilage 128
criminal codes 58
critical language study 397
critical period 265, 375
Cro-Magnon man 292
cross-examination 391
cross-reference 95
cross-sectional study 231,
    377
crosswords 64, 104
cry (baby) 128, 238–9
cryptanalysis 58

cryptic clues 64
cryptogram 58
cryptography 58, 196, 352,
    354
cryptology 58
cryptophasia 249
Cuba 327, 359
cued speech 227
cultural factors affecting
    language 29, **34–65**,
    118, 174, 237, 296,
    333, 345–6, 362,
    367–8, 372, 386, 406
cultural pluralism 369
Cuná 50, 58
cuneiform writing **200**,
    302–3, 318, 329
cup vs *glass* 247
curing ritual 50
curriculum 250, 256
cursing 12, 60, **61**
    tablet 61
cursive writing 188, 255
cycle (acoustic) 133
Cyprus 187, 303, 359
Czech critics 78
Czechoslovakia 302, 359,
    412

dactyl 74
dactylology 226–7
dance 407
dash (punctuation) 207
data banks 353
date conventions 57, 184
dative 299
Dead Sea Scrolls 34
deaf and dumb 269
deaf-blind communication
    403, 405
deafness 19, 133, 142, 213,
    221–7, 266–7, **268–71**,
    272, 279, 281, 363, 407
    types of 268
death taboos 8–9
debates 41
decibels 134
deciphering 58
declaratives (speech act) 121
deconstruction 79
decreolization 338
deep vs surface structure
    98, 413
deficiency vs difference 40
definitions 100, 102, 111,
    247
degree (semantic) 105
De interpretatione 408
deixis **106**, 120, 183, 233,
    246
delayed auditory feedback
    280
Delayed Oral Practice 379
deletion (graphological)
    214
deletion (phonological)
    165, 265
De lingua latina 409
delivery (rhetorical) 70
Delphi oracle 63

dementia 272
demographic trends 288,
    335
demonstratives 99
demotic script 201
Denmark 36, 359
dental consonants *see*
    consonants
De Oratore 70
dependency grammar 412
deprivation (verbal) 35
derivation **90**, 97, 265
derivational errors (dyslexic)
    274
descender 192
description in linguistics **2**,
    66, 82, 177, 411
    in literature 182, 250–1
    in science 384
desuggestion 379
determinative 201–2
determiner 96–7
determinism, linguistic 15
de-umming 396
deviance 52, 62, 71–2, 281
dez 223
diachronic vs synchronic
    approach 106, **411**
diacritics **156**, 160–1, 192,
    204, 253, 348, 367
diagnostic tests 381
diagramming sentences 96,
    251
diagrams 385
dialect
    accent vs 24
    international 360
    language vs 25, **286**,
    307, 309–11, 313–16,
    319, 324, 364, 400
    popular notions of 24
    regional 23, **24–33**, 35,
    39, 51, 68, 71, 77, 99,
    108, 111, 155, 206,
    223, 250, 286, 302–4,
    308, 334, 347, 357,
    366–7, 386, 396, 418
    rural 24, 26–7, 30–1
    urban 24, 26, **32**, 35
dialect chain 25, 33
dialect continuum **25**, 223,
    287
dialect geography 26
dialect surveys 26–7, 30–1
dialectic 410
dialectology 26, 32, 84
dialogue 55–7, 75, 77, 116
Diamond Sutra, The 194
diaphragm 124
diaries 55
    in child-language study
    230–1
dichotic listening 142, **261**,
    265
dictation 184
diction *see* poetry
dictionaries 2, 4, 87–8,
    102, 104–6, **108–11**,
    348, 358, 366, 416, 418
    bilingual 110–11, 352–3

historical 111, 332, 335
history of 110–11, **410**
    size of 108, 202, 384
*Dictionary of Modern English
    Usage* 88
*Dictionary of Slang and
    Unconventional English*
    61
*Dictionary of the English
    Language* 109
Dictionary Society of North
    America 111
Dictionnaire françois-latin
    111
differentiation (in writing)
    214
diffusion (lexical) 334
digital techniques 138
diglossia 43, 364
digraphs 367
diminutives 237
ding-dong theory 291
diphthongs **156**, 169, 242,
    334
diplomatics 189
direct/indirect speech 77
direction (stage) 76
directional reception 400–1
directives 121
direct method 378
direct selection 282
disadvantage (linguistic) 35
discourse 57, 71, 82, 107,
    116–19, 149, 173, 181,
    296, 353, 366, 416–19
    analysis 116, 120
discreteness (of language)
    401
displacement (of language)
    401
dispositio 70
dissimilation 330
distance zones 405
distinctive features 164,
    271
divergence 51, 294–6
Djibouti 359
doctor-patient interaction
    50
doctrinal statements 389
documentary hand 188
do-it-yourself instructions
    383
Domesday Book 12
dominance (brain) 21, 23,
    45, 60, **260–1**, 276, 280
    mixed 261
Dominica 340, 359, 361
Dominican Republic 359
dord 111
dot-matrix characters 367
Doublespeak Awards 383
doublets 65
downdrift 174
Down's syndrome 238
drama 39, 50, 63, 71, 73,
    75–7, 89, 124, 250
Dreaming (aboriginal) 327
drills 379, 381
drum signalling 404

duality of patterning 401
dual number 92
dubbing 346, **396**
Duden series 110
dullness in legal documents
    390
Dunlop 115
duration (phonological) 74,
    161, **171**
DynaVox 283
dyne 134
dysarthria 273
dysgraphia 274
dyslexia 211, 274–7
dysphasia 272, 281
    see also aphasia
dysphonia 278
dyspraxia 273

ear 142–3, 268
ear–voice span 351
Easter Island 187, 199,
    319, 321
East Germany 302, 359
Ecuador 359
Edda 11
Edinburgh, HMS 57
editing 396
education 3, 4–5, 23, 26,
    34–7, 40, 43, 186,
    250–7, 326, 362, 366,
    368–9, 373
educational linguistics 250,
    418
effort, law of least 87
eggy-peggy speech 59
egressive air **125–7**, 154,
    157
Egypt 199–201, 316, 318,
    359
ejectives **126–7**, 154, 159,
    168
elaborated code 40
electro-aerometer 139
electroencephalography
    261, 280
electrolaryngography 141,
    270
electromagnetic midsagittal
    articulography 140
electromyography 139
electronic composition 175
electronic larynx 278
electronic media 187, 195
electropalatography 140,
    158
elicitation (of language data)
    414
elision 166
ELIZA 416
ellative 92
ellipsis 55, 69, 94, **119**,
    392
elocutio 70
elocution 66, 70
El Salvador 359
e-mail 181, 283
'-emes' 79, 412
emotional appeals (Greek)
    70

emotional factors 2, **10**, 14, 281, 377, 406
emotive function **10**, 61, 173, 384
emphasis 3, 171, 173, **182–3**, 195, 383, 391, 406
Empire Strikes Back, The 98
empiricists 410
enciphering 58
encyclopedic information 108, 111
endangered languages 370–1
endocentric construction 95
endolymph 143
energy (sound) 133, 155
Eneydos (1490) 5
English
  opposition to 360
  plain 366, 382–3
  speakers of 361
  world language status of 360, 368
  see also Appendix VI
English Academy 4
English Dialect Dictionary 27
English Dialect Survey 27
English Grammar (1794) 3
English Place-Name Society 114
Enigma machine 58
epenthesis 330
epiglottis 128, 157
epigraphy 189
equality (linguistic) 6–7
Equalizer™ 283
Equatorial Guinea 359
equipotentiality 262, 265
erlebte Rede 77
errors 2–5, 66, 189, 214–15, 245, 247, 254, 257, 265, 273–7, **376–7**
essays 257
Essay towards Establishing the Melody and Measure of Speech 172
essive 92
Ethiopia 288, 318, 341, 359
ethnicity 23, **34–7**, 42, 51, 250, 338, 362, 418
  boom in 36
ethnographic translation 347
ethnography of communication 48, 54, 116
ethnolinguistics 34, 38, 324, 418
etic units 412
Etymologicon magnum 111
etymology 9, 106, 109, 111, 113–15, **332**, 408–9
euphemisms 8, 61, 101
Eurasia 294–5, 298, 306
eurhythmy 407

EURODICAUTOM 349
Europe
  languages of 2, 112, 120, 126–7, 298, **302–5**, 328
  language teaching in 251, 409
  linguistics in 411
  writing systems of 187, 188, 190
European Association for Lexicography 111
European Bureau for Lesser-Used Languages 370
European Commission for Democracy through Law 371
European Parliament resolutions 371
European Union 36, 344, 347, 352, 368, 370
European Union of Associations of Translation Companies 347
EUROTRA 352
Eustachian tube 142
evaluation 379
evaluative style 66
evidence, laws of 391
evolution and language 5, 6, 124, 128, 145, 210, **292–3**, 296, 402
exclamation 21
exclamation marks 196, 207
excretion vocabulary 61
Exeter Book 63
exhalation 124–5
existentials 35
Exner's centre 263
exocentric construction 95
expansions (grammatical) 233, 237
experimental methods 145, 147, 230–1, 415
expert systems 416
explanations 193, 386
expletives 61
explication de texte 79
Expolangues 345
expressive function **10**, 237, 256
expressive handicap 267
expressives 121
extension (historical) 332
external auditory canal 142
extraversion 22
extrinsic vs intrinsic muscles 131
eye 210, 276–7
eye contact 50, 118, **404**
eye movements 210–11, 224
eyebrow flashing 406
facial expression 173, 224, 233, **406–7**, 414
facial nerve 131
false friends *see faux amis*
familiar pronouns 45

family of languages 85, 226, 289, **294–327**, 328
family tree 294, 334
Farr's Law of Mean Familiarity 45
fascism, senses of 397
'father' (words for) 177
faux amis 349, 356
feature detectors 148, 240
feature geometry 164
Fédération Internationale des Traducteurs 347
feedback
  in conversation **118**, 181, 267
  internal 264, 267, 280
  total 401
felicity conditions 121
female speech 21
feminine *see* gender
feminism 46–7
Fernando Po 340
festination 280
fieldwork 26–7, 414–15
figurative change 332
figurative language 2, 22, 60, **70**, 247, 357, 384, 394
figures of speech 70
Fiji 321, 341, 359, 361
fillers 181
film (recording) 231
Find a Story 89
fine-tuning hypothesis 237
finger spelling **226–7**, 315, 405
Finland 37, 306, 359
First Five Minutes, The 171
'first grammarian' 410
'fis' phenomenon 242
fissures (of cortex) 260
fixation 210
flaps 159, 168
fluency 19, 23, 60, 280, 364
  disorders *see* non-fluency
fluorescent octons 22
flyting 60
Flyting of Dunbar and Kennedie, The 60
focal areas 28
Fog Index 254
folklore 9, 116
Follow me 360
foot (poetry) 74
football results intonation 243
foregrounding 71
foreigner talk 51, 339, 377
foreign languages 81, 181, 217, **344–81**, 414, 418
forensic linguistics 66, 69
forensic science 20
forgery 189
form (vs meaning) 67, 70, 82
formalists 78–9
formal language 2–3, 32, 39–40, **42–3**, 49–50,

54, 61, 68, 77, 93, 120, 181, 207, 250, 347, 365–6, 391, 396
formants 20, **135**, 146
forms (paper) 55, 383
formulae 12, 38, **52–3**, 56, 58–60, 63, 93, 385
  historical 295
Förster's syndrome 63
fossilized errors 377
fossils 292
Foundation for Endangered Languages 370
four-letter words 61
Four III 72
fovea 210
frames 417
France 29, **36–7**, 55, 63, 113, 303, 328, 359–60, 368, 373, 406
Franks Casket 205
free association 105
Freemasonry 407
free morpheme 90
free variation **163**, 206, 334
free verse 74
French Academy 1, 4
French Guiana 340, 359
frequency (acoustic) **133**, 136–7, 143–4, 146, 159, 175
  fundamental 19, **133**, 141
  fundamental, missing 144
  loss (high) of 270
  pitch vs 133
  theory of pitch 144
frequency (statistical) 21, 67–9, 71, **86–7**, 167–9
fricatives 29, 33, 137, **159**, 161, 168, 238, 242, 271, 279, 299
friction 129, 154, 156, 159
frictionless continuants 159
full stop 207
function (textual) 79
functional grammar 413
functional sentence perspective 412
functional syllabus 378
function words *see* grammatical words
Fundamento de Esperanto 356
fusion 166
fusional languages 295
futhark 205

g, dropping of 39
Gabon 359
Gadsby 65
Gallaudet University 269
Gambia 340, 359, 361
games 11, 58, 63, **64–5**, 239, 241, 248
Gargantua 61
Gastarbeiter **36**, 351, 362
gaze 406
gematria 8, **59**
gender 85, **93**, 95, 299, 332

genealogy (language) 84, **295**
generalized phrase structure grammar 413
general semantics 397
generative grammar *see* grammar
generic *man* 46–7
Genesis, Book of 388
genetic classification 84, **295**
genitive 92–3, 299
genres (stylistic) 52, 73–8
geographical identity 24–33
geographical linguistics 418
geographical reasons for language change 335
Germanic peoples 60
Germany *see* East Germany, West Germany
gesture 6, 40, 222, 233, 244, 272–3, 293, 376, **406–7**
  oral 291
Ghana 318, 340, 359, 361
ghoti 216
Gibraltar 361
Gilbert Is. 321
given/new information 107
global aphasia 273
glossai 110–11
glossematics 412
glossaries 56, **110–11**, 345
glosses 305
glossogenetics 292
glossographia 11
glossolalia **11**, 42, 389
glossopharyngeal nerve 131
glottalic sounds 126–7, 167
glottal sounds **128**, 154, **157**, 159, 167, 299
glottis 126–9, 154
glottochronology 333, 339
glottograph 141
gobbledegook 382–3
God is for Real, Man 51
God, names of 9
Golden Bull Awards 382
gradability 105
gradience 92
graffiti 55, 63, 189
Grammaire générale et raisonnée 84
grammar 2, 19, 82, **88–99**, 104, 111, 120, 147, 165, 172, 176, 185, 196, 207, 214, 264, 352, 366, 375, 377, 384, 400, 408–9, 412–13, 415
  acquisition of 234–5, **244–5**, 265
  categories of 93, 299
  changes in **332**, 335, 409
  handicaps in 267, 269, 272–3, 281
  hierarchy in **95**, 207, 352, 413

patterns in 6, 10, 24, 32–3, 35, 38, 40–3, 51, 55–8, 62–3, 69, 71, 73, 77, **95–7**, 181, 234, 247, 254, 295, 299, 377, 394
types of: case 413; core 85; dependency 412; functional 413; general 84, 355, 410; generalized phrase structure 413; generative 13, 84, **97**, 162, 164, 236, **413**, 414; Montague 413; network 413; pedagogical 88–9; realistic 413; reference 88; relational 413; speculative 410; stratificational 83, 412; traditional 3, 52, 70, 88–9, 91, 94, 97, 180, 409–10; transformational 97, 413
universal 84, 410
within the *trivium* 410
see also prescriptivism, rules
grammars 2–4, 109, 298, 409–10
grammar translation method 378
grammaticality 46, 88
grammatical meaning 107, 173
grammatical words 166, 245, 274–5
graphemes **196–207**, 212–18, 274, 367
graphetic handicap 267, 275
graphetics **187**, 196
graphical user interface 195
graphic expression 11, 13, 181, **184–95**, 206
graphic language 184
graphic symbolism 186
graphic translatability 195
graphological handicap 267
graphology (handwriting) 66, **191**
graphology (linguistic) 111, 119, 187, **196–209**, 267, 275, 384, 390, 400
Grassman's law 331
Gray's Anatomy 387
Great Illustrated Dictionary 111
Great Vowel Shift 216
Greece 9, 23, 43, 61, 68, 75, 88, 110, 208, 223, 302, 359, **408**, 410
Greenland 9, 60, 322, 359
greetings 40, 49, 52, 60, 120, 241
cards 180
Grenada 340, 361
grid games 64
Grimm's law 299, 330
Guadeloupe 340, 359
Guam 321, 361

Guardian, The 12, 181
Guatemala 359
Guiana 338, 340
Guinea 359
Guinea-Bissau 359
Gulliver's Travels 65
guó-yǔ 315
GUS 417
guslars 53
Guyana 340, 359, 361
gwoyeu romatzyh 315
gyri 260

h, dropping of 32
habituation experiments 240
hair cells 143
Haiti 43, 340, 359
HAL 417
half-uncial writing 188, 305
hammer 143
Handbook for Chemical Society Authors 385
Handbook of American Indian Languages 411
handedness 260, 277
hand-eye coordination 214
handicap 19, 173, 235, 259, 265, **266–83**, 418
classification of 266–7, 278–9
mental 22, 226, 238, 249, 266, **281–2**
physical 150, 266, 281–83
prevalence vs incidence 266
treatment of *see* speech therapy
hand-shaking 405
handwriting 66, 184, **187–8**, 190–1, 194, 212, 214, 252, 255
hapax legomena 67
haplology 330
hard palate *see* palate
hare lip 279
harmonics 133
harmony 91, **163**, 242
Haskins Laboratories 146
Hawaii 319, 340
he (sexist use) 47
head (grammatical) 95
headings 192
headlines 206, 336, **392**
head nods 118
headwords 108
hearing 142–5, 279
loss of *see* deafness
theories of 144
types of 142, 268, 270
hearing aids 270
hearsay 391
Hebrew Academy 4
Heineken advertisement 394
hemisphere *see* cerebral hemispheres
hemispherectomy 261
heraldry, language of 56

hertz 133–4
Heschl's gyri 263
hesitation 23, 52, 75, **174**, 182, 280
heuresis 70
hieroglyphic **201**, 302, 318, 328
high variety *see* diglossia
Hinduism 388
hiragana 197, 380
Hittites 200–1
hole, words for 15
holophrase 244
Homaranismo 356
Homeric epics 53
homographs 106
homo loquens 402
homonyms 106
homophones 58, **106**, 212, 274
homunculi 263
Honduras 359
Honest to God 51
Hong Kong 312, 341, 361
honorifics 21, 44, **99**, 120
hospital slang 53
humanistic language teaching 379
humanistic writing 188
humility, expression of 406
humour, and language 53, **62–3**, 72, 89, 186, 384
Hungarian Academy 4
Hungary 306, 359
Hung Society 407
hwyl 389
hypercreolization 338
hyperlexia 277
hyphenation 91, 183, 196, **207**, 254
hypnosis 379
hypocrisis 70
hypoglossal nerve 131
hyponymy 105

I (vs *me*) 3, 5
iamb 74
Iceland 359
iconicity 222
ideational function 10, 12–13, 180
identifying function 55
identity *see* language
ideographic writing 200–2, 354
ideology (of signs) 354
idioglossia 249
idiolect 24
idioms 62, **104–5**, 108, 111, 346, 352–3, 357–8
semi- 107
illative 92
illiteracy 211
illocutionary act 121
illustrations 192
imitation
by children 234, **236**, 238, 376, 378
by chimps 402
elicited 234

immediate constituents 96
immersion *see* language
immigrants 18, **34–7**, 266, 335, 351, 368, 372, 377, 386
imperative 121, 402
imperfective 93
impersonal language 384
impersonators 20
implicational universals 85, 167
implicatures 117
implosives **126–7**, 154, 159, 167–8
inanimateness 93
incompatibility 105
incongruity 62
incorporating languages 295
incus 143
indention 207
indexical function 173
indexing 56, 348, 416
semantic 397
indicative *see* mood
India 33–5, 38, 42, 58, 187, 204, 288–9, 303, **310-11**, 313, 329, 341, 359–61, 367, 409
individual differences in language use **233**, 238, 274, 282
indivisibility of words 91
Indonesia 310–12, 319–20, 341, 359
Indus Valley 200–1, 329
inessive 92
infant speech perception 147, 230
infixes 90
inflecting languages 90, **295**
inflectional morphology 90
inflections 5, 85, **90–1**, 95, 111, 224, 244–5, 295, 299, 332, 355–6
omission of 281, 338–9
informal language 3, 32, 43, **52–3**, 59, 62, 77, 94
informant 27–8, 30, 32, 403, **414**
information
function 54
retrieval 418
structure 120, 173, 412
technology 282
theory 267, 352
-ing ending 244
ingressive sounds **125–7**, 157, 161
inhalation 124–5
initials 59, 112
innateness 84, **236**, 410
inscriptions **189**, 198, 205, 302–4, 311, 320, 328–9
institutional style 67
Institutiones grammaticae 409
Institutio oratoria 70
instructional materials 54
instructive case 92

instrumental analysis *see* phonetics
instrumental case 299
insular writing 188
insults 60, 248
integrated pluralism 369
intelligence **22**, 233, 238, 255, 275–7, 281–2, 292–3
verbal vs non-verbal 22
intelligent programs 416
intelligibility 3, 5, 8, 11, 72, **382-13**
mutual 25, 286, 314
intelligibility gap 385
intensifiers 21
intensity (acoustic) **134**, 136, 146
interaction 50, **120–1**, 181, 195, 241, 248–50, 381, 406, 418
in machine translation 353
interchangeability 401
intercostals 124
diaphragmatic method 125
interference 376
interjections 10, 21, **91**, 291
interlanguage 376
interlevels 83
interlinear transcription 172
interlingual distance 375
International Auxiliary Language Association 355
International Computer Archive of Modern English 415
International Organization for Standardization 184
International Phonetic Alphabet 30, 160–1
International Translations Centre 347
Internet 195, 360, 370
interpreting 184, 344, 346, **351**, 414
consecutive vs simultaneous 351
deaf 269
interruptions 21, 391
intimate language 42, 45, 53, 68, 120
intonation 21, 41, 53, 56–7, 74, 83, 94, 133, 141, 149–50, **171–5**, 237, 241, 244–5, 264, 412
abnormal 270, 280
acquisition of 243
functions of 173, 181
stylized 175
intraoral devices 140
intrinsic muscles of tongue 131
introversion 23
intuition 106, **414–15**
inventio 70
inversions 215, 245, 265

inverted commas   207, 385
Ionia   61
Iran   303, 309, 329, 359
Iraq   318, 328, 359
Irian Jaya   1
Irish Republic   62, 188,
    223, **304–5**, 340, 359,
    361, 370
irregularity *see* regularity
Islam   318, 388
iso-   29
isochrony   171
isoglosses   28–9
isolate, language   169, 297,
    322, 324, **328–9**
isolating language   91,
    295–6
Israel   34, 318, 359, 368
i.t.a.   217, 219, 253
Italian-Americans/Australians
    34
italics   **182–3**, 188, 195,
    206
Italy   187, 302–4, 328, 359,
    368, 406
Ivory Coast   340, 359

Jabberwocky   177
Jainism   303
Jamaica   340, 359, 361
Japan   18, 56, 61, 103, 190,
    308, 329, 341, 347,
    359, 406
jargon   2, 56, 383
    aphasic   273
Java   320
jaw   130, 154, 158
Jewish background   8, 35, 59
Joint Interpreting and
    Conference Service   344
jokes   42, **62**, 66, 117–18,
    121, 248
Jordan   62, 359
Joseph Andrews   77
journalese   392
journalism   72, 186, 392
Judaism   8, 318, 388
Jugoslavia *see* Yugoslavia
juncture   166
Junggrammatiker   331
jury judgments   23
justified setting   185, 194,
    216, 254

kabary   41
Kabbala   59KAL   250
Kampuchea *see* Cambodia
kana   197, 203, 378
kanji   197, 202, 213, 282,
    308, 348
Kan-U-Go   64
katakana   197, 203, 380
Kay Elemetrics Corporation
    135
Kells, Book of   188
Kenya   318, 341, 359, 361
kinegraphs   406
kinesics   403, 406–7
kinship relations   40, 44,
    102, 106

Kiribati   361
knock-knock jokes   62
knowledge about language
    250
knowledge-based machine
    translation   353
Knowledge of Language   413
knowledge-testing
    (translation)   348
koine   303, 408
Koran *see* Qur'an
Korea (N and S)   190, 194,
    308, 341, 359
Kurgans   298
Kurzweil Reading Machine
    282
Kuthadaw book   313
Kuwait   359

l, clear vs dark   163
    dropping of   32
labialization   158
labials   209, 238–9, 299
labio-dental sounds   157, 161
labio-velar sounds   159,
    167, 299
Lady Chatterley's Lover   8, 61
la-la theory   291
laminagraphy   140
Lancaster-Oslo/Bergen   87,
    415
landscape printing   193
langage   411
language
    attitudes towards   **1–5**,
        36, 369
    awareness of   251, **256–7**,
        345, 375
    beliefs about   2–9
    changes in   2, **4–5**, 21,
        32, 45–7, 53, 84, 204,
        216, 222, 264, 294–7,
        330–6, 338, 366, 389,
        408–9, 418
    codification of   366
    crooked   41
    definition of   400
    edges of   72, 89
    functions of   **10–15**, 61,
        336, 338, 357, 386,
        400, 409
    genetics and   18, 33
    hidden   58–9
    identity and   13, **17–79**,
        334, 357, 359, 364–9,
        403, 414
    input   237, 377
    in the world   343–79
    models of   82, 184, 264
    origins of   7, 8, 84, 101,
        180, 222, 230, **290–3**,
        388, 408, 418
    power   8–9, 45, **397**
    speech vs   267
    structure of   **81–121**,
        251, 375, 378,
        399–400, 412
    systems in   411–12
    thought and   13, **14–15**,
        355, 357

use of   3, **16–79**, 251,
    296, 334, 336, 338,
    377–8, **382–97**
see also communication;
    dialect; handicap;
    literary language;
    speech; standard
    language; written
    language
Language (Bloomfield)   101,
    412
Language (Sapir)   411
language acquisition device
    236, 377
*Language Awareness and
    Reading Readiness*   254
language barrier   5, 34–5,
    344–5, 354, 358–9,
    372, 374, 382
language contact   309, 336,
    338–9, 362
language death   286, 362
language delay   249, 265–6,
    268, 277, 279, **301**
language experience
    programmes   253
Language for Life   250
Language from Within   379
language illiteracy   344
language immersion   **369**,
    375, 379
language laboratories   381
language learning   7, 18, 21,
    58, 181, 217, **250–7**,
    268, 282, 293, 357,
    368–81, 418
    theories of   376–7
language loyalty   43, 368–9
language maintenance   362,
    368–9
language mixing   364–5
language pathology   266,
    415
language play   59, 64–5
language policy
    implementation   366
language reform   314–15,
    397
language riots   1, 37, 43
languages
    adaptation vs adoption of
        360
    classification of   295
    critical   344
    distance between   375
    dominant/dormant   364
    equality of   6–7, 35
    first vs second   372
    modernization of   366
    modified natural   358
    names of   25, **287**, 306,
        319
    numbers of   15, 84–5,
        286–7
    official   288, 344,
        359–62
    primitive   **6–7**, 24, 327
    second   15, 360–1, **372**
    source vs target   346–9
    speakers of   288–9, 361

universal   104, 208,
    354–8, 384, 410
    world   359–61, 410
see also
    agglutinating/agglutina-
        tive; analytic; artificial;
        auxiliary; avoidance;
        click; family of; foreign;
        fusional; incorporating;
        inflecting; isolated;
        minority; oriental;
        pitch-accent;
        polysynthetic; tone;
        Appendix VI
language selection   366, 373
language shift   51, 362, 369
language switching   364–5
language teaching   3, 7, 26,
    36–7, 50, 82, 88–9,
    163, 174, 207, **250–7**,
    345, 360, **368–81**, 397,
    409, 418
    materials in   375, 376,
        380
    methods in   375, 376,
        378–9
language trains   368
langue   79, **411**, 413
langue d'oïl/langue d'oc   29
Langue Musicale Universelle
    355
Laos   311–13, 359
Lapland   37
Larousse dictionaries
    110–11
LARSP   235
laryngealization   159
laryngeal mirror   129, 141
laryngeal theory   299
laryngectomy   127, 266,
    278
laryngograph *see*
    electrolaryngography
laryngopharynx   130
laryngoscope, fibre-optic
    129, 141
larynx   19, 124, **128–9**,
    141, 155, 278, 292–3
    artificial   278
La Tène   303
lateralization   260–1, 265,
    277
laterals   74, **159**, 161
Latinate expressions   390
laughter   183, 238
law and the legal profession
    cases in   20, 35, 46, 66,
        115
    language of   8, 20, 61,
        181, 383, **390–1**
    mannerisms of   390
    procedures in   189,
        208–9, 391
layout   76, 191
leading (print)   192
learning disability   275
leavetaking   49, 52, 60, 120
Leave Your Language Alone
    180
Lebanon   359

lect   24
legasthenia   275
legibility   214, 392
leisure   373
*Leksys...synonima
    slovenorosskaia*   111
leptosomic type   18
Lern yerself Scouse   27
lesions   261
Lesotho   359, 361
Let Stalk Strine   27
letters (of alphabet)   57,
    182–3, 188, 191–2,
    194–6, **204–6**, 254–5,
    283, 356, 367
    frequency of   86, 194
    games with   59, **64–5**, 62
    mystical   59
    perception of   210–12
    repetition of   183
levels (linguistic)   **82–3**, 85,
    120, 234, 364, 412
levels (social)   40, 52
lexemes   28–30, **104–7**
    see also vocabulary
lexical diffusion   334
lexical fields *see* semantic
    fields
lexical gap   107
lexical items *see* lexemes
lexicalized sentence stems
    107
lexicography   4, **108–11**,
    410, 418
    see also dictionaries
lexicon *see* vocabulary
Lexicon   64
lexicostatistics   333
lexis   70
liaison   166
Liberia   340, 359, 361
Libya   359
Lightwriter   283
line   185, 191–2, **254**
    poetic   67, 74
linear branching   186
linearity   185, 215
lingua franca   34, 42, 309,
    316, 318–19, 324, 336,
    340–1, **359–61**, 366,
    373
lingualabials   161
linguist   418
Linguistic Atlas of England
    30
*Linguistic Atlas of the United
    States*   31
Linguistic Circle of Prague
    412
linguistician   418
linguistics
    applied   89, 372, **418**
    areal   33
    biological   418
    diachronic   106, 294–5,
        411, 418
    educational   250, 418
    forensic   66, 69
    general   418
    history of   70, 408–10

mathematical 418
methodology in 32, 94, 221, 230–1, 240, **414–15**
philosophical 418
schools of 412–13
statistical 67, **86–7**, 113, 418
structural 79, **96**, 104, 412
synchronic 106, **411**, 418
theoretical 296, 352, **411–13**, 418
18th-century 2–3, 5, 7, 15, 34, 410
19th-century 5–7, 34, **294–7**, 410
20th-century 2–3, 6–7, 66, 71, 78–9, 84, 88, 98, 100, 102, 111, 116, 120, 149, 164, 187, 273, 292, 338, 352, 399, 408, **411–18**
Linguistic Society of Paris 290
Linguistics of Visual English 226
linguistic stylistics *see* stylistics
linkage *see* connectivity
linotype 194
lipograms 65
lip reading 227
lips 130, 154, 156–8
rounding vs spreading 33, 130, **154–8**, 162–3, 169, 171, 237
liquid consonants 168
listening 118, **145–8**, 250, 263, 345, 365, 375, 378
active vs passive 148
handicaps in 266, 272
selective 147
lists, language of 185
litany 11
literacy **250**, 252, 366, 377, 388, 390
literary criticism 66, 78–9
literary language 2, 10, 34, 61, **70–9**, 109, 119, 180, 182–3, 286, 346–50, 366, 378
vs non-literary 71–2
liturgy 42, 50, 302, **389**
loan translation 332
loan words *see* borrowing
localization (brain) 262–3
localization (sound) 142
locative 299, 402
locutionary act 121
logic 70, 100, 107, 413
language and **3**, 7, 84, 384
logocentrism 79
logogen 213
logographic writing 65, 183, 197, **202**, 206, 213, 282, 350, 384
logopaedist 266
Logos Corporation 353

loi Bas-Lauriol 4
loi Toubon 4
London-Lund corpus 86–7, **415**
longitudinal study 231, 377
Longman dictionaries 108, 111
look-and-say 152, 219, **253**
Lore and Language of Schoolchildren, The 11
loss of sound 330
loudness 18–19, 23, 118, 128, 134, 163, **171**, 278
perception of 144
low variety *see* diglossia
ludic function *see* language play
lungs 124, **126–7**, 154, 157–8, 161
Luxembourg 36–7, 359
Lyrical Ballads 73
lyrics 11

Macau 341
machine translation *see* translation, machine
Macintosh 195
macro-phylum 294
macrostructures 119
Madagascar 319–20, 341, 359
magic, and language **8–9**, 58–9, 65
Magna Carta 189
magnetic resonance imaging 123, 140
Mahabarata 321
Maître Phonétique, Le 160
majuscule 188
makaris 60
Make-a-story charts 256
Malawi 359, 361
Malaysia 310–12, 320, 341, 359, 361
Maldives 359
Mali 359
malleus 143
Malta 37, 318, 359, 361
Manual English 226
manualism 269
Manual of graphology 191
margins (page) 185, 192
Marisat 57
marking (essay) 257
marking (linguistic) 85, 98
marriage request 41
Marshall Islands 361
Martha's Vineyard 334
Martinique 340, 359
masculine form *see* gender
masking 280
mass communication/media 50, 70, 366, **397**
matched guise 23
mathematical linguistics 418
mathematics 3, 13, 384–5
matrices 164, 185
matronymics 44
Mauritania 359

Mauritius 341, 359, 361
maxims *see* conversation
Mayan culture 201
meaning 67, 79, 82, 88, **100–3**, 116, 211, 243, 408, 412
abstract vs concrete 274
theories of 101
see also semantics
Meaning of Meaning, The 100
mean length of utterance (MLU) 235
Measurement of Meaning, The 103
media *see* mass communication/media
median longitudinal fissure 260
medicine 349, 383, **386–7**
language and 41, 50, 366, **386–7**
medium of transmission 83
medulla oblongata 260
Melanesia 18, 319–21
melodic utterance 239
memoria 70
memory, and language 15, 22, 238, 266, 275, 277, 281, 375
meningitis 238
mental handicap *see* handicap
mental processing 14–15, 22–3, 79
mental prodigies 13
mentalism 84, 162, 378, **413**
merger 330
Meso-America 60, 198, 287
Mesopotamia 198–9
message form 48
metabolic rate 261
metalanguage 250, 253, **254**
metaphor 2, 41, 51, **70**
metathesis 330
metonymy 70
metre (poetry) **74–5**, 78, 171, 331, 412
metronymics 44
Mexico 199, 287, **322–4**, 329, 359
mezzo-soprano 19
mhm 118
Micronesia 319–21, 361
Microsoft Corporation 195
mid-brain 260
middle ages 70, 410
Middle East 60, 189, 198, 302, 318, 340
minimal brain dysfunction 275
minimal free forms 91
minimal pairs 162
minim confusion 189
Minoan culture 199
minority languages 36–7, 51, 266, 288, 302, 335, 359, **362–9**, 370–1

minor sentence 94
minuscule 188
Minute on Education (1835) 7
mismatch (lexical) 246
missionary work 110–11, 316, 324, 410
misunderstandings 118
mneme 70
models (structural) 385
modem 195
Modern English Grammar 88
modernization 366
modes of address 44
modistae 410
modulations (in sign) 225
monastic signing 407
Mongolian People's Republic 309, 359
monitoring (by brain) 261
monitoring (of broadcasts) 346
monitor model 376
monogenesis 293, 339
monolingualism 362, 372
monophthongs 156
monosyllables 86
Montague grammar 413
Montreal accent 32
Montserrat 361
mood (verbs) 92, **93**, 299, 356
moon, place names on 114
Mornings 49
Morocco 318, 359
morphemes **90**, 95, 150, 176, 202, 211, 235, 346, 377, 412
free vs bound 90
index of 296
morphographic characters 202
morphology 28, 30, 62, 82, **90–1**, 95, 98–9, 104, 162, 196, 225, 244, 295–6, 352, 357, 377, 409, 412
disorder of 281
inflectional vs derivational 90
Morse Code 86, 405, 416
'mother' (words for) 177
motherese 51, 237, 375
mother-in-law languages 42
mother tongues 357, **372**
claiming of 36
motivation (for language) 359, 375
motor functions 131, 255, **263–4**, 273, 277, 279–80, 282
motor theory
of speech perception 148
of syllable production 166
mouse 195
mouthing 161
movement (on screen) 195
Mozambique 341, 359

Muhlenberg legend 367
multi-ethnic society 5, 34–7
multilingualism 42, 50, 73, 288–9, **362–5**, 368, 370
multimedia 195
murmured sound 159
muscle movement in speech 139
music 14, 71, 133, **175**, 261, 354–5, 403
myoelastic-aerodynamic theory 129
myth 8–9, 11, 79, 116
mythemes 79

names **112–15**, 348, 358
types of: apotropaic 112; brand 115, 348, 394; by- 112; car 350; city 9, 114; country 9, 114; dance- 44; days 196; family 112; first 113; foreign 350; geographical 114; given 112–13; holy 189; language 196; longest 115; male vs female 113; months 196; moon 114; ox- 44; people 44; personal **112–13**, 348, 350; place 9, **114–15**, 295, 304, 328; proper 9, 68, 109, **112**, 150, 196, 216, 218, 227, 402; public 9; secret 9; theophoric 112
Namibia 317, 341, 361
narrative style 19, 77–**9**, 119, 391
narrowing (phonetic) 159
narrowing (semantic) 332
nasal cavity **130**, 171, 278–9
nasalization 130, 154–5
nasals 85, 130, 154, 157–8, **159**, 161, 167–9, 238, 270, 292, 299
nasopharynx 130
National Council of Teachers of English 383
national identity **34–7**, 286, 357, 364–9
nationalism 7, **34**, 37, 43, 305, 362
National Translations Center 347
NATO alphabet 57
natural disasters 362
naturalism 101, 408
natural language learning 372
natural language processing 353, 416–19
natural method of language learning 378
natural-order hypothesis 377
Natural Approach 379
nature vs nurture 22

Nauru 361
Nazis 9
Neanderthal man 292–3
negation **99**, 245, 356, 402
    double 3, 35, 236, 245
Negroes 18
Neogrammarians 331
neologism 73, 366, 384
Nepal 359, 361
nerves, cranial 131
Netherlands 37, 359
network grammar 413
neural pacemaker 280
neurochronaxiac theory 129
neuroimaging 261–2
neurolinguistics 262–5, 418
neurology 260–5, 273, 292
neuropsychology 260–5, 274
neuter form *see* gender
New Caledonia 341
New Criticism 78
New English Dictionary 109
New Guinea 85, 106, 319–21, 370
New National First Reader 252
newspapers 13, 43, 54, 67, 86, 206, 208, 309, 366, **392–3**
New Spelling 217–18
news reading 50, 173
New Zealand 319, 321, 341, 359, 361
naming customs 9
-*ng*, use of 32
Nicaragua 324, 340, 359
Nicobar Is. 311
Niger 359
Nigeria 200, 288, 316, 341, 359, 361
Noblesse Oblige 38–9
nodes/nodules 278
noise **137–8**, 148, 151, 270, 280
    ambient 134
    loud 268, 407
nominative 92–3, 299, 356
non-fluency 50, 52, 245, 267, 273, 277, **280**, 396, 413
    normal 280
nongradable terms 105
non-linear phonology 164
non-linear viewing 186
nonsense verse 177, **251**
nonsense words 52, 59, 213, 274, 277
Non-SLIP 282
non-standard language *see* standard language
non-U, and U language 39
non-verbal communication 183, 233, 261, 385, **399–407**, 414
non-verbal intelligence 22
Norfolk Is. 341
norms (linguistic) 48, 52, 62, 67, **71–2**, 109, 366, 415

Northern Mariana Islands 361
Norway 306, 359
Norwich accent 32
nose 124
notional definitions 91
notional syllabus 378
noun 43, 68, 85, **91–3**, 196, 244, 299, 356, 402, 408
    common vs proper 112
    tense of 92
noun phrase 95–7, 385
novel 39, 71, 73, 75–6, 77–**8**
Nuba 404
Nuer 44
Nue Spelling 217
number 90, 92, **93**, 236, 244, 299, 356
    systems 99
numerals 15, 55, 57–8, **99**, 196, 218, 354, 356
numismatics 189
Nu Vois 278

object (grammatical) **95**, 98, 360
object-initial languages 98
objections (legal) 391
objective *see* accusative
object permanence 237
obscenity 8, 10, **61**, 181
observer effects 233, 414
observer's paradox 414
obsolescence 332
obviative 92
occipital lobe 260, 263
occupation 40, 42, **52–3**, 173, 334, 384–96
octave shift 19
Odin 388
oesophageal voice 127, 278
Oman 359
omissions 215, 265, 279
one 46
One-upmanship 45
onomastics 112
onomatopoeia 74, 101, **176–7**, 291
ontogenesis 230
opinion (legal) 391
opposites *see* antonymy
Optacon 282
optative *see* mood
optical character-recognition 282
optional features of language 67, 97
ORAC 283
Oracle 195
oracle bone 314
oracy 58, 250, 366
oral cavity **130–1**, 171
    sounds in 130, 154–9, 292
oralism vs manualism 269
oral literature 319
oral method of language teaching 378

oratory 11, 41, 43, 48–9, 66, 325
orbicularis oris 130
organ of Corti 143
oriental languages 171
Originum sive etymologiarum 101
oropharynx 130
orthoepists 331
Orthographie 331
orthography *see* writing, system of
orthophonist 266
oscillation 132
oscilloscope 135, 138
ossicles 143
otitis media 268
oval window 143
overextension 246–7
overheard speech 50
overtones *see* harmonics
Oxford English Dictionary 109, 332, 384
oxymoron 70

paedography 196
PageMaker 195
Paget-Gorman Sign System 226
Pakistan 329, 359, 361
palaeography 189
palaeontology 292
palantype 271
palatal consonants *see* consonants
palatalization 158
palate 18–19, 124, **130**, 140, 154–5, 157–9
palato-alveolar consonants 157
palatography 140
Palau 361
Pali Canon 388
palindrome 64–5
Paliyan culture 11
Panama 359
panda (talking) 232
Pandas 58
pangram 65
Pan South African Language Board 316
Pantagruel 61
pantomime 407
Papua New Guinea 5, 321, 341, 359, 361
paradigmatic relations 105, **411**
paradox 70
paragraphs 119, 181, **207**, 383
Paraguay 42, 324, 359, 362
paralanguage **171**, 173, 175, 403
parallelism 53, 60, 63
paraphrase 237, 375
pararhyme 74
parentese 237
parentheses 207
parietal lobe 260, 263, 275

parole 411, 413
parsing **89**, 251, 352
participants 48, **50**
participles 91
particles 21, **95**, 101, 338
partitive 92–3
parts of speech *see* word class
passive voice *see* articulators; voice (grammar)
patents 345
patronymics **44**, 112
Pattern Playback 146
pattern recognition 20
pause 51–3, 74–5, 91, 161, **174**, 181, 214, 224, 241, 273
PCs 195
pejoration 332
Penguin English Dictionary 108
perception 15, 247
    see also auditory perception; speech; visual perception
perceptual span 210–11
perfective 93, 176
performance (vs competence) 52, **413**
performance testing in translation 348
performative language 12, 121
perilymph 143
period (punctuation) 207
periodicity 133
periphery (of eye) 210
perlocutionary act 121, 214
perseveration 265
person (grammar) 78, 92, **93**, 106, 224, 299
personal computers 195
personal identity **20**, 51, **66**, 77, 173, 396
personality **23**, 182, 191, 233, 238, 255, 266, 375, 406, 414
personification 70
Peru 324, 359
petroglyphs 198
Phaistos disc 185
pharyngeal consonants 157, 167
pharyngealization 130, **158**, 171
pharynx **124**, 130, 155, 278
phatic communion 10, 180
Philippines 41, 320, 341, 359, 361
philological circle 78
philologist, vs linguist 295
philology, comparative 84, 111, 180, **294–7**, 299, 330, 408–11, 415
philosophical linguistics 418
philosophy 100, 102, 107, 116, 120, 408, 410, 418
phonation 128–9, 278
phone 196, 243
    tree 243

phonemes **162–3**, 167, 172, 175, 196, 204, 212, 215–16, 227, 274, 283, 367, 412
    perception of 145, 148
phonetic alphabet 160–1
phonetic boundaries 91, 145, 166
Phonetic Lexicon 163
phonetics 18, 74, 82, **154-61**, 162, 187, 408–10, 412
    acoustic **132–41**, 154, 164, 172
    articulatory **124–31**, 154–61, 164, 292
    auditory **142–8**, 172, 375
    experimental/instrumental 129, **138–41**, 270, 415
    historical 295, 299
    laboratory 138
    linguistics vs 418
    parametric 158
    physiological 139
phonetic similarity 163
Phonetic Teachers' Association 160
phonetic transcription 27, 57, 111, 116, 137, 155, **160–1**, 162, 172, 233, 314–15, 367, 378, 415; *see also* Appendix II
phonetic variants 90, 162–3
phoniatrist 266
phonic approaches to reading 219, **253**
phonic decoding 150, 274
phonic mediation 212–13
phonograms 201
phonological reading 212–13
phonological systems 155, **165–70**, 173, 292, 295, 335, 355
phonological theory 162, 410
phonological universals 85, **162**, 167
phonological writing 199, 202–5
    see also sound change
phonology 24, 28–30, 33, 35, 38, 43, 58, 60, 62–3, 71, 74, 82, 85, 88, 104, 120, 154, **162–70**, 187, 196, 212–13, 215, 223, 264, 291, 296, 375, 400, 412, 415
    abstract vs concrete 162, 165
    acquisition of 234, **242–3**, 265, 279
    comparative 167–70, 177
    errors in 273, 277, 377
    handicaps in **267**, 279, 281

historical 299
  phonetics vs **162**, 166, 172, 267, 279
  rules in 150, **165**, 282
  schools of 163–5
  suprasegmental 41, 82, 163, **171–5**, 207, 273, 403, 415
phonostylistics 74
Phonotypy 217
photocomposition 192, 194
photography (of vocal tract) 140
phrase **95**, 163, 283
phrase book 353
phrase marker 96–7
phrase structure 96–7, 413
phylacteries 8
phylogenesis 230
phylum 294
physical handicap 258, 283
physical identity 18–21
physiological phonetics *see* phonetics
Pictogram System, The 186
pictographic writing **199–201**, 329, 403
pidginization 336
pidgins 7, 223, 316, 319–21, 326, **336–41**, 362, 377–8
  expanded 336
Pig Latin 59
pīnyīn 197, 315, 367
Pitcairn Is. 340
pitch 18, 51, 118, 128, 133, 141, 163, **171**, 237–8, 278
  perception of 144
pitch-accent languages 174
place theory of pitch perception 144
plain language 2, 366, **382–3**
Plains Indians 42
planning 5, 34–7, 314–15, **366–9**, 390, 418
  corpus vs status 366
  educational policies in 368–9
plaster casts of vocal tract 140
plastographic techniques 140
play (linguistic) 41, 59, 62, 249
play (theatrical) *see* drama
playing the dozens 60
plethysmograph 125
plosives 29, 137, **159**, 161, 167–8, 279, 299
plot 71, 77, 119
pluralism 368–9
plurality *see* number
pneumotachograph 125, 139
poetic writing style 256
poetry 10, 11, 41, 43, 53, 60, 63, 70, **71–5**, 79, 163, 176, 186, 206–7, 251, 331

point size 192
Poland 302, 359
politeness 21, **41**, 45, 50, 52, 99, 107, 117, 120, 248, 417
politeness duels 60
politics, and language 11, 25, 34, 36–7, 42–3, 310, 362, **366–9**
Politics and the English Language 2
polyalphabetic ciphers 58
polygenesis 293, 339
Polynesia 7, 9, 61, 167, 319–21
polyp 278
polyphony 175
polysemy 106
polysyllables 87, 181, 384
polysynthetic languages 91, **295**
polysystemicism 412
pomposity 390
pons 260
pooh-pooh theory 291
Pope, the 355
Port-Royal grammar 84, 410, 413
Portugal 359
positron emission tomography 262
possessives 402
postalveolar consonants 157
post-creole continuum 338
poster pillars 394
postmodification 89, 95
PostScript 192, 195
post-structuralism 79
Poto and Cabenga 249
pragmatics 52, 83, 107, **120–1**, 412–13
  acquisition of 234, **248–9**, 265
  handicap in 281
pragmatic translation 347
Prague School 412
Prakrits 303
prayers 12, 41, 50, 389
preaching 389
predicate 89, 94
Preface (Johnson's) 4
prefixation 57, **90**, 99, 112, 165, 356
prelanguage 230
premodification 95
prepositions **91–3**, 235, 244, 247, 356
prescriptivism **2–5**, 38–9, 84, 88, 97, 180, 184, 315, 366, 409–10
Prestel 195
prestige, in language use 335, 338, 396
presupposition 417
primates 230, **292**, 402
print 11, 192–4
printing 111, 187, 192, **194–5**, 216, 332, 367, 389–90, 409–10
press 184, 194

Prisoner, The 76
prison slang 53
production *see* speech
productivity 401
profanity 61
proficiency tests 381
profiles (linguistic) 235
prognostic tests 381
Promptuarium parvulorum 111
pronounceability 115
pronouns 21, 85, **91–3**, 99, 106, 224, 356, 402
  sex-neutral 46–7
  T vs V 45, 120
pronunciation 2, 39, **122–78**, 180, 242–3, 377–8
  in dialects 26, 32, 77
  see also phonetics; phonology
propaganda 397
proper names *see* names
Proposal...(Swift's) 4
Proposed British Alphabet 217
propositions 10, 100, 107
proprioceptive feedback 264
proscription 2
prose 75
Prose Edda 410
prosodic features *see* prosody
prosody 10, 22–3, 41–2, 50, 52–3, 74, **171–5**, 181, 243–4, 291, 396
  sentence 107, 173
prosthetic devices 279
prothesis 330
proto-language 294
proverbs 40, 43, **53**, 60, 111, 315
proxemics 403, 405
pseudolinguistic behaviour 11, 42
psychiatry 66, 105
psycholinguistics 15, 22, 120, 177, 277, **418**
psychological reality 165, 413
psychology **22–3**, 102–3, 116, 119, 149, 173, 187, 191, 210–13, 230–1, 254, 273, 376, 405, 418
psychoneurotic theory 280
psychopathology 23
psychotherapy 66, 397
puberty, and language 19
publishing 366
Pueblo 323
Puerto Rico 35, 359, 361
pulmonic *see* lungs
punch lines 62, 72
punctuation 94, 171, 182, 184, 192, 196, **207**, 218
  absence of 390–1
  rules for 214, 366
puns 41, 62, **63**, 64, 331, 346, 392
pure tones *see* tone (acoustic)
purism 1, **3–4**, 330

Puritan names 113
purr words 397
pūtōnghuà 315, 367
Pygmies 317
pyknic type 18

Qatar 359
Quakerism 389
quantitative expression 402
Quebec 360, 369
Queens' English, The 5
question marks 183, 196, 207
questionnaires 26–7, 30, 31, 55, 288, **414**
questions 21, 57, 85, **99**, 149, 224, 237, 241, 243, **245**, 250, 386, 391
  tag- 40, 57, 173, 360
quotation marks 207
quotations 68, 176
Qur'an 7, 43, 52, 190, 356, **388**, 410
QWERTY keyboard 194

r, use of 32, 334–5
race, and language 18, 35
radicals 202
radio language 366, 396
radio microphones 230, 233, 246
radio telescope signals 403
ragged-edge margin 185
Random House Dictionary of the English Language 108
ranks (grammar) 95
rapid fading of speech 400–1
rate (speech) 19, 23, 51–3, 60, 74, 118, **125**, 145–6, 166, 212, 237, 248–9, 280, 351, 377
rationalists 410
readability 254, 383
Reader's Digest 111
reading 79, **179–219**, **252–9**, 263, 288, 389
  by ear vs by eye 212–13
  letter-by-letter 274
  process of 210–13, 215, **252–3**, 263
  speed of 212–13, 282
  teaching of 46, 187, 217, 250, **252–4**, 378
  theories of 211–13
reading disability 211, 213, 254, 266, 272, **274–7**
reading readiness 254
readings (religious) 389
reading schemes 252–3
reading tests 276
real books 252
realistic grammar 413
rearrangement (in writing) 214
rebus 65, 201, 258, 282
RECAP 271
received pronunciation 32, **39**, 50, 51, 156, 166
receptive handicap 267
reconstruction **294**, 331, 415

recording techniques 140, 231, 246, 405, **414**
record-keeping function 12, 180
Recuyell of the Historyes of Troye 194
redundancy 146
reduplicated babbling 239
reduplication 90, 176–7, 224, 237, 243
Reed and Kellogg diagrams 96
reference (semantic) 102
reference books 54
referential function 10
reflexes 145, 403
reflexive noises 238
regional speech *see* accent (speech variety); dialect
register (variety) 52
register (voice) 19
regularity 6, 90, 92, 108, 226, 236, 244, 332, 335, 354, 357, **408**
Regularized English 218
reinforcement 236, 376
relational grammar 413
relativity, linguistic 15
relay language 344
relevance theory 117
relexification 339
relic areas 27
religious language 7–8, 11, 34, 40, 42–3, 50–4, 59, 61, 66, 71–2, 86, 113–14, 181, 302–3, 313, 316, 347, 362, 366, **388–9**, 407–9
Renaissance 70, 88, 409, **410**
repetition 8, 11, 53, 59, 67, 74, 119, 181, 237, 273, 280, 338, 377, 390–1
rephrasing 181
reported speech 77
representatives (speech act) 121
resonance 130, 278
resonance theory of pitch perception 144
respect language 40
respiration 19, **124–5**, 131
respiratory cycle 125
response 2, 99, 101, **118**, 248
restricted code 35, **40**
restricted language 54, **56–7**, 407
resuggestion 379
retina 210
retroflex consonants *see* consonants
Réunion 341, 359
reverberation time 134, 138
reversal (consonant) 265
reverse lexicon 414
reverse rhyme 74
revision 214, 257
rewriting 214
Rhenish fan 29

rhetoric 70, 75, 116, 410
Rhetorica 70
rhotic areas 28
rhoticization 155
rhyme 11, 53, 60, 63, 66, 74, 331, 394
rhyming slang 53
rhythm 21, 41, 53, 63, 74, 94, 149, 163, 166, **171**, 175, 238–9, 244, 248–9, 264, 280–1, 346, 390–1, 394, 404
riddles 41, 62, **63**
ritual 41, 49–50, 52, 54, 60, 116, 127, 239, **389**, 406
Rochester method 227
Rolando, fissure of 260–3
role (social) 21, **41**, 52, 120, 174, 256
rolled consonant 159
Romania 37, 359
romanization 315, 318, 367
Roman Lipi Parishad 367
Romansch League 37
Rome (Ancient) 9, 61, 68, 88, 110, 189, 191, 208, 223, 303, **409**
root languages 295
roots 41, **90**, 299, 356
Rosencrantz and Guildenstern are Dead 76
Rosetta Stone 201
rounding *see* lips
round window 143
routines (linguistic) 57, 116
Rowntree Mackintosh 345
Rudiments of English Grammar 2
rules **2–4**, 6, 57, 72, 85, 88, **97**, 120, 148, 150, 165, 180, 196, 204, 206, 214, 222, 236, 244, 251, 265, 282, 356, 365, 378, 408–9, 413
runes 8, 187, 205, 302, 309, 388
Russian criticism 78
Rwanda 359

saccades 210
sagas 303, 388
Sahitya Akadami 367
Saint Christopher and Nevis 361
Saint Helena 341
Saint Lucia 340, 361
Saint Vincent and the Grenadines 361
Sakalava naming customs 9
Samoa 321
samples, language 67–9, 85, 87, 230–1, 233, 235, 413, **414–15**
sandhi 176, 409
San Serriffe 13
Sao Tomé and Principe 340, 359
Sapir–Whorf hypothesis 15
Saudi Arabia 318, 359

scala tympani/vestibuli 143
Scandinavia 36–7, 205
scanning 253, 282
scheme (rhetoric) 70
schools *see* education
science 79, 344, 349, 359–60, 408
language of 2, 86, 109, 181, 184, 196, 202, 344–5, 346, 347, 358, 366, **384–5**
Science and Sanity 397
Scouse 27
Scrabble 64, 108, 163
Screening Test of Spanish Grammar 235
screenplays 396
Seaspeak 57
secrecy 53, **58–9**, 249
Seeing Essential English 226
Sefer ha-zohar 59
segmentation (grammatical) 96
segments (speech) 163, 167–9
semantic
change 104, **332**
components 107
content 147, 237, 346, 357
differential 103
features 107
fields **104–6**, 226, 246
roles **107**, 245, 413
space 103
structure 104–7, 264
semanticity 401
semantics 28, 82, 88, 91, **100–7**, 118, 120, 147, 151, 172, 185, 211, 352–3, 397, 400, 412, 415
acquisition of 234, **246–7**, 265
dyslexic errors in 274, 277
handicaps in **267**, 272, 274, 281
semi-circular canals 143
semi-colon 207
semi-consonants 155, **159**, 299
semilingualism 365
semiology 403
semiotics 292, **403–7**, 412
semiotic triangle 101
semi-vowels 137, 155, **159**
Senegal 340, 359
Senegambia 361
sense 102, **105–6**, 111, 119
sensori-motor intelligence 237
sensorineural deafness 268
sensory functions 131, **263**, 273
sentence frames 237
Sentence Maker 252
sentences 88, **94–7**, 163, 173, 181, 244–5, 383–4, 396
definition of 94
length of 67, 99, 234,

237, **244–5**, 254, 365, 383–4, 390, 396
meaning of 107
patterns in 21, 52, 57, 60, 78, **95–7**, 116, 244–5, 251, 412
sequencing 277
Sequenza III 175
sermons 42–3, 48, 53, 208, 388
setting 40, 42, 44, **48**, 119
sex and language 19, **21**, 23, 32, 38–9, 40, 42, 44, **46–7**, 61, 93, 118, 128–9, 175, 233, 366, 395
Sex Discrimination Act 47, 395
Seychelles 341, 359, 361
shading 191
shadowing 147–8
shadow-puppet plays 320
Shakespeare/Bacon question 69
Shavian 218
shibboleth 26
shift (semantic) 332
shorthand 189, **208–9**, 218, 282, 354, 410
Short Introduction to English Grammar 3
SHRDLU 416
sibilants 137, **159**, 168
Sierra Leone 340, 359, 361
sig 223
sign (linguistic) 411
signatures 191
Signed English 226
signifiant/signifié 411
'signifying' 60
Signing Exact English 226
sign language **221–7**, 263, 266–7, 269, 272, 291, 293, 402–3, 407
modulations in 225
teaching of 269
types of 226–7, 282
sign space 224
silence 38, 41, 75, 117, 161, **174**, 391
Silent Way, The 379
simile 2, **70**
Simpler Spelling Association 218
simplification 237, 339, 357, 377, 390
Simplified Spelling Board 217
Simplified Spelling Society 217–18
sine wave 132–3
Singapore 312, 341, 359, 361
singular *see* number
situational syllabus 378
skimming 253
skywriting 187
slang **53**, 56, 59, 108, 181, 364
Slang Today and Yesterday 53

slips of the tongue 166, 264–5
slogans 63, 67, 174, **394–5**
snarl words 397
sneezing 10
snow, words for 15
social change 5, 36, 50–2, **335**
social class *see* class
social function of language 10, 61, 409
social history 26, 29, 33, 338
social identity **38–47**, 51, 53, 61, 173, 233, 248, 250, 281, 334, 357, 362–9, 386
social psychology 23, 51
social situation 32, **48**, 184, 334, 364, 377, 414
Society Is. 321
sociobiology 292
socioeconomic status 32, 334
sociolinguistics 2, 24, 26, 38, 120, 330, 334–5, 366–9, **418**
sociolinguistic translation 347
sociology 116, 405, 416
soft palate *see* palate
solidarity (social) 13, **42–5**, 58, 61–2, 365
Solomon Is. 341, 361
Somali 318
Somali Is. 341, 361
song 11, 19, 41, 49, 60, 125, **175**, 291
song duels 60
sonority 166
soprano voice 18, 19
sound 122–77, 238–43, 400–1, 404
localization of 142
recognition of 145
see also auditory perception; phonetics; phonology; spectrograph
sound change 204, 216, **330–1**, 334–5
'sounding' 60
sound laws 330
sound pressure level 134
sound shift 330
sound spectrum 137
sound symbolism **176–7**, 250–1, 291, 346, 407
sound wave 132–4
South Africa 34, **316**, 317, 341, 359, 361, 368
Soviet Union *see* USSR
spacing, in written language 91, 185, 189, **207**, 255, 383
spa effect 379
Spain 34, 37, 198, 303–4, 328, 340, 359, 368
Spanish Academy 4
Speakeasy Voice Output Communication Aid 283
speaker identity **20**, 66, 135, 146

Speaker's Corner 397
specialization 401
special purposes (language) 111, 288, 357, **382–97**
specific reading disability 75
spectral analyser 135
spectrograph 20, **135–7**, 146, 166, 172, 238, 271
speech
autonomous 249
backward 248
comprehension of 15, 19, 22, 231–2, 234–5, 240, 243, 246, 250–1, **263–5**, 268, 272–3, 277, 281, 291, 345, 395
disguised 58
female vs male 21
inner 12
language vs 267
medium of 65, 79, **123–77**, 375, 388, 403–4
physiology of 124–31, 264
speech acts 57, **121**
Speech Development of a Bilingual Child 230
speech making *see* oratory
speech pathology 148, 161, 265, **266–83**
speech perception **145–8**, 240, 265, 279
speech presentation (in novel) 77
speech production 19, 22, 132, 148, **152–61**, 231, 234, 236, 243, 246, 263–5, 267–8, 271, 272–3, 278–81, 291, 345, 376
speech reception 132, **142–8**, 267, 270
speech recognition 149, 151
speech synthesis 145–6, **149–51**, 270, 283
speech therapy 125, 163, 249, **266**, 278–81
spelling 59, 73, 109, 182, 204, 206, 208, 214, **215–19**, 227, 257, 355, 366–7, 375
errors in 215, 266, 274, 277
handicaps in 215, 277
non-standard 181, 206, 394
pronunciation and 39, 182
reform of **217–19**, 320, 366, 410
regularity in 216, 274, 357
Spelling Reform Association 217
spinal nerves 131
spirometer 125
split (sound) 330
spoken language
vs speech 267
vs written language 3,

39, 47, 52–3, 79, 86, 91, 94, 111, 116, 123, **179–84**, 250, 257, 267, 335, 378, 395
spoonerisms 264
sports reporting 56, 243
Sprachatlas des Deutschen Reichs 26
spreading *see* lips
sputnik 335
Sri Lanka 310, 341, 359, 361
Stammbaumtheorie 294
stammering *see* stuttering
standardization 5, 57, 357, **366**
    of spelling 217
standard language 2–**3**, 5, 10, 21–3, **24**, 26, 35, 43, 53, 180–1, 250, 257, 286, 302, 314–15, 332, 335, 338, 396, 408–9
    non-/sub- 35, 40, 52–3, 108, 206, 332
stapes 143
statistics 67–9, 416
status (social) **41–2**, 49–50, 52, 60, 117, 120, 223, 334, 396
steganography 58
Stenographic Soundhand 209
stenography 196, 208–9
stenotype machine 209
stereotyped language 265, 269, 273, 377
sticker books 252
stimulus-response 101
stirrup 143
Stoics 408
stops 159, 168, 209
story-grammars 119
Stoudion Gospels 188
strata 83
stratification (social) 38–40, 334–5
stratificational grammar 83, 412
stream of consciousness 77, 78
stress 41, 74, 91, 107, 146, 150, 163, **171**, 174, 196, 242–3, 251, 264–5, 280, 330–1
stress-timed language 171
Strine 27
stroboscope 141
stroke 272–3
structural linguistics *see* linguistics
structuralism (literary) 77, **79**, 119, 391, 412
studio (recording) 138
stuttering 266–7, **280**
style 3, 19, 21–2, 32, 40, 42, **66–79**, 86, 89, 98, 111, 116, 206, 257, 338, 364, 408–9
    'macro' approach to 71
    manuals 4, 67, 94, 207,

366, 392
    'micro' approach to 71, 78–9
    statistics and 67–69
style indirect libre 77
stylistics **66**, 71, 120, 416
stylolinguistics 78
stylometrics/stylostatistics 67
subject (grammatical) 89, **94–5**, 98
subject matter 40, 42, **48**, 52, 62
subjunctive *see* mood
sublanguages 351
submucous cleft palate 279
subordination **95**, 245, 332, 351
sub-standard language *see* standard language
substantive universals 85, 91
substitution 92, 119, 215, 265, 279, **411**
substratum 335
subtitling 271, 346
sub-vocal language 13, 148, 212
Suda 111
Sudan 316, 341, 359
suffixation **90**, 92, 99, 112, 356
Suggestopedia 379
sulci 260, 292
Sumatra 320
Sumerians 200
Summer Institute of Linguistics 370
supernatural 61
supplanting vs supplementing 217
suprasegmental *see* phonology
surface structure 98, 162, **413**
Suriname 340, 359
surnames 112–13
Survey of English Dialects 30
Survey of English Usage 415
suspension (in writing) 189
Swaziland 359, 361
swearing 10, **61**
Sweden **37**, 306, 359, 362, 368
Swedish Academy 4
switching 50, 52, **364–5**
Switzerland **37**, 303–4, 359, 362
syllabary *see* syllabic writing
syllabary curriculum 252
syllabic teaching 252
syllabic writing 197, **203**, 340, 380
syllables 59, 87, 150, 163, **166**, 171, 212, 238–9, 252, 280, 355, 404
    prominence vs pulse theory of 166
    structure 86, 152, **166**, 265, 299

syllable-timed rhythm 171
syllabus, types of 377–8
Sylvian fissure 260–3, 273
symbolism 74, 176–7, 272
symbols 55–6, 192, 194, 196, **198**, 206–7, 267, 282, 354
synchrony 411
syncope 330
synonymy **105**, 111, 391
Syntactic Structures 97, 413
syntagmatic relations 105, **411**
syntax 30, 53, 55–7, 75, 82, 88, **94–9**, 104, 107, 120, 151, 162, 235, 264–5, 280–1, 295–6, 352, 355–6, 377, 412
synthesis by rule 150
synthesis, index of 296
synthetic languages 295
synthetic speech *see* speech
Syria 302, 318, 359
systemic linguistics 412
SYSTRAN 352

T (address forms) 45
tab 223
Table Alphabeticall, A 109
tables 180, 193
taboo 9, 42, **61**, 115, 167, 174, 346
tachistoscope 210–11
tachygraphy 208–9
tactile communication 403, 405
Tadoma communication 405
tagging (corpus) 415
tagmemics 412
tag-questions *see* questions
Taiwan 315, 319, 359
talking books 180, 282
talking dolls 232
tally marks 327
Tanzania 317, 359, 361
tap consonants 168
tape recorders 26, 30, 32, 66, 69, 75, 116, 230–1, 233, 246, 251, 325, 331, **414**
task effects 232
Tasmania 319–21
tautology 390
taxis 70
teacher training 375
technical language 51, 55, 111, 185, 366, **384–5**
technography 196
Teeline 209
teeth 130, 157
teknonymy 44, 112
telegrammatic/telegraphic speech 56, 224, **245**, 273, 392
telephone conversation **48**, 86, 118, 353
telephone directories 367
telestich 64
teletex(t) 54, **195**, 271
television 305, 350

template matching 148–9
tempo 163, 171
    see also rate
temporal lobe 143, 260, 263
temporal theory of pitch 144
tenor voice 18–19
tenses 15, 35, 71, 90, 92, **93**, 174, 181, 224, 226, 236, 244–5, 299, 338, 356, 392
tense vs lax articulation 161
term banks 349, 353
terminal illness 386
terminology 2, 181, 251, 266, 349, 391
terms of art 391
Tesoro de la lengua castellana o española 111
tests 235, 268, 276, 381
tetragrammaton 9
Teutsch lateinisches Wörter-Büchlein 110
text 71, 78–9, 82, **116–19**, 173
textlinguistics 77, **116**
Thailand 311–13, 359
thalamus 262, 264
themes 52, 71, 119
theography 51
theolinguistics 418
theology 51, 72, 335, 389
theophoric names 112
Thesaurus (Roget's) 104
thinking *see* language
Third New International Dictionary 108–9
thoracic cage/cavity 124
Thoth 388
thou/you 389
thresholds 145
Thresor de la langue francoyse 111
Through the Looking Glass 100
Thumb English Dictionary 108
thyroid cartilage 128
Tibet 312
tick-tack talk 407
'T-ing in i' 59
timbre 19, 23, **133**, 171, 278
time depth 333
time line 224
tinnitus 268
title pages 189, 194
titles 44
Toda naming customs 9
Togo 340, 359
tokens 198, 282, 402
Tokyo, name of 9
tomography 140
tone (acoustic) 132–3
tone (linguistic) 74, **171**, 174
    of voice 163, **171**, 239, 243
    playing with 59, 62
    sandhi 174
tone languages 174, 347, 367, 404

contour vs register 174
tonemes 174
tonetic system 173
Tonga 62, 321, 361
tongue 124, **130–1**, 140, 155–6, 158, 238
    length of 18, 292
    slips of 166, 264–5
tongue twisters 65, 174
tongues, speaking in 11
tool using, and language 293, 402
topic (conversational) **116–18**, 386, 414
topic (sentence) 94
toponomastics/toponymy 112
Torah 59
total communication 269
Total Physical Response 379
trachea 124, 278
tracheostomy 278
trade marks 55, 67, 115, 345
traditional grammar *see* grammar
traditional transmission 401
traits (personality) 23
transactional style 256
transcription 348, 414–15
    see also phonetic transcription
transfer 376
transformation 85, 97
transformational grammar 413
transition (acoustic) 137, 146
transition areas 28
transition network 119
translation 15, 42, 51, 68, 104, 344–5, **346–50**, 352, 357, 375, 378, 388–9, 410, 414, 418
    back- 348
    editing of 347, 352–3
    loan 332
    machine 347, **352–3**, 416
    machine-aided 353
    types of 224, **346–7**, 352
translative case 92
Translators' Guild 347
transliteration 348
transpositions (of sounds) 279
Trappist signs 407
travel agency computer 417
travelling-wave theory 144
tree diagram **96**, 186, 193
tremor 19
trial number 92
trigeminal nerve 131
trills 159, 161, 168
Trinidad and Tobago 340, 359, 361
triphthongs 156
tripod grip (in writing) 254
trivium 70, 410
Trobriand Islanders 12
trochee 74
trope 70

trucker talk 56, 407
truth-conditional semantics 107, 120
Tuareg 318
tuning fork 132
Tunisia 359
Turkey 302–3, 309, 359
Turkistan 303
Tuvalu 361
twins 44, 249, 290
tympanic cavity 142–3
typeface 13, 193–4
types (personality) 23
typesetting 194
type-token distinction 87, 216, 246
typewriter 149, 184, **194**, 367
  Chinese 315
  electronic **194**, 367
  keyboard of 194
typing **194**, 214, 356
Typographical Printing Surfaces 192
typography 55, 56, 73, 183–4, 187, **192–4**, 254
  contrasts in 194, 211–12, 383, 390
  measurement in 192
typology 84–5, 98, 295
Tyranny of Words, The 397

U, and non-U language 39
Uganda 316, 359, 361
ultrasonics 140
Ulysses 77
uncial script 188
underextension 246
Under Mild Wood 76
UNESCO Committee on Language Endangerment 370
Unifon 253
unilateral hearing 142
United Arab Emirates 359
United Kingdom *see* Britain
United Nations 351
United Nations Declaration (1992) 371
United States of America 34, 36, 47, 53, 56, 63, 113–14, 190, 223, 227, 253, 302–3, 308, 312, 318, 321, **322–3**, 328–9, 340–1, 359, 361–3, 367–8, 373, 411
  Pacific territories 361
universal language 104, 208, **354–8**, 384, 410
universals 48, 62, 67, 79, **84–5**, 88, 106, 177, 236, 293, 296, 339, 357, 377, **400–1**, 406, 413
  formal 85
  statistical 85–7
  substantive 85, 91
univocalics 65
UPSID survey 166–70
Uruguay 359
usage **1–2**, 39, 46–7, 52, 88, 111, 207, 366

USSR 114, 223, 227, 302, **306–9**, 322, 329, 359, 368
utterance length 51, 67–9, 235
uvula 130
uvular consonants *see* consonants

V (address forms) 45
vagueness 391, 394
vagus nerve 131
valencies 412
Vanuatu 341, 361
variable (linguistic) 32, **234**
variegated babbling 239
variety of language **16–79**, 104, 336, 343, 345, 359–60, 366, 375, **382–97**, 414–15
  see also dialect
Vatican City 359
Vaupés Indians 42
Vedas 303, 388, 409
vegetative noises 238
vehicles, words for 15
velar consonants *see* consonants
velaric sounds 126–7
velarization 158
velocity 133
velopharyngeal closure 130
velum **126**, 130, 141, 158
Venezuela 276, 324, 340, 359
ventricular folds 128
verb 6, 21, **91–3**, 95–8, 107, 226, 244–7, 299, 332, 351, 356, 395, 402
verb phrase 95–7, 385
verbal (vs non-verbal) communication 14, 171, 403
verbal apraxia 273
verbal art/duelling 60–3
Vercingetorixe 63
vernacular 35
Verner's law 330–1
vibration 128–9, 132–3, 141, 154
vibro-tactile aids 270
video technology 230, 233, 381, 414
Vietnam 310–13, 319, 341, 359
viewdata 195
Virgin Is. 340
visual agnosia 273
visual aids (in deafness) 270–1
visual language 54–5, 75, 179–227
visual medium 403, 406–7
visual pattern identification 211, 277
visual perception 187, 263, 276–7
visual thinking 14
Vocabolista italiano-tedesco 111
Vocabulaire 111

vocabulary 2, 10, 19, 22, 24, 30–2, 38–9, 40–3, 46, 52, 55, 57–8, 62, 71, 73, 75, 82, **102–7**, 120, 174, 181, 214, 217, 246, 295, 298, 305, 340–1, 360, 375, 377, 384, 394
  acquisition of 234, **246–7**, 265, 365
  changes in 5, 51, **332–3**, 335, 339
  frequency of 67, 86–7, 212
  selection of 149, 282–3, 333, 355–6, 366, 378, 392
  size of 22, 56–7, 67–8, 150, 234, 246–7, 281, 283, 336, 338, 358, 402
vocal abuse 278
vocal folds 19, 124, **128–9**, 137, 141, 154, 157–8, 161, 238
  abnormality in 266, 278
  true vs false 128
vocalization 51, 183, 230
vocal organs 18–19, **124–31**, 154–61, 281, 292, 331, 402
vocal play 238
vocal tract 18, 20, **130**, 149, 154, 157, 230, 263–4, 278, 292, 403
vocative 93, 299
vocoid 155
Voder 150
voice (grammar) 2, **93**, 97–8, 231, 245, 299, 383–5
voice (phonetics)
  disorders 19, 125, 267, **278**
  male vs female 128, 133, 146
  mutation of 19
  quality of **19**, 66, 67, 125, 128, 145, 149, 171, 175, **278–9**, 403
  range of 19
voice-activated systems 149, 282
voice onset time 137, 147
voiceprints **20**, 66, 162
voice stereotypes 23
Voice Visualizer 271
voicing 50, **128–9**, **154**, 157, 159, 161, 164–5, 168, 203, 209, 218, 270–1, 279, 299, 409
Voiscope 141
volley theory of pitch 144
vowel gradation 299
vowel harmony 163, 242
vowels 33, 65, 74, 85, 128, 131, **154–8**, 169, 175, 196, 227, 238, 242–3, 265, 279, 292, 331
  acoustics of 133, 135, **137**, 154, 156
  cardinal 135, **156**, 169

dispersion of 169
English system of 163
intensity of 134
length of 145, **155**, 169, 299
perception of **148**, 240, 242
semi- 137, 155, **159**
symbolism of 176–7
systems of **169**, 299, 404
written 197, 204, 209
Vulgate 388

Wada technique 261
Wade-Giles transcription 315
Wales 51, 305, 368
Walloons 37, 51
Wantok 336–7
Waste Land, The 71
wave (theory of change) 334
waveforms **132–3**, 141, 145, 148–9, 268
wavelength 133
Webster's Third New International Dictionary 61, 400
Weidner Communications 353
Welsh Dialect Survey 31
wén-yán 314–15
Wernicke's aphasia 273
Wernicke's area 262–3, 273
Western Samoa 49, 321, 361
West Germany **36–7**, 56, 63, 113, 188, 194, 359, 373
West Indies 35, 60
whisper 128, 171
whistled speech 404
White Hotel, The 77
white space 383
whole-word reading *see* look-and-say
whom vs *who* 3, 335
widening (pharynx) 155
wild/wolf children 291
winding speech 41
Windows 195
window size (in reading) 211
witnesses' use of language 391
Wolf Children 291
'woofing' 60
word class 62, 67–8, **91–4**, 108, 111, 196, 236, 244, 251, 408–9, 415
word-finding problems 273
word games 64–5, 201
Word Geography of the Eastern United States 31
wordiness 390
word order 5, 56, 73, 82, 84–5, 95, **98**, 226, 236, 281, 295, 332, 392
word play *see* puns
word processing 194–5, 214, 315, 353, 381

words 68, 85, **91**, 95, 101, 104, 163, 234, 265, 352, 397
  identification of **91**, 147, 196, 207
  length of 2, 67–9, 210, 254, 383, 385
  proto- 239
  spaces between **91**, 185, 189, 255
  structure of *see* morphology
Word Search 64
word spectra 68
word superiority effect 213
World English 360
World English Spelling 218
World Esperanto Association 356
World Wide Web 370
writing 13, 104, **179–219**, 255–7, 263
  art of 190
  developmental stages in 257
  direction of 187, 214
  history of 187–9, **198–205**, 327, 388
  implements for 187, 189, 198
  marking of 257
  non-phonological 199–202
  phonological 199, 202–5
  physical factors in 214, 255
  styles of 256
  system of 77, 160, 171, 187, **196–209**, 214, 388
  teaching of 187, 250–1, **255–7**, 375
  see also handwriting
written language 2–3, 5, 8, 11, 25, 39, 43, 47, 54–5, 64–5, 79, 91, **180–219**, 282, 286, 295, 309, 390, 403, 408–9, 411
  handicaps in 266, 269, 272, **274–7**, 281
  see also spoken language
wugs 244

X-bar theory 413
xenoglossia 11
x height 192
X-rays 130, 140, 143, 156

Yahweh 9
Yemen 359
Yoda-speak 98
yo-he-ho theory 291
Yugoslavia 37, 197, 288, 302–3, 359, 362

Zaire 359
Zambia 341, 359, 361
Zimbabwe 341, 359, 361
Zipf's Law 87
zöosemiotics 402

ACKNOWLEDGEMENTS

The publishers gratefully acknowledge the help of the many individuals and organizations who cannot all be named in collecting the illustrations for this volume. Every effort has been made to obtain permission to use copyright materials; the publishers apologise for any omissions and would welcome these being brought to their attention.

The appearance of logos and trademarks in the Encyclopedia in no way affects their legal status as trademarks.

Note: Sources and copyright holders for materials used are given in order of their appearance in the volume (page numbers in bold type). The following abbreviations have been used: *b* bottom; *c* centre; *l* left; *r* right; *t* top; *x* text; BAL: Bridgeman Art Library, London; British Library: by permission of the British Library; CUL: by permission of the Syndics of Cambridge University Library. MEPL: Mary Evans Picture Library; NPG: reproduced by courtesy of the National Portrait Gallery, London; RHPL: Robert Harding Picture Library; SPL: Science Photo Library; TCL: Telegraph Colour Library.

0 *t* Colorific!; photo by Patrick Morrow/Black Star. *bl* Institut de France, Paris. *br* Ancient Art & Architecture Collection. **2** George Orwell Archive, University College London; photo by Vernon Richards. **3** *l* Hulton Deutsch Collection. *r* Cambridge University Library. **4** *l* Life File; photo by Emma Lee. *tr* MEPL. *br* Philip Mould, Historical Portraits Ltd., London/BAL. **5** The Mansell Collection. **6** *l* Royal Anthropological Institute, London. *r* Monumenti Musei E Gallerie Pontificie, Città del Vaticano; photo by Berri. **7** Bildarchiv Preussischer Kulturbesitz, Berlin; photo by Lutz Braun. **8** Colorific!; photo by Sylvain Grandadam. **9** TCL; photo by B. Tanaka. **11** *l* Life File; photo by Nicola Sutton. *r* G. Apollinaire *Calligrammes* 1925 © Editions Gallimard. **12** *l* Cephas; photo by Mick Rock. *r* Alecto Historical Editions. **13** *t* MEPL. *b* The *Guardian*. **14** *t* Cambridge University Aerial Photography. **16** Canapress, Toronto; photo by Ryan Remiorz. **18** After M. Nadoleczny *Untersuchungen uber den Kunstgesang* Springer 1923. **19** After R. D. Kent & R. Burkard 'Changes in the Acoustic Correlates of Speech Production' in D. S. Beasley & G. A. Davis (eds.) *Aging: Communication Processes and Disorders* Grune & Stratton 1981, p. 50, fig. 3.2. **20** Reprinted with permission from *Nature* **196** (4861) pp.1253-7. Copyright © 1962, Macmillan Magazines Ltd. **21** Life File; photo by Jeremy Hoare. **22** Galt Educational. **23** After H. J. Eysenck & S. B. G. Eysenck *The Eysenck Personality Inventory* University of London Press 1963. **25** *b* After J. K. Chambers & P. Trudgill *Dialectology* Cambridge University Press 1980. **26** British Library/portrait from *Bibliographie des Travaux de Jules Gillieron* AC 9807. **27** *tl*, *tr* University of Leeds Survey of English Dialects. *bl* British Library. *x* A. Lauder *Let Stalk Strine* Ure Smith/Lansdowne Press 1965 © Alastair Morrison. *x* F. Shaw *et al. Lern Yerself Scouse* Scouse Press 1966. **29** After J. K. Chambers & P. Trudgill *Dialectology* Cambridge University Press 1980. **30** University of Leeds Survey of English Dialects. **31** *t* A. R. Thomas *The Linguistic Geography of Wales* University of Wales Press 1973. *b* H. Kurath *A Word Geography of the Eastern United States* Copyright © 1949 by The University of Michigan, renewed 1977. Used by permission of The University of Michigan Press. **33** *t* After J. K. Chambers & P. Trudgill

Dialectology Cambridge University Press 1980. *b* After C. D. Darlington 1974, reprinted in L. F. Brosnahan *The Sounds of Language* Heffer 1961. **34** The Government Press Office, Jerusalem. **38** *x* J. Betjeman, 'How to Get on in Society' in N. Mitford (ed.) *Noblesse Oblige* Futura 1980. Reproduced by permission of Peters Fraser & Dunlop. **41** Hilary Bradt. **43** Basler Zeitung. **44** After S. Ervin-Tripp 'On Sociolinguistic Rules: Alternation and Co-occurence' in J. J. Gumperz & D. Hymes (eds.) *Directions in Sociolinguistics* Holt, Reinhart & Winston 1972. **45** *t* After S. Ervin-Tripp 'On Sociolinguistic Rules: Alternation and Co-occurence' in J. J. Gumperz & D. Hymes (eds.) *Directions in Sociolinguistics* Holt, Reinhart & Winston 1972. *x* S. Potter *One-upmanship* Hart Davis 1952. **46** *At Home* Beacon Readers, Ginn & Company, 2nd edn. **47** *t* *Children's Letters to God* Harper-Collins Publishers Ltd. *b* © 1977 United Feature Syndicate Inc. **49** *t* Photobank, Auckland; photo by Dallas and John Heaton. *b* Photobank, Auckland. **50** After A. Bell 'Language Style as Audience Design' *Language in Society* **13** Cambridge University Press 1984. **51** John Walmsley. *x* C. Burke *God is for Real, Man* Fontana 1967 © 1966 by National Board of Young Men's Associations, USA. **54** *bc* Jarrold Publishing, Norwich. *br* St Peter Mancroft Church, Norwich. **55** *c* Punch. *bcl* Life File; photo by Lionel Moss. *bcr* Life File; photo by Emma Lee. *br* Life File; photo by Emma Lee./Life File; photo by Emma Lee/James Duffell. **57** Surface Flotilla Photographic Unit, Portsmouth. **58** Times Newspapers Ltd; photo by Peter Trievnor. **60** Nigel Luckhurst, Cambridge. **61** *t* Punch. *b* Michael Holford. **63** Reproduced by permission of the Dean and Chapter of Exeter Cathedral. **64** *x* C. Wood 'Death of a Scrabble Master' in W. R. Espy *Another Almanac of Words at Play* Crown Publications Inc. 1980. SCRABBLE ® is the registered trademark of J. W. Spear and Sons plc, Enfield, Middlesex. **65** *t* Puzzle Mania © 1994, Henderson Publishing plc. *b* Courtesy of Morland plc. **67** *t* Life File; photo by Emma Lee. *r* The Master and Fellows of St John's College, Cambridge. *b* MEPL. **68** *t* MEPL. *b* NPG. **69** After J. Svartik 'The Evans Statements' *Gothenburg Studies in English 20* University of Gothenburg 1968. *b* After C. B. Williams *Style and Vocabulary: Numerical Studies* Charles Griffin and Co. Ltd. 1970. **70** *x* S. Spender 'The Prisoners' 1934 in *Collected Poems 1928–85*, Faber & Faber 1985. **71** *t* MEPL. *b* NPG. **72** *t* Corbis-Bettman/UPI. *b* National Museum of Wales, Cardiff/BAL. **73** MEPL. *x* S. Spender 'The Exiles' 1934 in *Collected Poems 1928–85*, Faber & Faber 1985. *x* T. S. Eliot *The Waste Land* ed. C. B. Cox & A. P. Hinchliffe, Macmillan 1968. **74** *x* T. S. Eliot 'East Coker' *The Waste Land* ed. C. B. Cox & A. P. Hinchliffe, Macmillan 1968. **75** *l* Ian Hamilton Finlay 'Au Pair Girl' taken from S. Bann (Ed) *Concrete Poetry*, London Magazine Edition. Reproduced by permission of London Magazine Edition. *r* Photostage; photo Donald Cooper. *x* H. Pinter *The Caretaker* Methuen, London 1960. **76** *l* Dickens House Museum, London/BAL. *r* 'The Prisoner' ™ & © 1997 PolyGram. *x* T. Stoppard *Rosencrantz & Guildenstern are Dead* Faber & Faber 1968. *x* D. Thomas *Under Milk Wood* Dent 1954; Copyright 1954 by New Directions Publishing Corporation. All rights reserved. **77** *x* E. Hemingway *For Whom the Bell Tolls* Penguin 1940. **78** *x* A. Solzhenitsyn *Cancer Ward* Bodley Head 1968 © Editions YMCA Press, Paris. *x* J. Joyce *Ulysses* Bodley Head 1986. © The Estate of James Joyce. **79** Sygma. **84** British Library, 626d 17 (2). **86** *x* A. Zettersten *A Statistical Study of the Graphic System*

of Present-day American English Studentlitteratur 1969. **87** Courtesy of the Harvard University Archives. **88** Quirk *et al. A Comprehensive Grammar of the English Language* Longman 1985. **89** *Find a Story 3* devised by Maureen Vidler (Penguin Education, 1974). Copyright © Maureen Vidler, 1974. Reproduced by permission of Penguin Books Ltd. **91** British Library MS 8650488. **94** *t* TCL; photo by Martin Goddard. *c* TCL *b* TCL; photo by S. Griggs Agency. **98** Courtesy of Lucasfilm Ltd. ™ & © Lucasfilm Ltd. (LCL) 1980. All rights reserved. **99** *Punch*. **101** Biblioteca Nacional, Madrid. Mss.Vit. 14-3 f.27. **103** *tl* After C. E. Osgood 'The Nature and Measurement of Meaning' *Psychological Bulletin 49*. Copyright 1952 by the American Psychological Association. Adapted by permission of the publisher and author. *tr* Institute of Communications Research, University of Illinois at Urbana-Champaign. *br* After H. Maclay & E. E. Ware 'Cross-cultural use of the Semantic Differential' *Behavioural Science 6*. Reprinted with permission from *Behavioural Science*, a publication of the Society for General Systems Research. **104** NPG. **108** *x* The *Random House Dictionary of the English Language*, 2nd edn. – unabridged. Copyright © 1987 by Random House Inc. *x* Longman *Dictionary of the English Language* Longman 1984. Reprinted by permission of Addison Wesley Longman Ltd. *x* Penguin *English Dictionary* Penguin Books 1969. **109** *tl* Private Collection/BAL. *tc*, *tr* Cambridge University Library. *bl* Oxford University Press Archives. *br* Mead Art Museum, Amherst College, MA; bequest of Waldo Hutchins, Jr. 1989. **147**, Samuel F. B. Morse, Portrait of Noah Webster, oil on canvas, 1823. **110** *t* Grand *Larousse Universel*, Larousse, Paris. *bl* Bibliographisches Institut & F. A. Brockhause AG. *Duden-Oxford Bildwöterbuch deutsch/english* by permission of Oxford University Press. *br* Cambridge University Library. **112** *t* Surface Flotilla Photographic Unit, Portsmouth. *b* Life File; photo by Juliet Highet. **114–115** North Wales Coast Light Railway Ltd. **117** *l* MTM. *tr* Popperfoto. *br* Life File; photo by Nicola Sutton. **119** Coherence diagram from R. de Beaugrande & W. Dressler *Introduction to Text Linguistics* Longman 1981. Reprinted by permission of Addison Wesley Longman Ltd. **121** James Duffell. **122** Dr Carol Gracco, Haskins Laboratories, Connecticut. **124** Crystal. **125** *tr* After J. Tarneaud *Le Chant, sa Construction et sa Destruction* Malouie. *c* Watson & Wood; photo by Peter Murray, Queen Margaret College, Edinburgh. *bl* Dr Linda Flack, Queen Margaret College, Edinburgh; photo by Richard Hardcastle, Edinburgh College of Art. *br* R. Menzies *Testamen Physiologioum Inaugurale de Respiratione* Creech 1790; reproduced in C. Code & H. Ball (eds.) *Experimental Clinical Phonetics* Croom Helm 1984. **126** *t* London Features; photo by S. Rapport/LFI. **128** Crystal. **129** *t* Dr Hiroya Yamaguchi, Tokyo Senbai Hospital. *bl* James Duffell. *br* Professor Hajime Hirose, Kitasato University. **130** Norfolk and Norwich Health Care NHS Trust. **132** *br* James Duffell. **133** *b* D. B. Fry *The Physics of Speech* Cambridge University Press 1979. **134** *x* D. B. Fry *The Physics of Speech* Cambridge University Press 1979. **135** *br* Kay Elemetrics Corp, Lincoln Park, NJ. **136** Dr James Scobbie, Queen Margaret College, Edinburgh; photos by Richard Hardcastle, Edinburgh College of Art. **138** *l* Kay Elemetrics Corp, Lincoln Park, NJ. *r* David MacKenzie, Heriot Watt University, Edinburgh; photo by Richard Hardcastle, Edinburgh College of Art. **139** Professor Seiji Niimi, University of Tokyo. **140** Professor Maureen Stone, John Hopkins University, Baltimore. **141** *tl*, *c* W. J. Hardcastle,

Queen Margaret College, Edinburgh. *tr* W. J. Hardcastle & R. Morgan in *British Journal of Disorders of Communication* 17 (1) 1982. *cr* Wendy Cohen, Queen Margaret College, Edinburgh; photo by Richard Hardcastle, Edinburgh College of Art. *bl* E. Abberton & A. Fourcin 'Electrolaryngography' in C. Code & H. Ball (eds.) *Experimental Clinical Phonetics* Croom Helm 1984. *br* Richard Hardcastle, Edinburgh College of Art. **142** SPL; photo by Peter Cull. *inset* BSIP VEM/SPL. **143** *t* SPL; photo by Dave Roberts. *br* After J.L. Northern & M. P. Downs *Hearing in Children* Williams & Wilkins 1978. **144** *tr* After O. Stuhlman *An Introduction to Biophysics* Wiley 1952. *bl* MEPL. *br* Courtesy of the Harvard University Archives. **145** Dr Patricia Sonkson, Institute of Child Health. **146** *t* A. M. Liberman *et al. Journal of Experimental Psychology 54* 1957 © 1957 by the American Psychological Association. Reprinted by permission of the author. *b* Borden & Harris. **147** *l* L. Lisker & A. Abramson 'The Voicing Dimension: Some Experiments in Comparative Phonetics'. Reproduced in *Proc. VIth Int. Cong. Phon. Sci.* Prague 1967; Academia 1970. **148** After G. Fant 'Auditory Patterns of Speech' in W. Walthen-Dunn (ed.) *Models for the Perception of Speech and Visual Form* MIT Press 1967. **149** Courtesy of the Library of Congress. **150** James Duffell. **151** *t* Courtesy of AT&T Archives, Warren, NJ; photo by R. L. Shepherd. *b* MEPL. **154** Kenneth L. Pike. **155** *t* Jiro Saito, Tokyo. *b* Department of Phonetics, University College London. **158** *b* L. F. Brosnahan & B. Malmberg *Introduction to Phonetics* Heffer 1970. **159** After *A Course in Phonetics*, 2nd edn., by Peter Ladefoged, copyright © 1982 by Harcourt Brace Jovanovich, Inc. Reprinted by permission of the publisher. **160** *t* Photograph reproduced from *Le Maître Phonétique*, janvier-mars 1941. *bl, cr* International Phonetics Association. *br* Kay Elemetrics Corp, Lincoln Park, NJ. **161** *t* International Phonetics Association. *br* C. Bush *et al.* 1973, Child Language Project, Stanford University Working Paper; reproduced in D. Ingram *Phonological Disability in Children* Edward Arnold 1976. **163** After D. Rockey *Phonetic Lexicon* Heyden 1973. **167** South African High Commission. **172** tl, *bl* Scolar Press Facsimile edn. 1969. **174** Reproduced in V. Fromkin & R. Rodman *An Introduction to Language* Holt Saunders. **175** © 1968 by Universal Edition (London) Ltd, London. **176** © 1996 - Les Éditions Albert René/Goscinny-Uderzo *Asterix y Galiad* Gwasg y Dref Wen. **177** The Governing Body, Christ Church, Oxford. **178** *background:* MEPL. **180** Proliance Ltd./Hammond Gower Publications Ltd/Second Generation Ltd. **181** The *Guardian* 1963. **182** Hergé/Moulinsart - 1996. **183** Reproduced by permission of PAWS, Inc. *x* A. Bester *The Demolished Man* Penguin Books. Copyright © 1953 by Alfred Bester, reprinted by permission of Tessa Sayle Agency. **185** *tl* Ancient Art & Architecture Collection. *tr* Savoy, London. *bl* D. Crystal & J. Foster *Electricity* Edward Arnold 1983. *br* The F. A. Premier League. **186** *tr* Gratten plc. *cr* Lynn Wendon. *bl* Michael Twyman. *br* McLachlan cartoons *Punch*. **187** *l* D. Diringer. *r* Rex; photo by Gerry Whitmont. **188** *t* Ancient Art & Architecture Collection. *tl* Lyn Davies. *tr* Ancient Art & Architecture Collection. *bl* National Library of Russia, St Petersburg. *bc* Cambridge University Press MS. Ee. 2.4(922), fo 121r, detail. *cr* Biblioteca Medicea Laurenziana, Firenze. Ms. Laur. Plut. 50.31, c.166 *br* Biblioteca Nazionale Centrale, Firenze. Conv. Soppre. J.I.14c.32r. **189** *l* British Library Add CH 19 792. *br* Ancient Art and Architecture Collection. **190** t, *cl* P. Struck *The Universal Penman* 1941 (facsimile edn.) Dover Publications Inc., New York. *b* Ancient Art & Architecture Collection. *cr, br* National Palace Museum, Taipei, Taiwan, Republic of China. **191** *c* E. Singer *A Manual of Graphology* Duckworth 1953. **193** *bl* A. E. Morton *Modern Typewriting and Manual of Office Procedure* 12th edn., London 1929; British Library. *r* After P. Wright 'Behavioural Research and the Technical Communicator' *The Communicator of Scientific and Technical Information 32* 1977. **194** *t* The Mansell Collection. *l inset* British Library C9d4, The Gutenberg Bible, Pages: Parabola. *l* Gutenberg-Museum der Stadt Mainz, Weltmuseum der Druckkunst. **195** From James L. Harner (ed.) *The World Shakespeare Bibliography on CD ROM*, Cambridge University Press 1996. **197** *b* D. Diringer. **198** *t* D. Diringer. *c* Musée du Louvre. **199** *t* D. Diringer. *c* D. Diringer, *Writing* Thames & Hudson 1962. *c* From 'Zapotec Writing', Joyce Marcus. Copyright © 1980 by Scientific American, Inc. All rights reserved. **199** *br* W. Haas *Writing Without Letters* Manchester University Press 1976. **200** tl, *bl* D. Diringer. *br* Copyright British Museum. **201** *tr, cr* D. Diringer. *bl, br* Copyright British Museum. **202** *r* D. Diringer. **203** *l* O. Masson *Les Inscriptions Chypriotes Syllabiques* Paris 1961, reproduced in W. Haas *Writing Without letters* Manchester University Press 1976. *tr Japanese for Beginners* Gakken Co. Ltd. *br* H. A. Gleason *An Introduction to Descriptive Linguistics* Holt, Rinehart, Winston 1955. **204** D. Diringer, *Writing* Thames & Hudson 1962. **205** *r* Copyright British Museum. **206** *t* Toys 'R' Us. *l* Jeyes UK, Thetford. *r* Life File; photo by Andrew Ward. *b* Kwik-Fit. **207** *x* José Paolo Paes 'The Suicide, or Descartes à Rebours', trans. E. Morgan. Reproduced from T*he Times Literary Supplement*, 3 September 1964. **208** Master and Fellows, Magdalene College, Cambridge. **209** *tl* Pitman Education & Training Ltd. *tr* Freeman *et al. Secretarial Skills* Longman. Reprinted by permission of Addison Wesley Longman Ltd. *bl* 'Shorthand' in *Encyclopaedia Britannica*, 15th edn., 1974. *br* National Archives and Records Administration; photo United Nations. *inset* Paramount (courtesy Kobal). **211** *t, b* L. Brooks 'Visual Pattern in Fluent Word Identification' in A. Reber & D. Scarborough (eds.) *Toward a Psychology of Reading* Wiley 1977. **214** After A. Matsuhashi 'Explorations in the Real-time Production of Written Discourse' in M. Nystrand (ed.) *What Writers Know* Academic Press 1982. **215** After A. M. Wing & A. D. Baddeley 'Spelling Errors in Handwriting: a Corpus and Distributional Analysis' in U. Frith (ed.) *Cognitive Processes in Spelling* Academic Press 1980. **216** British Library. *x* G. Dewey *English Spelling: Roadblock to Reading* Columbia University Press 1971. **218** George Bernard Shaw *Androcles and the Lion*, Penguin Books. *inset* MEPL. **219** *tl* 'The i.t.a. alphabet' from J. Mountford *I.t.a. as a Grading Device* University of London Institute of Education, Reading Research Document No 5 1965. *tr* University of London Institute of Education. *b* Noah Webster Foundation & Historical Society of West Hertford Inc, CT. **220** Signer: Mary Brand; photos by Geoff Staff. **222** *t* E. Klima & U. Bellugi *The Signs of Language* Harvard University Press © 1979 by the President and Fellows of Harvard College. Illustrations by Frank A. Paul. *b* Photos by Geoff Staff. **223** Photos by Geoff Staff. **224** *t, b* E. Klima & U. Bellugi *The Signs of Language* Harvard University Press © 1979 by the President and Fellows of Harvard College. Illustrations by Frank A. Paul. **225** *l* E. Klima & U. Bellugi T*he Signs of Language* Harvard University Press © 1979 by the President and Fellows of Harvard College. Illustrations by Frank A. Paul. *r* S. K. Liddell *American Sign Language Syntax* Mouton: The Hague 1980. **226** *l* E. Klima & U. Bellugi *The Signs of Language* Harvard University Press © 1979 by the President and Fellows of Harvard College. Illustrations by Frank A. Paul. *r* M. Skelly *Amer-Ind Gestural Code Based on Universal American Indian Hand Talk* 1979 Elsevier Science Publishing Co., Inc. **228** Cambridge Central Library; photo by Nigel Luckhurst, Cambridge. **230** Michael Holford. **231** John Walmsley. **232** *t* By permission of P. Lloyd and M. C. Donaldson. **233** James Duffell. **234** After M. E. Smith 'An Investigation of the Development of the Sentence and the Extent of Vocabulary in Young Children' *University of Iowa Studies in Child Welfare 3*. **235** *tl* After R. Brown *A First Language* Harvard University Press 1973. *tr* Item 4 from A. S. Toronto *Screening Test of Spanish Grammar* Northwestern University Press 1973. *b* © D. Crystal, P. Fletcher & M. Garman, 1981 revision, University of Reading. **236** Jean Mohr, Geneva. **238** O. Wasz-Höckert *et al. The Infant Cry: A Spectrographic and Auditory Analysis* Spastics International Medical Publications in Association with William Heinemann Medical Books Ltd. 1968. **239** *t* After B. L. Smith & D. K. Oller 'A Comparative Study of Premeaningful Vocalizations Produced by Normally Developing and Down's Syndrome Infants' *Journal of Speech and Hearing Disorders 46* © American Speech-Language-Hearing Association. *b* After J. L. Locke *Phonological Acquisition and Change* Academic Press 1983. **240** *l* Guy Devart; by kind permission of Jacques Mehler, Centre National de la Recherche Scientifique, Paris. *r* After P. D. Eimas *et al.* 'Speech Perception in Infants' *Science 171* 1971. **241** Saskia van Rees. **242** *x* J. Berko & R. Brown 'Psycholinguistic Research Methods' in P. H. Mussen (ed.) *Handbook of Research Methods in Child Development* Wiley 1960. **243** After C. A. Ferguson & C. B. Farwell 'Words and Sounds in Early Language Acquisition' *Language 51* 1975. **244** *t* After J. Berko 'The Child's Learning of English Morphology' *Word 14* 1958. *b* After R. Brown *A First Language* Harvard University Press 1973. **246** *x* K. R. Wagner *Journal of Child Language* Cambridge University Press 1985. *x* C. Stoel Gammon & J. A. Cooper *Journal of Child Language* Cambridge University Press 1984. **247** E. S. Anderson 'Cups and Glasses: Learning that Boundaries are Vague' *Journal of Child Language 2* Cambridge University Press 1975. **248** *x* P. Fletcher *A Child's Learning of English* Blackwell 1985. *x* M. McTear *Children's Conversation* Blackwell 1985. **249** *t* Colorific!; photo by Carl Skalak/DOT Pictures. *b* San Diego Children's Hospital. **250, 251** *l* R. James & R. G. Gregory *Imaginative Speech and Writing* Kemble Press Ltd., Banbury. **251** *br* D. P. Mettig & M. L. L. Magalhaes *Primeiras Nočoes de grammatica Portuguesa*, Editora do Brasil. *br* T. R. W. Alpin *et al. Introduction to Language* Hodder & Stoughton, 1981. **252** *t* Extract taken from *Rosie & Jim Sticker Book* Text copyright © Scholastic Children's Books 1993 Illustrations copyright © Joan Hickson 1993. Design of the Rosie and Jim puppets copyright © Ragdoll Publications UK Ltd. 1991. *br* Addison Wesley Longman Ltd. **254** *x* B. Raban & A. Jack *Mr West and his Monkey* University of Reading School of Education 1979 © B. Raban. *x* J. Downing, D. Ayres & B. Schaefer *Linguistic Awareness in Reading Readiness*; reproduced by permission of the publishers NFER–NELSON, Windsor, England. **255** *t, br* D. Mackay & J. Simo *Help Your Child to Read and Write and More* Penguin Books 1976 © David Mackay & Joseph Simo. **256** Fay Howat 'Make a Story' chart from *Junior Education* Oct. 1981 Scholastic Ltd. **257** P. Gannon *Assessing Writing* Edward Arnold, 1985. **258** Sarah Yarrow, a pupil at Meldreth Manor School; photo by Nigel Luckhurst, Cambridge. **260** After Crystal. **262** *t* Cambridge University Library; W. Penfield & L. Roberts *Speech and Brain-Mechanisms* Princeton University Press, New Jersey, 1959. *b* Wellcome Dept. of Cognitive Neurology/SPL. **263** *tl, tr* W. Penfield & L. Roberts *Speech and Brain-Mechanisms* Princeton University Press, New Jersey 1959. *br* After N. Geschwind 'Specializations of the Human

Brain', *Scientific American*, 1979. Copyright © 1979 Scientific American, Inc. All rights reserved. **264** MEPL. **265** Russ Rymer *Genie Escape from a Silent Childhood* Michael Joseph Ltd. 1993. **266** Table from *Speech Therapy Services* HMSO, reproduced with the permission of the Controller of Her Majesty's Stationery Office. **267** *r* After Crystal. **268** SPL; photo by James King-Holmes. **269** Gallaudet University, Washington. **270** M. M. Merzenich 'Studies on Electrical Stimulation of the Auditory Nerve in Animals and Man: Cochlear Implants' in D. B. Tower (ed.) *Human Communication and its Disorders* Raven Press, New York 1975. **271** *tl* W. Pronowost *et al.* 'ßThe Voice Visualizer' *American Annals of the Deaf 113* March 1968. *bl* From original research conducted by G. Bristow and F. Fallside into the visual display of sounds to assist speech therapy of the deaf. *tr, br* Copyright © BBC. **272** *t* Private Collection/BAL. *b* MEPL. **273** The Stroke Association; photo by Doug McKenzie, Beckenham. *x* A. R. Lecours & F. Lhermitte 'Clinical Forms of Aphasia' in A. R. Lecours *et al.* (eds.) *Aphasiology* Ballière Tindall 1983. **275** *l* S. J. Diamond & J. G. Beaumont (eds.) *Hemisphere Function in the Human Brain* Grafton Books, a Division of the Collins Publishing Group. *c* T. M. Hatfield & K. E. Patterson 'Interpretation of Spelling Disorders in Aphasia: Impact of Recent Developments in Cognitive Psychology' in F. Clifford Rose (ed.) *Progress in Aphasiology* Raven Press, New York 1984. *r* Aquarius. *x* S. Hampshire *Susan's Story* Sidgwick & Jackson 1981. **276** *t* L. Bradley 'ßThe organization of visual, phonological and motor strategies in learning to read and to spell' in U. Kirk (ed.) *Neurophysiology of Language, Reading and Spelling* Academic Press 1983. *b* M. Thomson *Developmental Dyslexia* Edward Arnold, 1984. **277** L. Tarnpol & M. Tarnpol *Reading Disabilities: an International Perspective* University Park Press 1976. **278** *t,c* After Crystal. *b* Kapitex Healthcare Ltd., Wetherby. **279** Brian C. Sommerlad. **281** SPL; photo by Hattie Young. *x* M. McTear *Children's Conversation* Blackwell 1985. **282** Widget Software. **283** *b* Manni Mason's Pictures. **284** Kunsthistorisches Museum, Vienna/BAL. **286** The Hutchison Library; photo by J. von Puttkamer. **288** Statistics Canada, Ottawa. **290** *t* Copyright British Museum. *c* AKG Photo, London; photo by Jon Burbank. *b* Scottish National Portrait Gallery, Edinburgh. **291** MEPL. **292** *l, c* P. Lieberman *The Speech of Primates* Mouton 1972. *r* After V. E. Negus *Comparative Anatomy and Physiology of the Larynx.* **294** Bildarchiv Preussischer Kulturbesitz, Berlin. **296–7** Map after C. Moseley & R. E. Asher (gen. eds.) *Atlas of the World's Languages* Routledge 1994. **298** Michael Nicholson/Corbis. **299** AKG London. **300–1** Map after C. Moseley & R. E. Asher (gen. eds.) *Atlas of the World's Languages* Routledge 1994. **302** *t* Copyright British Museum. *b* Universitetsbiblioteket, Uppsala, Sweden. Codex Argenteus, Lucas XIV: 19-24. **303** *t* British Library. *b* Kelsey Museum of Archaeology, University of Michigan, Ann Arbor. **304** *t* Copyright British Museum. **305** *b* Wales Tourist Board, Cardiff. **306** Map after C. Moseley & R. E. Asher (gen. eds.) *Atlas of the World's Languages* Routledge 1994. **307** *t* Map after C. Moseley & R. E. Asher (gen. eds.) *Atlas of the World's Languages* Routledge 1994. *b* Cambridge University Library; E. S. Takaishvili *Materialy po Arkeologii* Kavkaza Moscow 1909. **308** Hutchison Library. **308–9** Map after C. Moseley & R. E. Asher (gen. eds.) *Atlas of the World's Languages* Routledge 1994. **310** *t* Map after C. Moseley & R. E. Asher (gen. eds.) *Atlas of the World's Languages* Routledge 1994. *b* Popperfoto/Reuter. **311** *l* Howard J. Davies, Brighton. *r* Map after C. Moseley & R. E. Asher (gen. eds.) *Atlas of the World's Languages* Routledge 1994. **312** t, *b* Maps after C. Moseley & R. E. Asher (gen. eds.)

Atlas of the World's Languages Routledge 1994. *inset* Life File; photo by Andrew Watson. **313** Life File; photos by Stuart Norgrove. **314** *t* Werner Forman Archive/British Library, London. *b* Map after C. Moseley & R. E. Asher (gen. eds.) *Atlas of the World's Languages* Routledge 1994. **315** Science Museum/Science & Society Picture Library. **316** *b* The Egypt Exploration Society. **317**t Map after C. Moseley & R. E. Asher (gen. eds.) *Atlas of the World's Languages* Routledge 1994. *b* Panos Pictures; photo by David Reed. **318** *bl* RHPL. **319** Copyright British Museum. **320–1** Map after C. Moseley & R. E. Asher (gen. eds.) *Atlas of the World's Languages* Routledge 1994. **321** Life File; photo by Juliet Highet. **322-323** Map after W. Bright (ed.) *International Encyclopedia of Linguistics,* Oxford University Press 1992. **323** *tl* Panos Pictures; photo by Liba Taylor. *tr* Ancient Art & Architecture Collection. *b* RHPL; photo by C. & J. Lenars/Explorer. **324** Embajada del Paraguay en Londres. **325** *l* TCL Stock Directory UK; photo by R. Beliel/GLMR. *r* Map after C. Moseley & R. E. Asher (gen. eds.) *Atlas of the World's Languages* Routledge 1994. **327** Coo-ee Picture Library, Melbourne. **328** Michael Holford. **329** *t* Life File; photo by M. O. Khan. *bl* Copyright British Museum. *br* RHPL; photo by Gavin Hellier. **331** The Shakespeare Birthplace Trust, Stratford-upon-Avon. **332** Hutchison Library; photo by Jon Burbank. **334** Martha's Vineyard Chamber of Commerce; photo by Peter Simon, Chilmark, MA. **335** Novosti/SPL. **336** Papua New Guinea Government. **337** *t* *Wantok* World Publishing Co., Hohola, Papua New Guinea. **338** *t* Magnum; photo by Jean Gaumy. *b* Life File; photo by Juliet Highet. **339** Hutchison Library; photo by J. Henderson. **344** *t* European Commission. *b* C. M. Louttit 'The Use of Foreign Languages by Psychologists, Chemists and Physicists' *American Journal of Psychology 70* 1957. **345** *t* The Bell School of Languages, Cambridge, UK; photo by Unit 18 Photography, Norwich, UK. *bl, br* Expolangues, OIP, Paris. **346** Life File; photo by Emma Lee. **349** The Commission of the European Communities. **350** RHPL; photo by R. Dorel. *x* I. F. Finlay *Translating* Hodder & Stoughton. **351** United Nations/DPI Photos. **352** *x* F. Knowles 'Error Analysis of SYSTRAN Output – a Suggested Criterion for the International Evaluation of Translation Quality' in B. M. Shell (ed.) *Translating and the Computer* Elsevier 1979. **353** Logos Corporation, Stuttgart. **354** *bl* F. Lodwick *A Common Writing* Longman. **356** *l* The Borough of Hove and the British Tourist Authority. *r* MEPL. **358** *l, tr* Cambridge University Library; C. K. Ogden *Basic Dictionary* Kegan Paul, Trench, Trubner & Co. 1932. *br* Master and Fellows, Magdalene College, Cambridge. **360** Panos Pictures; photo by Jeremy Hartley. **361** *b* R. W. Bailey & M. Görlach *English as a World Language* University of Michigan Press and Cambridge University Press 1984. **362** Saint Pol-de-Leon Parish Church, Paul. **363** Image Bank; photo by Jay Freis. *x* S. Grosjean *Life with Two Languages* Harvard University Press 1982. **364** Biblioteca Vaticana. **367** New China News Agency. **368** SNCB, Brussels. **369** Canapress Photo Service; photo by Robert Galbraith. **370** The European Bureau for Lesser Used Languages: *t* photo by Augusta Cerruti. *b* W. Gregorini. **372** Cephas. Picture Library; photo by Mick Rock. **373** Life File; photo by Jeremy Hoare. **374** European Commission. **379** Stuart Cumberpatch, Reading. **380** *t* Reproduced from Kana Card, *Naoe Naganuma* copyright 1961 by Chōfūsha Co., Tokyo, Japan and reproduced with their permission. *l* D. E. Ager *Styles and Registers in Contemporary French* University of London Press 1970. *r* A. S. Macpherson *Deutsches Leben: Erster Teil* Ginn & Co. 1931, 17th edn. 1951 *br* M. Swann & C. Walter *Cambridge English Course* Cambridge University Press, split edn., 1986. **381** *t* John Walmsley. *b* K. Morrow

Advanced Conversational English Workbook Longman 1978. Reprinted by permission of Addison Wesley Longman Ltd. **382** King Features Syndicate. **384** By courtesy of the Royal Institution. **385** *t* SPL; photo by Dr Jeremy Burgess. *b* SPL; photo by Giani Tortoli. **387** *t* *Gray's Anatomy* 1901, reprinted by Bounty Books 1977. *b* Magnum Photos; photo by Burt Glinn. *x* P. S. Byrne & B. E. Long *Doctors Talking to Patients* HMSO 1976, reproduced with the permission of the Controller of Her Majesty's Stationery Office. **388** Copyright British Museum. **389** AKG London. **390** *t* D. Hayton *Cases and Commentary on the Law of Trusts* 8th edn. Stevens & Sons 1986. **393** 'Chronicles', Reubeni Foundation, Jerusalem, Israel. **394** *tr* Hutchison Library; photo by Robert Francis. *bl* Private Collection/BAL. *br* The Whitbread Beer Company/Lowe Howard-Spink. **395** *t* Equal Opportunities Commission, Manchester. *b* Cephas; photo by Nigel Blythe. **396** *bl* Copyright © BBC. *br* Screenplay by Dennis Spooner quoted in M. Hulke *Writing for Television* Black 1982. **397** *t* Institute of General Semantics, Englewood, NJ. *b* Cephas; photo by Mick Rock. **398** CIRAL, Université Laval. **400** Charles F. Hockett. **401** From 'Dialects in the Language of Bees' Karl von Frisch. Copyright © 1962 by Scientific American, Inc. All rights reserved. **402** *l* D. & A. J. Premack *The Mind of an Ape* Norton & Co. Inc. 1983. *r* From 'Teaching Language to an Ape' A. J. & D. Premack. Copyright © 1972 by Scientific American, Inc. All rights reserved. **403** From 'The Search for Extraterrestrial Intelligence' Carl Sagan and Frank Drake. Copyright © 1975 by Scientific American, Inc. All rights reserved. **404** *t* Magnum; photo by George Rodger. *b* G. Herzog 'Drum Signalling in a West African Tribe' *Word 1* 1945. **405** *t* D. Morris *Manwatching* © 1977 Equinox (Oxford) Ltd. and Jonathan Cape Ltd. *b* National Deafblind League. **406** *t* I. Eibl-Eibesfeldt 'Similarities and Differences Between Cultures in Expressive Movements' in R. A. Hinde (ed.) *Non-verbal Communication* Cambridge University Press 1972. *b* R. L. Birdwhistell *Kinesics and Context* University of Pennsylvania Press 1971 © The Trustees of the University of Pennsylvania Press. **407** *t* Courtesy of Rudolf Steiner Press. *b* National Horseracing Museum, Newmarket. **408** *t* Fitzwilliam Museum, University of Cambridge/BAL. *b* The Mansell Collection. **409** *t* India Office Library & Records, Sanskrit Ms. Egg 567: IO 2139. *bl, br* MEPL. **410** *t* The National and University Library of Iceland, Reykjavik; image by Kjartan Guôjónsson 1978. *b* Werner Forman Archive, Universitetsbiblioteket, Uppsala, Sweden. *x* E. Haugen (ed.) *First Grammatical Treatise* © Linguistic Society of America. **411** *l* AKG London. *r* Philip Sapir. **412** *t* Courtesy of the Harvard University Archives. *c* *Acta Linguistica Hafniensia* (International Journal of Structural Linguistics) Volume IX, Number 1. University of Copenhagen, 1965. *bl* BSOAS XVIII, 3, 1956. School of Oriental Studies, University of London. *bc* Charles F. Hockett. *br* University College London. **413** Massachusetts Institute of Technology, Cambridge, USA; photo by Donna Coveney. **414** *br* Brown Standard Corpus. *x* J. A. Loewen 'Culture, Meaning and Translation' *The Bible Translator 15* 1964. **417** *t* Halifax Building Society. *bl* Link Picture Library. *br* MGM (Courtesy Kobal) Personality: Dullea Keir.

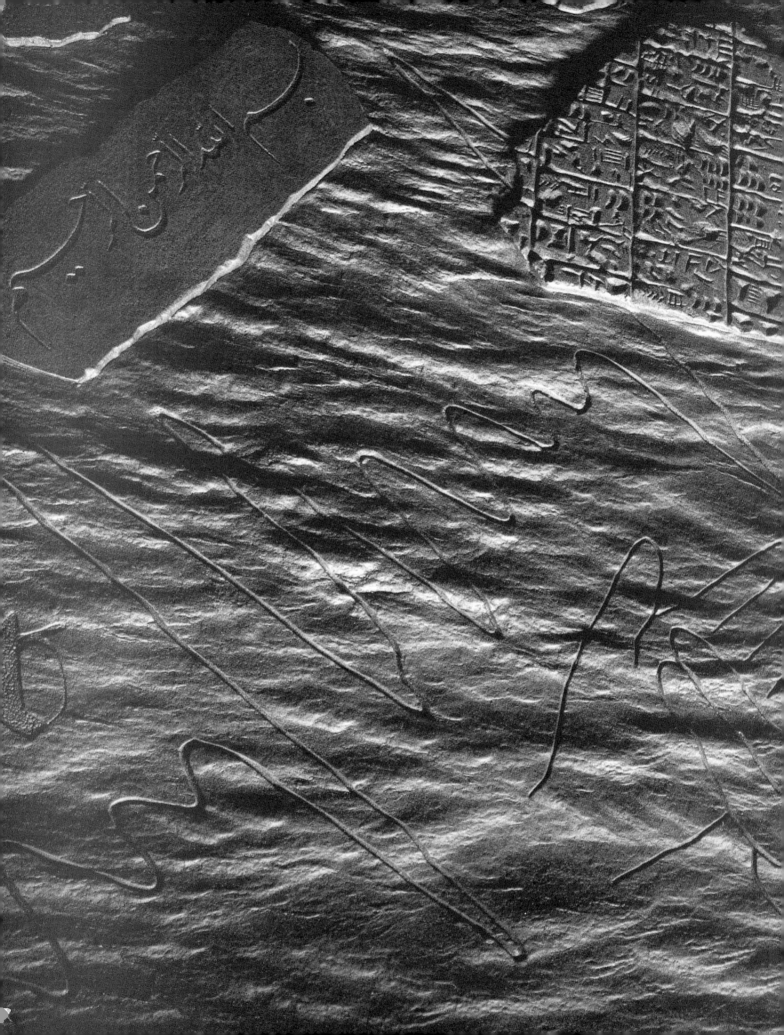